02/2010
#15.00

HarperCollins

STUDENT WORLD ATLAS

SECOND EDITION

OFFICIALLY WITHDRAWN

EDEN LAKE MEDIA CENTER

Collins

EDEN LAKE SCHOOL
12000 ANDERSON LAKES PKWY
EDEN PRAIRIE, MN 55344

Contents

Title	Scale	Page
Map Symbols		4
World States and Territories		5–9

World		**10–35**
Countries		10–11
Landscapes		12–13
Earthquakes and Volcanoes		14–15
Climate and Weather		16–17
Land Cover		18–19
Population		20–21
Urbanization and Cities		22–23
Communications		24–25
Social Indicators		26–27
Economy and Wealth		28–29
Conflict		30–31
Global Issues		32–33
Environmental Threats		34–35

Europe		**36–59**
Landscapes		36–37
Countries		38–39
Northern Europe	1:10 000 000	40–41
Western Russian Federation	1:7 500 000	42–43
Scandinavia and the Baltic States	1:5 000 000	44–45
Inset: Iceland	1:6 000 000	
Inset: Faroe Islands	1:5 000 000	
Northwest Europe	1:5 000 000	46–47
England and Wales	1:2 000 000	48–49
Scotland	1:2 000 000	50
Inset: Shetland Islands	1:2 000 000	
Ireland	1:2 000 000	51
Belgium, Netherlands, Luxembourg and Northwest Germany	1:2 000 000	52–53
Southern Europe and the Mediterranean	1:10 000 000	54–55
France	1:5 000 000	56
Spain and Portugal	1:5 000 000	57
Italy and the Balkans	1:5 000 000	58–59

Asia		**60–91**
Landscapes		60–61
Countries		62–63
Northern Asia	1:20 000 000	64–65
Eastern and Southeast Asia	1:20 000 000	66–67
Southeast Asia	1:15 000 000	68–69
Myanmar, Thailand, Peninsular Malaysia and Indo-China	1:7 000 000	70–71
Inset: Singapore	1:550 000	
Eastern Asia	1:15 000 000	72–73
Japan, North Korea and South Korea	1:7 000 000	74–75
Southeast China	1:7 000 000	76–77
Inset: Hong Kong	1:700 000	
Central and Southern Asia	1:20 000 000	78–79
Southern Asia	1:13 000 000	80–81
Northern India, Nepal, Bhutan and Bangladesh	1:7 000 000	82–83
Southern India and Sri Lanka	1:7 000 000	84
Middle East	1:3 000 000	85
Southwest Asia	1:13 000 000	86–87
The Gulf, Iran, Afghanistan and Pakistan	1:7 000 000	88–89
Eastern Mediterranean, the Caucasus and Iraq	1:7 000 000	90–91

Contents

Africa		92–101
Landscapes		92–93
Countries		94–95
Northern Africa	1:16 000 000	96–97
Inset: Cape Verde	1:16 000 000	
Central and Southern Africa	1:16 000 000	98–99
Republic of South Africa	1:5 000 000	100–101

Oceania		102–113
Landscapes		102–103
Countries		104–105
Australia, New Zealand and Southwest Pacific	1:20 000 000	106–107
Western Australia	1:8 000 000	108–109
Eastern Australia	1:8 000 000	110–111
Inset: Tasmania	1:8 000 000	
Southeast Australia	1:5 000 000	112
New Zealand	1:5 250 000	113

North America		114–137
Landscapes		114–115
Countries		116–117
Canada	1:16 000 000	118–119
Western Canada	1:7 000 000	120–121
Eastern Canada	1:7 000 000	122–123
United States of America	1:12 000 000	124–125
Western United States	1:7 000 000	126–127
Inset: Hawaiian Islands	1:7 000 000	
Southwest United States	1:3 500 000	128–129
Central United States	1:7 000 000	130–131
Eastern United States	1:7 000 000	132–133
Northeast United States	1:3 500 000	134–135
Central America and the Caribbean	1:14 000 000	136–137

South America		138–145
Landscapes		138–139
Countries		140–141
Northern South America	1:14 000 000	142–143
Inset: Galapagos Islands	1:14 000 000	
Southern South America	1:14 000 000	144
Southeast Brazil	1:7 000 000	145

Oceans and Poles		146–153
Features		146–147
Atlantic Ocean and Indian Ocean	1:50 000 000	148–149
Pacific Ocean	1:50 000 000	150–151
Antarctica	1:26 000 000	152
The Arctic	1:26 000 000	153

World Statistics	154–160
Index	161–239
Acknowledgements	240

Map Symbols

Southern Europe

Japan

Antarctica

Settlements

Population	National capital	Administrative capital	Other city or town
over 10 million	BEIJING	Karachi	New York
5 million to 10 million	JAKARTA	Tianjin	Nova Iguaçu
1 million to 5 million	KĀBUL	Sydney	Kaohsiung
500 000 to 1 million	BANGUI	Trujillo	Jeddah
100 000 to 500 000	WELLINGTON	Mansa	Apucarana
50 000 to 100 000	PORT OF SPAIN	Potenza	Arecibo
10 000 to 50 000	MALABO	Chinhoyi	Ceres
under 10 000	VALLETTA	Ati	Venta

Built-up area

Relief

Contour intervals and layer colours

Height metres	feet
5000	16404
3000	9843
2000	6562
1000	3281
500	1640
200	656
0	0
below sea level	
0	0
200	656
2000	6562
4000	13124
6000	19686
Depth	

1234 Summit
height in metres

-123 Spot height
height in metres

123 Ocean deep
depth in metres

Boundaries

- International boundary
- Disputed international boundary or alignment unconfirmed
- Administrative boundary
- Ceasefire line

Miscellaneous

- National park
- Reserve or Regional park
- Site of specific interest
- Wall

Land and sea features

- Desert
- Oasis
- Lava field
- Marsh
- 1234 Volcano
height in metres
- Ice cap or Glacier
- Escarpment
- Coral reef
- 1234 Pass
height in metres

Lakes and rivers

- Lake
- Impermanent lake
- Salt lake or lagoon
- Impermanent salt lake
- Dry salt lake or salt pan
- 123 Lake height
surface height above sea level, in metres
- River
- Impermanent river or watercourse
- Waterfall
- Dam
- Barrage

Transport

- Motorway (tunnel; under construction)
- Main road (tunnel; under construction)
- Secondary road (tunnel; under construction)
- Track
- Main railway (tunnel; under construction)
- Secondary railway (tunnel; under construction)
- Other railway (tunnel; under construction)
- Canal
- Main airport
- Regional airport

Satellite imagery - The thematic pages in the atlas contain a wide variety of photographs and images. These are a mixture of terrestrial and aerial photographs and satellite imagery. All are used to illustrate specific themes and to give an indication of the variety of imagery available today. The main types of imagery used in the atlas are described in the table below. The sensor for each satellite image is detailed on the acknowledgements page.

Main satellites/sensors

Satellite/sensor name	Launch dates	Owner	Aims and applications	Internet links	Additional internet links
Landsat 1, 2, 3, 4, 5, 7	July 1972–April 1999	National Aeronautics and Space Administration (NASA), USA	The first satellite to be designed specifically for observing the Earth's surface. Originally set up to produce images of use for agriculture and geology. Today is of use for numerous environmental and scientific applications.	landsat.gsfc.nasa.gov	asterweb.jpl.nasa.gov earth.jsc.nasa.gov earthnet.esrin.esa.it
SPOT 1, 2, 3, 4, 5 (Satellite Pour l'Observation de la Terre)	February 1986–March 1998	Centre National d'Etudes Spatiales (CNES) and Spot Image, France	Particularly useful for monitoring land use, water resources research, coastal studies and cartography.	www.spotimage.fr	earthobservatory.nasa.gov eol.jsc.nasa.gov
Space Shuttle	Regular launches from 1981	NASA, USA	Each shuttle mission has separate aims. Astronauts take photographs with high specification hand held cameras. The Shuttle Radar Topography Mission (SRTM) in 2000 obtained the most complete near-global high-resolution database of the earth's topography.	science.ksc.nasa.gov/shuttle/countdown www.jpl.nasa.gov/srtm	gs.mdacorporation.com modis.gsfc.nasa.gov seawifs.gsfc.nasa.gov topex-www.jpl.nasa.gov
IKONOS	September 1999	GeoEye	First commercial high-resolution satellite. Useful for a variety of applications mainly Cartography, Defence, Urban Planning, Agriculture, Forestry and Insurance.	www.geoeye.com	visibleearth.nasa.gov www.usgs.gov

Amsterdam, Netherlands

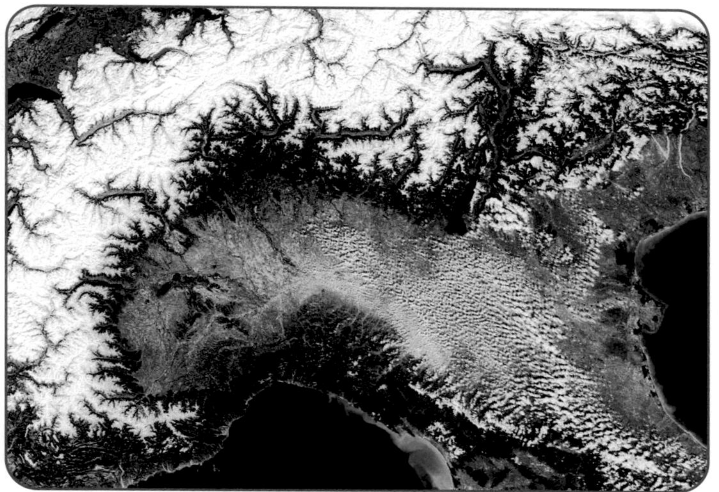

The Alps

Europe	Area sq km	Area sq miles	Population	Capital	Languages	Religions	Currency
ALBANIA	28 748	11 100	3 190 000	Tirana	Albanian, Greek	Sunni Muslim, Albanian Orthodox, Roman Catholic	Lek
ANDORRA	465	180	75 000	Andorra la Vella	Spanish, Catalan, French	Roman Catholic	Euro
AUSTRIA	83 855	32 377	8 361 000	Vienna	German, Croatian, Turkish	Roman Catholic, Protestant	Euro
BELARUS	207 600	80 155	9 689 000	Minsk	Belorussian, Russian	Belorussian Orthodox, Roman Catholic	Belarus rouble
BELGIUM	30 520	11 784	10 457 000	Brussels	Dutch (Flemish), French (Walloon), German	Roman Catholic, Protestant	Euro
BOSNIA-HERZEGOVINA	51 130	19 741	3 935 000	Sarajevo	Bosnian, Serbian, Croatian	Sunni Muslim, Serbian Orthodox, Roman Catholic, Protestant	Marka
BULGARIA	110 994	42 855	7 639 000	Sofia	Bulgarian, Turkish, Romany, Macedonian	Bulgarian Orthodox, Sunni Muslim	Lev
CROATIA	56 538	21 829	4 555 000	Zagreb	Croatian, Serbian	Roman Catholic, Serbian Orthodox, Sunni Muslim	Kuna
CZECH REPUBLIC	78 864	30 450	10 186 000	Prague	Czech, Moravian, Slovak	Roman Catholic, Protestant	Czech koruna
DENMARK	43 075	16 631	5 442 000	Copenhagen	Danish	Protestant	Danish krone
ESTONIA	45 200	17 452	1 335 000	Tallinn	Estonian, Russian	Protestant, Estonian and Russian Orthodox	Kroon
FINLAND	338 145	130 559	5 277 000	Helsinki	Finnish, Swedish	Protestant, Greek Orthodox	Euro
FRANCE	543 965	210 026	61 647 000	Paris	French, Arabic	Roman Catholic, Protestant, Sunni Muslim	Euro
GERMANY	357 022	137 849	82 599 000	Berlin	German, Turkish	Protestant, Roman Catholic	Euro
GREECE	131 957	50 949	11 147 000	Athens	Greek	Greek Orthodox, Sunni Muslim	Euro
HUNGARY	93 030	35 919	10 030 000	Budapest	Hungarian	Roman Catholic, Protestant	Forint
ICELAND	102 820	39 699	301 000	Reykjavík	Icelandic	Protestant	Icelandic króna
IRELAND	70 282	27 136	4 301 000	Dublin	English, Irish	Roman Catholic, Protestant	Euro
ITALY	301 245	116 311	58 877 000	Rome	Italian	Roman Catholic	Euro
KOSOVO	10 908	4 212	2 070 000	Prishtinë (Priština)	Albanian, Serbian	Sunni Muslim, Serbian Orthodox	Euro
LATVIA	63 700	24 595	2 277 000	Rīga	Latvian, Russian	Protestant, Roman Catholic, Russian Orthodox	Lats
LIECHTENSTEIN	160	62	35 000	Vaduz	German	Roman Catholic, Protestant	Swiss franc
LITHUANIA	65 200	25 174	3 390 000	Vilnius	Lithuanian, Russian, Polish	Roman Catholic, Protestant, Russian Orthodox	Litas
LUXEMBOURG	2 586	998	467 000	Luxembourg	Letzeburgish, German, French	Roman Catholic	Euro
MACEDONIA (F.Y.R.O.M.)	25 713	9 928	2 038 000	Skopje	Macedonian, Albanian, Turkish	Macedonian Orthodox, Sunni Muslim	Macedonian denar
MALTA	316	122	407 000	Valletta	Maltese, English	Roman Catholic	Euro
MOLDOVA	33 700	13 012	3 794 000	Chişinău	Romanian, Ukrainian, Gagauz, Russian	Romanian Orthodox, Russian Orthodox	Moldovan leu
MONACO	2	1	33 000	Monaco-Ville	French, Monegasque, Italian	Roman Catholic	Euro
MONTENEGRO	13 812	5 333	598 000	Podgorica	Serbian (Montenegrin), Albanian	Montenegrin Orthodox, Sunni Muslim	Euro
NETHERLANDS	41 526	16 033	16 419 000	Amsterdam/The Hague	Dutch, Frisian	Roman Catholic, Protestant, Sunni Muslim	Euro
NORWAY	323 878	125 050	4 698 000	Oslo	Norwegian	Protestant, Roman Catholic	Norwegian krone
POLAND	312 683	120 728	38 082 000	Warsaw	Polish, German	Roman Catholic, Polish Orthodox	Złoty
PORTUGAL	88 940	34 340	10 623 000	Lisbon	Portuguese	Roman Catholic, Protestant	Euro
ROMANIA	237 500	91 699	21 438 000	Bucharest	Romanian, Hungarian	Romanian Orthodox, Protestant, Roman Catholic	Romanian leu
RUSSIAN FEDERATION	17 075 400	6 592 849	142 499 000	Moscow	Russian, Tatar, Ukrainian, local languages	Russian Orthodox, Sunni Muslim, Protestant	Russian rouble
SAN MARINO	61	24	31 000	San Marino	Italian	Roman Catholic	Euro
SERBIA	77 453	29 904	7 788 000	Belgrade	Serbian, Hungarian	Serbian Orthodox, Roman Catholic, Sunni Muslim	Serbian dinar
SLOVAKIA	49 035	18 933	5 390 000	Bratislava	Slovak, Hungarian, Czech	Roman Catholic, Protestant, Orthodox	Euro
SLOVENIA	20 251	7 819	2 002 000	Ljubljana	Slovene, Croatian, Serbian	Roman Catholic, Protestant	Euro
SPAIN	504 782	194 897	44 279 000	Madrid	Castilian, Catalan, Galician, Basque	Roman Catholic	Euro
SWEDEN	449 964	173 732	9 119 000	Stockholm	Swedish	Protestant, Roman Catholic	Swedish krona
SWITZERLAND	41 293	15 943	7 484 000	Bern	German, French, Italian, Romansch	Roman Catholic, Protestant	Swiss franc
UKRAINE	603 700	233 090	46 205 000	Kiev	Ukrainian, Russian	Ukrainian Orthodox, Ukrainian Catholic, Roman Catholic	Hryvnia
UNITED KINGDOM	243 609	94 058	60 769 000	London	English, Welsh, Gaelic	Protestant, Roman Catholic, Muslim	Pound sterling
VATICAN CITY	0.5	0.2	557	Vatican City	Italian	Roman Catholic	Euro

Dependent territories	Territorial status	Area sq km	Area sq miles	Population	Capital	Languages	Religions	Currency
Azores	Autonomous Region of Portugal	2 300	888	242 000	Ponta Delgada	Portuguese	Roman Catholic, Protestant	Euro
Faroe Islands	Self-governing Danish Territory	1 399	540	49 000	Tórshavn	Faroese, Danish	Protestant	Danish krone
Gibraltar	United Kingdom Overseas Territory	7	3	29 000	Gibraltar	Engllish, Spanish	Roman Catholic, Protestant, Sunni Muslim	Gibraltar pound
Guernsey	United Kingdom Crown Dependency	78	30	64 000	St Peter Port	English, French	Protestant, Roman Catholic	Pound sterling
Isle of Man	United Kingdom Crown Dependency	572	221	79 000	Douglas	English	Protestant, Roman Catholic	Pound sterling
Jersey	United Kingdom Crown Dependency	116	45	88 000	St Helier	English, French	Protestant, Roman Catholic	Pound sterling

World

States and Territories

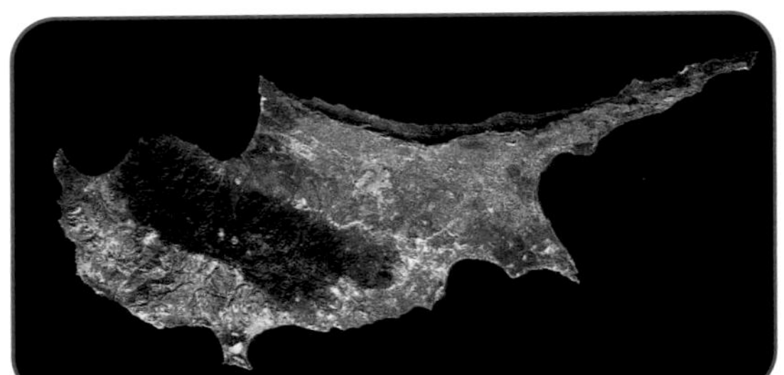

Cyprus, eastern Mediterranean

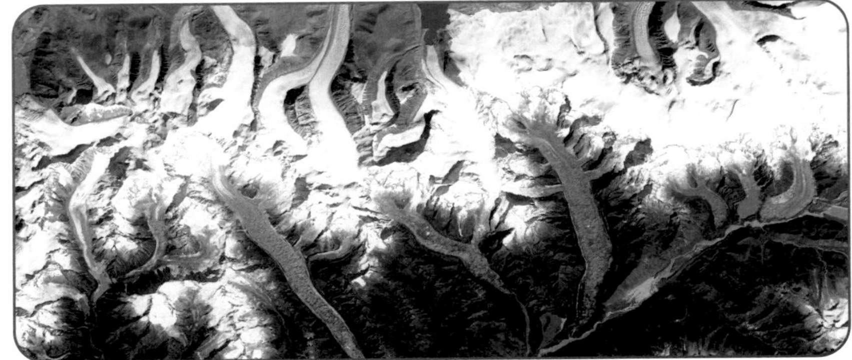

Bhutan, Himalayas

Asia	Area sq km	Area sq miles	Population	Capital	Languages	Religions	Currency
AFGHANISTAN	652 225	251 825	27 145 000	Kābul	Dari, Pushtu, Uzbek, Turkmen	Sunni Muslim, Shi'a Muslim	Afghani
ARMENIA	29 800	11 506	3 002 000	Yerevan	Armenian, Azeri	Armenian Orthodox	Dram
AZERBAIJAN	86 600	33 436	8 467 000	Baku	Azeri, Armenian, Russian, Lezgian	Shi'a Muslim, Sunni Muslim, Russian and Armenian Orthodox	Azerbaijani manat
BAHRAIN	691	267	753 000	Manama	Arabic, English	Shi'a Muslim, Sunni Muslim, Christian	Bahrain dinar
BANGLADESH	143 998	55 598	158 665 000	Dhaka	Bengali, English	Sunni Muslim, Hindu	Taka
BHUTAN	46 620	18 000	658 000	Thimphu	Dzongkha, Nepali, Assamese	Buddhist, Hindu	Ngultrum, Indian rupee
BRUNEI	5 765	2 226	390 000	Bandar Seri Begawan	Malay, English, Chinese	Sunni Muslim, Buddhist, Christian	Brunei dollar
CAMBODIA	181 035	69 884	14 444 000	Phnom Penh	Khmer, Vietnamese	Buddhist, Roman Catholic, Sunni Muslim	Riel
CHINA	9 584 492	3 700 593	1 313 437 000	Beijing	Mandarin, Wu, Cantonese, Hsiang, regional languages	Confucian, Taoist, Buddhist, Christian, Sunni Muslim	Yuan, HK dollar**, Macau pataca
CYPRUS	9 251	3 572	855 000	Nicosia	Greek, Turkish, English	Greek Orthodox, Sunni Muslim	Euro
EAST TIMOR	14 874	5 743	1 155 000	Dili	Portuguese, Tetun, English	Roman Catholic	United States dollar
GEORGIA	69 700	26 911	4 395 000	T'bilisi	Georgian, Russian, Armenian, Azeri, Ossetian, Abkhaz	Georgian Orthodox, Russian Orthodox, Sunni Muslim	Lari
INDIA	3 064 898	1 183 364	1 169 016 000	New Delhi	Hindi, English, many regional languages	Hindu, Sunni Muslim, Shi'a Muslim, Sikh, Christian	Indian rupee
INDONESIA	1 919 445	741 102	231 627 000	Jakarta	Indonesian, local languages	Sunni Muslim, Protestant, Roman Catholic, Hindu, Buddhist	Rupiah
IRAN	1 648 000	636 296	71 208 000	Tehrān	Farsi, Azeri, Kurdish, regional languages	Shi'a Muslim, Sunni Muslim	Iranian rial
IRAQ	438 317	169 235	28 993 000	Baghdād	Arabic, Kurdish, Turkmen	Shi'a Muslim, Sunni Muslim, Christian	Iraqi dinar
ISRAEL	20 770	8 019	6 928 000	Jerusalem (Yerushalayim) (El Quds)*	Hebrew, Arabic	Jewish, Sunni Muslim, Christian, Druze	Shekel
JAPAN	377 727	145 841	127 967 000	Tōkyō	Japanese	Shintoist, Buddhist, Christian	Yen
JORDAN	89 206	34 443	5 924 000	'Ammān	Arabic	Sunni Muslim, Christian	Jordanian dinar
KAZAKHSTAN	2 717 300	1 049 155	15 422 000	Astana	Kazakh, Russian, Ukrainian, German, Uzbek, Tatar	Sunni Muslim, Russian Orthodox, Protestant	Tenge
KUWAIT	17 818	6 880	2 851 000	Kuwait	Arabic	Sunni Muslim, Shi'a Muslim, Christian, Hindu	Kuwaiti dinar
KYRGYZSTAN	198 500	76 641	5 317 000	Bishkek	Kyrgyz, Russian, Uzbek	Sunni Muslim, Russian Orthodox	Kyrgyz som
LAOS	236 800	91 429	5 859 000	Vientiane	Lao, local languages	Buddhist, traditional beliefs	Kip
LEBANON	10 452	4 036	4 099 000	Beirut	Arabic, Armenian, French	Shi'a Muslim, Sunni Muslim, Christian	Lebanese pound
MALAYSIA	332 965	128 559	26 572 000	Kuala Lumpur/Putrajaya	Malay, English, Chinese, Tamil, local languages	Sunni Muslim, Buddhist, Hindu, Christian, traditional beliefs	Ringgit
MALDIVES	298	115	306 000	Male	Divehi (Maldivian)	Sunni Muslim	Rufiyaa
MONGOLIA	1 565 000	604 250	2 629 000	Ulan Bator	Khalka (Mongolian), Kazakh, local languages	Buddhist, Sunni Muslim	Tugrik (tögrög)
MYANMAR	676 577	261 228	48 798 000	Nay Pyi Taw/Rangoon	Burmese, Shan, Karen, local languages	Buddhist, Christian, Sunni Muslim	Kyat
NEPAL	147 181	56 827	28 196 000	Kathmandu	Nepali, Maithili, Bhojpuri, English, local languages	Hindu, Buddhist, Sunni Muslim	Nepalese rupee
NORTH KOREA	120 538	46 540	23 790 000	P'yŏngyang	Korean	Traditional beliefs, Chondoist, Buddhist	North Korean won
OMAN	309 500	119 499	2 595 000	Muscat	Arabic, Baluchi, Indian languages	Ibadhi Muslim, Sunni Muslim	Omani riyal
PAKISTAN	803 940	310 403	163 902 000	Islamabad	Urdu, Punjabi, Sindhi, Pushtu, English	Sunni Muslim, Shi'a Muslim, Christian, Hindu	Pakistani rupee
PALAU	497	192	20 000	Melekeok	Palauan, English	Roman Catholic, Protestant, traditional beliefs	United States dollar
PHILIPPINES	300 000	115 831	87 960 000	Manila	English, Filipino, Tagalog, Cebuano, local languages	Roman Catholic, Protestant, Sunni Muslim, Aglipayan	Philippine peso
QATAR	11 437	4 416	841 000	Doha	Arabic	Sunni Muslim	Qatari riyal
RUSSIAN FEDERATION	17 075 400	6 592 849	142 499 000	Moscow	Russian, Tatar, Ukrainian, local languages	Russian Orthodox, Sunni Muslim, Protestant	Russian rouble
SAUDI ARABIA	2 200 000	849 425	24 735 000	Riyadh	Arabic	Sunni Muslim, Shi'a Muslim	Saudi Arabian riyal
SINGAPORE	639	247	4 436 000	Singapore	Chinese, English, Malay, Tamil	Buddhist, Taoist, Sunni Muslim, Christian, Hindu	Singapore dollar
SOUTH KOREA	99 274	38 330	48 224 000	Seoul	Korean	Buddhist, Protestant, Roman Catholic	South Korean won
SRI LANKA	65 610	25 332	19 299 000	Sri Jayewardenepura Kotte	Sinhalese, Tamil, English	Buddhist, Hindu, Sunni Muslim, Roman Catholic	Sri Lankan rupee
SYRIA	185 180	71 498	19 929 000	Damascus	Arabic, Kurdish, Armenian	Sunni Muslim, Shi'a Muslim, Christian	Syrian pound
TAIWAN*	36 179	13 969	22 880 000	T'aipei	Mandarin, Min, Hakka, local languages	Buddhist, Taoist, Confucian, Christian	Taiwan dollar
TAJIKISTAN	143 100	55 251	6 736 000	Dushanbe	Tajik, Uzbek, Russian	Sunni Muslim	Somoni
THAILAND	513 115	198 115	63 884 000	Bangkok	Thai, Lao, Chinese, Malay, Mon-Khmer languages	Buddhist, Sunni Muslim	Baht
TURKEY	779 452	300 948	74 877 000	Ankara	Turkish, Kurdish	Sunni Muslim, Shi'a Muslim	Lira
TURKMENISTAN	488 100	188 456	4 965 000	Aşgabat	Turkmen, Uzbek, Russian	Sunni Muslim, Russian Orthodox	Turkmen manat
UNITED ARAB EMIRATES	77 700	30 000	4 380 000	Abu Dhabi	Arabic, English	Sunni Muslim, Shi'a Muslim	United Arab Emirates dirham
UZBEKISTAN	447 400	172 742	27 372 000	Toshkent	Uzbek, Russian, Tajik, Kazakh	Sunni Muslim, Russian Orthodox	Uzbek som
VIETNAM	329 565	127 246	87 375 000	Ha Nôi	Vietnamese, Thai, Khmer, Chinese, local languages	Buddhist, Taoist, Roman Catholic, Cao Dai, Hoa Hao	Dong
YEMEN	527 968	203 850	22 389 000	Ṣan'ā'	Arabic	Sunni Muslim, Shi'a Muslim	Yemeni rial

Dependent and disputed territories	Territorial status	Area sq km	Area sq miles	Population	Capital	Languages	Religions	Currency
Christmas Island	Australian External Territory	135	52	1 500	The Settlement	English	Buddhist, Sunni Muslim, Protestant, Roman Catholic	Australian dollar
Cocos Islands	Australian External Territory	14	5	621	West Island	English	Sunni Muslim, Christian	Australian dollar
Gaza	Semi-autonomous region	363	140	1 586 000	Gaza	Arabic	Sunni Muslim, Shi'a Muslim	Israeli shekel
Jammu and Kashmir	Disputed territory (India/Pakistan)	222 236	85 806	13 000 000	Srinagar			
West Bank	Disputed territory	5 860	2 263	2 676 000		Arabic, Hebrew	Sunni Muslim, Jewish, Shi'a Muslim, Christian	Jordanian dinar, Israeli shekel

*China claims Taiwan as its 23rd province

*De facto capital. Disputed

**Hong Kong dollar

Victoria Falls, Zambia/Zimbabwe

Africa	Area sq km	Area sq miles	Population	Capital	Languages	Religions	Currency
ALGERIA	2 381 741	919 595	33 858 000	Algiers	Arabic, French, Berber	Sunni Muslim	Algerian dinar
ANGOLA	1 246 700	481 354	17 024 000	Luanda	Portuguese, Bantu, local languages	Roman Catholic, Protestant, traditional beliefs	Kwanza
BENIN	112 620	43 483	9 033 000	Porto-Novo	French, Fon, Yoruba, Adja, local languages	Traditional beliefs, Roman Catholic, Sunni Muslim	CFA franc*
BOTSWANA	581 370	224 468	1 882 000	Gaborone	English, Setswana, Shona, local languages	Traditional beliefs, Protestant, Roman Catholic	Pula
BURKINA	274 200	105 869	14 784 000	Ouagadougou	French, Moore (Mossi), Fulani, local languages	Sunni Muslim, traditional beliefs, Roman Catholic	CFA franc*
BURUNDI	27 835	10 747	8 508 000	Bujumbura	Kirundi (Hutu, Tutsi), French	Roman Catholic, traditional beliefs, Protestant	Burundian franc
CAMEROON	475 442	183 569	18 549 000	Yaoundé	French, English, Fang, Bamileke, local languages	Roman Catholic, traditional beliefs, Sunni Muslim, Protestant	CFA franc*
CAPE VERDE	4 033	1 557	530 000	Praia	Portuguese, creole	Roman Catholic, Protestant	Cape Verde escudo
CENTRAL AFRICAN REPUBLIC	622 436	240 324	4 343 000	Bangui	French, Sango, Banda, Baya, local languages	Protestant, Roman Catholic, traditional beliefs, Sunni Muslim	CFA franc*
CHAD	1 284 000	495 755	10 781 000	Ndjamena	Arabic, French, Sara, local languages	Sunni Muslim, Roman Catholic, Protestant, traditional beliefs	CFA franc*
COMOROS	1 862	719	839 000	Moroni	Comorian, French, Arabic	Sunni Muslim, Roman Catholic	Comoros franc
CONGO	342 000	132 047	3 768 000	Brazzaville	French, Kongo, Monokutuba, local languages	Roman Catholic, Protestant, traditional beliefs, Sunni Muslim	CFA franc*
CONGO, DEM. REP. OF THE	2 345 410	905 568	62 636 000	Kinshasa	French, Lingala, Swahili, Kongo, local languages	Christian, Sunni Muslim	Congolese franc
CÔTE D'IVOIRE	322 463	124 504	19 262 000	Yamoussoukro	French, creole, Akan, local languages	Sunni Muslim, Roman Catholic, traditional beliefs, Protestant	CFA franc*
DJIBOUTI	23 200	8 958	833 000	Djibouti	Somali, Afar, French, Arabic	Sunni Muslim, Christian	Djibouti franc
EGYPT	1 000 250	386 199	75 498 000	Cairo	Arabic	Sunni Muslim, Coptic Christian	Egyptian pound
EQUATORIAL GUINEA	28 051	10 831	507 000	Malabo	Spanish, French, Fang	Roman Catholic, traditional beliefs	CFA franc*
ERITREA	117 400	45 328	4 851 000	Asmara	Tigrinya, Tigre	Sunni Muslim, Coptic Christian	Nakfa
ETHIOPIA	1 133 880	437 794	83 099 000	Addis Ababa	Oromo, Amharic, Tigrinya, local languages	Ethiopian Orthodox, Sunni Muslim, traditional beliefs	Birr
GABON	267 667	103 347	1 331 000	Libreville	French, Fang, local languages	Roman Catholic, Protestant, traditional beliefs	CFA franc*
THE GAMBIA	11 295	4 361	1 709 000	Banjul	English, Malinke, Fulani, Wolof	Sunni Muslim, Protestant	Dalasi
GHANA	238 537	92 100	23 478 000	Accra	English, Hausa, Akan, local languages	Christian, Sunni Muslim, traditional beliefs	Cedi
GUINEA	245 857	94 926	9 370 000	Conakry	French, Fulani, Malinke, local languages	Sunni Muslim, traditional beliefs, Christian	Guinea franc
GUINEA-BISSAU	36 125	13 948	1 695 000	Bissau	Portuguese, crioulo, local languages	Traditional beliefs, Sunni Muslim, Christian	CFA franc*
KENYA	582 646	224 961	37 538 000	Nairobi	Swahili, English, local languages	Christian, traditional beliefs	Kenyan shilling
LESOTHO	30 355	11 720	2 008 000	Maseru	Sesotho, English, Zulu	Christian, traditional beliefs	Loti, S. African rand
LIBERIA	111 369	43 000	3 750 000	Monrovia	English, creole, local languages	Traditional beliefs, Christian, Sunni Muslim	Liberian dollar
LIBYA	1 759 540	679 362	6 160 000	Tripoli	Arabic, Berber	Sunni Muslim	Libyan dinar
MADAGASCAR	587 041	226 658	19 683 000	Antananarivo	Malagasy, French	Traditional beliefs, Christian, Sunni Muslim	Malagasy ariary, Malagasy franc
MALAWI	118 484	45 747	13 925 000	Lilongwe	Chichewa, English, local languages	Christian, traditional beliefs, Sunni Muslim	Malawian kwacha
MALI	1 240 140	478 821	12 337 000	Bamako	French, Bambara, local languages	Sunni Muslim, traditional beliefs, Christian	CFA franc*
MAURITANIA	1 030 700	397 955	3 124 000	Nouakchott	Arabic, French, local languages	Sunni Muslim	Ouguiya
MAURITIUS	2 040	788	1 262 000	Port Louis	English, creole, Hindi, Bhojpurī, French	Hindu, Roman Catholic, Sunni Muslim	Mauritius rupee
MOROCCO	446 550	172 414	31 224 000	Rabat	Arabic, Berber, French	Sunni Muslim	Moroccan dirham
MOZAMBIQUE	799 380	308 642	21 397 000	Maputo	Portuguese, Makua, Tsonga, local languages	Traditional beliefs, Roman Catholic, Sunni Muslim	Metical
NAMIBIA	824 292	318 261	2 074 000	Windhoek	English, Afrikaans, German, Ovambo, local languages	Protestant, Roman Catholic	Namibian dollar
NIGER	1 267 000	489 191	14 226 000	Niamey	French, Hausa, Fulani, local languages	Sunni Muslim, traditional beliefs	CFA franc*
NIGERIA	923 768	356 669	148 093 000	Abuja	English, Hausa, Yoruba, Ibo, Fulani, local languages	Sunni Muslim, Christian, traditional beliefs	Naira
RWANDA	26 338	10 169	9 725 000	Kigali	Kinyarwanda, French, English	Roman Catholic, traditional beliefs, Protestant	Rwandan franc
SÃO TOMÉ AND PRÍNCIPE	964	372	158 000	São Tomé	Portuguese, creole	Roman Catholic, Protestant	Dobra
SENEGAL	196 720	75 954	12 379 000	Dakar	French, Wolof, Fulani, local languages	Sunni Muslim, Roman Catholic, traditional beliefs	CFA franc*
SEYCHELLES	455	176	87 000	Victoria	English, French, creole	Roman Catholic, Protestant	Seychelles rupee
SIERRA LEONE	71 740	27 699	5 866 000	Freetown	English, creole, Mende, Temne, local languages	Sunni Muslim, traditional beliefs	Leone
SOMALIA	637 657	246 201	8 699 000	Mogadishu	Somali, Arabic	Sunni Muslim	Somali shilling
SOUTH AFRICA, REPUBLIC OF	1 219 090	470 693	48 577 000	Pretoria/Cape Town	Afrikaans, English, nine official local languages	Protestant, Roman Catholic, Sunni Muslim, Hindu	Rand
SUDAN	2 505 813	967 500	38 560 000	Khartoum	Arabic, Dinka, Nubian, Beja, Nuer, local languages	Sunni Muslim, traditional beliefs, Christian	Sudanese pound (Sudani)
SWAZILAND	17 364	6 704	1 141 000	Mbabane	Swazi, English	Christian, traditional beliefs	Emalangeni, South African rand
TANZANIA	945 087	364 900	40 454 000	Dodoma	Swahili, English, Nyamwezi, local languages	Shi'a Muslim, Sunni Muslim, traditional beliefs, Christian	Tanzanian shilling
TOGO	56 785	21 925	6 585 000	Lomé	French, Ewe, Kabre, local languages	Traditional beliefs, Christian, Sunni Muslim	CFA franc*
TUNISIA	164 150	63 379	10 327 000	Tunis	Arabic, French	Sunni Muslim	Tunisian dinar
UGANDA	241 038	93 065	30 884 000	Kampala	English, Swahili, Luganda, local languages	Roman Catholic, Protestant, Sunni Muslim, traditional beliefs	Ugandan shilling
ZAMBIA	752 614	290 586	11 922 000	Lusaka	English, Bemba, Nyanja, Tonga, local languages	Christian, traditional beliefs	Zambian kwacha
ZIMBABWE	390 759	150 873	13 349 000	Harare	English, Shona, Ndebele	Christian, traditional beliefs	Zimbabwean dollar

Dependent and disputed territories	Territorial status	Area sq km	Area sq miles	Population	Capital	Languages	Religions	Currency
Canary Islands	Autonomous Community of Spain	7 447	2 875	1 996 000	Santa Cruz de Tenerife/Las Palmas	Spanish	Roman Catholic	Euro
Madeira	Autonomous Region of Portugal	779	301	245 000	Funchal	Portuguese	Roman Catholic, Protestant	Euro
Mayotte	French Territorial Collectivity	373	144	186 000	Dzaoudzi	French, Mahorian	Sunni Muslim, Christian	Euro
Réunion	French Overseas Department	2 551	985	807 000	St-Denis	French, creole	Roman Catholic	Euro
St Helena and Dependencies	United Kingdom Overseas Territory	121	47	7 000	Jamestown	English	Protestant, Roman Catholic	St Helena pound
Western Sahara	Disputed territory (Morocco)	266 000	102 703	480 000	Laâyoune	Arabic	Sunni Muslim	Moroccan dirham

*Communauté Financière Africaine franc

World
States and Territories

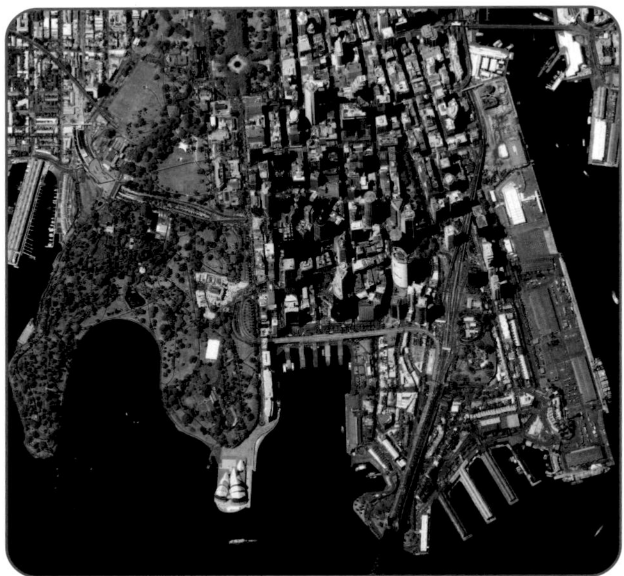

Sydney, Australia

Uluru (Ayers Rock), Australia

Oceania	Area sq km	Area sq miles	Population	Capital	Languages	Religions	Currency
AUSTRALIA	7 692 024	2 969 907	20 743 000	Canberra	English, Italian, Greek	Protestant, Roman Catholic, Orthodox	Australian dollar
FIJI	18 330	7 077	839 000	Suva	English, Fijian, Hindi	Christian, Hindu, Sunni Muslim	Fiji dollar
KIRIBATI	717	277	95 000	Bairiki	Gilbertese, English	Roman Catholic, Protestant	Australian dollar
MARSHALL ISLANDS	181	70	59 000	Delap-Uliga-Djarrit	English, Marshallese	Protestant, Roman Catholic	United States dollar
MICRONESIA, FEDERATED STATES OF	701	271	111 000	Palikir	English, Chuukese, Pohnpeian, local languages	Roman Catholic, Protestant	United States dollar
NAURU	21	8	10 000	Yaren	Nauruan, English	Protestant, Roman Catholic	Australian dollar
NEW ZEALAND	270 534	104 454	4 179 000	Wellington	English, Maori	Protestant, Roman Catholic	New Zealand dollar
PAPUA NEW GUINEA	462 840	178 704	6 331 000	Port Moresby	English, Tok Pisin (creole), local languages	Protestant, Roman Catholic, traditional beliefs	Kina
SAMOA	2 831	1 093	187 000	Apia	Samoan, English	Protestant, Roman Catholic	Tala
SOLOMON ISLANDS	28 370	10 954	496 000	Honiara	English, creole, local languages	Protestant, Roman Catholic	Solomon Islands dollar
TONGA	748	289	100 000	Nuku'alofa	Tongan, English	Protestant, Roman Catholic	Pa'anga
TUVALU	25	10	11 000	Vaiaku	Tuvaluan, English	Protestant	Australian dollar
VANUATU	12 190	4 707	226 000	Port Vila	English, Bislama (creole), French	Protestant, Roman Catholic, traditional beliefs	Vatu

Dependent territories	Territorial status	Area sq km	Area sq miles	Population	Capital	Languages	Religions	Currency
American Samoa	United States Unincorporated Territory	197	76	67 000	Fagatogo	Samoan, English	Protestant, Roman Catholic	United States dollar
Cook Islands	Self-governing New Zealand Territory	293	113	13 000	Avarua	English, Maori	Protestant, Roman Catholic	New Zealand dollar
French Polynesia	French Overseas Country	3 265	1 261	263 000	Papeete	French, Tahitian, Polynesian languages	Protestant, Roman Catholic	CFP franc*
Guam	United States Unincorporated Territory	541	209	173 000	Hagåtña	Chamorro, English, Tapalog	Roman Catholic	United States dollar
New Caledonia	French Overseas Collectivity	19 058	7 358	242 000	Nouméa	French, local languages	Roman Catholic, Protestant, Sunni Muslim	CFP franc*
Niue	Self-governing New Zealand Territory	258	100	2 000	Alofi	English, Niuean	Christian	New Zealand dollar
Norfolk Island	Australian External Territory	35	14	2 500	Kingston	English	Protestant, Roman Catholic	Australian Dollar
Northern Mariana Islands	United States Commonwealth	477	184	84 000	Capitol Hill	English, Chamorro, local languages	Roman Catholic	United States dollar
Pitcairn Islands	United Kingdom Overseas Territory	45	17	48	Adamstown	English	Protestant	New Zealand dollar
Tokelau	New Zealand Overseas Territory	10	4	1 000		English, Tokelauan	Christian	New Zealand dollar
Wallis and Futuna Islands	French Overseas Collectivity	274	106	15 000	Matā'utu	French, Wallisian, Futunian	Roman Catholic	CFP franc*

*Franc des Comptoirs Français du Pacifique

Aoraki (Mount Cook), New Zealand

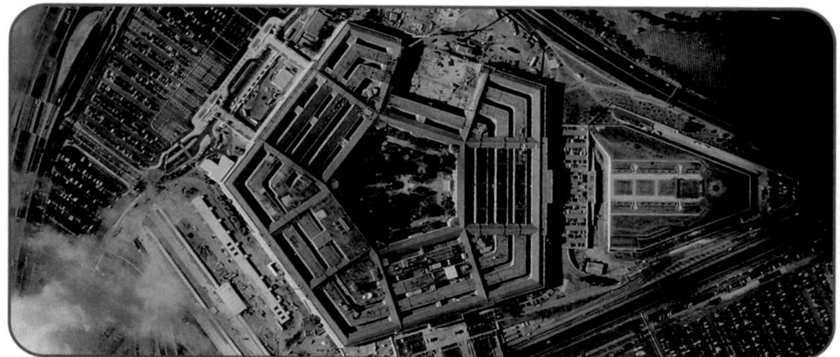

The Pentagon, Washington DC, USA

Cuba, Caribbean Sea

North America

North America	Area sq km	Area sq miles	Population	Capital	Languages	Religions	Currency
ANTIGUA AND BARBUDA	442	171	85 000	St John's	English, creole	Protestant, Roman Catholic	East Caribbean dollar
THE BAHAMAS	13 939	5 382	331 000	Nassau	English, creole	Protestant, Roman Catholic	Bahamian dollar
BARBADOS	430	166	294 000	Bridgetown	English, creole	Protestant, Roman Catholic	Barbados dollar
BELIZE	22 965	8 867	288 000	Belmopan	English, Spanish, Mayan, creole	Roman Catholic, Protestant	Belize dollar
CANADA	9 984 670	3 855 103	32 876 000	Ottawa	English, French, local languages	Roman Catholic, Protestant, Eastern Orthodox, Jewish	Canadian dollar
COSTA RICA	51 100	19 730	4 468 000	San José	Spanish	Roman Catholic, Protestant	Costa Rican colón
CUBA	110 860	42 803	11 268 000	Havana	Spanish	Roman Catholic, Protestant	Cuban peso
DOMINICA	750	290	67 000	Roseau	English, creole	Roman Catholic, Protestant	East Caribbean dollar
DOMINICAN REPUBLIC	48 442	18 704	9 760 000	Santo Domingo	Spanish, creole	Roman Catholic, Protestant	Dominican peso
EL SALVADOR	21 041	8 124	6 857 000	San Salvador	Spanish	Roman Catholic, Protestant	El Salvador colón, United States dollar
GRENADA	378	146	106 000	St George's	English, creole	Roman Catholic, Protestant	East Caribbean dollar
GUATEMALA	108 890	42 043	13 354 000	Guatemala City	Spanish, Mayan languages	Roman Catholic, Protestant	Quetzal, United States dollar
HAITI	27 750	10 714	9 598 000	Port-au-Prince	French, creole	Roman Catholic, Protestant, Voodoo	Gourde
HONDURAS	112 088	43 277	7 106 000	Tegucigalpa	Spanish, Amerindian languages	Roman Catholic, Protestant	Lempira
JAMAICA	10 991	4 244	2 714 000	Kingston	English, creole	Protestant, Roman Catholic	Jamaican dollar
MEXICO	1 972 545	761 604	106 535 000	Mexico City	Spanish, Amerindian languages	Roman Catholic, Protestant	Mexican peso
NICARAGUA	130 000	50 193	5 603 000	Managua	Spanish, Amerindian languages	Roman Catholic, Protestant	Córdoba
PANAMA	77 082	29 762	3 343 000	Panama City	Spanish, English, Amerindian languages	Roman Catholic, Protestant, Sunni Muslim	Balboa
ST KITTS AND NEVIS	261	101	50 000	Basseterre	English, creole	Protestant, Roman Catholic	East Caribbean dollar
ST LUCIA	616	238	165 000	Castries	English, creole	Roman Catholic, Protestant	East Caribbean dollar
ST VINCENT AND THE GRENADINES	389	150	120 000	Kingstown	English, creole	Protestant, Roman Catholic	East Caribbean dollar
TRINIDAD AND TOBAGO	5 130	1 981	1 333 000	Port of Spain	English, creole, Hindi	Roman Catholic, Hindu, Protestant, Sunni Muslim	Trinidad and Tobago dollar
UNITED STATES OF AMERICA	9 826 635	3 794 085	305 826 000	Washington DC	English, Spanish	Protestant, Roman Catholic, Sunni Muslim, Jewish	United States dollar

Dependent territories	Territorial status	Area sq km	Area sq miles	Population	Capital	Languages	Religions	Currency
Anguilla	United Kingdom Overseas Territory	155	60	13 000	The Valley	English	Protestant, Roman Catholic	East Caribbean dollar
Aruba	Self-governing Netherlands Territory	193	75	104 000	Oranjestad	Papiamento, Dutch, English	Roman Catholic, Protestant	Arubian florin
Bermuda	United Kingdom Overseas Territory	54	21	65 000	Hamilton	English	Protestant, Roman Catholic	Bermuda dollar
Cayman Islands	United Kingdom Overseas Territory	259	100	47 000	George Town	English	Protestant, Roman Catholic	Cayman Islands dollar
Greenland	Self-governing Danish Territory	2 175 600	840 004	58 000	Nuuk	Greenlandic, Danish	Protestant	Danish krone
Guadeloupe	French Overseas Department	1 780	687	445 000	Basse-Terre	French, creole	Roman Catholic	Euro
Martinique	French Overseas Department	1 079	417	399 000	Fort-de-France	French, creole	Roman Catholic, traditional beliefs	Euro
Montserrat	United Kingdom Overseas Territory	100	39	6 000	Brades	English	Protestant, Roman Catholic	East Caribbean dollar
Netherlands Antilles	Self-governing Netherlands Territory	800	309	192 000	Willemstad	Dutch, Papiamento, English	Roman Catholic, Protestant	Neth. Antilles guilder
Puerto Rico	United States Commonwealth	9 104	3 515	3 991 000	San Juan	Spanish, English	Roman Catholic, Protestant	United States dollar
St Pierre and Miquelon	French Territorial Collectivity	242	93	6 000	St-Pierre	French	Roman Catholic	Euro
Turks and Caicos Islands	United Kingdom Overseas Territory	430	166	26 000	Grand Turk	English	Protestant	United States dollar
Virgin Islands (U.K.)	United Kingdom Overseas Territory	153	59	23 000	Road Town	English	Protestant, Roman Catholic	United States dollar
Virgin Islands (U.S.A.)	United States Unincorporated Territory	352	136	111 000	Charlotte Amalie	English, Spanish	Protestant, Roman Catholic	United States dollar

South America

South America	Area sq km	Area sq miles	Population	Capital	Languages	Religions	Currency
ARGENTINA	2 766 889	1 068 302	39 531 000	Buenos Aires	Spanish, Italian, Amerindian languages	Roman Catholic, Protestant	Argentinian peso
BOLIVIA	1 098 581	424 164	9 525 000	La Paz/Sucre	Spanish, Quechua, Aymara	Roman Catholic, Protestant, Baha'i	Boliviano
BRAZIL	8 514 879	3 287 613	191 791 000	Brasília	Portuguese	Roman Catholic, Protestant	Real
CHILE	756 945	292 258	16 635 000	Santiago	Spanish, Amerindian languages	Roman Catholic, Protestant	Chilean peso
COLOMBIA	1 141 748	440 831	46 156 000	Bogotá	Spanish, Amerindian languages	Roman Catholic, Protestant	Colombian peso
ECUADOR	272 045	105 037	13 341 000	Quito	Spanish, Quechua, other Amerindian languages	Roman Catholic	US dollar
GUYANA	214 969	83 000	738 000	Georgetown	English, creole, Amerindian languages	Protestant, Hindu, Roman Catholic, Sunni Muslim	Guyana dollar
PARAGUAY	406 752	157 048	6 127 000	Asunción	Spanish, Guaraní	Roman Catholic, Protestant	Guaraní
PERU	1 285 216	496 225	27 903 000	Lima	Spanish, Quechua, Aymara	Roman Catholic, Protestant	Sol
SURINAME	163 820	63 251	458 000	Paramaribo	Dutch, Surinamese, English, Hindi	Hindu, Roman Catholic, Protestant, Sunni Muslim	Suriname guilder
URUGUAY	176 215	68 037	3 340 000	Montevideo	Spanish	Roman Catholic, Protestant, Jewish	Uruguayan peso
VENEZUELA	912 050	352 144	27 657 000	Caracas	Spanish, Amerindian languages	Roman Catholic, Protestant	Bolívar fuerte

Dependent territories	Territorial status	Area sq km	Area sq miles	Population	Capital	Languages	Religions	Currency
Falkland Islands	United Kingdom Overseas Territory	12 170	4 699	3 000	Stanley	English	Protestant, Roman Catholic	Falkland Islands pound
French Guiana	French Overseas Department	90 000	34 749	202 000	Cayenne	French, creole	Roman Catholic	Euro

World
Countries

The current pattern of the world's countries and territories is a result of a long history of exploration, colonialism, conflict and politics. The fact that there are currently 195 independent countries in the world – the most recent, Kosovo, only being created in February 2008 – illustrates the significant political changes which have occurred since 1950 when there were only eighty-two. There has been a steady progression away from colonial influences over the last fifty years, although many dependent overseas territories remain.

The shapes of countries and the pattern of international boundaries reflect both physical and political processes. Some borders follow natural features – rivers, mountain ranges, etc – others are defined according to political agreement or as a result of war. Some are still subject to dispute between two or more countries, and many remain undefined on the ground.

Facts

- The longest single continuous land border stretches for 6 416 kilometres between Canada and the USA
- Both China and the Russian Federation have land borders with 14 different countries
- Vatican City, the smallest independent country, was created in 1929 as an enclave within Rome, the capital of Italy
- All countries of the world are members of the United Nations except Kosovo, Taiwan and Vatican City

Internet Links

United Nations	**www.un.org**
Foreign and Commonwealth Office	**www.fco.gov.uk**
International Boundaries Research Unit	**www.dur.ac.uk/ibru**
Permanent Committee on Geographical Names	**www.pcgn.org.uk**
U.S. Board on Geographic Names	**geonames.usgs.gov**

Abbreviation Key

A.	ANDORRA	HUN.	HUNGARY	R.F.	RUSSIAN FEDERATION
AL.	ALBANIA	ISR.	ISRAEL	ROM.	ROMANIA
ARM.	ARMENIA	JOR.	JORDAN	S.	SERBIA
AUST.	AUSTRIA	K.	KOSOVO	SL.	SLOVENIA
AZER.	AZERBAIJAN	L.	LUXEMBOURG	SLA.	SLOVAKIA
B.	BURUNDI	LAT.	LATVIA	SUR.	SURINAME
BE.	BENIN	LEB.	LEBANON	SW.	SWITZERLAND
BEL.	BELGIUM	LITH.	LITHUANIA	T.	TOGO
B.H.	BOSNIA-HERZEGOVINA	M.	MONTENEGRO	TAJIK.	TAJIKISTAN
BULG.	BULGARIA	MA.	MACEDONIA	TURKM.	TURKMENISTAN
CR.	CROATIA	MOL.	MOLDOVA	U.A.E.	UNITED ARAB EMIRATES
CZ.R.	CZECH REPUBLIC	NETH.	NETHERLANDS	U.K.	UNITED KINGDOM
EST.	ESTONIA	N.Z.	NEW ZEALAND	U.S.A.	UNITED STATES OF AMERICA
GEOR.	GEORGIA	R.	RWANDA	UZBEK.	UZBEKISTAN

Geo Eye

High-resolution satellite image of **Vatican City**, the world's smallest country by both population and area.

World extremes

Countries			
Largest country (area)	**Russian Federation**	17 075 400 sq km	6 592 849 sq miles
Smallest country (area)	**Vatican City**	0.5 sq km	0.2 sq miles
Largest country (population)	**China**	1 313 437 000	
Smallest country (population)	**Vatican City**	557	
Most densely populated country	**Monaco**	17 500 per sq km	35 000 per sq mile
Least densely populated country	**Mongolia**	1.7 per sq km	4.4 per sq mile
Capitals			
Largest national capital (population)	**Tōkyō, Japan**	35 676 000	
Smallest national capital (population)	**Melekeok, Palau**	391	
Most northerly national capital	**Reykjavík, Iceland**	64° 08'N	
Most southerly national capital	**Wellington, New Zealand**	41° 18'S	
Highest national capital	**La Paz, Bolivia**	3 636 m	11 910 ft

World
Landscapes

The Earth's physical features, both on land and on the sea bed, closely reflect its geological structure. The current shapes of the continents and oceans have evolved over millions of years. Movements of the tectonic plates which make up the Earth's crust have created some of the best-known and most spectacular features. The processes which have shaped the Earth continue today with earthquakes, volcanoes, erosion, climatic variations and man's activities all affecting the Earth's landscapes.

The total topographic range of the Earth's surface is nearly 20 000 metres, from the highest point Mount Everest, to the lowest point in the Mariana Trench. Major mountain ranges include the Himalaya, the Andes and the Rocky Mountains, each of which give rise to some of the world's greatest rivers. In contrast, the deserts of the Sahara, Australia, the Arabian Peninsula and the Gobi cover vast areas and each provide unique landscapes.

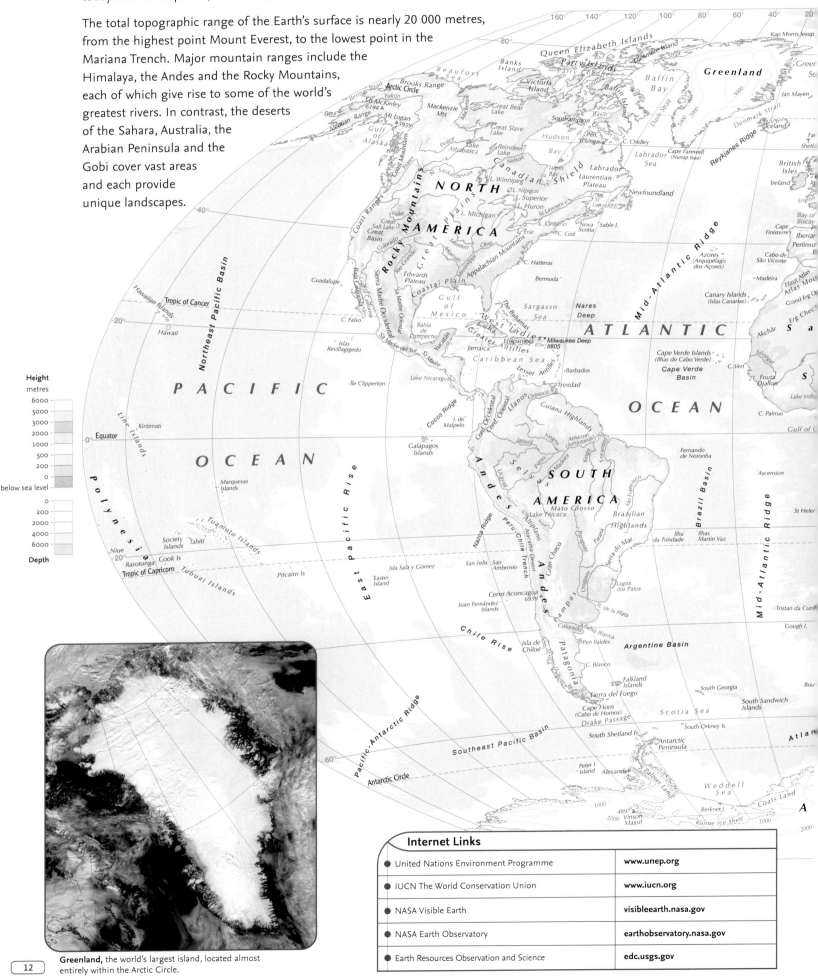

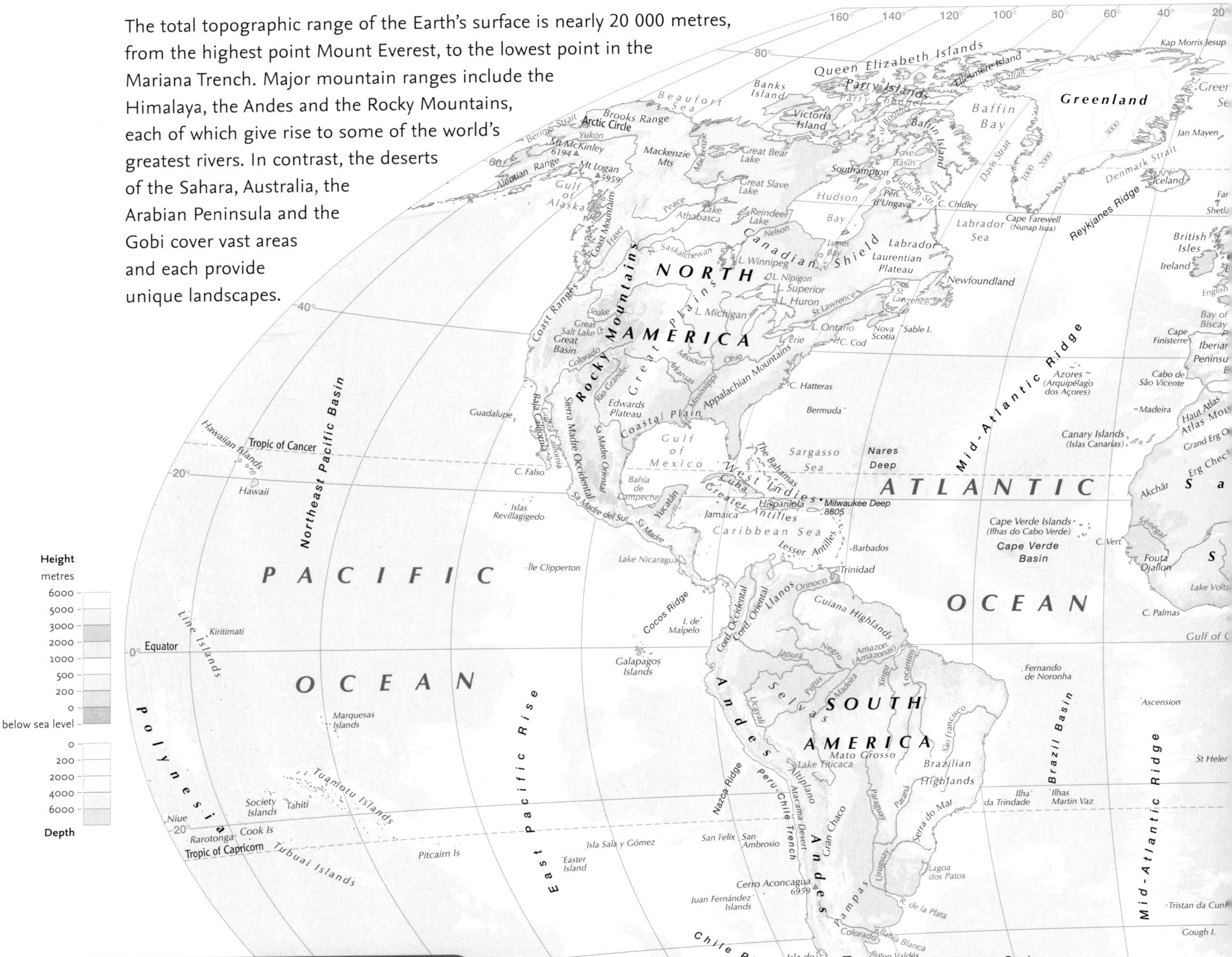

Height
metres
6000
5000
3000
2000
1000
500
200
0
below sea level
0
200
2000
4000
6000
Depth

Greenland, the world's largest island, located almost entirely within the Arctic Circle.

Internet Links	
United Nations Environment Programme	**www.unep.org**
IUCN The World Conservation Union	**www.iucn.org**
NASA Visible Earth	**visibleearth.nasa.gov**
NASA Earth Observatory	**earthobservatory.nasa.gov**
Earth Resources Observation and Science	**edc.usgs.gov**

Earth's dimensions

Mass	5.974 x 10^{21} tonnes
Total area	509 450 000 sq km / 196 698 645 sq miles
Land area	149 450 000 sq km / 57 702 645 sq miles
Water area	360 000 000 sq km / 138 996 000 sq miles
Volume	1 083 207 x 10^{6} cubic km / 259 911 x 10^{6} cubic miles
Equatorial diameter	12 756 km / 7 927 miles
Polar diameter	12 714 km / 7 901 miles
Equatorial circumference	40 075 km / 24 903 miles
Meridional circumference	40 008 km / 24 861 miles

Facts

- Approximately 10% of the Earth's land surface is permanently covered by ice
- The Pacific Ocean is larger than all the continents' land areas combined
- The world's highest waterfall, 979 metres high, is Angel Falls, Venezuela
- 52% of the Earth's land surface is below 500 metres
- The mean elevation of the Earth's land surface is 840 metres
- Lake Baikal is the world's deepest lake with a maximum depth of 1 741 metres

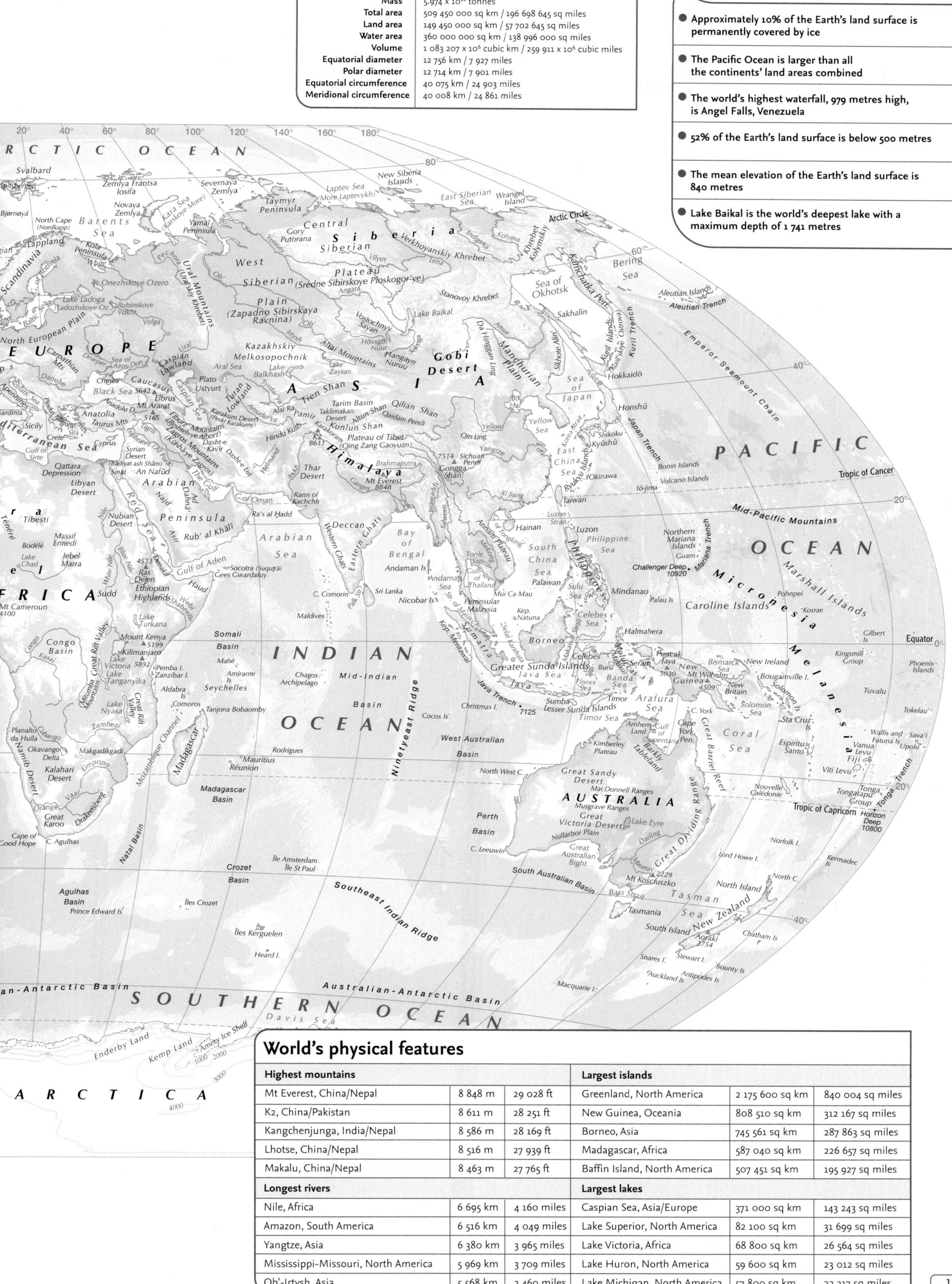

World's physical features

Highest mountains			Largest islands		
Mt Everest, China/Nepal	8 848 m	29 028 ft	Greenland, North America	2 175 600 sq km	840 004 sq miles
K2, China/Pakistan	8 611 m	28 251 ft	New Guinea, Oceania	808 510 sq km	312 167 sq miles
Kangchenjunga, India/Nepal	8 586 m	28 169 ft	Borneo, Asia	745 561 sq km	287 863 sq miles
Lhotse, China/Nepal	8 516 m	27 939 ft	Madagascar, Africa	587 040 sq km	226 657 sq miles
Makalu, China/Nepal	8 463 m	27 765 ft	Baffin Island, North America	507 451 sq km	195 927 sq miles
Longest rivers			**Largest lakes**		
Nile, Africa	6 695 km	4 160 miles	Caspian Sea, Asia/Europe	371 000 sq km	143 243 sq miles
Amazon, South America	6 516 km	4 049 miles	Lake Superior, North America	82 100 sq km	31 699 sq miles
Yangtze, Asia	6 380 km	3 965 miles	Lake Victoria, Africa	68 800 sq km	26 564 sq miles
Mississippi-Missouri, North America	5 969 km	3 709 miles	Lake Huron, North America	59 600 sq km	23 012 sq miles
Ob'-Irtysh, Asia	5 568 km	3 460 miles	Lake Michigan, North America	57 800 sq km	22 317 sq miles

World

Earthquakes and Volcanoes

Earthquakes and volcanoes hold a constant fascination because of their power, their beauty, and the fact that they cannot be controlled or accurately predicted. Our understanding of these phenomena relies mainly on the theory of plate tectonics. This defines the Earth's surface as a series of 'plates' which are constantly moving relative to each other, at rates of a few centimetres per year. As plates move against each other enormous pressure builds up and when the rocks can no longer bear this pressure they fracture, and energy is released as an earthquake. The pressures involved can also melt the rock to form magma which then rises to the Earth's surface to form a volcano. The distribution of earthquakes and volcanoes therefore relates closely to plate boundaries. In particular, most active volcanoes and much of the Earth's seismic activity are centred on the 'Ring of Fire' around the Pacific Ocean.

Facts

- Over 900 earthquakes of magnitude 5.0 or greater occur every year
- An earthquake of magnitude 8.0 releases energy equivalent to 1 billion tons of TNT explosive
- Ground shaking during an earthquake in Alaska in 1964 lasted for 3 minutes
- Indonesia has more than 120 volcanoes and over 30% of the world's active volcanoes
- Volcanoes can produce very fertile soil and important industrial materials and chemicals

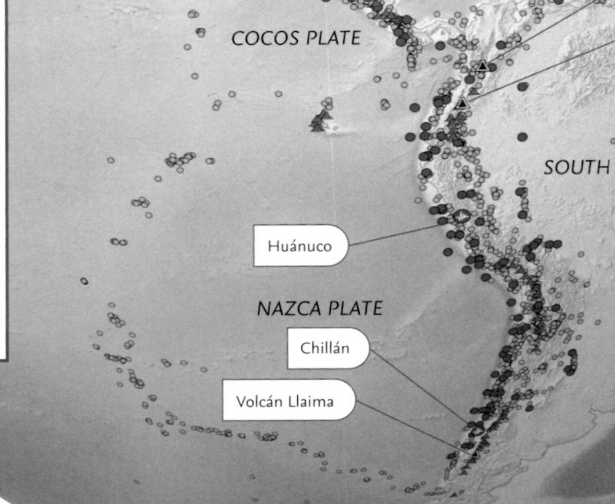

Earthquakes

Earthquakes are caused by movement along fractures or 'faults' in the Earth's crust, particularly along plate boundaries. There are three types of plate boundary: constructive boundaries where plates are moving apart; destructive boundaries where two or more plates collide; conservative boundaries where plates slide past each other. Destructive and conservative boundaries are the main sources of earthquake activity.

The epicentre of an earthquake is the point on the Earth's surface directly above its source. If this is near to large centres of population, and the earthquake is powerful, major devastation can result. The size, or magnitude, of an earthquake is generally measured on the Richter Scale.

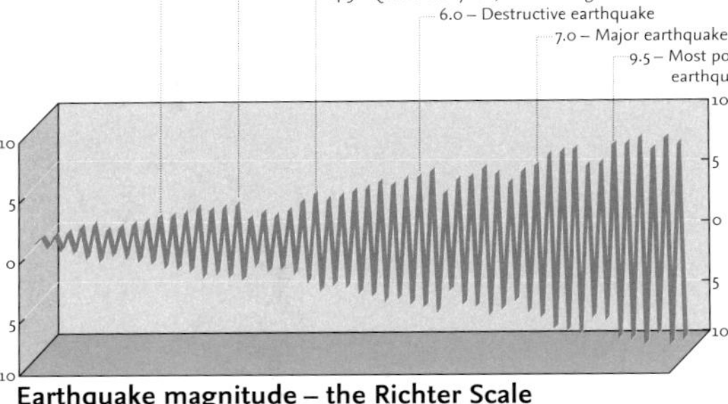

Earthquake magnitude – the Richter Scale

The scale measures the energy released by an earthquake. It is a logarithmic scale: an earthquake measuring 5 is thirty times more powerful than one measuring 4.

Plate boundaries

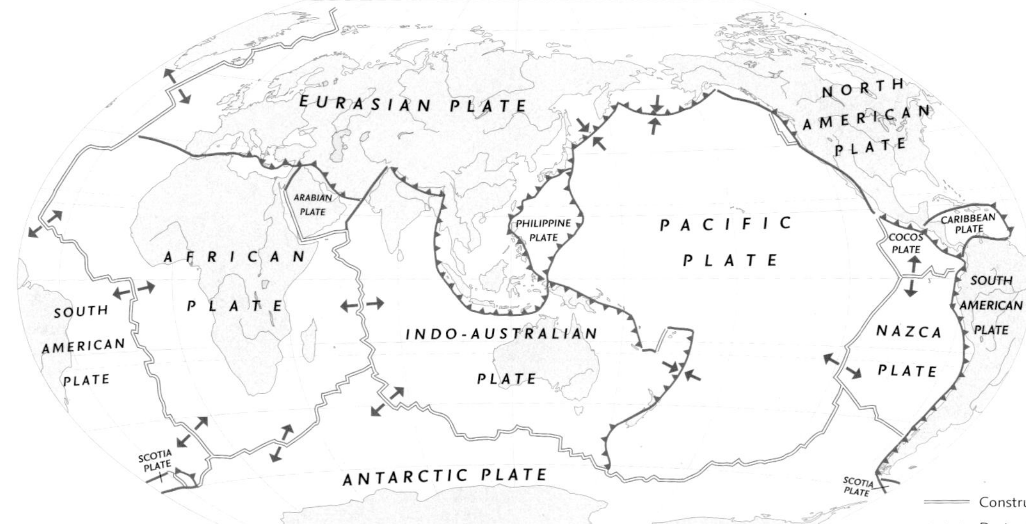

Volcanoes

The majority of volcanoes occur along destructive plate boundaries in the 'subduction zone' where one plate passes under another. The friction and pressure causes the rock to melt and to form magma which is forced upwards to the Earth's surface where it erupts as molten rock (lava) or as particles of ash or cinder. This process created the numerous volcanoes in the Andes, where the Nazca Plate is passing under the South American Plate. Volcanoes can be defined by the nature of the material they emit. 'Shield' volcanoes have extensive, gentle slopes formed from free-flowing lava, while steep-sided 'continental' volcanoes are created from thicker, slow-flowing lava and ash.

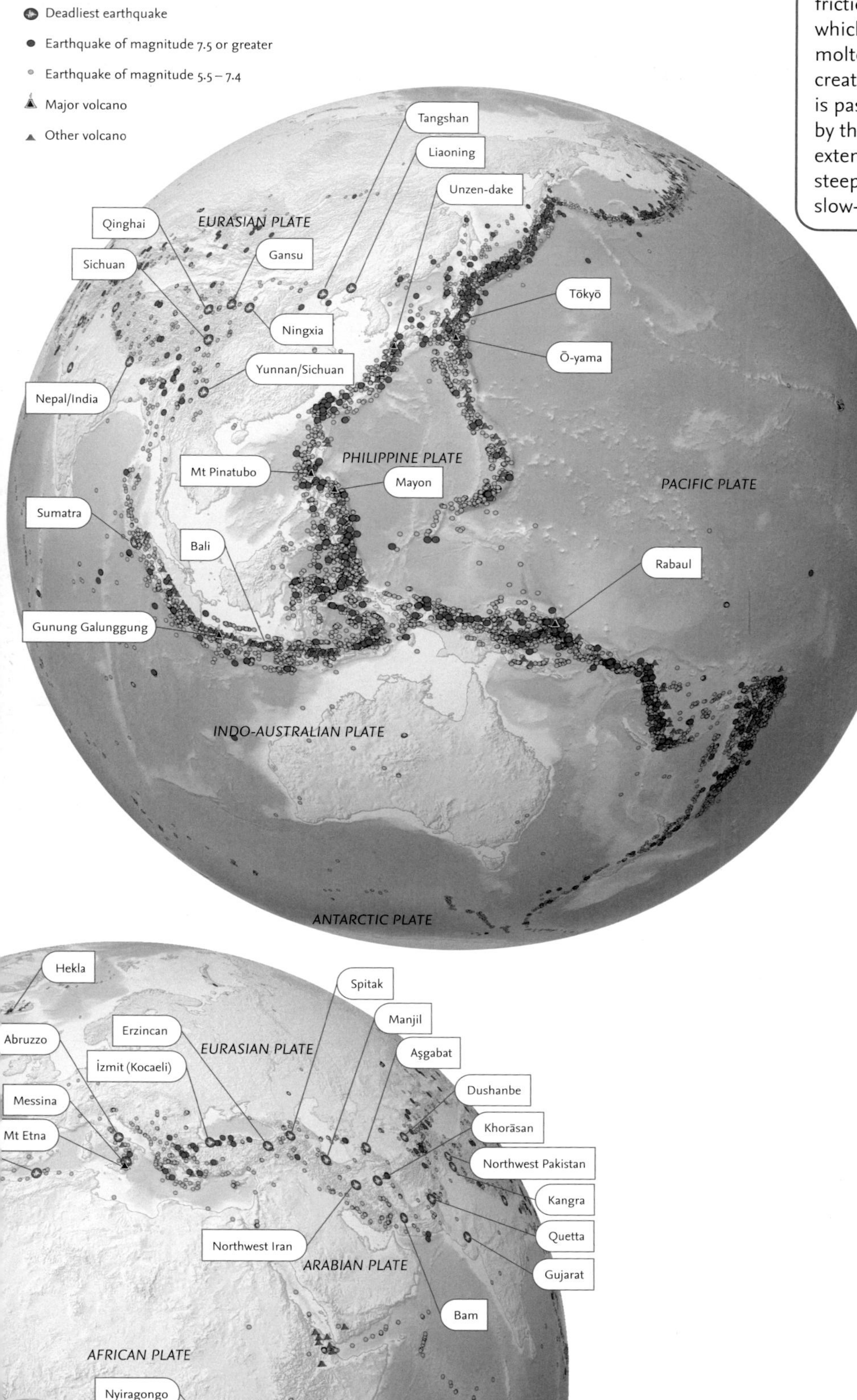

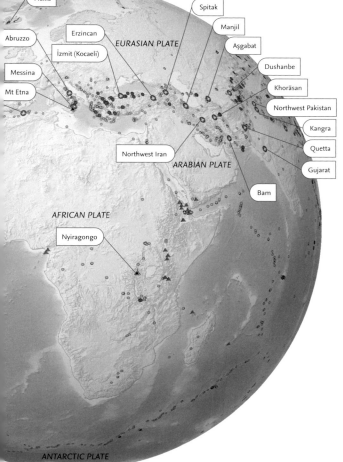

Major volcanic eruptions since 1980

Volcano	Country	Date
Mt St Helens	USA	1980
El Chichónal	Mexico	1982
Gunung Galunggung	Indonesia	1982
Kilauea	Hawaii, USA	1983
Ō-yama	Japan	1983
Nevado del Ruiz	Colombia	1985
Mt Pinatubo	Philippines	1991
Unzen-dake	Japan	1991
Mayon	Philippines	1993
Volcán Galeras	Colombia	1993
Volcán Llaima	Chile	1994
Rabaul	Papua New Guinea	1994
Soufrière Hills	Montserrat	1997
Hekla	Iceland	2000
Mt Etna	Italy	2001
Nyiragongo	Democratic Republic of the Congo	2002

Deadliest earthquakes since 1900

Year	Location	Deaths
1905	**Kangra,** India	19 000
1907	west of **Dushanbe,** Tajikistan	12 000
1908	**Messina,** Italy	110 000
1915	**Abruzzo,** Italy	35 000
1917	**Bali,** Indonesia	15 000
1920	**Ningxia Province,** China	200 000
1923	**Tōkyō,** Japan	142 807
1927	**Qinghai Province,** China	200 000
1932	**Gansu Province,** China	70 000
1933	**Sichuan Province,** China	10 000
1934	**Nepal/India**	10 700
1935	**Quetta,** Pakistan	30 000
1939	**Chillán,** Chile	28 000
1939	**Erzincan,** Turkey	32 700
1948	**Aşgabat,** Turkmenistan	19 800
1962	northwest **Iran**	12 225
1970	**Huánuco Province,** Peru	66 794
1974	**Yunnan** and **Sichuan Provinces,** China	20 000
1975	**Liaoning Province,** China	10 000
1976	central **Guatemala**	22 778
1976	**Tangshan,** Hebei Province, China	255 000
1978	**Khorāsan Province,** Iran	20 000
1980	**Chlef,** Algeria	11 000
1988	**Spitak,** Armenia	25 000
1990	**Manjil,** Iran	50 000
1999	**İzmit (Kocaeli),** Turkey	17 000
2001	**Gujarat,** India	20 000
2003	**Bam,** Iran	26 271
2004	off **Sumatra,** Indian Ocean	225 000
2005	northwest **Pakistan**	74 648
2008	**Sichuan Province,** China	> 60 000

Internet Links

USGS National Earthquake Hazards Program	**earthquake.usgs.gov/regional/neic**
USGS Volcano Hazards Program	**volcanoes.usgs.gov**
British Geological Survey	**www.bgs.ac.uk**
NASA Natural Hazards	**earthobservatory.nasa.gov/NaturalHazards**
Volcano World	**volcano.und.nodak.edu**

World

Climate and Weather

The climate of a region is defined by its long-term prevailing weather conditions. Classification of Climate Types is based on the relationship between temperature and humidity and how these factors are affected by latitude, altitude, ocean currents and winds. Weather is the specific short term condition which occurs locally and consists of events such as thunderstorms, hurricanes, blizzards and heat waves. Temperature and rainfall data recorded at weather stations can be plotted graphically and the graphs shown here, typical of each climate region, illustrate the various combinations of temperature and rainfall which exist worldwide for each month of the year. Data used for climate graphs are based on average monthly figures recorded over a minimum period of thirty years.

World Statistics: see pages **154–160**

Major climate regions, ocean currents and sea surface temperatures

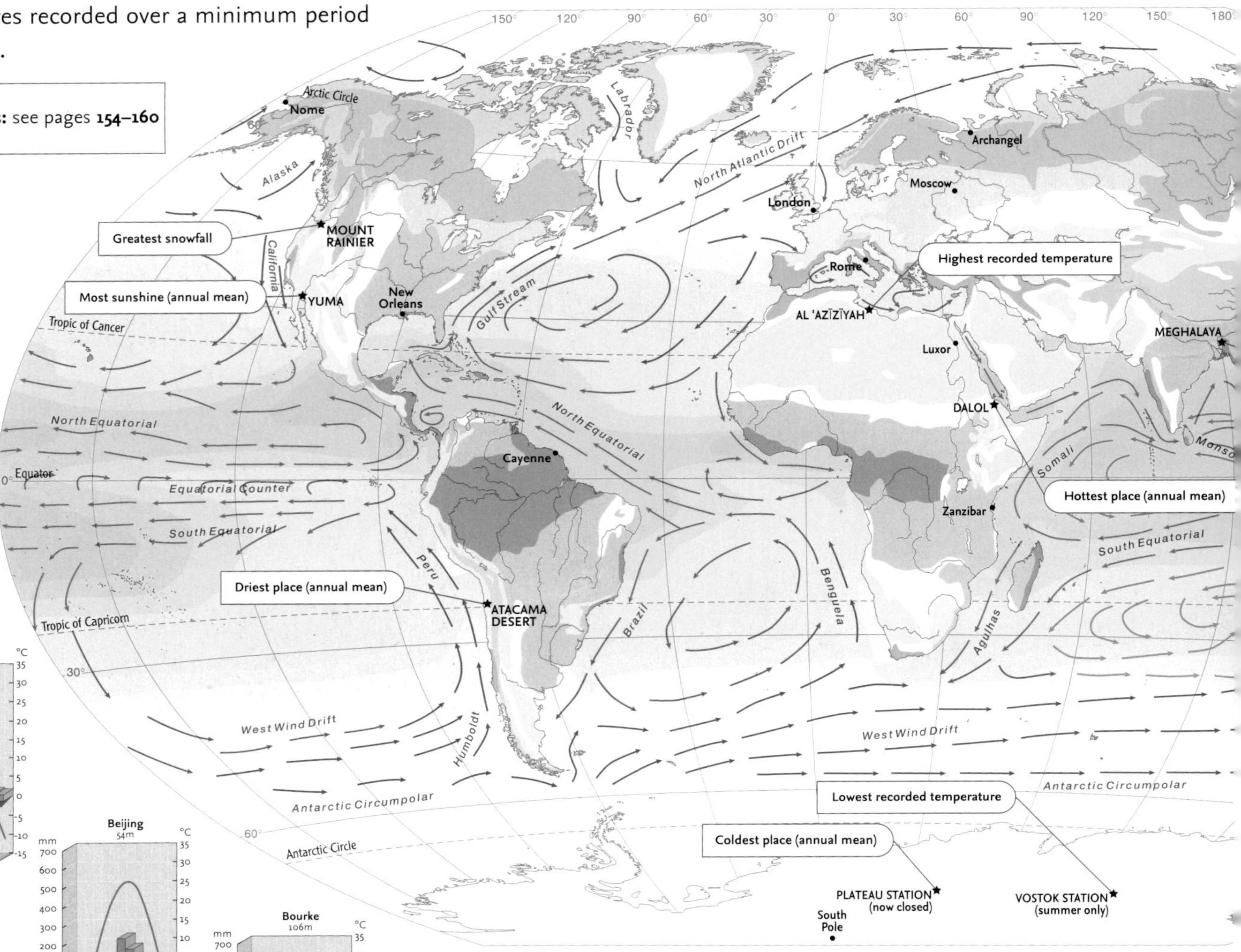

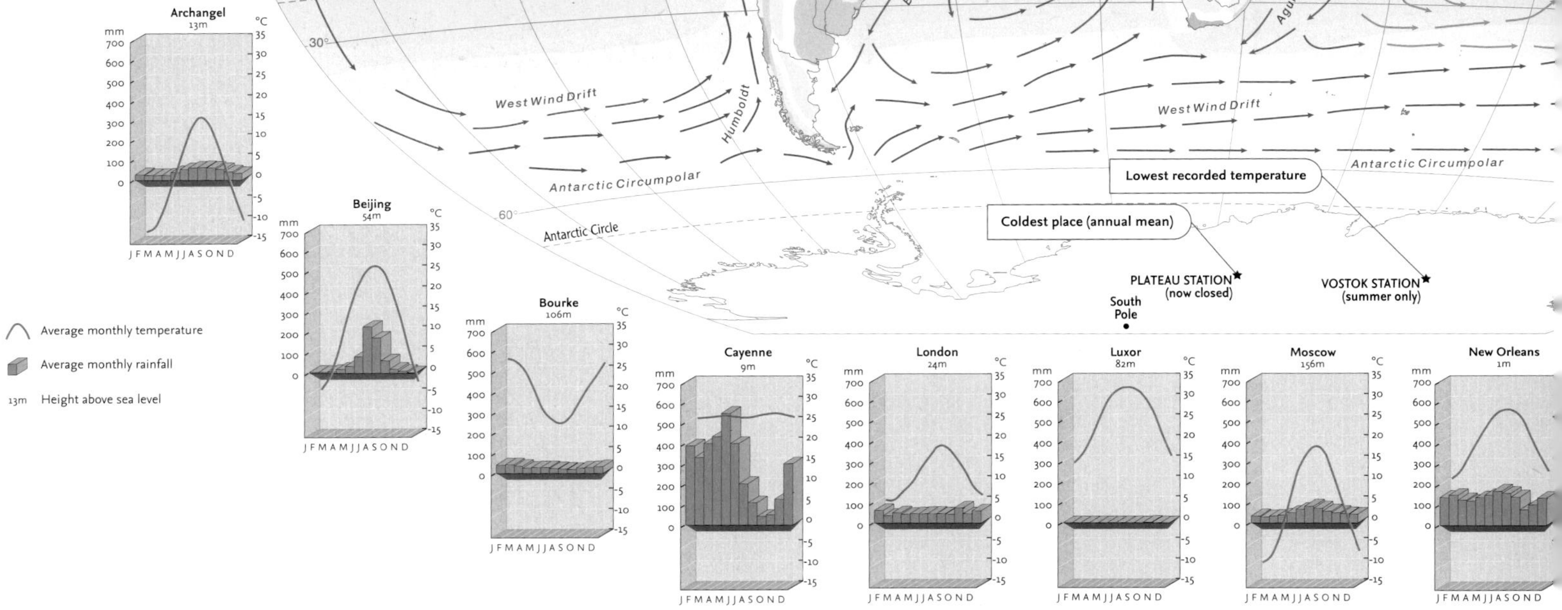

Average monthly temperature

Average monthly rainfall

13m Height above sea level

Climate change

In 2004 the global mean temperature was over 0.6°C higher than that at the end of the nineteenth century. Most of this warming is caused by human activities which result in a build-up of greenhouse gases, mainly carbon dioxide, allowing heat to be trapped within the atmosphere. Carbon dioxide emissions have increased since the beginning of the industrial revolution due to burning of fossil fuels, increased urbanization, population growth, deforestation and industrial pollution.

Annual climate indicators such as number of frost-free days, length of growing season, heat wave frequency, number of wet days, length of dry spells and frequency of weather extremes are used to monitor climate change. The map opposite shows how future changes in temperature will not be spread evenly around the world. Some regions will warm faster than the global average, while others will warm more slowly.

Facts

- Arctic Sea ice thickness has declined 40% in the last 40 years
- El Niño and La Niña episodes occur at irregular intervals of 2–7 years
- Sea levels are rising by one centimetre per decade
- Precipitation in the northern hemisphere is increasing
- Droughts have increased in frequency and intensity in parts of Asia and Africa

Projection of global temperatures 2090–2099

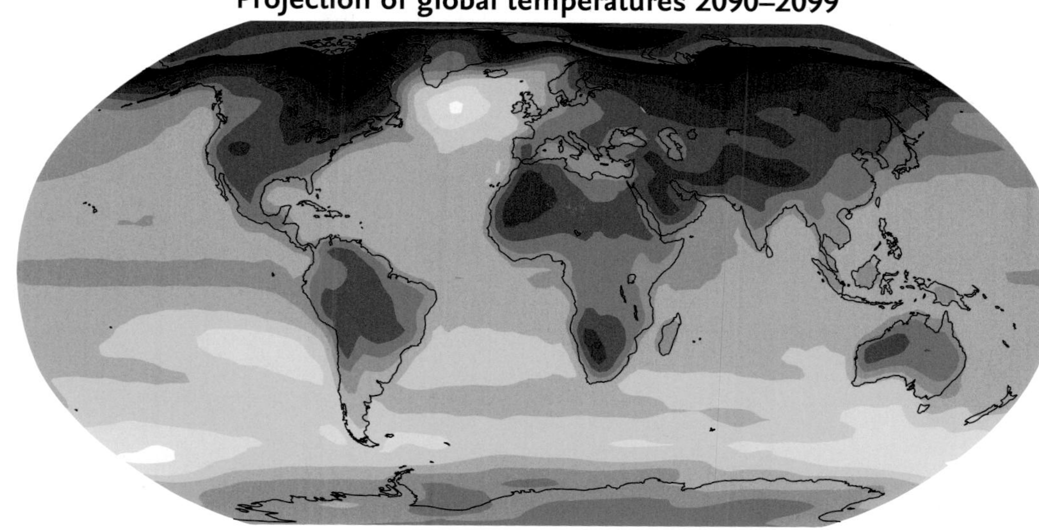

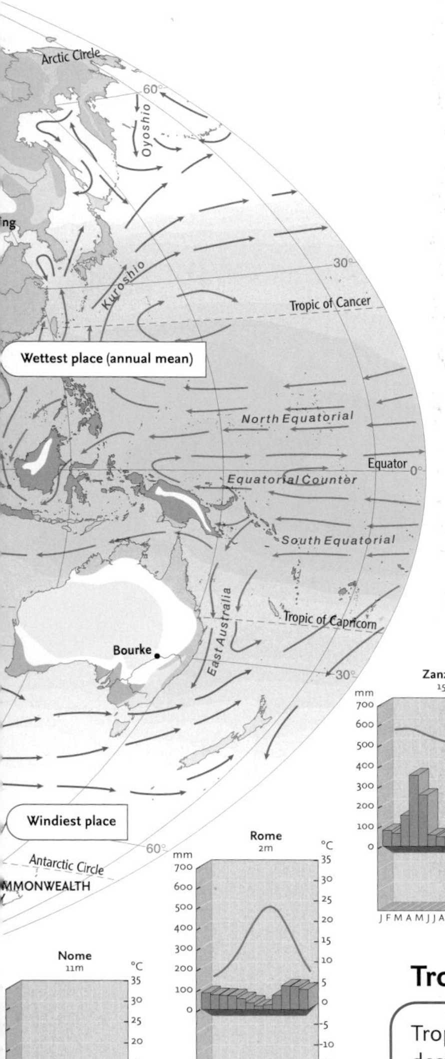

Tracks of tropical storms

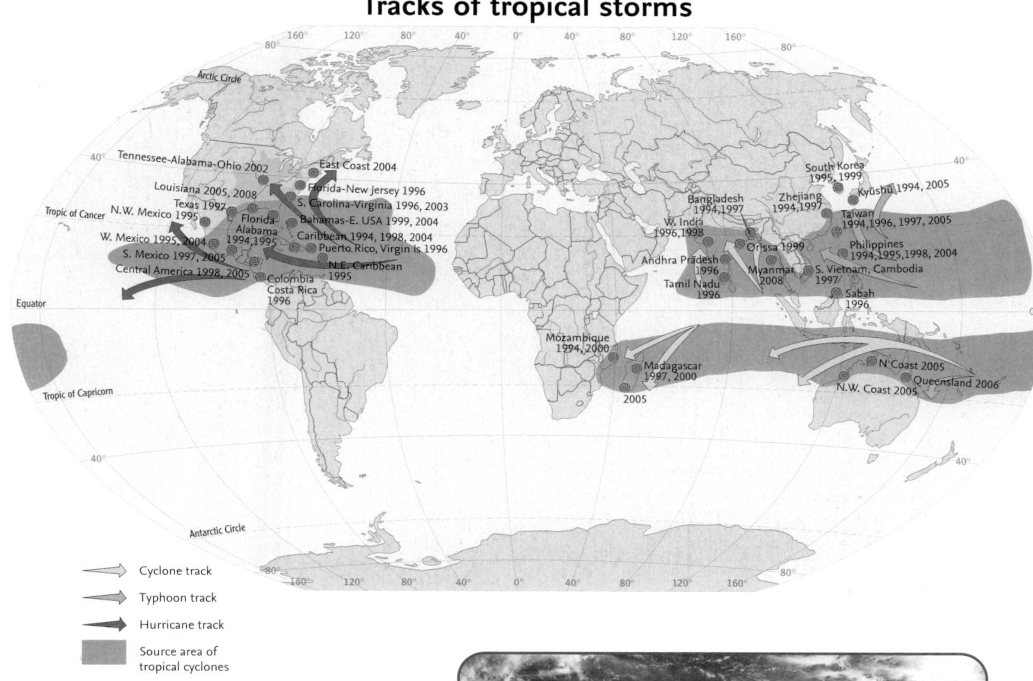

Tropical storms

Tropical storms are among the most powerful and destructive weather systems on Earth. Of the eighty to one hundred which develop annually over the tropical oceans, many make landfall and cause considerable damage to property and loss of life as a result of high winds and heavy rain. Although the number of tropical storms is projected to decrease, their intensity, and therefore their destructive power, is likely to increase.

Tropical storm Dina, January 2002.

Weather extremes

Highest recorded temperature	**57.8°C/136°F** Al'Azīzīyah, Libya (September 1922)
Hottest place - annual mean	**34.4°C/93.9°F** Dalol, Ethiopia
Driest place - annual mean	**0.1mm/0.004 inches** Atacama Desert, Chile
Most sunshine - annual mean	**90%** Yuma, Arizona, USA (over 4000 hours)
Lowest recorded temperature	**-89.2°C/-128.6°F** Vostok Station, Antarctica (July 1983)
Coldest place - annual mean	**-56.6°C/-69.9°F** Plateau Station, Antarctica
Wettest place annual mean	**11 873 mm/467.4 inches** Meghalaya, India
Greatest snowfall	**31 102 mm/1 224.5 inches** Mount Rainier, Washington, USA (February 1971 – February 1972)
Windiest place	**322 km per hour/200 miles per hour** (in gales) Commonwealth Bay, Antarctica

Internet Links

Met Office	**www.metoffice.gov.uk**
BBC Weather Centre	**www.bbc.co.uk/weather**
National Oceanic and Atmospheric Administration	**www.noaa.gov**
National Climatic Data Center	**www.ncdc.noaa.gov**
United Nations World Meteorological Organization	**www.wmo.ch**

World

Land Cover

The oxygen- and water-rich environment of the Earth has helped create a wide range of habitats. Forest and woodland ecosystems form the predominant natural land cover over most of the Earth's surface. Tropical rainforests are part of an intricate land-atmosphere relationship that is disturbed by land cover changes. Forests in the tropics are believed to hold most of the world's bird, animal, and plant species. Grassland, shrubland and deserts collectively cover most of the unwooded land surface, with tundra on frozen subsoil at high northern latitudes. These areas tend to have lower species diversity than most forests, with the notable exception of Mediterranean shrublands, which support some of the most diverse floras on the Earth. Humans have extensively altered most grassland and shrubland areas, usually through conversion to agriculture, burning and introduction of domestic livestock. They have had less immediate impact on tundra and true desert regions, although these remain vulnerable to global climate change.

World land cover

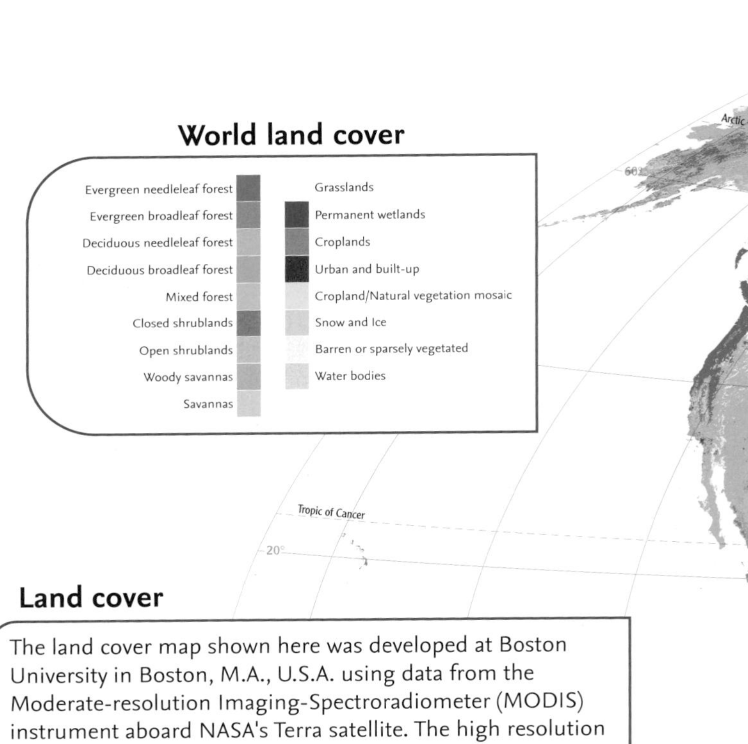

Land cover

The land cover map shown here was developed at Boston University in Boston, M.A., U.S.A. using data from the Moderate-resolution Imaging-Spectroradiometer (MODIS) instrument aboard NASA's Terra satellite. The high resolution (ground resolution of 1km) of the imagery used to compile the data set and map allows detailed interpretation of land cover patterns across the world. Important uses include managing forest resources, improving estimates of the Earth's water and energy cycles, and modelling climate change.

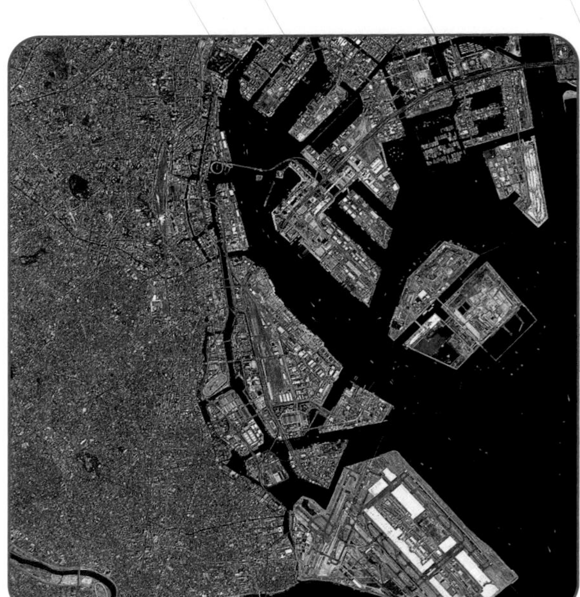

Urban, Tōkyō, capital of Japan and the largest city in the world.

Internet Links

World Resources Institute	**www.wri.org**
World Conservation Monitoring Centre	**www.unep-wcmc.org**
United Nations Environment Programme (UNEP)	**www.unep.org**
IUCN The World Conservation Union	**www.iucn.org**
Land Cover at Boston University	**www-modis.bu.edu/landcover/index.html**

Cropland, near Consuegra, Spain.

Barren/Shrubland, Mojave Desert, California, United States of America.

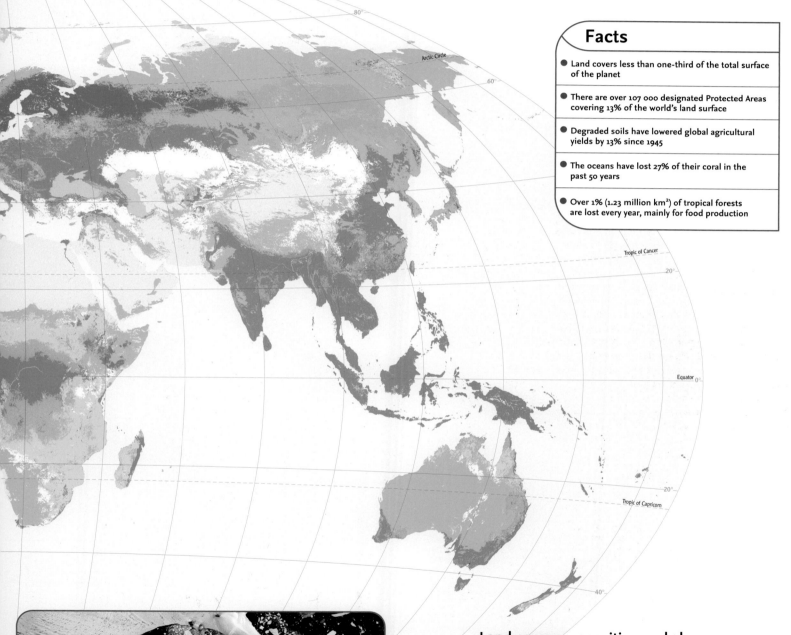

Facts

- Land covers less than one-third of the total surface of the planet
- There are over 107 000 designated Protected Areas covering 13% of the world's land surface
- Degraded soils have lowered global agricultural yields by 13% since 1945
- The oceans have lost 27% of their coral in the past 50 years
- Over 1% (1.23 million km²) of tropical forests are lost every year, mainly for food production

Land cover composition and change

The continents all have different characteristics. There are extensive croplands in North America and eastern Europe, while south of the Sahara are belts of grass/shrubland which are at risk from desertification. Tropical forests are not pristine areas either as they show signs of human activity in deforestation of land for crops or grazing.

Snow and ice, Larsen Ice Shelf, Antarctica.

World
Population

After increasing very slowly for most of human history, world population more than doubled in the last half century. Whereas world population did not pass the one billion mark until 1804 and took another 123 years to reach two billion in 1927, it then added the third billion in 33 years, the fourth in 14 years and the fifth in 13 years. Just twelve years later on October 12, 1999 the United Nations announced that the global population had reached the six billion mark. It is expected that another 2.5 billion people will have been added to the world's population by 2050.

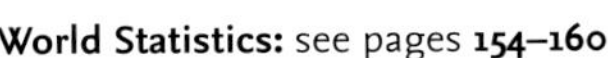

World Statistics: see pages **154–160**

World population distribution

Population density, continental populations (2005) and continental population change (2000–2005)

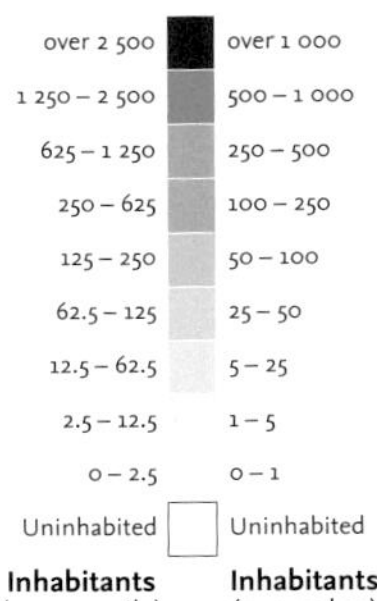

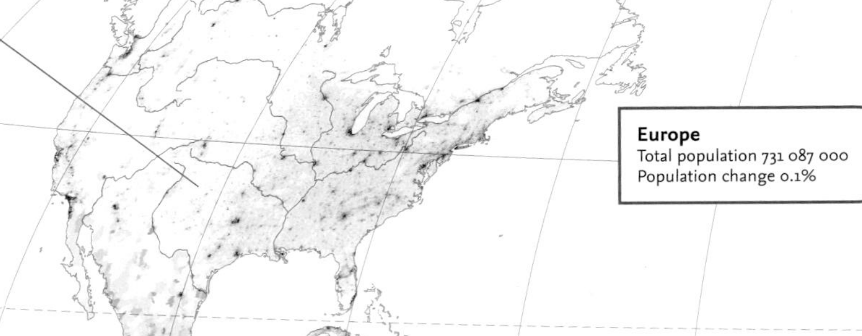

North America
Total population 332 245 000
Population change 1.0%

Europe
Total population 731 087 000
Population change 0.1%

Latin America and the Caribbean
Total population 557 979 000
Population change 1.3%

World
Total population 6 514 751 000
Population change 1.2%

World population change

Population growth since 1950 has been spread very unevenly between the continents. While overall numbers have been growing rapidly since 1950, a massive 89 per cent increase has taken place in the less developed regions, especially southern and eastern Asia. In contrast, Europe's population level has been almost stationary and is expected to decrease in the future. India and China alone are responsible for over one-third of current growth. Most of the highest rates of growth are to be found in Sub-Saharan Africa and, until population growth is brought under tighter control, the developing world in particular will continue to face enormous problems of supporting a rising population.

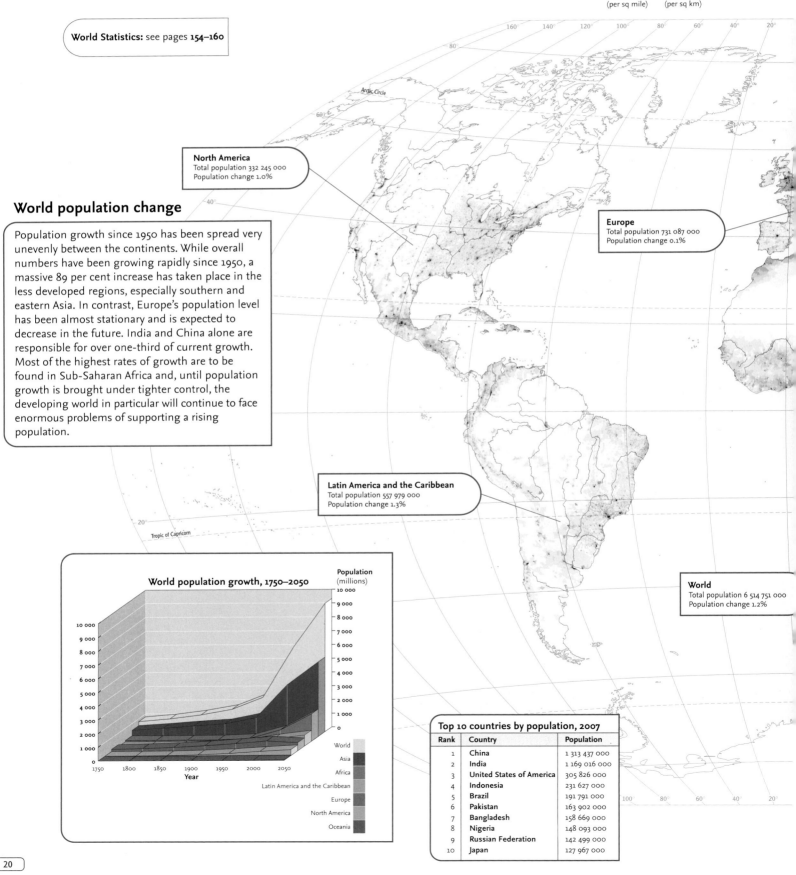

World population growth, 1750–2050

Population (millions): 0 – 10 000; Year: 1750, 1800, 1850, 1900, 1950, 2000, 2050

World, Asia, Africa, Latin America and the Caribbean, Europe, North America, Oceania

Top 10 countries by population, 2007

Rank	Country	Population
1	China	1 313 437 000
2	India	1 169 016 000
3	United States of America	305 826 000
4	Indonesia	231 627 000
5	Brazil	191 791 000
6	Pakistan	163 902 000
7	Bangladesh	158 669 000
8	Nigeria	148 093 000
9	Russian Federation	142 499 000
10	Japan	127 967 000

The island nation of **Singapore,** the world's second most densely populated country.

Kuna Indians inhabit this congested island off the north coast of Panama.

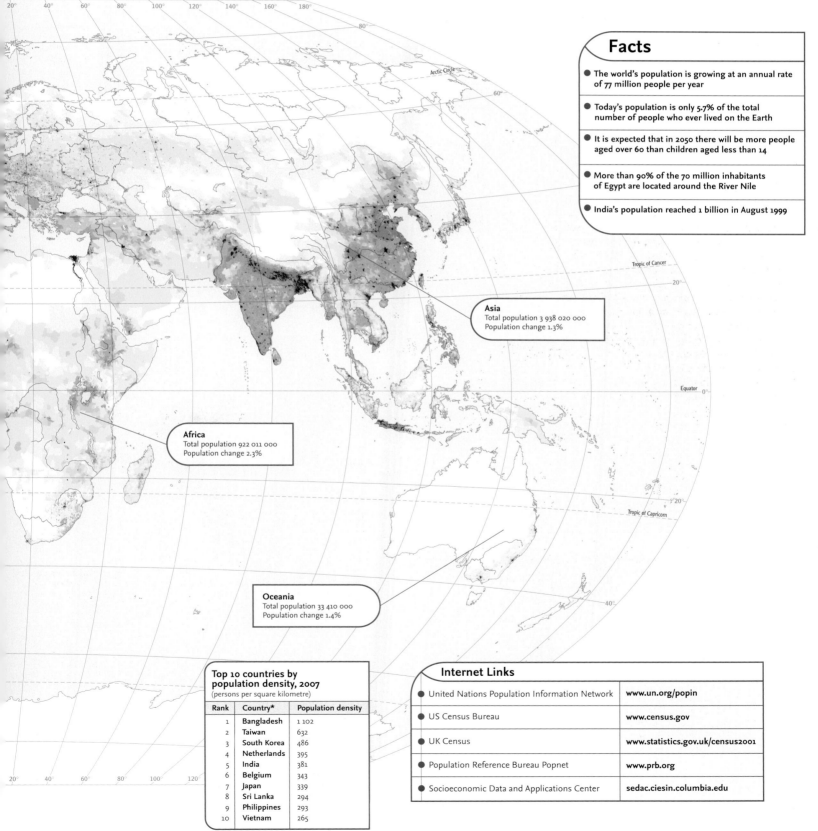

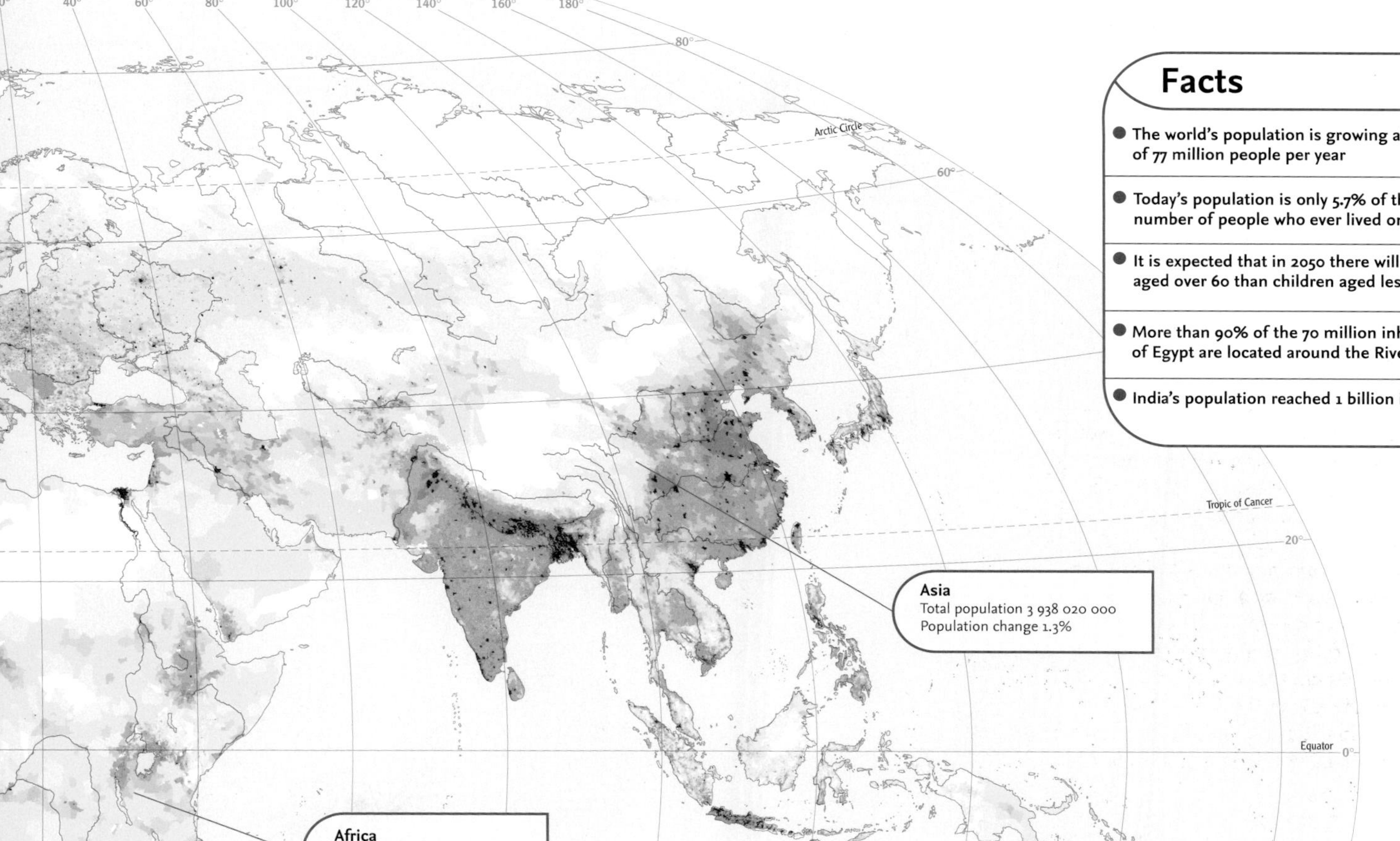

Facts

- The world's population is growing at an annual rate of 77 million people per year
- Today's population is only 5.7% of the total number of people who ever lived on the Earth
- It is expected that in 2050 there will be more people aged over 60 than children aged less than 14
- More than 90% of the 70 million inhabitants of Egypt are located around the River Nile
- India's population reached 1 billion in August 1999

Top 10 countries by population density, 2007

(persons per square kilometre)

Rank	Country*	Population density
1	Bangladesh	1 102
2	Taiwan	632
3	South Korea	486
4	Netherlands	395
5	India	381
6	Belgium	343
7	Japan	339
8	Sri Lanka	294
9	Philippines	293
10	Vietnam	265

*Only countries with a population of over 10 million are considered

Internet Links

United Nations Population Information Network	**www.un.org/popin**
US Census Bureau	**www.census.gov**
UK Census	**www.statistics.gov.uk/census2001**
Population Reference Bureau Popnet	**www.prb.org**
Socioeconomic Data and Applications Center	**sedac.ciesin.columbia.edu**

World

Urbanization and Cities

The world is becoming increasingly urban but the level of urbanization varies greatly between and within continents. At the beginning of the twentieth century only fourteen per cent of the world's population was urban and by 1950 this had increased to thirty per cent. In the more developed regions and in Latin America and the Caribbean over seventy per cent of the population is urban while in Africa and Asia the figure is forty per cent. In recent decades urban growth has increased rapidly to fifty per cent and there are now nearly 400 cities with over 1 000 000 inhabitants. It is in the developing regions that the most rapid increases are taking place and it is expected that by 2030 over half of urban dwellers worldwide will live in Asia. Migration from the countryside to the city in the search for better job opportunities is the main factor in urban growth.

World Statistics: see pages **154–160**

Characteristic high-rise urban development **Hong Kong,** China.

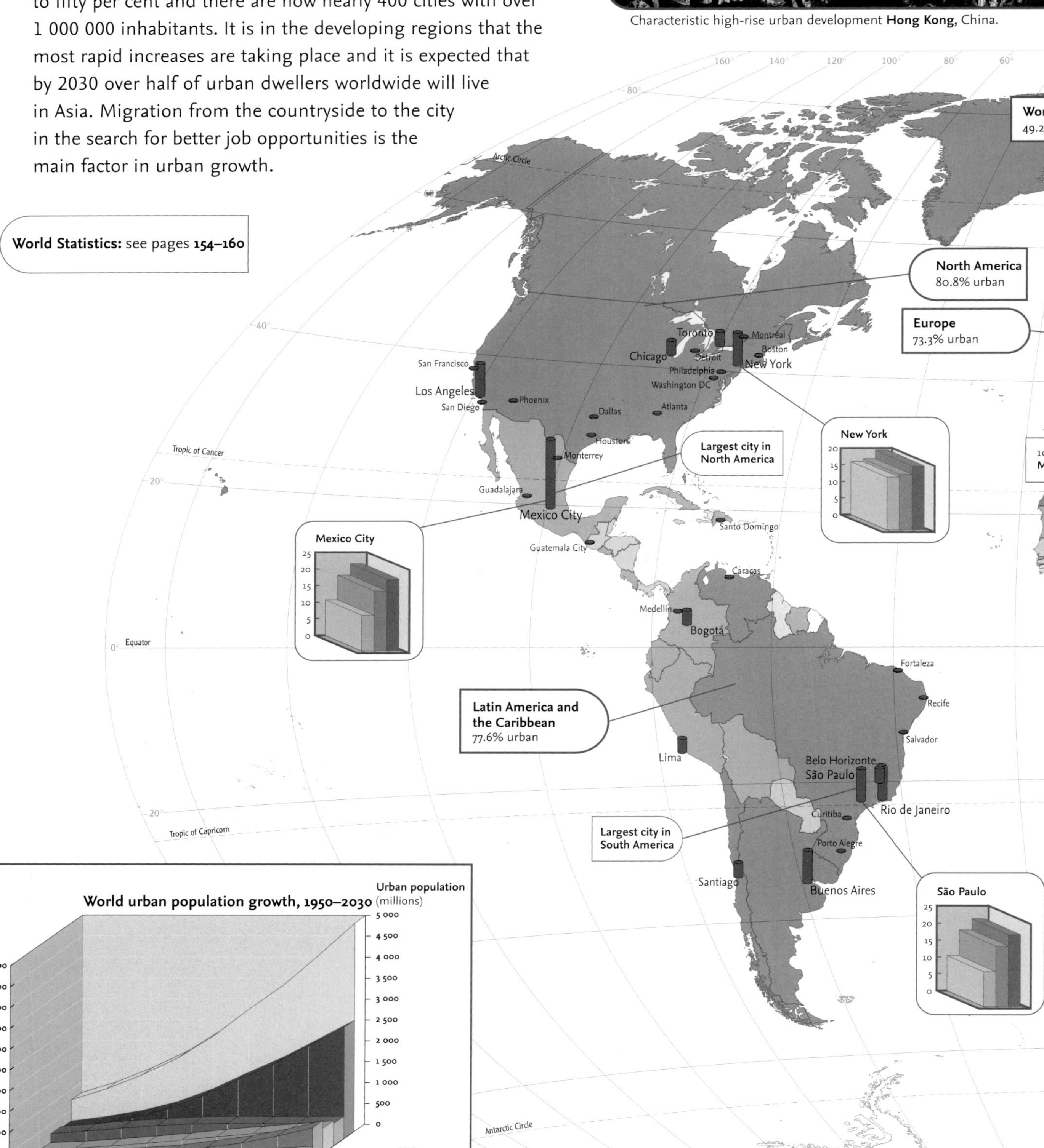

World urban population growth, 1950–2030

Urban population (millions)

0, 500, 1 000, 1 500, 2 000, 2 500, 3 000, 3 500, 4 000, 4 500, 5 000

Year: 1950, 1960, 1970, 1980, 1990, 2000, 2010, 2020, 2030

World
Asia
Europe
Latin America and the Caribbean
Africa
North America
Oceania

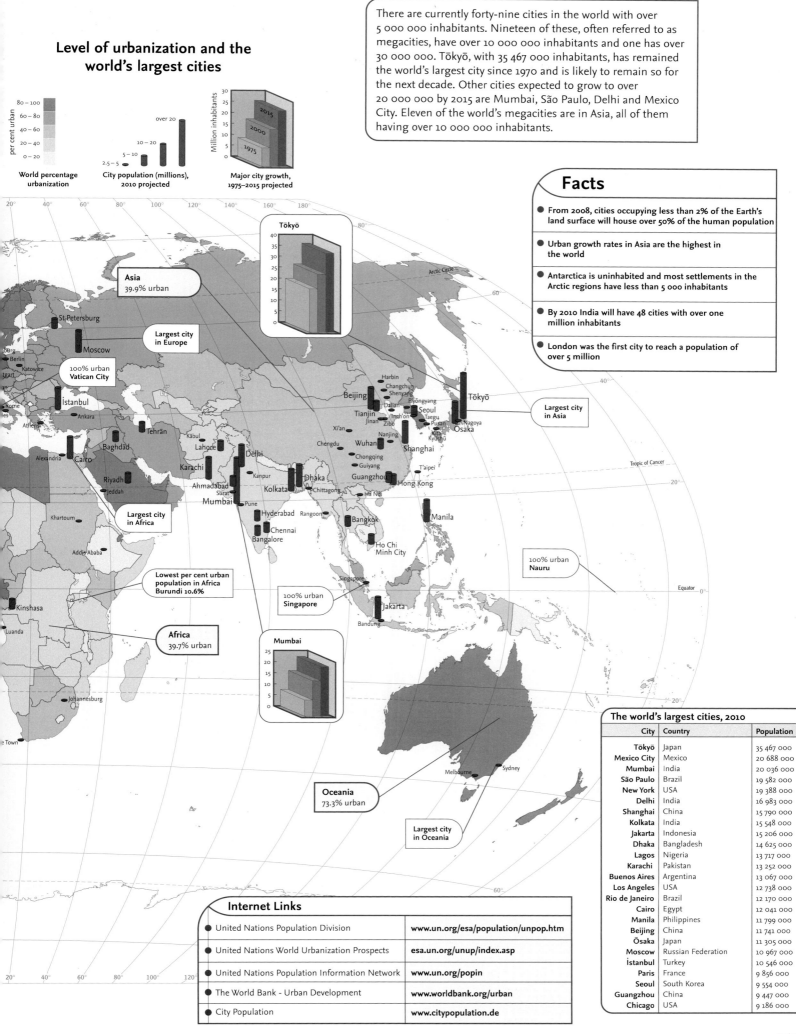

Level of urbanization and the world's largest cities

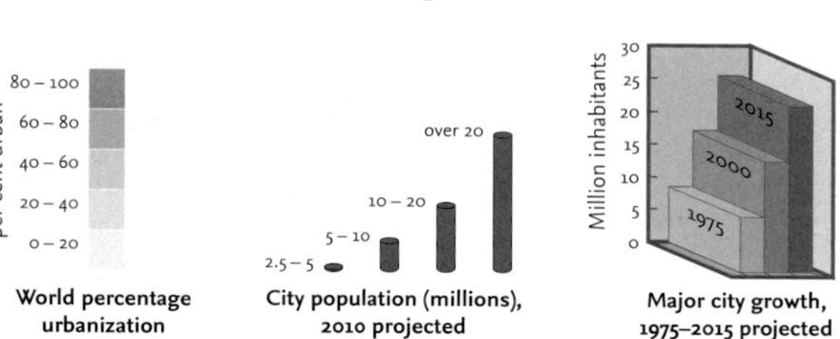

Megacities

There are currently forty-nine cities in the world with over 5 000 000 inhabitants. Nineteen of these, often referred to as megacities, have over 10 000 000 inhabitants and one has over 30 000 000. Tōkyō, with 35 467 000 inhabitants, has remained the world's largest city since 1970 and is likely to remain so for the next decade. Other cities expected to grow to over 20 000 000 by 2015 are Mumbai, São Paulo, Delhi and Mexico City. Eleven of the world's megacities are in Asia, all of them having over 10 000 000 inhabitants.

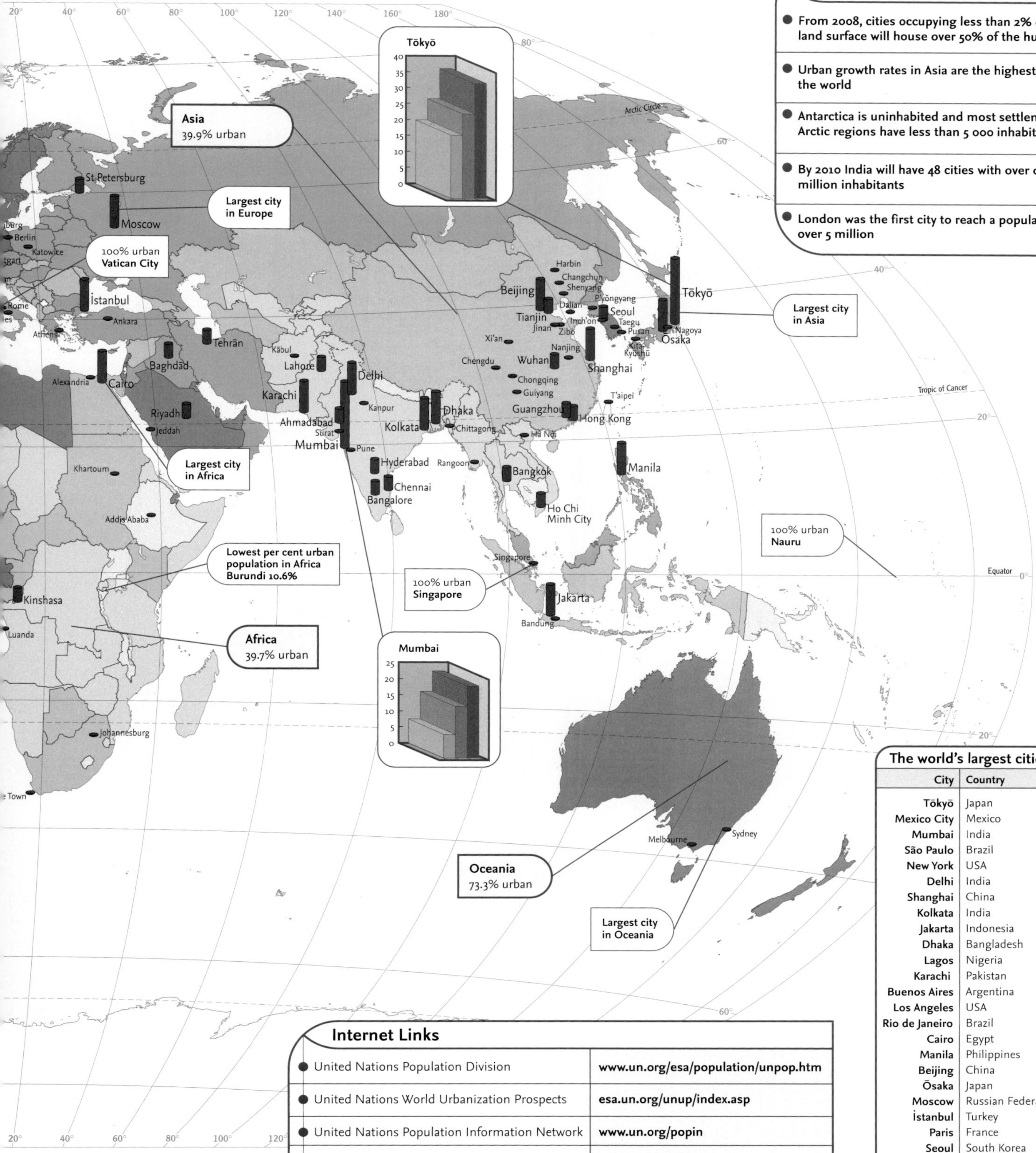

Facts

- **From 2008, cities occupying less than 2% of the Earth's land surface will house over 50% of the human population**
- **Urban growth rates in Asia are the highest in the world**
- **Antarctica is uninhabited and most settlements in the Arctic regions have less than 5 000 inhabitants**
- **By 2010 India will have 48 cities with over one million inhabitants**
- **London was the first city to reach a population of over 5 million**

Asia 39.9% urban

Largest city in Europe Moscow

100% urban Vatican City

Largest city in Asia Tōkyō

Largest city in Africa Cairo

Lowest per cent urban population in Africa Burundi 10.6%

100% urban Singapore

100% urban Nauru

Africa 39.7% urban

Oceania 73.3% urban

Largest city in Oceania Sydney

The world's largest cities, 2010

City	Country	Population
Tōkyō	Japan	35 467 000
Mexico City	Mexico	20 688 000
Mumbai	India	20 036 000
São Paulo	Brazil	19 582 000
New York	USA	19 388 000
Delhi	India	16 983 000
Shanghai	China	15 790 000
Kolkata	India	15 548 000
Jakarta	Indonesia	15 206 000
Dhaka	Bangladesh	14 625 000
Lagos	Nigeria	13 717 000
Karachi	Pakistan	13 252 000
Buenos Aires	Argentina	13 067 000
Los Angeles	USA	12 738 000
Rio de Janeiro	Brazil	12 170 000
Cairo	Egypt	12 041 000
Manila	Philippines	11 799 000
Beijing	China	11 741 000
Ōsaka	Japan	11 305 000
Moscow	Russian Federation	10 967 000
İstanbul	Turkey	10 546 000
Paris	France	9 856 000
Seoul	South Korea	9 554 000
Guangzhou	China	9 447 000
Chicago	USA	9 186 000

Internet Links

United Nations Population Division	**www.un.org/esa/population/unpop.htm**
United Nations World Urbanization Prospects	**esa.un.org/unup/index.asp**
United Nations Population Information Network	**www.un.org/popin**
The World Bank - Urban Development	**www.worldbank.org/urban**
City Population	**www.citypopulation.de**

World
Communications

Increased availability and ownership of telecommunications equipment since the beginning of the 1970s has aided the globalization of the world economy. Over half of the world's fixed telephone lines have been installed since the mid-1980s and the majority of the world's internet hosts have come on line since 1997. There are now over one billion fixed telephone lines in the world. The number of mobile cellular subscribers has grown dramatically from sixteen million in 1991 to well over one billion today.

The internet is the fastest growing communications network of all time. It is relatively cheap and now links over 140 million host computers globally. Its growth has resulted in the emergence of hundreds of Internet Service Providers (ISPs) and internet traffic is now doubling every six months. In 1993 the number of internet users was estimated to be just under ten million, there are now over half a billion.

Facts

- The first transatlantic telegraph cable came into operation in 1858
- Fibre-optic cables can now carry approximately 20 million simultaneous telephone calls
- The internet is the fastest growing communications network of all time and now has over 267 million host computers
- Bermuda has the world's highest density of internet and broadband subscribers
- Sputnik, the world's first artificial satellite, was launched in 1957

Internet users and major Internet routes

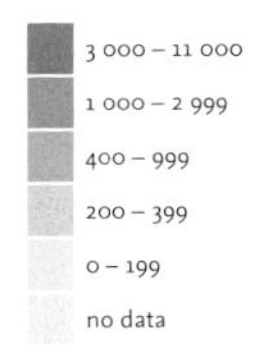

Internet users per 10 000 inhabitants 2006

150 50 15

Gigabytes per second

© TeleGeography Research www.telegeography.com

Aggregate international internet capacity 20

The Internet

The Internet is a global network of millions of computers around the world, all capable of being connected to each other. Internet Service Providers (ISPs) provide access via 'host' computers, of which there are now over 267 million. It has become a vital means of communication and data transfer for businesses, governments and financial and academic institutions, with a steadily increasing proportion of business transactions being carried out on-line. Personal use of the Internet – particularly for access to the World Wide Web information network, and for e-mail communication – has increased enormously and there are now estimated to be over half a billion users worldwide.

Top Broadband Economies 2006
Countries with the highest broadband penetration rate – subscribers per 100 inhabitants

	Top Economies	Rate
1	Denmark	29.3
2	Netherlands	28.8
3	Iceland	27.3
4	South Korea	26.4
5	Switzerland	26.2
6	Finland	25.0
7	Norway	24.6
8	Sweden	22.7
9	Canada	22.4
10	United Kingdom	19.4
11	Belgium	19.3
12	USA	19.2
13	Japan	19.0
14	Luxembourg	17.9
15	France	17.7
16	Austria	17.7
17	Australia	17.4
18	Germany	15.1
19	Spain	13.6
20	Italy	13.2

Internet users 1999 and 2006

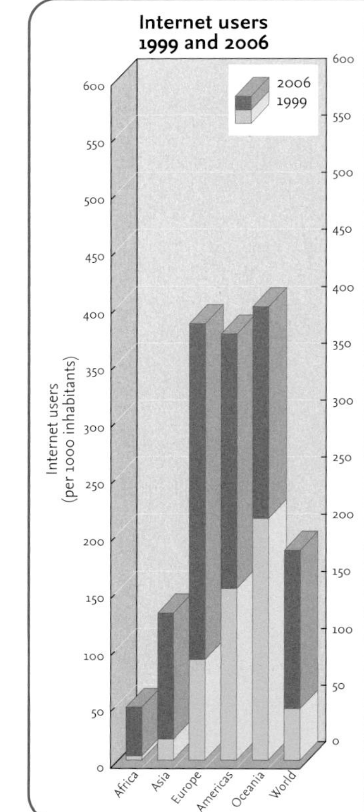

Internet Links

OECD Information and Communication Technologies	www.oecd.org
TeleGeography Research	www.telegeography.com
International Telecommunication Union	www.itu.int

Satellite communications

International telecommunications use either fibre-optic cables or satellites as transmission media. Although cables carry the vast majority of traffic around the world, communications satellites are important for person-to-person communication, including cellular telephones, and for broadcasting. The positions of communications satellites are critical to their use, and reflect the demand for such communications in each part of the world. Such satellites are placed in 'geostationary' orbit 36 000 km above the equator. This means that they move at the same speed as the Earth and remain fixed above a single point on the Earth's surface.

Mobile phone subscribers and communications satellites

over 100
80 – 100
60 – 79.9
40 – 59.9
20 – 39.9
0 – 19.9
no data

Cellular mobile subscribers per 100 inhabitants 2006

Geostationary communications satellites

In service
Inclined orbit
Planned

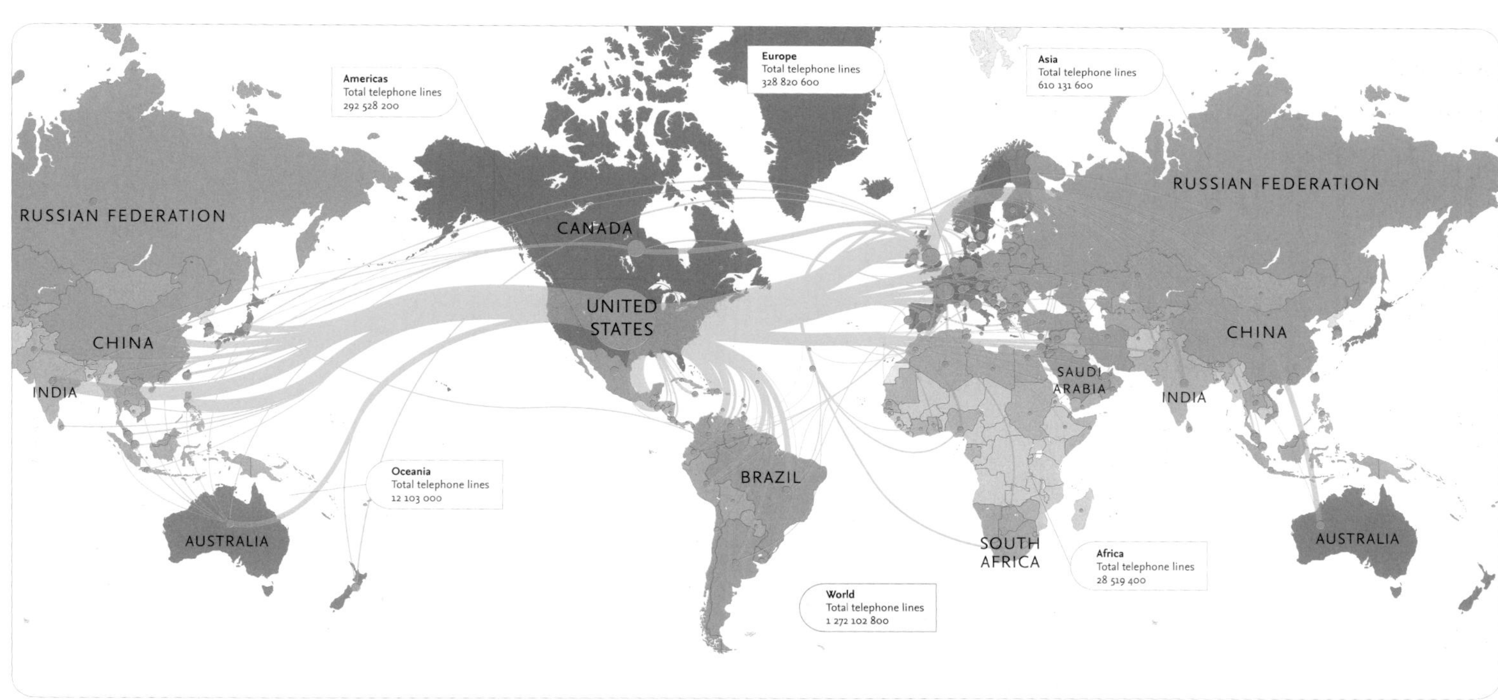

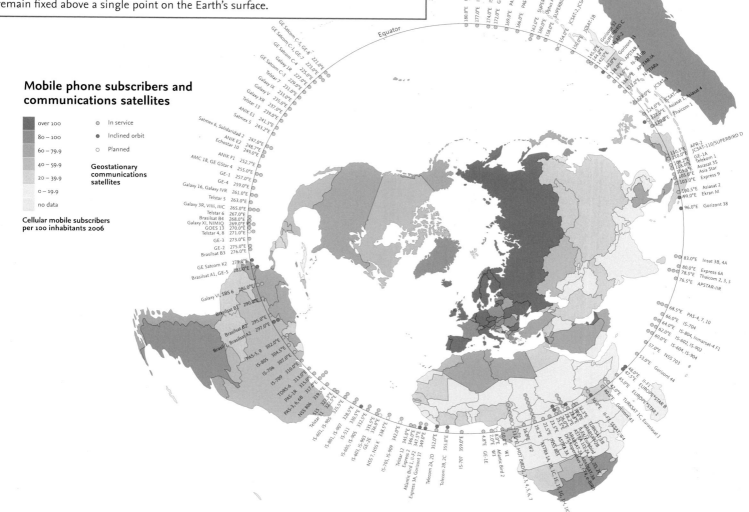

International telecommunications traffic

Each band is proportional to the total annual TDM (Time Division Multiplexed) traffic on the public telephone network in both directions between each pair of countries.

15 000 7 500 2 500

The main projection depicts inter-continental flows greater than 100 Mbps.

Millions of minutes of telecommunications traffic

The area of each circle is proportional to the volume of the total annual outgoing TDM traffic from each country.

10 001 – 20 000
5 001 – 10 000
1 001 – 5 000
101–1000
> 100

over 50.0
35.0 – 50.0
15.0 – 34.9
10.0 – 14.9
5.0 – 9.9
1.0 – 4.9
0 – 0.9
no data

Telephone lines per 100 inhabitants 2006

World
Social Indicators

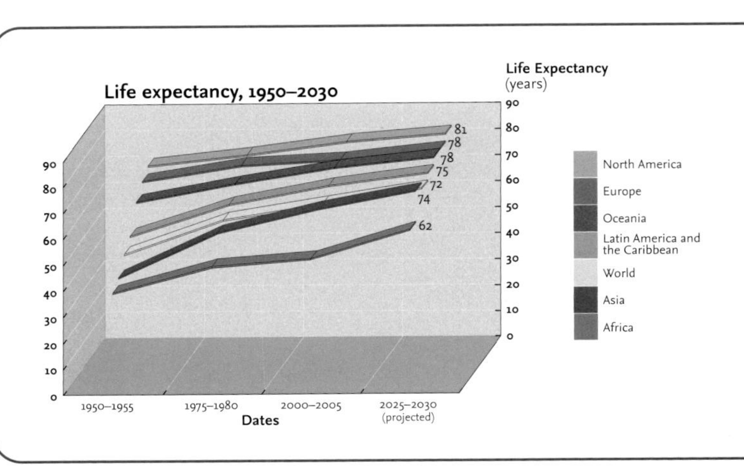

Countries are often judged on their level of economic development, but national and personal wealth are not the only measures of a country's status. Numerous other indicators can give a better picture of the overall level of development and standard of living achieved by a country. The availability and standard of health services, levels of educational provision and attainment, levels of nutrition, water supply, life expectancy and mortality rates are just some of the factors which can be measured to assess and compare countries.

While nations strive to improve their economies, and hopefully also to improve the standard of living of their citizens, the measurement of such indicators often exposes great discrepancies between the countries of the 'developed' world and those of the 'less developed' world. They also show great variations within continents and regions and at the same time can hide great inequalities within countries.

World Statistics: see pages **154–160**

Under-five mortality rate, 2006 and life expectancy by continent, 2005–2010

Europe = 75
World = 67
Europe
Life expectancy 2005–2010 (years)

Asia = 67
World = 67
Asia
Life expectancy 2005–2010 (years)

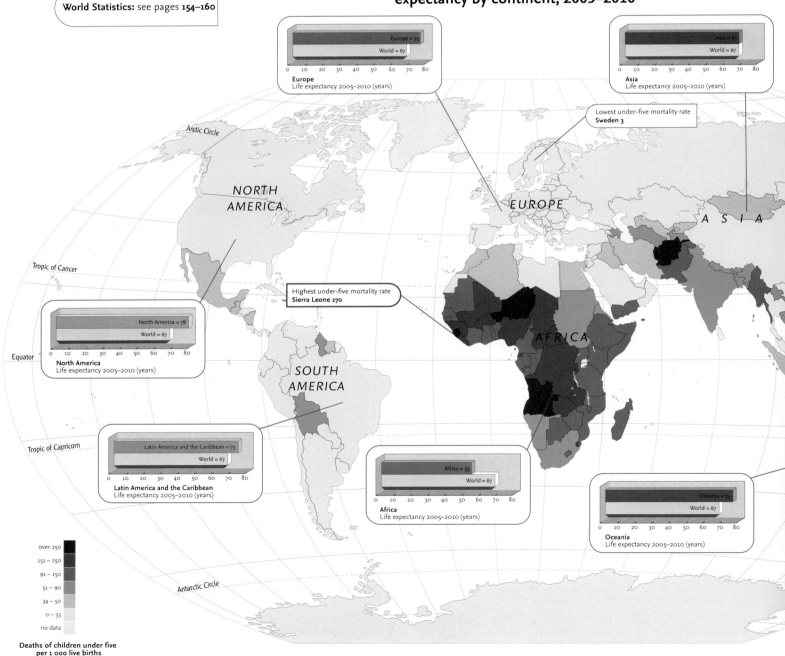

Lowest under-five mortality rate
Sweden 3

Highest under-five mortality rate
Sierra Leone 270

North America = 78
World = 67
North America
Life expectancy 2005–2010 (years)

Latin America and the Caribbean = 73
World = 67
Latin America and the Caribbean
Life expectancy 2005–2010 (years)

Africa = 53
World = 67
Africa
Life expectancy 2005–2010 (years)

Oceania = 75
World = 67
Oceania
Life expectancy 2005–2010 (years)

Arctic Circle
NORTH AMERICA
EUROPE
ASIA
AFRICA
SOUTH AMERICA
Tropic of Cancer
Equator
Tropic of Capricorn
Antarctic Circle

over 250
151 – 250
91 – 150
51 – 90
34 – 50
0 – 33
no data

Deaths of children under five per 1 000 live births

Facts

- Of the 11 countries with under-5 mortality rates of more than 200 per 1000 live births, 10 are in Africa
- Many western countries believe they have achieved satisfactory levels of education and no longer closely monitor levels of literacy
- Children born in Nepal have only a 12% chance of their birth being attended by trained health personnel; for most European countries the figure is 100%
- The illiteracy rate among young women in the Middle East and north Africa is almost twice the rate for young men

Health and education

Perhaps the most important indicators used for measuring the level of national development are those relating to health and education. Both of these key areas are vital to the future development of a country, and if there are concerns in standards attained in either (or worse, in both) of these, then they may indicate fundamental problems within the country concerned. The ability to read and write (literacy) is seen as vital in educating people and encouraging development, while easy access to appropriate health services and specialists is an important requirement in maintaining satisfactory levels of basic health.

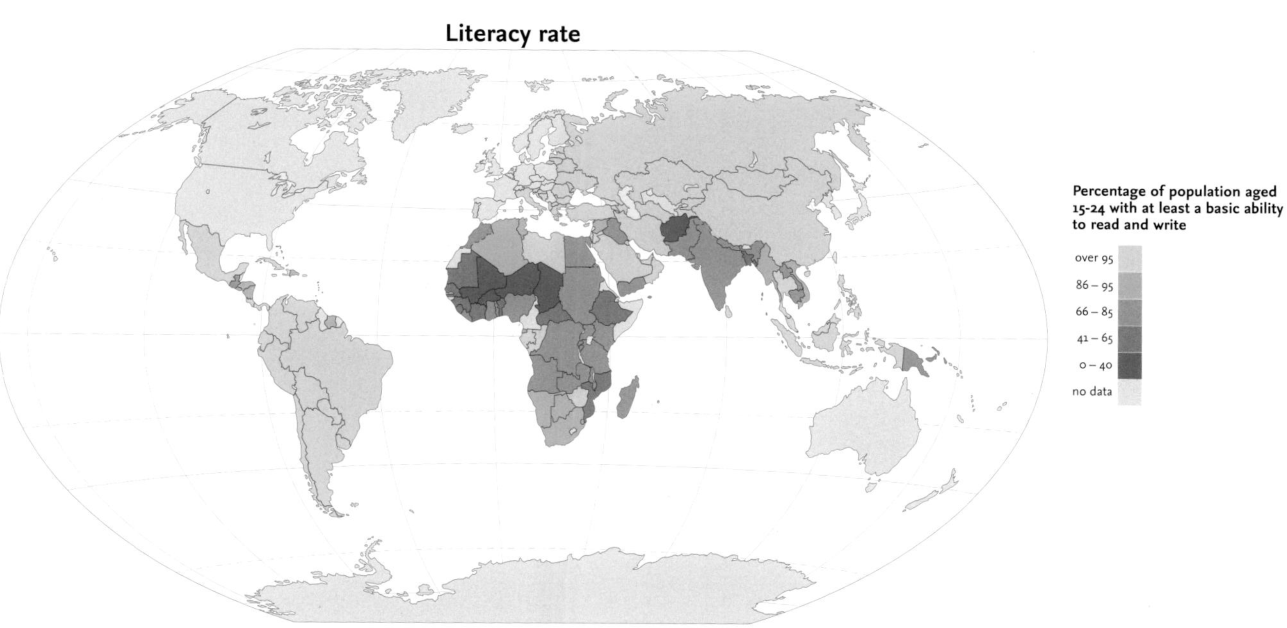

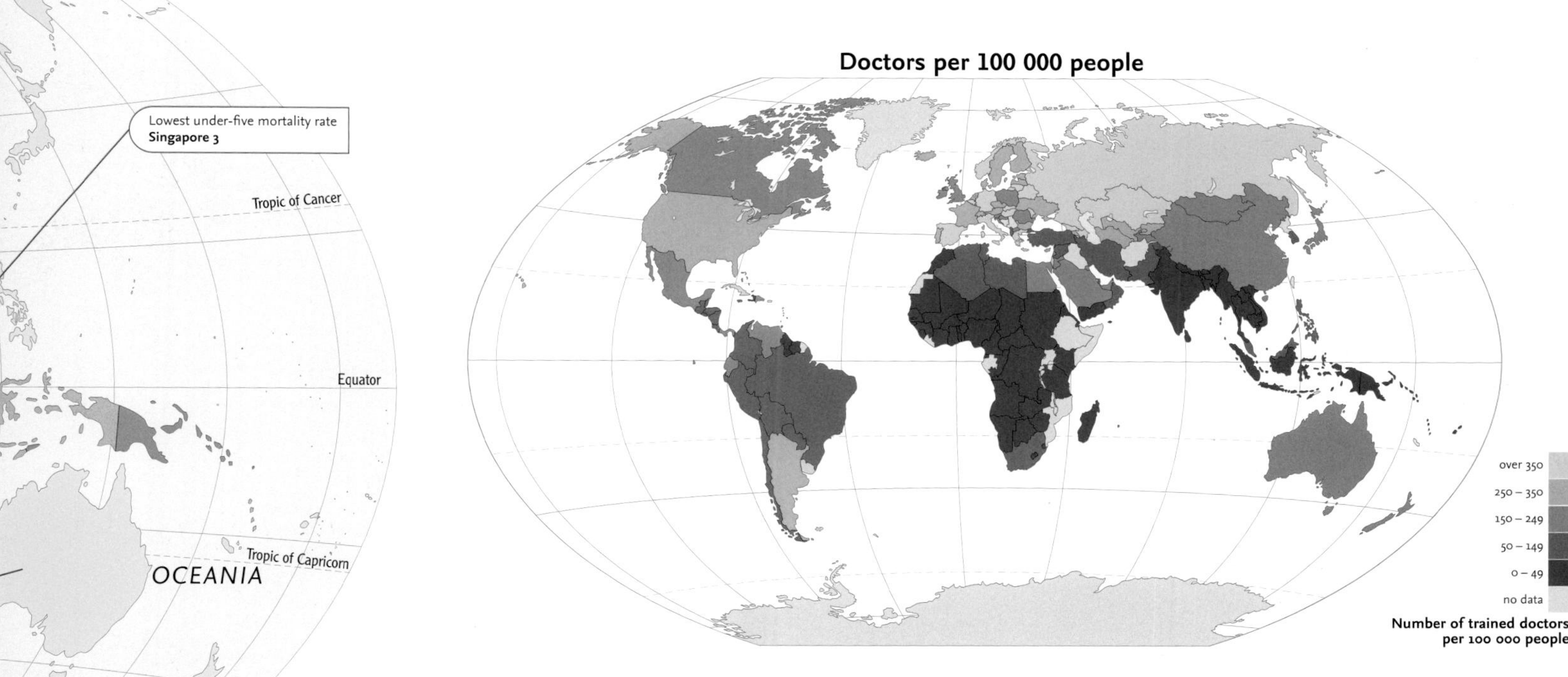

UN Millennium Development Goals

From the Millennium Declaration, 2000

Goal 1	Eradicate extreme poverty and hunger
Goal 2	Achieve universal primary education
Goal 3	Promote gender equality and empower women
Goal 4	Reduce child mortality
Goal 5	Improve maternal health
Goal 6	Combat HIV/AIDS, malaria and other diseases
Goal 7	Ensure environmental sustainability
Goal 8	Develop a global partnership for development

Internet Links

United Nation Development Programme	**www.undp.org**
World Health Organization	**www.who.int**
United Nations Statistics Division	**unstats.un.org**
United Nations Millennium Development Goals	**www.un.org/millenniumgoals**

World

Economy and Wealth

The globalization of the economy is making the world appear a smaller place. However, this shrinkage is an uneven process. Countries are being included in and excluded from the global economy to differing degrees. The wealthy countries of the developed world, with their market-led economies, access to productive new technologies and international markets, dominate the world economic system. Great inequalities exist between and within countries. There may also be discrepancies between social groups within countries due to gender and ethnic divisions. Differences between countries are evident by looking at overall wealth on a national and individual level.

Facts

- The City, one of 33 London boroughs, is the world's largest financial centre and contains Europe's biggest stock market
- Half the world's population earns only 5% of the world's wealth
- During the second half of the 20th century rich countries gave over US$1 trillion in aid
- For every £1 in grant aid to developing countries, more than £13 comes back in debt repayments
- On average, The World Bank distributes US$30 billion each year between 100 countries

World Statistics: see pages **154–160**

Personal wealth

A poverty line set at $1 a day has been accepted as the working definition of extreme poverty in low-income countries. It is estimated that a total of 1.2 billion people live below that poverty line. This indicator has also been adopted by the United Nations in relation to their Millennium Development Goals. The United Nations goal is to halve the proportion of people living on less than $1 a day in 1990 to 14.5 per cent by 2015. Today, over 80 per cent of the total population of Ethiopia, Uganda and Nicaragua live on less than this amount.

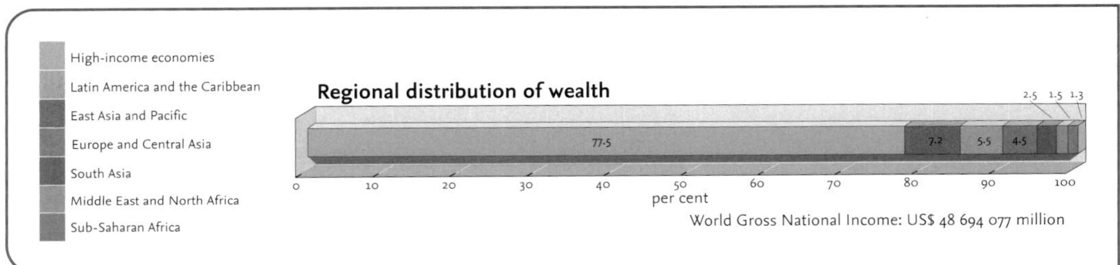

Percentage of population living on less than $1 a day

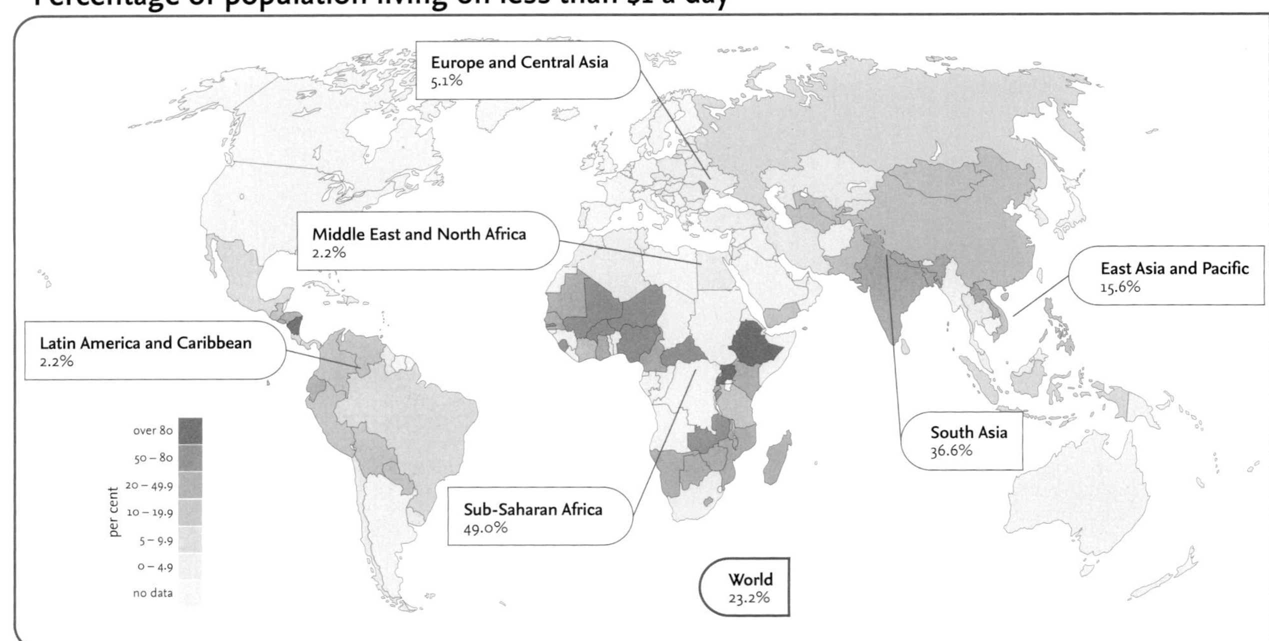

The world's biggest companies		
Rank	**Name**	**Sales (US$ millions)**
1	Wal-Mart Stores	351 139
2	ExxonMobil	347 254
3	Royal Dutch/Shell Group	318 845
4	BP	274 316
5	General Motors	207 349
6	Toyota Motor	204 746
7	Chevron	200 567
8	DaimlerChrysler	190 191
9	ConocoPhillips	172 451
10	Total	168 357

Rural homesteads, **Sudan** – most of the world's poorest countries are in Africa.

Gross National Income per capita

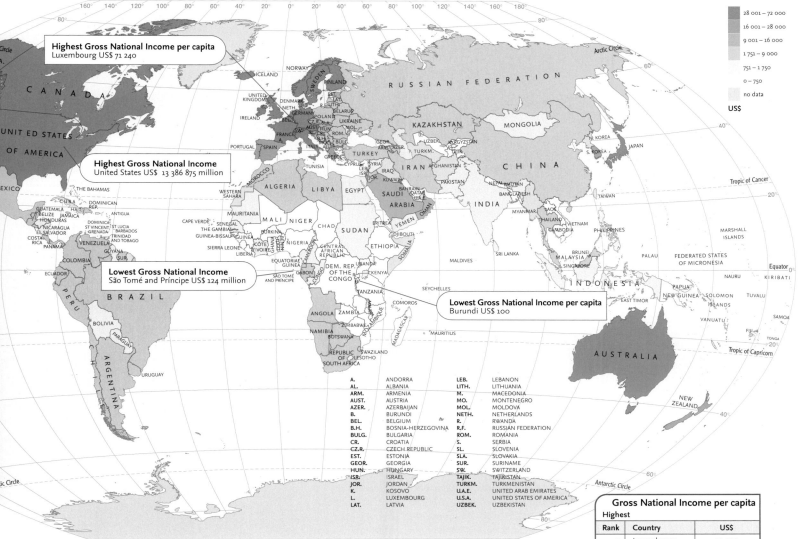

Highest Gross National Income per capita
Luxembourg US$ 71 240

Highest Gross National Income
United States US$ 13 386 875 million

Lowest Gross National Income
São Tomé and Príncipe US$ 124 million

Lowest Gross National Income per capita
Burundi US$ 100

US$
28 001 – 72 000
16 001 – 28 000
9 001 – 16 000
1 751 – 9 000
751 – 1 750
0 – 750
no data

A.	ANDORRA	LEB.	LEBANON
AL.	ALBANIA	LITH.	LITHUANIA
ARM.	ARMENIA	M.	MACEDONIA
AUST.	AUSTRIA	MO.	MONTENEGRO
AZER.	AZERBAIJAN	MOL.	MOLDOVA
B.	BURUNDI	NETH.	NETHERLANDS
BEL.	BELGIUM	R.	RWANDA
B.H.	BOSNIA-HERZEGOVINA	R.F.	RUSSIAN FEDERATION
BULG.	BULGARIA	ROM.	ROMANIA
CR.	CROATIA	S.	SERBIA
CZ.R.	CZECH REPUBLIC	SL.	SLOVENIA
EST.	ESTONIA	SLA.	SLOVAKIA
GEOR.	GEORGIA	SUR.	SURINAME
HUN.	HUNGARY	SW.	SWITZERLAND
ISR.	ISRAEL	TAJIK.	TAJIKISTAN
JOR.	JORDAN	TURKM.	TURKMENISTAN
K.	KOSOVO	U.A.E.	UNITED ARAB EMIRATES
L.	LUXEMBOURG	U.S.A.	UNITED STATES OF AMERICA
LAT.	LATVIA	UZBEK.	UZBEKISTAN

Gross National Income per capita		
Highest		
Rank	**Country**	**US$**
1	Luxembourg	71 240
2	Norway	68 440
3	Switzerland	58 050
4	Denmark	52 110
5	Iceland	49 960
6	San Marino	45 130
7	Ireland	44 830
8	United States	44 710
9	Sweden	43 530
10	Netherlands	43 050
Lowest		
Rank	**Country**	**US$**
156	Niger	270
157	Rwanda	250
158	Sierra Leone	240
159	Malawi	230
160=	Eritrea	190
160=	Guinea-Bissau	190
161	Ethiopia	170
162=	Dem. Rep. Congo	130
162=	Liberia	130
163	Burundi	100

Measuring wealth

One of the indicators used to determine a country's wealth is its Gross National Income (GNI). This gives a broad measure of an economy's performance. This is the value of the final output of goods and services produced by a country plus net income from non-resident sources. The total GNI is divided by the country's population to give an average figure of the GNI per capita. From this it is evident that the developed countries dominate the world economy with the United States having the highest GNI. China is a growing world economic player with the fourth highest GNI figure and a relatively high GNI per capita (US$2 000) in proportion to its huge population.

Internet Links	
United Nations Statistics Division	**unstats.un.org**
The World Bank	**www.worldbank.org**
International Monetary Fund	**www.imf.org**
Organisation for Economic Co-operation and Development	**www.oecd.org**

World
Conflict

Geo-political issues shape the countries of the world and the current political situation in many parts of the world reflects a long history of armed conflict. Since the Second World War conflicts have been fairly localized, but there are numerous 'flash points' where factors such as territorial claims, ideology, religion, ethnicity and access to resources can cause friction between two or more countries. Such factors also lie behind the recent growth in global terrorism.

Military expenditure can take up a disproportionate amount of a country's wealth – Eritrea, with a Gross National Income (GNI) per capita of only US$190 spends twenty-four per cent of its total GDP on military activity. There is an encouraging trend towards wider international cooperation, mainly through the United Nations (UN) and the North Atlantic Treaty Organization (NATO), to prevent escalation of conflicts and on peacekeeping missions.

Military spending, 2006 and conflicts, 1946–2003

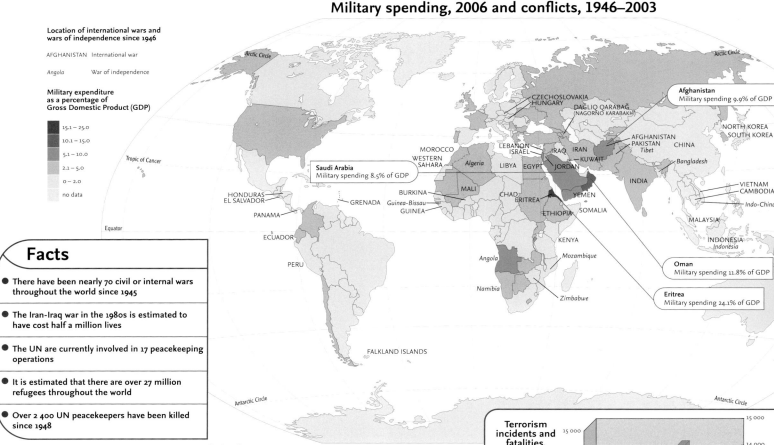

Location of international wars and wars of independence since 1946

AFGHANISTAN International war

Angola War of independence

Military expenditure as a percentage of Gross Domestic Product (GDP)

15.1 – 25.0
10.1 – 15.0
5.1 – 10.0
2.1 – 5.0
0 – 2.0
no data

Arctic Circle
Tropic of Cancer
Equator
Antarctic Circle

CZECHOSLOVAKIA
HUNGARY
DAĞLIQ QARABAĞ (NAGORNO KARABAKH)
Afghanistan Military spending 9.9% of GDP
NORTH KOREA
SOUTH KOREA
AFGHANISTAN
PAKISTAN
Tibet
CHINA
Bangladesh
INDIA
MOROCCO
WESTERN SAHARA
Algeria
LIBYA
EGYPT
LEBANON
ISRAEL
IRAQ
IRAN
KUWAIT
JORDAN
Saudi Arabia Military spending 8.5% of GDP
MALI
BURKINA
Guinea-Bissau
GUINEA
GRENADA
HONDURAS
EL SALVADOR
PANAMA
ECUADOR
PERU
CHAD
ERITREA
YEMEN
ETHIOPIA
SOMALIA
KENYA
Angola
Namibia
Mozambique
Zimbabwe
VIETNAM
CAMBODIA
Indo-China
MALAYSIA
INDONESIA
Indonesia
Oman Military spending 11.8% of GDP
Eritrea Military spending 24.1% of GDP
FALKLAND ISLANDS

Facts

- **There have been nearly 70 civil or internal wars throughout the world since 1945**
- **The Iran-Iraq war in the 1980s is estimated to have cost half a million lives**
- **The UN are currently involved in 17 peacekeeping operations**
- **It is estimated that there are over 27 million refugees throughout the world**
- **Over 2 400 UN peacekeepers have been killed since 1948**

Global terrorism

Terrorism is defined by the United Nations as "All criminal acts directed against a State and intended or calculated to create a state of terror in the minds of particular persons or a group of persons or the general public". The world has become increasingly concerned about terrorism and the possibility that terrorists could acquire and use nuclear, chemical and biological weapons. One common form of terrorist attack is suicide bombing. Pioneered by Tamil secessionists in Sri Lanka, it has been widely used by Palestinian groups fighting against Israeli occupation of the West Bank and Gaza. In recent years it has also been used by the Al Qaida network in its attacks on the western world.

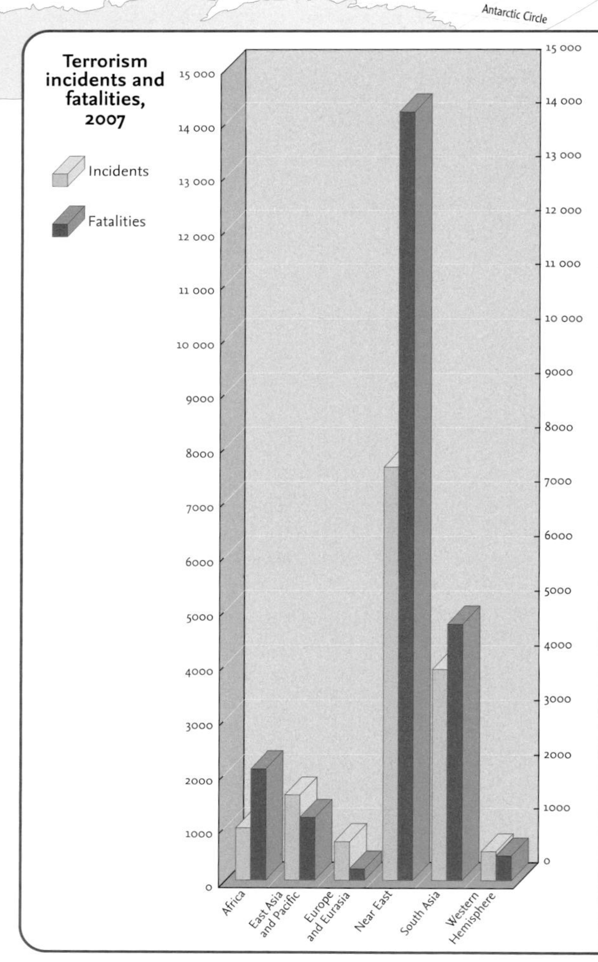

Internet Links

United Nations Peace and Security	**www.un.org/peace**
United Nations Refugee Agency	**www.unhcr.org**
NATO	**www.nato.int**
BBC News	**news.bbc.co.uk**
International Boundaries Research Unit	**www.dur.ac.uk/ibru**
International Peace Research Institute	**www.prio.no**

United Nations peacekeeping

United Nations peacekeeping was developed by the Organization as a way to help countries torn by conflict create the conditions for lasting peace. The first UN peacekeeping mission was established in 1948, when the Security Council authorized the deployment of UN military observers to the Middle East to monitor the Armistice Agreement between Israel and its Arab neighbours. Since then, there have been a total of 63 UN peacekeeping operations around the world.

UN peacekeeping goals were primarily limited to maintaining ceasefires and stabilizing situations on the ground, so that efforts could be made at the political level to resolve the conflict by peaceful means. Today's peacekeepers undertake a wide variety of complex tasks, from helping to build sustainable institutions of governance, to human rights monitoring, to security sector reform, to the disarmament, demobilization and reintegration of former combatants.

United Nations peacekeeping operations 1948–2008

Current peacekeeping operations are named on the map

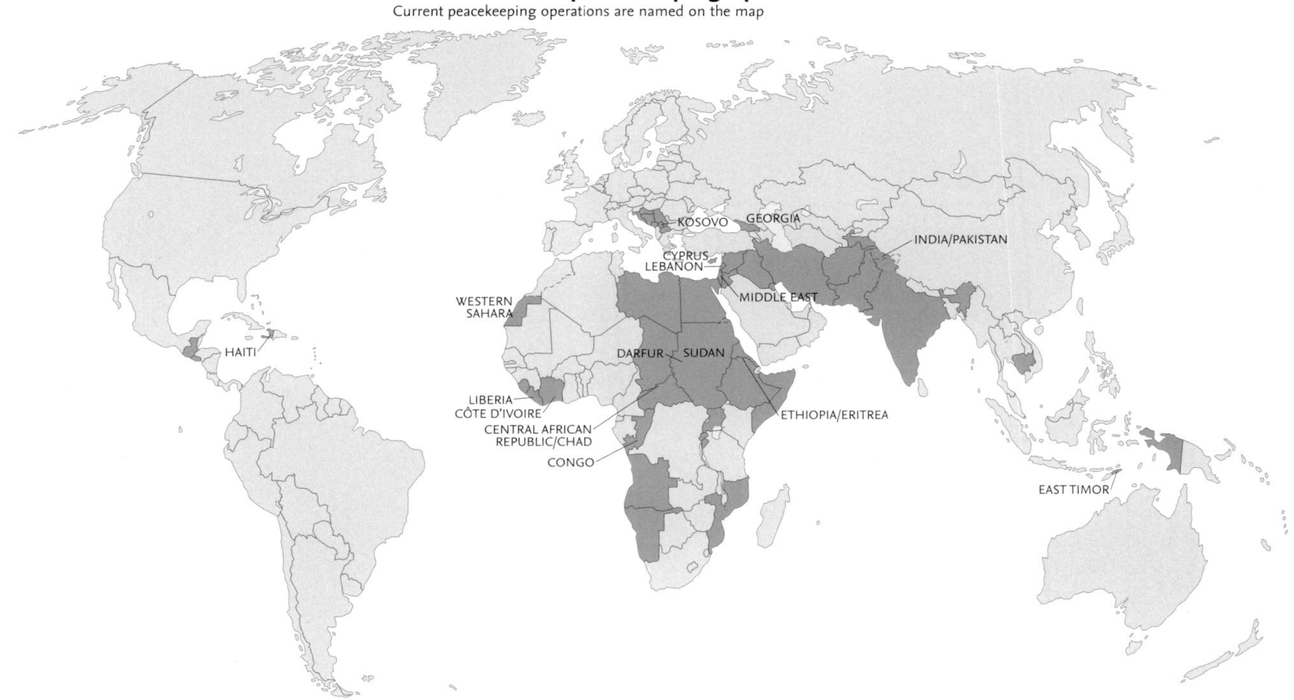

Refugees from **Darfur** in Iridmi refugee camp, Sudan.

Major terrorist incidents

Date	Location	Summary	Killed	Injured
December 1988	**Lockerbie, Scotland**	Airline bombing	270	5
March 1995	**Tōkyō, Japan**	Sarin gas attack on subway	12	5 510
April 1995	**Oklahoma City, USA**	Bomb in the Federal building	168	over 800
August 1998	**Nairobi, Kenya and Dar es Salaam, Tanzania**	US Embassy bombings	225	over 4 000
August 1998	**Omagh, Northern Ireland**	Town centre bombing	29	220
September 2001	**New York and Washington D.C., USA**	Airline hijacking and crashing	3 018	over 6 200
October 2002	**Bali, Indonesia**	Car bomb outside nightclub	202	over 200
October 2002	**Moscow, Russian Federation**	Theatre siege	170	over 600
March 2004	**Bāghdad and Karbalā', Iraq**	Suicide bombing of pilgrims	181	over 400
March 2004	**Madrid, Spain**	Train bombings	191	1 800
September 2004	**Beslan, Russian Federation**	School siege	385	over 700
July 2005	**London, UK**	Underground and bus bombings	56	700
July 2005	**Sharm ash Shaykh, Egypt**	Bombs at tourist sites	88	200
July 2006	**Mumbai, India**	Train bombings	209	700
August 2007	**Qahtaniya, Iraq**	Suicide bombing in town centres	796	over 1 500

Terrorist incidents

Number of terrorist incidents 2000-2006

- over 600
- 200–600
- 50–199
- 5–49
- 0–4
- no data

☆ Major terrorist incident location

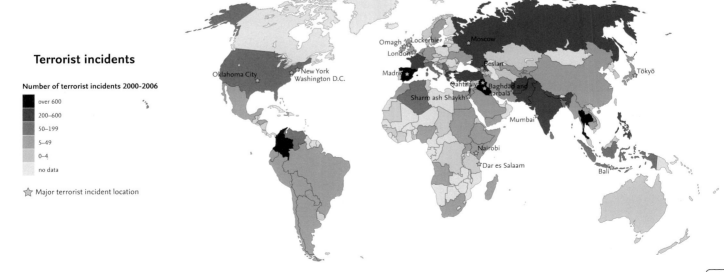

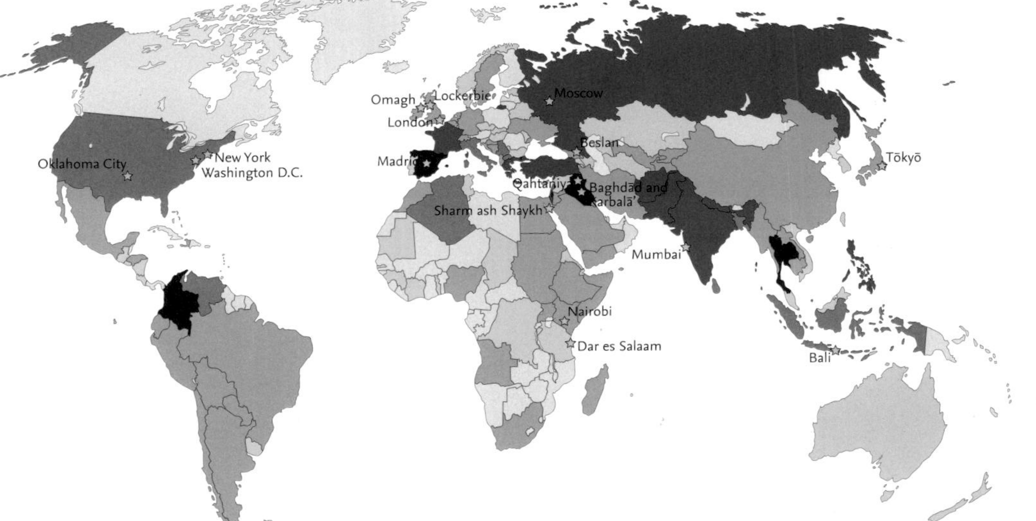

With the process of globalization has come an increased awareness of, and direct interest in, issues which have global implications. Social issues can now affect large parts of the world and can impact on large sections of society. Perhaps the current issues of greatest concern are those of national security, including the problem of international terrorism, health, crime and natural resources. The three issues highlighted here reflect this and are of immediate concern.

The international drugs trade, and the crimes commonly associated with it, can impact on society and individuals in devastating ways; scarcity of water resources and lack of access to safe drinking water can have major economic implications and cause severe health problems; and the AIDS epidemic is having disastrous consequences in large parts of the world, particularly in sub-Saharan Africa.

The drugs trade

The international trade in illegal drugs is estimated to be worth over US$400 billion. While it may be a lucrative business for the criminals involved, the effects of the drugs on individual users and on society in general can be devastating. Patterns of drug production and abuse vary, but there are clear centres for the production of the most harmful drugs – the opiates (opium, morphine and heroin) and cocaine. The 'Golden Triangle' of Laos, Myanmar and Thailand, and western South America respectively are the main producing areas for these drugs. Significant efforts are expended to counter the drugs trade, and there have been signs recently of downward trends in the production of heroin and cocaine.

Soldiers in **Colombia**, a major producer of cocaine, destroy an illegal drug processing laboratory.

The international drugs trade

Main producers and trafficking routes for opiates (opium, morphine, heroin) and cocaine

Cocaine producer
Opiate producer
Cocaine trafficking route
Opiate trafficking route

Arctic Circle
Tropic of Cancer
Equator
Tropic of Capricorn
Antarctic Circle
UNITED STATES OF AMERICA
MEXICO
CARIBBEAN
CENTRAL AMERICA
COLOMBIA
PERU
BOLIVIA
SOUTH AMERICA
WESTERN EUROPE
EASTERN EUROPE
WEST AFRICA
SOUTH AFRICA
AFGHANISTAN
PAKISTAN
INDIA
MYANMAR
LAOS
THAILAND
VIETNAM
JAPAN
AUSTRALIA

Colombia
Cocaine production 2006:
610 metric tonnes

Peru
Cocaine production 2006:
280 metric tonnes

Afghanistan
Opiate production 2006:
6 100 metric tonnes

Myanmar
Opiate production 2006:
315 metric tonnes

World
Opiate production 2006: 6 610 metric tonnes
Cocaine production 2006: 984 metric tonnes

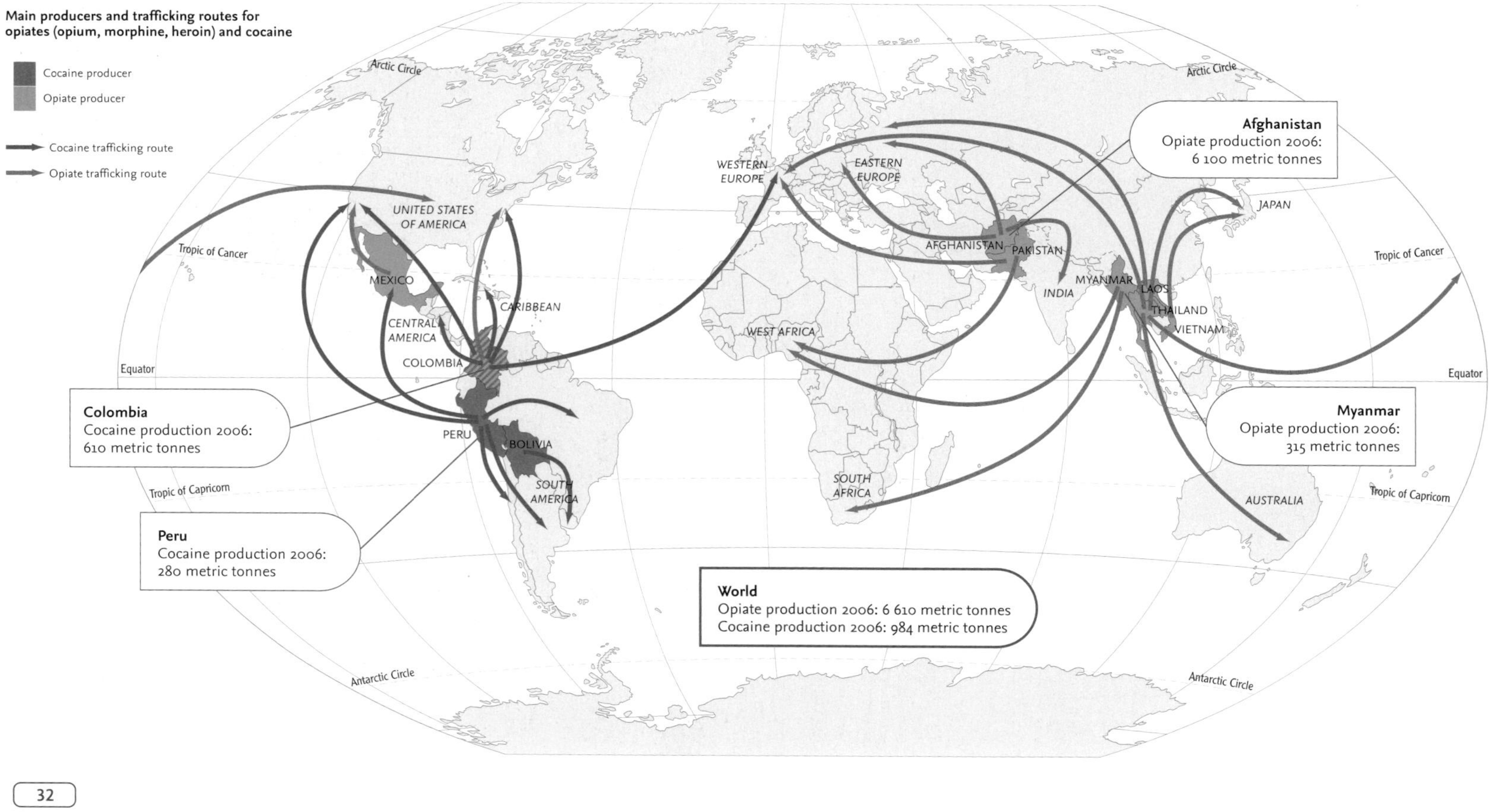

AIDS epidemic

With over 30 million people living with HIV/AIDS (Human Immunodeficiency Virus/Acquired Immune Deficiency Syndrome) and more than 20 million deaths from the disease, the AIDS epidemic poses one of the biggest threats to public health. The UNAIDS project estimated that 2.5 million people were newly infected in 2007 and that 2.1 million AIDS sufferers died. Estimates into the future look bleak, especially for poorer developing countries where an additional 45 million people are likely to become infected by 2010. The human cost is huge. As well as the death count itself, more than 11 million African children, half of whom are between the ages of 10 and 14, have been orphaned as a result of the disease.

Facts

- **The majority of people infected with HIV, if not treated, develop signs of AIDS within 8 to 10 years**
- **One in five developing countries will face water shortages by 2030**
- **Over 5 million people die each year from water-related diseases such as cholera and dysentery**
- **Estimates suggest that 200 million people consume illegal drugs around the world**

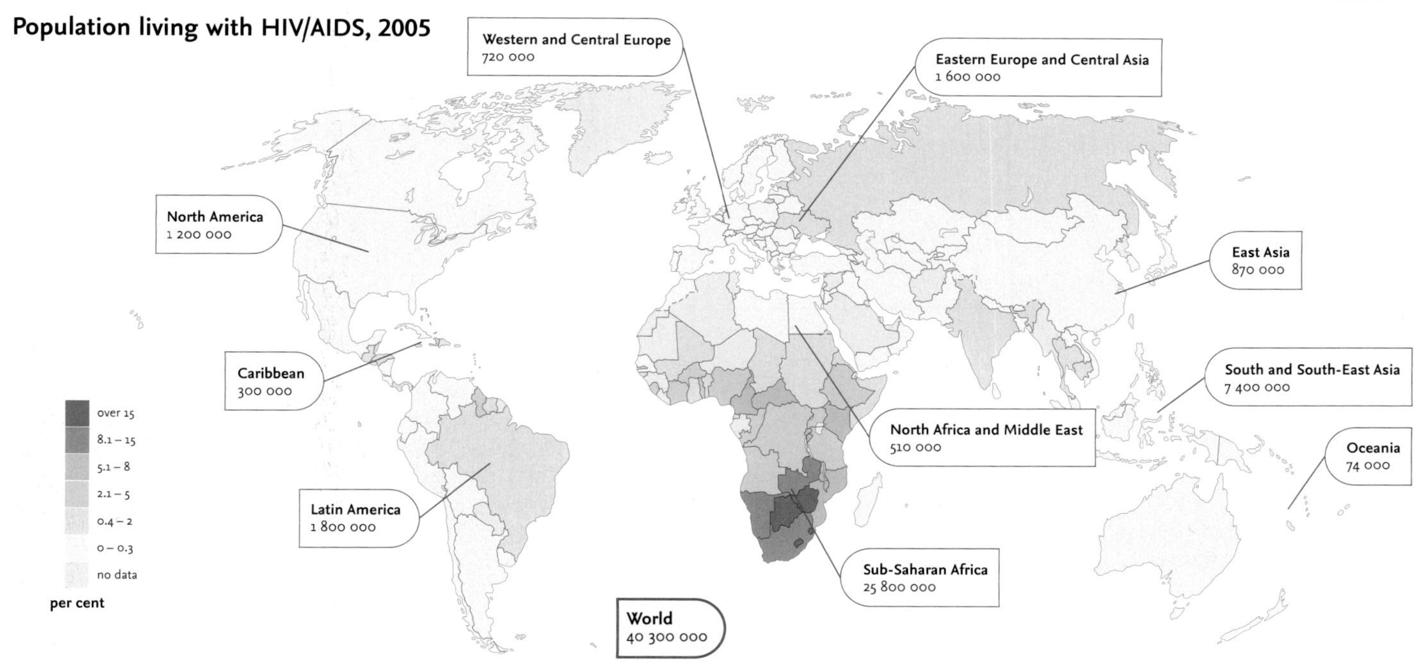

Water resources

Water is one of the fundamental requirements of life, and yet in some countries it is becoming more scarce due to increasing population and climate change. Safe drinking water, basic hygiene, health education and sanitation facilities are often virtually nonexistent for impoverished people in developing countries throughout the world. WHO/UNICEF estimate that the combination of these conditions results in 6 000 deaths every day, most of these being children. Currently over 1.2 billion people drink untreated water and expose themselves to serious health risks, while political struggles over diminishing water resources are increasingly likely to be the cause of international conflict.

Domestic use of **untreated water** in Kathmandu, Nepal

Access to safe water, 2004
Percentage of population with access to improved drinking water

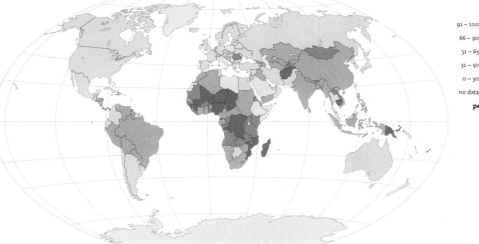

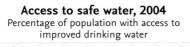

91 – 100
66 – 90
51 – 65
31 – 50
0 – 30
no data
per cent

Internet Links

UNESCO	**www.unesco.org**
UNAIDS	**www.unaids.org**
WaterAid	**www.wateraid.org.uk**
World Health Organization	**www.who.int**
United Nations Office on Drugs and Crime	**www.unodc.org**

World
Environmental Threats

The Earth has a rich and diverse environment which is under threat from both natural and man-induced forces. Forests and woodland form the predominant natural land cover with tropical rain forests – currently disappearing at alarming rates – believed to be home to the majority of animal and plant species. Grassland and scrub tend to have a lower natural species diversity but have suffered the most impact from man's intervention through conversion to agriculture, burning and the introduction of livestock. Wherever man interferes with existing biological and environmental processes degradation of that environment occurs to varying degrees. This interference also affects inland water and oceans where pollution, over-exploitation of marine resources and the need for fresh water has had major consequences on land and sea environments.

Facts

- The Sundarbans stretching across the Ganges delta is the largest area of mangrove forest in the world, covering 10 000 square kilometres (3 861 square miles) and forming an important ecological area, home to 260 species of birds, the Bengal tiger and other threatened species
- Over 90 000 square kilometres of precious tropical forest and wetland habitats are lost each year
- The surface level of the Dead Sea has fallen by more than 25 metres over the last 50 years
- Climate change and mismanagement of land areas can lead to soils becoming degraded and semi-arid grasslands becoming deserts – a process known as desertification

Environmental change

Whenever natural resources are exploited by man, the environment is changed. Approximately half the area of post-glacial forest has been cleared or degraded, and the amount of old-growth forest continues to decline. Desertification caused by climate change and the impact of man can turn semi-arid grasslands into arid desert. Regions bordering tropical deserts, such as the Sahel region south of the Sahara and regions around the Thar Desert in India, are most vulnerable to this process. Coral reefs are equally fragile environments, and many are under threat from coastal development, pollution and over-exploitation of marine resources.

Water resources in certain parts of the world are becoming increasingly scarce and competition for water is likely to become a common cause of conflict. The Aral Sea in central Asia was once the world's fourth largest lake but it now ranks only sixteenth after shrinking by almost 40 000 square kilometres. This shrinkage has been due to climatic change and to the diversion, for farming purposes, of the major rivers which feed the lake. The change has had a devastating effect on the local fishing industry and the exposure of chemicals on the lake bed has caused health problems for the local population.

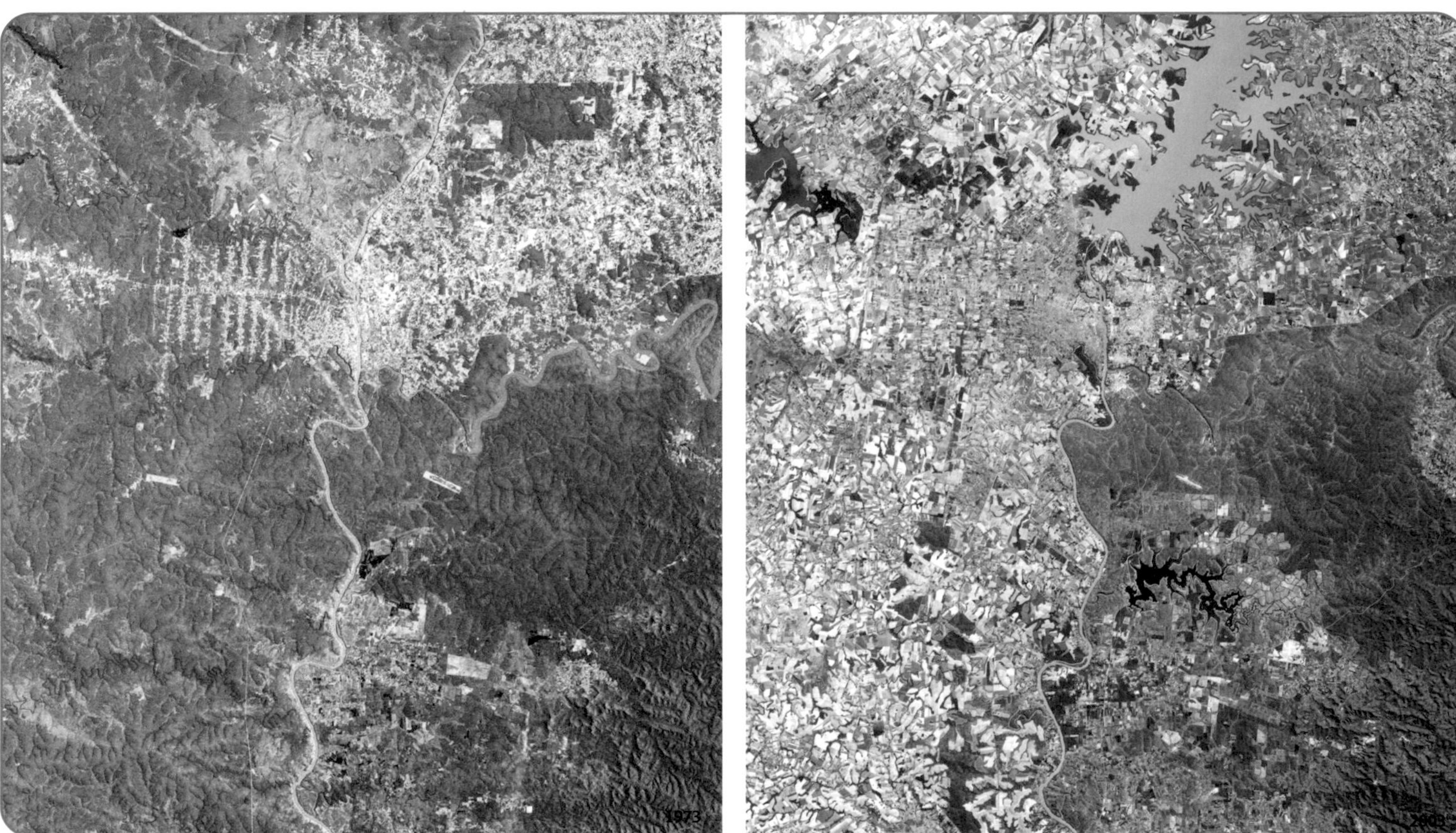

Deforestation and the creation of the **Itaipu Dam** on the Paraná river in Brazil have had a dramatic effect on the landscape and ecosystems of this part of South America. Some forest on the right of the images lies within Iguaçu National Park and has been protected from destruction.

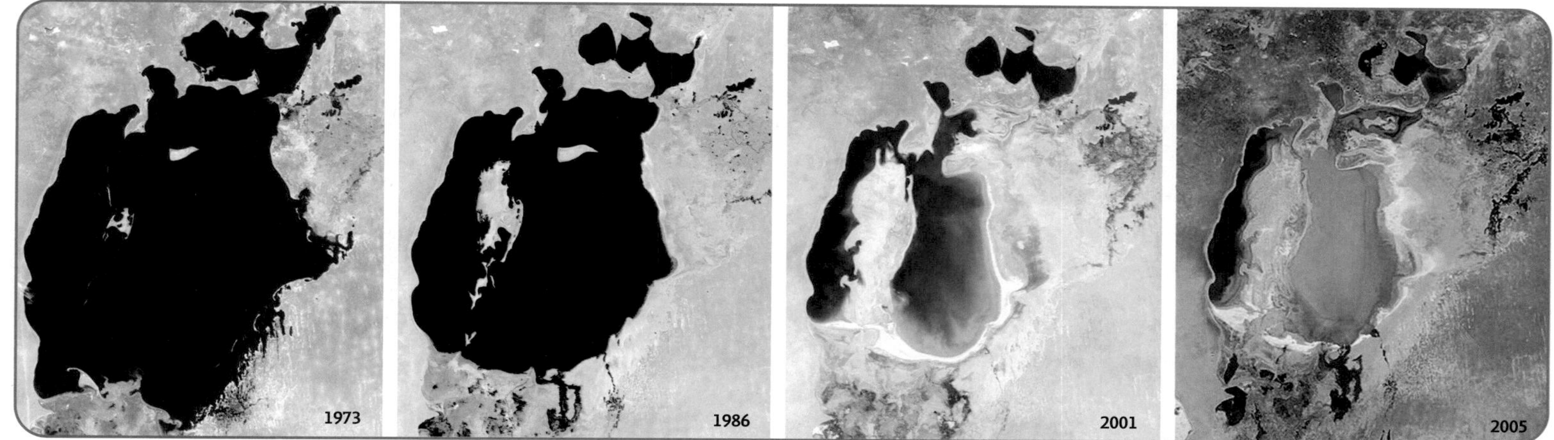

Aral Sea, Kazakhstan/Uzbekistan 1973-2005 Climate change and the diversion of rivers have caused its dramatic shrinkage.

Environmental Impacts

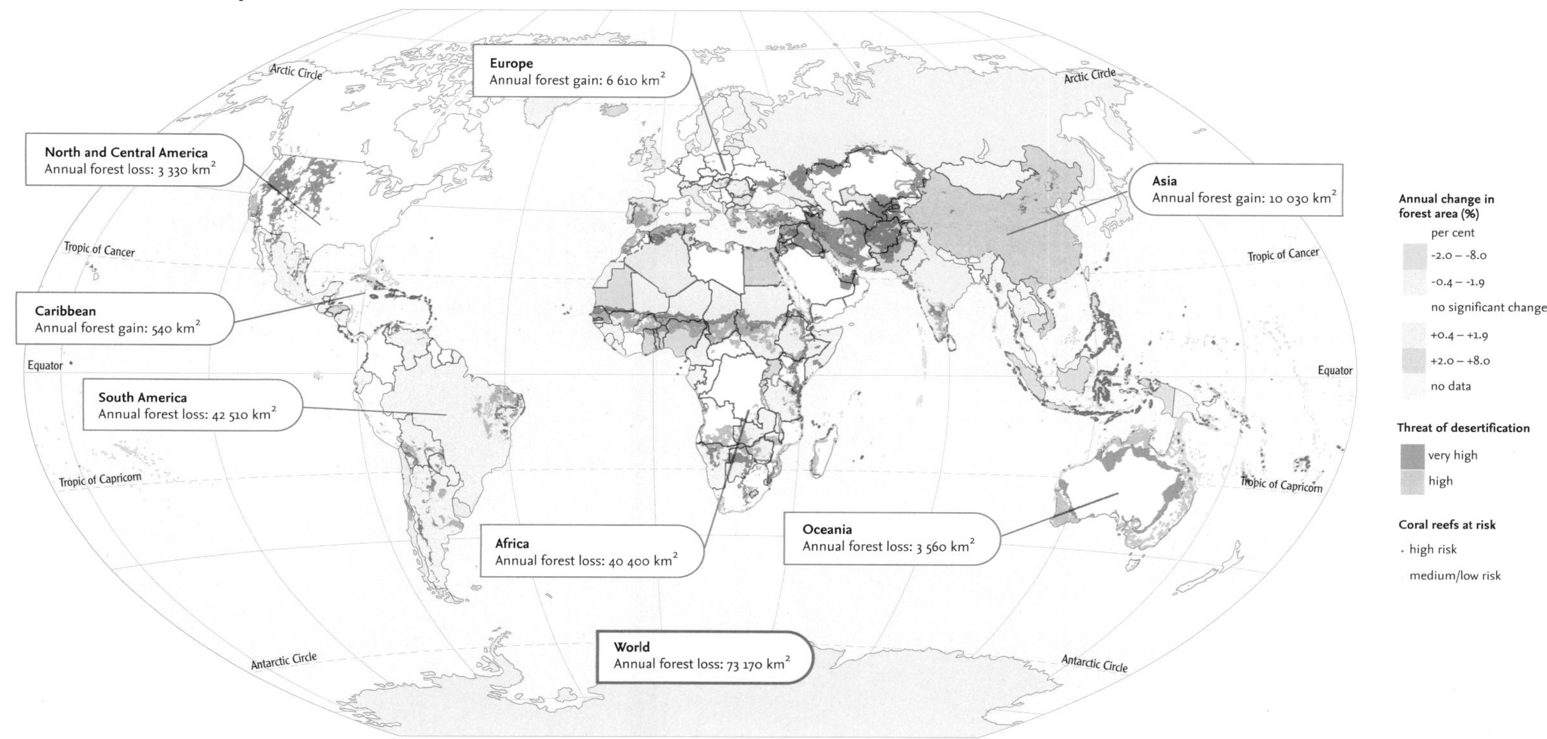

Internet links

UN Environment Programme	**www.unep.org**
IUCN World Conservation Union	**www.iucn.org**
UNESCO World Heritage Sites	**whc.unesco.org**

Environmental protection

Top 10 protected areas by size

Rank	Protected area	Country	Size (sq km)	Designation
1	**Northeast Greenland**	Greenland	972 000	National Park
2	**Rubʻ al-Khālī**	Saudi Arabia	640 000	Wildlife Management Area
3	**Phoenix Islands**	Kiribati	410 500	Protected Area
4	**Great Barrier Reef**	Australia	344 400	Marine Park
5	**Papahānaumokuākea Marine National Monument**	United States	341 362	Coral Reef Ecosystem Reserve
6	**Qiangtang**	China	298 000	Nature Reserve
7	**Macquarie Island**	Australia	162 060	Marine Park
8	**Sanjiangyuan**	China	152 300	Nature Reserve
9	**Galápagos**	Ecuador	133 000	Marine Reserve
10	**Northern Wildlife Management Zone**	Saudi Arabia	100 875	Wildlife Management Area

Great Barrier Reef, Australia, the world's third largest protected area.

Europe
Landscapes

Europe, the westward extension of the Asian continent and the second smallest of the world's continents, has a remarkable variety of physical features and landscapes. The continent is bounded by mountain ranges of varying character – the highlands of Scandinavia and northwest Britain, the Pyrenees, the Alps, the Carpathian Mountains, the Caucasus and the Ural Mountains. Two of these, the Caucasus and Ural Mountains, define the eastern limits of Europe, with the Black Sea and the Bosporus defining its southeastern boundary with Asia.

Across the centre of the continent stretches the North European Plain, broken by some of Europe's greatest rivers, including the Volga and the Dnieper and containing some of its largest lakes. To the south, the Mediterranean Sea divides Europe from Africa. The Mediterranean region itself has a very distinct climate and landscape.

Facts

- The Danube flows through 7 countries and has 7 different name forms
- Lakes cover almost 10% of the total land area of Finland
- The Strait of Gibraltar, separating the Atlantic Ocean from the Mediterranean Sea and Europe from Africa, is only 13 kilometres wide at its narrowest point
- The highest mountain in the Alps is Mont Blanc, 4 808 metres, on the France/Italy border

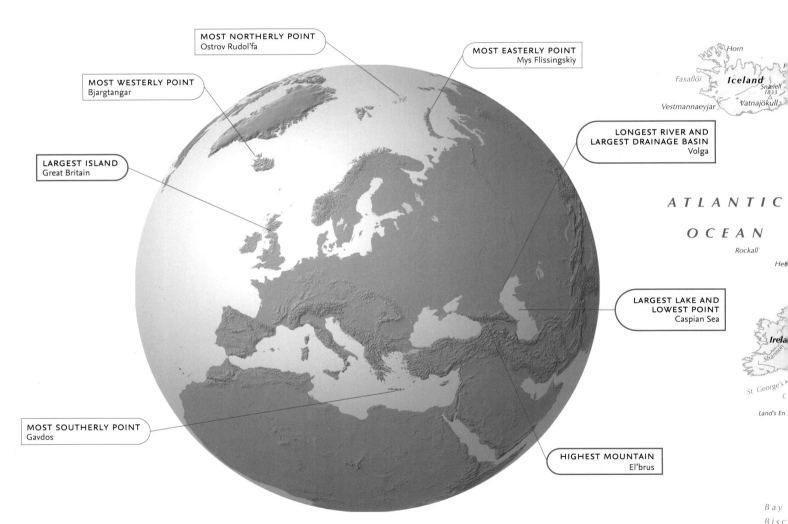

MOST NORTHERLY POINT
Ostrov Rudol'fa

MOST EASTERLY POINT
Mys Flissingskiy

MOST WESTERLY POINT
Bjargtangar

LONGEST RIVER AND LARGEST DRAINAGE BASIN
Volga

LARGEST ISLAND
Great Britain

LARGEST LAKE AND LOWEST POINT
Caspian Sea

MOST SOUTHERLY POINT
Gavdos

HIGHEST MOUNTAIN
El'brus

Europe's greatest physical features

Highest mountain	El'brus, Russian Federation	5 642 metres	18 510 feet
Longest river	Volga, Russian Federation	3 688 km	2 292 miles
Largest lake	Caspian Sea	371 000 sq km	143 243 sq miles
Largest island	Great Britain, United Kingdom	218 476 sq km	84 354 sq miles
Largest drainage basin	Volga, Russian Federation	1 380 000 sq km	532 818 sq miles

Europe's extent

TOTAL LAND AREA	9 908 599 sq km / 3 825 710 sq miles
Most northerly point	Ostrov Rudol'fa, Russian Federation
Most southerly point	Gavdos, Crete, Greece
Most westerly point	Bjargtangar, Iceland
Most easterly point	Mys Flissingskiy, Russian Federation

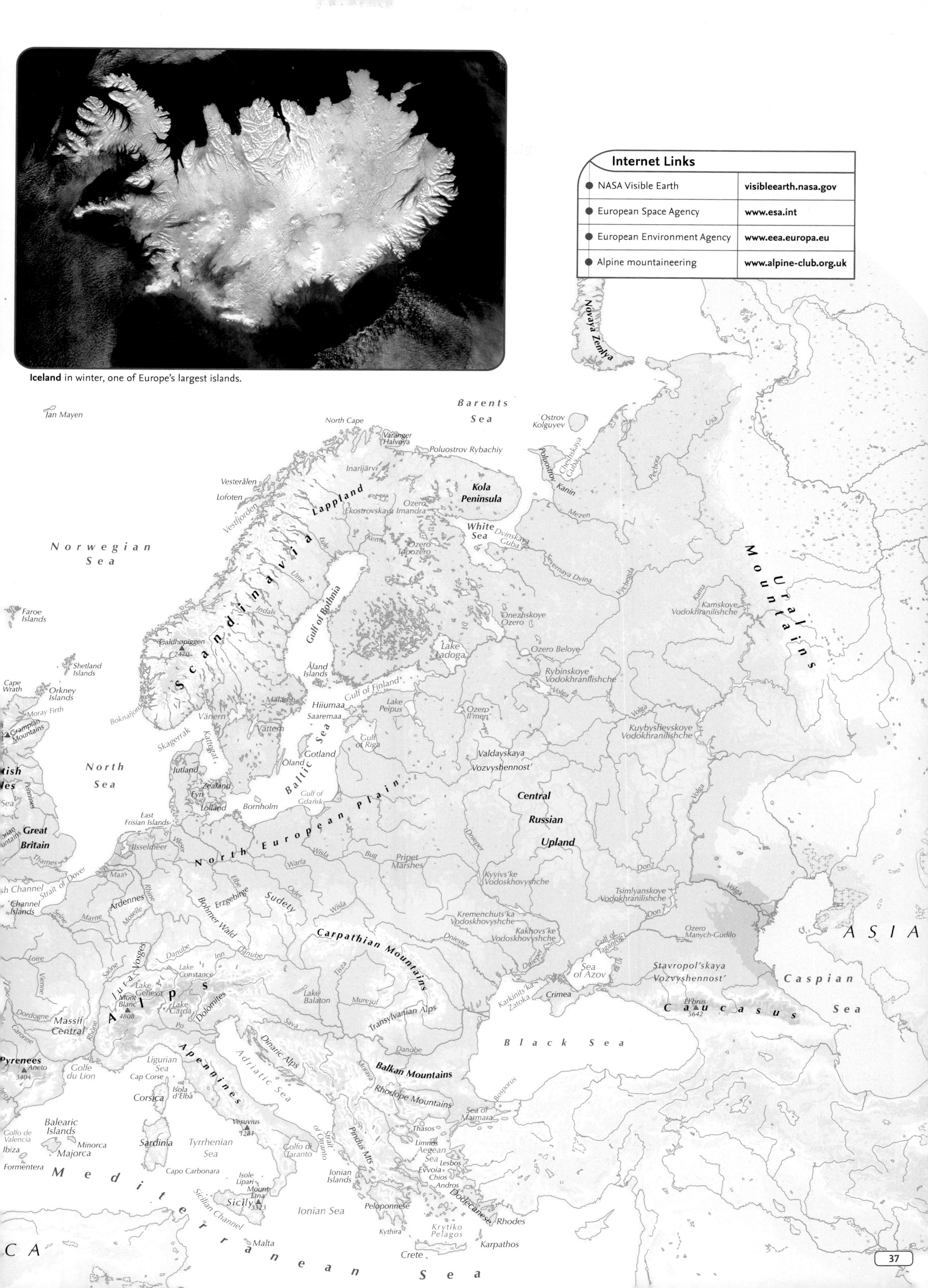

Internet Links

NASA Visible Earth	**visibleearth.nasa.gov**
European Space Agency	**www.esa.int**
European Environment Agency	**www.eea.europa.eu**
Alpine mountaineering	**www.alpine-club.org.uk**

Iceland in winter, one of Europe's largest islands.

Europe
Countries

The predominantly temperate climate of Europe has led to it becoming the most densely populated of the continents. It is highly industrialized, and has exploited its great wealth of natural resources and agricultural land to become one of the most powerful economic regions in the world.

The current pattern of countries within Europe is a result of numerous and complicated changes throughout its history. Ethnic, religious and linguistic differences have often been the cause of conflict, particularly in the Balkan region which has a very complex ethnic pattern. Current boundaries reflect, to some extent, these divisions which continue to be a source of tension. The historic distinction between 'Eastern' and 'Western' Europe is no longer made, following the collapse of Communism and the break up of the Soviet Union in 1991.

Facts

- **The European Union was founded by six countries: Belgium, France, Germany, Italy, Luxembourg, and the Netherlands. It now has 27 members**
- **The newest members of the European Union, Bulgaria and Romania joined in 2007**
- **Europe has the 2 smallest independent countries in the world – Vatican City and Monaco**
- **Vatican City is an independent country entirely within the city of Rome, and is the centre of the Roman Catholic Church**

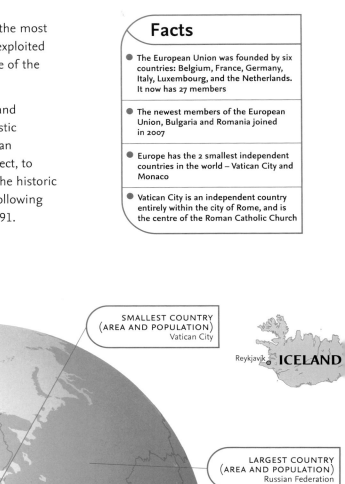

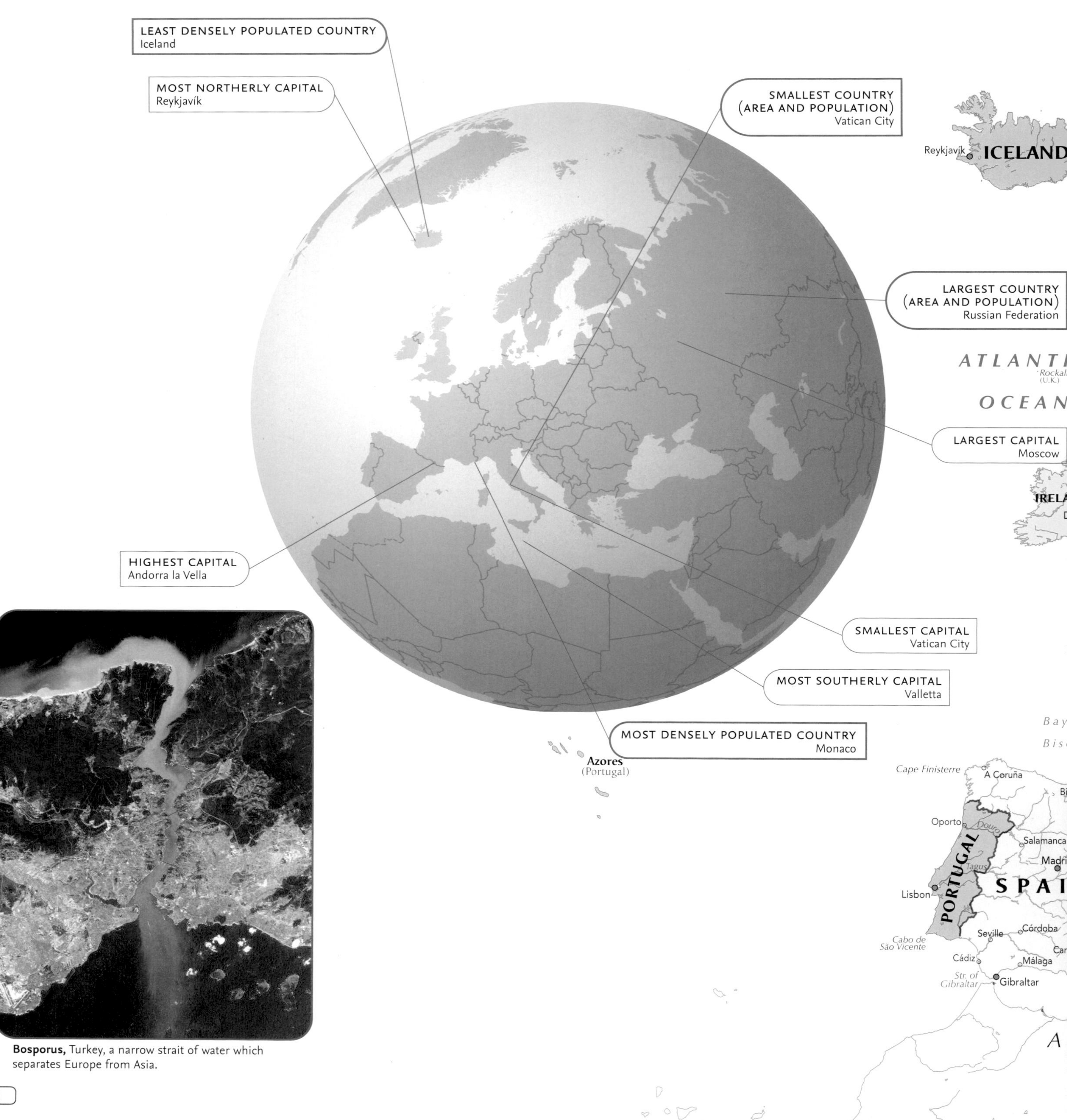

Bosporus, Turkey, a narrow strait of water which separates Europe from Asia.

Europe's capitals

Largest capital (population)	Moscow, Russian Federaton	10 452 000
Smallest capital (population)	Vatican City	557
Most northerly capital	Reykjavík, Iceland	64° 39'N
Most southerly capital	Valletta, Malta	35° 54'N
Highest capital	Andorra la Vella, Andorra	1 029 metres 3 376 feet

Europe's countries

Largest country (area)	Russian Federation	17 075 400 sq km	6 592 849 sq miles
Smallest country (area)	Vatican City	0.5 sq km	0.2 sq miles
Largest country (population)	Russian Federation	143 202 000	
Smallest country (population)	Vatican City	557	
Most densely populated country	Monaco	17 000 per sq km	34 000 per sq mile
Least densely populated country	Iceland	3 per sq km	7 per sq mile

Internet Links

European Union	**europa.eu**
UK Foreign and Commonwealth Office	**www.fco.gov.uk**
CIA World Factbook	**www.cia.gov/library/publications/the-world-factbook/index.html**

Denmark Strait
Arctic Circle
ICELAND
REYKJAVIK
Akureyri
Vatnajökull
ATLANTIC OCEAN
Faroe Islands (Denmark)
TÓRSHAVN
Norwegian Sea
Shetland Islands
Lerwick
Orkney Islands
Outer Hebrides
British Isles
North Sea
Rockall (U.K.)
IRELAND
DUBLIN
Cork
Belfast
UNITED KINGDOM
Glasgow
Edinburgh
Aberdeen
Newcastle upon Tyne
Manchester
Liverpool
Leeds
Birmingham
LONDON
Cardiff
Plymouth
Isle of Man (U.K.)
Irish Sea
St George's Channel
English Channel (La Manche)
Channel Islands (U.K.)
Strait of Dover
NORWAY
OSLO
Bergen
Trondheim
Stavanger
SWEDEN
STOCKHOLM
Gothenburg
Skagerrak
Kattegat
DENMARK
COPENHAGEN
Bornholm (Denmark)
Baltic Sea
Gotland (Sweden)
Öland
NETHERLANDS
AMSTERDAM
THE HAGUE
Rotterdam
BELGIUM
BRUSSELS
LUX.
LUXEMBOURG
GERMANY
BERLIN
Hamburg
Bremen
Hannover
Cologne
Düsseldorf
Frankfurt am Main
Stuttgart
Munich
Leipzig
Dresden
POLAND
Poznań
Wrocław
Gdańsk
CZECH REPUBLIC
PRAGUE
FRANCE
PARIS
Le Havre
Rennes
Nantes
Bordeaux
Lyon
Strasbourg
Dijon
Massif Central
Bay of Biscay
Gulf of Gascony
SWITZERLAND
BERN
Zürich
LIECHTENSTEIN
AUSTRIA
VIENNA
Salzburg
Innsbruck
SLOVENIA
SLOVAKIA
BRATISLAVA
HUNGARY
ITALY
SPAIN
Oviedo
Gijón-Xixón
Santander
↓ 54
Conic Equidistant Projection
1:10 000 000
0 100 200 300 400 miles
0 100 200 300 400 500 600 km

Europe

Northern Europe

Conic Equidistant Projection

1:7 500 000 0 100 200 300 miles
0 100 200 300 400 500 km

RUSSIAN FEDERATION
BELARUS
UKRAINE
POLAND
SLOVAKIA
HUNGARY
ROMANIA
MOLDOVA
BULGARIA
GREECE
TURKEY
GEORGIA
ARMENIA
AZER.
KAZAKHSTAN
ZAPADNYY KAZAKHSTAN
Black Sea
Sea of Azov
Caspian Sea
Crimea
Central Russian Upland
Carpathian Mountains
Caspian Lowland
MINSK
KIEV (Kyiv)
WARSAW (Warszawa)
BUCHAREST (București)
SOFIA (Sofiya)
CHIȘINĂU (Kishinev)
T'BILISI
↑ 91
↓ 47
↓ 59
90 ↓

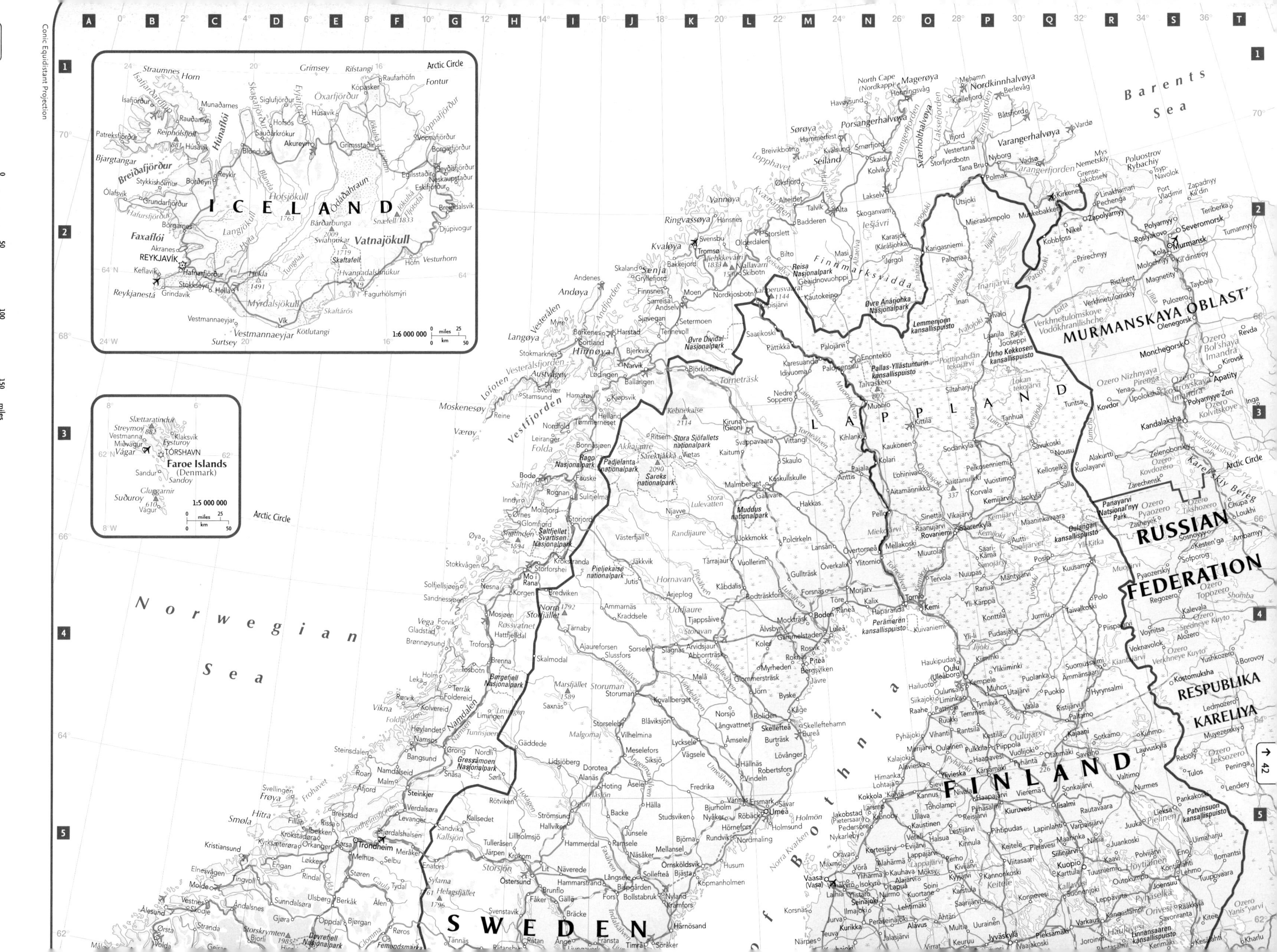

1:5 000 000 — 0 50 100 150 miles; 0 50 100 150 200 250 km

Europe

Scandinavia and the Baltic States

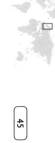

ATLANTIC OCEAN
North Sea
Celtic Sea
Irish Sea
English Channel (La Manche)
British Isles
UNITED KINGDOM
IRELAND
Great Britain
FRANCE
BELGIUM
NETHERLANDS
Outer Hebrides
Orkney Islands
Isle of Lewis
South Harris
North Uist
Benbecula
South Uist
Barra
St Kilda
Skye
Rum
Coll
Mull
Colonsay
Jura
Islay
Arran
Kintyre
Isle of Man (U.K.)
DOUGLAS
Anglesey
Isles of Scilly
Isle of Wight
Channel Islands (Îles Normandes)
Guernsey (U.K.)
Jersey (U.K.)
ST PETER PORT
ST HELIER
Golfe de St-Malo
Baie de Seine
Strait of Dover (Pas de Calais)
Bristol Channel
Cardigan Bay
St George's Channel
North Channel
The Minch
Little Minch
Moray Firth
Firth of Forth
Solway Firth
Pentland Firth
Cape Wrath
Butt of Lewis
Dunnet Head
John o'Groats
Land's End
Lizard Point
Start Point
Cap de la Hague
Pointe du Raz
Île d'Ouessant
Belle-Île
Île de Noirmoutier
Île d'Yeu
Île de Groix
Grampian Mountains
Cairngorms National Park
Loch Lomond & the Trossachs National Park
Southern Uplands
Cheviot Hills
Northumberland National Park
Lake District National Park
North York Moors National Park
Yorkshire Dales National Park
Peak District National Park
Snowdonia National Park
Cambrian Mountains
Brecon Beacons National Park
Pembrokeshire Coast National Park
Exmoor National Park
Dartmoor National Park
New Forest National Park
Pennines
Ben Nevis 1344
Ben Macdui 1309
Snowdon (Yr Wyddfa) 1085
Scafell Pike 977
Wicklow Mountains National Park
Lugnaquilla 926
Glenveagh National Park
Connemara National Park
Killarney National Park
MacGillycuddy's Reeks
Carrauntoohil 1041
ULSTER
CONNAUGHT
LEINSTER
MUNSTER
DUBLIN (Baile Átha Cliath)
Dún Laoghaire
Belfast
Londonderry
Cork (Corcaigh)
Limerick (Luimneach)
Galway (Gaillimh)
Waterford (Port Láirge)
Sligo (Sligeach)
LONDON
Edinburgh
Glasgow
Aberdeen
Dundee
Inverness
Perth
Newcastle upon Tyne
Sunderland
Middlesbrough
Leeds
Bradford
Manchester
Liverpool
Sheffield
Kingston upon Hull
Nottingham
Leicester
Birmingham
Coventry
Norwich
Cambridge
Oxford
Bristol
Cardiff (Caerdydd)
Swansea (Abertawe)
Newport (Casnewydd)
Southampton
Portsmouth
Brighton
Plymouth
Exeter
Dover
Ipswich
Peterborough
Great Yarmouth
PARIS
Lille
Rouen
Le Havre
Caen
Cherbourg
Rennes
Brest
Nantes
Le Mans
Orléans
Tours
Angers
Reims
Amiens
Calais
Boulogne-sur-Mer
Dunkirk (Dunkerque)
Poitiers
Bourges
BRITTANY
NORMANDY
PICARDY
ARTOIS
ANJOU
POITOU
BRIE
CHAMPAGNE POUILLEUSE
CHAMPAGNE HUMIDE
BURGUNDY
Collines de Normandie
AMSTERDAM
THE HAGUE ('s-Gravenhage) (Den Haag)
Rotterdam
BRUSSELS (Bruxelles)
Antwerp
Ghent (Gent)
Brugge (Bruges)
Conic Equidistant Projection
1:5 000 000
0 50 100 150 miles
0 50 100 150 200 250 km

NORWAY
SWEDEN
DENMARK
GERMANY
POLAND
CZECH REPUBLIC
SLOVAKIA
AUSTRIA
HUNGARY
SWITZERLAND
LIECHTENSTEIN
SLOVENIA
CROATIA
ITALY
SERBIA
ESTONIA
LATVIA
LITHUANIA
RUSSIAN FEDERATION
Skagerrak
Kattegat
Baltic Sea
Gulf of Riga
Gulf of Gdańsk
German Bight
Jutland
Zealand
Fyn
Lolland
Falster
Møn
Bornholm (Denmark)
Gotland (Sweden)
Öland
Saaremaa
Vänern
Vättern
COPENHAGEN (København)
Gothenburg (Göteborg)
BERLIN
WARSAW (Warszawa)
PRAGUE (Praha)
VIENNA (Wien)
BRATISLAVA
BUDAPEST
BERN
Hamburg
Munich (München)
Frankfurt am Main
Cologne (Köln)
Dresden
Leipzig
Hannover
Bremen
Gdańsk
Poznań
Wrocław
Kraków
Łódź
Stuttgart
Nuremberg
Zürich
Vosges
Black Forest (Schwarzwald)
Schwäbische Alb
Harz
Erzgebirge
Bohmer Wald
BAVARIA
ALSACE
Sudety
Malé Karpaty
Lake Constance (Bodensee)
↑ 45
↓ 58
→ 43

Conic Equidistant Projection

1:2 000 000
0 25 50 75 miles
0 25 50 75 100 125 km

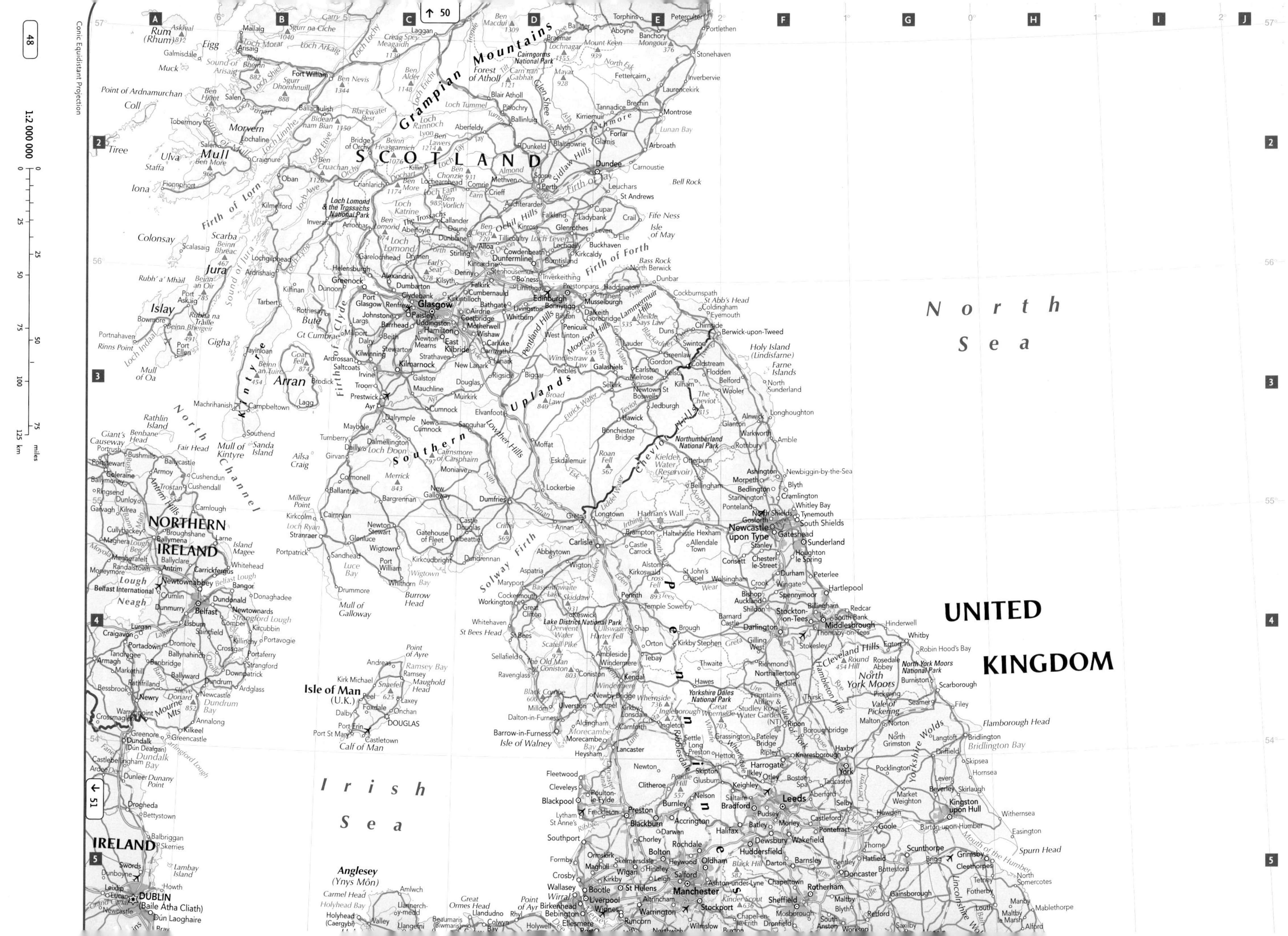

↑ 52

Europe
England and Wales

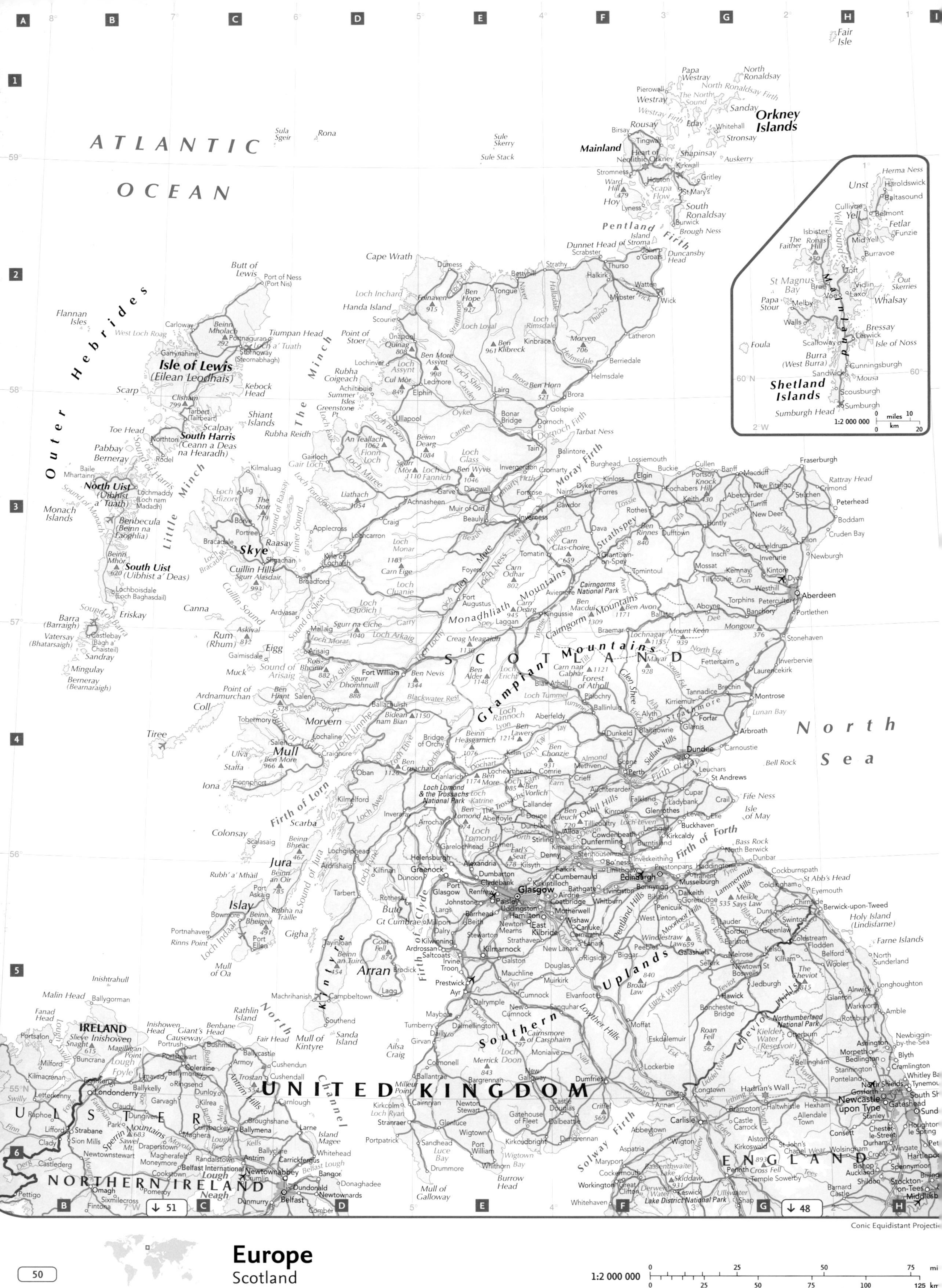

Conic Equidistant Projection

Europe
Scotland

1:2 000 000

onic Equidistant Projection

1:2 000 000 0 25 50 75 miles
0 25 50 75 100 125 km

Europe
Ireland

North Sea
West Frisian Islands
Waddenzee
IJsselmeer
Markermeer
NETHERLANDS
AMSTERDAM
THE HAGUE ('s-Gravenhage) (Den Haag)
Rotterdam
UNITED KINGDOM
ENGLAND
Strait of Dover (Pas de Calais)
BELGIUM
BRUSSELS (Bruxelles)
Antwerp
Ghent (Gent)
Bruges (Brugge)
Liège
Ardennes
LUXEMBOURG
FRANCE
PARIS
ÎLE-DE-FRANCE
NORD-PAS-DE-CALAIS
PICARDIE
PICARDY
FLANDRE
ARTOIS
HAINAUT
HAUTE-NORMANDIE
CHAMPAGNE-ARDENNE
LORRAINE
Côtes de Meuse
Eifel
SAARLAND
Düsseldorf
Conic Equidistant Projection
1:2 000 000
0 25 50 75 miles
0 25 50 75 100 125 km
49

↑ 45
↑ 47
GERMANY
CZECH REPUBLIC
MECKLENBURG-VORPOMMERN
SCHLESWIG-HOLSTEIN
HAMBURG
NIEDERSACHSEN
BREMEN
BRANDENBURG
BERLIN
SACHSEN-ANHALT
NORDRHEIN-WESTFALEN
HESSEN
THÜRINGEN
SACHSEN
RHEINLAND-PFALZ
BADEN-WÜRTTEMBERG
BAVARIA
BAYERN
ALSACE
OSTFRIESLAND
AMMERLAND
LÜNEBURGER HEIDE
ALTMARK
PRIGNITZ
UCKERMARK
ZAUCHE
MÜNSTER LAND
OBERWÄLDER LAND
BERGISCHES LAND
GOLDENE AUE
NORDPFÄLZER BERGLAND
ODENWALD
Harz
Thüringer Wald
Fränkische Alb
Bayerischer Wald
Böhmer Wald
Oberpfälzer Wald
Erzgebirge
Krušné hory
Český les
Hamburg
Bremen
Hannover
Magdeburg
Leipzig
Dresden
Erfurt
Frankfurt am Main
Nuremberg (Nürnberg)
Stuttgart
Karlsruhe
Mannheim
Würzburg
Regensburg
Kassel
Göttingen
Dortmund
Münster
Osnabrück

Conic Equidistant Projection

1:10 000 000

0 100 200 300 400 miles

0 100 200 300 400 500 600 km

↑ 41

→ 86

↓ 97

Europe

Southern Europe and the Mediterranean

Europe

France

onic Equidistant Projection

1:5 000 000

0 50 100 150 miles

0 50 100 150 200 250 km

Europe

Spain and Portugal

1:5 000 000 — 0 50 100 150 miles; 0 50 100 150 200 250 km

Europe

Italy and the Balkans

Asia

Landscapes

Asia is the world's largest continent and occupies almost one-third of the world's total land area. Stretching across approximately 165° of longitude from the Mediterranean Sea to the easternmost point of the Russian Federation on the Bering Strait, it contains the world's highest and lowest points and some of the world's greatest physical features. Its mountain ranges include the Himalaya, Hindu Kush, Karakoram and the Ural Mountains and its major rivers – including the Yangtze, Tigris-Euphrates, Indus, Ganges and Mekong – are equally well-known and evocative.

Asia's deserts include the Gobi, the Taklimakan, and those on the Arabian Peninsula, and significant areas of volcanic and tectonic activity are present on the Kamchatka Peninsula, in Japan, and on Indonesia's numerous islands. The continent's landscapes are greatly influenced by climatic variations, with great contrasts between the islands of the Arctic Ocean and the vast Siberian plains in the north, and the tropical islands of Indonesia.

The **Yangtze,** China, Asia's longest river, flowing into the East China Sea near Shanghai.

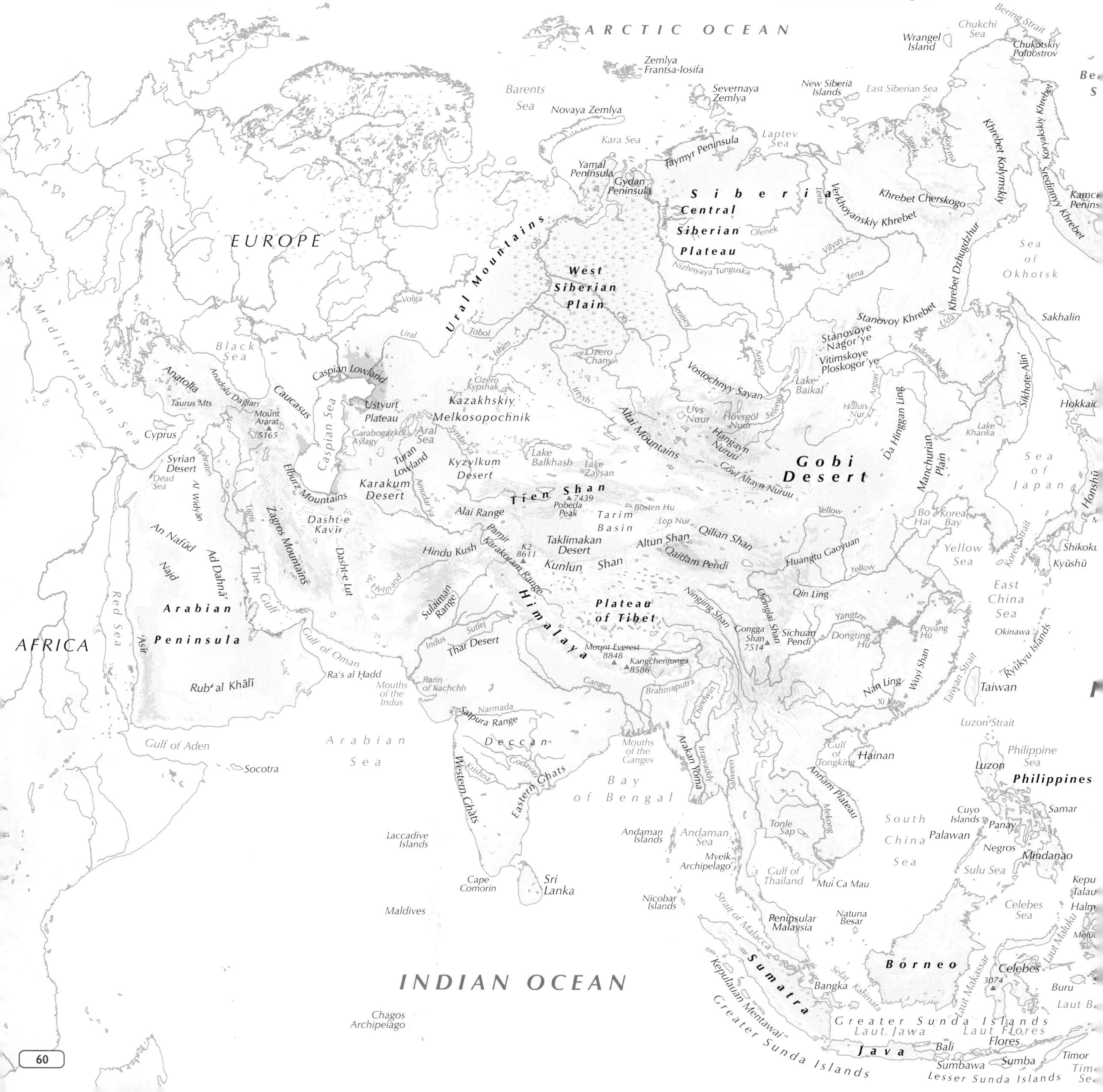

Internet Links	
NASA Visible Earth	visibleearth.nasa.gov
NASA Earth Observatory	earthobservatory.nasa.gov
Peakware World Mountain Encyclopedia	www.peakware.com
The Himalaya	www.alpine-club.org.uk

Asia's physical features

Highest mountain	Mt Everest, China/Nepal	8 848 metres	29 028 feet
Longest river	Yangtze, China	6 380 km	3 965 miles
Largest lake	Caspian Sea	371 000 sq km	143 243 sq miles
Largest island	Borneo	745 561 sq km	287 861 sq miles
Largest drainage basin	Ob'-Irtysh, Kazakhstan/Russian Federation	2 990 000 sq km	1 154 439 sq miles
Lowest point	Dead Sea	-421 metres	-1 381 feet

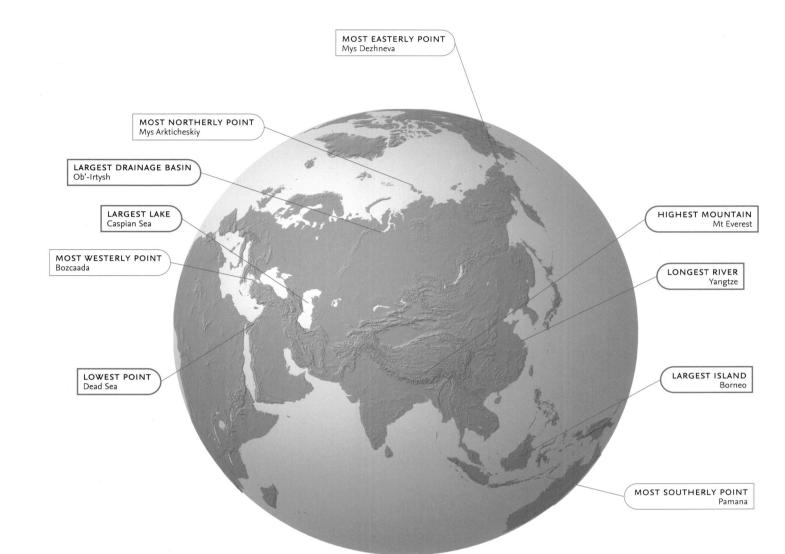

MOST EASTERLY POINT
Mys Dezhneva

MOST NORTHERLY POINT
Mys Arkticheskiy

LARGEST DRAINAGE BASIN
Ob'-Irtysh

LARGEST LAKE
Caspian Sea

MOST WESTERLY POINT
Bozcaada

LOWEST POINT
Dead Sea

HIGHEST MOUNTAIN
Mt Everest

LONGEST RIVER
Yangtze

LARGEST ISLAND
Borneo

MOST SOUTHERLY POINT
Pamana

Asia's extent

TOTAL LAND AREA	45 036 492 sq km / 17 388 686 sq miles
Most northerly point	Mys Arkticheskiy, Russian Federation
Most southerly point	Pamana, Indonesia
Most westerly point	Bozcaada, Turkey
Most easterly point	Mys Dezhneva, Russian Federation

Facts

- **90 of the world's 100 highest mountains are in Asia**
- **The Indonesian archipelago is made up of over 13 500 islands**
- **The height of the land in Nepal ranges from 60 metres to 8 848 metres**
- **The deepest lake in the world is Lake Baikal, Russian Federation, with a maximum depth of 1 741 metres**

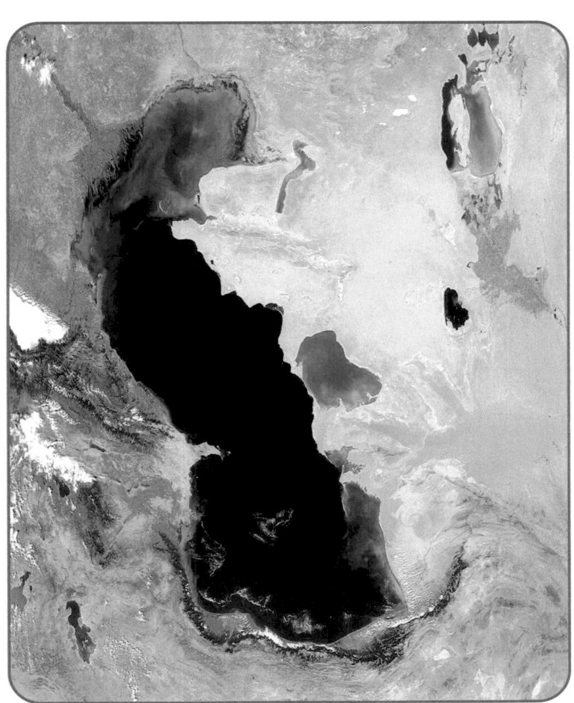
Caspian Sea, Europe/Asia, the world's largest expanse of inland water.

Asia

Countries

With approximately sixty per cent of the world's population, Asia is home to numerous cultures, people groups and lifestyles. Several of the world's earliest civilizations were established in Asia, including those of Sumeria, Babylonia and Assyria. Cultural and historical differences have led to a complex political pattern, and the continent has been, and continues to be, subject to numerous territorial and political conflicts – including the current disputes in the Middle East and in Jammu and Kashmir.

Separate regions within Asia can be defined by the cultural, economic and political systems they support. The major regions are: the arid, oil-rich, mainly Islamic southwest; southern Asia with its distinct cultures, isolated from the rest of Asia by major mountain ranges; the Indian- and Chinese-influenced monsoon region of southeast Asia; the mainly Chinese-influenced industrialized areas of eastern Asia; and Soviet Asia, made up of most of the former Soviet Union.

Timor island in southeast Asia, on which East Timor, Asia's newest independent state, is located.

ARCTIC OCEAN
Barents Sea
Laptev Sea
Ugol'nyye Kopi
Tiksi
EUROPE
St Petersburg
Noril'sk
Magadan
Petropavlovsk-Kamchatskiy
Sea of Okhotsk
Moscow
Nizhniy Novgorod
Urengoy
Yakutsk
Ural Mountains
Ob'
Yenisey
Lena
RUSSIAN FEDERATION
Kazan'
Perm'
Surgut
Aldan
Ufa
Yekaterinburg
Saratov
Samara
Chelyabinsk
Tobol'sk
Bodaybo
Tynda
Volgograd
Ural'sk
Orenburg
Tomsk
Ust'-Kut
Bratsk
Komsomol'sk-na-Amure
Bursa
Black Sea
Krasnodar
Omsk
Novosibirsk
Krasnoyarsk
Lake Baikal
Heilong Jiang
Yuzhno-Sakhalinsk
İzmir
Ankara
Samsun
Astrakhan'
Aktobe
Barnaul
Novokuznetsk
Irkutsk
Chita
Blagoveshchensk
Khabarovsk
TURKEY
Atyrau
Astana
Ulan-Ude
Antalya
Konya
Sivas
GEORGIA
Karaganda
Semipalatinsk
Ust'-Kamenogorsk
Kyzyl
Sapporo
Hakodate
CYPRUS
Adana
ARMENIA
T'bilisi
Aktau
Aral'sk
KAZAKHSTAN
Hulun Buir
Qiqihar
Nicosia
Gaziantep
Yerevan
AZERBAIJAN
Caspian Sea
Aral Sea
Ulaangom
Darhan
Ulan Bator
Harbin
Beirut
Aleppo
Baku
Altay
Jargalant
Vladivostok
LEBANON
Damascus
Euphrates
Mosul
Tabriz
Türkmenbashy
UZBEKISTAN
Lake Balkhash
MONGOLIA
Changchun
Jilin
Akita
Amman
SYRIA
Gobi Desert
Chongjin
Sea of Japan
JAPAN
Tōkyō
ISRAEL
Jerusalem
Kirkuk
Shymkent
Bishkek
Almaty
Yining
NORTH KOREA
JORDAN
IRAQ
TURKMENISTAN
Toshkent
Ürümqi
Dalandzadgad
Shenyang
Kanazawa
Kermānshāh
Aşgabat
KYRGYZSTAN
Tien Shan
P'yŏngyang
Yokohama
Baghdād
Tehrān
Gorgān
Samarqand
Korla
Jining
Beijing
Dalian
Seoul
Kyōto
An Najaf
Mashhad
Dushanbe
Yellow River
Baotou
Yantai
SOUTH KOREA
Kōbe
Ōsaka
Basra
Ahvāz
Eşfahān
TAJIKISTAN
Kashi
Yumen
Wuhai
Yinchuan
Taiyuan
Jinan
Zibo
Pusan
Hiroshima
Kuwait
Ābādān
IRAN
Herāt
Hotan
Qingdao
Yellow Sea
Medina
KUWAIT
Shīrāz
Birjand
Kābul
Golmud
Xining
Lanzhou
Nagasaki
Kagoshima
SAUDI
Būshehr
AFGHANISTAN
Peshawar
Islamabad
Yellow River
Zhengzhou
East China Sea
BAHRAIN
Dammam
Kandahār
Himalaya
CHINA
Xi'an
Huainan
Nanjing
Shanghai
Jeddah
Mecca
Red Sea
Riyadh
Manama
The Gulf
Zāhedān
Quetta
Faisalabad
Lahore
Plateau of Tibet
Wuhu
Wuhan
Ningbo
QATAR
Doha
Bandar-e 'Abbās
Chandigarh
Yangtze
Nanchong
ARABIA
U.A.E.
Dubai
Abu Dhabi
Gulf of Oman
PAKISTAN
Delhi
New Delhi
Mount Everest 8848
Chengdu
Changde
Nanchang
Wenzhou
AFRICA
Muscat
Pasni
Hyderabad
Jaipur
Agra
NEPAL
Lhasa
Yibin
Chongqing
Changsha
Fuzhou
Sūr
Karachi
Jodhpur
Lucknow
Kathmandu
Thimphu
BHUTAN
Dibrugarh
Hengyang
PACIFIC
Hodeidah
Şan'ā'
Kota
Ganges
Darjiling
Panzhihua
Guiyang
Xiamen
T'aipei
TAIWAN
YEMEN
OMAN
Ahmadabad
Bhopal
Varanasi
Patna
BANGLADESH
Guwahati
Kunming
Liuzhou
Kaohsiung
OCEAN
Ta'izz
Jabalpur
Dhaka
Myitkyina
Guangzhou
Shantou
Aden
Mukalla
Şalālah
Surat
Nagpur
Jamshedpur
Kolkata
MYANMAR (BURMA)
Nanning
Hong Kong
Macao
Luzon Strait
Gulf of Aden
Arabian Sea
Mumbai
Chittagong
Mandalay
Ha Nôi
Hai Phong
Haikou
Aparri
Pune
INDIA
Cuttack
Nay Pyi Taw
LAOS
Socotra (Yemen)
Hyderabad
Vishakhapatnam
Sittwe
Pyè
Irrawaddy
Louangphabang
VIETNAM
PHILIPPINES
Bay of Bengal
Vientiane
Dharwad
Rangoon
Quezon City
THAILAND
Mekong
Đa Nang
Manila
Kurnool
Mawlamyaing
Mangalore
Bangalore
Chennai
Bangkok
Nha Trang
South China Sea
Laccadive Islands (India)
Andaman Islands (India)
Andaman Sea
CAMBODIA
Calicut
Tiruchchirappalli
Myeik
Phnom Penh
Surigao
Madurai
Jaffna
Sihanoukville
Dapitan
Davao
Trivandrum
Trincomalee
Nakhon Si Thammarat
Gulf of Thailand
Ho Chi Minh City
Zamboanga
SRI LANKA
Colombo
Sri Jayewardenepura Kotte
Nicobar Islands (India)
Kota Bharu
Kota Kinabalu
Sandakan
George Town
Bandar Seri Begawan
Celebes Sea
Male
Ipoh
BRUNEI
MALDIVES
Banda Aceh
Strait of Malacca
MALAYSIA
Manado
Kuala Lumpur
Sibu
Medan
Putrajaya
Kuching
Palu
Singapore
SINGAPORE
Borneo
Sumatra
INDIAN OCEAN
Padang
Ketapang
Balikpapan
Parepare
Laut Banda
Palembang
INDONESIA
Bengkulu
Laut Jawa
Jakarta
Java
Surabaya
Raba
Dili
EAST TIMOR
British Indian Ocean Territory
Christmas Island (Australia)
Kupang

Internet Links

UK Foreign and Commonwealth Office	www.fco.gov.uk
CIA World Factbook	www.cia.gov/library/publicaions/the-world-factfile/index.html
Asian Development Bank	www.adb.org
Association of Southeast Asian Nations (ASEAN)	www.aseansec.org
Asia-Pacific Economic Cooperation	www.apecsec.org

Asia's countries

Largest country (area)	Russian Federation	17 075 400 sq km	6 592 849 sq miles
Smallest country (area)	Maldives	298 sq km	115 sq miles
Largest country (population)	China	1 313 437 000	
Smallest country (population)	Palau	20 000	
Most densely populated country	Singapore	6 770 per sq km	17 534 per sq mile
Least densely populated country	Mongolia	2 per sq km	5 per sq mile

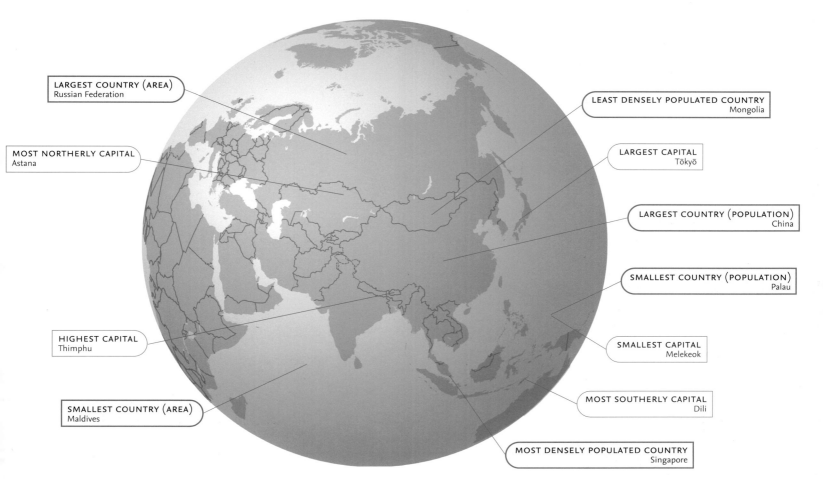

LARGEST COUNTRY (AREA)
Russian Federation

MOST NORTHERLY CAPITAL
Astana

HIGHEST CAPITAL
Thimphu

SMALLEST COUNTRY (AREA)
Maldives

LEAST DENSELY POPULATED COUNTRY
Mongolia

LARGEST CAPITAL
Tōkyō

LARGEST COUNTRY (POPULATION)
China

SMALLEST COUNTRY (POPULATION)
Palau

SMALLEST CAPITAL
Melekeok

MOST SOUTHERLY CAPITAL
Dili

MOST DENSELY POPULATED COUNTRY
Singapore

Asia's capitals

Largest capital (population)	Tōkyō, Japan	35 676 000	
Smallest capital (population)	Melekeok, Palau	391	
Most northerly capital	Astana, Kazakhstan	51° 10'N	
Most southerly capital	Dili, East Timor	8° 35'S	
Highest capital	Thimphu, Bhutan	2 423 metres	7 949 feet

Facts

- **Over 60% of the world's population live in Asia**
- **Asia has 11 of the world's 20 largest cities**
- **The Korean peninsula was divided into North Korea and South Korea in 1948 approximately along the 38th parallel**

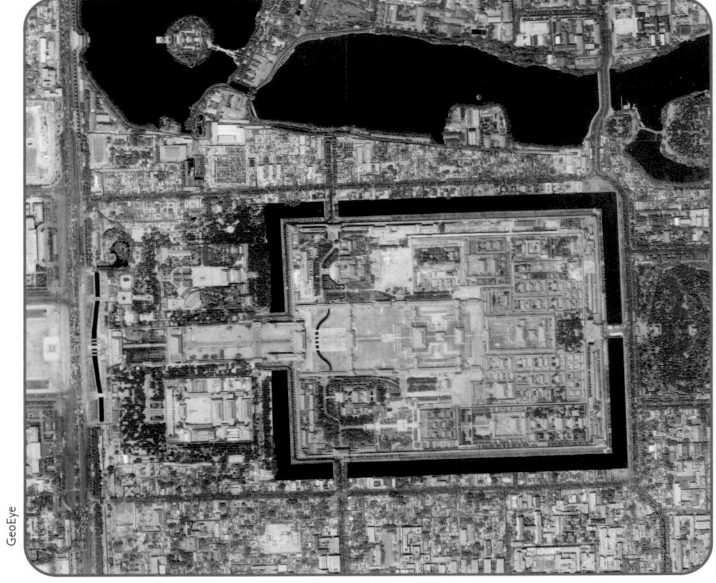

GeoEye

Beijing, capital of China, the most populous country in the world.

← 41
← 78
↓ 79

1:20 000 000

0 200 400 600 miles
0 200 400 600 800 1000 km

↑ 118
↓ 66
OCEAN
Severnaya Zemlya
New Siberia Islands
(Novosibirskiye Ostrova)
East Siberian Sea
(Vostochno-Sibirskoye More)
Laptev Sea
(More Laptevykh)
Chukchi Sea
Wrangel Island
(Ostrov Vrangelya)
Arctic Circle
Seward Peninsula
U.S.A.
Bering Strait
Chukotskiy Poluostrov
St. Lawrence Island
Bering Sea
Aleutian Islands
Koryakskoye Nagor'ye
Khrebet Kolymskiy
Khrebet Cherskogo
Verkhoyanskiy Khrebet
Kolymskaya Nizmennost'
Yukagirskoye Ploskogor'ye
Kamchatka Peninsula
(Poluostrov Kamchatka)
Petropavlovsk-Kamchatskiy
Sredinnyy Khrebet
Sea of Okhotsk
(Okhotskoye More)
Magadan
SIBERIA
(SIBIR')
Central Siberian Plateau
(Sredne-Sibirskoye Ploskogor'ye)
RUSSIAN FEDERATION
Yakutsk
Stanovoy Khrebet
Stanovoye Nagor'ye
Sakhalin
Kuril Islands
(Kuril'skiye Ostrova)
ADMINISTERED BY RUSSIAN FEDERATION, CLAIMED BY JAPAN
Khabarovsk
Sikhote-Alin'
Vladivostok
Irkutsk
Lake Baikal
Ulan-Ude
Chita
Harbin
MANCHURIA
Da Hinggan Ling
ULAN BATOR
(Ulaanbaatar)
MONGOLIA
Gobi Desert
INNER MONGOLIA
CHINA
BEIJING
(Peking)
Tianjin
Shenyang
Changchun
Dalian
NORTH KOREA
P'YONGYANG
SEOUL
SOUTH KOREA
Pusan
Yellow Sea
(Huang Hai)
Sea of Japan
(East Sea)
JAPAN
Hokkaido
Sapporo
Sendai
TOKYO
Yokohama
Nagoya
Kyoto
Osaka
Kobe
Hiroshima
Fukuoka
PACIFIC OCEAN

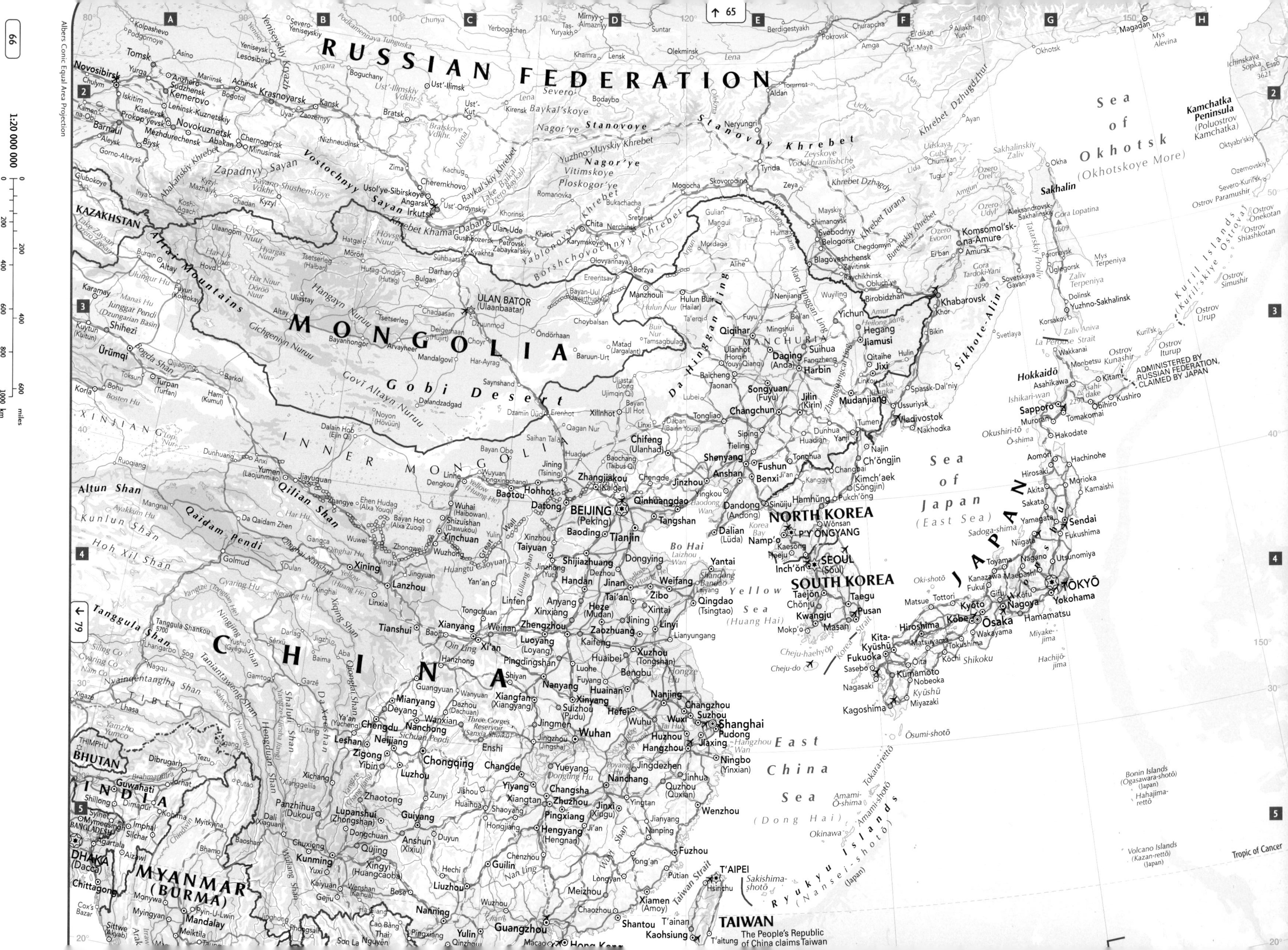

Albers Conic Equal Area Projection

1:20 000 000

0 200 400 600 miles

0 200 400 600 800 1000 km

Asia

Eastern and Southeast Asia

1:15 000 000

0 200 400 miles

0 200 400 600 800 km

PACIFIC
OCEAN
Philippine Sea
PHILIPPINES
TAIWAN
The People's Republic of China claims Taiwan as its 23rd province
T'AIPEI
Chilung (Keelung)
Ilan
Hualien
T'aitung
Lan Yü
Sakishima-shotō
Ishigaki
Yaeyama-retto
Ryukyu Islands (Nansei-shotō) (Japan)
Okino-Daitō-jima
Kita-Iō-jima
Volcano Islands (Kazan-retto) (Japan)
Minami-Iō-jima
Tropic of Cancer
Okino-Tori-shima (Japan)
Batan Islands
Itbayat
Batan
Luzon Strait
Babuyan
Babuyan Islands
Fuga
Babuyan Channel
Tuguegarao
Ilagan
Bontoc
Santiago
Bayombong
Baler
Luzon
Cabanatuan
Polillo Islands
Quezon City
MANILA
San Pablo
Lucena
Calapan
Daet
Lopez
Naga
Iriga
Catanduanes
Virac
Legaspi
Sorsogon
Irosin
Marinduque
Sibuyan Sea
Romblon
Sibuyan
Burias
Masbate
Laoang
Catarman
Calbayog
Catbalogan
Samar
Tacloban
Leyte
Roxas
Panay
Visayan Sea
Iloilo
Cadiz
Ormoc
Bacolod
Danao
Baybay
Bago
Talisay
Cebu
Maasin
Dinagat
Negros
Carcar
Surigao
Siargao
Cauayan
Bohol
Tanjay
Cebu
Bohol Sea
Dumaguete
Tandag
Butuan
Cagayan de Oro
Dipolog
Oroquieta
Ozamiz
Iligan
Bislig
Malaybalay
Lake Lanao
Mindanao
Pagadian
Cotabato
Davao
Mount Apo 2954
Zamboanga
Isabela
Moro Gulf
Davao Gulf
Mati
Basilan
Jolo
Norala
Digos
Malita
General Santos
Cape San Agustin
Sarangani Islands
Sulu Archipelago
Celebes Sea
Kepulauan Nanusa
Karakelong
Kepulauan Talaud
Salibabu
Niampak
Tahuna
Kaburuang
Sangir
Siau
Kepulauan Sangir
Tahulandang
Tanjung Sopi
Morotai
Susupu
Daruba
Tobelo
Tanjung Lelai
Loloda
Akelamo
Manado
Bitung
Tondano
Semenanjung Minahasa
Kotamobagu
Gorontalo
Taman Nasional Bogani Nani Wartabone
Ternate
Laut Maluku (Molucca Sea)
Halmahera
Marisa
Kepulauan Togian
Togian
Batudaka
Tanjung Pangkalsiang
Luwuk
Ampoa
Gebe
Laut Halmahera (Halmahera Sea)
Labuha
Gani
Bacan
Tg Libobo
Laiwui
Bisa
Banggai
Taliabu
Mangole
Moluccas (Maluku)
Obi
Kepulauan Banggai
Lekitobi
Kepulauan Sula
Kolonedale
Bahomonte
Waigeo
Selat Dampir
Sorong
Kwoka 3000
Kaironi
Manokwari
Salawati
Megamo
Sajam
Kep. Raja Ampat
Kep. Boo
Atkri
Misoöl
Tg Winsop
Kep. Pisang
Teminabuan
Jazirah Doberai
Arandai
Moderi
Laut Seram (Ceram Sea)
Wahai
Seram
Taman Nasional Manusela
Buru
Fogi
Ambelau
Ambon
Fakfak
Rufrufua
Semenanjung Bomberai
Selassi
Kaimana
Undur
Kepulauan Gorong
Nusawulan
Kepulauan Watubela
Adi
Teluk Kamrau
Kepulauan Banda
Kepulauan Tayandu
Kepulauan Kai
Kai Besar
Kai Kecil
Tual
Kepulauan Lucipara
Laut Banda (Banda Sea)
Kepulauan Tukangbesi
Wowoni
Kendari
Manui
Kolaka
Raha
Buton
Muna
Wangiwangi
Baubau
Siumpu
Laut Flores (Flores Sea)
Kepulauan Alor
Kepulauan Barat Daya
Pulau Romang
Damar
Kepulauan Babar
Babar
Wetar
Selat Wetar
Moa
Sermata
Kepulauan Leti
Kalabahi
Alor
Komba
Tanjung Kapondai
Larantuka
Maumere
Lomblen
Kepulauan Solor
Ende
Flores
Atambua
DILI
Tutuala
Foho Tatamailau 2960
EAST TIMOR
Laut Sawu (Savu Sea)
Savu
Raijua
Soë
Kefamenanu
Timor
Kupang
Rote
Timor Sea
Ashmore and Cartier Islands (Australia)
Molu
Larat
Kepulauan Tanimbar
Yamdena
Watmuri
Selaru
Dobo
Benjina
Kola
Wokam
Kobroör
Kepulauan Aru
Trangan
Workai
Sia
Arafura Sea
Cape Van Diemen
Milikapiti
Melville I.
Bathurst Island
Mitchell Point
Garig National Park
Croker Island
Cobourg Peninsula
Goulburn Is
Maningrida
Elcho I.
Wessel Islands
Cape Wessel
AUSTRALIA
110
Numfoor
Supiori
Biak
Num
Pom
Yapen
Serui
Rori
Tanjung d'Urville
Teba
Sarmi
Rumberpon
Maswaar
Taman Nasional Teluk Cenderawasih
Teluk Cenderawasih
2252
Asori
Gariau
Nabire
Pegunungan Van Rees
Ansudu
Demta
Jayapura
Lereh
Tariku
Taritatu
Mamberamo
Pegunungan Maoke
3892
Mulia
Tembagapura
Pk Jaya 5030
Puncak Yamin 4595
Puncak Mandala 4700
Pk Trikora 4730
Peg. Jayawijaya
Taman Nasional Lorentz
Amamapare
Agats
New Guinea
Tanjung Deyong
Yomuka
Pembre
Pulau Dolok
Komoran
Tanjung Vals
Kumbe
Merauke
Mombum
Muting
Digul
Vanimo
Sissano
Bewani
Lumi 1859
Aitape
Amanab
Wewak
Green River
Ambunti
Pagwi
Maprik
Sepik
Watam
Manam I.
Mount Kanangio
Karkar Island
Madang
Bismarck Sea
Aua Island
Ninigo Group
Wuvulu Island
Pelleluhu Is
Hermit Islands
Admiralty Islands
Kabuli
Lorengau
Manus Island
Rambutyo Island
Bismarck Archipelago
Mussau Island
Tabalo
St Matthias Group
Schouten Islands
Kairiru I.
Long I.
Umboi
Dampier Str.
New Britain
Nukuhu
Anepmete
Wasum
Walingai
Kandrian
Lae
Finschhafen
Central Ra. 3711
Wabag
Mount Wilhelm 4509
Bismarck Ra.
Lake Kopiago
Mt Hagen
Goroka
Tari
Mendi
Kikori
Kratke Ra.
Bulolo
Wau
PAPUA NEW GUINEA
Lake Murray
Fly
Aramia
Komaio
Balimo
Baimuru
Kerema
Morobe
Cape Ward Hunt
Gulf of Papua
Wasua
Weam
Morehead
Daru
Kiwai Island
Popondetta
Mount Victoria 4073
Kokoda
Cape Nelson
Bereina
Hisiu
PORT MORESBY
Owen Stanley Ra.
3676
Kwikila
Hood Point
Abau
Tais
Sibidiri
Bula
Boigu I.
Torres Strait
Badu Island
Moa Island
Prince of Wales Island
Ashmore Reefs
Endeavour Strait
Cape York
Jardine River National Park
Great Barrier Reef Marine Park (Far North Section)
Mapoon
Cape Grenville
Bramwell
Northern Mariana Islands (U.S.A.)
Farallon de Pajaros (Uracas)
Maug Islands
Asuncion
Agrihan
Pagan
Alamagan
Guguan
Sarigan
Anatahan
Farallon de Medinilla
CAPITOL HILL
Saipan
Tinian
Aguijan
Rota
HAGÅTÑA
Guam (U.S.A.)
Ulithi
Colonia
Yap
Fais
Ngulu
Sorol
FEDERATED STATES OF MICRONESIA
Gaferut
Faraulep
Namonuito
West Fayu
Pikelot
Olimarao
Lamotrek
Pulap
Woleai
Elato
Satawal
Puluwat
Eauripik
Ifalik
Pulusuk
Caroline Islands
Ngeruangel
PALAU
MELEKEOK
Koror
Eil Malk
Angaur
Palau Islands
Sonsorol Islands
Pulo Anna
Merir
Tobi
Helen
Helen Reef
Equator
106
G
H
I
J
K
L
1
2
3
4
5
6
7
8
9
125°
130°
135°
140°
145°
25°
20°
15°
10°
5°
0°

1:7 000 000 — 0, 100, 200 miles; 0, 100, 200, 300, 400 km

Asia

Myanmar, Thailand, Peninsular Malaysia and Indo-China

RUSSIAN FE
KAZAKHSTAN
KYRGYZSTAN
TAJIKISTAN
AFGHANISTAN
PAKISTAN
JAMMU AND KASHMIR
LINE OF CONTROL
AKSAI CHIN
INDIA
NEPAL
BHUTAN
BANGLADESH
MYANMAR (BURMA)
THAILAND
LAOS
VIETNAM
CHINA
MONGO
XINJIANG UYGUR ZIZHIQU (SINKIANG)
XIZANG ZIZHIQU (TIBET)
QINGHAI
GANSU
SICHUAN
YUNNAN
Taklimakan Desert (Taklimakan Shamo)
Tarim Basin (Tarim Pendi)
Plateau of Tibet (Qingzang Gaoyuan)
Kunlun Shan
Altun Shan
Tien Shan
Himalaya
Hindu Kush
Qaidam Pendi
Bay of Bengal
Mouths of the Ganges
Eastern Ghats
Altai Mountains
ASTANA (Akmola)
Almaty (Alma-Ata)
BISHKEK
TOSHKENT
DUSHANBE
ISLAMABAD
KATHMANDU
THIMPHU
DHAKA (Dacca)
NAY PYI TAW
HA NOI
ULAN BAT (Ulaanbaa
Delhi
NEW DELHI
Kolkata (Calcutta)
Hyderabad
Lhasa
Ürümqi
Lanzhou
Xining
Chengdu
Kunming
Mandalay
Chittagong
A
B
C
D
E
F
G
H
I
3
4
5
6
7
8
9
10
1:15 000 000
Albers Conic Equal Area Projection

↑ 64
← 80
← 81
↓ 68

↑ 65
RATION
JAPAN
NORTH KOREA
SOUTH KOREA
TAIWAN
PHILIPPINES
HEILONGJIANG
JILIN
LIAONING
HEBEI
SHANXI
SHANDONG
HENAN
JIANGSU
ANHUI
HUBEI
HUNAN
JIANGXI
ZHEJIANG
FUJIAN
GUANGDONG
HAINAN
NEI MONGGOL ZIZHIQU (INNER MONGOLIA)
MANCHURIA
Sea of Okhotsk (Okhotskoye More)
Sea of Japan (East Sea)
Yellow Sea (Huang Hai)
East China Sea (Dong Hai)
South China Sea
PACIFIC OCEAN
Bo Hai
Korea Bay
Sakhalin
Hokkaidō
Honshū
Shikoku
Kyūshū
Ryukyu Islands (Nansei-shotō) (Japan)
Tropic of Cancer
ADMINISTERED BY RUSSIAN FEDERATION, CLAIMED BY JAPAN
Kuril Islands (Kuril'skiye Ostrova)
The People's Republic of China claims Taiwan as its 23rd province
BEIJING (Peking)
TIANJIN
SHANGHAI
P'YŎNGYANG
SEOUL (Sŏul)
TŌKYŌ
T'AIPEI
Hong Kong
Macao (Aomen)
Shenzhen (Bao'an)
Guangzhou
Harbin
Shenyang
Dalian (Lüda)
Qingdao (Tsingtao)
Nanjing
Wuhan
Vladivostok
Khabarovsk
Pusan
Ōsaka
Nagoya
Yokohama
Sapporo
Sendai
Fukuoka
Kaohsiung
Bashi Channel
Luzon Strait
Korea Strait
La Pérouse Strait

RUSSIAN FEDERATION
AMURSKAYA OBLAST'
KHABAROVSKIY KRAY
YEVREYSKAYA AVTONOMNAYA OBLAST'
PRIMORSKIY KRAY
SAKHALINSKAYA OBLAST'
CHITINSKAYA OBLAST'
CHINA
HEILONGJIANG
JILIN
LIAONING
NEI MONGOL ZIZHIQU
MANCHURIA
Sea of Okhotsk (Okhotskoye More)
Sakhalin
Hokkaidō
Kuril Islands (Kuril'skiye Ostrova)
ADMINISTERED BY RUSSIAN FEDERATION, CLAIMED BY JAPAN
La Pérouse Strait
Tatarskiy Proliv
Amurskiy Liman
Sikhote-Alin'
Xiao Hinggan Ling
Da Hinggan Ling
Zhangguangcai Ling
Changbai Shan
Khabarovsk
Komsomol'sk-na-Amure
Blagoveshchensk
Birobidzhan
Vladivostok
Ussuriysk
Nakhodka
Yuzhno-Sakhalinsk
Harbin
Qiqihar
Daqing
Changchun
Jilin
Jiamusi
Mudanjiang
Shenyang
Sapporo
Hakodate
Asahikawa
Kushiro
Ch'ŏngjin
Conic Equidistant Projection
1:7 000 000
0 100 200 miles
0 100 200 300 400 km
↑ 65
73 ↓

77 ↓

↓ 73

Asia

Japan, North Korea and South Korea

Conic Equidistant Projection

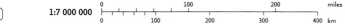

1:7 000 000

↑ 73
↓ 69
Yellow Sea
(Huang Hai)
East China Sea
(Dong Hai)
South China Sea
Taiwan Strait
SHANXI
SHANDONG
HENAN
JIANGSU
ANHUI
HUBEI
ZHEJIANG
JIANGXI
HUNAN
FUJIAN
GUANGDONG
HAINAN
TAIWAN
HONG KONG
MACAO
Tropic of Cancer
The People's Republic of China claims Taiwan as its 23rd province
Shanghai
Nanjing
Hangzhou
Wuhan
Changsha
Nanchang
Fuzhou
Guangzhou
Shenzhen
Hong Kong
Xiamen (Amoy)
T'AIPEI
Kaohsiung
Zhengzhou
Hefei
Haikou
GUANGDONG Shenzhen
SHENZHEN SPECIAL ECONOMIC ZONE
Deep Bay (Shenzhen Wan)
Lantau Island (Tai Yue Shan)
Kowloon
Lamma Island (Pok Liu Chau)
South China Sea
Mirs Bay (Tai Pang Wan)
Tolo Harbour
Hong Kong International
22° 30' N
114° 00' E
miles 0 5
km 0 10

↑ 64

↑ 55
↑ 97
↓ 98

Albers Conic Equal Area Projection

1:20 000 000

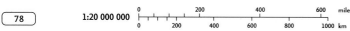

0 200 400 600 miles

0 200 400 600 800 1000 km

↑ 65
→ 66
→ 67
↓ 81
RUSSIAN FEDERATION
MONGOLIA
CHINA
INNER MONGOLIA
XINJIANG
TIBET
KYRGYZSTAN
NEPAL
BHUTAN
BANGLADESH
INDIA
MYANMAR (BURMA)
THAILAND
LAOS
VIETNAM
CAMBODIA
MALAYSIA
INDONESIA
SRI LANKA
SINGAPORE
MALDIVES
JAMMU AND KASHMIR
AKSAI CHIN CLAIMED BY INDIA, UNDER CHINESE ADMIN.
Gobi Desert
Altai Mountains
Tien Shan
Kunlun Shan
Altun Shan
Qilian Shan
Tarim Basin (Tarim Pendi)
Taklimakan Desert (Taklimakan Shamo)
Plateau of Tibet (Qingzang Gaoyuan)
Tanggula Shan
Gangdisê Shan
Nyainqêntanglha Shan
Qaidam Pendi
Hoh Xil Shan
Hengduan Shan
Deccan
Western Ghats
Eastern Ghats
Thar Desert
Bay of Bengal
Andaman Sea
Gulf of Thailand
South China Sea
Bo Hai
Strait of Malacca
Gulf of Tongking
Gulf of Mannar
Coromandel Coast
Malabar Coast
Mouths of the Ganges
Mouths of the Mekong
Andaman Islands (India)
Nicobar Islands (India)
Hainan
Ten Degree Channel
Nine Degree Channel
Eight Degree Channel
Tropic of Cancer
Equator
ULAN BATOR (Ulaanbaatar)
BEIJING (Peking)
NEW DELHI
Delhi
KATHMANDU
THIMPHU
DHAKA (Dacca)
Kolkata (Calcutta)
Mumbai (Bombay)
Chennai (Madras)
Bangalore
Hyderabad
NAY PYI TAW
RANGOON (Yangon)
BANGKOK (Krung Thep)
VIENTIANE (Viangchan)
HA NOI
PHNOM PENH
Ho Chi Minh City (Saigon)
KUALA LUMPUR
PUTRAJAYA
SRI JAYEWARDENEPURA KOTTE
Colombo
BISHKEK (Frunze)
Almaty (Alma-Ata)
ISLAMABAD
Lahore
Ürümqi
Lhasa
Chongqing
Chengdu
Kunming
Xi'an
Lanzhou
Wuhan
Tianjin
Hong Kong
Macao
Guangzhou
Novosibirsk
Omsk
Irkutsk
Chittagong
Mandalay
Medan

Albers Equal Area Conic Projection

1:13 000 000

INDIA
BANGLADESH
MYANMAR (BURMA)
SRI LANKA
MALDIVES
INDONESIA
Arabian Sea
Bay of Bengal
Andaman Sea
INDIAN OCEAN
Laccadive Islands (India)
Andaman Islands (India)
Nicobar Islands (India)
Nine Degree Channel
Eight Degree Channel
Ten Degree Channel
One and a Half Degree Channel
Gulf of Mannar
Gulf of Khambhat
Gulf of Kachchh
Coromandel Coast
Malabar Coast
Mouths of the Ganges
Mouths of the Indus
Mouths of the Irrawaddy
Deccan
Western Ghats
Eastern Ghats
Tropic of Cancer
Equator
Mumbai (Bombay)
Kolkata (Calcutta)
Chennai (Madras)
Hyderabad
Bangalore
DHAKA (Dacca)
RANGOON (Yangon)
NAY PYI TAW
Mandalay
Colombo
SRI JAYEWARDENEPURA KOTTE
MALE
Pune (Poona)
Ahmadabad
Nagpur
Varanasi
Patna
Chittagong
Cochin (Kochi)
Trivandrum (Thiruvananthapuram)
Madurai
Vishakhapatnam
Port Blair
Jaffna
→ 68

Conic Equidistant Projection

1:7 000 000

0 100 200 miles

0 100 200 300 400 km

Asia

Northern India, Nepal, Bhutan and Bangladesh

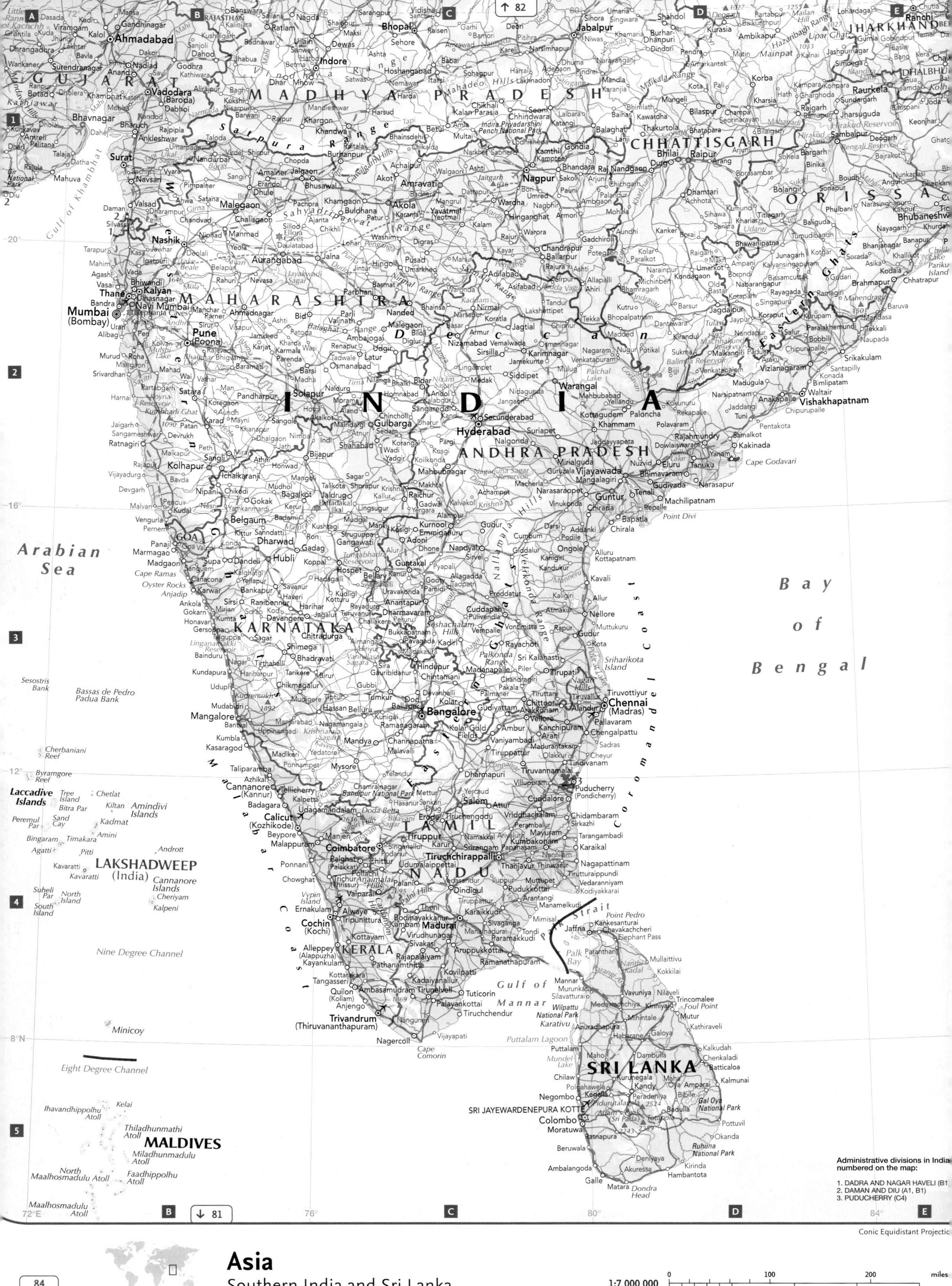

↑ 82
↓ 81

Conic Equidistant Projection

Asia
Southern India and Sri Lanka

1:7 000 000

TURKEY
MERSIN
ADANA
KARAMAN
HATAY
GAZIANTEP
KILIS
ŞANLIURFA
CYPRUS
NICOSIA (Lefkosia)
Akrotiri Sovereign Base Area (U.K.)
Dhekelia Sovereign Base Area (U.K.)
Mediterranean Sea
SYRIA
Aleppo (Halab)
Homs
Hamāh
DAMASCUS (Dimashq)
LEBANON
BEIRUT (Beyrouth)
Tripoli (Trâblous)
IRAQ
Syrian Desert (Bādiyat ash Shām)
Haifa (Ḥefa)
Tel Aviv-Yafo
WEST BANK
JERUSALEM (Yerushalayim) (El Quds)
GAZA
ISRAEL
JORDAN
AMMĀN
SAUDI ARABIA
EGYPT
SHAMĀL SĪNĀ'
JANŪB SĪNĀ'
Sinai (Shibh Jazīrat Sīnā')
Negev
Dead Sea
Gulf of Aqaba
Gulf of Suez
A
B
C
D
1
2
3
4
5
↑ 90
↑ 91
↓ 86
Conic Equidistant Projection
1:3 000 000
0 25 50 75 100 miles
0 25 50 75 100 125 150 175 km
Asia
Middle East

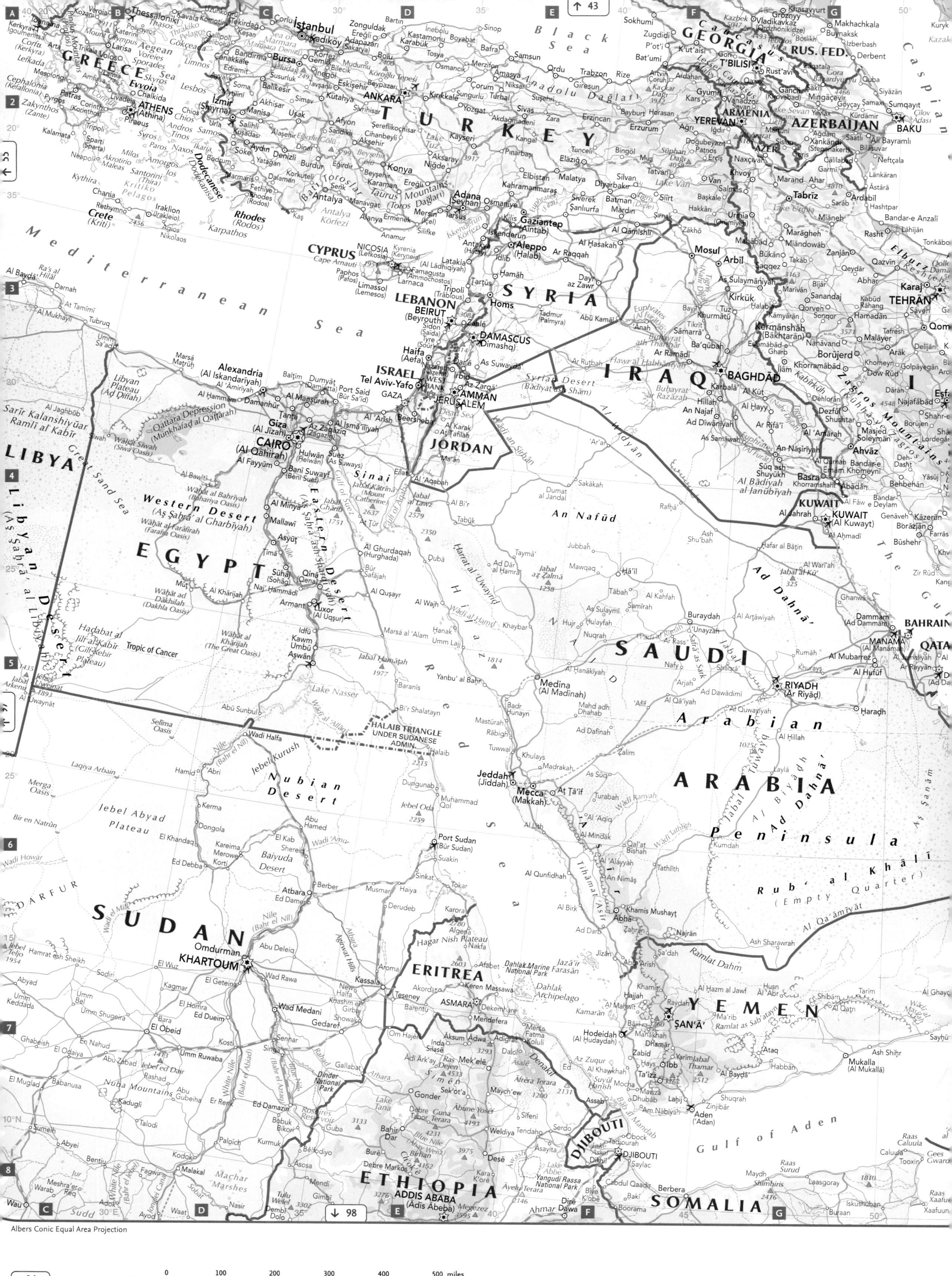

Albers Conic Equal Area Projection

1:13 000 000

↑ 80
→ 80
→ 81
KAZAKHSTAN
KYRGYZSTAN
UZBEKISTAN
TURKMENISTAN
TAJIKISTAN
AFGHANISTAN
PAKISTAN
INDIA
CHINA
NEPAL
OMAN
UNITED ARAB EMIRATES
XINJIANG UYGUR ZIZHIQU (SINKIANG)
XIZANG ZIZHIQU (TIBET)
JAMMU AND KASHMIR
AKSAI CHIN CLAIMED BY INDIA UNDER CHINESE ADMINISTRATION
LINE OF CONTROL
Tarim Basin (Tarim Pendi)
Taklimakan Desert (Taklimakan Shamo)
Kunlun Shan
Karakoram Range
Hindu Kush
Pamir
Himalaya
Siwalik Range
Gangdisê Shan
Alai Range
Turan Lowland
Karakum Desert (Peski Karakumy)
Dasht-e Kavīr
Dasht-e Lut
Dasht-e Mārgow
Thar Desert
Makran Coast Range
Central Makran Range
Toba and Kakar Ranges
Sulaiman Range
Vindhya Range
Satpura Range
Western Ghats
Deccan
Malabar Coast
Rann of Kachchh
Gulf of Kachchh
Gulf of Khambhat
Mouths of the Indus
Gulf of Oman
Strait of Hormuz
Arabian Sea
Laccadive Islands (India)
Amindivi Islands
Nine Degree Channel
Socotra (Suquṭrā) (Yemen)
Juzur al Ḥalāniyāt (Kuria Muria Islands)
TOSHKENT (Tashkent)
DUSHANBE
ASGABAT (Ashkhabad)
KĀBUL
ISLAMABAD
NEW DELHI
MUSCAT (Masqaṭ)
Mashhad
Herāt
Kandahār
Quetta
Peshawar
Rawalpindi
Lahore
Faisalabad
Multan
Hyderabad
Karachi
Amritsar
Delhi
Agra
Jaipur
Lucknow
Kanpur
Ahmadabad
Surat
Mumbai (Bombay)
Pune (Poona)
Nagpur
Bhopal
Indore
Bangalore
Mangalore
Calicut (Kozhikode)
Cochin (Kochi)
Trivandrum (Thiruvananthapuram)
Coimbatore
Dubai (Dubayy)
Sharjah (Ash Shāriqah)
Samarqand
Buxoro (Bukhara)
Zāhedān
Kermān
Bandar-e 'Abbās
55°
60°
65°
70°
75°
80°
85°
I
J
K
L
M
N
O
1
2
3
4
5
6
7
8

↑ 91

← 91

← 86

↓ 86

Conic Equidistant Projection

1:7 000 000 — 0 100 200 miles; 0 100 200 300 400 km

80
82
UZBEKISTAN
TAJIKISTAN
KYRGYZSTAN
CHINA
XINJIANG UYGUR ZIZHIQU
AFGHANISTAN
PAKISTAN
INDIA
NORTHERN AREAS
NORTH WEST FRONTIER
TRIBAL AREAS
PUNJAB
JAMMU AND KASHMIR
BALOCHISTAN
SINDH
RAJASTHAN
GUJARAT
HARYANA
LINE OF CONTROL
Arabian Sea
Dushanbe
Kābul
Islamabad
Peshawar
Rawalpindi
Lahore
Multan
Quetta
Karachi
Hyderabad
Kandahār
Herāt
Mazār-e Sharīf
Srinagar
Amritsar
Jodhpur
Ahmadabad
Samarqand
Hindu Kush
Rann of Kachchh
Gulf of Kachchh
Mouths of the Indus

Conic Equidistant Projection

1:7 000 000 — 0, 100, 200 miles; 0, 100, 200, 300, 400 km

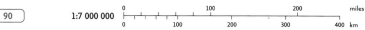

RUSSIAN FEDERATION
STAVROPOL'SKIY KRAY
GEORGIA
T'BILISI
ARMENIA
YEREVAN
AZERBAIJAN
BAKU
KAZAKHSTAN
MANGISTAUSKAYA OBLAST'
UZBEKISTAN
TURKMENISTAN
Ustyurt Plateau
Caspian Sea
Garabogazköl
IRAN
TEHRĀN
Elburz Mountains
Zagros Mountains
IRAQ
BAGHDĀD
MESOPOTAMIA
KUWAIT
KUWAIT (Al Kuwayt)
ARABIA
The Gulf
Dasht-e Kavīr
Toroslar
Caucasus
Tabrīz
Mosul
Arbīl
Kirkūk
Basra
Ahvāz
Eşfahān (Isfahan)
Shīrāz
Qom
Hamadān
Kermānshāh (Bākhtarān)
Rasht
Derbent
Makhachkala
Groznyy
Sumqayit
Türkmenbaşy
Erzurum
Van
Lake Van (Van Gölü)
Lake Urmia (Daryācheh-ye Orūmīyeh)
↑ 64
↓ 86
→ 88

Africa
Landscapes

Some of the world's greatest physical features are in Africa, the world's second largest continent. Variations in climate and elevation give rise to the continent's great variety of landscapes. The Sahara, the world's largest desert, extends across the whole continent from west to east, and covers an area of over nine million square kilometres. Other significant African deserts are the Kalahari and the Namib. In contrast, some of the world's greatest rivers flow in Africa, including the Nile, the world's longest, and the Congo.

The Great Rift Valley is perhaps Africa's most notable geological feature. It stretches for nearly 3 000 kilometres from Jordan, through the Red Sea and south to Mozambique, and contains many of Africa's largest lakes. Significant mountain ranges on the continent are the Atlas Mountains and the Ethiopian Highlands in the north, the Ruwenzori in east central Africa, and the Drakensberg in the far southeast.

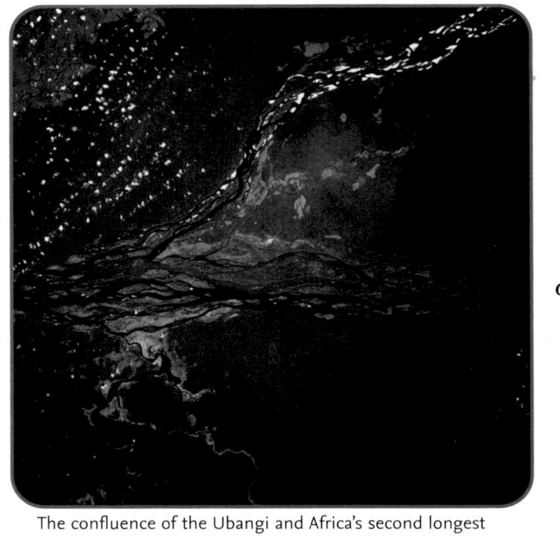

The confluence of the Ubangi and Africa's second longest river, the **Congo**.

Canary Islands
Tenerife
Gran Canaria
Akchâr
Cape Verde
Santo Antão
Boa Vista
Ilhas do Cabo Verde
Fogo
Santiago
Cap Vert
Sénégal
Gambia
Fouta Djallon
Ascension

Africa's extent

TOTAL LAND AREA	30 343 578 sq km / 11 715 655 sq miles
Most northerly point	La Galite, Tunisia
Most southerly point	Cape Agulhas, South Africa
Most westerly point	Santo Antão, Cape Verde
Most easterly point	Raas Xaafuun, Somalia

Internet Links

NASA Visible Earth	**visibleearth.nasa.gov**
NASA Astronaut Photography	**eol.jsc.nasa.gov**
Peace Parks Foundation	**www.peaceparks.org**

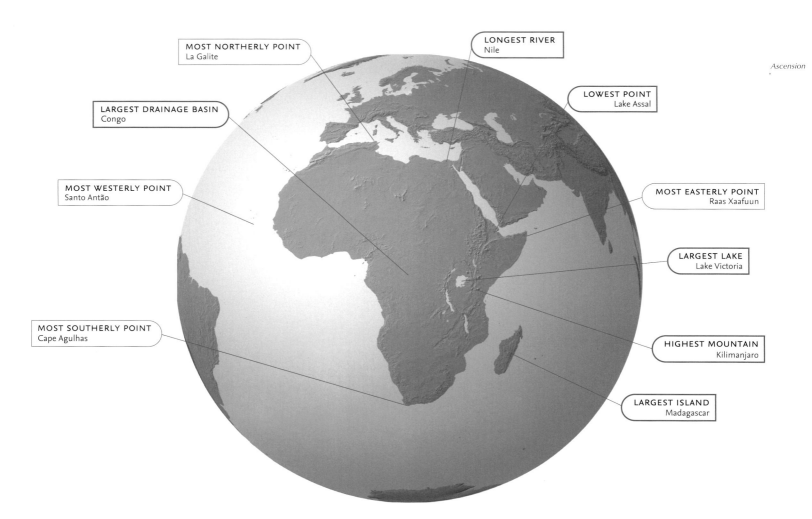

MOST NORTHERLY POINT
La Galite

LONGEST RIVER
Nile

LOWEST POINT
Lake Assal

LARGEST DRAINAGE BASIN
Congo

MOST WESTERLY POINT
Santo Antão

MOST EASTERLY POINT
Raas Xaafuun

LARGEST LAKE
Lake Victoria

MOST SOUTHERLY POINT
Cape Agulhas

HIGHEST MOUNTAIN
Kilimanjaro

LARGEST ISLAND
Madagascar

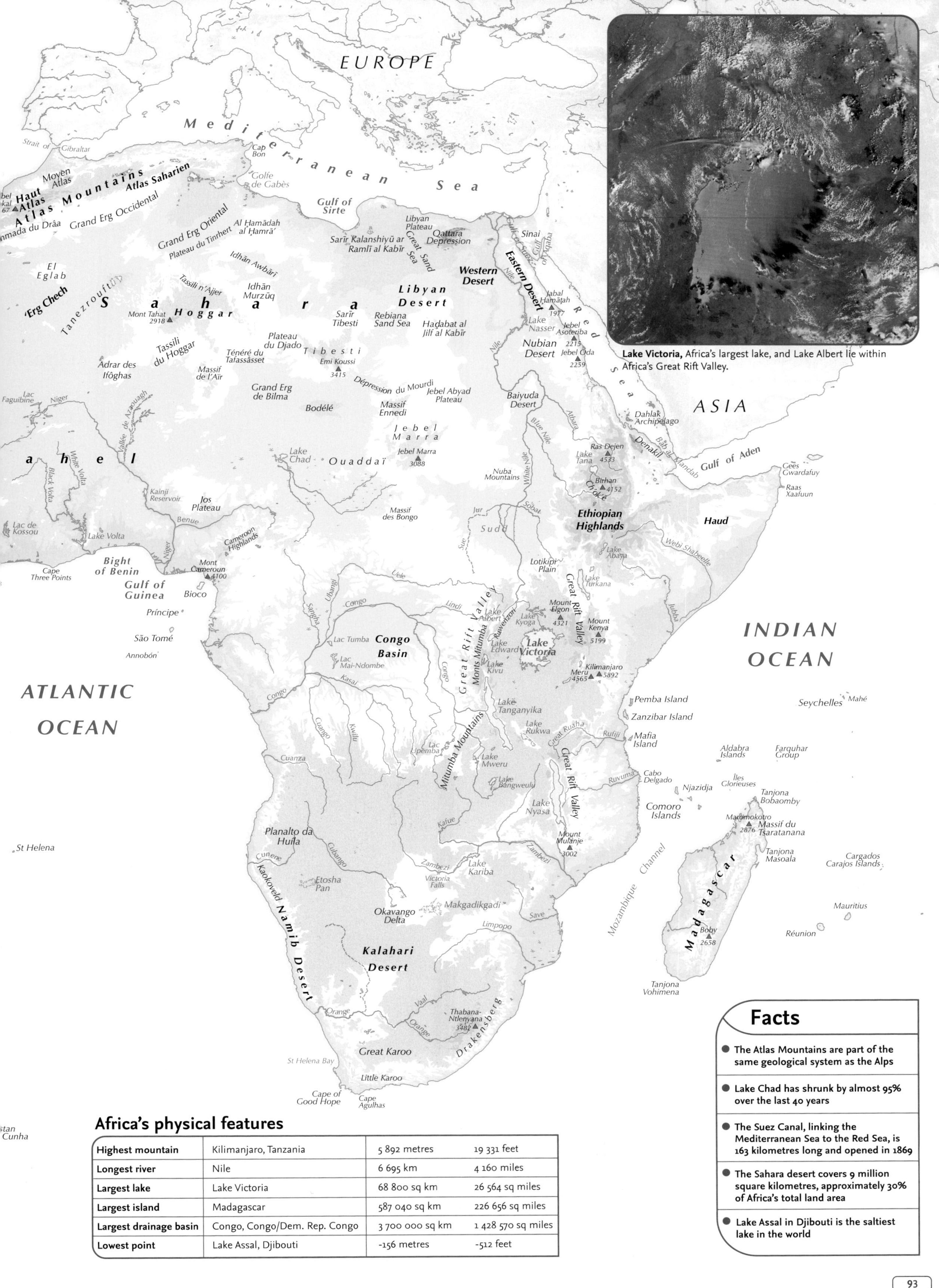

Lake Victoria, Africa's largest lake, and Lake Albert lie within Africa's Great Rift Valley.

Africa's physical features

Highest mountain	Kilimanjaro, Tanzania	5 892 metres	19 331 feet
Longest river	Nile	6 695 km	4 160 miles
Largest lake	Lake Victoria	68 800 sq km	26 564 sq miles
Largest island	Madagascar	587 040 sq km	226 656 sq miles
Largest drainage basin	Congo, Congo/Dem. Rep. Congo	3 700 000 sq km	1 428 570 sq miles
Lowest point	Lake Assal, Djibouti	-156 metres	-512 feet

Facts

- **The Atlas Mountains are part of the same geological system as the Alps**
- **Lake Chad has shrunk by almost 95% over the last 40 years**
- **The Suez Canal, linking the Mediterranean Sea to the Red Sea, is 163 kilometres long and opened in 1869**
- **The Sahara desert covers 9 million square kilometres, approximately 30% of Africa's total land area**
- **Lake Assal in Djibouti is the saltiest lake in the world**

Africa
Countries

Africa is a complex continent, with over fifty independent countries and a long history of political change. It supports a great variety of ethnic groups, with the Sahara creating the major divide between Arab and Berber groups in the north and a diverse range of groups, including the Yoruba and Masai, in the south.

The current pattern of countries in Africa is a product of a long and complex history, including the colonial period, which saw European control of the vast majority of the continent from the fifteenth century until widespread moves to independence began in the 1950s. Despite its great wealth of natural resources, Africa is by far the world's poorest continent. Many of its countries are heavily dependent upon foreign aid and many are also subject to serious political instability.

Facts

- Africa has over 1 000 linguistic and cultural groups
- Only Liberia and Ethiopia have remained free from colonial rule throughout their history
- Over 30% of the world's minerals, and over 50% of the world's diamonds, come from Africa
- 9 of the 10 poorest countries in the world are in Africa

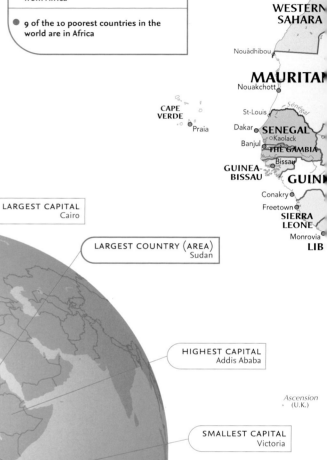

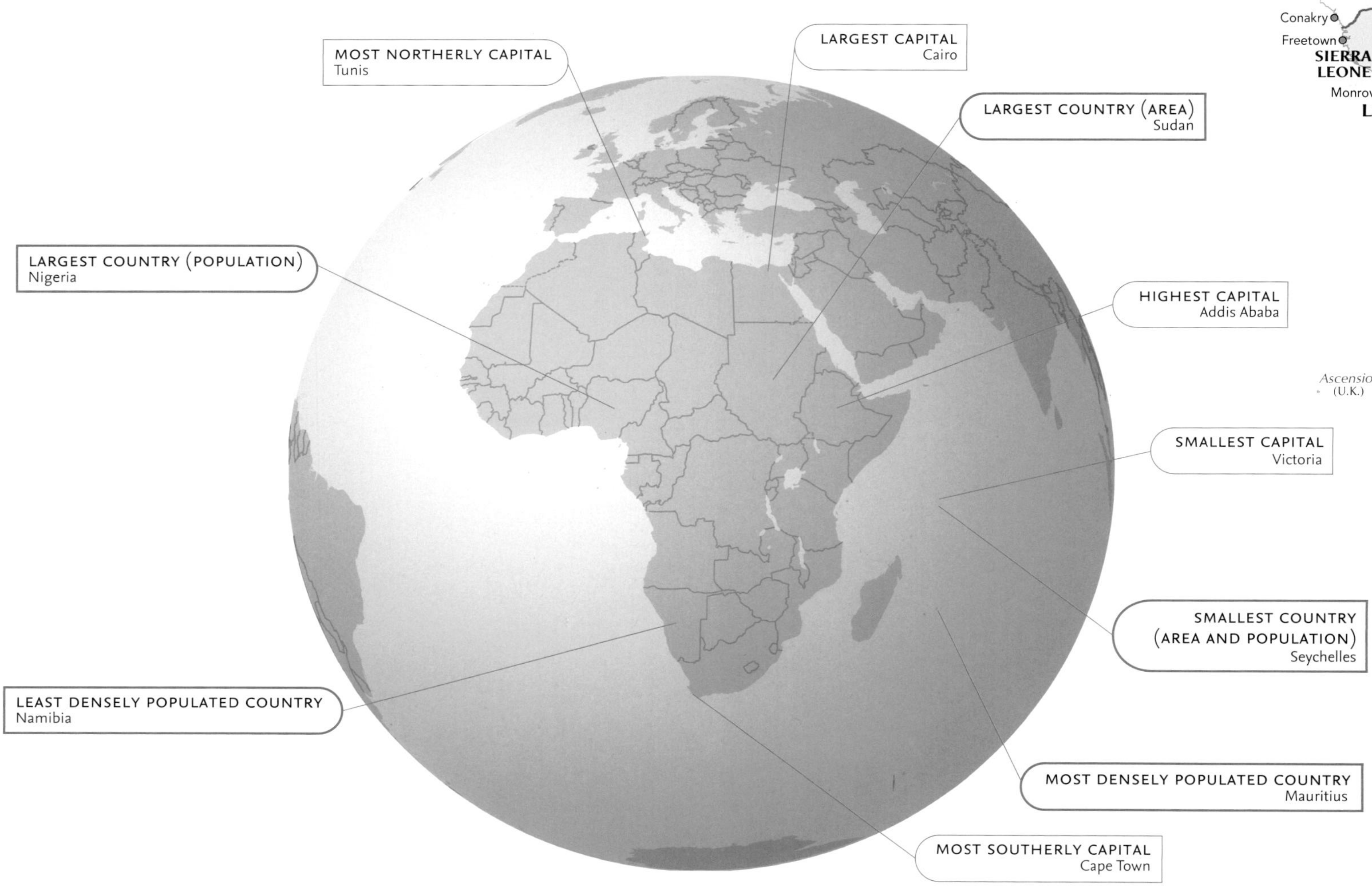

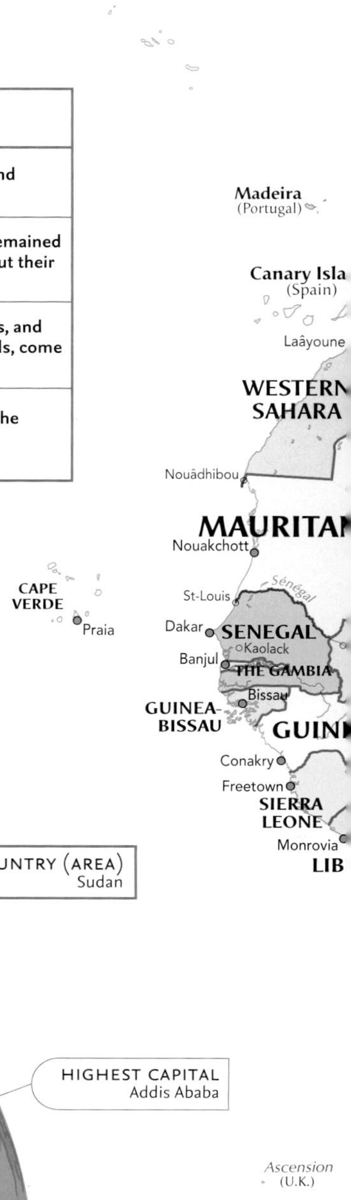

MOST NORTHERLY CAPITAL
Tunis

LARGEST CAPITAL
Cairo

LARGEST COUNTRY (AREA)
Sudan

LARGEST COUNTRY (POPULATION)
Nigeria

HIGHEST CAPITAL
Addis Ababa

SMALLEST CAPITAL
Victoria

SMALLEST COUNTRY (AREA AND POPULATION)
Seychelles

LEAST DENSELY POPULATED COUNTRY
Namibia

MOST DENSELY POPULATED COUNTRY
Mauritius

MOST SOUTHERLY CAPITAL
Cape Town

Internet Links

UK Foreign and Commonwealth Office	**www.fco.gov.uk**
CIA World Factbook	**www.cia.gov/library/publications/the-world-factbook/index.html**
Southern African Development Community	**www.sadc.int**
GeoEye	**www.GeoEye.com**

Cape Town, legislative capital of the Republic of South Africa and the most southerly African capital city.

Africa's capitals

Largest capital (population)	Cairo, Egypt	11 893 000
Smallest capital (population)	Victoria, Seychelles	25 500
Most northerly capital	Tunis, Tunisia	36° 46'N
Most southerly capital	Cape Town, Republic of South Africa	33° 57'S
Highest capital	Addis Ababa, Ethiopia	2 408 metres 7 900 feet

Africa's countries

Largest country (area)	Sudan	2 505 813 sq km	967 500 sq miles
Smallest country (area)	Seychelles	455 sq km	176 sq miles
Largest country (population)	Nigeria	131 530 000	
Smallest country (population)	Seychelles	81 000	
Most densely populated country	Mauritius	599 per sq km	1 549 per sq mile
Least densely populated country	Namibia	2 per sq km	6 per sq mile

Lambert Azimuthal Equal Area Projection

1:16 000 000 — 0, 200, 400 miles; 0, 200, 400, 600, 800 km

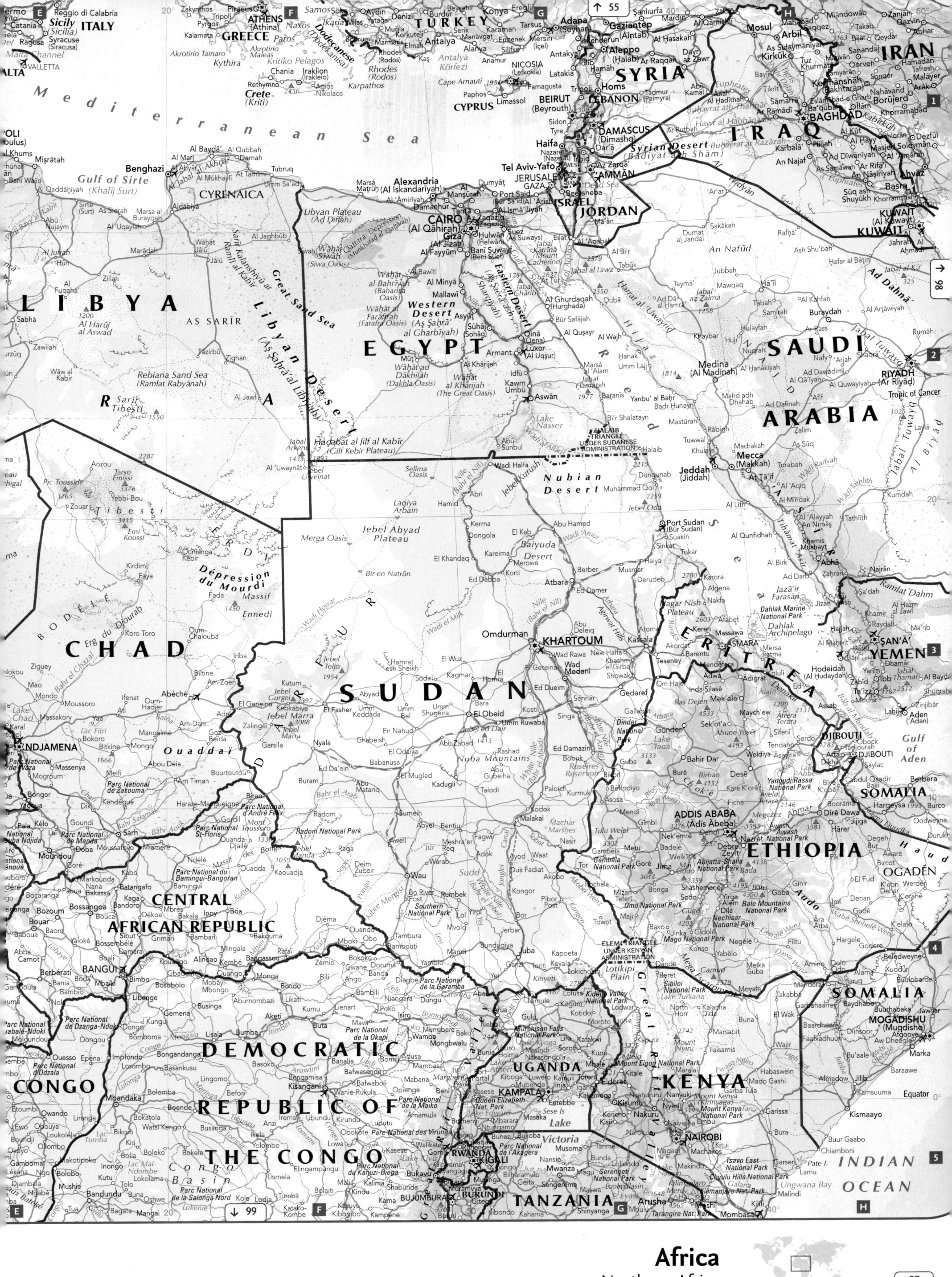

Africa
Northern Africa

Lambert Azimuthal Equal Area Projection

1:16 000 000

0 200 400 miles

0 200 400 600 800 km

Africa

Central and Southern Africa

↑ 99
NAMIBIA
BOTSWANA
REPUBLIC OF SOUTH AFRICA
ATLANTIC OCEAN
ERONGO
KHOMAS
OMAHEKE
HARDAP
KARAS
GHANZI
KGALAGADI
KWENENG
SOUTHERN
NORTH
GRIQUALAND WEST
GREAT NAMAQUALAND
NAMAQUALAND
NORTHERN CAPE
WESTERN CAPE
Kalahari
Kalahari Desert
Namib Desert
Great Karoo
Little Karoo
Central Kalahari Game Reserve
Khutse Game Reserve
Mabuasehube Game Reserve
Gemsbok National Park
Kalahari Gemsbok National Park
Kgalagadi Transfrontier Park
Namib-Naukluft Game Park
National West Coast Tourist Recreation Area
Ai-Ais Hot Springs Game Park
Ai-Ais/Richtersveld Transfrontier Park
Richtersveld National Park
Richtersveld Cultural and Botanical Landscape
Augrabies Falls National Park
Goegap Nature Reserve
Namaqua National Park
Tankwa-Karoo National Park
Karoo National Park
West Coast National Park
Table Mountain Nature Reserve
Bontebok National Park
De Hoop Nature Reserve
Tsitsikamma Forest and Coastal National Park
Wilderness National Park
Camdeboo National Park
Tropic of Capricorn
WINDHOEK
CAPE TOWN
Walvis Bay
Swakopmund
Rehoboth
Lüderitz
Keetmanshoop
Upington
Kimberley
Kuruman
Springbok
Port Nolloth
Oranjemund
Alexander Bay
Calvinia
Beaufort West
Worcester
Stellenbosch
Paarl
Bellville
Khayelitsha
Saldanha
Vredenburg
George
Knysna
Mossel Bay
Oudtshoorn
Cape of Good Hope
Cape Agulhas
Orange
Molopo
Nossob
Auob
Fish
Olifants
Kalahari
Dolphin Head
Hottentots Point
Diaz Point
Elizabeth Point
Possession Island
Cape Dernberg
Wreck Point
Cape Columbine
Cape St Martin
Danger Point
Quoin Point
Struis Bay
Lambert Azimuthal Equal Area Projection
1:5 000 000
0 50 100 150 miles
0 50 100 150 200 250 km

ZIMBABWE
MATABELELAND SOUTH
MASVINGO
CENTRAL
KGATLENG
GABORONE
LIMPOPO
GAZA
INHAMBANE
MOZAMBIQUE
MPUMALANGA
GAUTENG
PRETORIA (Tshwane)
Johannesburg
Soweto
Vereeniging
MAPUTO
SWAZILAND
MBABANE
Manzini
FREE STATE
Bloemfontein
Welkom
KWAZULU-NATAL
Pietermaritzburg
Durban
Richards Bay
LESOTHO
MASERU
Drakensberg
EASTERN CAPE
East London
Port Elizabeth
Mthatha
Port Shepstone
Kruger National Park
Great Limpopo Transfrontier Park
Parque Nacional de Banhine
Tropic of Capricorn
Polokwane (Pietersburg)
Nelspruit
Newcastle
Ladysmith
Kimberley
Bethlehem
Grahamstown
INDIAN OCEAN
Cape Hermes
South Sand Bluff
Great Fish Point
Cape Recife
Algoa Bay
Lake St Lucia
Kosi Bay
Isimangaliso Wetland Park

Oceania
Landscapes

Oceania comprises Australia, New Zealand, New Guinea and the islands of the Pacific Ocean. It is the smallest of the world's continents by land area. Its dominating feature is Australia, which is mainly flat and very dry. Australia's western half consists of a low plateau, broken in places by higher mountain ranges, which has very few permanent rivers or lakes. The narrow, fertile coastal plain of the east coast is separated from the interior by the Great Dividing Range, which includes the highest mountain in Australia.

The numerous Pacific islands of Oceania are generally either volcanic in origin or consist of coral. They can be divided into three main regions - Micronesia, north of the equator between Palau and the Gilbert islands; Melanesia, stretching from mountainous New Guinea to Fiji; and Polynesia, covering a vast area of the eastern and central Pacific Ocean.

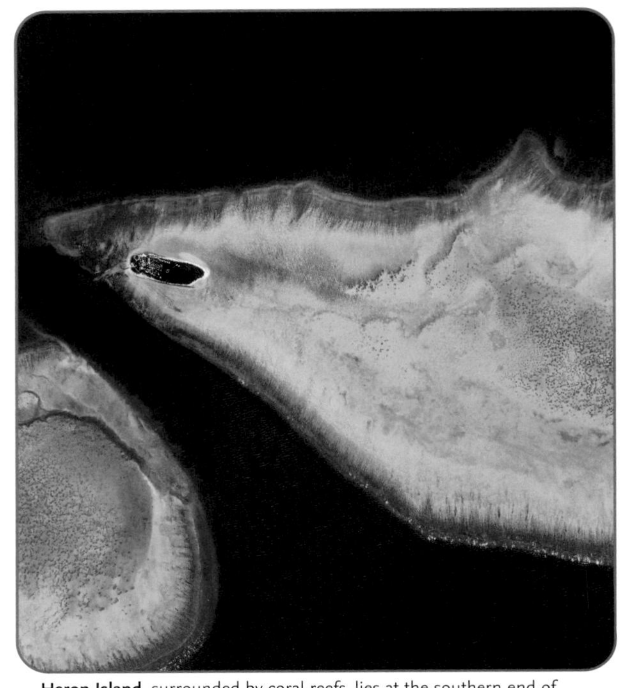

Heron Island, surrounded by coral reefs, lies at the southern end of Australia's Great Barrier Reef.

Facts

- **Australia's Great Barrier Reef is the world's largest coral reef and stretches for over 2 000 kilometres**
- **The highest point of Tuvalu is only 5 metres above sea level**
- **New Zealand lies directly on the boundary between the Pacific and Indo-Australian tectonic plates**
- **The Mariana Trench in the Pacific Ocean contains the earth's deepest point – Challenger Deep, 10 920 metres below sea level**

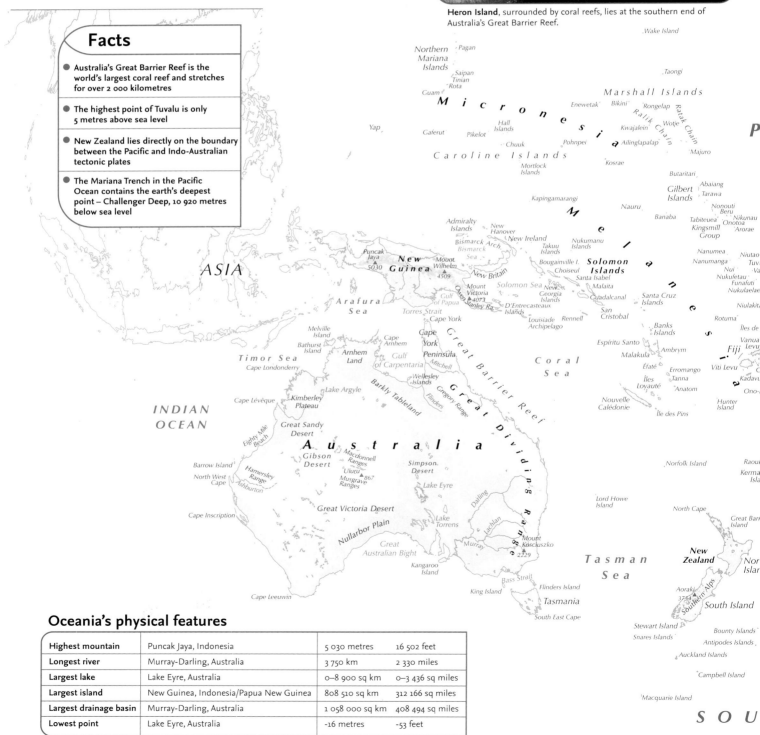

Oceania's physical features

Highest mountain	Puncak Jaya, Indonesia	5 030 metres	16 502 feet
Longest river	Murray-Darling, Australia	3 750 km	2 330 miles
Largest lake	Lake Eyre, Australia	0–8 900 sq km	0–3 436 sq miles
Largest island	New Guinea, Indonesia/Papua New Guinea	808 510 sq km	312 166 sq miles
Largest drainage basin	Murray-Darling, Australia	1 058 000 sq km	408 494 sq miles
Lowest point	Lake Eyre, Australia	-16 metres	-53 feet

Internet Links

NASA Visible Earth	**visibleearth.nasa.gov**
NASA Astronaut Photography	**eol.jsc.nasa.gov**
Great Barrier Reef Marine Park Authority	**www.gbrmpa.gov.au**

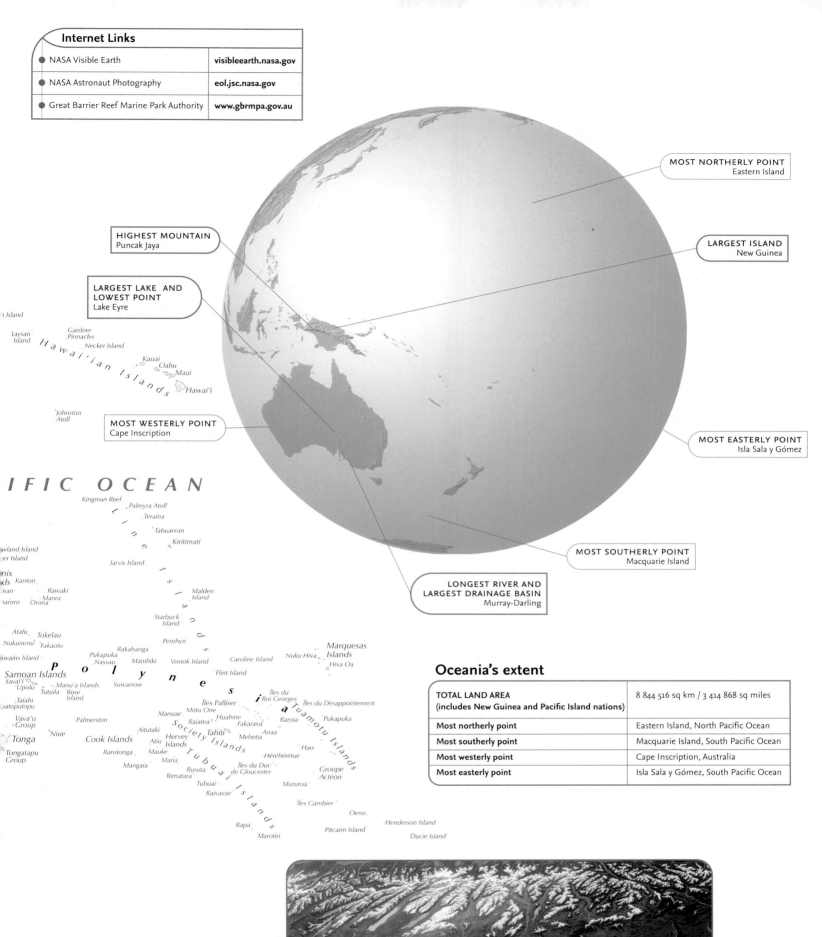

MOST NORTHERLY POINT
Eastern Island

HIGHEST MOUNTAIN
Puncak Jaya

LARGEST ISLAND
New Guinea

LARGEST LAKE AND LOWEST POINT
Lake Eyre

MOST WESTERLY POINT
Cape Inscription

MOST EASTERLY POINT
Isla Sala y Gómez

MOST SOUTHERLY POINT
Macquarie Island

LONGEST RIVER AND LARGEST DRAINAGE BASIN
Murray-Darling

Oceania's extent

TOTAL LAND AREA (includes New Guinea and Pacific Island nations)	8 844 516 sq km / 3 414 868 sq miles
Most northerly point	Eastern Island, North Pacific Ocean
Most southerly point	Macquarie Island, South Pacific Ocean
Most westerly point	Cape Inscription, Australia
Most easterly point	Isla Sala y Gómez, South Pacific Ocean

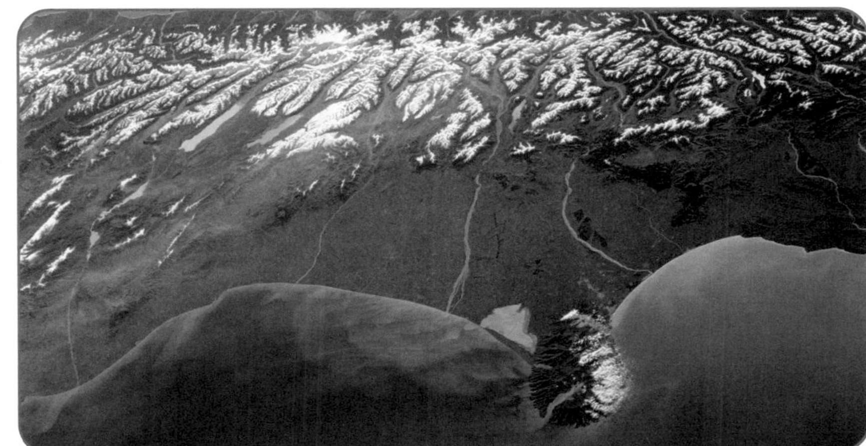

Banks Peninsula, Canterbury Plains and the **Southern Alps,** South Island, New Zealand.

Oceania
Countries

Stretching across almost the whole width of the Pacific Ocean, Oceania has a great variety of cultures and an enormously diverse range of countries and territories. Australia, by far the largest and most industrialized country in the continent, contrasts with the numerous tiny Pacific island nations which have smaller, and more fragile economies based largely on agriculture, fishing and the exploitation of natural resources.

The division of the Pacific island groups into the main regions of Micronesia, Melanesia and Polynesia – often referred to as the South Sea islands – broadly reflects the ethnological differences across the continent. There is a long history of colonial influence in the region, which still contains dependent territories belonging to Australia, France, New Zealand, the UK and the USA.

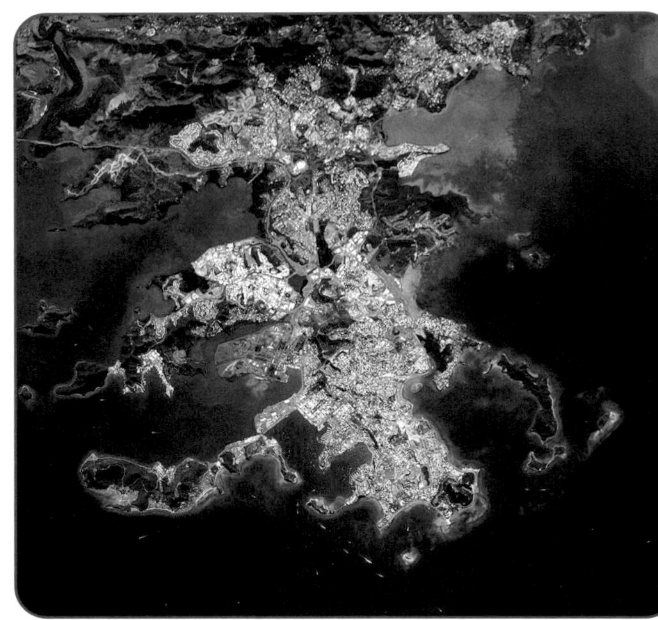

Nouméa, capital of the French dependency of New Caledonia in the southern Pacific Ocean.

Facts

- **Over 91% of Australia's population live in urban areas**
- **The Maori name for New Zealand is Aotearoa, meaning 'land of the long white cloud'**
- **Auckland, New Zealand, has the largest Polynesian population of any city in Oceania**
- **Over 800 different languages are spoken in Papua New Guinea**

ASIA
INDIAN OCEAN
Northern Mariana Islands (U.S.A.)
Pagan
Saipan
Tinian
Rota
Guam (U.S.A.)
Wake Island (U.S.A.)
MARSHALL ISLANDS
Taongi
Enewetak
Bikini
Rongelap
Ratak Chain
Ralik Chain
Wotje
Kwajalein
Ailinglapalap
Delap-Uliga-Djarrit
Majuro
Yap
Gaferut
Pikelot
Hall Islands
Chuuk
Palikir
Pohnpei
Kosrae
Caroline Islands
Mortlock Islands
FEDERATED STATES OF MICRONESIA
Bairiki
Tarawa
Gilbert Islands
Kingsmill Group
Yaren
NAURU
Admiralty Islands
New Ireland
Rabaul
Vanimo
Wewak
Bismarck Sea
New Guinea
Mount Wilhelm 4509
Lae
New Britain
Bougainville I.
Balimo
Kerema
Gulf of Papua
Solomon Sea
PAPUA NEW GUINEA
Daru
Port Moresby
Torres Strait
Arafura Sea
SOLOMON ISLANDS
Malaita
Honiara
Guadalcanal
Santa Cruz Islands
Nanumea
Niutao
TUVALU
Nukufetau
Nukulaelae
Rotuma
VANUATU
Banks Islands
Espíritu Santo
Malakula
Port Vila
Éfaté
Tanna
New Caledonia (France)
Nouméa
Îles Loyauté
FIJI
Vanua Levu
Viti Levu
Coral Sea
Coral Sea Islands Territory (Australia)
Melville Island
Bathurst Island
Timor Sea
Darwin
Gulf of Carpentaria
Cooktown
Cairns
Ashmore and Cartier Islands (Australia)
Wyndham
Normanton
Townsville
Cape Lévêque
Halls Creek
Broome
NORTHERN TERRITORY
Mackay
Cloncurry
Longreach
Rockhampton
Port Hedland
Alice Springs
QUEENSLAND
Maryborough
Charleville
Brisbane
Gold Coast
Barrow Island
North West Cape
Newman
AUSTRALIA
Lake Eyre
Grafton
Tamworth
WESTERN AUSTRALIA
SOUTH AUSTRALIA
Darling
NEW SOUTH WALES
Meekatharra
Lake Torrens
Broken Hill
Orange
Newcastle
Sydney
Port Augusta
Port Pirie
JERVIS BAY TERR.
Canberra
A.C.T.
Geraldton
Kalgoorlie
Great Australian Bight
Adelaide
Murray
Albury
VICTORIA
Perth
Kangaroo Island
Geelong
Melbourne
Fremantle
Esperance
Mount Gambier
Bass Strait
Cape Leeuwin
Albany
Launceston
TASMANIA
Hobart
South East Cape
Norfolk Island (Australia)
Lord Howe Island (Australia)
Tasman Sea
North Cape
Whangarei
Auckland
Rotorua
NEW ZEALAND
Blenheim
Wellington
Greymouth
Christchurch
South Island
Invercargill
Dunedin
Stewart Island
Bounty Islands (N.Z.)
Antipodes Islands (N.Z.)
Auckland Islands (N.Z.)
Campbell Island (N.Z.)
Macquarie Island (Australia)
SOUTHERN
PAC

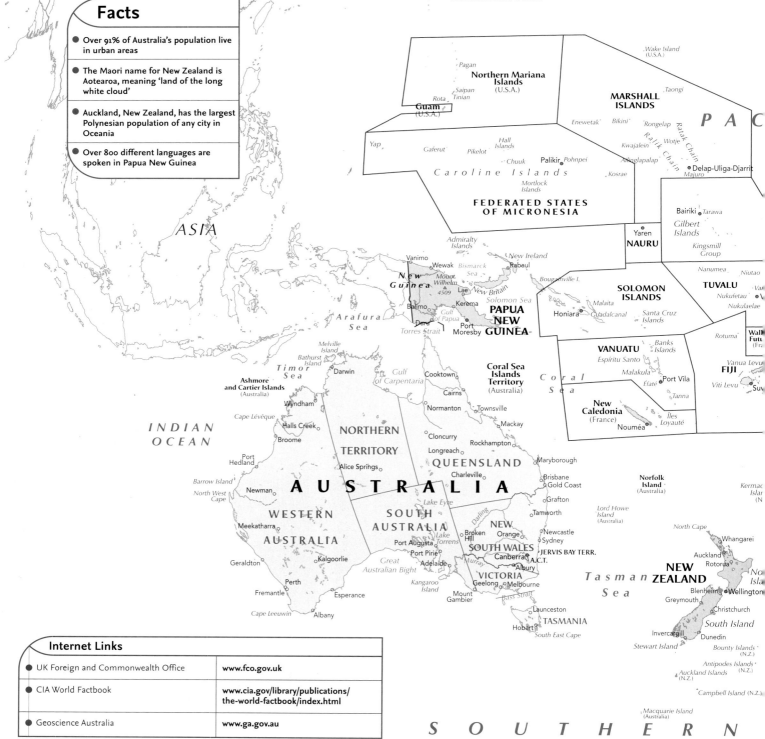

Internet Links

UK Foreign and Commonwealth Office	**www.fco.gov.uk**
CIA World Factbook	**www.cia.gov/library/publications/the-world-factbook/index.html**
Geoscience Australia	**www.ga.gov.au**

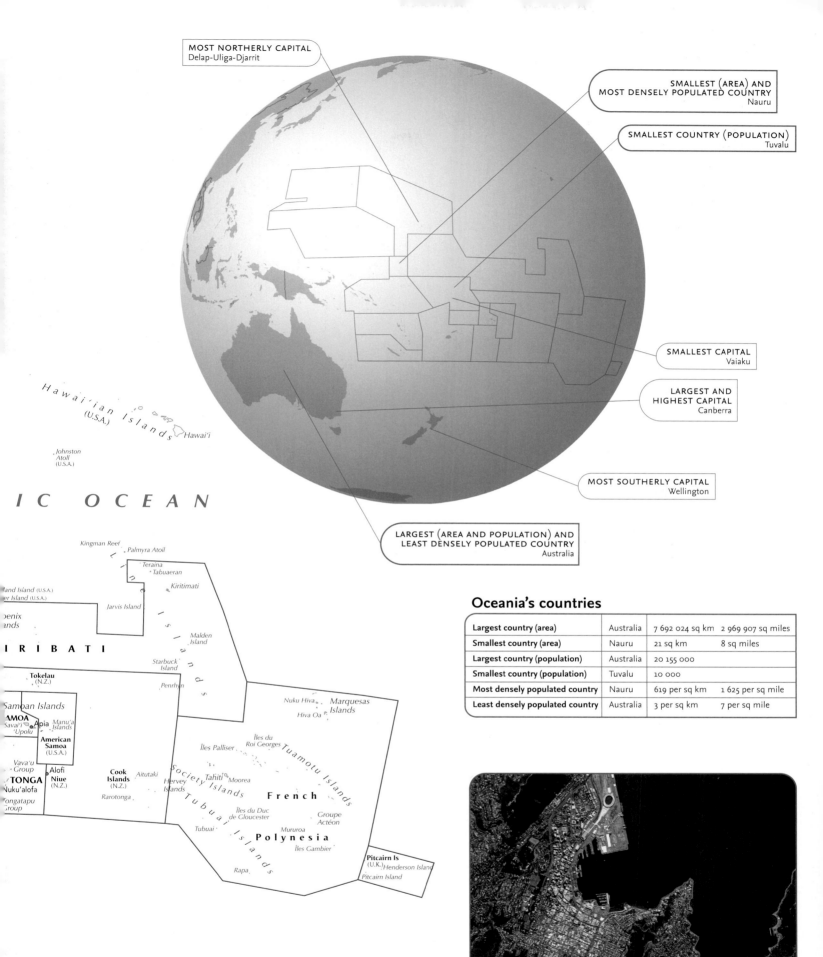

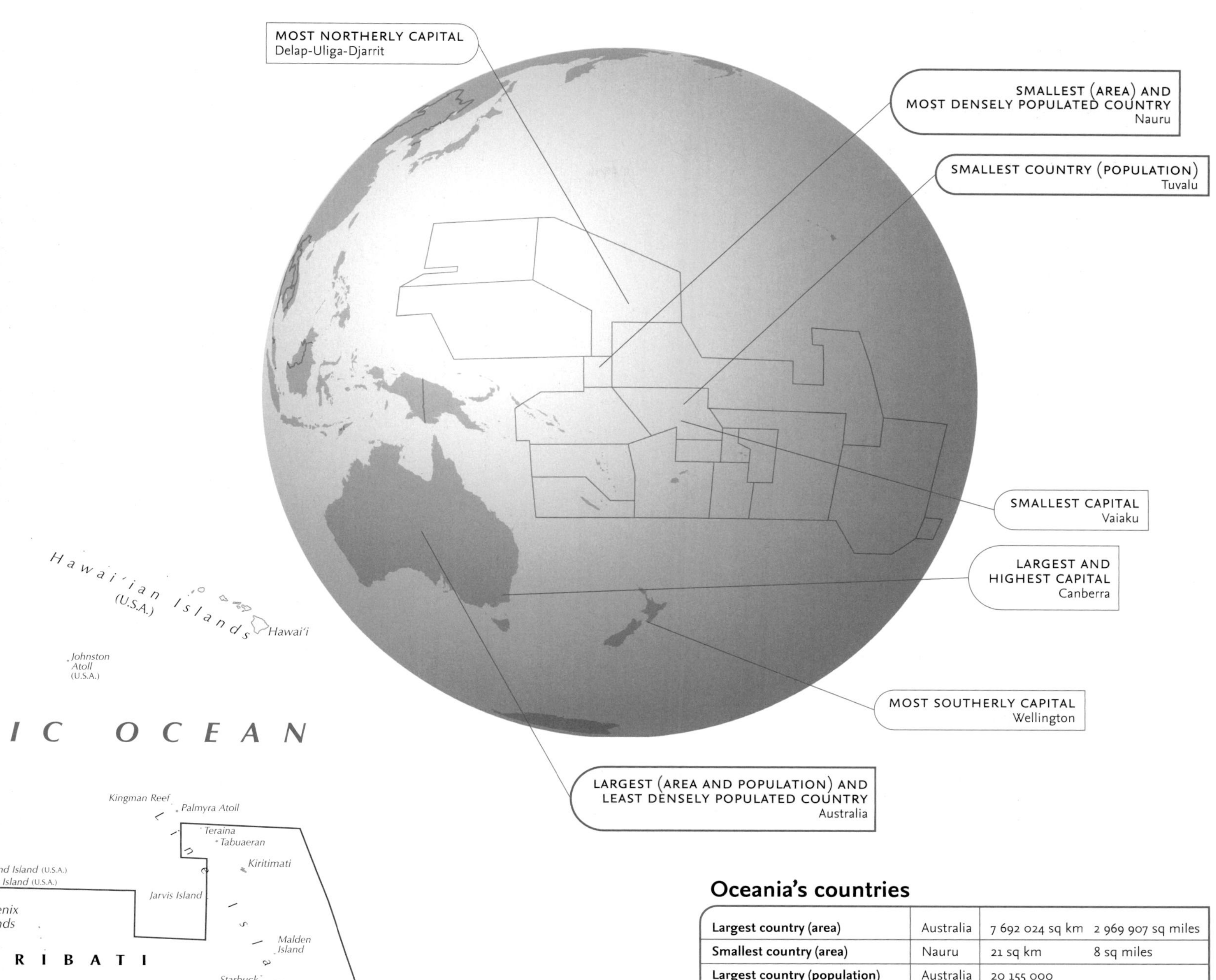

Oceania's countries

Largest country (area)	Australia	7 692 024 sq km	2 969 907 sq miles
Smallest country (area)	Nauru	21 sq km	8 sq miles
Largest country (population)	Australia	20 155 000	
Smallest country (population)	Tuvalu	10 000	
Most densely populated country	Nauru	619 per sq km	1 625 per sq mile
Least densely populated country	Australia	3 per sq km	7 per sq mile

Wellington, capital of New Zealand.

Oceania's capitals

Largest capital (population)	Canberra, Australia	381 000
Smallest capital (population)	Vaiaku, Tuvalu	516
Most northerly capital	Delap-Uliga-Djarrit, Marshall Islands	7° 7'N
Most southerly capital	Wellington, New Zealand	41° 18'S
Highest capital	Canberra, Australia	581 metres 1 906 feet

OCEAN

↑ 67

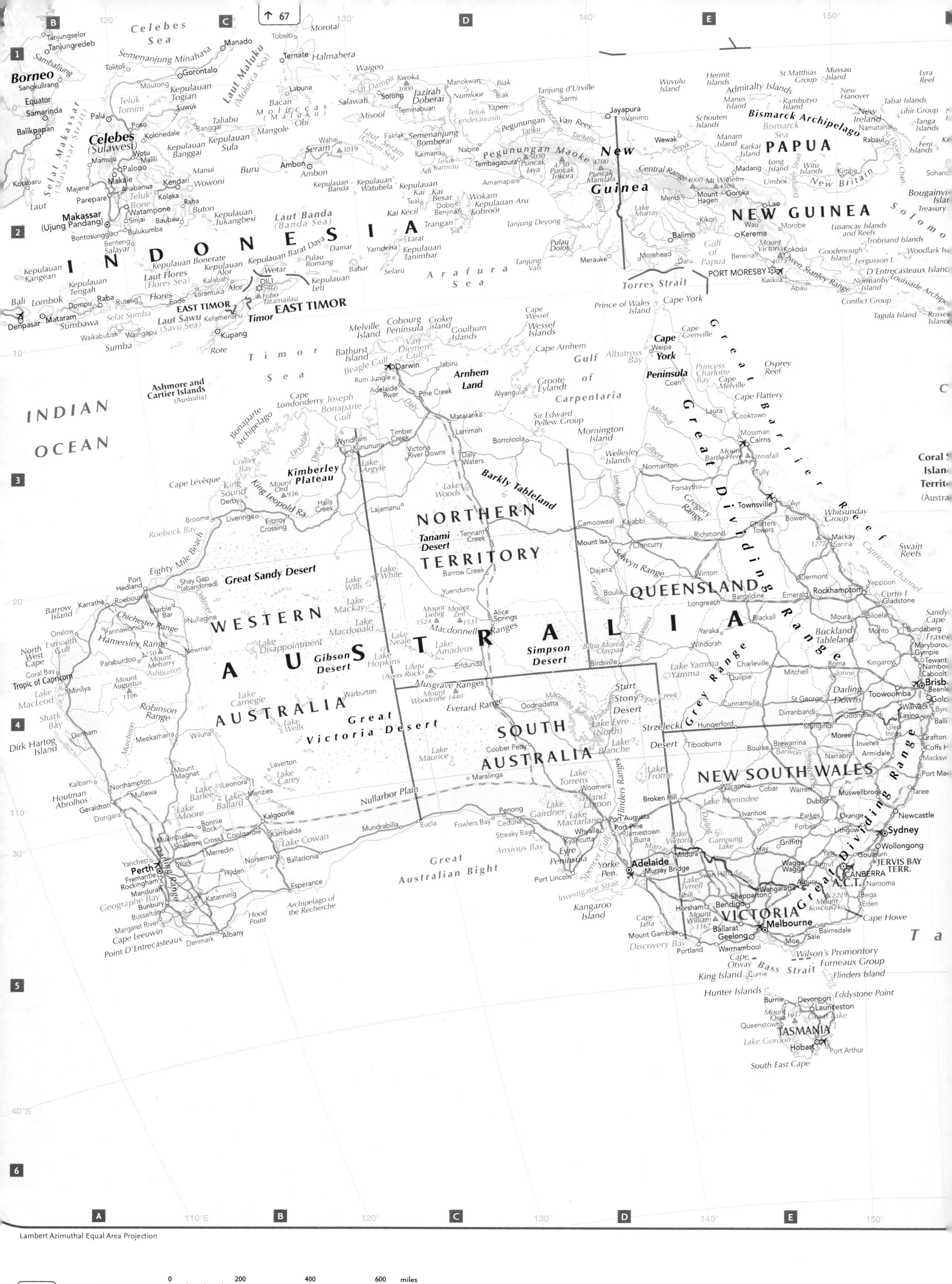

1:20 000 000

0 200 400 600 miles

0 200 400 600 800 1000 km

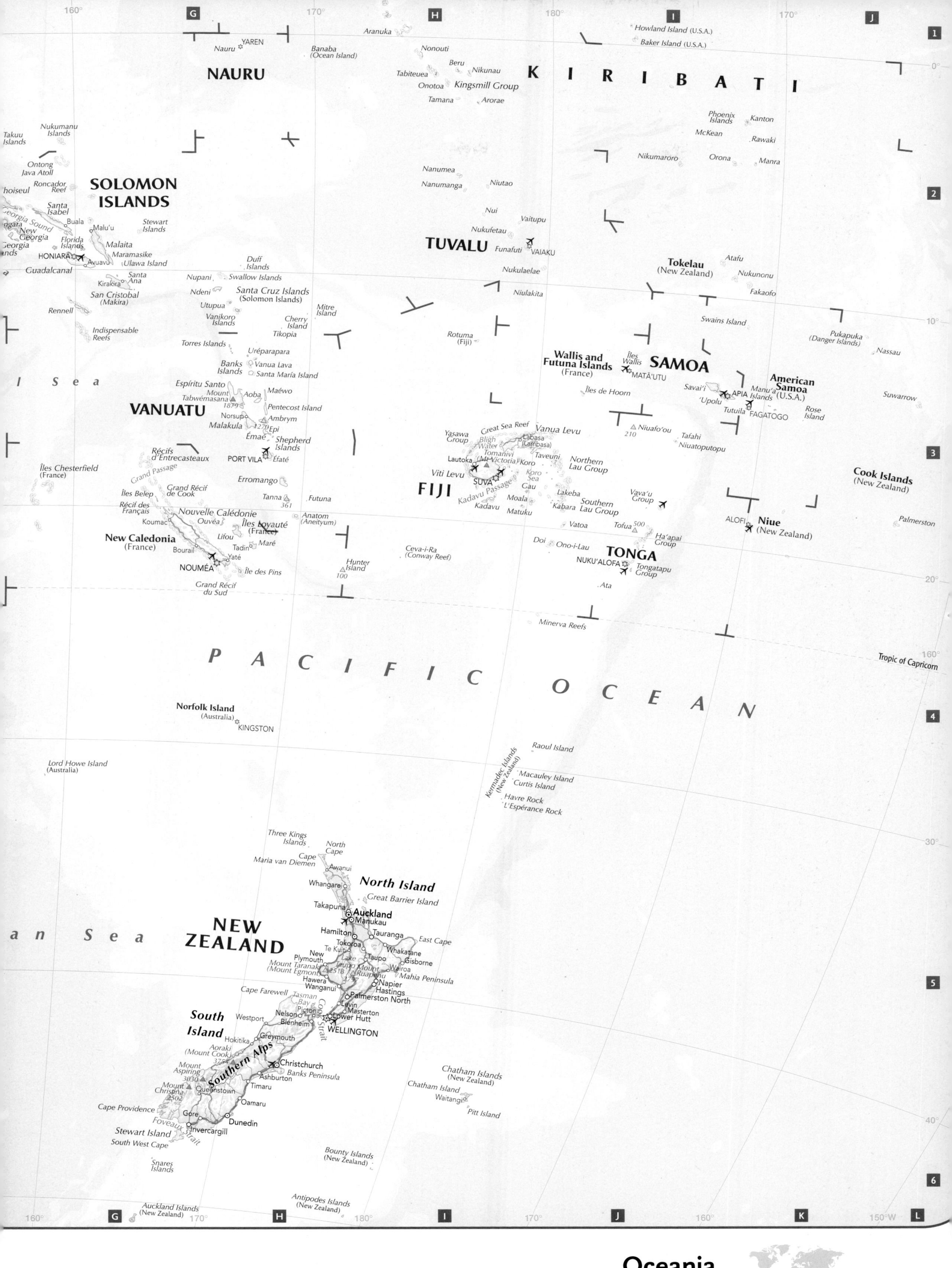

Oceania

Australia, New Zealand and Southwest Pacific

Lambert Azimuthal Equal Area Projection

1:8 000 000
0 100 200 300 miles
0 100 200 300 400 500 km

↑ 69
↑ 110

WESTERN AUSTRALIA
SOUTH AUSTRALIA
Great Victoria Desert
Gibson Desert
Little Sandy Desert
Simpson Desert
Nullarbor Plain
Great Australian Bight
Darling Range
Macdonnell Ranges
Musgrave Ranges
Everard Range
Stuart Range
Gawler Ranges
Eyre Peninsula
Spencer Gulf
Kangaroo Island
Lake Gairdner
Woomera Prohibited Area
Nullarbor National Park
Nullarbor Regional Reserve
Hampton Tableland
Roe Plains
Archipelago of the Recherche
Geographe Bay
Cape Leeuwin
Cape Naturaliste
Rottnest Island
Houtman Abrolhos
Geelvink Channel
Shark Bay
Dirk Hartog Island
Dorre Island
Bernier Island
Kennedy Range
Robinson Range
Carnarvon Range
Kimberley Range
Hutton Range
Alfred and Marie Range
Browne Range
Mann Ranges
Petermann Ranges
Tomkinson Ranges
Birksgate Range
Barrow Range
Rawlinson Range
Doctor Hicks Range
Bailey Range
Fraser Range
Russell Range
Tropic of Capricorn
Perth
Fremantle
Mandurah
Bunbury
Busselton
Albany
Esperance
Geraldton
Carnarvon
Kalgoorlie
Boulder
Coolgardie
Norseman
Leonora
Laverton
Meekatharra
Wiluna
Eucla
Ceduna
Port Lincoln
Whyalla
Coober Pedy
Oodnadatta
Alice Springs
Uluru (Ayers Rock)
Lake Amadeus
Lake Everard
Lake Torrens
Cape Catastrophe
Investigator Strait
Point Culver
Point Malcolm
Cape Arid
Pollock Reef
Scorpion Bight
Head of Bight
Fowlers Bay
Streaky Bay
Anxious Bay
Investigator Group

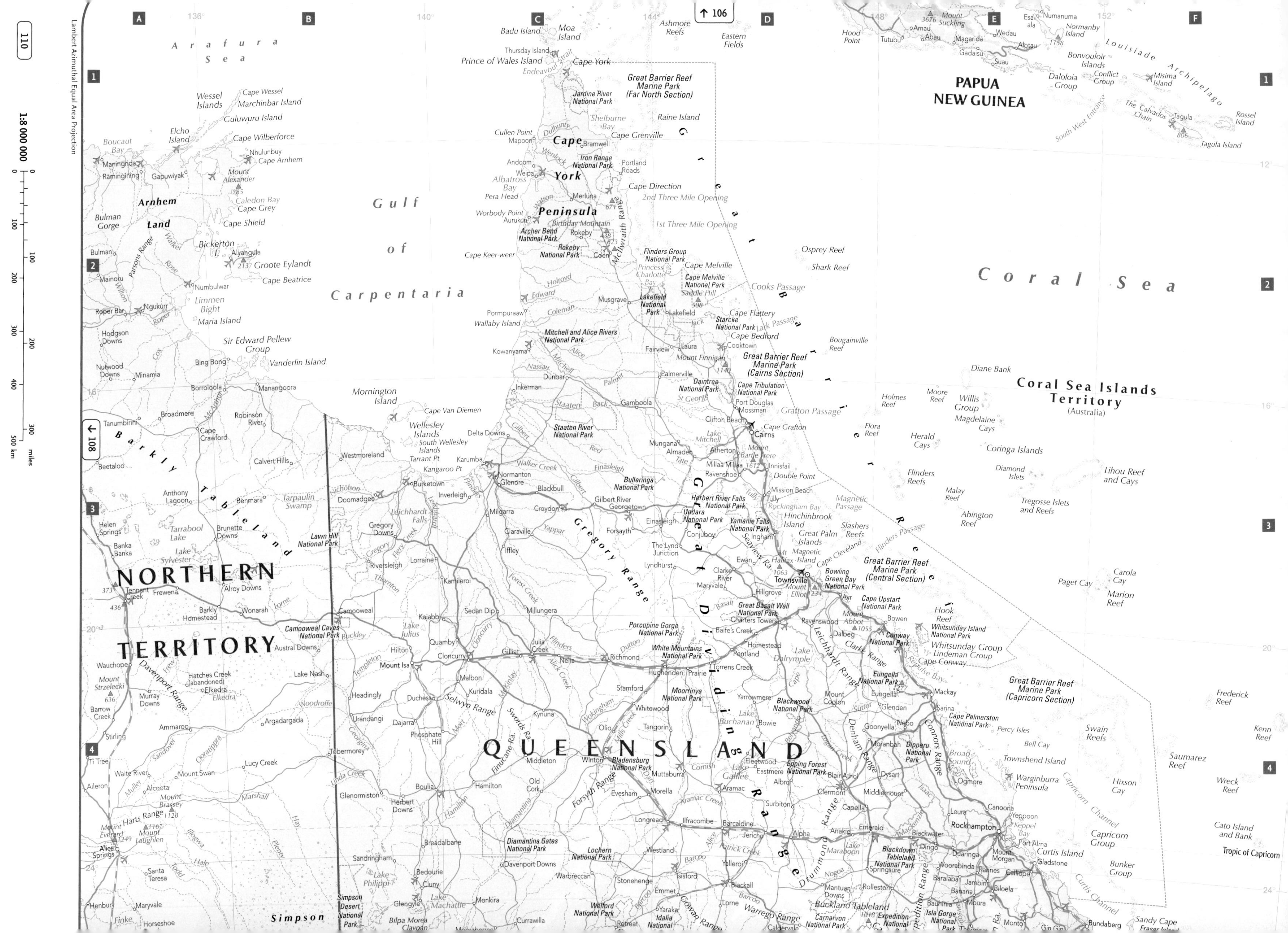
PAPUA NEW GUINEA
Coral Sea
Coral Sea Islands Territory (Australia)
Great Barrier Reef
Gulf of Carpentaria
Arafura Sea
QUEENSLAND
NORTHERN TERRITORY
Great Dividing Range
Gregory Range
Barkly Tableland
Cape York Peninsula
Arnhem Land
Louisiade Archipelago
Simpson
Mornington Island
Wellesley Islands
Groote Eylandt
Sir Edward Pellew Group
Wessel Islands
Thursday Island
Prince of Wales Island
Moa Island
Badu Island
Cape York
Cooktown
Cairns
Townsville
Mackay
Rockhampton
Gladstone
Bundaberg
Mount Isa
Cloncurry
Normanton
Karumba
Weipa
Longreach
Barcaldine
Emerald
Charters Towers
Hughenden
Winton
Tennant Creek
Alice Springs
Borroloola
Ngukurr
Tropic of Capricorn
Lambert Azimuthal Equal Area Projection
↑ 106
← 108
1:8 000 000
0 100 200 300 miles
0 100 200 300 400 500 km

AUSTRALIA
SOUTH AUSTRALIA
NEW SOUTH WALES
VICTORIA
TASMANIA
AUSTRALIAN CAPITAL TERRITORY
JERVIS BAY TERRITORY
Tasman Sea
Bass Strait
Brisbane
Sydney
Melbourne
Adelaide
CANBERRA
Hobart
Newcastle
Wollongong
Geelong
Launceston
Gold Coast
Toowoomba
Broken Hill
Port Augusta
Mildura
Bendigo
Ballarat
Wagga Wagga
Albury
Dubbo
Tamworth
Lake Eyre (North)
Lake Torrens
Lake Gairdner
Kangaroo Island
Eyre Peninsula
Spencer Gulf
Gulf St Vincent
Darling Downs
Flinders Ranges
Mount Lofty Ranges
Sturt Stony Desert
Strzelecki Desert
Simpson Desert Regional Reserve
Grey Range
Flinders Island
King Island
Wilson's Promontory
Cape Howe
Ninety Mile Beach
Riverina
Gippsland
1:8 000 000
↓ 109

Lambert Azimuthal Equal Area Projection

Oceania

Southeast Australia

1:5 000 000

0 50 100 150 mi
0 50 100 150 200 250 km

Tasman Sea

NEW ZEALAND

North Island

South Island

PACIFIC OCEAN

Three Kings Islands
Cape Maria van Diemen
North Cape
Te Paki
Ninety Mile Beach
Cape Karikari
Doubtless Bay
Ahipara Bay
Tauroa Point
Awanui
Kaitaia
Kerikeri
Bay of Islands
Cape Brett
Russell
Broadwood
Tahoke
Kawakawa
Poor Knights Islands
Donnellys Crossing
Whangarei
Dargaville
Bream Bay
Mokohinau Islands
Maungaturoto
Little Barrier
Port Fitzroy
Great Barrier Island
North Head
Kaipara Harbour
Wellsford
Leigh
Kawau Island
Colville Channel
Hauraki Gulf
Orewa
East Coast Bays
Takapuna
Waiheke Island
Colville
Mercury Islands
Auckland
Manukau
Whitianga
Coromandel Peninsula
Manukau Harbour
Papakura
Pukekohe
Waiuku
Thames
The Aldermen Islands
Port Waikato
Waitakaruru
Whangamata
Mayor Island
Huntly
Matakana Island
Motiti Island
Whakaari 1075
Cape Runaway
Hamilton
Tauranga
Cambridge
Bay of Plenty
Hicks Bay
Te Araroa
East Cape
Kawhia Harbour
Te Awamutu
Kawhia
Whakatane
Otorohanga
Te Kuiti
Rotorua
Tokoroa
Opotiki
Raukumara Range
Ruatoria
Piopio
Mangakino
Urewera National Park
Tokomaru Bay
Awakino
Mokau
Matawai
Tolaga Bay
North Taranaki Bight
Okahukura
Ohura
Taupo
Waitahanui
Lake Taupo
New Plymouth
Tongariro National Park
Gisborne
Mount Taranaki (Mount Egmont)
Whanganui National Park
Huiarau Range
Poverty Bay
Cape Egmont
Egmont National Park
Ohakune
Kaimanawa Mountains
Tarawera
Nuhaka
Opunake
Raetihi
Waiouru
Wairoa
Table Cape
Mahia Peninsula
Hawera
Hawke Bay
South Taranaki Bight
Bay View
Napier
Patea
Taihape
Hastings
Cape Kidnappers
Wanganui
Havelock North
Waimarama
Turakina
Marton
Apiti
Ruahine Range
Waipawa
Tikokino
Feilding
Waipukurau
Cape Farewell
Farewell Spit
Collingwood
Golden Bay
Kahurangi Point
Cape Stephens
Cook Strait
D'Urville Island
Palmerston North
Dannevirke
Porangahau
Abel Tasman National Park
Tasman Bay
French Pass
Levin
Otaki
Kapiti Island
Eketahuna
Pongaroa
Cape Turnagain
Tasman Mountains
Kahurangi National Park
Karamea
Karamea Bight
Riwaka
Paraparaumu
Upper Hutt
Porirua
Tararua Range
Mt Hector 1571
Masterton
Castlepoint
Richmond
Nelson
Havelock
Picton
Lower Hutt
Featherston
Seddonville
Wakefield
WELLINGTON
Blenheim
Waimangaroa
Hope Saddle
Owen River
Westport
Palliser Bay
Mount Ross 983
Cape Palliser
Charleston
Victoria Range
Seddon
Cape Campbell
Paparoa National Park
Reefton
St Arnaud Range
Mount Travers
2131
Inland Kaikoura Range
Tapuaenuku
Manakau
Clarence
Greymouth
Ahaura
Springs Junction
Nelson Lakes Nat. Park
Lewis Pass
Kaikoura
Hokitika
Lake Brunner
Rotomanu
Lake Sumner
Oaro
Ross
Otira
Arthur's Pass National Park
Culverden
Parnassus
Cheviot
Abut Head
Harihari
Southern Alps
Waikari
Westland National Park
Franz Josef Glacier
Fox Glacier
Waipara
Mount Arrowsmith 2795
Oxford
Pegasus Bay
Rangiora
Kaiapoi
Sheffield
Christchurch
Aoraki (Mount Cook) 3754
Lake Paringa
Aoraki/Mount Cook National Park
Canterbury Plains
Aylesbury
Sumner
Te Pirita
Tai Tapu
Banks Peninsula
Akaroa
Jackson Head
Cascade Point
Lake Tekapo
Mayfield
Ashburton
Lake Ellesmere
Awarua Point
Mount Aspiring National Park
Mount Aspiring 3030
Burkes Pass
Fairlie
Geraldine
Temuka
Longbeach
Canterbury Bight
Pleasant Point
Twizel
Timaru
Milford Sound
Richardson Mts
Mount Alta
Lake Hawea
Lake Benmore
The Hunters Hills
Pareora
Milford Sound
Mount Christina
Lake Wanaka
Wanaka
Hawkdun Range
Otematata
George Sound
Kinloch
Kurow
Studholme Junction
Waimate
Queenstown
Dunstan Mts
Duntroon
Secretary Island
Doubtful Sound
Fiordland National Park
Lake Wakatipu
Lake Te Anau
Ranfurly
Oamaru
Pukeuri Junction
Cape Wanbrow
James Peak
Alexandra
Hyde
Breaksea Sound
Te Anau
Eyre Mountains
Lake Manapouri
Athol
Moeraki Point
Shag Point
Palmerston
Waikouaiti
Resolution Island
Middlemarch
Mossburn
Roxburgh
Lammerlaw Range
Takitimu Mts
Lumsden
Warrington
Port Chalmers
Otago Peninsula
Caroline Peak 1722
Ohai
Beaumont
Mosgiel
Dunedin
Mandeville
Waitahuna
Milton
Cape Providence
Puysegur Point
Gore
Waipahi
Waiwera South
Henley
Te Waewae Bay
Winton
Orepuki
Edendale
Mataura
Balclutha
Riverton
Invercargill
Mount Pye 720
Kaitangata
Nugget Point
Solander Island
Foveaux Strait
Bluff
Fortrose
Long Point
Chaslands Mistake
Codfish Island
Mason Bay
Ruapuke Island
Stewart Island
Halfmoon Bay
Titi Islands (Muttonbird Islands)
Shelter Point
South West Cape
North Trap

nic Equidistant Projection

1:5 250 000 — 0 50 100 150 miles — 0 50 100 150 200 250 km

Oceania

New Zealand

North America
Landscapes

Internet Links	
NASA Visible Earth	**visibleearth.nasa.gov**
U.S. Geological Survey	**www.usgs.gov**
Natural Resources Canada	**www.nrcan-rncan.gc.ca**
SPOT Image satellite imagery	**www.spotimage.fr**

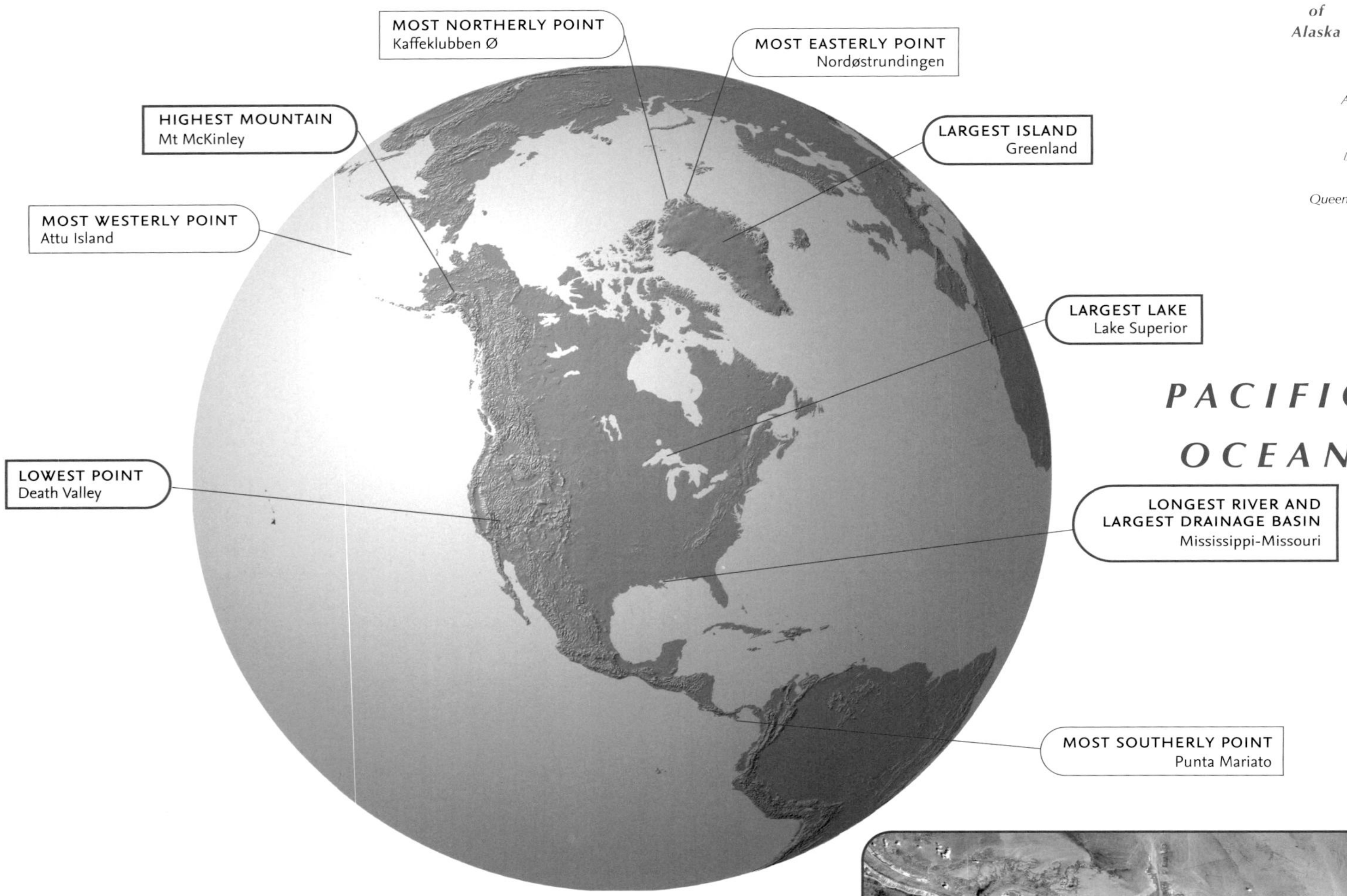

North America, the world's third largest continent, supports a wide range of landscapes from the Arctic north to sub-tropical Central America. The main physiographic regions of the continent are the mountains of the west coast, stretching from Alaska in the north to Mexico and Central America in the south; the vast, relatively flat Canadian Shield; the Great Plains which make up the majority of the interior; the Appalachian Mountains in the east; and the Atlantic coastal plain.

These regions contain some significant physical features, including the Rocky Mountains, the Great Lakes – three of which are amongst the five largest lakes in the world – and the Mississippi-Missouri river system which is the world's fourth longest river. The Caribbean Sea contains a complex pattern of islands, many volcanic in origin, and the continent is joined to South America by the narrow Isthmus of Panama.

MOST NORTHERLY POINT
Kaffeklubben Ø

MOST EASTERLY POINT
Nordøstrundingen

HIGHEST MOUNTAIN
Mt McKinley

LARGEST ISLAND
Greenland

MOST WESTERLY POINT
Attu Island

LARGEST LAKE
Lake Superior

PACIFIC OCEAN

LOWEST POINT
Death Valley

LONGEST RIVER AND LARGEST DRAINAGE BASIN
Mississippi-Missouri

MOST SOUTHERLY POINT
Punta Mariato

North America's physical features

Highest mountain	Mt McKinley, USA	6 194 metres	20 321 feet
Longest river	Mississippi-Missouri, USA	5 969 km	3 709 miles
Largest lake	Lake Superior, Canada/USA	82 100 sq km	31 699 sq miles
Largest island	Greenland	2 175 600 sq km	839 999 sq miles
Largest drainage basin	Mississippi-Missouri, USA	3 250 000 sq km	1 254 825 sq miles
Lowest point	Death Valley, USA	-86 metres	-282 feet

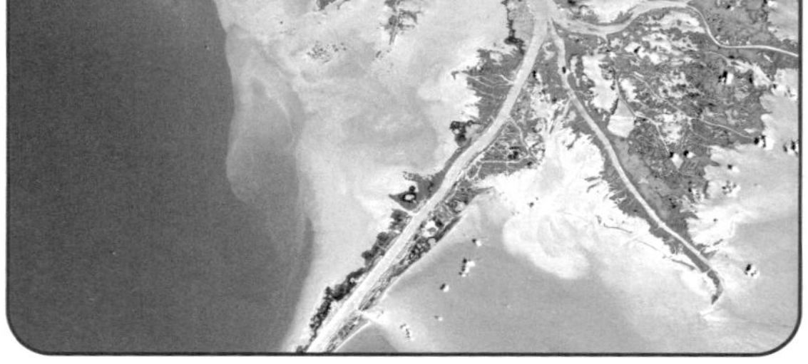

North America's longest river system, the **Mississippi-Missouri,** flows into the Gulf of Mexico through the Mississippi Delta.

North America's extent

TOTAL LAND AREA (including Hawai'ian Islands)	24 680 331 sq km / 9 529 076 sq miles
Most northerly point	Kaffeklubben Ø, Greenland
Most southerly point	Punta Mariato, Panama
Most westerly point	Attu Island, USA
Most easterly point	Nordøstrundingen, Greenland

The **Panama Canal,** Panama, linking the Pacific Ocean to the Atlantic Ocean.

Facts

- Devon Island, Canada, is the world's largest uninhabited island
- Canada has the longest coastline of any country in the world
- Lake Superior is the world's largest freshwater lake
- Over 320 000 square kilometres of the USA is protected for conservation purposes

North America
Countries

North America has been dominated economically and politically by the USA since the nineteenth century. Before that, the continent was subject to colonial influences, particularly of Spain in the south and of Britain and France in the east. The nineteenth century saw the steady development of the western half of the continent. The wealth of natural resources and the generally temperate climate were an excellent basis for settlement, agriculture and industrial development which has led to the USA being the richest nation in the world today.

Although there are twenty-three independent countries and fourteen dependent territories in North America, Canada, Mexico and the USA have approximately eighty-five per cent of the continent's population and eighty-eight per cent of its land area. Large parts of the north remain sparsely populated, while the most densely populated areas are in the northeast USA, and the Caribbean.

North America's capitals

Largest capital (population)	Mexico City, Mexico	19 028 000	
Smallest capital (population)	Belmopan, Belize	13 500	
Most northerly capital	Ottawa, Canada	45° 25'N	
Most southerly capital	Panama City, Panama	8° 56'N	
Highest capital	Mexico City, Mexico	2 300 metres	7 546 feet

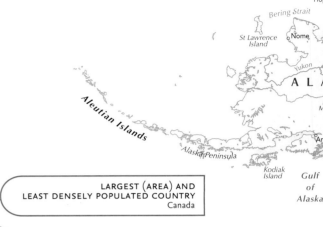

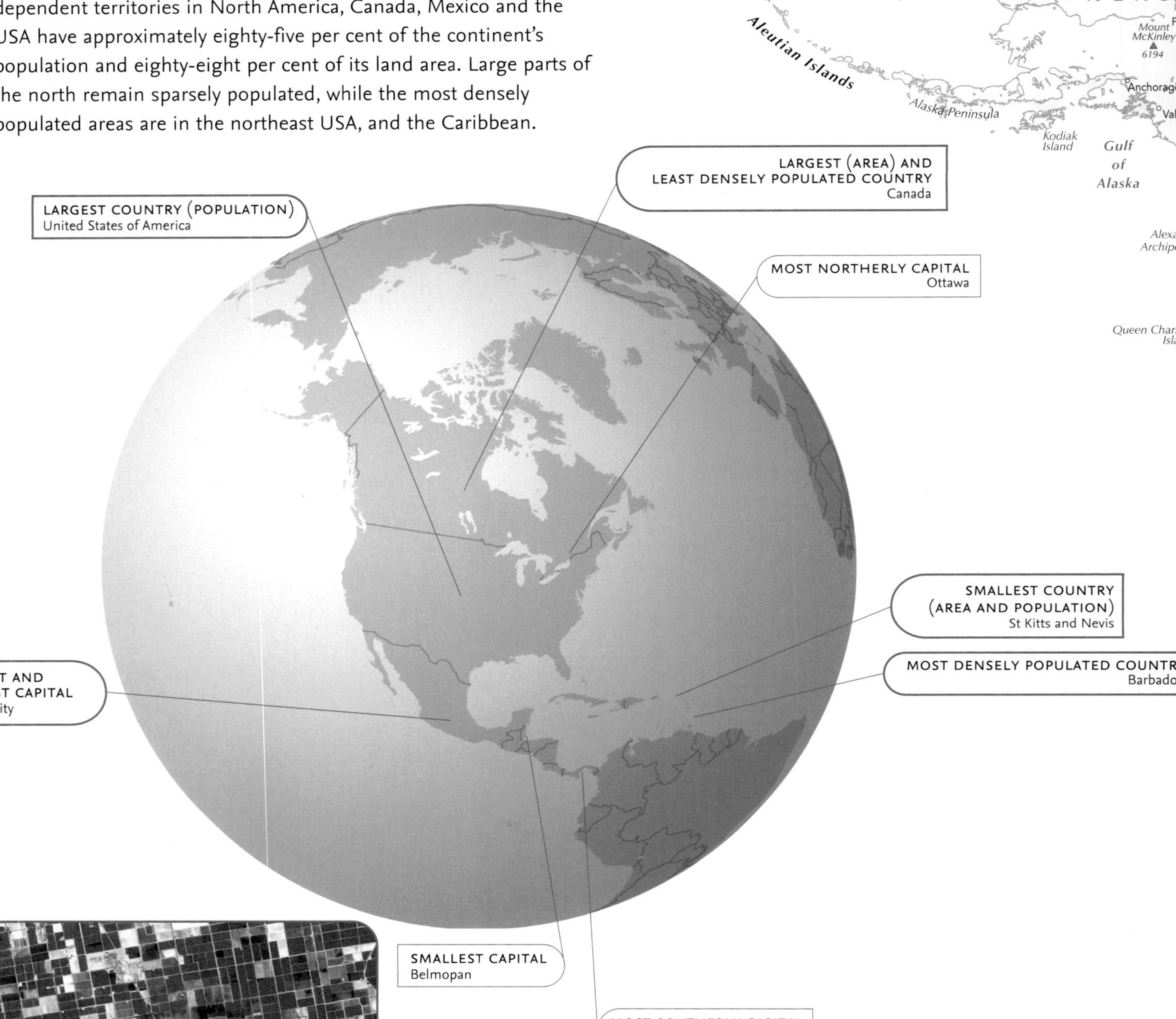

False-colour satellite image of the **Mexico-USA** boundary at Mexicali.

North America's countries

Largest country (area)	Canada	9 984 670 sq km	3 855 103 sq miles
Smallest country (area)	St Kitts and Nevis	261 sq km	101 sq miles
Largest country (population)	United States of America	298 213 000	
Smallest country (population)	St Kitts and Nevis	43 000	
Most densely populated country	Barbados	628 per sq km	1 627 per sq mile
Least densely populated country	Canada	3 per sq km	8 per sq mile

Internet Links

UK Foreign and Commonwealth Office	www.fco.gov.uk
CIA World Factbook	www.cia.gov/library/publications/the-world-factbook/index.html
U.S. Board on Geographic Names	geonames.usgs.gov
NASA Astronaut Photography	eol.jsc.nasa.gov

The Bahamas, a chain of islands in the North Atlantic Ocean, lying southeast of Florida, USA.

Facts

- The Panama Canal, opened in 1914, cut the journey between the Atlantic and the Pacific by over 14 000 km
- Mexico City is the highest city in North America and houses approximately 18% of Mexico's population
- The state of Alaska was bought by the USA from Russia in 1867
- The territory of Nunavut is Canada's newest administrative division, created in 1999 from the eastern part of Northwest Territories

Lambert Conformal Conic Projection

1:16 000 000

0 200 400 miles

0 200 400 600 800 km

North America
Canada

1:7 000 000

0 100 200 miles

0 100 200 300 400 km

North America

Western Canada

Conic Equidistant Projection

1:7 000 000

0 100 200 miles

0 100 200 300 400 km

Ungava Bay
Labrador Sea
Labrador
NEWFOUNDLAND AND LABRADOR
Torngat Mountains
Torngat Mountains National Park Reserve
Smallwood Reservoir
Churchill Falls
Happy Valley-Goose Bay
Mealy Mountains
Hamilton Inlet
Lake Melville
QUÉBEC
Réservoir Manicouagan
Île d'Anticosti
Gulf of St Lawrence
Détroit de Jacques-Cartier
Détroit d'Honguedo
Péninsule de la Gaspésie
Monts Notre-Dame
Monts Chic-Chocs
Chaleur Bay
NEW BRUNSWICK
PRINCE EDWARD ISLAND
Northumberland Strait
NOVA SCOTIA
Bay of Fundy
Cape Breton Island
Cabot Strait
Îles de la Madeleine
Newfoundland
Long Range Mountains
Strait of Belle Isle
Avalon Peninsula
St Pierre and Miquelon (France)
MAINE
NEW HAMPSHIRE
VERMONT
Gulf of Maine
ATLANTIC OCEAN
Sable Island
St John's
Halifax
Québec
Moncton
Fredericton
Charlottetown
Sydney
Sept-Îles
Gaspé
Nain
Hopedale
Kuujjuaq (Fort Chimo)

Lambert Conformal Conic Projection

1:12 000 000

0 100 200 300 400 miles

0 100 200 300 400 500 600 700 km

CANADA
UNITED STATES OF AMERICA
ONTARIO
QUÉBEC
NEW BRUNSWICK
NOVA SCOTIA
PRINCE EDWARD ISLAND
MAINE
VERMONT
NEW HAMPSHIRE
MASSACHUSETTS
RHODE ISLAND
CONNECTICUT
NEW YORK
NEW JERSEY
PENNSYLVANIA
DELAWARE
MARYLAND
WASHINGTON D.C.
WEST VIRGINIA
VIRGINIA
NORTH CAROLINA
SOUTH CAROLINA
GEORGIA
FLORIDA
ALABAMA
MISSISSIPPI
LOUISIANA
ARKANSAS
TENNESSEE
KENTUCKY
OHIO
INDIANA
ILLINOIS
MICHIGAN
WISCONSIN
MINNESOTA
IOWA
MISSOURI
THE BAHAMAS
CUBA
ATLANTIC OCEAN
Gulf of Mexico
Gulf of Maine
Gulf of St Lawrence
James Bay
Lake Superior
Lake Michigan
Lake Huron
Lake Erie
Lake Ontario
Appalachian Mountains
Allegheny Mountains
Cumberland Plateau
Ozark Plateau
Coastal Plain
Straits of Florida
Great Bahama Bank
Tropic of Cancer
Chicago
Detroit
Toronto
Montréal
OTTAWA
Boston
New York
Philadelphia
Baltimore
WASHINGTON
Pittsburgh
Cleveland
Columbus
Cincinnati
Indianapolis
St Louis
Memphis
Nashville
Atlanta
Charlotte
Jacksonville
Orlando
Tampa
Miami
New Orleans
Houston
Dallas
Milwaukee
Minneapolis
NASSAU
↑ 119
↓ 137

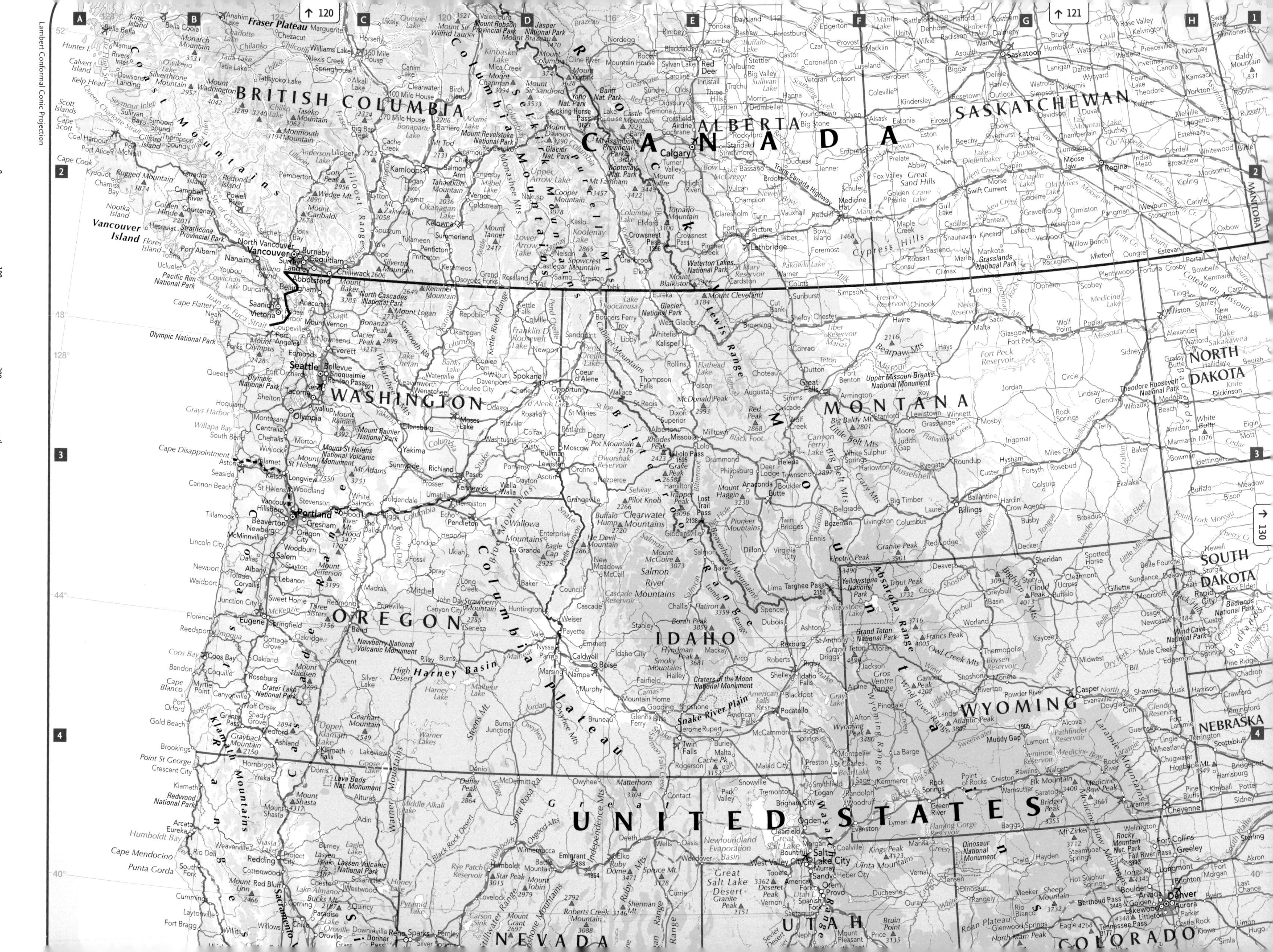

↑ 120
↑ 121
↑ 130

Lambert Conformal Conic Projection

1:7 000 000 — 0, 100, 200 miles; 0, 100, 200, 300, 400 km

↑ 131

OF AMERICA
CALIFORNIA
ARIZONA
NEW MEXICO
TEXAS
MEXICO
SONORA
CHIHUAHUA
DURANGO
SINALOA
BAJA CALIFORNIA
BAJA CALIFORNIA SUR
PACIFIC OCEAN
Gulf of California
Baja California
Sonoran Desert
Mojave Desert
Colorado Plateau
Sierra Madre Occidental
Sierra Nevada
San Joaquin Valley
Sangre de Cristo Range
Sacramento Mts
Death Valley
Grand Canyon
Los Angeles
San Diego
San Francisco
San Jose
Las Vegas
Phoenix
Tucson
Albuquerque
El Paso
Ciudad Juárez
Chihuahua
Hermosillo
Tijuana
Mexicali
HAWAII (U.S.A.)
Hawai'i
Maui
O'ahu
Honolulu
Kaua'i
Moloka'i
Lāna'i
Ni'ihau
Kaho'olawe
PACIFIC OCEAN
1:7 000 000

↓ 136

↑ 126

Lambert Conformal Conic Projection

1:3 500 000

0 50 100 miles

0 50 100 150 200 km

UTAH
COLORADO
ARIZONA
NEW MEXICO
D STATES
AMERICA
XICO
SONORA
Great Salt Lake
Salt Lake City
West Valley City
South Salt Lake
Murray
Sandy
Orem
Provo
Springville
Great Salt Lake Desert
Newfoundland Evaporation Basin
Sevier Desert
Uinta Mountains
Roan Plateau
East Tavaputs Plateau
Book Cliffs
Grand Junction
Colorado National Monument
Arches National Park
Canyonlands National Park
Capitol Reef National Park
Natural Bridges National Monument
Bryce Canyon National Park
Zion National Park
Great Basin National Park
Grand Staircase-Escalante National Monument
Kaiparowits Plateau
Aquarius Plateau
Glen Canyon
Vermilion Cliffs
Canyons of the Ancients National Monument
Mesa Verde National Park
Black Canyon of the Gunnison National Park
San Juan Mountains
Uncompahgre Plateau
Durango
Cortez
Farmington
Gallup
Shiprock
Chaco Culture National Historical Park
Chuska Mountains
Defiance Plateau
Canyon de Chelly National Monument
Black Mesa
Kaibab Plateau
Grand Canyon
Grand Canyon Parashant National Monument
Coconino Plateau
Colorado Plateau
Painted Desert
Petrified Forest National Park
Wupatki National Monument
Flagstaff
Sedona
Prescott
Kingman
Lake Mead
Las Vegas
North Las Vegas
Henderson
Boulder City
Lake Havasu City
Bullhead City
Mogollon Plateau
El Malpais National Monument
Zuni Mountains
Gallo Mountains
Plains of San Agustin
Mogollon Mountains
Black Range
Phoenix
Glendale
Peoria
Tempe
Mesa
Chandler
Gilbert
Tucson
Casa Grande
Saguaro National Park
Organ Pipe Cactus National Monument
Ironwood Forest Nat. Monument
Sonoran Desert Nat. Monument
Agua Fria National Monument
Chiricahua National Monument
Sonoran Desert
Yuma
Yuma Desert
Mexicali
El Centro
Brawley
Safford
Silver City
Lordsburg
Willcox
Benson
Nogales

↑ 127
↓ 136

Lambert Conformal Conic Projection

1:7 000 000

0 100 200 miles

0 100 200 300 400 km

North America
Central United States

Lambert Conformal Conic Projection

1:7 000 000

0 100 200 miles

0 100 200 300 400 km

ATLANTIC
OCEAN
Gulf
of
Mexico
OF AMERICA
SOUTH CAROLINA
GEORGIA
ALABAMA
MISSISSIPPI
FLORIDA
THE BAHAMAS
CUBA
MEXICO
Turks and Caicos Island (U.K.)
Great Bahama Bank
Little Bahama Bank
Straits of Florida
Tropic of Cancer
Yucatan Channel
Old Bahama Channel
Nicholas Channel
Northeast Providence Channel
Northwest Providence Channel
Tongue of the Ocean
Exuma Sound
Grand Bahama
Great Abaco
Andros
Eleuthera
Cat Island
San Salvador
Long Island
Great Exuma
Acklins Island
Crooked Island
Mayaguana
Little Inagua Island
NASSAU
HAVANA (La Habana)
Atlanta
Birmingham
Montgomery
Mobile
Pensacola
Tallahassee
Jacksonville
Savannah
Charleston
Columbia
Wilmington
Orlando
Tampa
St Petersburg
Miami
Fort Lauderdale
West Palm Beach
Key West
Cape Canaveral
Cape Fear
Cape Lookout
Cape Romano
Cape Sable
Everglades
Lake Okeechobee
Mississippi Delta
Chandeleur Islands
Apalachee Bay
Coastal Plain
Isla de la Juventud
Golfo de Batabanó
Archipiélago de Camagüey
Archipiélago de Sabana
↓ 131
↓ 137

Lambert Conformal Conic Projection

1:3 500 000

0	50	100	miles
0	50	100	150	200	km

↑ 123
CANADA
U.S.A.
QUÉBEC
ONTARIO
MAINE
VERMONT
NEW HAMPSHIRE
MASSACHUSETTS
RHODE ISLAND
CONNECTICUT
NEW YORK
PENNSYLVANIA
NEW JERSEY
DELAWARE
MARYLAND
VIRGINIA
D.C.
WASHINGTON
OTTAWA
Lake Ontario
Adirondack Mountains
Catskill Mountains
Green Mountains
White Mountains
Appalachian Mountains
Finger Lakes
Gulf of Maine
Long Island Sound
Long Island
Block Island Sound
Cape Cod Bay
Massachusetts Bay
Nantucket Sound
Delaware Bay
Chesapeake Bay
ATLANTIC OCEAN
New York
Philadelphia
Boston
Baltimore
Providence
Hartford
Albany
Syracuse
Rochester
Buffalo
Richmond
Norfolk
Virginia Beach
Atlantic City
Portland
Cape Cod
Nantucket Island
Martha's Vineyard
74°
72°
70°
42°
40°
38°

Lambert Conformal Conic Projection

1:14 000 000

0 200 400 miles
0 200 400 600 800 km

↑ 125

↓ 142

North America
Central America and the Caribbean

South America

Landscapes

South America is a continent of great contrasts, with landscapes varying from the tropical rainforests of the Amazon Basin, to the Atacama Desert, the driest place on earth, and the sub-Antarctic regions of southern Chile and Argentina. The dominant physical features are the Andes, stretching along the entire west coast of the continent and containing numerous mountains over 6 000 metres high, and the Amazon, which is the second longest river in the world and has the world's largest drainage basin.

The Altiplano is a high plateau lying between two of the Andes ranges. It contains Lake Titicaca, the world's highest navigable lake. By contrast, large lowland areas dominate the centre of the continent, lying between the Andes and the Guiana and Brazilian Highlands. These vast grasslands stretch from the Llanos of the north through the Selvas and the Gran Chaco to the Pampas of Argentina.

Confluence of the **Amazon** and **Negro** rivers at Manaus, northern Brazil.

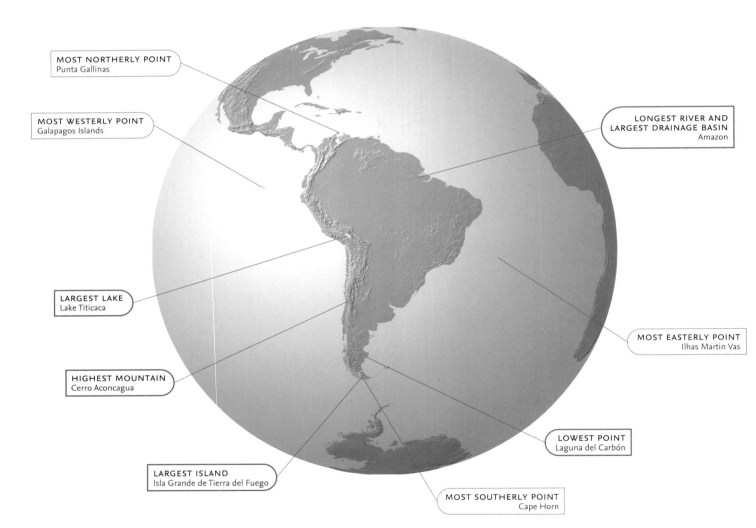

MOST NORTHERLY POINT
Punta Gallinas

MOST WESTERLY POINT
Galapagos Islands

LONGEST RIVER AND LARGEST DRAINAGE BASIN
Amazon

LARGEST LAKE
Lake Titicaca

MOST EASTERLY POINT
Ilhas Martin Vas

HIGHEST MOUNTAIN
Cerro Aconcagua

LOWEST POINT
Laguna del Carbón

LARGEST ISLAND
Isla Grande de Tierra del Fuego

MOST SOUTHERLY POINT
Cape Horn

South America's physical features

Highest mountain	Cerro Aconcagua, Argentina	6 959 metres	22 831 feet
Longest river	Amazon	6 516 km	4 049 miles
Largest lake	Lake Titicaca, Bolivia/Peru	8 340 sq km	3 220 sq miles
Largest island	Isla Grande de Tierra del Fuego, Argentina/Chile	47 000 sq km	18 147 sq miles
Largest drainage basin	Amazon	7 050 000 sq km	2 722 005 sq miles
Lowest point	Laguna del Carbón, Argentina	-105 metres	-345 feet

Internet Links

NASA Visible Earth	**visibleearth.nasa.gov**
NASA Astronaut Photography	**eol.jsc.nasa.gov**
World Rainforest Information Portal	**www.rainforestweb.org**
Peakware World Mountain Encyclopedia	**www.peakware.com**

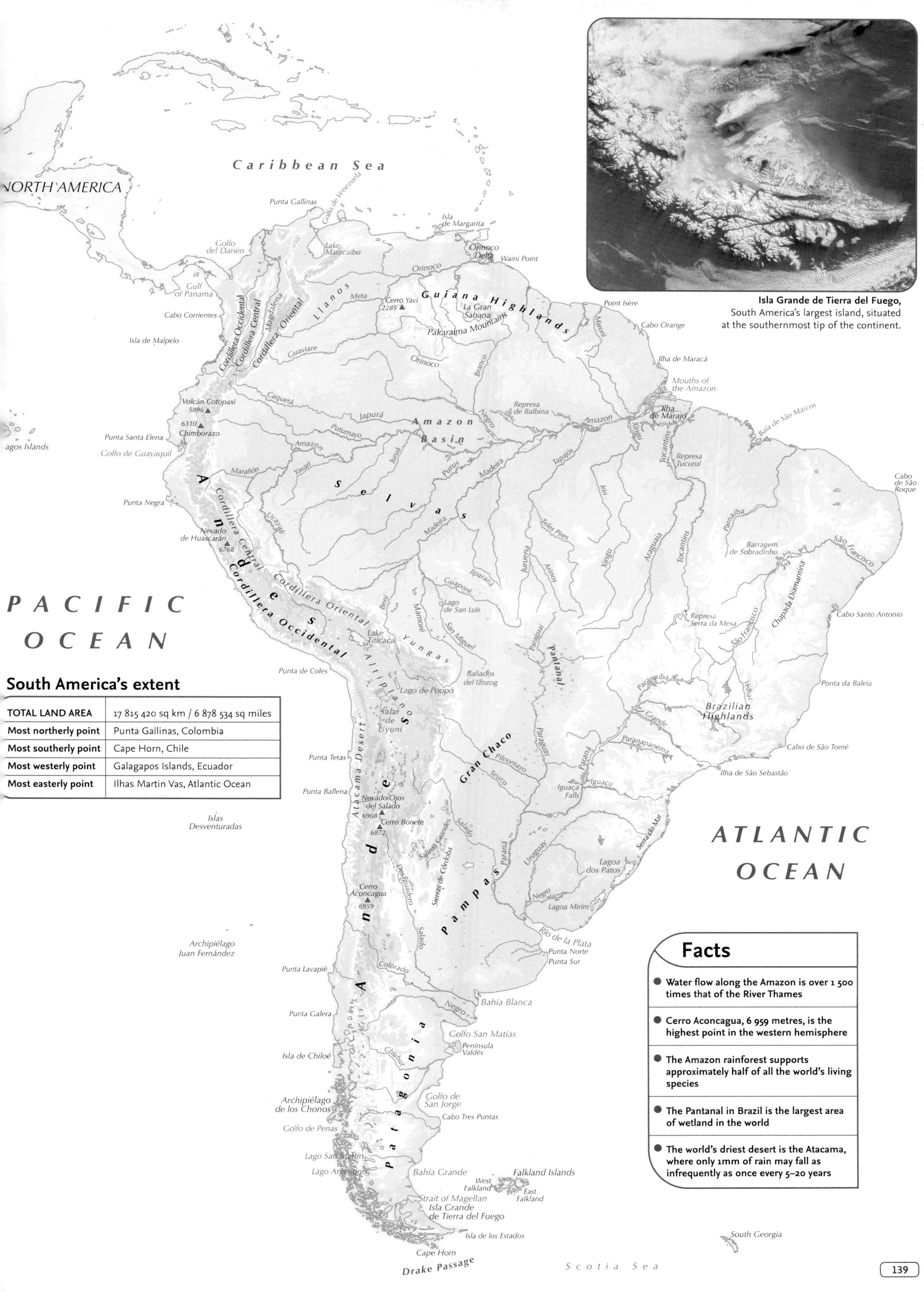

Isla Grande de Tierra del Fuego, South America's largest island, situated at the southernmost tip of the continent.

South America's extent

TOTAL LAND AREA	17 815 420 sq km / 6 878 534 sq miles
Most northerly point	Punta Gallinas, Colombia
Most southerly point	Cape Horn, Chile
Most westerly point	Galagapos Islands, Ecuador
Most easterly point	Ilhas Martin Vas, Atlantic Ocean

Facts

- Water flow along the Amazon is over 1 500 times that of the River Thames
- Cerro Aconcagua, 6 959 metres, is the highest point in the western hemisphere
- The Amazon rainforest supports approximately half of all the world's living species
- The Pantanal in Brazil is the largest area of wetland in the world
- The world's driest desert is the Atacama, where only 1mm of rain may fall as infrequently as once every 5–20 years

South America
Countries

French Guiana, a French Department, is the only remaining territory under overseas control on a continent which has seen a long colonial history. Much of South America was colonized by Spain in the sixteenth century, with Britain, Portugal and the Netherlands each claiming territory in the northeast of the continent. This colonization led to the conquering of ancient civilizations, including the Incas in Peru. Most countries became independent from Spain and Portugal in the early nineteenth century.

The population of the continent reflects its history, being composed primarily of indigenous Indian peoples and mestizos – reflecting the long Hispanic influence. There has been a steady process of urbanization within the continent, with major movements of the population from rural to urban areas. The majority of the population now lives in the major cities and within 300 kilometres of the coast.

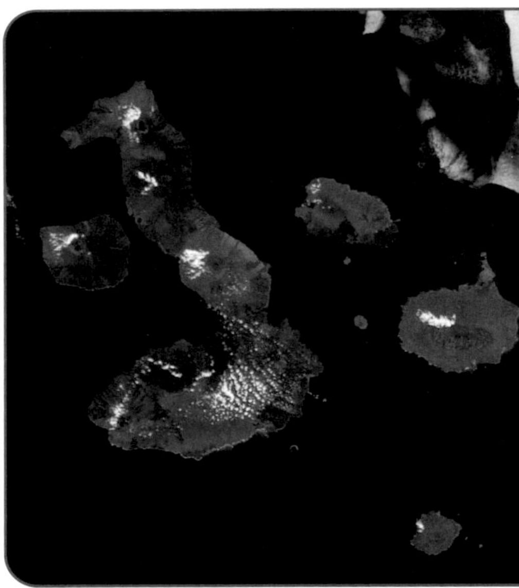

Galapagos Islands, an island territory of Ecuador which lies on the equator in the eastern Pacific Ocean over 900 kilometres west of the coast of Ecuador.

SMALLEST COUNTRY (POPULATION AND AREA) AND LEAST DENSELY POPULATED COUNTRY
Suriname

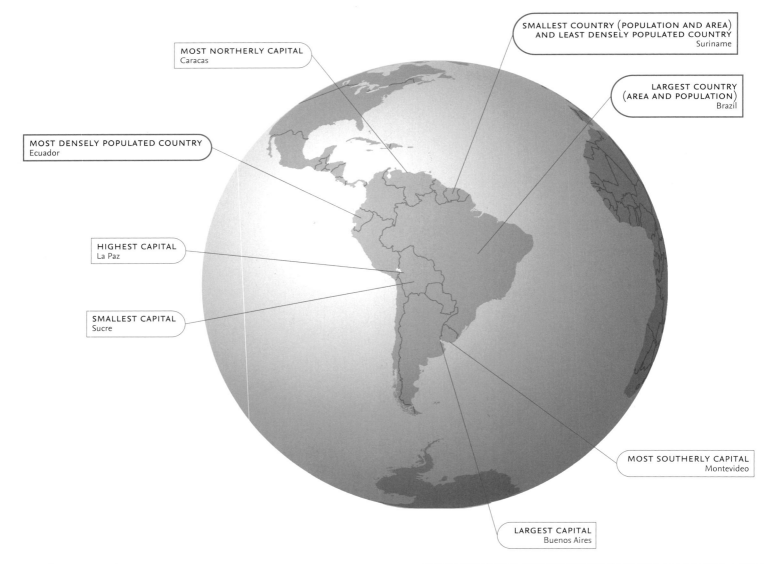

MOST NORTHERLY CAPITAL
Caracas

LARGEST COUNTRY (AREA AND POPULATION)
Brazil

MOST DENSELY POPULATED COUNTRY
Ecuador

HIGHEST CAPITAL
La Paz

SMALLEST CAPITAL
Sucre

MOST SOUTHERLY CAPITAL
Montevideo

LARGEST CAPITAL
Buenos Aires

South America's countries

Largest country (area)	Brazil	8 514 879 sq km	3 287 613 sq miles
Smallest country (area)	Suriname	163 820 sq km	63 251 sq miles
Largest country (population)	Brazil	186 405 000	
Smallest country (population)	Suriname	449 000	
Most densely populated country	Ecuador	48 per sq km	124 per sq mile
Least densely populated country	Suriname	3 per sq km	7 per sq mile

Internet Links

UK Foreign and Commonwealth Office	**www.fco.gov.uk**
CIA World Factbook	**www.cia.gov/library/publications/the-world-factbook/index.html**
Caribbean Community (Caricom)	**www.caricom.org**
Latin American Network Information Center	**lanic.utexas.edu**

South America's capitals

Largest capital (population)	Buenos Aires, Argentina	13 349 000
Smallest capital (population)	Sucre, Bolivia	231 000
Most northerly capital	Caracas, Venezuela	10° 28'N
Most southerly capital	Montevideo, Uruguay	34° 52'S
Highest capital	La Paz, Bolivia	3 630 metres 11 909 feet

Facts

- South America is often referred to as 'Latin America', reflecting the historic influences of Spain and Portugal
- The largest city in each South American country is the capital, except in Brazil and Ecuador
- South America has only two landlocked countries – Bolivia and Paraguay
- Chile is over 4 000 kilometres long but has an average width of only 177 kilometres

Falkland Islands, an overseas UK territory in the South Atlantic Ocean.

↑ 137
NICARAGUA
MANAGUA
COSTA RICA
SAN JOSE
PANAMA
PANAMA CITY
Gulf of Panama
Isthmus of Panama
COLOMBIA
BOGOTÁ
VENEZUELA
CARACAS
ECUADOR
QUITO
PERU
LIMA
BOLIVIA
LA PAZ
SUCRE
CHILE
ARGENTINA
Netherlands Antilles
GRENADA
PORT OF SPAIN
Aruba
ORANJESTAD
WILLEMSTAD
Barranquilla
Cartagena
Maracaibo
Medellín
Cali
Guayaquil
Iquitos
Arequipa
Cusco (Cuzco)
Callao
Trujillo
Chiclayo
Cochabamba
Santa Cruz
Manizales
Bucaramanga
Cúcuta
Valencia
Barquisimeto
Maracay
Ciudad Guayana
Llanos
Selvas
Andes
Cordillera Occidental
Cordillera Central
Cordillera Oriental
Guiana Highlands
Lake Titicaca
Equator
Tropic of Capricorn
PACIFIC OCEAN
Galapagos Islands (Islas Galápagos) (Ecuador)
Isla Isabela
Isla Fernandina
Isla San Salvador
Isla Santa Cruz
Isla San Cristóbal
Isla Santa María
Puerto Baquerizo Moreno
1:14 000 000
Lambert Azimuthal Equal Area Projection
1:14 000 000
0 200 400 miles
0 200 400 600 800 km

South America
Northern South America

South America

Southern South America

Lambert Azimuthal Equal Area Projection

1:7 000 000

0 100 200 miles

0 100 200 300 400 km

South America

Southeast Brazil

Oceans and Poles

Features

Between them, the world's oceans and polar regions cover approximately seventy per cent of the Earth's surface. The oceans contain ninety-six per cent of the Earth's water and a vast range of flora and fauna. They are a major influence on the world's climate, particularly through ocean currents. The Arctic and Antarctica are the coldest and most inhospitable places on the Earth. They both have vast amounts of ice which, if global warming continues, could have a major influence on sea level across the globe.

Our understanding of the oceans and polar regions has increased enormously over the last twenty years through the development of new technologies, particularly that of satellite remote sensing, which can generate vast amounts of data relating to, for example, topography (both on land and the seafloor), land cover and sea surface temperature.

Pacific Ocean
World's largest ocean: 166 241 000 sq km
Average depth: 4 200m
Challenger Deep: 10 920 metres
Mariana Trench
Deepest point
PACIF
OCEA
AUSTRALIA
South Pacific Ocean
Average depth: 3 935 metres

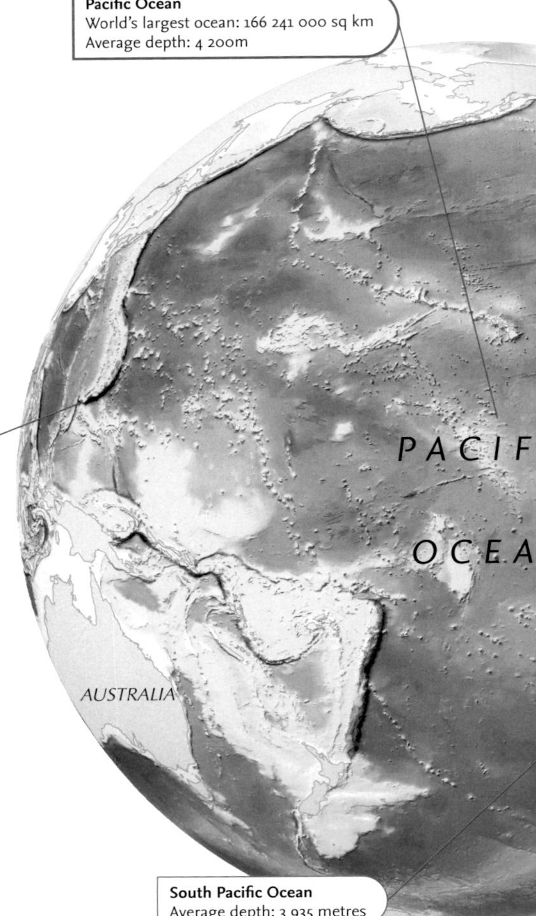

The oceans

The world's major oceans are the Pacific, the Atlantic and the Indian Oceans. The Arctic Ocean is generally considered as part of the Atlantic, and the Southern Ocean, which stretches around the whole of Antarctica is usually treated as an extension of each of the three major oceans.

One of the most important factors affecting the earth's climate is the circulation of water within and between the oceans. Differences in temperature and surface winds create ocean currents which move enormous quantities of water around the globe. These currents re-distribute heat which the oceans have absorbed from the sun, and so have a major effect on the world's climate system. El Niño is one climatic phenomenon directly influenced by these ocean processes.

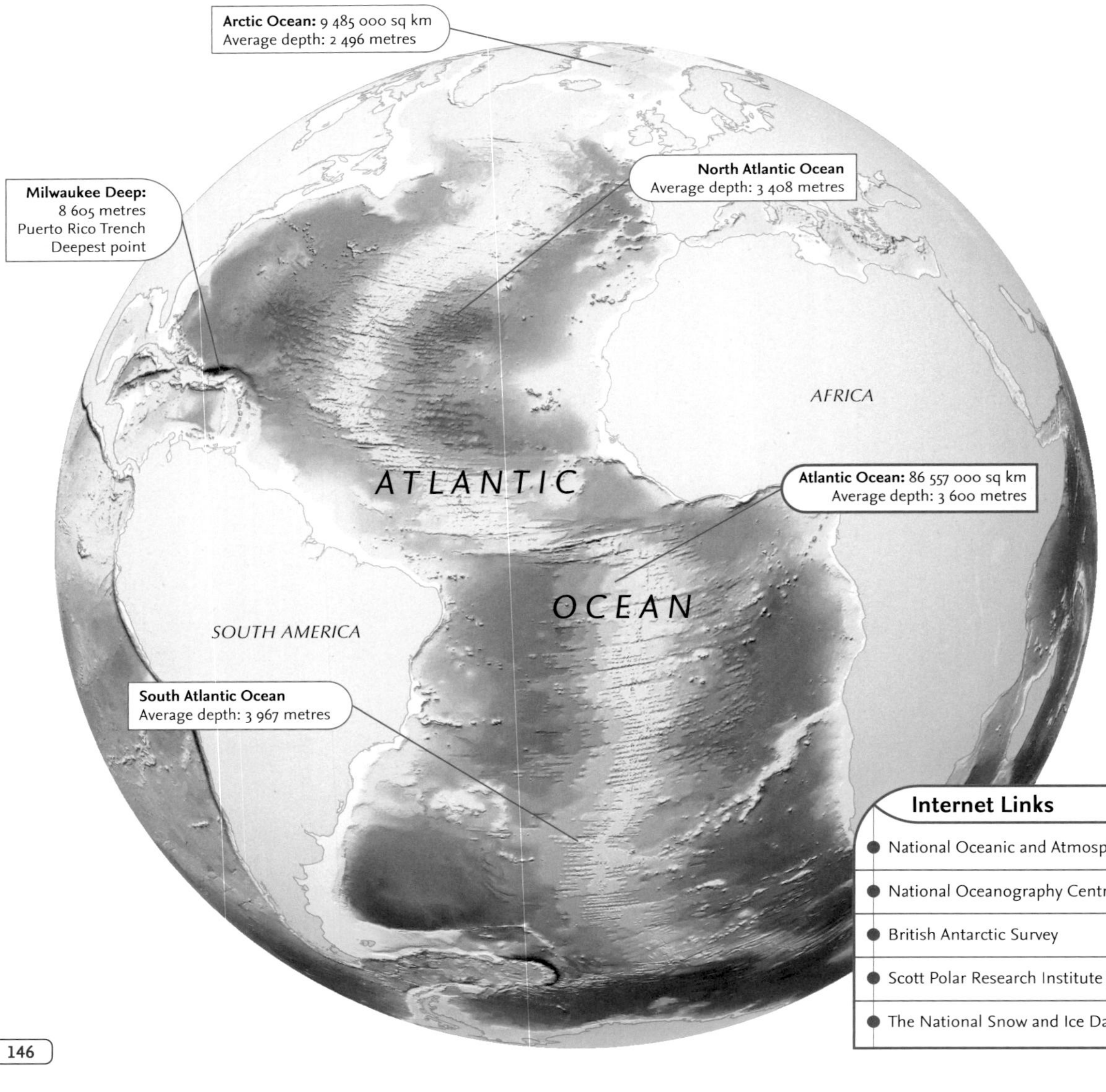

Arctic Ocean: 9 485 000 sq km
Average depth: 2 496 metres
Milwaukee Deep:
8 605 metres
Puerto Rico Trench
Deepest point
North Atlantic Ocean
Average depth: 3 408 metres
AFRICA
ATLANTIC
OCEAN
Atlantic Ocean: 86 557 000 sq km
Average depth: 3 600 metres
SOUTH AMERICA
South Atlantic Ocean
Average depth: 3 967 metres

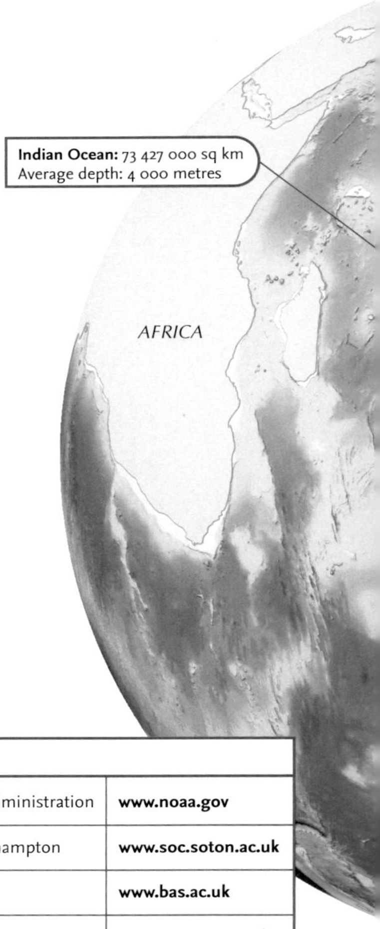

Indian Ocean: 73 427 000 sq km
Average depth: 4 000 metres
AFRICA

Internet Links

National Oceanic and Atmospheric Administration	**www.noaa.gov**
National Oceanography Centre, Southampton	**www.soc.soton.ac.uk**
British Antarctic Survey	**www.bas.ac.uk**
Scott Polar Research Institute (SPRI)	**www.spri.cam.ac.uk**
The National Snow and Ice Data Center (NSIDC)	**nsidc.org**

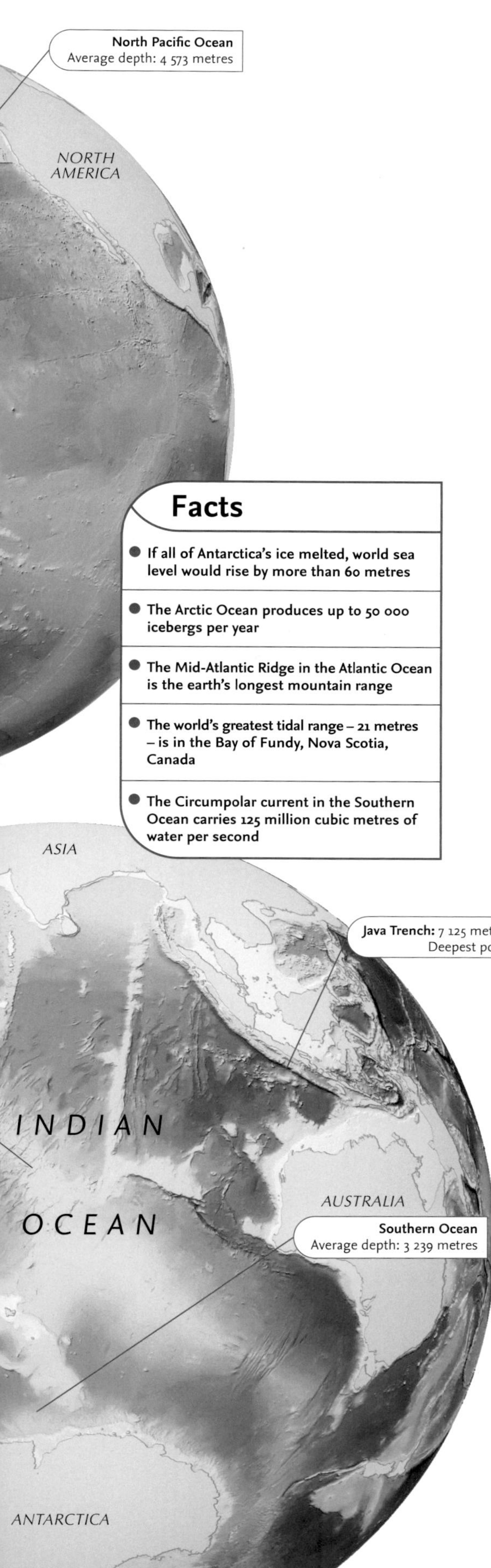

Facts

- If all of Antarctica's ice melted, world sea level would rise by more than 60 metres
- The Arctic Ocean produces up to 50 000 icebergs per year
- The Mid-Atlantic Ridge in the Atlantic Ocean is the earth's longest mountain range
- The world's greatest tidal range – 21 metres – is in the Bay of Fundy, Nova Scotia, Canada
- The Circumpolar current in the Southern Ocean carries 125 million cubic metres of water per second

Polar regions

Although a harsh climate is common to the two polar regions, there are major differences between the Arctic and Antarctica. The North Pole is surrounded by the Arctic Ocean, much of which is permanently covered by sea ice, while the South Pole lies on the huge land mass of Antarctica. This is covered by a permanent ice cap which reaches a maximum thickness of over four kilometres. Antarctica has no permanent population, but Europe, Asia and North America all stretch into the Arctic region which is populated by numerous ethnic groups. Antarctica is subject to the Antarctic Treaty of 1959 which does not recognize individual land claims and protects the continent in the interests of international scientific cooperation.

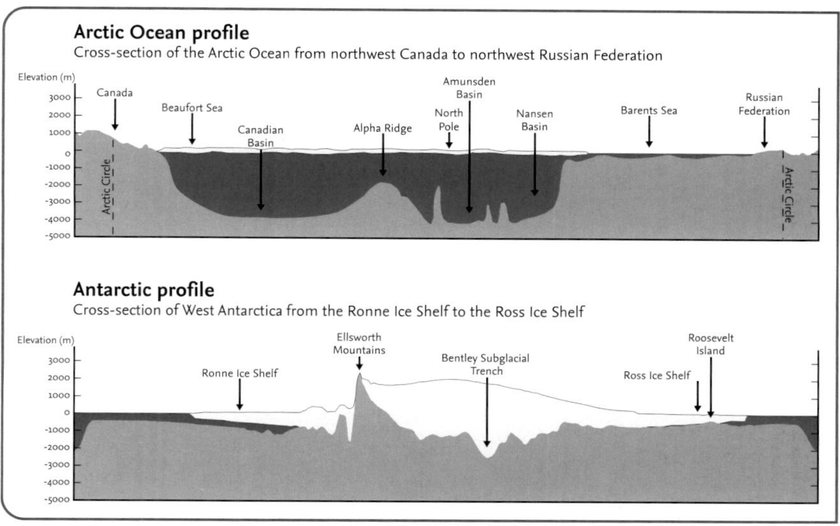

Antarctica's physical features

Highest mountain: Vinson Massif	4 897 m	16 066 ft
Total land area (excluding ice shelves)	12 093 000 sq km	4 669 107 sq miles
Ice shelves	1 559 000 sq km	601 930 sq miles
Exposed rock	49 000 sq km	18 919 sq miles
Lowest bedrock elevation (Bentley Subglacial Trench)	2 496 m below sea level	8 189 ft below sea level
Maximum ice thickness (Astrolabe Subglacial Basin)	4 776 m	15 669 ft
Mean ice thickness (including ice shelves)	1 859 m	6 099 ft
Volume of ice sheet (including ice shelves)	25 400 000 cubic km	6 094 628 cubic miles

The **Antarctic Peninsula** and the **Larsen Ice Shelf** in western Antarctica.

CANADA
UNITED STATES OF AMERICA
Rocky Mountains
Appalachian Mountains
OTTAWA
Toronto
Montréal
Québec
Chicago
Milwaukee
Detroit
Cleveland
Pittsburgh
Buffalo
Boston
New York
Philadelphia
Baltimore
WASHINGTON D.C.
Richmond
Raleigh
Charlotte
Atlanta
Nashville
Memphis
St Louis
Indianapolis
Columbus
Dallas
Houston
San Antonio
Austin
El Paso
Albuquerque
Tucson
New Orleans
Jacksonville
Orlando
Tampa
Miami
Halifax
Newfoundland
St John's
Grand Banks of Newfoundland
St Pierre and Miquelon (France)
Labrador
Greenland (Denmark)
ICELAND
REYKJAVIK
Faroe Islands (Denmark)
TÓRSHAVN
Reykjanes Ridge
Irminger Basin
Iceland Basin
Eirik Ridge
Rockall Bank
British Isles
UNITED KINGDOM
IRELAND
DUBLIN
Edinburgh
LONDON
PARIS
BRUSSELS
AMSTERDAM
THE HAGUE
FRANCE
Bordeaux
Toulouse
Marseille
Rennes
Nantes
Biscay Abyssal Plain
Bay of Biscay
Celtic Shelf
English Channel
Porcupine Abyssal Plain
A Coruña
Oporto
PORTUGAL
LISBON
MADRID
SPAIN
Barcelona
Seville
Cádiz
Gibraltar (U.K.)
Strait of Gibraltar
Oran
ALGIERS
TUNIS
Corsica
Sardinia
Azores (Portugal)
PONTA DELGADA
São Miguel
Azores-Biscay Rise
Horseshoe Seamounts
Madeira (Portugal)
FUNCHAL
RABAT
Casablanca
MOROCCO
Fès
Marrakech
Atlas Mountains
Las Palmas de Gran Canaria
LAÂYOUNE
WESTERN SAHARA
ALGERIA
Sahara
Hoggar
MAURITANIA
NOUAKCHOTT
Nouâdhibou
MALI
NIGER
NIAMEY
Gao
Mopti
Ségou
Bobo-Dioulasso
BURKINA
OUAGADOUGOU
Kayes
SENEGAL
DAKAR
St-Louis
BANJUL
THE GAMBIA
BISSAU
GUINEA-BISSAU
GUINEA
BAMAKO
CONAKRY
FREETOWN
SIERRA LEONE
MONROVIA
LIBERIA
YAMOUSSOUKRO
CÔTE D'IVOIRE
Abidjan
ACCRA
GHANA
Kumasi
LOMÉ
TOGO
BENIN
PORTO-NOVO
NIGERIA
ABUJA
Lagos
Ibadan
Ogbomosho
Kano
Zaria
Sokoto
Port Harcourt
MALABO
Bioco
Gulf of Guinea
SÃO TOMÉ AND PRÍNCIPE
SÃO TOMÉ
Príncipe
Annobón
CAPE VERDE
PRAIA
Cape Verde Plateau
Cape Verde Basin
Sierra Leone Rise
Sierra Leone Basin
Guinea Basin
Romanche Gap
Mid-Atlantic Ridge
Great Meteor Tablemount
Monaco Basin
Krylov Seamount
Corner Seamounts
New England Seamounts
Bermuda (U.K.)
Bermuda Rise
Hatteras Abyssal Plain
Sargasso Sea
Nares Deep
Nares Abyssal Plain
Gulf of Mexico
MEXICO
MEXICO CITY
Monterrey
Guadalajara
San Luis Potosí
León
Puebla
Veracruz
Acapulco
Oaxaca
Mérida
Tampico
Hermosillo
Ciudad Juárez
Baja California
Tropic of Cancer
Yucatán Channel
Straits of Florida
THE BAHAMAS
NASSAU
HAVANA
CUBA
Cayman Islands (U.K.)
Cayman Trench
Turks and Caicos Islands (U.K.)
PORT-AU-PRINCE
HAITI
SANTO DOMINGO
DOMINICAN REP.
Puerto Rico (U.S.A.)
KINGSTON
JAMAICA
BELMOPAN
BELIZE
GUATEMALA
GUATEMALA CITY
SAN SALVADOR
EL SALVADOR
HONDURAS
TEGUCIGALPA
NICARAGUA
MANAGUA
COSTA RICA
SAN JOSÉ
PANAMA
PANAMA CITY
Caribbean Sea
Venezuelan Basin
Colombian Basin
ANTIGUA AND BARBUDA
ST KITTS AND NEVIS
Guadeloupe (France)
DOMINICA
Martinique (France)
ST LUCIA
ST VINCENT AND THE GRENADINES
BARBADOS
GRENADA
PORT OF SPAIN
TRINIDAD AND TOBAGO
Aruba (Neth.)
Netherlands Antilles
Demerara Abyssal Plain
Milwaukee Deep
Puerto Rico Trench
Maracaibo
Barranquilla
Cartagena
CARACAS
VENEZUELA
Barquisimeto
Ciudad Bolívar
GEORGETOWN
GUYANA
PARAMARIBO
SURINAME
CAYENNE
French Guiana
Amazon Cone
Guiana Basin
Guiana Highlands
Llanos
Orinoco
Medellín
BOGOTÁ
COLOMBIA
Cali
Ibagué
Tunja
Pasto
Esmeraldas
Equator
QUITO
ECUADOR
Guayaquil
Galapagos Islands (Ecuador)
Isla de Coco (Costa Rica)
Cocos Ridge
Isla de Malpelo (Colombia)
PACIFIC OCEAN
Galapagos Rise
Iquitos
Manaus
Santarém
Belém
São Luís
Fortaleza
Natal
João Pessoa
Recife
Maceió
Aracaju
Salvador
Teresina
Marabá
Parnaíba
Amazon
Selvas
BRAZIL
Porto Velho
Rio Branco
Cruzeiro do Sul
Tarapoto
Chiclayo
Trujillo
Sullana
PERU
LIMA
Huancayo
Cusco
Pucallpa
Arequipa
Juliaca
LA PAZ
BOLIVIA
SUCRE
Santa Cruz
Potosí
Trinidad
Cuiabá
Goiânia
BRASÍLIA
Belo Horizonte
Vitória
Rio de Janeiro
São Paulo
Campinas
Curitiba
Florianópolis
Porto Alegre
Santa Maria
PARAGUAY
ASUNCIÓN
Campo Grande
Uberaba
Ribeirão Preto
Araçatuba
Maringá
Posadas
Corrientes
Resistencia
Formosa
Encarnación
San Miguel de Tucumán
San Salvador de Jujuy
Salta
Arica
Iquique
Antofagasta
Copiapó
Catamarca
La Rioja
Córdoba
Rosario
Paraná
Santa Fe
Concordia
Paysandú
URUGUAY
BUENOS AIRES
MONTEVIDEO
Río de la Plata
Mendoza
San Juan
San Luis
SANTIAGO
Valparaíso
Talca
Chillán
Concepción
Neuquén
Valdivia
Puerto Montt
Isla de Chiloé
Archipiélago de los Chonos
Golfo de Penas
Santa Rosa
Mar del Plata
Bahía Blanca
Viedma
Golfo San Matías
Trelew
Comodoro Rivadavia
Golfo de San Jorge
Río Gallegos
Punta Arenas
Ushuaia
Puerto Natales
Isla Grande de Tierra del Fuego
Isla de los Estados
Cape Horn
Drake Passage
ARGENTINA
CHILE
Andes
Atacama Desert
Pampas
Chaco
Nazca Ridge (South-West Peru Ridge)
Peru-Chile Trench
Peru Basin
Chile Basin
Chile Rise
Roggeveen Basin
Archipiélago Juan Fernández (Chile)
Islas Desventuradas (Chile)
Isla Sala y Gomez (Chile)
Easter Island (Isla de Pascua) (Chile)
Tropic of Capricorn
ATLANTIC OCEAN
Fernando de Noronha (Brazil)
São Pedro e São Paulo (Brazil)
Pernambuco Plain
Ascension (U.K.)
Brazil Basin
Ilhas Martin Vas (Brazil)
Ilha da Trindade (Brazil)
Vitória Seamount
Abrolhos Bank
Santos Plateau
Rio Grande Rise
Argentine Rise
Argentine Basin
Argentine Abyssal Plain
Falkland Escarpment
Falkland Islands (U.K.)
STANLEY
Falkland Plateau
Bahía Grande
Scotia Ridge
Scotia Sea
Shag Rocks
South Georgia (U.K.)
Meteor Depth
South Sandwich Islands (U.K.)
South Sandwich Trench
South Orkney Islands (U.K.)
Yaghan Basin
Mornington Abyssal Plain
Elephant Island
South Shetland Islands (U.K.)
Bransfield Strait
Joinville Island
Graham Land
Jason Pen.
Larsen Ice Shelf
Antarctic Peninsula
Weddell Sea
Weddell Abyssal Plain
Riiser-Larsen Ice Shelf
Brunt Ice Shelf
Cape Norvegia
Fimbull Ice Shelf
Maud Seamount
American-Antarctic Ridge
Atlantic-Indian Ridge
Bouvetøya (Norway)
Shona Ridge
Agulhas
Cape Basin
Gough Island (U.K.)
Tristan da Cunha (U.K.)
Vema Seamount
Walvis Ridge
Namibia Abyssal Plain
Angola Basin
JAMESTOWN
St Helena
St Helena and Dependencies (U.K.)
BRAZZAVILLE
Pointe-Noire
LUANDA
Congo Cone
Lambert Azimuthal Equal Area Projection
1:50 000 000
0 500 1000 1500 miles
0 500 1000 1500 2000 2500 km

Atlantic Ocean
Indian Ocean

PAKISTAN
INDIA
NEPAL
CHINA
MONGOLIA
Gobi Desert
BEIJING
Tianjin
Shanghai
Hong Kong
T'AIPEI
TAIWAN
NORTH KOREA
P'YONGYANG
SOUTH KOREA
SEOUL
JAPAN
TŌKYŌ
Ōsaka
Sapporo
Vladivostok
Sea of Okhotsk
Kamchatka Peninsula
Petropavlovsk-Kamchatskiy
Bering Sea
Aleutian Islands
Aleutian Basin
Kuril Islands
Kuril Trench
Emperor Seamount Chain
Emperor Trough
Chinook Trough
Northwest Pacific Basin
Mapmakers Seamounts
Midway Islands
Hawaiian Ridge
Mid-Pacific Mountains
Wake Island (U.S.A.)
Johnston Atoll (U.S.A.)
Mumbai
Pune
Hyderabad
Bangalore
Chennai
Kolkata
DHAKA
SRI LANKA
Colombo
MYANMAR
RANGOON
BANGKOK
THAILAND
LAOS
VIENTIANE
VIETNAM
HANOI
Ho Chi Minh City
CAMBODIA
PHNOM PENH
South China Sea
PHILIPPINES
MANILA
Philippine Basin
Philippine Trench
MALAYSIA
KUALA LUMPUR
SINGAPORE
BRUNEI
BANDAR SERI BEGAWAN
Borneo
Sumatra
Java
INDONESIA
JAKARTA
EAST TIMOR
DILI
Northern Mariana Islands (U.S.A.)
Guam (U.S.A.)
Mariana Trench
Challenger Deep 10920
East Mariana Basin
PALAU
MELEKEOK
FEDERATED STATES OF MICRONESIA
Caroline Islands
West Caroline Basin
East Caroline Basin
MICRONESIA
MARSHALL ISLANDS
MAJURO
Central Pacific Basin
MELANESIA
NAURU
PAPUA NEW GUINEA
PORT MORESBY
New Guinea
Bismarck Sea
SOLOMON ISLANDS
HONIARA
Solomon Sea
KIRIBATI
TUVALU
VAIAKU
Wallis and Futuna Islands (France)
SAMOA
APIA
American Samoa (U.S.A.)
Tokelau (N.Z.)
Niue (N.Z.)
TONGA
FIJI
SUVA
VANUATU
PORT VILA
New Caledonia (France)
NOUMÉA
Coral Sea
Coral Sea Basin
Great Barrier Reef
AUSTRALIA
Great Sandy Desert
Great Victoria Desert
Nullarbor Plain
Great Australian Bight
Darwin
Brisbane
Sydney
CANBERRA
Melbourne
Adelaide
Perth
Tasmania
Bass Strait
Tasman Sea
Tasman Basin
Lord Howe Rise
South Fiji Basin
Kermadec Trench
Louisville Ridge
Norfolk Island (Australia)
NEW ZEALAND
Auckland
WELLINGTON
Christchurch
North Island
South Island
Chatham Rise
Campbell Plateau
INDIAN OCEAN
Mid-Indian Basin
Cocos Basin
Ninetyeast Ridge
Java Trench (Sunda Trench)
Christmas Island (Australia)
Cocos Islands (Australia)
North Australian Basin
West Australian Basin
Perth Basin
Broken Plateau
South Australian Basin
South Tasman Rise
Southeast Indian Ridge
Indian-Antarctic Ridge
Australian-Antarctic Basin
Tropic of Capricorn
Equator
Antarctic Circle
Wilkes Land
Adélie Land
George V Land
Transantarctic Mountains
Dumont d'Urville Sea
ANTARCTICA
SOUTHERN OCEAN
PACIFIC OCEAN
POLYNESIA
Lambert Azimuthal Equal Area Projection
1:50 000 000
0 500 1000 1500 miles
0 500 1000 1500 2000 2500 km

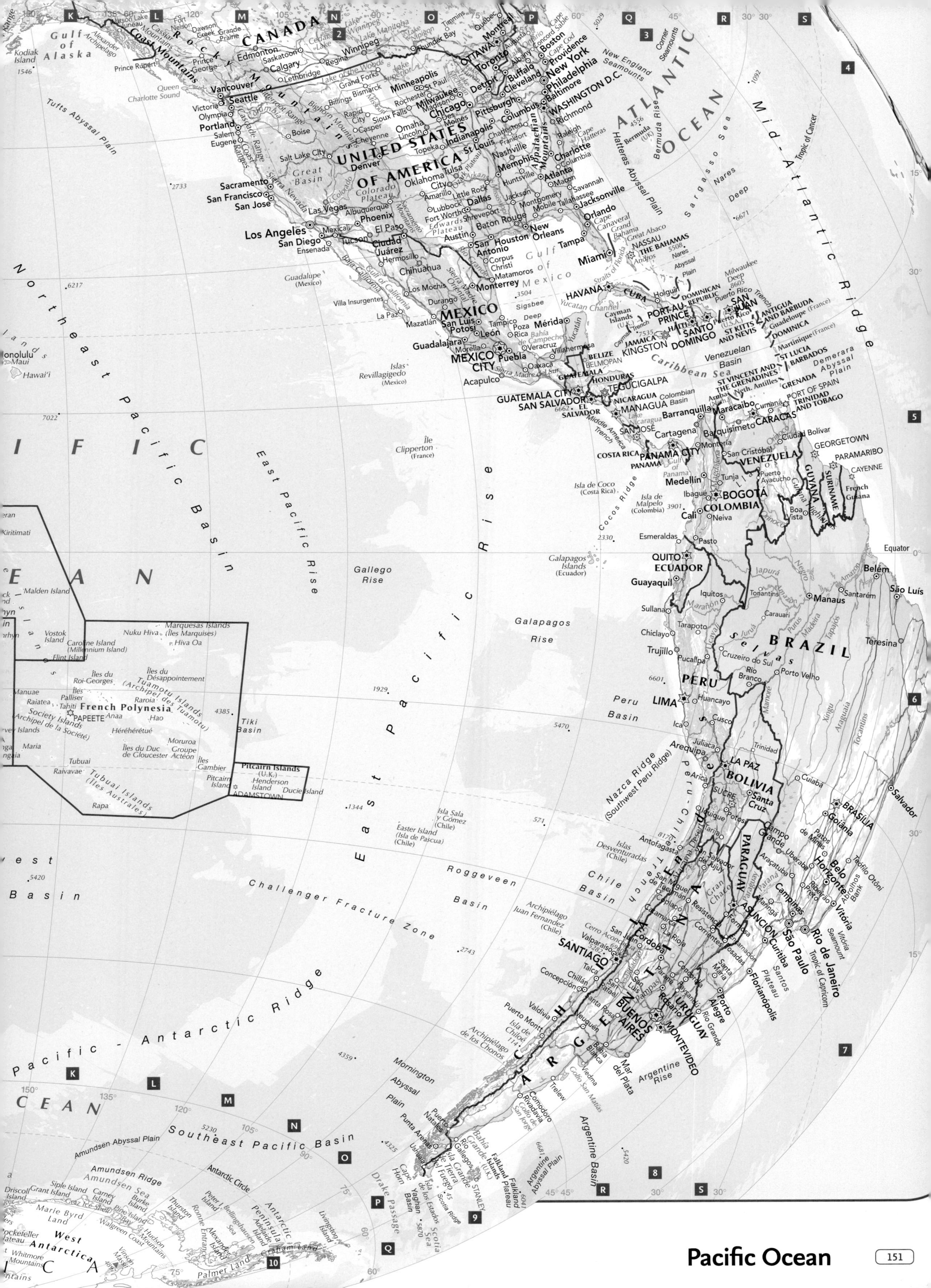
CANADA
Gulf of Alaska
Alexander Archipelago
Kodiak Island
Prince Rupert
Coast Mountains
Rocky Mountains
Edmonton
Calgary
Saskatoon
Regina
Winnipeg
Lethbridge
Thunder Bay
OTTAWA
Montréal
Québec
Toronto
Boston
Providence
New York
Philadelphia
Baltimore
WASHINGTON D.C.
Richmond
Vancouver
Seattle
Victoria
Olympia
Portland
Salem
Eugene
Boise
Queen Charlotte Sound
Tufts Abyssal Plain
Minneapolis
St Paul
Grand Forks
Bismarck
Billings
Rapid City
Sioux Falls
Milwaukee
Madison
Chicago
Detroit
Cleveland
Buffalo
Pittsburgh
Columbus
Omaha
Lincoln
Des Moines
Casper
Cheyenne
Denver
Salt Lake City
Great Basin
UNITED STATES OF AMERICA
Indianapolis
St Louis
Topeka
Charleston
Frankfort
Nashville
Appalachian Mountains
Raleigh
Charlotte
Columbia
Atlanta
Macon
Savannah
Jacksonville
Tallahassee
Memphis
Huntsville
Montgomery
Mobile
Jackson
Little Rock
Oklahoma City
Tulsa
Amarillo
Lubbock
Dallas
Fort Worth
Shreveport
Baton Rouge
New Orleans
Austin
San Antonio
Houston
Corpus Christi
Matamoros
Monterrey
Sacramento
San Francisco
San Jose
Sierra Nevada
Colorado Plateau
Las Vegas
Albuquerque
Phoenix
Los Angeles
San Diego
Ensenada
Mexicali
Tucson
El Paso
Ciudad Juárez
Hermosillo
Chihuahua
Los Mochis
Durango
Edwards Plateau
Orlando
Cape Canaveral
Tampa
Miami
Gulf of Mexico
Great Abaco
NASSAU
THE BAHAMAS
Andros
New England Seamounts
Corner Seamounts
ATLANTIC OCEAN
Bermuda (UK)
Bermuda Rise
Hatteras Abyssal Plain
Sargasso Sea
Nares Deep
Nares Abyssal Plain
Mid-Atlantic Ridge
Tropic of Cancer
Milwaukee Deep 8605
Puerto Rico Trench
HAVANA
CUBA
Holguín
Cayman Islands (U.K.)
Cayman Trench
Yucatan Channel
Sigsbee Deep
Mérida
Tampico
Poza Rica
Bahía de Campeche
Veracruz
Villahermosa
MEXICO
San Luis Potosí
León
Guadalajara
Morelia
MEXICO CITY
Puebla
Oaxaca
Acapulco
Mazatlán
La Paz
Villa Insurgentes
Gulf of California
Baja California
Guadalupe (Mexico)
Islas Revillagigedo (Mexico)
PORT-AU-PRINCE
HAITI
DOMINICAN REPUBLIC
SANTO DOMINGO
Puerto Rico (U.S.)
SAN JUAN
JAMAICA
KINGSTON
ST KITTS AND NEVIS
ANTIGUA AND BARBUDA
Guadeloupe (France)
DOMINICA
Martinique (France)
ST LUCIA
BARBADOS
ST VINCENT AND THE GRENADINES
GRENADA
PORT OF SPAIN
TRINIDAD AND TOBAGO
Caribbean Sea
Venezuelan Basin
Demerara Abyssal Plain
BELIZE
BELMOPAN
GUATEMALA
GUATEMALA CITY
HONDURAS
TEGUCIGALPA
SAN SALVADOR
EL SALVADOR
NICARAGUA
MANAGUA
Colombian Basin
Middle America Trench
SAN JOSÉ
COSTA RICA
PANAMA
PANAMA CITY
Gulf of Panama
Barranquilla
Cartagena
Maracaibo
Barquisimeto
CARACAS
Cumaná
Ciudad Bolívar
VENEZUELA
GEORGETOWN
GUYANA
PARAMARIBO
SURINAME
CAYENNE
French Guiana
Montería
San Cristóbal
Medellín
Tunja
Puerto Ayacucho
Ibagué
BOGOTÁ
COLOMBIA
Cali
Neiva
Pasto
Boa Vista
Île Clipperton (France)
Isla de Coco (Costa Rica)
Isla de Malpelo (Colombia)
Cocos Ridge
Esmeraldas
QUITO
ECUADOR
Guayaquil
Galapagos Islands (Ecuador)
Equator
Belém
São Luís
Manaus
Santarém
Iquitos
Sullana
Chiclayo
Trujillo
Tarapoto
Pucallpa
Cruzeiro do Sul
Rio Branco
Porto Velho
Teresina
BRAZIL
Selvas
PERU
LIMA
Huancayo
Ica
Cusco
Juliaca
Arequipa
Arica
Trinidad
LA PAZ
BOLIVIA
SUCRE
Santa Cruz
Potosí
Iquique
Cuiabá
Salvador
BRASÍLIA
Goiânia
Campo Grande
Uberaba
Belo Horizonte
Abrolhos Bank
Vitória
Vitória Seamount
Rio de Janeiro
São Paulo
Campinas
Ribeirão Preto
Curitiba
Florianópolis
Santos Plateau
Tropic of Capricorn
PARAGUAY
ASUNCIÓN
Gran Chaco
Antofagasta
San Miguel de Tucumán
Salta
San Salvador de Jujuy
Resistencia
Corrientes
Posadas
Santa Maria
Porto Alegre
Rio Grande
Catamarca
La Rioja
Córdoba
Santa Fe
Rosario
San Juan
Mendoza
Cerro Aconcagua
Valparaíso
SANTIAGO
Talca
Concepción
Chillán
Temuco
Valdivia
Puerto Montt
Isla de Chiloé
Archipiélago de los Chonos
Santa Rosa
Neuquén
BUENOS AIRES
MONTEVIDEO
URUGUAY
Mar del Plata
Bahía Blanca
Viedma
Golfo San Matías
Trelew
Comodoro Rivadavia
Golfo San Jorge
ARGENTINA
CHILE
Puerto Natales
Punta Arenas
Río Gallegos
Isla Grande de Tierra del Fuego
Ushuaia
Cape Horn
Isla de los Estados
Falkland Islands (U.K.)
STANLEY
Falkland Plateau
Argentine Rise
Argentine Basin
Argentine Abyssal Plain
Peru-Chile Trench
Nazca Ridge (Southwest Peru Ridge)
Peru Basin
Chile Basin
Islas Desventuradas (Chile)
Isla Sala y Gómez (Chile)
Easter Island (Isla de Pascua) (Chile)
Archipiélago Juan Fernández (Chile)
Roggeveen Basin
Challenger Fracture Zone
East Pacific Rise
Galapagos Rise
Gallego Rise
Northeast Pacific Basin
Hawaiian Islands
Honolulu
Maui
Hawai'i
PACIFIC OCEAN
Kiritimati
Malden Island
Vostok Island
Caroline Island (Millennium Island)
Flint Island
Marquesas Islands (Îles Marquises)
Nuku Hiva
Hiva Oa
Îles du Désappointement
Îles du Roi-Georges
Tuamotu Islands (Archipel des Tuamotu)
French Polynesia
Manuae
Raiatea
Tahiti
PAPEETE
Anaa
Raroia
Hao
Society Islands (Archipel de la Société)
Hérèhérètué
Îles du Duc de Gloucester
Moruroa
Groupe Actéon
Îles Gambier
Tiki Basin
Tubuai
Raivavae
Tubuai Islands (Îles Australes)
Rapa
Pitcairn Islands (U.K.)
Pitcairn Island
ADAMSTOWN
Henderson Island
Ducie Island
Southwest Pacific Basin
Pacific-Antarctic Ridge
Mornington Abyssal Plain
Southeast Pacific Basin
Amundsen Abyssal Plain
Amundsen Ridge
Antarctic Circle
Drake Passage
Yaghan Basin
Scotia Sea
Scotia Ridge
Amundsen Sea
Siple Island
Carney Island
Grant Island
Burke Island
Thurston Island
Peter I Island
Marie Byrd Land
Getz Ice Shelf
Walgreen Coast
Hudson Mountains
Bellingshausen Sea
Alexander Island
Ronne Entrance
Antarctic Peninsula
Adelaide Island
Graham Land
Palmer Land
Livingston Island
West Antarctica
Rockefeller Plateau
Whitmore Mountains
Vinson Massif
ANTARCTICA

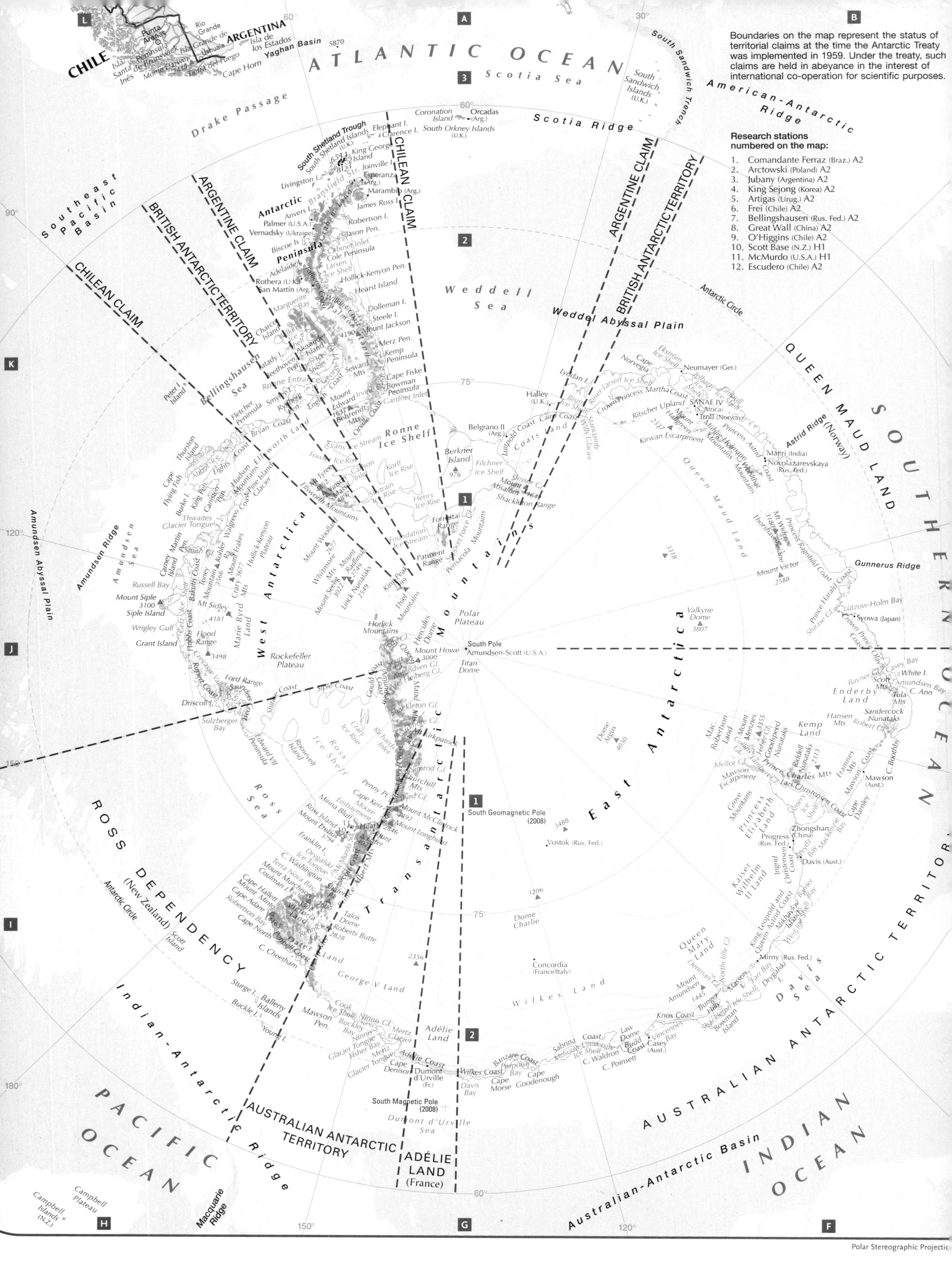

Polar Stereographic Projection

1:26 000 000

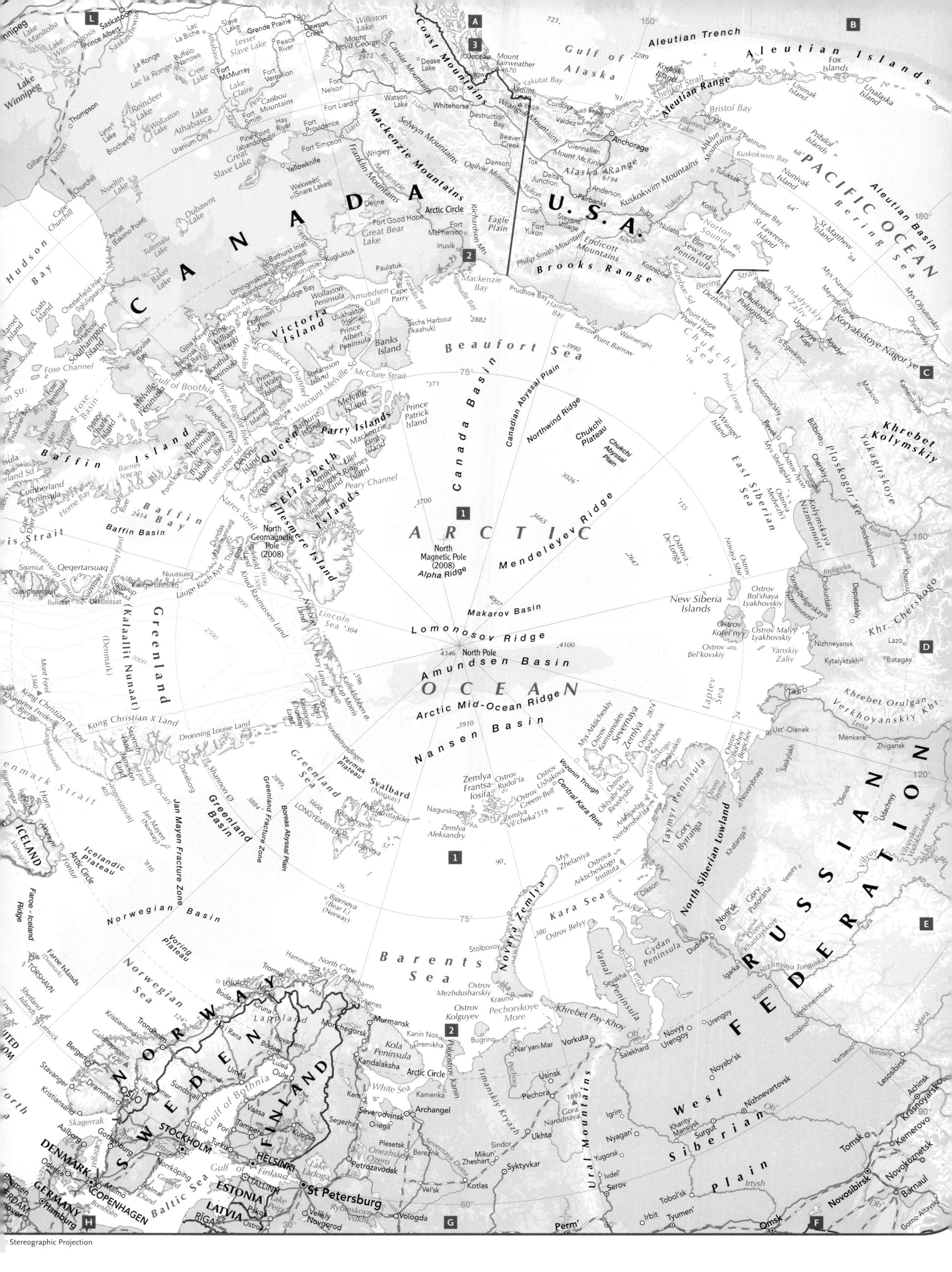

CANADA
U.S.A.
RUSSIAN FEDERATION
ARCTIC OCEAN
PACIFIC OCEAN
Beaufort Sea
Chukchi Sea
East Siberian Sea
Laptev Sea
Kara Sea
Barents Sea
Greenland Sea
Norwegian Sea
Baffin Bay
Hudson Bay
Gulf of Alaska
Bering Sea
Aleutian Islands
Aleutian Trench
Aleutian Basin
Canada Basin
Makarov Basin
Amundsen Basin
Nansen Basin
Lomonosov Ridge
Arctic Mid-Ocean Ridge
Mendeleyev Ridge
Alpha Ridge
Northwind Ridge
Chukchi Plateau
Canadian Abyssal Plain
North Pole
North Magnetic Pole (2008)
North Geomagnetic Pole (2008)
Arctic Circle
Greenland (Kalaallit Nunaat) (Denmark)
Baffin Island
Victoria Island
Banks Island
Ellesmere Island
Queen Elizabeth Islands
Parry Islands
Svalbard (Norway)
Zemlya Frantsa-Iosifa
Novaya Zemlya
Severnaya Zemlya
New Siberia Islands
Wrangel Island
ICELAND
NORWAY
SWEDEN
FINLAND
ESTONIA
LATVIA
DENMARK
GERMANY
Brooks Range
Alaska Range
Mackenzie Mountains
Ural Mountains
West Siberian Plain
North Siberian Lowland
Taymyr Peninsula
Anchorage
Murmansk
Archangel
St Petersburg
HELSINKI
STOCKHOLM
OSLO
COPENHAGEN
TALLINN
RIGA
Stereographic Projection

World

Statistics

See page 160 for explanatory table and sources

	Population							Economy					
	Total population	Population change (%)	% urban	Total fertility	Population by age (%) 0–14	Population by age (%) 60 or over	2050 projected population	Total Gross National Income (GNI) (US$M)	GNI per capita (US$)	Debt service ratio (% GNI)	Total debt service (US$)	Aid receipts (% GNI)	Military spending (% GDP)
WORLD	6 671 226 000	1.2	49.2	2.6	28.2	10.4	9 075 903 000	48 694 077	7 448	...	...	...	2.5
AFGHANISTAN	27 145 000	3.9	24.3	7.1	46.5	4.4	97 324 000	8 092	...	0.1	9 260 000	35.7	9.9
ALBANIA	3 190 000	0.6	45.0	2.1	27.0	12.0	3 458 000	9 295	2 930	1.4	132 034 000	3.5	1.6
ALGERIA	33 858 000	1.5	60.0	2.4	29.6	6.5	49 500 000	101 206	3 030	12.4	13 351 425 000	0.2	2.7
ANDORRA	75 000	0.4	91.1	...	...	...	58 000	...	...	...	...	...	...
ANGOLA	17 024 000	2.8	37.2	6.4	46.5	3.9	43 501 000	32 646	1 970	10.8	4 296 094 000	0.4	5.4
ANTIGUA AND BARBUDA	85 000	1.2	38.4	...	...	...	112 000	929	11 050	...	...	0.4	...
ARGENTINA	39 531 000	1.0	90.6	2.3	26.4	13.9	51 382 000	201 347	5 150	9.1	18 993 819 000	0.1	0.9
ARMENIA	3 002 000	-0.2	64.1	1.4	20.8	14.5	2 506 000	5 788	1 920	2.6	167 008 000	3.3	2.8
AUSTRALIA	20 743 000	1.0	92.7	1.8	19.6	17.3	27 940 000	742 254	35 860	...	...	...	1.8
AUSTRIA	8 361 000	0.4	65.8	1.4	15.5	22.7	8 073 000	329 183	39 750	...	...	...	0.8
AZERBAIJAN	8 467 000	0.8	49.9	1.8	25.8	9.2	9 631 000	15 639	1 840	1.4	241 872 000	1.2	3.3
THE BAHAMAS	331 000	1.2	90.0	2.0	28.3	9.3	466 000	...	...	...	...	...	0.7
BAHRAIN	753 000	1.8	90.2	2.3	27.1	4.5	1 155 000	14 022	19 350	...	...	...	3.0
BANGLADESH	158 665 000	1.7	25.0	2.8	35.5	5.7	242 937 000	70 475	450	1.0	684 513 000	1.9	1.1
BARBADOS	294 000	0.3	52.9	1.5	18.9	13.2	255 000	...	...	...	...	...	...
BELARUS	9 689 000	-0.6	71.6	1.2	15.2	18.6	7 017 000	33 760	3 470	2.0	733 327 000	0.2	1.7
BELGIUM	10 457 000	0.2	97.3	1.7	16.8	22.4	10 302 000	405 419	38 460	...	...	...	1.1
BELIZE	288 000	2.1	48.6	2.9	36.8	5.9	442 000	1 114	3 740	12.3	134 775 000	0.7	...
BENIN	9 033 000	3.0	46.1	5.4	44.2	4.3	22 123 000	4 665	530	1.8	82 763 000	8.0	...
BHUTAN	658 000	1.4	9.1	2.2	38.4	7.0	4 393 000	928	1 430	1.1	10 105 000	10.2	...
BOLIVIA	9 525 000	1.8	64.4	3.5	38.1	6.7	14 908 000	10 293	1 100	4.0	430 341 000	5.4	1.5
BOSNIA-HERZEGOVINA	3 935 000	0.1	45.3	1.2	16.5	19.2	3 170 000	12 689	3 230	4.6	589 095 000	4.2	1.6
BOTSWANA	1 882 000	1.2	52.5	2.9	37.6	5.1	1 658 000	10 358	5 570	0.6	54 861 000	0.7	3.0
BRAZIL	191 791 000	1.3	84.2	2.3	27.9	8.8	253 105 000	892 639	4 710	6.0	62 144 534 000	0.0	1.5
BRUNEI	390 000	2.1	77.6	2.3	29.6	4.7	681 000	10 287	26 930	...	...	...	2.4
BULGARIA	7 639 000	-0.7	70.5	1.3	13.8	22.4	5 065 000	30 669	3 990	8.7	2 743 215 000	...	2.3
BURKINA	14 784 000	2.9	18.6	6.0	47.2	4.2	39 093 000	6 249	440	0.8	51 765 000	14.0	1.4
BURUNDI	8 508 000	3.9	10.6	6.8	45.0	4.2	25 812 000	815	100	4.5	39 523 000	52.8	5.5
CAMBODIA	14 444 000	1.7	19.7	3.2	37.1	5.6	25 972 000	6 990	490	0.4	30 584 000	7.7	1.7
CAMEROON	18 549 000	2.0	52.9	4.3	41.2	5.6	26 891 000	18 060	990	2.9	518 897 000	9.3	1.4
CANADA	32 876 000	0.9	81.1	1.5	17.6	17.9	42 844 000	1 196 626	36 650	...	...	...	1.2
CAPE VERDE	530 000	2.2	57.6	3.4	39.5	5.5	1 002 000	1 105	2 130	2.9	31 361 000	12.6	0.7
CENTRAL AFRICAN REPUBLIC	4 343 000	1.8	43.8	4.6	43.0	6.1	6 747 000	1 499	350	4.7	70 406 000	9.0	1.1
CHAD	10 781 000	2.9	25.8	6.2	47.3	4.7	31 497 000	4 708	450	1.3	67 834 000	5.5	0.9
CHILE	16 635 000	1.0	87.7	1.9	24.9	11.6	20 657 000	111 869	6 810	10.9	13 792 891 000	0.1	3.6
CHINA	1 313 437 000	0.6	40.5	1.7	21.4	10.9	1 402 062 000	2 620 951	2 000	1.0	27 876 906 000	0.1	1.9
COLOMBIA	46 156 000	1.3	77.4	2.2	31.0	7.5	65 679 000	141 982	3 120	7.2	10 639 506 000	0.8	3.5
COMOROS	839 000	2.5	36.3	4.3	42.0	4.3	1 781 000	406	660	0.9	3 616 000	7.6	...
CONGO	3 768 000	2.1	54.4	4.5	47.1	4.5	13 721 000	3 806	1 050	2.7	101 220 000	...	1.1
CONGO, DEM. REPUBLIC OF THE	62 636 000	3.2	32.7	6.7	47.3	4.3	177 271 000	7 742	130	3.9	319 345 000	25.2	0.0
COSTA RICA	4 468 000	1.5	61.7	2.1	28.4	8.3	6 426 000	21 894	4 980	2.8	597 316 000	0.1	...
CÔTE D'IVOIRE	19 262 000	1.8	45.8	4.5	41.9	5.3	33 959 000	16 578	880	0.8	126 329 000	1.6	1.6
CROATIA	4 555 000	-0.1	59.9	1.4	15.5	22.1	3 686 000	41 348	9 310	18.5	7 680 306 000	0.5	1.6
CUBA	11 268 000	0.0	76.0	1.5	19.1	15.3	9 749 000	...	...	...	...	...	...
CYPRUS	855 000	1.1	69.5	1.6	19.9	16.8	1 174 000	17 948	23 270	...	...	...	1.4
CZECH REPUBLIC	10 186 000	0.0	74.5	1.2	14.6	20.0	8 452 000	131 404	12 790	...	...	...	1.7
DENMARK	5 442 000	0.2	85.5	1.8	18.8	21.1	5 851 000	283 316	52 110	...	...	...	1.4
DJIBOUTI	833 000	1.7	84.6	4.0	41.5	4.7	1 547 000	864	1 060	2.6	22 564 000	14.0	...
DOMINICA	67 000	-0.3	72.7	...	...	...	98 000	300	4 160	6.9	21 255 000	7.0	...
DOMINICAN REPUBLIC	9 760 000	1.5	60.1	2.8	32.7	6.2	12 668 000	27 954	2 910	4.5	1 345 913 000	0.2	0.5
EAST TIMOR	1 155 000	3.5	7.8	6.5	41.1	5.0	3 265 000	865	840	...	...	24.7	...
ECUADOR	13 341 000	1.1	62.8	2.6	32.4	8.3	19 214 000	38 481	2 910	10.5	4 157 073 000	0.5	2.3
EGYPT	75 498 000	1.8	42.3	2.9	33.6	7.1	125 916 000	100 912	1 360	2.1	2 201 406 000	0.8	2.7
EL SALVADOR	6 857 000	1.4	60.1	2.7	34.0	7.6	10 823 000	18 096	2 680	6.2	1 133 017 000	0.9	0.6
EQUATORIAL GUINEA	507 000	2.4	50.0	5.4	44.4	6.0	1 146 000	4 216	8 510	0.1	4 307 000	0.5	...
ERITREA	4 851 000	3.2	20.8	5.1	44.8	4.0	11 229 000	888	190	1.2	12 682 000	12.0	24.1
ESTONIA	1 335 000	-0.4	69.6	1.5	15.2	21.6	1 119 000	15 302	11 400	...	...	...	1.4
ETHIOPIA	83 099 000	2.5	16.2	5.3	44.5	4.7	170 190 000	12 874	170	1.2	163 799 000	14.7	2.6
FIJI	839 000	0.6	53.2	2.8	31.7	6.4	934 000	3 098	3 720	0.5	16 360 000	2.0	1.2
FINLAND	5 277 000	0.3	60.9	1.8	17.3	21.3	5 329 000	217 803	41 360	...	...	...	1.4
FRANCE	61 647 000	0.5	76.7	1.9	18.2	21.1	63 116 000	2 306 714	36 560	...	...	...	2.4
GABON	1 331 000	1.5	85.2	3.1	40.0	6.2	2 279 000	7 032	5 360	1.1	84 901 000	0.4	1.2
THE GAMBIA	1 709 000	2.6	26.1	4.7	40.1	6.0	3 106 000	488	290	6.6	33 137 000	14.8	0.5
GEORGIA	4 395 000	-0.8	51.5	1.4	18.9	17.9	2 985 000	7 008	1 580	3.6	268 375 000	4.9	3.1

Social Indicators					Environment				Communications				
Child mortality rate	Life expectancy	Literacy rate (%)	Access to safe water (%)	Doctors per 100 000 people	Forest area (%)	Annual change in forest area (%)	Protected land area (%)	CO_2 emissions (metric tonnes per capita)	Main telephone lines per 100 people	Cellular phone subscribers per 100 people	Internet users per 10 000 people	International dialling code	Time zone
72	**67.2**	**87.6**	**83**	**152**	**30.3**	**0.2**	**10.8**	**4.3**	**19.7**	**42.0**	**1 853**	**...**	**...**
257	43.8	34.3	39	19	1.3	-3.1	0.3	...	0.3	8.1	172	93	+4.5
17	76.4	99.4	96	139	29.0	0.6	0.7	1.2	11.3	60.4	1 498	355	+1
38	72.3	90.1	85	85	1.0	1.2	5.1	6.0	8.5	63.0	738	213	+1
3	...	...	100	259	35.6	0.0	9.7	...	51.3	96.9	3 257	376	+1
260	42.7	72.2	53	8	47.4	-0.2	10.0	0.5	0.6	14.3	60	244	+1
11	...	...	91	17	21.4	0.0	0.0	5.1	45.5	133.6	6 424	1 268	-4
16	75.3	98.9	96	301	12.1	-0.4	6.3	3.7	24.2	80.5	2 091	54	-3
24	72.0	99.8	92	353	10.0	-1.5	8.1	1.2	19.7	10.5	575	374	+4
6	81.2	...	100	249	21.3	-0.1	9.5	16.2	48.8	97.0	4 713	61	+8 to +10.5
5	79.8	...	100	324	46.7	0.1	28.3	8.5	43.4	112.8	5 131	43	+1
88	67.5	99.9	77	354	11.3	0.0	2.4	3.8	14.0	39.2	979	994	+4
14	73.5	...	97	106	51.5	0.0	0.1	6.3	40.2	77.3	3 188	1 242	-5
10	75.6	97.0	...	160	0.6	3.8	3.4	23.8	26.3	122.9	2 844	973	+3
69	64.1	63.6	74	23	6.7	-0.3	0.7	0.2	0.8	13.3	31	880	+6
12	77.3	...	100	121	4.0	0.0	0.1	4.4	50.1	87.8	5 948	1 246	-4
13	69.0	99.8	100	450	38.0	0.1	5.2	6.6	34.7	61.4	5 647	375	+2
4	79.4	...	...	418	22.0	0.0	3.2	9.7	45.2	92.6	5 260	32	+1
16	76.1	...	91	105	72.5	0.0	36.0	2.8	12.3	44.1	1 236	501	-6
148	56.7	45.3	67	6	21.3	-2.5	22.0	0.3	0.9	12.1	144	229	+1
70	65.6	...	62	5	68.0	0.3	31.5	0.7	3.8	9.8	357	975	+6
61	65.6	97.3	85	73	54.2	-0.5	20.0	0.8	7.1	30.8	620	591	-4
15	74.9	99.8	97	134	43.1	0.0	0.5	4.0	25.3	48.3	2 428	387	+1
124	50.7	94.0	95	29	21.1	-1.0	30.1	2.4	7.8	46.8	455	267	+2
20	72.4	96.8	90	206	57.2	-0.6	17.8	1.8	20.5	52.9	2 255	55	-2 to -5
9	77.1	98.9	...	101	52.8	-0.7	53.3	24.1	21.0	78.9	4 169	673	+8
14	73.0	98.2	99	338	32.8	1.4	10.0	5.5	31.3	107.6	2 166	359	+2
204	52.3	33.0	61	4	29.0	-0.3	14.0	0.1	0.7	7.5	59	226	GMT
181	49.6	73.3	79	5	5.9	-5.2	5.7	0.0	0.4	2.0	77	257	+2
82	59.7	83.4	41	16	59.2	-2.0	22.8	0.0	0.2	7.9	31	855	+7
149	50.4	...	66	7	45.6	-1.0	8.6	0.2	0.8	18.9	223	237	+1
6	80.7	...	100	209	33.6	0.0	4.8	20.0	64.5	57.6	6 789	1	-3.5 to -8
34	71.7	96.3	80	17	20.7	0.4	...	0.6	13.8	21.0	636	238	-1
175	44.7	58.5	75	4	36.5	-0.1	15.3	0.1	0.3	2.5	32	236	+1
209	50.7	37.6	42	3	9.5	-0.7	9.0	0.0	0.1	4.7	60	235	+1
9	78.6	99.0	95	109	21.5	0.4	3.9	3.9	20.2	75.6	2 524	56	-4
24	73.0	98.9	77	164	21.2	2.2	15.3	3.9	27.8	34.8	1 035	86	+8
21	72.9	98.0	93	135	58.5	-0.1	24.7	1.2	17.0	64.3	1 449	57	-5
68	65.2	...	86	7	2.9	-7.4	...	0.1	2.3	4.5	256	269	+3
126	55.3	97.4	58	25	65.8	-0.1	14.1	1.0	0.4	12.3	170	242	+1
205	46.5	70.4	46	7	58.9	-0.2	8.4	0.0	0.0	7.4	30	243	+1 to +2
12	78.8	97.6	97	172	46.8	0.1	21.1	1.5	30.7	32.8	2 761	506	-6
127	48.3	60.7	84	9	32.7	0.1	12.1	0.3	1.4	22.0	163	225	GMT
6	75.7	99.6	100	237	38.2	0.1	5.9	5.3	40.1	96.5	3 698	385	+1
7	78.3	100.0	91	591	24.7	2.2	1.4	2.3	8.6	1.4	213	53	-5
4	79.0	99.8	100	298	18.9	0.2	9.0	9.1	48.3	102.8	4 222	357	+2
4	76.5	...	100	343	34.3	0.1	15.9	11.5	28.3	116.4	3 469	420	+1
5	78.3	...	100	366	11.8	0.6	6.0	9.8	56.9	107.0	5 823	45	+1
130	54.8	...	73	13	0.2	0.0	...	0.5	1.6	6.4	136	253	+3
15	...	...	97	49	61.3	-0.6	46.8	1.5	29.4	58.7	3 722	1 767	-4
29	72.2	94.2	95	188	28.4	0.0	25.0	2.1	9.9	51.1	2 217	1 809	-4
55	60.8	...	58	...	53.7	-1.3	6.1	0.2	0.2	4.9	12	670	+9
24	75.0	96.4	94	148	39.2	-1.7	24.6	2.3	13.1	63.2	1 154	593	-5
35	71.3	84.9	98	212	0.1	2.6	5.3	2.2	14.3	23.9	795	20	+2
25	71.9	88.5	84	127	14.4	-1.7	1.0	0.9	14.8	55.0	1 000	503	-6
206	51.6	94.9	43	25	58.2	-0.9	17.1	11.5	2.0	19.3	155	240	+1
74	58.0	...	60	3	15.4	-0.3	4.2	0.2	0.8	1.4	219	291	+3
7	71.4	99.8	100	316	53.9	0.4	43.9	14.0	34.1	125.2	5 736	372	+2
123	52.9	49.9	22	3	11.9	-1.1	16.4	0.1	0.9	1.1	21	251	+3
18	68.8	...	47	34	54.7	0.0	0.9	1.3	13.3	15.9	936	679	+12
4	79.3	...	100	311	73.9	...	8.9	12.6	36.3	107.8	5 560	358	+2
4	80.7	...	100	329	28.3	0.3	10.2	6.2	55.8	85.1	4 957	33	+1
91	56.7	96.0	88	29	84.5	...	13.3	1.1	2.6	54.4	576	241	+1
113	59.4	...	82	4	41.7	0.4	...	0.2	3.0	26.0	529	220	GMT
32	71.0	...	82	391	39.7	...	3.9	0.9	12.5	38.4	749	995	+4

World
Statistics

See page 160 for explanatory table and sources

	Population							Economy					
	Total population	Population change (%)	% urban	Total fertility	Population by age (%) 0 – 14	Population by age (%) 60 or over	2050 projected population	Total Gross National Income (GNI) (US$M)	GNI per capita (US$)	Debt service ratio (% GNI)	Total debt service (US$)	Aid receipts (% GNI)	Military spending (% GDP)
GERMANY	82 599 000	-0.1	88.5	1.4	14.3	25.1	78 765 000	3 032 617	36 810	...	...	...	1.3
GHANA	23 478 000	2.0	46.3	3.8	39.0	5.7	40 573 000	11 778	510	2.0	261 043 000	9.2	0.7
GREECE	11 147 000	0.2	61.4	1.3	14.3	23.0	10 742 000	305 308	27 390	...	...	...	3.2
GRENADA	106 000	0.0	42.2	2.3	...	...	157 000	495	4 650	2.2	15 321 000	5.6	...
GUATEMALA	13 354 000	2.5	47.2	4.2	43.2	6.1	25 612 000	33 725	2 590	1.6	550 958 000	1.4	0.4
GUINEA	9 370 000	2.2	36.5	5.4	43.7	5.6	22 987 000	3 713	400	5.0	164 764 000	5.0	2.0
GUINEA-BISSAU	1 695 000	3.0	35.6	7.1	47.5	4.7	5 312 000	307	190	11.5	33 831 000	27.9	4.0
GUYANA	738 000	-0.2	38.5	2.3	29.3	7.4	488 000	849	1 150	3.8	32 940 000	20.1	...
HAITI	9 598 000	1.6	38.8	3.5	37.5	6.0	12 996 000	4 044	430	1.3	56 732 000	13.4	...
HONDURAS	7 106 000	2.0	46.4	3.3	39.2	5.6	12 776 000	8 844	1 270	3.6	325 235 000	6.6	0.6
HUNGARY	10 030 000	-0.3	65.9	1.3	15.7	20.8	8 262 000	109 461	10 870	29.4	30 827 896 000	...	1.2
ICELAND	301 000	0.8	93.0	2.1	22.0	15.8	370 000	15 078	49 960	...	...	...	0.0
INDIA	1 169 016 000	1.5	28.7	2.8	32.1	7.9	1 592 704 000	909 138	820	2.0	17 878 568 000	0.2	2.7
INDONESIA	231 627 000	1.2	47.9	2.2	28.3	8.4	284 640 000	315 845	1 420	5.9	20 434 246 000	0.4	1.2
IRAN	71 208 000	1.4	68.1	2.0	28.7	6.4	101 944 000	205 040	2 930	1.2	2 555 530 000	0.1	4.8
IRAQ	28 993 000	1.8	66.8	4.3	41.0	4.5	63 693 000	...	...	...	...	...	...
IRELAND	4 301 000	1.8	60.4	2.0	20.2	15.1	5 762 000	191 315	44 830	...	...	...	0.5
ISRAEL	6 928 000	1.7	91.7	2.8	27.8	13.3	10 403 000	142 199	20 170	...	...	...	8.4
ITALY	58 877 000	0.1	67.5	1.4	14.0	25.6	50 912 000	1 882 544	31 990	...	...	...	1.7
JAMAICA	2 714 000	0.5	52.2	2.4	31.2	10.2	2 586 000	9 504	3 560	8.8	824 547 000	0.4	0.6
JAPAN	127 967 000	0.0	65.7	1.3	14.0	26.3	112 198 000	4 934 676	38 630	...	...	...	0.9
JORDAN	5 924 000	3.0	79.3	3.1	37.2	5.1	10 225 000	14 653	2 650	4.7	688 206 000	3.9	4.9
KAZAKHSTAN	15 422 000	0.7	55.9	2.3	23.1	11.3	13 086 000	59 175	3 870	20.3	14 531 967 000	0.3	0.9
KENYA	37 538 000	2.7	41.6	5.0	42.8	4.1	83 073 000	21 335	580	1.9	432 974 000	4.5	1.6
KIRIBATI	95 000	1.6	50.2	...	...	...	177 000	124	1 240	...	...	-37.6	...
KOSOVO*	2 069 989	...	...	...	...	...	...	...	...	...	...	...	...
KUWAIT	2 851 000	2.4	96.4	2.2	24.3	3.1	5 279 000	77 660	30 630	...	...	...	4.8
KYRGYZSTAN	5 317 000	1.1	33.7	2.5	31.5	7.6	6 664 000	2 609	500	3.5	96 608 000	11.8	3.1
LAOS	5 859 000	1.7	21.6	3.2	40.9	5.3	11 586 000	2 890	500	5.6	169 326 000	12.1	...
LATVIA	2 277 000	-0.5	65.9	1.3	14.7	22.5	1 678 000	18 525	8 100	16.9	3 279 260 000	...	1.6
LEBANON	4 099 000	1.1	88.0	2.2	28.6	10.3	4 702 000	22 640	5 580	19.8	4 433 178 000	3.2	4.1
LESOTHO	2 008 000	0.6	18.2	3.4	38.6	7.5	1 601 000	1 957	980	2.5	47 040 000	4.0	2.4
LIBERIA	3 750 000	4.5	47.9	6.8	47.1	3.6	10 653 000	469	130	0.2	809 000	54.4	...
LIBYA	6 160 000	2.0	86.9	2.7	30.1	6.5	9 553 000	44 011	7 290	...	...	0.1	1.5
LIECHTENSTEIN	35 000	0.9	21.8	...	...	...	44 000	...	...	...	...	...	...
LITHUANIA	3 390 000	-0.5	66.6	1.3	16.7	20.7	2 565 000	26 917	7 930	15.3	4 215 870 000	...	1.2
LUXEMBOURG	467 000	1.1	92.4	1.7	18.9	18.3	721 000	32 904	71 240	...	...	...	0.8
MACEDONIA (F.Y.R.O.M.)	2 038 000	0.1	59.7	1.4	19.6	15.5	1 884 000	6 260	3 070	8.4	522 292 000	3.2	2.0
MADAGASCAR	19 683 000	2.7	27.0	4.8	44.0	4.8	43 508 000	5 343	280	1.2	67 571 000	13.9	1.0
MALAWI	13 925 000	2.6	17.2	5.6	47.3	4.7	29 452 000	3 143	230	2.9	90 044 000	30.5	0.5
MALAYSIA	26 572 000	1.7	65.1	2.6	32.4	7.0	38 924 000	146 754	5 620	5.2	7 630 086 000	0.2	2.0
MALDIVES	306 000	1.8	29.7	2.6	40.7	5.1	682 000	903	3 010	3.9	34 588 000	4.4	...
MALI	12 337 000	3.0	33.7	6.5	48.2	4.2	41 976 000	5 546	460	1.5	80 175 000	13.4	2.2
MALTA	407 000	0.4	92.1	1.4	17.6	18.8	428 000	6 216	15 310	...	...	...	0.6
MARSHALL ISLANDS	59 000	2.2	66.7	...	...	...	150 000	195	2 980	...	...	28.5	...
MAURITANIA	3 124 000	2.5	64.3	4.4	43.0	5.3	7 497 000	2 325	760	3.5	97 426 000	6.8	2.5
MAURITIUS	1 262 000	0.8	43.8	1.9	24.6	9.6	1 465 000	6 812	5 430	4.8	308 955 000	0.3	0.2
MEXICO	106 535 000	1.1	76.0	2.2	31.0	7.8	139 015 000	815 741	7 830	6.8	56 068 050 000	0.0	0.4
MICRONESIA, FED. STATES OF	111 000	0.5	30.0	3.7	39.0	4.9	99 000	264	2 390	...	...	41.4	...
MOLDOVA	3 794 000	-0.9	46.3	1.4	18.3	13.7	3 312 000	3 650	1 080	8.9	334 842 000	6.0	0.3
MONACO	33 000	0.3	100.0	...	...	...	55 000	...	...	...	...	...	...
MONGOLIA	2 629 000	1.0	57.0	1.9	30.5	5.7	3 625 000	2 576	1 000	1.6	48 462 000	7.8	1.3
MONTENEGRO*	598 000	-0.3	...	1.8	...	...	...	2 481	4 130	0.5	13 260 000	4.2	...
MOROCCO	31 224 000	1.2	58.8	2.4	31.1	6.8	46 397 000	65 793	2 160	5.3	3 404 801 000	1.8	3.7
MOZAMBIQUE	21 397 000	2.0	38.0	5.1	44.0	5.2	37 604 000	6 453	310	0.9	55 018 000	23.3	0.0
MYANMAR	48 798 000	0.9	30.6	2.1	29.5	7.5	63 657 000	...	...	...	86 428 000	...	...
NAMIBIA	2 074 000	1.3	33.5	3.2	41.5	5.3	3 060 000	6 573	3 210	...	...	2.3	2.9
NAURU	10 000	0.3	100.0	...	...	...	18 000	...	...	...	...	...	...
NEPAL	28 196 000	2.0	15.8	3.3	39.0	5.8	51 172 000	8 790	320	1.6	139 842 000	6.3	1.9
NETHERLANDS	16 419 000	0.2	66.8	1.7	18.2	19.2	17 139 000	703 484	43 050	...	...	...	1.5
NEW ZEALAND	4 179 000	0.9	86.0	2.0	21.3	16.7	4 790 000	111 958	26 750	...	...	...	1.0
NICARAGUA	5 603 000	1.3	58.1	2.8	38.9	4.9	9 371 000	5 163	930	2.4	122 997 000	13.9	0.7
NIGER	14 226 000	3.5	23.3	7.2	49.0	3.3	50 156 000	3 665	270	5.0	181 178 000	11.0	1.1
NIGERIA	148 093 000	2.3	48.3	5.3	44.3	4.8	258 108 000	90 025	620	6.8	6 805 053 000	11.1	0.7
NORTH KOREA	23 790 000	0.3	61.7	1.9	25.0	11.2	24 192 000	...	...	...	...	...	...

* See Serbia for figures prior to formation of independent states

Social Indicators					Environment				Communications				
Child mortality rate	Life expectancy	Literacy rate (%)	Access to safe water (%)	Doctors per 100 000 people	Forest area (%)	Annual change in forest area (%)	Protected land area (%)	CO_2 emissions (metric tonnes per capita)	Main telephone lines per 100 people	Cellular phone subscribers per 100 people	Internet users per 10 000 people	International dialling code	Time zone
4	79.4	...	100	362	31.7	0.0	21.3	9.8	65.9	103.6	4 667	49	+1
120	60.0	70.7	75	9	24.2	-2.0	15.1	0.3	1.6	23.1	270	233	GMT
4	79.5	98.9	...	440	29.1	0.8	3.2	8.7	55.4	98.6	1 838	30	+2
20	68.7	...	95	50	12.2	0.0	3.5	2.0	26.7	44.6	1 864	1 473	-4
41	70.3	82.2	95	90	36.3	-1.3	32.2	1.0	10.5	55.6	1 022	502	-6
161	56.0	46.6	50	9	27.4	-0.5	6.1	0.2	0.3	2.4	52	224	GMT
200	46.4	...	59	17	73.7	-0.5	9.1	0.2	0.4	9.2	226	245	GMT
62	66.8	...	83	48	76.7	0.0	2.3	2.0	14.7	37.5	2 130	592	-4
80	60.9	...	54	25	3.8	-0.7	0.3	0.2	1.7	13.9	751	509	-5
27	70.2	88.9	87	83	41.5	-3.1	19.4	1.1	9.7	30.4	467	504	-6
7	73.3	...	99	316	21.5	0.7	5.7	5.7	33.4	99.0	3 475	36	+1
3	81.8	...	100	347	0.5	3.9	3.9	7.6	63.5	108.7	6 530	354	GMT
76	64.7	76.4	86	51	22.8	...	4.8	1.2	3.6	14.8	1 072	91	+5.5
34	70.7	98.7	77	16	48.8	-2.0	11.0	1.7	6.6	28.3	469	62	+7 to +9
34	71.0	97.4	94	105	6.8	0.0	6.2	6.4	31.2	21.8	2 554	98	+3.5
46	59.5	84.8	81	54	1.9	0.1	...	...	4.0	15.5	16	964	+3
5	78.9	...	...	237	9.7	1.9	1.2	10.4	49.9	112.6	3 423	353	GMT
5	80.7	99.8	100	391	8.3	0.8	14.9	10.5	43.9	122.7	2 774	972	+2
4	80.5	99.8	...	606	33.9	1.1	6.4	7.7	46.3	135.1	5 291	39	+1
31	72.6	...	93	85	31.3	-0.1	14.8	4.0	12.9	93.7	2 942	1 876	-5
4	82.6	...	100	201	68.2	...	9.3	9.8	43.0	79.3	6 827	81	+9
25	72.5	99.0	97	205	0.9	0.0	10.7	3.1	10.5	74.4	1 365	962	+2
29	67.0	99.8	86	330	1.2	-0.2	2.7	13.3	19.8	52.9	842	7	+5 to +6
121	54.1	80.3	61	13	6.2	-0.3	11.8	0.3	0.8	20.9	789	254	+3
64	...	...	65	30	3.0	0.0	...	0.3	5.1	0.7	215	686	+12 to +14
...	...	...	...	...	...	...	...	...	...	...	...	381	+1
11	77.6	99.7	...	153	0.3	2.7	0.0	40.4	18.7	91.5	2 953	965	+3
41	65.9	99.7	77	268	4.5	0.3	3.1	1.1	8.6	23.7	560	996	+6
75	64.4	78.5	51	59	69.9	-0.5	16.3	0.2	1.5	16.7	116	856	+7
9	72.7	99.8	99	291	47.4	0.4	16.1	3.1	28.6	95.1	4 665	371	+2
30	72.0	...	100	325	13.3	0.8	0.4	4.1	18.9	30.6	2 628	961	+2
132	42.6	...	79	5	0.3	2.7	0.2	...	3.0	20.0	287	266	+2
235	45.7	67.4	61	2	32.7	-1.8	15.9	0.1	0.2	4.9	...	231	GMT
18	74.0	98.0	...	129	0.1	0.0	0.1	10.3	8.1	65.8	436	218	+2
3	...	...	...	...	43.1	0.0	57.4	...	57.2	81.8	6 398	423	+1
8	73.0	99.7	...	403	33.5	0.8	5.5	3.9	23.2	138.1	3 169	370	+2
4	78.7	...	100	255	33.5	0.0	16.7	24.9	52.4	116.8	7 201	352	+1
17	74.2	98.7	...	219	35.8	0.0	7.2	5.1	24.1	69.6	1 315	389	+1
115	59.4	70.2	50	9	22.1	-0.3	2.6	0.2	0.7	5.5	58	261	+3
120	48.3	76.0	73	1	36.2	-0.9	15.7	0.1	0.8	3.3	45	265	+2
12	74.2	97.2	99	70	63.6	-0.7	18.2	7.0	16.8	75.5	5 423	60	+8
30	68.5	98.2	83	78	3.0	0.0	...	2.5	10.9	87.9	664	960	+5
217	54.5	24.2	50	4	10.3	-0.8	2.1	0.1	0.6	10.9	64	223	GMT
6	79.4	96.0	100	293	1.1	0.0	21.4	6.1	50.1	86.0	3 173	356	+1
56	...	...	87	47	...	0.0	...	...	8.3	1.1	...	692	+12
125	64.2	61.3	53	14	0.3	-3.4	...	0.9	1.1	33.6	95	222	GMT
14	72.8	94.5	100	85	18.2	-0.5	4.8	2.6	28.5	61.5	2 548	230	+4
35	76.2	97.6	97	171	33.7	-0.4	5.2	4.3	18.3	52.6	1 898	52	-6 to -8
41	68.5	...	94	60	90.6	0.0	32.7	...	11.2	12.7	1 439	691	+10 to +11
19	68.9	99.7	92	269	10.0	0.2	1.4	2.0	24.3	32.4	1 735	373	+2
4	...	...	100	586	0.0	0.0	...	...	96.8	51.6	5 634	377	+1
43	66.8	97.7	62	267	6.5	-0.8	14.0	3.4	5.9	28.9	1 157	976	+8
10	74.5	...	...	...	...	...	...	...	58.9	107.3	4 434	382	+1
37	71.2	70.5	81	48	9.8	0.2	1.2	1.4	4.1	52.1	1 985	212	GMT
138	42.1	47.0	43	2	24.6	-0.3	5.7	0.1	0.3	11.6	90	258	+2
104	62.1	94.5	78	30	49.0	-1.4	5.4	0.2	0.9	0.4	18	95	+6.5
61	52.9	92.3	87	30	9.3	-0.9	5.2	1.2	6.8	24.4	397	264	+1
30	...	...	...	...	0.0	0.0	...	...	...	...	...	674	+12
59	63.8	70.1	90	5	25.4	-1.4	15.4	0.1	2.2	4.2	114	977	+5.75
5	79.8	...	100	329	10.8	0.3	12.4	8.7	46.6	106.9	10 998	31	+1
6	80.2	...	...	223	31.0	0.2	24.2	7.7	44.1	94.0	7 877	64	+12
36	72.9	86.2	79	164	42.7	-1.3	16.4	0.7	4.4	32.7	277	505	-6
253	56.9	36.5	46	3	1.0	-1.0	7.1	0.1	0.2	3.4	28	227	+1
191	46.9	84.2	48	27	12.2	-3.3	6.2	0.8	1.3	24.1	595	234	+1
55	67.3	...	100	297	51.4	-1.9	2.6	3.4	4.4	...	...	850	+9

World
Statistics

See page 160 for explanatory table and sources

	Population							Economy					
	Total population	Population change (%)	% urban	Total fertility	Population by age (%) 0 – 14	60 or over	2050 projected population	Total Gross National Income (GNI) (US$M)	GNI per capita (US$)	Debt service ratio (% GNI)	Total debt service (US$)	Aid receipts (% GNI)	Military spending (% GDP)
NORWAY	4 698 000	0.6	80.5	1.9	19.6	20.0	5 435 000	318 919	68 440	...	...	...	1.5
OMAN	2 595 000	2.0	78.6	3.0	34.5	4.2	4 958 000	27 887	11 120	5.1	310 065 000	...	11.8
PAKISTAN	163 902 000	1.8	34.8	3.5	38.3	5.8	304 700 000	126 711	800	1.8	2 282 421 000	1.7	3.8
PALAU	20 000	0.4	68.2	...	...	...	21 000	161	7 990	...	...	23.5	...
PANAMA	3 343 000	1.7	57.8	2.6	30.4	8.8	5 093 000	16 442	5 000	21.5	3 458 784 000	0.2	...
PAPUA NEW GUINEA	6 331 000	2.0	13.2	3.8	40.3	3.9	10 619 000	4 603	740	5.8	293 913 000	5.5	0.5
PARAGUAY	6 127 000	1.8	58.5	3.1	37.6	5.6	12 095 000	8 461	1 410	4.5	420 751 000	0.6	0.8
PERU	27 903 000	1.2	74.6	2.5	32.2	7.8	42 552 000	82 201	2 980	4.4	3 745 566 000	0.6	1.2
PHILIPPINES	87 960 000	1.9	62.6	3.2	35.1	6.1	127 068 000	120 190	1 390	10.7	13 680 640 000	0.4	0.9
POLAND	38 082 000	-0.2	62.0	1.2	16.3	16.8	31 916 000	312 994	8 210	11.1	36 044 403 000	...	2.0
PORTUGAL	10 623 000	0.4	55.6	1.5	15.9	22.3	10 723 000	189 017	17 850	...	...	...	2.1
QATAR	841 000	2.1	92.3	2.7	21.7	2.6	1 330 000	...	...	...	...	...	...
ROMANIA	21 438 000	-0.5	54.7	1.3	15.4	19.3	16 757 000	104 382	4 830	7.3	8 678 183 000	...	1.9
RUSSIAN FEDERATION	142 499 000	-0.5	73.3	1.3	15.3	17.1	111 752 000	822 328	5 770	5.2	50 222 974 000	...	4.0
RWANDA	9 725 000	2.8	21.8	5.9	43.5	3.9	18 153 000	2 341	250	1.2	30 612 000	23.6	2.7
SAMOA	187 000	0.9	22.5	3.9	40.7	6.5	157 000	421	2 270	7.0	29 506 000	11.3	...
SAN MARINO	31 000	0.8	88.7	...	...	...	30 000	1 291	45 130	...	...	...	...
SÃO TOMÉ AND PRÍNCIPE	158 000	1.6	37.9	3.9	39.5	5.7	295 000	124	800	7.8	9 337 000	18.0	...
SAUDI ARABIA	24 735 000	2.2	88.5	3.4	37.3	4.6	49 464 000	331 041	13 980	...	...	...	8.5
SENEGAL	12 379 000	2.5	51.0	4.7	42.6	4.9	23 108 000	9 117	760	2.2	202 197 000	9.3	1.6
SERBIA	7 788 448	0.1	52.3*	1.8	18.3*	18.5*	9 426 000*	29 961	4 030	8.5	2 679 730 000	5.1	2.1
SEYCHELLES	87 000	0.5	50.2	...	...	...	99 000	751	8 870	24.8	181 083 000	2.0	1.8
SIERRA LEONE	5 866 000	2.0	40.2	6.5	42.8	5.5	13 786 000	1 353	240	2.4	33 899 000	25.7	1.0
SINGAPORE	4 436 000	1.2	100.0	1.3	19.5	12.2	5 213 000	128 816	28 730	...	...	...	4.7
SLOVAKIA	5 390 000	0.0	58.0	1.3	16.7	16.2	4 612 000	51 807	9 610	7.8	4 125 305 000	...	1.7
SLOVENIA	2 002 000	0.0	50.8	1.3	13.9	20.5	1 630 000	37 445	18 660	...	...	...	1.7
SOLOMON ISLANDS	496 000	2.3	17.1	3.9	40.6	4.2	921 000	333	690	1.3	4 276 000	60.6	...
SOMALIA	8 699 000	2.9	35.9	6.0	44.1	4.2	21 329 000	...	...	...	19 000	...	...
SOUTH AFRICA, REPUBLIC OF	48 577 000	0.6	57.9	2.6	32.6	6.8	48 660 000	255 389	5 390	2.2	5 472 200 000	0.3	1.4
SOUTH KOREA	48 224 000	0.3	80.8	1.2	18.6	13.7	44 629 000	856 565	17 690	...	...	...	2.7
SPAIN	44 279 000	0.8	76.7	1.4	14.3	21.4	42 541 000	1 206 169	27 340	...	...	...	1.0
SRI LANKA	19 299 000	0.5	21.0	1.9	24.1	10.7	23 554 000	26 001	1 310	3.6	957 927 000	3.0	2.4
ST KITTS AND NEVIS	50 000	1.3	31.9	...	...	...	59 000	406	8 460	12.3	46 585 000	1.2	...
ST LUCIA	165 000	1.1	31.3	2.2	28.8	9.7	188 000	833	5 060	4.1	34 456 000	2.2	...
ST VINCENT AND THE GRENADINES	120 000	0.5	60.5	2.2	29.2	8.9	105 000	395	3 320	7.0	35 627 000	1.0	...
SUDAN	38 560 000	2.2	40.8	4.2	39.2	5.6	66 705 000	30 086	800	0.8	292 431 000	6.0	2.2
SURINAME	458 000	0.6	77.2	2.4	30.1	9.0	429 000	1 918	4 210	...	...	4.1	...
SWAZILAND	1 141 000	0.6	23.9	3.5	41.0	5.4	1 026 000	2 737	2 400	1.7	44 704 000	1.3	1.9
SWEDEN	9 119 000	0.5	83.4	1.8	17.5	23.4	10 054 000	395 411	43 530	...	...	...	1.4
SWITZERLAND	7 484 000	0.4	67.5	1.4	16.5	21.8	7 252 000	434 844	58 050	...	...	...	0.9
SYRIA	19 929 000	2.5	50.3	3.1	36.9	4.7	35 935 000	30 333	1 560	0.6	186 679 000	0.1	3.8
TAIWAN	22 880 000	...	...	...	19.8	9.2*	...	...	...	...	...	...	...
TAJIKISTAN	6 736 000	1.5	24.2	3.4	39.0	5.1	10 423 000	2 572	390	5.0	136 859 000	8.8	2.2
TANZANIA	40 454 000	2.5	37.5	5.2	42.6	5.1	66 845 000	13 404	350	0.9	113 148 000	14.5	1.1
THAILAND	63 884 000	0.7	32.5	1.9	23.8	10.5	74 594 000	193 734	3 050	7.3	14 685 762 000	-0.1	1.1
TOGO	6 585 000	2.7	36.3	4.8	43.5	4.9	13 544 000	2 265	350	0.7	15 432 000	3.6	1.6
TONGA	100 000	0.5	34.0	3.8	35.9	8.8	75 000	225	2 250	1.4	3 203 000	9.6	1.1
TRINIDAD AND TOBAGO	1 333 000	0.4	76.2	1.6	21.5	10.7	1 230 000	16 612	12 500	...	...	0.1	...
TUNISIA	10 327 000	1.1	64.4	1.9	25.9	8.6	12 927 000	30 091	2 970	8.8	2 520 202 000	1.5	1.4
TURKEY	74 877 000	1.3	67.3	2.1	29.2	8.0	101 208 000	393 903	5 400	10.1	40 511 288 000	0.1	2.9
TURKMENISTAN	4 965 000	1.3	45.8	2.5	31.8	6.2	6 780 000	...	...	2.6	254 770 000	0.3	...
TUVALU	11 000	0.4	57.0	...	...	...	12 000	...	...	...	...	...	...
UGANDA	30 884 000	3.2	12.4	6.5	50.5	3.8	126 950 000	8 996	300	1.2	114 694 000	16.9	2.1
UKRAINE	46 205 000	-0.8	67.3	1.2	14.9	20.9	26 393 000	90 740	1 940	9.0	9 388 953 000	0.5	2.1
UNITED ARAB EMIRATES	4 380 000	2.9	85.5	2.3	22.0	1.6	9 056 000	...	...	...	...	...	2.0
UNITED KINGDOM	60 769 000	0.4	89.2	1.8	17.9	21.2	67 143 000	2 455 691	40 560	...	...	...	2.6
UNITED STATES OF AMERICA	305 826 000	1.0	80.8	2.1	20.8	16.7	394 976 000	13 386 875	44 710	...	...	...	4.1
URUGUAY	3 340 000	0.3	93.0	2.1	24.3	17.4	4 043 000	17 591	5 310	30.3	5 689 614 000	0.1	1.2
UZBEKISTAN	27 372 000	1.4	36.4	2.5	33.2	6.2	38 665 000	16 179	610	5.4	923 830 000	0.9	0.5
VANUATU	226 000	2.4	23.7	3.7	39.9	5.1	375 000	373	1 690	1.0	3 725 000	13.6	...
VATICAN CITY	557	0.1	100.0	...	...	...	1 000	...	...	...	...	...	...
VENEZUELA	27 657 000	1.7	88.1	2.6	31.2	7.6	41 991 000	163 959	6 070	5.5	9 964 936 000	0.0	1.1
VIETNAM	87 375 000	1.3	26.7	2.1	29.5	7.5	116 654 000	58 506	700	1.5	918 307 000	3.1	...
YEMEN	22 389 000	3.0	26.3	5.5	46.4	3.6	59 454 000	16 444	760	1.3	225 869 000	1.6	6.0
ZAMBIA	11 922 000	1.9	36.5	5.2	45.8	4.6	22 781 000	7 413	630	1.6	153 699 000	14.3	2.3
ZIMBABWE	13 349 000	1.0	35.9	3.2	40.0	5.4	15 805 000	4 466	340	7.0	83 389 000	...	0.0

* Figures are for Serbia and Montenegro (including Kosovo) prior to formation of independent states

Social Indicators					Environment				Communications				
Child mortality rate	Life expectancy	Literacy rate (%)	Access to safe water (%)	Doctors per 100 000 people	Forest area (%)	Annual change in forest area (%)	Protected land area (%)	CO_2 emissions (metric tonnes per capita)	Main telephone lines per 100 people	Cellular phone subscribers per 100 people	Internet users per 10 000 people	International dialling code	Time zone
4	80.2	...	100	356	30.7	0.2	5.1	19.1	44.3	108.6	8 168	47	+1
12	75.6	97.3	...	126	0.0	0.0	0.1	12.5	10.3	69.6	1 222	968	+4
97	65.5	65.1	91	66	2.5	-2.1	7.4	0.8	3.3	22.0	764	92	+5
11	...	...	85	109	87.6	0.4	0.0	11.9	...	...	...	680	+9
23	75.5	96.1	90	168	57.7	-0.1	10.3	1.8	14.9	66.1	669	507	-5
73	57.2	66.7	39	5	65.0	-0.5	7.9	0.4	1.1	1.3	183	675	+10
22	71.8	95.9	86	117	46.5	-0.9	5.8	0.7	5.3	51.3	413	595	-4
25	71.4	97.1	83	117	53.7	-0.1	13.6	1.2	8.5	30.9	2 581	51	-5
32	71.7	95.1	85	116	24.0	-2.1	10.7	1.0	4.3	50.8	548	63	+8
7	75.6	...	...	220	30.0	0.3	24.2	8.0	29.8	95.5	3 658	48	+1
5	78.1	99.6	...	324	41.3	1.1	5.1	5.6	40.2	116.0	3 025	351	GMT
21	75.6	95.9	100	221	0.0	0.0	0.0	69.2	27.2	109.6	3 455	974	+3
18	72.5	97.8	57	189	27.7	...	2.2	4.2	19.4	80.5	5 224	40	+2
16	65.5	99.7	97	417	47.9	...	6.6	10.6	30.8	105.7	1 802	7	+2 to +12
160	46.2	77.6	74	2	19.5	6.9	8.0	0.1	0.2	3.4	55	250	+2
28	71.5	99.3	88	70	60.4	0.0	2.8	0.8	10.9	25.4	446	685	-11
3	...	...	...	251	1.6	0.0	...	...	77.8	64.4	5 704	378	+1
96	65.5	95.4	79	47	28.4	0.0	...	0.6	4.7	11.5	1 811	239	GMT
25	72.8	95.8	...	140	1.3	0.0	42.3	13.7	15.7	78.1	1 866	966	+3
116	63.1	49.1	76	8	45.0	-0.5	10.9	0.4	2.4	25.0	545	221	GMT
8	74.0	99.4*	...	...	26.4*	...	3.2*	...	25.9	63.3	1 334	381	+1
13	...	99.1	88	132	88.9	0.0	17.2	6.6	25.4	86.5	3 567	248	+4
270	42.6	47.9	57	7	38.5	-0.7	4.0	0.2	0.5	2.2	19	232	GMT
3	80.0	99.5	100	140	3.4	0.0	7.3	12.3	42.3	109.3	4 362	65	+8
8	74.7	...	100	325	40.1	0.1	19.8	6.7	21.6	90.6	4 176	421	+1
4	77.9	99.8	...	219	62.8	0.4	6.5	8.1	42.6	92.6	6 362	386	+1
73	63.6	...	70	13	77.6	-1.7	1.0	0.4	1.6	1.3	163	677	+11
145	48.2	...	29	4	11.4	-1.0	0.3	...	1.2	6.1	111	252	+3
69	49.3	93.9	88	69	7.6	0.0	6.0	9.4	10.0	83.3	1 075	27	+2
5	78.6	...	92	181	63.5	-0.1	3.7	9.7	49.8	83.8	7 275	82	+9
4	80.9	...	100	320	35.9	1.7	8.2	7.7	42.4	106.4	4 283	34	+1
13	72.4	95.6	79	43	29.9	-1.5	17.5	0.6	9.0	25.9	169	94	+5.5
19	...	...	100	118	14.7	0.0	0.1	2.7	59.3	23.7	2 428	1 869	-4
14	73.7	...	98	518	27.9	0.0	29.3	2.3	32.6	65.7	6 169	1 758	-4
20	71.6	...	...	88	27.4	0.8	18.6	1.7	19.0	73.6	840	1 784	-4
89	58.6	77.2	70	16	28.4	-0.8	4.6	0.3	1.7	12.7	946	249	+3
39	70.2	94.9	92	45	94.7	0.0	12.9	5.1	18.0	70.8	712	597	-3
164	39.6	88.4	62	18	31.5	0.9	3.2	0.9	4.3	24.3	408	268	+2
3	80.9	...	100	305	66.9	...	9.6	5.9	59.5	105.9	7 697	46	+1
5	81.7	...	100	352	30.9	0.4	28.2	5.5	66.9	99.0	5 807	41	+1
14	74.1	92.5	93	140	2.5	1.3	0.7	3.7	16.6	24.0	794	963	+2
...	...	...	...	...	...	...	...	...	63.6	102.0	6 368	886	+8
68	66.7	99.8	59	218	2.9	0.0	13.6	0.8	4.3	4.1	30	992	+5
118	52.5	78.4	62	2	39.9	-1.1	36.4	0.1	0.4	14.8	100	255	+3
8	70.6	98.0	99	30	28.4	-0.4	19.7	4.3	10.9	62.9	1 307	66	+7
108	58.4	74.4	52	6	7.1	-4.5	10.7	0.4	1.3	11.2	507	228	GMT
24	73.3	99.3	100	34	5.0	0.0	24.4	1.2	13.7	29.8	302	676	+13
38	69.8	99.5	91	79	44.1	-0.2	5.5	24.7	24.9	126.4	1 248	1 868	-4
23	73.9	94.3	93	70	6.8	1.9	1.5	2.3	12.4	71.9	1 268	216	+1
26	71.8	95.6	96	124	13.2	0.2	1.6	3.2	25.4	71.0	1 773	90	+2
51	63.2	99.8	72	317	8.8	0.0	2.3	8.7	8.2	4.4	132	993	+5
38	...	...	100	...	33.3	0.0	...	...	10.3	15	4 673	688	+12
134	51.5	76.6	60	5	18.4	-2.2	25.6	0.1	0.4	6.7	251	256	+3
24	67.9	99.8	96	297	16.5	0.1	3.3	6.9	26.8	106.7	1 206	380	+2
8	78.7	97.0	100	202	3.7	0.1	0.3	37.8	28.1	118.5	3 669	971	+4
6	79.4	...	100	166	11.8	0.4	20.0	9.8	56.2	116.6	6 316	44	GMT
8	78.2	...	100	549	33.1	0.1	14.6	20.6	57.2	77.4	6 983	1	-5 to -10
12	76.4	98.6	100	365	8.6	1.3	0.3	1.7	28.3	66.8	2 055	598	-3
43	67.2	...	82	289	8.0	0.5	2.0	5.3	6.7	9.3	630	998	+5
36	70.0	...	60	11	36.1	0.0	1.0	0.4	3.2	5.9	346	678	+11
...	...	...	...	...	0.0	0.0	...	...	...	...	...	39	+1
21	73.7	97.2	83	194	54.1	-0.6	69.9	6.6	15.8	69.0	1 521	58	-4.5
17	74.2	93.9	85	53	39.7	2.0	5.0	1.2	18.8	18.2	1 721	84	+7
100	62.7	75.2	67	22	1.0	0.0	0.0	1.0	4.5	13.8	125	967	+3
182	42.4	69.5	58	7	57.1	-1.0	39.9	0.2	0.8	14.0	422	260	+2
105	43.5	97.7	81	6	45.3	-1.7	14.6	0.8	2.6	6.5	932	263	+2

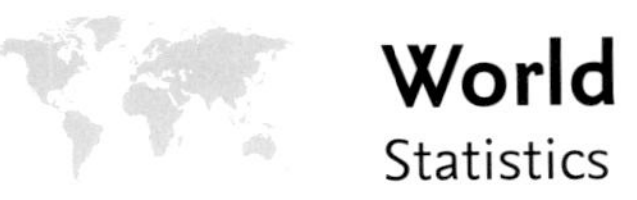

Definitions

Indicator	Definition
Population	
Total population	Interpolated mid-year population, 2005.
Population change	Percentage average annual rate of change, 2005–2010.
% urban	Urban population as a percentage of the total population, 2005.
Total fertility	Average number of children a woman will have during her child-bearing years, 2005–2010.
Population by age	Percentage of population in age groups 0–14 and 60 or over, 2005.
2050 projected population	Projected total population for the year 2050.
Economy	
Total Gross National Income (GNI)	The sum of value added to the economy by all resident producers plus taxes, less subsidies, plus net receipts of primary income from abroad. Data are in U.S. dollars (millions), 2006. Formerly known as Gross National Product (GNP).
GNI per capita	Gross National Income per person in U.S. dollars using the World Bank Atlas method, 2006.
Debt service ratio	Debt service as a percentage of GNI, 2006.
Total debt service	Sum of principal repayments and interest paid on long-term debt, interest paid on short-term debt and repayments to the International Monetary Fund (IMF), 2006.
Aid receipts	Aid received as a percentage of GNI from the Development Assistance Committee (DAC) countries of the Organization for Economic Co-operation and Development (OECD), 2006.
Military spending	Military-related spending, including recruiting, training, construction and the purchase of military supplies and equipment, as a percentage of Gross National Income, 2006.
Social Indicators	
Child mortality rate	Number of deaths of children aged under 5 per 1 000 live births, 2006.
Life expectancy	Average life expectancy, at birth in years, male and female, 2005–2010.
Literacy rate	Percentage of population aged 15–24 with at least a basic ability to read and write, 2005.
Access to safe water	Percentage of population using improved drinking water, 2004.
Doctors	Number of trained doctors per 100 000 people, 2004.
Environment	
Forest area	Percentage of total land area covered by forest, 2005.
Change in forest area	Average annual percentage change in forest area, 2000-2005.
Protected land area	Percentage of total land area designated as protected land, 2006.
CO_2 emissions	Emissions of carbon dioxide from the burning of fossil fuels and the manufacture of cement, divided by the population, expressed in metric tons per capita, 2004.
Communications	
Telephone lines	Main (fixed) telephone lines per 100 inhabitants, 2006.
Cellular phone subscribers	Cellular mobile subscribers per 100 inhabitants, 2006.
Internet users	Internet users per 10 000 inhabitants, 2006.
International dialling code	The country code prefix to be used when dialling from another country.
Time zone	Time difference in hours between local standard time and Greenwich Mean Time.

Main Statistical Sources	Internet Links
● United Nations Department of Economic and Social Affairs (UDESA) World Population Prospects: The 2006 Revision. World Urbanization Prospects: The 2005 Revision.	www.un.org/esa/population/unpop
● UNESCO Education Data Centre	stats.uis.unesco.org
● UN Human Development Report 2004	hdr.undp.org
● World Bank World Development Indicators online	www.worldbank.org/data
● OECD: Development Co-operation Report 2007	www.oecd.org
● UNICEF: The State of the World's Children 2008	www.unicef.org
● Food and Agriculture Organization (FAO) of the UN: Global Forest Resources Assessment 2005	www.fao.org
● World Resources Institute Biodiversity and Protected Areas Database	www.wri.org
● International Telecommunications Union (ITU)	www.itu.int

Index

ntroduction to the index

e index includes all names shown on the reference maps in the as. Each entry includes the country or geographical area in which e feature is located, a page number and an alphanumeric ference. Additional entry details and aspects of the index are plained below.

me forms
e names policy in this atlas is generally to use local name forms ich are officially recognized by the governments of the countries ncerned. Rules established by the Permanent Committee on ographical Names for British Official Use (PCGN) are applied to e conversion of non-roman alphabet names, for example in the ssian Federation, into the roman alphabet used in English.

owever, English conventional name forms are used for the most ll-known places for which such a form is in common use. In these ses, the local form is included in brackets on the map and appears a cross-reference in the index. Other alternative names, such as ll-known historical names or those in other languages, may also included in brackets on the map and as cross-references in the ex. All country names and those for international physical tures appear in their English forms. Names appear in full in the ex, although they may appear in abbreviated form on the maps.

ferencing
mes are referenced by page number and by grid reference. The d reference relates to the alphanumeric values which appear on e edges of each map. These reflect the graticule on the map – the ter relates to longitude divisions, the number to latitude divisions. mes are generally referenced to the largest scale map page on ich they appear. For large geographical features, including untries, the reference is to the largest scale map on which the ture appears in its entirety, or on which the majority of it appears.

Rivers are referenced to their lowest downstream point – either their mouth or their confluence with another river. The river name will generally be positioned as close to this point as possible.

Alternative names
Alternative names appear as cross-references and refer the user to the index entry for the form of the name used on the map.

For rivers with multiple names - for example those which flow through several countries - all alternative name forms are included within the main index entries, with details of the countries in which each form applies.

Administrative qualifiers
Administrative divisions are included in entries to differentiate duplicate names - entries of exactly the same name and feature type within the one country - where these division names are shown on the maps. In such cases, duplicate names are alphabetized in the order of the administrative division names.

Additional qualifiers are included for names within selected geographical areas, to indicate more clearly their location.

Descriptors
Entries, other than those for towns and cities, include a descriptor indicating the type of geographical feature. Descriptors are not included where the type of feature is implicit in the name itself, unless there is a town or city of exactly the same name.

Insets
Where relevant, the index clearly indicates [inset] if a feature appears on an inset map.

Alphabetical order
The Icelandic characters Þ and þ are transliterated and alphabetized as 'Th' and 'th'. The German character ß is alphabetized as 'ss'. Names beginning with Mac or Mc are alphabetized exactly as they appear. The terms Saint, Sainte, etc, are abbreviated to St, Ste, etc, but alphabetized as if in the full form.

Numerical entries
Entries beginning with numerals appear at the beginning of the index, in numerical order. Elsewhere, numerals are alphabetized before 'a'.

Permuted terms
Names beginning with generic geographical terms are permuted - the descriptive term is placed after, and the index alphabetized by, the main part of the name. For example, Mount Everest is indexed as Everest, Mount; Lake Superior as Superior, Lake. This policy is applied to all languages. Permuting has not been applied to names of towns, cities or administrative divisions beginning with such geographical terms. These remain in their full form, for example, Lake Isabella, USA.

Gazetteer entries
Selected entries have been extended to include gazetteer-style information. Important geographical facts which relate specifically to the entry are included within the entry.

bbreviations

dmin. dist.	administrative district	IL	Illinois	plat.	plateau
dmin. div.	administrative division	imp. l.	impermanent lake	P.N.G.	Papua New Guinea
dmin. reg.	administrative region	IN	Indiana	Port.	Portugal
fgh.	Afghanistan	Indon.	Indonesia	pref.	prefecture
K	Alaska	Kazakh.	Kazakhstan	prov.	province
L	Alabama	KS	Kansas	pt	point
lg.	Algeria	KY	Kentucky	Qld	Queensland
R	Arkansas	Kyrg.	Kyrgyzstan	Que.	Québec
rg.	Argentina	l.	lake	r.	river
ut. comm.	autonomous community	LA	Louisiana	reg.	region
ut. reg.	autonomous region	lag.	lagoon	res.	reserve
ut. rep.	autonomous republic	Lith.	Lithuania	resr	reservoir
Z	Arizona	Lux.	Luxembourg	RI	Rhode Island
zer.	Azerbaijan	MA	Massachusetts	Rus. Fed.	Russian Federation
.	bay	Madag.	Madagascar	S.	South, Southern
angl.	Bangladesh	Man.	Manitoba	S.A.	South Australia
.C.	British Columbia	MD	Maryland	salt l.	salt lake
ol.	Bolivia	ME	Maine	Sask.	Saskatchewan
os.-Herz.	Bosnia-Herzegovina	Mex.	Mexico	SC	South Carolina
ulg.	Bulgaria	MI	Michigan	SD	South Dakota
.	cape	MN	Minnesota	sea chan.	sea channel
A	California	MO	Missouri	Sing.	Singapore
ent. Afr. Rep.	Central African Republic	Moz.	Mozambique	Switz.	Switzerland
O	Colorado	MS	Mississippi	Tajik.	Tajikistan
ol.	Colombia	MT	Montana	Tanz.	Tanzania
T	Connecticut	mt.	mountain	Tas.	Tasmania
zech Rep.	Czech Republic	mts	mountains	terr.	territory
C	District of Columbia	N.	North, Northern	Thai.	Thailand
E	Delaware	nat. park	national park	TN	Tennessee
em. Rep. Congo	Democratic Republic of the Congo	N.B.	New Brunswick	Trin. and Tob.	Trinidad and Tobago
epr.	depression	NC	North Carolina	Turkm.	Turkmenistan
es.	desert	ND	North Dakota	TX	Texas
om. Rep.	Dominican Republic	NE	Nebraska	U.A.E.	United Arab Emirates
.	East, Eastern	Neth.	Netherlands	U.K.	United Kingdom
quat. Guinea	Equatorial Guinea	NH	New Hampshire	Ukr.	Ukraine
sc.	escarpment	NJ	New Jersey	U.S.A.	United States of America
st.	estuary	NM	New Mexico	UT	Utah
th.	Ethiopia	N.S.	Nova Scotia	Uzbek.	Uzbekistan
in.	Finland	N.S.W.	New South Wales	VA	Virginia
L	Florida	N.T.	Northern Territory	Venez.	Venezuela
or.	forest	NV	Nevada	Vic.	Victoria
r. Guiana	French Guiana	N.W.T.	Northwest Territories	vol.	volcano
.Y.R.O.M.	Former Yugoslav Republic of Macedonia	NY	New York	vol. crater	volcanic crater
.	gulf	N.Z.	New Zealand	VT	Vermont
A	Georgia	OH	Ohio	W.	West, Western
uat.	Guatemala	OK	Oklahoma	WA	Washington
I	Hawaii	OR	Oregon	W.A.	Western Australia
.K.	Hong Kong	PA	Pennsylvania	WI	Wisconsin
ond.	Honduras	Para.	Paraguay	WV	West Virginia
	island	P.E.I.	Prince Edward Island	WY	Wyoming
	Iowa	pen.	peninsula	Y.T.	Yukon Territory
	Idaho	Phil.	Philippines		

1st Three Mile Opening *sea chan.* Australia 110 D2
2nd Three Mile Opening *sea chan.* Australia 110 C2
3-y Severnyy Rus. Fed. 41 S3
5 de Outubro Angola *see* Xá-Muteba
9 de Julio Arg. 144 D5
25 de Mayo *Buenos Aires* Arg. 144 D5
25 de Mayo *La Pampa* Arg. 144 C5
70 Mile House Canada 120 F5
100 Mile House Canada 120 F5
150 Mile House Canada 120 F4

Aabenraa Denmark 45 F9
Aachen Germany 52 G4
Aalborg Denmark 45 F8
Aalborg Bugt *b.* Denmark 45 G8
Aalen Germany 53 K6
Aalesund Norway *see* Ålesund
Aaley Lebanon *see* Aley
Aalst Belgium 52 E4
Aanaar Fin. *see* Inari
Aarhus Denmark *see* Århus
Aarlen Belgium *see* Arlon
Aars Denmark 45 F8
Aarschot Belgium 52 E4
Aasiaat Greenland 119 M3
Aath Belgium *see* Ath
Aba China 76 D1
Aba Dem. Rep. Congo 98 D3
Aba Nigeria 96 D4
Abacaxis *r.* Brazil 143 G4
Ābādān Iran 88 C4
Abadan Turkm. 88 E2
Ābādeh Iran 88 D4
Ābādeh Ṭashk Iran 88 D4
Abadla Alg. 54 D5
Abaeté Brazil 145 B2
Abaetetuba Brazil 143 I4
Abagnar Qi China *see* Xilinhot
Abaiang *atoll* Kiribati 150 H5
Abajo Peak U.S.A. 129 I3
Abakaliki Nigeria 96 D4
Abakan Rus. Fed. 72 G2
Abakanskiy Khrebet *mts* Rus. Fed. 72 F2
Abalak Niger 96 D3
Abana Turkey 90 D2
Abancay Peru 142 D6
Abariringa *atoll* Kiribati *see* Kanton
Abarkūh, Kavīr-e *des.* Iran 88 D4
Abarqū Iran 88 D4
Abarshahr Iran *see* Neyshābūr
Abashiri Japan 74 G3
Abashiri-wan *b.* Japan 74 G3
Abasolo Mex. 131 D7
Abau P.N.G. 110 E1
Abaya, Lake Eth. 98 D3
Ābaya Hāyk' *l.* Eth. *see* Abaya, Lake
Ābay Wenz *r.* Eth./Sudan 98 D2 *see* Blue Nile
Abaza Rus. Fed. 72 G2
Abba Cent. Afr. Rep. 98 B3
'Abbāsābād Iran 88 D3
'Abbāsābād Iran 88 E2
Abbasanta *Sardinia* Italy 58 C4
Abbatis Villa France *see* Abbeville
Abbe, Lake Djibouti/Eth. 86 F7
Abbeville France 52 B4
Abbeville *AL* U.S.A. 133 C6
Abbeville *GA* U.S.A. 133 D6
Abbeville *LA* U.S.A. 131 E6
Abbeville *SC* U.S.A. 133 D5
Abbey Canada 121 I5
Abbeyfeale Ireland 51 C5
Abbeytown U.K. 48 D4
Abborrträsk Sweden 44 K4
Abbot, Mount Australia 110 D4
Abbot Ice Shelf Antarctica 152 K2
Abbotsford Canada 120 F5
Abbott *NM* U.S.A. 127 G5
Abbott *VA* U.S.A. 134 E5
Abbottabad Pak. 89 I3
'Abd al 'Azīz, Jabal *hill* Syria 91 F3
'Abd al Kūrī *i.* Yemen 86 H7
'Abd Allah, Khawr *sea chan.* Iraq/Kuwait 88 C4
Abd al Ma'asīr *well* Saudi Arabia 85 D4
Ābdānān Iran 88 B3
'Abdollāhābād Iran 88 D3
Abdulino Rus. Fed. 41 Q5
Abéché Chad 97 F3
Abellinum Italy *see* Avellino
Abel Tasman National Park N.Z. 113 D5
Abengourou Côte d'Ivoire 96 C4
Åbenrå Denmark *see* Aabenraa
Abensberg Germany 53 L6
Abeokuta Nigeria 96 D4
Aberaeron U.K. 49 C6
Aberchirder U.K. 50 G3
Abercorn Zambia *see* Mbala
Abercrombie *r.* Australia 112 D4
Aberdare U.K. 49 D7
Aberdaron U.K. 49 C6
Aberdaugleddau U.K. *see* Milford Haven
Aberdeen Australia 112 E4
Aberdeen H.K. China 77 [inset]
Aberdeen S. Africa 100 G7
Aberdeen U.K. 50 G3
Aberdeen U.S.A. 130 D2
Aberdeen Lake Canada 121 L1
Aberdovey U.K. 49 C6
Aberdyfi *Wales* U.K. *see* Aberdovey
Aberfeldy U.K. 50 F4
Aberford U.K. 48 F5
Aberfoyle U.K. 50 E4
Abergavenny U.K. 49 D7
Abergwaun U.K. *see* Fishguard
Aberhonddu U.K. *see* Brecon
Abermaw U.K. *see* Barmouth
Abernathy U.S.A. 131 C5
Aberporth U.K. 49 C6
Abersoch U.K. 49 C6
Abertawe U.K. *see* Swansea
Aberteifi U.K. *see* Cardigan
Aberystwyth U.K. 49 C6
Abeshr Chad *see* Abéché
Abez' Rus. Fed. 41 S2
Āb Gāh Iran 89 E5
Abhā Saudi Arabia 86 F6
Abhar Iran 88 C2
Abiad, Bahr el *r.* Sudan/Uganda 86 D6 *see* White Nile

▶Abidjan Côte d'Ivoire 96 C4
Former capital of Côte d'Ivoire.

Abijatta-Shalla National Park Eth. 98 D3
Ab-i-Kavīr *salt flat* Iran 88 E3
Abilene *KS* U.S.A. 130 D4
Abilene *TX* U.S.A. 131 D5
Abingdon U.K. 49 F7
Abingdon U.S.A. 134 D5
Abington Reef Australia 110 E3
Abinsk Rus. Fed. 90 E1
Abitau Lake Canada 121 J2
Abitibi, Lake Canada 122 E4
Ab Khūr Iran 88 E3
Abminga Australia 109 F6
Abnūb Egypt 90 C6
Åbo Fin. *see* Turku
Abohar India 82 C3
Aboisso Côte d'Ivoire 96 C4
Aboite U.S.A. 134 C3
Abomey Benin 96 D4
Abongabong, Gunung *mt.* Indon. 71 B6
Abong Mbang Cameroon 96 E4
Abou Déia Chad 97 E3
Abovyan Armenia 91 G2
Aboyne U.K. 50 G3
Abqaiq Saudi Arabia 88 C5
Abraham's Bay Bahamas 133 F8
Abramov, Mys *pt* Rus. Fed. 42 I2
Abrantes Port. 57 B4
Abra Pampa Arg. 144 C2
Abreojos, Punta *pt* Mex. 127 E8
'Abri Sudan 86 D5
Abrolhos Bank *sea feature* S. Atlantic Ocean 148 F7
Abruzzo, Parco Nazionale d' *nat. park* Italy 58 E4
Absalom, Mount Antarctica 152 B1
Absaroka Range *mts* U.S.A. 126 F3
Abtar, Jabal al *hills* Syria 85 C2
Abtsgmünd Germany 53 J6
Abū aḍ Ḍuhūr Syria 85 C2
Abū al Abyaḍ *i.* U.A.E. 88 D5
Abū al Ḥusayn, Qā' *imp. l.* Jordan 85 D3
Abū 'Alī *i.* Saudi Arabia 88 C5
Abū 'Āmūd, Wādī *watercourse* Jordan 85 C4
Abū 'Arīsh Saudi Arabia 86 F6
Abu 'Aweigīla *well* Egypt *see* Abū 'Uwayqilah
Abu Deleiq Sudan 86 D6

▶Abu Dhabi U.A.E. 88 D5
Capital of the United Arab Emirates.

Abū Du'ān Syria 85 D1
Abu Gubeiha Sudan 86 D7
Abū Ḥafnah, Wādī *watercourse* Jordan 85 D3
Abu Haggag Egypt *see* Ra's al Ḥikmah
Abū Ḥallūfah, Jabal *hill* Jordan 85 C4
Abu Hamed Sudan 86 D6

▶Abuja Nigeria 96 D4
Capital of Nigeria.

Abū Jifān *well* Saudi Arabia 88 B5
Abū Jurdhān Jordan 85 B4
Abū Kamāl Syria 91 F4
Abu Matariq Sudan 97 F3
Abumombazi Dem. Rep. Congo 98 C3
Abu Musa *i.* The Gulf 88 D5
Abū Mūsá, Jazīreh-ye *i.* The Gulf *see* Abu Musa
Abunã *r.* Bol. 142 E5
Abunã Brazil 142 E5
Ābune Yosēf *mt.* Eth. 86 E7
Abū Nujaym Libya 97 E1
Abū Qa'ṭūr Syria 85 C2
Abū Rawthah, Jabal *mt.* Egypt 85 B5
Aburo *mt.* Dem. Rep. Congo 98 D3
Abu Road India 79 G4
Abū Rujmayn, Jabal *mts* Syria 85 D2
Abu Rûtha, Gebel *mt.* Egypt *see* Abū Rawthah, Jabal
Abū Sawādah *well* Saudi Arabia 88 C5
Abu Simbil Egypt *see* Abū Sunbul
Abū Sunbul Egypt 86 D5
Abū Ṭarfā', Wādī *watercourse* Egypt 85 A5
Abut Head *hd* N.Z. 113 C6
Abū 'Uwayqilah *well* Egypt 85 B4
Abu Zabad Sudan 86 C7
Abū Ẓabī U.A.E. *see* Abu Dhabi
Abūzam Iran 88 C4
Abū Zanīmah Egypt 90 D5
Abu Zenîma Egypt *see* Abū Zanīmah
Abyad Sudan 86 C7
Abyaḍ, Jabal al *mts* Syria 85 C2
Abyār al Hakīm *well* Libya 90 A5
Abydos Australia 108 B5
Abyei Sudan 86 C8
Abyssinia *country* Africa *see* Ethiopia
Academician Vernadskiy *research station* Antarctica *see* Vernadsky
Academy Bay Rus. Fed. *see* Akademii, Zaliv
Acadia *prov.* Canada *see* Nova Scotia
Acadia National Park U.S.A. 132 G2
Açailândia Brazil 143 I5
Acamarachi *mt.* Chile *see* Pili, Cerro
Acampamento de Caça do Mucusso Angola 99 C5
Acandí Col. 142 C2
A Cañiza Spain 57 B2
Acaponeta Mex. 136 C4
Acapulco Mex. 136 E5
Acapulco de Juárez Mex. *see* Acapulco
Acará Brazil 143 I4
Acarai Mountains *hills* Brazil/Guyana 143 G3
Acaraú Brazil 143 J4
Acaray, Represa de *resr* Para. 144 E3
Acarigua Venez. 142 E2
Acatlán Mex. 136 E5
Accho Israel *see* 'Akko
Accomac U.S.A. 135 H5
Accomack U.S.A. *see* Accomac

▶Accra Ghana 96 C4
Capital of Ghana.

Accrington U.K. 48 E5
Ach *r.* Germany 53 L6
Achacachi Bol. 142 E7
Achaguas Venez. 142 E2
Achalpur India 82 D5
Achampet India 84 C2
Achan Rus. Fed. 74 E2
Achayvayam Rus. Fed. 65 S3
Acheng China 74 B3
Achhota India 84 D1
Achicourt France 52 C4
Achill Ireland 51 C4
Achillbeg Island Ireland 51 C4
Achill Island Ireland 51 B4
Achiltibuie U.K. 50 D2
Achim Germany 53 J1
Achinsk Rus. Fed. 64 K4
Achit Rus. Fed. 41 R4
Achit Nuur *l.* Mongolia 80 H2
Achkhoy-Martan Rus. Fed. 91 G2
Achna Cyprus 85 A2
Achnasheen U.K. 50 D3
Acıgöl *l.* Turkey 59 M6
Acıpayam Turkey 59 M6
Acireale *Sicily* Italy 58 F6
Ackerman U.S.A. 131 F5
Ackley U.S.A. 130 E3
Acklins Island Bahamas 133 F8
Acle U.K. 49 I6

▶Aconcagua, Cerro *mt.* Arg. 144 B4
Highest mountain in South America.

Acopiara Brazil 143 K5
A Coruña Spain 57 B2
Acqui Terme Italy 58 C2
Acra U.S.A. 135 H2
Acragas *Sicily* Italy *see* Agrigento
Acraman, Lake *salt flat* Australia 111 A7
Acre *r.* Brazil 142 E6
Acre Israel *see* 'Akko
Acre, Bay of Israel *see* Haifa, Bay of
Acri Italy 58 G5
Ács Hungary 47 Q7
Actaeon Group *is* Fr. Polynesia *see* Actéon, Groupe
Actéon, Groupe *is* Fr. Polynesia 151 K7
Acton Canada 134 E2
Acton U.S.A. 128 D4
Acungui Brazil 145 A4
Acunum Acusio France *see* Montélimar
Ada *MN* U.S.A. 130 D2
Ada *OH* U.S.A. 134 D3
Ada *OK* U.S.A. 131 D5
Ada *WI* U.S.A. 134 B2
Adabazar *Sakarya* Turkey *see* Adapazarı
Adaja *r.* Spain 57 D3
Adalia Turkey *see* Antalya
Adam Oman 87 I5
Adam, Mount *hill* Falkland Is 144 E8
Adamantina Brazil 145 A3
Adams *IN* U.S.A. 134 C4
Adams *KY* U.S.A. 134 D4
Adams *MA* U.S.A. 135 I2
Adams *NY* U.S.A. 135 G2
Adams, Mount U.S.A. 126 C3
Adams Center U.S.A. 135 G2
Adams Lake Canada 120 G5
Adams Mountain U.S.A. 120 D4
Adam's Peak Sri Lanka 84 D5
Adams Peak U.S.A. 128 C2

▶Adamstown Pitcairn Is 151 L7
Capital of the Pitcairn Islands.

'Adan Yemen *see* Aden
Adana Turkey 85 B1
Adana *prov.* Turkey 85 B1
Adana Yemen *see* Aden
Adapazarı Turkey 59 N4
Adare Ireland 51 D5
Adare, Cape Antarctica 152 H2
Adavale Australia 111 D5
Adban Afgh. 89 H2
Ad Dabbah Sudan *see* Ed Debba
Ad Ḍabbīyah *well* Saudi Arabia 88 C5
Ad Dafīnah Saudi Arabia 86 F5
Ad Dahnā' *des.* Saudi Arabia 86 G5
Ad Dakhla W. Sahara 96 B2
Ad Damir Sudan *see* Ed Damer
Ad Dammām Saudi Arabia *see* Dammam
Addanki India 84 C3
Ad Dār al Ḥamrā' Saudi Arabia 86 E4
Ad Darb Saudi Arabia 86 F6
Ad Dawādimī Saudi Arabia 86 F5
Ad Dawḥah Qatar *see* Doha
Ad Dawr Iraq 91 F4
Ad Daww *plain* Syria 85 C2
Ad Dayr Iraq 91 G5
Ad Dibdibah *plain* Saudi Arabia 88 B5
Aḍ Ḍiffah *plat.* Egypt *see* Libyan Plateau

▶Addis Ababa Eth. 98 D3
Capital of Ethiopia.

Addison U.S.A. 135 G2
Ad Dīwānīyah Iraq 91 G5
Addlestone U.K. 49 G7
Addo Elephant National Park S. Africa 101 G7
Addoo Atoll Maldives *see* Addu Atoll
Addu Atoll Maldives 81 D12
Ad Duwayd *well* Saudi Arabia 91 F5
Ad Duwaym Sudan *see* Ed Dueim
Ad Duwayris *well* Saudi Arabia 88 C6
Adegaon India 82 D5
Adel *GA* U.S.A. 133 D6
Adel *IA* U.S.A. 130 E3

▶Adelaide Australia 111 B7
Capital of South Australia.

Adelaide *r.* Australia 108 E3
Adelaide Bahamas 133 E7
Adelaide Island Antarctica 152 L2
Adelaide River Australia 108 E3
Adele Island Australia 108 C3
Adélie Coast Antarctica 152 G2
Adélie Land *reg.* Antarctica 152 G2
Adelong Australia 112 D5
Aden Yemen 86 F7
Aden, Gulf of Somalia/Yemen 86 G7
Adena U.S.A. 134 E3
Adenau Germany 52 G4
Adendorf Germany 53 K1
Aderbissinat Niger 96 D3
Aderno *Sicily* Italy *see* Adrano
Adesar India 82 B5
Adhan, Jabal *mt.* U.A.E. 88 E5
Adh Dhāyūf *well* Saudi Arabia 91 G6
'Adhfā' *well* Saudi Arabia 91 F5
'Ādhirīyāt, Jibāl al *mts* Jordan 85 C4
Adi *i.* Indon. 69 I7
Ādī Ārk'ay Eth. 86 E7
Adige *r.* Italy 58 E2
Ādīgrat Eth. 98 D2
Adilabad India 84 C2
Adilcevaz Turkey 91 F3
Adin U.S.A. 126 C4
Adīrī Libya 97 E2
Adirondack Mountains U.S.A. 135 H1
Ādīs Ābeba Eth. *see* Addis Ababa
Adi Ugri Eritrea *see* Mendefera
Adıyaman Turkey 90 E3
Adjud Romania 59 L1
Adlavik Islands Canada 123 K3
Admiralty Island Canada 119 H3
Admiralty Island U.S.A. 120 C3
Admiralty Island National Monument-Kootznoowoo Wilderness *nat. park* U.S.A. 120 C3
Admiralty Islands P.N.G. 69 L7
Ado-Ekiti Nigeria 96 D4
Adok Sudan 86 D8
Adolfo L. Mateos Mex. 127 E8
Adolphus U.S.A. 134 B5
Adonara *i.* Indon. 108 C2
Adoni India 84 C3
Adorf Germany 53 M4
Adorf (Diemelsee) Germany 53 I3
Ado-Tymovo Rus. Fed. 74 F2
Adour *r.* France 56 D5
Adra Spain 57 E5
Adramyttium Turkey *see* Edremit
Adramyttium, Gulf of Turkey *see* Edremit Körfezi
Adrano *Sicily* Italy 58 F6
Adrar Alg. 96 C2
Adrar *hills* Mali *see* Ifôghas, Adrar des
Adraskand *r.* Afgh. 89 F3
Adré Chad 97 F3
Adrian *MI* U.S.A. 134 C3
Adrian *TX* U.S.A. 131 C5
Adrianople Turkey *see* Edirne
Adrianopolis Turkey *see* Edirne
Adriatic Sea Europe 58 E2
Adua Eth. *see* Ādwa
Adunara *i.* Indon. *see* Adonara
Adusa Dem. Rep. Congo 98 C3
Aduwa Eth. *see* Ādwa
Adverse Well Australia 108 C5
Ādwa Eth. 98 D2
Adycha *r.* Rus. Fed. 65 O3
Adyk Rus. Fed. 43 J7
Adzopé Côte d'Ivoire 96 C4
Aegean Sea Greece/Turkey 59 K5
Aegina *i.* Greece *see* Aigina
Aegyptus *country* Africa *see* Egypt
Aela Jordan *see* Al 'Aqabah
Aelana Jordan *see* Al 'Aqabah
Aelia Capitolina Israel/West Bank *see* Jerusalem
Aelönlaplap *atoll* Marshall Is *see* Ailinglaplap
Aenus Turkey *see* Enez
Aerzen Germany 53 J2
Aesernia Italy *see* Isernia
A Estrada Spain 57 B2
Afabet Eritrea 86 E6
Afanas'yevo Rus. Fed. 42 L4
Affreville Alg. *see* Khemis Miliana
Afghānestān *country* Asia *see* Afghanistan
Afghanistan *country* Asia 89 G3
Afgooye Somalia 98 E3
'Afīf Saudi Arabia 86 F5
Afiun Karahissar Turkey *see* Afyon
Åfjord Norway 44 G5
Aflou Alg. 54 E5
Afmadow Somalia 98 E3
Afogados da Ingazoira Brazil 143 K5
A Fonsagrada Spain 57 C2
Afonso Cláudio Brazil 145 C3
Āfrēra Terara *vol.* Eth. 86 F7
Africa Nova *country* Africa *see* Tunisia
'Afrīn Syria 85 C1
'Afrīn, Nahr *r.* Syria/Turkey 85 C1
Afşin Turkey 90 E3
Afsluitdijk *barrage* Neth. 52 F2
Afton U.S.A. 126 F4
Afuá Brazil 143 H4
'Afula Israel 85 B3
Afyon Turkey 59 N5
Afyonkarahisar Turkey *see* Afyon
Aga Germany 53 M4
Agadès Niger *see* Agadez
Agadez Niger 96 D3
Agadir Morocco 96 C1
Agadyr' Kazakh. 80 D2
Agalega Islands Mauritius 149 L6
Agana Guam *see* Hagåtña
Agara Georgia 91 F2
Agartala India 83 G5
Agashi India 84 B2
Agate Canada 122 E4
Agathe France *see* Agde
Agathonisi *i.* Greece 59 L6
Agats Indon. 69 J8
Agatti *i.* India 84 B4
Agboville Côte d'Ivoire 96 C4
Ağcabädi Azer. 91 G2
Ağdam Azer. 91 G3
Ağdaş Azer. 91 G2
Agdash Azer. *see* Ağdaş
Agde France 56 F5
Agdzhabedi Azer. *see* Ağcabädi
Agedabia Libya *see* Ajdābiyā
Agen France 56 E4
Aggeneys S. Africa 100 D5
Aggteleki *nat. park* Hungary 47 R6
Aghil Pass China 82 D1
Agiabampo Mex. 127 F8
Agiguan *i.* N. Mariana Is *see* Aguijan
Ağın Turkey 90 E3
Aginskoye Rus. Fed. 72 G1
Aginum France *see* Agen
Agios Dimitrios Greece 59 J6
Agios Efstratios *i.* Greece 59 K5
Agios Georgios *i.* Greece 59 J6
Agios Nikolaos Greece 59 K7
Agios Theodoros Cyprus 85 B2
Agiou Orous, Kolpos *b.* Greece 59 J4
Agirwat Hills Sudan 86 E6
Agisanang S. Africa 101 G4
Agnes, Mount *hill* Australia 109 E6
Agnew Australia 109 C6
Agnibilékrou Côte d'Ivoire 96 C4
Agnita Romania 59 K2
Agniye-Afanas'yevsk Rus. Fed. 74 E2
Agra India 82 D4
Agrakhanskiy Poluostrov *pen.* Rus. Fed. 91 G2
Agram Croatia *see* Zagreb
Ağrı Turkey 91 F3
Agria Gramvousa *i.* Greece 59 J7
Agrigan *i.* N. Mariana Is *see* Agrihan
Agrigento *Sicily* Italy 58 E6
Agrigentum *Sicily* Italy *see* Agrigento
Agrihan *i.* N. Mariana Is 69 L3
Agrinio Greece 59 I5
Agropoli Italy 58 F4
Agryz Rus. Fed. 41 Q4
Ağsu Azer. 91 H2
Agua, Volcán de *vol.* Guat. 136 F6
Água Clara Brazil 144 F2
Aguadilla Puerto Rico 137 K5
Agua Escondida Arg. 144 C5
Agua Fria *r.* U.S.A. 129 G5
Agua Fria National Monument *nat. park* U.S.A. 129 G4
Aguanaval *r.* Mex. 131 C7
Aguanga U.S.A. 128 E5
Aguanish *r.* Canada 123 J4
Aguapeí *r.* Brazil 145 A3
Agua Prieta Mex. 127 F7
Aguaro-Guariquito, Parque Nacional *nat. park* Venez. 142 E2
Aguascalientes Mex. 136 D4
Agudos Brazil 145 A3
Águeda Port. 57 B3
Aguemour *reg.* Alg. 96 D2
Aguié Niger 96 D3
Aguijan *i.* N. Mariana Is 69 L4
Aguilar U.S.A. 127 G5
Aguilar de Campóo Spain 57 D2
Águilas Spain 57 F5

▶Agulhas, Cape S. Africa 100 E8
Most southerly point of Africa.

Agulhas Basin *sea feature* Southern Ocean 149 J9
Agulhas Negras *mt.* Brazil 145 B3
Agulhas Plateau *sea feature* Southern Ocean 149 J8
Agulhas Ridge *sea feature* S. Atlantic Ocean 148 I8
Ağva Turkey 59 M4
Agvali Rus. Fed. 91 G2
Ahaggar *plat.* Alg. *see* Hoggar
Āhangarān Iran 89 F3
Ahar Iran 88 B2
Ahaura N.Z. 113 C6
Ahaus Germany 52 H2
Ahipara Bay N.Z. 113 D2
Ahiri India 84 D2
Ahklun Mountains U.S.A. 118 B4
Ahlen Germany 53 H3
Ahmadabad India 82 C5
Aḥmadābād Iran 89 E3
Aḥmad al Bāqir, Jabal *mt.* Jordan 85 B5
Aḥmadī Iran 88 E5
Ahmadnagar India 84 B2
Ahmadpur East Pak. 89 H4
Ahmar *mts* Eth. 98 E3
Ahmar Mountains Eth. *see* Ahmar
Ahmedabad India *see* Ahmadabad
Ahmednagar India *see* Ahmadnagar
Ahorn Germany 53 K4
Ahr *r.* Germany 52 H4
Ahram Iran 88 C4
Ahrensburg Germany 53 K1
Ähtäri Fin. 44 N5
Ahtme Estonia 45 O7
Ahu China 77 H1
Āhū Iran 88 C4
Ahun France 56 F3
Ahuzhen China *see* Ahu
Ahvāz Iran 88 C4
Ahwa India 84 B1
Ahwāz Iran *see* Ahvāz
Ai-Ais Namibia 100 C4
Ai-Ais Hot Springs Game Park *nature res.* Namibia 100 C4
Aichwara India 82 D4
Aid U.S.A. 134 D4
Aigialousa Cyprus 85 B2
Aigina *i.* Greece 59 J6
Aigio Greece 59 J5
Aigle de Chambeyron *mt.* France 56 H4
Aigües Tortes i Estany de Sant Maurici, Parc Nacional d' *nat. park* Spain 57 G2
Ai He *r.* China 74 B4
Aihua China *see* Yunxian
Aihui China *see* Heihe
Aijal India *see* Aizawl
Aikawa Japan 75 E5
Aiken U.S.A. 133 D5
Ailao Shan *mts* China 76 D3
Aileron Australia 108 F5
Ailinglabelab *atoll* Marshall Is *see* Ailinglaplap
Ailinglaplap *atoll* Marshall Is 150 H5
Ailly-sur-Noye France 52 C5
Ailsa Craig Canada 134 E2
Ailsa Craig *i.* U.K. 50 D5
Ailt an Chorráin Ireland 51 D3
Aimangala India 84 C3
Aimorés, Serra dos *hills* Brazil 145 C2
Aïn Beïda Alg. 58 B7
'Aïn Ben Tili Mauritania 96 C2
'Ain Dâlla *spring* Egypt *see* 'Ayn Dällah
Aïn Defla Alg. 57 H5
Aïn Deheb Alg. 57 G6
Aïn el Hadjel Alg. 57 H6
'Ain el Maqfi *spring* Egypt *see* 'Ayn al Ma…
Aïn el Melh Alg. 57 I6
Aïn Mdila *well* Alg. 58 B7
Aïn-M'Lila Alg. 54 F4
Aïn Oussera Alg. 57 H6
Ain Salah Alg. *see* In Salah
Aïn Sefra Alg. 54 D5
Ainsworth U.S.A. 130 D3
Aintab Turkey *see* Gaziantep
Aïn Taya Alg. 57 H5
Aïn Tédélès Alg. 57 G6
Aïn Temouchent Alg. 57 F6
'Ain Tibaghbagh *spring* Egypt *see* 'Ayn Tabaghbugh
'Ain Timeira *spring* Egypt *see* 'Ayn Tumay…
'Ain Zeitûn Egypt *see* 'Ayn Zaytūn
Aiquile Bol. 142 E7
Air *i.* Indon. 71 D7
Airaines France 52 B5
Airdrie Canada 120 H5
Airdrie U.K. 50 F5
Aire *r.* France 52 E5
Aire, Canal d' France 52 C4
Aire-sur-l'Adour France 56 D5
Air Force Island Canada 119 K3
Airpanas Indon. 108 D1
Aisatung Mountain Myanmar 70 A2
Aisch *r.* Germany 53 L5
Aishihik Canada 120 B2
Aishihik Lake Canada 120 B2
Aisne *r.* France 52 C5
Aïssa, Djebel *mt.* Alg. 54 D5
Aitamännikkö Fin. 44 N3
Aitana *mt.* Spain 57 F4
Aït Benhaddou *tourist site* Morocco 54 …
Aiterach *r.* Germany 53 M6
Aitkin U.S.A. 130 E2
Aiud Romania 59 J1
Aix France *see* Aix-en-Provence
Aix-en-Provence France 56 G5
Aix-la-Chapelle Germany *see* Aachen
Aix-les-Bains France 56 G4
Aíyina *i.* Greece *see* Aigina
Aíyion Greece *see* Aigio
Aizawl India 83 H5
Aizkraukle Latvia 45 N8
Aizpute Latvia 45 L8
Aizu-Wakamatsu Japan 75 E5
Ajaccio *Corsica* France 56 I6
Ajanta India 84 B1
Ajanta Range *hills* India *see* Sahyadriparvat Range
Ajaureforsen Sweden 44 I4
Ajax Canada 134 F2
Ajayameru India *see* Ajmer
Ajban U.A.E. 88 D5
Aj Bogd Uul *mt.* Mongolia 80 I3
Ajdābiyā Libya 97 F1
a-Jiddét *des.* Oman *see* Ḥarāsīs, Jiddat a…
'Ajlūn Jordan 85 B3
'Ajman U.A.E. 88 D5
Ajmer India 82 C4
Ajmer-Merwara India *see* Ajmer
Ajnala India 82 C3
Ajo U.S.A. 129 G5
Ajo, Mount U.S.A. 129 G5
Ajrestan Afgh. 89 G3
Ajyyap Turkm. 88 D2
Akademii, Zaliv *b.* Rus. Fed. 74 E1
Akademii Nauk, Khrebet *mt.* Tajik. *see* Akademiyai Fanho, Qatorkŭhi
Akademiyai Fanho, Qatorkŭhi *mt.* Tajik. 89 H2
Akagera National Park Rwanda 98 D4
Akalkot India 84 C2
Akama, Akra *c.* Cyprus *see* Arnauti, Cape
Akamagaseki Japan *see* Shimonoseki
Akan Kokuritsu-kōen *nat. park* Japan 74…
Akaroa N.Z. 113 D6
Akas *reg.* India 76 B3
Akāshat Iraq 91 E4
Akbarābād Iran 91 I5
Akbarpur *Uttar Prad.* India 82 E4
Akbarpur *Uttar Prad.* India 83 E4
Akbaytal, Pereval *pass* Tajik. 89 I2
Akbaytal Pass Tajik. *see* Akbaytal, Pereva…
Akbez Turkey 85 C1
Akçadağ Turkey 90 E3
Akçakale Turkey 85 D1
Akçakoca Turkey 59 N4
Akçakoca Dağları *mts* Turkey 59 N4
Akçakoyunlu Turkey 85 C1
Akçalı Dağları *mts* Turkey 85 A1
Akchâr *reg.* Mauritania 96 B3
Akchi Kazakh. *see* Akshiy
Akdağlar *mts* Turkey 59 M6
Akdağmadeni Turkey 90 D3
Akdere Turkey 85 A1
Akelamo Indon. 69 H6
Åkersberga Sweden 45 K7
Akersloot Neth. 52 E2
Aketi Dem. Rep. Congo 98 C3
Akgyr Erezi *hills* Turkm. 88 D1
Akhali-Afoni Georgia *see* Akhali Ap'oni
Akhali Ap'oni Georgia 91 F2
Akhḍar, Al Jabal al *mts* Libya 97 F1
Akhḍar, Jabal *mts* Oman 88 E6
Akhisar Turkey 59 L5
Akhnoor India 82 C2
Akhsu Azer. *see* Ağsu
Akhta Armenia *see* Hrazdan
Akhtarīn Syria 85 C1
Akhtubinsk Rus. Fed. 43 J6
Akhty Rus. Fed. 91 G2
Akhtyrka Ukr. *see* Okhtyrka
Aki Japan 75 D6
Akiéni Gabon 98 B4
Akimiski Island Canada 122 E3
Akishma *r.* Rus. Fed. 74 D1
Akita Japan 75 F5
Akjoujt Mauritania 96 B3
Akkajaure *l.* Sweden 44 J3
Akkerman Ukr. *see* Bilhorod-Dnistrovs'k…
Akkeshi Japan 74 G4
'Akko Israel 85 B3
Akkol' *Akmolinskaya Oblast'* Kazakh. 80 …
Akkol' *Atyrauskaya Oblast'* Kazakh. 43 K…

ku Kazakh. 80 E1
kul' Kazakh. see Akkol'
kuş Turkey 90 E2
kyr, Gory hills Turkm. see Akgyr Erezi
lavik Canada 118 E3
lera India 82 D4
-Mechet Kazakh. see Kyzylorda
menrags pt Latvia 45 L8
meqit China 82 D1
mola Kazakh. see Astana
molinsk Kazakh. see Astana
obo Sudan 97 G4
obo Wenz r. Eth./Sudan 98 D3
okan Niger 96 D3
ola India 84 C1
om II Cameroon 96 E4
onolinga Cameroon 96 E4
ordat Eritrea 86 E6
ören Turkey 90 D3
ot India 82 D5
patok Island Canada 123 I1
qi China 80 E3
ra, Jabal mt. Syria/Turkey see
Aqra', Jabal al
ranes Iceland 44 [inset]
rehamn Norway 45 D7
rérèb Niger 96 D3
ron CO U.S.A. 130 C3
ron IN U.S.A. 134 B3
ron OH U.S.A. 134 E3
rotiri Bay Cyprus 85 A2
rotirion Bay Cyprus see Akrotiri Bay
rotiriou, Kolpos b. Cyprus see
Akrotiri Bay
rotiri Sovereign Base Area military base
Cyprus 85 A2

Aksai Chin terr. Asia 82 D2
Disputed territory (China/India).

saray Turkey 90 D3
say China 80 H4
say Kazakh. 41 Q5
-Say r. Kyrg. 87 M1
say Rus. Fed. 43 H7
şehir Turkey 59 N5
şehir Gölü l. Turkey 59 N5
seki Turkey 90 C3
sha Rus. Fed. 73 K2
shiganak Kazakh. 80 B2
shiy Kazakh. 80 E3
shukur Kazakh. 91 H2
su China 80 F3
su Kazakh. 80 E1
su r. Tajik. see Oqsu
su r. Turkey 59 N6
suat Kazakh. 80 F2
su-Ayuly Kazakh. 80 D2
subayevo Rus. Fed. 43 K5
sum Eth. 86 E7
tag mt. China 83 F1
tas Dağı mt. Turkey 91 G3
tau Kazakh. 78 E2
to China 89 J2
tobe Kazakh. 78 E1
togay Karagandinskaya Oblast' Kazakh.
80 E2
togay Vostochnyy Kazakhstan Kazakh.
80 E2
tsyabrski Belarus 43 F5
tyubinsk Kazakh. see Aktobe
ulivik Canada 119 K3
une Japan 75 C6
ure Nigeria 96 D4
uressa Sri Lanka 84 D5
ureyri Iceland 44 [inset]
usha Rus. Fed. 43 J8
wanga Nigeria 96 D4
xokesay China 83 G1
yab Myanmar see Sittwe
yatan Gölü salt l. Turkey 85 B1
yazı Turkey 59 N4
zhaykyn, Ozero salt l. Kazakh. 80 C3
Norway 45 F6
, Jabal al hills Syria 85 C2
bama r. U.S.A. 133 C6
bama state U.S.A. 133 C5
baster AL U.S.A. 133 C5
baster MI U.S.A. 134 D1
'Abţīyah well Iraq 91 G5
ca Turkey 90 D2
cahan Turkey 90 E3
çam Turkey 90 D2
çam Dağları mts Turkey 59 M5
cant Valencia Spain see Alicante
çatı Turkey 59 L5
dağ Turkey 90 D3
Dağlar mts Turkey 91 F3
Dağları mts Turkey 90 D3
'Adam Libya 90 A5
'er China 80 F3
Aflāj reg. Saudi Arabia 88 B6
g Hu l. China 76 C1
gir Rus. Fed. 91 G2
goinhas Brazil 145 D1
härmä Fin. 44 M5
Aḩmadī Kuwait 88 C4
Range mts Asia 89 H2
ivān Iran 88 D3
jah Syria 85 B2
järvi Fin. 44 M5
Ajrūd well Egypt 85 B4
kanuk U.S.A. 118 B3
Akhḑar Saudi Arabia 90 E5
kol', Ozero salt l. Kazakh. 80 F2
Kul salt l. Kazakh. see Alakol', Ozero
kurtti Rus. Fed. 44 Q3
Alamayn Egypt 90 C5
Alayyah Saudi Arabia 86 F6
ma Somalia 98 E3
Amādīyah Iraq 91 F3
magan i. N. Mariana Is 69 L3
maguan i. N. Mariana Is see Alamagan
Amārah Iraq 91 G5
m ar Rūm, Ra's pt Egypt 90 B5
marvdasht watercourse Iran 88 D4
meda U.S.A. 128 B3
m el Rûm, Râs pt Egypt see
Alam ar Rūm, Ra's
Amghar waterhole Iraq 91 G5
Āmirīyah Egypt 90 C5
mitos, Sierra de los mt. Mex. 131 C7

Alamo GA U.S.A. 133 D5
Alamo NV U.S.A. 129 F3
Alamo Dam U.S.A. 129 G4
Alamogordo U.S.A. 127 G6
Alamo Heights U.S.A. 131 D6
Alamos Sonora Mex. 127 F7
Alamos Sonora Mex. 127 F8
Alamos r. Mex. 131 C7
Alamos, Sierra mts Mex. 127 F8
Alamosa U.S.A. 127 G5
Alamos de Peña Mex. 127 G7
Alampur India 84 C3
Alan Myanmar see Aunglan
Alanäs Sweden 44 I4
Åland is Fin. see Åland Islands
Aland r. Germany 53 L1
Aland India 84 C2
Al Andarīn Syria 85 C2
Åland Islands Fin. 45 K6
Alando China 76 B2
Alandur India 84 D3
Alanson U.S.A. 134 C1
Alanya Turkey 90 D3
Alapli Turkey 59 N4
Alappuzha India see Alleppey
Alapuzha India see Alleppey
Al 'Aqabah Jordan 85 B5
Al 'Aqīq Saudi Arabia 86 F5
Al 'Arabīyah as Sa'ūdīyah country Asia see
Saudi Arabia
Alarcón, Embalse de resr Spain 57 E4
Al 'Arīsh Egypt 85 A4
Al Arţāwīyah Saudi Arabia 86 G4
Alas, Selat sea chan. Indon. 108 B2
Alaşehir Turkey 59 M5
Alashiya country Asia see Cyprus
Al Ashmūnayn Egypt 90 C6
Alaska state U.S.A. 118 D3
Alaska, Gulf of U.S.A. 118 D4
Alaska Highway Canada/U.S.A. 120 A2
Alaska Peninsula U.S.A. 118 B4
Alaska Range mts U.S.A. 118 D3
Älät Azer. 91 H3
Alat Uzbek. see Olot
Alataw Shankou pass China/Kazakh. see
Dzungarian Gate
Al Atwā' well Saudi Arabia 91 F5
Alatyr' Rus. Fed. 43 J5
Alatyr' r. Rus. Fed. 43 J5
Alausí Ecuador 142 C4
Alaverdi Armenia 91 G2
'Alavī Iran 88 C3
Alavieska Fin. 44 N4
Alavus Fin. 44 M5
Alawbum Myanmar 70 B1
Alawoona Australia 111 C7
Alay Kyrka Toosu mts Asia see Alai Range
Al 'Ayn Oman 88 E6
Al 'Ayn U.A.E. 88 D5
Alayskiy Khrebet mts Asia see Alai Range
Al 'Azīzīyah Iraq 91 G4

▶Al 'Azīzīyah Libya 55 G5
Highest recorded shade temperature in the world.

Al Azraq al Janūbī Jordan 85 C4
Alba Italy 58 C2
Alba U.S.A. 134 C1
Al Bāb Syria 85 C1
Albacete Spain 57 F4
Al Badī' Saudi Arabia 88 B6
Al Bādiyah al Janūbīyah hill Iraq 91 G5
Al Bahrayn country Asia see Bahrain
Alba Iulia Romania 59 J1
Al Bajā' well U.A.E. 88 C5
Albājī Iran 88 C4
Al Bakhrā well Saudi Arabia 88 B5
Albanel, Lac l. Canada 123 G4
Albania country Europe 59 H4
Albany Australia 109 B8
Albany r. Canada 122 E3
Albany GA U.S.A. 133 C6
Albany IN U.S.A. 134 C3
Albany KY U.S.A. 134 C5
Albany MO U.S.A. 130 E3

▶Albany NY U.S.A. 135 I2
Capital of New York state.

Albany OH U.S.A. 134 D4
Albany OR U.S.A. 126 C3
Albany TX U.S.A. 131 D5
Albany Downs Australia 112 D1
Albardão do João Maria coastal area Brazil
144 F4
Al Bardī Libya 90 B5
Al Bāridah hills Saudi Arabia 85 D5
Al Başrah Iraq see Basra
Al Baţḩa' marsh Iraq 91 G5
Al Bāţinah reg. Oman 88 E5
Albatross Bay Australia 110 C2
Albatross Island Australia 111 [inset]
Al Bawīţī Egypt 90 C6
Al Bayḑā' Libya 86 B3
Al Bayḑā' Yemen 86 G7
Albemarle U.S.A. 133 D5
Albemarle Island Galápagos Ecuador see
Isabela, Isla
Albemarle Sound sea chan. U.S.A. 132 E5
Albenga Italy 58 C2
Alberche r. Spain 57 D4
Alberga Australia 111 A5
Alberga watercourse Australia 111 A5
Albergaria-a-Velha Port. 57 B3
Albert Australia 112 C4
Albert France 52 C5
Albert, Lake Dem. Rep. Congo/Uganda
98 D3
Albert, Parc National nat. park
Dem. Rep. Congo see
Virunga, Parc National des
Alberta prov. Canada 120 H4
Alberta U.S.A. 135 G5
Albert Kanaal canal Belgium 52 F4
Albert Lea U.S.A. 130 E3
Albert Nile r. Sudan/Uganda 97 G4
Alberto de Agostini, Parque Nacional
nat. park Chile 144 B8
Alberton S. Africa 101 I4
Alberton U.S.A. 126 E3
Albert Town Bahamas 133 F8

Albertville Dem. Rep. Congo see Kalemie
Albertville France 56 H4
Albertville U.S.A. 133 C5
Albestroff France 52 G6
Albi France 56 F5
Albia U.S.A. 130 E3
Al Biḑah des. Saudi Arabia 88 C5
Albina Suriname 143 H2
Albino Italy 58 C2
Albion CA U.S.A. 128 B2
Albion IL U.S.A. 130 F4
Albion IN U.S.A. 134 C3
Albion MI U.S.A. 134 C2
Albion NE U.S.A. 130 D3
Albion NY U.S.A. 135 F2
Albion PA U.S.A. 134 E3
Al Biqā' valley Lebanon see El Béqaa
Al Bi'r Saudi Arabia 90 E5
Al Birk Saudi Arabia 86 F6
Al Biyāḑh reg. Saudi Arabia 86 G5
Alborán, Isla de i. Spain 57 E6
Ålborg Denmark see Aalborg
Ålborg Bugt b. Denmark see
Aalborg Bugt
Albro Australia 110 D4
Al Budayyi' Bahrain 88 C5
Albufeira Port. 57 B5
Al Buḩayrāt al Murrah lakes Egypt see
Bitter Lakes
Albuquerque U.S.A. 127 G6
Al Burayj Syria 85 C2
Al Buraymī Oman 88 D5
Al Burj Jordan 85 B5
Alburquerque Spain 57 C4
Albury Australia 112 C6
Al Buşayrah Syria 91 F4
Al Busayţā' plain Saudi Arabia 85 D4
Al Bushūk well Saudi Arabia 88 B4
Alcácer do Sal Port. 57 B4
Alcalá de Henares Spain 57 E3
Alcalá la Real Spain 57 E5
Alcamo Sicily Italy 58 E6
Alcañiz Spain 57 F3
Alcántara Spain 57 C4
Alcantara Lake Canada 121 I2
Alcaraz Spain 57 E4
Alcázar de San Juan Spain 57 E4
Alcazarquivir Morocco see Ksar el Kebir
Alchevs'k Ukr. 43 H6
Alcobaça Brazil 145 D2
Alcoi Spain see Alcoy-Alcoi
Alcoota Australia 108 F5
Alcova U.S.A. 126 G4
Alcoy Spain see Alcoy-Alcoi
Alcoy-Alcoi Spain 57 F4
Alcúdia Spain 57 H4
Aldabra Islands Seychelles 99 E4
Aldan Rus. Fed. 65 N4
Aldan r. Rus. Fed. 65 N3
Alde r. U.K. 49 I6
Aldeboarn Neth. 52 F1
Aldeburgh U.K. 49 I6
Alder Creek U.S.A. 135 H2
Alderney i. Channel Is 49 E9
Alder Peak U.S.A. 128 C4
Aldershot U.K. 49 G7
Al Dhafrah reg. U.A.E. 88 D6
Aldingham U.K. 48 D4
Aldridge U.K. 49 F6
Aleg Mauritania 96 B3
Alegre Espírito Santo Brazil 145 C3
Alegre Minas Gerais Brazil 145 B2
Alegrete Brazil 144 E3
Alegros Mountain U.S.A. 129 I4
Aleksandra, Mys hd Rus. Fed. 74 E1
Aleksandriya Ukr. see Oleksandriya
Aleksandro-Nevskiy Rus. Fed. 43 I5
Aleksandropol Armenia see Gyumri
Aleksandrov Rus. Fed. 42 H4
Aleksandrov Gay Rus. Fed. 43 K6
Aleksandrovsk Rus. Fed. 41 R4
Aleksandrovsk Ukr. see Zaporizhzhya
Aleksandrovskiy Rus. Fed. see
Aleksandrovsk
Aleksandrovskoye Rus. Fed. 91 F1
Aleksandrovsk-Sakhalinskiy Rus. Fed.
74 F2
Aleksandry, Zemlya i. Rus. Fed. 64 F1
Alekseyevka Akmolinskaya Oblast' Kazakh.
see Akkol'
Alekseyevka Vostochnyy Kazakhstan Kazakh.
see Terekty
Alekseyevka Amurskaya Oblast' Rus. Fed.
74 B1
Alekseyevka Belgorodskaya Oblast'
Rus. Fed. 43 H6
Alekseyevka Belgorodskaya Oblast'
Rus. Fed. 43 H6
Alekseyevskaya Rus. Fed. 43 I6
Alekseyevskoye Rus. Fed. 42 K5
Aleksin Rus. Fed. 43 H5
Aleksinac Serbia 59 I3
Alèmbé Gabon 98 B4
Ålen Norway 44 G5
Alençon France 56 E2
Alenquer Brazil 143 H4
'Alenuihāhā Channel U.S.A. 127 [inset]
Alep Syria see Aleppo
Aleppo Syria 85 C1
Alert Canada 119 L1
Alerta Peru 142 D6
Alès France 56 G4
Aleşd Romania 59 J1
Aleshki Ukr. see Tsyurupyns'k
Aleşkirt Turkey see Eleşkirt
Alessandria Italy 58 C2
Alessio Albania see Lezhë
Ålesund Norway 44 E5
Aleutian Basin sea feature Bering Sea
150 H2
Aleutian Islands U.S.A. 118 A4
Aleutian Range mts U.S.A. 118 C4
Aleutian Trench sea feature
N. Pacific Ocean 150 I2
Alevina, Mys c. Rus. Fed. 65 Q4
Alevişik Turkey see Samandağı
Alexander U.S.A. 130 C2
Alexander, Kap c. Greenland see Ullersuaq
Alexander, Mount hill Australia 110 B2
Alexander Archipelago is U.S.A. 120 B3
Alexander Bay b. Namibia/S. Africa 100 C5
Alexander Bay S. Africa 100 C5

Alexander City U.S.A. 133 C5
Alexander Island Antarctica 152 L2
Alexandra Australia 112 B6
Alexandra N.Z. 113 B7
Alexandra, Cape S. Georgia 144 I8
Alexandra Channel India 71 A4
Alexandra Land i. Rus. Fed. see
Aleksandry, Zemlya
Alexandreia Greece 59 J4
Alexandretta Turkey see İskenderun
Alexandria Afgh. see Ghaznī
Alexandria Canada 135 H1

▶Alexandria Egypt 90 C5
5th most populous city in Africa.

Alexandria Romania 59 K3
Alexandria S. Africa 101 H7
Alexandria Turkm. see Mary
Alexandria U.K. 50 E5
Alexandria IN U.S.A. 134 C3
Alexandria KY U.S.A. 134 C4
Alexandria LA U.S.A. 131 E6
Alexandria VA U.S.A. 135 G4
Alexandria Arachoton Afgh. see Kandahār
Alexandria Areion Afgh. see Herāt
Alexandria Bay U.S.A. 135 H1
Alexandria Prophthasia Afgh. see Farāh
Alexandrina, Lake Australia 111 B7
Alexandroupoli Greece 59 K4
Alexis r. Canada 123 K3
Alexis Creek Canada 120 F4
Aley Lebanon 85 B3
Aleyak Iran 88 E2
Aleysk Rus. Fed. 72 E2
Alf Germany 52 H4
Al Farwānīyah Kuwait 88 B4
Al Fas Morocco see Fès
Al Fatḩah Iraq 91 F4
Al Fāw Iraq 91 H5
Al Fayyūm Egypt 90 C5
Alfeld (Leine) Germany 53 J3
Alfenas Brazil 145 B3
Alford U.K. 48 H5
Alfred ME U.S.A. 135 J2
Alfred NY U.S.A. 135 G2
Alfred and Marie Range hills Australia
109 D6
Al Fujayrah U.A.E. see Fujairah
Al Fuqahā' Libya 97 E2
Al Furāt r. Asia 85 D2 see Euphrates
Alga Kazakh. 80 A2
Ålgård Norway 45 D7
Algarrobo del Aguilla Arg. 144 C5
Algarve reg. Port. 57 B5
Algeciras Spain 57 D5
Algemesí Spain 57 F4
Algena Eritrea 86 E6
Alger Alg. see Algiers
Alger U.S.A. 134 C1

▶Algeria country Africa 96 C2
2nd largest country in Africa.

Algérie country Africa see Algeria
Algermissen Germany 53 J2
Algha Kazakh. see Alga
Al Ghāfāt Oman 88 E6
Al Ghammās Iraq 91 G5
Al Ghardaqah Egypt see Al Ghurdaqah
Al Ghawr plain Jordan/West Bank 85 B4
Al Ghayḑah Yemen 86 H6
Alghero Sardinia Italy 58 C4
Al Ghurdaqah Egypt 86 D4
Al Ghuwayr well Qatar 88 C5

▶Algiers Alg. 57 H5
Capital of Algeria.

Algoa Bay S. Africa 101 G7
Algoma U.S.A. 134 B1
Algona U.S.A. 130 E3
Algonac U.S.A. 134 D2
Algonquin Park Canada 135 F1
Algonquin Provincial Park Canada 135 F1
Algorta Spain 57 E2
Algueirao Moz. see Hacufera
Al Habakah well Saudi Arabia 91 F5
Al Ḩabbānīyah Iraq 91 F4
Al Ḩadaqah well Saudi Arabia 88 B4
Al Ḩadd Bahrain 88 C5
Al Hadhālīl plat. Saudi Arabia 91 F5
Al Ḩadīdīyah Syria 85 C2
Al Ḩadīthah Iraq 91 F4
Al Ḩadīthah Saudi Arabia 85 C4
Al Ḩaḑr Iraq see Hatra
Al Ḩafār well Saudi Arabia 91 F5
Al Ḩaffah Syria 85 C2
Al Haggounia W. Sahara 96 B2
Al Ḩajar al Gharbī mts Oman 88 E5
Al Ḩajar ash Sharqī mts Oman 88 E6
Al Ḩamād plain Asia 90 E5
Al Ḩamādah al Ḩamrā' plat. Libya 96 E2
Alhama de Murcia Spain 57 F5
Al Ḩamar Saudi Arabia 88 B6
Al Ḩamīdīyah Syria 85 B2
Al Ḩammām Egypt 90 C5
Al Ḩanākīyah Saudi Arabia 86 F5
Al Haniyah esc. Iraq 91 G5
Al Hariq Saudi Arabia 88 B6
Al Ḩarrah Egypt 90 C5
Al Harūj al Aswad hills Libya 97 E2
Al Hasa reg. Saudi Arabia 88 C5
Al Ḩasakah Syria 91 F3
Al Hawi salt pan Saudi Arabia 85 D5
Al Hawjā' Saudi Arabia 90 E5
Al Ḩawţah reg. Saudi Arabia 88 B6
Al Ḩayy Iraq 91 G4
Al Ḩayz Egypt 90 C5
Al Hazīm Jordan 85 C4
Al Ḩazm Saudi Arabia 90 E5
Al Ḩazm al Jawf Yemen 86 F6
Al Ḩibāk des. Saudi Arabia 87 H6
Al Hījānah Syria 85 C3
Al Ḩillah Iraq see Hillah
Al Ḩillah Saudi Arabia 86 G5
Al Ḩinnāh Saudi Arabia 98 E1
Al Ḩinw mt. Saudi Arabia 85 D4
Al Hirrah well Saudi Arabia 88 C6
Al Hīshah Syria 85 D1
Al Ḩismā plain Saudi Arabia 90 D5
Al Ḩişn Jordan 85 B3

Al Hoceima Morocco 57 E6
Al Ḩudaydah Yemen see Hodeidah
Al Ḩufrah reg. Saudi Arabia 90 E5
Al Hūj hills Saudi Arabia 90 E5
Al Husayfīn Oman 88 E5
Al Huwwah Saudi Arabia 88 B6
Ali China 82 D2
'Alīābād Afgh. 89 H2
'Alīābād Golestān Iran 88 D2
'Alīābād Hormozgan Iran 88 D4
'Alīābād Khorāsān Iran 89 F4
'Alīābād Kordestān Iran 88 B2
'Alīābād, Kūh-e mt. Iran 88 C3
Aliağa Turkey 59 L5
Aliakmonas r. Greece 59 J4
Alibag India 84 B2
Āli Bayramlı Azer. 91 H3
Alicante Spain 57 F4
Alice r. Australia 110 C2
Alice watercourse Australia 110 D5
Alice U.S.A. 131 D7
Alice, Punta pt Italy 58 G5
Alice Springs Australia 109 F5
Alice Town Bahamas 133 E7
Aliceville U.S.A. 131 F5
Alichur Tajik. 89 I2
Alichur r. Tajik. 89 I2
Alick Creek r. Australia 110 C4
Alifu Atoll Maldives see Ari Atoll
Al Ifzi'iyyah i. U.A.E. 88 C5
Aliganj India 82 D4
Aligarh Rajasthan India 82 D4
Aligarh Uttar Prad. India 82 D4
Alīgūdarz Iran 88 C3
Alihe China 74 A2
Alījūq, Kūh-e mt. Iran 88 C4
'Alī Kheyl Afgh. 89 H3
Al Imārāt al 'Arabīyah at Muttaḩidah
country Asia see United Arab Emirates
Alimia i. Greece 59 L6
Alindao Cent. Afr. Rep. 98 C3
Alingsås Sweden 45 H8
Aliova r. Turkey 59 M5
Alipura India 82 D4
Alipur Duar India 83 G4
Alirajpur India 82 C5
Al 'Irāq country Asia see Iraq
Al 'Īsāwīyah Saudi Arabia 85 C4
Al Iskandarīyah Egypt see Alexandria
Al Iskandarīyah Iraq 91 G4
Al Ismā'īlīyah Egypt 90 D5
Al Ismā'īlīyah governorate Egypt 85 A4
Aliveri Greece 59 K5
Aliwal North S. Africa 101 H6
Alix Canada 120 H4
Al Jafr Jordan 85 C4
Al Jāfūrah des. Saudi Arabia 88 C5
Al Jaghbūb Libya 90 B5
Al Jahrah Kuwait 88 B4
Al Jamalīyah Qatar 88 C5
Al Jarāwī well Saudi Arabia 85 D4
Al Jauf Saudi Arabia see Dumat al Jandal
Al Jawb reg. Saudi Arabia 88 C6
Al Jawf Libya 97 F2
Al Jawsh Libya 96 E1
Al Jaza'ir country Africa see Algeria
Al Jaza'ir Alg. see Algiers
Aljezur Port. 57 B5
Al Jībān reg. Saudi Arabia 88 C5
Al Jil well Iraq 91 F5
Al Jilh esc. Saudi Arabia 88 B5
Al Jithāmīyah Saudi Arabia 91 F6
Al Jīzah Egypt see Giza
Al Jīzah Jordan 85 B4
Al Jubayl hills Saudi Arabia 88 B5
Al Jubaylah Saudi Arabia 88 B5
Al Jufrah Libya 97 E2
Al Julayqah well Saudi Arabia 88 C5
Aljustrel Port. 57 B5
Al Juwayf depr. Syria 85 C3
Al Kahfah Al Qaşīm Saudi Arabia 86 F4
Al Kahfah Ash Sharqīyah Saudi Arabia 88 C5
Alkali Lake Canada 120 F5
Al Karak Jordan 85 B4
Al Khābūrah Oman 88 E6
Al Khalīl West Bank see Hebron
Al Khāliş Iraq 91 G4
Al Khārijah Egypt 86 D4
Al Kharj reg. Saudi Arabia 88 B6
Al Kharrārah Qatar 88 C5
Al Kharrūbah Egypt 85 A4
Al Khaşab Oman 88 E5
Al Khatam reg. U.A.E. 88 D5
Al Khawkhah Yemen 86 F7
Al Khawr Qatar 88 C5
Al Khizāmī well Saudi Arabia 88 C5
Al Khums Libya 97 E1
Al Khunfah sand area Saudi Arabia 90 E5
Al Khunn Saudi Arabia 98 E1
Al Kifl Iraq 91 G4
Al Kir'ānah Qatar 88 C5
Al Kiswah Syria 85 C3
Alkmaar Neth. 52 E2
Al Kūbrī Egypt 85 A4
Al Kumayt Iraq 91 G4
Al Kuntillah Egypt 85 B5
Al Kusūr hills Saudi Arabia 85 D4
Al Kūt Iraq 91 G4
Al Kuwayt country Asia see Kuwait
Al Kuwayt Kuwait see Kuwait
Al Labbah plain Saudi Arabia 91 F5
Al Lādhiqīyah Syria see Latakia
Allagadda India 84 C3
Allahabad India 83 E4
Al Lajā lava field Syria 85 C3
Allakaket U.S.A. 118 C3
Allakh-Yun' Rus. Fed. 65 O3
Allanmyo Myanmar see Aunglan
Allanridge S. Africa 101 H4
Allapalli India 84 D2
'Allāqī, Wādī al watercourse Egypt 86 D5
'Allāqi, Wâdi el watercourse Egypt see
'Allāqī, Wādī al
Allardville Canada 123 I5
Alldays S. Africa 101 I2
Allegan U.S.A. 134 C2
Allegheny r. U.S.A. 134 F3
Allegheny Mountains U.S.A. 134 D5
Allegheny Reservoir U.S.A. 135 F3
Allen, Lough l. Ireland 51 D3
Allendale U.S.A. 133 D5
Allendale Town U.K. 48 E4

Allende Coahuila Mex. 131 C6
Allende Nuevo León Mex. 131 C7
Allendorf (Lumda) Germany 53 I4
Allenford Canada 134 E1
Allenstein Poland see Olsztyn
Allensville U.S.A. 134 B5
Allentown U.S.A. 135 H3
Alleppey India 84 C4
Aller r. Germany 53 J2
Alliance NE U.S.A. 130 C3
Alliance OH U.S.A. 134 E3
Al Lībīyah country Africa see Libya
Allier r. France 56 F3
Al Līhābah well Saudi Arabia 88 B5
Allinge-Sandvig Denmark 45 I9
Al Lişāfah well Saudi Arabia 88 B5
Al Lisān pen. Jordan 85 B4
Alliston Canada 134 F1
Al Līth Saudi Arabia 86 F5
Al Liwā' oasis U.A.E. 88 D6
Alloa U.K. 50 F4
Allons U.S.A. 134 C5
Allora Australia 112 F2
Allur India 84 D3
Alluru Kottapatnam India 84 D3
Al Lussuf well Iraq 91 F5
Alma Canada 123 H4
Alma MI U.S.A. 134 C2
Alma NE U.S.A. 130 D3
Alma WI U.S.A. 130 F2
Al Ma'ānīyah Iraq 91 F5
Alma-Ata Kazakh. see Almaty
Almada Port. 57 B4
Al Madāfi' plat. Saudi Arabia 90 E5
Al Ma'danīyāt well Iraq 91 G5
Almaden Australia 110 D3
Almadén Spain 57 D4
Al Madīnah Saudi Arabia see Medina
Al Mafraq Jordan 85 C3
Al Maghrib country Africa see Morocco
Al Maghrib reg. U.A.E. 88 D6
Al Mahākīk reg. Saudi Arabia 88 C6
Al Mahdum Syria 85 C1
Al Maḩiā depr. Saudi Arabia 90 E6
Al Maḩwīt Yemen 86 F6
Al Malsūnīyah reg. Saudi Arabia 88 C5
Almalyk Uzbek. see Olmaliq
Al Manadir reg. Oman 88 D6
Al Manāmah Bahrain see Manama
Al Manjūr well Saudi Arabia 88 B6
Almanor, Lake U.S.A. 128 C1
Almansa Spain 57 F4
Al Manşūrah Egypt 90 C5
Almanzor mt. Spain 57 D3
Al Mariyyah U.A.E. 88 D6
Al Marj Libya 97 F1
Almas, Rio das r. Brazil 145 A1
Al Maţarīyah Egypt 90 D5

▶Almaty Kazakh. 80 E3
Former capital of Kazakhstan.

Al Mawşil Iraq see Mosul
Al Mayādīn Syria 91 F4
Al Mazār Egypt 85 A4
Almaznyy Rus. Fed. 65 M3
Almeirim Brazil 143 H4
Almeirim Port. 57 B4
Almelo Neth. 52 G2
Almenara Brazil 145 C2
Almendra, Embalse de resr Spain 57 C3
Almendralejo Spain 57 C4
Almere Neth. 52 F2
Almería Spain 57 E5
Almería, Golfo de b. Spain 57 E5
Al'metievsk Rus. Fed. see Al'met'yevsk
Al'met'yevsk Rus. Fed. 41 Q5
Älmhult Sweden 45 I8
Almina, Punta pt Spain 57 D6
Al Mindak Saudi Arabia 86 F5
Al Minyā Egypt 90 C5
Almirós Greece see Almyros
Al Mish'āb Saudi Arabia 88 C4
Almodôvar Port. 57 B5
Almond r. U.K. 50 F4
Almont U.S.A. 134 D2
Almonte Spain 57 C5
Almora India 82 D3
Al Mu'ayzīlah hill Saudi Arabia 85 D5
Al Mubarrez Saudi Arabia 86 G4
Al Muḑaibī Oman 87 I5
Al Muḑairib Oman 88 E6
Al Muḩarraq Bahrain 88 C5
Al Mukallā Yemen see Mukalla
Al Mukhā Yemen see Mocha
Al Mukhaylī Libya 86 B3
Al Munbaţiḩ des. Saudi Arabia 88 C6
Almuñécar Spain 57 E5
Al Muqdādīyah Iraq 91 G4
Al Mūrītānīyah country Africa see
Mauritania
Al Murūt well Saudi Arabia 91 E5
Almus Turkey 90 E2
Al Musannāh ridge Saudi Arabia 88 B4
Al Musayyib Iraq 88 B3
Al Muwaqqar Jordan 85 C4
Almyros Greece 59 J5
Almyrou, Ormos b. Greece 59 K7
Alnwick U.K. 48 F3

▶Alofi Niue 107 J3
Capital of Niue.

Aloja Latvia 45 N8
Alon Myanmar 70 A2
Along India 83 H3
Alongshan China 74 A2
Alonnisos i. Greece 59 J5
Alor i. Indon. 108 D2
Alor, Kepulauan is Indon. 108 D2
Alor Setar Malaysia 71 C6
Alor Star Malaysia see Alor Setar
Alost Belgium see Aalst
Aloysius, Mount Australia 109 E6
Alozero Rus. Fed. 44 Q4
Alpen Germany 52 G3
Alpena U.S.A. 134 D1
Alpercatas, Serra das hills Brazil 143 J5
Alpha Australia 110 D4
Alpha Ridge sea feature Arctic Ocean
153 A1
Alpine AZ U.S.A. 129 I5

Alpine NY U.S.A. 135 G2
Alpine TX U.S.A. 131 C6
Alpine WY U.S.A. 126 F4
Alpine National Park Australia 112 C6
Alps mts Europe 56 H4
Al Qa'āmīyāt reg. Saudi Arabia 86 G6
Al Qaddāḥīyah Libya 97 E1
Al Qadmūs Syria 85 C2
Al Qaffay i. U.A.E. 88 D5
Al Qāhirah Egypt see Cairo
Al Qā'īyah Saudi Arabia 86 F5
Al Qā'īyah well Saudi Arabia 88 B5
Al Qal'a Beni Hammad tourist site Alg. 57 I6
Al Qalibah Saudi Arabia 90 E5
Al Qāmishlī Syria 91 F3
Al Qar'ah Libya 90 B5
Al Qar'ah well Saudi Arabia 88 B5
Al Qar'ah lava field Syria 85 C3
Al Qardāḥah Syria 85 C2
Al Qarqar Saudi Arabia 85 C4
Al Qaryatayn Syria 85 C2
Al Qaşab Ar Riyāḍ Saudi Arabia 88 B5
Al Qaşab Ash Sharqīyah Saudi Arabia 88 C6
Al Qaṭīf Saudi Arabia 88 C5
Al Qaṭn Yemen 86 G6
Al Qaṭrānah Jordan 85 C4
Al Qaṭrūn Libya 97 E2
Al Qāyṣūmah well Saudi Arabia 91 F5
Alqueva, Barragem de resr 57 C4
Al Qumur country Africa see Comoros
Al Qunayṭirah Syria 85 B3
Al Qunfidhah Saudi Arabia 86 F6
Al Qurayyāt Saudi Arabia 85 C4
Al Qurnah Iraq 91 G5
Al Quşaymah Egypt 85 B4
Al Quşayr Egypt 86 D4
Al Quşayr Syria 85 C2
Al Qūṣīyah Egypt 90 C6
Al Quşūrīyah Saudi Arabia 88 B6
Al Quṭayfah Syria 85 C3
Al Quwayi' Saudi Arabia 88 B6
Al Quwayīyah Saudi Arabia 86 G5
Al Quwayrah Jordan 85 B5
Al Rabbād reg. U.A.E. 88 D6
Alroy Downs Australia 110 B3
Alsace admin. reg. France 53 H6
Alsace reg. France 56 H2
Alsager U.K. 49 E5
Al Samīt well Iraq 91 F5
Alsask Canada 121 I5
Alsatia reg. France see Alsace
Alsek r. U.S.A. 120 B3
Alsfeld Germany 53 J4
Alsleben (Saale) Germany 53 L3
Alston U.K. 48 E4
Alstonville Australia 112 F2
Alsunga Latvia 45 L8
Alta Norway 44 M2
Alta, Mount N.Z. 113 B7
Altaelva r. Norway 44 M2
Altafjorden sea chan. Norway 44 M1
Alta Floresta Brazil 143 G5
Altai Mountains Asia 72 F3
Altamaha r. U.S.A. 133 D6
Altamira Brazil 143 H4
Altamura Italy 58 G4
Altan Shiret China 73 J5
Altan Xiret China see Altan Shiret
Alta Paraiso de Goiás Brazil 145 B1
Altar r. Mex. 127 F7
Altar, Desierto de des. Mex. 129 F6
Altavista U.S.A. 134 F5
Altay China 80 G2
Altay Mongolia 80 H3
Altay Mongolia 80 I2
Altayskiy Rus. Fed. 80 G1
Altayskiy Khrebet mts Asia see Altai Mountains
Altdorf Switz. 56 I3
Altea Spain 57 F4
Alteidet Norway 44 M1
Altenahr Germany 52 G4
Altenberge Germany 53 H2
Altenburg Germany 53 M4
Altenkirchen (Westerwald) Germany 53 H4
Altenqoke China 83 H1
Altin Köprü Iraq 91 G4
Altınoluk Turkey 59 L5
Altınözü Turkey 85 C1
Altıntaş Turkey 59 N5
Altiplano plain Bol. 142 E7
Altmark reg. Germany 53 L2
Altmühl r. Germany 53 L6
Alto, Monte hill Italy 58 D2
Alto Chicapa Angola 99 B5
Alto del Moncayo mt. Spain 57 F3
Alto de Pencoso hills Arg. 144 C4
Alto Garças Brazil 143 H7
Alto Madidi, Parque Nacional nat. park Bol. 142 E6
Alton CA U.S.A. 128 A1
Alton IL U.S.A. 130 F4
Alton MO U.S.A. 131 F4
Alton NH U.S.A. 135 J2
Altona Canada 120 F3
Altoona U.S.A. 135 F3
Alto Parnaíba Brazil 143 I5
Alto Taquarí Mato Grosso Brazil 143 H7
Altötting Germany 47 N6
Altrincham U.K. 48 E5
Alt Schwerin Germany 53 M1
Altun Kübrī Iraq see Altin Köprü
Altun Shan mts China 80 G4
Alturas U.S.A. 126 C4
Altus U.S.A. 131 D5
Al 'Ubaylah Saudi Arabia 98 F1
Alucra Turkey 90 E2
Alūksne Latvia 45 O8
Alūm Iran 88 C3
Alum Bridge U.S.A. 134 E4
Al 'Uqaylah Libya 97 E1
Al 'Uqaylah Saudi Arabia see An Nabk
Al Uqşur Egypt see Luxor
Alur India 84 C3
Al 'Urayq des. Saudi Arabia 90 E5
Al 'Urdun country Asia see Jordan
Alur Setar Malaysia see Alor Setar
'Ālūt Iran 88 B3
Aluva India see Alwaye
Al 'Uwayjā' well Saudi Arabia 88 C6
Al 'Uwaynāt Libya 86 B5
Al 'Uwayqīlah Saudi Arabia 91 F5
Al 'Uzayr Iraq 91 G5
Alva U.S.A. 131 D4
Alvand, Kūh-e mt. Iran 88 C3
Alvarães Brazil 142 F4
Alvaton U.S.A. 134 B5
Alvdal Norway 44 G5
Älvdalen Sweden 45 I6
Alvesta Sweden 45 I8
Ålvik Norway 45 E6
Alvik Sweden 44 J5
Alvin U.S.A. 131 E6
Alvorada do Norte Brazil 145 B1
Älvsbyn Sweden 44 L4
Al Wafrah Kuwait 88 B4
Al Wajh Saudi Arabia 86 E4
Al Wakrah Qatar 88 C5
Al Waqbá well Saudi Arabia 88 B4
Alwar India 82 D4
Al Wari'ah Saudi Arabia 86 G4
Al Wāṭiyah well Egypt 90 B5
Alwaye India 84 C4
Al Widyān plat. Iraq/Saudi Arabia 91 F4
Al Wusayṭ well Saudi Arabia 88 B4
Alxa Youqi China see Ehen Hudag
Alxa Zuoqi China see Bayan Hot
Al Yamāmah Saudi Arabia 88 B5
Al Yaman country Asia see Yemen
Alyangula Australia 110 B2
Al Yāsāt i. U.A.E. 88 C5
Alyth U.K. 50 F4
Alytus Lith. 45 N9
Alzette r. Lux. 52 G5
Alzey Germany 53 I5
Amacayacu, Parque Nacional nat. park Col. 142 D4
Amadeus, Lake salt flat Australia 109 E6
Amadjuak Lake Canada 119 K3
Amadora Port. 57 B4
Amakusa-nada b. Japan 75 C6
Åmål Sweden 45 H7
Amalia S. Africa 101 G4
Amaliada Greece 59 I6
Amalner India 82 C5
Amamapare Indon. 69 J7
Amambaí Brazil 144 E2
Amambaí, Serra de hills Brazil/Para. 144 E2
Amami-Ō-shima i. Japan 75 C7
Amami-shotō is Japan 75 C8
Amamula Dem. Rep. Congo 98 C4
Amanab P.N.G. 69 K7
Amangel'dy Kazakh. 80 C1
Amankeldi Kazakh. see Amangel'dy
Amantea Italy 58 G5
Amanzimtoti S. Africa 101 J6
Amapá Brazil 143 H3
Amarante Brazil 143 J5
Amarapura Myanmar 70 B2
Amareleja Port. 57 C4
Amargosa Brazil 145 D1
Amargosa watercourse U.S.A. 128 E3
Amargosa Desert U.S.A. 128 E3
Amargosa Range mts U.S.A. 128 E3
Amargosa Valley U.S.A. 128 E3
Amarillo U.S.A. 131 C5
Amarillo, Cerro mt. Arg. 144 C4
Amarkantak India 83 E5
Amarpur Madh. Prad. India 82 E5
Amasia Turkey see Amasya
Amasine W. Sahara 96 B2
Amasra Turkey 90 D2
Amasya Turkey 90 D2
Amata Australia 109 E6
Amatulla India 83 H4
Amau P.N.G. 110 E1
Amay Belgium 52 F4
Amazar Rus. Fed. 74 A1
Amazar r. Rus. Fed. 74 A1

▶Amazon r. S. America 142 F4
Longest river and largest drainage basin in South America and 2nd longest river in the world.
Also known as Amazonas or Solimões

Amazon, Mouths of the Brazil 143 I3
Amazonas r. S. America 142 F4 see Amazon
Amazon Cone sea feature S. Atlantic Ocean 148 E5
Amazônia, Parque Nacional nat. park Brazil 143 G4
Ambajogai India 84 C2
Ambala India 82 D3
Ambalangoda Sri Lanka 84 D5
Ambalavao Madag. 99 E6
Ambam Cameroon 98 B3
Ambar Iran 88 E4
Ambarchik Rus. Fed. 65 R3
Ambarnyy Rus. Fed. 44 R4
Ambasa India see Ambassa
Ambasamudram India 84 C4
Ambassa India 83 G5
Ambathala Australia 111 D5
Ambato Ecuador 142 C4
Ambato Boeny Madag. 99 E5
Ambato Finandrahana Madag. 99 E6
Ambatolampy Madag. 99 E5
Ambatomainty Madag. 99 E5
Ambatondrazaka Madag. 99 E5
Ambejogai India see Ambajogai
Ambelau i. Indon. 69 H7
Ambeno enclave East Timor see Ocussi
Amberg Germany 53 L5
Ambergris Cay i. Belize 136 G5
Ambérieu-en-Bugey France 56 G4
Amberley Canada 134 E1
Ambgaon India 84 D1
Ambianum France see Amiens
Ambikapur India 83 E5
Ambilobe Madag. 99 E5
Ambition, Mount Canada 120 D3
Amble U.K. 48 F3
Ambler U.S.A. 118 C3
Ambleside U.K. 48 E4
Amblève r. Belgium 52 F4
Ambo India 83 F5
Amboasary Madag. 99 E6
Ambodifotatra Madag. 99 E5
Ambohimahasoa Madag. 99 E6
Ambohitra mt. Madag. 99 E5
Amboina Indon. see Ambon
Ambon Indon. 69 H7
Ambon i. Indon. 69 H7
Amboró, Parque Nacional nat. park Bol. 142 F7
Ambositra Madag. 99 E6
Ambovombe Madag. 99 E6
Amboy U.S.A. 129 F4
Ambre, Cap d' c. Madag. see Bobaomby, Tanjona
Ambrim i. Vanuatu see Ambrym
Ambriz Angola 99 B4
Ambrizete Angola see N'zeto
Ambrosia Lake U.S.A. 129 J4
Ambrym i. Vanuatu 107 G3
Ambunti P.N.G. 69 K7
Ambur India 84 C3
Am-Dam Chad 97 F3
Amded, Oued watercourse Alg. 96 D2
Amdo China see Lharigarbo
Ameland i. Neth. 52 F1
Amelia Court House U.S.A. 135 G5
Amenia U.S.A. 135 I3
Amer, Erg d' des. Alg. 98 A1
Amereli India see Amreli
American, North Fork r. U.S.A. 128 C2
Americana Brazil 145 B3
American-Antarctic Ridge sea feature S. Atlantic Ocean 148 G9
American Falls U.S.A. 126 E4
American Falls Reservoir U.S.A. 126 E4
American Fork U.S.A. 129 H1

▶American Samoa terr. S. Pacific Ocean 107 J3
United States Unincorporated Territory.

Americus U.S.A. 133 C5
Amersfoort Neth. 52 F2
Amersfoort S. Africa 101 I4
Amersham U.K. 49 G7
Amery Canada 121 M3
Amery Ice Shelf Antarctica 152 E2
Ames U.S.A. 130 E3
Amesbury U.K. 49 F7
Amesbury U.S.A. 135 J2
Amet India 82 C4
Amethi India 83 E4
Amfissa Greece 59 J5
Amga Rus. Fed. 65 O3
Amgalang China 73 L3
Amgu Rus. Fed. 74 E3
Amguid Alg. 96 D2
Amgun' r. Rus. Fed. 74 E1
Amherst Canada 123 I5
Amherst Myanmar see Kyaikkami
Amherst MA U.S.A. 135 I2
Amherst OH U.S.A. 134 D3
Amherst VA U.S.A. 134 F5
Amherstburg Canada 134 D2
Amherst Island Canada 135 G1
Amiata, Monte mt. Italy 58 D3
Amida Turkey see Diyarbakır
Amidon U.S.A. 130 C2
Amiens France 52 C5
'Amīj, Wādī watercourse Iraq 91 F4
Amik Ovası marsh Turkey 85 C1
'Amīnābād Iran 88 D4
Amindivi atoll India see Amini
Amindivi Islands India 84 B4
Amini atoll India 84 B4
Amino Eth. 98 E3
Aminuis Namibia 100 D2
Amīrābād Iran 88 B3
Amirante Islands Seychelles 149 L6
Amirante Trench sea feature Indian Ocean 149 L6
Amisk Lake Canada 121 K4
Amistad, Represa de resr Mex./U.S.A. see Amistad Reservoir
Amistad Reservoir Mex./U.S.A. 131 C6
Amisus Turkey see Samsun
Amite U.S.A. 131 F6
Amity Point Australia 112 F1
Amla India 82 D5
Amlapura Indon. see Karangasem
Amlash Iran 88 C2
Amlekhganj Nepal 83 F4
Åmli Norway 45 F7
Amlia Island U.S.A. 118 A4
Amlwch U.K. 48 C5

▶'Ammān Jordan 85 B4
Capital of Jordan.

Ammanazar Turkm. 88 D2
Ammanford U.K. 49 D7
Ämmänsaari Fin. 44 P4
'Ammār, Tall hill Syria 85 C3
Ammarnäs Sweden 44 J4
Ammaroo Australia 110 A4
Ammassalik Greenland 153 J2
Ammerland reg. Germany 53 H1
Ammern Germany 53 K3
Ammochostos Cyprus see Famagusta
Ammochostos Bay Cyprus 85 B2
Am Nābiyah Yemen 86 F7
Amne Machin Range mts China see A'nyêmaqên Shan
Amnok-kang r. China/N. Korea see Yalu Jiang
Amo Jiang r. China 76 D4
Amol Iran 88 D2
Amorbach Germany 53 J5
Amorgos i. Greece 59 K6
Amory U.S.A. 131 F5
Amos Canada 122 F4
Amourj Mauritania 96 C3
Amoy China see Xiamen
Ampani India 84 D2
Ampanihy Madag. 99 E6
Amparai Sri Lanka 84 D5
Amparo Brazil 145 B3
Ampasimanolotra Madag. 99 E5
Amphitheatre Australia 112 A6
Amphitrite Group is Paracel Is 68 E3
Ampoa Indon. 69 G7
Amraoti India see Amravati
Amravati India 84 C1
Amrawad India 82 D5
Amreli India 82 B5
Amri Pak. 89 H5
Amring India 83 H4
'Amrīt Syria 85 B2
Amritsar India 82 C3
Amroha India 82 D3
Amsden U.S.A. 134 D3
Åmsele Sweden 44 K4
Amstelveen Neth. 52 E2

▶Amsterdam Neth. 52 E2
Official capital of the Netherlands.

Amsterdam S. Africa 101 J4
Amsterdam U.S.A. 135 H2
Amsterdam, Île i. Indian Ocean 149 N8
Amstetten Austria 47 O6
Am Timan Chad 97 F3
Amudar'ya r. Asia 89 F2
Amudaryo r. Asia see Amudar'ya
Amund Ringnes Island Canada 119 I2
Amundsen, Mount Antarctica 152 F2
Amundsen Abyssal Plain sea feature Southern Ocean 152 J2
Amundsen Basin sea feature Arctic Ocean 153 H1
Amundsen Bay Antarctica 152 D2
Amundsen Coast Antarctica 152 J1
Amundsen Glacier Antarctica 152 I1
Amundsen Gulf Canada 118 F2
Amundsen Ridges sea feature Southern Ocean 152 J2
Amundsen-Scott research station Antarctica 152 C1
Amundsen Sea Antarctica 152 K2
Amuntai Indon. 68 F7
Amur r. China/Rus. Fed. 74 D2
also known as Heilong Jiang (China)
Amur r. Rus. Fed. 74 F1
'Amur, Wadi watercourse Sudan 86 D6
Amur Oblast admin. div. Rus. Fed. see Amurskaya Oblast'
Amursk Rus. Fed. 74 E2
Amurskaya Oblast' admin. div. Rus. Fed. 74 C1
Amurskiy Liman strait Rus. Fed. 74 F1
Amurzet Rus. Fed. 74 C3
Amvrosiyivka Ukr. 43 H7
Amyderya r. Asia see Amudar'ya
Am-Zoer Chad 97 F3
An Myanmar 70 A3
Anaa atoll Fr. Polynesia 151 K7
Anabanua Indon. 69 G7
Anabar r. Rus. Fed. 65 M2
Anacapa Islands U.S.A. 128 D4
Anaconda U.S.A. 126 E3
Anacortes U.S.A. 126 C2
Anadarko U.S.A. 131 D5
Anadolu reg. Turkey 90 D3
Anadolu Dağları mts Turkey 90 E2
Anadyr' Rus. Fed. 65 S3
Anadyr, Gulf of Rus. Fed. see Anadyrskiy Zaliv
Anadyrskiy Zaliv b. Rus. Fed. 65 T3
Anafi i. Greece 59 K6
Anagé Brazil 145 C1
'Ānah Iraq 91 F4
Anaheim U.S.A. 128 E5
Anahim Lake Canada 120 E4
Anáhuac Mex. 131 C7
Anahuac U.S.A. 131 E6
Anaimalai Hills India 84 C4
Anaiteum i. Vanuatu see Anatom
Anajás Brazil 143 I4
Anakie Australia 110 D4
Analalava Madag. 99 E5
Anamã Brazil 142 F4
Anambas, Kepulauan is Indon. 71 D7
Anamosa U.S.A. 130 F3
Anamur Turkey 85 A1
Anan Japan 75 D6
Anand India 82 C5
Anandapur India 83 F5
Anantapur India 84 C3
Ananthapur India see Anantapur
Anantnag India 82 C2
Anant Peth India 82 D4
Anantpur India see Anantapur
Ananyev Ukr. see Anan'yiv
Anan'yiv Ukr. 43 F7
Anapa Rus. Fed. 90 E1
Anápolis Brazil 145 A2
Anār Fin. see Inari
Anār Iran 88 D4
Anardara Afgh. 89 F3
Anatahan i. N. Mariana Is 69 L3
Anatajan i. N. Mariana Is see Anatahan
Anatom i. Vanuatu 107 G4
Añatuya Arg. 144 D3
Anaypazari Turkey see Gülnar
An Baile Breac Ireland 51 B6
An Bun Beag Ireland 51 D2
Anbūr-e Kālārī Iran 88 D5
Anbyon N. Korea 75 B5
Ancenis France 56 D3
Anchorage U.S.A. 118 D3
Anchorage Island atoll Cook Is see Suwarrow
Anchor Bay U.S.A. 134 D2
Anchuthengu India see Anjengo
Anci China see Langfang
An Clochán Liath Ireland 51 D3
An Cóbh Ireland see Cobh
Ancona Italy 58 E3
Ancud, Golfo de g. Chile 144 B6
Ancyra Turkey see Ankara
Anda Heilong. China see Daqing
Anda Heilong. China 74 B3
Andacollo Chile 144 B4
Andado Australia 110 A5
Andahuaylas Peru 142 D6
An Daingean Ireland 51 B5
Andal India 83 F5
Åndalsnes Norway 44 E5
Andalucía aut. comm. Spain 57 D5
Andalusia aut. comm. Spain see Andalucía
Andalusia U.S.A. 133 C6
Andaman Basin sea feature Indian Ocean 149 O5
Andaman Islands India 71 A4
Andaman Sea Indian Ocean 71 A5
Andaman Strait India 71 A4
Andamooka Australia 111 B6
Andapa Madag. 99 E5
Andarāb reg. Afgh. 89 H3
Ande China 76 E4
Andegavum France see Angers
Andelle r. France 52 B5
Andenes Norway 44 J2
Andenne Belgium 52 F4
Andéramboukane Mali 96 D3
Anderlecht Belgium 52 E4
Andermatt Switz. 56 I3
Andernos-les-Bains France 56 D4
Anderson r. Canada 118 F3
Anderson AK U.S.A. 118 D3
Anderson IN U.S.A. 134 C3
Anderson SC U.S.A. 133 D5
Anderson TX U.S.A. 131 E6
Anderson Bay Australia 111 [inset]
Anderson Lake Canada 120 F5
Andes mts S. America 144 C4
Andfjorden sea chan. Norway 44 J2
Andhíparos i. Greece see Antiparos
Andhra Lake India 84 B2
Andhra Pradesh state India 84 C2
Andijon Uzbek. 80 D3
Andikíthira i. Greece see Antikythira
Andilamena Madag. 99 E5
Andilanatoby Madag. 99 E5
Andīmeshk Iran 88 C3
Andímilos i. Greece see Antimilos
Andípsara i. Greece see Antipsara
Andırın Turkey 90 E3
Andirlangar China 83 E1
Andizhan Uzbek. see Andijon
Andkhvoy Afgh. 89 G2
Andoany Madag. 99 E5
Andoas Peru 142 C4
Andogskaya Gryada hills Rus. Fed. 42 H4
Andol India 84 C2
Andong China see Dandong
Andong S. Korea 75 C5
Andongwei China 77 H1
Andoom Australia 110 C2
Andorra country Europe 57 G2

▶Andorra la Vella Andorra 57 G2
Capital of Andorra.

Andorra la Vieja Andorra see Andorra la Vella
Andover U.K. 49 F7
Andover NY U.S.A. 135 G2
Andover OH U.S.A. 134 E3
Andøya i. Norway 44 I2
Andrade U.S.A. 129 F5
Andradina Brazil 145 A3
Andranomavo Madag. 99 E5
Andranopasy Madag. 99 E6
Andreanof Islands U.S.A. 150 I2
Andreapol' Rus. Fed. 42 G4
Andreas Isle of Man 48 C4
André Félix, Parc National d' nat. park Cent. Afr. Rep. 98 C3
Andrelândia Brazil 145 B3
Andrew Canada 121 H4
Andrew Bay Myanmar 70 A3
Andrews SC U.S.A. 133 E5
Andrews TX U.S.A. 131 C5
Andria Italy 58 G4
Androka Madag. 99 E6
Andropov Rus. Fed. see Rybinsk
Andros i. Bahamas 133 E7
Andros i. Greece 59 K6
Androscoggin r. U.S.A. 135 K2
Andros Town Bahamas 133 E7
Androtti i. India 84 B4
Andselv Norway 44 K2
Andújar Spain 57 D4
Andulo Angola 99 B5
Anec, Lake salt flat Australia 109 E5
Āneen-Kio terr. N. Pacific Ocean see Wake Island
Anéfis Mali 96 D3
Anegada, Bahía b. Arg. 144 D6
Anegada Passage Virgin Is (U.K.) 137 L5
Aného Togo 96 D4
Aneityum i. Vanuatu see Anatom
'Aneiza, Jabal hill Iraq see 'Unayzah, Jabal
Anemourion tourist site Turkey 85 A1
Anepmete P.N.G. 69 L8
Anet France 52 B6
Anetchom, Île i. Vanuatu see Anatom
Aneto mt. Spain 57 G2
Ānewetak atoll Marshall Is see Enewetak
Aney Niger 96 E3
Aneytioum, Île i. Vanuatu see Anatom
Anfu China 77 G3
Angalarri r. Australia 108 E3
Angamos, Punta pt Chile 144 B2
Ang'angxi China 74 A3

▶Angara r. Rus. Fed. 72 G1
Part of the Yenisey-Angara-Selenga, 3rd longest river in Asia.

Angarsk Rus. Fed. 72 I2
Angas Downs Australia 109 F6
Angatuba Brazil 145 A3
Angaur i. Palau 69 I5
Ånge Sweden 44 I5
Ángel, Salto waterfall Venez. see Angel Falls
Ángel de la Guarda, Isla i. Mex. 127 E7

▶Angel Falls waterfall Venez. 142 F2
Highest waterfall in the world.

Ängelholm Sweden 45 H8
Angellala Creek r. Australia 112 C1
Angels Camp U.S.A. 128 C2
Ångermanälven r. Sweden 44 J5
Angers France 56 D3
Angikuni Lake Canada 121 L2
Angiola U.S.A. 128 D4
Angkor tourist site Cambodia 71 C4
Anglesea Australia 112 B7
Anglesey i. U.K. 48 C5
Angleton U.S.A. 131 E6
Anglo-Egyptian Sudan country Africa see Sudan
Angmagssalik Greenland see Ammassalik
Ang Mo Kio Sing. 71 [inset]
Ango Dem. Rep. Congo 98 C3
Angoche Moz. 99 D5
Angohrān Iran 88 E5
Angol Chile 144 B5
Angola country Africa 99 B5
Angola IN U.S.A. 134 C3
Angola NY U.S.A. 134 F2
Angola Basin sea feature S. Atlantic Ocean 148 H7
Angora Turkey see Ankara
Angostura Mex. 127 F8
Angoulême France 56 E4
Angra dos Reis Brazil 145 B3
Angren Uzbek. 80 D3
Ang Thong Thai. 71 C4
Anguang China 74 A3

▶Anguilla terr. West Indies 137 L5
United Kingdom Overseas Territory.

Anguilla Cays is Bahamas 133 E8
Anguille, Cape Canada 123 K5
Angul India 84 E1
Angus Canada 134 F1
Angutia Char i. Bangl. 83 G5
Anholt i. Denmark 45 G8
Anhua China 77 F2
Anhui prov. China 77 H1
Anhumas Brazil 143 H7
Anhwei prov. China see Anhui
Aniak U.S.A. 118 C3
Aniakchak National Monument and Preserve nat. park U.S.A. 118 C4
Anin Myanmar 70 B4
Anitápolis Brazil 145 A4
Anıtlı Turkey 85 A1
Aniva Rus. Fed. 74 F3
Aniva, Mys c. Rus. Fed. 74 F3
Aniva, Zaliv b. Rus. Fed. 74 F3
Anizy-le-Château France 52 D5
Anjadip i. India 84 B3
Anjalankoski Fin. 45 O6
Anjengo India 84 C4
Anji China 77 H2
Anjir Avand Iran 88 D3
Anjoman Iran 88 E3
Anjou reg. France 56 D3
Anjouan i. Comoros see Nzwani
Anjozorobe Madag. 99 E5
Anjuman reg. Afgh. 89 H3
Anjuthengu India see Anjengo
Ankang China 77 F1

▶Ankara Turkey 90 D3
Capital of Turkey.

Ankaratra mt. Madag. 99 E5
Ankazoabo Madag. 99 E6
Ankeny U.S.A. 130 E3
An Khê Vietnam 71 E4
Ankleshwar India 82 C5
Anklesvar India see Ankleshwar
Ankola India 84 B3
Ankouzhen China 76 E1
An Lôc Vietnam 71 D5
Anlong China 76 E3
Anlu China 77 G2
Anmoore U.S.A. 134 E4
An Muileann gCearr Ireland see Mullingar
Anmyŏn-do i. S. Korea 75 B5
Ann, Cape Antarctica 152 D2
Ann, Cape U.S.A. 135 J2
Anna Rus. Fed. 43 I6
Anna, Lake U.S.A. 135 G4
Annaba Alg. 58 B6
Annaberg-Buchholtz Germany 53 N4
An Nabk Saudi Arabia 85 C4
An Nabk Syria 85 C2
An Nafūd des. Saudi Arabia 91 F5
Annalee r. Ireland 51 E3
Annalong U.K. 51 G3
Annam reg. Vietnam 68 D3
Annam Highlands mts Laos/Vietnam 70 D3
Annan U.K. 50 F6
Annan r. U.K. 50 F6
'Annān, Wādī al watercourse Syria 85 D2
Annandale U.S.A. 135 G4
Anna Plains Australia 108 C4

▶Annapolis U.S.A. 135 G4
Capital of Maryland.

Annapurna Conservation Area nature res. Nepal 83 F3

▶Annapurna I mt. Nepal 83 E3
10th highest mountain in the world and in Asia.

Ann Arbor U.S.A. 134 D2
Anna Regina Guyana 143 G2
An Nás Ireland see Naas
An Naşrānī, Jabal mts Syria 85 C3
Annean, Lake salt flat Australia 109 B6
Anne Arundel Town U.S.A. see Annapolis
Annecy France 56 H4
Anne Marie Lake Canada 123 J3
Annen Neth. 52 G1
Annette Island U.S.A. 120 D4
An Nimārah Syria 85 C3
An Nimāş Saudi Arabia 86 F6
Anning China 76 D3
Anniston U.S.A. 133 C5
Annobón i. Equat. Guinea 96 D5
Annonay France 56 G4
An Nu'mānīyah Iraq 91 G4
An Nuşayrīyah, Jabal mts Syria 85 C2
Anonima atoll Micronesia see Namonuito
Anoón de Sardinas, Bahía de b. Col. 142 C3
Anorontany, Tanjona hd Madag. 99 E5
Ano Viannos Kriti Greece see Viannos
Anpu Gang b. China 77 F4
Anqing China 77 H2
Anren China 77 G3
Ans Belgium 52 F4
Ansbach Germany 53 K5
Anser Group is Australia 112 C7
Anshan China 74 A4
Anshun China 76 E3
Anshunchang China 76 D2
An Sirhān, Wādī watercourse Saudi Arabia 90 E5
Ansley U.S.A. 130 D3
Anson U.S.A. 131 D5
Anson Bay Australia 108 E3

nsongo Mali 96 D3
nsonville Canada 122 E4
nsted U.S.A. 134 E4
nsudu Indon. 69 J7
ntabamba Peru 142 D6
ntakya Turkey 85 C1
ntalaha Madag. 99 F5
ntalya Turkey 59 N6
ntalya prov. Turkey 85 A1
ntalya Körfezi g. Turkey 59 N6

Antananarivo Madag. 99 E5
Capital of Madagascar.

n tAonach Ireland see Nenagh

Antarctica 152
Most southerly and coldest continent, and the continent with the highest average elevation.

ntarctic Peninsula Antarctica 152 L2
ntas r. Brazil 145 A5
n Teallach mt. U.K. 50 D3
ntelope Island U.S.A. 129 G1
ntelope Range mts U.S.A. 128 E2
ntequera Spain 57 D5
nthony Lagoon Australia 110 A3
nti Atlas mts Morocco 54 C6
ntibes France 56 H5
nticosti, Île d' i. Canada 123 J4
nticosti Island Canada see Anticosti, Île d'
ntifer, Cap d' c. France 49 H9
ntigo U.S.A. 130 F2
ntigonish Canada 123 J5
ntigua i. Antigua and Barbuda 137 L5
ntigua country West Indies see Antigua and Barbuda
ntigua and Barbuda country West Indies 137 L5
ntikythira i. Greece 59 J7
ntikythiro, Steno sea chan. Greece 59 J7
nti Lebanon mts Lebanon/Syria see Sharqī, Jabal ash
ntimilos i. Greece 59 K6
ntimony U.S.A. 129 H2
n tInbhear Mór Ireland see Arklow
ntioch Turkey see Antakya
ntioch U.S.A. 128 C2
ntiocheia ad Cragum tourist site Turkey 85 A1
ntiochia Turkey see Antakya
ntiparos i. Greece 59 K6
ntipodes Islands N.Z. 107 H6
ntipsara i. Greece 59 K5
ntium Italy see Anzio
ntlers U.S.A. 131 E5
ntofagasta Chile 144 B2
ntofagasta de la Sierra Arg. 144 C3
ntofalla, Volcán vol. Arg. 144 C3
ntoing Belgium 52 D4
ntónio Enes Moz. see Angoche
ntri India 82 D4
ntrim U.K. 51 F3
ntrim Hills U.K. 51 F2
ntrim Plateau Australia 108 E4
ntropovo Rus. Fed. 42 I4
ntsalova Madag. 99 E5
ntseranana Madag. see Antsirañana
ntsirabe Madag. 99 E5
ntsirañana Madag. 99 E5
ntsla Estonia 45 O8
ntsohihy Madag. 99 E5
nttis Sweden 44 M3
nttola Fin. 45 O6
n Tuc Vietnam see An Khê
ntwerp Belgium 52 E3
ntwerp U.S.A. 135 H1
ntwerpen Belgium see Antwerp
n Uaimh Ireland see Navan
nuc, Lac l. Canada 122 G2
nuchino Rus. Fed. 74 D4
nugul India see Angul
nupgarh India 82 C3
nuradhapura Sri Lanka 84 D4
nveh Iran 88 D5
nvers Island Antarctica 152 L2
nvik U.S.A. 118 B3
nvil Range mts Canada 120 C2
nxi Fujian China 77 H3
nxi Gansu China 80 I3
nxiang China 77 G2
nxious Bay Australia 109 F8
nyang Guangxi China see Du'an
nyang Henan China 73 K5
nyang S. Korea 75 B5
nyêmaqên Shan mts China 76 C1
nyuan Jiangxi China 77 G3
nyuan Jiangxi China 77 G3
nyue China 76 E2
nyuy r. Rus. Fed. 74 E2
nyuysk Rus. Fed. 65 R3
nzac Alta Canada 121 I3
nzac B.C. Canada 120 F4
nzhero-Sudzhensk Rus. Fed. 64 J4
nzi Dem. Rep. Congo 98 C4
nzio Italy 58 E4
oba i. Vanuatu 107 G3
oga-shima i. Japan 75 E6
o Kham, Laem pt Thai. 71 B5
omen China see Macao
omen Tebie Xingzhengqu aut. reg. China see Macao
omori Japan 74 F4
o Phang Nga National Park Thai. 71 B5

Aoraki mt. N.Z. 113 C6
Highest mountain in New Zealand.

oraki/Mount Cook National Park N.Z. 113 C6
oral, Phnum mt. Cambodia 71 D4
orangi mt. N.Z. see Aoraki
orangi mt. N.Z. see Aoraki
osta Italy 58 B2
otearoa country Oceania see New Zealand
ouk, Bahr r. Cent. Afr. Rep./Chad 97 E4
oukâr reg. Mali/Mauritania 96 C2
oulef Alg. 96 D2
ozou Chad 97 E2
pa r. Brazil 144 E2
pache Creek U.S.A. 129 I5

Apache Junction U.S.A. 129 H5
Apaiang atoll Kiribati see Abaiang
Apalachee Bay U.S.A. 133 C6
Apalachicola U.S.A. 133 C6
Apalachicola r. U.S.A. 133 C6
Apalachin U.S.A. 135 G2
Apamea Turkey see Dinar
Apaporis r. Col. 142 E4
Aparecida do Tabuado Brazil 145 A3
Aparima N.Z. see Riverton
Aparri Phil. 150 E4
Apatity Rus. Fed. 44 R3
Apatzingán Mex. 136 D5
Ape Latvia 45 O8
Apeldoorn Neth. 52 F2
Apelern Germany 53 J2
Apennines mts Italy 58 D2
Apensen Germany 53 J1
Apex Mountain Canada 120 B2
Api mt. Nepal 82 E3
Api i. Vanuatu see Epi
Apia atoll Kiribati see Abaiang

▶Apia Samoa 107 I3
Capital of Samoa.

Apiacas, Serra dos hills Brazil 143 G6
Apiaí Brazil 145 A4
Apishapa r. U.S.A. 130 C4
Apiti N.Z. 113 E4
Apizolaya Mex. 131 C7
Aplao Peru 142 D7
Apo, Mount vol. Phil. 69 H5
Apoera Suriname 143 G2
Apolda Germany 53 L3
Apollo Bay Australia 112 A7
Apollonia Bulg. see Sozopol
Apolo Bol. 142 E6
Aporé Brazil 145 A2
Aporé r. Brazil 145 A2
Apostle Islands U.S.A. 130 F2
Apostolens Tommelfinger mt. Greenland 119 N3
Apostolos Andreas, Cape Cyprus 85 B2
Apoteri Guyana 143 G3
Apozai Pak. 89 H4
Appalachian Mountains U.S.A. 134 D5
Appalla i. Fiji see Kabara
Appennino mts Italy see Apennines
Appennino Abruzzese mts Italy 58 E3
Appennino Tosco-Emiliano mts Italy 58 D3
Appennino Umbro-Marchigiano mts Italy 58 E3
Appingedam Neth. 52 G1
Applecross U.K. 50 D3
Appleton MN U.S.A. 130 D2
Appleton WI U.S.A. 134 A1
Apple Valley U.S.A. 128 E4
Appomattox U.S.A. 135 F5
Aprilia Italy 58 E4
Aprunyi India 76 B2
Apsheronsk Rus. Fed. 91 E1
Apsheronskaya Rus. Fed. see Apsheronsk
Apsley Canada 135 F1
Apt France 56 G5
Apucarana Brazil 145 A3
Apucarana, Serra da hills Brazil 145 A3
Apulum Romania see Alba Iulia
Aq"a Georgia see Sokhumi
'Aqaba Jordan see Al 'Aqabah
Aqaba, Gulf of Asia 90 D5
'Aqaba, Wādī el watercourse Egypt see 'Aqabah, Wādī al
'Aqabah, Birkat al well Iraq 88 A4
'Aqabah, Wādī al watercourse Egypt 85 A4
Aqadyr Kazakh. see Agadyr'
Aqdoghmish r. Iran 88 B2
Aqköl Akmolinskaya Oblast' Kazakh. see Akkol'
Aqköl Atyrauskaya Oblast' Kazakh. see Akkol'
Aqmola Kazakh. see Astana
Aqqan China 83 F1
Aqqikkol Hu salt l. China 83 G1
Aqra', Jabal al mt. Syria/Turkey 85 B2
'Aqran hill Saudi Arabia 85 D4
Aqsay Kazakh. see Aksay
Aqsayqin Hit terr. Asia see Aksai Chin
Aqshī Kazakh. see Akshiy
Aqshuqyr Kazakh. see Akshukur
Aqsū Kazakh. see Aksu
Aqsūat Kazakh. see Aksuat
Aqsū-Ayuly Kazakh. see Aksu-Ayuly
Aqtaū Kazakh. see Aktau
Aqtöbe Kazakh. see Aktobe
Aqtoghay Kazakh. see Aktogay
Aquae Grani Germany see Aachen
Aquae Gratianae France see Aix-les-Bains
Aquae Sextiae France see Aix-en-Provence
Aquae Statiellae Italy see Acqui Terme
Aquarius Mountains U.S.A. 129 G4
Aquarius Plateau U.S.A. 129 H3
Aquaviva delle Fonti Italy 58 G4
Aquidauana Brazil 144 E2
Aquiles Mex. 127 G7
Aquincum Hungary see Budapest
Aquiry r. Brazil see Acre
Aquisgranum Germany see Aachen
Aquitaine reg. France 56 D5
Aquitania reg. France see Aquitaine
Aqzhayqyn Köli salt l. Kazakh. see Akzhaykyn, Ozero
Ara India 83 F4
Āra Āreba Eth. 98 E3
Arab Afgh. 89 G4
Arab, Bahr el watercourse Sudan 97 F4
'Arab, Khalīg el b. Egypt see 'Arab, Khalīj al
'Arab, Khalīj al b. Egypt 90 C5
'Arabah, Wādī al watercourse Israel/Jordan 85 B5
Arabian Basin sea feature Indian Ocean 149 M5
Arabian Gulf Asia see The Gulf
Arabian Peninsula Asia 86 G5
Arabian Sea Indian Ocean 87 K6
Araç Turkey 90 D2
Araça r. Brazil 142 F4
Aracaju Brazil 143 K6
Aracati Brazil 143 K4
Aracatu Brazil 145 C1
Araçatuba Brazil 145 A3
Aracena Spain 57 C5

Aracruz Brazil 145 C2
Araçuaí Brazil 145 C2
Araçuaí r. Brazil 145 C2
'Arad Israel 85 B4
Arad Romania 59 I1
'Arādah U.A.E. 88 D6
Arafura Sea Australia/Indon. 106 D2
Arafura Shelf sea feature Australia/Indon. 150 E6
Aragarças Brazil 143 H7
Aragón r. Spain 57 F2
Araguaçu Brazil 145 A1
Araguaia r. Brazil 145 A1
Araguaia, Parque Nacional do nat. park Brazil 143 H6
Araguaiana Brazil 145 A1
Araguaína Brazil 143 I5
Araguari Brazil 145 A2
Araguari r. Brazil 143 H3
Araguatins Brazil 143 I5
Arai Brazil 145 B1
'Arâif el Naga, Gebel hill Egypt see 'Urayf an Nāqah, Jabal
Araiosos Brazil 143 J4
Arak Alg. 96 D2
Arāk Iran 88 C3
Arak Syria 85 D2
Arakan reg. Myanmar 70 A2
Arakan Yoma mts Myanmar 70 A2
Arakkonam India 84 C3
Araks r. Azer. see Araz
Araku India 84 D2
Aral Kazakh. see Aral'sk
Aral Tajik. see Vose

▶Aral Sea salt l. Kazakh./Uzbek. 80 B2
4th largest lake in Asia.

Aral'sk Kazakh. 80 B2
Aral'skoye More salt l. Kazakh./Uzbek. see Aral Sea
Aralsor, Ozero l. Kazakh. 43 K6
Aral Tengizi salt l. Kazakh./Uzbek. see Aral Sea
Aramac Australia 110 D4
Aramac Creek watercourse Australia 110 D4
Aramah plat. Saudi Arabia 88 B5
Aramberri Mex. 131 D7
Aramia r. P.N.G. 69 K8
Aran r. India 84 C2
Aranda de Duero Spain 57 E3
Arandai Indon. 69 I7
Aranđelovac Serbia 59 I2
Arandis Namibia 100 B2
Arang India 83 E5
Arani India 84 C3
Aran Islands Ireland 51 C4
Aranjuez Spain 57 E3
Aranos Namibia 100 D3
Aransas Pass U.S.A. 131 D7
Arantangi India 84 C4
Aranuka atoll Kiribati 107 H1
Aranyaprathet Thai. 71 C4
Arao Japan 75 C6
Araouane Mali 96 C3
Arapaho U.S.A. 131 D5
Arapgir Turkey 90 E3
Arapiraca Brazil 143 K5
Arapis, Akra pt Greece see Arapis, Akrotirio
Arapis, Akrotirio pt Greece 59 K4
Arapkir Turkey see Arapgir
Arapongas Brazil 145 A3
Araquari Brazil 145 A4
'Ar'ar Saudi Arabia 91 F5
Araracuara Col. 142 D4
Araranguá Brazil 145 A5
Araraquara Brazil 145 A3
Araras Brazil 143 H5
Ararat Armenia 91 G3
Ararat Australia 112 A6
Ararat, Mount Turkey 91 G3
Araria India 83 F4
Araripina Brazil 143 J5
Aras r. Azer. see Araz
Aras Turkey 91 F3
Arataca Brazil 145 D1
Arauca Col. 142 D2
Arauca r. Venez. 142 E2
Aravalli Range mts India 82 C4
Aravete Estonia 45 N7
Arawa P.N.G. 106 F2
Araxá Brazil 145 B2
Araxes r. Azer. see Araz
Arayıt Dağı mt. Turkey 59 N5
Araz r. Azer. 91 H2
also spelt Araks (Armenia), Aras (Turkey), formerly known as Araxes
Arbailu Iraq see Arbīl
Arbat Iraq 91 G4
Arbela Iraq see Arbīl
Arberth U.K. see Narberth
Arbīl Iraq 91 G3
Arboga Sweden 45 I7
Arborfield Canada 121 K4
Arborg Canada 121 L5
Arbroath U.K. 50 G4
Arbuckle U.S.A. 128 B2
Arbu Lut, Dasht-e des. Afgh. 89 F4
Arcachon France 56 D4
Arcade U.S.A. 135 F2
Arcadia FL U.S.A. 133 D7
Arcadia LA U.S.A. 131 E5
Arcadia MI U.S.A. 134 B1
Arcanum U.S.A. 134 C4
Arcata U.S.A. 126 B4
Arc Dome mt. U.S.A. 128 E2
Arcelia Mex. 136 D5
Archangel Rus. Fed. 42 I2
Archer r. Australia 67 G9
Archer Bend National Park Australia 110 C2
Archer City U.S.A. 131 D5
Arches National Park U.S.A. 129 I2
Archipiélago Los Roques nat. park Venez. 142 E1
Ärçivan Azer. 91 H3
Arckaringa watercourse Australia 111 A6
Arco U.S.A. 126 E4
Arcos Brazil 145 B3
Arcos de la Frontera Spain 57 D5
Arctic Bay Canada 119 J2
Arctic Institute Islands Rus. Fed. see Arkticheskogo Instituta, Ostrova

Arctic Mid-Ocean Ridge sea feature Arctic Ocean 153 H1
Arctic Ocean 153 B1
Arctic Red r. Canada 118 E3
Arctowski research station Antarctica 152 A2
Arda r. Bulg. 59 L4
also known as Ardas (Greece)
Ardabīl Iran 88 C2
Ardahan Turkey 91 F2
Ardakān Iran 88 D3
Årdalstangen Norway 45 E6
Ardara Ireland 51 D3
Ardas r. Bulg. see Arda
Arḍ aş Şawwān plain Jordan 85 C4
Ardatov Nizhegorodskaya Oblast' Rus. Fed. 43 I5
Ardatov Respublika Mordoviya Rus. Fed. 43 J5
Ardee Ireland 51 F4
Ardennes plat. Belgium 52 E5
Ardennes, Canal des France 52 E5
Arden Town U.S.A. 128 C2
Arderin hill Ireland 51 E4
Ardestān Iran 88 D3
Ardglass U.K. 51 G3
Ardila r. Port. 57 C4
Ardlethan Australia 112 C5
Ardmore U.S.A. 131 D5
Ardnamurchan, Point of U.K. 50 C4
Ardon Rus. Fed. 91 G2
Ardrishaig U.K. 50 D4
Ardrossan U.K. 50 E5
Ardvasar U.K. 50 D3
Areia Branca Brazil 143 K4
Arel Belgium see Arlon
Arelas France see Arles
Arelate France see Arles
Aremberg hill Germany 52 G4
Arena, Point U.S.A. 128 B2
Arenas de San Pedro Spain 57 D3
Arendal Norway 45 F7
Arendsee (Altmark) Germany 53 L2
Areopoli Greece 59 J6
Arequipa Peru 142 D7
Arere Brazil 143 H4
Arévalo Spain 57 D3
Arezzo Italy 58 D3
'Arfajah well Saudi Arabia 85 D4
Argadargada Australia 110 B4
Arganda del Rey Spain 57 E3
Argel Alg. see Algiers
Argentan France 56 D2
Argentario, Monte hill Italy 58 D3
Argentera, Cima dell' mt. Italy 58 B2
Argenthal Germany 53 H5

▶Argentina country S. America 144 C5
2nd largest and 3rd most populous country in South America, and 8th largest in the world.

Argentine Abyssal Plain sea feature S. Atlantic Ocean 148 E9
Argentine Basin sea feature S. Atlantic Ocean 148 F8
Argentine Republic country S. America see Argentina
Argentine Rise sea feature S. Atlantic Ocean 148 E8
Argentino, Lago l. Arg. 144 B8
Argenton-sur-Creuse France 56 E3
Argentoratum France see Strasbourg
Argeş r. Romania 59 L2
Arghandab r. Afgh. 89 G4
Argi r. Rus. Fed. 74 C1
Argolikos Kolpos b. Greece 59 J6
Argos Greece 59 J6
Argos U.S.A. 134 B3
Argostoli Greece 59 I5
Arguís Spain 57 F2
Argun' r. China/Rus. Fed. 73 M2
Argun Rus. Fed. 91 G2
Argungu Nigeria 96 D3
Argus Range mts U.S.A. 128 E4
Argyle Canada 123 I6
Argyle, Lake Australia 108 E4
Argyrokastron Albania see Gjirokastër
Ar Horqin Qi China see Tianshan
Århus Denmark 45 G8
Ariah Park Australia 112 C5
Ariamsvlei Namibia 100 D5
Ariana Tunisia see L'Ariana
Ariano Irpino Italy 58 F4
Ari Atoll Maldives 81 D11
Aribinda Burkina 96 C3
Arica Chile 142 D7
Arid, Cape Australia 109 C8
Arigza China 76 C1
Arīḥā Syria 85 C2
Arīḥā West Bank see Jericho
Arikaree r. U.S.A. 130 C3
Arima Trin. and Tob. 137 L6
Ariminum Italy see Rimini
Arinos Brazil 145 B1
Aripuanã Brazil 143 G6
Aripuanã r. Brazil 142 F5
Ariquemes Brazil 142 F5
Aris Namibia 100 C2
Arisaig U.K. 50 D4
Arisaig, Sound of sea chan. U.K. 50 D4
'Arīsh, Wādī al watercourse Egypt 85 A4
Aristazabal Island Canada 120 D4
Arixang China see Wenquan
Ariyalur India 84 C4
Arizaro, Salar de salt flat Arg. 144 C2
Arizona Arg. 144 C5
Arizona state U.S.A. 127 F6
Arizpe Mex. 127 F7
'Arjah Saudi Arabia 86 F5
Arjasa Indon. 68 F8
Arjeplog Sweden 44 J3
Arjuni Chhattisgarh India 84 D1
Arjuni India 82 E5
Arkadak Rus. Fed. 43 I6
Arkadelphia U.S.A. 131 E5
Arkaig, Loch l. U.K. 50 D4
Arkalyk Kazakh. 80 C1
Arkansas r. U.S.A. 131 F5
Arkansas state U.S.A. 131 E5
Arkansas City AR U.S.A. 131 F5
Arkansas City KS U.S.A. 131 D4
Arkatag Shan mts China 83 G1

Arkell, Mount Canada 120 C2
Arkenu, Jabal mt. Libya 86 B5
Arkhangel'sk Rus. Fed. see Archangel
Arkhara Rus. Fed. 74 C2
Arkhipovka Rus. Fed. 74 D4
Árki i. Greece see Arkoi
Arklow Ireland 51 F5
Arkoi i. Greece 59 L6
Arkona Canada 134 E2
Arkona, Kap c. Germany 47 N3
Arkonam India see Arakkonam
Arkport U.S.A. 135 G2
Arkticheskogo Instituta, Ostrova is Rus. Fed. 64 J2
Arkul' Rus. Fed. 42 K4
Arlandag mt. Turkm. 88 D2
Arles France 56 G5
Arlington S. Africa 101 H5
Arlington NY U.S.A. 135 I3
Arlington OH U.S.A. 134 D3
Arlington SD U.S.A. 130 D2
Arlington VA U.S.A. 135 G4
Arlington Heights U.S.A. 134 A2
Arlit Niger 96 D3
Arlon Belgium 52 F5
Arm r. Canada 121 J5
Armadale Australia 109 A8
Armagh U.K. 51 F3
Armant Egypt 86 D4
Armavir Armenia 91 G2
Armavir Rus. Fed. 91 F1
Armenia country Asia 91 G2
Armenia Col. 142 C3
Armenopolis Romania see Gherla
Armeria Mex. 136 D5
Armidale Australia 112 E3
Armington U.S.A. 126 F3
Armit Lake Canada 121 N1
Armori India 84 D1
Armour U.S.A. 130 D3
Armoy U.K. 51 F2
Armstrong r. Australia 108 E4
Armstrong Canada 122 C4
Armstrong, Mount Canada 120 C2
Armstrong Island Cook Is see Rarotonga
Armu r. Rus. Fed. 74 E3
Armur India 84 C2
Armutçuk Dağı mts Turkey 59 L5
Armyanskaya S.S.R. country Asia see Armenia
Arnaoutis, Cape Cyprus see Arnauti, Cape
Arnaud r. Canada 123 H2
Arnauti, Cape Cyprus 85 A2
Årnes Norway 45 G6
Arnett U.S.A. 131 D4
Arnhem Neth. 52 F3
Arnhem, Cape Australia 110 B2
Arnhem Land reg. Australia 108 F3
Arno r. Italy 58 D3
Arno Bay Australia 111 B7
Arnold U.K. 49 F5
Arnold's Cove Canada 123 L5
Arnon r. Jordan see Mawjib, Wādī al
Arnprior Canada 135 G1
Arnsberg Germany 53 I3
Arnstadt Germany 53 K4
Arnstein Germany 53 J5
Arnstorf Germany 53 M6
Aroab Namibia 100 D4
Aroland Canada 122 D4
Arolsen Germany 53 J3
Aroma Sudan 86 E6
Arona Italy 58 C2
Arorae i. Kiribati 107 H2
Arore i. Kiribati see Arorae
Aros r. Mex. 127 F7
Arossi i. Solomon Is see San Cristobal
Arqalyq Kazakh. see Arkalyk
Arquipélago da Madeira aut. reg. Port. 96 B1
Arrabury Australia 111 C5
Arrah India see Ara
Arraias Brazil 145 B1
Arraias, Serra de hills Brazil 145 B1
Ar Ramlah Jordan 85 B5
Ar Ramthā Jordan 85 C3
Arran i. U.K. 50 D5
Arranmore Island Ireland 51 D3
Ar Raqqah Syria 85 D2
Arras France 52 C4
Ar Rass Saudi Arabia 86 F4
Ar Rastān Syria 85 C2
Ar Rayyān Qatar 88 C5
Arrecife Canary Is 96 B2
Arretium Italy see Arezzo
Arriagá Mex. 136 F5
Ar Rifā'ī Iraq 91 G5
Ar Rihāb salt flat Iraq 91 G5
Ar Rimāl reg. Saudi Arabia 98 F1
Arrington U.S.A. 135 F5
Ar Riyāḍ Saudi Arabia see Riyadh
Arrochar U.K. 50 E4
Arrojado r. Brazil 145 B1
Arrow, Lough l. Ireland 51 D3
Arrowsmith, Mount N.Z. 113 C6
Arroyo Grande U.S.A. 128 C4
Ar Rubay'iyah Saudi Arabia 88 B5
Ar Rummān Jordan 85 B3
Ar Ruq'ī well Saudi Arabia 88 B4
Ar Ruşāfah Syria 85 D2
Ar Ruşayfah Jordan 85 C3
Ar Rustāq Oman 88 E6
Ar Ruṭbah Iraq 91 F4
Ar Ruwaydah Saudi Arabia 88 B5
Ar Ruwaydah Saudi Arabia 88 B6
Ar Ruwayḍah Syria 85 C2
Års Denmark see Aars
Ars Iran 88 B2
Arseno Lake Canada 120 H1
Arsen'yev Rus. Fed. 74 D3
Arsk Rus. Fed. 42 K4
Arta Greece 59 I5
Artem Rus. Fed. 74 D4
Artemisa Cuba 133 D8
Artemivs'k Ukr. 43 H6
Artemovsk Ukr. see Artemivs'k
Artenay France 56 E2
Artesia AZ U.S.A. 129 I5
Artesia NM U.S.A. 127 G6
Arthur Canada 134 E2
Arthur NE U.S.A. 130 C3
Arthur TN U.S.A. 134 D5

Arthur, Lake U.S.A. 134 E3
Arthur's Pass National Park N.Z. 113 C6
Arthur's Town Bahamas 133 F7
Arti Rus. Fed. 41 R4
Artigas research station Antarctica 152 A2
Artigas Uruguay 144 E4
Art'ik Armenia 91 F2
Artillery Lake Canada 121 I2
Artisia Botswana 101 H3
Artois reg. France 52 B4
Artois, Collines d' hills France 52 B4
Artos Dağı mt. Turkey 91 F3
Artova Turkey 90 E2
Artsakh aut. reg. Azer. see Dağlıq Qarabağ
Artsiz Ukr. see Artsyz
Artsyz Ukr. 59 M2
Artur de Paiva Angola see Kuvango
Artux China 80 E4
Artvin Turkey 91 F2
Artyk Turkm. 88 E2
Aru, Kepulauan is Indon. 108 F1
Arua Uganda 98 D3
Aruanã Brazil 145 A1

▶Aruba terr. West Indies 137 K6
Self-governing Netherlands territory.

Arunachal Pradesh state India 83 H4
Arundel U.K. 49 G8
Arun Gol r. China 74 B3
Arun He r. China see Arun Gol
Arun Qi China see Naji
Aruppukkottai India 84 C4
Arusha Tanz. 98 D4
Aruwimi r. Dem. Rep. Congo 98 C3
Arvada U.S.A. 126 G5
Arvagh Ireland 51 E4
Arvayheer Mongolia 80 J2
Arviat Canada 121 M2
Arvidsjaur Sweden 44 K4
Arvika Sweden 45 H7
Arvonia U.S.A. 135 F5
Arwā' Saudi Arabia 88 B6
Arwād i. Syria 85 B2
Arwala Indon. 108 D1
Arxan China 73 L3
Aryanah Tunisia see L'Ariana
Arys' Kazakh. 80 C3
Arzamas Rus. Fed. 43 I5
Arzanah i. U.A.E. 88 D5
Arzberg Germany 53 M4
Arzew Alg. 57 F6
Arzgir Rus. Fed. 91 G1
Arzila Morocco see Asilah
Aš Czech Rep. 53 M4
Asaba Nigeria 96 D4
Asad, Buḥayrat al resr Syria 85 D1
Asadābād Afgh. 89 H3
Asadābād Iran 88 C3
Asahi-dake vol. Japan 74 F4
Asahikawa Japan 74 F4
'Asal Egypt 85 A5
Āsalē l. Eth. 98 E2
Asālem Iran 88 C2
'Asalūyeh Iran 88 D5
Asan-man b. S. Korea 75 B5
Asansol India 83 F5
Āsayita Eth. 98 E2
Asbach Germany 53 H4
Asbestos Mountains S. Africa 100 F5
Asbury Park U.S.A. 135 H3
Ascalon Israel see Ashqelon
Ascea Italy 58 F4
Ascensión Bol. 142 F7
Ascensión Mex. 127 G7
Ascension atoll Micronesia see Pohnpei

▶Ascension i. S. Atlantic Ocean 148 H6
Dependency of St Helena.

Aschaffenburg Germany 53 J5
Ascheberg Germany 53 H3
Aschersleben Germany 53 L3
Ascoli Piceno Italy 58 E3
Asculum Italy see Ascoli Piceno
Asculum Picenum Italy see Ascoli Piceno
Ascutney U.S.A. 135 I2
Āseb Eritrea see Assab
Āseda Sweden 45 I8
Āsele Sweden 44 J4
Asenovgrad Bulg. 59 K3
Aşfar, Jabal al mt. Jordan 85 C3
Aşfar, Tall al hill Syria 85 C3

▶Aşgabat Turkm. 88 E2
Capital of Turkmenistan.

Asha Rus. Fed. 41 R5
Ashburn U.S.A. 133 D6
Ashburton watercourse Australia 108 A5
Ashburton N.Z. 113 C6
Ashburton Range hills Australia 108 F4
Ashdod Israel 85 B4
Ashdown U.S.A. 131 E5
Asheboro U.S.A. 132 E5
Asher U.S.A. 131 D5
Ashern Canada 121 L5
Asheville U.S.A. 132 D5
Asheweig r. Canada 122 D3
Ashford Australia 112 E2
Ashford U.K. 49 H7
Ash Fork U.S.A. 129 G4
Ashgabat Turkm. see Aşgabat
Ashibetsu Japan 74 F4
Ashikaga Japan 75 E5
Ashington U.K. 48 F3
Ashizuri-misaki pt Japan 75 D6
Ashkelon Israel see Ashqelon
Ashkhabad Turkm. see Aşgabat
Ashkum U.S.A. 134 B3
Ashkun reg. Afgh. 89 H3
Ashland AL U.S.A. 133 C5
Ashland ME U.S.A. 132 G2
Ashland NH U.S.A. 135 J2
Ashland OH U.S.A. 134 D3
Ashland OR U.S.A. 126 C4
Ashland VA U.S.A. 135 G5
Ashland WI U.S.A. 130 F2
Ashland City U.S.A. 134 B5
Ashley Australia 112 D2
Ashley MI U.S.A. 134 C2
Ashley ND U.S.A. 130 D2

▶Ashmore and Cartier Islands terr. Australia 108 C3
Australian External Territory.
Ashmore Reef Australia 108 C3
Ashmore Reefs Australia 110 D1
Ashmyany Belarus 45 N9
Ashqelon Israel 85 B4
Ash Shabakah Iraq 91 F5
Ash Shaddādah Syria 91 F3
Ash Shallūfah Egypt 85 A4
Ash Sham Syria see Damascus
Ash Shanāfīyah Iraq 91 G5
Ash Shaqīq well Saudi Arabia 91 F5
Ash Sharāh mts Jordan 85 B4
Ash Sharawrah Saudi Arabia 86 G6
Ash Shāriqah U.A.E. see Sharjah
Ash Sharqāţ Iraq 91 F4
Ash Shaţrah Iraq 91 G5
Ash Shaţţ Egypt 85 A5
Ash Shawbak Jordan 85 B4
Ash Shaybānī well Saudi Arabia 91 F5
Ash Shaykh Ibrāhīm Syria 85 D2
Ash Shiblīyāt hill Saudi Arabia 85 C5
Ash Shiḩr Yemen 86 G7
Ash Shu'āybah Saudi Arabia 91 F6
Ash Shu'bah Saudi Arabia 86 F4
Ash Shurayf Saudi Arabia see Khaybar
Ashta India 82 D5
Ashtabula U.S.A. 134 E3
Ashtarak Armenia 91 G2
Ashti Mahar. India 82 D5
Ashti Mahar. India 84 B2
Ashti Mahar. India 84 C2
Āshtīān Iran 88 C3
Ashton S. Africa 100 E7
Ashton U.S.A. 126 F3
Ashton-under-Lyne U.K. 48 E5
Ashuanipi r. Canada 123 I3
Ashuanipi Lake Canada 123 I3
Ashur Iraq see Ash Sharqāţ
Ashville U.S.A. 133 C5
Ashwaubenon U.S.A. 134 A1
Asi r. Asia 90 E3 see 'Āşī, Nahr al
'Āşī r. Lebanon/Syria see Orontes
'Āşī, Nahr al r. Asia 90 E3
also known as Asi or Orontes
Āsīā Bak Iran 88 C3
Asifabad India 84 C2
Asika India 84 E2
Asilah Morocco 57 C6
Asinara, Golfo dell' b. Sardinia Italy 58 C4
Asino Rus. Fed. 64 J4
Asipovichy Belarus 43 F5
Asīr Iran 88 D5
'Asīr reg. Saudi Arabia 86 F5
Asisium Italy see Assisi
Askale Pak. 82 C2
Aşkale Turkey 91 F3
Asker Norway 45 G7
Askersund Sweden 45 I7
Askim Norway 45 G7
Askī Mawşil Iraq 91 F3
Askino Rus. Fed. 41 R4
Askival hill U.K. 50 C4
Asl Egypt see 'Asal
Aslanköy r. Turkey 85 B1
Asmar reg. Afgh. 89 H3
▶Asmara Eritrea 86 E6
Capital of Eritrea.
Āsmera Eritrea see Asmara
Åsnen l. Sweden 45 I8
Aso-Kuju Kokuritsu-kōen nat. park Japan 75 C6
Asonli India 76 B2
Asop India 82 C4
Asori Indon. 69 J7
Āsosa Eth. 98 D2
Asotin U.S.A. 126 D3
Aspang-Markt Austria 47 P7
Aspatria U.K. 48 D4
Aspen U.S.A. 126 G5
Asperg Germany 53 J6
Aspermont U.S.A. 131 C5
Aspiring, Mount N.Z. 113 B7
Aspro, Cape Cyprus 85 A2
Aspromonte, Parco Nazionale dell' nat. park Italy 58 F5
Aspron, Cape Cyprus see Aspro, Cape
Aspur India 89 I6
Asquith Canada 121 J4
As Sa'an Syria 85 C2
Assab Eritrea 86 F7
As Sabsab well Saudi Arabia 88 C5
Assad, Lake resr Syria see Asad, Buḩayrat al
Aş Şadr U.A.E. 88 D5
Aş Şafā lava field Syria 85 C3
Aş Şafāqis Tunisia see Sfax
Aş Şaff Egypt 90 C5
As Safirah Syria 85 C1
Aş Şaḩrā' al Gharbīyah des. Egypt see Western Desert
Aş Şaḩrā' ash Sharqīyah des. Egypt see Eastern Desert
Assake-Audan, Vpadina depr. Kazakh./Uzbek. 91 J2
'Assal, Lac l. Djibouti see Assal, Lake
▶Assal, Lake Djibouti 86 F7
Lowest point in Africa.
Aş Şāliḩīyah Syria 91 F4
As Sallūm Egypt 90 B5
As Salmān Iraq 91 G5
As Salţ Jordan 85 B3
Assam state India 83 G4
Assamakka Niger 96 D3
As Samāwah Iraq 91 G5
As Samrā' Jordan 85 C3
Aş Şanām reg. Saudi Arabia 86 H5
As Sarīr reg. Libya 97 F2
Assateague Island U.S.A. 135 H4
As Sawādah reg. Saudi Arabia 88 B6
Assayeta Eth. see Āsayita
As Sayḩ Saudi Arabia 88 B6
Assen Neth. 52 G1
Assenede Belgium 52 D3
Assesse Belgium 52 F4
As Sidrah Libya 97 E1
As Sīfah Oman 88 E6
Assigny, Lac l. Canada 123 I3
As Sikak Saudi Arabia 88 C5
Assiniboia Canada 121 J5
Assiniboine r. Canada 121 L5
Assiniboine, Mount Canada 118 G4
Assis Brazil 145 A3
Assisi Italy 58 E3
Aßlar Germany 53 I4
Aş Şubayḩīyah Kuwait 88 B4
Aş Şufayrī well Saudi Arabia 88 B4
As Sukhnah Syria 85 D2
As Sulaymī Saudi Arabia 86 F4
Aş Şulb reg. Saudi Arabia 88 C5
Aş Şummān plat. Saudi Arabia 88 B5
Aş Şummān plat. Saudi Arabia 88 C6
As Sūq Saudi Arabia 86 F5
As Sūrīyah country Asia see Syria
Aş Şuwar Syria 91 F4
As Suwaydā' Syria 85 C3
As Suways Egypt see Suez
As Suways governorate Egypt 85 A4
Assynt, Loch l. U.K. 50 D2
Astacus Kocaeli Turkey see İzmit
Astakida i. Greece 59 L7
Astakos Greece 59 I5
Astalu Island Pak. see Astola Island
▶Astana Kazakh. 80 D1
Capital of Kazakhstan.
Astaneh Iran 88 C2
Astara Azer. 91 H3
Āstārā Iran 86 G2
Asterabad Iran see Gorgān
Asti Italy 58 C2
Astillero Peru 142 E6
Astin Tag mts China see Altun Shan
Astipálaia i. Greece see Astypalaia
Astola Island Pak. 89 F5
Astor r. Pak. 89 I3
Astorga Spain 57 C2
Astoria U.S.A. 126 C3
Åstorp Sweden 45 H8
Astrabad Iran see Gorgān
Astrakhan' Rus. Fed. 43 K7
Astrakhan' Bazar Azer. see Cälilabad
Astravyets Belarus 45 N9
Astrida Rwanda see Butare
Asturias aut. comm. Spain 57 C2
Asturias, Principado de aut. comm. Spain see Asturias
Asturica Augusta Spain see Astorga
Astypalaia i. Greece 59 L6
Asuncion i. N. Mariana Is 69 L3
▶Asunción Para. 144 E3
Capital of Paraguay.
Aswad Oman 88 E5
Aswān Egypt 86 D5
Aswân Egypt see Aswān
Asyût Egypt see Asyūţ
Asyūţ Egypt 90 C6
Ata i. Tonga 107 I4
Atacama, Desierto de des. Chile see Atacama Desert
Atacama, Salar de salt flat Chile 144 C2
▶Atacama Desert Chile 144 C3
Driest place in the world.
Atafu atoll Tokelau 107 I2
Atafu i. Tokelau 150 I6
'Aţā'iţah, Jabal al mt. Jordan 85 B4
Atakent Turkey 85 B1
Atakpamé Togo 96 D4
Atalándi Greece see Atalanti
Atalanti Greece 59 J5
Atalaya Peru 142 D6
Ataléia Brazil 145 C2
Atambua Indon. 108 D2
Atamyrat Turkm. 89 G2
Ataniya Turkey see Adana
'Ataq Yemen 86 G7
Atâr Mauritania 96 B2
Atari Pak. 89 I4
Atascadero U.S.A. 128 C4
Atasu Kazakh. 80 D2
Ataúro, Ilha de i. East Timor 108 D2
Atáviros mt. Greece see Attavyros
Atayurt Turkey 85 A1
Atbara Sudan 86 D6
Atbara r. Sudan 86 D6
Atbasar Kazakh. 80 C1
Atchison U.S.A. 130 E4
Atebubu Ghana 96 C4
Ateransk Kazakh. see Atyrau
Āteshān Iran 88 D3
Āteshkhāneh, Kūh-e hill Afgh. 89 F3
Atessa Italy 58 F3
Ath Belgium 52 D4
Athabasca r. Canada 121 I3
Athabasca, Lake Canada 121 I3
Athalia U.S.A. 134 D4
'Athāmīn, Birkat al well Iraq 88 A4
Atharan Hazari Pak. 89 I4
Athboy Ireland 51 F4
Athenae Greece see Athens
Athenry Ireland 51 D4
Athens Canada 135 H1
▶Athens Greece 59 J6
Capital of Greece.
Athens AL U.S.A. 133 C5
Athens GA U.S.A. 133 D5
Athens MI U.S.A. 134 C2
Athens OH U.S.A. 134 D4
Athens PA U.S.A. 135 G3
Athens TN U.S.A. 132 C5
Athens TX U.S.A. 131 E5
Atherstone U.K. 49 F6
Atherton Australia 110 D3
Athies France 52 C5
Athina Greece see Athens
Athínai Greece see Athens
Athleague Ireland 51 D4
Athlone Ireland 51 E4
Athnā', Wādī al watercourse Jordan 85 D3
Athni India 84 B2
Athol N.Z. 113 B7
Athol U.S.A. 135 I2
Atholl, Forest of reg. U.K. 50 E4
Athos mt. Greece 59 K4
Ath Thamad Egypt 85 B5
Ath Thāyat mt. Saudi Arabia 85 C5
Ath Thumāmī well Saudi Arabia 88 B5
Athy Ireland 51 F5
Ati Chad 97 E3
Aţīābād Iran 88 E3
Atico Peru 142 D7
Atikameg Canada 120 H4
Atikameg r. Canada 122 E3
Atik Lake Canada 121 M4
Atikokan Canada 119 I5
Atikonak Lake Canada 123 I3
Atka Rus. Fed. 65 Q3
Atka Island U.S.A. 118 A4
Atkarsk Rus. Fed. 43 J6
Atkri Indon. 69 I7
▶Atlanta GA U.S.A. 133 C5
Capital of Georgia.
Atlanta IN U.S.A. 134 B3
Atlanta MI U.S.A. 134 C1
Atlantic IA U.S.A. 130 E3
Atlantic NC U.S.A. 133 E5
Atlantic City U.S.A. 135 H4
Atlantic-Indian-Antarctic Basin sea feature S. Atlantic Ocean 148 H10
Atlantic-Indian Ridge sea feature Southern Ocean 148 H9
▶Atlantic Ocean 148
2nd largest ocean in the world.
Atlantic Peak U.S.A. 126 F4
Atlantis S. Africa 100 D7
Atlas Méditerranéen mts Alg. see Atlas Tellien
Atlas Mountains Africa 54 C5
Atlas Saharien mts Alg. 54 E5
Atlas Tellien mts Alg. 57 H6
Atlin Lake Canada 120 C3
Atmakur India 84 C3
Atmore U.S.A. 133 C6
Atnur India 84 C2
Atocha Bol. 142 E8
Atoka U.S.A. 131 D5
Atouat mt. Laos 70 D3
Atouila, Erg des. Mali 96 C2
Atqan China see Aqqan
Atrak r. Iran/Turkm. see Atrek
Atrato r. Col. 142 C2
Atrek r. Iran/Turkm. 88 D2
also known as Atrak, alt. Etrek
Atropatene country Asia see Azerbaijan
Atsonupuri vol. Rus. Fed. 74 G3
Aţ Ţafīlah Jordan 85 B4
Aţ Ţā'if Saudi Arabia 86 F5
Attalea Turkey see Antalya
Attalia Turkey see Antalya
At Tamīmī Libya 90 A4
Attapu Laos 70 D4
Attavyros mt. Greece 59 L6
Attawapiskat Canada 122 E3
Attawapiskat r. Canada 122 E3
Attawapiskat Lake Canada 122 D3
Aţ Ţawīl mts Saudi Arabia 91 E5
At Taysīyah plat. Saudi Arabia 91 F5
Attendorn Germany 53 H3
Attersee l. Austria 47 N7
Attica IN U.S.A. 134 B3
Attica NY U.S.A. 135 F2
Attica OH U.S.A. 134 D3
Attigny France 52 E5
Attikamagen Lake Canada 123 I3
Attila Line Cyprus 85 A2
Attleborough U.K. 49 I6
Attopeu Laos see Attapu
Attu Greenland 119 M3
Aţ Ţubayq reg. Saudi Arabia 85 C5
▶Attu Island U.S.A. 65 S4
Most westerly point of North America.
At Tūnisīyah country Africa see Tunisia
Aţ Ţūr Egypt 90 D5
Attur India 84 C4
Aţ Ţuwayyah well Saudi Arabia 91 F6
Atuk Mountain hill U.S.A. 118 A3
Åtvidaberg Sweden 45 I7
Atwater U.S.A. 128 C3
Atwood U.S.A. 130 C4
Atwood Lake U.S.A. 134 E3
Atyashevo Rus. Fed. 43 J5
Atyrau Kazakh. 78 E2
Atyraū admin. div. Kazakh. see Atyrauskaya Oblast'
Atyrau Oblast admin. div. Kazakh. see Atyrauskaya Oblast'
Atyrauskaya Oblast' admin. div. Kazakh. 41 Q6
Aua Island P.N.G. 69 K7
Aub Germany 53 K5
Aubagne France 56 G5
Aubange Belgium 52 F5
Aubenas France 56 G4
Aubergenville France 52 B6
Auboué France 52 F5
Aubrey Cliffs mts U.S.A. 129 G4
Aubry Lake Canada 118 F3
Auburn r. Australia 111 E5
Auburn Canada 134 E2
Auburn AL U.S.A. 133 C5
Auburn CA U.S.A. 128 C2
Auburn IN U.S.A. 134 C3
Auburn KY U.S.A. 134 B5
Auburn ME U.S.A. 135 J1
Auburn NE U.S.A. 130 E3
Auburn NY U.S.A. 135 G2
Auburn Range hills Australia 110 E5
Aubusson France 56 F4
Auch France 56 E5
Auche Myanmar 70 B1
Auchterarder U.K. 50 F4
▶Auckland N.Z. 113 E3
5th most populous city in Oceania.
Auckland Islands N.Z. 107 G7
Auden Canada 122 D4
Audenarde Belgium see Oudenaarde
Audo mts Eth. 98 E3
Audo Range mts Eth. see Audo
Audruicq France 52 C4
Audubon U.S.A. 130 E3
Aue Germany 53 M4
Auerbach Germany 53 M4
Auerbach in der Oberpfalz Germany 53 L5
Auersberg mt. Germany 53 M4
Augathella Australia 111 D5
Augher U.K. 51 E3
Aughnacloy U.K. 51 F3
Aughrim Ireland 51 F5
Augrabies S. Africa 100 E5
Augrabies Falls S. Africa 100 E5
Augrabies Falls National Park S. Africa 100 E5
Au Gres U.S.A. 134 D1
Augsburg Germany 47 M6
Augusta Australia 109 A8
Augusta Sicily Italy 58 F6
Augusta AR U.S.A. 131 F5
Augusta GA U.S.A. 133 D5
Augusta KY U.S.A. 134 C4
▶Augusta ME U.S.A. 135 K1
Capital of Maine.
Augusta MT U.S.A. 126 E3
Augusta Auscorum France see Auch
Augusta Taurinorum Italy see Turin
Augusta Treverorum Germany see Trier
Augusta Vindelicorum Germany see Augsburg
Augusto de Lima Brazil 145 B2
Augustus, Mount Australia 109 B6
Auke Bay U.S.A. 120 C3
Aukštaitijos nacionalinis parkas nat. park Lith. 45 O9
Aulavik National Park Canada 118 G2
Auld, Lake salt flat Australia 108 C5
Auliye Ata Kazakh. see Taraz
Aulnoye-Aymeries France 52 D4
Aulon Albania see Vlorë
Ault France 52 B4
Aumale Alg. see Sour el Ghozlane
Aumale France 52 B5
Aundh India 84 B2
Aundhi India 84 D1
Aunglan Myanmar 70 A3
Auob watercourse Namibia/S. Africa 100 E4
Aupaluk Canada 123 H2
Aur i. Malaysia 71 D7
Aura Fin. 45 M6
Auraiya India 82 D4
Aurangabad Bihar India 83 F4
Aurangabad Mahar. India 84 B2
Aure r. France 49 F9
Aurich Germany 53 H1
Aurigny i. Channel Is see Alderney
Aurilândia Brazil 145 A2
Aurillac France 56 F4
Aurora CO U.S.A. 126 G5
Aurora IL U.S.A. 134 A3
Aurora MO U.S.A. 131 E4
Aurora NE U.S.A. 130 D3
Aurora UT U.S.A. 129 H2
Aurora Island Vanuatu see Maéwo
Aurukun Australia 110 C2
Aus Namibia 100 C4
Au Sable U.S.A. 134 D1
Au Sable Point U.S.A. 134 D1
Auskerry i. U.K. 50 G1
Austin IN U.S.A. 134 C4
Austin MN U.S.A. 130 E3
Austin NV U.S.A. 128 E2
▶Austin TX U.S.A. 131 D6
Capital of Texas.
Austin, Lake salt flat Australia 109 B6
Austintown U.S.A. 134 E3
Austral Downs Australia 110 B4
Australes, Îles is Fr. Polynesia see Tubuai Islands
▶Australia country Oceania 106 C4
Largest and most populous country in Oceania, and 6th largest in the world.
Australian-Antarctic Basin sea feature S. Atlantic Ocean 150 C9
Australian Antarctic Territory reg. Antarctica 152 G2
Australian Capital Territory admin. div. Australia 112 D5
Austria country Europe 47 N7
Austvågøy i. Norway 44 I2
Autazes Brazil 143 G4
Autesiodorum France see Auxerre
Authie r. France 52 B4
Autti Fin. 44 O3
Auvergne reg. France 56 F4
Auvergne, Monts d' mts France 56 F4
Auxerre France 56 F3
Auxi-le-Château France 52 C4
Auxonne France 56 G3
Auyuittuq National Park Canada 119 L3
Auzangate, Nevado mt. Peru 142 D6
Ava MO U.S.A. 131 E4
Ava NY U.S.A. 135 H2
Avallon France 56 F3
Avalon U.S.A. 128 D5
Avalon Peninsula Canada 123 L5
Avān Iran 91 G3
Avarau atoll Cook Is see Palmerston
Avaré Brazil 145 A3
Avaricum France see Bourges
▶Avarua Cook Is 151 J7
Capital of the Cook Islands, on Rarotonga.
Avawam U.S.A. 134 D5
Avaz Iran 89 F3
Aveiro Port. 57 B3
Aveiro, Ria de est. Port. 57 B3
Āvej Iran 88 C3
Avellino Italy 58 F4
Avenal U.S.A. 128 C3
Avenhorn Neth. 52 E2
Avenio France see Avignon
Aversa Italy 58 F4
Avesnes-sur-Helpe France 52 D4
Avesta Sweden 45 J6
Aveyron r. France 56 E4
Avezzano Italy 58 E3
Aviemore U.K. 50 F3
Avignon France 56 G5
Ávila Spain 57 D3
Avilés Spain 57 D2
Avion France 52 C4
Avis U.S.A. 135 G3
Avlama Dağı mt. Turkey 85 A1
Avlama Dağı mt. Turkey 85 A1
Avlona Albania see Vlorë
Avnyugskiy Rus. Fed. 42 J3
Avoca Australia 112 A6
Avoca r. Australia 112 A5
Avoca Ireland 51 F5
Avoca IA U.S.A. 130 E3
Avoca NY U.S.A. 135 G2
Avola Sicily Italy 58 F6
Avon r. England U.K. 49 E6
Avon r. England U.K. 49 E7
Avon r. England U.K. 49 F8
Avon r. Scotland U.K. 50 F3
Avon U.S.A. 135 G2
Avondale U.S.A. 129 G5
Avonmore r. Ireland 51 F5
Avonmore U.S.A. 134 F3
Avonmouth U.K. 49 E7
Avranches France 56 D2
Avre r. France 52 C5
Avsuyu Turkey 85 C1
Avuavu Solomon Is 107 G2
Avveel Fin. see Ivalo
Avvil Fin. see Ivalo
A'waj r. Syria 85 B3
Awakino N.Z. 113 E4
'Awālī Bahrain 88 C5
Awanui N.Z. 113 D2
Āwarē Eth. 98 E3
'Awārid, Wādī al watercourse Syria 85 D2
Awarua Point N.Z. 113 B7
Āwash Eth. 98 E3
Āwash r. Eth. 98 E2
Awa-shima i. Japan 75 E5
Āwash National Park Eth. 98 D3
Awasib Mountains Namibia 100 B3
Awat China 80 F3
Awatere r. N.Z. 113 E5
Awbārī Libya 96 E2
Awbeg r. Ireland 51 D5
'Awdah well Saudi Arabia 88 C6
'Awdah, Hawr al imp. l. Iraq 91 G5
Aw Dheegle Somalia 97 H4
Awe, Loch l. U.K. 50 D4
Aweil Sudan 97 F4
Awka Nigeria 96 D4
Awserd W. Sahara 96 B2
Axe r. England U.K. 49 D8
Axe r. England U.K. 49 E7
Axedale Australia 112 B6
Axel Heiberg Glacier Antarctica 152 I1
Axel Heiberg Island Canada 119 I2
Axim Ghana 96 C4
Axminster U.K. 49 E8
Axum Eth. see Āksum
Ay France 52 E5
Ayachi, Jbel mt. Morocco 54 D5
Ayacucho Arg. 144 E5
Ayacucho Peru 142 D6
Ayadaw Myanmar 70 A2
Ayagoz Kazakh. 80 F2
Ayaguz Kazakh. see Ayagoz
Ayakkum Hu salt l. China 83 G1
Ayaköz Kazakh. see Ayagoz
Ayan Rus. Fed. 65 O4
Ayancık Turkey 90 D2
Ayang N. Korea 75 B5
Ayaş Turkey 90 D2
Āybak Afgh. 89 H2
Aybas Kazakh. 43 K7
Aydar r. Ukr. 43 H6
Aydarko'l ko'li l. Uzbek. 80 C3
Aydere Turkm. 88 E2
Aydın Turkey 59 L6
Aydıncık Turkey 85 A1
Aydın Dağları mts Turkey 59 L5
Aýdyň Turkm. 88 D2
Āyelu Terara vol. Eth. 86 F7
Ayer U.S.A. 135 J2
Ayers Rock hill Australia see Uluru
Ayeyarwady r. Myanmar see Irrawaddy
Ayila Ri'gyü mts China 82 D2
Áyios Dhimítrios Greece see Agios Dimitrios
Áyios Evstrátios i. Greece see Agios Efstratios
Áyios Nikólaos Greece see Agios Nikolaos
Áyios Yeóryios i. Greece see Agios Georgios
Aylesbury N.Z. 113 D6
Aylesbury U.K. 49 G7
Aylett U.S.A. 135 G5
Ayllón Spain 57 E3
Aylmer Ont. Canada 134 E2
Aylmer Que. Canada 135 H1
Aylmer Lake Canada 121 I1
'Ayn al 'Abd well Saudi Arabia 88 C4
'Ayn al Baidā' Saudi Arabia 85 C4
'Ayn al Bayḑā' well Syria 85 C2
'Ayn al Ghazalah well Libya 90 A4
'Ayn al Maqfī spring Egypt 90 C6
'Ayn Dāllah spring Egypt 90 B6
Aynī Tajik. 89 H2
'Ayn 'Īsá Syria 85 D1
'Ayn Tabaghbugh spring Egypt 90 B5
'Ayn Tumayrah spring Egypt 90 B5
'Ayn Zaytūn Egypt 90 B5
Ayod Sudan 86 D8
Ayon, Ostrov i. Rus. Fed. 65 R3
'Ayoûn el 'Atroûs Mauritania 96 C3
Ayr Australia 110 D3
Ayr Canada 134 E2
Ayr U.K. 50 E5
Ayr r. U.K. 50 E5
Ayr, Point of U.K. 48 D5
Ayrancı Turkey 90 D3
Ayre, Point of Isle of Man 48 C4
Aytos Bulg. 59 L3
A Yun Pa Vietnam 71 E4
Ayuthia Thai. see Ayutthaya
Ayutthaya Thai. 71 C4
Ayvacık Turkey 59 L5
Ayvalı Turkey 90 E3
Ayvalık Turkey 59 L5
Azak Rus. Fed. see Azov
Azalia U.S.A. 134 C4
Azamgarh India 83 E4
Azaouâd reg. Mali 96 C3
Azaouagh, Vallée de watercourse Mali/Nig
96 D3
Azaran Iran see Hashtrud
Azärbaycan country Asia see Azerbaijan
Azärbaijan country Asia see Azerbaijan
Azare Nigeria 96 E3
A'zāz Syria 85 C1
Azbine mts Niger see L'Aïr, Massif de
Azdavay Turkey 90 D2
Azerbaijan country Asia 91 G2
Azerbaydzhanskaya S.S.R. country Asia see Azerbaijan
Azhikal India 84 B4
Aziscohos Lake U.S.A. 135 J1
'Azīzābād Iran 88 E4
Aziziye Turkey see Pınarbaşı
Azogues Ecuador 142 C4
▶Azores terr. N. Atlantic Ocean 148 G3
Autonomous region of Portugal.
Azores-Biscay Rise sea feature N. Atlantic Ocean 148 G3
Azotus Israel see Ashdod
Azov Rus. Fed. 43 H7
Azov, Sea of Rus. Fed./Ukr. 43 H7
Azovs'ke More sea Rus. Fed./Ukr. see Azov, Sea of
Azovskoye More sea Rus. Fed./Ukr. see Azov, Sea of
Azraq, Bahr el r. Eth./Sudan 86 D6 see Blue Nile
Azraq ash Shīshān Jordan 85 C4
Azrou Morocco 54 C5
Aztec U.S.A. 129 I3
Azuaga Spain 57 D4
Azuero, Península de pen. Panama 137 H
Azul, Cordillera mts Peru 142 C5
Azuma-san vol. Japan 75 F5
'Azza Gaza see Gaza
Azzaba Alg. 58 B6
Aẓ Ẓahrān Saudi Arabia see Dhahran
Az Zaqāzīq Egypt 90 C5
Az Zarbah Syria 85 C1
Az Zarqā' Jordan 85 C3
Az Zawr, Ra's pt Saudi Arabia 91 H6
Azzeffâl hills Mauritania/W. Sahara 96 B2
Az Zubayr Iraq 91 G5
Az Zuqur i. Yemen 86 F7

B

Ba, Sông r. Vietnam 71 E4
Baa Indon. 108 C2
Baabda Lebanon 85 B3
Ba'albek Lebanon 85 C2
Ba'al Ḩazor mt. West Bank 85 B4
Baan Baa Australia 112 D3
Baardheere Somalia 98 E3
Bab India 82 D4
Bābā, Kūh-e mts Afgh. 89 H3
Baba Burnu pt Turkey 59 L5
Babadağ mt. Azer. 91 H2
Babadag Romania 59 M2
Babadurmaz Turkm. 88 E2
Babaeski Turkey 59 L4
Babahoyo Ecuador 142 C4
Babai India 82 D5
Babai r. Nepal 83 E3
Bābā Kalān Iran 88 C4
Bāb al Mandab strait Africa/Asia 86 F7
Babanusa Sudan 86 C7
Babao Qinghai China see Qilian
Babao Yunnan China 76 E4
Babar i. Indon. 108 E1
Babar, Kepulauan is Indon. 108 E1
Babati Tanz. 99 D4
Babayevo Rus. Fed. 42 G4
Babayurt Rus. Fed. 91 G2
B'abdā Lebanon see Baabda
Bab el Mandeb, Straits of Africa/Asia see Bāb al Mandab
Babi, Pulau i. Indon. 71 B7
Babian Jiang r. China 76 D4
Babine r. Canada 120 E4
Babine Lake Canada 120 E4
Babine Range mts Canada 120 E4
Bābol Iran 88 D2
Bābol Sar Iran 88 D2
Babongo Cameroon 97 E4
Baboon Point S. Africa 100 D7
Baboua Cent. Afr. Rep. 98 B3
Babruysk Belarus 43 F5
Babstovo Rus. Fed. 74 D2
Babu China see Hezhou
Babuhri India 82 B4
Babusar Pass Pak. 89 I3
Babuyan i. Phil. 69 G3
Babuyan Channel Phil. 69 G3
Babuyan Islands Phil. 69 G3
Bacaadweyn Somalia 98 E3
Bacabal Brazil 143 J4
Bacan i. Indon. 69 H7
Bacanora Mex. 127 F7
Bacău Romania 59 L1
Baccaro Point Canada 123 I6
Băc Giang Vietnam 70 D2
Bacha China 74 D2
Bach Ice Shelf Antarctica 152 L2
Bach Long Vi, Đao i. Vietnam 70 D2
Bachu China 80 E4
Bachuan China see Tongliang
Back r. Australia 110 C3
Back r. Canada 121 M1
Bačka Palanka Serbia 59 H2
Backbone Mountain U.S.A. 134 F4
Backbone Ranges mts Canada 120 D2
Backe Sweden 44 J5
Backstairs Passage Australia 111 B7
Bắc Liêu Vietnam 71 D5
Bắc Ninh Vietnam 70 D2
Bacoachi Mex. 127 F7
Bacoachi watercourse Mex. 127 F7

acobampo Mex. 127 F8
acolod Phil. 69 G4
acqueville, Lac l. Canada 122 G2
acqueville-en-Caux France 49 H9
acubirito Mex. 127 G8
ad Iran 88 D3
ada China see Xilin
ada mt. Eth. 98 D3
ada i. Myanmar 71 B5
adabaýhan Turkm. 89 F2
ad Abbach Germany 53 M6
adagara India 84 B4
adain Jaran Shamo des. China 80 J3
adajoz Spain 57 C4
adami India 84 B3
adampaharh India 83 F5
adanah Saudi Arabia 91 F5
adanjilin Shamo des. China see
Badain Jaran Shamo
adaojiang China see Baishan
adarpur India 83 H4
adaun India see Budaun
ad Axe U.S.A. 134 D2
ad Bederkesa Germany 53 I1
ad Bergzabern Germany 53 H5
ad Berleburg Germany 53 I3
d Bevensen Germany 53 K1
d Blankenburg Germany 53 L4
d Camberg Germany 53 I4
dderen Norway 44 M2
d Driburg Germany 53 J3
d Düben Germany 53 M3
d Dürkheim Germany 53 I5
d Dürrenberg Germany 53 M3
ademli Turkey see Aladağ
ademli Geçidi pass Turkey 90 C3
d Ems Germany 53 H4
aden Austria 47 P6
aden Switz. 56 I3
aden-Baden Germany 53 I6
aden-Württemberg land Germany 53 I6
d Essen Germany 53 I2
d Grund (Harz) Germany 53 K3
d Harzburg Germany 53 K3
d Hersfeld Germany 53 J4
d Hofgastein Austria 47 N7
d Homburg vor der Höhe Germany
53 I4
dia Polesine Italy 58 D2
din Pak. 89 H5
d Ischl Austria 47 N7
diyat ash Shām des. Asia see
Syrian Desert
d Kissingen Germany 53 K4
d Königsdorff Poland see
Jastrzębie-Zdrój
d Kösen Germany 53 L3
d Kreuznach Germany 53 H5
d Laasphe Germany 53 I4
dlands reg. ND U.S.A. 130 C2
dlands reg. SD U.S.A. 130 C3
dlands National Park U.S.A. 130 C3
d Langensalza Germany 53 K3
d Lauterberg im Harz Germany 53 K3
d Liebenwerda Germany 53 N3
d Lippspringe Germany 53 I3
d Marienberg (Westerwald) Germany
53 H4
d Mergentheim Germany 53 J5
d Nauheim Germany 53 I4
dnawar India 82 C5
dnera India 84 C1
d Neuenahr-Ahrweiler Germany 52 H4
d Neustadt an der Saale Germany 53 K4
dnor India 82 C4
dong China 77 F2
Đông Vietnam 71 D5
dou Togo 96 D4
d Pyrmont Germany 53 J3
drah Iraq 91 G4
d Reichenhall Germany 47 N7
dr Ḥunayn Saudi Arabia 86 E5
d Sachsa Germany 53 K3
d Salzdetfurth Germany 53 K2
d Salzuflen Germany 53 I2
d Salzungen Germany 53 K4
d Schwalbach Germany 53 I4
d Schwartau Germany 47 M4
d Segeberg Germany 47 M4
d Sobernheim Germany 53 H5
du Island Australia 110 C1
dulla Sri Lanka 84 D5
d Vilbel Germany 53 I4
d Wilsnack Germany 53 L2
d Windsheim Germany 53 K5
dzhal Rus. Fed. 74 D2
dzhal'skiy Khrebet mts Rus. Fed. 74 D2
d Zwischenahn Germany 53 I1
e Colwyn U.K. see Colwyn Bay
esweiler Germany 52 G4
eza Spain 57 E5
fatá Guinea-Bissau 96 B3
ffa Pak. 89 I3
ffin Bay sea Canada/Greenland 119 L2

Baffin Island Canada 119 L3
2nd largest island in North America, and 5th in the world.

fia Cameroon 96 E4
filo Togo 96 D4
fing r. Africa 96 B3
foulabé Mali 96 B3
foussam Cameroon 96 E4
fq Iran 88 D4
fra Turkey 90 D2
fra Burnu pt Turkey 90 D2
ft Iran 88 E4
fwaboli Dem. Rep. Congo 98 C3
fwasende Dem. Rep. Congo 98 C3
gaha India 83 F4
galkot India 84 B2
galkote India see Bagalkot
gamoyo Tanz. 99 D4
gan China 76 C1
gan Datoh Malaysia see Bagan Datuk
gan Datuk Malaysia 71 C7
gansiapiapi Indon. 71 C7
gata Dem. Rep. Congo 98 B4
gdad U.S.A. 129 G4
gdarin Rus. Fed. 73 K2
gé Brazil 144 F4
Bagenalstown Ireland 51 F5
Bagerhat Bangl. 83 G5
Bageshwar India 82 D3
Baggs U.S.A. 126 G4
Baggy Point U.K. 49 C7
Bagh India 82 C5
Bàgh a' Chaisteil U.K. see Castlebay
Baghak Pak. 89 G4
Baghbaghū Iran 89 F2

▶Baghdād Iraq 91 G4
Capital of Iraq.

Bāgh-e Malek Iran 88 C4
Bagherhat Bangl. see Bagerhat
Bāghīn Iran 88 E4
Baghlān Afgh. 89 H2
Baghrān Afgh. 89 G3
Bağirsak r. Turkey 85 C1
Bağırsak Deresi r. Syria/Turkey see
Sājūr, Nahr
Bagley U.S.A. 130 E2
Baglung Nepal 83 E3
Bagnères-de-Luchon France 56 E5
Bago Myanmar see Pegu
Bago Phil. 69 G4
Bagong China see Sansui
Bagor India 89 I5
Bagrationovsk Rus. Fed. 45 L9
Bagrax China see Bohu
Bagrax Hu l. China see Bosten Hu
Baguio Phil. 69 G3
Bagur, Cabo c. Spain see Begur, Cap de
Bagzane, Monts mts Niger 96 D3
Bahādorābād-e Bālā Iran 88 E4
Bahalda India 83 F5
Bahāmabād Iran see Rafsanjān
Bahamas, The country West Indies 133 E7
Bahara Pak. 89 G5
Baharampur India 83 G4
Bahardipur Pak. 89 H5
Bahariya Oasis oasis Egypt see
Bahrīyah, Wāḥāt al
Bahau Malaysia 71 C7
Bahawalnagar Pak. 89 I4
Bahawalpur Pak. 89 H4
Bahçe Adana Turkey 85 B1
Bahçe Osmaniye Turkey 90 E3
Baher Dar Eth. see Bahir Dar
Baheri India 82 D3
Bahia Brazil see Salvador
Bahia state Brazil 145 C1
Bahía, Islas de la is Hond. 137 G5
Bahía Asunción Mex. 127 E8
Bahía Blanca Arg. 144 D5
Bahía Kino Mex. 127 F7
Bahía Laura Arg. 144 C7
Bahía Negra Para. 144 E2
Bahía Tortugas Mex. 127 E8
Bahir Dar Eth. 98 D2
Bahl India 82 C3
Bahlā Oman 88 E6
Bahomonte Indon. 69 G7
Bahraich India 83 E4
Bahrain country Asia 88 C5
Bahrain, Gulf of Asia 88 C5
Bahrām Beyg Iran 88 C2
Bahrāmjerd Iran 88 E4
Bahrīyah, Wāḥāt al oasis Egypt 90 C6
Bahuaja-Sonene, Parque Nacional
nat. park Peru 142 E6
Baia Mare Romania 59 J1
Baiazeh Iran 88 D3
Baicang China 83 G3
Baicheng Henan China see Xiping
Baicheng Jilin China 74 A3
Baicheng Xinjiang China 80 F3
Baidoa Somalia see Baydhabo
Baidoi Co l. China 83 F2
Baidu China 77 H3
Baie-aux-Feuilles Canada see Tasiujaq
Baie-Comeau Canada 123 H4
Baie-du-Poste Canada see Mistissini
Baie-St-Paul Canada 123 H5
Baie-Trinité Canada 123 I4
Baie Verte Canada 123 K4
Baiguan China see Shangyu
Baiguo Hubei China 77 G2
Baiguo Hunan China 77 G3
Baihanchang China 76 C3
Baihar India 82 E5
Baihe Jilin China 74 C4
Baihe Shaanxi China 77 F1
Baiji Iraq see Bayjī

▶Baikal, Lake Rus. Fed. 72 J2
Deepest and 2nd largest lake in Asia, and 8th largest in the world.

Baikunthpur India 83 E5
Baile Átha Cliath Ireland see Dublin
Baile Átha Luain Ireland see Athlone
Baile Mhartainn U.K. 50 B3
Baile na Finne Ireland 51 D3
Băileşti Romania 59 J2
Bailey Range hills Australia 109 C7
Bailianhe Shuiku resr China 77 G2
Bailieborough Ireland 51 F4
Bailleul France 52 C4
Baillie r. Canada 121 J1
Bailong China see Hadapu
Bailong Jiang r. China 76 E1
Baima Qinghai China 76 D1
Baima Xizang China see Baxoi
Baima Jian mt. China 77 H2
Baimuru P.N.G. 69 K8
Bain r. U.K. 48 G5
Bainang China see Norkyung
Bainbridge GA U.S.A. 133 C6
Bainbridge IN U.S.A. 134 B4
Bainbridge NY U.S.A. 135 H2
Bainduru India 84 B3
Baingoin China see Porong
Baini China see Yuqing
Baiona Spain 57 B2
Baiqên China 76 D1
Baiquan China 74 B3
Bā'ir Jordan 85 C4
Bā'ir, Wādī watercourse Jordan/Saudi Arabia
85 C4
Bairab Co l. China 83 E2
Bairat India 82 D4
Baird U.S.A. 131 D5
Baird Mountains U.S.A. 118 C3

▶Bairiki Kiribati 150 H5
Capital of Kiribati, on Tarawa atoll.

Bairin Youqi China see Daban
Bairnsdale Australia 112 C6
Baisha Chongqing China 76 E2
Baisha Hainan China 77 F5
Baisha Sichuan China 77 F2
Baishan Guangxi China see Mashan
Baishan Jilin China 74 B4
Baishan Jilin China see Baishanzhen
Baishanzhen China 74 B4
Baishui Shaanxi China 77 F1
Baishui Sichuan China 76 E1
Baishui Jiang r. China 76 E1
Baisogala Lith. 45 M9
Baitadi Nepal 82 E3
Baitang China 76 C1
Bai Thương Vietnam 70 D3
Baixi China see Yibin
Baiyashi China see Dong'an
Baiyin China 72 I5
Baiyü China 76 C2
Baiyuda Desert Sudan 86 D6
Baja Hungary 58 H1
Baja, Punta pt Mex. 127 E7
Baja California pen. Mex. 127 E7
Baja California state Mex. 127 E7
Baja California Norte state Mex. see
Baja California
Baja California Sur state Mex. 127 E8
Bajan Mex. 131 C7
Bajau i. Indon. 71 D7
Bajaur reg. Pak. 89 H3
Bajawa Indon. 108 C2
Baj Baj India 83 G5
Bājgīrān Iran 88 E2
Bājil Yemen 86 F7
Bajo Caracoles Arg. 144 B7
Bajoga Nigeria 96 E3
Bajoi China 76 D2
Bajrakot India 83 F5
Bakala Cent. Afr. Rep. 97 F4
Bakanas Kazakh. 80 E3
Bakar Pak. 89 H5
Bakel Senegal 96 B3
Baker CA U.S.A. 128 E4
Baker ID U.S.A. 126 E3
Baker LA U.S.A. 131 F6
Baker MT U.S.A. 126 G3
Baker NV U.S.A. 129 F2
Baker OR U.S.A. 126 D3
Baker WV U.S.A. 135 F4
Baker, Mount vol. U.S.A. 126 C2
Baker Butte mt. U.S.A. 129 H4

▶Baker Island terr. N. Pacific Ocean 107 I1
United States Unincorporated Territory.

Baker Island U.S.A. 120 C4
Baker Lake salt flat Australia 109 D6
Baker Lake Canada 121 M1
Baker Lake l. Canada 121 M1
Baker's Dozen Islands Canada 122 F2
Bakersfield U.S.A. 128 D4
Bakersville U.S.A. 132 D4
Bâ Kêv Cambodia 71 D4
Bakhardok Turkm. see Bokurdak
Bākharz mts Iran 89 F3
Bakhasar India 82 B4
Bakhirevo Rus. Fed. 74 C2
Bakhmach Ukr. 43 G6
Bakhma Dam Iraq see Bēkma, Sadd
Bakhmut Ukr. see Artemivs'k
Bākhtarān Iran see Kermānshāh
Bakhtegan, Daryācheh-ye l. Iran 88 D4
Bakhtiari Country reg. Iran 88 C3
Bakı Azer. see Baku
Baki Awdal 98 E2
Bakırköy Turkey 59 M4
Bakkejord Norway 44 K2
Bakloh India 82 C2
Bako Eth. 98 D3
Bakongan Indon. 71 B7
Bakouma Cent. Afr. Rep. 98 C3
Baksan Rus. Fed. 91 F2

▶Baku Azer. 91 H2
Capital of Azerbaijan.

Baku Dem. Rep. Congo 98 D3
Bakutis Coast Antarctica 152 J2
Baky Azer. see Baku
Balâ Turkey 90 D3
Bala U.K. 49 D6
Bala, Cerros de mts Bol. 142 E6
Balabac i. Phil. 68 F5
Balabac Strait Malaysia/Phil. 68 F5
Baladeh Māzandarān Iran 88 C2
Baladeh Māzandarān Iran 88 C2
Baladek Rus. Fed. 74 D1
Balaghat India 82 E5
Balaghat Range hills India 84 B2
Bālā Ḥowẓ Iran 88 E4
Balaka Malawi 99 D5
Balakän Azer. 91 G2
Balakhna Rus. Fed. 42 I4
Balakhta Rus. Fed. 72 G1
Balaklava Australia 111 B7
Balaklava Ukr. 90 D1
Balakleya Ukr. see Balakliya
Balakliya Ukr. 43 H6
Balakovo Rus. Fed. 43 J5
Bala Lake l. U.K. 49 D6
Balaman India 82 E4
Balan India 82 B4
Balanda Rus. Fed. see Kalininsk
Balanda r. Rus. Fed. 43 J6
Balan Dağı hill Turkey 59 M6
Balanga Phil. 69 G4
Balangir India see Bolangir
Balaözen r. Kazakh./Rus. Fed. see
Malyy Uzen'
Balarampur India see Balrampur
Balashov Rus. Fed. 43 I6
Balasore India see Baleshwar
Balaton, Lake Hungary 58 G1
Balatonboglár Hungary 58 G1
Balatonfüred Hungary 58 G1
Balbina Brazil 143 G4
Balbina, Represa de resr Brazil 143 G4
Balbriggan Ireland 51 F4
Balchik Bulg. 59 M3
Balclutha N.Z. 113 B8
Balcones Escarpment U.S.A. 131 C6
Bald Knob U.S.A. 134 E5
Bald Mountain U.S.A. 129 F3
Baldock Lake Canada 121 L3
Baldwin Canada 134 F1
Baldwin FL U.S.A. 133 D6
Baldwin MI U.S.A. 134 C2
Baldwin PA U.S.A. 134 F3
Baldy Mount Canada 126 D2
Baldy Mountain hill Canada 121 K5
Baldy Peak U.S.A. 129 I5
Bale Indon. 68 C7
Bâle Switz. see Basel
Baléa Mali 96 B3
Baleares is Spain see Balearic Islands
Baleares, Islas is Spain see Balearic Islands
Baleares Insulae is Spain see
Balearic Islands
Balearic Islands is Spain 57 G4
Balears is Spain see Balearic Islands
Balears, Illes is Spain see Balearic Islands
Baleia, Ponta da pt Brazil 145 D2
Bale Mountains National Park Eth. 98 D3
Baler Phil. 69 G3
Baleshwar India 83 F5
Balestrand Norway 45 E6
Baléyara Niger 96 D3
Balezino Rus. Fed. 41 Q4
Balfe's Creek Australia 110 D4
Balfour Downs Australia 108 C5
Balgo Australia 108 D5
Balguntay China 80 G3
Bali India 82 C4
Bali i. Indon. 108 A2
Bali, Laut sea Indon. 108 A1
Balia India see Ballia
Baliapal India 83 F5
Balige Indon. 71 B7
Baliguda India 84 D1
Balıkesir Turkey 59 L5
Balīkh r. Syria/Turkey 85 D2
Balikpapan Indon. 68 F7
Balimila Reservoir India 84 D2
Balimo P.N.G. 69 K8
Balin China 74 A2
Baling Malaysia 71 C6
Balingen Germany 47 L6
Balintore U.K. 50 F3
Bali Sea Indon. see Bali, Laut
Balk Neth. 52 F2
Balkanabat Turkm. 88 D2
Balkan Mountains Bulg./Serbia 59 J3
Balkassar Pak. 89 I3
Balkhash Kazakh. 80 D2

▶Balkhash, Lake Kazakh. 80 D2
3rd largest lake in Asia.

Balkhash, Ozero l. Kazakh. see
Balkhash, Lake
Balkuduk Kazakh. 43 J7
Ballachulish U.K. 50 D4
Balladonia Australia 109 C8
Balladoran Australia 112 D3
Ballaghaderreen Ireland 51 D4
Ballan Australia 112 B6
Ballangen Norway 44 J2
Ballantine U.S.A. 126 F3
Ballantrae U.K. 50 E5
Ballarat Australia 112 A6
Ballard, Lake salt flat Australia 109 C7
Ballarpur India 84 C2
Ballater U.K. 50 F3
Ballé Mali 96 C3
Ballena, Punta pt Chile 144 B3
Balleny Islands Antarctica 152 H2
Ballia India 83 F4
Ballina Australia 112 F2
Ballina Ireland 51 C3
Ballinafad Ireland 51 D3
Ballinalack Ireland 51 E4
Ballinamore Ireland 51 E3
Ballinasloe Ireland 51 D4
Ballindine Ireland 51 D4
Ballinger U.S.A. 131 D6
Ballinluig U.K. 50 F4
Ballinrobe Ireland 51 C4
Ballston Spa U.S.A. 135 I2
Ballybay Ireland 51 F3
Ballybunion Ireland 51 C5
Ballycanew Ireland 51 F5
Ballycastle Ireland 51 C3
Ballycastle U.K. 51 F2
Ballyclare U.K. 51 G3
Ballyconnell Ireland 51 E3
Ballygar Ireland 51 D4
Ballygawley U.K. 51 E3
Ballygorman Ireland 51 E2
Ballyhaunis Ireland 51 D4
Ballyheigue Ireland 51 C5
Ballykelly U.K. 51 E2
Ballylynan Ireland 51 E5
Ballymacmague Ireland 51 E5
Ballymahon Ireland 51 E4
Ballymena U.K. 51 F3
Ballymoney U.K. 51 F2
Ballymote Ireland 51 D3
Ballynahinch U.K. 51 G3
Ballyshannon Ireland 51 D3
Ballyteige Bay Ireland 51 F5
Ballyvaughan Ireland 51 C4
Ballyward U.K. 51 F3
Balmartin U.K. see Baile Mhartainn
Balmer India see Barmer
Balmertown Canada 121 M5
Balmorhea U.S.A. 131 C6
Balochistan prov. Pak. 89 G4
Balombo Angola 99 B5
Balonne r. Australia 112 D2
Balotra India 82 C4
Balqash Kazakh. see Balkhash
Balqash Köli l. Kazakh. see Balkhash, Lake
Balrampur India 83 E4
Balranald Australia 112 A5
Balş Romania 59 K2
Balsam Lake Canada 135 F1
Balsas Brazil 143 I5
Balta Ukr. 43 F7
Baltasound U.K. 50 [inset]
Baltay Rus. Fed. 43 J5
Bălţi Moldova 43 E7
Baltic U.S.A. 134 E3
Baltic Sea g. Europe 45 J9
Balṭīm Egypt 90 C5
Balṭim Egypt see Balṭīm
Baltimore S. Africa 101 I2
Baltimore MD U.S.A. 135 G4
Baltimore OH U.S.A. 134 D4
Baltinglass Ireland 51 F5
Baltistan reg. Pak. 82 C2
Baltiysk Rus. Fed. 45 K9
Balu India 76 B3
Baluarte, Arroyo watercourse U.S.A. 131 D7
Baluch Ab well Iran 88 E4
Balumundam Indon. 71 B7
Balurghat India 83 G4
Balve Germany 53 H3
Balvi Latvia 45 O8
Balya Turkey 59 L5
Balykchy Kyrg. 80 E3
Balykshi Kazakh. 78 E2
Balyqshy Kazakh. see Balykshi
Bam Iran 88 E4
Bām Iran 88 E2
Bama China 76 E3

▶Bamako Mali 96 C3
Capital of Mali.

Bamba Mali 96 C3
Bambari Cent. Afr. Rep. 98 C3
Bambel Indon. 71 B7
Bamberg Germany 53 K5
Bamberg U.S.A. 133 D5
Bambili Dem. Rep. Congo 98 C3
Bambio Cent. Afr. Rep. 98 B3
Bamboesberg mts S. Africa 101 H6
Bamboo Creek Australia 108 C5
Bambouti Cent. Afr. Rep. 98 C3
Bambuí Brazil 145 B3
Bamda China 76 C2
Bamenda Cameroon 96 E4
Bāmīān Afgh. 89 G3
Bamiantong China see Muling
Bamingui Cent. Afr. Rep. 98 C3
Bamingui-Bangoran, Parc National du
nat. park Cent. Afr. Rep. 98 B3
Bâmnak Cambodia 71 D4
Bamnet Narong Thai. 70 C4
Bamor India 82 D4
Bamori India 84 C1
Bam Posht reg. Iran 89 F5
Bam Posht, Kūh-e mts Iran 89 F5
Bampton U.K. 49 D8
Bampūr Iran 89 F5
Bampūr watercourse Iran 89 E5
Bamrūd Iran 89 F3
Bam Tso l. China 83 G3
Bamyili Australia 108 F3
Banaba i. Kiribati 107 G2
Banabuiu, Açude resr Brazil 143 K5
Bañados del Izozog swamp Bol. 142 F7
Banagher Ireland 51 E4
Banalia Dem. Rep. Congo 98 C3
Banamana, Lagoa l. Moz. 101 K2
Banamba Mali 96 C3
Banámichi Mex. 127 F7
Banana Australia 110 E5
Bananal, Ilha do i. Brazil 143 H6
Bananga India 71 A6
Banapur India 84 E2
Banas r. India 82 D4
Banaz Turkey 59 M5
Ban Ban Laos 70 C3
Banbar China see Domartang
Ban Bo Laos 70 C3
Banbridge U.K. 51 F3
Ban Bua Chum Thai. 70 C4
Ban Bua Yai Thai. 70 C4
Ban Bungxai Laos 70 D4
Banbury U.K. 49 F6
Ban Cang Vietnam 70 C2
Banc d'Arguin, Parc National du nat. park
Mauritania 96 B2
Ban Channabot Thai. 70 C3
Banchory U.K. 50 G3
Bancroft Canada 135 G1
Bancroft Zambia see Chililabombwe
Banda Dem. Rep. Congo 98 C3
Banda India 82 E4
Banda, Kepulauan is Indon. 69 H7
Banda, Laut sea Indon. 69 H8
Banda Aceh Indon. 71 A6
Banda Banda, Mount Australia 112 F3
Banda Daud Shah Pak. 89 H3
Bandahara, Gunung mt. Indon. 71 B7
Bandama r. Côte d'Ivoire 96 C4
Bandān Kūh mts Iran 89 F4
Bandar India see Machilipatnam
Bandar Moz. 99 D5
Bandar Abbas Iran see Bandar-e 'Abbās
Bandarban Bangl. 83 H5
Bandar-e 'Abbās Iran 88 E5
Bandar-e Anzalī Iran 88 C2
Bandar-e Deylam Iran 88 C4
Bandar-e Emām Khomeynī Iran 88 C4
Bandar-e Lengeh Iran 88 D5
Bandar-e Ma'shur Iran 88 C4
Bandar-e Nakhīlū Iran 88 D5
Bandar-e Pahlavī Iran see Bandar-e Anzalī
Bandar-e Shāh Iran see Bandar-e Torkeman
Bandar-e Shāhpūr Iran see
Bandar-e Emām Khomeynī
Bandar-e Shīū' Iran 88 D5
Bandar-e Torkeman Iran 88 D2
Bandar Labuan Malaysia see Labuan
Bandar Lampung Indon. 68 D8
Bandarpunch mt. India 82 D3

▶Bandar Seri Begawan Brunei 68 E6
Capital of Brunei.

Banda Sea sea Indon. see Banda, Laut
Band-e Amīr r. Afgh. 89 G3
Band-e Amīr, Daryā-ye r. Afgh. 89 G2
Band-e Bābā mts Afgh. 89 F3
Bandeira Brazil 145 C1
Bandeirante Brazil 145 A1
Bandeiras, Pico de mt. Brazil 145 C3
Bandelierkop S. Africa 101 I2
Banderas Mex. 131 B6
Banderas, Bahía de b. Mex. 136 C4
Band-e Sar Qom Iran 88 D3
Band-e Torkestān mts Afgh. 89 F3
Bandhi Pak. 89 H5
Bandhogarh India 82 E5
Bandi r. India 82 C4
Bandiagara Mali 96 C3
Bandikui India 82 D4
Bandipur National Park India 84 C4
Bandırma Turkey 59 L4
Bandjarmasin Indon. see Banjarmasin
Bandon Ireland 51 D6
Bandon r. Ireland 51 D6
Ban Don Thai. see Surat Thani
Bandon U.S.A. 126 B4
Band Qīr Iran 88 C4
Bandra India 84 B2
Bandundu Dem. Rep. Congo 98 B4
Bandung Indon. 68 D8
Bandya Australia 109 C6
Bāneh Iran 88 B3
Banera India 82 C4
Banes Cuba 137 I4
Banff Canada 120 H5
Banff U.K. 50 G3
Banff National Park Canada 120 G5
Banfora Burkina 96 C3
Banga Dem. Rep. Congo 99 C4
Bangalore India 84 C3
Bangalow Australia 112 F2
Bangaon India 83 G5
Bangar Brunei 68 F6
Bangassou Cent. Afr. Rep. 98 C3
Bangdag Co salt l. China 83 E2
Banggai Indon. 69 G7
Banggai, Kepulauan is Indon. 69 G7
Banggi i. Malaysia 68 F5
Banghāzī Libya see Benghazi
Banghiang, Xé r. Laos 70 D3
Bangka i. Indon. 68 D7
Bangka, Selat sea chan. Indon. 68 D7
Bangkalan Indon. 68 E8
Bangkaru i. Indon. 71 B7
Bangko Indon. 68 C7

▶Bangkok Thai. 71 C4
Capital of Thailand.

Bangkok, Bight of b. Thai. 71 C4
Bangkor China 83 F3
Bangla state India see West Bengal

▶Bangladesh country Asia 83 G4
7th most populous country in the world.

Bangma Shan mts China 76 C4
Bang Mun Nak Thai. 70 C3
Ba Ngoi Vietnam 71 E5
Bangolo Côte d'Ivoire 96 C4
Bangong Co salt l. China/India 82 D2
Bangor Ireland 51 C3
Bangor Northern Ireland U.K. 51 G3
Bangor Wales U.K. 48 C5
Bangor ME U.S.A. 132 G2
Bangor MI U.S.A. 134 B2
Bangor PA U.S.A. 135 H3
Bangs, Mount U.S.A. 129 G3
Bang Saphan Yai Thai. 71 B5
Bangsund Norway 44 G4
Bangued Phil. 69 G3

▶Bangui Cent. Afr. Rep. 98 B3
Capital of the Central African Republic.

Bangweulu, Lake Zambia 99 C5
Banhā Egypt 90 C5
Banhine, Parque Nacional de nat. park
Moz. 101 K2
Ban Hin Heup Laos 70 C3
Ban Houei Sai Laos see Huayxay
Ban Huai Khon Thai. 70 C3
Ban Huai Yang Thai. 71 B5
Bani, Jbel ridge Morocco 54 C6
Bania Cent. Afr. Rep. 98 B3
Bani-Bangou Niger 96 D3
Banifing r. Mali 96 C3
Banī Forūr, Jazīreh-ye i. Iran 88 D5
Banihal Pass and Tunnel India 82 C2
Banister r. U.S.A. 134 F5
Banī Suwayf Egypt 90 C5
Banī Walīd Libya 97 E1
Banī Wuṭayfān well Saudi Arabia 88 C5
Bāniyās Al Qunayṭirah Syria 85 B3
Bāniyās Ṭarṭūs Syria 85 B2
Bani Yas reg. U.A.E. 88 D6
Banja Luka Bos.-Herz. 58 G2
Banjarmasin Indon. 68 E7
Banjes, Liqeni i resr Albania 59 I4

▶Banjul Gambia 96 B3
Capital of The Gambia.

Banka India 83 F4
Banka Banka Australia 108 F4
Bankapur India 84 B3
Bankass Mali 96 C3
Ban Kengkabao Laos 70 D3
Ban Khao Yoi Thai. 71 B4
Ban Khok Kloi Thai. 71 B5
Bankilaré Niger 96 D3
Banks Island B.C. Canada 120 D4
Banks Island N.W.T. Canada 118 F2
Banks Islands Vanuatu 107 G3
Banks Lake Canada 121 M2
Banks Lake U.S.A. 126 D3
Banks Peninsula N.Z. 113 D6
Banks Strait Australia 111 [inset]
Bankura India 83 F5
Ban Lamduan Thai. 71 C4
Banlan China 77 F3
Ban Mae La Luang Thai. 70 B3
Banmaw Myanmar see Bhamo
Banmo Myanmar see Bhamo
Bann r. Ireland 51 F5
Bann r. U.K. 51 F2
Ban Nakham Laos 70 D3
Bannerman Town Bahamas 133 E7
Banning U.S.A. 128 E5
Banningville Dem. Rep. Congo see
Bandundu

Ban Noi Myanmar 70 B3
Ban Nong Kung Thai. 70 D3
Bannu Pak. 89 H3
Bano India 83 F5
Bañolas Spain see Banyoles
Ban Phai Thai. 70 C3
Ban Phôn Laos see Lamam
Ban Phôn-Hông Laos 70 C3
Banqiao Yunnan China 76 C3
Banqiao Yunnan China 76 E3
Bansi Bihar India 83 F4
Bansi Rajasthan India 82 C4
Bansi Uttar Prad. India 82 D4
Bansi Uttar Prad. India 83 E4
Bansihari India 83 G4
Banská Bystrica Slovakia 47 Q6
Banspani India 83 F5
Bansur India 82 D4
Ban Sut Ta Thai. 70 B3
Ban Suwan Wari Thai. 70 D4
Banswara India 82 C5
Banteer Ireland 51 D5
Ban Tha Song Yang Thai. 70 B3
Banthat mts Cambodia/Thai. see Cardamom Range
Ban Tha Tum Thai. 70 C4
Ban Tôp Laos 70 D3
Bantry Ireland 51 C6
Bantry Bay Ireland 51 C6
Bantval India 84 B3
Ban Wang Chao Thai. 70 B3
Ban Woen Laos 70 C3
Ban Xepian Laos 70 D4
Banyak, Pulau-pulau is Indon. 71 B7
Ban Yang Yong Thai. 71 B4
Banyo Cameroon 96 E4
Banyoles Spain 57 H2
Banyuwangi Indon. 108 A2
Banzare Coast Antarctica 152 G2
Banzare Seamount sea feature Indian Ocean 149 N9
Banzart Tunisia see Bizerte
Banzkow Germany 53 L1
Banzyville Dem. Rep. Congo see Mobayi-Mbongo
Bao'an China see Shenzhen
Baochang China 73 L4
Baocheng China 76 E1
Baoding China 73 L5
Baofeng China 77 G1
Baohe China see Weixi
Baoji Shaanxi China 76 E1
Baoji Shaanxi China 76 E1
Baokang Hubei China 77 F2
Baokang Nei Mongol China 74 A3
Bao Lac Vietnam 70 D2
Baolin China 74 C3
Bao Lôc Vietnam 71 D5
Baoqing China 74 D3
Baoro Cent. Afr. Rep. 98 B3
Baoshan China 76 C3
Baotou China 73 K4
Baotou Shan mt. China/N. Korea 74 C4
Baoulé r. Mali 96 C3
Baoxing China 76 D2
Baoying China 77 H1
Baoyou China see Ledong
Bap India 82 C4
Bapatla India 84 D3
Bapaume France 52 C4
Baptiste Lake Canada 135 F1
Bapu China see Meigu
Baq'ā' oasis Saudi Arabia 91 F6
Baqbaq Egypt see Buqbuq
Baqên Xizang China 76 B1
Baqên Xizang China 76 B2
Baqiu China 77 G3
Ba'qūbah Iraq 91 G4
Bar Montenegro 59 H3
Bara Sudan 86 D7
Baraawe Somalia 98 E3
Bara Banki India see Barabanki
Barabanki India 82 E4
Baraboo U.S.A. 130 F3
Baracaju r. Brazil 145 A1
Baracaldo Spain see Barakaldo
Baracoa Cuba 137 J4
Baradá, Nahr r. Syria 85 C3
Baradine Australia 112 D3
Baradine r. Australia 112 D3
Baragarh India see Bargarh
Barahona Dom. Rep. 137 J5
Barail Range mts India 83 H4
Baraka watercourse Eritrea/Sudan 97 G3
Barakaldo Spain 57 E2
Barakī Barak Afgh. 89 H3
Baralaba Australia 110 E5
Bara Lacha Pass India 82 D2
Baralzon Lake Canada 121 L3
Baram India 83 F5
Baram r. Malaysia 68 E6
Baramati India 84 B2
Baramula India see Baramulla
Baramulla India 82 C2
Baran India 82 D4
Baran r. Pak. 89 H5
Bārān, Kūh-e mts Iran 89 F3
Baranavichy Belarus 45 O10
Barang, Dasht-i des. Afgh. 89 F3
Baranikha Rus. Fed. 65 R3
Baranîs Egypt 86 E5
Baranîs Egypt see Baranīs
Barannda India 82 E4
Baranof Island U.S.A. 120 C3
Baranovichi Belarus see Baranavichy
Baranowicze Belarus see Baranavichy
Baraouéli Mali 96 C3
Baraque de Fraiture hill Belgium 52 F4
Barasat India 83 G5
Barat Daya, Kepulauan is Indon. 108 D1
Baraut India 82 D3
Barbacena Brazil 145 C3
Barbados country West Indies 137 M6
Barbar, Gebel el mt. Egypt see Barbar, Jabal
Barbar, Jabal mt. Egypt 85 A5
Barbara Lake Canada 122 D4
Barbastro Spain 57 G2
Barbate Spain 57 D5
Barberton S. Africa 101 J3
Barberton U.S.A. 134 E3
Barbezieux-St-Hilaire France 56 D4
Barbour Bay Canada 121 M2
Barbourville U.S.A. 134 D5
Barboza Phil. 69 G4
Barbuda i. Antigua and Barbuda 137 L5
Barby (Elbe) Germany 53 L3
Barcaldine Australia 110 D4
Barce Libya see Al Marj
Barcelona Spain 57 H3
Barcelona Venez. 142 F1
Barcelonnette France 56 H4
Barcelos Brazil 142 F4
Barchfeld Germany 53 K4
Barcino Spain see Barcelona
Barclay de Tolly atoll Fr. Polynesia see Raroia
Barclayville Liberia 96 C4
Barcoo watercourse Australia 110 C5
Barcoo Creek watercourse Australia see Cooper Creek
Barcoo National Park Australia see Welford National Park
Barcs Hungary 58 G2
Bärdä Azer. 91 G2
Bárðarbunga mt. Iceland 44 [inset]
Bardaskan Iran 88 E3
Bardawil, Khabrat al salt pan Saudi Arabia 85 D4
Bardawīl, Sabkhat al lag. Egypt 85 A4
Barddhaman India 83 F5
Bardejov Slovakia 43 D6
Bardera Somalia see Baardheere
Bardhaman India see Barddhaman
Bardsey Island U.K. 49 C6
Bardsīr Iran 88 E4
Barðsneshorn pt Iceland 40 D2
Bardstown U.S.A. 134 C5
Barduli Italy see Barletta
Bardwell U.S.A. 131 F4
Bareilly India 82 D3
Barellan Australia 112 C5
Barentin France 49 H9
Barentsburg Svalbard 64 C2
Barents Sea Arctic Ocean 42 I1
Barentu Eritrea 86 E6
Barfleur, Pointe de pt France 49 F9
Bārgāh Iran 88 E5
Bargarh India 83 E5
Barghamad Iran 88 E2
Bargrennan U.K. 50 E5
Bargteheide Germany 53 K1
Barguna Bangl. 83 G5
Barhaj India 83 E4
Barham Australia 112 B5
Bari Italy 58 G4
Bari Doab lowland Pak. 89 I4
Barika Alg. 54 F4
Barinas Venez. 142 D2
Baripada India 83 F5
Bariri Brazil 145 A3
Bari Sadri India 82 C4
Barisal Bangl. 83 G5
Barisan, Pegunungan mts Indon. 68 C7
Barito r. Indon. 68 E7
Barium Italy see Bari
Barkal Bangl. 83 H5
Barkam China 76 D2
Barkan, Ra's-e pt Iran 88 C4
Barkava Latvia 45 O8
Bark Lake Canada 135 G1
Barkly East S. Africa 101 H6
Barkly Homestead Australia 110 A3
Barkly-Oos S. Africa see Barkly East
Barkly Tableland reg. Australia 110 A3
Barkly-Wes S. Africa see Barkly West
Barkly West S. Africa 100 G5
Barkol China 80 H3
Barla Turkey 59 N5
Bârlad Romania 59 L1
Bar-le-Duc France 52 F6
Barlee, Lake salt flat Australia 109 B7
Barlee Range hills Australia 109 A5
Barletta Italy 58 G4
Barlow Canada 120 B2
Barlow Lake Canada 121 K2
Barmah Forest Australia 112 B5
Barmedman Australia 112 C5
Barmen-Elberfeld Germany see Wuppertal
Barmer India 82 B4
Barm Fīrūz, Kūh-e mt. Iran 88 C4
Barmouth U.K. 49 C6
Barnala India 82 C3
Barnard Castle U.K. 48 F4
Barnato Australia 112 B3
Barnaul Rus. Fed. 72 E2
Barnegat Bay U.S.A. 135 H4
Barnes Icecap Canada 119 K2
Barnesville GA U.S.A. 133 D5
Barnesville MN U.S.A. 130 D2
Barneveld Neth. 52 F2
Barneville-Carteret France 49 F9
Barneys Lake imp. l. Australia 112 B4
Barney Top mt. U.S.A. 129 H3
Barnsley U.K. 48 F5
Barnstable U.S.A. 135 J3
Barnstaple U.K. 49 C7
Barnstaple Bay U.K. 49 C7
Barnstorf Germany 53 I2
Baro Nigeria 96 D4
Baroda Gujarat India see Vadodara
Baroda Madh. Prad. India 82 D4
Barong China 76 C2
Barons Range hills Australia 109 D6
Barowghīl, Kowtal-e Afgh. 89 I2
Barpathar India 76 B3
Barpeta India 83 G4
Bar Pla Soi Thai. see Chon Buri
Barques, Point Aux U.S.A. 134 D1
Barquisimeto Venez. 142 E1
Barra Brazil 143 J6
Barra i. U.K. 50 B4
Barra, Ponta da pt Moz. 101 L2
Barra, Sound of sea chan. U.K. 50 B3
Barraba Australia 112 E3
Barra Bonita Brazil 145 A3
Barracão do Barreto Brazil 143 G5
Barra do Bugres Brazil 143 G7
Barra do Corda Brazil 143 I5
Barra do Cuieté Brazil 145 C2
Barra do Garças Brazil 143 H7
Barra do Piraí Brazil 145 C3
Barra do São Manuel Brazil 143 G5
Barra do Turvo Brazil 145 A4
Barra Falsa, Ponta da pt Moz. 101 L2
Barraigh i. U.K. see Barra
Barra Mansa Brazil 145 B3
Barrana Pak. 89 I4
Barranca Peru 142 C4
Barranqueras Arg. 144 E3
Barranquilla Col. 142 D1
Barre MA U.S.A. 135 I2
Barre VT U.S.A. 135 I1
Barre des Écrins mt. France 56 H4
Barreiras Brazil 143 J6
Barreirinha Brazil 143 G4
Barreirinhas Brazil 143 J4
Barreiro Port. 57 B4
Barreiros Brazil 143 K5
Barren Island India 71 A4
Barren Island Kiribati see Starbuck Island
Barren River Lake U.S.A. 134 B5
Barretos Brazil 145 A3
Barrett, Mount hill Australia 108 D4
Barrhead Canada 120 H4
Barrhead U.K. 50 E5
Barrie Canada 134 F1
Barrier Bay Antarctica 152 E2
Barrière Canada 120 F5
Barrier Range hills Australia 111 C6
Barrington Canada 123 I6
Barrington, Mount Australia 112 E4
Barrington Tops National Park Australia 112 E4
Barringun Australia 112 B2
Barro Alto Brazil 145 A1
Barrocão Brazil 145 C2
Barron U.S.A. 130 F2
Barrow r. Ireland 51 F5
Barrow U.S.A. 118 C2
Barrow, Point U.S.A. 118 C2
Barrow Creek Australia 108 F5
Barrow-in-Furness U.K. 48 D4
Barrow Island Australia 108 A5
Barrow Range hills Australia 109 D6
Barrow Strait Canada 119 I2
Barr Smith Range hills Australia 109 C6
Barry U.K. 49 D7
Barrydale S. Africa 100 E7
Barry Mountains Australia 112 C6
Barrys Bay Canada 135 G1
Barryville U.S.A. 135 H3
Barsalpur India 82 C3
Barshatas Kazakh. 80 E2
Barshi India see Barsi
Barsi India 84 B2
Barsinghausen Germany 53 J2
Barstow U.S.A. 128 E4
Barsur India 84 D2
Bar-sur-Aube France 56 G2
Bartang Tajik. 89 H2
Barth Germany 47 N3
Bartica Guyana 143 G2
Bartın Turkey 90 D2
Bartle Frere, Mount Australia 110 D3
Bartlett U.S.A. 130 D3
Bartlett Reservoir U.S.A. 129 H5
Barton U.S.A. 135 I1
Barton-upon-Humber U.K. 48 G5
Bartoszyce Poland 47 R3
Bartow U.S.A. 133 D7
Barú, Volcán vol. Panama 137 H7
Barung i. Indon. 68 E8
Barunga Australia see Bamyili
Barun-Torey, Ozero l. Rus. Fed. 73 L2
Barus Indon. 71 B7
Baruunturuun Mongolia 80 H2
Baruun-Urt Mongolia 73 K3
Baruva India 84 E2
Barwani India 82 C5
Barwéli Mali see Baraouéli
Barwon r. Australia 112 C3
Barygaza India see Bharuch
Barysaw Belarus 45 P9
Barysh Rus. Fed. 43 J5
Basaga Turkm. 89 G2
Basăk, Tônlé r. Cambodia 71 D5
Basalt r. Australia 110 D3
Basalt Island H.K. China 77 [inset]
Basankusu Dem. Rep. Congo 98 B3
Basar India 84 C2
Basarabi Romania 59 M2
Basargechar Armenia see Vardenis
Bascuñán, Cabo c. Chile 144 B3
Basel Switz. 56 H3
Bashākerd, Kūhhā-ye mts Iran 88 E5
Bashanta Rus. Fed. see Gorodovikovsk
Bashaw Canada 120 H4
Bashee r. S. Africa 101 I7
Bāshī Iran 88 C4
Bashi Channel Phil./Taiwan 69 G2
Bashmakovo Rus. Fed. 43 I5
Bāsht Iran 88 C4
Bashtanka Ukr. 43 G7
Basi Punjab India 82 D3
Basi Rajasthan India 82 D4
Basia India 83 F5
Basilan i. Phil. 69 G5
Basildon U.K. 49 H7
Basile, Pico mt. Equat. Guinea 96 D4
Basin U.S.A. 126 F3
Basingstoke U.K. 49 F7
Basin Lake Canada 121 J4
Basirhat India 83 G5
Basīṭ, Ra's al pt Syria 85 B2
Başkale Turkey 91 G3
Baskatong, Réservoir resr Canada 122 G5
Baskerville, Cape Australia 108 C4
Başkomutan Tarıhı Milli Parkı nat. park Turkey 59 N5
Başköy Turkey 85 A1
Baskunchak, Ozero l. Rus. Fed. 43 J6
Basle Switz. see Basel
Basmat India 84 C2
Basoko Dem. Rep. Congo 98 C3
Basra Iraq 91 G5
Bassano Canada 121 H5
Bassano del Grappa Italy 58 D2
Bassar Togo 96 D4
Bassas da India reef Indian Ocean 99 D6
Bassas de Pedro Padua Bank sea feature India 84 B3
Bassein Myanmar 70 A3
Bassein r. Myanmar 70 A3
Basse-Normandie admin. reg. France 49 F9
Bassenthwaite Lake U.K. 48 D4
Basse Santa Su Gambia 96 B3

▶Basse-Terre Guadeloupe 137 L5
Capital of Guadeloupe.

▶Basseterre St Kitts and Nevis 137 L5
Capital of St Kitts and Nevis.

Bassett NE U.S.A. 130 D3
Bassett VA U.S.A. 134 F5
Bassikounou Mauritania 96 C3
Bass Rock i. U.K. 50 G4
Bass Strait Australia 111 D8
Bassum Germany 53 I2
Basswood Lake Canada 122 C4
Båstad Sweden 45 H8
Bastānābād Iran 88 B2
Bastheim Germany 53 K4
Basti India 83 E4
Bastia Corsica France 56 I5
Bastioes r. Brazil 143 K5
Bastogne Belgium 52 F4
Bastrop LA U.S.A. 131 F5
Bastrop TX U.S.A. 131 D6
Basul r. Pak. 89 G5
Basuo China see Dongfang
Basutoland country Africa see Lesotho
Başyayla Turkey 85 A1
Bata Equat. Guinea 96 D4
Batabanó, Golfo de b. Cuba 137 H4
Batagay Rus. Fed. 65 O3
Batala India 82 C3
Batalha Port. 57 B4
Batam i. Indon. 71 D7
Batamay Rus. Fed. 65 N3
Batamshinskiy Kazakh. 80 A1
Batamshy Kazakh. see Batamshinskiy
Batan Jiangsu China 77 I1
Batan Qinghai China 76 D1
Batan i. Phil. 69 G2
Batan is Phil. 69 G2
Batang China 76 C2
Batangafo Cent. Afr. Rep. 98 B3
Batangas Phil. 69 G4
Batangtoru Indon. 71 B7
Batan Islands Phil. 69 G2
Batavia Indon. see Jakarta
Batavia NY U.S.A. 135 F2
Batavia OH U.S.A. 134 C4
Bataysk Rus. Fed. 43 H7
Batchawana Mountain hill Canada 122 D5
Bătdâmbâng Cambodia 71 C4
Bateemeucica, Gunung mt. Indon. 71 A6
Batéké, Plateaux Congo 98 B4
Batemans Bay Australia 112 E5
Bates Range hills Australia 109 C6
Batesville AR U.S.A. 131 F5
Batesville IN U.S.A. 134 C4
Batesville MS U.S.A. 131 F5
Batetskiy Rus. Fed. 42 F4
Bath N.B. Canada 123 I5
Bath Ont. Canada 135 G1
Bath U.K. 49 E7
Bath ME U.S.A. 135 K2
Bath NY U.S.A. 135 G2
Bath PA U.S.A. 135 H3
Batha watercourse Chad 97 E3
Bathgate U.K. 50 F5
Bathinda India 82 C3
Bathurst Australia 112 D4
Bathurst Canada 123 I5
Bathurst Gambia see Banjul
Bathurst S. Africa 101 H7
Bathurst, Cape Canada 118 F2
Bathurst, Lake Australia 112 D5
Bathurst Inlet inlet Canada 118 H3
Bathurst Inlet (abandoned) Canada 118 H3
Bathurst Island Australia 108 E2
Bathurst Island Canada 119 I2
Bathyz Döwlet Gorugy nature res. Turkm. 89 F3
Batié Burkina 96 C4
Batı Menteşe Dağları mts Turkey 59 L6
Batı Toroslar mts Turkey 59 N6
Batken Kyrg. 80 D4
Batkes Indon. 108 E1
Bāṭlāq-e Gavkhūnī marsh Iran 88 D3
Batley U.K. 48 F5
Batlow Australia 112 D5
Batman Turkey 91 F3
Batna Alg. 54 F4
Batok, Bukit hill Sing. 71 [inset]

▶Baton Rouge U.S.A. 131 F6
Capital of Louisiana.

Batopilas Mex. 127 G8
Batouri Cameroon 97 E4
Batrā' tourist site Jordan see Petra
Batrā', Jabal al mt. Jordan 85 B5
Batroûn Lebanon 85 B2
Båtsfjord Norway 44 P1
Battambang Cambodia see Bătdâmbâng
Batticaloa Sri Lanka 84 D5
Batti Malv i. India 71 A5
Battipaglia Italy 58 F4
Battle r. Canada 121 I4
Battle Creek U.S.A. 134 C2
Battleford Canada 121 I4
Battle Mountain U.S.A. 128 E1
Battle Mountain mt. U.S.A. 128 E1
Battura Glacier Pak. 82 C1
Batu mt. Eth. 98 D3
Batu, Pulau-pulau is Indon. 68 B7
Batudaka i. Indon. 69 G7
Batu Gajah Malaysia 71 C6
Batum Georgia see Bat'umi
Bat'umi Georgia 91 F2
Batu Pahat Malaysia 71 C7
Batu Putih, Gunung mt. Malaysia 71 C6
Baturaja Indon. 68 C7
Baturité Brazil 143 K4
Batyrevo Rus. Fed. 43 J5
Batys Qazaqstan admin. div. Kazakh. see Zapadnyy Kazakhstan
Bau Sarawak Malaysia 68 E6
Baubau Indon. 69 G8
Baucau East Timor 108 D2
Bauchi Nigeria 96 D3
Bauda India see Boudh
Baudette U.S.A. 130 E1
Baudh India see Boudh
Baugé France 56 D3
Bauhinia Australia 110 E5
Baukau East Timor see Baucau
Bauld, Cape Canada 123 L4
Baume-les-Dames France 56 H3
Baunach r. Germany 53 K5
Baundal India 82 C2
Baura Bangl. 83 G4
Bauru Brazil 145 A3
Bausendorf Germany 52 G4
Bauska Latvia 45 N8
Bautino Kazakh. 91 H1
Bautzen Germany 47 O5
Bavānāt Iran 88 D4
Bavaria land Germany see Bayern
Bavaria reg. Germany 53 L6
Bavda India 84 B2
Baviaanskloofberge mts S. Africa 100 F7
Bavispe r. Mex. 127 F7
Bavla India 82 C5
Bavly Rus. Fed. 41 Q5
Baw Myanmar 70 A2
Bawal India 82 D3
Baw Baw National Park Australia 112 C6
Bawdeswell U.K. 49 I6
Bawdwin Myanmar 70 B2
Bawean i. Indon. 68 E8
Bawinkel Germany 53 H2
Bawlake Myanmar 70 B3
Bawolung China 76 D2
Baxi China 76 D1
Baxley U.S.A. 133 D6
Baxoi China 76 C2
Baxter Mountain U.S.A. 129 J2
Bay China see Baicheng
Bayamo Cuba 137 I4
Bayan Heilong. China 74 B3
Bayan Qinghai China 76 C1
Bayana India 82 D4
Bayan-Adraga Mongolia 73 K3
Bayanaul Kazakh. 80 E1
Bayanbulak China 80 F3
Bayanday Rus. Fed. 72 J2
Bayan Gol China see Dengkou
Bayan Har Shan mts China 76 B1
Bayan Har Shankou pass China 76 C1
Bayanhongor Mongolia 80 J2
Bayan Hot China 72 J5
Bayan Mod China 72 I4
Bayan Obo China 73 J4
Bayantsagaan Mongolia 80 I2
Bayan Ul Hot China 73 L4
Bayan-Uul Mongolia 73 K3
Bayard U.S.A. 129 I5
Bayat Turkey 59 N5
Bayāẓ Iran 88 E4
Baybay Phil. 69 G4
Bayboro U.S.A. 133 E5
Bayburt Turkey 91 F2
Bay Canh, Hon i. Vietnam 71 D5
Bay City MI U.S.A. 134 D2
Bay City TX U.S.A. 131 D6
Baydaratskaya Guba Rus. Fed. 64 H3
Baydhabo Somalia 98 E3
Bayerischer Wald mts Germany 53 M5
Bayerischer Wald nat. park Germany 53 M5
Bayerischer Wald, Nationalpark nat. park Germany 47 N6
Bayern land Germany 53 L6
Bayeux France 49 G9
Bayfield Canada 134 E2
Bayındır Turkey 59 L5
Bay Islands is Hond. see Bahía, Islas de la
Bayizhen China 76 B2
Bayjī Iraq 91 F4
Baykal, Ozero l. Rus. Fed. see Baikal, Lake
Baykal-Amur Magistral Rus. Fed. 74 C1
Baykal Range mts Rus. Fed. see Baykal'skiy Khrebet
Baykal'skiy Khrebet mts Rus. Fed. 73 J2
Baykan Turkey 91 F3
Bay-Khaak Rus. Fed. 80 H1
Baykibashevo Rus. Fed. 41 R4
Baykonur Kazakh. see Baykonyr
Baykonyr Kazakh. 80 B2
Baymak Rus. Fed. 64 G4
Bay Minette U.S.A. 133 C6
Baynūna'h reg. U.A.E. 88 D6
Bayombong Phil. 69 G3
Bayona Spain see Baiona
Bayonne France 56 D5
Bayonne U.S.A. 135 H3
Bay Port U.S.A. 134 D2
Bayqongyr Kazakh. see Baykonyr
Bayram-Ali Turkm. see Baýramaly
Baýramaly Turkm. 89 F2
Bayramiç Turkey 59 L5
Bayreuth Germany 53 L5
Bayrūt Lebanon see Beirut
Bays, Lake of Canada 134 F1
Bayshore U.S.A. 134 C1
Bay Shore U.S.A. 135 I3
Bay Springs U.S.A. 131 F6
Bayston Hill U.K. 49 E6
Baysun Uzbek. see Boysun
Bayt Lahm West Bank see Bethlehem
Baytown U.S.A. 131 E6
Bay View N.Z. 113 F4
Bayy al Kabīr, Wādī watercourse Libya 97 E1
Baza Spain 57 E5
Baza, Sierra de mts Spain 57 E5
Bāzārak Afgh. 89 G3
Bazardüzü Dağı mt. Azer./Rus. Fed. see Bazardyuzyu, Gora
Bazardyuzyu, Gora mt. Azer./Rus. Fed. 91 G2
Bāzār-e Māsāl Iran 88 C2
Bazarnyy Karabulak Rus. Fed. 43 J5
Bazaruto, Ilha do i. Moz. 99 D6
Bazdar Pak. 89 G5
Bazhong China 76 E2
Bazhou China see Bazhong
Bazin r. Canada 122 G5
Bazmān Iran 89 F5
Bazmān, Kūh-e mt. Iran 89 F4
Bcharré Lebanon 85 C2
Be, Sông r. Vietnam 71 D5
Beach U.S.A. 130 C2
Beachy Head hd U.K. 49 H8
Beacon U.S.A. 135 I3
Beacon Bay S. Africa 101 H7
Beaconsfield U.K. 49 G7
Beagle, Canal sea chan. Arg. 144 C8
Beagle Bank reef Australia 108 C3
Beagle Bay Australia 108 C4
Beagle Gulf Australia 108 E3
Bealanana Madag. 99 E5
Béal an Átha Ireland see Ballina
Béal an Mhuirthead Ireland 51 C3
Béal Átha na Sluaighe Ireland see Ballinasloe
Beale, Lake India 84 B2
Beaminster U.K. 49 E8
Bear r. U.S.A. 126 E4
Bearalváhki Norway see Berlevåg
Bear Cove Point Canada 121 O2
Beardmore Canada 122 D4
Beardmore Glacier Antarctica 152 H1
Bear Island Arctic Ocean see Bjørnøya
Bear Island Canada 122 E3
Bear Lake l. Canada 122 A3
Bear Lake U.S.A. 134 B1
Bear Lake l. U.S.A. 126 F4
Bearma r. India 82 D4
Bear Mountain U.S.A. 130 C3
Bearnaraigh i. U.K. see Berneray
Bear Paw Mountain U.S.A. 126 F2
Bearpaw Mountains U.S.A. 126 F2
Bearskin Lake Canada 121 N4
Beas Dam India 82 C3
Beata, Cabo c. Dom. Rep. 137 J5
Beatrice U.S.A. 130 D3
Beatrice, Cape Australia 110 B2
Beatton r. Canada 120 F3
Beatton River Canada 120 F3
Beatty U.S.A. 128 E3
Beattyville Canada 122 F4
Beattyville U.S.A. 134 D5
Beaucaire France 56 G5
Beauchene Island Falkland Is 144 E8
Beaufort Australia 112 A6
Beaufort NC U.S.A. 133 E5
Beaufort SC U.S.A. 133 D5
Beaufort Island H.K. China 77 [inset]
Beaufort Sea Canada/U.S.A. 118 D2
Beaufort West S. Africa 100 F7
Beaulieu r. Canada 121 H2
Beauly U.K. 50 E3
Beauly r. U.K. 50 E3
Beaumaris U.K. 48 C5
Beaumont Belgium 52 E4
Beaumont N.Z. 113 B7
Beaumont MS U.S.A. 131 F6
Beaumont TX U.S.A. 131 E6
Beaune France 56 G3
Beaupréau France 56 D3
Beauquesne France 52 C4
Beauraing Belgium 52 E4
Beauséjour Canada 121 L5
Beauvais France 52 C5
Beauval France 52 C4
Beaver r. Alberta/Saskatchewan Canada 121 J4
Beaver r. Ont. Canada 122 D3
Beaver r. Y.T. Canada 120 E3
Beaver OK U.S.A. 131 C4
Beaver PA U.S.A. 134 E3
Beaver UT U.S.A. 129 G2
Beaver r. U.S.A. 129 G2
Beaver Creek Canada 153 A2
Beavercreek U.S.A. 134 C4
Beaver Creek r. MT U.S.A. 130 B1
Beaver Creek r. ND U.S.A. 130 C2
Beaver Dam KY U.S.A. 134 B5
Beaver Dam WI U.S.A. 130 F3
Beaver Falls U.S.A. 134 E3
Beaverhead Mountains U.S.A. 126 E3
Beaverhill Lake Alta Canada 121 H4
Beaver Hill Lake Canada 121 M4
Beaverhill Lake N.W.T. Canada 121 J2
Beaver Island U.S.A. 132 C2
Beaverlodge Canada 120 G4
Beaverton Canada 134 F1
Beaverton MI U.S.A. 134 C2
Beaverton OR U.S.A. 126 C3
Beawar India 82 C4
Beazley Arg. 144 C4
Bebedouro Brazil 145 A3
Bebington U.K. 48 D5
Bebra Germany 53 J4
Bêca China 76 C2
Bécard, Lac l. Canada 123 G1
Beccles U.K. 49 I6
Bečej Serbia 59 I2
Becerreá Spain 57 C2
Béchar Alg. 54 D5
Bechhofen Germany 53 K5
Bechuanaland country Africa see Botswana
Beckley U.S.A. 134 E5
Beckum Germany 53 I3
Becky Peak U.S.A. 129 F2
Bečov nad Teplou Czech Rep. 53 M4
Bedale U.K. 48 F4
Bedburg Germany 52 G4
Bedelē Eth. 98 D3
Bedford N.S. Canada 123 J5
Bedford Que. Canada 135 I1
Bedford E. Cape S. Africa 101 H7
Bedford Kwazulu-Natal S. Africa 101 J5
Bedford U.K. 49 G6
Bedford IN U.S.A. 134 B4
Bedford KY U.S.A. 134 C4
Bedford PA U.S.A. 135 F3
Bedford VA U.S.A. 134 F5
Bedford, Cape Australia 110 D2
Bedford Downs Australia 108 D4
Bedgerebong Australia 112 C4
Bedi India 82 B5
Bedla India 82 C4
Bedlington U.K. 48 F3
Bedok Sing. 71 [inset]
Bedok Jetty Sing. 71 [inset]
Bedok Reservoir Sing. 71 [inset]
Bedou China 77 F3
Bedourie Australia 110 B5
Bedum Neth. 52 G1
Bedworth U.K. 49 F6
Beechworth Australia 112 C6
Beechy Canada 121 J5
Beecroft Peninsula Australia 112 E5
Beed India see Bid
Beelitz Germany 53 M2
Beenleigh Australia 112 F1

eernem Belgium 52 D3
eersheba Israel 85 B4
e'ér Sheva' Israel see Beersheba
e'ér Sheva' watercourse Israel 85 B4
eervlei Dam S. Africa 100 F7
eerwah Australia 112 F1
eetaloo Australia 108 F4
eethoven Peninsula Antarctica 152 L2
eeville U.S.A. 131 D6
efori Dem. Rep. Congo 98 C3
eg, Lough l. U.K. 51 F3
ega Australia 112 D6
egari r. Pak. 89 H4
egicheva, Ostrov i. Rus. Fed. see Bol'shoy Begichev, Ostrov
egur, Cap de c. Spain 57 H3
egusarai India 83 F4
éhague, Pointe pt Fr. Guiana 143 H3
ehbehān Iran 88 C4
ehchokô Canada 120 G2
ehrendt Mountains Antarctica 152 L2
ehrūsī Iran 88 D4
ehshahr Iran 88 D2
ehsūd Afgh. 89 G3
ei'an China 74 B2
ei'ao China see Dongtou
eibei China 76 E2
eichuan China 76 E2
eida Libya see Al Bayḑā'
eigang Taiwan see Peikang
eiguan China see Anyang
eihai China 77 F4
ei Hulsan Hu salt l. China 83 H1

Beijing China 73 L5
Capital of China.

eijing municipality China 73 L4
eik Myanmar see Myeik
eilen Neth. 52 G2
eiliu China 77 F4
eilngries Germany 53 L5
eiluheyan China 76 B1
einn an Oir hill U.K. 50 D5
einn an Tuirc hill U.K. 50 D5
einn Bheigeir hill U.K. 50 C5
einn Bhreac hill U.K. 50 D4
inn Dearg mt. U.K. 50 E3
inn Heasgarnich mt. U.K. 50 E4
einn Mholach hill U.K. 50 C2
einn Mhòr hill U.K. 50 B3
inn na Faoghlia i. U.K. see Benbecula
eipan Jiang r. China 76 E3
eipiao China 73 M4
ira Moz. 99 D5

Beirut Lebanon 85 B3
Capital of Lebanon.

i Shan mts China 80 I3
itbridge Zimbabwe 99 C6
ith U.K. 50 E5
eit Jālā West Bank 85 B4
ja Port. 57 C4
ja Tunisia 58 C6
jaïa Alg. 57 I5
jar Spain 57 D3
ji r. Pak. 80 C6
kaa valley Lebanon see El Béqaa
kés Hungary 59 I1
késcsaba Hungary 59 I1
kily Madag. 99 E6
kkai Japan 74 G4
kma, Sadd dam Iraq 91 G3
kovo Rus. Fed. 43 I5
kwai Ghana 96 C4
la India 83 E4
la Pak. 89 G5
lab r. Pak. 89 H4
la-Bela S. Africa 101 I3
labo Cameroon 96 E4
la Crkva Serbia 59 I2
Air U.S.A. 135 G4
lalcázar Spain 57 D4
lá nad Radbuzou Czech Rep. 53 M5
lapur India 84 B2
larus country Europe 43 E5
lau country N. Pacific Ocean see Palau
la Vista Brazil 144 E2
la Vista Moz. 101 K4
la Vista de Goiás Brazil 145 A2
lawan Indon. 71 B7
laya r. Rus. Fed. 65 S3
also known as Bila
laya Glina Rus. Fed. 43 I7
laya Kalitva Rus. Fed. 43 I6
laya Kholunitsa Rus. Fed. 42 K4
laya Tserkva Ukr. see Bila Tserkva
lbédji Niger 96 D3
lchatów Poland 47 Q5
lcher U.S.A. 134 D5
lcher Islands Canada 122 F2
lchiragh Afgh. 89 G3
lcoo U.K. 51 E3
lden U.S.A. 128 C1
lding U.S.A. 134 C2
eapani reef India see Cherbaniani Reef
ebey Rus. Fed. 41 Q5
ledweyne Somalia 98 E3
lém Brazil 143 I4
lém Novo Brazil 145 A5
lén Arg. 144 C3
len Antalya Turkey 85 A1
en Hatay Turkey 85 C1
len U.S.A. 127 G6
lep, Îles is New Caledonia 107 G3
lev Rus. Fed. 43 H5
lfast S. Africa 101 J3

Belfast U.K. 51 G3
Capital of Northern Ireland.

fast U.S.A. 132 G2
fast Lough inlet U.K. 51 G3
fodiyo Eth. 98 D2
ford U.K. 48 F3
fort France 56 H3
gaum India 84 B3
gern Germany 53 N3
gian Congo country Africa see
Congo, Democratic Republic of the
gië country Europe see Belgium

Belgique country Europe see Belgium
Belgium country Europe 52 E4
Belgorod Rus. Fed. 43 H6
Belgorod-Dnestrovskyy Ukr. see Bilhorod-Dnistrovs'kyy

▶Belgrade Serbia 59 I2
Capital of Serbia.

Belgrade ME U.S.A. 135 K1
Belgrade MT U.S.A. 126 F3
Belgrano II research station Antarctica 152 A1
Belice r. Sicily Italy 58 E6
Belinskiy Rus. Fed. 43 I5
Belinyu Indon. 68 D7
Belitung i. Indon. 68 D7
Belize Angola 99 B4

▶Belize Belize 136 G5
Former capital of Belize.

Belize country Central America 136 G5
Beljak Austria see Villach
Belkina, Mys pt Rus. Fed. 74 E3
Bel'kovskiy, Ostrov i. Rus. Fed. 65 O2
Bell Australia 112 E1
Bell r. Australia 112 D4
Bell r. Canada 122 F4
Bella Bella Canada 120 D4
Bellac France 56 E3
Bella Coola Canada 120 E4
Bellaire U.S.A. 134 C1
Bellary India 84 C3
Bellata Australia 112 D2
Bella Unión Uruguay 144 E4
Bella Vista U.S.A. 128 B1
Bellbrook Australia 112 F3
Bell Cay reef Australia 110 E4
Belledonne mts France 56 G4
Bellefontaine U.S.A. 134 D3
Bellefonte U.S.A. 135 G3
Belle Fourche U.S.A. 130 C2
Belle Fourche r. U.S.A. 130 C2
Belle Glade U.S.A. 133 D7
Belle-Île i. France 56 C3
Belle Isle i. Canada 123 L4
Belle Isle, Strait of Canada 123 K4
Belleville Canada 135 G1
Belleville IL U.S.A. 130 F4
Belleville KS U.S.A. 130 D4
Bellevue IA U.S.A. 130 F3
Bellevue MI U.S.A. 134 C2
Bellevue OH U.S.A. 134 D3
Bellevue WA U.S.A. 126 C3
Bellin Canada see Kangirsuk
Bellingham U.K. 48 E3
Bellingham U.S.A. 126 C2
Bellingshausen research station Antarctica 152 A2
Bellingshausen Sea Antarctica 152 L2
Bellinzona Switz. 56 I3
Bellows Falls U.S.A. 135 I2
Bellpat Pak. 89 H4
Belluno Italy 58 E1
Belluru India 84 C3
Bell Ville Arg. 144 D4
Bellville S. Africa 100 D7
Belm Germany 53 I2
Belmont Australia 112 E4
Belmont U.K. 50 [inset]
Belmont U.S.A. 135 F2
Belmonte Brazil 145 D1

▶Belmopan Belize 136 G5
Capital of Belize.

Belmore, Mount hill Australia 112 F2
Belo Madag. 99 E6
Belo Campo Brazil 145 C1
Belœil Belgium 52 D4
Belogorsk Rus. Fed. 74 C2
Belogorsk Ukr. see Bilohirs'k
Beloha Madag. 99 E6
Belo Horizonte Brazil 145 C2
Beloit KS U.S.A. 130 D4
Beloit WI U.S.A. 130 F3
Belokurikha Rus. Fed. 80 F1
Belo Monte Brazil 143 H4
Belomorsk Rus. Fed. 42 G2
Belonia India 83 G5
Belorechensk Rus. Fed. 91 E1
Belorechenskaya Rus. Fed. see Belorechensk
Belören Turkey 90 D3
Beloretsk Rus. Fed. 64 G4
Belorussia country Europe see Belarus
Belorusskaya S.S.R. country Europe see Belarus
Belostok Poland see Białystok
Belot, Lac l. Canada 118 F3
Belo Tsiribihina Madag. 99 E5
Belovo Rus. Fed. 72 F2
Beloyarskiy Rus. Fed. 41 T3
Beloye, Ozero l. Rus. Fed. 42 H3
Beloye More sea Rus. Fed. see White Sea
Belozersk Rus. Fed. 42 H3
Belpre U.S.A. 134 E4
Beltana Australia 111 B6
Belted Range mts U.S.A. 128 E3
Belton U.S.A. 131 D6
Bel'ts' Moldova see Bălţi
Bel'tsy Moldova see Bălţi
Belukha, Gora mt. Kazakh./Rus. Fed. 80 G2
Belush'ye Rus. Fed. 42 J2
Belvidere IL U.S.A. 130 F3
Belvidere NJ U.S.A. 135 H3
Belyando r. Australia 110 D4
Belyayevka Ukr. see Bilyayivka
Belyy Rus. Fed. 42 G5
Belyy, Ostrov i. Rus. Fed. 64 I2
Belzig Germany 53 M2
Belzoni U.S.A. 131 F5
Bemaraha, Plateau du Madag. 99 E5
Bembe Angola 99 B4
Bemidji U.S.A. 130 E2
Béna Burkina 96 C3
Bena Dibele Dem. Rep. Congo 98 C4
Ben Alder mt. U.K. 50 E4
Benalla Australia 112 B6
Benares India see Varanasi
Ben Arous Tunisia 58 D6

Benavente Spain 57 D2
Ben Avon mt. U.K. 50 F3
Benbane Head hd U.K. 51 F2
Benbecula i. U.K. 50 B3
Ben Boyd National Park Australia 112 E6
Benburb U.K. 51 F3
Bencha China 77 I1
Ben Chonzie hill U.K. 50 F4
Ben Cleuch hill U.K. 50 F4
Ben Cruachan mt. U.K. 50 D4
Bend U.S.A. 126 C3
Bendearg mt. S. Africa 101 H6
Bender Moldova see Tighina
Bender-Bayla Somalia 98 F3
Bendery Moldova see Tighina
Bendigo Australia 112 B6
Bendoc Australia 112 D6
Bene Moz. 99 D5
Benedict, Mount hill Canada 123 K3
Benenitra Madag. 99 E6
Benešov Czech Rep. 47 O6
Bénestroff France 52 G6
Benevento Italy 58 F4
Beneventum Italy see Benevento
Benezette U.S.A. 135 F3
Beng, Nam r. Laos 70 C3
Bengal, Bay of sea Indian Ocean 81 G8
Bengamisa Dem. Rep. Congo 98 C3
Bengbu China 77 H1
Benghazi Libya 97 F1
Bengkalis Indon. 71 C7
Bengkalis i. Indon. 71 C7
Bengkulu Indon. 68 C7
Bengtsfors Sweden 45 H7
Benguela Angola 99 B5
Benha Egypt see Banhā
Ben Hiant hill U.K. 50 C4
Ben Hope hill U.K. 50 E2
Ben Horn hill U.K. 50 E2
Beni r. Bol. 142 E6
Beni Dem. Rep. Congo 98 C3
Beni Nepal 83 E3
Beni Abbès Alg. 54 D5
Beniah Lake Canada 121 H2
Benidorm Spain 57 F4
Beni Mellal Morocco 54 C5
Benin country Africa 96 D4
Benin, Bight of g. Africa 96 D4
Benin City Nigeria 96 D4
Beni Saf Alg. 57 F6
Beni Snassen, Monts des mts Morocco 57 E6
Beni Suef Egypt see Banī Suwayf
Benito, Islas is Mex. 127 E7
Benito Juárez Arg. 144 E5
Benito Juárez Mex. 129 F5
Benjamim Constant Brazil 142 E4
Benjamin U.S.A. 131 D5
Benjamín Hill Mex. 127 F7
Benjina Indon. 69 I8
Benkelman U.S.A. 130 C3
Ben Klibreck hill U.K. 50 E2
Ben Lavin Nature Reserve S. Africa 101 I2
Ben Lawers mt. U.K. 50 E4
Ben Lomond mt. Australia 112 E3
Ben Lomond hill U.K. 50 E4
Ben Lomond National Park Australia 111 [inset]
Ben Macdui mt. U.K. 50 F3
Benmara Australia 110 B3
Ben More hill U.K. 50 C4
Ben More mt. U.K. 50 E4
Benmore, Lake N.Z. 113 C7
Ben More Assynt hill U.K. 50 E2
Bennetta, Ostrov i. Rus. Fed. 65 P2
Bennett Island Rus. Fed. see Bennetta, Ostrov
Bennett Lake Canada 120 C3
Bennettsville U.S.A. 133 E5
Ben Nevis mt. U.K. 50 D4
Bennington NH U.S.A. 135 J2
Bennington VT U.S.A. 135 I2
Benoni S. Africa 101 I4
Ben Rinnes hill U.K. 50 F3
Bensheim Germany 53 I5
Benson AZ U.S.A. 129 H6
Benson MN U.S.A. 130 E2
Benta Seberang Malaysia 71 C6
Benteng Indon. 69 G8
Bentinck Island Myanmar 71 B5
Bentiu Sudan 86 C8
Bent Jbaïl Lebanon 85 B3
Bentley U.K. 48 F5
Bento Gonçalves Brazil 145 A5
Benton AR U.S.A. 131 E5
Benton CA U.S.A. 128 D3
Benton IL U.S.A. 130 F4
Benton KY U.S.A. 131 F4
Benton LA U.S.A. 131 E5
Benton MO U.S.A. 131 F4
Benton PA U.S.A. 135 G3
Bentong Malaysia see Bentung
Benton Harbor U.S.A. 134 B2
Bentonville U.S.A. 131 E4
Bên Tre Vietnam 71 D5
Bentung Malaysia 71 C7
Benue r. Nigeria 96 D4
Benum, Gunung mt. Malaysia 71 C7
Ben Vorlich hill U.K. 50 E4
Benwee Head hd Ireland 51 C3
Benwood U.S.A. 134 E3
Ben Wyvis mt. U.K. 50 E3
Benxi Liaoning China 74 A4
Benxi Liaoning China 74 B4
Beograd Serbia see Belgrade
Béoumi Côte d'Ivoire 96 C4
Beppu Japan 75 C6
Béqaa valley Lebanon see El Béqaa
Berach r. India 82 C4
Beraketa Madag. 99 E6
Bérard, Lac l. Canada 123 H2
Berasia India 82 D5
Berat Albania 59 H4
Beravina Madag. 99 E5
Berbak, Taman Nasional Indon. 68 C7
Berber Sudan 86 D6
Berbera Somalia 98 E2
Berbérati Cent. Afr. Rep. 98 B3
Berchtesgaden, Nationalpark nat. park Germany 47 N7
Berck France 52 B4
Berdichev Ukr. see Berdychiv

Berdigestyakh Rus. Fed. 65 N3
Berdyans'k Ukr. 43 H7
Berdychiv Ukr. 43 F6
Berea KY U.S.A. 134 C5
Berea OH U.S.A. 134 E3
Beregovo Ukr. see Berehove
Beregovoy Rus. Fed. 74 B1
Berehove Ukr. 43 D6
Bereina P.N.G. 69 L8
Bere Island Ireland 51 C6
Bereket Turkm. 88 D2
Berekum Ghana 96 C4
Berenice Egypt see Baranīs
Berenice Libya see Benghazi
Berens r. Canada 121 L4
Berens Island Canada 121 L4
Berens River Canada 121 L4
Beresford U.S.A. 130 D3
Bereza Belarus see Byaroza
Berezino Belarus see Byerazino
Berezivka Ukr. 43 F7
Berezne Ukr. 43 E6
Bereznik Rus. Fed. 42 I3
Berezniki Rus. Fed. 41 R4
Berezov Rus. Fed. see Berezovo
Berezovka Rus. Fed. 74 B2
Berezovka Ukr. see Berezivka
Berezovo Rus. Fed. 41 T3
Berezovyy Rus. Fed. 74 D2
Berga Germany 53 L3
Berga Spain 57 G2
Bergama Turkey 59 L5
Bergamo Italy 58 C2
Bergby Sweden 45 J6
Bergen Mecklenburg-Vorpommern Germany 47 N3
Bergen Niedersachsen Germany 53 J2
Bergen Norway 45 D6
Bergen U.S.A. 135 G2
Bergen op Zoom Neth. 52 E3
Bergerac France 56 E4
Bergères-lès-Vertus France 52 E6
Bergheim (Erft) Germany 52 G4
Bergisches Land reg. Germany 53 H4
Bergisch Gladbach Germany 52 H4
Bergland Namibia 100 C2
Bergomum Italy see Bergamo
Bergoo U.S.A. 134 E4
Bergsjö Sweden 45 J6
Bergsviken Sweden 44 L4
Bergtheim Germany 53 K5
Bergues France 52 C4
Bergum Neth. see Burgum
Bergville S. Africa 101 I5
Berhampur India see Baharampur
Beringa, Ostrov i. Rus. Fed. 65 R4
Beringen Belgium 52 F3
Beringovskiy Rus. Fed. 65 S3
Bering Sea N. Pacific Ocean 65 S4
Bering Strait Rus. Fed./U.S.A. 65 U3
Berīs, Ra's pt Iran 89 F5
Berislav Ukr. see Beryslav
Berkåk Norway 44 G5
Berkane Morocco 57 E6
Berkel r. Neth. 52 G2
Berkeley U.S.A. 128 B3
Berkeley Springs U.S.A. 135 F4
Berkhout Neth. 52 F2
Berkner Island Antarctica 152 A1
Berkovitsa Bulg. 59 J3
Berkshire Downs hills U.K. 49 F7
Berkshire Hills U.S.A. 135 I2
Berland r. Canada 120 G4
Berlare Belgium 52 E3
Berlevåg Norway 44 P1

▶Berlin Germany 53 N2
Capital of Germany.

Berlin land Germany 53 N2
Berlin MD U.S.A. 135 H4
Berlin NH U.S.A. 135 J1
Berlin PA U.S.A. 135 F4
Berlin Lake U.S.A. 134 E3
Bermagui Australia 112 E6
Bermejo r. Arg./Bol. 144 E3
Bermejo Bol. 142 F8
Bermen, Lac l. Canada 123 H3

▶Bermuda terr. N. Atlantic Ocean 137 L2
United Kingdom Overseas Territory.
north america 9, 116–117

Bermuda Rise sea feature N. Atlantic Ocean 148 D4

▶Bern Switz. 56 H3
Capital of Switzerland.

Bernalillo U.S.A. 127 G6
Bernardino de Campos Brazil 145 A3
Bernardo O'Higgins, Parque Nacional nat. park Chile 144 B7
Bernasconi Arg. 144 D5
Bernau Germany 53 N2
Bernburg (Saale) Germany 53 L3
Berne Germany 53 I1
Berne Switz. see Bern
Berne U.S.A. 134 C3
Berner Alpen mts Switz. 56 H3
Bernera i. Scotland U.K. 50 B3
Bernera i. Scotland U.K. 50 B4
Bernier Island Australia 109 A6
Bernina Pass Switz. 56 J3
Bernkastel-Kues Germany 52 H5
Beroea Greece see Veroia
Beroea Syria see Aleppo
Beroroha Madag. 99 E6
Beroun Czech Rep. 47 O6
Berounka r. Czech Rep. 47 O6
Berovina Madag. see Beravina
Berri Australia 111 C7
Berriane Alg. 54 E5
Berridale Australia 112 D6
Berriedale U.K. 50 F2
Berrigan Australia 112 B5
Berrima Australia 112 E5
Berrouaghia Alg. 57 H5
Berry Australia 112 E5
Berry U.S.A. 134 C4
Berryessa, Lake U.S.A. 128 B2
Berry Head hd U.K. 49 D8

Berry Islands Bahamas 133 E7
Berryville U.S.A. 135 G4
Berseba Namibia 100 C4
Bersenbrück Germany 53 H2
Bertam Malaysia 71 C6
Berté, Lac l. Canada 123 H4
Berthoud Pass U.S.A. 126 G5
Bertolinía Brazil 143 J5
Bertoua Cameroon 96 E4
Bertraghboy Bay Ireland 51 C4
Beru atoll Kiribati 107 H2
Beruri Brazil 142 F4
Beruwala Sri Lanka 84 C5
Berwick Australia 112 B7
Berwick U.S.A. 135 G3
Berwick-upon-Tweed U.K. 48 E3
Berwyn hills U.K. 49 D6
Beryslav Ukr. 59 O1
Berytus Lebanon see Beirut
Besalampy Madag. 99 E5
Besançon France 56 H3
Besar, Gunung mt. Malaysia 71 C7
Besbay Kazakh. 80 A2
Beserah Malaysia 71 C7
Beshkent Uzbek. 89 G2
Beshneh Iran 88 D4
Besikama Indon. 108 D2
Besitang Indon. 71 B6
Beskra Alg. see Biskra
Beslan Rus. Fed. 91 G2
Besnard Lake Canada 121 J4
Besni Turkey 90 E3
Besor watercourse Israel 85 B4
Beşparmak Dağları mts Cyprus see Pentadaktylos Range
Bessbrook U.K. 51 F3
Bessemer U.S.A. 133 C5
Besshoky, Gora hill Kazakh. 91 I1
Besskorbnaya Rus. Fed. 43 I7
Bessonovka Rus. Fed. 43 J5
Betanzos Spain 57 B2
Bethal S. Africa 101 I4
Bethanie Namibia 100 C4
Bethany U.S.A. 130 E3
Bethel U.S.A. 123 H5
Bethel Park U.S.A. 134 E3
Bethesda U.K. 48 C5
Bethesda MD U.S.A. 135 G4
Bethesda OH U.S.A. 134 E3
Bethlehem S. Africa 101 I5
Bethlehem U.S.A. 135 H3
Bethlehem West Bank 85 B4
Bethulie S. Africa 101 G6
Béthune France 52 C4
Beti Pak. 89 H4
Betim Brazil 145 B2
Bet Lehem West Bank see Bethlehem
Betma India 82 C5
Betong Thai. 71 C6
Betoota Australia 110 C5
Betpak-Dala plain Kazakh. 80 D2
Betroka Madag. 99 E6
Bet She'an Israel 85 B3
Betsiamites Canada 123 H4
Betsiamites r. Canada 123 H4
Bettiah India 83 F4
Bettyhill U.K. 50 E2
Bettystown Ireland 51 F4
Betul India 82 D5
Betung Kerihun, Taman Nasional Indon. 68 E6
Betwa r. India 82 D4
Betws-y-coed U.K. 49 D5
Betzdorf Germany 53 H4
Beulah Australia 111 C7
Beulah MI U.S.A. 134 B1
Beulah ND U.S.A. 130 C2
Beult r. U.K. 49 H7
Beuthen Poland see Bytom
Bever r. Germany 53 H2
Beverley U.K. 48 G5
Beverly MA U.S.A. 135 J2
Beverly OH U.S.A. 134 E4
Beverly Hills U.S.A. 128 D4
Beverly Lake Canada 121 K1
Beverstedt Germany 53 I1
Beverungen Germany 53 J3
Beverwijk Neth. 52 E2
Bewani P.N.G. 69 K7
Bexbach Germany 53 H5
Bexhill U.K. 49 H8
Bexley, Cape Canada 118 G3
Beyānlū Iran 88 B3
Beyce Turkey see Orhaneli
Bey Dağları mts Turkey 59 N6
Beykoz Turkey 59 M4
Beyla Guinea 96 C4
Beylagan Azer. see Beyläqan
Beyläqan Azer. 91 G3
Beyneu Kazakh. 78 E2
Beypazarı Turkey 59 N4
Beypınarı Turkey 90 E3
Beypore India 84 B4
Beyrouth Lebanon see Beirut
Beyşehir Turkey 90 C3
Beyşehir Gölü l. Turkey 90 C3
Beytonovo Rus. Fed. 74 B1
Beytüşşebap Turkey 91 F3
Bezameh Iran 88 E3
Bezbozhnik Rus. Fed. 42 K4
Bezhanitsy Rus. Fed. 42 F4
Bezhetsk Rus. Fed. 42 H4
Béziers France 56 F5
Bezmein Turkm. see Abadan
Bezwada India see Vijayawada
Bhabha India see Bhabhua
Bhabhar India 82 B4
Bhabhua India 83 E4
Bhabua India see Bhabhua
Bhachau India 82 B5
Bhachbhar India 82 B4
Bhadgaon Nepal see Bhaktapur
Bhadohi India 83 E4
Bhadra India 82 C3
Bhadrachalam Road Station India see Kottagudem
Bhadrak India 83 F5
Bhadrakh India see Bhadrak
Bhadravati India 84 B3
Bhag Pak. 89 G4
Bhagalpur India 83 F4
Bhainsa India 84 C2

Bhainsdehi India 82 D5
Bhairab Bazar Bangl. 83 G4
Bhairi Hol mt. Pak. 89 G5
Bhaktapur Nepal 83 F4
Bhalki India 84 C2
Bhamo Myanmar 70 B1
Bhamragarh India 84 D2
Bhandara India 82 D5
Bhanjanagar India 84 E2
Bhanrer Range hills India 82 D5
Bhaptiahi India 83 F4
Bharat country Asia see India
Bharatpur India 82 D4
Bhareli r. India 83 H4
Bharuch India 82 C5
Bhatapara India 83 E5
Bhatarsaigh i. U.K. see Vatersay
Bhatghar Lake India 84 B2
Bhatinda India see Bathinda
Bhatnair India see Hanumangarh
Bhatpara India 83 G5
Bhaunagar India see Bhavnagar
Bhavani r. India 84 C4
Bhavani Sagar l. India 84 C4
Bhavnagar India 82 C5
Bhawana Pak. 89 I4
Bhawanipatna India 84 D2
Bhearnaraigh, Eilean i. U.K. see Berneray
Bheemavaram India see Bhimavaram
Bhekuzulu S. Africa 101 J4
Bhera Pak. 89 I3
Bhigvan India 84 B2
Bhikhna Thori Nepal 83 F4
Bhilai India 82 E5
Bhildi India 82 C4
Bhilwara India 82 C4
Bhima r. India 84 C2
Bhimar India 82 B4
Bhimavaram India 84 D2
Bhimlath India 82 E5
Bhind India 82 D4
Bhinga India 83 E4
Bhisho S. Africa 101 H7
Bhiwandi India 84 B2
Bhiwani India 82 D3
Bhogaipur India 82 D4
Bhojpur Nepal 83 F4
Bhola Bangl. 83 G5
Bhongweni S. Africa 101 I6
Bhopal India 82 D5
Bhopalpatnam India 84 D2
Bhrigukaccha India see Bharuch
Bhuban India 84 E1
Bhubaneshwar India 84 E1
Bhubaneswar India see Bhubaneshwar
Bhuj India 82 B5
Bhusawal India 82 C5
Bhutan country Asia 83 G4
Bhuttewala India 82 B4
Bia r. Ghana 96 C4
Bia, Phou mt. Laos 70 C3
Biābān mts Iran 88 E5
Biafo Glacier Pak. 82 C2
Biafra, Bight of g. Africa see Benin, Bight of
Biak Indon. 69 J7
Biak i. Indon. 69 J7
Biała Podlaska Poland 43 D5
Białogard Poland 47 O4
Białystok Poland 43 D5
Bianco, Monte mt. France/Italy see Mont Blanc
Biandangang Kou r. mouth China 77 I1
Bianzhao China 74 A3
Bianzhuang China see Cangshan
Biaora India 82 D5
Biarritz France 56 D5
Bi'ār Tabrāk well Saudi Arabia 88 B5
Bibai Japan 74 F4
Bibbenluke Australia 112 D6
Bibbiena Italy 58 D3
Bibby Island Canada 121 M2
Biberach an der Riß Germany 47 L6
Bibile Sri Lanka 84 D5
Biblis Germany 53 I5
Biblos Lebanon see Jbail
Bicas Brazil 145 C3
Biçer Turkey 59 N5
Bicester U.K. 49 F7
Bichabhera India 82 C4
Bicheng China see Bishan
Bichevaya Rus. Fed. 74 D3
Bichi r. Rus. Fed. 74 E1
Bickerton Island Australia 110 B2
Bickleigh U.K. 49 D8
Bicknell U.S.A. 134 B4
Bicuari, Parque Nacional do nat. park Angola 99 B5
Bid India 84 B2
Bida Nigeria 96 D4
Bidar India 84 C2
Biddeford U.S.A. 135 J2
Biddinghuizen Neth. 52 F2
Bidean nam Bian mt. U.K. 50 D4
Bideford U.K. 49 C7
Bideford Bay U.K. see Barnstaple Bay
Bidokht Iran 88 E3
Bidzhan Rus. Fed. 74 C3
Bié Angola see Kuito
Bié, Planalto do Angola 99 B5
Biebrzański Park Narodowy nat. park Poland 45 M10
Biedenkopf Germany 53 I4
Biel Switz. 56 H3
Bielawa Poland 47 P5
Bielefeld Germany 53 I2
Bielitz Poland see Bielsko-Biała
Biella Italy 58 C2
Bielsko-Biała Poland 47 Q6
Bielstein hill Germany 53 J3
Bienenbüttel Germany 53 K1
Biên Hoa Vietnam 71 D5
Bienne Switz. see Biel
Bienville, Lac l. Canada 123 G3
Bierbank Australia 112 B1
Biesiesvlei S. Africa 101 G4
Bietigheim-Bissingen Germany 53 J6
Bièvre Belgium 52 F5
Bifoun Gabon 98 B4
Big r. Canada 123 K3
Biga Turkey 59 L4
Bigadiç Turkey 59 M5

Biga Yarımadası pen. Turkey 59 L5
Big Baldy Mountain U.S.A. 126 F3
Big Bar Creek Canada 120 F5
Big Bear Lake U.S.A. 128 E4
Big Belt Mountains U.S.A. 126 F3
Big Bend Swaziland 101 J4
Big Bend National Park U.S.A. 131 C6
Bigbury-on-Sea U.K. 49 D8
Big Canyon watercourse U.S.A. 131 C6
Biger Nuur salt l. Mongolia 80 I2
Big Falls U.S.A. 130 E1
Big Fork r. U.S.A. 130 E1
Biggar Canada 121 J4
Biggar U.K. 50 F5
Biggar, Lac l. Canada 122 G4
Bigge Island Australia 108 D3
Biggenden Australia 111 F5
Bigger, Mount Canada 120 B3
Biggesee l. Germany 53 H3
Biggleswade U.K. 49 G6
Biggs CA U.S.A. 128 C2
Biggs OR U.S.A. 126 C3
Big Hole r. U.S.A. 126 E3
Bighorn r. U.S.A. 126 G3
Bighorn Mountains U.S.A. 126 G3
Big Island Nunavut Canada 119 K3
Big Island N.W.T. Canada 120 G2
Big Island Ont. Canada 121 M5
Big Kalzas Lake Canada 120 C2
Big Lake l. Canada 121 H1
Big Lake U.S.A. 131 C6
Bignona Senegal 96 B3
Big Pine U.S.A. 128 D3
Big Pine Peak U.S.A. 128 D4
Big Raccoon r. U.S.A. 134 B4
Big Rapids U.S.A. 134 C2
Big River Canada 121 J4
Big Sable Point U.S.A. 134 B1
Big Salmon r. Canada 120 C2
Big Sand Lake Canada 121 L3
Big Sandy r. U.S.A. 126 F4
Big Sandy Lake Canada 121 J4
Big Smokey Valley U.S.A. 128 E2
Big South Fork National River and Recreation Area park U.S.A. 134 C5
Big Spring U.S.A. 131 C5
Big Stone Canada 121 I5
Big Stone Gap U.S.A. 134 D5
Bigstone Lake Canada 121 M4
Big Timber U.S.A. 126 F3
Big Trout Lake Canada 121 N4
Big Trout Lake l. Canada 121 N4
Big Valley Canada 121 H4
Big Water U.S.A. 129 H3
Bihać Bos.-Herz. 58 F2
Bihar state India 83 F4
Bihariganj India 83 F4
Bihar Sharif India 83 F4
Bihor, Vârful mt. Romania 59 J1
Bihoro Japan 74 G4
Bijagós, Arquipélago dos is Guinea-Bissau 96 B3
Bijaipur India 82 D4
Bijapur India 84 B2
Bījār Iran 88 B3
Bijbehara India 82 C2
Bijeljina Bos.-Herz. 59 H2
Bijelo Polje Montenegro 59 H3
Bijeraghogarh India 82 E5
Bijiang China see Zhiziluo
Bijie China 76 E3
Bijji India 84 D2
Bijnor India 82 D3
Bijnore India see Bijnor
Bijnot Pak. 89 H4
Bijrān well Saudi Arabia 88 C5
Bijrān, Khashm hill Saudi Arabia 88 C5
Bikampur India 82 C4
Bikaner India 82 C3
Bīkhūyeh Iran 88 D5
Bikin Rus. Fed. 74 D3
Bikin r. Rus. Fed. 74 D3
Bikini atoll Marshall Is 150 H5
Bikori Sudan 86 D7
Bikoro Dem. Rep. Congo 98 B4
Bikou China 76 E1
Bikramganj India 83 F4
Bilād Banī Bū 'Alī Oman 87 I5
Bilaigarh India 84 D1
Bilara India 82 C4
Bilaspur Chhattisgarh India 83 E5
Bilaspur Hima. Prad. India 82 D3
Biläsuvar Azer. 91 H3
Bila Tserkva Ukr. 43 F6
Bilauktaung Range mts Myanmar/Thai. 71 B4
Bilbao Spain 57 E2
Bilbays Egypt 90 C5
Bilbeis Egypt see Bilbays
Bilbo Spain see Bilbao
Bilecik Turkey 59 M4
Biłgoraj Poland 43 D6
Bilharamulo Tanz. 98 D4
Bilhaur India 82 E4
Bilhorod-Dnistrovs'kyy Ukr. 59 N1
Bili Dem. Rep. Congo 98 C3
Bilibino Rus. Fed. 65 R3
Bilin Myanmar 70 B3
Bill U.S.A. 126 G4
Billabalong Australia 109 A6
Billabong Creek r. Australia see Moulamein Creek
Billericay U.K. 49 H7
Billiluna Australia 108 D4
Billingham U.K. 48 F4
Billings U.S.A. 126 F3
Billiton i. Indon. see Belitung
Bill of Portland hd U.K. 49 E8
Bill Williams r. U.S.A. 129 F4
Bill Williams Mountain U.S.A. 129 G4
Bilma Niger 96 E3
Bilo r. Rus. Fed. see Belaya
Biloela Australia 110 E5
Bilohirs'k Ukr. 90 D1
Bilohir"ya Ukr. 43 E6
Biloku Guyana 143 G3
Biloli India 84 C2
Bilovods'k Ukr. 43 H6
Biloxi U.S.A. 131 F6
Bilpa Morea Claypan salt flat Australia 110 B5
Bilston U.K. 50 F5
Biltine Chad 97 F3
Bilto Norway 44 L2
Bilugyun Island Myanmar 70 B3
Bilyayivka Ukr. 59 N1
Bilzen Belgium 52 F4
Bima Indon. 108 B2
Bimberi, Mount Australia 112 D5
Bimbo Ombella-Mpoko 97 E4
Bimini Islands Bahamas 133 E7
Bimlipatam India 84 D2
Bināb Iran 88 C2
Bina-Etawa India 82 D4
Binaija, Gunung mt. Indon. 67 E8
Bīnālūd, Kūh-e mts Iran 88 E2
Binboğa Daği mt. Turkey 90 E3
Bincheng China see Binzhou
Binchuan China 76 D3
Bindebango Australia 112 C1
Bindle Australia 112 D1
Bindu Dem. Rep. Congo 99 B4
Bindura Zimbabwe 99 D5
Binefar Spain 57 G3
Binga Zimbabwe 99 C5
Binga, Monte mt. Moz. 99 D5
Bingara Australia 112 E2
Bingaram i. India 84 B4
Bing Bong Australia 110 B2
Bingen am Rhein Germany 53 H5
Bingham U.S.A. 135 K1
Binghamton U.S.A. 135 H2
Bingmei China see Congjiang
Bingöl Turkey 91 F3
Bingöl Dağı mt. Turkey 91 F3
Bingxi China see Yushan
Bingzhongluo China 76 C2
Binh Gia Vietnam 70 D2
Binika India 83 E5
Binjai Indon. 71 B7
Bin Mürkhan well U.A.E. 88 D5
Binnaway Australia 112 D3
Binpur India 83 F5
Bintan i. Indon. 71 D7
Bint Jbeil Lebanon see Bent Jbaïl
Bintulu Sarawak Malaysia 68 E6
Binxian Heilong. China 74 B3
Binxian Shaanxi China 77 F1
Binya Australia 112 C5
Binyang China 77 F4
Bin-Yauri Nigeria 96 D3
Binzhou Guangxi China see Binyang
Binzhou Heilong. China see Binxian
Binzhou Shandong China 73 L5
Bioco i. Equat. Guinea 96 D4
Biograd na Moru Croatia 58 F3
Bioko i. Equat. Guinea see Bioco
Biokovo mts Croatia 58 G3
Biquinhas Brazil 145 B2
Bir India see Bid
Bira Rus. Fed. 74 D2
Bi'r Abū Jady oasis Syria 85 D1
Birag, Kūh-e mts Iran 89 F5
Birāk Libya 97 E2
Birakan Rus. Fed. 74 C2
Bi'r al 'Abd Egypt 85 A4
Bi'r al Ḥalbā well Syria 85 D2
Bi'r al Jifjāfah well Egypt 85 A4
Bi'r al Khamsah well Egypt 90 B5
Bi'r al Māliḥah well Egypt 85 A5
Bi'r al Mulūsi Iraq 91 F4
Bi'r al Munbaṭiḥ well Syria 85 D2
Bi'r al Qaṭrānī well Egypt 90 B5
Bi'r al Ubbayiḍ well Egypt 90 B6
Birandozero Rus. Fed. 42 H3
Bi'r an Nuṣf well Egypt see Bi'r an Nuṣṣ
Bi'r an Nuṣṣ well Egypt 90 B5
Bir Anzarane W. Sahara 96 B2
Birao Cent. Afr. Rep. 98 C2
Bi'r ar Rābiyah well Egypt 90 B5
Birata Turkm. 89 F1
Biratnagar Nepal 83 F4
Bi'r aṭ Ṭarfāwī well Libya 90 B5
Bi'r Başīrī well Syria 85 C2
Bi'r Bayḍā' well Egypt 85 B4
Bi'r Baylī well Egypt 90 B5
Bîr Beïda well Egypt see Bi'r Bayḍā'
Bi'r Buṭaymān Syria 91 E3
Birch r. Canada 121 H3
Birch Hills Canada 121 J4
Birch Island Canada 120 G5
Birch Lake N.W.T. Canada 120 G2
Birch Lake Ont. Canada 121 M5
Birch Lake Sask. Canada 121 I4
Birch Mountains Canada 120 H3
Birch River U.S.A. 134 E4
Birch Run U.S.A. 134 D2
Bircot Eth. 98 E3
Birdaard Neth. see Burdaard
Bîr Dignâsh well Egypt see Bi'r Diqnāsh
Bi'r Diqnāsh well Egypt 90 B5
Bird Island N. Mariana Is see Farallon de Medinilla
Birdseye U.S.A. 129 H2
Birdsville Australia 111 B5
Birecik Turkey 90 E3
Bir el 'Abd Egypt see Bi'r al 'Abd
Bir el Arbi well Alg. 57 I6
Bîr el Istabl well Egypt see Bi'r Iṣṭabl
Bîr el Khamsa well Egypt see Bi'r al Khamsah
Bîr el Nuşş well Egypt see Bi'r an Nuşş
Bîr el Obeiyid well Egypt see Bi'r al Ubbayiḍ
Bîr el Qaţrâni well Egypt see Bi'r al Qaṭrānī
Bîr el Râbia well Egypt see Bi'r ar Rābiyah
Birendranagar Nepal see Surkhet
Bir en Natrûn well Sudan 86 C6
Bireun Indon. 71 B6
Bi'r Fāḍil well Saudi Arabia 88 C6
Bi'r Fajr well Saudi Arabia 90 E5
Bi'r Fu'ād well Egypt 90 B5
Bîr Gifgâfa well Egypt see Bi'r al Jifjāfah
Bi'r Ḥajal well Syria 85 D2
Birhan mt. Eth. 98 D2
Bi'r Ḥasanah well Egypt 85 A4
Bi'r Ḥayzān well Saudi Arabia 90 E6
Bi'r Ibn Hirmās Saudi Arabia see Al Bi'r
Bir Ibn Juhayyim Saudi Arabia 88 C6
Birigüi Brazil 145 A3
Bīrīn Syria 85 C2
Bi'r Iṣṭabl well Egypt 90 B5
Bīrjand Iran 88 E3
Bi'r Jubnī well Libya 90 B5
Birkát Hamad well Iraq 91 G5
Birkenfeld Germany 53 H5
Birkenhead U.K. 48 D5
Birkirkara Malta 58 F7
Birksgate Range hills Australia 109 E6
Bîrlad Romania see Bârlad
Bi'r Lahfān well Egypt 85 A4
Birlik Kazakh. 80 D3
Birmal reg. Afgh. 89 H3
Birmingham U.K. 49 F6
Birmingham U.S.A. 133 C5
Bîr Mogreïn Mauritania 96 B2
Bi'r Muḥaymid al Wazwaz well Syria 85 D2
Bi'r Nāḥid oasis Egypt 90 C5
Birnin-Gwari Nigeria 96 D3
Birnin-Kebbi Nigeria 96 D3
Birnin Konni Niger 96 D3
Birobidzhan Rus. Fed. 74 D2
Bi'r Qaşīr as Sirr well Egypt 90 B5
Birr Ireland 51 E4
Bi'r Rawḍ Sālim well Egypt 85 A4
Birrie r. Australia 112 C2
Birrindudu Australia 108 E4
Bîr Rôd Sâlim well Egypt see Bi'r Rawḍ Sālim
Birsay U.K. 50 F1
Bi'r Shalatayn Egypt 86 E5
Bîr Shalatein Egypt see Bi'r Shalatayn
Birsk Rus. Fed. 41 R4
Birstall U.K. 49 F6
Birstein Germany 53 J4
Bir Ṭalḥah well Saudi Arabia 88 B6
Birthday Mountain hill Australia 110 C2
Birtle Canada 121 K5
Biru China 76 B2
Birur India 84 B3
Bi'r Usaylīlah well Saudi Arabia 88 B6
Biruxiong China see Biru
Biržai Lith. 45 N8
Bisa India 70 A1
Bisa i. Indon. 69 H7
Bisalpur India 82 D3
Bisau India 82 C3
Bisbee U.S.A. 127 F7
Biscay, Bay of sea France/Spain 56 B4
Biscay Abyssal Plain sea feature N. Atlantic Ocean 148 H3
Biscayne National Park U.S.A. 133 D7
Biscoe Islands Antarctica 152 L2
Biscotasi Lake Canada 122 E5
Biscotasing Canada 122 E5
Bisezhai China 76 D4
Bishan China 76 E2
Bishbek Kyrg. see Bishkek
Bishenpur India see Bishnupur

▶Bishkek Kyrg. 80 D3
Capital of Kyrgyzstan.

Bishnath India 76 B3
Bishnupur Manipur India 83 H4
Bishnupur W. Bengal India 83 F5
Bishop U.S.A. 128 D3
Bishop Auckland U.K. 48 F4
Bishop Lake Canada 120 G1
Bishop's Stortford U.K. 49 H7
Bishopville U.S.A. 133 D5
Bishrī, Jabal hills Syria 85 D2
Bishui Heilong. China 74 A1
Bishui Henan China see Biyang
Biskra Alg. 54 F5
Bislig Phil. 69 H5

▶Bismarck U.S.A. 130 C2
Capital of North Dakota.

Bismarck Archipelago is P.N.G. 69 L7
Bismarck Range mts P.N.G. 69 K7
Bismarck Sea P.N.G. 69 L7
Bismark (Altmark) Germany 53 L2
Bismil Turkey 91 F3
Bismo Norway 44 F6
Bison U.S.A. 130 C2
Bispgården Sweden 44 J5
Bispingen Germany 53 K1
Bissa, Djebel mt. Alg. 57 G5
Bissamcuttak India 84 D2

▶Bissau Guinea-Bissau 96 B3
Capital of Guinea-Bissau.

Bissaula Nigeria 96 E4
Bissett Canada 121 M5
Bistcho Lake Canada 120 G3
Bistrița Romania 59 K1
Bistrița r. Romania 59 L1
Bitburg Germany 52 G5
Bitche France 53 H5
Bithur India 82 E4
Bithynia reg. Turkey 59 M4
Bitkine Chad 97 E3
Bitlis Turkey 91 F3
Bitola Macedonia 59 I4
Bitolj Macedonia see Bitola
Bitonto Italy 58 G4
Bitrān, Jabal hill Saudi Arabia 88 B6
Bitra Par reef India 84 B4
Bitter Creek r. U.S.A. 129 I2
Bitterfeld Germany 53 M3
Bitterfontein S. Africa 100 D6
Bitter Lakes Egypt 90 D5
Bitterroot r. U.S.A. 126 E3
Bitterroot Range mts U.S.A. 126 E3
Bitterwater U.S.A. 128 C3
Bittkau Germany 53 L2
Bitung Indon. 69 H6
Biu Nigeria 96 E3
Biwa-ko l. Japan 75 D6
Biwmaris U.K. see Beaumaris
Biyang China 77 G1
Biye K'obē Eth. 98 E2
Biysk Rus. Fed. 72 F2
Bizana S. Africa 101 I6
Bizerta Tunisia see Bizerte
Bizerte Tunisia 58 C6
Bīzhanābād Iran 88 E5

▶Bjargtangar hd Iceland 44 [inset]
Most westerly point of Europe.

Bjästa Sweden 44 K5
Bjelovar Croatia 58 G2
Bjerkvik Norway 44 J2
Bjerringbro Denmark 45 F8
Bjørgan Norway 44 G5
Björkliden Sweden 44 K2
Björklinge Sweden 45 J6
Bjorli Norway 44 F5
Björna Sweden 44 K5
Björneborg Fin. see Pori

▶Bjørnøya i. Arctic Ocean 64 C2
Part of Norway.

Bjurholm Sweden 44 K5
Bla Mali 96 C3
Black r. Man. Canada 121 L5
Black r. Ont. Canada 122 E4
Black r. AR U.S.A. 131 F5
Black r. AR U.S.A. 131 F5
Black r. AZ U.S.A. 129 H5
Black r. Vietnam 70 D2
Blackadder Water r. U.K. 50 G5
Blackall Australia 110 D5
Blackbear r. Canada 121 N4
Black Birch Lake Canada 121 J3
Black Bourton U.K. 49 F7
Blackbull Australia 110 C3
Blackburn U.K. 48 E5
Blackbutt Australia 112 F1
Black Butte mt. U.S.A. 128 B2
Black Butte Lake U.S.A. 128 B2
Black Canyon gorge U.S.A. 129 F4
Black Canyon of the Gunnison National Park U.S.A. 129 J2
Black Combe hill U.K. 48 D4
Black Creek watercourse U.S.A. 129 I4
Black Donald Lake Canada 135 G1
Blackdown Tableland National Park Australia 110 E4
Blackduck U.S.A. 130 E2
Blackfalds Canada 120 H4
Blackfoot U.S.A. 126 E4
Black Foot r. U.S.A. 126 E3
Black Forest mts Germany 47 L7
Black Hill hill U.K. 48 F5
Black Hills SD U.S.A. 124 G3
Black Hills SD U.S.A. 126 G3
Black Island Canada 121 L5
Black Lake Canada 121 J3
Black Lake l. Canada 121 J3
Black Lake l. U.S.A. 134 C1
Black Mesa mt. U.S.A. 129 I5
Black Mesa ridge U.S.A. 129 H3
Black Mountain Pak. 89 I3
Black Mountain hill U.K. 49 D7
Black Mountain AK U.S.A. 118 B3
Black Mountain CA U.S.A. 128 E4
Black Mountain KY U.S.A. 134 D5
Black Mountain NM U.S.A. 129 I5
Black Mountains hills U.K. 49 D7
Black Mountains U.S.A. 129 F4
Black Nossob watercourse Namibia 100 D2
Black Pagoda India see Konarka
Blackpool U.K. 48 D5
Black Range mts U.S.A. 129 I5
Black River MI U.S.A. 134 D1
Black River NY U.S.A. 135 H1
Black River Falls U.S.A. 130 F2
Black Rock hill Jordan see 'Unāb, Jabal al
Black Rock Desert U.S.A. 126 D4
Blacksburg U.S.A. 134 E5
Black Sea Asia/Europe 43 H8
Blacks Fork r. U.S.A. 126 F4
Blackshear U.S.A. 133 D6
Blacksod Bay Ireland 51 B3
Black Springs U.S.A. 128 D2
Blackstairs Mountains hills Ireland 51 F5
Blackstone U.S.A. 135 F5
Black Sugarloaf mt. Australia 112 E3
Black Tickle Canada 123 L3
Blackville Australia 112 E3
Blackwater Australia 110 E4
Blackwater Ireland 51 F5
Blackwater r. Ireland 51 E5
Blackwater r. Ireland/U.K. 51 F3
Blackwater watercourse U.S.A. 131 C5
Blackwater Lake Canada 120 F2
Blackwater Reservoir U.K. 50 E4
Blackwood r. Australia 109 A8
Blackwood National Park Australia 110 D4
Bladensburg National Park Australia 110 C4
Blaenavon U.K. 49 D7
Blagodarnyy Rus. Fed. 91 F1
Blagoevgrad Bulg. 59 J3
Blagoveshchensk Amurskaya Oblast' Rus. Fed. 74 B2
Blagoveshchensk Respublika Bashkortostan Rus. Fed. 41 R4
Blaikiston, Mount Canada 120 H5
Blaine Lake Canada 121 J4
Blair U.S.A. 130 D3
Blair Athol Australia 110 D4
Blair Atholl U.K. 50 F4
Blairgowrie U.K. 50 F4
Blairsden U.S.A. 128 C2
Blairsville U.S.A. 133 D5
Blakang Mati, Pulau i. Sing. see Sentosa
Blakely U.S.A. 133 C6
Blakeney U.K. 49 I6

▶Blanc, Mont mt. France/Italy 56 H4
5th highest mountain in Europe.

Blanca, Bahía b. Arg. 144 D5
Blanca, Sierra mt. U.S.A. 127 G6
Blanca Peak U.S.A. 127 G5
Blanche, Lake salt flat S.A. Australia 111 B6
Blanche, Lake salt flat W.A. Australia 108 C5
Blanchester U.S.A. 134 D4
Blanc Nez, Cap c. France 52 B4
Blanco r. Bol. 142 F6
Blanco U.S.A. 129 J3
Blanco, Cape U.S.A. 126 B4
Blanc-Sablon Canada 123 K4
Bland r. Australia 112 C4
Bland U.S.A. 134 E5
Blanda r. Iceland 44 [inset]
Blandford Forum U.K. 49 E8
Blanding U.S.A. 129 I3
Blanes Spain 57 H3
Blangah, Telok Sing. 71 [inset]
Blangkejeren Indon. 71 B7
Blangpidie Indon. 71 B7
Blankenberge Belgium 52 D3
Blankenheim Germany 52 G4
Blanquilla, Isla i. Venez. 142 F1
Blansko Czech Rep. 47 P6
Blantyre Malawi 99 D5
Blarney Ireland 51 D6
Blaufelden Germany 53 J5
Blåviksjön Sweden 44 K4
Blaye France 56 D4
Blayney Australia 112 D4
Blaze, Point Australia 108 E3
Bleckede Germany 53 K1
Bleilochtalsperre resr Germany 53 L4
Blenheim Canada 134 E2
Blenheim N.Z. 113 D5
Blenheim Palace tourist site U.K. 49 F7
Blerick Neth. 52 G3
Blessington Lakes Ireland 51 F4
Bletchley U.K. 49 G6
Blida Alg. 57 H5
Blies r. Germany 53 H5
Bligh Water b. Fiji 107 H3
Blind River Canada 122 E5
Bliss U.S.A. 126 E4
Blissfield U.S.A. 134 D3
Blitta Togo 96 D4
Blocher U.S.A. 134 C4
Block Island U.S.A. 135 J3
Block Island Sound sea chan. U.S.A. 135 J3
Bloemfontein S. Africa 101 H5
Bloemhof S. Africa 101 G4
Bloemhof Dam S. Africa 101 G4
Bloemhof Dam Nature Reserve S. Africa 101 G4
Blomberg Germany 53 J3
Blönduós Iceland 44 [inset]
Blongas Indon. 108 B2
Bloods Range mts Australia 109 E6
Bloodsworth Island U.S.A. 135 G4
Bloodvein r. Canada 121 L5
Bloody Foreland pt Ireland 51 D2
Bloomer U.S.A. 130 F2
Bloomfield Canada 135 G2
Bloomfield IA U.S.A. 130 E3
Bloomfield IN U.S.A. 134 B4
Bloomfield MO U.S.A. 131 F4
Bloomfield NM U.S.A. 129 J3
Blooming Prairie U.S.A. 130 E3
Bloomington IL U.S.A. 130 F3
Bloomington IN U.S.A. 134 B4
Bloomington MN U.S.A. 130 E2
Bloomsburg U.S.A. 135 G3
Blossburg U.S.A. 135 G3
Blosseville Kyst coastal area Greenland 119 P3
Blouberg S. Africa 101 I2
Blouberg Nature Reserve S. Africa 101 I2
Blountstown U.S.A. 133 C6
Blountville U.S.A. 134 D5
Bloxham U.K. 49 F6
Blue r. Canada 120 D3
Blue watercourse U.S.A. 129 I5
Blue Bell Knoll mt. U.S.A. 129 H2
Blueberry r. Canada 120 F3
Blue Diamond U.S.A. 129 F3
Blue Earth U.S.A. 130 E3
Bluefield VA U.S.A. 132 D4
Bluefield WV U.S.A. 134 E5
Bluefields Nicaragua 137 H6
Blue Hills Turks and Caicos Is 133 F8
Blue Knob hill U.S.A. 135 F3
Blue Mesa Reservoir U.S.A. 129 J2
Blue Mountain hill Canada 123 K4
Blue Mountain India 83 H5
Blue Mountain Lake U.S.A. 135 H2
Blue Mountain Pass Lesotho 101 H5
Blue Mountains Australia 112 D4
Blue Mountains U.S.A. 126 D3
Blue Mountains National Park Australia 112 E4
Blue Nile r. Eth./Sudan 86 D6
also known as Ābay Wenz (Ethiopia), Bahr el Azraq (Sudan)
Bluenose Lake Canada 118 G3
Blue Ridge GA U.S.A. 133 C5
Blue Ridge VA U.S.A. 134 F5
Blue Ridge mts U.S.A. 134 E5
Blue Stack hill Ireland 51 D3
Blue Stack Mts hills Ireland 51 D3
Bluestone Lake U.S.A. 134 E5
Bluewater U.S.A. 129 J4
Bluff N.Z. 113 B8
Bluff U.S.A. 129 I3
Bluffdale U.S.A. 129 H1
Bluff Island H.K. China 77 [inset]
Bluff Knoll mt. Australia 109 B8
Bluffton IN U.S.A. 134 C3
Bluffton OH U.S.A. 134 D3
Blumenau Brazil 145 A4
Blustry Mountain Canada 126 C2
Blyde River Canyon Nature Reserve S. Africa 101 J3
Blyth Canada 134 E2
Blyth England U.K. 48 F3
Blyth England U.K. 48 F5
Blythe U.S.A. 129 F5
Blytheville U.S.A. 131 F5
Bø Norway 45 F7
Bo Sierra Leone 96 B4
Boa Esperança Brazil 145 B3
Bo'ai Henan China 77 G1
Bo'ai Yunnan China 76 E4
Boali Cent. Afr. Rep. 98 B3
Boalsert Neth. see Bolsward
Boane Moz. 101 K4
Boa Nova Brazil 145 C1
Boardman U.S.A. 134 E3
Boatlaname Botswana 101 G2
Boa Viagem Brazil 143 K5
Boa Vista Brazil 142 F3
Boa Vista i. Cape Verde 96 [inset]
Bobadah Australia 112 C4
Bobai China 77 F4
Bobaomby, Tanjona c. Madag. 99 E5
Bobbili India 84 D2
Bobcaygeon Canada 135 F1
Bobo-Dioulasso Burkina 96 C3
Bobotov Kuk mt. Montenegro see Durmitor
Bobriki Rus. Fed. see Novomoskovsk
Bobrinets Ukr. see Bobrynets'
Bobrov Rus. Fed. 43 I6
Bobrovitsa Ukr. see Bobrovytsya
Bobrovytsya Ukr. 43 F6
Bobruysk Belarus see Babruysk
Bobrynets' Ukr. 43 G6
Bobs Lake Canada 135 G1
Bobuk Sudan 86 D7
Bobures Venez. 142 D2
Boby mt. Madag. 99 E6
Boca de Macareo Venez. 142 F2
Boca do Acre Brazil 142 E5
Boca do Jari Brazil 143 H4
Bocaiúva Brazil 145 C2
Bocaranga Cent. Afr. Rep. 98 B3
Boca Raton U.S.A. 133 D7
Bocas del Toro Panama 137 H7
Bochnia Poland 47 R6
Bocholt Germany 52 G3
Bochum Germany 53 H3
Bockenem Germany 53 K2
Bocoio Angola 99 B5
Bocoyna Mex. 127 G8
Boda Cent. Afr. Rep. 98 B3
Bodalla Australia 112 E6
Bodallin Australia 109 B7
Bodaybo Rus. Fed. 65 M4
Boddam U.K. 50 H3
Bode r. Germany 53 L3
Bodega Head hd U.S.A. 128 B2
Bodélé reg. Chad 97 E3
Boden Sweden 44 L4
Bodenham U.K. 49 E6
Bodensee l. Germany/Switz. see Constance, Lake
Bodenteich Germany 53 K2
Bodenwerder Germany 53 J3
Bodie (abandoned) U.S.A. 128 D2
Bodinayakkanur India 84 C4
Bodmin U.K. 49 C8
Bodmin Moor moorland U.K. 49 C8
Bodø Norway 44 I3
Bodoquena Brazil 143 G7
Bodoquena, Serra da hills Brazil 144 E2
Bodrum Turkey 59 L6
Bodträskfors Sweden 44 L3
Boechout Belgium 52 E3
Boende Dem. Rep. Congo 97 F5
Boerne U.S.A. 131 D6
Boeuf r. U.S.A. 131 F6
Boffa Guinea 96 B3
Bogalay Myanmar see Bogale
Bogale Myanmar 70 A3
Bogale r. Myanmar 70 A4
Bogalusa U.S.A. 131 F6
Bogan r. Australia 112 C2
Bogandé Burkina 96 C3
Bogan Gate Australia 112 C4
Bogani Nani Wartabone, Taman Nasional Indon. 69 G6
Boğazlıyan Turkey 90 D3
Bogcang Zangbo r. China 83 F3
Bogd Övörhangay Mongolia 80 J3
Bogda Shan mts China 80 G3
Boggabilla Australia 112 E2
Boggabri Australia 112 E3
Boggeragh Mts hills Ireland 51 C5
Boghar Alg. 57 H6
Boghari Alg. see Ksar el Boukhari
Bognor Regis U.K. 49 G8
Bogodukhov Ukr. see Bohodukhiv
Bog of Allen reg. Ireland 51 E4
Bogong, Mount Australia 112 C6
Bogopol' Rus. Fed. 74 D3
Bogor Indon. 68 D8
Bogoroditsk Rus. Fed. 43 H5
Bogorodsk Rus. Fed. 42 I4
Bogorodskoye Khabarovskiy Kray Rus. Fed. 74 F1
Bogorodskoye Kirovskaya Oblast' Rus. Fed. 42 K4

▶Bogotá Col. 142 D3
Capital of Colombia. 4th most populous city in South America.

Bogotol Rus. Fed. 64 J4
Bogoyavlenskoye Rus. Fed. see Pervomayskiy
Bogra Bangl. 83 G4
Boguchany Rus. Fed. 65 K4
Boguchar Rus. Fed. 43 I6
Bogué Mauritania 96 B3
Bo Hai g. China 73 L5
Bohain-en-Vermandois France 52 D5
Bohai Wan b. China 66 D4
Bohemian Forest mts Germany see Böhmer Wald
Böhlen Germany 53 M3
Bohlokong S. Africa 101 I5
Böhme r. Germany 53 J2
Böhmer Wald mts Germany 53 M5
Bohmte Germany 53 I2
Bohodukhiv Ukr. 43 G6
Bohol i. Phil. 69 G5
Bohol Sea Phil. 69 G5
Bohu China 80 G3
Boiaçu Brazil 142 F4
Boichoko S. Africa 100 F5
Boigu Island Australia 69 K8
Boikhutso S. Africa 101 H4
Boileau, Cape Australia 108 C4
Boim Brazil 143 G4
Boipeba, Ilha i. Brazil 145 D1
Bois r. Brazil 145 A2
Bois Blanc Island U.S.A. 132 C2

▶Boise U.S.A. 126 D4
Capital of Idaho.

Boise City U.S.A. 131 C4
Boissevain Canada 121 K5
Boitumelong S. Africa 101 G4
Boizenburg Germany 53 K1
Bojd Iran 88 E3
Bojnūrd Iran 88 E2
Bokaak atoll Marshall Is see Taongi
Bokajan India 83 H4
Bokaro India 83 F5

karo Reservoir India 83 F5
katola Dem. Rep. Congo 98 B4
ké Guinea 96 B3
kele Dem. Rep. Congo 98 C4
khara r. Australia 112 C2
Kheo Cambodia see Bâ Kêv
knafjorden sea chan. Norway 45 D7
koko Dem. Rep. Congo 98 C3
koro Chad 97 E3
kovskaya Rus. Fed. 43 I6
kspits S. Africa 100 E4
ktor Rus. Fed. 74 E2
kurdak Turkm. 88 E2
l Chad 97 E3
laiti Dem. Rep. Congo 97 F5
lama Guinea-Bissau 96 B3
langir India 84 D1
lan Pass Pak. 89 G4
lavén, Phouphiang plat. Laos 70 D4
lbec France 56 E2
le China 80 F3
le Ghana 96 C4
leko Dem. Rep. Congo 98 B4
len Rus. Fed. 74 D2
lgar Rus. Fed. 43 K5
lgatanga Ghana 96 C3
lgrad Ukr. see Bolhrad
lhrad Ukr. 59 M2
li China 74 C3
lia Dem. Rep. Congo 98 B4
liden Sweden 44 L4
lingbrook U.S.A. 134 A3
lintin-Vale Romania 59 K2
lívar Peru 142 C5
livar NY U.S.A. 135 F2
livar TN U.S.A. 131 F5
lívar, Pico mt. Venez. 142 D2
livia Cuba 133 E8

olivia country S. America 142 E7
th largest country in South America.

khov Rus. Fed. 43 H5
lène France 56 G4
lnäs Sweden 45 J6
lon Australia 112 C2
lstabruk Sweden 44 J5
lmen l. Sweden 45 H8
lobo Dem. Rep. Congo 98 B4
logna Italy 58 D2
lognesi Peru 142 D5
logoye Rus. Fed. 42 G4
lokanang S. Africa 101 G5
lomba Dem. Rep. Congo 98 B3
lon' Rus. Fed. see Achan
lpur India 83 F5
lsena, Lago di l. Italy 58 D3
'shakovo Rus. Fed. 45 L9
'shaya Chernigovka Rus. Fed. 41 Q5
'shaya Glushitsa Rus. Fed. 43 K5
'shaya Imandra, Ozero l. Rus. Fed.
4 R3
'shaya Martinovka Rus. Fed. 43 I7
'shaya Tsarevshchina Rus. Fed. see
olzhskiy
'shenarymskoye Kazakh. 80 F2
'shevik, Ostrov i. Rus. Fed. 65 L2
'shezemel'skaya Tundra lowland
us. Fed. 42 L2
'shiye Barsuki, Peski des. Kazakh.
0 A2
'shiye Chirki Rus. Fed. 42 J3
'shiye Kozly Rus. Fed. 42 H2
'shoy Begichev, Ostrov i. Rus. Fed.
53 E2
'shoye Murashkino Rus. Fed. 42 J5
'shoy Irgiz r. Rus. Fed. 43 J6
'shoy Kamen' Rus. Fed. 74 D4
'shoy Kavkaz mts Asia/Europe see
aucasus
'shoy Kundysh r. Rus. Fed. 42 J4
'shoy Lyakhovskiy, Ostrov i. Rus. Fed.
5 P2
'shoy Tokmak Kyrg. see Tokmok
'shoy Tokmak Ukr. see Tokmak
són de Mapimí des. Mex. 131 B7
sward Neth. 52 F1
ton Canada 134 F2
ton U.K. 48 E5
u Turkey 59 N4
untay China 83 H1
uo China 77 G4
us Head hd Ireland 51 B6
vadin Turkey 59 N5
zano Italy 58 D1
na Dem. Rep. Congo 99 B4
naderry Australia 112 E5
nbala Australia 112 D6
nbay India see Mumbai
nbay Beach U.S.A. 129 F5
nberai, Semenanjung pen. Indon. 69 I7
nboma Dem. Rep. Congo 98 B3
n Comércio Brazil 142 E5
ndila India 83 H4
ni China 76 B2
nili Dem. Rep. Congo 98 C3
n Jardim Brazil 145 D1
n Jardim de Goiás Brazil 145 A2
n Jesus Brazil 145 A5
n Jesus da Gurgueia, Serra do hills
razil 143 J5
n Jesus da Lapa Brazil 145 C1
n Jesus do Norte Brazil 145 C3
nlo i. Norway 45 D7
nokandi r. Dem. Rep. Congo 98 C3
n Retiro Brazil 145 A4
n Sucesso Brazil 145 B3
, Cap c. Tunisia 58 D6
, Ko i. Thai. 71 B5
a Alg. see Annaba
a, Mount U.S.A. 120 A2
āb Iran 88 B2
Air U.S.A. 135 G5
aire i. Neth. Antilles 137 K6
anza Peak U.S.A. 126 C2
aparte Archipelago is Australia 108 D3
aparte Lake Canada 120 F5
ar Bridge U.K. 50 E3
avista Canada 123 L4
avista Bay Canada 123 L4
chester Bridge U.K. 50 G5
do Dem. Rep. Congo 98 C3

Bondokodi Indon. 68 F8
Bondoukou Côte d'Ivoire 96 C4
Bonduel U.S.A. 134 A1
Bondyuzhskiy Rus. Fed. see Mendeleyevsk
Bône Alg. see Annaba
Bone, Teluk b. Indon. 69 G8
Bönen Germany 53 H3
Bonerate, Kepulauan is Indon. 108 C1
Bo'ness U.K. 50 F4

▶Bonete, Cerro mt. Arg. 144 C3
3rd highest mountain in South America.

Bonga Eth. 98 D3
Bongaigaon India 83 G4
Bongandanga Dem. Rep. Congo 98 C3
Bongani S. Africa 100 F5
Bongao Phil. 68 F5
Bongba China 82 E2
Bong Co l. China 83 G3
Bongo, Massif des mts Cent. Afr. Rep. 98 C3
Bongo, Serra do mts Angola 99 B4
Bongolava mts Madag. 99 E5
Bongor Chad 97 E3
Bông Sơn Vietnam 71 E4
Bonham U.S.A. 131 D5
Bonheiden Belgium 52 E3
Boni Mali 96 C3
Bonifacio Corsica France 56 I6
Bonifacio, Bocche di strait France/Italy see Bonifacio, Strait of
Bonifacio, Bouches de strait France/Italy see Bonifacio, Strait of
Bonifacio, Strait of France/Italy 56 I6

▶Bonin Islands Japan 75 F8
Part of Japan.

▶Bonn Germany 52 H4
Former capital of Germany.

Bonna Germany see Bonn
Bonnåsjøen Norway 44 I3
Bonners Ferry U.S.A. 126 D2
Bonnet, Lac du resr Canada 121 M5
Bonneville France 56 H3
Bonneville Salt Flats U.S.A. 129 G1
Bonnières-sur-Seine France 52 B5
Bonnie Rock Australia 109 B7
Bonnieville U.S.A. 134 C5
Bonnyrigg U.K. 50 F5
Bonnyville Canada 121 I4
Bonobono Phil. 68 F5
Bononia Italy see Bologna
Bonorva Sardinia Italy 58 C4
Bonshaw Australia 112 E2
Bontebok National Park S. Africa 100 E8
Bonthe Sierra Leone 96 B4
Bontoc Phil. 77 I5
Bontosunggu Indon. 68 F8
Bontrug S. Africa 101 G7
Bonvouloir Islands P.N.G. 110 E1
Bonwapitse Botswana 101 H2
Boo, Kepulauan is Indon. 69 H7
Book Cliffs ridge U.S.A. 129 I2
Booker U.S.A. 131 C4
Boolba Australia 112 D2
Booligal Australia 112 B4
Boomer U.S.A. 134 E4
Boomi Australia 112 D2
Boon U.S.A. 134 C1
Boonah Australia 112 F1
Boone CO U.S.A. 127 G5
Boone IA U.S.A. 130 E3
Boone NC U.S.A. 132 D4
Boone Lake U.S.A. 134 D5
Boones Mill U.S.A. 134 F5
Booneville AR U.S.A. 131 E5
Booneville KY U.S.A. 134 D5
Booneville MS U.S.A. 131 F5
Böön Tsagaan Nuur salt l. Mongolia 80 I2
Boonville CA U.S.A. 128 B2
Boonville IN U.S.A. 134 B4
Boonville MO U.S.A. 130 E4
Boonville NY U.S.A. 135 H2
Boorabin National Park Australia 109 C7
Boorama Somalia 98 E3
Booroorban Australia 112 B5
Boorowa Australia 112 D5
Boort Australia 112 A6
Boothby, Cape Antarctica 152 D2
Boothia, Gulf of Canada 119 J3
Boothia Peninsula Canada 119 I2
Bootle U.K. 48 E5
Booué Gabon 98 B4
Boppard Germany 53 H4
Boqê China 83 G3
Boqueirão, Serra do hills Brazil 143 J6
Bor Czech Rep. 53 M5
Bor Rus. Fed. 42 J4
Bor Sudan 97 G4
Bor Turkey 90 D3
Boraha, Nosy i. Madag. 99 F5
Borah Peak U.S.A. 126 E3
Borai India 84 D1
Borakalalo Nature Reserve S. Africa 101 H3
Boran Kazakh. see Buran
Boraphet, Bung l. Thai. 70 C4
Boraphet, Nong l. Thai. see Boraphet, Bung
Borås Sweden 45 H8
Borasambar India 84 D1
Borāzjān Iran 88 C4
Borba Brazil 143 G4
Borba China 76 C1
Borborema, Planalto da plat. Brazil 143 K5
Borchen Germany 53 I3
Borçka Turkey 91 F2
Bor Dağı mt. Turkey 59 M6
Bordeaux France 56 D4
Borden Island Canada 119 G2
Borden Peninsula Canada 119 J2
Border Ranges National Park Australia 112 F2
Borðeyri Iceland 44 [inset]

Bordj Bou Arréridj Alg. 57 I5
Bordj Bounaama Alg. 57 G6
Bordj Flye Ste-Marie Alg. 96 C2
Bordj Messaouda Alg. 54 F5
Bordj Mokhtar Alg. 96 D2
Bordj Omar Driss Alg. see Bordj Omer Driss
Bordj Omer Driss Alg. 96 D2
Boreas Abyssal Plain sea feature Arctic Ocean 153 H1
Borel r. Canada 123 H2
Borgå Fin. see Porvoo
Borgarfjörður Iceland 44 [inset]
Borgarnes Iceland 44 [inset]
Børgefjell Nasjonalpark nat. park Norway 44 H4
Borger U.S.A. 131 C5
Borgholm Sweden 45 J8
Borgne, Lake b. U.S.A. 131 F6
Borgo San Lorenzo Italy 58 D3
Bori India 84 C1
Bori r. India 82 C5
Borikhan Laos 70 C3
Borislav Ukr. see Boryslav
Borisoglebsk Rus. Fed. 43 I6
Borisov Belarus see Barysaw
Borisovka Rus. Fed. 43 H6
Borispol' Ukr. see Boryspil'
Bo River Post Sudan 97 F4
Borja Peru 142 C4
Borken Germany 52 G3
Borkenes Norway 44 J2
Borkovskaya Rus. Fed. 42 K2
Borkum Germany 52 G1
Borkum i. Germany 52 G1
Borlänge Sweden 45 I6
Borlaug Norway 45 E6
Borlu Turkey 59 M5
Borna Germany 53 M3
Born-Berge hill Germany 53 K3
Borndiep sea chan. Neth. 52 F1
Borne Neth. 52 G2

▶Borneo i. Asia 68 E6
Largest island in Asia, and 3rd in the world.

Bornholm county Denmark 153 H3
Bornholm i. Denmark 45 I9
Bornova Turkey 59 L5
Borodino Rus. Fed. 64 J3
Borodinskoye Rus. Fed. 45 P6
Borogontsy Rus. Fed. 65 O3
Borohoro Shan mts China 80 F3
Borok-Sulezhskiy Rus. Fed. 42 H4
Boromo Burkina 96 C3
Boron U.S.A. 128 E4
Borondi India 84 D2
Boroughbridge U.K. 48 F4
Borovichi Rus. Fed. 42 G4
Borovoy Kirovskaya Oblast' Rus. Fed. 42 K4
Borovoy Respublika Kareliya Rus. Fed. 44 R4
Borovoy Respublika Komi Rus. Fed. 42 L3
Borpeta India see Barpeta
Borrisokane Ireland 51 D5
Borroloola Australia 110 B3
Børsa Norway 44 G5
Borşa Romania 43 E7
Borsakelmas sho'rxogi salt marsh Uzbek. 91 J2
Borshchiv Ukr. 43 E6
Borshchovochnyy Khrebet mts Rus. Fed. 73 J3
Bortala China see Bole
Borton U.S.A. 134 B4
Borūjen Iran 88 C4
Borūjerd Iran 88 C3
Borun Iran 88 E3
Borve U.K. 50 C3
Boryslav Ukr. 43 D6
Boryspil' Ukr. 43 F6
Borzna Ukr. 43 G6
Borzya Rus. Fed. 73 L2
Bosanska Dubica Bos.-Herz. 58 G2
Bosanska Gradiška Bos.-Herz. 58 G2
Bosanska Krupa Bos.-Herz. 58 G2
Bosanski Novi Bos.-Herz. 58 G2
Bosansko Grahovo Bos.-Herz. 58 G2
Boscawen Island Tonga see Niuatoputopu
Bose China 76 E4
Boshof S. Africa 101 G5
Boshruyeh Iran 88 E3
Bosna i Hercegovina country Europe see Bosnia-Herzegovina
Bosna Saray Bos.-Herz. see Sarajevo
Bosnia-Herzegovina country Europe 58 G2
Bosobogolo Pan salt pan Botswana 100 F3
Bosobolo Dem. Rep. Congo 98 B3
Bōsō-hantō pen. Japan 75 F6
Bosporus strait Turkey 59 M4
Bossaga Turkm. see Basaga
Bossangoa Cent. Afr. Rep. 98 B3
Bossembélé Cent. Afr. Rep. 98 B3
Bossier City U.S.A. 131 E5
Bossiesvlei Namibia 100 C3
Bossut, Cape Australia 108 C4
Bostan China 83 F1
Bostān Iran 88 B4
Bostan Pak. 89 G4
Bostāneh, Ra's-e pt Iran 88 D5
Bosten Hu l. China 80 G3
Boston U.K. 49 G6

▶Boston U.S.A. 135 J2
Capital of Massachusetts.

Boston Mountains U.S.A. 131 E5
Boston Spa U.K. 48 F5
Boswell U.S.A. 134 B3
Botad India 82 B5
Botany Bay Australia 112 E4
Botev mt. Bulg. 59 K3
Botevgrad Bulg. 59 J3
Bothaville S. Africa 101 H4
Bothnia, Gulf of Fin./Sweden 45 K6
Bothwell Canada 134 E2
Botkins U.S.A. 134 C3
Botlikh Rus. Fed. 91 G2
Botoşani Romania 43 E7
Botou China 73 L5
Botshabelo S. Africa 101 H5

Botswana country Africa 99 C6
Botte Donato, Monte mt. Italy 58 G5
Bottesford U.K. 48 G5
Bottrop Germany 52 G3
Botucatu Brazil 145 A3
Botuporã Brazil 145 C1
Botwood Canada 123 L4
Bouaflé Côte d'Ivoire 96 C4
Bouaké Côte d'Ivoire 96 C4
Bouar Cent. Afr. Rep. 98 B3
Bouârfa Morocco 54 D5
Bouba Ndjida, Parc National de nat. park Cameroon 97 E4
Bouca Cent. Afr. Rep. 98 B3
Boucaut Bay Australia 108 F3
Bouchain France 52 D4
Bouctouche Canada 123 I5
Boudh India 84 E1
Bougaa Alg. 57 I5
Bougainville, Cape Australia 108 D3
Bougainville Island P.N.G. 106 F2
Bougainville Reef Australia 110 D2
Boughessa Mali 96 D3
Bougie Alg. see Bejaïa
Bougouni Mali 96 C3
Bougtob Alg. 54 E5
Bouillon Belgium 52 F5
Bouira Alg. 57 H5
Bou Izakarn Morocco 96 C2
Boujdour W. Sahara 96 B2
Boulder Australia 109 C7
Boulder CO U.S.A. 126 G4
Boulder MT U.S.A. 126 E3
Boulder UT U.S.A. 129 H3
Boulder Canyon gorge U.S.A. 129 F3
Boulder City U.S.A. 129 F4
Boulevard U.S.A. 128 E5
Boulia Australia 110 B4
Boulogne France see Boulogne-sur-Mer
Boulogne-Billancourt France 52 C6
Boulogne-sur-Mer France 52 B4
Boumerdes Alg. 57 H5
Bouna Côte d'Ivoire 96 C4
Bou Naceur, Jbel mt. Morocco 54 D5
Boû Nâga Mauritania 96 B3
Boundary Mountains U.S.A. 135 J1
Boundary Peak U.S.A. 128 D3
Boundiali Côte d'Ivoire 96 C4
Boundji Congo 98 B4
Boun Nua Laos 70 C2
Bountiful U.S.A. 129 H1
Bounty Islands N.Z. 107 H6
Bounty Trough sea feature S. Pacific Ocean 150 H9
Bourail New Caledonia 107 G4
Bourbon reg. France see Bourbonnais
Bourbon terr. Indian Ocean see Réunion
Bourbon U.S.A. 134 B3
Bourbonnais reg. France 56 F3
Bourem Mali 96 C3
Bouressa Mali see Boughessa
Bourg-Achard France 49 H9
Bourganeuf France 56 E4
Bourg-en-Bresse France 56 G3
Bourges France 56 F3
Bourget Canada 135 H1
Bourgogne reg. France see Burgundy
Bourgogne, Canal de France 56 G3
Bourke Australia 112 B3
Bourne U.K. 49 G6
Bournemouth U.K. 49 F8
Bourtoutou Chad 97 F3
Bou Saâda Alg. 57 I6
Bou Salem Tunisia 58 C6
Bouse U.S.A. 129 F5
Bouse Wash watercourse U.S.A. 129 F4
Boussu Belgium 52 D4
Boutilimit Mauritania 96 B3
Bouvet Island terr. S. Atlantic Ocean see Bouvetøya

▶Bouvetøya terr. S. Atlantic Ocean 148 I9
Dependency of Norway.

Bouy France 52 E5
Bova Marina Italy 58 F6
Bovenden Germany 53 J3
Bow r. Alta Canada 121 I5
Bow r. Alta Canada 126 F2
Bowa China see Muli
Bowbells U.S.A. 130 C1
Bowden U.S.A. 134 F4
Bowditch atoll Tokelau see Fakaofo
Bowen Australia 110 E4
Bowen, Mount Australia 112 D6
Bowenville Australia 112 E1
Bowers Ridge sea feature Bering Sea 150 H2
Bowie Australia 110 D4
Bowie AZ U.S.A. 129 I5
Bowie TX U.S.A. 131 D5
Bow Island Canada 121 I5
Bowling Green KY U.S.A. 134 B5
Bowling Green MO U.S.A. 130 F4
Bowling Green OH U.S.A. 134 D3
Bowling Green VA U.S.A. 135 G4
Bowling Green Bay National Park Australia 110 D3
Bowman U.S.A. 130 C2
Bowman, Mount Canada 126 C2
Bowman Island Antarctica 152 F2
Bowman Peninsula Antarctica 152 L2
Bowmore U.K. 50 C5
Bowo China see Bomi
Bowral Australia 112 E5
Bowser Lake Canada 120 D3
Boxberg Germany 53 J5
Box Elder U.S.A. 130 C2
Box Elder r. U.S.A. 130 C2
Boxtel Neth. 52 F3
Boyabat Turkey 90 D2
Boyana tourist site Bulg. 59 J3
Boyang China 77 H2
Boyd r. Australia 112 F2
Boyd Lagoon salt flat Australia 109 D6
Boyd Lake Canada 121 K2
Boydton U.S.A. 135 F5
Boyers U.S.A. 134 F3
Boykins U.S.A. 135 G5
Boyle Canada 121 H4
Boyle Ireland 51 D4

Boyne r. Ireland 51 F4
Boyne City U.S.A. 134 C1
Boysen Reservoir U.S.A. 126 F4
Boysun Uzbek. 89 G2
Boyuibe Bol. 142 F8
Böyük Qafqaz mts Asia/Europe see Caucasus

▶Bozcaada i. Turkey 59 L5
Most westerly point of Asia.

Bozdağ mt. Turkey 59 L5
Bozdağ mt. Turkey 85 C1
Boz Dağları mts Turkey 59 L5
Bozdoğan Turkey 59 M6
Bozeat U.K. 49 G6
Bozeman U.S.A. 126 F3
Bozen Italy see Bolzano
Bozhou China 77 G1
Bozoum Cent. Afr. Rep. 98 B3
Bozova Turkey 90 E3
Bozqūsh, Kūh-e mts Iran 88 B2
Bozüyük Turkey 59 N5
Bozyazı Turkey 85 A1
Bra Italy 58 B2
Brač i. Croatia 58 G3
Bracadale U.K. 50 C3
Bracadale, Loch b. U.K. 50 C3
Bracara Port. see Braga
Bracciano, Lago di l. Italy 58 E3
Bracebridge Canada 134 F1
Bräcke Sweden 44 I5
Brackenheim Germany 53 J5
Brackettville U.S.A. 131 C6
Bracknell U.K. 49 G7
Bradano r. Italy 58 G4
Bradenton U.S.A. 133 D7
Bradford Canada 134 F1
Bradford U.K. 48 F5
Bradford OH U.S.A. 134 C3
Bradford PA U.S.A. 135 F3
Bradley U.S.A. 134 B3
Brady U.S.A. 131 D6
Brady Glacier U.S.A. 120 B3
Brae U.K. 50 [inset]
Braemar U.K. 50 F3
Braga Port. 57 B3
Bragado Arg. 144 D5
Bragança Brazil 143 I4
Bragança Port. 57 C3
Bragança Paulista Brazil 145 B3
Brahin Belarus 43 F6
Brahlstorf Germany 53 K1
Brahmanbaria Bangl. 83 G5
Brahmapur India 84 E2
Brahmaputra r. Asia 83 H4
also known as Dihang (India) or Jamuna (Bangladesh) or Siang (India) or Yarlung Zangbo (China)
Brahmaur India 82 D2
Brăila Romania 59 L2
Braine France 52 D5
Braine-le-Comte Belgium 52 E4
Brainerd U.S.A. 130 E2
Braintree U.K. 49 H7
Braithwaite Point Australia 108 F2
Brak r. S. Africa 101 I2
Brake (Unterweser) Germany 53 I1
Brakel Belgium 52 D4
Brakel Germany 53 J3
Brakwater Namibia 100 C2
Bramfield Australia 109 F8
Bramming Denmark 45 F9
Brämön i. Sweden 44 J5
Brampton Canada 134 F2
Brampton England U.K. 48 E4
Brampton England U.K. 49 I6
Bramsche Germany 53 I2
Bramwell Australia 110 C2
Brancaster U.K. 49 H6
Branch Canada 123 L5
Branco r. Brazil 142 F4
Brandberg mt. Namibia 99 B6
Brandbu Norway 45 G6
Brande Denmark 45 F9
Brandenburg Germany 53 M2
Brandenburg land Germany 53 N2
Brandenburg U.S.A. 134 B5
Brandfort S. Africa 101 H5
Brandis Germany 53 N3
Brandon Canada 121 L5
Brandon U.K. 49 H6
Brandon MS U.S.A. 131 F5
Brandon VT U.S.A. 135 I2
Brandon Head hd Ireland 51 B5
Brandon Mountain hill Ireland 51 B5
Brandvlei S. Africa 100 E6
Braniewo Poland 47 Q3
Bransfield Strait Antarctica 152 L2
Branson U.S.A. 131 C4
Brantford Canada 134 E2
Branxton Australia 112 E4
Bras d'Or Lake Canada 123 J5
Brasil country S. America see Brazil
Brasileia Brazil 142 E6

▶Brasília Brazil 145 B1
Capital of Brazil.

Brasília de Minas Brazil 145 B2
Braslav Belarus see Braslaw
Braslaw Belarus 45 O9
Braşov Romania 59 K2
Brassey, Mount Australia 109 F5
Brassey Range hills Australia 109 C6
Brasstown Bald mt. U.S.A. 133 D5

▶Bratislava Slovakia 47 P6
Capital of Slovakia.

Bratsk Rus. Fed. 72 I1
Bratskoye Vodokhranilishche resr Rus. Fed. 72 I1
Brattleboro U.S.A. 135 I2
Braunau am Inn Austria 47 N6
Braunfels Germany 53 I4
Braunlage Germany 53 K3
Braunsbedra Germany 53 L3
Braunschweig Germany 53 K2
Brava i. Cape Verde 96 [inset]
Brave U.S.A. 134 E4
Bråviken inlet Sweden 45 J7

Bravo, Cerro mt. Bol. 142 F7
Bravo del Norte, Río r. Mex./U.S.A. 127 G7 see Rio Grande
Brawley U.S.A. 129 F5
Bray Ireland 51 F4
Bray Island Canada 119 K3
Brazeau r. Canada 120 H4
Brazeau, Mount Canada 120 G4

▶Brazil country S. America 143 G5
Largest and most populous country in South America, and 5th largest and 5th most populous in the world.

Brazil U.S.A. 134 B4
Brazil Basin sea feature S. Atlantic Ocean 148 G7
Brazilian Highlands plat. Brazil 143 J7
Brazos r. U.S.A. 131 E6

▶Brazzaville Congo 99 B4
Capital of Congo.

Brčko Bos.-Herz. 58 H2
Bré Ireland see Bray
Breadalbane Australia 110 B4
Breaksea Sound inlet N.Z. 113 A7
Bream Bay N.Z. 113 E2
Brechfa U.K. 49 C7
Brechin U.K. 50 G4
Brecht Belgium 52 E3
Breckenridge MI U.S.A. 134 C2
Breckenridge MN U.S.A. 130 D2
Breckenridge TX U.S.A. 131 D5
Břeclav Czech Rep. 47 P6
Brecon U.K. 49 D7
Brecon Beacons reg. U.K. 49 D7
Brecon Beacons National Park U.K. 49 D7
Breda Neth. 52 E3
Bredasdorp S. Africa 100 E8
Bredbo Australia 112 D5
Breddin Germany 53 M2
Bredevoort Neth. 52 G3
Bredviken Sweden 44 I3
Bree Belgium 52 F3
Breed U.S.A. 134 A1
Bregenz Austria 47 L7
Breiðafjörður b. Iceland 44 [inset]
Breiðdalsvík Iceland 44 [inset]
Breidenbach Germany 53 I4
Breien U.S.A. 130 C2
Breitenfelde Germany 53 K1
Breitengüßbach Germany 53 K5
Breiter Luzinsee l. Germany 53 N1
Breivikbotn Norway 44 M1
Breizh reg. France see Brittany
Brejo Velho Brazil 145 C1
Brekstad Norway 44 F5
Bremen Germany 53 I1
Bremen land Germany 53 I1
Bremen IN U.S.A. 134 B3
Bremen OH U.S.A. 134 D4
Bremer Bay Australia 109 B8
Bremerhaven Germany 53 I1
Bremer Range hills Australia 109 C8
Bremersdorp Swaziland see Manzini
Bremervörde Germany 53 J1
Bremm Germany 52 H4
Brenham U.S.A. 131 D6
Brenna Norway 44 H4
Brennero, Passo di pass Austria/Italy see Brenner Pass
Brennerpaß pass Austria/Italy see Brenner Pass
Brenner Pass Austria/Italy 58 D1
Brentwood U.K. 49 H7
Brescia Italy 58 D2
Breslau Poland see Wrocław
Bresle r. France 52 B4
Brésolles, Lac l. Canada 123 H3
Bressanone Italy 58 D1
Bressay i. U.K. 50 [inset]
Bressuire France 56 D3
Brest Belarus 45 M10
Brest France 56 B2
Brest-Litovsk Belarus see Brest
Bretagne reg. France see Brittany
Breteuil France 52 C5
Brétigny-sur-Orge France 52 C6
Breton Canada 120 H4
Breton Sound b. U.S.A. 131 F6
Brett, Cape N.Z. 113 E2
Bretten Germany 53 I5
Bretton U.K. 48 E5
Breueh, Pulau i. Indon. 71 A6
Brevard U.S.A. 133 D5
Breves Brazil 143 H4
Brewarrina Australia 112 C2
Brewer U.S.A. 132 G4
Brewster NE U.S.A. 130 D3
Brewster OH U.S.A. 134 E3
Brewster, Kap c. Greenland see Kangikajik
Brewster, Lake imp. l. Australia 112 B4
Brewton U.S.A. 133 C6
Breyten S. Africa 101 I4
Breytovo Rus. Fed. 42 H4
Brezhnev Rus. Fed. see Naberezhnyye Chelny
Brezno Slovakia 47 Q6
Brezovo Bulg. 59 K3
Brezovo Polje hill Croatia 58 G2
Bria Cent. Afr. Rep. 98 C3
Briançon France 56 H4
Brian Head mt. U.S.A. 129 G3
Bribbaree Australia 112 C5
Bribie Island Australia 112 F1
Briceni Moldova 43 E6
Brichany Moldova see Briceni
Brichen' Moldova see Briceni
Bridgend U.K. 49 D7
Bridge of Orchy U.K. 50 E4
Bridgeport CA U.S.A. 128 D2
Bridgeport CT U.S.A. 135 I3
Bridgeport IL U.S.A. 134 B4
Bridgeport NE U.S.A. 130 C3
Bridger Peak U.S.A. 126 G4
Bridgeton U.S.A. 135 H4
Bridgetown Australia 109 B8

▶Bridgetown Barbados 137 M6
Capital of Barbados.

Bridgetown Canada 123 I5
Bridgeville U.S.A. 135 H4
Bridgewater Canada 123 I5
Bridgewater U.S.A. 135 H2
Bridgnorth U.K. 49 E6
Bridgton U.S.A. 135 J1
Bridgwater U.K. 49 D7
Bridgwater Bay U.K. 49 D7
Bridlington U.K. 48 G4
Bridlington Bay U.K. 48 G4
Bridport Australia 111 [inset]
Bridport U.K. 49 E8
Brie *reg.* France 56 F2
Brie-Comte-Robert France 52 C6
Brieg Poland *see* **Brzeg**
Briery Knob *mt.* U.S.A. 134 E4
Brig Switz. 56 H3
Brigg U.K. 48 G5
Brigham City U.S.A. 126 E4
Brightlingsea U.K. 49 I7
Brighton Canada 135 G1
Brighton U.K. 49 G8
Brighton *CO* U.S.A. 126 G5
Brighton *MI* U.S.A. 134 D2
Brighton *NY* U.S.A. 135 G2
Brighton *WV* U.S.A. 134 D4
Brignoles France 56 H5
Brikama Gambia 96 B3
Brillion U.S.A. 134 A1
Brilon Germany 53 I3
Brindisi Italy 58 G4
Brinkley U.S.A. 131 F5
Brion, Île *i.* Canada 123 J5
Brioude France 56 F4
Brisay Canada 123 H3

▶**Brisbane** Australia 112 F1
Capital of Queensland. 3rd most populous city in Oceania.

Brisbane Ranges National Park Australia 112 B6
Bristol U.K. 49 E7
Bristol *CT* U.S.A. 135 I3
Bristol *FL* U.S.A. 133 C6
Bristol *NH* U.S.A. 135 J2
Bristol *RI* U.S.A. 135 J3
Bristol *TN* U.S.A. 134 D5
Bristol *VT* U.S.A. 135 I1
Bristol Bay U.S.A. 118 B4
Bristol Channel *est.* U.K. 49 C7
Bristol Lake U.S.A. 129 F4
Britannia Island New Caledonia *see* **Maré**
British Antarctic Territory *reg.* Antarctica 152 L2
British Columbia *prov.* Canada 120 F5
British Empire Range *mts* Canada 119 J1
British Guiana *country* S. America *see* **Guyana**
British Honduras *country* Central America *see* **Belize**

▶**British Indian Ocean Territory** *terr.* Indian Ocean 149 M6
United Kingdom Overseas Territory.

British Solomon Islands *country* S. Pacific Ocean *see* **Solomon Islands**
Brito Godins Angola *see* **Kiwaba N'zogi**
Brits S. Africa 101 H3
Britstown S. Africa 100 F6
Brittany *reg.* France 56 C2
Britton U.S.A. 130 D2
Brive-la-Gaillarde France 56 E4
Briviesca Spain 57 E2
Brixham U.K. 49 D8
Brixia Italy *see* **Brescia**
Brlik Kazakh. *see* **Birlik**
Brno Czech Rep. 47 P6
Broach India *see* **Bharuch**
Broad *r.* U.S.A. 133 D5
Broadalbin U.S.A. 135 H2
Broad Arrow Australia 109 C7
Broadback *r.* Canada 122 F4
Broad Bay U.K. *see* **Tuath, Loch a'**
Broadford Australia 112 B6
Broadford Ireland 51 D5
Broadford U.K. 50 D3
Broad Law *hill* U.K. 50 F5
Broadmere Australia 110 A3
Broad Peak China/Pakistan 89 J3
Broad Sound *sea chan.* Australia 110 E4
Broadstairs U.K. 49 I7
Broadus U.S.A. 126 G3
Broadview Canada 121 K5
Broadway U.S.A. 135 F4
Broadwood N.Z. 113 D2
Brochet Canada 121 K3
Brochet, Lac *l.* Canada 121 K3
Brochet, Lac au *l.* Canada 123 H4
Brocken *mt.* Germany 53 K3
Brockman, Mount Australia 108 B5
Brockport *NY* U.S.A. 135 G2
Brockport *PA* U.S.A. 135 F3
Brockton U.S.A. 135 J2
Brockville Canada 135 H1
Brockway U.S.A. 135 F3
Brodeur Peninsula Canada 119 J2
Brodhead U.S.A. 134 C5
Brodick U.K. 50 D5
Brodnica Poland 47 Q4
Brody Ukr. 43 E6
Broken Arrow U.S.A. 131 E4
Broken Bay Australia 112 E4
Broken Bow *NE* U.S.A. 130 D3
Broken Bow *OK* U.S.A. 131 E5
Brokenhead *r.* Canada 121 L5
Broken Hill Australia 111 C6
Broken Hill Zambia *see* **Kabwe**
Broken Plateau *sea feature* Indian Ocean 149 O8
Brokopondo Suriname 143 G2
Brokopondo Stuwmeer *resr* Suriname *see* **Professor van Blommestein Meer**
Bromberg Poland *see* **Bydgoszcz**
Brome Germany 53 K2
Bromsgrove U.K. 49 E6
Brønderslev Denmark 45 F8
Brønnøysund Norway 44 H4
Bronson *FL* U.S.A. 133 D6
Bronson *MI* U.S.A. 134 C3
Brooke U.K. 49 I6
Brookfield U.S.A. 134 A2
Brookhaven U.S.A. 131 F6
Brookings *OR* U.S.A. 126 B4
Brookings *SD* U.S.A. 130 D2
Brookline U.S.A. 135 J2
Brooklyn U.S.A. 134 C2
Brooklyn Park U.S.A. 130 E2
Brookneal U.S.A. 135 F5
Brooks Canada 121 I5
Brooks Brook Canada 120 C2
Brooks Range *mts* U.S.A. 118 D3
Brookston U.S.A. 134 B3
Brooksville *FL* U.S.A. 133 D6
Brooksville *KY* U.S.A. 134 C4
Brookton Australia 109 B8
Brookville *IN* U.S.A. 134 C4
Brookville *PA* U.S.A. 134 F3
Brookville Lake U.S.A. 134 C4
Broom, Loch *inlet* U.K. 50 D3
Broome Australia 108 C4
Brora U.K. 50 F2
Brora *r.* U.K. 50 F2
Brösarp Sweden 45 I9
Brosna *r.* Ireland 51 E4
Brosville U.S.A. 134 F5
Brothers *is* India 71 A5
Brough U.K. 48 E4
Brough Ness *pt* U.K. 50 G2
Broughshane U.K. 51 F3
Broughton Island Canada *see* **Qikiqtarjuaq**
Broughton Islands Australia 112 F4
Brovary Ukr. 43 F6
Brovinia Australia 111 E5
Brovst Denmark 45 F8
Brown City U.S.A. 134 D2
Brown Deer U.S.A. 134 B2
Browne Range *hills* Australia 109 D6
Brownfield U.S.A. 131 C5
Browning U.S.A. 126 E2
Brown Mountain U.S.A. 128 E4
Brownstown U.S.A. 134 B4
Brownsville *KY* U.S.A. 134 B5
Brownsville *PA* U.S.A. 134 F3
Brownsville *TN* U.S.A. 131 F5
Brownsville *TX* U.S.A. 131 D7
Brownwood U.S.A. 131 D6
Browse Island Australia 108 C3
Bruay-la-Bussière France 52 C4
Bruce Peninsula Canada 134 E1
Bruce Peninsula National Park Canada 134 E1
Bruce Rock Australia 109 B7
Bruchsal Germany 53 I5
Brück Germany 53 M2
Bruck an der Mur Austria 47 O7
Brue *r.* U.K. 49 E7
Bruges Belgium *see* **Brugge**
Brugge Belgium 52 D3
Brühl *Baden-Württemberg* Germany 53 I5
Brühl *Nordrhein-Westfalen* Germany 52 G4
Bruin *KY* U.S.A. 134 D4
Bruin *PA* U.S.A. 134 F3
Bruin Point *mt.* U.S.A. 129 H2
Bruint India 83 I3
Brûk, Wâdi el *watercourse* Egypt *see* **Burūk, Wādī al**
Brukkaros Namibia 100 D3
Brûlé Canada 120 G4
Brûlé, Lac *l.* Canada 123 J3
Brûly Belgium 52 E5
Brumado Brazil 145 C1
Brumath France 53 H6
Brumunddal Norway 45 G6
Brunau Germany 53 L2
Brundisium Italy *see* **Brindisi**
Bruneau U.S.A. 126 E4
Brunei *country* Asia 68 E6
Brunei Brunei *see* **Bandar Seri Begawan**
Brunette Downs Australia 110 A3
Brunflo Sweden 44 I5
Brunico Italy 58 D1
Brünn Czech Rep. *see* **Brno**
Brunner, Lake N.Z. 113 C6
Bruno Canada 121 J4
Brunswick Germany *see* **Braunschweig**
Brunswick *GA* U.S.A. 133 D6
Brunswick *MD* U.S.A. 135 G4
Brunswick *ME* U.S.A. 135 K2
Brunswick, Península de *pen.* Chile 144 B8
Brunswick Bay Australia 108 D3
Brunswick Lake Canada 122 E4
Bruntál Czech Rep. 47 P6
Brunt Ice Shelf Antarctica 152 B2
Bruntville S. Africa 101 J5
Bruny Island Australia 111 [inset]
Brusa Turkey *see* **Bursa**
Brusenets Rus. Fed. 42 I3
Brushton U.S.A. 135 H1
Brusque Brazil 145 A4
Brussel Belgium *see* **Brussels**

▶**Brussels** Belgium 52 E4
Capital of Belgium.

Bruthen Australia 112 C6
Bruxelles Belgium *see* **Brussels**
Bruzual Venez. 142 E2
Bryan *OH* U.S.A. 134 C3
Bryan *TX* U.S.A. 131 D6
Bryan, Mount *hill* Australia 111 B7
Bryan Coast Antarctica 152 L2
Bryansk Rus. Fed. 43 G5
Bryanskoye Rus. Fed. 91 G1
Bryant Pond U.S.A. 135 J1
Bryantsburg U.S.A. 134 C4
Bryce Canyon National Park U.S.A. 129 G3
Bryce Mountain U.S.A. 129 I5
Brynbuga U.K. *see* **Usk**
Bryne Norway 45 D7
Bryukhovetskaya Rus. Fed. 43 H7
Brzeg Poland 47 P5
Brześć nad Bugiem Belarus *see* **Brest**
Bua *r.* Malawi 99 D5
Bu'aale Somalia 98 E3
Buala Solomon Is 107 F2
Bu'ayj *well* Saudi Arabia 88 C5
Būbiyān, Jazīrat Kuwait 88 C4
Bucak Turkey 59 N6
Bucaramanga Col. 142 D2
Buccaneer Archipelago *is* Australia 108 C4
Buchanan Liberia 96 B4
Buchanan *MI* U.S.A. 134 B3
Buchanan *VA* U.S.A. 134 F5
Buchanan, Lake *salt flat* Australia 110 D4
Buchan Gulf Canada 119 K2

▶**Bucharest** Romania 59 L2
Capital of Romania.

Büchen Germany 53 K1
Buchen (Odenwald) Germany 53 J5
Buchholz Germany 53 M1
Bucholz in der Nordheide Germany 53 J1
Buchon, Point U.S.A. 128 C4
Buchy France 52 B5
Bucin, Pasul *pass* Romania 59 K1
Buckambool Mountain *hill* Australia 112 B3
Bückeburg Germany 53 J2
Bücken Germany 53 J2
Buckeye U.S.A. 129 G5
Buckhannon U.S.A. 134 E4
Buckhaven U.K. 50 F4
Buckhorn Lake Canada 135 F1
Buckie U.K. 50 G3
Buckingham U.K. 49 G6
Buckingham U.S.A. 135 F5
Buckingham Bay Australia 67 F9
Buckland Tableland *reg.* Australia 110 E5
Buckleboo Australia 109 G8
Buckle Island Antarctica 152 H2
Buckley *watercourse* Australia 110 B4
Buckley Bay Antarctica 152 G2
Bucklin U.S.A. 130 D4
Buckskin Mountains U.S.A. 129 G4
Bucks Mountain U.S.A. 128 C2
Bucksport U.S.A. 123 H5
Bückwitz Germany 53 M2
București Romania *see* **Bucharest**
Bucyrus U.S.A. 134 D3
Buda-Kashalyova Belarus 43 F5
Budalin Myanmar 70 A2

▶**Budapest** Hungary 59 H1
Capital of Hungary.

Budaun India 82 D3
Budawang National Park Australia 112 E5
Budda Australia 112 B3
Budd Coast Antarctica 152 F2
Buddusò *Sardinia* Italy 58 C4
Bude U.K. 49 C8
Bude U.S.A. 131 F6
Budennovsk Rus. Fed. 91 G1
Buderim Australia 112 F1
Būding Iran 88 E5
Büdingen Germany 53 J4
Budīyah, Jabal *hills* Egypt 85 A5
Budongquan China 83 H2
Budoni *Sardinia* Italy 58 C4
Budū, Ḩadabat al *plain* Saudi Arabia 88 C6
Budū', Sabkhat al *salt pan* Saudi Arabia 88 C6
Budweis Czech Rep. *see* **České Budějovice**
Buenaventura Col. 142 C3
Buena Vista *i.* N. Mariana Is *see* **Tinian**
Buena Vista *CO* U.S.A. 126 G5
Buena Vista *VA* U.S.A. 134 F5
Buendia, Embalse de *resr* Spain 57 E3

▶**Buenos Aires** Arg. 144 E4
Capital of Argentina. 2nd most populous city in South America.

Buenos Aires, Lago *l.* Arg./Chile 144 B7
Buerarema Brazil 145 D1
Buet *r.* Canada 123 H1
Búfalo Mex. 131 B7
Buffalo *r.* Canada 120 H2
Buffalo *KY* U.S.A. 134 C5
Buffalo *MO* U.S.A. 130 E4
Buffalo *NY* U.S.A. 135 F2
Buffalo *OK* U.S.A. 131 D4
Buffalo *SD* U.S.A. 130 C2
Buffalo *TX* U.S.A. 131 D6
Buffalo *WY* U.S.A. 126 G3
Buffalo Head Hills Canada 120 G3
Buffalo Head Prairie Canada 120 G3
Buffalo Hump *mt.* U.S.A. 126 E3
Buffalo Lake *Alta* Canada 121 H4
Buffalo Lake *N.W.T.* Canada 120 H2
Buffalo Narrows Canada 121 I4
Buffels *watercourse* S. Africa 100 C5
Buffels Drift S. Africa 101 H2
Buftea Romania 59 K2
Bug *r.* Poland 47 S5
Buga Col. 142 C3
Bugaldie Australia 112 D3
Bugdaýly Turkm. 88 D2
Buggenhout Belgium 52 E3
Bugojno Bos.-Herz. 58 G2
Bugrino Rus. Fed. 42 K1
Bugsuk *i.* Phil. 68 F5
Bugt China 74 A2
Bugul'ma Rus. Fed. 41 Q5
Bugun' Kazakh. 80 B2
Bügür China *see* **Luntai**
Buguruslan Rus. Fed. 41 Q5
Būhābād Iran 88 D4
Buḩayrat Dahūk *res.* Iraq 91 F3
Buhera Zimbabwe 99 D5
Bühl Germany 53 I6
Buhuși Romania 59 L1
Buick Canada 120 F3
Builth Wells U.K. 49 D6
Bui National Park Ghana 96 C4
Buinsk Rus. Fed. 43 K5
Bu'in Zahrā Iran 88 C3
Buir Nur *l.* Mongolia 73 L3
Buitepos Namibia 100 D2
Bujanovac Serbia 59 I3

▶**Bujumbura** Burundi 98 C4
Capital of Burundi.

Bukachacha Rus. Fed. 73 L2
Buka Daban *mt.* China 83 G1
Buka Island P.N.G. 106 F2
Būkān Iran 88 B2
Būkand Iran 88 D4
Bukavu Dem. Rep. Congo 98 C4
Bukhara *Buxoro* Uzbek. *see* **Buxoro**
Bukhoro Uzbek. *see* **Buxoro**
Bukit Baka-Bukit Raya, Taman Nasional Indon. 68 E7
Bukit Timah Sing. 71 [inset]
Bukittinggi Indon. 68 C7
Bukkapatnam India 84 C3
Bukoba Tanz. 98 D4
Bükreş Romania *see* **Bucharest**
Būl, Kūh-e *mt.* Iran 88 D4
Bula P.N.G. 69 K8
Bülach Switz. 56 I3
Bulan *i.* Indon. 71 C7
Bulancak Turkey 90 E2
Bulandshahr India 82 D3
Bulanık Turkey 91 F3
Bulava Rus. Fed. 74 F2
Bulawayo Zimbabwe 99 C6
Buldan Turkey 59 M5
Buldana India *see* **Buldhana**
Buldhana India 84 C1
Buleda *reg.* Pak. 89 F5
Bulembu Swaziland 101 J3
Bulgan *Bulgan* Mongolia 80 J2
Bulgan Mongolia 80 H2
Bulgar Rus. Fed. *see* **Bolgar**
Bulgaria *country* Europe 59 K3
Bŭlgariya *country* Europe *see* **Bulgaria**
Bulkley Ranges *mts* Canada 120 D4
Bullawarra, Lake *salt flat* Australia 112 A1
Bullen *r.* Canada 121 K1
Buller *r.* N.Z. 113 C5
Buller, Mount Australia 112 C6
Bulleringa National Park Australia 110 C3
Bullfinch Australia 109 B7
Bullhead City U.S.A. 129 F4
Bulli Australia 112 E5
Bullion Mountains U.S.A. 128 E4
Bullo *r.* Australia 108 E3
Bulloo Downs Australia 111 C6
Bulloo Lake *salt flat* Australia 111 C6
Büllsport Namibia 100 C3
Bully Choop Mountain U.S.A. 128 B1
Bulman Australia 108 F3
Bulman Gorge Australia 108 F3
Bulmer Lake Canada 120 F2
Buloh, Pulau *i.* Sing. 71 [inset]
Buloke, Lake *dry lake* Australia 112 A6
Bulolo P.N.G. 69 L8
Bulsar India *see* **Valsad**
Bultfontein S. Africa 101 H5
Bulukumba Indon. 69 G8
Bulun Rus. Fed. 65 N2
Bulungu Dem. Rep. Congo 99 C4
Bulung'ur Uzbek. 89 G2
Bumba Dem. Rep. Congo 98 C3
Būmbah Libya 90 A4
Bumbah, Khalīj *b.* Libya 90 A4
Bumhkang Myanmar 70 B1
Bumpha Bum *mt.* Myanmar 70 B1
Buna Dem. Rep. Congo 98 B4
Buna Kenya 98 D3
Bunayyān *well* Saudi Arabia 88 C6
Bunazi Tanz. 98 D4
Bunbury Australia 109 A8
Bunclody Ireland 51 F5
Buncrana Ireland 51 E2
Bunda Tanz. 98 D4
Bundaberg Australia 110 F5
Bundaleer Australia 112 C2
Bundarra Australia 112 E3
Bundi India 82 C4
Bundjalung National Park Australia 112 F2
Bundoran Ireland 51 D3
Bunduqiya Sudan 97 G4
Buner *reg.* Pak. 89 I3
Bungalaut, Selat *sea chan.* Indon. 68 B7
Bungay U.K. 49 I6
Bungendore Australia 112 D5
Bunger Hills Antarctica 152 F2
Bungle Bungle National Park Australia *see* **Purnululu National Park**
Bungo-suidō *sea chan.* Japan 75 D6
Bunguran, Kepulauan *is* Indon. *see* **Natuna, Kepulauan**
Bunguran, Pulau *i.* Indon. *see* **Natuna Besar**
Bunia Dem. Rep. Congo 98 D3
Buniangа Dem. Rep. Congo 98 C4
Buningonia *well* Australia 109 C7
Bunji Pak. 82 C2
Bunker Group *atolls* Australia 110 F4
Bunkeya Dem. Rep. Congo 99 C5
Bunnell U.S.A. 133 D6
Bünsum China 83 E3
Bunya Mountains National Park Australia 112 E1
Bünyan Turkey 90 D3
Bunyu *i.* Indon. 68 F6
Buôn Đôn Vietnam 71 D4
Buôn Ma Thuôt Vietnam 71 E4
Buorkhaya, Guba *b.* Rus. Fed. 65 O2
Bup *r.* China 83 F3
Buqayq Saudi Arabia *see* **Abqaiq**
Buqbuq Egypt 90 B5
Bura Kenya 98 D4
Buraan Somalia 98 E2
Buram Sudan 97 F3
Buran Kazakh. 80 G2
Buranhaém Brazil 145 C2
Buranhaém *r.* Brazil 145 D2
Burāq Syria 85 C3
Buray *r.* India 82 C5
Buraydah Saudi Arabia 86 F4
Burbach Germany 53 I4
Burbank U.S.A. 128 D4
Burcher Australia 112 C4
Burco Somalia 98 E3
Burdaard Neth. 52 F1
Burdalyk Turkm. 89 G2
Burdigala France *see* **Bordeaux**
Burdur Turkey 59 N6
Burdur Gölü *l.* Turkey 59 N6
Burdwan India *see* **Barddhaman**
Burē Eth. 98 D2
Bure *r.* U.K. 49 I6
Bureå Sweden 44 L4
Bureinskiy Khrebet *mts* Rus. Fed. 74 D2
Bureinskiy Zapovednik *nature res.* Rus. Fed. 74 D2
Bureya *r.* Rus. Fed. 74 C2
Bureya Range *mts* Rus. Fed. *see* **Bureinskiy Khrebet**
Burford Canada 134 E2
Burgas Bulg. 59 L3
Burgaw U.S.A. 133 E5
Burg bei Magdeburg Germany 53 L2
Burgbernheim Germany 53 K5
Burgdorf Germany 53 K2
Burgeo Canada 123 K5
Burgersdorp S. Africa 101 H6
Burgersfort S. Africa 101 J3
Burges, Mount *hill* Australia 109 C7
Burgess Hill U.K. 49 G8
Burghaun Germany 53 J4
Burghausen Germany 47 N6
Burghead U.K. 50 F3
Burgh-Haamstede Neth. 52 D3
Burgio, Serra di *hill Sicily* Italy 58 F6
Burglengenfeld Germany 53 M5
Burgos Mex. 131 D7
Burgos Spain 57 E2
Burgstädt Germany 53 M4
Burgsvik Sweden 45 K8
Burgum Neth. 52 G1
Burgundy *reg.* France 56 G3
Burhan Budai Shan *mts* China 80 H4
Burhaniye Turkey 59 L5
Burhanpur India 82 D5
Burhar-Dhanpuri India 83 E5
Buri Brazil 145 A3
Burias *i.* Phil. 69 G4
Burin Canada 123 L5
Burin Peninsula Canada 123 L5
Buriram Thai. 70 C4
Buritama Brazil 145 A3
Buriti Alegre Brazil 145 A2
Buriti Bravo Brazil 143 J5
Buritirama Brazil 143 J6
Buritis Brazil 145 B1
Burj Aziz Khan Pak. 89 G4
Burke U.S.A. 130 D3
Burke Island Antarctica 152 K2
Burke Pass N.Z. *see* **Burkes Pass**
Burkes Pass N.Z. 113 C7
Burkesville U.S.A. 134 C5
Burketown Australia 110 B3
Burkeville U.S.A. 135 F5
Burkina *country* Africa 96 C3
Burkina Faso *country* Africa *see* **Burkina**
Burk's Falls Canada 122 F5
Burley U.S.A. 126 E4
Burlington Canada 134 F2
Burlington *CO* U.S.A. 130 C4
Burlington *IA* U.S.A. 130 F3
Burlington *KS* U.S.A. 130 E4
Burlington *KY* U.S.A. 134 C4
Burlington *VT* U.S.A. 135 I1
Burlington *WI* U.S.A. 134 A2
Burmantovo Rus. Fed. 41 S3
Burnaby Canada 120 F5
Burnet U.S.A. 131 D6
Burney U.S.A. 128 C1
Burney, Monte *vol.* Chile 144 B8
Burnham U.S.A. 135 G3
Burnie Australia 111 [inset]
Burniston U.K. 48 G4
Burnley U.K. 48 E5
Burns U.S.A. 126 D4
Burnside *r.* Canada 118 H3
Burnside U.S.A. 134 C5
Burnside, Lake *salt flat* Australia 109 C6
Burns Junction U.S.A. 126 D4
Burns Lake Canada 120 E4
Burntisland U.K. 50 F4
Burnt Lake Canada *see* **Brûlé, Lac**
Burntwood *r.* Canada 121 L4
Burog Co *l.* China 83 F2
Buron *r.* Canada 123 H2
Burovoy Uzbek. 89 F1
Burqin China 80 G2
Burqu' Jordan 85 D3
Burra Australia 111 B7
Burra *i.* U.K. 50 [inset]
Burravoe U.K. 50 [inset]
Burrel Albania 59 I4
Burrel U.S.A. 128 D3
Burren *reg.* Ireland 51 C4
Burrendong, Lake Australia 112 D4
Burren Junction Australia 112 D3
Burrewarra Point Australia 112 E5
Burrinjuck Australia 112 D5
Burrinjuck Reservoir Australia 112 D5
Burro, Serranías del *mts* Mex. 131 C6
Burr Oak Reservoir U.S.A. 134 D4
Burro Creek *watercourse* U.S.A. 129 G4
Burro Peak U.S.A. 129 I5
Burrowa Pine Mountain National Park Australia 112 C6
Burrow Head *hd* U.K. 50 E6
Burrows U.S.A. 134 B3
Burrundie Australia 108 E3
Bursa Turkey 59 M4
Būr Safāga Egypt *see* **Būr Safājah**
Būr Safājah Egypt 86 D4
Būr Sa'īd Egypt *see* **Port Said**
Būr Sa'īd Egypt *see* **Port Said**
Būr Sa'īd *governorate* Egypt *see* **Būr Sa'īd**
Būr Sa'īd *governorate* Egypt 85 A4
Bursinskoye Vodokhranilishche *resr* Rus. Fed. 74 C2
Bürstadt Germany 53 I5
Būr Sudan Sudan *see* **Port Sudan**
Burt Lake U.S.A. 132 C2
Burton U.S.A. 134 D2
Burton, Lac *l.* Canada 122 F3
Burton upon Trent U.K. 49 F6
Burträsk Sweden 44 L4
Burt Well Australia 109 F5
Buru *i.* Indon. 69 H7
Burūk, Wādī al *watercourse* Egypt 85 A4
Burullus, Baḩra el *lag.* Egypt *see* **Burullus, Lake**
Burullus, Buḩayrat al *lag.* Egypt *see* **Burullus, Lake**
Burullus, Lake *lag.* Egypt 90 C5
Burultokay China *see* **Fuhai**
Burūn, Ra's *pt* Egypt 85 A4
Burundi *country* Africa 98 C4
Burunniy Rus. Fed. *see* **Tsagan Aman**
Bururi Burundi 98 C4
Burwash Landing Canada 120 B2
Burwick U.K. 50 G2
Buryn' Ukr. 43 G6
Bury St Edmunds U.K. 49 H6
Burzil Pass Pak. 82 C2
Busan S. Korea *see* **Pusan**
Busanga Dem. Rep. Congo 98 C4
Busby U.S.A. 126 G3
Buseire Syria *see* **Al Buşayrah**
Bush *r.* U.K. 51 F2
Būshehr Iran 88 C4
Bushêngcaka China 83 E2
Bushenyi Uganda 98 D4
Bushire Iran *see* **Būshehr**
Bushmills U.K. 51 F2
Bushnell U.S.A. 133 D6
Businga Dem. Rep. Congo 98 C3
Buşrá ash Shām Syria 85 C3
Busse Rus. Fed. 74 B2
Busselton Australia 109 A8
Bussum Neth. 52 F2
Bustillos, Lago *l.* Mex. 127 G7
Busto Arsizio Italy 58 C2
Buta Dem. Rep. Congo 98 C3
Butare Rwanda 98 C4
Butaritari *atoll* Kiribati 150 H5
Bute Australia 111 B7
Bute *i.* U.K. 50 D5
Butedale Canada 120 D4
Butha Buthe Lesotho 101 I5
Butha Qi China *see* **Zalantun**
Buthidaung Myanmar 70 A2
Butler *AL* U.S.A. 131 F5
Butler *GA* U.S.A. 133 C5
Butler *IN* U.S.A. 134 C3
Butler *KY* U.S.A. 134 C4
Butler *MO* U.S.A. 130 E4
Butler *PA* U.S.A. 134 F3
Butlers Bridge Ireland 51 E3
Buton *i.* Indon. 69 G7
Bütow Germany 53 M1
Butte *MT* U.S.A. 126 E3
Butte *NE* U.S.A. 130 D3
Buttelstedt Germany 53 L3
Butterworth Malaysia 71 C6
Butterworth S. Africa 101 I7
Buttes, Sierra *mt.* U.S.A. 128 C2
Buttevant Ireland 51 D5
Butt of Lewis *hd* U.K. 50 C2
Button Bay Canada 121 M3
Butuan Phil. 69 H5
Butuo China 76 D3
Buturlinovka Rus. Fed. 43 I6
Butwal Nepal 83 E4
Butzbach Germany 53 I4
Buulobarde Somalia 98 E3
Buur Gaabo Somalia 98 E4
Buurhabaka Somalia 98 E3
Buutsagaan Mongolia 80 I2
Buxar India 83 F4
Buxoro Uzbek. 89 G2
Buxtehude Germany 53 J1
Buxton U.K. 48 F5
Buy Rus. Fed. 42 I4
Buynaksk Rus. Fed. 91 G2
Büyükçekmece Turkey 90 C2
Büyük Egri Dağ *mt.* Turkey 85 A1
Büyükmenderes *r.* Turkey 59 L6
Buzancy France 52 E5
Buzău Romania 59 L2
Buzdyak Rus. Fed. 41 Q5
Búzi Moz. 99 D5
Büzmeýin Turkm. *see* **Abadan**
Buzuluk Rus. Fed. 41 Q5
Buzuluk *r.* Rus. Fed. 43 I6
Buzzards Bay U.S.A. 135 J3
Byakar Bhutan *see* **Jakar**
Byala Bulg. 59 K3
Byala Slatina Bulg. 59 J3
Byalynichy Belarus 43 F5
Byarezina *r.* Belarus 43 F5
Byaroza Belarus 45 N10
Byblos *tourist site* Lebanon 85 B2
Bydgoszcz Poland 47 Q4
Byelorussia *country* Europe *see* **Belarus**
Byerazino Belarus 43 F5
Byers U.S.A. 126 G5
Byeshankovichy Belarus 43 F5
Byesville U.S.A. 134 E4
Bygland Norway 45 E7
Bykhaw Belarus 43 F5
Bykhov Belarus *see* **Bykhaw**
Bykle Norway 45 E7
Bykovo Rus. Fed. 43 J6
Bylas U.S.A. 129 H5
Bylot Island Canada 119 K2
Byramgore Reef India 84 A4
Byrd Glacier Antarctica 152 H1
Byrdstown U.S.A. 134 C5
Byrkjelo Norway 45 E6
Byrock Australia 112 C3
Byron U.S.A. 135 J1
Byron, Cape Australia 112 F2
Byron Bay Australia 112 F2
Byron Island Kiribati *see* **Nikunau**
Byrranga, Gory *mts* Rus. Fed. 65 K2
Byske Sweden 44 L4
Byssa Rus. Fed. 74 C1
Byssa *r.* Rus. Fed. 74 C1
Bytom Poland 47 Q5
Bytów Poland 47 P3
Byurgyutli Turkm. 88 D2
Byzantium Turkey *see* **İstanbul**

C

Ca, Sông *r.* Vietnam 70 D3
Caacupé Para. 144 E3
Caatinga Brazil 145 B2
Caazapá Para. 144 E3
Cabaiguán Cuba 133 E8
Caballas Peru 142 C6
Caballococha Peru 142 D4
Caballos Mesteños, Llano de los *plain* Mex. 131 B6
Cabanaconde Peru 142 D7
Cabanatuan Phil. 69 G3
Cabano Canada 123 H5
Cabdul Qaadir Somalia 98 E2
Cabeceira Rio Manso Brazil 143 G7
Cabeceiras Brazil 145 B1
Cabeza del Buey Spain 57 D4
Cabezas Bol. 142 F7
Cabimas Venez. 142 D1

binda Angola 99 B4
binda *prov.* Angola 99 B5
binet Inlet Antarctica 152 L2
binet Mountains U.S.A. 126 E2
bistra Turkey *see* Ereğli
bo Frio Brazil 145 C3
bo Frio, Ilha do *i.* Brazil 145 C3
bonga, Réservoir *resr* Canada 122 F5
bool U.S.A. 131 E4
boolture Australia 112 F1
bo Orange, Parque Nacional de
at. park Brazil 143 H3
bo Pantoja Peru 142 C4
bora Bassa, Lake *resr* Moz. 99 D5
bo Raso Arg. 144 C6
borca Mex. 127 E7
bot Head *hd* Canada 134 E1
bot Strait Canada 123 J5
bourg France 49 G9
bo Verde *country* N. Atlantic Ocean *see*
ape Verde
bo Verde, Ilhas do *is* N. Atlantic Ocean
6 [inset]
bo Yubi Morocco *see* Tarfaya
bral, Serra do *mts* Brazil 145 B2
brayıl Azer. 91 G3
brera, Illa de *i.* Spain 57 H4
bri Canada 121 I5
bullona Mex. 127 F7
cador Brazil 145 A4
cagoin China *see* Qagca
čak Serbia 59 I3
ccia, Capo *c. Sardinia* Italy 58 C4
e Turkm. 89 F2
cequi Brazil 144 F3
ceres Brazil 143 G7
ceres Spain 57 C4
che Creek Canada 120 F5
che Peak U.S.A. 126 E4
cheu Guinea-Bissau 96 B3
chi, Nevados de *mts* Arg. 144 C2
chimbo, Serra do *hills* Brazil 143 H5
choeira Brazil 145 D1
choeira Alta Brazil 145 A2
choeira de Goiás Brazil 145 A2
hoeira do Arari Brazil 143 I4
choeiro de Itapemirim Brazil 145 C3
cine Guinea-Bissau 96 B3
ciporé, Cabo *c.* Brazil 143 H3
colo Angola 99 B5
congo Angola 99 B4
ctus U.S.A. 131 C4
çu Brazil 145 A2
ulé Brazil 145 C1
ca Slovakia 47 Q6
ereyta Mex. 131 C7
dibarrawirracanna, Lake *salt flat*
ustralia 111 A6
dillac Canada 121 J5
dillac U.S.A. 134 C1
diz Phil. 69 G4
diz Spain 57 C5
diz *IN* U.S.A. 134 C4
diz *KY* U.S.A. 132 C4
diz *OH* U.S.A. 134 E3
diz, Golfo de *g.* Spain 57 C5
diz Lake U.S.A. 129 F4
domin Canada 120 G4
dotte *r.* Canada 120 G3
dotte Lake Canada 120 G3
en France 56 D2
erdydd U.K. *see* Cardiff
erffili U.K. *see* Caerphilly
erfyrddin U.K. *see* Carmarthen
ergybi U.K. *see* Holyhead
ernarfon U.K. 49 C5
ernarfon Bay U.K. 49 C5
ernarvon U.K. *see* Caernarfon
erphilly U.K. 49 D7
esaraugusta Spain *see* Zaragoza
esarea Alg. *see* Cherchell
esarea Cappadociae Turkey *see* Kayseri
esarea Philippi Syria *see* Bāniyās
esarodunum France *see* Tours
esaromagus U.K. *see* Chelmsford
etité Brazil 145 C1
ayate Arg. 144 C3
elândia Brazil 145 A3
fa Ukr. *see* Feodosiya
gayan de Oro Phil. 69 G5
gayan de Tawi-Tawi *i.* Phil. 68 F5
gles Mill Lake U.S.A. 134 B4
gli Italy 58 E3
gliari *Sardinia* Italy 58 C5
gliari, Golfo di *b. Sardinia* Italy 58 C5
ğyl Turkm. 91 I2
ama Angola 99 B5
a Mts *hills* Ireland 51 C6
ermore Ireland 51 B6
ersiveen Ireland *see* Cahirsiveen
ir Ireland 51 E5
irsiveen Ireland 51 B6
ora Bassa, Lago de *resr* Moz. *see*
abora Bassa, Lake
ore Point Ireland 51 F5
ors France 56 E4
uapanas Peru 142 C5
ul Moldova 59 M2
a Moz. 99 D5
abis, Serra dos *hills* Brazil 143 G6
anda Angola 99 C5
apó *r.* Brazil 145 A1
apó, Serra do *mts* Brazil 145 A2
apônia Brazil 145 A2
barién Cuba 133 E8
Bâu, Đao *i.* Vietnam 70 D2
cara Venez. 142 E2
cos Islands Turks and Caicos Is 137 J4
cos Passage
ahamas/Turks and Caicos Is 133 F8
dian China 77 G2
guna Australia 109 D8
modorro *mt.* Spain 57 F3
nnyigoin China 76 D1
ns Store U.S.A. 134 C5
be Arg. 144 C2
d Coast Antarctica 152 B1
ngorm Mountains U.K. 50 F3
ngorms National Park *nat. park*
cotland 46 F2
ngorms National Park *nat. park*
cotland 48 D2

Cairngorms National Park *nat. park*
Scotland 50 F3
Cairnryan U.K. 50 D6
Cairns Australia 110 D3
Cairnsmore of Carsphairn *hill* U.K. 50 E5

►Cairo Egypt 90 C5
Capital of Egypt. 2nd most populous city in Africa.

Cairo U.S.A. 133 C6
Caisleán an Bharraigh Ireland *see* Castlebar
Caiundo Angola 99 B5
Caiwarro (abandoned) Australia 112 B2
Caiyuanzhen China *see* Shengsi
Caizi Hu *l.* China 77 H2
Cajamarca Peru 142 C5
Cajati Brazil 145 A4
Cajuru Brazil 145 B3
Caka'lho China *see* Yanjing
Čakovec Croatia 58 G1
Çal *Denizli* Turkey 59 M5
Çal *Hakkâri* Turkey *see* Çukurca
Cala S. Africa 101 H6
Calabar Nigeria 96 D4
Calabogie Canada 135 G1
Calabria, Parco Nazionale della *nat. park*
Italy 58 G5
Calafat Romania 59 J3
Calagua Mex. 127 F8
Calagurris Spain *see* Calahorra
Calahorra Spain 57 F2
Calai Angola 99 B5
Calais France 52 B4
Calais U.S.A. 123 I5
Calalasteo, Sierra de *mts* Arg. 144 C3
Calama Brazil 142 F5
Calama Chile 144 C2
Calamajué Mex. 127 E7
Calamar Col. 142 D1
Calamian Group *is* Phil. 68 F4
Calamocha Spain 57 F3
Calandula Angola 99 B4
Calang Indon. 71 A6
Calapan Phil. 69 G4
Călărași Romania 59 L2
Calatayud Spain 57 F3
Calayan *i.* Phil. 69 G3
Calbayog Phil. 69 G4
Calbe (Saale) Germany 53 L3
Calçoene Brazil 143 H3
Calcutta India *see* Kolkata
Caldas da Rainha Port. 57 B4
Caldas Novas Brazil 143 I7
Calden Germany 53 J3
Calder *r.* Canada 120 G1
Caldera Chile 144 B3
Caldervale Australia 110 D5
Caldew *r.* U.K. 48 E4
Caldwell *ID* U.S.A. 126 D4
Caldwell *KS* U.S.A. 131 D4
Caldwell *OH* U.S.A. 134 E4
Caldwell *TX* U.S.A. 131 D6
Caledon *r.* Lesotho/S. Africa 101 H6
Caledon S. Africa 100 D8
Caledon Bay Australia 110 B2
Caledonia Canada 134 F2
Caledonia *admin. div.* U.K. *see* Scotland
Caledonia U.S.A. 135 G2
Caleta el Cobre Chile 144 B2
Calexico U.S.A. 129 F5
Calf of Man *i.* Isle of Man 48 C4
Calgary Canada 120 H5
Calhoun U.S.A. 134 B5
Cali Col. 142 C3
Calicut India 84 B4
Caliente U.S.A. 129 F3
California U.S.A. 134 F3
California *state* U.S.A. 127 C4
California, Gulf of Mex. 127 E7
California Aqueduct *canal* U.S.A. 128 C3
Cälilabad Azer. 91 H3
Calingasta Arg. 144 C4
Calipatria U.S.A. 129 F5
Calistoga U.S.A. 128 B2
Calkiní Mex. 136 F4
Callabonna, Lake *salt flat* Australia 111 C6
Callaghan, Mount U.S.A. 128 E2
Callan Ireland 51 E5
Callan *r.* U.K. 51 F3
Callander Canada 122 F5
Callander U.K. 50 E4
Callang Phil. 77 I5
Callao Peru 142 C6
Callao U.S.A. 129 G2
Callicoon U.S.A. 135 H3
Calling Lake Canada 120 H4
Callington U.K. 49 C8
Calliope Australia 110 E5
Callipolis Turkey *see* Gallipoli
Calmar U.S.A. 130 F3
Caloosahatchee *r.* U.S.A. 133 D7
Caloundra Australia 112 F1
Caltagirone *Sicily* Italy 58 F6
Caltanissetta *Sicily* Italy 58 F6
Calucinga Angola 99 B5
Calulo Angola 99 B4
Calunga Angola 99 B5
Caluquembe Angola 99 B5
Caluula Somalia 98 F2
Caluula, Raas *pt* Somalia 98 F2
Calvert Hills Australia 110 B3
Calvert Island Canada 120 D5
Calvi *Corsica* France 56 I5
Calvià Spain 57 H4
Calvinia S. Africa 100 D6
Calvo, Monte *mt.* Italy 58 F4
Cam *r.* U.K. 49 H6
Camaçari Brazil 145 D1
Camache Reservoir U.S.A. 128 C2
Camachigama *r.* Canada 122 F5
Camacho Mex. 131 C7
Camacuio Angola 99 B5
Camacupa Angola 99 B5
Camagüey Cuba 137 I4
Camagüey, Archipiélago de *is* Cuba
137 I4
Camamu Brazil 145 D1
Camana Peru 142 D7
Camanongue Angola 99 C5
Camapuã Brazil 143 H7
Camaquã Brazil 144 F4

Çamardı Turkey 90 D3
Camargo Bol. 142 E8
Camargue *reg.* France 56 G5
Camarillo U.S.A. 128 D4
Camarones Arg. 144 C6
Camarones, Bahía *b.* Arg. 144 C6
Camas *r.* U.S.A. 126 E4
Ca Mau Vietnam 71 D5
Cambay India *see* Khambhat
Cambay, Gulf of India *see* Khambhat, Gulf of
Camberley U.K. 49 G7
Cambodia *country* Asia 71 D4
Camboriú Brazil 145 A4
Camborne U.K. 49 B8
Cambrai France 52 D4
Cambria *admin. div.* U.K. *see* Wales
Cambrian Mountains *hills* U.K. 49 D6
Cambridge Canada 134 E2
Cambridge N.Z. 113 E3
Cambridge U.K. 49 H6
Cambridge *MA* U.S.A. 135 J2
Cambridge *MD* U.S.A. 135 G4
Cambridge *MN* U.S.A. 130 E2
Cambridge *NY* U.S.A. 135 I2
Cambridge *OH* U.S.A. 134 E3
Cambridge Bay Canada 119 H3
Cambridge City U.S.A. 134 C4
Cambridge Springs U.S.A. 134 E3
Cambrien, Lac *l.* Canada 123 H2
Cambulo Angola 99 C4
Cambundi-Catembo Angola 99 B5
Cambuquira Brazil 145 B3
Cam Co *l.* China 83 E2
Camdeboo National Park S. Africa 100 G7
Camden *AL* U.S.A. 133 C5
Camden *AR* U.S.A. 131 E5
Camden *NJ* U.S.A. 135 H4
Camden *NY* U.S.A. 135 H2
Camden *SC* U.S.A. 133 D5
Camdenton U.S.A. 130 E4
Cameia Angola 99 C5
Cameia, Parque Nacional da *nat. park*
Angola 99 C5
Cameron *AZ* U.S.A. 129 H4
Cameron *LA* U.S.A. 131 E6
Cameron *MO* U.S.A. 130 E4
Cameron *TX* U.S.A. 131 D6
Cameron Highlands *mts* Malaysia 71 C6
Cameron Hills Canada 120 G3
Cameron Island Canada 119 H2
Cameron Park U.S.A. 128 C2
Cameroon *country* Africa 96 E4
Cameroon, Mount *vol.* Cameroon *see*
Cameroun, Mont
Cameroon Highlands *slope*
Cameroon/Nigeria 96 E4
Caméroun *country* Africa *see*
Cameroon
Cameroun, Mont *vol.* Cameroon 96 D4
Cametá Brazil 143 I4
Camiña Chile 142 E7
Camiri Bol. 142 F8
Camisea Peru 142 D6
Camocim Brazil 143 J4
Camooweal Australia 110 B3
Camooweal Caves National Park
Australia 110 B4
Camorta *i.* India 81 H10
Campana Mex. 131 C7
Campana, Isla *i.* Chile 144 A7
Campania Island Canada 120 D4
Campbell S. Africa 100 F5
Campbell, Cape N.Z. 113 E5
Campbell, Mount *hill* Australia 108 E5
Campbellford Canada 135 G1
Campbell Hill *hill* U.S.A. 134 D3
Campbell Island N.Z. 150 H9
Campbell Lake Canada 121 J2
Campbell Plateau *sea feature*
S. Pacific Ocean 150 H9
Campbell Range *hills* Australia 108 D3
Campbell River Canada 120 E5
Campbellsville U.S.A. 134 C5
Campbellton Canada 123 I5
Campbelltown Australia 112 E5
Campbeltown U.K. 50 D5
Campeche Mex. 136 F5
Campeche, Bahía de *g.* Mex. 136 F5
Camperdown Australia 112 A7
Câmpina Romania 59 K2
Campina Grande Brazil 143 K5
Campinas Brazil 145 B3
Campina Verde Brazil 145 A2
Campo Cameroon 96 D4
Campobasso Italy 58 F4
Campo Belo Brazil 145 B3
Campo Belo do Sul Brazil 145 A4
Campo de Diauarum Brazil 143 H6
Campo Florido Brazil 145 A2
Campo Gallo Arg. 144 D3
Campo Grande Brazil 144 F2
Campo Largo Brazil 145 A4
Campo Maior Brazil 143 J4
Campo Maior Port. 57 C4
Campo Mourão Brazil 144 F2
Campos Brazil 145 C3
Campos Altos Brazil 145 B2
Campos Novos Brazil 145 A4
Campos Sales Brazil 143 J5
Campton U.S.A. 134 D5
Câmpulung Romania 59 K2
Câmpulung Moldovenesc Romania 59 K1
Camp Verde U.S.A. 129 H4
Camrose Canada 121 H4
Camrose U.K. 49 B7
Camsell Lake Canada 121 I2
Camsell Portage Canada 121 I3
Camsell Range *mts* Canada 120 F2
Camulodunum U.K. *see* Colchester
Çan Turkey 59 L4
Ca Na, Mui *hd* Vietnam 71 E5
Canaan *r.* Canada 123 I5
Canaan U.S.A. 135 I2
Canaan Peak U.S.A. 129 H3
Canabrava Brazil 145 B2
Canacona India 84 B3

►Canada *country* N. America 118 H4
Largest country in North America and 2nd in the world. 3rd most populous country in North America.

Canada Basin *sea feature* Arctic Ocean
153 A1
Canadian U.S.A. 131 C5
Canadian *r.* U.S.A. 131 E5
Canadian Abyssal Plain *sea feature* Arctic
Ocean 153 A1
Cañadon Grande, Sierra *mts* Arg. 144 C7
Canaima, Parque Nacional *nat. park* Venez.
142 F2
Çanakkale Turkey 59 L4
Çanakkale Boğazı *strait* Turkey *see*
Dardanelles
Canalejas Arg. 144 C5
Cañamares Spain 57 E3
Canandaigua U.S.A. 135 G2
Cananea Mex. 127 F7
Cananéia Brazil 145 B4
Canápolis Brazil 145 A2
Cañar Ecuador 142 C4
Canarias *terr.* N. Atlantic Ocean *see*
Canary Islands
Canárias, Ilha das *i.* Brazil 143 J4
Canarias, Islas *terr.* N. Atlantic Ocean *see*
Canary Islands

►Canary Islands *terr.* N. Atlantic Ocean
96 B2
Autonomous Community of Spain.

Canaseraga U.S.A. 135 G2
Canastota U.S.A. 135 H2
Canastra, Serra da *mts* Brazil 145 B2
Canastra, Serra da *mts* Brazil 145 A1
Canatiba Brazil 145 C1
Canatlán Mex. 131 B7
Canaveral, Cape U.S.A. 133 D6
Cañaveras Spain 57 E3
Canavieiras Brazil 145 D1
Canbelego Australia 112 C3

►Canberra Australia 112 D5
Capital of Australia and Australian Capital Territory.

Cancún Mex. 137 G4
Çandar Turkey *see* Kastamonu
Çandarlı Turkey 59 L5
Candela Mex. 131 C7
Candela *r.* Mex. 131 C7
Candelaria Mex. 127 G7
Candia Greece *see* Iraklion
Cândido de Abreu Brazil 145 A4
Çandır Turkey 90 D2
Candle Lake Canada 121 J4
Candlewood, Lake U.S.A. 135 I3
Cando U.S.A. 130 D1
Candon Phil. 77 I5
Cane *r.* Australia 108 A5
Canea Greece *see* Chania
Canela Brazil 145 A5
Canelones Uruguay 144 E4
Cane Valley U.S.A. 134 C5
Cangallo Peru 142 D6
Cangamba Angola 99 B5
Cangandala, Parque Nacional de *nat. park*
Angola 99 B4
Cango Caves S. Africa 100 F7
Cangola Angola 99 B4
Cangshan China 77 H1
Canguaretama Brazil 143 K5
Canguçu Brazil 144 F4
Canguçu, Serra do *hills* Brazil 144 F4
Cangwu China 77 F4
Cangzhou China 73 L5
Caniapiscau Canada 123 H3
Caniapiscau *r.* Canada 123 H2
Caniapiscau, Réservoir de *l.* Canada
123 H3
Caniçado Moz. *see* Guija
Canicattì *Sicily* Italy 58 E6
Canim Lake Canada 120 F5
Canindé Brazil 143 K4
Canisteo U.S.A. 135 G2
Canisteo *r.* U.S.A. 135 G2
Canisteo Peninsula Antarctica 152 K2
Cañitas de Felipe Pescador Mex. 131 C8
Çankırı Turkey 90 D2
Canna Australia 109 A7
Canna *i.* U.K. 50 C3
Cannanore India 84 B4
Cannanore Islands India 84 B4
Cannelton U.S.A. 134 B5
Cannes France 56 H5
Cannock U.K. 49 E6
Cannon Beach U.S.A. 126 C3
Cann River Australia 112 D6
Canoas Brazil 145 A5
Canõas, Rio das *r.* Brazil 145 A4
Canoeiros Brazil 145 B2
Canoe Lake Canada 121 I4
Canoe Lake *l.* Canada 121 I4
Canoinhas Brazil 145 A4
Canon City U.S.A. 127 G5
Cañon Largo *watercourse* U.S.A. 129 J3
Canoona Australia 110 E4
Canora Canada 121 K5
Canowindra Australia 112 D4
Canso Canada 123 J5
Canso, Cape Canada 123 J5
Cantabrian Mountains Spain *see*
Cantábrica, Cordillera
Cantábrica, Cordillera *mts* Spain 57 D2
Cantábrico, Mar *sea* Spain 57 C2
Canterbury U.K. 49 I7
Canterbury Bight *b.* N.Z. 113 C7
Canterbury Plains N.Z. 113 C6
Cân Thơ Vietnam 71 D5
Cantil U.S.A. 128 E4
Canton *GA* U.S.A. 133 C5
Canton *IL* U.S.A. 130 F3
Canton *MO* U.S.A. 130 F3
Canton *MS* U.S.A. 131 F5
Canton *NY* U.S.A. 135 H1
Canton *OH* U.S.A. 134 E3
Canton *PA* U.S.A. 135 G3
Canton *SD* U.S.A. 130 D3
Canton *TX* U.S.A. 131 E5
Canton Island *atoll* Kiribati *see* Kanton
Cantuaria U.K. *see* Canterbury
Canunda National Park Australia 111 C8
Canutama Brazil 142 F5
Canutillo Mex. 131 B7

Canvey Island U.K. 49 H7
Canwood Canada 121 J4
Cany-Barville France 49 H9
Canyon U.S.A. 131 C5
Canyon (abandoned) Canada 120 B2
Canyon City U.S.A. 126 D3
Canyondam U.S.A. 128 C1
Canyon de Chelly National Monument
nat. park U.S.A. 129 I3
Canyon Ferry Lake U.S.A. 126 F3
Canyon Lake U.S.A. 129 H5
Canyonlands National Park U.S.A. 129 I2
Canyon Ranges *mts* Canada 120 E2
Canyons of the Ancients National
Monument *nat. park* U.S.A. 129 I3
Canyonville U.S.A. 126 C4
Cao Băng Vietnam 70 D2
Caocheng China *see* Caoxian
Caohai China *see* Weining
Caohe China *see* Qichun
Caohu China 80 F3
Caojiahe China *see* Qichun
Caojian China 76 C3
Caoshi China 74 B4
Caoxian China 77 G1
Caozhou China *see* Heze
Capac U.S.A. 134 D2
Çapakçur Turkey *see* Bingöl
Capanaparo *r.* Venez. 142 E2
Capanema Brazil 143 I4
Capão Bonito Brazil 145 A4
Caparaó, Serra do *mts* Brazil 145 C3
Cap-aux-Meules Canada 123 J5
Cap-de-la-Madeleine Canada 123 G5
Cape *r.* Australia 110 D4
Cape Arid National Park Australia 109 C8
Cape Barren Island Australia 111 [inset]
Cape Basin *sea feature* S. Atlantic Ocean
148 I8
Cape Breton Highlands National Park
Canada 123 J5
Cape Breton Island Canada 123 J5
Cape Charles Canada 123 L3
Cape Charles U.S.A. 135 G5
Cape Coast Ghana 96 C4
Cape Coast Castle Ghana *see* Cape Coast
Cape Cod Bay U.S.A. 135 J3
Cape Cod National Seashore *nature res.*
U.S.A. 135 K3
Cape Coral U.S.A. 133 D7
Cape Crawford Australia 110 A3
Cape Dorset Canada 119 K3
Cape Fanshaw U.S.A. 120 C3
Cape Fear *r.* U.S.A. 133 E5
Cape George Canada 123 J5
Cape Girardeau U.S.A. 131 F4
Cape Johnson Depth *sea feature*
N. Pacific Ocean 150 E5
Cape Juby Morocco *see* Tarfaya
Cape Krusenstern National Monument
nat. park U.S.A. 118 B3
Capel Australia 109 A8
Cape Le Grand National Park Australia
109 C8
Capelinha Brazil 145 C2
Capella Australia 110 E4
Capelle aan de IJssel Neth. 52 E3
Capelongo Angola *see* Kuvango
Cape May U.S.A. 135 H4
Cape May Court House U.S.A. 135 H4
Cape May Point U.S.A. 135 H4
Cape Melville National Park Australia
110 D2
Capenda-Camulemba Angola 99 B4
Cape Palmerston National Park Australia
110 E4
Cape Range National Park Australia 108 A5
Cape St George Canada 123 K4

►Cape Town S. Africa 100 D7
Legislative capital of South Africa.

Cape Tribulation National Park
Australia 110 D2
Cape Upstart National Park
Australia 110 D3
Cape Verde *country* N. Atlantic Ocean
96 [inset]
Cape Verde Basin *sea feature*
N. Atlantic Ocean 148 F5
Cape Verde Plateau *sea feature*
N. Atlantic Ocean 148 F4
Cape Vincent U.S.A. 135 G1
Cape York Peninsula Australia 110 C2
Cap-Haïtien Haiti 137 J5
Capim *r.* Brazil 143 I4
Capitán Arturo Prat *research station*
Antarctica 152 A2

►Capitol Hill N. Mariana Is 69 L3
Capital of the Northern Mariana Islands, on Saipan.

Capitol Reef National Park U.S.A. 129 H2
Capivara, Represa *resr* Brazil 145 A3
Čapljina Bos.-Herz. 58 G3
Cappoquin Ireland 51 E5
Capraia, Isola di *i.* Italy 58 C3
Caprara, Punta *pt Sardinia* Italy 58 C4
Capri, Isola di *i.* Italy 58 F4
Capricorn Channel Australia 110 E4
Capricorn Group *atolls* Australia 110 F4
Caprivi Strip *reg.* Namibia 99 C5
Cap Rock Escarpment U.S.A. 131 C5
Capsa Tunisia *see* Gafsa
Captain Cook U.S.A. 127 [inset]
Captina *r.* U.S.A. 134 E4
Capuava Brazil 145 B4
Caquetá *r.* Col. 142 E4
Caracal Romania 59 K2

►Caracas Venez. 142 E1
Capital of Venezuela.

Caraguatatuba Brazil 145 B3
Caraí Brazil 145 C2
Carajás Brazil 143 H5
Carajás, Serra dos *hills* Brazil 143 H5
Carales *Sardinia* Italy *see* Cagliari
Caralis *Sardinia* Italy *see* Cagliari
Carandaí Brazil 145 C3
Caransebeș Romania 59 J2

Caraquet Canada 123 I5
Caratasca, Laguna de *lag.* Hond. 137 H5
Caratinga Brazil 145 C2
Carauari Brazil 142 E4
Caravaca de la Cruz Spain 57 F4
Caravelas Brazil 145 D2
Carberry Canada 121 L5
Carbó Mex. 127 F7
Carbon, Cap *hd* Alg. 57 F6

►Carbón, Laguna del Arg. 144 C7
Lowest point in South America.

Carbonara, Capo *c. Sardinia* Italy 58 C5
Carbondale *CO* U.S.A. 129 J2
Carbondale *PA* U.S.A. 135 H3
Carboneras Mex. 131 D7
Carbonia *Sardinia* Italy 58 C5
Carbonita Brazil 145 C2
Carcaixent Spain 57 F4
Carcajou Canada 120 G3
Carcajou *r.* Canada 120 D1
Carcar Phil. 69 G4
Carcassonne France 56 F5
Cardamomes, Chaîne des *mts*
Cambodia/Thai. *see* Cardamom Range
Cardamom Hills India 84 C4
Cardamom Range *mts* Cambodia/Thai.
71 C4
Cárdenas Cuba 137 H4
Cárdenas Mex. 136 E4
Cardenyabba *watercourse* Australia 112 A2
Çardi Turkey *see* Harmancık
Cardiel, Lago *l.* Arg. 144 B7

►Cardiff U.K. 49 D7
Capital of Wales.

Cardiff U.S.A. 135 G4
Cardigan U.K. 49 C6
Cardigan Bay U.K. 49 C6
Cardinal Lake Canada 120 G3
Cardington U.S.A. 134 D3
Cardón, Cerro *hill* Mex. 127 E8
Cardoso Brazil 145 A3
Cardoso, Ilha do *i.* Brazil 145 B4
Cardston Canada 120 H5
Careen Lake Canada 121 I3
Carei Romania 59 J1
Carentan France 56 D2
Carey U.S.A. 134 D3
Carey, Lake *salt flat* Australia 109 C7
Carey Lake Canada 121 K2
Cargados Carajos Islands Mauritius 149 L7
Carhaix-Plouguer France 56 C2
Cariacica Brazil 145 C3
Cariamanga Ecuador 142 C4
Caribbean Sea N. Atlantic Ocean 137 H5
Cariboo Mountains Canada 120 F4
Caribou *r. Man.* Canada 121 M3
Caribou *r. N.W.T.* Canada 120 E2
Caribou U.S.A. 132 G2
Caribou Lake Canada 119 J4
Caribou Mountains Canada 120 H3
Carichic Mex. 127 G8
Carignan France 52 F5
Carinda Australia 112 C3
Cariñena Spain 57 F3
Carinhanha *r.* Brazil 145 C1
Carlabhagh U.K. *see* Carloway
Carleton U.S.A. 134 D2
Carleton, Mount *hill* Canada 123 I5
Carletonville S. Africa 101 H4
Carlin U.S.A. 128 E1
Carlingford Lough *inlet* Ireland/U.K. 51 F3
Carlinville U.S.A. 130 F4
Carlisle U.K. 48 E4
Carlisle *IN* U.S.A. 134 B4
Carlisle *KY* U.S.A. 134 C4
Carlisle *NY* U.S.A. 135 H2
Carlisle *PA* U.S.A. 135 G3
Carlisle Lakes *salt flat* Australia 109 D7
Carlit, Pic *mt.* France 56 E5
Carlos Chagas Brazil 145 C2
Carlow Ireland 51 F5
Carloway U.K. 50 C2
Carlsbad Czech Rep. *see* Karlovy Vary
Carlsbad *CA* U.S.A. 128 E5
Carlsbad *NM* U.S.A. 127 G6
Carlsbad Caverns National Park U.S.A.
127 G6
Carlsberg Ridge *sea feature* Indian Ocean
149 L5
Carlson Inlet Antarctica 152 L1
Carlton U.S.A. 130 E2
Carlton Hill Australia 108 E3
Carluke U.K. 50 F5
Carlyle Canada 121 K5
Carmacks Canada 120 B2
Carmagnola Italy 58 B2
Carman Canada 121 L5
Carmana Iran *see* Kermān
Carmarthen U.K. 49 C7
Carmarthen Bay U.K. 49 C7
Carmaux France 56 F4
Carmel *IN* U.S.A. 134 B4
Carmel *NY* U.S.A. 135 I3
Carmel, Mount *hill* Israel 85 B3
Carmel Head *hd* U.K. 48 C5
Carmel Valley U.S.A. 128 C3
Carmen *r.* Mex. 131 B6
Carmen U.S.A. 127 F7
Carmen, Isla *i.* Mex. 127 F8
Carmen de Patagones Arg. 144 D6
Carmi U.S.A. 130 F4
Carmichael U.S.A. 128 C2
Carmo da Cachoeira Brazil 145 B3
Carmo do Paranaíba Brazil 145 B2
Carmona Angola *see* Uíge
Carmona Spain 57 D5
Carnac France 56 C3
Carnamah Australia 109 A7
Carnarvon Australia 109 A6
Carnarvon S. Africa 100 F6
Carnarvon National Park Australia 110 D5
Carnarvon Range *hills* Australia 109 C6
Carnarvon Range *mts* Australia 110 E5
Carn Dearg *hill* U.K. 50 E3
Carndonagh Ireland 51 E2
Carnegie Australia 109 C6
Carnegie, Lake *salt flat* Australia 109 C6
Carn Eige *mt.* U.K. 50 D3

Carnes Australia 109 F7
Carney Island Antarctica 152 J2
Carnforth U.K. 48 E4
Carn Glas-choire hill U.K. 50 F3
Car Nicobar i. India 71 A5
Carnlough U.K. 51 G3
Carn nan Gabhar mt. U.K. 50 F4
Carn Odhar hill U.K. 50 E3
Carnot Cent. Afr. Rep. 98 B3
Carnoustie U.K. 50 G4
Carnsore Point Ireland 51 F5
Carnwath U.K. 50 F5
Caro U.S.A. 134 D2
Carola Cay reef Australia 110 F3
Carol City U.S.A. 133 D7
Carolina Brazil 143 I5
Carolina S. Africa 101 J4
Carolina Beach U.S.A. 133 E5
Caroline Canada 120 H4
Caroline Island atoll Kiribati 151 J6
Caroline Islands N. Pacific Ocean 69 K5
Caroline Peak N.Z. 113 A7
Caroline Range hills Australia 108 D4
Caroní r. Venez. 142 F2
Carp Canada 135 G1
Carpathian Mountains Europe 43 C6
Carpații mts Europe see Carpathian Mountains
Carpații Meridionali mts Romania see Transylvanian Alps
Carpații Occidentali mts Romania 59 J2
Carpentaria, Gulf of Australia 110 B2
Carpentras France 56 G4
Carpi Italy 58 D2
Carpinteria U.S.A. 128 D4
Carpio U.S.A. 130 C1
Carra, Lough l. Ireland 51 C4
Carraig na Siuire Ireland see Carrick-on-Suir
Carrantuohill mt. Ireland 51 C6
Carrara Italy 58 D2
Carrasco, Parque Nacional nat. park Bol. 142 F7
Carrathool Australia 112 B5
Carrhae Turkey see Harran
Carrickfergus U.K. 51 G3
Carrickmacross Ireland 51 F4
Carrick-on-Shannon Ireland 51 D4
Carrick-on-Suir Ireland 51 E5
Carrigallen Ireland 51 E4
Carrigtohill Ireland 51 D6
Carrillo Mex. 131 C7
Carrington U.S.A. 130 D2
Carrizal Mex. 127 G7
Carrizal Bajo Chile 144 B3
Carrizo U.S.A. 129 H4
Carrizo Creek r. U.S.A. 131 C4
Carrizo Springs U.S.A. 131 D6
Carrizo Wash watercourse U.S.A. 129 I4
Carrizozo U.S.A. 127 G6
Carroll U.S.A. 130 E3
Carrollton AL U.S.A. 131 F5
Carrollton GA U.S.A. 133 C5
Carrollton IL U.S.A. 130 F4
Carrollton KY U.S.A. 134 C4
Carrollton MO U.S.A. 130 E4
Carrollton OH U.S.A. 134 E3
Carrolltown U.S.A. 135 F3
Carron r. U.K. 50 E3
Carrot r. Canada 121 K4
Carrothers U.S.A. 134 D3
Carrot River Canada 121 K4
Carrowmore Lake Ireland 51 C3
Carrsville U.S.A. 135 G5
Carruthers Lake Canada 121 K2
Carruthersville U.S.A. 131 F4
Carry Falls Reservoir U.S.A. 135 H1
Çarşamba Turkey 90 E2
Carson r. U.S.A. 128 D2
Carson City MI U.S.A. 134 C2
▶Carson City NV U.S.A. 128 D2
Capital of Nevada.
Carson Escarpment Australia 108 D3
Carson Lake U.S.A. 128 D2
Carson Sink l. U.S.A. 128 D2
Carstensz Pyramid mt. Indon. see Jaya, Puncak
Carstensz-top mt. Indon. see Jaya, Puncak
Carswell Lake Canada 121 I3
Cartagena Col. 142 C1
Cartagena Spain 57 F5
Carteret Group is P.N.G. see Kilinailau Islands
Carteret Island Solomon Is see Malaita
Cartersville U.S.A. 133 C5
Carthage tourist site Tunisia 58 D6
Carthage MO U.S.A. 131 E4
Carthage NC U.S.A. 133 E5
Carthage NY U.S.A. 135 H2
Carthage TX U.S.A. 131 E5
Carthago tourist site Tunisia see Carthage
Carthago Nova Spain see Cartagena
Cartier Island Australia 108 C3
Cartmel U.K. 48 E4
Cartwright Man. Canada 121 L5
Cartwright Nfld. and Lab. Canada 123 K3
Caruarú Brazil 143 K5
Carúpano Venez. 142 F1
Carver U.S.A. 134 D5
Carvin France 52 C4
Cary U.S.A. 132 E5
Caryapundy Swamp Australia 111 C6
Casablanca Morocco 54 C5
Casa Branca Brazil 145 B3
Casa de Piedra, Embalse resr Arg. 144 C5
Casa Grande U.S.A. 129 H5
Casale Monferrato Italy 58 C2
Casalmaggiore Italy 58 D2
Casas Grandes Mex. 127 G7
Casca Brazil 145 A5
Cascada de Bassaseachic, Parque Nacional nat. park Mex. 127 F7
Cascade Australia 109 C8
Cascade r. N.Z. 113 B7
Cascade ID U.S.A. 126 D3
Cascade MT U.S.A. 126 F3
Cascade Point N.Z. 113 B7
Cascade Range mts Canada/U.S.A. 126 C4
Cascade Reservoir U.S.A. 126 D3
Cascais Port. 57 B4
Cascavel Brazil 144 F2
Casco Bay U.S.A. 135 K2
Caserta Italy 58 F4
Casey research station Antarctica 152 F2
Casey Bay Antarctica 152 D2
Caseyr, Raas c. Somalia see Gwardafuy, Gees
Cashel Ireland 51 E5
Cashmere Australia 112 D1
Casino Australia 112 F2
Casiquiare, Canal r. Venez. 142 E3
Casita Mex. 127 F7
Casnewydd U.K. see Newport
Caspe Spain 57 F3
Casper U.S.A. 126 G4
Caspian Lowland Kazakh./Rus. Fed. 78 D2
▶Caspian Sea l. Asia/Europe 91 H1
Largest lake in the world and in Asia/Europe, and lowest point in Europe.
Cass U.S.A. 134 F4
Cass r. U.S.A. 134 D2
Cassacatiza Moz. 99 D5
Cassadaga U.S.A. 134 F2
Cassaigne Alg. see Sidi Ali
Cassamba Angola 99 C5
Cass City U.S.A. 134 D2
Cassel France 52 C4
Casselman Canada 135 H1
Cássia Brazil 145 B3
Cassiar Mountains Canada 120 D2
Cassilândia Brazil 145 A2
Cassilis Australia 112 D4
Cassino Italy 58 E4
Cassley r. U.K. 50 E3
Cassongue Angola 99 B5
Cassopolis U.S.A. 134 B3
Cassville U.S.A. 131 E4
Castanhal Brazil 143 I4
Castanho Brazil 142 F5
Castaños Mex. 131 C7
Castelfranco Veneto Italy 58 D2
Castell-nedd U.K. see Neath
Castell Newydd Emlyn U.K. see Newcastle Emlyn
Castellón Spain see Castellón de la Plana
Castellón de la Plana Spain 57 F4
Castelo Branco Port. 57 C4
Castelo de Vide Port. 57 C4
Casteltermini Sicily Italy 58 E6
Castelvetrano Sicily Italy 58 E6
Castiglione della Pescaia Italy 58 D3
Castignon, Lac l. Canada 123 H2
Castilla y León reg. Spain 56 B6
Castlebar Ireland 51 C4
Castlebay U.K. 50 B4
Castlebellingham Ireland 51 F4
Castleblayney Ireland 51 F3
Castlebridge Ireland 51 F5
Castle Carrock U.K. 48 E4
Castle Cary U.K. 49 E7
Castle Dale U.S.A. 129 H2
Castlederg U.K. 51 E3
Castledermot Ireland 51 F5
Castle Dome Mountains U.S.A. 129 F5
Castle Donington U.K. 49 F6
Castle Douglas U.K. 50 F6
Castleford U.K. 48 F5
Castlegar Canada 120 G5
Castlegregory Ireland 51 B5
Castle Island Bahamas 133 F8
Castleisland Ireland 51 C5
Castlemaine Australia 112 B6
Castlemaine Ireland 51 C5
Castlemartyr Ireland 51 D6
Castle Mountain Alta Canada 120 H5
Castle Mountain Y.T. Canada 120 C1
Castle Mountain U.S.A. 128 C4
Castle Peak hill H.K. China 77 [inset]
Castle Peak Bay H.K. China 77 [inset]
Castlepoint N.Z. 113 F5
Castlepollard Ireland 51 E4
Castlerea Ireland 51 D4
Castlereagh r. Australia 112 C3
Castle Rock U.S.A. 126 G5
Castletown Ireland 51 E5
Castletown Isle of Man 48 C4
Castor Canada 121 I4
Castor r. U.S.A. 131 F4
Castor, Rivière du r. Canada 122 F3
Castra Regina Germany see Regensburg
Castres France 56 F5
Castricum Neth. 52 E2
▶Castries St Lucia 137 L6
Capital of St Lucia.
Castro Brazil 145 A4
Castro Chile 144 B6
Castro Alves Brazil 145 D1
Castro Verde Port. 57 B5
Castroville U.S.A. 128 C3
Çat Turkey 91 F3
Catacaos Peru 142 B5
Cataguases Brazil 145 C3
Catahoula Lake U.S.A. 131 E6
Çatak Turkey 91 F3
Catalão Brazil 145 B2
Çatalca Yarımadası pen. Turkey 59 M4
Catalina U.S.A. 129 H5
Catalonia aut. comm. Spain see Cataluña
Cataluña aut. comm. Spain 57 G3
Catalunya aut. comm. Spain see Cataluña
Catamarca Arg. 144 C3
Catana Sicily Italy see Catania
Catanduanes i. Phil. 69 G4
Catanduva Brazil 145 A3
Catania Sicily Italy 58 F6
Catanzaro Italy 58 G5
Cataract Creek watercourse U.S.A. 129 G3
Catarina U.S.A. 131 D6
Catarino Rodríguez Mex. 131 C7
Catarman Phil. 69 G4
Catastrophe, Cape Australia 111 A7
Catawba r. U.S.A. 133 D5
Cataxa Moz. 99 D5
Cat Ba, Đao i. Vietnam 70 D2
Catbalogan Phil. 69 G4
Catembe Moz. 101 K4
Catengue Angola 99 B5
Catete Angola 99 B4
Cathair Dónall Ireland 51 B6
Cathcart Australia 112 D6
Cathcart S. Africa 101 H7
Cathedral Peak S. Africa 101 I5
Cathedral Rock National Park Australia 112 F3
Catherine, Mount U.S.A. 129 G2
Catheys Valley U.S.A. 128 C3
Cathlamet U.S.A. 126 C3
Catió Guinea-Bissau 96 B3
Catisimiña Venez. 142 F3
Cat Island Bahamas 133 F7
Cat Lake Canada 121 N5
Catlettsburg U.S.A. 134 D4
Catoche, Cabo c. Mex. 133 C8
Cato Island and Bank reef Australia 110 F4
Catriló Arg. 144 D5
Cats, Mont des hill France 52 C4
Catskill U.S.A. 135 I2
Catskill Mountains U.S.A. 135 H2
Catuane Moz. 101 K4
Cauayan Phil. 69 G5
Caubvick, Mount Canada 123 J2
Cauca r. Col. 137 J7
Caucaia Brazil 143 K4
Caucasia Col. 142 C2
Caucasus mts Asia/Europe 91 F2
Cauchon Lake Canada 121 L4
Caudry France 52 D4
Câu Giat Vietnam 70 D3
Caulonia Italy 58 G5
Caungula Angola 99 B4
Cauquenes Chile 144 B5
Causapscal Canada 123 I4
Cavaglià Italy 58 C2
Cavalcante, Serra do hills Brazil 145 B1
Cavalier U.S.A. 130 D1
Cavan Ireland 51 E4
Çavdır Turkey 59 M6
Cave City U.S.A. 134 C5
Cave Creek U.S.A. 129 H5
Caveira r. Brazil 145 C1
Cavern Island Myanmar 71 B5
Cave Run Lake U.S.A. 134 D4
Caviana, Ilha i. Brazil 143 H3
Cawdor U.K. 50 F3
Cawnpore India see Kanpur
Cawston U.K. 49 I6
Caxias Brazil 143 J4
Caxias do Sul Brazil 145 A5
Caxito Angola 99 B4
Çay Turkey 59 N5
Cayambe, Volcán vol. Ecuador 142 C3
Çaybaşı Turkey see Çayeli
Çaycuma Turkey 59 O4
Çayeli Turkey 91 F2
▶Cayenne Fr. Guiana 143 H3
Capital of French Guiana.
Cayeux-sur-Mer France 52 B4
Çayırhan Turkey 59 N4
Cayman Brac i. Cayman Is 137 I5
▶Cayman Islands terr. West Indies 137 H5
United Kingdom Overseas Territory.
Cayman Trench sea feature Caribbean Sea 148 C4
Caynabo Somalia 98 E3
Cay Sal i. Bahamas 133 D8
Cay Sal Bank sea feature Bahamas 133 D8
Cay Santa Domingo i. Bahamas 133 F8
Cayucos U.S.A. 128 C4
Cayuga Canada 134 F2
Cayuga Lake U.S.A. 135 G2
Cay Verde i. Bahamas 133 F8
Cazê China 83 F3
Cazenovia U.S.A. 135 H2
Cazombo Angola 99 C5
Ceadâr-Lunga Moldova see Ciadîr-Lunga
Ceanannus Mór Ireland see Kells
Ceann a Deas na Hearadh pen. U.K. see South Harris
Ceará Brazil see Fortaleza
Ceara Abyssal Plain sea feature S. Atlantic Ocean 148 F6
Ceatharlach Ireland see Carlow
Ceballos Mex. 131 B7
Cebu Phil. 69 G4
Cebu i. Phil. 69 G4
Čechy reg. Czech Rep. 47 N6
Cecil Plains Australia 112 E1
Cecil Rhodes, Mount hill Australia 109 C6
Cecina Italy 58 D3
Cedar r. ND U.S.A. 130 C2
Cedar r. NE U.S.A. 130 D3
Cedar City U.S.A. 129 G3
Cedaredge U.S.A. 129 J2
Cedar Falls U.S.A. 130 E3
Cedar Grove U.S.A. 134 B2
Cedar Hill NM U.S.A. 129 J3
Cedar Hill TN U.S.A. 134 B5
Cedar Island U.S.A. 135 H5
Cedar Lake Canada 121 K4
Cedar Point U.S.A. 134 D3
Cedar Rapids U.S.A. 130 F3
Cedar Run U.S.A. 135 H4
Cedar Springs U.S.A. 134 C2
Cedartown U.S.A. 133 C5
Cedarville S. Africa 101 I6
Cedros Mex. 127 F8
Cedros, Cerro mt. Mex. 127 E7
Cedros, Isla i. Mex. 127 E7
Ceduna Australia 109 F8
Ceeldheere Somalia 98 E3
Ceerigaabo Somalia 98 E2
Cefalù Sicily Italy 58 F5
Cegléd Hungary 59 H1
Cêgnê China 76 B1
Ceheng China 76 E3
Çekerek Turkey 90 D2
Çekiçler Turkm. 88 D2
Celaya Mex. 136 D4
Celbridge Ireland 51 F4
▶Celebes i. Indon. 69 G7
4th largest island in Asia.
Celebes Basin sea feature Pacific Ocean 150 E5
Celebes Sea Indon./Phil. 69 G6
Celestún Mex. 136 F4
Celina OH U.S.A. 134 C3
Celina TN U.S.A. 134 C5
Celje Slovenia 58 F1
Celle Germany 53 K2
Celovec Austria see Klagenfurt
Celtic Sea Ireland/U.K. 46 D5
Celtic Shelf sea feature N. Atlantic Ocean 148 H2
Çemenibit Turkm. 89 F3
Cenderawasih, Teluk b. Indon. 69 J7
Çendir r. Turkm. 88 D2
Centane S. Africa see Kentani
Centenary Zimbabwe 99 D5
Center NE U.S.A. 130 D3
Center TX U.S.A. 131 E6
Centereach U.S.A. 135 I3
Center Point U.S.A. 133 C5
Centerville IA U.S.A. 130 E3
Centerville MO U.S.A. 131 F4
Centerville TX U.S.A. 131 E6
Centerville WV U.S.A. 134 E4
Centrafricaine, République country Africa see Central African Republic
Central admin. dist. Botswana 101 H2
Central U.S.A. 129 I5
Central, Cordillera mts Col. 142 C3
Central, Cordillera mts Peru 142 C6
Central African Empire country Africa see Central African Republic
Central African Republic country Africa 98 B3
Central Brahui Range mts Pak. 89 G4
Central Butte Canada 126 G2
Central City U.S.A. 130 D3
Centralia IL U.S.A. 130 F4
Centralia WA U.S.A. 126 C3
Central Kalahari Game Reserve nature res. Botswana 100 F2
Central Kara Rise sea feature Arctic Ocean 153 F1
Central Makran Range mts Pak. 89 G5
Central Mount Stuart hill Australia 108 F5
Central Pacific Basin sea feature Pacific Ocean 150 H5
Central Provinces state India see Madhya Pradesh
Central Range mts P.N.G. 69 K7
Central Russian Upland hills Rus. Fed. 43 H5
Central Siberian Plateau Rus. Fed. 65 M3
Central Square U.S.A. 135 G2
Centre U.S.A. 133 C5
Centreville AL U.S.A. 133 C5
Centreville U.S.A. 135 G4
Cenxi China 77 F4
Cenyang China see Hengfeng
Ceos i. Greece see Tzia
Ceos i. Notio Aigaio Greece see Tzia
Cephaloedium Sicily Italy see Cefalù
Cephalonia i. Greece 59 I5
Ceram i. Indon. see Seram
Ceram Sea Indon. see Seram, Laut
Cerbat Mountains U.S.A. 129 F4
Čerchov mt. Czech Rep. 53 M5
Ceres Arg. 144 D3
Ceres Brazil 145 A1
Ceres S. Africa 100 D7
Ceres U.S.A. 128 C3
Céret France 56 F5
Cerezo de Abajo Spain 57 E3
Cerignola Italy 58 F4
Cerigo i. Greece see Kythira
Cêringgolêb China see Dongco
Çerkeş Turkey 90 D2
Çerkeşli Turkey 59 M4
Çermik Turkey 91 E3
Cernăuți Ukr. see Chernivtsi
Cernavodă Romania 59 M2
Cerralvo, Isla i. Mex. 136 C4
Cërrik Albania 59 H4
Cerritos Mex. 136 D4
Cerro Azul Brazil 145 A4
Cerro de Pasco Peru 142 C6
Cerros Colorados, Embalse resr Arg. 144 C5
Cervantes, Cerro mt. Arg. 144 B8
Cervati, Monte mt. Italy 58 F4
Cervione Corsica France 56 I5
Cervo Spain 57 C2
Cesena Italy 58 E2
Cēsis Latvia 45 N8
Česká Republika country Europe see Czech Republic
České Budějovice Czech Rep. 47 O6
Českomoravská vysočina hills Czech Rep. 47 O6
Český Krumlov Czech Rep. 47 O6
Český les mts Czech Rep./Germany 53 M5
Çeşme Turkey 59 L5
Cessnock Australia 112 E4
Cetatea Albă Ukr. see Bilhorod-Dnistrovs'kyy
Cetinje Montenegro 58 H3
Cetraro Italy 58 F5
▶Ceuta N. Africa 57 D6
Autonomous Community of Spain.
Ceva-i-Ra reef Fiji 107 H4
Cévennes mts France 56 F5
Cévennes, Parc National des nat. park France 56 F4
Cevizli Turkey 85 C1
Cevizlik Turkey see Maçka
Ceyhan Turkey 90 D3
Ceyhan r. Turkey 85 B1
Ceyhan Boğazı r. mouth Turkey 85 B1
Ceylanpınar Turkey 91 F3
Ceylon country Asia see Sri Lanka
Chābahār Iran 89 F5
Chabrol i. New Caledonia see Lifou
Chabug China 83 E2
Chabyêr Caka salt l. China 83 F3
Chachapoyas Peru 142 C5
Chacharan Pak. 89 H4
Chäche Turkm. see Çäçe
Chachoengsao Thai. 71 C4
Chachro Pak. 89 H5
Chaco r. U.S.A. 129 I3
Chaco Boreal reg. Para. 144 E2
Chaco Culture National Historical Park nat. park U.S.A. 129 J3
Chaco Mesa plat. U.S.A. 129 J4
▶Chad country Africa 97 E3
5th largest country in Africa.
Chad, Lake Africa 97 E3
Chadaasan Mongolia 72 I3
Chadan Rus. Fed. 80 H1
Chadibe Botswana 101 H2
Chadron U.S.A. 130 C3
Chadyr-Lunga Moldova see Ciadîr-Lunga
Chae Hom Thai. 70 B3
Chaeryŏng N. Korea 75 B5
Chae Son National Park Thai. 70 B3
Chagai Pak. 89 G4
Chagai Hills Afgh./Pak. 89 F4
Chagdo Kangri mt. China 83 F2
Chaghā Khūr mt. Iran 88 C4
Chaghcharān Afgh. 89 G3
Chagny France 56 G3
Chagoda Rus. Fed. 42 G4
Chagos Archipelago is B.I.O.T. 149 M6
Chagos-Laccadive Ridge sea feature Indian Ocean 149 M6
Chagos Trench sea feature Indian Ocean 149 M6
Chagoyan Rus. Fed. 74 C1
Chagrayskoye Plato plat. Kazakh. see Shagyray, Plato
Chāh Ākhvor Iran 89 E3
Chāh 'Ali Akbar Iran 88 E3
Chahbounia Alg. 57 H6
Chahchaheh Turkm. 89 F2
Chāh-e Āb Afgh. 89 H2
Chāh-e Bāgh well Iran 88 D4
Chāh-e Bāzargānī Iran 88 D4
Chāh-e Dow Chāhī Iran 88 D4
Chāh-e Gonbad well Iran 88 D3
Chāh-e Kavīr well Iran 88 E3
Chāh-e Khorāsān well Iran 88 D3
Chāh-e Khoshāb Iran 88 E3
Chāh-e Malek well Iran 88 D3
Chāh-e Malek Mīrzā well Iran 88 D4
Chāh-e Mūjān well Iran 88 D3
Chāh-e Qeyşar well Iran 88 D4
Chāh-e Qobād well Iran 88 D3
Chāh-e Rāh Iran 88 D4
Chāh-e Raḩmān well Iran 89 E4
Chāh-e Shūr well Iran 88 D3
Chāh-e Tūnī well Iran 88 E3
Chāh Kūh Iran 88 D4
Chāh Lak Iran 88 E5
Chāh Pās well Iran 88 D3
Chah Sandan Pak. 89 F4
Chaibasa India 83 F5
Chaigneau, Lac l. Canada 123 I3
Chainat Thai. 70 C4
Chainjoin Co l. China 83 F2
Chai Prakan Thai. 70 B3
Chaitén Chile 144 B6
Chai Wan H.K. China 77 [inset]
Chaiya Thai. 71 B5
Chaiyaphum Thai. 70 C4
Chajarí Arg. 144 E4
Chakai India 83 F4
Chak Amru Pak. 89 I3
Chakar r. Pak. 89 H4
Chakaria Bangl. 83 H5
Chakdarra Pak. 89 I3
Chakku Pak. 89 G5
Chakonipau, Lac l. Canada 123 H2
Chakoria Bangl. see Chakaria
Ch'ak'vi Georgia 91 F2
Chala Peru 142 D7
Chalap Dalan mts Afgh. 89 G3
Chalatenango El Salvador 136 G6
Chaláua Moz. 99 D5
Chalaxung China 76 C1
Chalcedon Turkey see Kadıköy
Chalengkou China 80 H4
Chaleur Bay inlet Canada 123 I4
Chaleurs, Baie des inlet Canada see Chaleur Bay
Chali China 76 C2
Chaling China 77 G3
Chalisgaon India 84 B1
Chalki i. Greece 59 L6
Chalkida Greece 59 J5
Challakere India 84 C3
Challans France 56 D3
Challapata Bol. 142 E7
▶Challenger Deep sea feature N. Pacific Ocean 150 F5
Deepest point in the world (Mariana Trench).
Challenger Fracture Zone sea feature S. Pacific Ocean 150 M8
Challis U.S.A. 126 E3
Chalmette U.S.A. 131 F6
Châlons-en-Champagne France 52 E6
Châlons-sur-Marne France see Châlons-en-Champagne
Chalon-sur-Saône France 56 G3
Chaltan Pass Azer. 91 H2
Chālūs Iran 88 C2
Cham Germany 53 M5
Cham, Kūh-e hill Iran 88 C3
Chamah, Gunung mt. Malaysia 71 C6
Chamaico Arg. 144 D5
Chamais Bay Namibia 100 B4
Chaman Pak. 78 F3
Chaman Bid Iran 88 E2
Chamao, Khao mt. Thai. 71 C4
Chamba India 82 D2
Chamba Tanz. 99 D5
Chambal r. India 82 D4
Chambas Cuba 133 E8
Chambeaux, Lac l. Canada 123 H3
Chamberlain r. Australia 108 D4
Chamberlain Canada 121 J5
Chamberlain U.S.A. 130 D3
Chamberlain Lake U.S.A. 132 G2
Chambers U.S.A. 129 I4
Chambersburg U.S.A. 135 G4
Chambers Island U.S.A. 134 B1
Chambéry France 56 G4
Chambeshi r. Zambia 99 C5
Chambi, Jebel mt. Tunisia 58 C7
Chamdo China see Qamdo
Chamechaude mt. France 56 G4
Chamiss Bay Canada 120 E5
Chamoli India see Gopeshwar
Chamonix-Mont-Blanc France 56 H4
Champa India 83 E5
Champagne-Ardenne admin. reg. France 52 E6
Champagne Castle mt. S. Africa 101 I5
Champagne Humide reg. France 56 G2
Champagne Pouilleuse reg. France 56 F2
Champagnole France 56 G3
Champagny Islands Australia 108 D3
Champaign U.S.A. 130 F3
Champasak Laos 70 D4
Champdoré, Lac l. Canada 123 I3
Champhai India 83 H5
Champion Canada 120 H5
Champlain U.S.A. 135 G4
Champlain, Lake Canada/U.S.A. 135 I1
Champotón Mex. 136 F5
Chamrajnagar India 84 C4
Chamzinka Rus. Fed. 43 J5
Chana Thai. 71 C6
Chanak Turkey see Çanakkale
Chañaral Chile 144 B3
Chanārān Iran 88 E2
Chanda India see Chandrapur
Chandalar r. U.S.A. 118 D3
Chandausi India 82 D3
Chandbali India 83 F5
Chandeleur Islands U.S.A. 131 F6
Chanderi India 82 D4
Chandigarh India 82 D3
Chandil India 83 F5
Chandir Uzbek. 89 G2
Chandler Canada 123 I4
Chandler AZ U.S.A. 129 H5
Chandler IN U.S.A. 134 B4
Chandler OK U.S.A. 131 D5
Chandod India 82 C5
Chandos Lake Canada 135 G1
Chandpur Bangl. 83 G5
Chandpur India 82 D3
Chandragiri India 84 C3
Chandrapur India 84 C2
Chandvad India 84 B1
Chang, Ko i. Thai. 71 C4
Chang'an China 77 F1
Changane r. Moz. 101 K3
Changbai China 74 C4
Changbai Shan mts China/N. Korea 74 B
Chang Cheng research station Antarctica Great Wall
Changcheng China 77 F5
Changchow Fujian China see Zhangzhou
Changchow Jiangsu China see Changzho
Changchun China 74 B4
Changchunling China 74 B3
Changde China 77 F2
Changgang China 77 G3
Changge China 77 G1
Changgi-ap pt S. Korea 75 C5
Changgo China 83 F3
Chang Hu l. China 77 G2
Changhua Taiwan 77 I3
Changhŭng S. Korea 75 B6
Changhwa Taiwan see Changhua
Changi Sing. 71 [inset]
Changji China 80 G3
Changjiang China 77 F5
Chang Jiang r. China 77 I2 see Yangtze
Changjiang Kou China see Mouth of the Yangtze
Changjin-ho resr N. Korea 75 B4
Changkiang China see Zhanjiang
Changlang India 83 H4
Changleng China see Xinjian
Changling China 74 A3
Changlung India 87 M3
Changma China 80 I4
Changning Jiangxi China see Xunwu
Changning Sichuan China 76 E2
Changnyŏn N. Korea 75 B5
Ch'ang-pai Shan mts China/N. Korea see Changbai Shan
Changpu China see Suining
Changp'yŏng S. Korea 75 C5
Changsan-got pt N. Korea 75 B5
Changsha China 77 G2
Changshan China 77 H2
Changshi China 76 E3
Changshoujie China 77 G2
Changshu China 77 I2
Changtai China 77 H3
Changteh China see Changde
Changting Fujian China 77 H3
Changting Heilong. China 74 C3
Ch'angwŏn S. Korea 75 C6
Changxing China 77 H2
Changyang China 77 F2
Changyŏn N. Korea 75 B5
Changyuan China 77 G1
Changzhi China 73 K5
Changzhou China 77 H2
Chañi, Nevado de mt. Arg. 144 C2
Chania Greece 59 K7
Chanion, Kolpos b. Greece 59 J7
Chankou China 76 E1
Channahon U.S.A. 134 A3
Channapatna India 84 C3
Channel Islands English Chan. 49 E9
Channel Islands U.S.A. 128 D5
Channel Islands National Park U.S.A. 128 D4
Channel-Port-aux-Basques Canada 123
Channel Rock i. Bahamas 133 E8
Channel Tunnel France/U.K. 49 I7
Channing U.S.A. 131 C5
Chantada Spain 57 C2
Chanthaburi Thai. 71 C4
Chantilly France 52 C5
Chanumla India 71 A5
Chanute U.S.A. 130 E4
Chanuwala Pak. 89 I3
Chany, Ozero salt l. Rus. Fed. 64 I4
Chaohu China 77 H2
Chao Hu l. China 77 H2
Chaor He r. China see Qulin Gol
Chaouèn Morocco 57 D6
Chaowula Shan mt. China 76 C1
Chaoyang Guangdong China 77 H4

aoyang Heilong. China see Jiayin
aoyang Liaoning China 73 M4
aoyangcun China 74 B2
aoyang Hu l. China 83 F2
aozhong China 74 A2
aozhou China 77 H4
apada Diamantina, Parque Nacional
nat. park Brazil 145 C1
apada dos Veadeiros, Parque Nacional
da nat. park Brazil 145 B1
apais Canada 122 G4
apak Guzar Afgh. 89 G2
apala, Laguna de l. Mex. 136 D4
āpārī, Kowtal-e Afgh. 89 G3
apayevo Kazakh. 78 E1
apayevsk Rus. Fed. 43 K5
apecó Brazil 144 F3
apecó r. Brazil 144 F3
apel-en-le-Frith U.K. 48 F5
apelle-lez-Herlaimont Belgium 52 E4
apeltown U.K. 48 F5
apleau Canada 122 E5
aplin Canada 121 J5
aplin Lake Canada 121 J5
aplygin Rus. Fed. 43 H5
apman, Mount Canada 120 G5
apmanville U.S.A. 134 D5
appell U.S.A. 130 C3
appell Islands Australia 111 [inset]
apra Bihar India see Chhapra
apra Jharkhand India see Chatra
aqmaqtīn, Kowl-e Afgh. 89 I2
aragua Bol. 142 F7
aray Mex. 127 F8
arcas Mex. 136 D4
arcot Island Antarctica 152 L2
ard Canada 121 I4
ard U.K. 49 E8
ardara Kazakh. see Shardara
ardara, Step' plain Kazakh. 80 C3
ardon U.S.A. 134 E3
ardzhev Lebap Turkm. see Türkmenabat
ardzhev Turkm. see Türkmenabat
ardzhou Lebap Turkm. see Türkmenabat
ardzhou Turkm. see Türkmenabat
aref Alg. 57 H6
aref, Oued watercourse Morocco 54 D5
arente r. France 56 D4
ari r. Cameroon/Chad 97 E3
ārī Iran 88 E4
ārīkār Afgh. 89 H3
ariton U.S.A. 130 E3
ärjew Lebap Turkm. see Türkmenabat
ärjew Turkm. see Türkmenabat
arkayuvom Rus. Fed. 42 L2
ar Kent Afgh. 89 G2
arkhlik China see Ruoqiang
arleroi Belgium 52 E4
arles, Cape U.S.A. 135 H5
arlesbourg Canada 123 H5
arles City IA U.S.A. 130 E3
arles City VA U.S.A. 135 G5
arles Hill Botswana 100 E2
arles Island Galápagos Ecuador see
anta María, Isla
arles Lake Canada 121 I3
arles Point Australia 108 E3
arleston N.Z. 113 C5
arleston IL U.S.A. 130 F4
arleston MO U.S.A. 131 F4
arleston SC U.S.A. 133 E5

Charleston WV U.S.A. 134 E4
Capital of West Virginia.

arleston Peak U.S.A. 129 F3
arlestown Ireland 51 D4
arlestown IN U.S.A. 134 C4
arlestown NH U.S.A. 135 I2
arlestown RI U.S.A. 135 J3
arles Town U.S.A. 135 G4
arleville Australia 111 D5
arleville Ireland 51 D5
arleville-Mézières France 52 E5
arlevoix U.S.A. 134 C1
arlie Lake Canada 120 F3
arlotte MI U.S.A. 134 C2
arlotte NC U.S.A. 133 D5
arlotte TN U.S.A. 134 B5

Charlotte Amalie Virgin Is (U.S.A.) 137 L5
Capital of the U.S. Virgin Islands.

arlotte Harbor b. U.S.A. 133 D7
arlotte Lake Canada 120 E4
arlottesville U.S.A. 135 F4

Charlottetown Canada 123 J5
Capital of Prince Edward Island.

arlton Australia 112 A6
arlton Island Canada 122 F3
arron Lake Canada 121 M4
arsadda Pak. 89 H3
arshanga Turkm. see Köýtendag
arshangngy Turkm. see Köýtendag
arters Towers Australia 110 D4
artres France 56 E2
as India 83 F5
ase Canada 120 G5
ase U.S.A. 134 C2
ase City U.S.A. 135 F5
ashmeh Nūrī Iran 88 E3
ashmeh-ye Ab-e Garm spring Iran 88 E3
ashmeh-ye Magu well Iran 88 E3
ashmeh-ye Mūkīk spring Iran 88 E3
ashmeh-ye Palasi Iran 88 D3
ashmeh-ye Safīd spring Iran 88 E3
ashmeh-ye Shotoran well Iran 88 D3
ashniki Belarus 43 F5
aska U.S.A. 130 E2
aslands Mistake c. N.Z. 113 B8
asŏng N. Korea 74 B4
asseral mt. Switz. 47 K7
assiron, Pointe de pt France 56 D3
astab, Kūh-e mts Iran 88 D3
at Iran 88 D2
atanika U.S.A. 118 D3
ateaubriant France 56 D3
ateau-du-Loir France 56 E3
ateaudun France 56 E2
ateaugay U.S.A. 135 H1

Châteauguay Canada 135 I1
Châteauguay r. Canada 123 H2
Châteauguay, Lac l. Canada 123 H2
Châteaulin France 56 B2
Châteaumeillant France 56 F3
Châteauneuf-en-Thymerais France 52 B6
Châteauneuf-sur-Loire France 56 F3
Chateau Pond l. Canada 123 K3
Châteauroux France 56 E3
Château-Salins France 52 G6
Château-Thierry France 52 D5
Chateh Canada 120 G3
Châtelet Belgium 52 E4
Châtellerault France 56 E3
Chatfield U.S.A. 122 B6
Chatham Canada 134 D2
Chatham U.K. 49 H7
Chatham MA U.S.A. 135 K3
Chatham NY U.S.A. 135 I2
Chatham PA U.S.A. 135 H4
Chatham VA U.S.A. 134 F5
Chatham, Isla i. Chile 144 B8
Chatham Island Galápagos Ecuador see
San Cristóbal, Isla
Chatham Island N.Z. 107 I6
Chatham Island Samoa see Savai'i
Chatham Islands N.Z. 107 I6
Chatham Rise sea feature S. Pacific Ocean
150 I8
Chatham Strait U.S.A. 120 C3
Châtillon-sur-Seine France 56 G3
Chatkal Range mts Kyrg./Uzbek. 80 D3
Chatom U.S.A. 131 F6
Chatra India 83 F4
Chatra Nepal 83 F4
Chatsworth Canada 134 E1
Chatsworth U.S.A. 135 H4
Chattagam Bangl. see Chittagong
Chattanooga U.S.A. 133 C5
Chattarpur India see Chhatarpur
Chatteris U.K. 49 H6
Chattisgarh state India see Chhattisgarh
Chatturat Thai. 70 C4
Chatyr-Tash Kyrg. 80 E3
Châu Đôc Vietnam 71 D5
Chauhtan India 82 B4
Chauk Myanmar 70 A2
Chaumont France 56 G2
Chauncey U.S.A. 134 D4
Chaungzon Myanmar 70 B3
Chaunskaya Guba b. Rus. Fed. 65 R3
Chauny France 52 D5
Chau Phu Vietnam see Châu Đôc
Chausy Belarus see Chavusy
Chautauqua, Lake U.S.A. 134 F2
Chauter Pak. 89 G4
Chauvin Canada 121 I4
Chavakachcheri Sri Lanka 84 D4
Chaves Port. 57 C3
Chavigny, Lac l. Canada 122 G2
Chavusy Belarus 43 F5
Chawal r. Pak. 89 G4
Chay, Sông r. Vietnam 70 D2
Chayatyn, Khrebet ridge Rus. Fed. 74 E1
Chayevo Rus. Fed. 42 H4
Chaykovskiy Rus. Fed. 41 Q4
Chazhegovo Rus. Fed. 42 L3
Chazy U.S.A. 135 I1
Cheadle U.K. 49 F6
Cheaha Mountain hill U.S.A. 133 C5
Cheat r. U.S.A. 134 F4
Cheatham Lake U.S.A. 134 B5
Cheb Czech Rep. 53 M4
Chebba Tunisia 58 D7
Cheboksarskoye Vodokhranilishche resr
Rus. Fed. 42 J5
Cheboksary Rus. Fed. 42 J4
Cheboygan U.S.A. 132 C2
Chechen', Ostrov i. Rus. Fed. 91 G2
Chech'ŏn S. Korea 75 C5
Chedabucto Bay Canada 123 J5
Cheddar U.K. 49 E7
Cheduba Myanmar see Man-aung
Cheduba Island i. Myanmar see
Man-aung Kyun
Chée r. France 52 E6
Cheektowaga U.S.A. 135 F2
Cheepie Australia 112 B1
Cheetham, Cape Antarctica 152 H2
Chefoo China see Yantai
Chefornak U.S.A. 118 B3
Chefu Moz. 101 K2
Chegdomyn Rus. Fed. 74 D2
Chegga Mauritania 96 C2
Chegutu Zimbabwe 99 D5
Chehalis U.S.A. 126 C3
Chehar Burj Iran 88 E2
Chehardeh Iran 88 E3
Chehel Chashmeh, Kūh-e hill Iran 88 B3
Chehel Dokhtarān, Kūh-e mt. Iran 89 F4
Chehell'āyeh Iran 88 E4
Cheju S. Korea 75 B6
Cheju-do i. S. Korea 75 B6
Cheju-haehyŏp sea chan. S. Korea 75 B6
Chek Chue H.K. China see Stanley
Chekhov Moskovskaya Oblast' Rus. Fed.
43 H5
Chekhov Sakhalinskaya Oblast' Rus. Fed.
74 F3
Chekiang prov. China see Zhejiang
Chekichler Turkm. see Çekiçler
Chek Lap Kok reg. H.K. China 77 [inset]
Chek Mun Hoi Hap H.K. China see
Tolo Channel
Chekunda Rus. Fed. 74 D2
Chela, Serra da mts Angola 99 B5
Chelan, Lake U.S.A. 126 C2
Cheleken Turkm. see Hazar
Cheline Moz. 101 L2
Chelkar Kazakh. see Shalkar
Chełm Poland 43 D6
Chelmer r. U.K. 49 H7
Chełmno Poland 47 Q4
Chelmsford U.K. 49 H7
Chelsea MI U.S.A. 134 C2
Chelsea VT U.S.A. 135 I2
Cheltenham U.K. 49 E7
Chelva Spain 57 F4
Chelyabinsk Rus. Fed. 64 H4
Chelyuskin Rus. Fed. 153 E1
Chemba Moz. 99 D5
Chêm Co l. China 82 D2

Chemnitz Germany 53 M4
Chemulpo S. Korea see Inch'ŏn
Chenab r. India/Pak. 82 B3
Chenachane, Oued watercourse Alg. 96 C2
Chendir r. Turkm. see Çendir
Cheney U.S.A. 126 D3
Cheney Reservoir U.S.A. 130 D4
Chengalpattu India 84 D3
Chengbu China 77 F3
Chengchow China see Zhengzhou
Chengde China 73 L4
Chengdu China 76 E2
Chengele India 76 C2
Chenggong China 76 D3
Chenghai China 77 H4
Cheng Hai l. China 76 D3
Chengjiang China see Taihe
Chengmai China 77 F5
Chengtu China see Chengdu
Chengwu China 77 G1
Chengxian China 76 E1
Chengxiang Chongqing China see Wuxi
Chengxiang Jiangxi China see Quannan
Chengzhong China see Ningming
Cheniu Shan i. China 77 H1
Chenkaladi Sri Lanka 84 D5
Chennai India 84 D3
Chenqian Shan i. China 77 I2
Chenqing China 74 B2
Chenqingqiao China see Chenqing
Chenstokhov Poland see Częstochowa
Chentejn Nuruu mts Mongolia 73 J3
Chenxi China 77 F3
Chenyang China see Chenxi
Chenying China see Wannian
Chenzhou China 77 G3
Chepén Peru 142 C5
Chepes Arg. 144 C4
Chepo Panama 137 I7
Chepstow U.K. 49 E7
Cheptsa r. Rus. Fed. 42 K4
Chequamegon Bay U.S.A. 130 F2
Cher r. France 56 E3
Chera state India see Kerala
Cheraw U.S.A. 133 E5
Cherbaniani Reef India 84 A3
Cherbourg France 56 D2
Cherchell Alg. 57 H5
Cherchen China see Qiemo
Cherdakly Rus. Fed. 43 K5
Cherdyn' Rus. Fed. 41 R3
Chereapani reef India see Byramgore Reef
Cheremkhovo Rus. Fed. 72 I2
Cheremshany Rus. Fed. 74 D3
Cheremukhovka Rus. Fed. 42 K4
Cherepanovo Rus. Fed. 72 E2
Cherepovets Rus. Fed. 42 H4
Cherevkovo Rus. Fed. 42 J3
Chergui, Chott ech imp. l. Alg. 54 D5
Chéria Alg. 58 B7
Cheriton U.S.A. 135 H5
Cheriyam atoll India 84 B4
Cherkassy Ukr. see Cherkasy
Cherkasy Ukr. 43 G6
Cherkessk Rus. Fed. 91 F1
Cherla India 84 D2
Chernaya Rus. Fed. 42 M1
Chernaya r. Rus. Fed. 42 M1
Chernigov Ukr. see Chernihiv
Chernigovka Rus. Fed. 74 D3
Chernihiv Ukr. 43 F6
Cherninivka Ukr. 43 H7
Chernivtsi Ukr. 43 E6
Chernobyl' Ukr. see Chornobyl'
Chernogorsk Rus. Fed. 72 G2
Chernovtsy Ukr. see Chernivtsi
Chernoye More sea Asia/Europe see
Black Sea
Chernushka Rus. Fed. 41 R4
Chernyakhiv Ukr. 43 F6
Chernyakhovsk Rus. Fed. 45 L9
Chernyanka Rus. Fed. 43 H6
Chernyayevo Rus. Fed. 74 B1
Chernyshevsk Rus. Fed. 73 L2
Chernyshevskiy Rus. Fed. 65 M3
Chernyshkovskiy Rus. Fed. 43 I6
Chernyye Zemli reg. Rus. Fed. 43 J7
Chernyy Irtysh r. China/Kazakh. see
Ertix He
Chernyy Porog Rus. Fed. 42 G3
Chernyy Yar Rus. Fed. 43 J6
Cherokee U.S.A. 130 E3
Cherokee Sound Bahamas 133 E7

▶Cherrapunji India 83 G4
Highest recorded annual rainfall in the world.

Cherry Creek r. U.S.A. 130 C2
Cherry Creek Mountains U.S.A. 129 F1
Cherry Hill U.S.A. 135 H4
Cherry Island Solomon Is 107 G3
Cherry Lake U.S.A. 128 D2
Cherskiy Rus. Fed. 153 C2
Cherskiy Range mts Rus. Fed. see
Cherskogo, Khrebet
Cherskogo, Khrebet mts Rus. Fed. 65 P3
Cherskogo, Khrebet mts Rus. Fed. 73 K2
Chertkov Ukr. see Chortkiv
Chertkovo Rus. Fed. 43 I6
Cherven Bryag Bulg. 59 K3
Chervonoarmeyskoye Ukr. see
Vil'nyans'k
Chervonoarmiys'k Donets'ka Oblast' Ukr.
see Krasnoarmiys'k
Chervonoarmiys'k Rivnens'ka Oblast' Ukr.
see Radyvyliv
Chervonograd Ukr. see Chervonohrad
Chervonohrad Ukr. 43 E6
Chervyen' Belarus 43 F5
Cherwell r. U.K. 49 F7
Cherykaw Belarus 43 F5
Chesapeake U.S.A. 135 G5
Chesapeake Bay U.S.A. 135 G4
Chesham U.K. 49 G7
Cheshire Plain U.K. 48 E5
Cheshme Vtoroy Turkm. 89 F2
Cheshskaya Guba b. Rus. Fed. 42 J2
Cheshtebe Tajik. 89 I2
Cheshunt U.K. 49 G7
Chesnokovka Rus. Fed. see Novoaltaysk
Chester Canada 123 I5

Chester U.K. 48 E5
Chester CA U.S.A. 128 C1
Chester IL U.S.A. 130 F4
Chester MT U.S.A. 126 F2
Chester OH U.S.A. 134 E4
Chester SC U.S.A. 133 D5
Chester r. U.S.A. 135 G4
Chesterfield U.K. 48 F5
Chesterfield U.S.A. 135 G5
Chesterfield, Îles is New Caledonia 107 F3
Chesterfield Inlet Canada 121 N2
Chesterfield Inlet inlet Canada 121 M2
Chester-le-Street U.K. 48 F4
Chestertown MD U.S.A. 135 G4
Chestertown NY U.S.A. 135 I2
Chesterville Canada 135 H1
Chestnut Ridge U.S.A. 134 F3
Chesuncook Lake U.S.A. 132 G2
Chetaïbi Alg. 58 B6
Chéticamp Canada 123 J5
Chetlat i. India 84 B4
Chetumal Mex. 136 G5
Chetwynd Canada 120 F4
Cheung Chau H.K. China 77 [inset]
Chevelon Creek r. U.S.A. 129 H4
Cheviot N.Z. 113 D6
Cheviot Hills U.K. 48 E3
Cheviot Range hills Australia 110 C5
Chevreulx r. Canada 122 G3
Cheyenne OK U.S.A. 131 D5

▶Cheyenne WY U.S.A. 126 G4
Capital of Wyoming.

Cheyenne r. U.S.A. 130 C2
Cheyenne Wells U.S.A. 130 C4
Cheyne Bay Australia 109 B8
Cheyur India 84 D3
Chezacut Canada 120 E4
Chhapra India 83 F4
Chhata India 82 D4
Chhatak Bangl. 83 G4
Chhatarpur Jharkhand India 83 F4
Chhatarpur Madh. Prad. India 82 D4
Chhatr Pak. 89 H4
Chhatrapur India 84 E2
Chhattisgarh state India 83 E5
Chhay Arêng, Stœng r. Cambodia 71 C5
Chhindwara India 82 D5
Chhitkul India 82 D3
Chhukha Bhutan 83 G4
Chi, Lam r. Thai. 71 C4
Chi, Mae Nam r. Thai. 70 D4
Chiai Taiwan 77 I4
Chiamboni Somalia 98 E4
Chiange Angola 99 B5
Chiang Kham Thai. 70 C3
Chiang Khan Thai. 70 C3
Chiang Mai Thai. 70 B3
Chiang Rai Thai. 70 B3
Chiang Saen Thai. 70 C2
Chiari Italy 58 C2
Chiautla Mex. 136 E5
Chiavenna Italy 58 C1
Chiayi Taiwan see Chiai
Chiba Japan 75 F6
Chibi China 77 G2
Chibia Angola 99 B5
Chibizovka Rus. Fed. see Zherdevka
Chiboma Moz. 99 D6
Chibougamau Canada 122 G4
Chibougamau, Lac l. Canada 122 G4
Chibuto Moz. 101 K3
Chicacole India see Srikakulam

▶Chicago U.S.A. 134 B3
4th most populous city in North America.

Chic-Chocs, Monts mts Canada 123 I4
Chichagof U.S.A. 120 B3
Chichagof Island U.S.A. 120 C3
Chichak r. Pak. 89 G5
Chichaoua Morocco 54 C5
Chichatka Rus. Fed. 74 A1
Chicheng China see Pengxi
Chichester U.K. 49 G8
Chichester Range mts Australia 108 B5
Chichgarh India 84 D1
Chichibu Japan 75 E6
Chichibu-Tama Kokuritsu-kōen nat. park
Japan 75 E6
Chichijima-rettō is Japan 75 F8
Chickasha U.S.A. 131 D5
Chiclana de la Frontera Spain 57 C5
Chiclayo Peru 142 C5
Chico r. Arg. 144 C6
Chico U.S.A. 128 C2
Chicomo Moz. 101 L3
Chicopee U.S.A. 135 I2
Chicoutimi Canada 123 H4
Chicualacuala Moz. 101 J2
Chidambaram India 84 C4
Chidenguele Moz. 101 L3
Chidley, Cape Canada 119 L3
Chido China see Sêndo
Chido S. Korea 75 B6
Chiducuane Moz. 101 L3
Chiefland U.S.A. 133 D6
Chiemsee l. Germany 47 N7
Chiengmai Thai. see Chiang Mai
Chiers r. France 52 F5
Chieti Italy 58 F3
Chifeng China 73 L4
Chifre, Serra do mts Brazil 145 C2
Chiganak Kazakh. 80 D2
Chiginagak Volcano, Mount U.S.A. 118 C4
Chigu China 83 G3
Chigubo Moz. 101 K2
Chigu Co l. China 83 G3
Chihli, Gulf of China see Bo Hai
Chihuahua Mex. 127 G7
Chihuahua state Mex. 127 G7
Chihuahua, Desierto de des. Mex. 127 G7
Chiili Kazakh. 80 C3
Chikalda India 82 D5
Chikan China 77 F4
Chikaskia r. U.S.A. 131 D4
Chikhali Kalan Parasia India 82 D5
Chikhli India 84 C1
Chikishlyar Turkm. see Çekiçler
Chikmagalur India 84 B3
Chikodi India 84 B2

Chilanko r. Canada 120 F4
Chilas Pak. 82 C2
Chilaw Sri Lanka 84 C5
Chilcotin r. Canada 120 F5
Childers Australia 110 F5
Childress U.S.A. 131 C5
Chile country S. America 144 B4
Chile Basin sea feature S. Pacific Ocean
151 O8
Chile Chico Chile 144 B7
Chile Rise sea feature S. Pacific Ocean
151 O8
Chilgir Rus. Fed. 43 J7
Chilhowie U.S.A. 134 E5
Chilia-Nouă Ukr. see Kiliya
Chilik Kazakh. 80 E3
Chilika Lake India 84 E2
Chililabombwe Zambia 99 C5
Chilko r. Canada 120 F4
Chilko Lake Canada 120 E5
Chilkoot Pass Canada/U.S.A. 120 C3
Chilkoot Trail National Historic Site
nat. park Canada 120 C3
Chillán Chile 144 B5
Chillicothe MO U.S.A. 130 E4
Chillicothe OH U.S.A. 134 D4
Chilliwack Canada 120 F5
Chilo India 82 C4
Chiloé, Isla de i. Chile 144 B6
Chiloé, Isla Grande de i. Chile see
Chiloé, Isla de
Chilpancingo Mex. 136 E5
Chilpancingo de los Bravos Mex. see
Chilpancingo
Chilpi Pak. 82 C1
Chiltern Hills U.K. 49 G7
Chilton U.S.A. 134 A1
Chiluage Angola 99 C4
Chilubi Zambia 99 C5
Chilung Taiwan 77 I3
Chilwa, Lake Malawi 99 D5
Chimala Tanz. 99 D4
Chimaltenango Guat. 136 F6
Chi Ma Wan H.K. China 77 [inset]
Chimay Belgium 52 E4
Chimbas Arg. 144 C4
Chimbay Uzbek. see Chimboy
Chimborazo mt. Ecuador 142 C4
Chimbote Peru 142 C5
Chimboy Uzbek. 80 A3
Chimian Pak. 89 I4
Chimishliya Moldova see Cimişlia
Chimkent Kazakh. see Shymkent
Chimney Rock U.S.A. 129 J3
Chimoio Moz. 99 D5
Chimtargha, Qullai mt. Tajik. 89 H2
Chimtorga, Gora mt. Tajik. see
Chimtargha, Qullai

▶China country Asia 72 H5
Most populous country in the world and in Asia. 2nd largest country in Asia and 4th largest in the world.

China Mex. 131 D7
China, Republic of country Asia see Taiwan
China Bakir r. Myanmar see To
China Lake CA U.S.A. 128 E4
China Lake ME U.S.A. 135 K1
Chinandega Nicaragua 136 G6
China Point U.S.A. 128 D5
Chinati Peak U.S.A. 131 B6
Chincha Alta Peru 142 C6
Chinchaga r. Canada 120 G3
Chinchilla Australia 112 E1
Chincholi India 84 C2
Chinchorro, Banco sea feature Mex. 137 G5
Chincoteague Bay U.S.A. 135 H5
Chinde Moz. 99 D5
Chindo S. Korea 75 B6
Chin-do i. S. Korea 75 B6
Chindwin r. Myanmar 70 A2
Chinese Turkestan aut. reg. China see
Xinjiang Uygur Zizhiqu
Chinghai prov. China see Qinghai
Chingiz-Tau, Khrebet mts Kazakh. 80 E2
Chingleput India see Chengalpattu
Chingola Zambia 99 C5
Chinguar Angola 99 B5
Chinguetti Mauritania 96 B2
Chinhae S. Korea 75 C6
Chinhoyi Zimbabwe 99 D5
Chini India see Kalpa
Chining China see Jining
Chiniot Pak. 89 I4
Chinipas Mex. 127 F8
Chinit, Stœng r. Cambodia 71 D4
Chinju S. Korea 75 C6
Chinle U.S.A. 129 I3
Chinmen Taiwan 77 H3
Chinmen Tao i. Taiwan 77 H3
Chinnamp'o N. Korea see Namp'o
Chinnur India 84 C2
Chino Creek watercourse U.S.A. 129 G4
Chinon France 56 E3
Chinook U.S.A. 126 F2
Chinook Trough sea feature
N. Pacific Ocean 150 I3
Chino Valley U.S.A. 129 G4
Chin-shan China see Zhujing
Chintamani India 84 C3
Chioggia Italy 58 E2
Chios Greece 59 L5
Chios i. Greece 59 K5
Chipata Zambia 99 D5
Chipchihua, Sierra de mts Arg. 144 C6
Chiphu Cambodia 71 D5
Chipindo Angola 99 B5
Chipinga Zimbabwe see Chipinge
Chipinge Zimbabwe 99 D6
Chipley U.S.A. 133 C6
Chipman Canada 123 I5
Chippenham U.K. 49 E7
Chippewa, Lake U.S.A. 130 F2
Chippewa Falls U.S.A. 130 F2
Chipping Norton U.K. 49 F7
Chipping Sodbury U.K. 49 E7
Chipurupalle Andhra Prad. India 84 D2
Chipurupalle Andhra Prad. India 84 D2
Chiquilá Mex. 133 C8
Chiquinquira Col. 142 D2
Chir r. Rus. Fed. 43 I6

Chirada India 84 D3
Chirala India 84 D3
Chiras Afgh. 89 G3
Chirchiq Uzbek. 80 C3
Chiredzi Zimbabwe 99 D6
Chirfa Niger 96 E2
Chiricahua National Monument nat. park
U.S.A. 129 I5
Chiricahua Peak U.S.A. 129 I6
Chirikof Island U.S.A. 118 C4
Chiriquí, Golfo de b. Panama 137 H7
Chiriquí, Volcán de vol. Panama see
Barú, Volcán
Chiri-san mt. S. Korea 75 B6
Chirk U.K. 49 D6
Chirnside U.K. 50 G5
Chirripó mt. Costa Rica 137 H7
Chisamba Zambia 99 C5
Chisana r. U.S.A. 120 A2
Chisasibi Canada 122 F3
Chishima-retto is Rus. Fed. see
Kuril Islands
Chisholm Canada 120 H4
Chishtian Mandi Pak. 89 I4
Chishui China 76 E2
Chishuihe China 76 E3
Chisimaio Somalia see Kismaayo

▶Chişinău Moldova 59 M1
Capital of Moldova.

Chistopol' Rus. Fed. 42 K5
Chita Rus. Fed. 73 K2
Chitado Angola 99 B5
Chitaldrug India see Chitradurga
Chitalwana India 82 B4
Chitambo Zambia 99 D5
Chita Oblast admin. div. Rus. Fed. see
Chitinskaya Oblast'
Chitato Angola 99 C4
Chitek Lake Canada 121 J4
Chitek Lake l. Canada 121 L4
Chitembo Angola 99 B5
Chitina U.S.A. 118 D3
Chitinskaya Oblast' admin. div.
Rus. Fed. 74 A1
Chitipa Malawi 99 D4
Chitkul India see Chhitkul
Chitobe Moz. 99 D6
Chitoor India see Chittoor
Chitor India see Chittaurgarh
Chitose Japan 74 F4
Chitradurga India 84 C3
Chitrakoot India 82 E4
Chitrakut India see Chitrakoot
Chitral Pak. 89 H3
Chitral r. Pak. 89 H3
Chitravati r. India 84 C3
Chitré Panama 137 H7
Chitrod India 82 B5
Chittagong Bangl. 83 G5
Chittaurgarh India 82 C4
Chittoor India 84 C3
Chittor India see Chittoor
Chittorgarh India see Chittaurgarh
Chittur India 84 C4
Chitungwiza Zimbabwe 99 D5
Chiu Lung H.K. China see Kowloon
Chiume Angola 99 C5
Chivasso Italy 58 B2
Chívato, Punta pt Mex. 127 F8
Chivhu Zimbabwe 99 D5
Chixi China 77 G4
Chizarira National Park
Zimbabwe 99 C5
Chizha Vtoraya Kazakh. 43 K6
Chizhou China 77 H2
Chizu Japan 75 D6
Chkalov Rus. Fed. see Orenburg
Chkalovsk Rus. Fed. 42 I4
Chkalovskoye Rus. Fed. 74 D3
Chlef Alg. 57 G5
Chlef, Oued r. Alg. 57 G5
Chloride U.S.A. 129 F4
Chlya, Ozero l. Rus. Fed. 74 F1
Choa Chu Kang Sing. 71 [inset]
Choa Chu Kang hill Sing. 71 [inset]
Chobe National Park Botswana 99 C5
Chodov Czech Rep. 53 M4
Choele Choel Arg. 144 C5
Chogar r. Rus. Fed. 74 D1
Chogori Feng mt. China/Pakistan see K2
Chograyskoye Vodokhranilishche resr
Rus. Fed. 43 J7
Choiseul i. Solomon Is 107 F2
Choix Mex. 127 F8
Chojnice Poland 47 P4
Chōkai-san vol. Japan 75 F5
Ch'ok'ē mts Eth. 98 D2
Ch'ok'ē Mountains Eth. see Ch'ok'ē
Chokola mt. China 82 E3
Choksum China 83 F3
Chokue Moz. see Chókwé
Chokurdakh Rus. Fed. 65 P2
Chókwé Moz. 101 K3
Cho La pass China 76 C2
Cholame U.S.A. 128 C4
Chola Shan mts China 76 C1
Cholet France 56 D3
Cholpon-Ata Kyrg. 80 E3
Choluteca Hond. 137 G6
Choma Zambia 99 C5
Chomo Ganggar mt. China 83 G3
Chơ Moi Vietnam 70 D2
Chomo Lhari mt. China/Bhutan 83 G4
Chom Thong Thai. 70 B3
Chomutov Czech Rep. 47 N5
Ch'ŏnan S. Korea 75 B5
Chon Buri Thai. 71 C4
Ch'ŏnch'ŏn N. Korea 74 B4
Chone Ecuador 142 B4
Ch'ŏngch'ŏn-gang r. N. Korea 75 B5
Ch'ongdo S. Korea 75 C6
Chonggye China see Qonggyai
Ch'ŏngjin N. Korea 74 C4
Ch'ŏngju S. Korea 75 B5
Chông Kal Cambodia 71 C4
Chongkü China 76 C2
Chonglong China see Zizhong
Chongming Dao i. China 77 I2
Chongoroi Angola 99 B5
Chŏngp'yŏng N. Korea 75 B5

Chongqing China 76 E2
Chongqing *municipality* China 76 E2
Chonguene Moz. 101 K3
Chŏngŭp S. Korea 75 B6
Chongyang China 77 G2
Chongyi China 77 G3
Chongzuo China 76 E4
Chŏnju S. Korea 75 B6

▶Cho Oyu *mt.* China/Nepal 83 F3
6th highest mountain in the world and in Asia.

Chopda India 82 C5
Chor Pak. 89 H5
Chora Sfakion Greece 59 K7
Chorley U.K. 48 E5
Chornobyl' Ukr. 43 F6
Chornomors'ke Ukr. 59 O2
Chortkiv Ukr. 43 E6
Ch'osan N. Korea 74 B4
Chōshi Japan 75 F6
Chosŏn *country* Asia *see* South Korea
Chosŏn-minjujuŭi-inmin-konghwaguk *country* Asia *see* North Korea
Choszczno Poland 47 O4
Chota Peru 142 C5
Chota Sinchula *hill* India 83 G4
Choteau U.S.A. 126 E3
Choti Pak. 89 H4
Choûm Mauritania 96 B2
Chowchilla U.S.A. 128 C3
Chowghat India 84 B4
Chown, Mount Canada 120 G4
Choybalsan Mongolia 73 K3
Choyr Mongolia 73 J3
Chrétiens, Île aux *i.* Canada *see* Christian Island
Chřiby *hills* Czech Rep. 47 P6
Chrisman U.S.A. 134 B4
Chrissiesmeer S. Africa 101 J4
Christchurch N.Z. 113 D6
Christchurch U.K. 49 F8
Christian, Cape Canada 119 L2
Christiana S. Africa 101 G4
Christiania Norway *see* Oslo
Christian Island Canada 134 E1
Christiansburg U.S.A. 134 E5
Christianshåb Greenland *see* Qasigiannguit
Christie Bay Canada 121 I2
Christie Island Myanmar 71 B5
Christina *r.* Canada 121 I3
Christina, Mount N.Z. 113 B7

▶Christmas Island *terr.* Indian Ocean 68 D9
Australian External Territory.

Christopher, Lake *salt flat* Australia 109 D6
Chrudim Czech Rep. 47 O6
Chrysi *i.* Kriti Greece *see* Gaïdouronisi
Chrysochou Bay Cyprus 85 A2
Chrysochous, Kolpos *b.* Cyprus *see* Chrysochou Bay
Chu Kazakh. *see* Shu
Chu *r.* Kazakh./Kyrg. 80 C3
Chuadanga Bangl. 83 G5
Chuali, Lago *l.* Moz. 101 K3
Chuanhui China *see* Zhoukou
Chuansha China 77 I2
Chubalung China 76 C2
Chubarovka Ukr. *see* Polohy
Chubartau Kazakh. *see* Barshatas
Chūbu-Sangaku Kokuritsu-kōen *nat. park* Japan 75 E5
Chu-ching China *see* Zhujing
Chuchkovo Rus. Fed. 43 I5
Chuckwalla Mountains U.S.A. 129 F5
Chudniv Ukr. 43 F6
Chudovo Rus. Fed. 42 F4
Chudskoye, Ozero *l.* Estonia/Rus. Fed. *see* Peipus, Lake
Chugach Mountains U.S.A. 118 D3
Chūgoku-sanchi *mts* Japan 75 D6
Chugqênsumdo China *see* Jigzhi
Chuguchak China *see* Tacheng
Chuguyev Ukr. *see* Chuhuyiv
Chuguyevka Rus. Fed. 74 D3
Chugwater U.S.A. 126 G4
Chuhai China *see* Zhuhai
Chuhuyiv Ukr. 43 H6
Chu-Iliyskiye Gory *mts* Kazakh. 80 D3
Chujiang China *see* Shimen
Chukai Malaysia *see* Cukai
Chukchagirskoye, Ozero *l.* Rus. Fed. 74 E1
Chukchi Abyssal Plain *sea feature* Arctic Ocean 153 B1
Chukchi Peninsula Rus. Fed. *see* Chukotskiy Poluostrov
Chukchi Plateau *sea feature* Arctic Ocean 153 B1
Chukchi Sea Rus. Fed./U.S.A. 65 T3
Chukhloma Rus. Fed. 42 I4
Chukotskiy, Mys *c.* Rus. Fed. 118 A3
Chukotskiy Poluostrov *pen.* Rus. Fed. 65 T3
Chulakkurgan Kazakh. *see* Sholakkorgan
Chulaktau Kazakh. *see* Karatau
Chulasa Rus. Fed. 42 J2
Chula Vista U.S.A. 128 E5
Chulucanas Peru 142 B5
Chulung Pass Pak. 82 D2
Chulym Rus. Fed. 64 J4
Chumar India 82 D2
Chumbicha Arg. 144 C3
Chumda China 76 C1
Chumikan Rus. Fed. 65 O4
Chum Phae Thai. 70 C3
Chumphon Thai. 71 B5
Chum Saeng Thai. 70 C4
Chunar India 83 E4
Ch'unch'ŏn S. Korea 75 B5
Chunchura India 83 G5
Chundzha Kazakh. 80 E3
Chunga Zambia 99 C5
Chung-hua Jen-min Kung-ho-kuo *country* Asia *see* China
Chung-hua Min-kuo *country* Asia *see* Taiwan
Ch'ungju S. Korea 75 B5
Chungking China *see* Chongqing
Ch'ungmu S. Korea *see* T'ongyŏng
Chŭngsan N. Korea 75 B5
Chungyang Shanmo *mts* Taiwan 77 I4
Chunskiy Rus. Fed. 72 H1
Chunya *r.* Rus. Fed. 65 K3
Chuôi, Hon *i.* Vietnam 71 D5
Chuosijia China *see* Guanyinqiao
Chupa Rus. Fed. 44 R3
Chūplū Iran 88 B2
Chuquicamata Chile 144 C2
Chur Switz. 56 I3
Churachandpur India 83 H4
Chūrān Iran 88 D4
Churapcha Rus. Fed. 65 O3
Churchill Canada 121 M3
Churchill *r. Man.* Canada 121 M3
Churchill *r. Nfld. and Lab.* Canada 123 J3
Churchill, Cape Canada 121 M3
Churchill Falls Canada 123 I3
Churchill Lake Canada 121 I4
Churchill Mountains Antarctica 152 H1
Churchill Sound *sea chan.* Canada 122 F2
Churchs Ferry U.S.A. 130 D1
Churchville U.S.A. 134 F4
Churia Ghati Hills Nepal 83 F4
Churu India 82 C3
Churubusco U.S.A. 134 C3
Churún-Merú *waterfall* Venez. *see* Angel Falls
Chushul India 82 D2
Chuska Mountains U.S.A. 129 I3
Chusovaya *r.* Rus. Fed. 41 R4
Chusovoy Rus. Fed. 41 R4
Chust Ukr. *see* Khust
Chute-des-Passes Canada 123 H4
Chutia *Assam* India 83 H4
Chutia *Jharkhand* India 83 F5
Chutung Taiwan 77 I3
Chuuk *is* Micronesia 150 G5
Chuxiong China 76 D3
Chüy *r.* Kazakh./Kyrg. *see* Chu
Chư Yang Sin *mt.* Vietnam 71 E4
Chuzhou *Anhui* China 77 H1
Chuzhou *Jiangsu* China 77 H1
Chymyshliya Moldova *see* Cimişlia
Chyulu Hills National Park Kenya 98 D4
Ciadâr-Lunga Moldova *see* Ciadîr-Lunga
Ciadîr-Lunga Moldova 59 M1
Ciamis Indon. 68 D8
Cianjur Indon. 68 D8
Cianorte Brazil 144 F2
Cibecue U.S.A. 129 H4
Cibolo Creek *r.* U.S.A. 131 D6
Cibuta, Sierra *mt.* Mex. 127 F7
Čičarija *mts* Croatia 58 E2
Cicero U.S.A. 134 B3
Cide Turkey 90 D2
Ciechanów Poland 47 R4
Ciego de Ávila Cuba 137 I4
Ciénaga Col. 142 D1
Ciénega Mex. 131 C7
Ciénega de Flores Mex. 131 C7
Cienfuegos Cuba 137 H4
Cieza Spain 57 F4
Çiftlik Turkey *see* Kelkit
Cifuentes Spain 57 E3
Cigüela *r.* Spain 57 E4
Cihanbeyli Turkey 90 D3
Cijara, Embalse de *resr* Spain 57 D4
Cilacap Indon. 68 D8
Çıldır Turkey 91 F2
Çıldır Gölü *l.* Turkey 91 F2
Çıldıroba Turkey 85 C1
Cilento e del Vallo di Diano, Parco Nazionale del *nat. park* Italy 58 F4
Cili China 77 F2
Cilician Gates *pass* Turkey *see* Gülek Boğazı
Cill Airne Ireland *see* Killarney
Cill Chainnigh Ireland *see* Kilkenny
Cill Mhantáin Ireland *see* Wicklow
Çilmämmetgum *des.* Turkm. 88 D1
Cilo Dağı *mt.* Turkey 91 G3
Çilov Adası *i.* Azer. 91 H2
Cimarron *CO* U.S.A. 129 J2
Cimarron *KS* U.S.A. 130 C4
Cimarron *NM* U.S.A. 127 G5
Cimarron *r.* U.S.A. 131 D4
Cimişlia Moldova 59 M1
Cimone, Monte *mt.* Italy 58 D2
Cîmpina Romania *see* Câmpina
Cîmpulung Romania *see* Câmpulung
Cîmpulung Moldovenesc Romania *see* Câmpulung Moldovenesc
Cina, Tanjung *c.* Indon. 68 C8
Çınar Turkey 91 F3
Cinaruco-Capanaparo, Parque Nacional *nat. park* Venez. 142 E2
Cinca *r.* Spain 57 G3
Cincinnati U.S.A. 134 C4
Cinco de Outubro Angola *see* Xá-Muteba
Cinderford U.K. 49 E7
Çine Turkey 59 M6
Ciney Belgium 52 F4
Cintalapa Mex. 136 F5
Cinto, Monte *mt.* France 56 I5
Ciping China *see* Jinggangshan
Circeo, Parco Nazionale del *nat. park* Italy 58 E4
Circle *AK* U.S.A. 118 D3
Circle *MT* U.S.A. 126 G3
Circleville *OH* U.S.A. 134 D4
Circleville *UT* U.S.A. 129 G2
Cirebon Indon. 68 D8
Cirencester U.K. 49 F7
Cirò Marina Italy 58 G5
Cirta Alg. *see* Constantine
Cisco U.S.A. 129 I2
Cisne, Islas del *is* Caribbean Sea 137 H5
Citlaltépetl *vol.* Mex. *see* Orizaba, Pico de
Čitluk Bos.-Herz. 58 G3
Citronelle U.S.A. 131 F6
Citrus Heights U.S.A. 128 C2
Città di Castello Italy 58 E3
Ciucaş, Vârful *mt.* Romania 59 K2
Ciudad Acuña Mex. 131 C6
Ciudad Altamirano Mex. 136 D5
Ciudad Bolívar Venez. 142 F2
Ciudad Camargo Mex. 131 B7
Ciudad Constitución Mex. 136 B3
Ciudad del Carmen Mex. 136 F5
Ciudad Delicias Mex. 131 B6
Ciudad de Panamá Panama *see* Panama City
Ciudad de Valles Mex. 136 E4
Ciudad Flores Guat. *see* Flores
Ciudad Guayana Venez. 142 F2
Ciudad Guerrero Mex. 127 G7
Ciudad Guzmán Mex. 136 D5
Ciudad Juárez Mex. 127 G7
Ciudad Lerdo Mex. 131 C7
Ciudad Mante Mex. 136 E4
Ciudad Obregón Mex. 127 F8
Ciudad Real Spain 57 E4
Ciudad Río Bravo Mex. 131 D7
Ciudad Rodrigo Spain 57 C3
Ciudad Trujillo Dom. Rep. *see* Santo Domingo
Ciudad Victoria Mex. 131 D8
Ciutadella Spain 57 H3
Civa Burnu *pt* Turkey 90 E2
Cividale del Friuli Italy 58 E1
Civitanova Marche Italy 58 E3
Civitavecchia Italy 58 D3
Çivril Turkey 59 M5
Cixi China 77 I2
Cizre Turkey 91 F3
Clacton-on-Sea U.K. 49 I7
Clady U.K. 51 E3
Claire, Lake Canada 121 H3
Clairfontaine Alg. *see* El Aouinet
Clamecy France 56 F3
Clane Ireland 51 F4
Clanton U.S.A. 133 C5
Clanwilliam Dam S. Africa 100 D7
Clara Ireland 51 E4
Clara Island Myanmar 71 B5
Claraville Australia 110 C3
Clare *N.S.W.* Australia 112 A4
Clare *S.A.* Australia 111 B7
Clare *r.* Ireland 51 C4
Clare U.S.A. 134 C2
Clarecastle Ireland 51 D5
Clare Island Ireland 51 B4
Claremont U.S.A. 135 I2
Claremore U.S.A. 131 E4
Claremorris Ireland 51 D4
Clarence *r.* Australia 112 F2
Clarence N.Z. 113 D6
Clarence Island Antarctica 152 A2
Clarence Strait Iran *see* Khūran
Clarence Strait U.S.A. 120 C3
Clarence Town Bahamas 133 F8
Clarendon *AR* U.S.A. 131 F5
Clarendon *PA* U.S.A. 134 F3
Clarendon *TX* U.S.A. 131 C5
Clarenville Canada 123 L4
Claresholm Canada 120 H5
Clarie Coast Antarctica *see* Wilkes Coast
Clarinda U.S.A. 130 E3
Clarington U.S.A. 134 E4
Clarion *IA* U.S.A. 130 E3
Clarion *PA* U.S.A. 134 F3
Clarion *r.* U.S.A. 134 F3
Clarión, Isla *i.* Mex. 136 B5
Clark U.S.A. 130 D2
Clark, Mount Canada 120 F1
Clarkdale U.S.A. 129 G4
Clarkebury S. Africa 101 I6
Clarke Range *mts* Australia 110 D4
Clarke River Australia 110 D3
Clarke's Head Canada 123 L4
Clark Mountain U.S.A. 129 F4
Clark Point Canada 134 E1
Clarksburg U.S.A. 134 E4
Clarksdale U.S.A. 131 F5
Clarks Hill U.S.A. 134 B3
Clarksville *AR* U.S.A. 131 E5
Clarksville *TN* U.S.A. 134 B5
Clarksville *TX* U.S.A. 131 E5
Clarksville *VA* U.S.A. 135 F5
Claro *r. Goiás* Brazil 145 A2
Claro *r. Mato Grosso* Brazil 145 A1
Clashmore Ireland 51 E5
Claude U.S.A. 131 C5
Claudy U.K. 51 E3
Clavier Belgium 52 F4
Claxton U.S.A. 133 D5
Clay U.S.A. 134 E4
Clayburg U.S.A. 135 I1
Clay Center *KS* U.S.A. 130 D4
Clay Center *NE* U.S.A. 130 D3
Clay City *IN* U.S.A. 134 B4
Clay City *KY* U.S.A. 134 D5
Clayhole Wash *watercourse* U.S.A. 129 G3
Claypool U.S.A. 129 H5
Clay Springs U.S.A. 129 H4
Clayton *DE* U.S.A. 135 H4
Clayton *GA* U.S.A. 133 D5
Clayton *MI* U.S.A. 134 C3
Clayton *MO* U.S.A. 130 F4
Clayton *NM* U.S.A. 131 C4
Clayton *NY* U.S.A. 135 G1
Claytor Lake U.S.A. 134 E5
Clay Village U.S.A. 134 C4
Clear, Cape Ireland 51 C6
Clearco U.S.A. 134 E4
Clear Creek Canada 134 E2
Clear Creek *r.* U.S.A. 129 H4
Cleare, Cape U.S.A. 118 D4
Clearfield *PA* U.S.A. 135 F3
Clearfield *UT* U.S.A. 126 E4
Clear Fork Brazos *r.* U.S.A. 131 D5
Clear Hills Canada 120 G3
Clear Island Ireland 51 C6
Clear Lake *IA* U.S.A. 130 E3
Clear Lake *SD* U.S.A. 130 D2
Clear Lake *l. CA* U.S.A. 128 B2
Clear Lake *l. UT* U.S.A. 129 G2
Clearmont U.S.A. 126 G3
Clearwater Canada 120 G5
Clearwater *r. Alberta/Saskatchewan* Canada 121 I3
Clearwater *r. Alta* Canada 120 H4
Clearwater U.S.A. 133 D7
Clearwater Lake Canada 121 K4
Clearwater Mountains U.S.A. 126 E3
Cleaton U.S.A. 134 B5
Cleburne U.S.A. 131 D5
Cleethorpes U.K. 48 G5
Clementi Sing. 71 [inset]
Clendenin U.S.A. 134 E4
Clendening Lake U.S.A. 134 E3
Clères France 52 B5
Clerf Lux. *see* Clervaux
Clerke Reef Australia 108 B4
Clermont Australia 110 D4
Clermont France 52 C5
Clermont-en-Argonne France 52 F5
Clermont-Ferrand France 56 F4
Clervaux Lux. 52 G4
Cles Italy 58 D1
Clevedon U.K. 49 E7
Cleveland *MS* U.S.A. 131 F5
Cleveland *OH* U.S.A. 134 E3
Cleveland *TN* U.S.A. 133 C5
Cleveland *UT* U.S.A. 129 H2
Cleveland *WI* U.S.A. 134 B2
Cleveland, Cape Australia 110 D3
Cleveland, Mount U.S.A. 126 E2
Cleveland Heights U.S.A. 134 E3
Cleveland Hills U.K. 48 F4
Cleveleys U.K. 48 D5
Cleves Germany *see* Kleve
Clew Bay Ireland 51 C4
Clifden Ireland 51 B4
Cliff U.S.A. 129 I5
Cliffoney Ireland 51 D3
Clifton Australia 112 E1
Clifton U.S.A. 129 I5
Clifton Beach Australia 110 D3
Clifton Forge U.S.A. 134 F5
Clifton Park U.S.A. 135 I2
Climax Canada 121 I5
Climax U.S.A. 134 C2
Clinch Mountain *mts* U.S.A. 134 D5
Cline River Canada 120 G4
Clinton *B.C.* Canada 120 F5
Clinton *Ont.* Canada 134 E2
Clinton *IA* U.S.A. 130 F3
Clinton *IL* U.S.A. 130 F3
Clinton *IN* U.S.A. 134 B4
Clinton *KY* U.S.A. 131 F4
Clinton *MI* U.S.A. 134 D2
Clinton *MO* U.S.A. 130 E4
Clinton *MS* U.S.A. 131 F5
Clinton *NC* U.S.A. 133 E5
Clinton *OK* U.S.A. 131 D5
Clinton-Colden Lake Canada 121 J1
Clintwood U.S.A. 134 D5

▶Clipperton, Île *terr.* N. Pacific Ocean 151 M5
French Overseas Territory. Most easterly point of Oceania.

Clisham *hill* U.K. 50 C3
Clitheroe U.K. 48 E5
Clive Lake Canada 120 G2
Cliza Bol. 142 E7
Clocolan S. Africa 101 H5
Cloghan Ireland 51 E4
Clonakilty Ireland 51 D6
Clonbern Ireland 51 D4
Cloncurry Australia 110 C4
Cloncurry *r.* Australia 110 C3
Clones Ireland 51 E3
Clonmel Ireland 51 E5
Clonygowan Ireland 51 E4
Cloonbannin Ireland 51 C5
Clooneagh Ireland 51 E4
Cloppenburg Germany 53 I2
Cloquet U.S.A. 130 E2
Cloquet *r.* U.S.A. 130 E2
Cloud Peak *WY* U.S.A. 124 F3
Cloud Peak *WY* U.S.A. 126 G3
Clova Canada 122 G4
Clover U.S.A. 129 G1
Cloverdale *CA* U.S.A. 128 B2
Cloverdale *IN* U.S.A. 134 B4
Cloverport U.S.A. 134 B5
Clovis *CA* U.S.A. 128 D3
Clovis *NM* U.S.A. 131 C5
Cloyne Canada 135 G1
Cluain Meala Ireland *see* Clonmel
Cluanie, Loch *l.* U.K. 50 D3
Cluff Lake Mine Canada 121 I3
Cluj-Napoca Romania 59 J1
Clun U.K. 49 D6
Clunes Australia 112 A6
Cluny Australia 110 B5
Cluses France 56 H3
Cluster Springs U.S.A. 135 F5
Clut Lake Canada 120 G1
Clutterbuck Head *hd* Canada 123 H1
Clutterbuck Hills *hill* Australia 109 D6
Clwydian Range *hills* U.K. 48 D5
Clyde Canada 120 H4
Clyde *r.* U.K. 50 E5
Clyde *NY* U.S.A. 135 G2
Clyde *OH* U.S.A. 134 D3
Clyde, Firth of *est.* U.K. 50 E5
Clydebank U.K. 50 E5
Clyde River Canada 119 L2
Côa *r.* Port. 57 C3
Coachella U.S.A. 128 E5
Coahuila *state* Mex. 131 C7
Coahuila de Zaragoza *state* Mex. *see* Coahuila
Coal *r.* Canada 120 E3
Coal City U.S.A. 134 A3
Coaldale U.S.A. 128 E2
Coalgate U.S.A. 131 D5
Coal Harbour Canada 120 E5
Coalinga U.S.A. 128 C3
Coalport U.S.A. 135 F3
Coal River Canada 120 E3
Coal Valley U.S.A. 129 F3
Coalville U.K. 49 F6
Coalville U.S.A. 129 H1
Coari Brazil 142 F4
Coari *r.* Brazil 142 F4
Coarsegold U.S.A. 128 D3
Coastal Plain U.S.A. 131 E6
Coast Mountains Canada 120 E4
Coast Range *hills* Australia 111 E5
Coast Ranges *mts* U.S.A. 128 B1
Coatbridge U.K. 50 E5
Coatesville U.S.A. 135 H4
Coaticook Canada 135 J1
Coats Island Canada 119 J3
Coats Land *reg.* Antarctica 152 A1
Coatzacoalcos Mex. 136 F5
Cobar Australia 112 B3
Cobargo Australia 112 D6
Cobden Australia 112 A7
Cobh Ireland 51 D6
Cobham *r.* Canada 121 M4
Cobija Bol. 142 E6
Coblenz Germany *see* Koblenz
Cobleskill U.S.A. 135 H2
Cobourg Peninsula Australia 108 F2
Cobra Australia 109 B6
Cobram Australia 112 B5
Coburg Germany 53 K4
Coburg Island Canada 119 K2
Coca Ecuador 142 C4
Coca Spain 57 D3
Cocalinho Brazil 145 A1
Cocanada India *see* Kakinada
Cochabamba Bol. 142 E7
Cochem Germany 53 H4
Cochin India 84 C4
Cochin *reg.* Vietnam 71 D5
Cochinos, Bahía de *b.* Cuba *see* Pigs, Bay of
Cochise U.S.A. 129 I5
Cochise Head *mt.* U.S.A. 129 I5
Cochrane *Alta* Canada 120 H5
Cochrane *Ont.* Canada 122 E4
Cochrane *r.* Canada 121 K3
Cockburn Australia 111 C7
Cockburnspath U.K. 50 G5
Cockburn Town Bahamas 133 F7
Cockburn Town Turks and Caicos Is *see* Grand Turk
Cockermouth U.K. 48 D4
Cocklebiddy Australia 109 D8
Cockscomb *mt.* S. Africa 100 G7
Coco *r.* Hond./Nicaragua 137 H6
Coco, Cayo *i.* Cuba 133 E8
Coco, Isla de *i.* N. Pacific Ocean 137 G7
Cocobeach Gabon 98 A3
Coco Channel India 71 A4
Cocomórachic Mex. 127 G7
Coconino Plateau U.S.A. 129 G4
Cocopara National Park Australia 112 C5
Cocos Brazil 145 B1
Cocos Basin *sea feature* Indian Ocean 149 O5

▶Cocos Islands *terr.* Indian Ocean 68 B9
Australian External Territory.

Cocos Ridge *sea feature* N. Pacific Ocean 151 O5
Cocuy, Sierra Nevada del *mt.* Col. 142 D2
Cod, Cape U.S.A. 135 J3
Codajás Brazil 142 F4
Coderre Canada 121 J5
Codfish Island N.Z. 113 A8
Codigoro Italy 58 E2
Cod Island Canada 123 J2
Codlea Romania 59 K2
Codó Brazil 143 J4
Codsall U.K. 49 E6
Cod's Head *hd* Ireland 51 B6
Cody U.S.A. 126 F3
Coeburn U.S.A. 134 D5
Coen Australia 110 C2
Coesfeld Germany 53 H3
Coeur d'Alene U.S.A. 126 D3
Coeur d'Alene Lake U.S.A. 126 D3
Coevorden Neth. 52 G2
Coffee Bay S. Africa 101 I6
Coffeyville U.S.A. 131 E4
Coffin Bay Australia 111 A7
Coffin Bay National Park Australia 111 A7
Coffs Harbour Australia 112 F3
Cofimvaba S. Africa 101 H7
Cognac France 56 D4
Cogo Equat. Guinea 96 D4
Coguno Moz. 101 L3
Cohoes U.S.A. 135 I2
Cohuna Australia 112 B5
Coiba, Isla de *i.* Panama 137 H7
Coigeach, Rubha *pt* U.K. 50 D2
Coihaique Chile 144 B7
Coimbatore India 84 C4
Coimbra Port. 57 B3
Coipasa, Salar de *salt flat* Bol. 142 E7
Coire Switz. *see* Chur
Colac Australia 112 A7
Colair Lake India *see* Kolleru Lake
Colatina Brazil 145 C2
Colbitz Germany 53 L2
Colborne Canada 135 G2
Colby U.S.A. 130 C4
Colchester U.K. 49 H7
Colchester U.S.A. 135 I3
Cold Bay U.S.A. 118 B4
Coldingham U.K. 50 G5
Colditz Germany 53 M3
Cold Lake Canada 121 I4
Cold Lake *l.* Canada 121 I4
Coldspring U.S.A. 131 E6
Coldstream Canada 120 G5
Coldstream U.K. 50 G5
Coldwater Canada 134 F1
Coldwater *KS* U.S.A. 131 D4
Coldwater *MI* U.S.A. 134 C3
Coldwater *r.* U.S.A. 131 F5
Coleambally Australia 112 B5
Colebrook U.S.A. 135 J1
Coleman *r.* Australia 110 C2
Coleman U.S.A. 131 D6
Çölemerik Turkey *see* Hakkârı
Colenso S. Africa 101 I5
Cole Peninsula Antarctica 152 L2
Coleraine Australia 111 C8
Coleraine U.K. 51 F2
Coles, Punta de *pt* Peru 142 D7
Coles Bay Australia 111 [inset]
Colesberg S. Africa 101 G6
Coleville Canada 121 I5
Colfax *CA* U.S.A. 128 C2
Colfax *LA* U.S.A. 131 E6
Colfax *WA* U.S.A. 126 D3
Colhué Huapí, Lago *l.* Arg. 144 C7
Coligny S. Africa 101 H4
Colima Mex. 136 D5
Colima, Nevado de *vol.* Mex. 136 D5
Coll *i.* U.K. 50 C4
Collado Villalba Spain 57 E3
Collarenebri Australia 112 D2
College Station U.S.A. 131 D6
Collerina Australia 112 C2
Collie *N.S.W.* Australia 112 D3
Collie *W.A.* Australia 109 B8
Collier Bay Australia 108 D4
Collier Range National Park Australia 109 B6
Collingwood Canada 134 E1
Collingwood N.Z. 113 D5
Collins U.S.A. 131 F6
Collins Glacier Antarctica 152 E2
Collinson Peninsula Canada 119 H2
Collipulli Chile 144 B5
Collmberg *hill* Germany 53 N3
Collooney Ireland 51 D3
Colmar France 56 H2
Colmenar Viejo Spain 57 E3
Colmonell U.K. 50 E5
Colne *r.* U.K. 49 H7
Cologne Germany 52 G4
Coloma U.S.A. 134 B2
Colomb-Béchar Alg. *see* Béchar
Colômbia Brazil 145 A3
Colombia Mex. 131 D7

▶Colombia *country* S. America 142 D3
2nd most populous and 4th largest count in South America.

Colombian Basin *sea feature* S. Atlantic Ocean 148 C5

▶Colombo Sri Lanka 84 C5
Former capital of Sri Lanka.

Colomiers France 56 E5
Colón *Buenos Aires* Arg. 144 D4
Colón *Entre Ríos* Arg. 144 E4
Colón Cuba 133 D8
Colón Panama 137 I7
Colon U.S.A. 134 C3
Colón, Archipiélago de *is* Ecuador *see* Galapagos Islands
Colona Australia 109 F7
Colonelganj India 83 E4
Colonel Hill Bahamas 133 F8
Colonet, Cabo *c.* Mex. 127 D7
Colônia *r.* Brazil 145 D1
Colonia Micronesia 69 J5
Colonia Agrippina Germany *see* Cologne
Colonia Díaz Mex. 127 F7
Colonia Julia Fenestris Italy *see* Fano
Colonia Las Heras Arg. 144 C7
Colonial Heights U.S.A. 135 G5
Colonna, Capo *c.* Italy 58 G5
Colonsay *i.* U.K. 50 C4
Colorado *r.* Arg. 144 D5
Colorado *r.* Mex./U.S.A. 127 E7
Colorado *r.* U.S.A. 131 D6
Colorado *state* U.S.A. 126 G5
Colorado City *AZ* U.S.A. 129 G3
Colorado City *TX* U.S.A. 131 C5
Colorado Desert U.S.A. 128 E5
Colorado National Monument *nat. park* U.S.A. 129 I2
Colorado Plateau U.S.A. 129 I3
Colorado River Aqueduct *canal* U.S.A. 129 F4
Colorado Springs U.S.A. 126 G5
Colossae Turkey *see* Honaz
Colotlán Mex. 136 D4
Cölpin Germany 53 N1
Colquiri Bol. 142 E7
Colquitt U.S.A. 133 C6
Colson U.S.A. 134 D5
Colsterworth U.K. 49 G6
Colstrip U.S.A. 126 G3
Coltishall U.K. 49 I6
Colton *CA* U.S.A. 128 E4
Colton *NY* U.S.A. 135 H1
Colton *UT* U.S.A. 129 H2
Columbia *KY* U.S.A. 134 C5
Columbia *LA* U.S.A. 131 E5
Columbia *MD* U.S.A. 135 G4
Columbia *MO* U.S.A. 130 E4
Columbia *MS* U.S.A. 131 F6
Columbia *NC* U.S.A. 132 E5
Columbia *PA* U.S.A. 135 G3

▶Columbia *SC* U.S.A. 133 D5
Capital of South Carolina.

Columbia *TN* U.S.A. 132 C5
Columbia *r.* U.S.A. 126 C3
Columbia, District of *admin. dist.* U.S.A. 135 G4
Columbia, Mount Canada 120 G4
Columbia, Sierra *mts* Mex. 127 E7
Columbia City U.S.A. 134 C3
Columbia Lake Canada 120 H5
Columbia Mountains Canada 120 F4
Columbia Plateau U.S.A. 126 D3
Columbine, Cape S. Africa 100 C7
Columbus *GA* U.S.A. 133 C5
Columbus *IN* U.S.A. 134 C4
Columbus *MS* U.S.A. 131 F5
Columbus *MT* U.S.A. 126 F3
Columbus *NC* U.S.A. 133 D5
Columbus *NE* U.S.A. 130 D3
Columbus *NM* U.S.A. 127 G7

▶Columbus *OH* U.S.A. 134 D4
Capital of Ohio.

Columbus *TX* U.S.A. 131 D6
Columbus Grove U.S.A. 134 C3
Columbus Salt Marsh U.S.A. 128 D2
Colusa U.S.A. 128 B2
Colville N.Z. 113 E3
Colville U.S.A. 126 D2
Colville *r.* U.S.A. 118 C2
Colville Channel N.Z. 113 E3
Colville Lake Canada 118 F3
Colwyn Bay U.K. 48 D5
Comacchio Italy 58 E2
Comacchio, Valli di *lag.* Italy 58 E2
Comai China 83 G3
Comalcalco Mex. 136 F5
Comanche U.S.A. 131 D6
Comandante Ferraz *research station* Antarctica 152 A2
Comandante Salas Arg. 144 C4
Comăneşti Romania 59 L1
Combahee *r.* U.S.A. 133 D5
Combarbalá Chile 144 B4
Comber U.K. 51 G3
Combermere Bay Myanmar 70 A3
Combles France 52 C4
Combol *i.* Indon. 71 C7

mbomune Moz. 101 K2
mboyne Australia 112 F3
mencho, Lac *l.* Canada 122 G4
mendador Dom. Rep. *see* **Elías Piña**
mendador Gomes Brazil 145 A2
meragh Mountains *hills* Ireland 51 E5
mercinho Brazil 145 C2
metela Moz. 101 L1
mfort U.S.A. 131 D6
milla Bangl. 83 G5
mines Belgium 52 C4
mino, Capo *c. Sardinia* Italy 58 C4
mitán de Domínguez Mex. 136 F5
mmack U.S.A. 135 I3
mmentry France 56 F3
mmittee Bay Canada 119 J3
mmonwealth Territory *admin. div.*
ustralia *see* **Jervis Bay Territory**
mo Italy 58 C2
mo, Lago di Italy *see* **Como, Lake**
mo, Lake Italy 58 C2
mo Chamling *l.* China 83 G3
modoro Rivadavia Arg. 144 C7
mores *country* Africa *see* **Comoros**
morin, Cape India 84 C4
moro Islands *country* Africa *see*
omoros
moros *country* Africa 99 E5
mpiègne France 52 C5
mprida, Ilha *i.* Brazil 145 B4
mrat Moldova 59 M1
mrie U.K. 50 F4
mstock U.S.A. 131 C6
, Sông *r.* Vietnam 71 E4
a China 83 G4

onakry Guinea 96 B4
apital of Guinea.

a Niyeo Arg. 144 C6
ceição *r.* Brazil 145 B2
ceição da Barra Brazil 145 D2
ceição do Araguaia Brazil 143 I5
ceição do Mato Dentro Brazil 145 C2
cepción Chile 144 B5
cepción Mex. 131 C7
cepción *r.* Mex. 127 E7
cepción Para. 144 E2
cepción, Punta *pt* Mex. 127 F8
cepción de la Vega Dom. Rep. *see*
Vega
ception, Point U.S.A. 128 C4
ception Island Bahamas 133 F8
chas U.S.A. 127 G6
chas Lake U.S.A. 127 G6
cho U.S.A. 129 I4
chos *r. Nuevo León/Tamaulipas* Mex.
31 D7
chos *r.* Mex. 131 B6
cord *CA* U.S.A. 128 B3
cord *NC* U.S.A. 133 D5

oncord *NH* U.S.A. 135 J2
apital of New Hampshire.

cord *VT* U.S.A. 135 J1
cordia Arg. 144 E4
cordiá Mex. 131 B8
cordia Peru 142 D4
cordia S. Africa 100 C5
cordia *KS* U.S.A. 130 D4
cordia *KY* U.S.A. 134 B4
cordia *research stn* 152 G2
cord Peak Afgh. 89 I2
Cuông Vietnam 70 D3
damine Australia 112 E1
damine *r.* Australia 112 D1
Đao Vietnam 71 D5
deúba Brazil 145 C1
dobolin Australia 112 C4
dom France 56 E5
don U.S.A. 126 C3
dor, Cordillera del *mts* Ecuador/Peru
42 C4
droz *reg.* Belgium 52 E4
ecuh *r.* U.S.A. 133 C6
egliano Italy 58 E2
ejos Mex. 131 C7
ejos U.S.A. 127 G5
emaugh *r.* U.S.A. 134 F3
estogo Lake Canada 134 E2
esus Lake U.S.A. 135 G2
flict Group *is* P.N.G. 110 E1
foederatio Helvetica *country* Europe
e **Switzerland**
fusion Range *mts* U.S.A. 129 G2
gdü China 83 F3
ghua China 77 G4
gjiang China 77 F3
gleton U.K. 48 E5
go *country* Africa 98 B4

ongo *r.* Congo/Dem. Rep. Congo 98 B4
nd longest river in Africa, and 8th in
e world.
ormerly known as Zaïre.

go (Brazzaville) *country* Africa *see*
ongo
go (Kinshasa) *country* Africa *see*
ongo, Democratic Republic of the

ongo, Democratic Republic of the
untry Africa 98 C4
d largest and 4th most populous country
Africa.

go, Republic of *country* Africa *see*
ongo
go Basin Dem. Rep. Congo 98 C4
go Cone *sea feature* S. Atlantic Ocean
8 I6
go Free State *country* Africa *see*
ongo, Democratic Republic of the
gonhas Brazil 145 C3
gress U.S.A. 129 G4
mbla National Park Australia 112 D4
ingsby U.K. 49 G5
iston Canada 122 E5
iston U.K. 48 D4
juboy Australia 110 D3
klin Canada 121 I4

Conn *r.* Canada 122 F3
Conn, Lough *l.* Ireland 51 C3
Connacht *reg.* Ireland *see* **Connaught**
Connaught *reg.* Ireland 51 C4
Conneaut U.S.A. 134 E3
Connecticut *state* U.S.A. 135 I3
Connemara *reg.* Ireland 51 C4
Connemara National Park Ireland 51 C4
Connersville U.S.A. 134 C4
Connolly, Mount Canada 120 C2
Connors Range *hills* Australia 110 E4
Conoble Australia 112 B4
Conquista Brazil 145 B2
Conrad U.S.A. 126 F2
Conrad Rise *sea feature* Southern Ocean
149 K9
Conroe U.S.A. 131 E6
Conselheiro Lafaiete Brazil 145 C3
Consett U.K. 48 F4
Consolación del Sur Cuba 133 D8
Côn Sơn, Đao *i.* Vietnam 71 D5
Consort Canada 121 I4
Constance Germany *see* **Konstanz**
Constance, Lake Germany/Switz. 47 L7
Constância dos Baetas Brazil 142 F5
Constanța Romania 59 M2
Constantia *tourist site* Cyprus *see* **Salamis**
Constantia Germany *see* **Konstanz**
Constantina Spain 57 D5
Constantine Alg. 54 F4
Constantine, Cape U.S.A. 118 C4
Constantinople Turkey *see* **İstanbul**
Constitución de 1857, Parque Nacional
nat. park Mex. 129 F5
Consul Canada 121 I5
Contact U.S.A. 126 E4
Contagalo Brazil 145 C3
Contamana Peru 142 C5
Contas *r.* Brazil 145 D1
Contoy, Isla *i.* Mex. 133 C8
Contria Brazil 145 B2
Contwoyto Lake Canada 121 I1
Convención Col. 142 D2
Convent U.S.A. 131 F6
Conway U.K. *see* **Conwy**
Conway *AR* U.S.A. 131 E5
Conway *ND* U.S.A. 130 D1
Conway *NH* U.S.A. 135 J2
Conway *SC* U.S.A. 133 E5
Conway, Cape Australia 110 E4
Conway, Lake *salt flat* Australia 111 A6
Conway National Park Australia 110 E4
Conway Reef Fiji *see* **Ceva-i-Ra**
Conwy U.K. 48 D5
Conwy *r.* U.K. 49 D5
Coober Pedy Australia 109 F7
Cooch Behar India *see* **Koch Bihar**
Coochbehar India *see* **Koch Bihar**
Cook Australia 109 E7
Cook, Cape Canada 120 E5
Cook, Grand Récif de *reef* New Caledonia
107 G3
Cook, Mount *mt.* N.Z. *see* **Aoraki**
Cookes Peak U.S.A. 127 G6
Cookeville U.S.A. 132 C4
Cookhouse S. Africa 101 G7
Cook Ice Shelf Antarctica 152 H2
Cook Inlet *sea chan.* U.S.A. 118 C3

▶**Cook Islands** *terr.* S. Pacific Ocean 150 J7
Self-governing New Zealand Territory.

Cooksburg U.S.A. 135 H2
Cooks Passage Australia 110 D2
Cookstown U.K. 51 F3
Cook Strait N.Z. 113 E5
Cooktown Australia 110 D2
Coolabah Australia 112 C3
Cooladdi Australia 112 B1
Coolah Australia 112 D3
Coolamon Australia 112 C5
Coolgardie Australia 109 C7
Coolibah Australia 108 E3
Coolidge U.S.A. 129 H5
Cooloola National Park Australia 111 F5
Coolum Beach Australia 111 F5
Cooma Australia 112 D6
Coombah Australia 111 C7
Coonabarabran Australia 112 D3
Coonamble Australia 112 D3
Coondambo Australia 111 A6
Coondapoor India *see* **Kundapura**
Coongoola Australia 112 B1
Coon Rapids U.S.A. 130 E2
Cooper Creek *watercourse* Australia 111 B6
Cooper Mountain Canada 120 G5
Coopernook Australia 112 F3
Cooper's Town Bahamas 133 E7
Cooperstown *ND* U.S.A. 130 D2
Cooperstown *NY* U.S.A. 135 H2
Coopracambra National Park Australia
112 D6
Coorabie Australia 109 F7
Coorong National Park Australia 111 B8
Coorow Australia 109 B7
Coosa *r.* U.S.A. 133 C5
Coos Bay U.S.A. 126 B4
Coos Bay *b.* U.S.A. 126 B4
Cootamundra Australia 112 D5
Cootehill Ireland 51 E3
Cooyar Australia 112 E1
Copala Mex. 136 E5
Cope U.S.A. 130 C4
Copemish U.S.A. 134 C1

▶**Copenhagen** Denmark 45 H9
Capital of Denmark.

Copenhagen U.S.A. 135 H2
Copertino Italy 58 H4
Copeton Reservoir Australia 112 E2
Cô Pi, Phou *mt.* Laos/Vietnam 70 D3
Copiapó Chile 144 B3
Copley Australia 111 B6
Copparo Italy 58 D2
Copper Cliff Canada 122 E5
Copper Harbor U.S.A. 132 C2
Coppermine Canada *see* **Kugluktuk**
Coppermine *r.* Canada 120 H1
Coppermine Point Canada 122 D5
Copperton S. Africa 100 F5
Copp Lake Canada 120 H2

Coqên China 83 F3
Coqên *Xizang* China 83 F3
Coquilhatville Dem. Rep. Congo *see*
Mbandaka
Coquille *i.* Micronesia *see* **Pikelot**
Coquille U.S.A. 126 B4
Coquimbo Chile 144 B3
Coquitlam Canada 120 F5
Corabia Romania 59 K3
Coração de Jesus Brazil 145 B2
Coracesium Turkey *see* **Alanya**
Coraki Australia 112 F2
Coral Bay Australia 109 A5
Coral Harbour Canada 119 J3
Coral Sea S. Pacific Ocean 106 F3
Coral Sea Basin S. Pacific Ocean 150 G6

▶**Coral Sea Islands Territory** *terr.* Australia
106 F3
Australian External Territory.

Corangamite, Lake Australia 112 A7
Corat Azer. 91 H2
Corbeny France 52 D5
Corbett Inlet Canada 121 M2
Corbett National Park India 82 D3
Corbie France 52 C5
Corbin U.S.A. 134 C5
Corby U.K. 49 G6
Corcaigh Ireland *see* **Cork**
Corcoran U.S.A. 128 D3
Corcovado, Golfo de *sea chan.* Chile
144 B6
Corcyra *i.* Greece *see* **Corfu**
Cordele U.S.A. 133 D6
Cordelia U.S.A. 128 B2
Cordell U.S.A. 131 D5
Cordilheiras, Serra das *hills* Brazil 143 I5
Cordillera Azul, Parque Nacional *nat. park*
Peru 142 C5
Cordillera de los Picachos, Parque
Nacional *nat. park* Col. 142 D3
Cordillo Downs Australia 111 C5
Cordisburgo Brazil 145 B2
Córdoba Arg. 144 D4
Córdoba *Durango* Mex. 131 C7
Córdoba *Veracruz* Mex. 136 E5
Córdoba Spain 57 D5
Córdoba, Sierras de *mts* Arg. 144 D4
Cordova Spain *see* **Córdoba**
Cordova U.S.A. 118 D3
Corduba Spain *see* **Córdoba**
Corfu *i.* Greece 59 H5
Coria Spain 57 C4
Coribe Brazil 145 B1
Coricudgy *mt.* Australia 112 E4
Corigliano Calabro Italy 58 G5
Coringa Islands Australia 110 E3
Corinium U.K. *see* **Cirencester**
Corinth Greece 59 J6
Corinth *KY* U.S.A. 134 C4
Corinth *MS* U.S.A. 131 F5
Corinth *NY* U.S.A. 135 I2
Corinth, Gulf of *sea chan.* Greece 59 J5
Corinthus Greece *see* **Corinth**
Corinto Brazil 145 B2
Cork Ireland 51 D6
Corleone *Sicily* Italy 58 E6
Çorlu Turkey 59 L4
Cormeilles France 49 H9
Cornelia S. Africa 101 I4
Cornélio Procópio Brazil 145 A3
Cornélios Brazil 145 A5
Cornell U.S.A. 130 F2
Corner Brook Canada 123 K4
Corner Inlet *b.* Australia 112 C7
Corner Seamounts *sea feature*
N. Atlantic Ocean 148 E3
Corneto Italy *see* **Tarquinia**
Cornillet, Mont *hill* France 52 E5
Corning *AR* U.S.A. 131 F4
Corning *CA* U.S.A. 128 B2
Corning *NY* U.S.A. 135 G2
Cornish *watercourse* Australia 110 D4
Corn Islands *is* Nicaragua *see*
Maíz, Islas del
Corno, Monte *mt.* Italy 58 E3
Corno di Campo *mt.* Italy/Switz. 56 J3
Cornwall Canada 135 H1
Cornwallis Island Canada 119 I2
Cornwall Island Canada 119 I2
Coro Venez. 142 E1
Coroaci Brazil 145 C2
Coroatá Brazil 143 J4
Corofin Ireland 51 C5
Coromandel Brazil 145 B2
Coromandel Coast India 84 D4
Coromandel Peninsula N.Z. 113 E3
Coromandel Range *hills* N.Z. 113 E3
Corona *CA* U.S.A. 128 E5
Corona *NM* U.S.A. 127 G6
Coronado U.S.A. 128 E5
Coronado, Bahía de *b.* Costa Rica 137 H7
Coronation Canada 121 I4
Coronation Gulf Canada 118 G3
Coronation Island S. Atlantic Ocean 152 A2
Coronda Arg. 144 D4
Coronel Fabriciano Brazil 145 C2
Coronel Oviedo Para. 144 E3
Coronel Pringles Arg. 144 D5
Coronel Suárez Arg. 144 D5
Çorovodë Albania 59 I4
Corowa Australia 112 C5
Corpus Christi U.S.A. 131 D7
Corque Bol. 142 E7
Corral de Cantos *mt.* Spain 57 D4
Corrales Mex. 131 B7
Corralilla Cuba 133 D8
Corrandibby Range *hills* Australia 109 A6
Corrente Brazil 143 I6
Corrente *r. Bahia* Brazil 145 C1
Corrente *r. Minas Gerais* Brazil 145 A2
Correntes Brazil 143 H7
Correntina Brazil 145 B1
Correntina *r.* Brazil *see* **Éguas**
Corrib, Lough *l.* Ireland 51 C4
Corrientes Arg. 144 E3
Corrientes, Cabo *c.* Col. 142 C2
Corrientes, Cabo *c.* Cuba 133 C8
Corrientes, Cabo *c.* Mex. 136 C4
Corrigin Australia 109 B8
Corris U.K. 49 D6

Corry U.S.A. 134 F3
Corse *i.* France *see* **Corsica**
Corse, Cap *c. Corsica* France 56 I5
Corsham U.K. 49 E7
Corsica *i.* France 56 I5
Corsicana U.S.A. 131 D5
Corte *Corsica* France 56 I5
Cortegana Spain 57 C5
Cortes, Sea of *g.* Mex. *see*
California, Golfo de
Cortez U.S.A. 129 I3
Cortina d'Ampezzo Italy 58 E1
Cortland U.S.A. 135 G2
Corton U.K. 49 I6
Cortona Italy 58 D3
Coruche Port. 57 B4
Çoruh Turkey *see* **Artvin**
Çoruh *r.* Turkey 91 F2
Çorum Turkey 90 D2
Corumbá Brazil 143 G7
Corumbá *r.* Brazil 145 A2
Corumbá de Goiás Brazil 145 A1
Corumbaíba Brazil 145 A2
Corumbaú, Ponta *pt* Brazil 145 D2
Corunna Spain *see* **A Coruña**
Corunna U.S.A. 134 C2
Corvallis U.S.A. 126 C3
Corwen U.K. 49 D6
Corydon *IA* U.S.A. 130 E3
Corydon *IN* U.S.A. 134 B4
Coryville U.S.A. 135 F3
Cos *i.* Greece *see* **Kos**
Cosentia Italy *see* **Cosenza**
Cosenza Italy 58 G5
Coshocton U.S.A. 134 E3
Cosne-Cours-sur-Loire France 56 F3
Costa Blanca *coastal area* Spain 57 F4
Costa Brava *coastal area* Spain 57 H3
Costa de la Luz *coastal area* Spain 57 C5
Costa del Sol *coastal area* Spain 57 D5
Costa de Miskitos *coastal area* Nicaragua
see **Costa de Mosquitos**
Costa de Mosquitos *coastal area* Nicaragua
137 H6
Costa Marques Brazil 142 F6
Costa Rica Brazil 143 H7
Costa Rica *country* Central America 137 H6
Costa Rica Mex. 136 C4
Costa Verde *coastal area* Spain 57 C2
Costermansville Dem. Rep. Congo *see*
Bukavu
Costești Romania 59 K2
Costigan Lake Canada 121 J3
Coswig Germany 53 M3
Cotabato Phil. 69 G5
Cotagaita Bol. 142 E8
Cotahuasi Peru 142 D7
Cote, Mount U.S.A. 120 D3
Coteau des Prairies *slope* U.S.A. 130 D2
Coteau du Missouri *slope ND* U.S.A.
130 C1
Coteau du Missouri *slope SD* U.S.A. 130 C2
Côte d'Azur *coastal area* France 56 H5
Côte d'Ivoire *country* Africa 96 C4
Côte Française de Somalis *country* Africa
see **Djibouti**
Cotentin *pen.* France 49 F9
Côtes de Meuse *ridge* France 52 E5
Cothi *r.* U.K. 49 C7
Cotiaeum Turkey *see* **Kütahya**
Cotiella *mt.* Spain 57 G2
Cotonou Benin 96 D4
Cotopaxi, Volcán *vol.* Ecuador 142 C4
Cotswold Hills U.K. 49 E7
Cottage Grove U.S.A. 126 C4
Cottbus Germany 47 O5
Cottenham U.K. 49 H6
Cottian Alps *mts* France/Italy 56 H4
Cottica Suriname 143 H3
Cottiennes, Alpes *mts* France/Italy *see*
Cottian Alps
Cottonwood *AZ* U.S.A. 129 G4
Cottonwood *CA* U.S.A. 128 B1
Cottonwood *r.* U.S.A. 130 D4
Cottonwood Falls U.S.A. 130 D4
Cotulla U.S.A. 131 D6
Coudersport U.S.A. 135 F3
Couedic, Cape du Australia 111 B8
Coulee City U.S.A. 126 D3
Coulee Dam U.S.A. 126 D3
Coulman Island Antarctica 152 H2
Coulogne France 52 B4
Coulommiers France 52 D6
Coulonge *r.* Canada 122 F5
Coulterville U.S.A. 128 C3
Council U.S.A. 126 D3
Council Bluffs U.S.A. 130 E3
Council Grove U.S.A. 130 D4
Councillor Island Australia 111 [inset]
Counselor U.S.A. 129 J3
Coupeville U.S.A. 126 C2
Courageous Lake Canada 121 I1
Courland Lagoon *b.* Lith./Rus. Fed. 45 L9
Courtenay Canada 120 E5
Courtland U.S.A. 135 G5
Courtmacsherry Ireland 51 D6
Courtmacsherry Bay Ireland 51 D6
Courtown Ireland 51 F5
Courtrai Belgium *see* **Kortrijk**
Coushatta U.S.A. 131 E5
Coutances France 56 D2
Coutts Canada 121 I5
Couture, Lac *l.* Canada 122 G2
Couvin Belgium 52 E4
Cove Fort U.S.A. 129 G2
Cove Island Canada 134 E1
Cove Mountains *hills* U.S.A. 135 F4
Coventry U.K. 49 F6
Covered Wells U.S.A. 129 G5
Covesville U.S.A. 135 F5
Covilhã Port. 57 C3
Covington *GA* U.S.A. 133 D5
Covington *IN* U.S.A. 134 B3
Covington *KY* U.S.A. 134 C4
Covington *LA* U.S.A. 131 F6
Covington *MI* U.S.A. 130 F2
Covington *TN* U.S.A. 131 F5
Covington *VA* U.S.A. 134 E5
Cowal, Lake *dry lake* Australia 112 C4
Cowan, Lake *salt flat* Australia 109 C7
Cowansville Canada 135 I1
Cowargarzê China 76 C1

Cowcowing Lakes *salt flat*
Australia 109 B7
Cowdenbeath U.K. 50 F4
Cowell Australia 111 B7
Cowes U.K. 49 F8
Cowichan Lake Canada 120 E5
Cowley Australia 112 B1
Cowper Point Canada 119 G2
Cowra Australia 112 D4
Cox *r.* Australia 110 A2
Coxá *r.* Brazil 145 B1
Coxen Hole Hond. *see* **Roatán**
Coxilha de Santana *hills* Brazil/Uruguay
144 E4
Coxilha Grande *hills* Brazil 144 F3
Coxim Brazil 143 H7
Cox's Bazar Bangl. 83 G5
Coyame Mex. 131 B6
Coyhaique Chile *see* **Coihaique**
Coyote Lake U.S.A. 128 E4
Coyote Peak *hill* U.S.A. 129 F5
Cozhê China 83 F2
Cozie, Alpi *mts* France/Italy *see* **Cottian Alps**
Cozumel Mex. 137 G4
Cozumel, Isla de *i.* Mex. 137 G4
Craboon Australia 112 D4
Cracovia Poland *see* **Kraków**
Cracow Australia 110 E5
Cracow Poland *see* **Kraków**
Cradle Mountain Lake St Clair National
Park Australia 111 [inset]
Cradock S. Africa 101 G7
Craig U.K. 50 D3
Craig *AK* U.S.A. 120 C4
Craig *CO* U.S.A. 129 J1
Craigavon U.K. 51 F3
Craigieburn Australia 112 B6
Craig Island Taiwan *see* **Mienhua Yü**
Craignure U.K. 50 D4
Craigsville U.S.A. 134 E4
Crail U.K. 50 G4
Crailsheim Germany 53 K5
Craiova Romania 59 J2
Cramlington U.K. 48 F3
Cranberry Lake U.S.A. 135 H1
Cranberry Portage Canada 121 K4
Cranborne Chase *for.* U.K. 49 E8
Cranbourne Australia 112 B7
Cranbrook Canada 120 H5
Crandon U.S.A. 130 F2
Crane Lake Canada 121 I5
Cranston *KY* U.S.A. 134 D4
Cranston *RI* U.S.A. 135 J3
Cranz Rus. Fed. *see* **Zelenogradsk**
Crary Ice Rise Antarctica 152 I1
Crary Mountains Antarctica 152 J1
Crater Lake National Park U.S.A. 126 C4
Crater Peak U.S.A. 128 C1
Craters of the Moon National Monument
nat. park U.S.A. 126 E4
Crateús Brazil 143 J5
Crato Brazil 143 K5
Crawford *CO* U.S.A. 129 J2
Crawford *NE* U.S.A. 130 C3
Crawfordsville U.S.A. 134 B3
Crawfordville *FL* U.S.A. 133 C6
Crawfordville *GA* U.S.A. 133 D5
Crawley U.K. 49 G7
Crazy Mountains U.S.A. 126 F3
Creag Meagaidh *mt.* U.K. 50 E4
Crécy-en-Ponthieu France 52 B4
Credenhill U.K. 49 E6
Crediton U.K. 49 D8
Cree *r.* Canada 121 J3
Creel Mex. 127 G8
Cree Lake Canada 121 J3
Creemore Canada 134 E1
Creighton Canada 121 K4
Creil France 52 C5
Creil Neth. 52 F2
Crema Italy 58 C2
Cremlingen Germany 53 K2
Cremona Canada 120 H5
Cremona Italy 58 D2
Crépy-en-Valois France 52 C5
Cres *i.* Croatia 58 F2
Crescent U.S.A. 126 C4
Crescent City *CA* U.S.A. 126 B4
Crescent City *FL* U.S.A. 133 D6
Crescent Group *is* Paracel Is 68 E3
Crescent Head Australia 112 F3
Crescent Junction U.S.A. 129 I2
Crescent Valley U.S.A. 128 E1
Cressy Australia 112 A7
Crest Hill *hill H.K.* China 77 [inset]
Crestline U.S.A. 134 D3
Creston Canada 120 G5
Creston *IA* U.S.A. 130 E3
Creston *WY* U.S.A. 126 G4
Crestview U.S.A. 133 C6
Creswick Australia 112 A6
Creta *i.* Greece *see* **Crete**
Crete *i.* Greece 59 K7
Crete U.S.A. 130 D3
Creus, Cap de *c.* Spain 57 H2
Creuse *r.* France 56 E3
Creußen Germany 53 L5
Creutzwald France 52 G5
Creuzburg Germany 53 K3
Crevasse Valley Glacier Antarctica 152 J1
Crewe U.K. 49 E5
Crewe U.S.A. 135 F5
Crewkerne U.K. 49 E8
Crianlarich U.K. 50 E4
Criccieth U.K. 49 C6
Criciúma Brazil 145 A5
Crieff U.K. 50 F4
Criffel *hill* U.K. 50 F6
Criffell *hill* U.K. *see* **Criffel**
Crikvenica Croatia 58 F2
Crillon, Mount U.S.A. 120 B3
Crimea *pen.* Ukr. 90 D1
Crimmitschau Germany 53 M4
Crimond U.K. 50 H3
Crisfield U.S.A. 135 H5
Cristalândia Brazil 143 I6
Cristalina Brazil 145 B2
Cristalino *r.* Brazil *see* **Mariembero**
Cristóbal Colón, Pico *mt.* Col. 142 D1
Crixás Brazil 145 A1
Crixás Açu *r.* Brazil 145 A1
Crixás Mirim *r.* Brazil 145 A1

Crna Gora *country* Europe *see* **Montenegro**
Crni Vrh *mt.* Serbia 59 J2
Črnomelj Slovenia 58 F2
Croagh Patrick *hill* Ireland 51 C4
Croajingolong National Park Australia
112 D6
Croatia *country* Europe 58 G2
Crocker, Banjaran *mts* Malaysia 68 E6
Crockett U.S.A. 131 E6
Crofton *KY* U.S.A. 134 B5
Crofton *NE* U.S.A. 130 D3
Croghan U.S.A. 135 H2
Croisilles France 52 C4
Croker, Cape Canada 134 E1
Croker Island Australia 108 F2
Cromarty U.K. 50 E3
Cromarty Firth *est.* U.K. 50 E3
Cromer U.K. 49 I6
Crook U.K. 48 F4
Crooked Harbour *b. H.K.* China 77 [inset]
Crooked Island Bahamas 133 F8
Crooked Island *H.K.* China 77 [inset]
Crooked Island Passage Bahamas 133 F8
Crookston U.S.A. 130 D2
Crooksville U.S.A. 134 D4
Crookwell Australia 112 D5
Croom Ireland 51 D5
Croppa Creek Australia 112 E2
Crosby U.K. 48 D5
Crosby *MN* U.S.A. 130 E2
Crosby *ND* U.S.A. 130 C1
Crosbyton U.S.A. 131 C5
Cross Bay Canada 121 M2
Cross City U.S.A. 133 D6
Cross Fell *hill* U.K. 48 E4
Crossfield Canada 120 H5
Crossgar U.K. 51 G3
Crosshaven Ireland 51 D6
Cross Inn U.K. 49 C6
Cross Lake Canada 121 L4
Cross Lake *l.* Canada 121 L4
Cross Lake *l.* U.S.A. 135 G2
Crossmaglen U.K. 51 F3
Crossman Peak U.S.A. 129 F4
Crossville U.S.A. 132 C5
Crotch Lake Canada 135 G1
Croton Italy *see* **Crotone**
Crotone Italy 58 G5
Crouch *r.* U.K. 49 H7
Crow *r.* Canada 120 E3
Crow Agency U.S.A. 126 G3
Crowal *watercourse* Australia 112 C3
Crowborough U.K. 49 H7
Crowdy Bay National Park
Australia 112 F3
Crowell U.S.A. 131 D5
Crowland U.K. 49 G6
Crowley U.S.A. 131 E6
Crowley, Lake U.S.A. 128 D3
Crown Point *IN* U.S.A. 134 B3
Crownpoint U.S.A. 129 I4
Crown Point *NY* U.S.A. 135 I2
Crown Prince Olav Coast
Antarctica 152 D2
Crown Princess Martha Coast
Antarctica 152 B1
Crows Nest Australia 112 F1
Crowsnest Pass Canada 120 H5
Crowsnest Pass *pass* Canada 120 H5
Crow Wing *r.* U.S.A. 130 E2
Croydon Australia 110 C3
Crozet U.S.A. 135 F4
Crozet, Îles *is* Indian Ocean 149 L9
Crozet Basin *sea feature* Indian Ocean
149 M8
Crozet Plateau *sea feature* Indian Ocean
149 K8
Crozon France 56 B2
Cruces Cuba 133 D8
Cruden Bay U.K. 50 H3
Cruillas Mex. 131 D7
Crum U.S.A. 134 D5
Crumlin U.K. 51 F3
Crusheen Ireland 51 D5
Cruz Alta Brazil 144 F3
Cruz del Eje Arg. 144 D4
Cruzeiro Brazil 145 B3
Cruzeiro do Sul Brazil 142 D5
Cry Lake Canada 120 D3
Crysdale, Mount Canada 120 F4
Crystal U.S.A. 129 I3
Crystal City Canada 121 L5
Crystal City U.S.A. 131 D6
Crystal Falls U.S.A. 130 F2
Crystal Lake U.S.A. 134 A2
Crystal River U.S.A. 133 D6
Csongrád Hungary 59 I1
Cửa Lớn, Sông *r.* Vietnam 71 D5
Cuamba Moz. 99 D5
Cuando *r.* Angola/Zambia 99 C5
Cuangar Angola 99 B5
Cuango Angola 99 B4
Cuanza *r.* Angola 99 B4
Cuatro Ciénegas Mex. 131 C7
Cuauhtémoc Mex. 127 G7
Cuba *NM* U.S.A. 127 G5
Cuba *NY* U.S.A. 135 F2

▶**Cuba** *country* West Indies 137 H4
5th largest island and 5th most populous
country in North America.

Cubal Angola 99 B5
Cubango *r.* Angola/Namibia 99 C5
Cubatão Brazil 145 B3
Cub Hills Canada 121 J4
Çubuk Turkey 90 D2
Cucapa, Sierra *mts* Mex. 129 F5
Cuchi Angola 99 B5
Cuchilla Grande *hills* Uruguay 144 E4
Cucuí Brazil 142 E3
Cucurpe Mex. 127 F7
Cúcuta Col. 142 D2
Cudal Australia 112 D4
Cuddalore India 84 C4
Cuddapah India 84 C3
Cuddeback Lake U.S.A. 128 E4
Cue Australia 109 B6
Cuéllar Spain 57 D3
Cuemba Angola 99 B5
Cuenca Ecuador 142 C4
Cuenca Spain 57 E3

Cuenca, Serranía de mts Spain 57 E3
Cuencamé Mex. 131 C7
Cuernavaca Mex. 136 E5
Cuero U.S.A. 131 D6
Cuervos Mex. 129 F5
Cugir Romania 59 J2
Cuiabá Amazonas Brazil 143 G5
Cuiabá Mato Grosso Brazil 143 G7
Cuiabá r. Brazil 143 G7
Cuihua China see Daguan
Cuijiang China see Ninghua
Cuijk Neth. 52 F3
Cuilcagh hill Ireland/U.K. 51 E3
Cuillin Hills U.K. 50 C3
Cuillin Sound sea chan. U.K. 50 C3
Cuilo Angola 99 B4
Cuiluan China 74 C3
Cuité r. Brazil 145 C2
Cuito r. Angola 99 C5
Cuito Cuanavale Angola 99 B5
Cukai Malaysia 71 C6
Çukurca Turkey 88 A2
Çukurova plat. Turkey 85 B1
Cu Lao Cham i. Vietnam 70 E4
Cu Lao Xanh i. Vietnam 71 E4
Culcairn Australia 112 C5
Culfa Azer. 91 G3
Culgoa r. Australia 112 C2
Culiacán Mex. 136 C4
Culiacán Rosales Mex. see Culiacán
Culion Phil. 69 F4
Culion i. Phil. 68 F4
Cullen U.K. 50 G3
Cullen Point Australia 110 C1
Cullera Spain 57 F4
Cullivoe U.K. 50 [inset]
Cullman U.S.A. 133 C5
Cullybackey U.K. 51 F3
Cul Mòr hill U.K. 50 D2
Culpeper U.S.A. 135 G4
Culuene r. Brazil 143 H6
Culver, Point Australia 109 D8
Culverden N.Z. 113 D6
Cumaná Venez. 142 F1
Cumari Brazil 145 A2
Cumbal, Nevado de vol. Col. 142 C3
Cumberland KY U.S.A. 134 D5
Cumberland MD U.S.A. 135 F4
Cumberland VA U.S.A. 135 F5
Cumberland r. U.S.A. 132 C4
Cumberland, Lake U.S.A. 134 C5
Cumberland Lake Canada 121 K4
Cumberland Mountains U.S.A. 134 D5
Cumberland Peninsula Canada 119 L3
Cumberland Plateau U.S.A. 132 C5
Cumberland Point U.S.A. 130 F2
Cumberland Sound sea chan. Canada 119 L3
Cumbernauld U.K. 50 F5
Cumbres de Majalca, Parque Nacional nat. park Mex. 127 G7
Cumbres de Monterey, Parque Nacional nat. park Mex. 131 C7
Cumbum India 84 C3
Cumlosen Germany 53 L1
Cummings U.S.A. 128 B2
Cummins Australia 111 A7
Cummins Range hills Australia 108 D4
Cumnock Australia 112 D4
Cumnock U.K. 50 E5
Çumra Turkey 90 D3
Cumuruxatiba Brazil 145 D2
Cunagua Cuba see Bolivia
Cunderdin Australia 109 B7
Cunene r. Angola 99 B5
also known as Kunene
Cuneo Italy 58 B2
Cung Sơn Vietnam 71 E4
Cunnamulla Australia 112 B2
Cunningsburgh U.K. 50 [inset]
Cupar U.K. 50 F4
Cupica, Golfo de b. Col. 142 C2
Curaçá Brazil 143 K5
Curaçá r. Brazil 142 D4
Curaçao i. Neth. Antilles 137 K6
Curaray r. Ecuador 142 D4
Curdlawidny Lagoon salt flat Australia 111 B6
Curia Switz. see Chur
Curicó Chile 144 B4
Curitiba Brazil 145 A4
Curitibanos Brazil 145 A4
Curlewis Australia 112 E3
Curnamona Australia 111 B6
Currabubula Australia 112 E3
Currais Novos Brazil 143 K5
Curran U.S.A. 134 D1
Currane, Lough l. Ireland 51 B6
Currant U.S.A. 129 F2
Curranyalpa Australia 112 B3
Currawilla Australia 110 C5
Currawinya National Park Australia 112 B2
Currie Australia 106 E5
Currie U.S.A. 129 F1
Currituck U.S.A. 135 G5
Currockbilly, Mount Australia 112 E5
Curtis Channel Australia 110 F5
Curtis Island Australia 110 E4
Curtis Island N.Z. 107 I5
Curuá r. Brazil 143 H5
Curup Indon. 68 C7
Curupira, Serra mts Brazil/Venez. 142 F3
Cururupu Brazil 143 J4
Curvelo Brazil 145 B2
Curwood, Mount hill U.S.A. 130 F2
Cusco Peru 142 D6
Cushendall U.K. 51 F2
Cushendun U.K. 51 F2
Cushing U.S.A. 131 D4
Cusseta U.S.A. 133 C5
Custer MT U.S.A. 126 G3
Custer SD U.S.A. 130 C3
Cut Bank U.S.A. 126 E2
Cuthbert U.S.A. 133 C6
Cuthbertson Falls Australia 108 F3
Cut Knife Canada 121 I4
Cutler Ridge U.S.A. 133 D7
Cuttaburra Creek r. Australia 112 B2
Cuttack India 84 E1
Cuvelai Angola 99 B5
Cuxhaven Germany 47 L4
Cuya Chile 142 D7
Cuyahoga Falls U.S.A. 134 E3
Cuyama U.S.A. 128 D4
Cuyama r. U.S.A. 128 C4
Cuyo Islands Phil. 69 G4
Cuyuni r. Guyana 143 G2
Cuzco Peru see Cusco
Cwmbrân U.K. 49 D7
Cyangugu Rwanda 98 C4
Cyclades is Greece 59 K6
Cydonia Greece see Chania
Cygnet U.S.A. 134 D3
Cymru admin. div. U.K. see Wales
Cynthiana U.S.A. 134 C4
Cypress Hills Canada 121 I5
Cyprus country Asia 85 A2
Cyrenaica reg. Libya 97 F2
Cythera i. Greece see Kythira
Czar Canada 121 I4
Czechia country Europe see Czech Republic

▶Czechoslovakia
Divided in 1993 into the Czech Republic and Slovakia.

Czech Republic country Europe 47 O6
Czernowitz Ukr. see Chernivtsi
Czersk Poland 47 P4
Częstochowa Poland 47 Q5

Đa, Sông r. Vietnam see Black
Da'an China 74 B3
Ḑabāb, Jabal aḑ mt. Jordan 85 B4
Dabakala Côte d'Ivoire 96 C4
Daban China 73 L4
Dabao China 76 D2
Daba Shan mts China 77 F1
Dabba China see Daocheng
Dabein Myanmar 70 B3
Dabhoi India 82 C5
Ḑab'ī, Wādī aḑ watercourse Jordan 85 C4
Dabie Shan mts China 77 G2
Dablana India 82 C4
Dabola Guinea 96 B3
Dabqig China 73 J5
Dąbrowa Górnicza Poland 47 Q5
Dabsan Hu salt l. China 83 H1
Dabs Nur l. China 74 A3
Dabu Guangdong China 77 H3
Dabu Guangxi China see Liucheng
Dabusu Pao l. China see Dabs Nur
Dacca Bangl. see Dhaka
Dachau Germany 47 M6
Dachuan China see Dazhou
Dacre Canada 135 G1
Daday Turkey 90 D2
Dade City U.S.A. 133 D6
Dadeville U.S.A. 133 C5
Dādkān Iran 89 F5
Dadong China see Donggang
Dadra India see Achalpur
Dadu Pak. 89 G5
Daegu S. Korea see Taegu
Daejŏn S. Korea see Taejŏn
Daet Phil. 69 G4
Dafang China 76 E3
Dafeng China 77 I1
Dafengman China 74 B4
Dafla Hills India 83 H4
Dafoe Canada 121 J5
Dafoe r. Canada 121 M4
Dagana Senegal 96 B3
Dagcagoin China see Zoigê
Dagcanglhamo China 76 D1
Daghmar Oman 88 E6
Dağlıq Qarabağ aut. reg. Azer. 91 G3
Daglung China 83 G3
Dagö i. Estonia see Hiiumaa
Dagon Myanmar see Rangoon
Daguan China 76 D3
Daguokui Shan hill China 74 C3
Dagupan Phil. 69 G3
Dagxoi Sichuan China see Yidun
Dagxoi Sichuan China see Sowa
Dagzê China 83 G3
Dagzê Co salt l. China 83 F3
Dahadinni r. Canada 120 E2
Dahalach, Isole is Eritrea see Dahlak Archipelago
Dahana des. Saudi Arabia see Ad Dahnā'
Dahe China see Ziyuan
Daheiding Shan mt. China 74 C3
Dahei Shan mts China 74 B4
Dahej India 82 C5
Daheng China 77 H3
Dahezhen China 74 D3
Da Hinggan Ling mts China 74 A2
Dahlak Archipelago is Eritrea 86 F6
Dahlak Marine National Park Eritrea 86 F6
Daḩl al Furayy well Saudi Arabia 88 B5
Dahlem Germany 52 G4
Dahlenburg Germany 53 K1
Dahm, Ramlat des. Saudi Arabia/Yemen 86 G6
Dahmani Tunisia 58 C7
Dahme Germany 53 N3
Dahn Germany 53 H5
Dahnā' plain Saudi Arabia 88 B5
Dahod India 82 C5
Dahomey country Africa see Benin
Dahongliutan Aksai Chin 82 D2
Dahra Senegal see Dara
Dähre Germany 53 K2
Dahūk Iraq 91 F3
Dai i. Indon. 108 E1
Daik Indon. 68 C7
Daik-U Myanmar 70 B3
Đai Lanh, Mui pt Vietnam 71 E4
Dailekh Nepal 83 E3
Dailly U.K. 50 E5
Daimiel Spain 57 E4
Dainkog China 76 C1
Dainkognubma China 76 C1
Daintree National Park Australia 110 D3
Dair, Jebel ed mt. Sudan 86 D7
Dairen China see Dalian
Dai-sen vol. Japan 75 D6
Daisetsu-zan Kokuritsu-kōen nat. park Japan 74 F4
Daishan China 77 I2
Daiyun Shan mts China 77 H3
Dajarra Australia 110 B4
Dajin Chuan r. China 76 D2
Da Juh China 83 H1

▶Dakar Senegal 96 B3
Capital of Senegal.

Dākhilah, Wāḩāt ad oasis Egypt 86 C4
Dakhla W. Sahara see Ad Dakhla
Dakhla Oasis oasis Egypt see Dākhilah, Wāḩāt ad
Đăk Lăk, Cao Nguyên plat. Vietnam 71 E4
Dakoank India 71 A6
Dakol'ka r. Belarus 43 F5
Dakor India 82 C5
Dakoro Niger 96 D3
Dakota City IA U.S.A. 130 E3
Dakota City NE U.S.A. 130 D3
Đakovica Kosovo see Gjakovë
Đakovo Croatia 58 H2
Daktuy Rus. Fed. 74 B1
Dala Angola 99 C5
Dalaba Guinea 96 B3
Dalai China see Da'an
Dalain Hob China 80 J3
Dālakī Iran 88 C4
Dalälven r. Sweden 45 J6
Dalaman Turkey 59 M6
Dalandzadgad Mongolia 72 I4
Dalap-Uliga-Darrit Marshall Is see Delap-Uliga-Djarrit
Đa Lat Vietnam 71 E5
Dalatando Angola see N'dalatando
Dalaud India 82 C5
Dalauda India 82 C5
Dalbandin Pak. 89 G4
Dalbeattie U.K. 50 F6
Dalbeg Australia 110 D4
Dalby Australia 112 E1
Dalby Isle of Man 48 C4
Dale Hordaland Norway 45 D6
Dale Sogn og Fjordane Norway 45 D6
Dale City U.S.A. 135 G4
Dale Hollow Lake U.S.A. 134 C5
Dalen Neth. 52 G2
Dalet Myanmar 70 A3
Daletme Myanmar 70 A2
Dalfors Sweden 45 I6
Dalgān Iran 88 E5
Dalgety Australia 112 D6
Dalgety r. Australia 109 A6
Dalhart U.S.A. 131 C4
Dalhousie Canada 123 I4
Dalhousie, Cape Canada 118 F2
Dali Shaanxi China 77 F1
Dali Yunnan China 76 D3
Dalian China 73 M5
Daliang China see Shunde
Daliang Shan mts China 76 D2
Daliji China 77 H1
Dalin China 74 A4
Dalizi China 74 B4
Dalkeith U.K. 50 F5
Dallas OR U.S.A. 126 C3
Dallas TX U.S.A. 131 D5
Dalles City U.S.A. see The Dalles
Dall Island U.S.A. 120 C4
Dalmā i. U.A.E. 88 D5
Dalmacija reg. Bos.-Herz./Croatia see Dalmatia
Dalmas, Lac l. Canada 123 H3
Dalmatia reg. Bos.-Herz./Croatia 78 A2
Dalmau India 82 E4
Dalmellington U.K. 50 E5
Dalmeny Canada 121 J4
Dalmi India 83 F5
Dal'negorsk Rus. Fed. 74 D3
Dal'nerechensk Rus. Fed. 74 D3
Dal'niye Zelentsy Rus. Fed. 42 H1
Dalny China see Dalian
Daloa Côte d'Ivoire 96 C4

▶Dalol Eth. 86 F7
Highest recorded annual mean temperature in the world.

Daloloia Group is P.N.G. 110 E1
Dalou Shan mts China 76 E3
Dalqān well Saudi Arabia 88 B5
Dalry U.K. 50 E5
Dalrymple U.K. 50 E5
Dalrymple, Lake Australia 110 D4
Daltenganj India 83 F4
Dalton Canada 122 D4
Dalton S. Africa 101 J5
Dalton GA U.S.A. 133 C5
Dalton MA U.S.A. 135 I2
Dalton PA U.S.A. 135 H3
Daltonganj India see Daltenganj
Dalton-in-Furness U.K. 48 D4
Daludalu Indon. 71 C7
Daluo China 76 D4
Daly r. Australia 108 E3
Daly City U.S.A. 128 B3
Daly River Australia 108 E3
Daly Waters Australia 108 F4
Damagaram Takaya Niger 96 D3
Daman India 84 B1
Daman and Diu union terr. India 84 A1
Damanhūr Egypt 90 C5
Damanhûr Egypt see Damanhūr
Damant Lake Canada 121 J2
Damão India see Daman
Damar i. Indon. 108 E1
Damara Cent. Afr. Rep. 98 B3
Damaraland reg. Namibia 99 B6
Damas Syria see Damascus

▶Damascus Syria 85 C3
Capital of Syria.

Damascus U.S.A. 134 E5
Damaturu Nigeria 96 E3
Damāvand Iran 88 D3
Damāvand, Qolleh-ye mt. Iran 88 D3
Dambulla Sri Lanka 84 D5
Damdy Kazakh. 80 B1
Damghan Iran 88 D2
Damianópolis Brazil 145 B1
Damietta Egypt see Dumyāţ
Daming Shan mt. China 77 F4
Dāmiyā Jordan 85 B3
Damjong China 76 B1
Damlasu Turkey 85 D1
Dammam Saudi Arabia 86 H4
Damme Belgium 52 D3
Damme Germany 53 I2
Damoh India 82 D5
Damour Lebanon 85 B3
Dampar, Tasik l. Malaysia 71 C7
Dampier Archipelago is Australia 108 B5
Dampier Island P.N.G. see Karkar Island
Dampier Land reg. Australia 108 C4
Dampier Strait P.N.G. 69 L8
Dampir, Selat sea chan. Indon. 69 I7
Damqoq Zangbo r. China see Maquan He
Dam Qu r. China 76 B1
Dâmrei, Chuŏr Phnum mts Cambodia 71 D5
Damroh India 76 B2
Damwâld Neth. see Damwoude
Damwoude Neth. 52 G1
Damxoi China see Comai
Damxung China 83 G3
Ḑānā Jordan 85 B4
Dana Nepal 83 E3
Danakil reg. Africa see Denakil
Danané Côte d'Ivoire 96 C4
Đa Năng Vietnam 70 E3
Đa Năng, Vung b. Vietnam 70 E3
Danao Phil. 69 G4
Danata Turkm. 88 D2
Danba China 76 D2
Danbury CT U.S.A. 135 I3
Danbury NC U.S.A. 132 D4
Danby U.S.A. 135 I2
Danby Lake U.S.A. 129 F4
Dandaragan Australia 109 A7
Dande Eth. 98 D3
Dandeldhura Nepal 82 E3
Dandeli India 84 B3
Dandong China 75 B4
Dandot Pak. 89 I3
Dandridge U.S.A. 132 D4
Dane r. U.K. 48 E5
Daneborg Greenland 153 I2
Danese U.S.A. 134 E5
Danfeng China see Shizong
Dangan Liedao i. China 77 G4
Dangara Tajik. see Danghara
Dangbizhen Rus. Fed. 74 C3
Dangchang China 76 E1
Dangchengwan China see Subei
Danger Islands atoll Cook Is see Pukapuka
Danger Point S. Africa 100 D8
Danghara Tajik. 89 H2
Danghe Nanshan mts China 80 H4
Dang La pass China see Tanggula Shankou
Dangla Shan mts China see Tanggula Shan
Dangqên China 83 G3
Dângrêk, Chuŏr Phnum mts Cambodia/Thai. see Phanom Dong Rak, Thiu Khao
Dangriga Belize 136 G5
Dangshan China 77 H1
Dangtu China 77 H2
Daniel's Harbour Canada 123 K4
Daniëlskuil S. Africa 100 F5
Danilov Rus. Fed. 42 I4
Danilovka Rus. Fed. 43 J6
Danilovskaya Vozvyshennost' hills Rus. Fed. 42 H4
Danjiang China see Leishan
Danjiangkou China 77 F1
Danjiangkou Shuiku resr China 77 F1
Danjo-guntō is Japan 75 C6
Ḑank Oman 88 E6
Dankhar India 82 D2
Dankov Rus. Fed. 43 H5
Danlí Hond. 137 G6
Danmark country Europe see Denmark
Dannebrog Ø i. Greenland see Qillak
Dannenberg (Elbe) Germany 53 L1
Dannenwalde Germany 53 N1
Dannevirke N.Z. 113 F5
Dannhauser S. Africa 101 J5
Dano Burkina 96 C3
Danshui Taiwan see Tanshui
Dansville U.S.A. 135 G2
Danta India 82 C4
Dantan India 83 F5
Dantevada India see Dantewara
Dantewada India see Dantewara
Dantewara India 84 D2
Dantu China see Zhenjiang

▶Danube r. Europe 47 P6
2nd longest river in Europe.
Also spelt Donau (Austria/Germany) or Duna (Hungary) or Dunaj (Slovakia) or Dunărea (Romania) or Dunav (Bulgaria/Croatia/Serbia) or Dunay (Ukraine).

Danube Delta Romania/Ukr. 59 M2
Danubyu Myanmar 70 A3
Danville IL U.S.A. 134 B3
Danville IN U.S.A. 134 B4
Danville KY U.S.A. 134 C5
Danville OH U.S.A. 134 D3
Danville PA U.S.A. 135 G3
Danville VA U.S.A. 134 F5
Danville VT U.S.A. 135 I1
Danxian China see Danzhou
Danzhai China 76 E3
Danzhou Guangxi China 77 F3
Danzhou Hainan China 77 F5
Danzig Poland see Gdańsk
Danzig, Gulf of Poland/Rus. Fed. see Gdańsk, Gulf of
Daocheng China 76 D2
Daokou China see Huaxian
Dao Tay Sa is S. China Sea see Paracel Islands
Daoud Alg. see Aïn Beïda
Daoukro Côte d'Ivoire 96 C4
Daozhen China 76 E2
Dapaong Togo 96 D3
Dapeng Wan b. H.K. China see Mirs Bay
Daphabum mt. India 83 I4
Dapitan Phil. 69 G5
Daporijo India 83 H4
Dapu China see Liucheng
Da Qaidam Zhen China 80 I4
Daqiao China 76 D3
Daqing China 74 B3
Daqiu China 77 H3
Dāq Mashī Iran 88 E3
Daqq-e Patargān salt flat Iran 89 F3
Daqq-e Sorkh, Kavīr-e salt flat Iran 88 D3
Daqq-e Tundi, Dasht-e imp. l. Afgh. 89 F3
Daqu Shan i. China 77 I2
Dara Senegal 96 B3
Dar'ā Syria 85 C3
Dâra, Gebel mt. Egypt see Dārah, Jabal
Dārāb Iran 88 D4
Darāgāh Iran 88 D4
Dārah, Jabal mt. Egypt 90 D6
Daraj Libya 96 E1
Dārākūyeh Iran 88 D4
Dārān Iran 88 C3
Daraut-Korgon Kyrg. 89 I2
Darazo Nigeria 96 E3
Darband, Kūh-e mt. Iran 88 E4
Darband-e Hajjī Boland Turkm. 89 F2
Darbhanga India 83 F4
Darcang China 76 C1
Dardanelle U.S.A. 131 E5
Dardanelles strait Turkey 59 L4
Dardania prov. Europe see Kosovo
Dardesheim Germany 53 K3
Dardo China see Kangding
Dar el Beida Morocco see Casablanca
Darende Turkey 90 E3

▶Dar es Salaam Tanz. 99 D4
Former capital of Tanzania.

Darfo Boario Terme Italy 58 D2
Dargai Pak. 89 H3
Dargaville N.Z. 113 D2
Dargo Australia 112 C6
Dargo Zangbo r. China 83 F3
Darhan Mongolia 72 J3
Darien U.S.A. 133 D6
Darién, Golfo del g. Col. 142 C2
Darién, Parque Nacional de nat. park Panama 137 I7
Dariga Pak. 89 G5
Darīganga Mongolia 73 K3
Darjeeling India see Darjiling
Darjiling India 83 G4
Darkhazīneh Iran 88 C4
Darlag China 76 C1

▶Darling r. Australia 112 B3
2nd longest river in Oceania, and a major part of the longest (Murray-Darling)

Darling Downs hills Australia 112 D1
Darling Range hills Australia 109 A8
Darlington U.K. 48 F4
Darlington U.S.A. 130 F3
Darlington Point Australia 112 C5
Darlot, Lake salt flat Australia 109 C6
Darłowo Poland 47 P3
Darma Pass China/India 82 E3
Darmstadt Germany 53 I5
Darnah Libya 90 A4
Darnall S. Africa 101 J5
Darnick Australia 112 A4
Darnley, Cape Antarctica 152 E2
Daroca Spain 57 F3
Daroot-Korgon Kyrg. see Daraut-Korgon
Darovskoy Rus. Fed. 42 J4
Darr watercourse Australia 110 C4
Darreh Bīd Iran 88 E3
Darreh-ye Bāhābād Iran 88 D4
Darreh-ye Shahr Iran 88 B3
Darsi India 84 C3
Dart r. U.K. 49 D8
Dartang China see Baqên
Dartford U.K. 49 H7
Dartmoor Australia 111 C8
Dartmoor hills U.K. 49 C8
Dartmoor National Park U.K. 49 D8
Dartmouth Canada 123 J5
Dartmouth U.K. 49 D8
Dartmouth, Lake salt flat Australia 111 D5
Dartmouth Reservoir Australia 112 C6
Darton U.K. 48 F5
Daru P.N.G. 69 K8
Daru Sierra Leone 96 B4
Daruba Indon. 69 H6
Darvaza Turkm. see Derweze
Darvoz, Qatorkŭhi mts Tajik. 89 H2
Darwazgai Afgh. 89 G4
Darwen U.K. 48 E5
Darweshan Afgh. 89 G4

▶Darwin Australia 108 E3
Capital of Northern Territory.

Darwin, Monte mt. Chile 144 C8
Daryācheh-ye Orūmīyeh salt l. Iran see Urmia, Lake
Dar'yalyktakyr, Ravnina plain Kazakh. 80 B2
Dar"yoi Amu r. Asia see Amudar'ya
Dārzīn Iran 88 E4
Dās i. U.A.E. 88 D5
Dasada India 82 B5
Dashennongjia mt. China see Shennong Ding
Dashhowuz Daşoguz Turkm. see Daşoguz
Dashkesan Azer. see Daşkäsän
Dashkhovuz Daşoguz Turkm. see Daşoguz
Dashköpri Turkm. see Daşköpri
Dashoguz Daşoguz Turkm. see Daşoguz
Dasht Iran 88 E2
Dashtiari Iran 89 F5
Daska Pak. 89 I3
Daşkäsän Azer. 91 G2
Daşköpri Turkm. 89 F2
Daşoguz Turkm. 87 I1
Daşoguz Turkm. see Daşoguz
Dasongshu China 76 E3
Daspar mt. Pak. 89 I2
Dassel Germany 53 J3
Dastgardān Iran 88 E3
Datadian Indon. 68 F6
Datça Turkey 59 L6
Date Japan 74 F4
Date Creek watercourse U.S.A. 129 G4
Dateland U.S.A. 129 G5
Datha India 82 C5
Datia India 82 D4
Datian China 77 H3
Datian Ding mt. China 77 F4
Datil U.S.A. 129 J4
Datong Anhui China 77 H2
Datong Heilong. China 74 B3
Datong Shanxi China 73 K4
Datong He r. China 72 I5
Dattapur India 84 C1
Datu, Tanjung c. Indon./Malaysia 71 E7
Daudkandi Bangl. 83 G5
Daugava r. Latvia 45 N8
Daugavpils Latvia 45 O9
Daulatabad India 84 B2
Daulatabad Iran see Malāyer
Daulatpur Bangl. 83 G5
Daun Germany 52 G4
Daungyu r. Myanmar 70 A2
Dauphin Canada 121 K5
Dauphiné reg. France 56 G4
Dauphiné, Alpes du mts France 56 G4
Dauphin Lake Canada 121 L5
Daurie Creek r. Australia 109 A6
Dausa India 82 D4
Dầu Tiêng, Hồ resr Vietnam 71 D5
Dava U.K. 50 F3
Däväçi Azer. 91 H2
Davanagere India see Davangere
Davangere India 84 B3
Davao Phil. 69 H5
Davao Gulf Phil. 69 H5
Dāvarī Iran 88 E5
Dāvarzan Iran 88 E2
Davel S. Africa 101 I4
Davenport IA U.S.A. 130 F3
Davenport WA U.S.A. 126 D3
Davenport Downs Australia 110 C5
Davenport Range hills Australia 108 F5
Daventry U.K. 49 F6
Daveyton S. Africa 101 I4
David Panama 137 H7
David City U.S.A. 130 D3
Davidson Canada 121 J5
Davidson, Mount hill Australia 108 E5
Davis research station Antarctica 152 E2
Davis r. Australia 108 C5
Davis i. Myanmar see Than Kyun
Davis CA U.S.A. 128 C2
Davis WV U.S.A. 134 F4
Davis, Mount hill U.S.A. 134 F4
Davis Bay Antarctica 152 G2
Davis Dam U.S.A. 129 F4
Davis Inlet (abandoned) Canada 123 J3
Davis Sea Antarctica 152 F2
Davis Strait Canada/Greenland 119 M3
Davlekanovo Rus. Fed. 41 Q5
Davos Switz. 56 I3
Davy Lake Canada 121 I3
Dawa Co l. China 83 F3
Dawa Wenz r. Eth. 98 E3
Dawaxung China 83 F3
Dawê China 76 D2
Dawei Myanmar see Tavoy
Dawei r. mouth Myanmar see Tavoy
Dawera i. Indon. 108 E1
Dawna Range mts Myanmar/Thai. 70 B3
Dawna Taungdan mts Myanmar/Thai. see Dawna Range
Dawo China see Maqên
Dawqah Oman 87 H6
Dawson r. Australia 110 E4
Dawson Canada 120 B1
Dawson GA U.S.A. 133 C6
Dawson ND U.S.A. 130 D2
Dawson, Mount Canada 120 G5
Dawson Bay Canada 121 K4
Dawson Creek Canada 120 F4
Dawson Inlet Canada 121 M2
Dawson Range mts Canada 120 A2
Dawsons Landing Canada 120 E5
Dawu Hubei China 77 G2
Dawu Qinghai China see Maqên
Dawu Taiwan see Tawu
Dawukou China see Shizuishan
Dawu Shan hill China 77 G2
Dax France 56 D5
Daxian China see Dazhou
Daxiang Ling mts China 76 D2
Daxin China 76 E4
Daxing Yunnan China see Ninglang
Daxing Yunnan China see Lüchun
Daxing'an Ling mts China see Da Hinggan Ling
Da Xueshan mts China 76 D2
Dayan China see Lijiang
Dayangshu China 74 B2
Dayao China 76 D3
Dayao Shan mts China 77 F4
Daye China 77 G2
Daying China 76 E2
Daying Jiang r. China 76 C3
Dayishan China see Guanyun
Dāykundī Afgh. 89 G3
Daylesford Australia 112 B6
Daylight Pass U.S.A. 128 E3
Dayong China see Zhangjiajie
Dayr Abū Sa'īd Jordan 85 B3
Dayr az Zawr Syria 91 F4
Dayr Ḩāfir Syria 85 C1
Daysland Canada 121 H4
Dayton OH U.S.A. 134 C4
Dayton TN U.S.A. 132 C5
Dayton VA U.S.A. 135 F4
Dayton WA U.S.A. 126 D3
Daytona Beach U.S.A. 133 D6
Dayu Ling mts China 77 G3
Da Yunhe canal China 77 H1
Dayyer Iran 88 C5
Dayyīna i. U.A.E. 88 D5
Dazhongji China see Dafeng
Dazhou China 76 E2
Dazhou Dao i. China 77 F5
Dazhu China 76 E2
Dazu China 76 E2
Dazu Rock Carvings tourist site China 76 E2
De Aar S. Africa 100 G6
Dead r. Ireland 51 D5
Deadman Lake U.S.A. 128 E4
Deadman's Cay Bahamas 133 F8

ead Mountains U.S.A. 129 F4
Dead Sea salt l. Asia 85 B4
Lowest point in the world and in Asia.
eadwood U.S.A. 130 C2
eakin Australia 109 E7
eal U.K. 49 I7
ealesville S. Africa 101 G5
e'an China 77 G2
ean, Forest of U.K. 49 E7
eán Funes Arg. 144 D4
eanuvuotna inlet Norway see Tanafjorden
earborn U.S.A. 134 D2
earne r. U.K. 48 F5
eary U.S.A. 126 D3
ease r. Canada 120 D3
ease Lake Canada 120 D3
ease Lake l. Canada 120 D3
ease Strait Canada 118 H3
Death Valley depr. U.S.A. 128 E3
Lowest point in the Americas.
eath Valley Junction U.S.A. 128 E3
eath Valley National Park U.S.A. 128 E3
eauville France 56 E2
eaver U.S.A. 126 F3
Baai S. Africa see Port Elizabeth
ebao China 76 E4
ebar Macedonia 59 I4
ebden Canada 121 J4
ebenham U.K. 49 I6
Beque U.S.A. 129 I2
Biesbosch, Nationaal Park nat. park Neth. 52 E3
ebo, Lac l. Mali 96 C3
eborah East, Lake salt flat Australia 109 B7
eborah West, Lake salt flat Australia 109 B7
ebrecen Hungary 59 I1
ebre Markos Eth. 86 E7
ebre Tabor Eth. 86 E7
ebre Zeyit Eth. 98 D3
ecatur AL U.S.A. 133 C5
ecatur GA U.S.A. 133 C5
ecatur IL U.S.A. 130 F4
ecatur IN U.S.A. 134 C3
ecatur MI U.S.A. 134 C2
ecatur MS U.S.A. 131 F5
ecatur TX U.S.A. 131 D5
Deccan plat. India 84 C2
Plateau making up most of southern and central India.
ception Bay Australia 112 F1
chang China 76 D3
čín Czech Rep. 47 O5
cker U.S.A. 126 G3
corah U.S.A. 130 F3
dap i. Indon. see Penasi, Pulau
daye Myanmar 70 A3
ddington U.K. 49 F7
degöl Dağları mts Turkey 59 N6
deleben Germany 53 K2
delstorf Germany 53 K2
demsvaart Neth. 52 G2
do de Deus mt. Brazil 145 B4
dougou Burkina 96 C3
dovichi Rus. Fed. 42 F4
du China see Wudalianchi
e r. Ireland 51 F4
e est. U.K. 48 D5
e r. England/Wales U.K. 49 D5
e r. Scotland U.K. 50 G3
el r. Ireland 51 D5
el r. Ireland 51 F4
ep Bay H.K. China 77 [inset]
ep Creek Lake U.S.A. 134 F4
ep Creek Range mts U.S.A. 129 G2
ep River Canada 122 F5
epwater Australia 112 E2
eri Somalia 98 E3
ering U.S.A. 118 B3
ering, Mount Australia 109 E6
er Island U.S.A. 118 B4
er Lake Canada 121 M4
er Lake l. Canada 121 M4
er Lodge U.S.A. 126 E3
esa India see Disa
eth U.S.A. 126 E4
feng China see Liping
fensores del Chaco, Parque Nacional nat. park Para. 144 D2
fiance U.S.A. 134 C3
fiance Plateau U.S.A. 129 I4
gana India 82 C4
geh Bur Eth. 98 E3
gema Nigeria 96 D4
ggendorf Germany 53 M6
gh r. Pak. 89 I4
Grey r. Australia 108 B5
Groote Peel, Nationaal Park nat. park Neth. 52 F3
gtevo Rus. Fed. 43 I6
Haan Belgium 52 D3
Hamert, Nationaal Park nat. park Neth. 52 G3
hak Iran 89 F4
h-Dasht Iran 88 C4
heq Iran 88 C3
nestān Iran 88 D4
h Golān Iran 88 B3
ngon Afgh. 89 F3
hi Afgh. 89 G3
nkūyeh Iran 88 D5
hlorān Iran 88 B3
Hoge Veluwe, Nationaal Park nat. park Neth. 52 F2
Hoop Nature Reserve S. Africa 100 E8
hqonobod Uzbek. 89 G2
nra Dun India 82 D3
hradun India see Dehra Dun
hri India 83 F4
n Shū Afgh. 89 F4
'm Zubeir Sudan 97 F4
nze Belgium 52 D4
r-ez-Zor Syria see Dayr az Zawr
Romania 59 J1
i China see Rinbung
Dejiang China 77 F2
De Jouwer Neth. see Joure
De Kalb IL U.S.A. 130 F3
De Kalb MS U.S.A. 131 F5
De Kalb TX U.S.A. 131 E5
De Kalb Junction U.S.A. 135 H1
De-Kastri Rus. Fed. 74 F2
Dekemhare Eritrea 86 E6
Dekhkanabad Uzbek. see Dehqonobod
Dekina Nigeria 96 D4
Dékoa Cent. Afr. Rep. 98 B3
De Koog Neth. 52 E1
De Kooy Neth. 52 E2
Delaki Indon. 108 D2
Delamar Lake U.S.A. 129 F3
De Land U.S.A. 133 D6
Delano U.S.A. 128 D4
Delano Peak U.S.A. 129 G2
▶Delap-Uliga-Djarrit Marshall Is 150 H5
Capital of the Marshall Islands, on Majuro atoll.
Delārām Afgh. 89 F3
Delareyville S. Africa 101 G4
Delaronde Lake Canada 121 J4
Delavan U.S.A. 122 C6
Delaware U.S.A. 134 D3
Delaware r. U.S.A. 135 H4
Delaware state U.S.A. 135 H4
Delaware, East Branch r. U.S.A. 135 H3
Delaware Bay U.S.A. 135 H4
Delaware Lake U.S.A. 134 D3
Delaware Water Gap National Recreational Area park U.S.A. 135 H3
Delay r. Canada 123 H2
Delbarton U.S.A. 134 D5
Delbrück Germany 53 I3
Delburne Canada 120 H4
Dêlêg China 83 F3
Delegate Australia 112 D6
De Lemmer Neth. see Lemmer
Delémont Switz. 56 H3
Delevan CA U.S.A. 128 B2
Delevan NY U.S.A. 135 F2
Delfinópolis Brazil 145 B3
Delft Neth. 52 E2
Delfzijl Neth. 52 G1
Delgada, Point U.S.A. 128 A1
Delgado, Cabo c. Moz. 99 E5
Delgerhaan Mongolia 72 I3
Delhi Canada 134 E2
Delhi China 80 I4
▶Delhi India 82 D3
3rd most populous city in Asia and 6th in the world.
Delhi CO U.S.A. 127 G5
Delhi LA U.S.A. 131 F5
Delhi NY U.S.A. 135 H2
Delice Turkey 90 D3
Delice r. Turkey 90 D2
Delījān Iran 88 C3
Déline Canada 120 F1
Delingha China see Delhi
Delisle Canada 121 J5
Delitzsch Germany 53 M3
Delligsen Germany 53 J3
Dell Rapids U.S.A. 130 D3
Dellys Alg. 57 H5
Del Mar U.S.A. 128 E5
Delmenhorst Germany 53 I1
Delnice Croatia 58 F2
Del Norte U.S.A. 127 G5
Delong China see Ande
De-Longa, Ostrova is Rus. Fed. 65 Q2
De Long Islands Rus. Fed. see De-Longa, Ostrova
De Long Mountains U.S.A. 118 B3
De Long Strait Rus. Fed. see Longa, Proliv
Deloraine Canada 121 K5
Delphi U.S.A. 134 B3
Delphos U.S.A. 134 C3
Delportshoop S. Africa 100 G5
Delray Beach U.S.A. 133 D7
Delrey U.S.A. 134 A3
Del Río Mex. 127 F7
Del Rio U.S.A. 131 C6
Delsbo Sweden 45 J6
Delta CO U.S.A. 129 I2
Delta OH U.S.A. 134 C3
Delta UT U.S.A. 129 G2
Delta Downs Australia 110 C3
Delta Junction U.S.A. 118 D3
Deltona U.S.A. 133 D6
Delungra Australia 112 E2
Delvin Ireland 51 E4
Delvinë Albania 59 I5
Delwara India 82 C4
Demavend mt. Iran see Damāvand, Qolleh-ye
Demba Dem. Rep. Congo 99 C4
Dembī Dolo Eth. 86 D8
Demerara Guyana see Georgetown
Demerara Abyssal Plain sea feature S. Atlantic Ocean 148 E5
Demidov Rus. Fed. 43 F5
Deming U.S.A. 127 G6
Demirci Turkey 59 M5
Demirköy Turkey 59 L4
Demirtaş Turkey 85 A1
Demmin Germany 47 N4
Demopolis U.S.A. 133 C5
Demotte U.S.A. 134 B3
Dempo, Gunung vol. Indon. 68 C7
Dêmqog China 82 D2
Demta Indon. 69 K7
Dem'yanovo Rus. Fed. 42 J3
De Naawte S. Africa 100 E6
Denakil reg. Africa 98 E2
Denali mt. U.S.A. see McKinley, Mount
Denali National Park and Preserve U.S.A. 118 C3
Denan Eth. 98 E3
Denbigh Canada 135 G1
Denbigh U.K. 48 D5
Den Bosch Neth. see 's-Hertogenbosch
Den Burg Neth. 52 E1
Den Chai Thai. 70 C3
Dendāra Mauritania 96 C3
Dendermonde Belgium 52 E3
Dendi mt. Eth. 98 D3
Dendre r. Belgium 52 E3
Dendron S. Africa see Mogwadi
Denezhkin Kamen', Gora mt. Rus. Fed. 41 R3
Dêngka China see Têwo
Dêngkagoin China see Têwo
Dengkou China 72 J4
Dêngqên China 76 B2
Dengta China 77 G4
Dengxian China see Dengzhou
Dengzhou China 77 G1
Den Haag Neth. see The Hague
Denham Australia 109 A6
Denham r. Australia 108 E3
Den Ham Neth. 52 G2
Denham Range mts Australia 110 E4
Den Helder Neth. 52 E2
Denholm Canada 121 I4
Denia Spain 57 G4
Denial Bay Australia 111 A7
Deniliquin Australia 112 B5
Denio U.S.A. 126 D4
Denison IA U.S.A. 130 E3
Denison TX U.S.A. 131 D5
Denison, Cape Antarctica 152 G2
Denison Plains Australia 108 E4
Deniyaya Sri Lanka 84 D5
Denizli Turkey 59 M6
Denman Australia 112 E4
Denman Glacier Antarctica 152 F2
Denmark Australia 106 B5
Denmark country Europe 45 G8
Denmark U.S.A. 134 B1
Denmark Strait Greenland/Iceland 40 A2
Dennis, Lake salt flat Australia 108 E5
Dennison IL U.S.A. 134 B4
Dennison OH U.S.A. 134 E3
Denny U.K. 50 F4
Denov Uzbek. 89 G2
Denow Uzbek. see Denov
Denpasar Indon. 108 A2
Denton MD U.S.A. 135 H4
Denton TX U.S.A. 131 D5
D'Entrecasteaux, Point Australia 109 A8
D'Entrecasteaux, Récifs reef New Caledonia 107 G3
D'Entrecasteaux Islands P.N.G. 106 F2
D'Entrecasteaux National Park Australia 109 A8
▶Denver CO U.S.A. 126 G5
Capital of Colorado.
Denver PA U.S.A. 135 G3
Denys r. Canada 122 F3
Deo India 83 F4
Deoband India 82 D3
Deogarh Jharkhand India see Deoghar
Deogarh Orissa India 83 F5
Deogarh Rajasthan India 82 C4
Deogarh Uttar Prad. India 82 D4
Deogarh mt. India 83 E5
Deoghar India 83 F4
Deolali India 84 B2
Deoli India 83 F5
Deori Madh. Prad. India 82 D5
Deoria India 83 E4
Deosai, Plains of Pak. 82 C2
Deosil India 83 E5
Deothang Bhutan 83 G4
De Panne Belgium 52 C3
De Pere U.S.A. 134 A1
Deposit U.S.A. 135 H2
Depsang Point hill Aksai Chin 82 D2
Deputatskiy Rus. Fed. 65 O3
Dêqên Xizang China see Dagzê
Dêqên Xizang China 83 G3
Dêqên Xizang China 83 G3
De Queen U.S.A. 131 E5
Dera Ghazi Khan Pak. 89 H4
Dera Ismail Khan Pak. 89 H4
Derajat reg. Pak. 89 H4
Derawar Fort Pak. 89 H4
Derbent Rus. Fed. 91 H2
Derbesiye Turkey see Şenyurt
Derbur China 74 A2
Derby Australia 108 C4
Derby U.K. 49 F6
Derby CT U.S.A. 135 I3
Derby KS U.S.A. 131 D4
Derby NY U.S.A. 135 F2
Dereham U.K. 49 H6
Derg r. Ireland/U.K. 51 E3
Derg, Lough l. Ireland 51 D5
Dergachi Rus. Fed. 43 K6
Dergachi Ukr. see Derhachi
Derhachi Ukr. 43 H6
De Ridder U.S.A. 131 E6
Derik Turkey 91 F3
Derm Namibia 100 D2
Derna Libya see Darnah
Dernberg, Cape Namibia 100 B4
Dêrong China 76 C2
Derravaragh, Lough l. Ireland 51 E4
Derry U.K. see Londonderry
Derry U.S.A. 135 J2
Derryveagh Mts hills Ireland 51 D3
Dêrub China 82 D2
Derudeb Sudan 86 E6
De Rust S. Africa 100 F7
Derventa Bos.-Herz. 58 G2
Derwent r. England U.K. 48 F6
Derwent r. England U.K. 48 G5
Derwent Water l. U.K. 48 D4
Derweze Turkm. 88 E1
Derzhavinsk Kazakh. 80 C1
Derzhavinskiy Kazakh. see Derzhavinsk
Desaguadero r. Arg. 144 C4
Désappointement, Îles du is Fr. Polynesia 151 K6
Desatoya Mountains U.S.A. 128 E2
Deschambault Lake Canada 121 K4
Deschutes r. U.S.A. 126 C3
Desē Eth. 98 D2
Deseado Arg. 144 C7
Deseado r. Arg. 144 C7
Desengaño, Punta pt Arg. 144 C7
Deseret U.S.A. 129 G2
Deseret Peak U.S.A. 129 G1
Deseronto Canada 135 G1
Desert Canal Pak. 89 H4
Desert Center U.S.A. 129 F5
Desert Lake U.S.A. 129 F3
Desert View U.S.A. 129 H3
Deshler U.S.A. 134 D3
De Smet U.S.A. 130 D2
▶Des Moines IA U.S.A. 130 E3
Capital of Iowa.
Des Moines NM U.S.A. 131 C4
Des Moines r. U.S.A. 130 F3
Desna r. Rus. Fed./Ukr. 43 F6
Desnogorsk Rus. Fed. 43 G5
Desolación, Isla i. Chile 144 B8
Des Plaines U.S.A. 134 B2
Dessau Germany 53 M3
Dessye Eth. see Desē
Destelbergen Belgium 52 D3
Destruction Bay Canada 153 A2
Desventuradas, Islas is S. Pacific Ocean 151 O7
Desvres France 52 B4
Detah Canada 120 H2
Dete Zimbabwe 99 C5
Detmold Germany 53 I3
Detrital Wash watercourse U.S.A. 129 F3
Detroit U.S.A. 134 D2
Detroit Lakes U.S.A. 130 E2
Dett Zimbabwe see Dete
Deua National Park Australia 112 D5
Deuben Germany 53 M3
Deurne Neth. 52 F3
Deutschland country Europe see Germany
Deutschlandsberg Austria 47 O7
Deutzen Germany 53 M3
Deva Romania 59 J2
Deva U.K. see Chester
Devana U.K. see Aberdeen
Devangere India see Davangere
Devanhalli India 84 C3
Deve Bair pass Bulg./Macedonia see Velbŭzhdki Prokhod
Develi Turkey 90 D3
Deventer Neth. 52 G2
Deveron r. U.K. 50 G3
Devét Skal hill Czech Rep. 47 P6
Devgarh India 84 B2
Devghar India see Deoghar
Devikot India 82 B4
Devil's Bridge U.K. 49 D6
Devil's Gate pass U.S.A. 128 D2
Devil's Lake U.S.A. 130 D1
Devil's Paw mt. U.S.A. 120 C3
Devil's Peak U.S.A. 128 D3
Devil's Point Bahamas 133 F7
Devine U.S.A. 131 D6
Devizes U.K. 49 F7
Devli India 82 C4
Devnya Bulg. 59 L3
Devon r. U.K. 50 F4
Devon Island Canada 119 I2
Devonport Australia 111 [inset]
Devrek Turkey 59 N4
Devrukh India 84 B2
Dewa, Tanjung pt Indon. 71 A7
Dewas India 82 D5
De Weerribben, Nationaal Park nat. park Neth. 52 G2
Dewetsdorp S. Africa 101 H5
De Witt AR U.S.A. 131 F5
De Witt IA U.S.A. 130 F3
Dewsbury U.K. 48 F5
Dexing China 77 H2
Dexter ME U.S.A. 135 K1
Dexter MI U.S.A. 134 D2
Dexter MO U.S.A. 131 F4
Dexter NM U.S.A. 127 G6
Dexter NY U.S.A. 135 G1
Deyang China 76 E2
Dey-Dey Lake salt flat Australia 109 E7
Deyhuk Iran 88 E3
Deyong, Tanjung pt Indon. 69 J8
Dez r. Iran 86 G3
Dezadeash Lake Canada 120 B2
Dezfūl Iran 88 C3
▶Dezhneva, Mys c. Rus. Fed. 65 T3
Most easterly point of Asia.
Dezhou Shandong China 73 L5
Dezhou Sichuan China see Dechang
Dezh Shāhpūr Iran see Marīvān
Dhabarau India 83 E4
Dhahab, Wādī adh r. Syria 85 B3
Dhāhiriya West Bank 85 B4
Dhahran Saudi Arabia 88 C5
▶Dhaka Bangl. 83 G5
Capital of Bangladesh. 10th most populous city in the world.
Dhalbhum reg. India 83 F5
Dhalgaon India 84 B2
Dhamār Yemen 86 F7
Dhamoni India 82 D4
Dhamtari India 84 D1
Dhana Pak. 89 H5
Dhana Sar Pak. 89 H4
Dhanbad India 83 F5
Dhanera India 82 C4
Dhang Range mts Nepal 83 E3
Dhankuta Nepal 83 F4
Dhansia India 82 C3
Dhar India 82 C5
Dhar Adrar hills Mauritania 96 B3
Dharampur India 84 B1
Dharan Bazar Nepal 83 F4
Dharashiv India see Osmanabad
Dhari India 82 B5
Dharmapuri India 84 C3
Dharmavaram India 84 C3
Dharmsala Hima. Prad. India see Dharmshala
Dharmsala Orissa India 83 F5
Dharmshala India 82 D2
Dharnaoda India 82 D4
Dhar Oualâta hills Mauritania 96 C3
Dhar Tîchît hills Mauritania 96 C3
Dharug National Park Australia 112 E4
Dharur India 84 C2
Dharwad India 84 B3
Dharwar India see Dharwad
Dharwas India 82 D2
Dhasan r. India 82 D4
Dhāt al Ḩājj Saudi Arabia 90 E5
▶Dhaulagiri mt. Nepal 83 E3
7th highest mountain in the world and in Asia.
Dhaulpur India see Dholpur
Dhaura India 82 D4
Dhaurahra India 82 E4
Dhawlagiri mt. Nepal see Dhaulagiri
Dhebar Lake India see Jaisamand Lake
Dhekelia Sovereign Base Area military base Cyprus 85 A2
Dhemaji India 83 H4
Dhenkanal India 84 E1
Dhībān Jordan 85 B4
Dhidhimótikhon Greece see Didymoteicho
Dhing India 83 H4
Dhirwah, Wādī adh watercourse Jordan 85 C4
Dhodhekánisos is Greece see Dodecanese
Dhola India 82 B5
Dholera India 82 C5
Dholpur India 82 D4
Dhomokós Greece see Domokos
Dhone India 84 C3
Dhoraji India 82 B5
Dhori India 82 B5
Dhrangadhra India 82 B5
Dhubāb Yemen 86 F7
Dhubri India 83 G4
Dhuburi India see Dhubri
Dhudial Pak. 89 I3
Dhule India 84 B1
Dhulia India see Dhule
Dhulian India 83 F4
Dhulian Pak. 89 I3
Dhuma India 82 D5
Dhund r. India 82 D4
Dhurwai India 82 D4
Dhuusa Marreeb Somalia 98 E3
Dia i. Greece 59 K7
Diablo, Mount U.S.A. 128 C3
Diablo, Picacho del mt. Mex. 127 E7
Diablo Range mts U.S.A. 128 C3
Diagbe Dem. Rep. Congo 98 C3
Diamante Arg. 144 D4
Diamantina watercourse Australia 110 B5
Diamantina Brazil 145 C2
Diamantina, Chapada plat. Brazil 145 C1
Diamantina Deep sea feature Indian Ocean 149 O8
Diamantina Gates National Park Australia 110 C4
Diamantino Brazil 143 G6
Diamond Islets Australia 110 E3
Diamond Peak U.S.A. 129 F2
Dianbai China 77 F4
Diancang Shan mt. China 76 D3
Dian Chi l. China 76 D3
Diandioumé Mali 96 C3
Diane Bank sea feature Australia 110 E2
Dianjiang China 76 E2
Dianópolis Brazil 143 I6
Dianyang China see Shidian
Diaobingshan China 74 A4
Diaoling China 74 C3
Diapaga Burkina 96 D3
Diarizos r. Cyprus 85 A2
Diavolo, Mount hill India 71 A4
Diaz Point Namibia 100 B4
Dibaya Dem. Rep. Congo 99 C4
Dibella well Niger 96 E3
Dibeng S. Africa 100 F4
Dibete Botswana 101 H2
Dibrugarh India 83 H4
Dibse Syria see Dibsī
Dibsī Syria 85 D2
Dickens U.S.A. 131 C5
Dickinson U.S.A. 130 C2
Dicle r. Asia 91 F3 see Tigris
Dīdēsa Wenz r. Eth. 98 D3
Didiéni Mali 96 C3
Didsbury Canada 120 H5
Didwana India 82 C4
Didymoteicho Greece 59 L4
Die France 56 G4
Dieblich Germany 53 H4
Diébougou Burkina 96 C3
Dieburg Germany 53 I5
Diedenhofen France see Thionville
Diefenbaker, Lake Canada 121 I5
Diego de Almagro, Isla i. Chile 144 A8
Diégo Suarez Madag. see Antsirañana
Diekirch Lux. 52 G5
Diéma Mali 96 C3
Diemel r. Germany 53 J3
Điện Biên Vietnam see Điện Biên Phu
Điện Biên Phu Vietnam 70 C2
Diên Châu Vietnam 70 D3
Diên Khanh Vietnam 71 E4
Diepholz Germany 53 I2
Dieppe France 52 B5
Dierks U.S.A. 131 E5
Di'er Songhua Jiang r. China 74 B3
Diessen Neth. 52 F3
Diest Belgium 52 F4
Dietikon Switz. 56 I3
Diez Germany 53 I4
Diffa Niger 96 E3
Digby Canada 123 I5
Diggi India 82 C4
Diglur India 84 C2
Digne France see Digne-les-Bains
Digne-les-Bains France 56 H4
Digoin France 56 F3
Digos Phil. 69 H5
Digras India 84 C1
Digri Pak. 89 H5
Digul r. Indon. 69 K8
Digya National Park Ghana 96 C4
Dihang r. India 83 H4 see Brahmaputra
Dihōk Iraq see Dahūk
Dihourse, Lac l. Canada 123 I2
Diinsoor Somalia 98 E3
Dijon France 56 G3
Dik Chad 97 E4
Diken India 82 C4
Dikhil Djibouti 86 F7
Dikili Turkey 59 L5
Diklosmta mt. Rus. Fed. 43 J8
Diksmuide Belgium 52 C3
Dikson Rus. Fed. 64 J2
Dīla Eth. 98 D3
Dilaram Iran 88 E4
▶Dili East Timor 108 D2
Capital of East Timor.
Di Linh Vietnam 71 E5
Dillenburg Germany 53 I4
Dilley U.S.A. 131 D6
Dillingen (Saar) Germany 52 G5
Dillingen an der Donau Germany 47 M6
Dillingham U.S.A. 118 C4
Dillon r. Canada 121 I4
Dillon MT U.S.A. 126 E3
Dillon SC U.S.A. 133 E5
Dillwyn U.S.A. 135 F5
Dilolo Dem. Rep. Congo 99 C5
Dilsen Belgium 52 F3
Dimapur India 83 H4
Dimashq Syria see Damascus
Dimbokro Côte d'Ivoire 96 C4
Dimboola Australia 111 C8
Dimitrov Ukr. see Dymytrov
Dimitrovgrad Bulg. 59 K3
Dimitrovgrad Rus. Fed. 43 K5
Dimitrovo Bulg. see Pernik
Dimmitt U.S.A. 131 C5
Dīmona Israel 85 B4
Dimpho Pan salt pan Botswana 100 E3
Dinagat i. Phil. 69 H4
Dinajpur Bangl. 83 G4
Dinan France 56 C2
Dinant Belgium 52 E4
Dinapur India 83 F4
Dinar Turkey 59 N5
Dīnār, Kūh-e mt. Iran 88 C4
Dinara Planina mts Bos.-Herz./Croatia see Dinaric Alps
Dinaric Alps mts Bos.-Herz./Croatia 58 G2
Dinbych U.K. see Denbigh
Dinbych-y-pysgod U.K. see Tenby
Dinder National Park Sudan 97 G3
Dindi r. India 84 C2
Dindigul India 84 C4
Dindima Nigeria 96 E3
Dindiza Moz. 101 K2
Dindori India 82 E5
Dingcheng China see Dingyuan
Dingelstädt Germany 53 K3
Dingla Nepal 83 F4
Dingle Bay Ireland 51 B5
Dingnan China 77 G3
Dingo Australia 110 E4
Dingolfing Germany 53 M6
Dingping China see Linshui
Dingtao China 77 G1
Dinguiraye Guinea 96 B3
Dingwall U.K. 50 E3
Dingxi China 76 E1
Dingyuan China 77 H1
Dinh Lâp Vietnam 70 D2
Dinkelsbühl Germany 53 K5
Dinngyê China 83 F3
Dinokwe Botswana 101 H2
Dinosaur U.S.A. 129 I1
Dinosaur National Monument nat. park U.S.A. 129 I1
Dinslaken Germany 52 G3
Dinwiddie U.S.A. 135 G5
Dioïla Mali 96 C3
Dionísio Cerqueira Brazil 144 F3
Diorama Brazil 145 A2
Dioscurias Georgia see Sokhumi
Diouloulou Senegal 96 B3
Diourbel Senegal 96 B3
Dipayal Far Western 82 E3
Diphu India 83 H4
Dipkarpaz Cyprus see Rizokarpason
Diplo Pak. 89 H5
Dipperu National Park Australia 110 E4
Dipu China see Anji
Dir reg. Pak. 89 I3
Dirang India 83 H4
Diré Mali 96 C3
Direction, Cape Australia 110 C2
Dirē Dawa Eth. 98 E3
Dirico Angola 99 C5
Dirk Hartog Island Australia 109 A6
Dirranbandi Australia 112 D2
Ḑirs Saudi Arabia 98 E2
Dirschau Poland see Tczew
Dirty Devil r. U.S.A. 129 H3
Disa India 82 C4
Disang r. India 83 H4
Disappointment, Cape S. Georgia 144 I8
Disappointment, Cape U.S.A. 126 B3
Disappointment, Lake salt flat Australia 109 C5
Disappointment Islands Fr. Polynesia see Désappointement, Îles du
Disappointment Lake Canada 123 J3
Disaster Bay Australia 112 D6
Discovery Bay Australia 111 C8
Disko i. Greenland see Qeqertarsuaq
Disko Bugt b. Greenland see Qeqertarsuup Tunua
Dismal Swamp U.S.A. 132 E4
Dispur India 83 G4
Disputanta U.S.A. 135 G5
Disraëli Canada 123 H5
Diss U.K. 49 I6
Distrito Federal admin. dist. Brazil 145 B1
Disūq Egypt 90 C5
Ditloung S. Africa 100 F5
Dittaino r. Sicily Italy 58 F6
Diu India 84 A1
Dīvān Darreh Iran 88 B3
Divehi country Indian Ocean see Maldives
Divi, Point India 84 D3
Divichi Azer. see Däväçi
Divide Mountain U.S.A. 120 A2
Divinópolis Brazil 145 B3
Divnoye Rus. Fed. 43 I7
Divo Côte d'Ivoire 96 C4
Divriği Turkey 90 E3
Diwana Pak. 89 G5
Diwaniyah Iraq see Ad Dīwānīyah
Dixfield U.S.A. 135 J1
Dixon CA U.S.A. 128 C2

Dixon IL U.S.A. 130 F3
Dixon KY U.S.A. 134 B5
Dixon MT U.S.A. 126 E3
Dixon Entrance sea chan. Canada/U.S.A. 120 C4
Dixonville Canada 120 G3
Dixville Canada 135 J1
Diyadin Turkey 91 F3
Diyarbakır Turkey 91 F3
Diz Pak. 89 F5
Diz Chah Iran 88 D3
Dize Turkey see Yüksekova
Dizney U.S.A. 134 D5
Djado Niger 96 E2
Djado, Plateau du Niger 96 E2
Djaja, Puntjak mt. Indon. see Jaya, Puncak
Djakarta Indon. see Jakarta
Djakovica Kosovo see Gjakovë
Djakovo Croatia see Đakovo
Djambala Congo 98 B4
Djanet Alg. 96 D2
Djarrit-Uliga-Dalap Marshall Is see Delap-Uliga-Djarrit
Djelfa Alg. 57 H6
Djéma Cent. Afr. Rep. 98 C3
Djenné Mali 96 C3
Djerdap nat. park Serbia 59 J2
Djibo Burkina 96 C3
Djibouti country Africa 86 F7

▶Djibouti Djibouti 86 F7
Capital of Djibouti.

Djidjelli Alg. see Jijel
Djizak Uzbek. see Jizzax
Djougou Benin 96 D4
Djoum Cameroon 96 E4
Djourab, Erg du des. Chad 97 E3
Djúpivogur Iceland 44 [inset]
Djurås Sweden 45 I6
Djurdjura, Parc National du Alg. 57 I5
Dmitriya Lapteva, Proliv sea chan. Rus. Fed. 65 P2
Dmitriyev-L'govskiy Rus. Fed. 43 G5
Dmitriyevsk Ukr. see Makiyivka
Dmitrov Rus. Fed. 42 H4
Dmytriyevs'k Ukr. see Makiyivka
Dnepr r. Europe 43 F5 see Dnieper
Dneprodzerzhinsk Ukr. see Dniprodzerzhyns'k
Dnepropetrovsk Ukr. see Dnipropetrovs'k

▶Dnieper r. Europe 43 G7
3rd longest river in Europe.
Also spelt Dnepr (Rus. Fed.) or Dnipro (Ukraine) or Dnyapro (Belarus).

Dniester r. Ukr. 43 F6
also spelt Dnister (Ukraine) or Nistru (Moldova)
Dnipro r. Europe 43 G7 see Dnieper
Dniprodzerzhyns'k Ukr. 43 G6
Dnipropetrovs'k Ukr. 43 G6
Dnister r. Ukr. 43 F6 see Dniester
Dno Rus. Fed. 42 F4
Dnyapro r. Europe 43 F6 see Dnieper
Doāb Afgh. 89 G3
Doaba Pak. 89 H3
Doan Hung Vietnam 70 D2
Doba Chad 97 E4
Doba China see Toiba
Dobele Latvia 45 M8
Döbeln Germany 53 N3
Doberai, Jazirah pen. Indon. 69 I7
Doberai Peninsula Indon. see Doberai, Jazirah
Dobo Indon. 69 I8
Doboj Bos.-Herz. 58 H2
Do Borjī Iran 88 D4
Döbraberg hill Germany 53 L4
Dobrich Bulg. 59 L3
Dobrinka Rus. Fed. 43 I5
Dobroye Rus. Fed. 43 H5
Dobrudja reg. Romania see Dobruja
Dobruja reg. Romania 59 L3
Dobrush Belarus 43 F5
Dobryanka Rus. Fed. 41 R4
Dobzha China 83 G3
Doce r. Brazil 145 D2
Dochart r. U.K. 50 E4
Do China Qala Afgh. 89 H4
Docking U.K. 49 H6
Doctor Hicks Range hills Australia 109 D7
Doctor Pedro P. Peña Para. 144 D2
Doda India 82 C2
Doda Betta mt. India 84 C4
Dod Ballapur India 84 C3
Dodecanese is Greece 59 L7
Dodekanisa is Greece see Dodecanese
Dodekanisos is Greece see Dodecanese
Dodge City U.S.A. 130 C4
Dodgeville U.S.A. 130 F3
Dodman Point U.K. 49 C8

▶Dodoma Tanz. 99 D4
Capital of Tanzania.

Dodsonville U.S.A. 134 D4
Doetinchem Neth. 52 G3
Dog r. Canada 122 C4
Dogai Coring salt l. China 83 G2
Dogaicoring Qangco salt l. China 83 G2
Doğanşehir Turkey 90 E3
Dogên Co l. Xizang China 83 G3
Dogên Co l. Xizang China see Bam Tso
Doghārūn Iran 89 F3
Dog Island Canada 123 J2
Dog Lake Man. Canada 121 L5
Dog Lake Ont. Canada 122 C4
Dog Lake Ont. Canada 122 D4
Dōgo i. Japan 75 D5
Dogondoutchi Niger 96 D3
Dog Rocks is Bahamas 133 E7
Doğubeyazıt Turkey 91 G3
Doğu Menteşe Dağları mts Turkey 59 M6
Dogxung Zangbo r. China 83 F3
Do'gyaling China 83 G3

▶Doha Qatar 88 C5
Capital of Qatar.

Dohad India see Dahod
Dohazari Bangl. 83 H5
Dohrighat India 83 E4
Doi i. Fiji 107 I4
Doi Inthanon National Park Thai. 70 B3
Doi Luang National Park Thai. 70 B3
Doire U.K. see Londonderry
Doi Saket Thai. 70 B3
Dois Irmãos, Serra dos hills Brazil 143 J5
Dokan, Sadd Iraq 91 G4
Dok-do i. Asia see Liancourt Rocks
Dokhara, Dunes de des. Alg. 54 F5
Dokka Norway 45 G6
Dokkum Neth. 52 F1
Dokog He r. China 76 D2
Dokri Pak. 89 H5
Dokshukino Rus. Fed. see Nartkala
Dokshytsy Belarus 45 O9
Dokuchayeva, Mys c. Rus. Fed. 74 G3
Dokuchayevka Kazakh. see Karamendy
Dokuchayevs'k Ukr. 43 H7
Dolbeau-Mistassini Canada 123 G4
Dolbenmaen U.K. 49 C6
Dol-de-Bretagne France 56 D2
Dole France 56 G3
Dolgellau U.K. 49 D6
Dolgen Germany 53 N1
Dolgiy, Ostrov i. Rus. Fed. 42 L1
Dolgorukovo Rus. Fed. 43 H5
Dolina Ukr. see Dolyna
Dolinsk Rus. Fed. 74 F3
Dolisie Congo see Loubomo
Dolleman Island Antarctica 152 L2
Dollnstein Germany 53 L6
Dolok, Pulau i. Indon. 69 J8
Dolomites mts Italy 58 D2
Dolomiti mts Italy see Dolomites
Dolomiti Bellunesi, Parco Nazionale delle nat. park Italy 58 D1
Dolomitiche, Alpi mts Italy see Dolomites
Dolonnur China 73 L4
Dolo Odo Eth. 98 E3
Dolores Arg. 144 E5
Dolores Uruguay 144 E4
Dolores U.S.A. 129 I3
Dolphin and Union Strait Canada 118 G3
Dolphin Head hd Namibia 100 B3
Đô Lương Vietnam 70 D3
Dolyna Ukr. 43 D6
Domaila India 82 D3
Domaniç Turkey 59 M5
Domar China 80 F5
Domartang China 76 B2
Domažlice Czech Rep. 53 M5
Domba China 76 B1
Dom Bākh Iran 88 B3
Dombås Norway 44 F5
Dombóvár Hungary 58 H1
Dombrau Poland see Dąbrowa Górnicza
Dombrovitsa Ukr. see Dubrovytsya
Dombrowa Poland see Dąbrowa Górnicza
Domda China see Qingshuihe
Dome Argus ice feature Antarctica 152 E1
Dome Charlie ice feature Antarctica 152 F2
Dome Creek Canada 120 F4
Dome Rock Mountains U.S.A. 129 F5
Domeyko Chile 144 B3
Domfront France 56 D2
Dominica country West Indies 137 L5
Dominicana, República country West Indies see Dominican Republic
Dominican Republic country West Indies 137 J5
Dominion, Cape Canada 119 K3
Dominique i. Fr. Polynesia see Hiva Oa
Dömitz Germany 53 L1
Dom Joaquim Brazil 145 C2
Dommel r. Neth. 52 F3
Domo Eth. 98 E3
Domokos Greece 59 J5
Dompu Indon. 108 B2
Domula China see Duomula
Domuyo, Volcán vol. Arg. 144 B5
Domville, Mount hill Australia 112 E2
Don Mex. 127 F8

▶Don r. Rus. Fed. 43 H7
5th longest river in Europe.

Don r. U.K. 50 G3
Don, Xé r. Laos 70 D4
Donaghadee U.K. 51 G3
Donaghmore U.K. 51 F3
Donald Australia 112 A6
Donaldsonville U.S.A. 131 F6
Donalsonville U.S.A. 133 C6
Doñana, Parque Nacional de nat. park Spain 57 C5
Donau r. Europe 47 P6 see Danube
Donauwörth Germany 53 K6
Don Benito Spain 57 D4
Doncaster U.K. 48 F5
Dondo Angola 99 B4
Dondo Moz. 99 D5
Dondra Head hd Sri Lanka 84 D5
Donegal Ireland 51 D3
Donegal Bay Ireland 51 D3
Donets'k Ukr. 43 H7
Donetsko-Amrovsiyevka Ukr. see Amvrosiyivka
Donets'kyy Kryazh hills Rus. Fed./Ukr. 43 H6
Donga r. Cameroon/Nigeria 96 D4
Dong'an China 77 F3
Dongane, Lagoa lag. Moz. 101 L3
Dongara Australia 109 A7
Dongbo China see Mêdog
Dongchuan Yunnan China 76 D3
Dongchuan Yunnan China see Yao'an
Dongco China 83 F2
Dong Co l. China 83 F2
Dongfang China 77 F5
Dongfanghong China 74 D3
Donggang China 75 B5
Donggang Shandong China 77 H1
Donggi Conag l. China 76 C1
Donggou China see Donggang
Donggu China 77 G3
Dongguan China 77 G4
Dong Hai sea N. Pacific Ocean see East China Sea
Đông Hơi Vietnam 70 D3
Donghuang China see Xishui
Dongjiang Shuiku resr China 77 G3
Dongjug China 76 B2
Dongkou China 77 F3
Donglan China 76 E3
Dongliao He r. China 74 A4
Dongmen China see Luocheng
Dongminzhutun China 74 A3
Dongning China 74 C3
Dongo Angola 99 B5
Dongo Dem. Rep. Congo 98 B3
Dongola Sudan 86 D6
Dongou Congo 98 B3
Dong Phraya Yen esc. Thai. 70 C4
Dongping Guangdong China 77 G4
Dongping Hunan China see Anhua
Dongpo China see Meishan
Dongqiao China 83 G3
Dongshan Fujian China 77 H4
Dongshan Jiangsu China 77 I2
Dongshan Jiangxi China see Shangyou
Dongshao China 77 G3
Dongsha Qundao is China 68 F2
Dongsheng Nei Mongol China see Ordos
Dongsheng Sichuan China see Shuangliu
Dongshuan China see Tangdan
Dongtai China 77 I1
Dongting Hu l. China 77 G2
Dongtou China 77 I3
Đông Triêu Vietnam 70 D2
Dong Ujimqin Qi China see Uliastai
Đông Văn Vietnam 70 D2
Dongxiang China 77 H2
Dongxi Liandao i. China 77 H1
Dongxing Guangxi China 76 E4
Dongxing Heilong. China 74 B3
Dongyang China 77 I2
Dongying China 73 L5
Dongzhi China 77 H2
Donkerbroek Neth. 52 G1
Donnacona Canada 123 H5
Donnellys Crossing N.Z. 113 D2
Donner Pass U.S.A. 128 C2
Donnersberg hill Germany 53 H5
Donostia-San Sebastián Spain 57 F2
Donousa i. Greece 59 K6
Donoussa i. Greece see Donousa
Donskoye Rus. Fed. 43 I7
Donyztau, Sor dry lake Kazakh. 80 A2
Dooagh Ireland 51 B4
Doomadgee Australia 110 B3
Doon r. U.K. 50 E5
Doon, Loch l. U.K. 50 E5
Doonbeg r. Ireland 51 C5
Doorn Neth. 52 F2
Door Peninsula U.S.A. 134 B1
Doorwerth Neth. 52 F3
Dooxo Nugaaleed valley Somalia 98 E3
Doqêmo China 76 B2
Dor watercourse Afgh. 89 F4
Dor Israel 85 B3
Dora U.S.A. 131 C5
Dora, Lake salt flat Australia 108 C5
Dorado Mex. 131 B7
Dorah Pass Pak. 89 H2
Doran Lake Canada 121 I2
Dorbiljin China see Emin
Dorbod China see Taikang
Dorbod Qi China see Ulan Hua
Dorchester U.K. 49 E8
Dordabis Namibia 100 C2
Dordogne r. France 56 D4
Dordrecht Neth. 52 E3
Dordrecht S. Africa 101 H6
Doreenville Namibia 100 D2
Doré Lake Canada 121 J4
Doré Lake l. Canada 121 J4
Dores do Indaiá Brazil 145 B2
Dorgê Co l. China 83 H2
Dori r. Afgh. 89 G4
Dori Burkina 96 C3
Doring r. S. Africa 100 D6
Dorisvale Australia 108 E3
Dorking U.K. 49 G7
Dormagen Germany 52 G3
Dormans France 52 D5
Dormidontovka Rus. Fed. 74 D3
Dornoch U.K. 50 E3
Dornoch Firth est. U.K. 50 E3
Dornum Germany 53 H1
Doro Mali 96 C3
Dorogobuzh Rus. Fed. 43 G5
Dorogorskoye Rus. Fed. 42 J2
Dorohoi Romania 43 E7
Döröö Nuur salt l. Mongolia 80 H2
Dorostol Bulg. see Silistra
Dorotea Sweden 44 J4
Dorpat Estonia see Tartu
Dorre Island Australia 109 A6
Dorrigo Australia 112 F3
Dorris U.S.A. 126 C4
Dorset Canada 135 F1
Dorsoidong Co l. China 83 G2
Dortmund Germany 53 H3
Dörtyol Turkey 85 C1
Dorum Germany 53 I1
Doruma Dem. Rep. Congo 98 C3
Dorūneh, Kūh-e mts Iran 88 E3
Dörverden Germany 53 J2
Dorylaeum Turkey see Eskişehir
Dos Bahías, Cabo c. Arg. 144 C6
Dos de Mayo Peru 142 C5
Doshakh, Koh-i- mt. Afgh. see Do Shākh, Kūh-e
Do Shākh, Kūh-e mt. Afgh. 89 F3
Đo Sơn Vietnam 70 D2
Dos Palos U.S.A. 128 C3
Dosse r. Germany 53 M2
Dosso Niger 96 D3
Dothan U.S.A. 133 C6
Dotsero U.S.A. 129 J2
Douai France 52 D4
Douala Cameroon 96 D4
Douarnenez France 56 B2
Double Headed Shot Cays is Bahamas 133 D8
Double Island H.K. China 77 [inset]
Double Island Point Australia 111 F5
Double Mountain Fork r. U.S.A. 131 C5
Double Peak U.S.A. 128 D4
Double Point Australia 110 D3
Double Springs U.S.A. 133 C5
Doubs r. France/Switz. 56 G3
Doubtful Sound inlet N.Z. 113 A7
Doubtless Bay N.Z. 113 D2
Douentza Mali 96 C3
Dougga tourist site Tunisia 58 C6

▶Douglas Isle of Man 48 C4
Capital of the Isle of Man.

Douglas S. Africa 100 F5
Douglas U.K. 50 F5
Douglas AZ U.S.A. 127 F7
Douglas GA U.S.A. 133 D6
Douglas WY U.S.A. 126 G4
Douglas Reef i. Japan see Okino-Tori-shima
Douglasville U.S.A. 133 C5
Douhudi China see Gong'an
Doulatpur Bangl. see Daulatpur
Douliu Taiwan see Touliu
Doullens France 52 C4
Douna Mali 96 C3
Doune U.K. 50 E4
Doupovské hory mts Czech Rep. 53 N4
Dourada, Serra hills Brazil 145 A2
Dourada, Serra mts Brazil 145 A1
Dourados Brazil 144 F2
Douro r. Port. 57 B3
also known as Duero (Spain)
Doushi China see Gong'an
Doushui Shuiku resr China 77 G3
Douve r. France 49 F9
Douzy France 52 F5
Dove r. U.K. 49 F6
Dove Brook Canada 123 K3
Dove Creek U.S.A. 129 I3
Dover U.K. 49 I7

▶Dover DE U.S.A. 135 H4
Capital of Delaware.

Dover NH U.S.A. 135 J2
Dover NJ U.S.A. 135 H3
Dover OH U.S.A. 134 E3
Dover TN U.S.A. 132 C4
Dover, Strait of France/U.K. 56 E1
Dover-Foxcroft U.S.A. 135 K1
Dovey r. U.K. 49 D6
Dovrefjell Nasjonalpark nat. park Norway 44 F5
Dowagiac U.S.A. 134 B3
Dowi, Tanjung pt Indon. 71 B7
Dowlaiswaram India 84 D2
Dowlatābād Afgh. 89 F3
Dowlatābād Fārs Iran 88 C4
Dowlatābād Fārs Iran 88 D4
Dowlatābād Khorāsān Iran 88 E2
Dowlatābād Khorāsān Iran 89 F2
Dowl at Yār Afgh. 89 G3
Downieville U.S.A. 128 C2
Downpatrick U.K. 51 G3
Downsville U.S.A. 135 H2
Dow Rūd Iran 88 C3
Doyle U.S.A. 128 C1
Doylestown U.S.A. 135 H3
Dozdān r. Iran 88 E5
Dōzen is Japan 75 D5
Dozois, Réservoir resr Canada 122 F5
Dozulé France 49 G9
Drâa, Hamada du plat. Alg. 54 C6
Dracena Brazil 145 A3
Drachten Neth. 52 G1
Drăgănești-Olt Romania 59 K2
Drăgășani Romania 59 K2
Dragonera, Isla i. Spain see Sa Dragonera
Dragoon U.S.A. 129 H5
Dragsfjärd Fin. 45 M6
Draguignan France 56 H5
Drahichyn Belarus 45 N10
Drake Australia 112 F2
Drake U.S.A. 130 C2
Drakensberg mts S. Africa 101 I3
Drake Passage S. Atlantic Ocean 148 D9
Drakes Bay U.S.A. 128 B3
Drama Greece 59 K4
Drammen Norway 45 G7
Drang, Prêk r. Cambodia 71 D4
Drangedal Norway 45 F7
Dransfeld Germany 53 J3
Draper, Mount U.S.A. 120 B3
Draperstown U.K. 51 F3
Drapsaca Afgh. see Kunduz
Dras India 82 C2
Drasan Pak. 89 I2
Drau r. Europe 47 O7 see Drava
Drava r. Europe 58 H2
also known as Drau (Austria), Drave or Drava (Slovenia and Croatia), Dráva (Hungary)
Dráva r. Europe see Drava
Drave r. Europe see Drava
Drayton Valley Canada 120 H4
Drazinda Pak. 89 H4
Dréan Alg. 58 B6
Dreistelzberge hill Germany 53 J4
Drentse Hoofdvaart canal Neth. 52 G2
Drepano, Akra pt Greece see Laimos, Akrotirio
Dresden Canada 134 D2
Dresden Germany 47 N5
Dreux France 52 B6
Drevsjø Norway 45 H6
Drewryville U.S.A. 135 G5
Dri China 76 C2
Driffield U.K. 48 G4
Driftwood U.S.A. 135 F3
Driggs U.S.A. 126 F4
Drillham Australia 112 E1
Drimoleague Ireland 51 C6
Drina r. Bosnia-Herzegovina/Serbia 59 H2
Driscoll Island Antarctica 152 J1
Drissa Belarus see Vyerkhnyadzvinsk
Drniš Croatia 58 G3
Drobeta-Turnu Severin Romania 59 J2
Drochtersen Germany 53 J1
Drogheda Ireland 51 F4
Drogichin Belarus see Drahichyn
Drogobych Ukr. see Drohobych
Drohobych Ukr. 43 D6
Droichead Átha Ireland see Drogheda
Droichead Nua Ireland see Newbridge
Droitwich U.K. see Droitwich Spa
Droitwich Spa U.K. 49 E6
Dromedary, Cape Australia 112 E6
Dromod Ireland 51 E4
Dromore Northern Ireland U.K. 51 E3
Dromore Northern Ireland U.K. 51 F3
Dronfield U.K. 48 F5
Dronning Louise Land reg. Greenland 153 I1
Dronning Maud Land reg. Antarctica see Queen Maud Land
Dronten Neth. 52 F2
Druk-Yul country Asia see Bhutan
Drumheller Canada 121 H5
Drummond atoll Kiribati see Tabiteuea
Drummond U.S.A. 126 E3
Drummond Island Kiribati see McKean
Drummond, Lake U.S.A. 135 G5
Drummond Range hills Australia 110 D5
Drummondville Canada 123 G5
Drummore U.K. 50 E6
Drury Lake Canada 120 C2
Druskieniki Lith. see Druskininkai
Druskininkai Lith. 45 N10
Druzhina Rus. Fed. 65 P3
Druzhnaya Gorka Rus. Fed. 45 Q7
Dry r. Australia 108 F3
Dryanovo Bulg. 59 K3
Dryberry Lake Canada 121 M5
Dryden Canada 121 M5
Dryden U.S.A. 135 G2
Dry Fork r. U.S.A. 126 G4
Drygalski Ice Tongue Antarctica 152 H1
Drygalski Island Antarctica 152 F2
Dry Lake U.S.A. 129 F3
Dry Lake l. U.S.A. 130 D1
Drymen U.K. 50 E4
Dry Ridge U.S.A. 134 C4
Drysdale r. Australia 108 D3
Drysdale River National Park Australia 108 D3
Dry Tortugas is U.S.A. 133 D7
Du'an China 77 F4
Duaringa Australia 110 E4
Duarte, Pico mt. Dom. Rep. 137 J5
Duartina Brazil 145 A3
Ḍubā Saudi Arabia 86 E4
Dubai U.A.E. 88 D5
Dubakella Mountain U.S.A. 128 B1
Dubawnt r. Canada 121 L2
Dubawnt Lake Canada 121 K2
Dubayy U.A.E. see Dubai
Dubbo Australia 112 D4

▶Dublin Ireland 51 F4
Capital of Ireland.

Dublin U.S.A. 133 D5
Dubna Rus. Fed. 42 H4
Dubno Ukr. 43 E6
Dubois ID U.S.A. 126 E3
Dubois IN U.S.A. 134 B4
Du Bois U.S.A. 135 F3
Dubovka Rus. Fed. 43 J6
Dubovskoye Rus. Fed. 43 I7
Dubréka Guinea 96 B4
Dubris U.K. see Dover
Dubrovnik Croatia 58 H3
Dubrovytsya Ukr. 43 E6
Dubuque U.S.A. 130 F3
Dubysa r. Lith. 45 M9
Đức Bôn Vietnam 71 D5
Duc de Gloucester, Îles du is Fr. Polynesia 151 K7
Duchang China 77 H2
Ducheng China see Yunan
Duchesne U.S.A. 129 H1
Duchesne r. U.S.A. 129 I1
Duchess Australia 110 B4
Duchess Canada 121 I5
Ducie Island atoll Pitcairn Is 151 L7
Duck Bay Canada 121 K4
Duck Creek r. Australia 108 B5
Duck Lake Canada 121 J4
Duckwater Peak U.S.A. 129 F2
Duc Tho Vietnam 70 D3
Dudelange Lux. 52 G5
Duderstadt Germany 53 K3
Dudhi India 83 E4
Dudhwa India 82 E3
Dudinka Rus. Fed. 64 J3
Dudley U.K. 49 E6
Dudleyville U.S.A. 129 H5
Dudna r. India 84 C2
Dudu India 82 C4
Duékoué Côte d'Ivoire 96 C4
Duen, Bukit vol. Indon. 68 C7
Duero r. Spain 57 C3
also known as Douro (Portugal)
Duffel Belgium 52 E3
Dufferin, Cape Canada 122 F2
Duffer Peak U.S.A. 126 D4
Duff Islands Solomon Is 107 G2
Duffreboy, Lac l. Canada 123 H2
Dufftown U.K. 50 F3
Dufourspitze mt. Italy/Switz. 56 H4
Dufrost, Pointe pt Canada 122 F1
Dugi Otok i. Croatia 58 F2
Dugi Rat Croatia 58 G3
Du He r. China 77 F1
Duida-Marahuaca, Parque Nacional nat. park Venez. 142 E3
Duisburg Germany 52 G3
Duiwelskloof S. Africa 101 J2
Dujiangyan China 76 D2
Dukathole S. Africa 101 H6
Duke Island U.S.A. 120 D4
Duke of Clarence atoll Tokelau see Nukunonu
Duke of Gloucester Islands Fr. Polynesia see Duc de Gloucester, Îles du
Duke of York atoll Tokelau see Atafu
Duk Fadiat Sudan 97 G4
Dukhovnitskoye Rus. Fed. 43 K5
Duki Pak. 89 H4
Duki Rus. Fed. 74 D2
Duki r. Rus. Fed. 74 D2
Dukou China see Panzhihua
Dūkštas Lith. 45 O9
Dulac U.S.A. 131 F6
Dulan China 80 I4
Dulce r. Arg. 144 D4
Dulce U.S.A. 127 G5
Dul'durga Rus. Fed. 73 K2
Dulhunty r. Australia 110 C1
Dulishi Hu salt l. China 83 E2
Duliu Jiang r. China 77 F3
Dullewala Pak. 89 H4
Dullstroom S. Africa 101 J3
Dülmen Germany 53 H3
Dulmera India 82 C3
Dulovo Bulg. 59 L3
Duluth U.S.A. 130 E2
Dulverton U.K. 49 D7
Dūmā Syria 85 C3
Dumaguete Phil. 69 G5
Dumai Indon. 71 C7
Dumaran i. Phil. 68 G4
Dumaresq r. Australia 112 E2
Dumas U.S.A. 131 C5
Dumat al Jandal Saudi Arabia 91 E5
Ḑumayr Syria 85 C3
Ḑumayr, Jabal mts Syria 85 C3
Dumbakh Iran see Dom Bākh
Dumbarton U.K. 50 E5
Dumbe S. Africa 101 J4
Ďumbier mt. Slovakia 47 Q6
Dumchele India 82 D2
Dumdum i. Indon. 71 D7
Dum Duma India 83 H4
Dumfries U.K. 50 F5
Dumka India 83 F4
Dumont d'Urville research station Antarctica 152 G2
Dumont d'Urville Sea Antarctica 152 G2
Dümpelfeld Germany 52 G4
Dumyāṭ Egypt 90 C5
Dumyâṭ Egypt see Dumyāṭ
Duna r. Europe 58 H2 see Danube
Dünaburg Latvia see Daugavpils
Dunaj r. Europe see Danube
Dunajská Streda Slovakia 47 P7
Dunakeszi Hungary 59 H1
Dunany Point Ireland 51 F4
Dunărea r. Europe 59 L2 see Danube
Dunării, Delta Romania/Ukr. see Danube Delta
Dunaújváros Hungary 58 H1
Dunav r. Europe 58 L2 see Danube
Dunay r. Europe see Danube
Dunayivtsi Ukr. 43 E6
Dunbar Australia 110 C3
Dunbar U.K. 50 G4
Dunblane U.K. 50 F4
Dunboyne Ireland 51 F4
Duncan Canada 120 F5
Duncan AZ U.S.A. 129 I5
Duncan OK U.S.A. 131 D5
Duncan, Cape Canada 122 E3
Duncan, Lac l. Canada 122 F3
Duncan Lake Canada 120 H2
Duncan Passage India 71 A5
Duncansby Head hd U.K. 50 F2
Duncan Town Bahamas 133 F8
Duncormick Ireland 51 F5
Dundaga Latvia 45 M8
Dundalk Ireland 51 F3
Dundalk U.S.A. 135 G4
Dundalk Bay Ireland 51 F4
Dundas Canada 134 F2
Dundas Greenland 119 L2
Dundas, Lake salt flat Australia 109 C8
Dundas Island Canada 120 D4
Dundas Strait Australia 108 E2
Dún Dealgan Ireland see Dundalk
Dundee S. Africa 101 J5
Dundee U.K. 50 G4
Dundee MI U.S.A. 134 D3
Dundee NY U.S.A. 135 G2
Dundonald U.K. 51 G3
Dundoo Australia 112 B1
Dundrennan U.K. 50 F6
Dundrum U.K. 51 G3
Dundrum Bay U.K. 51 G3
Dundwa Range mts India/Nepal 83 E4
Dune, Lac l. Canada 122 G2
Dunedin N.Z. 113 C7
Dunedin U.S.A. 133 D6
Dunfermline U.K. 50 F4
Dungannon U.K. 51 F3
Dún Garbhán Ireland see Dungarvan
Dungarpur India 82 C5
Dungarvan Ireland 51 E5
Dung Co l. China 83 G3
Dungeness hd U.K. 49 H8
Dungeness, Punta pt Arg. 144 C8
Düngenheim Germany 53 H4
Dungiven U.K. 51 F3
Dungog Australia 112 E4
Dungu Dem. Rep. Congo 98 C3
Dungun Malaysia 71 C6
Dungunab Sudan 86 E5
Dunhua China 74 C4
Dunhuang China 80 H3
Dunkeld Australia 112 D1
Dunkeld U.K. 50 F4
Dunkellin r. Ireland 51 D4
Dunkerque France see Dunkirk
Dunkery Hill hill U.K. 49 D7
Dunkirk France 52 C3
Dunkirk U.S.A. 134 F2
Dún Laoghaire Ireland 51 F4
Dunlap IA U.S.A. 130 E3
Dunlap TN U.S.A. 132 C5
Dunlavin Ireland 51 F4
Dunleer Ireland 51 F4
Dunloy U.K. 51 F2
Dunmanway Ireland 51 C6
Dunmarra Australia 108 F4
Dunmor U.S.A. 134 B5
Dunmore Ireland 51 D4
Dunmore U.S.A. 135 H3
Dunmore Town Bahamas 133 E7
Dunmurry U.K. 51 G3
Dunnet Head hd U.K. 50 F2
Dunnigan U.S.A. 128 C2
Dunning U.S.A. 130 C3
Dunnville Canada 134 F2
Dunnville U.S.A. 134 C5
Dunolly Australia 112 A6
Dunoon U.K. 50 E5
Dunphy U.S.A. 128 E1
Duns U.K. 50 G5
Dunseith U.S.A. 130 C1
Dunstable U.K. 49 G7
Dunstan Mountains N.Z. 113 B7
Dun-sur-Meuse France 52 F5

untroon N.Z. 113 C7
unvegan Lake Canada 121 J2
unyapur Pak. 89 H4
uolun Nei Mongol China see Dolonnur
uomula China 83 E2
upang Ling mts China 77 F3
uperré Alg. see Aïn Defla
upnitsa Bulg. 59 J3
upree U.S.A. 130 C2
uque de Bragança Angola see Calandula
ūrā West Bank 85 B4
urack r. Australia 108 D3
urack Range hills Australia 108 D4
ura Europos Syria see Aş Şālihīyah
urağan Turkey 90 D2
urance r. France 56 G5
urand U.S.A. 130 F2
urango Mex. 131 B7
urango state Mex. 131 B7
urango Spain 57 E2
urango U.S.A. 129 J3
urani reg. Afgh. 89 G4
urant U.S.A. 131 D5
urazno Uruguay 144 E4
urazzo Albania see Durrës
urban S. Africa 101 J5
urban-Corbières France 56 F5
urbanville S. Africa 100 D7
urbin U.S.A. 134 F4
urbun Pak. 89 G4
urbuy Belgium 52 F4
üren Germany 52 G4
üren Iran 88 E3
uren, Kūh-e mt. Iran 88 E3
urg India 82 E5
urgapur Bangl. 83 G4
urgapur India 83 F5
urham Canada 134 E1
urham U.K. 48 F4
urham U.S.A. 132 E5
urham Downs Australia 111 C5
uri Indon. 71 C7
urlas Ireland see Thurles
urleşti Moldova 59 M1
urmersheim Germany 53 I6
urmitor mt. Montenegro 59 H3
urmitor nat. park Montenegro 58 H3
urness U.K. 50 E2
urocortorum France see Reims
urong South Australia 111 E5
urostorum Bulg. see Silistra
urour Island P.N.G. see Aua Island
urovernum U.K. see Canterbury
urrës Albania 59 H4
urrie Australia 110 C5
urrington U.K. 49 F7
ursey Island Ireland 51 B6
ursunbey Turkey 59 M5
uru China see Wuchuan
uruh Iran 89 F3
urukhsi Somalia 98 E3
urusu Gölü l. Turkey 59 M4
urūz, Jabal ad mt. Syria 85 C3
'Urville, Tanjung pt Indon. 69 J7
'Urville Island N.Z. 113 D5
urzab Afgh. 89 G3
uşak Turkm. 89 E2
ushai Pak. 89 G4
ushan China 76 E3

Dushanbe Tajik. 89 H2
Capital of Tajikistan.

ushet'i Georgia 91 G2
ushore U.S.A. 135 G3
usse-Alin', Khrebet mts Rus. Fed. 74 D2
üsseldorf Germany 52 G3
usty NM U.S.A. 129 J5
usty WA U.S.A. 126 D3
utch East Indies country Asia see Indonesia
utch Guiana country S. America see Suriname
utch Mountain U.S.A. 129 G1
utch West Indies terr. West Indies see Netherlands Antilles
utlwe Botswana 100 F2
utse Nigeria 96 D3
utsin-Ma Nigeria 96 D3
utton r. Australia 110 C4
utton Canada 134 E2
utton U.S.A. 126 F3
utton, Lake salt flat Australia 111 B6
utton, Mount U.S.A. 129 G2
uval Canada 121 J5
uvert, Lac l. Canada 123 H2
uvno Bos.-Herz. see Tomislavgrad
uwin Iraq 91 G3
uxanbibazar China 82 E1
uyun China 76 E3
uzab Pak. 89 F5
üzce Turkey 59 N4
uzdab Iran see Zāhedān
vina r. Europe see Zapadnaya Dvina
vina r. Rus. Fed. see Severnaya Dvina
vinsk Latvia see Daugavpils
vinskaya Guba g. Rus. Fed. 42 H2
warka India 82 B5
warsberg S. Africa 101 H3
wingelderveld, Nationaal Park nat. park Neth. 52 G2
worshak Reservoir U.S.A. 126 E3
wyka S. Africa 100 E7
yat'kovo Rus. Fed. 43 G5
yce U.K. 50 G3
yer, Cape Canada 119 L3
yer Bay Canada 134 E1
yersburg U.S.A. 131 F4
yffryn U.K. see Valley
yfi r. U.K. see Dovey
yfrdwy r. U.K. see Dee
yfrdwy r. England/Wales U.K. see Dee
yje r. Austria/Czech Rep. 47 P6
yke U.K. 50 F3

Dykh-Tau, Gora mt. Rus. Fed. 91 F2
2nd highest mountain in Europe.

yle r. Belgium 52 E4
yleň hill Czech Rep. 53 M5

Dylewska Góra hill Poland 47 Q4
Dymytrov Ukr. 43 H6
Dynevor Downs Australia 112 B2
Dyoki S. Africa 101 I6
Dyrrhachium Albania see Durrës
Dysart Australia 110 E4
Dysselsdorp S. Africa 100 F7
Dyurtyuli Rus. Fed. 41 Q4
Dzamīn Üüd Mongolia 73 K4
Dzanga-Ndoki, Parc National de nat. park Cent. Afr. Rep. 98 B3

▶Dzaoudzi Mayotte 99 E5
Capital of Mayotte.

Dzaudzhikau Rus. Fed. see Vladikavkaz
Dzavhan Mongolia 80 H2
Dzerzhinsk Belarus see Dzyarzhynsk
Dzerzhinsk Rus. Fed. 42 I4
Dzhagdy, Khrebet mts Rus. Fed. 74 C1
Dzhaki-Unakhta Yakbyyana, Khrebet mts Rus. Fed. 74 D2
Dzhalalabad Azer. see Cälilabad
Dzhalal-Abad Kyrg. see Jalal-Abad
Dzhalil' Rus. Fed. 41 Q4
Dzhalinda Rus. Fed. 74 A1
Dzhaltyr Kazakh. see Zhaltyr
Dzhambeyty Kazakh. see Zhympity
Dzhambul Kazakh. see Taraz
Dzhangala Kazakh. 41 Q6
Dzhankoy Ukr. 43 G7
Dzhanybek Kazakh. see Zhanibek
Dzharkent Kazakh. see Zharkent
Dzhava Georgia see Java
Dzhetygara Kazakh. see Zhitikara
Dzhezkazgan Kazakh. see Zhezkazgan
Dzhidinskiy, Khrebet mts Mongolia/Rus. Fed. 80 J1
Dzhirgatal' Tajik. see Jirgatol
Dzhizak Uzbek. see Jizzax
Dzhokhar Ghala Rus. Fed. see Groznyy
Dzhubga Rus. Fed. 90 E1
Dzhugdzhur, Khrebet mts Rus. Fed. 65 O4
Dzhul'fa Azer. see Culfa
Dzhuma Uzbek. see Juma
Dzhungarskiy Alatau, Khrebet mts China/Kazakh. 80 E3
Dzhusaly Kazakh. 80 B2
Działdowo Poland 47 R4
Dzūkija nat. park Lith. 45 N9
Dzungarian Basin China see Junggar Pendi
Dzungarian Gate pass China/Kazakh. 80 F2
Dzüünharaa Mongolia 72 J3
Dzuunmod Mongolia 72 J3
Dzyaniskavichy Belarus 45 O10
Dzyarzhynsk Belarus 45 O10
Dzyatlavichy Belarus 45 O10

Eabamet Lake Canada 122 D4
Eads U.S.A. 130 C4
Eagar U.S.A. 129 I4
Eagle r. Canada 123 K3
Eagle AK U.S.A. 118 D3
Eagle CO U.S.A. 126 G5
Eagle Cap mt. U.S.A. 126 D3
Eagle Crags mt. U.S.A. 128 E4
Eagle Creek r. Canada 121 J4
Eagle Lake Canada 121 M5
Eagle Lake CA U.S.A. 128 C1
Eagle Lake ME U.S.A. 132 G2
Eagle Mountain U.S.A. 129 F5
Eagle Mountain hill U.S.A. 130 F2
Eagle Pass U.S.A. 131 C6
Eagle Peak U.S.A. 127 G7
Eagle Plain Canada 118 E3
Eagle River U.S.A. 130 F2
Eagle Rock U.S.A. 134 F5
Eaglesham Canada 120 G4
Eap i. Micronesia see Yap
Ear Falls Canada 121 M5
Earlimart U.S.A. 128 D4
Earl's Seat hill U.K. 50 E4
Earlston U.K. 50 G5
Earn r. U.K. 50 F4
Earn, Loch l. U.K. 50 E4
Earp U.S.A. 129 F4
Earth U.S.A. 131 C5
Easington U.K. 48 H5
Easley U.S.A. 133 D5
East Alligator r. Australia 108 F3
East Antarctica reg. Antarctica 152 F1
East Ararat U.S.A. 135 H3
East Aurora U.S.A. 135 F2
East Bay inlet U.S.A. 133 C6
East Bengal country Asia see Bangladesh
Eastbourne U.K. 49 H8
East Branch Clarion River Reservoir U.S.A. 135 F3
East Caicos i. Turks and Caicos Is 133 G8
East Cape N.Z. 113 G3
East Carbon City U.S.A. 129 H2
East Caroline Basin sea feature N. Pacific Ocean 150 F5
East China Sea N. Pacific Ocean 73 N6
East Coast Bays N.Z. 113 E3
East Dereham England U.K. see Dereham
Eastend Canada 121 I5

▶Easter Island S. Pacific Ocean 151 M7
Part of Chile.

Eastern Cape prov. S. Africa 101 H6
Eastern Desert Egypt 86 D4
Eastern Fields reef Australia 110 D1
Eastern Ghats mts India 84 C4

▶Eastern Island U.S.A. 150 I4
Most northerly point of Oceania.

Eastern Nara canal Pak. 89 H5
Eastern Samoa terr. S. Pacific Ocean see American Samoa
Eastern Sayan Mountains Rus. Fed. see Vostochnyy Sayan

Eastern Taurus plat. Turkey see Güneydoğu Toroslar
Eastern Transvaal prov. S. Africa see Mpumalanga
Easterville Canada 121 L4
Easterwâlde Neth. see Oosterwolde
East Falkland i. Falkland Is 144 E8
East Falmouth U.S.A. 135 J3
East Frisian Islands Germany 47 K4
Eastgate U.S.A. 128 E2
East Greenwich U.S.A. 135 J3
East Grinstead U.K. 49 G7
Easthampton U.S.A. 135 I2
East Hampton U.S.A. 135 I3
East Hartford U.S.A. 135 I3
East Indiaman Ridge sea feature Indian Ocean 149 O7
East Jordan U.S.A. 134 C1
East Kilbride U.K. 50 E5
Eastlake U.S.A. 134 E3
East Lamma Channel H.K. China 77 [inset]
Eastland U.S.A. 131 D5
East Lansing U.S.A. 134 C2
Eastleigh U.K. 49 F8
East Liverpool U.S.A. 134 E3
East London S. Africa 101 H7
East Lynn Lake U.S.A. 134 D4
Eastmain Canada 122 F3
Eastmain r. Canada 122 F3
Eastman U.S.A. 133 D5
East Mariana Basin sea feature N. Pacific Ocean 150 G5
Eastmere Australia 110 D4
East Naples U.S.A. 133 D7
Easton MD U.S.A. 135 G4
Easton PA U.S.A. 135 H3
East Orange U.S.A. 135 H3
East Pacific Rise sea feature N. Pacific Ocean 151 M4
East Pakistan country Asia see Bangladesh
East Palestine U.S.A. 134 E3
East Park Reservoir U.S.A. 128 B2
East Point Canada 123 J5
Eastport U.S.A. 132 H2
East Providence U.S.A. 135 J3
East Range mts U.S.A. 128 E1
East Retford U.K. see Retford
East St Louis U.S.A. 130 F4
East Sea N. Pacific Ocean see Japan, Sea of
East Shoal Lake Canada 121 L5
East Siberian Sea Rus. Fed. 65 P2
East Side Canal r. U.S.A. 128 D4
East Stroudsburg U.S.A. 135 H3
East Tavaputs Plateau U.S.A. 129 I2

▶East Timor country Asia 108 D2
Former Portuguese territory. Gained independence from Indonesia in 2002.

East Toorale Australia 112 B3
East Troy U.S.A. 134 A2
East Verde r. U.S.A. 129 H4
Eastville U.S.A. 135 H5
East-Vlylân Neth. see Oost-Vlieland
East York Canada 134 F2
Eaton U.S.A. 134 C4
Eatonia Canada 121 I5
Eaton Rapids U.S.A. 134 C2
Eatonton U.S.A. 133 D5
Eau Claire U.S.A. 130 F2
Eauripik atoll Micronesia 69 K5
Eauripik Rise-New Guinea Rise sea feature N. Pacific Ocean 150 F5
Eaurypyg atoll Micronesia see Eauripik
Ebbw Vale U.K. 49 D7
Ebebiyin Equat. Guinea 96 E4
Ebenerde Namibia 100 C3
Ebensburg U.S.A. 135 F3
Eber Gölü l. Turkey 59 N5
Ebergötzen Germany 53 K3
Eberswalde-Finow Germany 47 N4
Ebetsu Japan 74 F4
Ebian China 76 D2
Ebi Nor salt l. China see Ebinur Hu
Ebinur Hu salt l. China 80 F3
Eboli Italy 58 F4
Ebolowa Cameroon 96 E4
Ebony Namibia 100 B2
Ebre r. Spain see Ebro
Ebro r. Spain 57 G3
Ebstorf Germany 53 K1
Eburacum U.K. see York
Ebusus i. Spain see Ibiza
Ecbatana Iran see Hamadān
Eceabat Turkey 59 L4
Ech Chélif Alg. see Chlef
Echegárate, Puerto pass Spain 57 E2
Echeng China see Ezhou
Echeverria, Pico mt. Mex. 127 E7
Echmiadzin Armenia see Ejmiatsin
Echo U.S.A. 126 D3
Echo Bay N.W.T. Canada 120 G1
Echo Bay Ont. Canada 122 D5
Echo Cliffs U.S.A. 129 H3
Echoing r. Canada 121 M4
Echt Neth. 52 F3
Echternach Lux. 52 G5
Echuca Australia 112 B6
Echzell Germany 53 I4
Écija Spain 57 D5
Eckental Germany 53 L5
Eckernförde Germany 47 L3
Eclipse Sound sea chan. Canada 119 J2
Écrins, Parc National des nat. park France 56 H4
Ecuador country S. America 142 C4
Écueils, Pointe aux pt Canada 122 F2
Ed Eritrea 86 F7
Ed Sweden 45 G7
Edam Neth. 52 F2
Eday i. U.K. 50 G1
Ed Da'ein Sudan 97 F3
Ed Damazin Sudan 86 D7
Ed Damer Sudan 86 D6
Ed Debba Sudan 86 D6
Eddies Cove Canada 123 K4
Ed Dueim Sudan 86 D7
Eddystone Point Australia 111 [inset]
Eddyville U.S.A. 131 F4
Ede Neth. 52 F2

Edéa Cameroon 96 E4
Edehon Lake Canada 121 L2
Edéia Brazil 145 A2
Eden Australia 112 D6
Eden r. U.K. 48 D4
Eden NC U.S.A. 134 F5
Eden TX U.S.A. 131 D6
Edenburg S. Africa 101 G5
Edendale N.Z. 113 B8
Edenderry Ireland 51 E4
Edenton U.S.A. 132 E4
Edenville S. Africa 101 H4
Eder r. Germany 53 J3
Eder-Stausee resr Germany 53 I3
Edessa Greece 59 J4
Edessa Turkey see Şanlıurfa
Edewecht Germany 53 H1
Edfu Egypt see Idfū
Edgar Ranges hills Australia 108 C4
Edgartown U.S.A. 135 J3
Edgecumbe Island Solomon Is see Utupua
Edgefield U.S.A. 133 D5
Edge Island Svalbard see Edgeøya
Edgemont U.S.A. 130 C3
Edgeøya i. Svalbard 64 D2
Edgerton Canada 121 I4
Edgerton U.S.A. 134 C3
Edgeworthstown Ireland 51 E4
Édhessa Greece see Edessa
Edina U.S.A. 130 E3
Edinboro U.S.A. 134 E3
Edinburg TX U.S.A. 131 D7
Edinburg VA U.S.A. 135 F4

▶Edinburgh U.K. 50 F5
Capital of Scotland.

Edirne Turkey 59 L4
Edith, Mount U.S.A. 126 F3
Edith Cavell, Mount Canada 120 G4
Edith Ronne Land ice feature Antarctica see Ronne Ice Shelf
Edjeleh Libya 96 D2
Edjudina Australia 109 C7
Edku Egypt see Idkū
Edmond U.S.A. 131 D5
Edmonds U.S.A. 126 C3

▶Edmonton Canada 120 H4
Capital of Alberta.

Edmonton U.S.A. 134 C5
Edmore MI U.S.A. 134 C2
Edmore ND U.S.A. 130 D1
Edmund Lake Canada 121 M4
Edmundston Canada 123 H5
Edna U.S.A. 131 D6
Edna Bay U.S.A. 120 C4
Edo Japan see Tōkyō
Edom reg. Israel/Jordan 85 B4
Édouard, Lac l. Dem. Rep. Congo/Uganda see Edward, Lake
Edremit Turkey 59 L5
Edremit Körfezi b. Turkey 59 L5
Edrengiyn Nuruu mts Mongolia 80 I3
Edsbyn Sweden 45 I6
Edson Canada 120 G4
Eduni, Mount Canada 120 D1
Edward r. N.S.W. Australia 112 B5
Edward r. Qld Australia 110 C2
Edward, Lake Dem. Rep. Congo/Uganda 98 C4
Edward, Mount Antarctica 152 L1
Edwardesabad Pak. see Bannu
Edwards U.S.A. 135 H1
Edward's Creek Australia 111 A6
Edwards Plateau U.S.A. 131 C6
Edwardsville U.S.A. 130 F4
Edward VII Peninsula Antarctica 152 I1
Edziza, Mount Canada 120 D3
Edzo Canada see Behchokǫ̀
Eeklo Belgium 52 D3
Eel r. U.S.A. 128 A1
Eel, South Fork r. U.S.A. 128 B1
Eem r. Neth. 52 F2
Eemshaven pt Neth. 52 G1
Eenrum Neth. 52 G1
Eenzamheid Pan salt pan S. Africa 100 E4
Eesti country Europe see Estonia
Éfaté i. Vanuatu 107 G3
Effingham U.S.A. 130 F4
Efsus Turkey see Afşin
Egadi, Isole is Sicily Italy 58 D5
Egan Range mts U.S.A. 129 F2
Eganville Canada 135 G1
Egedesminde Greenland see Aasiaat
Eger r. Germany 53 M4
Eger Hungary 47 R7
Egersund Norway 45 E7
Egerton, Mount hill Australia 109 B6
Eggegebirge hills Germany 53 I3
Egg Lake Canada 121 J4
Eggolsheim Germany 53 L5
Eghezée Belgium 52 E4
Egilsstaðir Iceland 44 [inset]
Eğin Turkey see Kemaliye
Eğirdir Turkey 59 N6
Eğirdir Gölü l. Turkey 59 N6
Eglinton U.K. 51 E2
Egmond aan Zee Neth. 52 E2
Egmont, Cape N.Z. 113 D4
Egmont, Mount vol. N.Z. see Taranaki, Mount
Egmont National Park N.Z. 113 E4
eGoli S. Africa see Johannesburg
Eğrigöz Dağı mts Turkey 59 M5
Egton U.K. 48 G4
Éguas r. Brazil 145 B1
Egvekinot Rus. Fed. 65 T3

▶Egypt country Africa 86 C4
3rd most populous country in Africa.

Ehden Lebanon 85 B2
Ehen Hudag China 72 I5
Ehingen (Donau) Germany 47 L6
Ehle r. Germany 53 L2
Ehra-Lessien Germany 53 K2
Ehrenberg U.S.A. 129 F5
Ehrenberg Range hills Australia 109 E5
Eibelstadt Germany 53 K5
Eibergen Neth. 52 G2

Eichenzell Germany 53 J4
Eichstätt Germany 53 L6
Eidfjord Norway 45 E6
Eidsvold Australia 110 E5
Eidsvoll Norway 45 G6
Eifel hills Germany 52 G4
Eigg i. U.K. 50 C4
Eight Degree Channel India/Maldives 84 B5
Eights Coast Antarctica 152 K2
Eighty Mile Beach Australia 108 C4
Eilat Israel 85 B5
Eildon Australia 112 B6
Eildon, Lake Australia 112 C6
Eileen Lake Canada 121 J2
Eilenburg Germany 53 M3
Eil Malk i. Palau 69 I5
Eimke Germany 53 K2
Einasleigh Australia 110 D3
Einasleigh r. Australia 110 C3
Einbeck Germany 53 J3
Eindhoven Neth. 52 F3
Einme Myanmar 70 A3
Einsiedeln Switz. 56 I3
Eirik Ridge sea feature N. Atlantic Ocean 148 F2
Eiriosgaigh i. U.K. see Eriskay
Eirunepé Brazil 142 E5
Eisberg hill Germany 53 J3
Eiseb watercourse Namibia 99 C5
Eisenach Germany 53 K4
Eisenberg Germany 53 L4
Eisenhower, Mount Canada see Castle Mountain
Eisenhüttenstadt Germany 47 O4
Eisenstadt Austria 47 P7
Eisfeld Germany 53 K4
Eisleben Lutherstadt Germany 53 L3
Eite, Loch inlet U.K. see Etive, Loch
Eiterfeld Germany 53 J4
Eivissa Spain see Ibiza
Eivissa i. Spain see Ibiza
Ejea de los Caballeros Spain 57 F2
Ejeda Madag. 99 E6
Ejin Horo Qi China see Altan Shiret
Ejin Qi China see Dalain Hob
Ejmiadzin Armenia see Ejmiatsin
Ejmiatsin Armenia 91 G2
Ekalaka U.S.A. 126 G3
Ekenäs Fin. 45 M7
Ekerem Turkm. 88 D2
Ekeren Belgium 52 E3
Eketahuna N.Z. 113 E5
Ekibastuz Kazakh. 80 E1
Ekimchan Rus. Fed. 74 D1
Ekinyazı Turkey 85 D1
Ekonda Rus. Fed. 65 L3
Ekostrovskaya Imandra, Ozero l. Rus. Fed. 44 R3
Ekshärad Sweden 45 H6
Eksjö Sweden 45 I8
Eksteenfontein S. Africa 100 C5
Ekström Ice Shelf Antarctica 152 B2
Ekwan r. Canada 122 E3
Ekwan Point Canada 122 E3
Ela Myanmar 70 B3
El Aaiún W. Sahara see Laâyoune
Elafonisou, Steno sea chan. Greece 59 J6
El 'Agrûd well Egypt see Al 'Ajrūd
Elaia, Cape Cyprus 85 B2
El 'Alamein Egypt see Al 'Alamayn
El 'Âmirîya Egypt see Al 'Āmirīyah
Elands r. S. Africa 101 I3
Elandsdoorn S. Africa 101 I3
El Aouinet Alg. 58 B7
Elar Armenia see Abovyan
El Araïche Morocco see Larache
El Arco Mex. 127 E7
El Ariana Tunisia see L'Ariana
El Aricha Alg. 54 D5
El 'Arîsh Egypt see Al 'Arīsh
El Arrouch Alg. 58 B6
El Ashmûnein Egypt see Al Ashmūnayn
El Asnam Alg. see Chlef
Elassona Greece 59 J5
Elat Israel see Eilat
Elato atoll Micronesia 69 L5
Elazığ Turkey 91 E3
Elba U.S.A. 133 C6
Elba, Isola d' i. Italy 58 D3
El'ban Rus. Fed. 74 E2
El Barco de Valdeorras Spain see O Barco
El Barreal salt l. Mex. 127 G7
Elbasan Albania 59 I4
El Batroun Lebanon see Batroûn
El Baúl Venez. 142 E2
El Bawiti Egypt see Al Bawītī
El Bayadh Alg. 54 E5
Elbe r. Germany 53 J1
also known as Labe (Czech Republic)
Elbe-Havel-Kanal canal Germany 53 L2
El Béqaa valley Lebanon 85 C2
Elbert, Mount U.S.A. 126 G5
Elberta U.S.A. 129 H2
Elberton U.S.A. 133 D5
Elbeuf France 56 E2
Elbeyli Turkey 85 C1
Elbing Poland see Elbląg
Elbistan Turkey 90 E3
Elbląg Poland 47 Q3
El Boulaïda Alg. see Blida
Elbow Canada 121 J5
Elbow Lake U.S.A. 130 D2
El Bozal Mex. 131 C8
El Brasil Mex. 131 C7

▶El'brus mt. Rus. Fed. 91 F2
Highest mountain in Europe.

Elburg Neth. 52 F2
El Burgo de Osma Spain 57 E3
Elburz Mountains Iran 88 C2
El Cajon U.S.A. 128 E5
El Callao Venez. 142 F2
El Campo U.S.A. 131 D6
El Capitan Mountain U.S.A. 127 G6
El Capulín r. Mex. 131 C7
El Casco Mex. 131 B7
El Centro U.S.A. 129 F5
El Cerro Bol. 142 F7
Elche Spain see Elche-Elx
Elche-Elx Spain 57 F4

El Chilicote Mex. 131 B6
Elcho Island Australia 110 A1
El Coca Orellana Ecuador see Coca
El Coca Ecuador see Coca
El Cocuy, Parque Nacional nat. park Col. 142 D2
El Cuyo Mex. 133 C8
Elda Spain 57 F4
El Dátil Mex. 127 E7
El Desemboque Mex. 127 E7
El Diamante Mex. 131 C6
El'dikan Rus. Fed. 65 O3
El Djezair country Africa see Algeria
El Djezair Alg. see Algiers
El Doctor Mex. 129 F6
Eldon U.S.A. 130 E4
Eldorado Arg. 144 F3
Eldorado Brazil 145 A4
El Dorado Col. 142 D3
El Dorado Mex. 124 F7
El Dorado AR U.S.A. 131 E5
El Dorado KS U.S.A. 130 D4
Eldorado U.S.A. 131 C6
El Dorado Venez. 142 F2
Eldorado Mountains U.S.A. 129 F4
Eldoret Kenya 98 D3
Elea, Cape Cyprus see Elaia, Cape
Eleanor U.S.A. 134 E4
Electric Peak U.S.A. 126 F3
Elefantes r. Moz./S. Africa see Olifants
El Eglab plat. Alg. 96 C2
El Ejido Spain 57 E5

▶Elemi Triangle terr. Africa 98 D3
Disputed territory (Ethiopia/Kenya/Sudan) administered by Kenya.

El Encanto Col. 142 D4
Elend Germany 53 K3
Elephanta Caves tourist site India 84 B2
Elephant Butte Reservoir U.S.A. 127 G6
Elephant Island Antarctica 152 A2
Elephant Pass Sri Lanka 84 D4
Elephant Point Bangl. 83 H5
Eleşkirt Turkey 91 F3
El Eulma Alg. 54 F4
Eleuthera i. Bahamas 133 E7
Eleven Point r. U.S.A. 131 F4
El Fahs Tunisia 58 C6
El Faiyûm Egypt see Al Fayyūm
El Fasher Sudan 97 F3
El Ferrol Spain see Ferrol
El Ferrol del Caudillo Spain see Ferrol
Elfershausen Germany 53 J4
El Fud Eth. 98 E3
El Fuerte Mex. 127 F8
El Gara Egypt see Qārah
El Geneina Sudan 97 F3
El Geteina Sudan 86 D7
El Ghardaqa Egypt see Al Ghurdaqah
El Ghor plain Jordan/West Bank see Al Ghawr
Elgin U.K. 50 F3
Elgin IL U.S.A. 130 F3
Elgin ND U.S.A. 130 C2
Elgin NV U.S.A. 129 F3
Elgin TX U.S.A. 131 D6
El'ginskiy Rus. Fed. 65 P3
El Gîza Egypt see Giza
El Goléa Alg. 54 E5
El Golfo de Santa Clara Mex. 127 E7
Elgon, Mount Kenya/Uganda 78 C6
El Hadjar Alg. 58 B6
El Ḥammâm Egypt see Al Ḥammām
El Ḥammâmi reg. Mauritania 96 B2
El Ḥank esc. Mali/Mauritania 96 C2
El Ḥarra Egypt see Al Ḥarrah
El Hazim Jordan see Al Hazīm
El Ḥeiz Egypt see Al Ḥayz
El Hierro i. Canary Is 96 B2
El Homr Alg. 54 E6
El Homra Sudan 86 D7
Eliase Indon. 108 E2
Elías Piña Dom. Rep. 137 J5
Elichpur India see Achalpur
Elida U.S.A. 134 C3
Elie U.K. 50 G4
Elila r. Dem. Rep. Congo 98 C4
Elim U.S.A. 118 B3
Elimberrum France see Auch
Eling China see Yinjiang
Elingampangu Dem. Rep. Congo 98 C4
Eliot, Mount Canada 123 J2
Élisabethville Dem. Rep. Congo see Lubumbashi
Eliseu Martins Brazil 143 J5
El Iskandarîya Egypt see Alexandria
Elista Rus. Fed. 43 J7
Elizabeth NJ U.S.A. 135 H3
Elizabeth WV U.S.A. 134 E4
Elizabeth, Mount hill Australia 108 D4
Elizabeth Bay Namibia 100 B4
Elizabeth City U.S.A. 132 E4
Elizabeth Island Pitcairn Is see Henderson Island
Elizabeth Point Namibia 100 B4
Elizabethton U.S.A. 132 D4
Elizabethtown IL U.S.A. 130 F4
Elizabethtown KY U.S.A. 134 C5
Elizabethtown NC U.S.A. 133 E5
Elizabethtown NY U.S.A. 135 I1
El Jadida Morocco 54 C5
El Jaralito Mex. 131 B7
El Jem Tunisia 58 D7
Elk r. Canada 120 H5
Ełk Poland 47 S4
Elk r. U.S.A. 135 H4
El Kaa Lebanon see Qaa
El Kab Sudan 86 D6
Elkader U.S.A. 130 F3
El Kala Alg. 58 C6
Elk City U.S.A. 131 D5
Elkedra Australia 110 A4
Elkedra watercourse Australia 110 B4
El Kef Tunisia see Le Kef
El Kelaâ des Srarhna Morocco 54 C5
Elkford Canada 120 H5
Elk Grove U.S.A. 128 C2
El Khalil West Bank see Hebron
El Khandaq Sudan 86 D6
El Khârga Egypt see Al Khārijah
El Kharrûba Egypt see Al Kharrūbah

Elkhart IN U.S.A. 134 C3
Elkhart KS U.S.A. 131 C4
El Kharṭûm Sudan see Khartoum
El Khenachich esc. Mali see El Khnâchîch
El Khnâchîch esc. Mali 96 C2
Elkhorn U.S.A. 130 F3
Elkhorn City U.S.A. 134 D5
Elkhovo Bulg. 59 L3
Elki Turkey see Beytüşşebap
Elkin U.S.A. 132 D4
Elkins U.S.A. 134 F4
Elk Island National Park Canada 121 H4
Elk Lake Canada 122 E5
Elk Lake l. U.S.A. 134 C1
Elkland U.S.A. 135 G3
Elk Mountain U.S.A. 126 G4
Elk Mountains U.S.A. 129 J2
Elko Canada 120 H5
Elko U.S.A. 129 F1
Elk Point Canada 121 I4
Elk Point U.S.A. 130 D3
Elk Springs U.S.A. 129 I1
Elkton MD U.S.A. 135 H4
Elkton VA U.S.A. 135 F4
El Kûbri Egypt see Al Kūbrī
El Kuntilla Egypt see Al Kuntillah
Elkview U.S.A. 134 E4
Ellas country Europe see Greece
Ellaville U.S.A. 133 C5
Ell Bay Canada 121 O1
Ellef Ringnes Island Canada 119 H2
Ellen, Mount U.S.A. 129 H2
Ellenburg Depot U.S.A. 135 I1
Ellendale U.S.A. 130 D2
Ellensburg U.S.A. 126 C3
Ellenville U.S.A. 135 H3
El León, Cerro mt. Mex. 131 B7
Ellesmere, Lake N.Z. 113 D6

▶Ellesmere Island Canada 119 J2
4th largest island in North America, and 10th in the world.

Ellesmere Island National Park Reserve Canada see Quttinirpaaq National Park
Ellesmere Port U.K. 48 E5
Ellettsville U.S.A. 134 B4
Ellice r. Canada 121 K1
Ellice Island atoll Tuvalu see Funafuti
Ellice Islands country S. Pacific Ocean see Tuvalu
Ellicott City U.S.A. 135 G4
Ellijay U.S.A. 133 C5
Ellingen Germany 53 K5
Elliot S. Africa 101 H6
Elliot, Mount Australia 110 D3
Elliotdale S. Africa 101 I6
Elliot Knob mt. U.S.A. 134 F4
Elliot Lake Canada 122 E5
Elliott Australia 108 F4
Elliston U.S.A. 134 E5
Ellon U.K. 50 G3
Ellora Caves tourist site India 84 B1
Ellsworth KS U.S.A. 130 D4
Ellsworth ME U.S.A. 132 G2
Ellsworth NE U.S.A. 130 C3
Ellsworth WI U.S.A. 130 E2
Ellsworth Land reg. Antarctica 152 K1
Ellsworth Mountains Antarctica 152 L1
Ellwangen (Jagst) Germany 53 K6
El Maghreb country Africa see Morocco
Elmakuz Dağı mt. Turkey 85 A1
Elmalı Turkey 59 M6
El Malpais National Monument nat. park U.S.A. 129 J4
El Manṣûra Egypt see Al Manṣūrah
El Maṭarîya Egypt see Al Maṭarīyah
El Mazâr Egypt see Al Mazār
El Meghaïer Alg. 54 F5
El Milia Alg. 54 F4
El Minya Egypt see Al Minyā
Elmira Ont. Canada 134 E2
Elmira P.E.I. Canada 123 J5
Elmira MI U.S.A. 134 C1
Elmira NY U.S.A. 135 G2
El Mirage U.S.A. 129 G5
El Moral Spain 57 E5
Elmore Australia 112 B6
El Mreyyé reg. Mauritania 96 C3
Elmshorn Germany 53 J1
El Muglad Sudan 86 C7
Elmvale Canada 134 F1
Elnesvågen Norway 44 E5
El Nevado, Cerro mt. Col. 142 D3
El Oasis Mex. 129 F5
El Obeid Sudan 86 D7
El Odaiya Sudan 86 C7
El Oro Mex. 131 C7
Elorza Venez. 142 E2
El Oued Alg. 54 F5
Eloy U.S.A. 129 H5
El Palmito Mex. 131 B7
El Paso IL U.S.A. 130 F3
El Paso KS U.S.A. see Derby
El Paso TX U.S.A. 127 G7
Elphin U.K. 50 D2
Elphinstone i. Myanmar see Thayawthadangyi Kyun
El Portal U.S.A. 128 D3
El Porvenir Mex. 131 B6
El Porvenir Panama 137 I7
El Prat de Llobregat Spain 57 H3
El Progreso Hond. 136 G5
El Puerto de Santa María Spain 57 C5
El Qâhira Egypt see Cairo
El Qasimiye r. Lebanon 85 B3
El Quds Israel/West Bank see Jerusalem
El Quṣeima Egypt see Al Quṣaymah
El Quṣeir Egypt see Al Quṣayr
El Qûṣîya Egypt see Al Qūṣīyah
El Regocijo Mex. 131 B8
El Reno U.S.A. 131 D5
Elrose Canada 121 I5
Elsa Canada 120 C2
El Ṣaff Egypt see Aṣ Ṣaff
El Sahuaro Mex. 127 E7
El Salado Mex. 131 C7
El Salto Mex. 131 B8
El Salvador country Central America 136 G6
El Salvador Chile 144 C3
El Salvador Mex. 131 C7
Elsass reg. France see Alsace
El Sauz Mex. 127 G7
Else r. Germany 53 I2
El Sellûm Egypt see As Sallūm
Elsey Australia 108 F3
El Shallûfa Egypt see Ash Shallūfah
El Sharana Australia 108 F3
El Shaṭṭ Egypt see Ash Shaṭṭ
Elsie U.S.A. 134 C2
Elsinore Denmark see Helsingør
Elsinore CA U.S.A. 128 E5
Elsinore UT U.S.A. 129 G2
Elsinore Lake U.S.A. 128 E5
El Sueco Mex. 127 G7
El Suweis Egypt see Suez
El Suweis governorate Egypt see As Suways
El Tama, Parque Nacional nat. park Venez. 142 D2
El Tarf Alg. 58 C6
El Teleno mt. Spain 57 C2
El Temascal Mex. 131 D7
El Ter r. Spain 57 H2
El Thamad Egypt see Ath Thamad
El Tigre Venez. 142 F2
Eltmann Germany 53 K5
El'ton Rus. Fed. 43 J6
El'ton, Ozero l. Rus. Fed. 43 J6
El Tren Mex. 127 E7
El Tuparro, Parque Nacional nat. park Col. 142 E2
El Tûr Egypt see Aṭ Ṭūr
El Turbio Arg. 144 B8
El Uqṣur Egypt see Luxor
Eluru India 84 D2
Elva Estonia 45 O7
Elvanfoot U.K. 50 F5
Elvas Port. 57 C4
Elverum Norway 45 G6
Elvira Brazil 142 D5
El Wak Kenya 98 E3
El Wâtya well Egypt see Al Wāṭiyah
Elwood IN U.S.A. 134 C3
Elwood NE U.S.A. 130 D3
El Wuz Sudan 86 D7
Elx Spain see Elche-Elx
Elxleben Germany 53 K3
Ely U.K. 49 H6
Ely MN U.S.A. 130 F2
Ely NV U.S.A. 129 F2
Elyria U.S.A. 134 D3
Elz Germany 53 I4
El Zagâzîg Egypt see Az Zaqāzīq
Elze Germany 53 J2
Émaé i. Vanuatu 107 G3
Emāmrūd Iran 88 D2
Emām Ṣaḥēb Afgh. 89 H2
Emām Taqī Iran 88 E2
Emån r. Sweden 45 J8
Emas, Parque Nacional das nat. park Brazil 143 H7
Emba Kazakh. 80 A2
Emba r. Kazakh. 80 A2
Embalenhle S. Africa 101 I4
Embarcación Arg. 144 D2
Embarras Portage Canada 121 I3
Embi Kazakh. see Emba
Embira r. Brazil see Envira
Emborcação, Represa de resr Brazil 145 B2
Embrun Canada 135 H1
Embu Kenya 98 D4
Emden Germany 53 H1
Emden Deep sea feature N. Pacific Ocean see Cape Johnson Depth
Emei China see Emeishan
Emeishan China 76 D2
Emei Shan mt. China 76 D2
Emerald Australia 110 E4
Emeril Canada 123 I3
Emerita Augusta Spain see Mérida
Emerson Canada 121 L5
Emerson U.S.A. 134 D4
Emery U.S.A. 129 H2
Emesa Syria see Homs
Emet Turkey 59 M5
eMgwenya S. Africa 101 J3
Emigrant Pass U.S.A. 128 E1
Emigrant Valley U.S.A. 129 F3
Emi Koussi mt. Chad 97 E3
Emile r. Canada 120 G2
Emiliano Zapata Mex. 136 F5
Emin China 80 F2
Emine, Nos pt Bulg. 59 L3
Eminence U.S.A. 134 C4
Eminska Planina hills Bulg. 59 L3
Emirdağ Turkey 59 N5
Emir Dağı mt. Turkey 59 N5
Emir Dağları mts Turkey 59 N5
eMjindini S. Africa 101 J3
Emmaboda Sweden 45 I8
Emmaste Estonia 45 M7
Emmaville Australia 112 E2
Emmeloord Neth. 52 F2
Emmelshausen Germany 53 H4
Emmen Neth. 52 G2
Emmen Switz. 56 I3
Emmerich Germany 52 G3
Emmet Australia 110 D5
Emmetsburg U.S.A. 130 E3
Emmett U.S.A. 126 D4
Emmiganuru India 84 C3
Emo Canada 121 M5
Emona Slovenia see Ljubljana
Emory Peak U.S.A. 131 C6
Empalme Mex. 127 F8
Empangeni S. Africa 101 J5
Emperor Seamount Chain sea feature N. Pacific Ocean 150 H2
Emperor Trough sea feature N. Pacific Ocean 150 H2
Empingham Reservoir U.K. see Rutland Water
Emplawas Indon. 108 E2
Empoli Italy 58 D3
Emporia KS U.S.A. 130 D4
Emporia VA U.S.A. 135 G5
Emporium U.S.A. 135 F3
Empress Canada 121 I5
Empty Quarter des. Saudi Arabia see Rub' al Khālī
Ems r. Germany 53 H1
Emsdale Canada 134 F1
Emsdetten Germany 53 H2
Ems-Jade-Kanal canal Germany 53 H1
eMzinoni S. Africa 101 I4
Enafors Sweden 44 H5
Encantadas, Serra das hills Brazil 144 F4
Encarnación Para. 144 E3
Enchi Ghana 96 C4
Encinal U.S.A. 131 D6
Encinitas U.S.A. 128 E5
Encino U.S.A. 127 G6
Encruzilhada Brazil 145 C1
Endako Canada 120 E4
Endau-Rompin National Park nat. park Malaysia 71 C7
Ende Indon. 108 C2
Endeavour Strait Australia 110 C1
Endeh Indon. see Ende
Enderby Canada 120 G5
Enderby atoll Micronesia see Puluwat
Enderby Land reg. Antarctica 152 D2
Endicott U.S.A. 135 G2
Endicott Mountains U.S.A. 118 C3
EnenKio terr. N. Pacific Ocean see Wake Island
Energodar Ukr. see Enerhodar
Enerhodar Ukr. 43 G7
Enewetak atoll Marshall Is 150 G5
Enez Turkey 59 L4
Enfe Lebanon 85 B2
Enfião, Ponta do pt Angola 99 B5
Enfidaville Tunisia 58 D6
Enfield U.S.A. 132 E4
Engan Norway 44 F5
Engaru Japan 74 F3
Engcobo S. Africa 101 H6
En Gedi Israel 85 B4
Engelhard U.S.A. 132 F5
Engel's Rus. Fed. 43 J6
Engelschmangat sea chan. Neth. 52 E1
Enggano i. Indon. 68 C8
Enghien Belgium 52 E4
England admin. div. U.K. 49 E6
Englee Canada 123 L4
Englehart Canada 122 F5
Englewood FL U.S.A. 133 D7
Englewood OH U.S.A. 134 C4
English r. Canada 121 M5
English U.S.A. 134 B4
English Bazar India see Ingraj Bazar
English Channel France/U.K. 49 F9
English Coast Antarctica 152 L2
Engozero Rus. Fed. 42 G2
Enhlalakahle S. Africa 101 J5
Enid U.S.A. 131 D4
Eniwa Japan 74 F4
Eniwetok atoll Marshall Is see Enewetak
Enjiang China see Yongfeng
Enkeldoorn Zimbabwe see Chivhu
Enkhuizen Neth. 52 F2
Enköping Sweden 45 J7
Enna Sicily Italy 58 F6
Ennadai Lake Canada 121 K2
En Nahud Sudan 86 C7
Ennedi, Massif mts Chad 97 F3
Ennell, Lough l. Ireland 51 E4
Enngonia Australia 112 B2
Enning U.S.A. 130 C2
Ennis Ireland 51 D5
Ennis MT U.S.A. 126 F3
Ennis TX U.S.A. 131 D5
Enniscorthy Ireland 51 F5
Enniskillen U.K. 51 E3
Ennistymon Ireland 51 C5
Enn Nâqoûra Lebanon 85 B3
Enns r. Austria 47 O6
Eno Fin. 44 Q5
Enoch U.S.A. 129 G3
Enontekiö Fin. 44 M2
Enosburg Falls U.S.A. 135 I1
Enosville U.S.A. 134 B4
Enping China 77 G4
Ens Neth. 52 F2
Ensay Australia 112 C6
Enschede Neth. 52 G2
Ense Germany 53 I3
Ensenada Mex. 127 D7
Enshi China 77 F2
Ensley U.S.A. 133 C6
Entebbe Uganda 98 D3
Enterprise Canada 120 G2
Enterprise AL U.S.A. 133 C6
Enterprise OR U.S.A. 126 D3
Enterprise UT U.S.A. 129 G3
Entre Ríos Bol. 142 F8
Entre Rios Brazil 143 H5
Entre Rios de Minas Brazil 145 B3
Entroncamento Port. 57 B4
Enugu Nigeria 96 D4
Enurmino Rus. Fed. 65 T3
Envira Brazil 142 D5
Envira r. Brazil 142 D5
'En Yahav Israel 85 B4
Enyamba Dem. Rep. Congo 98 C4
Eochaill Ireland see Youghal
Epe Neth. 52 F2
Epéna Congo 98 B3
Épernay France 52 D5
Ephraim U.S.A. 129 H2
Ephrata U.S.A. 135 G3
Epi i. Vanuatu 107 G3
Epidamnus Albania see Durrës
Épinal France 56 H2
Episkopi Bay Cyprus 85 A2
Episkopis, Kolpos b. Cyprus see Episkopi Bay
ePitoli S. Africa see Pretoria
Epomeo, Monte hill Italy 58 E4
Epping U.K. 49 H7
Epping Forest National Park Australia 110 D4
Eppstein Germany 53 I4
Eppynt, Mynydd hills U.K. 49 D6
Epsom U.K. 49 G7
Epte r. France 52 B5
Eqlīd Iran 88 D4
Equatorial Guinea country Africa 96 D4
Équeurdreville-Hainneville France 49 F9
Erac Creek watercourse Australia 112 B1
Erandol India 84 B1
Erawadi r. Myanmar see Irrawaddy
Erawan National Park Thai. 71 B4
Erbaa Turkey 90 E2
Erbendorf Germany 53 M5
Erbeskopf hill Germany 52 H5
Ercan airport Cyprus 85 A2
Erciş Turkey 91 F3
Erciyes Dağı mt. Turkey 90 D3
Érd Hungary 58 H1
Erdaobaihe China see Baihe
Erdaogou China 76 B1
Erdao Jiang r. China 74 B4
Erdek Turkey 59 L4
Erdemli Turkey 85 B1
Erdenedalay Mongolia 72 I3
Erdenet Mongolia 80 J2
Erdenetsagaan Mongolia 73 L3
Erdi reg. Chad 97 F3
Erdniyevskiy Rus. Fed. 43 J7

▶Erebus, Mount vol. Antarctica 152 H1
Highest active volcano in Antarctica.

Erechim Brazil 144 F3
Ereentsav Mongolia 73 L3
Ereğli Konya Turkey 90 D3
Ereğli Zonguldak Turkey 59 N4
Erego Moz. see Errego
Erei, Monti mts Sicily Italy 58 F6
Erementaū Kazakh. see Yereymentau
Erenhot China 73 K4
Erepucu, Lago de l. Brazil 143 G4
Erevan Armenia see Yerevan
Erfurt Germany 53 L4
Erfurt airport Germany 53 K4
Ergani Turkey 91 E3
'Erg Chech des. Alg./Mali 96 C2
Ergene r. Turkey 59 L4
Ērgļi Latvia 45 N8
Ergu China 74 C3
Ergun China 73 M2
Ergun He r. China/Rus. Fed. see Argun'
Ergun Youqi China see Ergun
Ergun Zuoqi China see Genhe
Er Hai l. China 76 D3
Erhulai China 74 B4
Eriboll, Loch inlet U.K. 50 E2
Ericht r. U.K. 50 F4
Ericht, Loch l. U.K. 50 E4
Erickson Canada 121 L5
Erie KS U.S.A. 131 E4
Erie PA U.S.A. 134 E2
Erie, Lake Canada/U.S.A. 134 E2
'Erîgât des. Mali 96 C3
Erik Eriksenstretet sea chan. Svalbard 64 D2
Eriksdale Canada 121 L5
Erimo-misaki c. Japan 74 F4
Erin Canada 134 E2
Erinpura Road India 82 C4
Eriskay i. U.K. 50 B3
Eritrea country Africa 86 E6
Erlangen Germany 53 L5
Erlangping China 77 F1
Erldunda Australia 109 F6
Erlistoun watercourse Australia 109 C6
Erlong Shan mt. China 74 C4
Erlongshan Shuiku resr China 74 B4
Ermak Kazakh. see Aksu
Ermelo Neth. 52 F2
Ermelo S. Africa 101 I4
Ermenek Turkey 85 A1
Ermenek r. Turkey 85 A1
Ermont Egypt see Armant
Ermoupoli Greece 59 K6
Ernakulam India 84 C4
Erne r. Ireland/U.K. 51 D3
Ernest Giles Range hills Australia 109 C6
Erode India 84 C4
Eromanga Australia 111 C5
Erongo admin. reg. Namibia 100 B1
Erp Neth. 52 F3
Erqu China see Zhouzhi
Errabiddy Hills Australia 109 A6
Er Rachidia Morocco 54 D5
Er Raoui des. Alg. 54 D6
Errego Moz. 99 D5
Er Remla Tunisia 58 D7
Er Renk Sudan 86 D7
Errigal hill Ireland 51 D2
Errinundra National Park Australia 112 D6
Erris Head hd Ireland 51 B3
Errol U.S.A. 135 J1
Erromango i. Vanuatu 107 G3
Erronan i. Vanuatu see Futuna
Erseka Albania see Ersekë
Ersekë Albania 59 I4
Erskine U.S.A. 130 D2
Ersmark Sweden 44 L5
Ertai China 80 H2
Ertil' Rus. Fed. 43 I6
Ertis r. Kazakh./Rus. Fed. see Irtysh
Ertix He r. China/Kazakh. 80 G2
Ērtra country Africa see Eritrea
Eruh Turkey 91 F3
Erwin U.S.A. 132 D4
Erwitte Germany 53 I3
Erxleben Sachsen-Anhalt Germany 53 L2
Erxleben Sachsen-Anhalt Germany 53 L2
Eryuan China 76 C3
Erzerum Turkey see Erzurum
Erzgebirge mts Czech Rep./Germany 53 N4
Erzhan China 74 B2
Erzin Turkey 85 C1
Erzincan Turkey 91 E3
Erzurum Turkey 91 F3
Esa-ala P.N.G. 110 E1
Esan-misaki pt Japan 74 F4
Esashi Japan 74 F3
Esbjerg Denmark 45 F9
Esbo Fin. see Espoo
Escalante U.S.A. 129 H3
Escalante r. U.S.A. 129 H3
Escalante Desert U.S.A. 129 G3
Escalón Mex. 131 B7
Escambia r. U.S.A. 133 C6
Escanaba U.S.A. 132 C2
Escárcega Mex. 136 F5
Escatrón Spain 57 F3
Escaut r. Belgium 52 D4
Esch Neth. 52 F3
Eschede Germany 53 K2
Eschscholtz atoll Marshall Is see Bikini
Esch-sur-Alzette Lux. 52 F5
Eschwege Germany 53 K3
Eschweiler Germany 52 G4
Escondido r. Mex. 131 C6
Escondido U.S.A. 128 E5
Escudilla mt. U.S.A. 129 I5
Escuinapa Mex. 136 C4
Escuintla Guat. 136 F6
Eséka Cameroon 96 E4
Eşen Turkey 59 M6
Esenguly Turkm. 88 D2
Esenguly Döwlet Gorugy nature res. Turkm. 88 D2
Esens Germany 53 H1
Eşfahān Iran 88 C3
Esfarayen, Reshteh-ye mts Iran 88 E2
Esfideh Iran 89 E3
Eshan China 76 D3
Eshāqābād Iran 88 E3
Eshkamesh Afgh. 89 H2
Eshkanān Iran 88 D5
Eshowe S. Africa 101 J5
Esikhawini S. Africa 101 K5
Esil Kazakh. see Yesil'
Esil r. Kazakh./Rus. Fed. see Ishim
Esk Australia 112 F1
Esk r. Australia 111 [inset]
Esk r. U.K. 48 D4
Eskdalemuir U.K. 50 F5
Esker Canada 123 I3
Eskifjörður Iceland 44 [inset]
Eski Gediz Turkey 59 M5
Eskilstuna Sweden 45 J7
Eskimo Lakes Canada 118 E3
Eskimo Point Canada see Arviat
Eskipazar Turkey 90 D2
Eskişehir Turkey 59 N5
Eski-Yakkabog' Uzbek. 89 G2
Esla r. Spain 57 C3
Eslāmābād-e Gharb Iran 88 B3
Esler Dağı mt. Turkey 59 M6
Eslohe (Sauerland) Germany 53 I3
Eslöv Sweden 45 H9
Esmā'īlī-ye Soflá Iran 88 E4
Eşme Turkey 59 M5
Esmeraldas Ecuador 142 C3
Esmont U.S.A. 135 F5
Esnagami Lake Canada 122 D4
Esnes France 52 D4
Espakeh Iran 89 F5
Espalion France 56 F4
España country Europe see Spain
Espanola Canada 122 E5
Espanola U.S.A. 131 B4
Espelkamp Germany 53 I2
Esperance Australia 109 C8
Esperance Bay Australia 109 C8
Esperanza research station Antarctica 152 A2
Esperanza Arg. 144 B8
Esperanza Mex. 127 F8
Espichel, Cabo c. Port. 57 B4
Espigão, Serra do mts Brazil 145 A4
Espigüete mt. Spain 57 D2
Espinazo Mex. 131 C7
Espinhaço, Serra do mts Brazil 145 C2
Espinosa Brazil 145 C1
Espírito Santo Brazil see Vila Velha
Espírito Santo state Brazil 145 C2
Espíritu Santo i. Vanuatu 107 G3
Espíritu Santo, Isla i. Mex. 124 E7
Espoo Fin. 45 N6
Espuña mt. Spain 57 F5
Esqueda Mex. 127 F7
Esquel Arg. 144 B6
Esquimalt Canada 120 F5
Essaouira Morocco 96 C1
Es Semara W. Sahara 96 B2
Essen Belgium 52 E3
Essen Germany 52 H3
Essen (Oldenburg) Germany 53 H2
Essequibo r. Guyana 143 G2
Essex Canada 134 D2
Essex CA U.S.A. 129 F4
Essex MD U.S.A. 135 G4
Essex NY U.S.A. 135 I1
Essexville U.S.A. 134 D2
Esslingen am Neckar Germany 53 J6
Esso Rus. Fed. 65 Q4
Essoyla Rus. Fed. 42 G3
Eşţahbān Iran 88 D4
Estância Brazil 143 K6
Estancia U.S.A. 127 G6
Estand, Kūh-e mt. Iran 89 F4
Estats, Pic d' mt. France/Spain 56 E5
Estcourt S. Africa 101 I5
Este r. Germany 53 J1
Estelí Nicaragua 137 G6
Estella Spain 57 E2
Estepa Spain 57 D5
Estepona Spain 57 D5
Esteras de Medinaceli Spain 57 E3
Esterhazy Canada 121 K5
Estero Bay U.S.A. 128 C4
Esteros Para. 144 D2
Estevan Canada 121 K5
Estevan Group is Canada 120 D4
Estherville U.S.A. 130 E3
Estill U.S.A. 133 D5
Eston Canada 121 I5
Estonia country Europe 45 N7
Estonskaya S.S.R. country Europe see Estonia
Estrées-St-Denis France 52 C5
Estrela Brazil 145 A5
Estrela, Serra da mts Port. 57 C3
Estrela do Sul Brazil 145 B2
Estrella mt. Spain 57 E4
Estrella, Punta pt Mex. 127 E7
Estremoz Port. 57 C4
Estrondo, Serra hills Brazil 143 I5
Etadunna Australia 111 B6
Etah India 82 D4
Étain France 52 F5
Étamamiou Canada 123 K4
Étampes France 56 F2
Étaples France 52 B4
Etawah Rajasthan India 82 D4
Etawah Uttar Prad. India 82 D4
Ethandakukhanya S. Africa 101 J4
Ethelbert Canada 121 K5
Ethel Creek Australia 109 C5
E'Thembini S. Africa 100 F5

▶Ethiopia country Africa 98 D3
2nd most populous country in Africa.

Etimesğut Turkey 90 D3
Etive, Loch inlet U.K. 50 D4

▶Etna, Mount vol. Sicily Italy 58 F6
Highest active volcano in Europe.

Etne Norway 45 D7
Etobicoke Canada 134 F2
Etolin Strait U.S.A. 118 B3
Etorofu-tō i. Rus. Fed. see Iturup, Ostrov
Etosha National Park Namibia 99 B5
Etosha Pan salt pan Namibia 99 B5
Etoumbi Congo 98 B3
Etrek r. Iran/Turkm. see Atrek
Etrek Turkm. 88 D2
Étrépagny France 52 B5
Étretat France 49 H9
Ettelbruck Lux. 52 G5
Etten-Leur Neth. 52 E3
Ettlingen Germany 53 I6
Ettrick Water r. U.K. 50 F5
Euabalong Australia 112 C4
Euboea i. Greece see Evvoia
Eucla Australia 109 E7
Euclid U.S.A. 134 E3
Euclides da Cunha Brazil 143 K6
Eucumbene, Lake Australia 112 D6
Eudistes, Lac des l. Canada 123 I4
Eudora U.S.A. 131 F5
Eudunda Australia 111 B7
Eufaula AL U.S.A. 133 C6
Eufaula OK U.S.A. 131 E5
Eufaula Lake resr U.S.A. 131 E5
Eugene U.S.A. 126 C3
Eugenia, Punta pt Mex. 127 E8
Eugowra Australia 112 D4
Eulo Australia 112 B2
Eumungerie Australia 112 D3
Eungella Australia 110 E4
Eungella National Park Australia 110 E4
Eunice LA U.S.A. 131 E6
Eunice NM U.S.A. 131 C5
Eupen Belgium 52 G4

▶Euphrates r. Asia 91 G5
Longest river in western Asia. Also known as Al Furāt (Iraq/Syria) or Fırat (Turkey).

Eura Fin. 45 M6
Eure r. France 52 B5
Eureka CA U.S.A. 126 B4
Eureka KS U.S.A. 130 D4
Eureka MT U.S.A. 126 E2
Eureka NV U.S.A. 129 F2
Eureka OH U.S.A. 134 D4
Eureka SD U.S.A. 130 D2
Eureka UT U.S.A. 129 G2
Eureka Sound sea chan. Canada 119 J2
Eureka Springs U.S.A. 131 E4
Eureka Valley U.S.A. 128 E3
Euriowie Australia 111 C6
Euroa Australia 112 B6
Eurombah Australia 111 E5
Eurombah Creek r. Australia 111 E5
Europa, Île i. Indian Ocean 99 E6
Europa, Punta de pt Gibraltar see Europa Point
Europa Point Gibraltar 57 D5
Euskirchen Germany 52 G4
Eutaw U.S.A. 133 C5
Eutsuk Lake Canada 120 E4
Eutzsch Germany 53 M3
Eva Downs Australia 108 F4
Evans, Lac l. Canada 122 F4
Evans, Mount U.S.A. 126 G5
Evansburg Canada 120 H4
Evans City U.S.A. 134 E3
Evans Head Australia 112 F2
Evans Head hd Australia 112 F2
Evans Ice Stream Antarctica 152 L1
Evans Strait Canada 121 P2
Evanston IL U.S.A. 134 B2
Evanston WY U.S.A. 126 F4
Evansville Canada 122 E5
Evansville IN U.S.A. 134 B5
Evansville WY U.S.A. 126 G4
Evant U.S.A. 131 D6
Eva Perón Arg. see La Plata
Evart U.S.A. 134 C2
Evaton S. Africa 101 H4
Evaz Iran 88 D5
Evening Shade U.S.A. 131 F4
Evensk Rus. Fed. 65 Q3
Everard, Lake salt flat Australia 111 A6
Everard, Mount Australia 109 F5
Everard Range hills Australia 109 F6
Everdingen Neth. 52 F3
Everek Turkey see Develi

▶Everest, Mount China/Nepal 83 F4
Highest mountain in the world and in Asia.

Everett PA U.S.A. 135 F3
Everett WA U.S.A. 126 C3
Evergem Belgium 52 D3
Everglades swamp U.S.A. 133 D7
Everglades National Park U.S.A. 133 D7
Evergreen U.S.A. 133 C6
Evesham Australia 110 C4
Evesham U.K. 49 F6
Evesham, Vale of valley U.K. 49 F6
Evijärvi Fin. 44 M5
Evje Norway 45 E7
Évora Port. 57 C4
Evoron, Ozero l. Rus. Fed. 74 E2
Évreux France 52 B5
Evros r. Bulg. see Maritsa
Evros r. Turkey see Meriç
Evrotas r. Greece 59 J6
Évry France 52 C6
Evrychou Cyprus 85 A2
Evrykhou Cyprus see Evrychou
Evvoia i. Greece 59 K5
Ewan Australia 110 D3
Ewaso Ngiro r. Kenya 98 E3
Ewe, Loch b. U.K. 50 D3

ving U.S.A. 134 D5
vo Congo 98 B4
altación Bol. 142 E6
celsior S. Africa 101 H5
celsior Mountain U.S.A. 128 D2
celsior Mountains U.S.A. 128 D2
e r. U.K. 49 D8
eter Australia 112 E5
eter Canada 134 E2
eter U.K. 49 D8
eter CA U.S.A. 128 D3
eter NH U.S.A. 135 J2
eter Lake Canada 121 I1
loo Neth. 52 G2
minster U.K. 49 D8
moor hills U.K. 49 D7
moor National Park U.K. 49 D7
more U.S.A. 135 H5
mouth Australia 108 A5
mouth U.K. 49 D8
mouth, Mount Australia 112 D3
mouth Gulf Australia 108 A5
mouth Lake Canada 120 H1
mouth Plateau sea feature Indian Ocean 149 P7
pedition National Park Australia 110 E5
pedition Range mts Australia 110 E5
ploits r. Canada 123 L4
ton U.S.A. 135 H3
tremadura aut. comm. Spain 57 D4
uma Cays is Bahamas 133 E7
uma Sound sea chan. Bahamas 133 F7
asi, Lake salt l. Tanz. 98 D4
awadi r. Myanmar see Irrawaddy
e U.K. 49 I6
eberry Lake Canada 121 J2
elenoborsk Rus. Fed. 41 S3
emouth U.K. 50 G5
afjörður inlet Iceland 44 [inset]
Somalia 98 E3
au Rus. Fed. see Bagrationovsk
nsham U.K. 49 F7
re (North), Lake Australia 111 B6
re (South), Lake Australia 111 B6

▶Eyre, Lake Australia 111 B6
Largest lake in Oceania and lowest point.

re Creek watercourse Australia 110 B5
re Mountains N.Z. 113 B7
re Peninsula Australia 111 A7
strup Germany 53 J2
sturoy i. Faroe Is 44 [inset]
akheni S. Africa 101 J5
el U.S.A. 134 D5
enzeleni S. Africa 101 I4
equiel Ramos Mexía, Embalse resr Arg. 144 C5
hou China 77 G2
hva Rus. Fed. 42 K3
ine Turkey 59 L5
o i. Japan see Hokkaidō
ousa r. Cyprus 85 A2

F

aborg Denmark 45 G9
adhippolhu Atoll Maldives 84 B5
afxadhuun Somalia 98 E3
bens U.S.A. 127 G7
ber, Mount hill Sing. 71 [inset]
ber Lake Canada 120 G2
borg Denmark see Faaborg
briano Italy 58 E3
ches-Thumesnil France 52 D4
chi Niger 96 E3
da Chad 97 F3
da-N'Gourma Burkina 96 D3
dghāmī Syria 91 F4
diffolu Atoll Maldives see Faadhippolhu Atoll
dippolu Atoll Maldives see Faadhippolhu Atoll
enza Italy 58 D2
roerne terr. N. Atlantic Ocean see Faroe Islands
eroes terr. N. Atlantic Ocean see Faroe Islands
găraş Romania 59 K2

Fagatogo American Samoa 107 I3
Capital of American Samoa.

gersta Sweden 45 I7
gne reg. Belgium 52 E4
gurhólsmýri Iceland 44 [inset]
gwir Sudan 86 D8
hraj Iran 88 D4
id Egypt 90 D5
irbanks U.S.A. 118 D3
irborn U.S.A. 134 C4
irbury U.S.A. 130 D3
irchance U.S.A. 134 F4
irfax U.S.A. 135 G4
irfield CA U.S.A. 128 B2
irfield IA U.S.A. 130 F3
irfield ID U.S.A. 126 E4
irfield IL U.S.A. 130 F4
irfield OH U.S.A. 134 C4
irfield TX U.S.A. 131 D6
r Haven U.S.A. 135 I2
r Head hd U.K. 51 F2
r Isle i. U.K. 50 H1
rlee U.S.A. 135 I2
rlie Canterbury 113 C7
rmont MN U.S.A. 130 E3
rmont WV U.S.A. 134 E4
r Oaks U.S.A. 134 B3
rview Australia 110 D2
rview Canada 120 G3
rview MI U.S.A. 134 C1
rview OK U.S.A. 131 D4
rview PA U.S.A. 134 E2
rview UT U.S.A. 129 H2
rview Park H.K. China 77 [inset]
rweather, Cape U.S.A. 120 B3
rweather, Mount Canada/U.S.A. 120 B3
is i. Micronesia 69 K5
salabad Pak. 89 I4

Faissault France 52 E5
Faith U.S.A. 130 C2
Faizabad Afgh. see Feyzābād
Faizabad India 83 E4
Fakaofo atoll Tokelau 107 I2
Fakaofu atoll Tokelau see Fakaofo
Fakenham U.K. 49 H6
Fåker Sweden 44 I5
Fakfak Indon. 69 I7
Fakhrābād Iran 88 D4
Fakiragram India 83 G4
Fako vol. Cameroon see Cameroun, Mont
Fal r. U.K. 49 C8
Falaba Sierra Leone 96 B4
Falaise Lake Canada 120 G2
Falam Myanmar 70 A2
Falavarjan Iran 88 C3
Falcon Lake Canada 121 M5
Falcon Lake l. Mex./U.S.A. 131 D7
Falenki Rus. Fed. 42 K4
Falfurrias U.S.A. 131 D7
Falher Canada 120 G4
Falkenberg Germany 53 N3
Falkenberg Sweden 45 H8
Falkenhagen Germany 53 M1
Falkenhain Germany 53 M3
Falkensee Germany 53 N2
Falkenstein Germany 53 M5
Falkirk U.K. 50 F5
Falkland U.K. 50 F4
Falkland Escarpment sea feature S. Atlantic Ocean 148 E9

▶Falkland Islands terr. S. Atlantic Ocean 144 E8
United Kingdom Overseas Territory.

Falkland Plateau sea feature S. Atlantic Ocean 148 E9
Falkland Sound sea chan. Falkland Is 144 D8
Falköping Sweden 45 H7
Fallbrook U.S.A. 128 E5
Fallieres Coast Antarctica 152 L2
Fallingbostel Germany 53 J2
Fallon U.S.A. 128 D2
Fall River U.S.A. 135 J3
Fall River Pass U.S.A. 126 G4
Falls City U.S.A. 130 E3
Falmouth U.K. 49 B8
Falmouth KY U.S.A. 134 C4
Falmouth VA U.S.A. 135 G4
False r. Canada 123 H2
False Bay S. Africa 100 D8
False Point India 83 F5
Falster i. Denmark 45 G9
Fălticeni Romania 43 E7
Falun Sweden 45 I6
Famagusta Cyprus 85 A2
Famagusta Bay Cyprus see Ammochostos Bay
Fameck France 52 G5
Famenin Iran 88 C3
Fame Range hills Australia 109 C6
Family Lake Canada 121 M5
Family Well Australia 108 D5
Fāmūr, Daryācheh-ye l. Iran 88 C4
Fana Mali 96 C3
Fanad Head hd Ireland 51 E2
Fandriana Madag. 99 E6
Fane r. Ireland 51 F4
Fang Thai. 70 B3
Fangcheng Guangxi China see Fangchenggang
Fangcheng Henan China 77 G1
Fangchenggang China 77 F4
Fangdou Shan mts China 77 F2
Fangliao Taiwan 77 I4
Fangshan Taiwan 77 I4
Fangxian China 77 F1
Fangzheng China 74 C3
Fankuai China 77 F2
Fankuaidian China see Fankuai
Fanling H.K. China 77 [inset]
Fannich, Loch l. U.K. 50 D3
Fannūj Iran 89 E5
Fano Italy 58 E3
Fanshan Anhui China 77 H2
Fanshan Zhejiang China 77 I3
Fanum Fortunae Italy see Fano
Faqīh Aḥmadān Iran 88 C4
Farab Turkm. see Farap
Faraba Mali 96 B3
Faradofay Madag. see Tôlañaro
Farafangana Madag. 99 E6
Farāfirah, Wāḥāt al oasis Egypt 86 C4
Farafra Oasis oasis Egypt see Farāfirah, Wāḥāt al
Farāh Afgh. 89 F3
Faraḥābād Iran see Khezerābād
Farallon de Medinilla i. N. Mariana Is 69 L3
Farallon de Pajaros vol. N. Mariana Is 69 K2
Farallones de Cali, Parque Nacional nat. park Col. 142 C3
Faranah Guinea 96 B3
Farap Turkm. 89 F2
Fararah Oman 87 I6
Farasān, Jazā'ir is Saudi Arabia 86 F6
Faraulep atoll Micronesia 69 K5
Fareham U.K. 49 F8
Farewell, Cape Greenland 119 N3
Farewell, Cape N.Z. 113 D5
Farewell Spit N.Z. 113 D5
Färgelanda Sweden 45 H7
Farghona Uzbek. see Farg'ona
Fargo U.S.A. 130 D2
Farg'ona Uzbek. 87 L1
Faribault U.S.A. 130 E2
Faribault, Lac l. Canada 123 H2
Faridabad India 82 D3
Faridkot India 82 C3
Faridpur Bangl. 83 G5
Farīmān Iran 89 E3
Farkhar Afgh. see Farkhato
Farkhato Afgh. 89 H2
Farkhor Tajik. 89 H2
Farmahin Iran 88 C3
Farmer Island Canada 122 E2
Farmerville U.S.A. 131 E5
Farmington Canada 120 F4

Farmington ME U.S.A. 135 J1
Farmington MO U.S.A. 130 F4
Farmington NH U.S.A. 135 J2
Farmington NM U.S.A. 129 I3
Farmington Hills U.S.A. 134 D2
Far Mountain Canada 120 E4
Farmville U.S.A. 135 F5
Farnborough U.K. 49 G7
Farne Islands U.K. 48 F3
Farnham U.K. 49 G7
Farnham, Lake salt flat Australia 109 D6
Farnham, Mount Canada 120 G5
Faro Brazil 143 G4
Faro Canada 120 C2
Faro Port. 57 C5
Fårö i. Sweden 45 K8
Faroe - Iceland Ridge sea feature Arctic Ocean 153 I2

▶Faroe Islands terr. N. Atlantic Ocean 44 [inset]
Self-governing Danish territory.

Fårösund Sweden 45 K8
Farquhar Group is Seychelles 99 F5
Farquharson Tableland hills Australia 109 C6
Farrāshband Iran 88 D4
Farr Bay Antarctica 152 F2
Farristown U.S.A. 134 C5
Farrukhabad India see Fatehgarh
Fārsī Afgh. 89 F3
Farsund Norway 45 E7
Fārūj Iran 88 E2
Farwell MI U.S.A. 134 C2
Farwell TX U.S.A. 131 C5
Fasā Iran 88 D4
Fasano Italy 58 G4
Faşikan Geçidi pass Turkey 85 A1
Faßberg Germany 53 K2
Fastiv Ukr. 43 F6
Fastov Ukr. see Fastiv
Fatehabad India 82 C3
Fatehgarh India 82 D4
Fatehpur Rajasthan India 82 C4
Fatehpur Uttar Prad. India 82 E4
Fatick Senegal 96 B3
Fattoilep atoll Micronesia see Faraulep
Faughan r. U.K. 51 E2
Faulkton U.S.A. 130 D2
Faulquemont France 52 G5
Fauresmith S. Africa 101 G5
Fauske Norway 44 I3
Faust Canada 120 H4
Fawcett Canada 120 H4
Fawley U.K. 49 F8
Fawn r. Canada 121 N4
Faxaflói b. Iceland 44 [inset]
Faxälven r. Sweden 44 J5
Faya Chad 97 E3
Fayette AL U.S.A. 133 C5
Fayette MO U.S.A. 130 E4
Fayette MS U.S.A. 131 F6
Fayette OH U.S.A. 134 C3
Fayetteville AR U.S.A. 131 E4
Fayetteville NC U.S.A. 133 E5
Fayetteville TN U.S.A. 133 C5
Fayetteville WV U.S.A. 134 E4
Fâyid Egypt see Fā'id
Faylakah i. Kuwait 88 C4
Fazao Malfakassa, Parc National de nat. park Togo 96 D4
Fazilka India 82 C3
Fazrān, Jabal hill Saudi Arabia 88 C5
Fdérik Mauritania 96 B2
Fead Group is P.N.G. see Nuguria Islands
Feale r. Ireland 51 C5
Fear, Cape U.S.A. 133 E5
Featherston N.Z. 113 E5
Feathertop, Mount Australia 112 C6
Fécamp France 56 E2
Federal District admin. dist. Brazil see Distrito Federal
Federalsburg U.S.A. 135 H4
Federated Malay States country Asia see Malaysia
Fedusar India 82 C4
Fehet Lake Canada 121 M1
Fehmarn i. Germany 47 M3
Fehrbellin Germany 53 M2
Feia, Lagoa lag. Brazil 145 C3
Feicheng China see Feixian
Feijó Brazil 142 D5
Feilding N.Z. 113 E5
Fei Ngo Shan hill H.K. China see Kowloon Peak
Feio r. Brazil see Aguapeí
Feira de Santana Brazil 145 D1
Feixi China 77 H2
Feixian China 77 H1
Fejd el Abiod pass Alg. 58 B6
Feke Turkey 90 D3
Felanitx Spain 57 H4
Feldberg Germany 53 N1
Feldberg mt. Germany 47 L7
Feldkirch Austria 47 L7
Feldkirchen in Kärnten Austria 47 O7
Felidhu Atoll Maldives 81 D11
Felidu Atoll Maldives see Felidhu Atoll
Felipe C. Puerto Mex. 136 G5
Felixlândia Brazil 145 B2
Felixstowe U.K. 49 I7
Felixton S. Africa 101 J5
Fellowsville U.S.A. 134 F4
Felsina Italy see Bologna
Felton U.S.A. 135 H4
Feltre Italy 58 D1
Femunden l. Norway 44 G5
Femundsmarka Nasjonalpark nat. park Norway 44 H5
Fenaio, Punta del pt Italy 58 D3
Fence Lake U.S.A. 129 I4
Fener Burnu hd Turkey 85 B1
Fénérive Madag. see Fenoarivo Atsinanana
Fengari mt. Greece 59 K4
Fengcheng Fujian China see Lianjiang
Fengcheng Fujian China see Yongding
Fengcheng Fujian China see Anxi
Fengcheng Guangdong China see Xinfeng
Fengcheng Guangxi China see Fengshan

Fengcheng Guizhou China see Tianzhu
Fengcheng Jiangxi China 77 G2
Fenggang Fujian China see Shaxian
Fenggang Guizhou China 76 E3
Fenggang Jiangxi China see Yihuang
Fengguang China 74 B3
Fenghuang China 77 F3
Fengjiaba China see Wangcang
Fengjie China 77 F2
Fengkai China 77 F4
Fenglin Taiwan 77 I4
Fengming Shaanxi China see Qishan
Fengming Sichuan China see Pengshan
Fengqing China 76 C3
Fengshan Fujian China see Luoyuan
Fengshan Guangxi China 76 E3
Fengshan Hubei China see Luotian
Fengshan Yunnan China see Fengqing
Fengshuba Shuiku resr China 77 G3
Fengshui Shan mt. China 74 A1
Fengtongzhai Giant Panda Reserve nature res. China 76 D2
Fengxian China 76 E1
Fengxiang Heilong. China see Luobei
Fengxiang Yunnan China see Lincang
Fengyang China 77 H1
Fengyüan Taiwan 77 I3
Fengzhen China 73 K4
Feni Bangl. 83 G5
Feni Islands P.N.G. 106 F2
Fennville U.S.A. 134 B2
Feno, Capo di c. Corsica France 56 I6
Fenoarivo Atsinanana Madag. 99 E5
Fenshui Guan pass China 77 H3
Fenton U.S.A. 134 D2
Fenua Ura atoll Fr. Polynesia see Manuae
Fenyi China 77 G3
Feodosiya Ukr. 90 D1
Fer, Cap de c. Alg. 58 B6
Férai Greece see Feres
Ferdows Iran 88 E3
Fère-Champenoise France 52 D6
Feres Greece 59 L4
Fergus Canada 134 E2
Fergus Falls U.S.A. 130 D2
Ferguson Lake Canada 121 L2
Fergusson Island P.N.G. 106 F2
Fériana Tunisia 58 C7
Ferijaz Kosovo 59 I3
Ferkessédougou Côte d'Ivoire 96 C4
Fermo Italy 58 E3
Fermont Canada 123 I3
Fermoselle Spain 57 C3
Fermoy Ireland 51 D5
Fernandina, Isla i. Galápagos Ecuador 142 [inset]
Fernandina Beach U.S.A. 133 D6
Fernando de Magallanes, Parque Nacional nat. park Chile 144 B8
Fernando de Noronha i. Brazil 148 F6
Fernandópolis Brazil 145 A3
Fernando Poó i. Equat. Guinea see Bioco
Fernão Dias Brazil 145 B2
Ferndale U.S.A. 128 A1
Ferndown U.K. 49 F8
Fernlee Australia 112 C2
Fernley U.S.A. 128 D2
Ferns Ireland 51 F5
Ferozepore India see Firozpur
Ferrara Italy 58 D2
Ferreira-Gomes Brazil 143 H3
Ferro, Capo c. Sardinia Italy 58 C4
Ferrol Spain 57 B2
Ferron U.S.A. 129 H2
Ferros Brazil 145 C2
Ferryland Canada 123 L5
Ferryville Tunisia see Menzel Bourguiba
Fertő-tavi nat. park Hungary 58 G1
Ferwerd Neth. see Ferwert
Ferwert Neth. 52 F1
Fès Morocco 54 D5
Feshi Dem. Rep. Congo 99 B4
Fessenden U.S.A. 130 D2
Festus U.S.A. 130 F4
Fété Bowé Senegal 96 B3
Fethard Ireland 51 E5
Fethiye Malatya Turkey see Yazıhan
Fethiye Muğla Turkey 59 M6
Fethiye Körfezi b. Turkey 59 M6
Fetisovo Kazakh. 91 I2
Fetlar i. U.K. 50 [inset]
Fettercairn U.K. 50 G4
Feucht Germany 53 L5
Feuchtwangen Germany 53 K5
Feuilles, Rivière aux r. Canada 123 H2
Fevral'sk Rus. Fed. 74 C1
Fevzipaşa Turkey 90 E3
Feyzābād Afgh. 89 H2
Feyzābād Kermān Iran 88 D4
Feyzābād Khorāsān Iran 88 E3
Fez Morocco see Fès
Ffestiniog U.K. 49 D6
Fianarantsoa Madag. 99 E6
Fichē Eth. 98 D3
Fichtelgebirge hills Germany 53 M4
Field U.S.A. 134 D5
Fier Albania 59 H4
Fiery Creek r. Australia 110 B3
Fife Lake U.S.A. 134 C1
Fife Ness pt U.K. 50 G4
Fifield Australia 112 C4
Fifth Meridian Canada 120 H3
Figeac France 56 F4
Figueira da Foz Port. 57 B3
Figueras Spain see Figueres
Figueres Spain 57 H2
Figuig Morocco 54 D5
Figuil Cameroon 97 E4

▶Fiji country S. Pacific Ocean 107 H3
4th most populous and 5th largest country in Oceania.

Fīk' Eth. 98 E3
Filadelfia Para. 144 D2
Filchner Ice Shelf Antarctica 152 A1
Filey U.K. 48 G4
Filibe Bulg. see Plovdiv
Filingué Niger 96 D3
Filipinas country Asia see Philippines
Filippiada Greece 59 I5
Filipstad Sweden 45 I7

Fillan Norway 44 F5
Fillmore CA U.S.A. 128 D4
Fillmore UT U.S.A. 129 G2
Fils r. Germany 53 J6
Filtu Eth. 98 E3
Fimbull Ice Shelf Antarctica 152 C2
Fin Iran 88 C3
Finch Canada 135 H1
Findhorn r. U.K. 50 F3
Fındık Turkey 88 A2
Findlay U.S.A. 134 D3
Fine U.S.A. 135 H1
Finger Lake Canada 121 M4
Finger Lakes U.S.A. 135 G2
Finike Turkey 59 N6
Finike Körfezi b. Turkey 59 N6
Finisterre Spain see Fisterra
Finisterre, Cabo c. Spain see Finisterre, Cape
Finisterre, Cape Spain 57 B2
Finke watercourse Australia 110 A5
Finke, Mount hill Australia 109 F7
Finke Bay Australia 108 E3
Finke Gorge National Park Australia 109 F6
Finland country Europe 44 O5
Finland, Gulf of Europe 45 M7

▶Finlay r. Canada 120 E3
Part of the Mackenzie-Peace-Finlay, the 2nd longest river in North America.

Finlay, Mount Canada 120 E3
Finlay Forks Canada 120 F4
Finley U.S.A. 130 D2
Finn r. Ireland 51 E3
Finne ridge Germany 53 L3
Finnigan, Mount Australia 110 D2
Finniss, Cape Australia 109 F8
Finnmarksvidda reg. Norway 44 H2
Finnsnes Norway 44 J2
Fins Oman 88 E6
Finschhafen P.N.G. 69 L8
Finspång Sweden 45 I7
Fintona U.K. 51 E3
Finucane Range hills Australia 110 C4
Fionn Loch l. U.K. 50 D3
Fionnphort U.K. 50 C4
Fiordland National Park N.Z. 113 A7
Fir reg. Saudi Arabia 88 B4
Firat r. Asia 90 E3 see Euphrates
Firebaugh U.S.A. 128 C3
Firedrake Lake Canada 121 J2
Firenze Italy see Florence
Fireside Canada 120 E3
Firk, Sha'īb watercourse Iraq 91 G5
Firmat Arg. 144 D4
Firminy France 56 G4
Firmum Italy see Fermo
Firmum Picenum Italy see Fermo
Firovo Rus. Fed. 42 G4
Firozabad India 82 D4
Firozkoh reg. Afgh. 89 G3
Firozpur India 82 C3
Fīrūzābād Iran 88 D4
Fīrūzkūh Iran 88 D3
Firyuza Turkm. see Pöwrize
Fischbach Germany 53 H5
Fischersbrunn Namibia 100 B3
Fish watercourse Namibia 100 C5
Fisher (abandoned) Australia 109 E7
Fisher Bay Antarctica 152 G2
Fisher Glacier Antarctica 152 E2
Fisher River Canada 121 L5
Fishers U.S.A. 134 B4
Fishers Island U.S.A. 135 J3
Fisher Strait Canada 119 J3
Fishguard U.K. 49 C7
Fishing Creek U.S.A. 135 G4
Fishing Lake Canada 121 M4
Fish Lake Canada 120 F2
Fish Point U.S.A. 134 D2
Fish Ponds H.K. China 77 [inset]
Fiske, Cape Antarctica 152 L2
Fiskenæsset Greenland see Qeqertarsuatsiaat
Fismes France 52 D5
Fisterra Spain 57 B2
Fisterra, Cabo c. Spain see Finisterre, Cape
Fitchburg U.S.A. 130 F3
Fitri, Lac l. Chad 97 E3
Fitzgerald Canada 121 I3
Fitzgerald U.S.A. 133 D6
Fitzgerald River National Park Australia 109 B8
Fitz Hugh Sound sea chan. Canada 120 D5
Fitz Roy Arg. 144 C7
Fitzroy r. Australia 108 C4
Fitz Roy, Cerro mt. Arg. 144 B7
Fitzroy Crossing Australia 108 D4
Fitzwilliam Island Canada 134 E1
Fiume Croatia see Rijeka
Fivemiletown U.K. 51 E3
Five Points U.S.A. 128 C3
Fizi Dem. Rep. Congo 99 C4
Fizuli Azer. see Füzuli
Flå Norway 45 F6
Flagstaff S. Africa 101 I6
Flagstaff U.S.A. 129 H4
Flagstaff Lake U.S.A. 132 G2
Flaherty Island Canada 122 F2
Flambeau r. U.S.A. 130 F2
Flamborough Head hd U.K. 48 G4
Fläming hills Germany 53 M2
Flaming Gorge Reservoir U.S.A. 126 F4
Flaminksvlei salt pan S. Africa 100 E6
Flanagan r. Canada 121 M4
Flandre reg. France 52 C4
Flannagan Lake U.S.A. 134 D5
Flannan Isles U.K. 50 B2
Flåsjön l. Sweden 44 I4
Flat r. Canada 120 E2
Flat r. U.S.A. 134 C2
Flat Creek Canada 120 B2
Flathead r. U.S.A. 124 E2
Flathead Lake U.S.A. 126 E3
Flatiron mt. U.S.A. 126 E3
Flat Island S. China Sea 68 F4
Flat Lick U.S.A. 134 D5
Flattery, Cape Australia 110 D2
Flattery, Cape U.S.A. 126 B2
Flat Top mt. Canada 120 B2
Flatwillow Creek r. U.S.A. 126 G3

Flatwoods U.S.A. 134 E4
Fleetmark Germany 53 L2
Fleetwood Australia 110 D4
Fleetwood U.K. 48 D5
Fleetwood U.S.A. 135 H3
Flekkefjord Norway 45 E7
Flemingsburg U.S.A. 134 D4
Flemington U.S.A. 135 H3
Flen Sweden 45 J7
Flensburg Germany 47 L3
Flers France 56 D2
Flesherton Canada 134 E1
Fletcher Lake Canada 121 I2
Fletcher Peninsula Antarctica 152 L2
Fleur de Lys Canada 123 K4
Fleur-de-May, Lac l. Canada 123 I4
Flinders r. Australia 110 C3
Flinders Chase National Park Australia 111 B7
Flinders Group National Park Australia 110 D2
Flinders Island Australia 111 [inset]
Flinders Passage Australia 110 E3
Flinders Ranges mts Australia 111 B7
Flinders Ranges National Park Australia 111 B6
Flinders Reefs Australia 110 E3
Flin Flon Canada 121 K4
Flint U.K. 48 D5
Flint U.S.A. 134 D2
Flint r. U.S.A. 133 C6
Flint Island Kiribati 151 J6
Flinton Australia 112 D1
Flisa Norway 45 H6

▶Flissingskiy, Mys c. Rus. Fed. 64 H2
Most easterly point of Europe.

Flixecourt France 52 C4
Flodden U.K. 48 E3
Flöha Germany 53 N4
Flood Range mts Antarctica 152 J1
Flora r. Australia 108 E3
Flora U.S.A. 134 B3
Florac France 56 F4
Florala U.S.A. 133 C6
Florange France 52 G5
Flora Reef Australia 110 D3
Florence Italy 58 D3
Florence AL U.S.A. 133 C5
Florence AZ U.S.A. 129 H5
Florence CO U.S.A. 127 G5
Florence OR U.S.A. 126 B4
Florence SC U.S.A. 133 E5
Florence WI U.S.A. 130 F2
Florence Junction U.S.A. 129 H5
Florencia Col. 142 C3
Florennes Belgium 52 E4
Florentia Italy see Florence
Florentino Ameghino, Embalse resr Arg. 144 C6
Flores r. Arg. 144 E5
Flores Guat. 136 G5
Flores i. Indon. 108 C2
Flores, Laut sea Indon. 108 B1
Flores Island Canada 120 E5
Flores Sea Indon. see Flores, Laut
Floresta Brazil 143 K5
Floresville U.S.A. 131 D6
Floriano Brazil 143 J5
Florianópolis Brazil 145 A4
Florida Uruguay 144 E4
Florida state U.S.A. 133 D6
Florida, Straits of Bahamas/U.S.A. 133 D8
Florida Bay U.S.A. 133 D7
Florida City U.S.A. 133 D7
Florida Islands Solomon Is 107 G2
Florida Keys is U.S.A. 133 D7
Florin U.S.A. 128 C2
Florina Greece 59 I4
Florissant U.S.A. 130 F4
Florø Norway 45 D6
Flour Lake Canada 123 I3
Floyd U.S.A. 134 E5
Floyd, Mount U.S.A. 129 G4
Floydada U.S.A. 131 C5
Fluessen l. Neth. 52 F2
Flushing Neth. see Vlissingen
Fly r. P.N.G. 69 K8
Flying Fish, Cape Antarctica 152 K2
Flying Mountain U.S.A. 129 I6
Flylân i. Neth. see Vlieland
Foam Lake Canada 121 K5
Foča Bos.-Herz. 58 H3
Foça Turkey 59 L5
Fochabers U.K. 50 F3
Focşani Romania 59 L2
Fogang China 77 G4
Foggia Italy 58 F4
Fogi Indon. 69 H7
Fogo i. Cape Verde 96 [inset]
Fogo Island Canada 123 L4
Foinaven hill U.K. 50 E2
Foix France 56 E5
Folda sea chan. Norway 44 I3
Foldereid Norway 44 H4
Foldfjorden sea chan. Norway 44 G4
Folegandros i. Greece 59 K6
Foleyet Canada 122 E4
Foley Island Canada 119 K3
Foligno Italy 58 E3
Folkestone U.K. 49 I7
Folkingham U.K. 49 G6
Folkston U.S.A. 133 D6
Folldal Norway 44 G5
Follonica Italy 58 D3
Folsom Lake U.S.A. 128 C2
Fomboni Comoros 99 E5
Fomento Cuba 133 E8
Fomin Rus. Fed. 43 I7
Fominskaya Rus. Fed. 42 K2
Fominskoye Rus. Fed. 42 I4
Fonda U.S.A. 135 H2
Fond-du-Lac Canada 121 J3
Fond du Lac r. Canada 121 J3
Fond du Lac U.S.A. 134 A2
Fondevila Spain 57 B3
Fondi Italy 58 E4
Fonni Sardinia Italy 58 C4
Fonsagrada Spain see A Fonsagrada
Fonseca, Golfo do b. Central America 136 G6

Fontaine Lake Canada 121 J3
Fontanges Canada 123 H3
Fontas Canada 120 F3
Fontas r. Canada 120 F3
Fonte Boa Brazil 142 E4
Fonteneau, Lac l. Canada 123 J4
Fontur pt Iceland 44 [inset]
Foochow China see **Fuzhou**
Foot's Bay Canada 134 F1
Foping China 77 F1
Foraker, Mount U.S.A. 118 C3
Foraulep atoll Micronesia see **Faraulep**
Forbes Australia 112 D4
Forbes, Mount Canada 120 G4
Forchheim Germany 53 L5
Ford r. U.S.A. 132 C2
Ford City U.S.A. 128 D4
Førde Norway 45 D6
Forde Lake Canada 121 L2
Fordham U.K. 49 H6
Fordingbridge U.K. 49 F8
Ford Range mts Antarctica 152 J1
Fords Bridge Australia 112 B2
Fordsville U.S.A. 134 B5
Fordyce U.S.A. 131 E5
Forécariah Guinea 96 B4
Forel, Mont mt. Greenland 119 O3
Foreland hd U.K. 49 F8
Foreland Point U.K. 49 D7
Foremost Canada 126 F2
Foresight Mountain Canada 120 E4
Forest Canada 134 E2
Forest MS U.S.A. 131 F5
Forest OH U.S.A. 134 D3
Forestburg Canada 121 H4
Forest Creek r. Australia 110 C3
Forest Hill Australia 112 C5
Forest Ranch U.S.A. 128 C2
Forestville Canada 123 H4
Forestville CA U.S.A. 128 B2
Forestville MI U.S.A. 134 D2
Forfar U.K. 50 G4
Forgan U.S.A. 131 C4
Forges-les-Eaux France 52 B5
Forillon, Parc National de nat. park Canada 123 I4
Forked River U.S.A. 135 H4
Forks U.S.A. 126 B3
Fork Union U.S.A. 135 F5
Forlì Italy 58 E2
Forman U.S.A. 130 D2
Formby U.K. 48 D5
Formentera i. Spain 57 G4
Formentor, Cap de c. Spain 57 H4
Formerie France 52 B5
Former Yugoslav Republic of Macedonia country Europe see **Macedonia**
Formiga Brazil 145 B3
Formosa Arg. 144 E3
Formosa country Asia see **Taiwan**
Formosa Brazil 145 B1
Formosa, Serra hills Brazil 143 G6
Formosa Bay Kenya see **Ungwana Bay**
Formosa Strait China/Taiwan see **Taiwan Strait**
Formoso r. Bahia Brazil 145 B1
Formoso r. Tocantins Brazil 145 A1
Fornos Moz. 101 L2
Forres U.K. 50 F3
Forrest Vic. Australia 112 A7
Forrest W.A. Australia 109 E7
Forrestal Range mts Antarctica 152 A1
Forrest City U.S.A. 131 F5
Forrest Lake Canada 121 I3
Forrest Lakes salt flat Australia 109 E7
Fors Sweden 44 J5
Forsayth Australia 110 C3
Forsnäs Sweden 44 M3
Forssa Fin. 45 M6
Forster Australia 112 F4
Forsyth GA U.S.A. 133 D5
Forsyth MT U.S.A. 126 G3
Forsyth Range hills Australia 110 C4
Fort Abbas Pak. 89 I4
Fort Albany Canada 122 E3
Fortaleza Brazil 143 K4
Fort Amsterdam U.S.A. see **New York**
Fort Archambault Chad see **Sarh**
Fort Ashby U.S.A. 135 F4
Fort Assiniboine Canada 120 H4
Fort Augustus U.K. 50 E3
Fort Beaufort S. Africa 101 H7
Fort Benton U.S.A. 126 F3
Fort Brabant Canada see **Tuktoyaktuk**
Fort Bragg U.S.A. 128 B2
Fort Branch U.S.A. 134 B4
Fort Carillon U.S.A. see **Ticonderoga**
Fort Charlet Alg. see **Djanet**
Fort Chimo Canada see **Kuujjuaq**
Fort Chipewyan Canada 121 I3
Fort Collins U.S.A. 126 G4
Fort-Coulonge Canada 122 F5
Fort Crampel Cent. Afr. Rep. see **Kaga Bandoro**
Fort-Dauphin Madag. see **Tôlañaro**
Fort Davis U.S.A. 131 C6

►**Fort-de-France** Martinique 137 L6
Capital of Martinique.

Fort de Kock Indon. see **Bukittinggi**
Fort de Polignac Alg. see **Illizi**
Fort Dodge U.S.A. 130 E3
Fort Duchesne U.S.A. 129 I1
Fort Edward U.S.A. 135 I2
Fortescue r. Australia 108 B5
Forte Veneza Brazil 143 H5
Fort Flatters Alg. see **Bordj Omer Driss**
Fort Foureau Cameroon see **Kousséri**
Fort Franklin Canada see **Déline**
Fort Gardel Alg. see **Zaouatallaz**
Fort Gay U.S.A. 134 D4
Fort George Canada see **Chisasibi**
Fort Good Hope Canada 118 F3
Fort Gouraud Mauritania see **Fdérik**
Forth r. U.K. 50 F4
Forth, Firth of est. U.K. 50 F4
Fort Hertz Myanmar see **Putao**
Fortification Range mts U.S.A. 129 F2
Fortín General Mendoza Para. 144 D2
Fortín Leonida Escobar Para. 144 D2
Fortín Madrejón Para. 144 E2
Fortín Pilcomayo Arg. 144 D2
Fortín Ravelo Bol. 142 F7
Fortín Sargento Primero Leyes Arg. 144 E2
Fortín Suárez Arana Bol. 142 F7
Fortín Teniente Juan Echauri López Para. 144 D2
Fort Jameson Zambia see **Chipata**
Fort Johnston Malawi see **Mangochi**
Fort Kent U.S.A. 132 G2
Fort Lamy Chad see **Ndjamena**
Fort Laperrine Alg. see **Tamanrasset**
Fort Laramie U.S.A. 126 G4
Fort Lauderdale U.S.A. 133 D7
Fort Liard Canada 120 F2
Fort Mackay Canada 121 I3
Fort Macleod Canada 120 H5
Fort Madison U.S.A. 130 F3
Fort Manning Malawi see **Mchinji**
Fort McMurray Canada 121 I3
Fort McPherson Canada 118 E3
Fort Meyers Beach U.S.A. 133 D7
Fort Morgan U.S.A. 130 C3
Fort Munro Pak. 89 H4
Fort Myers U.S.A. 133 D7
Fort Nelson Canada 120 F3
Fort Nelson r. Canada 120 F3
Fort Norman Canada see **Tulita**
Fort Orange U.S.A. see **Albany**
Fort Payne U.S.A. 133 C5
Fort Peck U.S.A. 126 G2
Fort Peck Reservoir U.S.A. 126 G3
Fort Pierce U.S.A. 133 D7
Fort Portal Uganda 98 D3
Fort Providence Canada 120 G2
Fort Randall U.S.A. see **Cold Bay**
Fort Resolution Canada 120 H2
Fortrose N.Z. 113 B8
Fortrose U.K. 50 E3
Fort Rosebery Zambia see **Mansa**
Fort Rousset Congo see **Owando**
Fort Rupert Canada see **Waskaganish**
Fort St James Canada 120 E4
Fort St John Canada 120 F3
Fort Sandeman Pak. see **Zhob**
Fort Saskatchewan Canada 120 H4
Fort Scott U.S.A. 130 E4
Fort Severn Canada 122 D2
Fort-Shevchenko Kazakh. 78 E2
Fort Simpson Canada 120 F2
Fort Smith Canada 121 H2
Fort Smith U.S.A. 131 E5
Fort Stockton U.S.A. 131 C6
Fort Sumner U.S.A. 127 G6
Fort Supply U.S.A. 131 D4
Fort Thomas U.S.A. 129 I5
Fort Trinquet Mauritania see **Bîr Mogreïn**
Fortuna U.S.A. 130 C1
Fortune Bay Canada 123 L5
Fort Valley U.S.A. 133 D5
Fort Vermilion Canada 120 G3
Fort Victoria Zimbabwe see **Masvingo**
Fort Ware Canada see **Ware**
Fort Wayne U.S.A. 134 C3
Fort William U.K. 50 D4
Fort Worth U.S.A. 131 D5
Fort Yates U.S.A. 130 C2
Fort Yukon U.S.A. 118 D3
Forum Iulii France see **Fréjus**
Forūr, Jazīreh-ye i. Iran 88 D5
Forvik Norway 44 H4
Foshan China 77 G4
Fo Shek Chau H.K. China see **Basalt Island**
Fossano Italy 58 B2
Fossil U.S.A. 126 C3
Fossil Downs Australia 108 D4
Foster Australia 112 C7
Foster U.S.A. 134 C4
Foster, Mount Canada/U.S.A. 120 C3
Foster Lakes Canada 121 J3
Fostoria U.S.A. 134 D3
Fotadrevo Madag. 99 E6
Fotherby U.K. 48 G5
Fotokol Cameroon 97 E3
Fotuna i. Vanuatu see **Futuna**
Fougères France 56 D2
Foula i. U.K. 50 [inset]
Foul Island Myanmar 70 A3
Foulness Point U.K. 49 H7
Foul Point Sri Lanka 84 D4
Foumban Cameroon 96 E4
Foundation Ice Stream glacier Antarctica 152 L1
Fount U.S.A. 134 D5
Fountains Abbey and Royal Water Garden (NT) tourist site U.K. 48 F4
Fourches, Mont des hill France 56 G2
Four Corners U.S.A. 128 E4
Fouriesburg S. Africa 101 I5
Fourmies France 52 E4
Fournier, Lac l. Canada 123 I4
Fournoi i. Greece 59 L6
Fourpeaked Mountain U.S.A. 118 C4
Fouta Djallon reg. Guinea 96 B3
Foveaux Strait N.Z. 113 A8
Fowey r. U.K. 49 C8
Fowler CO U.S.A. 127 G5
Fowler IN U.S.A. 134 B3
Fowler Ice Rise Antarctica 152 L1
Fowlers Bay Australia 106 D5
Fowlers Bay b. Australia 109 F8
Fowlerville U.S.A. 134 C2
Fox r. B.C. Canada 120 E3
Fox r. Man. Canada 121 M3
Fox r. U.S.A. 130 F3
Fox Creek Canada 120 G4
Fox Creek U.S.A. 134 C5
Foxdale Isle of Man 48 C4
Foxe Basin g. Canada 119 K3
Foxe Channel Canada 119 J3
Foxe Peninsula Canada 119 K3
Fox Glacier N.Z. 113 C6
Fox Islands U.S.A. 118 B4
Fox Lake Canada 120 H3
Fox Mountain Canada 120 C2
Fox Valley Canada 121 I5
Foyers U.K. 50 E3
Foyle r. Ireland/U.K. 51 E3
Foyle, Lough b. Ireland/U.K. 51 E2
Foynes Ireland 51 C5
Foz de Areia, Represa de resr Brazil 145 A4
Foz do Cunene Angola 99 B5
Foz do Iguaçu Brazil 144 F3
Fraga Spain 57 G3
Frakes, Mount Antarctica 152 K1
Framingham U.S.A. 135 J2
Framnes Mountains Antarctica 152 E2
Franca Brazil 145 B3
Français, Récif des reef New Caledonia 107 G3
Francavilla Fontana Italy 58 G4

►**France** country Europe 56 F3
3rd largest and 3rd most populous country in Europe.

Frances Australia 111 C8
Frances Lake Canada 120 D2
Frances Lake l. Canada 120 D2
Franceville Gabon 98 B4
Francis Canada 121 K5
Francis atoll Kiribati see **Beru**
Francis, Lake U.S.A. 135 J1
Francisco de Orellana Ecuador see **Coca**
Francisco de Orellana Orellana Ecuador see **Coca**
Francisco I. Madero Coahuila Mex. 131 C7
Francisco I. Madero Durango Mex. 131 B7
Francisco Zarco Mex. 128 E5
Francistown Botswana 99 C6
Francois Canada 123 K5
François Lake Canada 120 E4
Francois Peron National Park Australia 109 A6
Francs Peak U.S.A. 126 F4
Franeker Neth. 52 F1
Frankenberg Germany 53 N4
Frankenberg (Eder) Germany 53 I3
Frankenhöhe hills Germany 47 M6
Frankenmuth U.S.A. 134 D2
Frankenthal (Pfalz) Germany 53 I5
Frankenwald mts Germany 53 L4
Frankford Canada 135 G1
Frankfort IN U.S.A. 134 B3

►**Frankfort** KY U.S.A. 134 C4
Capital of Kentucky.

Frankfort MI U.S.A. 134 B1
Frankfort OH U.S.A. 134 D4
Frankfurt Germany see **Frankfurt am Main**
Frankfurt am Main Germany 53 I4
Frankfurt an der Oder Germany 47 O4
Frank Hann National Park Australia 109 C8
Frankin Lake U.S.A. 129 F1
Fränkische Alb hills Germany 53 K6
Fränkische Schweiz reg. Germany 53 L5
Frankland, Cape Australia 111 [inset]
Franklin AZ U.S.A. 129 I5
Franklin GA U.S.A. 133 C5
Franklin IN U.S.A. 134 B4
Franklin KY U.S.A. 134 B5
Franklin LA U.S.A. 131 F6
Franklin MA U.S.A. 135 J2
Franklin NC U.S.A. 133 D5
Franklin NE U.S.A. 130 D3
Franklin NH U.S.A. 135 J2
Franklin PA U.S.A. 134 F3
Franklin TN U.S.A. 132 C5
Franklin TX U.S.A. 131 D6
Franklin VA U.S.A. 135 G5
Franklin WV U.S.A. 134 F4
Franklin Bay Canada 153 A2
Franklin D. Roosevelt Lake resr U.S.A. 126 D2
Franklin Furnace U.S.A. 134 D4
Franklin-Gordon National Park Australia 111 [inset]
Franklin Island Antarctica 152 H1
Franklin Mountains Canada 120 F2
Franklin Strait Canada 119 I2
Franklinton U.S.A. 131 F6
Franklinville U.S.A. 135 F2
Frankston Australia 112 B7
Fränsta Sweden 44 J5
Frantsa-Iosifa, Zemlya is Rus. Fed. 64 G2
Franz Canada 122 D4
Franz Josef Glacier N.Z. 113 C6
Frasca, Capo della c. Sardinia Italy 58 C5
Frascati Italy 58 E4
Fraser r. Australia 108 C4
Fraser r. B.C. Canada 120 F5
Fraser r. Nfld. and Lab. Canada 123 J2
Fraser, Mount hill Australia 109 B6
Fraserburg S. Africa 100 E6
Fraserburgh U.K. 50 G3
Fraserdale Canada 122 E4
Fraser Island Australia 110 F5
Fraser Island National Park Australia 110 F5
Fraser Lake Canada 120 E4
Fraser National Park Australia 112 B6
Fraser Plateau Canada 120 E4
Fraser Range hills Australia 109 C8
Frauenfeld Switz. 56 I3
Fray Bentos Uruguay 144 E4
Frazeysburg U.S.A. 134 D3
Frechen Germany 52 G4
Freckleton U.K. 48 E5
Frederic U.S.A. 134 C1
Frederica U.S.A. 135 H4
Fredericia Denmark 45 F9
Frederick MD U.S.A. 135 G4
Frederick OK U.S.A. 131 D5
Frederick Reef Australia 110 F4
Fredericksburg TX U.S.A. 131 D6
Fredericksburg VA U.S.A. 135 G4
Fredericktown U.S.A. 130 F4

►**Fredericton** Canada 123 I5
Capital of New Brunswick.

Frederikshåb Greenland see **Paamiut**
Frederikshavn Denmark 45 G8
Frederiksværk Denmark 45 H9
Fredonia AZ U.S.A. 129 G3
Fredonia KS U.S.A. 131 E4
Fredonia NY U.S.A. 134 F2
Fredonia WI U.S.A. 134 B2
Fredrika Sweden 44 K4
Fredrikshamn Fin. see **Hamina**
Fredrikstad Norway 45 G7
Freedonyer Peak U.S.A. 128 C1
Freehold U.S.A. 135 H3
Freeland U.S.A. 135 H3
Freeling Heights hill Australia 111 B6
Freel Peak U.S.A. 128 D2
Freels, Cape Canada 123 L4
Freeman U.S.A. 130 D3
Freeman, Lake U.S.A. 134 B3
Freeport FL U.S.A. 133 C6
Freeport IL U.S.A. 130 F3
Freeport TX U.S.A. 131 E6
Freeport City Bahamas 133 E7
Freer U.S.A. 131 D7
Freesoil U.S.A. 134 B1
Free State prov. S. Africa 101 H5

►**Freetown** Sierra Leone 96 B4
Capital of Sierra Leone.

Fregenal de la Sierra Spain 57 C4
Fregon Australia 109 F6
Fréhel, Cap c. France 56 C2
Frei (Chile) research station Antarctica 152 A2
Freiberg Germany 53 N4
Freiburg Switz. see **Fribourg**
Freiburg im Breisgau Germany 47 K6
Freisen Germany 53 H5
Freising Germany 47 M6
Freistadt Austria 47 O6
Fréjus France 56 H5
Fremantle Australia 109 A8
Fremont CA U.S.A. 128 C3
Fremont IN U.S.A. 134 C3
Fremont MI U.S.A. 134 C2
Fremont NE U.S.A. 130 D3
Fremont OH U.S.A. 134 D3
Fremont r. U.S.A. 129 H2
Fremont Junction U.S.A. 129 H2
Frenchburg U.S.A. 134 D5
French Cay i. Turks and Caicos Is 133 F8
French Congo country Africa see **Congo**

►**French Guiana** terr. S. America 143 H3
French Overseas Department.

French Guinea country Africa see **Guinea**
French Island Australia 112 B7
French Lick U.S.A. 134 B4
Frenchman r. U.S.A. 126 G2
Frenchman Lake CA U.S.A. 128 C2
Frenchman Lake NV U.S.A. 129 F3
Frenchpark Ireland 51 D4
French Pass N.Z. 113 D5

►**French Polynesia** terr. S. Pacific Ocean 151 K7
French Overseas Country.

French Somaliland country Africa see **Djibouti**

►**French Southern and Antarctic Lands** terr. Indian Ocean 149 M8
French Overseas Territory.

French Sudan country Africa see **Mali**
French Territory of the Afars and Issas country Africa see **Djibouti**
Frenda Alg. 57 G6
Frentsjer Neth. see **Franeker**
Freren Germany 53 H2
Fresco r. Brazil 143 H5
Freshford Ireland 51 E5
Fresnillo Mex. 136 D4
Fresno U.S.A. 128 D3
Fresno r. U.S.A. 128 C3
Fresno Reservoir U.S.A. 126 F2
Fressel, Lac l. Canada 122 G3
Freu, Cap des c. Spain 57 H4
Freudenberg Germany 53 H4
Freudenstadt Germany 47 L6
Frévent France 52 C4
Frew watercourse Australia 110 A4
Frewena Australia 110 A3
Freycinet Estuary inlet Australia 109 A6
Freycinet Peninsula Australia 111 [inset]
Freyenstein Germany 53 M1
Freyming-Merlebach France 52 G5
Fria Guinea 96 B3
Fria, Cape Namibia 99 B5
Friant U.S.A. 128 D3
Frias Arg. 144 C3
Fribourg Switz. 56 H3
Friday Harbor U.S.A. 126 C2
Friedeburg Germany 53 H1
Friedens U.S.A. 135 F3
Friedland Rus. Fed. see **Pravdinsk**
Friedrichshafen Germany 47 L7
Friedrichskanal canal Germany 53 L2
Friend U.S.A. 130 D3
Friendly Islands country S. Pacific Ocean see **Tonga**
Friendship U.S.A. 130 F3
Friesack Germany 53 M2
Friese Wad tidal flat Neth. 52 F1
Friesoythe Germany 53 H1
Frinton-on-Sea U.K. 49 I7
Frio r. U.S.A. 131 D6
Frio watercourse U.S.A. 131 C5
Frisco Mountain U.S.A. 129 G2
Frissell, Mount hill U.S.A. 135 I2
Fritzlar Germany 53 J3
Frjentsjer Neth. see **Franeker**
Frobisher Bay Canada see **Iqaluit**
Frobisher Bay b. Canada 119 L3
Frobisher Lake Canada 121 I3
Frohavet b. Norway 44 F5
Frohburg Germany 53 M3
Froissy France 52 C5
Frolovo Rus. Fed. 43 I6
Frome watercourse Australia 111 B6
Frome U.K. 49 E7
Frome r. U.K. 49 E8
Frome, Lake salt flat Australia 111 B6
Frome Downs Australia 111 B6
Fröndenberg Germany 53 H3
Frontera Coahuila Mex. 131 C7
Frontera Tabasco Mex. 136 F5
Fronteras Mex. 127 F7
Front Royal U.S.A. 135 F4
Frosinone Italy 58 E4
Frostburg U.S.A. 135 F4
Frøya i. Norway 44 F5
Fruges France 52 C4
Fruita U.S.A. 129 I2
Fruitland U.S.A. 129 H1
Fruitvale U.S.A. 129 I2
Frunze Kyrg. see **Bishkek**
Frusino Italy see **Frosinone**
Fruska Gora nat. park Serbia 59 H2
Frýdek-Místek Czech Rep. 47 Q6
Fu'an China 77 H3
Fucheng Anhui China see **Fengyang**
Fucheng Shaanxi China see **Fuxian**
Fuchuan China 77 F3
Fuchun Jiang r. China 77 I2
Fude China 77 H3
Fuding China 77 I3
Fudul reg. Saudi Arabia 88 B6
Fuenlabrada Spain 57 E3
Fuerte r. Mex. 127 F8
Fuerte Olimpo Para. 144 E2
Fuerteventura i. Canary Is 96 B2
Fufeng China 76 E1
Fuga i. Phil. 69 G3
Fugong China 76 C3
Fugou China 77 G1
Fuhai China 80 G2
Fuḩaymī Iraq 91 F4
Fujairah U.A.E. 88 E5
Fujeira U.A.E. see **Fujairah**
Fuji Japan 75 E6
Fujian prov. China 77 H3
Fuji-Hakone-Izu Kokuritsu-kōen nat. park Japan 75 E6
Fujin China 74 C3
Fujinomiya Japan 75 E6
Fuji-san vol. Japan 75 E6
Fujiyoshida Japan 75 E6
Fûka Egypt see **Fūkah**
Fūkah Egypt 90 B5
Fukien prov. China see **Fujian**
Fukuchiyama Japan 75 D6
Fukue-jima i. Japan 75 C6
Fukui Japan 75 E5
Fukuoka Japan 75 C6
Fukushima Japan 75 F5
Fukuyama Japan 75 C7
Fûl, Gebel hill Egypt see **Fūl, Jabal**
Fūl, Jabal hill Egypt 85 A5
Fulchhari Bangl. 83 G4
Fulda Germany 53 J4
Fulda r. Germany 53 J3
Fulham U.K. 49 G7
Fuli China see **Jixian**
Fuliji China 77 H1
Fuling China 76 E2
Fulitun China see **Jixian**
Fullerton CA U.S.A. 128 E5
Fullerton NE U.S.A. 130 D3
Fullerton, Cape Canada 121 N2
Fulton IN U.S.A. 134 B3
Fulton MO U.S.A. 130 F4
Fulton MS U.S.A. 131 F5
Fulton NY U.S.A. 135 G2
Fumane Moz. 101 K3
Fumay France 52 E5
Fumin China 76 D3
Funabashi Japan 75 E6
Funafuti atoll Tuvalu 107 H2
Funan China 77 G1

►**Funchal** Madeira 96 B1
Capital of Madeira.

Fundão Brazil 145 C2
Fundão Port. 57 C3
Fundi Italy see **Fondi**
Fundición Mex. 127 F8
Fundy, Bay of g. Canada 123 I5
Fundy National Park Canada 123 I5
Fünen i. Denmark see **Fyn**
Funeral Peak U.S.A. 128 E3
Fünfkirchen Hungary see **Pécs**
Fung Wong Shan hill H.K. China see **Lantau Peak**
Funhalouro Moz. 101 L2
Funing Jiangsu China 77 H1
Funing Yunnan China 76 E4
Funiu Shan mts China 77 F1
Funtua Nigeria 96 D3
Funzie U.K. 50 [inset]
Fuqing China 77 H3
Fürgun, Kūh-e mt. Iran 88 E5
Furmanov Rus. Fed. 42 I4
Furmanovka Kazakh. see **Moyynkum**
Furmanovo Kazakh. see **Zhalpaktal**
Furnás hill Spain 57 G4
Furnas, Represa resr Brazil 145 B3
Furneaux Group is Australia 111 [inset]
Furnes Belgium see **Veurne**
Furong China see **Wan'an**
Fürstenau Germany 53 H2
Fürstenberg Germany 53 N1
Fürstenwalde Germany 47 O4
Fürth Germany 53 K5
Furth im Wald Germany 53 M5
Furukawa Japan 75 F5
Fury and Hecla Strait Canada 119 J3
Fusan S. Korea see **Pusan**
Fushun China 74 A4
Fushuncheng China see **Shuncheng**
Fusong China 74 B4
Fu Tau Pun Chau i. H.K. China 77 [inset]
Futuna i. Vanuatu 107 H3
Futuna Islands Wallis and Futuna Is see **Hoorn, Îles de**
Fuxian Liaoning China see **Wafangdian**
Fuxian Shaanxi China 73 J5
Fuxian Hu l. China 76 D3
Fuxin China 73 M4
Fuxing China see **Wangmo**
Fuxinzhen China see **Fuxin**
Fuyang Anhui China 77 G1
Fuyang Guangxi China see **Fuchuan**
Fuyang Zhejiang China 77 H2
Fuying Dao i. China 77 I3
Fuyu Anhui China see **Susong**
Fuyu Heilong. China 74 B3
Fuyu Jilin China see **Songyuan**
Fuyu Jilin China 74 B3
Fuyuan Heilong. China 74 D2
Fuyuan Yunnan China 76 E3
Fuyun China 80 G2
Fuzhou Fujian China 77 H3
Fuzhou Jiangxi China 77 H3
Füzuli Azer. 91 G3
Fyn i. Denmark 45 G9
Fyne, Loch inlet U.K. 50 D5
F.Y.R.O.M. (Former Yugoslav Republic of Macedonia) country Europe see **Macedon**

Gaaf Atoll Maldives see **Huvadhu Atoll**
Gaâfour Tunisia 58 C6
Gaalkacyo Somalia 98 E3
Gabakly Turkm. 89 F2
Gabasumdo China see **Tongde**
Gabbs U.S.A. 128 E2
Gabbs Valley Range mts U.S.A. 128 D2
Gabd Pak. 89 F5
Gabela Angola 99 B5
Gaberones Botswana see **Gaborone**
Gabès Tunisia 54 G5
Gabès, Golfe de g. Tunisia 54 G5
Gabo Island Australia 112 D6
Gabon country Africa 98 B4

►**Gaborone** Botswana 101 G3
Capital of Botswana.

Gābrīk Iran 88 E5
Gabrovo Bulg. 59 K3
Gabú Guinea-Bissau 96 B3
Gadag India 84 B3
Gadaisu P.N.G. 110 E1
Gadap Pak. 89 G5
Gadchiroli India 84 D1
Gäddede Sweden 44 I4
Gadê China 76 C1
Gades Spain see **Cádiz**
Gadhka India 89 H6
Gadhra India 82 B5
Gadra Pak. 89 H5
Gadsden U.S.A. 133 C5
Gadwal India 84 C2
Gadyach Ukr. see **Hadyach**
Gaer U.K. 49 D7
Găeşti Romania 59 K2
Gaeta Italy 58 E4
Gaeta, Golfo di g. Italy 58 E4
Gaferut i. Micronesia 69 L5
Gaffney U.S.A. 133 D5
Gafsa Tunisia 58 C7
Gagarin Rus. Fed. 43 G5
Gagnoa Côte d'Ivoire 96 C4
Gagnon Canada 123 H4
Gago Coutinho Angola see **Lumbala N'guimbo**
Gagra Georgia 43 I8
Gaiab watercourse Namibia 100 D5
Gaibanda Bangl. see **Gaibandha**
Gaibandha Bangl. 83 G4
Gaïdouronisi i. Greece 59 K7
Gaifi, Wâdi el watercourse Egypt see **Jayfī, Wādī al**
Gail U.S.A. 131 C5
Gaildorf Germany 53 J6
Gaillac France 56 E5
Gaillimh Ireland see **Galway**
Gaillon France 52 B5
Gaindainqoinkor China 83 G3
Gainesboro U.S.A. 134 C5
Gainesville FL U.S.A. 133 D6
Gainesville GA U.S.A. 133 D5
Gainesville MO U.S.A. 131 E4
Gainesville TX U.S.A. 131 D5
Gainsborough U.K. 48 G5
Gairdner, Lake salt flat Australia 111 A6
Gairloch U.K. 50 D3
Gair Loch b. U.K. 50 D3
Gajah Hutan, Bukit hill Malaysia 71 C6
Gajipur India see **Ghazipur**
Gajol India 83 G4
Gakarosa mt. S. Africa 100 F4
Gala China 83 G3
Galaasiya Uzbek. see **Galaosiyo**
Gala Co l. China 83 G3
Galâla el Baharîya, Gebel el plat. Egypt se **Jalālah al Baḩrīyah, Jabal**
Galana r. Kenya 98 E4
Galanta Slovakia 47 P6
Galaosiyo Uzbek. 89 G2

►**Galapagos Islands** is Ecuador 151 O6
Part of Ecuador. Most westerly point of South America.

Galapagos Rise sea feature Pacific Ocean 151 N6
Galashiels U.K. 50 G5
Galaţi Romania 59 M2
Galatina Italy 58 H4
Gala Water r. U.K. 50 G5
Galax U.S.A. 134 E5
Galaymor Turkm. see **Galaýmor**
Galaýmor Turkm. 89 F3
Galbally Ireland 51 D5
Galdhøpiggen mt. Norway 45 F6
Galeana Chihuahua Mex. 127 G7
Galeana Nuevo León Mex. 131 C7
Galena AK U.S.A. 118 C3
Galena IL U.S.A. 130 F3
Galena MD U.S.A. 135 H4
Galena MO U.S.A. 131 E4
Galera, Punta pt Chile 144 B6
Galesburg IL U.S.A. 130 F3
Galesburg MI U.S.A. 134 C2
Galeshewe S. Africa 100 G5
Galeton U.S.A. 135 G3
Galey r. Ireland 51 C5
Galheirão r. Brazil 145 B1
Galiano Island Canada 120 F5
Galich Rus. Fed. 42 I4
Galichskaya Vozvyshennost' hills Rus. Fed. 42 I4
Galicia aut. comm. Spain 57 C2
Galičica nat. park Macedonia 59 I4
Galilee, Lake salt flat Australia 110 D4
Galilee, Sea of l. Israel 85 B3
Galion U.S.A. 134 D3
Galiuro Mountains U.S.A. 129 H5
Galizia aut. comm. Spain see **Galicia**
Gallabat Sudan 86 E7

'allaorol Uzbek. 89 G1
allatin *MO* U.S.A. 130 E4
allatin *TN* U.S.A. 134 B5
alle Sri Lanka 84 D5
allego Rise *sea feature* Pacific Ocean 151 M6
allegos *r.* Arg. 144 C8
allia *country* Europe *see* **France**

Gallinas, Punta *pt* Col. 142 D1
Most northerly point of South America.

allipoli Italy 58 H4
allipoli Turkey 59 L4
allipolis U.S.A. 134 D4
illivare Sweden 44 L3
illö Sweden 44 I5
allo Island U.S.A. 135 G2
allo Mountains U.S.A. 129 I4
allup U.S.A. 129 I4
almisdale U.K. 50 C4
along Australia 112 D5
aloya Sri Lanka 84 D4
al Oya National Park Sri Lanka 84 D5
alston U.K. 50 E5
alt U.S.A. 128 C2
altat Zemmour W. Sahara 96 B2
altee Mountains *hills* Ireland 51 D5
altymore *hill* Ireland 46 C4
alūgāh, Kūh-e *mts* Iran 88 D4
alveston *IN* U.S.A. 134 B3
alveston *TX* U.S.A. 131 E6
alveston Bay U.S.A. 131 E6
alwa Nepal 83 E3
alway Ireland 51 C4
alway Bay Ireland 51 C4
im, Sông *r.* Vietnam 70 D2
amalakhe S. Africa 101 J6
amba China *see* **Gongbalou**
amba Gabon 98 A4
ambēla Eth. 98 D3
ambēla National Park Eth. 98 D3
ambell U.S.A. 118 A3
ambella Eth. *see* **Gambēla**
mbia, The *country* Africa 96 B3
mbier, Îles *is* Fr. Polynesia 151 L7
mbier Islands Australia 111 B7
mbier Islands Fr. Polynesia *see* **Gambier, Îles**
mbo Canada 123 L4
mboma Congo 98 B4
mboola Australia 110 C3
mboula Cent. Afr. Rep. 98 B3
mda China *see* **Zamtang**
mêtî Canada 120 G1
mlakarleby Fin. *see* **Kokkola**
mleby Sweden 45 J8
mmelstaden Sweden 44 M4
mmon Ranges National Park Australia 111 B6
mova, Mys *pt* Rus. Fed. 74 C4
mshadzai Kūh *mts* Iran 89 F4
mtog China 76 C2
mud *mt.* Eth. 98 D3
na China 76 D1
nado U.S.A. 129 I4
nanoque Canada 135 G1
ncā Azer. 91 G2
ncheng China 77 F5
nda Angola 99 B5
ndaingoin China 83 G3
ndajika Dem. Rep. Congo 99 C4
ndak Barrage Nepal 83 E4
ndari Mountain Pak. 89 H4
ndava Pak. 89 G4
nder Canada 123 L4
nderkesee Germany 53 I1
ndesa Spain 57 G3
ndhidham India 82 B5
ndhinagar India 82 C5
ndhi Sagar *resr* India 82 C4
ndia Spain 57 F4
ndzha Azer. *see* **Gäncä**
nga *r.* Bangl./India 83 G5 *see* **Ganges**
nga Cone *sea feature* Indian Ocean *see* **Ganges Cone**
ngán Arg. 144 C6
nganagar India 82 C3
ngapur India 82 D4
nga Sera India 82 B4
ngaw Myanmar 70 A2
ngawati India 84 C3
ngaw Range *mts* Myanmar 70 B2
ngca China 80 J4
ngdisê Shan *mts* China 83 E3
nges *r.* Bangl./India 83 G5
lso known as Ganga
nges France 56 F5
nges, Mouths of the Bangl./India 83 G5
nges Cone *sea feature* Indian Ocean 149 N4
ngouyi China 72 J5
ngra Turkey *see* **Çankırı**
ngtok India 83 G4
ngu China 76 E1
i Indon. 69 H7
n Jiang *r.* China 77 H2
njig China 73 M4
nluo China 76 D2
nmain Australia 112 C5
nnan China 74 A3
nnat France 56 F3
nnett Peak U.S.A. 126 F4
nq China 80 H4
nshui China 76 E2
nsu *prov.* China 76 D1
ntheaume Point Australia 108 C4
ntsevichi Belarus *see* **Hantsavichy**
nxian China 77 G3
nye Nigeria 96 E4
nyu China 77 H1
nyushkino Kazakh. 41 P6
nzhou China 77 G3
nzi Sudan 97 G4
o Mali 96 C3
ocheng China *see* **Litang**
ocun China *see* **Mayang**
ohe China *see* **Huaining**
ohebu China *see* **Huaining**
oleshan China *see* **Xianfeng**
oliangjian China *see* **Hongze**
omutang China 77 F3
Gaoping China 77 G1
Gaotai China 80 I4
Gaoth Dobhair Ireland 51 D2
Gaoting China *see* **Daishan**
Gaotingzhen China *see* **Daishan**
Gaoua Burkina 96 C3
Gaoual Guinea 96 B3
Gaoxiong Taiwan *see* **Kaohsiung**
Gaoyao China *see* **Zhaoqing**
Gaoyou China 77 H1
Gaoyou Hu *l.* China 77 H1
Gap France 56 H4
Gapuwiyak Australia 110 A2
Gaqoi China 83 E3
Gar China 82 E2
Gar Pak. 89 F5
Gar' *r.* Rus. Fed. 74 C1
Gara, Lough *l.* Ireland 51 D4
Garabekevyul Turkm. *see* **Garabekewül**
Garabekewül Turkm. 89 G2
Garabil Belentligi *hills* Turkm. 89 F2
Garabogaz Turkm. 91 I2
Garabogaz Aylagy *b.* Turkm. *see* **Garabogazköl Aýlagy**
Garabogazköl Aylagy *b.* Turkm. *see* **Garabogazköl Aýlagy**
Garabogazköl Aýlagy *b.* Turkm. 91 I2
Garabogazköl Bogazy *sea chan.* Turkm. 91 I2
Garāgheh Iran 89 F4
Garagum *des.* Turkm. 88 E2
Garagum *des.* Turkm. *see* **Karakum Desert**
Garagum Kanaly *canal* Turkm. 89 F2
Garah Australia 112 D2
Garalo Mali 96 C3
Garamätnyýaz Turkm. 89 G2
Garamätnyyaz Turkm. *see* **Garamätnyýaz**
Garamba *r.* Dem. Rep. Congo 98 C3
Garanhuns Brazil 143 K5
Ga-Rankuwa S. Africa 101 H3
Garapuava Brazil 145 B2
Gárasavvon Sweden *see* **Karesuando**
Garautha India 82 D4
Garba China *see* **Jiulong**
Garbahaarrey Somalia 98 E3
Garba Tula Kenya 98 D3
Garberville U.S.A. 128 B1
Garbo China *see* **Lhozhag**
Garbsen Germany 53 J2
Garça Brazil 145 A3
Garco China 83 G2
Garda, Lago di Italy *see* **Garda, Lake**
Garda, Lake Italy 58 D2
Garde, Cap de *c.* Alg. 58 B6
Gardelegen Germany 53 L2
Garden City U.S.A. 130 C4
Garden Hill Canada 121 M4
Garden Mountain U.S.A. 134 E5
Gardeyz Afgh. *see* **Gardēz**
Gardēz Afgh. 89 H3
Gardinas Belarus *see* **Hrodna**
Gardiner U.S.A. 135 K1
Gardiner, Mount Australia 108 F5
Gardiner Range *hills* Australia 108 E4
Gardiners Island U.S.A. 135 I3
Gardīz Afgh. *see* **Gardēz**
Gardner *atoll* Micronesia *see* **Faraulep**
Gardner U.S.A. 135 J2
Gardner Inlet Antarctica 152 L1
Gardner Island *atoll* Kiribati *see* **Nikumaroro**
Gardner Pinnacles *is* U.S.A. 150 I4
Gáregasnjárga Fin. *see* **Karigasniemi**
Garelochhead U.K. 50 E4
Garet el Djenoun *mt.* Alg. 96 D2
Gargano, Parco Nazionale del *nat. park* Italy 58 F4
Gargantua, Cape Canada 122 D5
Gargunsa China *see* **Gar**
Gargždai Lith. 45 L9
Garhchiroli India *see* **Gadchiroli**
Garhi *Madh. Prad.* India 84 C1
Garhi *Rajasthan* India 82 C5
Garhi Khairo Pak. 89 G4
Garhwa India 83 E4
Gari Rus. Fed. 41 S4
Gariau Indon. 69 I7
Garibaldi, Mount Canada 120 F5
Gariep Dam *resr* S. Africa 101 G6
Garies S. Africa 100 C6
Garigliano *r.* Italy 58 E4
Garissa Kenya 98 D4
Garkalne Latvia 45 N8
Garkung Caka *l.* China 83 F2
Garland U.S.A. 131 D5
Garm Tajik. *see* **Gharm**
Garm Āb Iran 89 E3
Garmāb Iran 88 E3
Garm Āb, Chashmeh-ye *spring* Iran 88 E3
Garmī Iran 88 C2
Garmsar Iran 88 D3
Garmsel *reg.* Afgh. 89 F4
Garner *IA* U.S.A. 130 E3
Garner *KY* U.S.A. 134 D5
Garnett U.S.A. 130 E4
Garnpung Lake *imp. l.* Australia 112 A4
Garo Hills India 83 G4
Garonne *r.* France 56 D4
Garoowe Somalia 98 E3
Garopaba Brazil 145 A5
Garoua Cameroon 96 E4
Garoua Boulai Cameroon 97 E4
Garqêntang China *see* **Sog**
Garré Arg. 144 D5
Garrett U.S.A. 134 C3
Garrison U.S.A. 130 E2
Garruk Pak. 89 G4
Garry *r.* U.K. 50 E3
Garrychyrla Turkm. *see* **Garryçyrla**
Garryçyrla Turkm. 89 F2
Garry Lake Canada 121 K1
Garrynahine U.K. 50 C2
Garsen Kenya 98 E4
Garshy Turkm. *see* **Garşy**
Garsila Sudan 97 F3
Garşy Turkm. 91 I2
Gartar China *see* **Qianning**
Garth U.K. 49 D6
Gartog China *see* **Markam**
Gartok China *see* **Garyarsa**
Gartow Germany 53 L1
Garub Namibia 100 C4
Garvagh U.K. 51 F3
Garve U.K. 50 E3
Garwa India *see* **Garhwa**
Garwha India *see* **Garhwa**
Gar Xincun China 82 E2
Gary *IN* U.S.A. 134 B3
Gary *WV* U.S.A. 134 E5
Garyarsa China 82 E3
Garyi China 76 C2
Garyū-zan *mt.* Japan 75 D6
Garza García Mex. 131 C7
Garzê China 76 C2
Gasan-Kuli Turkm. *see* **Esenguly**
Gas City U.S.A. 134 C3
Gascogne *reg.* France *see* **Gascony**
Gascogne, Golfe de *g.* France *see* **Gascony, Gulf of**
Gascony *reg.* France 56 D5
Gascony, Gulf of France 56 C5
Gascoyne *r.* Australia 109 A6
Gascoyne Junction Australia 109 A6
Gasherbrum I *mt.* China/Pakistan 82 D2
Gashua Nigeria 96 E3
Gask Iran 89 E3
Gaspar Cuba 133 E8
Gaspar, Selat *sea chan.* Indon. 68 D7
Gaspé Canada 123 I4
Gaspé, Cap *c.* Canada 123 I4
Gaspésie, Péninsule de la *pen.* Canada 123 I4
Gassan *vol.* Japan 75 F5
Gassaway U.S.A. 134 E4
Gasselte Neth. 52 G2
Gasteiz Spain *see* **Vitoria-Gasteiz**
Gastello Rus. Fed. 74 F2
Gaston U.S.A. 135 G5
Gaston, Lake U.S.A. 135 G5
Gastonia U.S.A. 133 D5
Gata, Cabo de *c.* Spain 57 E5
Gata, Cape Cyprus 85 A2
Gata, Sierra de *mts* Spain 57 C3
Gataga *r.* Canada 120 E3
Gatas, Akra *c.* Cyprus *see* **Gata, Cape**
Gatchina Rus. Fed. 45 Q7
Gate City U.S.A. 134 D5
Gatehouse of Fleet U.K. 50 E6
Gatentiri Indon. 69 K8
Gateshead U.K. 48 F4
Gates of the Arctic National Park and Preserve U.S.A. 118 C3
Gatesville U.S.A. 131 D6
Gateway U.S.A. 129 I2
Gatineau Canada 135 H1
Gatineau *r.* Canada 122 G5
Gatong China *see* **Jomda**
Gatooma Zimbabwe *see* **Kadoma**
Gatton Australia 112 F1
Gatvand Iran 88 C3
Gatyana S. Africa *see* **Willowvale**
Gau *i.* Fiji 107 H3
Gauer Lake Canada 121 L3
Gauhati India *see* **Guwahati**
Gaujas nacionālais parks *nat. park* Latvia 45 N8
Gaul *country* Europe *see* **France**
Gaula *r.* Norway 44 G5
Gaume *reg.* Belgium 52 F5
Gaurama Brazil 145 A4
Gauribidanur India 84 C3
Gauteng *prov.* S. Africa 101 I4
Gavarr Armenia 91 G2
Gāvbandī Iran 88 D5
Gāvbūs, Kūh-e *mts* Iran 88 D5

▶**Gavdos** *i.* Greece 59 K7
Most southerly point of Europe.

Gavião *r.* Brazil 145 C1
Gavīleh Iran 88 B3
Gav Khūnī Iran 88 D3
Gävle Sweden 45 J6
Gavrilovka Vtoraya Rus. Fed. 43 I5
Gavrilov-Yam Rus. Fed. 42 H4
Gawachab Namibia 100 C4
Gawai Myanmar 76 C3
Gawan India 83 F4
Gawilgarh Hills India 82 D5
Gawler Australia 111 B7
Gawler Ranges *hills* Australia 111 A7
Gaxun Nur *salt l.* China 80 J3
Gaya India 83 F4
Gaya Niger 96 D3
Gaya He *r.* China 74 C4
Gayéri Burkina 96 D3
Gaylord U.S.A. 134 C1
Gayndah Australia 111 E5
Gayny Rus. Fed. 42 L3
Gaysin Ukr. *see* **Haysyn**
Gayutino Rus. Fed. 42 H4
Gaz Iran 88 C3

▶**Gaza** *terr.* Asia 85 B4
Semi-autonomous region.

▶**Gaza** Gaza 85 B4
Capital of Gaza.

Gaza *prov.* Moz. 101 K2
Gazan Pak. 89 G4
Gazandzhyk Turkm. *see* **Bereket**
Gazanjyk Turkm. *see* **Bereket**
Gaza Strip *terr.* Asia *see* **Gaza**
Gaziantep Turkey 90 E3
Gaziantep *prov.* Turkey 85 C1
Gazibenli Turkey *see* **Yahyalı**
Gazīk Iran 89 F3
Gazimağusa Cyprus *see* **Famagusta**
Gazimurskiy Khrebet *mts* Rus. Fed. 73 L2
Gazimurskiy Zavod Rus. Fed. 73 L2
Gazipaşa Turkey 85 A1
Gazli Uzbek. 89 F1
Gaz Māhū Iran 88 E5
Gbarnga Liberia 96 C4
Gboko Nigeria 96 D4
Gcuwa S. Africa *see* **Butterworth**
Gdańsk Poland 47 Q3
Gdańsk, Gulf of Poland/Rus. Fed. 47 Q3
Gdańska, Zatoka *g.* Poland/Rus. Fed. *see* **Gdańsk, Gulf of**
Gdingen Poland *see* **Gdynia**
Gdov Rus. Fed. 45 O7
Gdynia Poland 47 Q3
Geaidnovuohppi Norway 44 M2
Gearhart Mountain U.S.A. 126 C4
Gearraidh na h-Aibhne U.K. *see* **Garrynahine**
Gebe *i.* Indon. 69 H6
Gebesee Germany 53 K3
Geçitkale Cyprus *see* **Lefkonikon**
Gedaref Sudan 86 E7
Gedern Germany 53 J4
Gedinne Belgium 52 E5
Gediz *r.* Turkey 59 L5
Gedney Drove End U.K. 49 H6
Gedong, Tanjong *pt* Sing. 71 [inset]
Gedser Denmark 45 G9
Geel Belgium 52 F3
Geelong Australia 112 B7
Geelvink Channel Australia 109 A7
Geel Vloer *salt pan* S. Africa 100 E5
Gees Gwardafuy *c.* Somalia *see* **Gwardafuy, Gees**
Geeste Germany 53 H2
Geesthacht Germany 53 K1
Ge Hu *l.* China 77 H2
Geidam Nigeria 96 E3
Geiersberg *hill* Germany 53 J5
Geikie *r.* Canada 121 K3
Geilenkirchen Germany 52 G4
Geilo Norway 45 F6
Geiranger Norway 44 E5
Geislingen an der Steige Germany 53 J6
Geisûm, Gezâ'ir *is* Egypt *see* **Qaysūm, Juzur**
Geita Tanz. 98 D4
Geithain Germany 53 M3
Gejiu China 76 D4
Gēkdepe Turkm. 88 E2
Gela *Sicily* Italy 58 F6
Gêladaindong *mt.* China 83 G2
Geladī Eth. 98 E3
Gelang, Tanjung *pt* Malaysia 71 C7
Geldern Germany 52 G3
Gelendzhik Rus. Fed. 90 E1
Gelibolu Turkey *see* **Gallipoli**
Gelidonya Burnu *pt* Turkey *see* **Yardımcı Burnu**
Gelincik Dağı *mt.* Turkey 59 N5
Gelmord Iran 88 E3
Gelnhausen Germany 53 J4
Gelsenkirchen Germany 52 H3
Gemas Malaysia 71 C7
Gemena Dem. Rep. Congo 98 B3
Geminokağı Cyprus *see* **Karavostasi**
Gemlik Turkey 59 M4
Gemona del Friuli Italy 58 E1
Gemsa Egypt *see* **Jamsah**
Gemsbok National Park Botswana 100 E3
Gemsbokplein *well* S. Africa 100 E4
Genalē Wenz *r.* Eth. 98 E3
Genappe Belgium 52 E4
Genāveh Iran 88 C4
General Acha Arg. 144 D5
General Alvear Arg. 144 C5
General Belgrano II *research station* Antarctica *see* **Belgrano II**
General Bravo Mex. 131 D7

▶**General Carrera, Lago** *l.* Arg./Chile 144 B7
Deepest lake in South America.

General Conesa Arg. 144 D6
General Freire Angola *see* **Muxaluando**
General Juan Madariaga Arg. 144 E5
General La Madrid Arg. 144 D5
General Machado Angola *see* **Camacupa**
General Pico Arg. 144 D5
General Pinedo Arg. 144 D3
General Roca Arg. 144 C5
General Salgado Brazil 145 A3
General San Martín *research station* Antarctica *see* **San Martín**
General Santos Phil. 69 H5
General Simón Bolívar Mex. 131 C7
General Trías Mex. 127 G7
General Villegas Arg. 144 D5
Genesee U.S.A. 135 G3
Geneseo U.S.A. 135 G2
Geneva S. Africa 101 H4
Geneva Switz. 56 H3
Geneva *AL* U.S.A. 133 C6
Geneva *IL* U.S.A. 134 A3
Geneva *NE* U.S.A. 130 D3
Geneva *NY* U.S.A. 135 G2
Geneva *OH* U.S.A. 134 E3
Geneva, Lake France/Switz. 56 H3
Genève Switz. *see* **Geneva**
Genf Switz. *see* **Geneva**
Gengda China *see* **Gana**
Gengma China 76 C4
Gengxuan China *see* **Gengma**
Genhe China 74 A2
Genichesk Ukr. *see* **Heniches'k**
Genji India 82 C5
Genk Belgium 52 F4
Gennep Neth. 52 F3
Genoa Australia 112 D6
Genoa Italy 58 C2
Genoa, Gulf of Italy 58 C2
Genova Italy *see* **Genoa**
Genova, Golfo di Italy *see* **Genoa, Gulf of**
Gent Belgium *see* **Ghent**
Genthin Germany 53 M2
Gentioux, Plateau de France 56 F4
Genua Italy *see* **Genoa**
Geographe Bay Australia 109 A8
Geographical Society Ø *i.* Greenland 119 P2
Geok-Tepe Turkm. *see* **Gëkdepe**
Georga, Zemlya *i.* Rus. Fed. 64 F1
George *r.* Canada 123 I2
George S. Africa 100 F7
George, Lake Australia 112 D5
George, Lake *FL* U.S.A. 133 D6
George, Lake *NY* U.S.A. 135 I2
George Land *i.* Rus. Fed. *see* **Georga, Zemlya**
Georges Mills U.S.A. 135 I2
George Sound *inlet* N.Z. 113 A7
Georgetown Australia 110 C3

▶**George Town** Cayman Is 137 H5
Capital of the Cayman Islands.

Georgetown Gambia 96 B3

▶**Georgetown** Guyana 143 G2
Capital of Guyana.

George Town Malaysia 71 C6
Georgetown *DE* U.S.A. 135 H4
Georgetown *GA* U.S.A. 133 C6
Georgetown *IL* U.S.A. 134 B4
Georgetown *KY* U.S.A. 134 C4
Georgetown *OH* U.S.A. 134 D4
Georgetown *SC* U.S.A. 133 E5
Georgetown *TX* U.S.A. 131 D6
George VI Sound *sea chan.* Antarctica 152 L2
George V Land *reg.* Antarctica 152 G2
George West U.S.A. 131 D6
Georgia *country* Asia 91 F2
Georgia *state* U.S.A. 133 D5
Georgia, Strait of Canada 120 E5
Georgiana U.S.A. 131 G6
Georgian Bay Canada 134 E1
Georgian Bay Islands National Park Canada 134 F1
Georgienne, Baie *b.* Canada *see* **Georgian Bay**
Georgina *watercourse* Australia 110 B5
Georgiu-Dezh Rus. Fed. *see* **Liski**
Georgiyevka *Vostochnyy Kazakhstan* Kazakh. 80 F2
Georgiyevka *Zhambylskaya Oblast'* Kazakh. *see* **Korday**
Georgiyevsk Rus. Fed. 91 F1
Georgiyevskoye Rus. Fed. 42 J4
Georg von Neumayer *research station* Antarctica *see* **Neumayer**
Gera Germany 53 M4
Geraardsbergen Belgium 52 D4
Geral, Serra *mts* Brazil 145 A4
Geral de Goiás, Serra *hills* Brazil 145 B1
Geraldine N.Z. 113 C7
Geral do Paraná, Serra *hills* Brazil 145 B1
Geraldton Australia 109 A7
Gerar *watercourse* Israel 85 B4
Gerber U.S.A. 128 B1
Gercüş Turkey 91 F3
Gerede Turkey 90 D2
Gereshk Afgh. 89 G4
Gerik Malaysia 71 C6
Gerlach U.S.A. 128 D1
Gerlachovský štít *mt.* Slovakia 47 R6
Germaine, Lac *l.* Canada 123 I3
Germania *country* Europe *see* **Germany**
Germanicea Turkey *see* **Kahramanmaraş**
Germansen Landing Canada 120 E4
German South-West Africa *country* Africa *see* **Namibia**
Germantown *OH* U.S.A. 134 C4
Germantown *WI* U.S.A. 134 A2

▶**Germany** *country* Europe 47 L5
2nd most populous country in Europe.

Germersheim Germany 53 I5
Gernsheim Germany 53 I5
Gerolstein Germany 52 G4
Gerolzhofen Germany 53 K5
Gerona Spain *see* **Girona**
Gerrit Denys *is* P.N.G. *see* **Lihir Group**
Gers *r.* France 56 E4
Gersfeld (Rhön) Germany 53 J4
Gersoppa India 84 B3
Gerstungen Germany 53 K4
Gerwisch Germany 53 L2
Géryville Alg. *see* **El Bayadh**
Gêrzê China 83 F2
Gerze Turkey 90 D2
Gescher Germany 52 H3
Gesoriacum France *see* **Boulogne-sur-Mer**
Gessie U.S.A. 134 B3
Gete *r.* Belgium 52 F4
Gettysburg *PA* U.S.A. 135 G4
Gettysburg *SD* U.S.A. 130 D2
Gettysburg National Military Park *nat. park* U.S.A. 135 G4
Getz Ice Shelf Antarctica 152 J2
Geumpang Indon. 71 B6
Geureudong, Gunung *vol.* Indon. 71 B6
Geurie Australia 112 D4
Gevaş Turkey 91 F3
Gevgelija Macedonia 59 J4
Gexto Spain *see* **Algorta**
Gey Iran *see* **Nikshahr**
Geyikli Turkey 59 L5
Geylegphug Bhutan 83 G4
Geysdorp S. Africa 101 G4
Geyserville U.S.A. 128 B2
Geyve Turkey 59 N4
Gezīr Iran 88 D5
Ghaap Plateau S. Africa 100 F4
Ghāb, Wādī al *r.* Syria 85 C2
Ghabāghib Syria 85 C3
Ghabeish Sudan 86 C7
Ghadaf, Wādī al *watercourse* Jordan 85 C4
Ghadamés Libya *see* **Ghadāmis**
Ghadāmis Libya 96 D1
Gha'em Shahr Iran 88 D2
Ghaghara *r.* India 83 F4
Ghaibi Dero Pak. 89 G5
Ghalend Iran 89 F4
Ghallaorol Uzbek. *see* **G'allaorol**
Ghana *country* Africa 96 C4
Ghanādah, Rās *pt* U.A.E. 88 D5
Ghantila India 82 B5
Ghanwā Saudi Arabia 86 G4
Ghanzi Botswana 99 C6
Ghanzi *admin. dist.* Botswana 100 F2
Ghap'an Armenia *see* **Kapan**
Ghār, Ras al *pt* Saudi Arabia 88 C5
Ghardaïa Alg. 54 E5
Gharghoda India 84 D1
Ghārib, Gebel *mt.* Egypt *see* **Ghārib, Jabal**
Ghārib, Jabal *mt.* Egypt 90 D5
Gharm Tajik. 89 H2
Gharq Ābād Iran 88 C3
Gharwa India *see* **Garhwa**
Gharyān Libya 97 E1
Ghāt Libya 96 E2
Ghatgan India 83 F5
Ghatol India 82 C5
Ghawdex *i.* Malta *see* **Gozo**
Ghazal, Bahr el *watercourse* Chad 97 E3
Ghazaouet Alg. 57 F6
Ghaziabad India 82 D3
Ghazi Ghat Pak. 89 H4
Ghazipur India 83 E4
Ghazna Afgh. *see* **Ghaznī**
Ghaznī Afgh. 89 H3
Ghaznī *r.* Afgh. 89 G3
Ghazoor Afgh. 89 G3
Ghazzah Gaza *see* **Gaza**
Ghebar Gumbad Iran 88 E3
Ghent Belgium 52 D3
Gheorghe Gheorghiu-Dej Romania *see* **Onești**
Gheorgheni Romania 59 K1
Gherla Romania 59 J1
Ghijduwon Uzbek. *see* **G'ijduvon**
Ghilzai *reg.* Afgh. 89 G4
Ghīnah, Wādī al *watercourse* Saudi Arabia 85 D4
Ghisonaccia *Corsica* France 56 I5
Ghorak Afgh. 89 G3
Ghost Lake Canada 120 H2
Ghotaru India 82 B4
Ghotki Pak. 89 H5
Ghudamis Libya *see* **Ghadāmis**
Ghugri *r.* India 83 F4
Ghurayfah *hill* Saudi Arabia 85 C4
Ghūrī Iran 88 D4
Ghurian Afgh. 89 F3
Ghurrab, Jabal *hill* Saudi Arabia 88 B5
Ghuzor Uzbek. *see* **G'uzor**
Ghyvelde France 52 C3
Giaginskaya Rus. Fed. 91 F1
Gialias *r.* Cyprus 85 A2
Gia Nghia Vietnam 71 D4
Gianisada *i.* Greece 59 L7
Giannitsa Greece 59 J4
Giant's Castle *mt.* S. Africa 101 I5
Giant's Causeway *lava field* U.K. 51 F2
Gianysada *i. Kriti* Greece *see* **Gianisada**
Gia Rai Vietnam 71 D5
Giarre *Sicily* Italy 58 F6
Gibb *r.* Australia 108 D3
Gibbonsville U.S.A. 126 E3
Gibeon Namibia 100 C3
Gibraltar *terr.* Europe 57 D5

▶**Gibraltar** Gibraltar 148 H3
United Kingdom Overseas Territory.

Gibraltar, Strait of Morocco/Spain 57 C6
Gibraltar Range National Park Australia 112 F2
Gibson Australia 109 C8
Gibson City U.S.A. 134 A3
Gibson Desert Australia 109 C6
Gichgeniyn Nuruu *mts* Mongolia 80 H2
Gidar Pak. 89 G4
Giddalur India 84 C3
Giddi, Gebel el *hill* Egypt *see* **Jiddī, Jabal al**
Giddings U.S.A. 131 D6
Gīdolē Eth. 97 G4
Gien France 56 F3
Gießen Germany 53 I4
Gīfan Iran 88 E2
Gifford *r.* Canada 119 J2
Gifhorn Germany 53 K2
Gift Lake Canada 120 H4
Gifu Japan 75 E6
Giganta, Cerro *mt.* Mex. 127 F8
Gigha *i.* U.K. 50 D5
Gīgīga Eth. *see* **Jijiga**
G'ijduvon Uzbek. 89 G1
Gijón Spain *see* **Gijón-Xixón**
Gijón-Xixón Spain 57 D2
Gila *r.* U.S.A. 129 F5
Gila Bend U.S.A. 129 G5
Gila Bend Mountains U.S.A. 129 G5
Gīlān-e Gharb Iran 88 B3
Gilbert *r.* Australia 110 C3
Gilbert *AZ* U.S.A. 129 H5
Gilbert *WV* U.S.A. 134 E5
Gilbert Islands Kiribati 150 H5
Gilbert Islands *country* Pacific Ocean *see* **Kiribati**
Gilbert Peak U.S.A. 129 H1
Gilbert Ridge *sea feature* Pacific Ocean 150 H6
Gilbert River Australia 110 C3
Gilbués Brazil 143 I5
Gil Chashmeh Iran 88 E3
Gilé Moz. 99 D5
Giles Creek *r.* Australia 108 E4
Gilford Island Canada 120 E5
Gilgai Australia 112 E2
Gilgandra Australia 112 D3
Gil Gil Creek *r.* Australia 112 D2
Gilgit Pak. 82 C2
Gilgit *r.* Pak. 87 L2
Gilgunnia Australia 112 C4
Gilindire Turkey *see* **Aydıncık**
Gillam Canada 121 M3
Gillen, Lake *salt flat* Australia 109 D6
Gilles, Lake *salt flat* Australia 111 B7
Gillett U.S.A. 135 G3
Gillette U.S.A. 126 G3
Gilliat Australia 110 C4
Gillingham *England* U.K. 49 E7
Gillingham *England* U.K. 49 H7
Gilling West U.K. 48 F4
Gilman U.S.A. 134 B3
Gilmer U.S.A. 131 E5
Gilmour Island Canada 122 F2
Gilroy U.S.A. 128 C3
Gīmbī Eth. 98 D3
Gimhae S. Korea *see* **Kimhae**
Gimli Canada 121 L5
Gimol'skoye, Ozero *l.* Rus. Fed. 42 G3
Ginebra, Laguna *l.* Bol. 142 E6
Gineifa Egypt *see* **Junayfah**
Gin Gin Australia 110 E5
Gingin Australia 109 A7
Gīnīr Eth. 98 E3
Ginosa Italy 58 G4
Ginzo de Limia Spain *see* **Xinzo de Limia**
Gioia del Colle Italy 58 G4
Gipouloux *r.* Canada 122 G3
Gippsland *reg.* Australia 112 B7

Girâ, Wâdi watercourse Egypt see Jirā', Wādī
Girān Rīg mt. Iran 88 E4
Girard U.S.A. 134 E2
Girardin, Lac l. Canada 123 I2
Girdab Iran 88 E3
Giresun Turkey 90 E2
Girgenti Sicily Italy see Agrigento
Giridh India see Giridih
Giridih India 83 F4
Girilambone Australia 112 C3
Girna r. India 82 C5
Gir National Park India 82 B5
Girne Cyprus see Kyrenia
Girón Ecuador 142 C4
Giron Sweden see Kiruna
Girona Spain 57 H3
Gironde est. France 56 D4
Girot Pak. 89 I3
Girral Australia 112 C4
Girraween National Park Australia 112 E2
Girvan U.K. 50 E5
Girvas Rus. Fed. 42 G3
Gisborne N.Z. 113 G4
Giscome Canada 120 F4
Gislaved Sweden 45 H8
Gisors France 52 B5
Gissar Tajik. see Hisor
Gissar Range mts Tajik./Uzbek. 89 G2
Gissarskiy Khrebet mts Tajik./Uzbek. see Gissar Range
Gitarama Rwanda 98 C4
Gitega Burundi 98 C4
Giuba r. Somalia see Jubba
Giulianova Italy 58 E3
Giurgiu Romania 59 K3
Giuvala, Pasul pass Romania 59 K2
Givar Iran 88 E2
Givet France 52 E4
Givors France 56 G4
Givry-en-Argonne France 52 E6
Giyani S. Africa 101 J2
Giza Egypt 90 C5
Gizhiga Rus. Fed. 65 R3
Gjakovë Kosovo 59 I3
Gjilan Kosovo 59 I3
Gjirokastër Albania 59 I4
Gjirokastra Albania see Gjirokastër
Gjoa Haven Canada 119 I3
Gjøra Norway 44 F5
Gjøvik Norway 45 G6
Gkinas, Akrotirio pt Greece 59 M6
Glace Bay Canada 123 K5
Glacier Bay National Park and Preserve U.S.A. 120 B3
Glacier National Park Canada 120 G5
Glacier National Park U.S.A. 126 E2
Glacier Peak vol. U.S.A. 126 C2
Gladstad Norway 44 G4
Gladstone Australia 110 E4
Gladstone Canada 121 L5
Gladwin U.S.A. 134 C2
Gladys U.S.A. 134 F5
Gladys Lake Canada 120 C3
Glamis U.K. 50 F4
Glamis U.S.A. 129 F5
Glamoč Bos.-Herz. 58 G2
Glan r. Germany 53 H5
Glandorf Germany 53 I2
Glanton U.K. 48 F3
Glasgow U.K. 50 E5
Glasgow KY U.S.A. 134 C5
Glasgow MT U.S.A. 126 G2
Glasgow VA U.S.A. 134 F5
Glaslyn Canada 121 I4
Glass, Loch l. U.K. 50 E3
Glass Mountain U.S.A. 128 D3
Glastonbury U.K. 49 E7
Glauchau Germany 53 M4
Glazov Rus. Fed. 42 L4
Gleiwitz Poland see Gliwice
Glen U.S.A. 135 J1
Glen Allen U.S.A. 135 G5
Glen Alpine Dam S. Africa 101 I2
Glenamaddy Ireland 51 D4
Glenamoy r. Ireland 51 C3
Glen Arbor U.S.A. 134 C1
Glenbawn, Lake Australia 112 E4
Glenboro Canada 121 L5
Glen Canyon gorge U.S.A. 129 H3
Glen Canyon Dam U.S.A. 129 H3
Glencoe Canada 134 E2
Glencoe S. Africa 101 J5
Glencoe U.S.A. 130 E2
Glendale AZ U.S.A. 129 G5
Glendale CA U.S.A. 128 D4
Glendale UT U.S.A. 129 G3
Glendale Lake U.S.A. 135 F3
Glen Davis Australia 112 E4
Glenden Australia 110 E4
Glendive U.S.A. 126 G3
Glendon Canada 121 I4
Glendo Reservoir U.S.A. 126 G4
Glenfield U.S.A. 135 H2
Glengavlen Ireland 51 E3
Glengyle Australia 110 B5
Glen Innes Australia 112 E2
Glenluce U.K. 50 E6
Glen Lyon U.S.A. 135 G3
Glenlyon Peak Canada 120 C2
Glen More valley U.K. 50 E3
Glenmorgan Australia 112 D1
Glenn U.S.A. 128 B2
Glennallen U.S.A. 118 D3
Glennie U.S.A. 134 D1
Glenns Ferry U.S.A. 126 E4
Glenora Canada 120 D3
Glenore Australia 110 C3
Glenormiston Australia 110 B4
Glenreagh Australia 112 F3
Glen Rose U.S.A. 131 D5
Glenrothes U.K. 50 F4
Glens Falls U.S.A. 135 I2
Glen Shee valley U.K. 50 F4
Glenties Ireland 51 D3
Glenveagh National Park Ireland 51 E2
Glenville U.S.A. 134 E4
Glenwood AR U.S.A. 131 E5
Glenwood IA U.S.A. 130 E3
Glenwood MN U.S.A. 130 E2
Glenwood NM U.S.A. 129 I5
Glenwood Springs U.S.A. 129 J2
Glevum U.K. see Gloucester
Glinde Germany 53 K1
Glittertinden mt. Norway 45 F6
Gliwice Poland 47 Q5
Globe U.S.A. 129 H5
Glogau Poland see Głogów
Głogów Poland 47 P5
Glomfjord Norway 44 H3
Glomma r. Norway 44 G7
Glommersträsk Sweden 44 K4
Glorieuses, Îles is Indian Ocean 99 E5
Glorioso Islands Indian Ocean see Glorieuses, Îles
Gloster U.S.A. 131 F6
Gloucester Australia 112 E3
Gloucester U.K. 49 E7
Gloucester MA U.S.A. 135 J2
Gloucester VA U.S.A. 135 G5
Gloversville U.S.A. 135 H2
Glovertown Canada 123 L4
Glöwen Germany 53 M2
Glubinnoye Rus. Fed. 74 D3
Glubokiy Krasnoyarskiy Kray Rus. Fed. 72 H2
Glubokiy Rostovskaya Oblast' Rus. Fed. 43 I6
Glubokoye Belarus see Hlybokaye
Glubokoye Kazakh. 80 F1
Gluggarnir hill Faroe Is 44 [inset]
Glukhov Ukr. see Hlukhiv
Glusburn U.K. 48 F5
Glynebwy U.K. see Ebbw Vale
Gmelinka Rus. Fed. 43 J6
Gmünd Austria 47 O6
Gmunden Austria 47 N7
Gnarp Sweden 45 J5
Gnarrenburg Germany 53 J1
Gnesen Poland see Gniezno
Gniezno Poland 47 P4
Gnjilane Kosovo see Gjilan
Gnowangerup Australia 109 B8
Gnows Nest Range hills Australia 109 B7
Goa India 84 B3
Goa state India 84 B3
Goageb Namibia 100 C4
Goalen Head hd Australia 112 E6
Goalpara India 83 G4
Goat Fell hill U.K. 50 D5
Goba Eth. 98 E3
Gobabis Namibia 100 D2
Gobannium U.K. see Abergavenny
Gobas Namibia 100 D4
Gobi Desert des. China/Mongolia 72 J4
Gobindpur India 83 F5
Gobles U.S.A. 134 C2
Gobō Japan 75 D6
Goch Germany 52 G3
Gochas Namibia 100 D3
Go Công Vietnam 71 D5
Godalming U.K. 49 G7
Godavari r. India 84 D2
Godavari, Cape India 84 D2
Godda India 83 F4
Godē Eth. 98 E3
Godere Eth. 98 E3
Goderich Canada 134 E2
Goderville France 49 H9
Godhavn Greenland see Qeqertarsuaq
Godhra India 82 C5
Godia Creek b. India 89 H6
Gods r. Canada 121 M3
Gods Lake Canada 121 M4
God's Mercy, Bay of Canada 121 O2
Godthåb Greenland see Nuuk
Godwin-Austen, Mount China/Pakistan see K2
Goedereede Neth. 52 D3
Goedgegun Swaziland see Nhlangano
Goegap Nature Reserve S. Africa 100 D5
Goélands, Lac aux l. Canada 123 J3
Goes Neth. 52 D3
Gogama Canada 122 E5
Gogebic Range hills U.S.A. 130 F2
Gogra r. India see Ghaghara
Goiana Brazil 143 L5
Goiandira Brazil 145 A2
Goianésia Brazil 145 A1
Goiânia Brazil 145 A2
Goiás Brazil 145 A1
Goiás state Brazil 145 A2
Goinsargoin China 76 C2
Goio-Erê Brazil 144 F2
Gojra Pak. 89 I4
Gokak India 84 B2
Gokarn India 84 B3
Gök Çay r. Turkey 85 A1
Gökçeada i. Turkey 59 K4
Gökdepe Turkm. see Gëkdepe
Gökdere r. Turkey 85 A1
Goklenkuy, Solonchak salt l. Turkm. 88 E1
Gökova Körfezi b. Turkey 59 L6
Gokprosh Hills Pak. 89 F5
Göksun Turkey 90 E3
Goksu Parkı Turkey 85 A1
Gokteik Myanmar 70 B2
Gokwe Zimbabwe 99 C5
Gol Norway 45 F6
Golaghat India 83 H4
Golbāf Iran 88 E4
Gölbaşı Turkey 90 E3
Golconda U.S.A. 128 E1
Gölcük Turkey 59 M4
Gold U.S.A. 135 G3
Gołdap Poland 47 S3
Gold Beach U.S.A. 126 B4
Goldberg Germany 53 M1
Gold Coast country Africa see Ghana
Gold Coast Australia 112 F2
Golden U.S.A. 126 G5
Golden Bay N.Z. 113 D5
Goldendale U.S.A. 126 C3
Goldene Aue reg. Germany 53 K3
Golden Gate Highlands National Park S. Africa 101 I5
Golden Hinde mt. Canada 120 E5
Golden Lake Canada 135 G1
Golden Prairie Canada 121 I5
Goldenstedt Germany 53 I2
Goldfield U.S.A. 128 E3
Goldsand Lake Canada 121 K3
Goldsboro U.S.A. 133 E5
Goldstone Lake U.S.A. 128 E4
Goldsworthy (abandoned) Australia 108 B5
Goldthwaite U.S.A. 131 D6
Goldvein U.S.A. 135 G4
Göle Turkey 91 F2
Golestān Afgh. 89 F3
Goleta U.S.A. 128 D4
Golets-Davydov, Gora mt. Rus. Fed. 73 J2
Golfo di Orosei Gennargentu e Asinara, Parco Nazionale del nat. park Sardinia Italy 58 C4
Gölgeli Dağları mts Turkey 59 M6
Goliad U.S.A. 131 D6
Golingka China see Gongbo'gyamda
Gölköy Turkey 90 E2
Gollel Swaziland see Lavumisa
Golm Germany 53 M2
Golmberg hill Germany 53 N2
Golmud China 80 H4
Golovnino Rus. Fed. 74 G4
Golpāyegān Iran 88 C3
Gölpazarı Turkey 59 N4
Golspie U.K. 50 F3
Gol Vardeh Iran 89 F3
Golyama Syutkya mt. Bulg. 59 K4
Golyam Persenk mt. Bulg. 59 K4
Golyshi Rus. Fed. see Vetluzhskiy
Golzow Germany 53 M2
Goma Dem. Rep. Congo 98 C4
Gomang Co salt l. China 83 G3
Gomati r. India 87 N4
Gombak, Bukit hill Sing. 71 [inset]
Gombe Nigeria 96 E3
Gombe r. Tanz. 99 D4
Gombi Nigeria 96 E3
Gombroon Iran see Bandar-e 'Abbās
Gomel' Belarus see Homyel'
Gómez Palacio Mex. 131 C7
Gomīshān Iran 88 D2
Gommern Germany 53 L2
Gomo Co salt l. China 83 F2
Gonābād Iran 88 E2
Gonaïves Haiti 137 J5
Gonarezhou National Park Zimbabwe 99 D6
Gonbad-e Kavus Iran 88 D2
Gonda India 83 E4
Gondal India 82 B5
Gondar Eth. see Gonder
Gonder Eth. 98 D2
Gondia India 82 E5
Gondiya India see Gondia
Gönen Turkey 59 L4
Gonfreville-l'Orcher France 49 H9
Gong'an China 77 G2
Gongbalou China 83 G3
Gongbo'gyamda China 76 B2
Gongchang China see Longxi
Gongcheng China 77 F3
Gongga Shan mt. China 76 D2
Gonghe Qinghai China 80 J4
Gonghe Yunnan China see Mouding
Gongjiang China see Yudu
Gongogi r. Brazil 145 D1
Gongolgon Australia 112 C3
Gongpoquan China 80 I3
Gongquan China 76 E2
Gongtang China see Damxung
Gongwang Shan mts China 76 D3
Gongxian China see Gongquan
Gonjo China see Kasha
Gonjog China see Coqên
Gonzales CA U.S.A. 128 C3
Gonzales TX U.S.A. 131 D6
Gonzha Rus. Fed. 74 B1
Goochland U.S.A. 135 G5
Goodenough, Cape Antarctica 152 G2
Goodenough Island P.N.G. 106 F2
Gooderham Canada 135 F1
Good Hope, Cape of S. Africa 100 D8
Good Hope Mountain Canada 126 B2
Gooding U.S.A. 126 E4
Goodland IN U.S.A. 134 B3
Goodland KS U.S.A. 130 C4
Goodlettsville U.S.A. 134 B5
Goodooga Australia 112 C2
Goodspeed Nunataks Antarctica 152 E2
Goole U.K. 48 G5
Goolgowi Australia 112 B5
Goolma Australia 112 D4
Gooloogong Australia 112 D4
Goomalling Australia 109 B7
Goombalie Australia 112 B2
Goondiwindi Australia 112 E2
Goongarrie, Lake salt flat Australia 109 C7
Goongarrie National Park Australia 109 C7
Goonyella Australia 110 D4
Goorly, Lake salt flat Australia 109 B7
Goose Bay Canada see Happy Valley-Goose Bay
Goose Creek U.S.A. 133 D5
Goose Lake U.S.A. 126 C4
Gooty India 84 C3
Gopalganj Bangl. 83 G5
Gopalganj India 83 F4
Gopeshwar India 82 D3
Göppingen Germany 53 J6
Gorakhpur India 83 E4
Goražde Bos.-Herz. 58 H3
Gorbernador U.S.A. 129 J3
Gorczański Park Narodowy nat. park Poland 47 R6
Gorda, Punta pt U.S.A. 128 A1
Gördes Turkey 59 M5
Gordil Cent. Afr. Rep. 98 C3
Gordon r. Canada 121 O1
Gordon U.K. 50 G5
Gordon U.S.A. 130 C3
Gordon, Lake Australia 111 [inset]
Gordon Downs (abandoned) Australia 108 E4
Gordon Lake Canada 121 I3
Gordon Lake U.S.A. 135 F4
Gordonsville U.S.A. 135 F4
Goré Chad 97 E4
Gorē Eth. 98 D3
Gore N.Z. 113 B8
Gore U.S.A. 135 F4
Gorebridge U.K. 50 F5
Gore Point U.S.A. 118 C4
Gorey Ireland 51 F5
Gorg Iran 89 E4
Gorgān Iran 88 D2
Gorgān, Khalīj-e Iran 88 D2
Gorge Range hills Australia 108 B5
Gorgona, Isla i. Col. 142 C3
Gorham U.S.A. 135 J1
Gori Georgia 86 F1
Gorinchem Neth. 52 E3
Goris Armenia 91 G3
Gorizia Italy 58 E2
Gorki Belarus see Horki
Gor'kiy Rus. Fed. see Nizhniy Novgorod
Gor'kovskoye Vodokhranilishche resr Rus. Fed. 42 I4
Gorlice Poland 43 D6
Görlitz Germany 47 O5
Gorlovka Ukr. see Horlivka
Gorna Dzhumaya Bulg. see Blagoevgrad
Gorna Oryakhovitsa Bulg. 59 K3
Gornji Milanovac Serbia 59 I2
Gornji Vakuf Bos.-Herz. 58 G3
Gorno-Altaysk Rus. Fed. 80 G1
Gornotrakiyska Nizina lowland Bulg. 59 K3
Gornozavodsk Permskaya Oblast' Rus. Fed. 41 R4
Gornozavodsk Sakhalinskaya Oblast' Rus. Fed. 74 F3
Gornyak Rus. Fed. 80 F1
Gornyy Rus. Fed. 43 K6
Gornyye Klyuchi Rus. Fed. 74 D3
Goro i. Fiji see Koro
Gorodenka Ukr. see Horodenka
Gorodets Rus. Fed. 42 I4
Gorodishche Penzenskaya Oblast' Rus. Fed. 43 J5
Gorodishche Volgogradskaya Oblast' Rus. Fed. 43 J6
Gorodok Belarus see Haradok
Gorodok Rus. Fed. see Zakamensk
Gorodok Khmel'nyts'ka Oblast' Ukr. see Horodok
Gorodok L'vivs'ka Oblast' Ukr. see Horodok
Gorodovikovsk Rus. Fed. 43 I7
Goroka P.N.G. 69 L8
Gorokhovets Rus. Fed. 42 I4
Gorom Gorom Burkina 96 C3
Gorong, Kepulauan is Indon. 69 I7
Gorongosa mt. Moz. 99 D5
Gorongosa, Parque Nacional de nat. park Moz. 99 D5
Gorontalo Indon. 69 G6
Gorshechnoye Rus. Fed. 43 H6
Gort Ireland 51 D4
Gort an Choirce Ireland 51 D2
Gorutuba r. Brazil 145 C1
Gorveh Iran 88 E4
Goryachiy Klyuch Rus. Fed. 91 E1
Görzke Germany 53 M2
Gorzów Wielkopolski Poland 47 O4
Gosainthan mt. China see Xixabangma Feng
Gosforth U.K. 48 F3
Goshen CA U.S.A. 128 D3
Goshen IN U.S.A. 134 C3
Goshen NH U.S.A. 135 I2
Goshen NY U.S.A. 135 H3
Goshen VA U.S.A. 134 F5
Goshoba Turkm. see Goşoba
Goslar Germany 53 K3
Goşoba Turkm. 91 I2
Gospić Croatia 58 F2
Gosport U.K. 49 F8
Gossi Mali 96 C3
Gostivar Macedonia 59 I4
Gosu China 76 C1
Göteborg Sweden see Gothenburg
Götene Sweden 45 H7
Gotenhafen Poland see Gdynia
Gotha Germany 53 K4
Gothenburg Sweden 45 G8
Gothenburg U.S.A. 130 C3
Gotland i. Sweden 45 K8
Gotō-rettō is Japan 75 C6
Gotse Delchev Bulg. 59 J4
Gotska Sandön i. Sweden 45 K7
Gōtsu Japan 75 D6
Göttingen Germany 53 J3
Gott Peak Canada 120 F5
Gottwaldow Czech Rep. see Zlín
Gouda Neth. 52 E2
Goudiri Senegal 96 B3
Goudoumaria Niger 96 E3
Goûgaram Niger 96 D3

▶Gough Island S. Atlantic Ocean 148 H8
Dependency of St Helena.

Gouin, Réservoir resr Canada 122 G4
Goulburn Australia 112 D5
Goulburn r. N.S.W. Australia 112 E4
Goulburn r. Vic. Australia 112 B6
Goulburn Islands Australia 108 F2
Goulburn River National Park Australia 112 E4
Gould Coast Antarctica 152 J1
Goulou atoll Micronesia see Ngulu
Goundam Mali 96 C3
Goundi Chad 97 E4
Goupil, Lac l. Canada 123 H3
Gouraya Alg. 57 G5
Gourcy Burkina 96 C3
Gourdon France 56 E4
Gouré Niger 96 E3
Gouripur Bangl. 83 G4
Gourits r. S. Africa 100 E8
Gourma-Rharous Mali 96 C3
Gournay-en-Bray France 52 B5
Goussainville France 52 C5
Gouverneur U.S.A. 135 H1
Governador Valadares Brazil 145 C2
Governor's Harbour Bahamas 133 E7
Govĭ Altayn Nuruu mts Mongolia 80 I3
Govind Ballash Pant Sagar resr India 83 E4
Gowanda U.S.A. 135 F2
Gowan Range hills Australia 110 D5
Gowārān Afgh. 89 G4
Gowd-e Mokh l. Iran 88 D4
Gowd-e Zereh plain Afgh. 89 F4
Gowmal Kalay Afgh. 89 H3
Gowna, Lough l. Ireland 51 E4
Goya Arg. 144 E3
Göyçay Azer. 91 G2
Goyder watercourse Australia 109 F6
Goymatdag hills Turkm. 88 D1
Goymatdag hills Turkm. see Goýmatdag
Göynük Turkey 59 N4
Goyoum Cameroon 96 E4
Gozareh Afgh. 89 F3
Goz-Beïda Chad 97 F3
Gozha Co salt l. China 82 E2
Gözkaya Turkey 85 C1
Gozo i. Malta 58 F6
Graaff-Reinet S. Africa 100 G7
Grabfeld plain Germany 53 K4
Grabo Côte d'Ivoire 96 C4
Grabouw S. Africa 100 D8
Grabow Germany 53 L1
Gračac Croatia 58 F2
Gracefield Canada 122 F5
Gracey U.S.A. 134 B5
Gradaús, Serra dos hills Brazil 143 H5
Gradiška Bos.-Herz. see Bosanska Gradiška
Grady U.S.A. 131 C5
Gräfenhainichen Germany 53 M3
Grafenwöhr Germany 53 L5
Grafton Australia 112 F2
Grafton ND U.S.A. 130 D1
Grafton WI U.S.A. 134 B2
Grafton WV U.S.A. 134 E4
Grafton, Cape Australia 110 D3
Grafton, Mount U.S.A. 129 F2
Grafton Passage Australia 110 D3
Graham NC U.S.A. 132 E4
Graham TX U.S.A. 131 D5
Graham, Mount U.S.A. 129 I5
Graham Bell Island Rus. Fed. see Greem-Bell, Ostrov
Graham Island B.C. Canada 120 C4
Graham Island Nunavut Canada 119 I2
Graham Land reg. Antarctica 152 L2
Grahamstown S. Africa 101 H7
Grahovo Bos.-Herz. see Bosansko Grahovo
Graigue Ireland 51 F5
Grajaú Brazil 143 I5
Grajaú r. Brazil 143 J4
Grammont Belgium see Geraardsbergen
Grammos mt. Greece 59 I4
Grampian Mountains U.K. 50 E4
Grampians National Park Australia 111 C8
Granada Nicaragua 137 G6
Granada Spain 57 E5
Granada U.S.A. 130 C4
Granard Ireland 51 E4
Granbury U.S.A. 131 D5
Granby Canada 123 G5
Gran Canaria i. Canary Is 96 B2
Gran Chaco reg. Arg./Para. 144 D3
Grand r. MO U.S.A. 134 B2
Grand r. SD U.S.A. 130 C2
Grand Atlas mts Morocco see Haut Atlas
Grand Bahama i. Bahamas 133 E7
Grand Ballon mt. France 47 K7
Grand Bank Canada 123 L5
Grand Banks of Newfoundland sea feature N. Atlantic Ocean 148 E3
Grand-Bassam Côte d'Ivoire 96 C4
Grand Bay-Westfield Canada 123 I5
Grand Bend Canada 134 E2
Grand Blanc U.S.A. 134 D2
Grand Canal Ireland 51 E4
Grand Canary i. Canary Is see Gran Canaria
Grand Canyon U.S.A. 129 G3
Grand Canyon gorge U.S.A. 129 G3
Grand Canyon National Park U.S.A. 129 G3
Grand Canyon - Parashant National Monument nat. park U.S.A. 129 G3
Grand Cayman i. Cayman Is 137 H5
Grand Drumont mt. France 47 K7
Grande r. Bahia Brazil 145 B1
Grande r. São Paulo Brazil 145 A3
Grande r. Nicaragua 137 H6
Grande, Bahía b. Arg. 144 C8
Grande, Ilha i. Brazil 145 B3
Grande Cache Canada 120 G4
Grande Comore i. Comoros see Njazidja
Grande Prairie Canada 120 G4
Grand Erg de Bilma des. Niger 96 E3
Grand Erg Occidental des. Alg. 54 D5
Grand Erg Oriental des. Alg. 54 F6
Grande-Rivière Canada 123 I4
Grandes, Salinas salt marsh Arg. 144 C4
Grande-Vallée Canada 123 I4
Grand Falls N.B. Canada 123 I5
Grand Falls-Windsor Nfld. and Lab. Canada 123 L4
Grand Forks Canada 120 G5
Grand Forks U.S.A. 130 D2
Grand Gorge U.S.A. 135 H2
Grand Haven U.S.A. 134 B2
Grandin, Lac l. Canada 120 G1
Grandioznyy, Pik mt. Rus. Fed. 72 H2
Grand Island U.S.A. 130 D3
Grand Isle U.S.A. 131 F6
Grand Junction U.S.A. 129 I2
Grand Lac Germain l. Canada 123 I4
Grand-Lahou Côte d'Ivoire 96 C4
Grand Lake N.B. Canada 123 I5
Grand Lake Nfld. and Lab. Canada 123 J3
Grand Lake Nfld. and Lab. Canada 123 K4
Grand Lake LA U.S.A. 131 E6
Grand Lake MI U.S.A. 134 D1
Grand Lake St Marys U.S.A. 134 C3
Grand Ledge U.S.A. 134 C2
Grand Manan Island Canada 123 I5
Grand Marais MI U.S.A. 132 C2
Grand Marais MN U.S.A. 130 F2
Grand-Mère Canada 123 G5
Grand Mesa U.S.A. 129 J2
Grândola Port. 57 B4
Grand Passage New Caledonia 107 G3
Grand Rapids Canada 121 L4
Grand Rapids MI U.S.A. 134 C2
Grand Rapids MN U.S.A. 130 E2
Grand-Sault Canada see Grand Falls
Grand St-Bernard, Col du pass Italy/Switz. see Great St Bernard Pass
Grand Teton mt. U.S.A. 126 F4
Grand Teton National Park U.S.A. 126 F4
Grand Traverse Bay U.S.A. 134 C1

▶Grand Turk Turks and Caicos Is 137 J4
Capital of the Turks and Caicos Islands.

Grandville U.S.A. 134 C2
Grandvilliers France 52 B5
Grand Wash Cliffs mts U.S.A. 129 F4
Grange Ireland 51 E6
Grängesberg Sweden 45 I6
Grangeville U.S.A. 126 D3
Granisle Canada 120 E4
Granite Falls U.S.A. 130 E2
Granite Mountain U.S.A. 128 E1
Granite Mountains CA U.S.A. 129 F4
Granite Mountains CA U.S.A. 129 F5
Granite Peak MT U.S.A. 126 F3
Granite Peak UT U.S.A. 129 G1
Granite Range mts AK U.S.A. 120 A3
Granite Range mts NV U.S.A. 128 D1
Granitola, Capo c. Sicily Italy 58 E6
Granja Brazil 143 J4
Gran Laguna Salada l. Arg. 144 C6
Gränna Sweden 45 I7
Gran Paradiso mt. Italy 58 B2
Gran Paradiso, Parco Nazionale del nat. park Italy 58 B2
Gran Pilastro mt. Austria/Italy 47 M7
Gran San Bernardo, Colle del pass Italy/Switz. see Great St Bernard Pass
Gran Sasso e Monti della Laga, Parco Nazionale del nat. park Italy 58 E3
Granschütz Germany 53 M3
Gransee Germany 53 N1
Grant U.S.A. 130 C3
Grant, Mount U.S.A. 128 E2
Grantham U.K. 49 G6
Grant Island Antarctica 152 J2
Grant Lake Canada 120 G1
Grantown-on-Spey U.K. 50 F3
Grant Range mts U.S.A. 129 F2
Grants U.S.A. 129 J4
Grants Pass U.S.A. 126 C4
Grantsville UT U.S.A. 129 G1
Grantsville WV U.S.A. 134 E4
Granville France 56 D2
Granville AZ U.S.A. 129 I5
Granville NY U.S.A. 135 I2
Granville TN U.S.A. 134 C5
Granville (abandoned) Canada 120 B2
Granville Lake Canada 121 K3
Grão Mogol Brazil 145 C2
Grapevine Mountains U.S.A. 128 E3
Gras, Lac de l. Canada 121 I1
Graskop S. Africa 101 J3
Grasplatz Namibia 100 B4
Grass r. Canada 121 L3
Grass r. U.S.A. 135 H1
Grasse France 56 H5
Grassflat U.S.A. 135 F3
Grassington U.K. 48 F4
Grasslands National Park Canada 121 J5
Grassrange U.S.A. 126 F3
Grass Valley U.S.A. 128 C2
Grassy Butte U.S.A. 130 C2
Grästorp Sweden 45 H7
Gratz U.S.A. 134 C4
Graudenz Poland see Grudziądz
Graus Spain 57 G2
Gravataí Brazil 145 A5
Grave, Pointe de pt France 56 D4
Gravelbourg Canada 121 J5
Gravel Hill Lake Canada 121 K2
Gravelines France 52 C4
Gravelotte S. Africa 101 J2
Gravenhurst Canada 134 F1
Grave Peak U.S.A. 126 E3
Gravesend Australia 112 E2
Gravesend U.K. 49 H7
Gravina in Puglia Italy 58 G4
Grawn U.S.A. 134 C1
Gray France 56 G3
Gray GA U.S.A. 133 D5
Gray KY U.S.A. 134 C5
Gray ME U.S.A. 135 J2
Grayback Mountain U.S.A. 126 C4
Gray Lake Canada 121 I2
Grayling r. Canada 120 E3
Grayling U.S.A. 134 C1
Grays U.K. 49 H7
Grays Harbor inlet U.S.A. 126 B3
Grays Lake U.S.A. 126 F4
Grayson U.S.A. 134 D4
Graz Austria 47 O7
Greasy Lake Canada 120 F2
Great Abaco i. Bahamas 133 E7
Great Australian Bight g. Australia 109 E8
Great Baddow U.K. 49 H7
Great Bahama Bank sea feature Bahamas 133 E7
Great Barrier Island N.Z. 113 E3
Great Barrier Reef Australia 110 D1
Great Barrier Reef Marine Park (Cairns Section) Australia 110 D3
Great Barrier Reef Marine Park (Capricorn Section) Australia 110 E4
Great Barrier Reef Marine Park (Central Section) Australia 110 E3
Great Barrier Reef Marine Park (Far North Section) Australia 110 D2
Great Barrington U.S.A. 135 I2
Great Basalt Wall National Park Australia 110 D3
Great Basin U.S.A. 128 E2
Great Basin National Park U.S.A. 129 F2
Great Bear r. Canada 120 E1

▶Great Bear Lake Canada 120 G1
4th largest lake in North America, and 7th in the world.

Great Belt sea chan. Denmark 45 G9
Great Bend U.S.A. 130 D4
Great Bitter Lake Egypt 85 A4
Great Blasket Island Ireland 51 B5

▶Great Britain i. U.K. 46 G4
Largest island in Europe, and 8th in the world.

Great Clifton U.K. 48 D4
Great Coco Island Cocos Is 68 A4
Great Cumbrae i. U.K. 50 E5

eat Dismal Swamp National Wildlife Refuge nature res. U.S.A. 135 G5
eat Dividing Range mts Australia 112 B6
eat Eastern Erg des. Alg. see Grand Erg Oriental
eater Antarctica reg. Antarctica see East Antarctica
eater Antilles is Caribbean Sea 137 H4
eater Khingan Mountains China see Da Hinggan Ling
eater Tunb i. The Gulf 88 D5
eat Exuma i. Bahamas 133 F8
eat Falls U.S.A. 126 F3
eat Fish r. S. Africa 101 H7
eat Fish Point S. Africa 101 H7
eat Fish River Reserve Complex ature res. S. Africa 101 H7
eat Gandak r. India 83 F4
eat Ganges atoll Cook Is see Manihiki
eat Guana Cay i. Bahamas 133 E7
eat Inagua i. Bahamas 137 J4
eat Karoo plat. S. Africa 100 F7
eat Kei r. S. Africa 101 I7
eat Lake Australia 111 [inset]
eat Limpopo Transfrontier Park 101 J2
eat Malvern U.K. 49 E6
eat Meteor Tablemount sea feature N. Atlantic Ocean 148 G4
eat Namaqualand reg. Namibia 100 C4
eat Nicobar i. India 71 A6
eat Ormes Head hd U.K. 48 D5
eat Ouse r. U.K. 49 H6
eat Oyster Bay Australia 111 [inset]
eat Palm Islands Australia 110 D3
eat Plain of the Koukdjuak Canada 119 K3
eat Plains U.S.A. 130 C3
eat Point U.S.A. 135 J3
eat Rift Valley Africa 98 D4
eat Ruaha r. Tanz. 99 D4
eat Sacandaga Lake U.S.A. 135 H2
eat St Bernard Pass Italy/Switz. 58 B2
eat Salt Lake U.S.A. 129 G1
eat Salt Lake Desert U.S.A. 129 G1
eat Sand Hills Canada 121 I5
eat Sand Sea des. Egypt/Libya 90 B5
eat Sandy Desert Australia 108 C5
eat Sandy Island Australia see Fraser Island
eat Sea Reef Fiji 107 H3

Great Slave Lake Canada 120 H2
Deepest and 5th largest lake in North America and 10th largest in the world.

eat Smoky Mountains U.S.A. 133 C5
eat Smoky Mountains National Park U.S.A. 132 D5
eat Snow Mountain Canada 120 E3
eatstone-on-Sea U.K. 49 H8
eat Stour r. U.K. 49 I7
eat Torrington U.K. 49 C8
eat Victoria Desert Australia 109 E7
eat Wall research station Antarctica 152 A2
eat Wall tourist site China 73 L4
eat Waltham U.K. 49 H7
eat Western Erg des. Alg. see Grand Erg Occidental
eat West Torres Islands Myanmar 71 B5
eat Whernside hill U.K. 48 F4
eat Yarmouth U.K. 49 I6
ebenkovskiy Ukr. see Hrebinka
ebyonka Ukr. see Hrebinka
eco, Cape Cyprus see Greko, Cape
edos, Sierra de mts Spain 57 D3
eece country Europe 59 I5
eece U.S.A. 135 G2
eeley U.S.A. 126 G4
eely Center U.S.A. 130 D3
em-Bell, Ostrov i. Rus. Fed. 64 H1
en r. KY U.S.A. 134 B5
en r. WY U.S.A. 129 I2
en Bay U.S.A. 134 A1
en Bay b. U.S.A. 134 B1
enbrier U.S.A. 134 B5
enbrier r. U.S.A. 134 E5
en Cape Australia 112 E6
encastle Bahamas 133 E7
encastle U.K. 51 F3
encastle U.S.A. 134 B4
en Cove Springs U.S.A. 133 D6
ene ME U.S.A. 135 J1
ene NY U.S.A. 135 H2
eneville U.S.A. 132 D4
enfield CA U.S.A. 128 C3
enfield IN U.S.A. 134 C4
enfield MA U.S.A. 135 I2
enfield OH U.S.A. 134 D4
en Head hd Australia 109 A7
enhill Island Australia 108 F2
en Island Taiwan see Lü Tao
en Lake Canada 121 J4

reenland terr. N. America 119 N3
elf-governing Danish territory. Largest land in North America and in the world, nd 3rd largest political entity in North merica.

enland Basin sea feature Arctic Ocean 53 I2
enland Fracture Zone sea feature ctic Ocean 153 I1
enland Sea Greenland/Svalbard 64 A2
enlaw U.K. 50 G5
en Mountains U.S.A. 135 I1
enock U.K. 50 E5
enore Ireland 51 F3
enport U.S.A. 135 I3
en River P.N.G. 69 K7
en River UT U.S.A. 129 H2
en River WY U.S.A. 126 F4
en River Lake U.S.A. 134 C5
ensboro U.S.A. 133 D5
ensburg IN U.S.A. 134 C4
ensburg KS U.S.A. 130 D4
ensburg KY U.S.A. 134 C5
ensburg LA U.S.A. 131 F6
ensburg PA U.S.A. 134 F3
ens Peak U.S.A. 129 I4
enstone Point U.K. 50 D3

Green Swamp U.S.A. 133 E5
Greentown U.S.A. 134 C3
Greenup IL U.S.A. 130 F4
Greenup KY U.S.A. 134 D4
Green Valley Canada 135 H1
Greenville Liberia 96 C4
Greenville AL U.S.A. 133 C6
Greenville IL U.S.A. 130 F4
Greenville KY U.S.A. 134 B5
Greenville ME U.S.A. 132 G2
Greenville MI U.S.A. 134 C2
Greenville MS U.S.A. 131 F5
Greenville NC U.S.A. 132 E5
Greenville NH U.S.A. 135 J2
Greenville OH U.S.A. 134 C3
Greenville PA U.S.A. 134 E3
Greenville SC U.S.A. 133 D5
Greenville TX U.S.A. 131 D5
Greenwich atoll Micronesia see Kapingamarangi
Greenwich CT U.S.A. 135 I3
Greenwich OH U.S.A. 134 D3
Greenwood AR U.S.A. 131 E5
Greenwood IN U.S.A. 134 B4
Greenwood MS U.S.A. 131 F5
Greenwood SC U.S.A. 133 D5
Gregory r. Australia 110 B3
Gregory, Lake salt flat S.A. Australia 111 B6
Gregory, Lake salt flat W.A. Australia 108 D5
Gregory, Lake salt flat W.A. Australia 109 B6
Gregory Downs Australia 110 B3
Gregory National Park Australia 108 E4
Gregory Range hills Qld Australia 110 C3
Gregory Range hills W.A. Australia 108 C5
Greifswald Germany 47 N3
Greiz Germany 53 M4
Greko, Cape Cyprus 85 B2
Gremikha Rus. Fed. 153 G2
Gremyachinsk Rus. Fed. 41 R4
Grenå Denmark 45 G8
Grenaa Denmark see Grenå
Grenada U.S.A. 131 F5
Grenada country West Indies 137 L6
Grenade France 56 E5
Grenen spit Denmark 45 G8
Grenfell Australia 112 D4
Grenfell Canada 121 K5
Grenoble France 56 G4
Grense-Jakobselv Norway 44 Q2
Grenville, Cape Australia 110 C1
Grenville Island Fiji see Rotuma
Greshak Pak. 89 G5
Gresham U.S.A. 126 C3
Gressåmoen Nasjonalpark nat. park Norway 44 H4
Greta r. U.K. 48 E4
Gretna U.K. 50 F6
Gretna LA U.S.A. 131 F6
Gretna VA U.S.A. 134 F5
Greußen Germany 53 K3
Grevelingen sea chan. Neth. 52 D3
Greven Germany 53 H2
Grevena Greece 59 I4
Grevenbicht Neth. 52 F3
Grevenbroich Germany 52 G3
Grevenmacher Lux. 52 G5
Grevesmühlen Germany 47 M4
Grey, Cape Australia 110 B2
Greybull U.S.A. 126 F3
Greybull r. U.S.A. 126 F3
Grey Hunter Peak Canada 120 C2
Grey Islands Canada 123 L4
Greylock, Mount U.S.A. 135 I2
Greymouth N.Z. 113 C6
Grey Range hills Australia 112 A2
Grey's Plains Australia 109 A6
Greytown S. Africa 101 J5
Grez-Doiceau Belgium 52 E4
Gribanovskiy Rus. Fed. 43 I6
Gridley U.S.A. 128 C2
Griffin U.S.A. 133 C5
Griffith Australia 112 C5
Grigan i. N. Mariana Is see Agrihan
Grik Malaysia see Gerik
Grim, Cape Australia 111 [inset]
Grimari Cent. Afr. Rep. 98 C3
Grimma Germany 53 M3
Grimmen Germany 47 N3
Grimnitzsee l. Germany 53 N2
Grimsby U.K. 48 G5
Grímsey i. Iceland 44 [inset]
Grimshaw Canada 120 G3
Grímsstaðir Iceland 44 [inset]
Grimstad Norway 45 F7
Grindavík Iceland 44 [inset]
Grindsted Denmark 45 F9
Grind Stone City U.S.A. 134 D1
Grindul Chituc spit Romania 59 M2
Grinnell Peninsula Canada 119 I2
Griqualand East reg. S. Africa 101 I6
Griqualand West reg. S. Africa 100 F5
Griquatown S. Africa 100 F5
Grise Fiord Canada 119 J2
Grishino Ukr. see Krasnoarmiys'k
Gris Nez, Cap c. France 52 B4
Gritley U.K. 50 G2
Grizzly Bear Mountain hill Canada 120 F1
Grmeč mts Bos.-Herz. 58 G2
Grobbendonk Belgium 52 E3
Groblersdal S. Africa 101 I3
Groblershoop S. Africa 100 F5
Grodno Belarus see Hrodna
Groen watercourse S. Africa 100 F6
Groen watercourse S. Africa 100 C6
Groix, Île de i. France 56 C3
Gromblia Tunisia 58 D6
Gronau (Westfalen) Germany 52 H2
Grong Norway 44 H4
Groningen Neth. 52 G1
Groninger Wad tidal flat Neth. 52 G1
Grønland terr. N. America see Greenland
Groom Lake U.S.A. 129 F3
Groot-Aar Pan salt pan S. Africa 100 E4
Groot Berg r. S. Africa 100 D7
Groot Brakrivier S. Africa 100 F8
Grootdraaidam dam S. Africa 101 I4
Grootdrink S. Africa 100 E5
Groote Eylandt i. Australia 110 B2
Grootfontein Namibia 99 B5
Groot Karas Berg plat. Namibia 100 D4

Groot Letaba r. S. Africa 101 J2
Groot Marico S. Africa 101 H3
Groot Swartberge mts S. Africa 100 E7
Grootvloer salt pan S. Africa 100 E5
Groot Winterberg mt. S. Africa 101 H7
Gros Morne National Park Canada 123 K4
Gross Barmen Namibia 100 C2
Große Aue r. Germany 53 J2
Große Laaber r. Germany 53 M6
Großengottern Germany 53 K3
Großenkneten Germany 53 I2
Großenlüder Germany 53 J4
Großer Arber mt. Germany 53 N5
Großer Beerberg hill Germany 53 K4
Großer Eyberg hill Germany 53 H5
Großer Gleichberg hill Germany 53 K4
Großer Kornberg hill Germany 53 M4
Großer Osser mt. Czech Rep./Germany 53 N5
Großer Rachel mt. Germany 47 N6
Grosser Speikkogel mt. Austria 47 O7
Grosseto Italy 58 D3
Grossevichi Rus. Fed. 74 E3
Groß-Gerau Germany 53 I5
Großglockner mt. Austria 47 N7
Groß Oesingen Germany 53 K2
Großrudestedt Germany 53 L3
Groß Schönebeck Germany 53 N2
Gross Ums Namibia 100 D2
Großvenediger mt. Austria 47 N7
Gros Ventre Range mts U.S.A. 126 F4
Groswater Bay Canada 123 K3
Groton U.S.A. 130 D2
Grottoes U.S.A. 135 F4
Grou Neth. 52 F1
Groundhog r. Canada 122 E4
Grouw Neth. see Grou
Grove U.S.A. 131 E4
Grove City U.S.A. 134 D4
Grove Hill U.S.A. 133 C6
Grove Mountains Antarctica 152 E2
Grover Beach U.S.A. 128 C4
Grovertown U.S.A. 134 B3
Groveton NH U.S.A. 135 J1
Groveton TX U.S.A. 131 E6
Growler Mountains U.S.A. 129 G5
Groznyy Rus. Fed. 91 G2
Grubišno Polje Croatia 58 G2
Grudovo Bulg. see Sredets
Grudziądz Poland 47 Q4
Grünau Namibia 100 D4
Grünberg Poland see Zielona Góra
Grundarfjörður Iceland 44 [inset]
Grundy U.S.A. 134 D5
Gruñidora Mex. 131 C7
Grünstadt Germany 53 I5
Gruver U.S.A. 131 C4
Gruzinskaya S.S.R. country Asia see Georgia
Gryazi Rus. Fed. 43 H5
Gryazovets Rus. Fed. 42 I4
Gryfice Poland 47 O4
Gryfino Poland 47 O4
Gryfów Śląski Poland 47 O5
Gryllefjord Norway 44 J2
Grytviken S. Georgia 144 I8
Gua India 83 F5
Guacanayabo, Golfo de b. Cuba 137 I4
Guachochi Mex. 127 G8
Guadajoz r. Spain 57 D5
Guadalajara Mex. 136 D4
Guadalajara Spain 57 E3
Guadalcanal i. Solomon Is 107 G2
Guadalete r. Spain 57 C5
Guadalope r. Spain 57 F3
Guadalquivir r. Spain 57 C5
Guadalupe Mex. 131 C7
Guadalupe i. Mex. 127 D7
Guadalupe watercourse Mex. 128 E5
Guadalupe U.S.A. 128 C4
Guadalupe, Sierra de mts Spain 57 D4
Guadalupe Aguilera Mex. 131 B7
Guadalupe Bravos Mex. 127 G7
Guadalupe Mountains National Park U.S.A. 127 G7
Guadalupe Peak U.S.A. 127 G7
Guadalupe Victoria Baja California Mex. 129 F5
Guadalupe Victoria Durango Mex. 131 B7
Guadarrama, Sierra de mts Spain 57 D3

▶Guadeloupe terr. West Indies 137 L5
French Overseas Department.

Guadeloupe Passage Caribbean Sea 137 L5
Guadiana r. Port./Spain 57 C5
Guadix Spain 57 E5
Guafo, Isla i. Chile 144 B6
Guaíba Brazil 145 A5
Guaiçuí Brazil 145 B2
Guaíra Brazil 144 F2
Guajaba, Cayo i. Cuba 133 E8
Guaje, Llano de plain Mex. 131 C7
Gualala U.S.A. 128 B2
Gualeguay Arg. 144 E4
Gualeguaychu Arg. 144 E4
Gualicho, Salina salt flat Arg. 144 C6

▶Guam terr. N. Pacific Ocean 69 K4
United States Unincorporated Territory.

Guamblin, Isla i. Chile 144 A6
Guampí, Sierra de mts Venez. 142 E2
Guamúchil Mex. 127 F8
Guanabacoa Cuba 133 D8
Guanacevi Mex. 131 B7
Guanahacabibes, Península de pen. Cuba 133 C8
Guanajay Cuba 133 D8
Guanajuato Mex. 136 D4
Guanambi Brazil 145 C1
Guanare Venez. 142 E2
Guandu China 77 G3
Guane Cuba 137 H4
Guang'an China 76 E2
Guangchang China 77 H3
Guangdong prov. China 77 [inset]
Guanghai China 77 G4
Guanghan China 76 E2
Guanghua China see Laohekou
Guangming China see Xide

Guangming Ding mt. China 77 H2
Guangnan China 76 E3
Guangshan China 77 G2
Guangxi aut. reg. China see Guangxi Zhuangzu Zizhiqu
Guangxi Zhuangzu Zizhiqu aut. reg. China 76 F4
Guangyuan China 76 E1
Guangze China 77 H3
Guangzhou China 77 G4
Guanhães Brazil 145 C2
Guanhe Kou r. mouth China 77 H1
Guanipa r. Venez. 142 F2
Guanling China 76 E3
Guanmian Shan mts China 77 F2
Guannan China 77 H1
Guanpo China 77 F1
Guanshui China 74 B4
Guansuo China see Guanling
Guantánamo Cuba 137 I4
Guanxian China see Dujiangyan
Guanyang China 77 F3
Guanyinqiao China 76 D2
Guanyun China 77 H1
Guapé Brazil 145 B3
Guapí Col. 142 C3
Guaporé r. Bol./Brazil 142 E6
Guaporé Brazil 145 A5
Guaqui Bol. 142 E7
Guará r. Brazil 145 B1
Guarabira Brazil 143 K5
Guaranda Ecuador 142 C4
Guarapari Brazil 145 C3
Guarapuava Brazil 145 A4
Guararapes Brazil 145 A3
Guaratinguetá Brazil 145 B3
Guaratuba Brazil 145 A4
Guaratuba, Baía de b. Brazil 145 A4
Guarda Port. 57 C3
Guardafui, Cape Somalia see Gwardafuy, Gees
Guardiagrele Italy 58 F3
Guardo Spain 57 D2
Guárico, del Embalse resr Venez. 142 E2
Guarujá Brazil 145 B3
Guasave Mex. 127 F8
Guasdualito Venez. 142 D2

▶Guatemala country Central America 136 F5
4th most populous country in North America.

▶Guatemala City Guat. 136 F6
Capital of Guatemala.

Guaviare r. Col. 142 E3
Guaxupé Brazil 145 B3
Guayaquil Ecuador 142 C4
Guayaquil, Golfo de g. Ecuador 142 B4
Guaymas Mex. 127 F8
Guba Eth. 98 D2
Gubakha Rus. Fed. 41 R4
Gubbi India 84 C3
Gubio Nigeria 96 E3
Gubkin Rus. Fed. 43 H6
Gucheng China 77 F1
Gudari India 84 D2
Gudbrandsdalen valley Norway 45 F6
Gudermes Rus. Fed. 91 G2
Gudivada India 84 D2
Gudiyattam India 84 C3
Gudur Andhra Prad. India 84 C3
Gudur Andhra Prad. India 84 C3
Gudvangen Norway 45 E6
Gudzhal r. Rus. Fed. 74 D2
Gué, Rivière du r. Canada 123 H2
Guecho Spain see Algorta
Guéckédou Guinea 96 B4
Guelma Alg. 58 B6
Guelmine Morocco 96 B2
Guelph Canada 134 E2
Guémez Mex. 131 D8
Guénange France 52 G5
Guerara Alg. 54 E5
Guérard, Lac l. Canada 123 I2
Guercif Morocco 54 D5
Guéret France 56 E3

▶Guernsey terr. Channel Is 49 E9
United Kingdom Crown Dependency.

Guernsey U.S.A. 126 G4
Guérou Mauritania 96 B3
Guerrah Et-Tarf salt pan Alg. 58 B7
Guerrero Negro Mex. 127 E8
Guers, Lac l. Canada 123 I2
Gueugnon France 56 G3
Gufeng China see Pingnan
Gufu China see Xingshan
Gugē mt. Eth. 98 D3
Gügerd, Küh-e mts Iran 88 D3
Guguan i. N. Mariana Is 69 L3
Guhakolak, Tanjung pt Indon. 68 D8
Guhe China 77 H2
Güh Küh mt. Iran 88 E5
Guhuai China see Pingyu
Guiana Basin sea feature N. Atlantic Ocean 148 E5
Guiana Highlands mts S. America 142 E2
Guichi China see Chizhou
Guidan-Roumji Niger 96 D3
Guider Cameroon 97 E4
Guiding China 76 E3
Guidong China 77 G3
Guidonia-Montecelio Italy 58 E4
Guigang China 77 F4
Guiglo Côte d'Ivoire 96 C4
Guignicourt France 52 D5
Guija Moz. 101 K3
Guiji Shan mts China 77 I2
Guildford U.K. 49 G7
Guilford U.S.A. 132 G2
Guilherme Capelo Angola see Cacongo
Guilin China 77 F3
Guillaume-Delisle, Lac l. Canada 122 F2
Guimarães Brazil 143 J4
Guimarães Port. 57 B3
Guinan China 76 D1

Guinea country Africa 96 B3
Guinea, Gulf of Africa 96 D4
Guinea Basin sea feature N. Atlantic Ocean 148 H5
Guinea-Bissau country Africa 96 B3
Guinea-Conakry country Africa see Guinea
Guinea Ecuatorial country Africa see Equatorial Guinea
Guiné-Bissau country Africa see Guinea-Bissau
Guinée country Africa see Guinea
Güines Cuba 137 H4
Guînes France 52 B4
Guines, Lac l. Canada 123 J3
Guingamp France 56 C2
Guipavas France 56 B2
Guiping China 77 F4
Güira de Melena Cuba 133 D8
Guiratinga Brazil 143 H7
Guiscard France 52 D5
Guise France 52 D5
Guishan China see Xinping
Guishun China 76 E3
Guixi Chongqing China see Dianjiang
Guixi Jiangxi China 77 H2
Guiyang Guizhou China 76 E3
Guiyang Hunan China 77 G3
Guizhou prov. China 76 E3
Guizi China 77 F4
Gujarat state India 82 C5
Gujar Khan Pak. 89 I3
Gujerat state India see Gujarat
Gujranwala Pak. 89 I3
Gujrat Pak. 89 I3
Gukovo Rus. Fed. 43 H6
Gulabgarh India 82 D2
Gulbarga India 84 C2
Gulbene Latvia 45 O8
Gul'cha Kyrg. see Gülchö
Gülchö Kyrg. 80 D3
Gülcihan Turkey 85 B1
Gülek Boğazı pass Turkey 90 D3
Gulf, The Asia 88 C4
Gulfport U.S.A. 131 F6
Gulian China 74 A1
Gulin China 76 E3
Gulistan Uzbek. see Guliston
Guliston Uzbek. 80 C3
Gülitz Germany 53 L1
Guliya Shan mt. China 74 A2
Gulja China see Yining
Gul Kach Pak. 89 H4
Gul'kevichi Rus. Fed. 91 F1
Gull Lake Canada 121 I5
Gullrock Lake Canada 121 M5
Gullträsk Sweden 44 L3
Güllük Körfezi b. Turkey 59 L6
Gülnar Turkey 85 A1
Gulu China see Xincai
Gulu Uganda 98 D3
Guluwuru Island Australia 110 B1
Gulyayevskiye Koshki, Ostrova is Rus. Fed. 42 L1
Guma China see Pishan
Gumal r. Pak. 89 H4
Gumare Botswana 99 C5
Gumbaz Pak. 89 H4
Gumbinnen Rus. Fed. see Gusev
Gumdag Turkm. 88 D2
Gumel Nigeria 96 D3
Gümgüm Turkey see Varto
Gumla India 83 F5
Gummersbach Germany 53 H3
Gümüşhacıköy Turkey 90 D2
Gümüşhane Turkey 91 E2
Guna India 82 D4
Gunan China see Qijiang
Guna Terara mt. Eth. 86 E7
Gunbar Australia 112 B5
Gunbower Australia 112 B5
Güncang China 76 B2
Gund r. Tajik. see Gunt
Gundagai Australia 112 D5
Gundelsheim Germany 53 J5
Güney Turkey 59 M5
Güneydoğu Toroslar plat. Turkey 90 F3
Gunglilap Myanmar 70 B1
Gungu Dem. Rep. Congo 99 B4
Gunib Rus. Fed. 91 G2
Gunisao r. Canada 121 L4
Gunisao Lake Canada 121 L4
Gunnaur India 82 D3
Gunnbjørn Fjeld nunatak Greenland 119 P3
Gunnedah Australia 112 E3
Gunning Australia 112 D5
Gunnison U.S.A. 127 G5
Gunnison r. U.S.A. 129 I2
Güns Hungary see Kőszeg
Gunt r. Tajik. 89 H2
Guntakal India 84 C3
Güntersberge Germany 53 K3
Guntur India 84 D2
Gunung Gading National Park Malaysia 71 E7
Gunung Leuser, Taman Nasional Indon. 71 B7
Gunung Niyut, Suaka Margasatwa nature res. Indon. 71 E7
Gunung Palung, Taman Nasional Indon. 68 E7
Gunungsitoli Indon. 71 B7
Günyüzü Turkey 90 C3
Gunza Angola see Porto Amboim
Günzburg Germany 47 M6
Gunzenhausen Germany 53 K5
Guo He r. China 77 H1
Guovdageaidnu Norway see Kautokeino
Guozhen China see Baoji
Gupis Pak. 82 C1
Gurbantünggüt Shamo des. China 80 G3
Gurdaspur India 82 C2
Gurdon U.S.A. 131 E5
Gurdzhaani Georgia see Gurjaani
Güre Turkey 59 M5
Gurgan Iran see Gorgān
Gurgaon India 82 D3
Gurgei, Jebel mt. Sudan 97 F3
Gurha India 82 B4

Guri, Embalse de resr Venez. 142 F2
Gurig National Park Australia 108 F2
Gurinhatã Brazil 145 A2
Gurjaani Georgia 91 G2
Gur Khar Iran 89 E4
Guro Moz. 99 D5
Gurşunmagdan Kärhanasy Turkm. 89 G2
Guru China 83 G3
Gürün Turkey 90 E3
Gurupá Brazil 143 H4
Gurupi Brazil 143 I6
Gurupi r. Brazil 143 I4
Gurupi, Serra do hills Brazil 143 I4
Guru Sikhar mt. India 82 C4
Guruzala India 84 C2
Gur'yev Kazakh. see Atyrau
Gur'yevsk Rus. Fed. 45 L9
Gur'yevskaya Oblast' admin. div. Kazakh. see Atyrauskaya Oblast'
Gurz Afgh. 89 G3
Gusau Nigeria 96 D3
Güsen Germany 53 L2
Gusev Rus. Fed. 45 M9
Gushan China 75 A5
Gushgy Turkm. see Serhetabat
Gushi China 77 G1
Gusino Rus. Fed. 43 F5
Gusinoozersk Rus. Fed. 72 J2
Gus'-Khrustal'nyy Rus. Fed. 42 I5
Guspini Sardinia Italy 58 C5
Gustav Holm, Kap c. Greenland see Tasiilap Karra
Gustavo Sotelo Mex. 127 E7
Güsten Germany 53 L3
Gustine U.S.A. 128 C3
Güstrow Germany 47 N4
Güterfelde Germany 53 N2
Gütersloh Germany 53 I3
Guthrie AZ U.S.A. 129 I5
Guthrie KY U.S.A. 134 B5
Guthrie OK U.S.A. 131 D5
Guthrie TX U.S.A. 131 C5
Gutian Fujian China 77 H3
Gutian Fujian China 77 H3
Gutian Shuiku resr China 77 H3
Guting China see Yutai
Gutsuo China 83 F3
Guwahati India 83 G4
Guwēr Iraq 91 F3
Guwlumaýak Turkm. 88 D1
Guwlumayak Turkm. see Guwlumaýak
Guxhagen Germany 53 J3
Guxian China 77 G3
Guyana country S. America 143 G2
Guyane Française terr. S. America see French Guiana
Guyang Hunan China see Guzhang
Guyang Nei Mongol China 73 K4
Guyenne reg. France 56 D4
Guy Fawkes River National Park Australia 112 F3
Guyi China see Sanjiang
Guymon U.S.A. 131 C4
Guyra Australia 112 E3
Guysborough Canada 123 J5
Guyuan Hebei China 73 L4
Guyuan Ningxia China 72 J5
Güzeloluk Turkey 85 B1
Güzelyurt Cyprus see Morfou
Guzhang China 77 F2
Guzhen China 77 H1
Guzhou China see Rongjiang
Guzmán Mex. 127 G7
Guzmán, Lago de l. Mex. 127 G7
G'uzor Uzbek. 89 G2
Gvardeysk Rus. Fed. 45 L9
Gvasyugi Rus. Fed. 74 E3
Gwa Myanmar 70 A3
Gwabegar Australia 112 D3
Gwadar West Bay Pak. 89 F5
Gwaii Haanas National Park Reserve Canada 120 D4
Gwal Haidarzai Pak. 89 H4
Gwalior India 82 D4
Gwanda Zimbabwe 99 C6
Gwane Dem. Rep. Congo 98 C3
Gwardafuy, Gees c. Somalia 98 F2
Gwash Pak. 89 G4
Gwatar Bay Pak. 89 F5
Gwedaukkon Myanmar 70 A1
Gweebarra Bay Ireland 51 D3
Gwelo Zimbabwe see Gweru
Gweru Zimbabwe 99 C5
Gweta Botswana 99 C6
Gwinner U.S.A. 130 D2
Gwoza Nigeria 96 E3
Gwydir r. Australia 112 D2
Gyablung China 76 B2
Gyaca China 76 B2
Gyagartang China 76 D1
Gya'gya China see Saga
Gyaijêpozhanggê China see Zhidoi
Gyai Qu r. China 76 B2
Gyairong China 76 C1
Gyaisi China see Jiulong
Gyali i. Greece 59 L6
Gyamotang China see Dêngqên
Gyamug China 82 E2
Gyandzha Azer. see Gäncä
Gyangkar China see Dinngyê
Gyangnyi Caka salt l. China 83 F2
Gyangrang China 83 F3
Gyangtse China see Gyangzê
Gyangzê China 83 G3
Gyaring China 76 C1
Gyaring Co l. China 83 G3
Gyaring Hu l. China 76 C1
Gyarishing India 76 B2
Gyaros i. Greece 59 K6
Gyarubtang China 76 B2
Gydan, Khrebet mts Rus. Fed. see Kolymskiy, Khrebet
Gydan Peninsula Rus. Fed. 64 I2
Gydanskiy Poluostrov pen. Rus. Fed. see Gydan Peninsula
Gyêgu China see Yushu
Gyêmdong China 76 B2
Gyigang China 76 C2
Gyimda China 76 B2
Gyirong Xizang China 83 F3
Gyirong Xizang China 83 F3

Gyiza China 76 B1
Gyldenløve Fjord inlet Greenland see Umiiviip Kangertiva
Gympie Australia 111 F5
Gyobingauk Myanmar 70 A3
Gyöngyös Hungary 47 Q7
Győr Hungary 58 G1
Gypsum Point Canada 120 H2
Gypsumville Canada 121 L5
Gyrfalcon Islands Canada 123 H2
Gytheio Greece 59 J6
Gyula Hungary 59 I1
Gyulafehérvár Romania see Alba Iulia
Gyümai China see Darlag
Gyumri Armenia 91 F2
Gyzylarbat Turkm. see Serdar
Gyzylbaydak Turkm. see Gyzylbaýdak
Gyzylbaýdak Turkm. 89 F2
Gzhatsk Rus. Fed. see Gagarin

Ha Bhutan 83 G4
Haa-Alif Atoll Maldives see Ihavandhippolhu Atoll
Ha'apai Group is Tonga 107 I3
Haapajärvi Fin. 44 N5
Haapavesi Fin. 44 N4
Haapsalu Estonia 45 M7
Ha 'Arava watercourse Israel/Jordan see 'Arabah, Wādī al
Ha'Arava, Nahal watercourse Israel/Jordan see Jayb, Wādī al
Haarlem Neth. 52 E2
Haarlem S. Africa 100 F7
Haarstrang ridge Germany 53 H3
Hab r. Pak. 89 G5
Habahe China 80 G2
Habana Cuba see Havana
Habarane Sri Lanka 84 D4
Habarūt well Saudi Arabia 88 C6
Habaswein Kenya 98 D3
Habay Canada 120 G3
Habbān Yemen 86 G7
Ḩabbānīyah, Hawr al l. Iraq 91 F4
Hab Chauki Pak. 89 G5
Habiganj Bangl. 83 G4
Habra India 83 G5
Hachijō-jima i. Japan 75 E6
Hachinohe Japan 74 F4
Hachita U.S.A. 129 I6
Hacıköy Turkey see Çekerek
Hack, Mount Australia 111 B6
Hackberry U.S.A. 129 G4
Hackensack U.S.A. 135 H3
Hacufera Moz. 99 D6
Hadabat al Jilf al Kabīr plat. Egypt see Jilf al Kabīr, Hadabat al
Hadagalli India 84 B3
Hada Mountains Afgh. 89 G4
Hadapu China 76 E1
Hadayang China 74 B2
Ḩadd, Ra's al pt Oman 89 E6
Haddington U.K. 50 G5
Haddumati Atoll Maldives see Hadhdhunmathi Atoll
Haddunmahti Atoll Maldives see Hadhdhunmathi Atoll
Hadejia Nigeria 96 E3
Hadera Israel 85 B3
Hadera r. Israel 85 B3
Haderslev Denmark 45 F9
Hadhdhunmathi Atoll Maldives 81 D11
Hadhramaut reg. Yemen see Ḩaḑramawt
Hādī, Jabal al mts Jordan 85 C4
Hadım Turkey 90 D3
Hadleigh U.K. 49 H6
Hadong S. Korea 75 B6
Ḩadraj, Wādī watercourse Saudi Arabia 85 C4
Ḩaḑramawt reg. Yemen 98 E2
Hadranum Sicily Italy see Adrano
Hadrian's Wall tourist site U.K. 48 E3
Hadrumetum Tunisia see Sousse
Hadsund Denmark 45 G8
Hadyach Ukr. 43 G6
Haeju N. Korea 75 B5
Haeju-man b. N. Korea 75 B5
Haenam S. Korea 75 B6
Haenertsburg S. Africa 101 I2
Ha'erbin China see Harbin
Ḩafar al 'Atk well Saudi Arabia 88 B5
Ḩafar al Bāţin Saudi Arabia 86 G4
Hafford Canada 121 J4
Hafik Turkey 90 E3
Ḩafirah, Qā' al salt pan Jordan 85 C4
Hafirat Nasah Saudi Arabia 88 B5
Hafizabad Pak. 89 I3
Haflong India 83 H4
Hafnarfjörður Iceland 44 [inset]
Hafren r. U.K. see Severn
Haft Gel Iran 88 C4
Hafursfjörður b. Iceland 44 [inset]
Haga Myanmar see Haka
Hagar Nish Plateau Eritrea 86 E6

▶Hagåtña Guam 69 K4
Capital of Guam.

Hagelberg hill Germany 53 M2
Hagen Germany 53 H3
Hagenow Germany 53 L1
Hagerhill U.S.A. 134 D5
Hagerstown U.S.A. 135 G4
Hagfors Sweden 45 H6
Haggin, Mount U.S.A. 126 E3
Hagi Japan 75 C6
Ha Giang Vietnam 70 D2
Hagley U.K. 49 E6
Hag's Head hd Ireland 51 C5
Hague U.S.A. 135 I2
Haguenau France 53 H6
Hahajima-rettō is Japan 75 F8
Hai Tanz. 97 G5
Hai'an China 77 F4
Haib watercourse Namibia 100 C5
Haibowan China see Wuhai
Haicheng Guangdong China see Haifeng
Haicheng Liaoning China 73 M4
Hai Dương Vietnam 70 D2
Haifa Israel 85 B3
Haifa, Bay of Israel 85 B3
Haifeng China 77 G4
Haig Australia 109 D7
Haiger Germany 53 I4
Haikakan country Asia see Armenia
Haikang China see Leizhou
Haikou China 77 F4
Ḩā'īl Saudi Arabia 91 F6
Ḩā'īl, Wādī watercourse Saudi Arabia 91 F6
Hai-la-erh Nei Mongol China see Hulun Buir
Hailar Nei Mongol China see Hulun Buir
Hailey U.S.A. 126 E4
Haileybury Canada 122 F5
Hailin China 74 C3
Hailong China see Meihekou
Hailsham U.K. 49 H8
Hailun China 74 B3
Hailuoto Fin. 44 N4
Hainan i. China 77 F5
Hainan prov. China 77 F5
Hai-nang Myanmar 70 B2
Hainan Strait China 77 F5
Hainaut reg. France 52 D4
Haines U.S.A. 120 C3
Haines Junction Canada 120 B2
Haines Road Canada/U.S.A. 120 B2
Hainichen Germany 53 N4
Hainleite ridge Germany 53 K3
Hai Phong Vietnam 70 D2
Haiphong Vietnam see Hai Phong
Haiqing China 74 D3
Haitan Dao i. China 77 H3
Haiti country West Indies 137 J5
Haitou China 77 F5
Hai Triêu Vietnam 71 E4
Haiwee Reservoir U.S.A. 128 E3
Haiya Sudan 86 E6
Haiyan Qinghai China 72 I5
Haiyan Zhejiang China 77 I2
Haiyang China see Xiuning
Haiyang Dao i. China 75 A5
Haiyou China see Sanmen
Haizhou Wan b. China 77 H1
Hāj Ali Qoli, Kavīr-e salt l. Iran 88 D3
Hajdúböszörmény Hungary 59 I1
Hajeb El Ayoun Tunisia 58 C7
Ḩajhir mt. Yemen 87 H7
Haji Mahesar Pak. 89 G4
Hajipur India 83 F4
Hajir reg. Saudi Arabia 88 C5
Ḩajjah Yemen 86 F6
Ḩājjīābād Fārs Iran 88 D4
Ḩājjīābād Hormozgan Iran 88 D4
Ḩājjīābād Iran 88 D3
Haka Myanmar 70 A2
Hakha Myanmar see Haka
Hakkâri Turkey 91 F3
Hakkas Sweden 44 L3
Hakken-zan mt. Japan 75 D6
Hako-dake mt. Japan 74 F3
Hakodate Japan 74 F4
Hakos Mountains Namibia 100 C2
Hakseen Pan salt pan S. Africa 100 E4
Hakui Japan 75 E5
Haku-san vol. Japan 75 E5
Hal Belgium see Halle
Hala Pak. 89 H5
Ḩalab Syria see Aleppo
Ḩalabja Iraq 91 G4
Halaç Turkm. 89 G2
Halaç Turkm. see Halaç
Halaha China 74 B3
Halahai China 74 B3
Halaib Sudan 86 E5

▶Halaib Triangle terr. Egypt/Sudan 86 E5
Disputed territory (Egypt/Sudan) administered by Sudan.

Halāl, Gebel hill Egypt see Hilāl, Jabal
Ha Lam Vietnam 70 E4
Ḩalānīyāt, Juzur al is Oman 87 I6
Hālawa U.S.A. 127 [inset]
Halba Lebanon 85 C2
Halberstadt Germany 53 L3
Halcon, Mount Phil. 69 G4
Halden Norway 45 G7
Haldensleben Germany 53 L2
Haldwani India 82 D3
Hale watercourse Australia 110 A5
Hale U.S.A. 134 D1
Ḩāleh Iran 88 D5
Haleparki Deresi r. Syria/Turkey see Quwayq, Nahr
Halesowen U.K. 49 E6
Halesworth U.K. 49 I6
Half Assini Ghana 96 C4
Halfmoon Bay N.Z. 113 B8
Halfway r. Canada 120 F3
Halfway Ireland 51 D6
Halfweg Neth. 52 E2
Halhgol Mongolia 73 L3
Halia India 83 E4
Ḩalībīyah Syria 91 E4
Haliburton Canada 135 F1
Haliburton Highlands hills Canada 135 F1
Halicarnassus Turkey see Bodrum

▶Halifax Canada 123 J5
Capital of Nova Scotia.

Halifax U.K. 48 F5
Halifax NC U.S.A. 132 E4
Halifax VA U.S.A. 135 F5
Halifax, Mount Australia 110 D3
Ḩalīmah mt. Lebanon/Syria 85 C2
Halkirk U.K. 50 F2
Hall U.S.A. 134 C5
Hälla Sweden 44 J5
Halladale r. U.K. 50 F2
Halla-san National Park S. Korea 75 B6
Hall Beach Canada 119 J3
Halle Belgium 52 E4
Halle Neth. 52 G3
Halle (Saale) Germany 53 L3
Halleck U.S.A. 129 F1
Hällefors Sweden 45 I7
Hallein Austria 47 N7
Halle-Neustadt Germany 53 L3
Hallett, Cape Antarctica 152 H2
Hallettsville U.S.A. 131 D6
Halley research station Antarctica 152 B1
Hallgreen, Mount Antarctica 152 B2
Halliday U.S.A. 130 C2
Halliday Lake Canada 121 I2
Hall Islands Micronesia 150 G5
Hällnäs Sweden 44 K4
Hallock U.S.A. 130 D1
Hall Peninsula Canada 119 L3
Hallsberg Sweden 45 I7
Halls Creek Australia 108 D4
Halls Gap U.S.A. 134 C5
Halls Lake Canada 135 F1
Hallstead U.S.A. 135 H3
Halluin Belgium 52 D4
Hallviken Sweden 44 I5
Halmahera i. Indon. 69 H6
Halmahera, Laut sea Indon. 69 H7
Halmahera Sea sea Indon. see Halmahera, Laut
Halmstad Sweden 45 H8
Ha Long Vietnam 70 D2
Hals Denmark 45 G8
Hälsingborg Sweden see Helsingborg
Halsua Fin. 44 N5
Haltern Germany 53 H3
Haltwhistle U.K. 48 E4
Ḩālūl i. Qatar 88 D5
Ḩalvān Iran 88 E3
Halver Germany 53 H3
Haly, Mount hill Australia 112 E1
Ham France 52 D5
Hamada Japan 75 D6
Ḩamâda El Ḩaricha des. Mali 96 C2
Hamadān Iran 88 C3
Ḩamādat Murzuq plat. Libya 98 B1
Ḩamāh Syria 85 C2
Hamam Turkey 85 C1
Hamamatsu Japan 75 E6
Hamar Norway 45 G6
Hamarøy Norway 44 I2
Ḩamâţa, Gebel mt. Egypt see Ḩamāţah, Jabal
Ḩamāţah, Jabal mt. Egypt 86 D5
Hamatonbetsu Japan 74 F3
Hambantota Sri Lanka 84 D5
Hambergen Germany 53 I1
Hambleton Hills U.K. 48 F4
Hamburg Germany 53 J1
Hamburg land Germany 53 J1
Hamburg S. Africa 101 H7
Hamburg AR U.S.A. 131 F5
Hamburg NY U.S.A. 135 F2
Hamburgisches Wattenmeer, Nationalpark nat. park Germany 47 L4
Ḩamḑ, Wādī al watercourse Saudi Arabia 86 E4
Hamden U.S.A. 135 I3
Hämeenlinna Fin. 45 N6
HaMelah, Yam salt l. Asia see Dead Sea
Hamelin Australia 109 A6
Hameln Germany 53 J2
Hamersley Lakes salt flat Australia 109 B7
Hamersley Range mts Australia 108 B5
Hamhŭng N. Korea 75 B5
Hami China 80 H3
Hamid Sudan 86 D5
Hamilton Qld Australia 110 C4
Hamilton S.A. Australia 111 A5
Hamilton Vic. Australia 111 C8
Hamilton watercourse Qld Australia 110 B4
Hamilton watercourse S.A. Australia 111 A5

▶Hamilton Bermuda 137 L2
Capital of Bermuda.

Hamilton Canada 134 F2
Hamilton r. Canada see Churchill
Hamilton N.Z. 113 E3
Hamilton U.K. 50 E5
Hamilton AL U.S.A. 133 C5
Hamilton CO U.S.A. 129 J1
Hamilton MI U.S.A. 134 B2
Hamilton MT U.S.A. 126 E3
Hamilton NY U.S.A. 135 H2
Hamilton OH U.S.A. 134 C4
Hamilton TX U.S.A. 131 D6
Hamilton, Mount CA U.S.A. 128 C3
Hamilton, Mount NV U.S.A. 129 F2
Hamilton City U.S.A. 128 B2
Hamilton Inlet Canada 123 K3
Hamilton Mountain hill U.S.A. 135 H2
Hamīm, Wādī al watercourse Libya 55 I5
Hamina Fin. 45 O6
Hamirpur Hima. Prad. India 82 D3
Hamirpur Uttar Prad. India 82 E4
Hamitabat Turkey see Isparta
Hamju N. Korea 75 B5
Hamlet U.S.A. 133 E5
Hamlin TX U.S.A. 131 C5
Hamlin WV U.S.A. 134 D4
Hamm Germany 53 H3
Ḩammām al 'Alīl Iraq 91 F3
Hammam Boughrara Alg. 57 F6
Hammamet Tunisia 58 D6
Hammamet, Golfe de g. Tunisia 58 D6
Ḩammār, Hawr al imp. l. Iraq 91 G5
Hammarstrand Sweden 44 J5
Hammelburg Germany 53 J4
Hammerdal Sweden 44 I5
Hammerfest Norway 44 M1
Hamminkeln Germany 52 G3
Hammond U.S.A. 134 B3
Hammone, Lac l. Canada 123 K4
Hammonton U.S.A. 135 H4
Ham Ninh Vietnam 71 D5
Hamoir Belgium 52 F4
Hampden Sydney U.S.A. 135 F5
Hampshire Downs hills U.K. 49 F7
Hampton AR U.S.A. 131 E5
Hampton IA U.S.A. 130 E3
Hampton NH U.S.A. 135 J2
Hampton SC U.S.A. 133 D5
Hampton VA U.S.A. 135 G5
Hampton Tableland reg. Australia 109 D8
Ḩamrā, Birkat al well Saudi Arabia 91 F5
Hamra, Vâdii watercourse Syria/Turkey see Ḩimār, Wādī al
Hamrā Jūdah plat. Saudi Arabia 88 C5
Hamrat esh Sheikh Sudan 86 C7
Ham Tân Vietnam 71 D5
Hamta Pass India 82 D2
Hāmūn-e Jaz Mūrīān salt marsh Iran 88 E5
Hāmūn-e Lowrah dry lake Afgh./Pak. see Hamun-i-Lora
Hāmūn Helmand salt flat Afgh./Iran 89 F4
Hamun-i-Lora dry lake Afgh./Pak. 89 G4
Hamun-i-Mashkel salt flat Pak. 89 F4
Hamunt Kūh hill Iran 89 F5
Hamur Turkey 91 F3
Hamwic U.K. see Southampton
Hāna U.S.A. 127 [inset]
Hanábana r. Cuba 133 D8
Hanahai watercourse Botswana/Namibia 100 F2
Ḩanak Saudi Arabia 86 E4
Hanakpınar Turkey see Çınar
Hanalei U.S.A. 127 [inset]
Hanamaki Japan 75 F5
Hanang mt. Tanz. 99 D4
Hanau Germany 53 I4
Hanbin China see Ankang
Hanchang China see Pingjiang
Hancheng China 77 F1
Hanchuan China 77 G2
Hancock MD U.S.A. 135 F4
Hancock NY U.S.A. 135 H3
Handa Island U.K. 50 D2
Handan China 73 K5
Handeni Tanz. 99 D4
HaNegev des. Israel see Negev
HaNeqarot watercourse Israel 85 B4
Hanfeng China see Kaixian
Hanford U.S.A. 128 D3
Hangan Myanmar 70 B4
Hangayn Nuruu mts Mongolia 80 I2
Hangchow China see Hangzhou
Hangchuan China see Guangze
Hangö Fin. see Hanko
Hangu China 73 L5
Hanguang China 77 G3
Hangya China 80 I4
Hangzhou China 77 I2
Hangzhou Wan b. China 77 I2
Hani Turkey 91 F3
Hanish Kabir i. Yemen see Suyūl Ḩanīsh
Hanjia China see Pengshui
Hankensbüttel Germany 53 K2
Hankey S. Africa 100 G7
Hanko Fin. 45 M7
Hanksville U.S.A. 129 H2
Hanle India 82 D2
Hanley Canada 121 J5
Hann, Mount hill Australia 108 D3
Hanna Canada 121 I5
Hannagan Meadow U.S.A. 129 I5
Hannah Bay Canada 122 E4
Hannibal MO U.S.A. 130 F4
Hannibal NY U.S.A. 135 G2
Hannover Germany 53 J2
Hannoversch Münden Germany 53 J3
Hann Range mts Australia 109 F5
Hannut Belgium 52 F4
Hanöbukten b. Sweden 45 I9

▶Ha Nôi Vietnam 70 D2
Capital of Vietnam.

Hanoi Vietnam see Ha Nôi
Hanover Canada 134 E1
Hanover Germany see Hannover
Hanover S. Africa 100 G6
Hanover NH U.S.A. 135 I2
Hanover PA U.S.A. 135 G4
Hanover VA U.S.A. 135 G5
Hansen Mountains Antarctica 152 D2
Hanshou China 77 F2
Han Shui r. China 77 G2
Hansi India 82 D3
Hansnes Norway 44 K2
Hanstholm Denmark 45 F8
Han-sur-Nied France 52 G6
Hantsavichy Belarus 45 O10
Hanumangarh India 82 C3
Hanwood Australia 112 C5
Hanyang China see Caidian
Hanyang Feng mt. China 77 G2
Hanyin China 77 F1
Hanzhong China 76 E1
Hao atoll Fr. Polynesia 151 K7
Haora India 83 G5
Haparanda Sweden 44 N4
Happy Jack U.S.A. 129 H4
Happy Valley-Goose Bay Canada 123 J3
Ḩaql Saudi Arabia 85 B5
Haqshah well Saudi Arabia 88 C6
Ḩaraḑ well Saudi Arabia 88 C5
Ḩarad, Jabal al mt. Jordan 85 B5
Ḩaraḑh Saudi Arabia 86 G5
Haradok Belarus 43 F5
Haramachi Japan 75 F5
Haramukh mt. India 82 C2
Haran Turkey see Harran
Harappa Road Pak. 89 I4
Harar Eth. see Hārer

▶Harare Zimbabwe 99 D5
Capital of Zimbabwe.

Ḩarāsīs, Jiddat al des. Oman 87 I6
Harāt Iran 88 D4
Har-Ayrag Mongolia 73 J3
Haraze-Mangueigne Chad 97 F3
Harb, Jabal mt. Saudi Arabia 90 D6
Harbin China 74 B3
Harboi Hills Pak. 89 G4
Harbor Beach U.S.A. 134 D2
Harchoka India 83 E5
Harda India 82 D5
Harda Khas India see Harda
Hardangerfjorden sea chan. Norway 45 D7
Hardangervidda plat. Norway 45 E6
Hardangervidda Nasjonalpark nat. park Norway 45 E6
Hardap admin. reg. Namibia 100 C3
Hardap nature res. Namibia 100 C3
Hardap Dam Namibia 100 C3
Hardenberg Neth. 52 G2
Harderwijk Neth. 52 F2
Hardeveld mts S. Africa 100 D6
Hardheim Germany 53 J5
Hardin U.S.A. 126 G3
Harding S. Africa 101 I6
Harding Range hills Australia 109 B6
Hardinsburg IN U.S.A. 134 B4
Hardinsburg KY U.S.A. 134 B5
Hardoi India 82 E4
Hardwar India see Haridwar
Hardwick U.S.A. 135 I1
Hardy U.S.A. 131 F4
Hardy Reservoir U.S.A. 134 C2
Hare Bay Canada 123 L4
Ḩareidīn, Wâdi watercourse Egypt see Ḩuraydīn, Wādī
Harelbeke Belgium 52 D4
Haren Neth. 52 G1
Haren (Ems) Germany 53 H2
Hārer Eth. 98 E3
Harf el Mreffi mt. Lebanon 85 B3
Hargeisa Somalia see Hargeysa
Hargele Eth. 98 E3
Hargeysa Somalia 98 E3
Harghita-Mădăraş, Vârful mt. Romania 59 K1
Harhorin Mongolia 80 J2
Har Hu l. China 80 I4
Haridwar India 82 D3
Ḩarif, Har mt. Israel 85 B4
Harihar India 84 B3
Harihari N.Z. 113 C6
Hariharpur India 84 B3
Ḩārim Syria 85 C1
Harīm, Jabal al mt. Oman 88 E5
Harima-nada b. Japan 75 D6
Haringhat r. Bangl. 83 G5
Haringvliet est. Neth. 52 E3
Ḩarīr, Wādī adh r. Syria 85 C3
Hari Rūd r. Afgh./Iran 89 F2
Harjavalta Fin. 45 M6
Harlan IA U.S.A. 130 E3
Harlan KY U.S.A. 134 D5
Harlan County Lake U.S.A. 130 D3
Harlech U.K. 49 C6
Harleston U.K. 49 I6
Harlingen Neth. 52 F1
Harlingen U.S.A. 131 D7
Harlow U.K. 49 H7
Harlowton U.S.A. 126 F3
Harly France 52 D5
Harman U.S.A. 134 F4
Harmancık Turkey 59 M5
Harmony U.S.A. 135 K1
Harmsdorf Germany 53 K1
Harnai India 84 B2
Harnai Pak. 89 G4
Harnes France 52 C4
Harney Basin U.S.A. 126 D4
Harney Lake U.S.A. 126 D4
Härnösand Sweden 44 J5
Harns Neth. see Harlingen
Har Nuur l. Mongolia 80 H2
Haroldswick U.K. 50 [inset]
Harper Liberia 96 C4
Harper U.S.A. 131 D4
Harper, Mount U.S.A. 118 D3
Harper Creek r. Canada 120 H3
Harper Lake U.S.A. 128 E4
Harp Lake Canada 123 J3
Harpstedt Germany 53 I2
Harquahala Mountains U.S.A. 127 E6
Harrai India 82 D5
Harran Turkey 85 D1
Harrand Pak. 89 H4
Harricana, Rivière d' r. Canada 122 F4
Harrington Australia 112 F3
Harrington U.S.A. 135 H4
Harris, Lake salt flat Australia 111 A6
Harris, Mount Australia 109 E6
Harris, Sound of sea chan. U.K. 50 B3
Harrisburg AR U.S.A. 131 F5
Harrisburg IL U.S.A. 130 F4
Harrisburg NE U.S.A. 130 C3

▶Harrisburg PA U.S.A. 135 G3
Capital of Pennsylvania.

Harrismith Australia 109 B8
Harrison AR U.S.A. 131 E4
Harrison MI U.S.A. 134 C1
Harrison NE U.S.A. 130 C3
Harrison OH U.S.A. 134 C4
Harrison, Cape Canada 123 K3
Harrison Bay U.S.A. 118 C2
Harrisonburg LA U.S.A. 131 F6
Harrisonburg VA U.S.A. 135 F4
Harrisonville U.S.A. 130 E4
Harriston Canada 134 E2
Harrisville MI U.S.A. 134 D1
Harrisville NY U.S.A. 135 H1
Harrisville PA U.S.A. 134 E3
Harrisville WV U.S.A. 134 E4
Harrodsburg IN U.S.A. 134 B4
Harrodsburg KY U.S.A. 134 C5
Harrodsville N.Z. see Otorohanga
Harrogate U.K. 48 F5
Harrowsmith Canada 135 G1
Harry S. Truman Reservoir U.S.A. 130 E4
Har Sai Shan mt. China 76 C1
Harsefeld Germany 53 J1
Harsīn Iran 88 B3
Harşit r. Turkey 90 E2
Hârşova Romania 59 L2
Harstad Norway 44 J2
Harsud India 82 D5
Harsum Germany 53 J2
Hart r. Canada 118 E3
Hart U.S.A. 134 B2
Hartbees watercourse S. Africa 100 E5
Hartberg Austria 47 O7
Harteigan mt. Norway 45 E6
Harter Fell hill U.K. 48 E4

▶Hartford CT U.S.A. 135 I3
Capital of Connecticut.

Hartford KY U.S.A. 134 B5
Hartford MI U.S.A. 134 B2
Hartford City U.S.A. 134 C3
Hartland U.K. 49 C8
Hartland U.S.A. 135 K1
Hartland Point U.K. 49 C7
Hartlepool U.K. 48 F4
Hartley U.S.A. 131 C5
Hartley Zimbabwe see Chegutu
Hartley Bay Canada 120 D4
Hartola Fin. 45 O6
Harts r. S. Africa 101 G5
Härtsfeld hills Germany 53 K6
Harts Range mts Australia 109 F5
Hartsville U.S.A. 134 B5
Hartswater S. Africa 100 G4
Hartville U.S.A. 131 E4
Hartwell U.S.A. 133 D5
Har Us Nuur l. Mongolia 80 H2
Harūz-e Bālā Iran 88 E4
Harvard, Mount U.S.A. 126 G5
Harvey Australia 109 A8
Harvey U.S.A. 130 C2
Harvey Mountain U.S.A. 128 C1
Harwich U.K. 49 I7
Haryana state India 82 D3
Harz hills Germany 47 M5
Har Zin Israel 85 B4
Ḩaşāh, Wādī al watercourse Jordan 85 B4
Ḩaşāh, Wādī al watercourse Jordan/Saudi Arabia 85 C4
Hasalbag China 89 J2
Ḩasanah, Wādī watercourse Egypt 85 A4
Hasan Dağı mts Turkey 90 D3
Hasan Guli Turkm. see Esenguly
Hasankeyf Turkey 91 F3
Hasan Küleh Afgh. 89 F3
Hasanur India 84 C4
Hasardag mt. Turkm. 88 E2
Hasbaïya Lebanon 85 B3
Hasbaya Lebanon see Hasbaïya
Hase r. Germany 53 H2
Haselünne Germany 53 H2
Hashak Iran 89 F5
HaSharon plain Israel 85 B3
Hashtgerd Iran 88 C3
Hashtpar Iran 88 C2
Hashtrud Iran 88 B2
Haskell U.S.A. 131 D5
Haslemere U.K. 49 G7
Hăşmaşul Mare mt. Romania 59 K1
Ḩaşş, Jabal al hills Syria 85 C1
Hassan India 84 C3
Hassayampa watercourse U.S.A. 129 G5
Haßberge hills Germany 53 K4
Hasselt Belgium 52 F4
Hasselt Neth. 52 G2
Hassi Bel Guebbour Alg. 96 D2
Hassi Messaoud Alg. 54 F5
Hässleholm Sweden 45 H8
Hastings Australia 112 B7
Hastings r. Australia 112 F3
Hastings Canada 135 G1
Hastings N.Z. 113 F4
Hastings U.K. 49 H8
Hastings MI U.S.A. 134 C2
Hastings MN U.S.A. 130 E2
Hastings NE U.S.A. 130 D3
Hata India 83 E4
Hatanbulag Mongolia 73 J4
Hatay Turkey see Antakya
Hatay prov. Turkey 85 C1
Hatch U.S.A. 129 G3
Hatches Creek (abandoned) Australia 110 A4
Hatchet Lake Canada 121 K3
Hatfield Australia 112 A4
Hatfield U.K. 48 G5
Hatgal Mongolia 80 J1
Hath India 84 D1
Hat Head National Park Australia 112 F3
Hathras India 82 D4
Ha Tiên Vietnam 71 D5
Ha Tinh Vietnam 70 D3
Hatisar Bhutan see Geylegphug
Hatod India 82 C5
Hato Hud East Timor see Hatudo
Hatra Iraq 91 F4
Hattah Australia 111 C7
Hattah Kulkyne National Park Australia 111 C7
Hatteras, Cape U.S.A. 133 F5
Hatteras Abyssal Plain sea feature S. Atlantic Ocean 148 D4
Hattfjelldal Norway 44 H4
Hattiesburg U.S.A. 131 F6
Hattingen Germany 53 H3
Hattras Passage Myanmar 71 B4
Hatudo East Timor 108 D2
Hat Yai Thai. 71 C6
Hau Bon Vietnam see A Yun Pa
Haubstadt U.S.A. 134 B4
Haud reg. Eth. 98 E3
Hauge Norway 45 E7
Haugesund Norway 45 D7
Haukeligrend Norway 45 E7
Haukipudas Fin. 44 N4
Haukivesi l. Fin. 44 P5
Haultain r. Canada 121 J4
Hauraki Gulf N.Z. 113 E3
Haut Atlas mts Morocco 54 C5
Haute-Normandie admin. reg. France 52 B5
Haute-Volta country Africa see Burkina
Haut-Folin hill France 56 G3
Hauts Plateaux Alg. 54 D5

▶Havana Cuba 137 H4
Capital of Cuba.

Havana U.S.A. 130 F3
Havant U.K. 49 G8
Havasu, Lake U.S.A. 129 F4
Havel r. Germany 53 L2
Havelange Belgium 52 F4
Havelberg Germany 53 M2
Havelock Canada 135 G1
Havelock N.Z. 113 D5

welock Swaziland *see* **Bulembu**
welock U.S.A. 133 E5
welock Falls Australia 108 F3
welock Island India 71 A5
welock North N.Z. 113 F4
werfordwest U.K. 49 C7
werhill U.S.A. 135 J2
weri India 84 B3
wersin Belgium 52 F4
wixbeck Germany 53 H3
vlíčkův Brod Czech Rep. 47 O6
øysund Norway 44 N1
wran Turkey 59 L5
wre U.S.A. 126 F2
wre Aubert, Île du *i.* Canada 123 J5
wre Rock *i.* Kermadec Is 107 I5
wre-St-Pierre Canada 123 J4
vza Turkey 90 D2
wai'i *i.* U.S.A. 127 [inset]
wai'ian Islands N. Pacific Ocean 150 I4
waiian Ridge *sea feature*
. Pacific Ocean 150 I4
wai'i Volcanoes National Park U.S.A.
27 [inset]
wallī Kuwait 88 C4
war *i.* Bahrain *see* **Ḥuwār**
warden U.K. 48 D5
wea, Lake N.Z. 113 B7
wera N.Z. 113 E4
wes U.K. 48 E4
wesville U.S.A. 134 B5
wi U.S.A. 127 [inset]
wick U.K. 50 G5
wizah, Hawr al *imp. l.* Iraq 91 G5
wkdun Range *mts* N.Z. 113 B7
wke Bay N.Z. 113 F4
wkes Bay Canada 123 K4
wkins Peak U.S.A. 129 G3
wlēr Iraq *see* **Arbīl**
wley U.S.A. 135 H3
wng Luk Myanmar 70 B2
wrān, Wādī *watercourse* Iraq 91 F4
wshah, Jibāl al *mts* Saudi Arabia 88 B6
wston S. Africa 100 D8
wthorne U.S.A. 128 D2
at China 74 B3
oy U.K. 48 F4
Australia 112 B5
watercourse Australia 110 B5
r. Canada 120 H2
achine-san *mt.* Japan 75 F5
astan *country* Asia *see* **Armenia**
dān, Wādī al *r.* Jordan 85 B4
den *AZ* U.S.A. 129 H5
den *CO* U.S.A. 129 J1
den *IN* U.S.A. 134 C4
es *r. Man.* Canada 121 M3
es *r. Nunavut* Canada 119 I3
es Halvø *pen.* Greenland 119 L2
field Reservoir U.S.A. 129 F5
ork U.S.A. 128 B1
, Wādī *watercourse* Syria 85 C3
, Wādī al *watercourse* Syria 85 D2
le U.K. 49 B8
mā' Oman 87 I6
mana Turkey 90 D3
market U.S.A. 135 G4
-on-Wye U.K. 49 D6
rabolu Turkey 59 L4
River Canada 118 G3
River Reserve Canada 120 H2
s *KS* U.S.A. 130 D4
s *MT* U.S.A. 126 F2
s Yemen 86 F7
sville U.S.A. 131 D4
syn Ukr. 43 F6
ţān, Jabal *hill* Egypt 85 A4
ward *CA* U.S.A. 128 B3
ward *WI* U.S.A. 130 F2
wards Heath U.K. 49 G8
ar Turkm. 88 D2
arajat *reg.* Afgh. 89 G3
ard U.S.A. 134 D5
aribag India *see* **Hazaribagh**
aribagh India 83 F5
aribagh Range *mts* India 83 E5
ār Masjed, Kūh-e *mts* Iran 88 E2
ebrouck France 52 C4
elton Canada 120 E4
en Strait Canada 119 G2
erswoude-Rijndijk Neth. 52 E2
ndanahr *reg.* Afgh. 89 G2
eton *IN* U.S.A. 134 B4
eton *PA* U.S.A. 135 H3
ett, Lake *salt flat* Australia 108 E5
rat-e Solţān Afgh. 89 G2
ouchard Arg. 144 D4
dford Ireland 51 C4
dingly Australia 110 B4
d of Bight *b.* Australia 109 E7
ldsburg U.S.A. 128 B2
esville Australia 112 B6
y U.S.A. 118 D3
nor U.K. 49 F5

eard and McDonald Islands *terr.*
dian Ocean 149 M9
stralian External Territory.

rd Island Indian Ocean 149 M9
rne U.S.A. 131 D6
rne Lake Canada 121 H2
rrenfean Neth. *see* **Heerenveen**
rst Canada 122 E4
rst Island Antarctica 152 L2
rt *r.* U.S.A. 130 C2
rt of Neolithic Orkney *tourist site* U.K.
F1
thcote Australia 112 B6
thfield U.K. 49 H8
thsville U.S.A. 135 G5
bardsville U.S.A. 134 B5
bronville U.S.A. 131 D7
ei *prov.* China 73 L5
el Australia 112 C2
er U.S.A. 129 H4
er City U.S.A. 129 H1
er Springs U.S.A. 131 E5
China 73 K5
ron Canada 123 J2
ron U.S.A. 130 D3
ron West Bank 85 B4

Hecate Strait Canada 120 D4
Hecheng *Jiangxi* China *see* **Zixi**
Hecheng *Zhejiang* China *see* **Qingtian**
Hechi China 77 F3
Hechuan *Chongqing* China 76 E2
Hechuan *Jiangxi* China *see* **Yongxing**
Hecla Island Canada 121 L5
Hede China *see* **Sheyang**
Hede Sweden 44 H5
Hedemora Sweden 45 I6
He Devil Mountain U.S.A. 126 D3
Hedi Shuiku *resr* China 77 F4
Heech Neth. *see* **Heeg**
Heeg Neth. 52 F2
Heek Germany 52 H2
Heer Belgium 52 E4
Heerde Neth. 52 G2
Heerenveen Neth. 52 F2
Heerhugowaard Neth. 52 E2
Heerlen Neth. 52 F4
Hefa Israel *see* **Haifa**
Hefa, Mifraz Israel *see* **Haifa, Bay of**
Hefei China 77 H2
Hefeng China 77 F2
Heflin U.S.A. 133 C5
Hegang China 74 C3
Heho Myanmar 70 B2
Heidan *r.* Jordan *see* **Haydān, Wādī al**
Heidberg *hill* Germany 53 L3
Heide Germany 47 L3
Heide Namibia 100 C2
Heidelberg Germany 53 I5
Heidelberg S. Africa 101 I4
Heidenheim an der Brenz Germany 53 K6
Heihe China 74 B2
Heilbron S. Africa 101 H4
Heilbronn Germany 53 J5
Heiligenhafen Germany 47 M3
Hei Ling Chau *i. H.K.* China 77 [inset]
Heilongjiang *prov.* China 74 C3
Heilong Jiang *r.* China/Rus. Fed. 74 D2
also known as Amur (Rus. Fed.)
Heilong Jiang *r.* Rus. Fed. *see* **Amur**
Heilsbronn Germany 53 K5
Heilungkiang *prov.* China *see* **Heilongjiang**
Heinola Fin. 45 O6
Heinze Islands Myanmar 71 B4
Heirnkut Myanmar 70 A1
Heishi Beihu *l.* China 83 E2
Heishui China 76 D1
Heisker Islands U.K. *see* **Monach Islands**
Heist-op-den-Berg Belgium 52 E3
Heiţān, Gebel *hill* Egypt *see* **Ḩayţān, Jabal**
Hejaz *reg.* Saudi Arabia *see* **Hijaz**
Hejiang China 76 E2
He Jiang *r.* China 77 F4
Hejing China 80 G3
Hekimhan Turkey 90 E3
Hekla *vol.* Iceland 44 [inset]
Hekou *Gansu* China 72 I5
Hekou *Hubei* China 77 G2
Hekou *Jiangxi* China *see* **Yanshan**
Hekou *Sichuan* China *see* **Yajiang**
Hekou *Yunnan* China 76 D4
Helagsfjället *mt.* Sweden 44 H5
Helam India 76 B3
Helan Shan *mts* China 72 J5
Helbra Germany 53 L3
Helen *atoll* Palau 69 I6
Helena *AR* U.S.A. 131 F5

▶**Helena** *MT* U.S.A. 126 E3
Capital of Montana.

Helen Reef Palau 69 I6
Helensburgh U.K. 50 E4
Helen Springs Australia 108 F4
Helez Israel 85 B4
Helgoland *i.* Germany 47 K3
Helgoländer Bucht *g.* Germany 47 L3
Heligoland *i.* Germany *see* **Helgoland**
Heligoland Bight *g.* Germany *see*
Helgoländer Bucht
Heliopolis Lebanon *see* **Ba'albek**
Helixi China *see* **Ningguo**
Hella Iceland 44 [inset]
Helland Norway 44 J2
Hellas *country* Europe *see* **Greece**
Helleh *r.* Iran 88 C4
Hellespont *strait* Turkey *see* **Dardanelles**
Hellevoetsluis Neth. 52 E3
Hellhole Gorge National Park Australia
110 D5
Hellín Spain 57 F4
Hellinikon *tourist site* Greece 90 A3
Hells Canyon *gorge* U.S.A. 126 D3
Hell-Ville Madag. *see* **Andoany**
Helmand *r.* Afgh. 89 F4
Helmantica Spain *see* **Salamanca**
Helmbrechts Germany 53 L4
Helme *r.* Germany 53 L3
Helmeringhausen Namibia 100 C3
Helmond Neth. 52 F3
Helmsdale U.K. 50 F2
Helmsdale *r.* U.K. 50 F2
Helmstedt Germany 53 L2
Helong China 74 C4
Helper U.S.A. 129 H2
Helpter Berge *hills* Germany 53 N1
Helsingborg Sweden 45 H8
Helsingfors Fin. *see* **Helsinki**
Helsingør Denmark 45 H8

▶**Helsinki** Fin. 45 N6
Capital of Finland.

Helston U.K. 49 B8
Helvécia Brazil 145 D2
Helvetic Republic *country* Europe *see*
Switzerland
Helwân Egypt *see* **Ḩulwān**
Hemel Hempstead U.K. 49 G7
Hemet U.S.A. 128 E5
Hemingford U.S.A. 130 C3
Hemlock Lake U.S.A. 135 G2
Hemmingen Germany 53 J2
Hemmingford Canada 135 I1
Hemmoor Germany 53 J1
Hempstead U.S.A. 131 D6
Hemsby U.K. 49 I6
Hemse Sweden 45 K8
Henan China 76 D1

Henan *prov.* China 77 G1
Henares *r.* Spain 57 E3
Henashi-zaki *pt* Japan 75 E4
Henbury Australia 109 F6
Hendek Turkey 59 N4
Henderson *KY* U.S.A. 134 B5
Henderson *NC* U.S.A. 132 E4
Henderson *NV* U.S.A. 129 F3
Henderson *NY* U.S.A. 135 G2
Henderson *TN* U.S.A. 131 F5
Henderson *TX* U.S.A. 131 E5
Henderson Island Pitcairn Is 151 L7
Hendersonville *NC* U.S.A. 133 D5
Hendersonville *TN* U.S.A. 134 B5
Henderville *atoll* Kiribati *see* **Aranuka**
Hendon U.K. 49 G7
Hendorābī *i.* Iran 88 D5
Hendy-Gwyn U.K. *see* **Whitland**
Hengām Iran 89 E5
Hengduan Shan *mts* China 76 C2
Hengelo Neth. 52 G2
Hengfeng China 77 H2
Hengnan China *see* **Hengyang**
Hengshan China 74 C3
Heng Shan *mt.* China 77 G3
Hengshui *Hebei* China 73 L5
Hengshui *Jiangxi* China *see* **Chongyi**
Hengxian China 77 F4
Hengyang *Hunan* China 77 G3
Hengyang *Hunan* China 77 G3
Hengzhou China *see* **Hengxian**
Heniches'k Ukr. 43 G7
Henley N.Z. 113 C7
Henley-on-Thames U.K. 49 G7
Henlopen, Cape U.S.A. 135 H4
Hennef (Sieg) Germany 53 H4
Hennenman S. Africa 101 H4
Hennepin U.S.A. 130 F3
Hennessey U.S.A. 131 D4
Hennigsdorf Berlin Germany 53 N2
Henniker U.S.A. 135 J2
Henning U.S.A. 134 B3
Henrietta U.S.A. 131 D5
Henrietta Maria, Cape Canada 122 E3
Henrieville U.S.A. 129 H3
Henrique de Carvalho Angola *see* **Saurimo**
Henry, Cape U.S.A. 135 G5
Henry Ice Rise Antarctica 152 A1
Henryk Arctowski *research station*
Antarctica *see* **Arctowski**
Henry Kater, Cape Canada 119 L3
Henry Mountains U.S.A. 129 H2
Hensall Canada 134 E2
Henshaw, Lake U.S.A. 128 E5
Hentiesbaai Namibia 100 B2
Henty Australia 112 C5
Henzada Myanmar *see* **Hinthada**
Heping *Guangdong* China 77 G3
Heping *Guizhou* China *see* **Huishui**
Heping *Guizhou* China *see* **Yanhe**
Hepo China *see* **Jiexi**
Heppner U.S.A. 126 D3
Heptanesus *is* Ionia Nisia Greece *see*
Ionian Islands
Heptanesus *is* Greece *see* **Ionian Islands**
Hepu China 77 F4
Heqing China 76 D3
Heraclea Turkey *see* **Ereğli**
Heraclea Pontica Turkey *see* **Ereğli**
Heraklion Greece *see* **Iraklion**
Herald Cays *atolls* Australia 110 E3
Herāt Afgh. 89 F3
Hérault *r.* France 56 F5
Herbertabad India 71 A5
Herbert Downs Australia 110 B4
Herbert River Falls National Park Australia
110 D3
Herbert Wash *salt flat* Australia 109 D6
Herborn Germany 53 I4
Herbstein Germany 53 J4
Hercules Dome *ice feature* Antarctica
152 K1
Herdecke Germany 53 H3
Herdorf Germany 53 H4
Hereford U.K. 49 E6
Hereford U.S.A. 131 C5
Héréhérétué *atoll* Fr. Polynesia 151 K7
Herent Belgium 52 E4
Herford Germany 53 I2
Heringen (Werra) Germany 53 K4
Herington U.S.A. 130 D4
Herīs Iran 88 B2
Herisau Switz. 56 I3
Herkimer U.S.A. 135 H2
Herlen Gol *r.* China/Mongolia 73 L3
Herlen He *r.* China/Mongolia *see*
Herlen Gol
Herleshausen Germany 53 K3
Herlong U.S.A. 128 C1
Herm *i.* Channel Is 49 E9
Hermanas Mex. 131 C7
Herma Ness *hd* U.K. 50 [inset]
Hermann U.S.A. 130 F4
Hermannsburg Germany 53 K2
Hermanus S. Africa 100 D8
Hermel Lebanon 85 C2
Hermes, Cape S. Africa 101 I6
Hermidale Australia 112 C3
Hermiston U.S.A. 126 D3
Hermitage *MO* U.S.A. 130 E4
Hermitage *PA* U.S.A. 134 E3
Hermitage Bay Canada 123 K5
Hermite, Islas *is* Chile 144 C9
Hermit Islands P.N.G. 69 L7
Hermon, Mount Lebanon/Syria 85 B3
Hermonthis Egypt *see* **Armant**
Hermopolis Magna Egypt *see*
Al Ashmūnayn
Hermosa U.S.A. 129 J3
Hermosillo Mex. 127 F7
Hernandarias Para. 144 F3
Hernando U.S.A. 131 F5
Herndon *CA* U.S.A. 128 D3
Herndon *PA* U.S.A. 135 G3
Herndon *WV* U.S.A. 134 E5
Herne Germany 53 H3
Herne Bay U.K. 49 I7
Herning Denmark 45 F8
Heroica Nogales Mex. *see* **Nogales**
Heroica Puebla de Zaragoza Mex. *see*
Puebla
Hérouville-St-Clair France 49 G9

Herowābād Iran *see* **Khalkhāl**
Herrera del Duque Spain 57 D4
Herrieden Germany 53 K5
Hershey U.S.A. 135 G3
Hertford U.K. 49 G7
Hertzogville S. Africa 101 G5
Herve Belgium 52 F4
Hervé, Lac *l.* Canada 123 H3
Hervey Islands Cook Is 151 J7
Herzberg *Brandenburg* Germany 53 M2
Herzberg *Brandenburg* Germany 53 N3
Herzlake Germany 53 H2
Herzliyya Israel 85 B3
Herzogenaurach Germany 53 K5
Herzsprung Germany 53 M1
Ḩeşār Iran 88 C4
Ḩeşār Iran 88 E5
Hesdin France 52 C4
Hesel Germany 53 H1
Heshan China 77 F4
Heshengqiao China 77 G2
Hesperia U.S.A. 128 E4
Hesperus U.S.A. 129 I3
Hesperus Peak U.S.A. 129 I3
Hesquiat Canada 120 E5
Hess *r.* Canada 120 C2
Heßdorf Germany 53 K5
Hesse *land* Germany *see* **Hessen**
Hesselberg *hill* Germany 53 K5
Hessen *land* Germany 53 J4
Hessisch Lichtenau Germany 53 J3
Hess Mountains Canada 120 C2
Het *r.* Laos 70 D2
Heteren Neth. 52 F3
Hetou China 77 F4
Hettinger U.S.A. 130 C2
Hetton U.K. 48 E4
Hettstedt Germany 53 L3
Heung Kong Tsai *H.K.* China *see* **Aberdeen**
Hevron West Bank *see* **Hebron**
Hexham U.K. 48 E4
Hexian *Anhui* China 77 H2
Hexian *Guangxi* China *see* **Hezhou**
Heyang China 77 F1
Ḩeydarābād Iran 88 B2
Ḩeydarābād Iran 89 F4
Heydebreck Poland *see* **Kędzierzyn-Koźle**
Heysham U.K. 48 E4
Heyshope Dam S. Africa 101 J4
Heyuan China 77 G4
Heywood U.K. 48 E5
Heze China 77 G1
Hezhang China 76 E3
Hezheng China 76 D1
Hezhou China 77 F3
Hezuo China 76 D1
Hezuozhen China *see* **Hezuo**
Hialeah U.S.A. 133 D7
Hiawassee U.S.A. 133 D5
Hiawatha U.S.A. 130 E4
Hibbing U.S.A. 130 E2
Hibbs, Point Australia 111 [inset]
Hibernia Reef Australia 108 C3
Hīchān Iran 89 F5
Hicks, Point Australia 112 D6
Hicks Bay N.Z. 113 G3
Hicks Lake Canada 121 K2
Hicksville U.S.A. 134 C3
Hico U.S.A. 131 D5
Hidaka-sanmyaku *mts* Japan 74 F4
Hidalgo Mex. 131 D7
Hidalgo del Parral Mex. 131 B7
Hidrolândia Brazil 145 A2
Hierosolyma Israel/West Bank *see*
Jerusalem
Higashi-suidō *sea chan.* Japan 75 C6
Higgins U.S.A. 131 C4
Higgins Bay U.S.A. 135 H2
Higgins Lake U.S.A. 134 C1
High Atlas *mts* Morocco *see* **Haut Atlas**
High Desert U.S.A. 126 C4
High Island *i. H.K.* China 77 [inset]
High Island U.S.A. 131 E6
High Island Reservoir *H.K.* China 77 [inset]
Highland Peak *CA* U.S.A. 128 D2
Highland Peak *NV* U.S.A. 129 F3
Highlands U.S.A. 135 I3
Highland Springs U.S.A. 135 G5
High Level Canada 120 G3
Highmore U.S.A. 130 D2
High Point U.S.A. 132 E5
High Point *hill* U.S.A. 135 H3
High Prairie Canada 120 G4
High River Canada 120 H5
Highrock Lake *Man.* Canada 121 K4
Highrock Lake *Sask.* Canada 121 J3
High Springs U.S.A. 133 D6
High Tatras *mts* Poland/Slovakia *see*
Tatra Mountains
High Wycombe U.K. 49 G7
Higuera de Zaragoza Mex. 127 F8
Higüey Dom. Rep. 137 K5
Hiiumaa *i.* Estonia 45 M7
Hijānah, Buḩayrat al *imp. l.* Syria 85 C3
Hijaz *reg.* Saudi Arabia 86 E4
Ḩikmah, Ra's al *pt* Egypt 90 B5
Hiko U.S.A. 129 F3
Hikone Japan 75 E6
Hikurangi *mt.* N.Z. 113 G3
Hila Indon. 108 D1
Hilāl, Jabal *hill* Egypt 85 A4
Hilāl, Ra's al *pt* Libya 86 B3
Hilary Coast Antarctica 152 H1
Hildale U.S.A. 129 G3
Hildburghausen Germany 53 K4
Hilders Germany 53 K4
Hildesheim Germany 53 J2
Hillah Iraq 91 G4
Hill City U.S.A. 130 D4
Hillegom Neth. 52 E2
Hill End Australia 112 D4
Hillerød Denmark 45 H9
Hillgrove Australia 110 D3
Hill Island Lake Canada 121 I2
Hillman U.S.A. 134 D1
Hillsboro *ND* U.S.A. 130 D2
Hillsboro *NM* U.S.A. 127 G6
Hillsboro *OH* U.S.A. 134 D4
Hillsboro *OR* U.S.A. 126 C3
Hillsboro *TX* U.S.A. 131 D5
Hillsdale *IN* U.S.A. 134 B4
Hillsdale *MI* U.S.A. 134 C3

Hillside Australia 108 B5
Hillston Australia 112 B4
Hillsville U.S.A. 134 E5
Hilo U.S.A. 127 [inset]
Hilton Australia 110 B4
Hilton S. Africa 101 J5
Hilton U.S.A. 135 G2
Hilton Head Island U.S.A. 133 D5
Hilvan Turkey 90 E3
Hilversum Neth. 52 F2
Himachal Pradesh *state* India 82 D3
Himalaya *mts* Asia 82 D2
Himalchul *mt.* Nepal 83 F3
Himanka Fin. 44 M4
Ḩimār, Wādī al *watercourse* Syria/Turkey
85 D1
Himarë Albania 59 H4
Himatnagar India 82 C5
Himeji Japan 75 D6
Ḩimş Syria *see* **Homs**
Ḩimş, Baḩrat *resr* Syria *see*
Qaţţīnah, Buḩayrat
Hinchinbrook Island Australia 110 D3
Hinckley U.K. 49 F6
Hinckley *MN* U.S.A. 130 E2
Hinckley *UT* U.S.A. 129 G2
Hinckley Reservoir U.S.A. 135 H2
Hindaun India 82 D4
Hinderwell U.K. 48 G4
Hindley U.K. 48 E5
Hindman U.S.A. 134 D5
Hindmarsh, Lake *dry lake* Australia 111 C8
Hindu Kush *mts* Afgh./Pak. 89 G3
Hindupur India 84 C3
Hines Creek Canada 120 G3
Hinesville U.S.A. 133 D6
Hinganghat India 84 C1
Hingoli India 84 C2
Hınıs Turkey 91 F3
Hinnøya *i.* Norway 44 I2
Hinojosa del Duque Spain 57 D4
Hinsdale U.S.A. 135 I2
Hinte Germany 53 H1
Hinthada Myanmar 70 A3
Hinton Canada 120 G4
Hinton U.S.A. 134 E5
Hiort *i.* U.K. *see* **St Kilda**
Hippolytushoef Neth. 52 E2
Hipponium Italy *see* **Vibo Valentia**
Hippo Regius Alg. *see* **Annaba**
Hippo Zarytus Tunisia *see* **Bizerte**
Hirabit Dağ *mt.* Turkey 91 G3
Hirakud Dam India 83 E5
Hirakud Reservoir India 83 E5
Hirapur India 82 D4
Hiriyur India 84 C3
Hirosaki Japan 74 F4
Hiroshima Japan 75 D6
Hirschaid Germany 53 L5
Hirschberg Germany 53 L4
Hirschberg *mt.* Germany 47 M7
Hirschberg Poland *see* **Jelenia Góra**
Hirschenstein *mt.* Germany 53 M6
Hirson France 52 E5
Hîrşova Romania *see* **Hârşova**
Hirta *is* U.K. *see* **St Kilda**
Hirtshals Denmark 45 F8
Hisar India 82 C3
Hisar Iran 88 C2
Hisarköy Turkey *see* **Domaniç**
Hisarönü Turkey 59 O4
Ḩisb, Sha'īb *watercourse* Iraq 91 G5
Ḩisbān Jordan 85 B4
Hisiu P.N.G. 69 L8
Hisor Tajik. 89 H2
Hisor Tizmasi *mts* Tajik./Uzbek. *see*
Gissar Range
Hispalis Spain *see* **Seville**
Hispania *country* Europe *see* **Spain**

▶**Hispaniola** *i.* Caribbean Sea 137 J4
Consists of the Dominican Republic and Haiti.

Hispur Glacier Pak. 82 C1
Hissar India *see* **Hisar**
Hisua India 83 F4
Ḩisyah Syria 85 C2
Hīt Iraq 91 F4
Hitachi Japan 75 F5
Hitachinaka Japan 75 F5
Hitra *i.* Norway 44 F5
Hitzacker Germany 53 L1
Hiva Oa *i.* Fr. Polynesia 151 K6
Hixon Canada 120 F4
Hixson Cay *reef* Australia 110 F4
Hiyyon *watercourse* Israel 85 B4
Hizan Turkey 91 F3
Hjälmaren *l.* Sweden 45 I7
Hjerkinn Norway 44 F5
Hjo Sweden 45 I7
Hjørring Denmark 45 G8
Hkakabo Razi *mt.* China/Myanmar 76 C2
Hlaingdet Myanmar 70 B2
Hlako Kangri *mt.* China *see* **Lhagoi Kangri**
Hlane Royal National Park Swaziland
101 J4
Hlatikulu Swaziland 101 J4
Hlegu Myanmar 70 B3
Hlohlowane S. Africa 101 H5
Hlotse Lesotho 101 I5
Hluhluwe-Umfolozi Park *nature res.*
S. Africa 101 J5
Hlukhiv Ukr. 43 G6
Hlung-Tan Myanmar 70 B2
Hlusha Belarus 43 F5
Hlybokaye Belarus 45 O9
Ho Ghana 96 D4
Hoa Binh Vietnam 70 D2
Hoa Binh Vietnam 70 D3
Hoachanas Namibia 100 D2
Hoagland U.S.A. 134 C3
Hoang Liên Sơn *mts* Vietnam 70 C2
Hoang Sa *is* S. China Sea *see*
Paracel Islands
Hoan Lao Vietnam 70 D3

▶**Hobart** Australia 111 [inset]
Capital of Tasmania.

Hobart U.S.A. 131 D5
Hobbs U.S.A. 131 C5

Hobbs Coast Antarctica 152 J1
Hobe Sound U.S.A. 133 D7
Hobiganj Bangl. *see* **Habiganj**
Hobro Denmark 45 F8
Hobyo Somalia 98 E3
Hoceima, Baie d'Al *b.* Morocco 57 E6
Höchberg Germany 53 J5
Hochfeiler *mt.* Austria/Italy *see*
Gran Pilastro
Hochfeld Namibia 99 B6
Hochharz *nat. park* Germany 53 K3
Hô Chi Minh Vietnam *see*
Ho Chi Minh City
Ho Chi Minh City Vietnam 71 D5
Hochschwab *mt.* Austria 47 O7
Hochschwab *mts* Austria 47 O7
Hockenheim Germany 53 I5
Ḩôḑ *reg.* Mauritania 96 C3
Hoddesdon U.K. 49 G7
Hodeidah Yemen 86 F7
Hodgenville U.S.A. 134 C5
Hodgson Downs Australia 108 F3
Hódmezővásárhely Hungary 59 I1
Hodna, Chott el *salt l.* Alg. 57 I6
Hodo-dan *pt* N. Korea 75 B5
Hoek van Holland Neth. *see*
Hook of Holland
Hoensbroek Neth. 52 F4
Hoeryŏng N. Korea 74 C4
Hof Germany 53 L4
Hoffman Mountain U.S.A. 135 I2
Hofheim in Unterfranken
Germany 53 K4
Hofmeyr S. Africa 101 G6
Höfn Iceland 44 [inset]
Hofors Sweden 45 J6
Hofsjökull *ice cap* Iceland 44 [inset]
Hofsós Iceland 44 [inset]
Hōfu Japan 75 C6
Hofūf Saudi Arabia 86 G4
Höganäs Sweden 45 H8
Hogan Group *is* Australia 112 C7
Hogansburg U.S.A. 135 H1
Hogback Mountain U.S.A. 130 C3
Hoge Vaart *canal* Neth. 52 F2
Hogg, Mount Canada 120 C2
Hoggar *plat.* Alg. 96 D2
Hog Island U.S.A. 135 H5
Högsby Sweden 45 J8
Hohenloher Ebene *plain* Germany 53 J5
Hohenmölsen Germany 53 M3
Hohennauen Germany 53 M2
Hohensalza Poland *see* **Inowrocław**
Hohenwald U.S.A. 132 C5
Hohenwartetalsperre *resr* Germany 53 L4
Hoher Dachstein *mt.* Austria 47 N7
Hohe Rhön *mts* Germany 53 J4
Hohe Tauern *mts* Austria 47 N7
Hohe Venn *moorland* Belgium 52 G4
Hohhot China 73 K4
Höhmorït Mongolia 80 H2
Hohneck *mt.* France 56 H2
Hoh Sai Hu *l.* China 83 H2
Hoh Xil Hu *salt l.* China 83 G2
Hoh Xil Shan *mts* China 83 G2
Hôi An Vietnam 70 E4
Hoima Uganda 98 D3
Hojagala Turkm. 88 E2
Hojai India 83 H4
Hojambaz Turkm. 89 G2
Højryggen *mts* Greenland 119 M2
Hokitika N.Z. 113 C6
Hokkaidō *i.* Japan 74 F4
Hokksund Norway 45 F7
Hol Norway 45 F6
Holbæk Denmark 45 G9
Holbeach U.K. 49 H6
Holbrook Australia 112 C5
Holbrook U.S.A. 129 H4
Holden U.S.A. 129 G2
Holdenville U.S.A. 131 D5
Holdrege U.S.A. 130 D3
Holgate U.S.A. 134 C3
Holguín Cuba 137 I4
Höljes Sweden 45 H6
Holland *country* Europe *see* **Netherlands**
Holland *MI* U.S.A. 134 B2
Holland *NY* U.S.A. 135 F2
Hollandia Indon. *see* **Jayapura**
Hollick-Kenyon Peninsula
Antarctica 152 L2
Hollick-Kenyon Plateau Antarctica 152 K1
Hollidaysburg U.S.A. 135 F3
Hollis *AK* U.S.A. 120 C4
Hollis *OK* U.S.A. 131 D5
Hollister U.S.A. 128 C3
Holly U.S.A. 134 D2
Hollyhill U.S.A. 134 C5
Holly Springs U.S.A. 131 F5
Hollywood *CA* U.S.A. 129 D4
Hollywood *FL* U.S.A. 133 D7
Holm Norway 44 H4
Holmes Reef Australia 110 D3
Holmestrand Norway 45 G7
Holmgard Rus. Fed. *see* **Velikiy Novgorod**
Holm Ø *i.* Greenland *see* **Kiatassuaq**
Holmön *i.* Sweden 44 L5
Holmsund Sweden 44 L5
Holon Israel 85 B3
Holoog Namibia 100 C4
Holothuria Banks *reef* Australia 108 D3
Holroyd *r.* Australia 110 C2
Holstebro Denmark 45 F8
Holstein U.S.A. 130 E3
Holsteinsborg Greenland *see* **Sisimiut**
Holston *r.* U.S.A. 132 D4
Holsworthy U.K. 49 C8
Holt U.K. 49 I6
Holt U.S.A. 134 C2
Holton U.S.A. 134 B2
Holwerd Neth. 52 F1
Holwert Neth. *see* **Holwerd**
Holycross Ireland 51 E5
Holy Cross U.S.A. 118 C3
Holy Cross, Mount of the U.S.A. 126 G5
Holyhead U.K. 48 C5
Holyhead Bay U.K. 48 C5
Holy Island *England* U.K. 48 F3
Holy Island *Wales* U.K. 48 C5
Holyoke U.S.A. 130 C3
Holy See Europe *see* **Vatican City**
Holywell U.K. 48 D5

Holzhausen Germany 53 M3
Holzkirchen Germany 47 M7
Holzminden Germany 53 J3
Homand Iran 89 E3
Homāyūnshahr Iran *see* **Khomeynīshahr**
Homberg (Efze) Germany 53 J3
Hombori Mali 96 C3
Homburg Germany 53 H5
Home Bay Canada 119 L3
Homécourt France 52 F5
Homer *GA* U.S.A. 133 D5
Homer *LA* U.S.A. 131 E5
Homer *MI* U.S.A. 134 C2
Homer *NY* U.S.A. 135 G2
Homerville U.S.A. 133 D6
Homestead Australia 110 D4
Homnabad India 84 C2
Homoine Moz. 101 L2
Homs Libya *see* **Al Khums**
Homs Syria 85 C2
Homyel' Belarus 43 F5
Honan *prov.* China *see* **Henan**
Honavar India 84 B3
Honaz Turkey 59 M6
Hon Chông Vietnam 71 D5
Hondeklipbaai S. Africa 100 C6
Hondo U.S.A. 131 D6
Hondsrug *reg.* Neth. 52 G1

▶**Honduras** *country* Central America 137 G6
5th largest country in Central and North America.

Hønefoss Norway 45 G6
Honesdale U.S.A. 135 H3
Honey Lake *salt l.* U.S.A. 128 C1
Honeyoye Lake U.S.A. 135 G2
Honfleur France 56 E2
Hong, Mouths of the Vietnam *see* **Red River, Mouths of the**
Hông, Sông *r.* Vietnam *see* **Red**
Hongchuan China *see* **Hongya**
Hongguo China *see* **Panxian**
Honghai Wan *b.* China 77 G4
Honghe China 76 D4
Hong He *r.* China 77 G1
Honghu China 77 G2
Hongjiang *Hunan* China 77 F3
Hongjiang *Sichuan* China *see* **Wangcang**
Hong Kong *H.K.* China 77 [inset]
Hong Kong *aut. reg.* China 77 [inset]
Hong Kong Harbour *sea chan. H.K.* China 77 [inset]
Hong Kong Island *H.K.* China 77 [inset]
Hongliuwan China *see* **Aksay**
Hongliuyuan China 80 I3
Hongqiao China *see* **Qidong**
Hongqizhen China *see* **Wuzhishan**
Hongqizhen *Hainan* China *see* **Wuzhishan**
Hongshi China 74 B4
Hongshui He *r.* China 76 F4
Honguedo, Détroit d' *sea chan.* Canada 123 I4
Hongwŏn N. Korea 75 B4
Hongxing China 74 A3
Hongya China 76 D2
Hongyuan China 76 D1
Hongze China 77 H1
Hongze Hu *l.* China 77 H1

▶**Honiara** Solomon Is 107 F2
Capital of the Solomon Islands.

Honiton U.K. 49 D8
Honjō Japan 75 F5
Honkajoki Fin. 45 M6
Honningsvåg Norway 44 N1
Honoka'a U.S.A. 127 [inset]

▶**Honolulu** U.S.A. 127 [inset]
Capital of Hawaii.

▶**Honshū** *i.* Japan 75 D6
Largest island in Japan, 3rd largest in Asia and 7th in the world.

Honwad India 84 B2
Hood, Mount *vol.* U.S.A. 126 C3
Hood Point Australia 109 B8
Hood Point P.N.G. 110 D1
Hood River U.S.A. 126 C3
Hoogeveen Neth. 52 G2
Hoogezand-Sappemeer Neth. 52 G1
Hooghly *r. mouth* India *see* **Hugli**
Hooker U.S.A. 131 C4
Hook Head *hd* Ireland 51 F5
Hook of Holland Neth. 52 E3
Hook Reef Australia 110 E3
Hoonah U.S.A. 120 C3
Hooper Bay U.S.A. 153 B2
Hooper Island U.S.A. 135 G4
Hoopeston U.S.A. 134 B3
Hoopstad S. Africa 101 G4
Höör Sweden 45 H9
Hoorn Neth. 52 F2
Hoorn, Îles de *is* Wallis and Futuna Is 107 I3
Hoosick U.S.A. 135 I2
Hoover Dam U.S.A. 129 F3
Hoover Memorial Reservoir U.S.A. 134 D3
Hopa Turkey 91 F2
Hope Canada 120 F5
Hope *r.* N.Z. 113 D6
Hope *AR* U.S.A. 131 E5
Hope *IN* U.S.A. 134 C4
Hope, Lake *salt flat* Australia 109 C8
Hope, Point U.S.A. 118 B3
Hopedale Canada 123 J3
Hopefield S. Africa 100 D7
Hopei *prov.* China *see* **Hebei**
Hope Mountains Canada 123 J3
Hope Saddle *pass* N.Z. 113 D5
Hopes Advance, Baie *b.* Canada 123 H2
Hopes Advance, Cap *c.* Canada 119 L3
Hopes Advance Bay Canada *see* **Aupaluk**
Hopetoun Australia 111 C7
Hopetown S. Africa 100 G5
Hopewell U.S.A. 135 G5
Hopewell Islands Canada 122 F2
Hopin Myanmar 70 B1
Hopkins *r.* Australia 111 C8
Hopkins, Lake *salt flat* Australia 109 E6
Hopkinsville U.S.A. 134 B5
Hopland U.S.A. 128 B2
Hoquiam U.S.A. 126 C3
Hor China 76 D1
Horasan Turkey 91 F2
Hörby Sweden 45 H9

▶**Horizon Deep** *sea feature* S. Pacific Ocean 150 I7
Deepest point in the Tonga Trench, and 2nd in the world.

Horki Belarus 43 F5
Horlick Mountains Antarctica 152 K1
Horlivka Ukr. 43 H6
Hormoz *i.* Iran 88 E5
Hormoz, Kūh-e *mt.* Iran 88 D5
Hormuz, Strait of Iran/Oman 88 E5
Horn Austria 47 O6
Horn *r.* Canada 120 G2
Horn *c.* Iceland 44 [inset]

▶**Horn, Cape** Chile 144 C9
Most southerly point of South America.

Hornavan *l.* Sweden 44 J3
Hornbrook U.S.A. 126 C4
Hornburg Germany 53 K2
Horncastle U.K. 48 G5
Horndal Sweden 45 J6
Horne, Îles de *is* Wallis and Futuna Is *see* **Hoorn, Îles de**
Horneburg Germany 53 J1
Hörnefors Sweden 44 K5
Hornell U.S.A. 135 G2
Hornepayne Canada 122 D4
Hornillos Mex. 127 F8
Hornisgrinde *mt.* Germany 47 L6
Hornkranz Namibia 100 C2
Horn Mountains Canada 120 F2
Hornos, Cabo de Chile *see* **Horn, Cape**
Hornoy-le-Bourg France 52 B5
Horn Peak Canada 120 D2
Hornsby Australia 112 E4
Hornsea U.K. 48 G5
Hornslandet *pen.* Sweden 45 J6
Horodenka Ukr. 43 E6
Horodnya Ukr. 43 F6
Horodok *Khmel'nyts'ka Oblast'* Ukr. 43 E6
Horodok *L'vivs'ka Oblast'* Ukr. 43 D6
Horokanai Japan 74 F3
Horoshiri-dake *mt.* Japan 74 F4
Horqin Youyi Qianqi China *see* **Ulanhot**
Horqin Zuoyi Houqi China *see* **Ganjig**
Horqin Zuoyi Zhongqi China *see* **Baokang**
Horrabridge U.K. 49 C8
Horrocks Australia 109 A7
Horru China 83 G3
Horse Cave U.S.A. 134 C5
Horsefly Canada 120 F4
Horseheads U.S.A. 135 G2
Horse Islands Canada 123 L4
Horseleap Ireland 51 D4
Horsens Denmark 45 F9
Horseshoe Bend Australia 109 F6
Horseshoe Reservoir U.S.A. 129 H4
Horseshoe Seamounts *sea feature* N. Atlantic Ocean 148 G3
Horsham Australia 111 C8
Horsham U.K. 49 G7
Horšovský Týn Czech Rep. 53 M5
Horst *hill* Germany 53 J4
Hörstel Germany 53 H2
Horten Norway 45 G7
Hortobágyi *nat. park* Hungary 59 I1
Horton *r.* Canada 118 F3
Horwood Lake Canada 122 E4
Hösbach Germany 53 J4
Hose, Pegunungan *mts* Malaysia 68 E6
Ḥoseynābād Iran 88 B3
Ḥoseynīyeh Iran 88 C4
Hoshab Pak. 89 F5
Hoshangabad India 82 D5
Hoshiarpur India 82 C3
Hospet India 84 C3
Hospital Ireland 51 D5
Hosséré Vokre *mt.* Cameroon 96 E4
Hosta Butte *mt.* U.S.A. 129 I4
Hotagen *r.* Sweden 44 I5
Hotahudo East Timor *see* **Hatudo**
Hotan China 82 E1
Hotazel S. Africa 100 F4
Hot Creek Range *mts* U.S.A. 128 E2
Hotgi India 84 C2
Hotham *r.* Australia 109 B8
Hoting Sweden 44 J4
Hot Springs *AR* U.S.A. 131 E5
Hot Springs *NM* U.S.A. *see* **Truth or Consequences**
Hot Springs *SD* U.S.A. 130 C3
Hot Sulphur Springs U.S.A. 126 G4
Hottah Lake Canada 120 G1
Hottentots Bay Namibia 100 B4
Hottentots Point Namibia 100 B4
Houdan France 52 B6
Houffalize Belgium 52 F4
Hougang Sing. 71 [inset]
Houghton *MI* U.S.A. 130 F2
Houghton *NY* U.S.A. 135 F2
Houghton Lake U.S.A. 134 C1
Houghton Lake *l.* U.S.A. 134 C1
Houghton le Spring U.K. 48 F4
Houie Moc, Phou *mt.* Laos 70 C2
Houlton U.S.A. 132 H2
Houma China 77 F1
Houma U.S.A. 131 F6
Houmen China 77 G4
House Range *mts* U.S.A. 129 G2
Houston Canada 120 E4
Houston *MO* U.S.A. 131 F4
Houston *MS* U.S.A. 131 F5
Houston *TX* U.S.A. 131 E6
Hout *r.* S. Africa 101 I2
Houtman Abrolhos *is* Australia 109 A7
Houton U.K. 50 F2
Houwater S. Africa 100 F6
Hovd *Hovd* Mongolia 80 H2
Hove U.K. 49 G8
Hoveton U.K. 49 I6
Hovmantorp Sweden 45 I8
Hövsgöl Nuur *l.* Mongolia 80 J1
Howar, Wadi *watercourse* Sudan 86 C6
Howard Australia 110 F5
Howard *PA* U.S.A. 135 G3
Howard *SD* U.S.A. 130 D2
Howard *WI* U.S.A. 134 A1
Howard City U.S.A. 134 C2
Howard Lake Canada 121 J2
Howden U.K. 48 G5
Howe, Cape Australia 112 D6
Howe, Mount Antarctica 152 J1
Howell U.S.A. 134 D2
Howick Canada 135 I1
Howick S. Africa 101 J5
Howland U.S.A. 132 G2

▶**Howland Island** *terr.* N. Pacific Ocean 107 I1
United States Unincorporated Territory.

Howlong Australia 112 C5
Howrah India *see* **Haora**
Howth Ireland 51 F4
Ḥowz̧ *well* Iran 88 E3
Ḥowz̧-e Khān *well* Iran 88 E3
Ḥowz̧-e Panj Iran 88 E4
Ḥowz̧-e Panj *waterhole* Iran 88 D3
Howz i-Mian i-Tak Iran 88 D3
Hô Xa Vietnam 70 D3
Höxter Germany 53 J3
Hoy *i.* U.K. 50 F2
Hoya Germany 53 J2
Høyanger Norway 45 E6
Hoyerswerda Germany 47 O5
Høylandet Norway 44 H4
Hoym Germany 53 L3
Höytiäinen *l.* Fin. 44 P5
Hoyt Peak U.S.A. 129 H1
Hpa-an Myanmar 70 B3
Hpapun Myanmar 70 B3
Hradec Králové Czech Rep. 47 O5
Hradiště *hill* Czech Rep. 53 N4
Hrasnica Bos.-Herz. 58 H3
Hrazdan Armenia 91 G2
Hrebinka Ukr. 43 G6
Hrodna Belarus 45 M10
Hrvatska *country* Europe *see* **Croatia**
Hrvatsko Grahovo Bos.-Herz. *see* **Bosansko Grahovo**
Hsenwi Myanmar 70 B2
Hsiang Chang *i. H.K.* China *see* **Hong Kong Island**
Hsiang Kang *H.K.* China *see* **Hong Kong**
Hsi-hseng Myanmar 70 B2
Hsin-chia-p'o *country* Asia *see* **Singapore**
Hsin-chia-p'o Sing. *see* **Singapore**
Hsinchu Taiwan 77 I3
Hsinking China *see* **Changchun**
Hsinying Taiwan 77 I4
Hsipaw Myanmar 70 B2
Hsi-sha Ch'ün-tao *is* S. China Sea *see* **Paracel Islands**
Hsiyüp'ing Yü *i.* Taiwan 77 H4
Hsü-chou *Jiangsu* China *see* **Xuzhou**
Hsüeh Shan *mt.* Taiwan 77 I3
Huab *watercourse* Namibia 99 B6
Huachinera Mex. 127 F7
Huacho Peru 142 C6
Huachuan China 74 C3
Huade China 73 K4
Huadian China 74 B4
Huadu China 77 G4
Hua Hin Thai. 71 B4
Huai'an *Jiangsu* China 77 H1
Huai'an *Jiangsu* China *see* **Chuzhou**
Huaibei China 77 H1
Huaibin China 77 G1
Huaicheng *Guangdong* China *see* **Huaiji**
Huaicheng *Jiangsu* China *see* **Chuzhou**
Huaidezhen China 74 B4
Huaidian China *see* **Shenqiu**
Huai Had National Park Thai. 70 D3
Huaihua China 77 F3
Huaiji China 77 G4
Huai Kha Khaeng Wildlife Reserve *nature res.* Thai. 70 B4
Huailillas *mt.* Peru 142 C5
Huainan China 77 H1
Huaining *Anhui* China 77 H2
Huaining *Anhui* China *see* **Shipai**
Huaiyang China 77 G1
Huaiyin *Jiangsu* China *see* **Huai'an**
Huaiyin *Jiangsu* China 77 H1
Huaiyuan China 77 H1
Huajialing China 76 E1
Huajuápan de León Mex. 136 E5
Hualapai Peak U.S.A. 129 G4
Hualian Taiwan *see* **Hualien**
Hualien Taiwan 77 I3
Huallaga *r.* Peru 142 C5
Huambo Angola 99 B5
Huanan China 74 C3
Huancane Peru 142 E7
Huancavelica Peru 142 C6
Huancayo Peru 142 C6
Huangbei China 77 G3
Huangcaoba China *see* **Xingyi**
Huang-chou *Hubei* China *see* **Huanggang**
Huangchuan China 77 G1
Huanggang China 77 G2
Huang Hai *sea* N. Pacific Ocean *see* **Yellow Sea**
Huang He *r.* China *see* **Yellow River**
Huangjiajian China 77 I1
Huang-kang *Hubei* China *see* **Huanggang**
Huangling China 77 F1
Huangliu China 77 F5
Huanglongsi China *see* **Kaifeng**
Huangmao Jian *mt.* China 77 H3
Huangmei China 77 G2
Huangpu China 77 G4
Huangqi China 77 H3
Huangshan China 77 H2
Huangshi China 77 G2
Huangtu Gaoyuan *plat.* China 73 J5
Huangyan China 77 I2
Huangzhou *Hubei* China *see* **Huanggang**
Huaning China 76 D3
Huanjiang China 77 F3
Huanren China 74 B4
Huanshan China *see* **Yuhuan**
Huánuco Peru 142 C5
Huaping China 76 D3
Huap'ing Yü *i.* Taiwan 77 I3
Huaqiao China 76 E2
Huaqiaozhen China *see* **Huaqiao**
Huaráz Peru 142 C5
Huarmey Peru 142 C6
Huarong China 77 G2
Huascarán, Nevado de *mt.* Peru 142 C5
Huasco Chile 144 B3
Hua Shan *mt.* China 77 F1
Huashixia China 76 C1
Huashugou China *see* **Jingtieshan**
Huashulinzi China 74 B4
Huatabampo Mex. 127 F8
Huaxian *Guangdong* China *see* **Huadu**
Huaxian *Henan* China 77 G1
Huayang China *see* **Jixi**
Huayin China 77 F1
Huayuan China 77 F2
Huayxay Laos 70 C2
Huazangsi China *see* **Tianzhu**
Hubbard, Mount Canada/U.S.A. 120 B2
Hubbard, Pointe *pt* Canada 123 I2
Hubbard Lake U.S.A. 134 D1
Hubbart Point Canada 121 M3
Hubei *prov.* China 77 G2
Hubli India 84 B3
Hückelhoven Germany 52 G3
Hucknall U.K. 49 F5
Huddersfield U.K. 48 F5
Huder China 74 A2
Hudiksvall Sweden 45 J6
Hudson *MA* U.S.A. 135 J2
Hudson *MD* U.S.A. 135 G4
Hudson *MI* U.S.A. 134 C3
Hudson *NH* U.S.A. 135 J2
Hudson *NY* U.S.A. 135 I2
Hudson *r.* U.S.A. 135 I3
Hudson, Baie d' *sea* Canada *see* **Hudson Bay**
Hudson, Détroit d' *strait* Canada *see* **Hudson Strait**
Hudson Bay Canada 121 K4
Hudson Bay *sea* Canada 119 J4
Hudson Falls U.S.A. 135 I2
Hudson Island Tuvalu *see* **Nanumanga**
Hudson Mountains Antarctica 152 K2
Hudson's Hope Canada 120 F3
Hudson Strait Canada 119 K3
Huê Vietnam 70 D3
Huehuetenango Guat. 136 F5
Huehueto, Cerro *mt.* Mex. 131 B7
Huelva Spain 57 C5
Huentelauquén Chile 144 B4
Huépac Mex. 127 F7
Huércal-Overa Spain 57 F5
Huertecillas Mex. 131 C7
Huesca Spain 57 F2
Huéscar Spain 57 E5
Hughenden Australia 110 D4
Hughes *r.* Canada 121 K3
Hughes (abandoned) Australia 109 E7
Hughson U.S.A. 128 C3
Hugli *r. mouth* India 83 F5
Hugo *CO* U.S.A. 130 C4
Hugo *OK* U.S.A. 131 E5
Hugo Lake U.S.A. 131 E5
Hugoton U.S.A. 131 C4
Huhehot China *see* **Hohhot**
Huhhot China *see* **Hohhot**
Huhudi S. Africa 100 G4
Hui'an China 77 H3
Hui'anpu China 72 J5
Huiarau Range *mts* N.Z. 113 F4
Huib-Hoch Plateau Namibia 100 C4
Huichang China 77 G3
Huicheng *Anhui* China *see* **Shexian**
Huicheng *Guangdong* China *see* **Huilai**
Huidong China 76 D3
Huijbergen Neth. 52 E3
Huila, Nevado de *vol.* Col. 142 C3
Huíla, Planalto da Angola 99 B5
Huilai China 77 H4
Huili China 76 D3
Huimanguillo Mex. 136 F5
Huinan China *see* **Nanhui**
Huining China 76 E1
Huishi China *see* **Huining**
Huishui China 76 E3
Huiten Nur *l.* China 83 G2
Huitong China 77 F3
Huittinen Fin. 45 M6
Huixian *Gansu* China 76 E1
Huixian *Henan* China 77 G1
Huiyang China *see* **Huizhou**
Huize China 76 D3
Huizhou China 77 G4
Hujr Saudi Arabia 86 F4
Hukawng Valley Myanmar 70 B1
Hukuntsi Botswana 100 E2
Hulan China 74 B3
Hulan Ergi China 74 A3
Ḥulayfah Saudi Arabia 86 F4
Ḥulayḥilah *well* Syria 85 D2
Huliao China *see* **Dabu**
Hulilan Iran 88 B3
Hulin China 74 D3
Hulin Gol *r.* China 74 B3
Hull Canada 135 H1
Hull U.K. *see* **Kingston upon Hull**
Hull Island *atoll* Kiribati *see* **Orona**
Hultsfred Sweden 45 I8
Hulun China *see* **Hulun Buir**
Hulun *Nei Mongol* China *see* **Hulun Buir**
Hulun Buir China 73 L3
Hulun Nur *l.* China 73 L3
Ḥulwān Egypt 90 C5
Huma China 74 B2
Humahuaca Arg. 144 C2
Humaitá Brazil 142 F5
Humaya *r.* Mex. 127 G8
Humaym *well* U.A.E. 88 D6
Humayyān, Jabal *hill* Saudi Arabia 88 B5
Humber, Mouth of the U.K. 48 H5
Humboldt Canada 121 J4
Humboldt *AZ* U.S.A. 129 G4
Humboldt *NE* U.S.A. 130 E3
Humboldt *NV* U.S.A. 128 D1
Humboldt *r.* U.S.A. 128 D1
Humboldt Bay U.S.A. 126 B4
Humboldt Range *mts* U.S.A. 128 D1
Humbolt Salt Marsh U.S.A. 128 E2
Hume *r.* Canada 120 D1
Humeburn Australia 112 B1
Hu Men *sea chan.* China 77 G4
Hume Reservoir Australia 112 C5
Humphrey Island *atoll* Cook Is *see* **Manihiki**
Humphreys, Mount U.S.A. 128 D3
Humphreys Peak U.S.A. 129 H4
Hūn Libya 97 E2
Húnaflói *b.* Iceland 44 [inset]
Hunan *prov.* China 77 F3
Hundeluft Germany 53 M3
Hunedoara Romania 59 J2
Hünfeld Germany 53 J4
Hungary *country* Europe 55 H2
Hungerford Australia 112 B2
Hung Fa Leng *hill H.K.* China *see* **Robin's Nest**
Hŭngnam N. Korea 75 B5
Hung Shui Kiu *H.K.* China 77 [inset]
Hưng Yên Vietnam 70 D2
Hunjiang China *see* **Baishan**
Huns Mountains Namibia 100 C4
Hunstanton U.K. 49 H6
Hunte *r.* Germany 53 I1
Hunter *r.* Australia 112 E4
Hunter Island Australia 111 [inset]
Hunter Island Canada 120 D5
Hunter Island S. Pacific Ocean 107 H4
Hunter Islands Australia 111 [inset]
Huntingburg U.S.A. 134 B4
Huntingdon Canada 135 H1
Huntingdon U.K. 49 G6
Huntingdon *PA* U.S.A. 135 G3
Huntingdon *TN* U.S.A. 131 F4
Huntington *IN* U.S.A. 134 C3
Huntington *OR* U.S.A. 126 D3
Huntington *WV* U.S.A. 134 D4
Huntington Beach U.S.A. 128 D5
Huntington Creek *r.* U.S.A. 129 F1
Huntly N.Z. 113 E3
Huntly U.K. 50 G3
Hunt Mountain U.S.A. 126 G3
Huntsville Canada 134 F1
Huntsville *AL* U.S.A. 133 C5
Huntsville *AR* U.S.A. 131 E4
Huntsville *TN* U.S.A. 134 C5
Huntsville *TX* U.S.A. 131 E6
Hunza *reg.* Pak. 82 C1
Huolin He *r.* China *see* **Hulin Gol**
Huolongmen China 74 B2
Hương Khê Vietnam 70 D3
Huonville Australia 111 [inset]
Huoqiu China 77 H1
Huoshan China 77 H2
Huo Shan *mt.* China *see* **Baima Jian**
Huoshao Tao *i.* Taiwan *see* **Lü Tao**
Hupeh *prov.* China *see* **Hubei**
Hupnik *r.* Turkey 85 C1
Hupu India 76 B2
Ḥūr Iran 88 E4
Hurault, Lac *l.* Canada 123 H3
Ḥuraydīn, Wādī *watercourse* Egypt 85 A4
Huraysān *reg.* Saudi Arabia 88 B6
Hurd, Cape Canada 134 E1
Hurd Island Kiribati *see* **Arorae**
Hurghada Egypt *see* **Al Ghurdaqah**
Hurler's Cross Ireland 51 D5
Hurley *NM* U.S.A. 129 I5
Hurley *WI* U.S.A. 130 F2
Hurmagai Pak. 89 G4
Huron *CA* U.S.A. 128 C3
Huron *SD* U.S.A. 130 D2

▶**Huron, Lake** Canada/U.S.A. 134 D1
2nd largest lake in North America, and 4th in the world.

Hurricane U.S.A. 129 G3
Hursley U.K. 49 F7
Hurst Green U.K. 49 H7
Husain Nika Pak. 89 H4
Húsavík *Norðurland eystra* Iceland 44 [inset]
Húsavík *Vestfirðir* Iceland 44 [inset]
Huseyinabat Turkey *see* **Alaca**
Huseyinli Turkey *see* **Kızılırmak**
Hushan *Zhejiang* China 77 H2
Hushan *Zhejiang* China *see* **Wuyi**
Hushan *Zhejiang* China *see* **Cixi**
Huşi Romania 59 M1
Huskvarna Sweden 45 I8
Husn Jordan *see* **Al Ḥiṣn**
Ḥuṣn Āl 'Abr Yemen 86 G6
Husnes Norway 45 D7
Husum Germany 47 L3
Husum Sweden 44 K5
Hutag-Öndör Mongolia 80 J2
Hutchinson *KS* U.S.A. 130 D4
Hutchinson *MN* U.S.A. 130 E2
Hutch Mountain U.S.A. 129 H4
Hutou China 74 D3
Hutsonville U.S.A. 134 B4
Hutton, Mount *hill* Australia 111 E5
Hutton Range *hills* Australia 109 C6
Huvadhu Atoll Maldives 81 D11
Hüvek Turkey *see* **Bozova**
Hūvīān, Kūh-e *mts* Iran 89 E5
Ḥuwār *i.* Bahrain 88 C5
Huwaytat *reg.* Saudi Arabia 85 C5
Huxi China 77 G3
Huzhong China 74 A2
Huzhou China 77 I2
Hvannadalshnúkur *vol.* Iceland 44 [inset]
Hvar *i.* Croatia 58 G3
Hvide Sande Denmark 45 F8
Hvíta *r.* Iceland 44 [inset]
Hwange Zimbabwe 99 C5
Hwange National Park Zimbabwe 99 C5
Hwang Ho *r.* China *see* **Yellow River**
Hwedza Zimbabwe 99 D5
Hwlffordd U.K. *see* **Haverfordwest**
Hyannis *MA* U.S.A. 135 J3
Hyannis *NE* U.S.A. 130 C3
Hyargas Nuur *salt l.* Mongolia 80 H2
Hyco Lake U.S.A. 134 F5
Hyde N.Z. 113 C7
Hyden Australia 109 B8
Hyden U.S.A. 134 D5
Hyde Park U.S.A. 135 I1
Hyderabad India 84 C2
Hyderabad Pak. 89 H5
Hydra *i.* Greece *see* **Ydra**
Hyères France 56 H5
Hyères, Îles d' *is* France 56 H5
Hyesan N. Korea 74 C4
Hyland, Mount Australia 112 F3
Hyland Post Canada 120 D3
Hyllestad Norway 45 D6
Hyltebruk Sweden 45 H8
Hyndman Peak U.S.A. 126 E4
Hyōno-sen *mt.* Japan 75 D6
Hyrcania Iran *see* **Gorgān**
Hyrynsalmi Fin. 44 P4
Hysham U.S.A. 126 G3
Hythe Canada 120 G4
Hythe U.K. 49 I7
Hyūga Japan 75 C6
Hyvinkää Fin. 45 N6

Iaciara Brazil 145 B1
Iaco *r.* Brazil 142 E5
Iaçu Brazil 145 C1
Iadera Croatia *see* **Zadar**
Iaeger U.S.A. 134 E5
Iakora Madag. 99 E6
Ialomița *r.* Romania 59 L2
Ianca Romania 59 L2
Iași Romania 59 L1
Iba Phil. 69 F3
Ibadan Nigeria 96 D4
Ibagué Col. 142 C3
Ibaiti Brazil 145 A3
Ibapah U.S.A. 129 G1
Ibarra Ecuador 142 C3
Ibb Yemen 86 F7
Ibbenbüren Germany 53 H2
Iberá, Esteros del *marsh* Arg. 144 E3
Iberia Peru 142 E6

▶**Iberian Peninsula** Europe 57
Consists of Portugal, Spain and Gibralta

Iberville, Lac d' *l.* Canada 123 G3
Ibeto Nigeria 96 D3
iBhayi S. Africa *see* **Port Elizabeth**
Ibi Indon. 71 B6
Ibi Nigeria 96 D4
Ibiá Brazil 145 B2
Ibiaí Brazil 145 B2
Ibiapaba, Serra da *hills* Brazil 143 J4
Ibiassucê Brazil 145 C1
Ibicaraí Brazil 145 D1
Ibiquera Brazil 145 C1
Ibirama Brazil 145 A4
Ibiranhém Brazil 145 C2
Ibitinga Brazil 145 A3
Ibiza Spain 57 G4
Ibiza *i.* Spain 57 G4
Iblei, Monti *mts Sicily* Italy 58 F6
Ibn Buşayyiş *well* Saudi Arabia 88 B5
Ibotirama Brazil 143 J6
Iboundji, Mont *hill* Gabon 98 B4
Ibrā' Oman 88 E6
İbradı Turkey 90 C3
Ibrī Oman 88 E6
Ica *r.* Col. *see* **Putumayo**
Ica Peru 142 C6
Içana Brazil 142 E3
Içana *r.* Brazil 142 E3
Icaria *i.* Greece *see* **Ikaria**
Icatu Brazil 143 J4
Iceberg Canyon *gorge* U.S.A. 129 F3
İçel *Mersin* Turkey *see* **Mersin**

▶**Iceland** *country* Europe 44 [inset]
2nd largest island in Europe.

Iceland Basin *sea feature* N. Atlantic Ocean 148 G2
Icelandic Plateau *sea feature* N. Atlantic Ocean 153 I2
Ichalkaranji India 84 B2
Ichifusa-yama *mt.* Japan 75 C6
Ichinomiya Japan 75 E6
Ichinoseki Japan 75 F5
Ichinskaya Sopka *vol.* Rus. Fed. 65 Q4
Ichkeul, Parc National de l' Tunisia 58 C6
Ichnya Ukr. 43 G6
Ichtegem Belgium 52 D3
Ichtershausen Germany 53 K4
Icó Brazil 143 K5
Iconha Brazil 145 C3
Iconium Turkey *see* **Konya**
Icosium Alg. *see* **Algiers**
Iculisma France *see* **Angoulême**
Icy Cape U.S.A. 118 B2
İd Turkey *see* **Narman**
Idabel U.S.A. 131 E5
Ida Grove U.S.A. 130 E3
Idah Nigeria 96 D4
Idaho *state* U.S.A. 126 E3
Idaho City U.S.A. 126 E4
Idaho Falls U.S.A. 126 E4
Idalia National Park Australia 110 D5
Idar India 82 C5
Idar-Oberstein Germany 53 H5
Ideriyn Gol *r.* Mongolia 80 J2
Idfū Egypt 86 D5
Idhān Awbārī *des.* Libya 96 E2
Idhān Murzūq *des.* Libya 96 E2
Idhra *i.* Greece *see* **Ydra**
Idi Amin Dada, Lake Dem. Rep. Congo/Uganda *see* **Edward, Lake**
Idiofa Dem. Rep. Congo 99 B4
Idivuoma Sweden 44 M2
Idkū Egypt 90 C5
Idle *r.* U.K. 48 G5
Idlewild *airport* U.S.A. *see* **John F. Kennedy**
Idlib Syria 85 C2
Idra *i.* Greece *see* **Ydra**

re Sweden 45 H6
stein Germany 53 I4
utywa S. Africa 101 I7
chevan Armenia see Ijevan
cava Latvia 45 N8
eê Brazil 145 A3
oer Belgium 52 C4
apetra Greece 59 K7
issou, Kolpos b. Greece 59 J4
ijávri l. Norway 44 N2
kara Tanz. 99 D4
lik atoll Micronesia 69 K5
luk atoll Micronesia see Ifalik
nadiana Madag. 99 E6
Nigeria 96 D4
nat Chad 97 E3
rouâne Niger 96 D3
ey Australia 110 C3
ord Norway 44 O1
ghas, Adrar des hills Mali 96 D3
ras, Adrar des hills Mali see
Ifôghas, Adrar des
n Sarawak Malaysia 68 E6
nga Uganda 97 G4
rapava Brazil 145 B3
rka Rus. Fed. 64 J3
tpuri India 84 B2
eti Nigeria see Igbetti
etti Nigeria 96 D4
ir Iran 88 B2
ir Turkey 91 G3
esund Sweden 45 J6
kpak, Mount U.S.A. 118 C3
yar China 89 J2
esias Sardinia Italy 58 C5
esiente reg. Sardinia Italy 58 C5
olik Canada 119 J3
uligaarjuk Canada see
Chesterfield Inlet
ace Canada 121 N5
acio Zaragosa Mex. 127 G7
acio Zaragoza Mex. 131 C8
alina Lith. 45 O9
eada Turkey 59 L4
eada Burnu pt Turkey 59 M4
oitijala India 71 A5
oli S. Africa see Johannesburg
oumenitsa Greece 59 I5
a Rus. Fed. 41 Q4
im Rus. Fed. 41 S3
açu r. Brazil 145 A4
açu, Saltos do waterfall Arg./Brazil see
guaçu Falls
açu Falls Arg./Brazil 144 F3
aí Brazil 145 C1
ala Mex. 136 E5
alada Spain 57 G3
ape Brazil 145 B4
araçu Brazil 145 A3
atama Brazil 145 B3
atemi Brazil 144 F2
atu Brazil 143 K5
azú, Cataratas do waterfall Arg./Brazil
ee Iguaçu Falls
éla Gabon 98 A4
idi, Erg des. Alg./Mauritania 96 C2
nga Tanz. 99 D4
raña Madag. 99 E5
vandhippolhu Atoll Maldives 84 B5
vandiffulu Atoll Maldives see
havandhippolhu Atoll
Bogd Uul mt. Mongolia 80 J3
sy Madag. 99 E6
e-san mt. Japan 75 E5
vi l. Fin. 44 O2
ki r. Fin. 44 N4
lmi Fin. 44 O5
ka Japan 75 C6
u-Ode Nigeria 96 D4
an Armenia 91 G2
uiden Neth. 52 E2
el r. Neth. 52 F2
selmeer l. Neth. 52 F2
r r. France see Yser
ahuk Canada see Sachs Harbour
alinen Fin. 45 M6
geleng S. Africa 101 H3
geng S. Africa 101 H4
pa S. Africa see Cape Town
re Nigeria 96 D4
ia i. Greece 59 L6
st Denmark 45 F8
da Japan 74 F4
a Dem. Rep. Congo 98 C4
timan Bulg. 59 J3
utseng S. Africa 100 G5
Burul Rus. Fed. 43 J7
n Nigeria 96 D4
an S. Korea 75 B6
ngu Tanz. 99 D4
an Phil. 77 I5
samis Kenya 98 D3
n Iran 88 B3
n Nepal 83 F4
Taiwan 77 I3
e Peru 142 E7
va Poland 47 Q4
ārān, Kūh-e mt. Iran 88 E4
à-la-Crosse Canada 121 J4
à-la-Crosse, Lac l. Canada 121 J4
o Dem. Rep. Congo 99 C4
de-France admin. reg. France 52 C6
Europa i. Indian Ocean see
uropa, Île
Kazakh. 41 Q5
r. Ireland 51 C6
et Kenya 98 D3
a Rus. Fed. 42 I3
d Germany 53 K3
d Canada 121 M3
rd U.K. 49 H7
combe Australia 110 D4
combe U.K. 49 C7
z Turkey 90 D2
Turkey 90 C3
Grande, Represa resr Brazil 144 F2
Solteira, Represa resr Brazil 145 A3
vo Port. 57 B3
us Brazil 145 D1
azakh. see Kapchagay
nna Lake U.S.A. 118 C4
Turkey 90 E3

Il'ichevsk Azer. see Şărur
Il'ichevsk Ukr. see Illichivs'k
Ilici Spain see Elche-Elx
Iligan Phil. 69 G5
Ilimananngip Nunaa i. Greenland 119 P2
Il'inka Rus. Fed. 43 J7
Il'inskiy Permskaya Oblast' Rus. Fed. 41 R4
Il'inskiy Sakhalinskaya Oblast'
Rus. Fed. 74 F3
Il'insko-Podomskoye Rus. Fed. 42 J3
Ilion U.S.A. 135 H2
Ilium tourist site Turkey see Troy
Iliysk Kazakh. see Kapchagay
Ilkal India 84 C3
Ilkeston U.K. 49 F6
Ilkley U.K. 48 F5
Illapel Chile 144 B4
Illéla Niger 96 D3
Iller r. Germany 47 L6
Illichivs'k Ukr. 59 N1
Illimani, Nevado de mt. Bol. 142 E7
Illinois r. U.S.A. 130 F4
Illinois state U.S.A. 134 A3
Illizi Alg. 96 D2
Illogwa watercourse Australia 110 A5
Ilm r. Germany 53 L3
Ilmajoki Fin. 44 M5
Il'men', Ozero l. Rus. Fed. 42 F4
Ilmenau Germany 53 K4
Ilmenau r. Germany 53 K1
Ilminster U.K. 49 E8
Ilo Peru 142 D7
Iloilo Phil. 69 G4
Ilomantsi Fin. 44 Q5
Ilong India 76 B3
Ilorin Nigeria 96 D4
Ilovlya Rus. Fed. 43 I6
Ilsede Germany 53 K2
Iluka Australia 112 F2
Ilulissat Greenland 119 M3
Iluppur India 84 C4
Ilva i. Italy see Elba, Isola d'
Imabari Japan 75 D6
Imaichi Japan 75 E5
Imala Moz. 99 D5
Imam-baba Turkm. 89 F2
İmamoğlu Turkey 90 D3
Iman Rus. Fed. see Dal'nerechensk
Iman r. Rus. Fed. 74 D3
Imari Japan 75 C6
Imaruí Brazil 145 A5
Imataca, Serranía de mts Venez. 142 F2
Imatra Fin. 45 P6
Imbituva Brazil 145 A4
imeni 26 Bakinskikh Komissarov Azer. see
Uzboy
imeni Babushkina Rus. Fed. 42 I4
imeni Chapayevka Turkm. see
S. A. Nyýazow Adyndaky
imeni Kalinina Tajik. see Cheshtebe
imeni Kirova Kazakh. see Kopbirlik
imeni Petra Stuchki Latvia see Aizkraukle
imeni Poliny Osipenko Rus. Fed. 74 E1
imeni Tel'mana Rus. Fed. 74 D2
Īmī Eth. 98 E3
Imishli Azer. see İmişli
İmişli Azer. 91 H3
Imit Pak. 82 C1
Imja-do i. S. Korea 75 B6
Imlay U.S.A. 128 D1
Imlay City U.S.A. 134 D2
Imola Italy 58 D2
iMonti S. Africa see East London
Impendle S. Africa 101 I5
Imperatriz Brazil 143 I5
Imperia Italy 58 C3
Imperial CA U.S.A. 129 F5
Imperial NE U.S.A. 130 C3
Imperial Beach U.S.A. 128 E5
Imperial Dam U.S.A. 129 F5
Imperial Valley plain U.S.A. 129 F5
Imperieuse Reef Australia 108 B4
Impfondo Congo 98 B3
Imphal India 83 H4
İmralı Adası i. Turkey 59 M4
İmroz Turkey 59 K4
İmroz i. Turkey see Gökçeada
Imtān Syria 85 C3
Imuris Mex. 127 F7
In r. Rus. Fed. 74 D2
Ina Japan 75 E6
Inambari r. Peru 142 E6
Inari Fin. 44 O2
Inarijärvi l. Fin. 44 O2
Inarijoki r. Fin./Norway 44 N2
Inca Spain 57 H4
İnce Burnu pt Turkey 59 L4
İnce Burun pt Turkey 90 D2
Inch Ireland 51 F5
Inchard, Loch b. U.K. 50 D2
Incheon S. Korea see Inch'ŏn
Inchicronan Lough l. Ireland 51 D5
Inch'ŏn S. Korea 75 B5
Incirli Turkey see Karasu
Indaal, Loch b. U.K. 50 C5
Indalsälven r. Sweden 44 J5
Indalstø Norway 45 D6
Inda Silasē Eth. 98 D2
Indaw Myanmar 70 A2
Indawgyi, Lake Myanmar 76 C3
Indé Mex. 131 B7
Indefatigable Island Galápagos Ecuador see
Santa Cruz, Isla
Independence CA U.S.A. 128 D3
Independence IA U.S.A. 130 F3
Independence KS U.S.A. 131 E4
Independence KY U.S.A. 134 C4
Independence MO U.S.A. 130 E4
Independence VA U.S.A. 134 E5
Independence Mountains U.S.A. 126 D4
Inder China 74 A3
Inderborskiy Kazakh. 78 E2
Indi India 84 C2

▶India country Asia 81 E7
2nd most populous country in the world and in Asia. 3rd largest country in Asia, and 7th in the world.

Indian r. Canada 120 B2
Indiana U.S.A. 134 F3
Indiana state U.S.A. 134 B3
Indian-Antarctic Ridge sea feature
Southern Ocean 150 D9

▶Indianapolis U.S.A. 134 B4
Capital of Indiana.

Indian Cabins Canada 120 G3
Indian Desert India/Pak. see Thar Desert
Indian Harbour Canada 123 K3
Indian Head Canada 121 K5
Indian Lake U.S.A. 135 H2
Indian Lake l. NY U.S.A. 135 H2
Indian Lake l. OH U.S.A. 134 D3
Indian Lake l. PA U.S.A. 135 F3

▶Indian Ocean 149
3rd largest ocean in the world.

Indianola IA U.S.A. 130 E3
Indianola MS U.S.A. 131 F5
Indian Peak U.S.A. 129 G2
Indian Springs IN U.S.A. 134 B4
Indian Springs NV U.S.A. 129 F3
Indian Wells U.S.A. 129 H4
Indiga Rus. Fed. 42 K2
Indigirka r. Rus. Fed. 65 P2
Indigskaya Guba b. Rus. Fed. 42 K2
Indija Serbia 59 I2
Indin Lake Canada 120 H1
Indio U.S.A. 128 E5
Indira Point India see Pygmalion Point
Indira Priyadarshini Pench National Park
India 82 D5
Indispensable Reefs Solomon Is 107 G3
Indjija Serbia see Inđija
Indo-China reg. Asia 70 D3

▶Indonesia country Asia 68 E7
4th most populous country in the world and 3rd in Asia.

Indore India 82 C5
Indrapura, Gunung vol. Indon. see
Kerinci, Gunung
Indravati r. India 84 D2
Indre r. France 56 E3
Indulkana Australia 109 F6
Indur India see Nizamabad
Indus r. China/Pakistan 89 G6
also known as Sênggê Zangbo (China) or Shiquan He (China)
Indus, Mouths of the Pak. 89 G5
Indus Cone sea feature Indian Ocean
149 M4
Indwe S. Africa 101 H6
İnebolu Turkey 90 D2
İnegöl Turkey 59 M4
Inevi Turkey see Cihanbeyli
Inez U.S.A. 134 D5
Infantes Spain see
Villanueva de los Infantes
Infiernillo, Presa resr Mex. 136 D5
Ing, Nam Mae r. Thai. 70 C2
Inga Rus. Fed. 44 S3
Ingalls, Mount U.S.A. 128 C2
Ingelmunster Belgium 52 D4
Ingenika r. Canada 120 E3
Ingersoll Canada 134 E2
Ingham Australia 110 D3
Ingichka Uzbek. 89 G2
Ingleborough hill U.K. 48 E4
Inglefield Land reg. Greenland 119 K2
Ingleton U.K. 48 E4
Inglewood Qld Australia 112 E2
Inglewood Vic. Australia 112 A6
Inglewood U.S.A. 128 D5
Ingoka Pum mt. Myanmar 70 B1
Ingoldmells U.K. 48 H5
Ingolstadt Germany 53 L6
Ingomar Australia 109 F7
Ingomar U.S.A. 126 G3
Ingonish Canada 123 J5
Ingraj Bazar India 83 G4
Ingram U.S.A. 134 F5
Ingray Lake Canada 120 G1
Ingrid Christensen Coast
Antarctica 152 E2
Ingwavuma S. Africa 101 K4
Ingwavuma r. S. Africa/Swaziland see
Ngwavuma
Ingwiller France 53 H6
Inhaca Moz. 101 K3
Inhaca, Península pen. Moz. 101 K4
Inhambane Moz. 101 L2
Inhambane prov. Moz. 101 L2
Inhaminga Moz. 99 D5
Inharrime Moz. 101 L3
Inhassoro Moz. 99 D6
Inhaúmas Brazil 145 B1
Inhobim Brazil 145 C1
Inhumas Brazil 145 A2
Inis Ireland see Ennis
Inis Córthaidh Ireland see Enniscorthy
Inishark i. Ireland 51 B4
Inishbofin i. Ireland 51 B4
Inisheer i. Ireland 51 C4
Inishkea North i. Ireland 51 B3
Inishkea South i. Ireland 51 B3
Inishmaan i. Ireland 51 C4
Inishmore i. Ireland 51 C4
Inishmurray i. Ireland 51 D3
Inishowen pen. Ireland 51 E2
Inishowen Head hd Ireland 51 F2
Inishtrahull i. Ireland 51 E2
Inishturk i. Ireland 51 B4
Injune Australia 111 E5
Inkerman Australia 110 C3
Inklin Canada 120 C3
Inklin r. Canada 120 C3
Inkylap Turkm. 89 F2
Inland Kaikoura Range mts N.Z. 113 D6
Inland Sea Japan see Seto-naikai
Inlet U.S.A. 135 H2
Inn r. Europe 47 M7
Innaanganeq c. Greenland 119 L2
Innamincka Australia 111 C5
Innamincka Regional Reserve nature res.
Australia 111 C5
Inndyr Norway 44 I3
Inner Sound sea chan. U.K. 50 D3
Innes National Park Australia 111 B7
Innisfail Australia 110 D3
Innisfail Canada 120 H4
Innokent'yevka Rus. Fed. 74 C2
Innoko r. U.S.A. 118 C3
Innsbruck Austria 47 M7
Innuksuak r. Canada 122 F2
Inny r. Ireland 51 E4
Inocência Brazil 145 A2
Inongo Dem. Rep. Congo 98 B4
İnönü Turkey 59 N5
Inoucdjouac Canada see Inukjuak
Inowrocław Poland 47 Q4
In Salah Alg. 96 D2
Insch U.K. 50 G3

▶Inscription, Cape Australia 110 B3
Most westerly point of Oceania.

Insein Myanmar 70 B3
Insterburg Rus. Fed. see Chernyakhovsk
Inta Rus. Fed. 41 S2
Interamna Italy see Teramo
Interlaken Switz. 56 H3
International Falls U.S.A. 130 E1
Interview Island India 71 A4
Intracoastal Waterway canal U.S.A. 131 E6
Intutu Peru 142 D4
Inubō-zaki pt Japan 75 F6
Inukjuak Canada 122 F2
Inuvik Canada 118 E3
Inveraray U.K. 50 D4
Inverbervie U.K. 50 G4
Invercargill N.Z. 113 B8
Inverell Australia 112 E2
Invergordon U.K. 50 E3
Inverkeithing U.K. 50 F4
Inverleigh Australia 110 C3
Invermay Canada 121 K5
Inverness Canada 123 J5
Inverness U.K. 50 E3
Inverness CA U.S.A. 128 B2
Inverness FL U.S.A. 133 D6
Inverurie U.K. 50 G3
Investigator Channel Myanmar 71 B4
Investigator Group is Australia 109 F8
Investigator Ridge sea feature Indian Ocean
149 O6
Investigator Strait Australia 111 B7
Inwood U.S.A. 135 F4
Inya Rus. Fed. 80 G1
Inyanga Zimbabwe see Nyanga
Inyangani mt. Zimbabwe 99 D5
Inyokern U.S.A. 128 E4
Inyo Mountains U.S.A. 128 D3
Inyonga Tanz. 99 D4
Inza Rus. Fed. 43 J5
Inzhavino Rus. Fed. 43 I5
Ioannina Greece 59 I5
Iokanga r. Rus. Fed. 42 H2
Iola U.S.A. 130 E4
Iolgo, Khrebet mts Rus. Fed. 80 G1
Iolotan' Turkm. see Ýolöten
Iona Canada 123 J5
Iona i. U.K. 50 C4
Iona, Parque Nacional do nat. park Angola
99 B5
Ione U.S.A. 128 E2
Iongo Angola 99 B4
Ionia U.S.A. 134 C2
Ionia Nisia is Ionia Nisia Greece see
Ionian Islands
Ionian Islands Greece 59 H5
Ionian Sea Greece/Italy 58 H5
Ionioi Nisoi is Ionia Nisia Greece see
Ionian Islands
Ionioi Nisoi is Greece see Ionian Islands
Ios i. Greece 59 K6
Iowa state U.S.A. 130 E3
Iowa City U.S.A. 130 F3
Iowa Falls U.S.A. 130 E3
Ipameri Brazil 145 A2
Ipanema Brazil 145 C2
Ipiría Peru 142 D5
Ipatinga Brazil 145 C2
Ipatovo Rus. Fed. 43 I7
Ipelegeng S. Africa 101 G4
Ipiales Col. 142 C3
Ipiaú Brazil 145 D1
Ipirá Brazil 145 D1
Ipiranga Brazil 145 A4
iPitoli S. Africa see Pretoria
Ipixuna r. Brazil 142 F5
Ipoh Malaysia 71 C6
Iporá Brazil 145 A2
Ippy Cent. Afr. Rep. 98 C3
Ipsala Turkey 59 L4
Ipswich Australia 112 F1
Ipswich U.K. 49 I6
Ipswich U.S.A. 130 D2
Ipu Brazil 143 J4

▶Iqaluit Canada 119 L3
Capital of Nunavut.

Iquique Chile 144 B2
Iquiri r. Brazil see Ituxi
Iquitos Peru 142 D4
Īrafshān reg. Iran 89 F5
Irai Brazil 144 F3
Irakleio Greece see Iraklion
Iraklion Greece 59 K7
Iramaia Brazil 145 C1
Iran country Asia 88 D3
Iran, Pegunungan mts Indon. 68 E6
Īrānshahr Iran 89 F5
Irapuato Mex. 136 D4
Iraq country Asia 91 F4
Irara Brazil 145 D1
Irati Brazil 145 A4
Irayel' Rus. Fed. 42 L2
Irazú, Volcán vol. Costa Rica 137 H7
Irbid Jordan 85 B3
Irbil Iraq see Arbīl
Irbit Rus. Fed. 64 H4
Irecê Brazil 143 J6
Ireland country Europe 51 E4

▶Ireland i. Ireland/U.K. 51
4th largest island in Europe.

Irema Dem. Rep. Congo 98 C4
Irgiz Kazakh. 80 B2
Irgiz r. Kazakh. 80 B2
Iri S. Korea see Iksan
Irian, Teluk b. Indon. see
Cenderawasih, Teluk
Iriba Chad 97 F3
Īrī Dāgh mt. Iran 88 B2
Iriga Phil. 69 G4
Irîgui reg. Mali/Mauritania 96 C3
Iringa Tanz. 99 D4
Iriri r. Brazil 143 H4
Irish Sea Ireland/U.K. 51 G4
Irituia Brazil 143 I4
'Irj well Saudi Arabia 88 C5
Irkutsk Rus. Fed. 72 I2
Irma Canada 121 I4
Irmak Turkey 90 D3
Irminger Basin sea feature
N. Atlantic Ocean 148 F2
Iron Baron Australia 111 B7
Irondequoit U.S.A. 135 G2
Iron Mountain U.S.A. 130 F2
Iron Mountain mt. U.S.A. 129 G3
Iron Range National Park Australia 110 C2
Iron River U.S.A. 130 F2
Ironton MO U.S.A. 130 F4
Ironton OH U.S.A. 134 D4
Ironwood Forest National Monument
nat. park U.S.A. 129 H5
Iroquois r. U.S.A. 134 B3
Iroquois Falls Canada 122 E4
Irosin Phil. 69 G4
Irpen' Ukr. see Irpin'
Irpin' Ukr. 43 F6
'Irq al Ḩarūrī des. Saudi Arabia 88 B5
'Irq Banbān des. Saudi Arabia 88 B5
Irrawaddy r. Myanmar 70 A4
Irrawaddy, Mouths of the Myanmar 70 A4
Irshad Pass Afgh./Pak. 89 I2
Irta Rus. Fed. 42 K3
Irthing r. U.K. 48 E4

▶Irtysh r. Kazakh./Rus. Fed. 80 E1
5th longest river in Asia and 10th in the world, and a major part of the 2nd longest in Asia (Ob'-Irtysh).

Irun Spain 57 F2
Iruña Spain see Pamplona
Iruñea Spain see Pamplona
Irvine U.K. 50 E5
Irvine CA U.S.A. 128 E5
Irvine KY U.S.A. 134 D5
Irvine Glacier Antarctica 152 L2
Irving U.S.A. 131 D5
Irvington U.S.A. 134 B5
Irwin r. Australia 109 A7
Irwinton U.S.A. 133 D5
Isa Nigeria 96 D3
Isaac r. Australia 110 E4
Isabel U.S.A. 130 C2
Isabela Phil. 69 G5
Isabela, Isla i. Galápagos Ecuador
142 [inset]
Isabelia, Cordillera mts Nicaragua 137 G6
Isabella Lake U.S.A. 128 D4
Isachsen, Cape Canada 119 H2
Ísafjarðardjúp est. Iceland 44 [inset]
Ísafjörður Iceland 44 [inset]
Isa Khel Pak. 89 H3
Isar r. Germany 53 M6
Isbister U.K. 50 [inset]
Ischia, Isola d' i. Italy 58 E4
Ise Japan 75 E6
Isère r. France 56 G4
Isère, Pointe pt Fr. Guiana 143 H2
Iserlohn Germany 53 H3
Isernhagen Germany 53 J2
Isernia Italy 58 F4
Ise-shima Kokuritsu-kōen nat. park Japan
75 E6
Ise-wan b. Japan 75 E6
Iseyin Nigeria 96 D4
Isfahan Iran see Eşfahān
Isfana Kyrg. 89 H2
Isheyevka Rus. Fed. 43 K5
Ishigaki Japan 73 M8
Ishikari-wan b. Japan 74 F4
Ishim r. Kazakh./Rus. Fed. 80 D1
Ishinomaki Japan 75 F5
Ishinomaki-wan b. Japan 73 Q5
Ishioka Japan 75 F5
Ishkoshim Tajik. 89 H2
Ishpeming U.S.A. 132 C2
Ishtikhon Uzbek. see Ishtixon
Ishtixon Uzbek. 89 G2
Ishtragh Afgh. 89 H2
Ishurdi Bangl. 83 G4
Ishwardi Bangl. see Ishurdi
Isiboro Sécure, Parque Nacional nat. park
Bol. 142 E7
Isigny-sur-Mer France 49 F9
Işıklar Dağı mts Turkey 59 L4
Işıklı Turkey 59 M5
Isil'kul' Rus. Fed. 64 I4
Isimangaliso Wetland Park nature res.
S. Africa 101 K4
Isipingo S. Africa 101 J5
Isiro Dem. Rep. Congo 98 C3
Isisford Australia 110 D5
Iskateley Rus. Fed. 42 L2
İskenderun Turkey 85 C1
İskenderun Körfezi b. Turkey 85 B1
İskilip Turkey 90 D2
Iskitim Rus. Fed. 64 J4
Iskŭr r. Bulg. 59 K3
Iskushuban Somalia 98 F2
Isla r. Scotland U.K. 50 F4
Isla r. Scotland U.K. 50 G3
Isla Gorge National Park Australia 110 E5
İslahiye Turkey 90 E3
Islamabad India see Anantnag

▶Islamabad Pak. 89 I3
Capital of Pakistan.

Islamgarh Pak. 89 H5
Islamkot Pak. 89 H5
Island r. Canada 120 F2
Ísland country Europe see Iceland
Island U.S.A. 134 B5
Island Falls U.S.A. 132 G2
Island Lagoon salt flat Australia 111 B6
Island Lake Canada 121 M4
Island Lake l. Canada 121 M4
Island Magee pen. U.K. 51 G3
Island Pond U.S.A. 135 J1
Islands, Bay of N.Z. 113 E2
Islay i. U.K. 50 C5

▶Isle of Man terr. Irish Sea 48 C4
United Kingdom Crown Dependency.

Isle of Wight U.S.A. 135 G5
Isle Royale National Park U.S.A. 130 F2
Ismail Ukr. see Izmayil
Ismâ'ilîya Egypt see Al Ismā'īlīyah
Ismâ'ilîya governorate Egypt see
Al Ismā'īlīyah
Ismailly Azer. see İsmayıllı
İsmayıllı Azer. 91 H2
Isojoki Fin. 44 L5
Isoka Zambia 99 D5
Isokylä Fin. 44 O3
Isokyrö Fin. 44 M5
Isola di Capo Rizzuto Italy 58 G5
Ispahan Iran see Eşfahān
Isparta Turkey 59 N6
Isperikh Bulg. 59 L3
Ispikan Pak. 89 F5
İspir Turkey 91 F2
Ispisar Tajik. see Khŭjand
Isplinji Pak. 89 G4
Israel country Asia 85 B4
Israelite Bay Australia 109 C8
Isra'il country Asia see Israel
Isselburg Germany 52 G3
Issia Côte d'Ivoire 96 C4
Issoire France 56 F4
Issyk-Kul' Kyrg. see Balykchy
Issyk-Kul', Ozero salt l. Kyrg. see Ysyk-Köl
Istalif Afgh. 89 H3

▶İstanbul Turkey 59 M4
2nd most populous city in Europe.

İstanbul Boğazı strait Turkey see Bosporus
Īstgāh-e Eznā Iran 88 C3
Istiaia Greece 59 J5
Istik r. Tajik. 89 I2
Istočni Drvar Bos.-Herz. 58 G2
Istra pen. Croatia see Istria
Istres France 56 G5
Istria pen. Croatia 58 E2
Iswardi Bangl. see Ishurdi
Itabapoana r. Brazil 145 C3
Itaberá Brazil 145 A3
Itaberaba Brazil 145 C1
Itaberaí Brazil 145 A2
Itabira Brazil 145 C2
Itabirito Brazil 145 C3
Itabuna Brazil 145 D1
Itacajá Brazil 143 I5
Itacarambi Brazil 145 B1
Itacoatiara Brazil 143 G4
Itaetê Brazil 145 C1
Itagmatana Iran see Hamadān
Itaguaçu Brazil 145 C2
Itaí Brazil 145 A3
Itaiópolis Brazil 145 A4
Itäisen Suomenlahden kansallispuisto
nat. park Fin. 45 O6
Itaituba Brazil 143 G4
Itajaí Brazil 145 A4
Itajubá Brazil 145 B3
Itajuipe Brazil 145 D1
Italia country Europe see Italy
Italia, Laguna l. Bol. 142 F6

▶Italy country Europe 58 E3
5th most populous country in Europe.

Itamarandiba Brazil 145 C2
Itambé Brazil 145 C1
Itambé, Pico de mt. Brazil 145 C2
It Amelân i. Neth. see Ameland
Itampolo Madag. 99 E6
Itanagar India 83 H4
Itanguari r. Brazil 145 B1
Itanhaém Brazil 145 B4
Itanhém Brazil 145 C2
Itanhém r. Brazil 145 D2
Itaobím Brazil 145 C2
Itapaci Brazil 145 A1
Itapajipe Brazil 145 A2
Itapebi Brazil 145 D1
Itapecerica Brazil 145 B3
Itapemirim Brazil 145 C3
Itaperuna Brazil 145 C3
Itapetinga Brazil 145 C1
Itapetininga Brazil 145 A3
Itapeva Brazil 145 A3
Itapeva, Lago l. Brazil 145 A5
Itapicuru Brazil 143 J6
Itapicuru, Serra de hills Brazil 143 I5
Itapicuru Mirim Brazil 143 J4
Itapipoca Brazil 143 K4
Itapira Brazil 145 B3
Itaporanga Brazil 145 A3
Itapuã Brazil 145 A5
Itaqui Brazil 144 E3
Itararé Brazil 145 A4
Itarsi India 82 D5
Itarumã Brazil 145 A2
Itatiba Brazil 145 B3
Itatuba Brazil 142 F5
Itaúna Brazil 145 B3
Itaúnas Brazil 145 D2
Itbayat i. Phil. 69 G2
Itchen Lake Canada 121 H1
Itea Greece 59 J5
Ithaca MI U.S.A. 134 C2
Ithaca NY U.S.A. 135 G2
It Hearrenfean Neth. see Heerenveen
iThekweni S. Africa see Durban
Ith Hils ridge Germany 53 J2
Ithrah Saudi Arabia 85 C4
Itilleq Greenland 119 M3
Itimbiri r. Dem. Rep. Congo 98 C3
Itinga Brazil 145 C2
Itiquira Brazil 143 H7
Itiruçu Brazil 145 C1
Itiúba, Serra de hills Brazil 143 K6
Itō Japan 75 E6
iTswane S. Africa see Pretoria
Ittiri Sardinia Italy 58 C4

Ittoqqortoormiit Greenland 119 P2
Itu Brazil 145 B3
Itu Abu Island Spratly Is 68 E4
Ituaçu Brazil 145 C1
Ituberá Brazil 145 D1
Ituí r. Brazil 142 D4
Ituiutaba Brazil 145 A2
Itumbiara Brazil 145 A2
Itumbiara, Barragem resr Brazil 145 A2
Ituni Guyana 143 G2
Itupiranga Brazil 143 I5
Ituporanga Brazil 145 A4
Iturama Brazil 145 A2
Iturbide Mex. 131 D7
Ituri r. Dem. Rep. Congo 98 C3
Iturup, Ostrov i. Rus. Fed. 74 G3
Itutinga Brazil 145 B3
Ituxi r. Brazil 142 F5
Ītyop'ia country Africa see Ethiopia
Itz r. Germany 53 K5
Itzehoe Germany 47 L4
Iuka U.S.A. 131 F5
Iul'tin Rus. Fed. 65 T3
Ivalo Fin. 44 O2
Ivalojoki r. Fin. 44 O2
Ivanava Belarus 45 N10
Ivanhoe Australia 112 B4
Ivanhoe U.S.A. 130 D2
Ivanhoe Lake Canada 121 J2
Ivankiv Ukr. 43 F6
Ivankovtsy Rus. Fed. 74 D2
Ivano-Frankivs'k Ukr. 43 E6
Ivano-Frankovsk Ukr. see Ivano-Frankivs'k
Ivanovka Rus. Fed. 74 B2
Ivanovo Belarus see Ivanava
Ivanovo tourist site Bulg. 59 K3
Ivanovo Rus. Fed. 42 I4
Ivanteyevka Rus. Fed. 43 K5
Ivantsevichi Belarus see Ivatsevichy
Ivatsevichy Belarus 45 N10
Ivaylovgrad Bulg. 59 L4
Ivdel' Rus. Fed. 41 S3
Ivittuut Greenland 119 N3
Iviza i. Spain see Ibiza
Ivory Coast country Africa see Côte d'Ivoire
Ivrea Italy 58 B2
İvrindi Turkey 59 L5
Ivris Ugheltekhili pass Georgia 91 G2
Ivry-la-Bataille France 52 B6
Ivugivik Canada see Ivujivik
Ivujivik Canada 119 K3
Ivyanyets Belarus 45 O10
Ivydale U.S.A. 134 E4
Iwaki Japan 75 F5
Iwaki-san vol. Japan 74 F4
Iwakuni Japan 75 D6
Iwamizawa Japan 74 F4
Iwo Nigeria 96 D4
Iwye Belarus 45 N10
Ixelles Belgium 52 E4
Ixiamas Bol. 142 E6
Ixmiquilpán Mex. 136 E4
Ixopo S. Africa 101 J6
Ixtlán Mex. 136 D4
Ixworth U.K. 49 H6
İyirmi Altı Bakı Komissarı Azer. see Uzboy
Izabal, Lago de l. Guat. 136 G5
Izberbash Rus. Fed. 91 G2
Izegem Belgium 52 D4
Īzeh Iran 88 C4
Izgal Pak. 89 I3
Izhevsk Rus. Fed. 41 Q4
Izhma Respublika Komi Rus. Fed. 42 L2
Izhma Respublika Komi Rus. Fed. see Sosnogorsk
Izhma r. Rus. Fed. 42 L2
Izmail Ukr. see Izmayil
Izmayil Ukr. 59 M2
İzmir Turkey 59 L5
İzmir Körfezi g. Turkey 59 L5
İzmit Turkey 59 M4
İzmit Körfezi b. Turkey 59 M4
Izozog Bol. 142 F7
Izra' Syria 85 C3
Iztochni Rodopi mts Bulg. 59 K4
Izu-hantō pen. Japan 75 E6
Izuhara Japan 75 C6
Izumo Japan 75 D6

▶Izu-Ogasawara Trench sea feature N. Pacific Ocean 150 F3
5th deepest trench in the world.

Izu-shotō is Japan 75 E6
Izyaslav Ukr. 43 E6
Iz"yayu Rus. Fed. 42 M2
Izyum Ukr. 43 H6

Jabal Dab Saudi Arabia 88 C6
Jabalón r. Spain 57 D4
Jabalpur India 82 D5
Jabbūl, Sabkhat al salt flat Syria 85 C2
Jabir reg. Oman 88 E6
Jabiru Australia 108 F3
Jablah Syria 85 B2
Jablanica Bos.-Herz. 58 G3
Jaboatão Brazil 143 L5
Jaboticabal Brazil 145 A3
Jabung, Tanjung pt Indon. 68 C7
Jacaraci Brazil 145 C1
Jacareacanga Brazil 143 G5
Jacareí Brazil 145 B3
Jacarézinho Brazil 145 A3
Jáchymov Czech Rep. 53 M4
Jacinto Brazil 145 C2
Jack r. Australia 110 D2
Jack Lake Canada 135 F1
Jackman U.S.A. 132 G2
Jacksboro U.S.A. 131 D5
Jackson Australia 112 D1
Jackson AL U.S.A. 133 C6
Jackson CA U.S.A. 128 C2
Jackson GA U.S.A. 133 D5
Jackson KY U.S.A. 134 D5
Jackson MI U.S.A. 134 C2
Jackson MN U.S.A. 130 E3

▶Jackson MS U.S.A. 131 F5
Capital of Mississippi.

Jackson NC U.S.A. 132 E4
Jackson OH U.S.A. 134 D4
Jackson TN U.S.A. 131 F5
Jackson WY U.S.A. 126 F4
Jackson, Mount Antarctica 152 L2
Jackson Head hd N.Z. 113 B6
Jacksonville AR U.S.A. 131 E5
Jacksonville FL U.S.A. 133 D6
Jacksonville IL U.S.A. 130 F4
Jacksonville NC U.S.A. 133 E5
Jacksonville OH U.S.A. 134 D4
Jacksonville TX U.S.A. 131 E6
Jacksonville Beach U.S.A. 133 D6
Jack Wade U.S.A. 118 D3
Jacmel Haiti 137 J5
Jacobabad Pak. 89 H4
Jacobina Brazil 143 J6
Jacob Lake U.S.A. 129 G3
Jacobsdal S. Africa 100 G5
Jacques-Cartier, Détroit de sea chan. Canada 123 I4
Jacques-Cartier, Mont mt. Canada 123 I4
Jacques Cartier Passage Canada see Jacques-Cartier, Détroit de
Jacuí Brazil 145 B3
Jacuípe r. Brazil 143 K6
Jacunda Brazil 143 I4
Jaddangi India 84 D2
Jaddi, Ras pt Pak. 89 F5
Jadebusen b. Germany 53 I1
J. A. D. Jensen Nunatakker nunataks Greenland 119 N3
Jadotville Dem. Rep. Congo see Likasi
Jādū Libya 96 E1
Jaén Spain 57 E5
Ja'farābād Iran 88 E2
Jaffa, Cape Australia 111 B8
Jaffna Sri Lanka 84 C4
Jafr, Qā' al imp. l. Jordan 85 C4
Jagadhri India 82 D3
Jagalur India 84 C3
Jagatsinghapur India see Jagatsinghpur
Jagatsinghpur India 83 F5
Jagdalpur India 84 D2
Jagdaqi China 74 B2
Jagersfontein S. Africa 101 G5
Jaggang China 82 D2
Jaggayyapeta India 84 D2
Jaghīn Iran 88 E5
Jagok Tso salt l. China see Urru Co
Jagsamka China see Luding
Jagst r. Germany 53 J5
Jagtial India 84 C2
Jaguariaíva Brazil 145 A4
Jaguaripe Brazil 145 D1
Jagüey Grande Cuba 133 D8
Jahām, 'Irq des. Saudi Arabia 88 B5
Jahanabad India see Jehanabad
Jahmah well Iraq 91 G5
Jahrom Iran 88 D4
Jaicós Brazil 143 J5
Jaigarh India 84 B2
Jailolo Gilolo i. Indon. see Halmahera
Jainpur India 83 E4
Jaintapur Bangl. see Jaintiapur
Jaintiapur Bangl. 83 H4
Jaipur India 82 C4
Jaipurhat Bangl. see Joypurhat
Jais India 83 E4
Jaisalmer India 82 B4
Jaisamand Lake India 82 C4
Jaitaran India 82 C4
Jaitgarh hill India 84 C1
Jajapur India see Jajpur
Jajarkot Nepal 87 N4
Jajce Bos.-Herz. 58 G2
Jajnagar state India see Orissa
Jajpur India 83 F5
Jakar Bhutan 83 G4

▶Jakarta Indon. 68 D8
Capital of Indonesia. 9th most populous city in the world.

Jakes Corner Canada 120 C2
Jakhau India 82 B5
Jakin mt. Afgh. 89 G4
Jakkī Kowr Iran 89 F5
Jäkkvik Sweden 44 J3
Jakliat India 82 C3
Jakobshavn Greenland see Ilulissat
Jakobstad Fin. 44 M5
Jal U.S.A. 131 C5
Jalaid China see Inder
Jalājil Saudi Arabia 88 B5
Jalālābād Afgh. 89 H3
Jalal-Abad Kyrg. 80 D3
Jalālah al Baḥrīyah, Jabal plat. Egypt 90 C5
Jalalpur Pirwala Pak. 89 H4
Jalāmīd, Ḥazm al ridge Saudi Arabia 91 E5
Jalandhar India 82 C3
Jalapa Mex. 136 E5
Jalapa Enríquez Mex. see Jalapa
Jalasjärvi Fin. 44 M5
Jalaun India 82 D4
Jalawlā' Iraq 91 G4
Jaldak Afgh. 89 G4
Jaldrug India 84 C2
Jales Brazil 145 A3
Jalesar India 82 D4
Jalgaon India 82 C5
Jalībah Iraq 91 G5
Jalingo Nigeria 96 E4
Jallābī Iran 88 E5
Jalna India 84 B2
Jālo Iran 89 F5
Jalón r. Spain 57 F3
Jalor India see Jalore
Jalore India 82 C4
Jalpa Mex. 136 D4
Jalpaiguri India 83 G4
Jālū Libya 97 F2
Jalūlā Iraq see Jalawlā'
Jām reg. Iran 89 F3
Jamaica country West Indies 137 I5
Jamaica Channel Haiti/Jamaica 137 I5
Jamalpur Bangl. 83 G4
Jamalpur India 83 F4
Jamanxim r. Brazil 143 G4
Jambi Indon. 68 C7
Jambin Australia 110 E5
Jambo India 82 C4
Jambuair, Tanjung pt Indon. 71 B6
Jamda India 83 F5
Jamekunte India 84 C2
James r. N. Dakota/S. Dakota U.S.A. 130 D3
James r. VA U.S.A. 135 G5
James, Baie b. Canada see James Bay
Jamesabad Pak. 89 H5
James Bay Canada 122 E3
Jamesburg U.S.A. 135 H3
James Island Galápagos Ecuador see San Salvador, Isla
Jameson Land reg. Greenland 119 P2
James Peak N.Z. 113 B7
James Ranges mts Australia 109 F6
James Ross Island Antarctica 152 A2
James Ross Strait Canada 119 I3
Jamestown Australia 111 B7
Jamestown Canada see Wawa
Jamestown S. Africa 101 H6

▶Jamestown St Helena 148 H7
Capital of St Helena.

Jamestown ND U.S.A. 130 D2
Jamestown NY U.S.A. 134 F2
Jamestown TN U.S.A. 134 C5
Jamkhed India 84 B2
Jammu India 82 C2

▶Jammu and Kashmir terr. Asia 82 D2
Disputed territory (India/Pakistan).

Jamnagar India 82 B5
Jampur Pak. 89 H4
Jamrud Pak. 89 H3
Jämsä Fin. 45 N6
Jamsah Egypt 90 D6
Jämsänkoski Fin. 44 N6
Jamshedpur India 83 F5
Jamtari Nigeria 96 E4
Jamui India 83 F4
Jamuna r. Bangl. see Raimangal
Jamuna r. India see Yamuna
Janā i. Saudi Arabia 88 C5
Janāb, Wādī al watercourse Jordan 85 C4
Janakpur India 83 E5
Janaúba Brazil 145 C1
Jand Pak. 89 I3
Jandaia Brazil 145 A2
Jandaq Iran 88 D3
Jandola Pak. 89 H3
Jandowae Australia 112 E1
Janesville CA U.S.A. 128 C1
Janesville WI U.S.A. 130 F3
Jangada Brazil 145 A4
Jangal Iran 88 E3
Jangamo Moz. 101 L3
Jangaon India 84 C2
Jangipur India 83 G4
Jangngai Ri mts China 83 F2
Jangnga Turkm. see Jaňňa
Jänickendorf Germany 53 N2
Jani Khel Pak. 89 H3

▶Jan Mayen terr. Arctic Ocean 153 I2
Part of Norway.

Jan Mayen Fracture Zone sea feature Arctic Ocean 153 I2
Jaňňa Turkm. 88 D1
Janos Mex. 127 F7
Jans Bay Canada 121 I4
Jansenville S. Africa 100 G7
Januária Brazil 145 B1
Janūb Sīnā' governorate Egypt 85 A5
Janūb Sīnā' governorate Egypt see Janūb Sīnā'
Janzar mt. Pak. 89 F5
Jaodar Pak. 89 F5

▶Japan country Asia 75 D5
10th most populous country in the world.

Japan, Sea of N. Pacific Ocean 75 D5
Japan Alps National Park Japan see Chūbu-Sangaku Kokuritsu-kōen
Japan Trench sea feature N. Pacific Ocean 150 F3
Japiim Brazil 142 D5
Japurá r. Brazil 142 F4
Japvo Mount India 83 H4
Jarābulus Syria 85 D1
Jaraguá Brazil 145 A1
Jaraguá, Serra mts Brazil 145 A4
Jaraguá do Sul Brazil 145 A4
Jarash Jordan 85 B3
Jarboesville U.S.A. see Lexington Park
Jardine River National Park Australia 110 C1
Jardinésia Brazil 145 A2
Jardinópolis Brazil 145 B3
Jargalang China 74 A4
Jargalant Bayanhongor Mongolia 80 I2
Jargalant Hovd Mongolia see Hovd
Jari r. Brazil 143 H4
Järna Sweden 45 J7
Jarocin Poland 47 P5
Jarosław Poland 43 D6
Järpen Sweden 44 H5
Jarqo'rg'on Uzbek. 89 G2
Jarqŭrghon Uzbek. see Jarqo'rg'on
Jarrettsville U.S.A. 135 G4
Jarú Brazil 142 F6
Jarud China see Lubei
Järvakandi Estonia 45 N7
Järvenpää Fin. 45 N6

▶Jarvis Island terr. S. Pacific Ocean 150 J6
United States Unincorporated Territory.

Jarwa India 83 E4
Jashpurnagar India 83 F5
Jāsk Iran 88 E5
Jāsk-e Kohneh Iran 88 E5
Jasliq Uzbek. 91 J2
Jasło Poland 43 D6
Jasol India 82 C4
Jason Islands Falkland Is 144 D8
Jason Peninsula Antarctica 152 L2
Jasonville U.S.A. 134 B4
Jasper Canada 120 G4
Jasper AL U.S.A. 133 C5
Jasper FL U.S.A. 133 D6
Jasper GA U.S.A. 133 C5
Jasper IN U.S.A. 134 B4
Jasper NY U.S.A. 135 G2
Jasper TN U.S.A. 133 C5
Jasper TX U.S.A. 131 E6
Jasper National Park Canada 120 G4
Jasrasar India 82 C4
Jaşşān Iraq 91 G4
Jassy Romania see Iaşi
Jastrzębie-Zdrój Poland 47 Q6
Jaswantpura India 82 C4
Jászberény Hungary 59 H1
Jataí Brazil 145 A2
Jatapu r. Brazil 143 G4
Jath India 84 B2
Jati Pak. 89 H5
Jatibonico Cuba 133 E8
Játiva Spain see Xàtiva
Jatoi Pak. 89 H4
Jat Poti Afgh. 89 G4
Jaú Brazil 145 A3
Jaú r. Brazil 142 F4
Jaú, Parque Nacional do nat. park Brazil 142 F4
Jaua Sarisariñama, Parque Nacional nat. park Venez. 142 F3
Jauja Peru 142 C6
Jaunlutriņi Latvia 45 M8
Jaunpiebalga Latvia 45 O8
Jaunpur India 83 E4
Jauri Iran 89 F4
Java Georgia 91 F2

▶Java i. Indon. 108 A1
5th largest island in Asia.

Javaés r. Brazil see Formoso
Javand Afgh. 89 G3
Javari r. Brazil/Peru see Yavari
Java Ridge sea feature Indian Ocean 149 P6
Java Sea Indon. see Jawa, Laut

▶Java Trench sea feature Indian Ocean 149 P6
Deepest point in the Indian Ocean.

Jävenitz Germany 53 L2
Jävre Sweden 44 L4
Jawa i. Indon. see Java
Jawa, Laut sea Indon. 68 E7
Jawhar India 84 B2
Jawhar Somalia 98 E3
Jawor Poland 47 P5
Jay U.S.A. 131 E4

▶Jaya, Puncak mt. Indon. 69 J7
Highest mountain in Oceania.

Jayakusumu mt. Indon. see Jaya, Puncak
Jayakwadi Sagar l. India 84 B2
Jayantiapur Bangl. see Jaintiapur
Jayapura Indon. 69 K7
Jayawijaya, Pegunungan mts Indon. 69 J7
Jayb, Wādī al watercourse Israel/Jordan 85 B4
Jayfī, Wādī al watercourse Egypt 85 B4
Jaypur India 84 D2
Jayrūd Syria 85 C3
Jayton U.S.A. 131 C5
Jazīreh-ye Shīf Iran 88 C4
Jazminal Mex. 131 C7
Jbail Lebanon 85 B2
J. C. Murphey Lake U.S.A. 134 B3
Jean U.S.A. 129 F4
Jean Marie River Canada 120 F2
Jeannin, Lac l. Canada 123 I2
Jebāl Bārez, Kūh-e mts Iran 88 E4
Jebel, Bahr el r. Sudan/Uganda see White Nile
Jebel Abyad Plateau Sudan 86 C6
Jech Doab lowland Pak. 89 I4
Jedburgh U.K. 50 G5
Jeddah Saudi Arabia 86 E5
Jedeida Tunisia 58 C6
Jeetze r. Germany 53 L1
Jefferson IA U.S.A. 130 E3
Jefferson NC U.S.A. 132 D4
Jefferson OH U.S.A. 134 E3
Jefferson TX U.S.A. 131 E5
Jefferson, Mount U.S.A. 128 E2
Jefferson, Mount vol. U.S.A. 126 C3

▶Jefferson City U.S.A. 130 E4
Capital of Missouri.

Jeffersonville GA U.S.A. 133 D5
Jeffersonville IN U.S.A. 134 C4
Jeffersonville OH U.S.A. 134 D4
Jeffreys Bay S. Africa 100 G8
Jehanabad India 83 F4
Jeju S. Korea see Cheju
Jejuí Guazú r. Para. 144 E2
Jēkabpils Latvia 45 N8
Jelbart Ice Shelf Antarctica 152 B2
Jelenia Góra Poland 47 O5
Jelep La pass China/India 83 G4
Jelgava Latvia 45 M8
Jellico U.S.A. 134 C5
Jellicoe Canada 122 D4
Jelloway U.S.A. 134 D3
Jemaja i. Indon. 71 D7
Jember Indon. 68 E8
Jempang, Danau l. Indon. 68 F7
Jena Germany 53 L4
Jena U.S.A. 131 E6
Jendouba Tunisia 58 C6
Jengish Chokusu mt. China/Kyrg. see Pobeda Peak
Jenīn West Bank 85 B3
Jenkins U.S.A. 134 D5
Jenne Mali see Djenné
Jenner Canada 121 I5
Jennings r. Canada 120 C3
Jennings U.S.A. 131 E6
Jenolan Caves Australia 112 E4
Jenpeg Canada 121 L4
Jensen U.S.A. 129 I1
Jens Munk Island Canada 119 K3
Jeparit Australia 111 C8
Jequié Brazil 145 C1
Jequitaí r. Brazil 145 B2
Jequitinhonha Brazil 145 C2
Jequitinhonha r. Brazil 145 D1
Jerba, Île de i. Tunisia 54 G5
Jerbar Sudan 97 G4
Jereh Iran 88 C4
Jérémie Haiti 137 J5
Jerez Mex. 136 D4
Jerez de la Frontera Spain 57 C5
Jergol Norway 44 N2
Jergucat Albania 59 I5
Jericho Australia 110 D4
Jericho West Bank 85 B4
Jerichow Germany 53 M2
Jerid, Chott el salt l. Tunisia 54 F5
Jerilderie Australia 112 B5
Jerimoth Hill hill U.S.A. 135 J3
Jeroaquara Brazil 145 A1
Jerome U.S.A. 126 E4
Jerruck Pak. 89 H5

▶Jersey terr. Channel Is 49 E9
United Kingdom Crown Dependency.

Jersey City U.S.A. 135 H3
Jersey Shore U.S.A. 135 G3
Jerseyville U.S.A. 130 F4
Jerumenha Brazil 143 J5

▶Jerusalem Israel/West Bank 85 B4
De facto capital of Israel, disputed.

Jervis Bay Australia 112 E5
Jervis Bay b. Australia 112 E5
Jervis Bay Territory admin. div. Australia 112 E5
Jesenice Slovenia 58 F1
Jesenice, Vodní nádrž resr Czech Rep. 53 M4
Jesi Italy 58 E3
Jesselton Sabah Malaysia see Kota Kinabalu
Jessen Germany 53 M3
Jessheim Norway 45 G6
Jessore Bangl. 83 G5
Jesteburg Germany 53 J1
Jesu Maria Island P.N.G. see Rambutyo Island
Jesup U.S.A. 133 D6
Jesús María, Barra spit Mex. 131 D7
Jetmore U.S.A. 130 D4
Jetpur India 82 B5
Jever Germany 53 H1
Jewell Ridge U.S.A. 134 E5
Jewish Autonomous Oblast admin. div. Rus. Fed. see Yevreyskaya Avtonomnaya Oblast'
Jeypur India see Jaypur
Jezzine Lebanon 85 B3
Jhabua India 82 C5
Jhajhar India see Jhajjar
Jhajjar India 82 D3
Jhal Pak. 89 G4
Jhalawar India 82 D4
Jhal Jhao Pak. 89 G5
Jhang Pak. 89 I4
Jhansi India 82 D4
Jhanzi r. India 70 A1
Jhapa Nepal 83 F4
Jharia India 83 F5
Jharkhand state India 83 F5
Jharsuguda India 83 F5
Jhawani Nepal 83 F4
Jhelum r. India/Pak. 89 I4
Jhelum Pak. 89 I3
Jhenaidah Bangl. 83 G5
Jhenaidaha Bangl. see Jhenaidah
Jhenida Bangl. see Jhenaidah
Jhimpir Pak. 89 H5
Jhudo Pak. 89 H5
Jhumritilaiya India 83 F4
Jhund India 82 B5
Jhunjhunun India 82 C3
Jiachuan China 76 E1
Jiachuanzhen China see Jiachuan
Jiading Jiangxi China see Xinfeng
Jiading Shanghai China 77 I2
Jiahe China 77 G3
Jiajiang China 76 D2
Jiamusi China 74 C3
Ji'an Jiangxi China 77 G3
Ji'an Jilin China 74 B4
Jianchuan China 76 C3
Jiande China 77 H2
Jiangbei China see Yubei
Jiangbiancun China 77 G3
Jiangcheng China 76 D4
Jiangcun China 77 F3
Jiangdu China 77 H1
Jiange China see Pu'an
Jianghong China 77 F4
Jiangjin China 76 E2
Jiangjunmiao China 80 G3
Jiangkou Guangdong China see Fengkai
Jiangkou Guizhou China 77 F3
Jiangkou Shaanxi China 76 E1
Jiangling China see Jingzhou
Jiangluozhen China 76 E1
Jiangmen China 77 G4
Jiangna China see Yanshan
Jiangshan China 77 H2
Jiangsi China see Dejiang
Jiangsu prov. China 77 H1
Jiangxi prov. China 77 G3
Jiangxia China 77 G2
Jiangyan China 77 I1
Jiangyin China 77 I2
Jiangyou China 76 E2
Jiangzhesongrong China 83 F3
Jianjun China see Yongshou
Jiankang China 76 D3
Jianli China 77 G2
Jian'ou China 77 H3
Jianping China see Langxi
Jianshe China see Baiyü
Jianshi China 77 F2
Jianshui China 76 D4
Jianshui Hu l. China 83 E2
Jianxing China 76 E2
Jianyang Fujian China 77 H3
Jianyang Sichuan China 76 E2
Jiaochang China 76 D1
Jiaochangba China see Jiaochang
Jiaocheng China see Jiaoling
Jiaohe China 74 B4
Jiaojiang China see Taizhou
Jiaokui China see Yiliang
Jiaoling China 77 H3
Jiaopingdu China 76 D3
Jiaowei China 77 H3
Jiaozuo China 77 G1
Jiasa China 76 D3
Jiashan China see Mingguang
Jia Tsuo La pass China 83 F3
Jiawang China 77 H1
Jiaxian China 77 G1
Jiaxing China 77 I2
Jiayi Taiwan see Chiai
Jiayin China 74 C2
Jiayuguan China 80 I4
Jiazi China 77 H4
Jībūtī country Africa see Djibouti
Jibuti Djibouti see Djibouti
Jiddah Saudi Arabia see Jeddah
Jiddī, Jabal al hill Egypt 85 A4
Jidong China 74 C3
Jiehkkevárri mt. Norway 44 K2
Jieshi China 77 G4
Jieshipu China 76 E1
Jieshi Wan b. China 77 G4
Jiexi China 77 G4
Jiexiu China 73 K5
Jieyang China 77 H4
Jieznas Lith. 45 N9
Jigzhi China 76 D1
Jiḥār, Wādī al watercourse Syria 85 C2
Jih-chao Shandong China see Donggang
Jih-chao Shandong China see Donggang
Jihlava Czech Rep. 47 O6
Jija Sarai Afgh. 89 F3
Jijel Alg. 54 F4
Jijiga Eth. 98 E3
Jījīrud Iran 88 C3
Jijū China 76 D2
Jil'ād reg. Jordan 85 B3
Jilf al Kabīr, Haḍabat al plat. Egypt 86 C5
Jilh al 'Ishār plain Saudi Arabia 88 B5
Jilib Somalia 98 E3
Jilin China 74 B4
Jilin prov. China 74 B4
Jilin Hada Ling mts China 74 B4
Jiliu He r. China 74 A2
Jilo India 82 C4
Jilong Taiwan see Chilung
Jima Eth. 98 D3
Jimda China see Zindo
Jiménez Chihuahua Mex. 131 B7
Jiménez Coahuila Mex. 131 C6
Jiménez Tamaulipas Mex. 131 D7
Jimía, Cerro mt. Hond. 136 G5
Jimsar China 80 G3
Jim Thorpe U.S.A. 135 H3
Jinan China 73 L5
Jin'an China see Songpan
Jinbi China see Dayao
Jinchang China 72 I5
Jincheng Shanxi China 77 G1
Jincheng Sichuan China see Yilong
Jincheng Yunnan China see Wuding
Jinchengjiang China see Hechi
Jinchuan Gansu China see Jinchang
Jinchuan Jiangxi China see Xingan
Jind India 82 D3
Jinding China see Lanping
Jindřichův Hradec Czech Rep. 47 O6
Jin'e China see Longchang
Jingbian China 73 J5
Jingchuan China 76 E1
Jingde China 77 H2
Jingdezhen China 77 H2
Jingellic Australia 112 C5
Jinggangshan China 77 G3
Jinggang Shan hill China 77 G3
Jinggongqiao China 77 H2
Jinggu China 76 D4
Jing He r. China 77 F1
Jinghong China 76 D4
Jingle China 73 K5
Jingmen China 77 G2
Jingpo China 74 C4
Jingpo Hu resr China 74 C4
Jingsha China see Jingzhou
Jingtai China 72 I5
Jingtieshan China 80 I4
Jingxi China 76 E4
Jingxian Anhui China 77 H2
Jingxian Hunan China see Jingzhou
Jingyang China see Jingde
Jingyu China 74 B4
Jingyuan China 72 I5
Jingzhou Hubei China 77 G2
Jingzhou Hubei China 77 G2
Jingzhou Hunan China 77 F3
Jinhe Nei Mongol China 74 A2
Jinhe Yunnan China see Jinping
Jinhu China 77 H1
Jinhua Yunnan China see Jianchuan
Jinhua Zhejiang China 77 H2
Jining Nei Mongol China 73 K4
Jining Shandong China 77 H1
Jinja Uganda 98 D3
Jinjiang Hainan China see Chengmai
Jinjiang Yunnan China 76 D3
Jin Jiang r. China 77 G2
Jinka Eth. 98 D3
Jinmen Taiwan see Chinmen
Jinmen Dao i. Taiwan see Chinmen Tao
Jinmu Jiao pt China 77 F5
Jinning China 76 D3
Jinotepe Nicaragua 137 G6
Jinping Guizhou China 77 F3
Jinping Yunnan China 76 D4
Jinping Yunnan China see Qiubei
Jinping Shan mts China 76 D3
Jinsen S. Korea see Inch'ŏn
Jinsha China 76 E3
Jinsha Jiang r. China 76 E2 see Yangtze
Jinshan Nei Mongol China see Guyang

shan China see **Zhujing**
shan *Yunnan* China see **Lufeng**
shi *Hunan* China **77** F2
shi *Hunan* China see **Xinning**
tur India **84** C2
xi *Anhui* China see **Taihu**
xi *Jiangxi* China **77** H3
xi *Liaoning* China see **Lianshan**
Xi r. China **77** H3
xian China **77** H2
xiang China **77** H1
yun China **77** I2
z, Qā' al *salt flat* Jordan **85** C4
zhai China **77** G2
zhong China **73** K5
zhou China **73** M4
zhu China see **Daocheng**
Paraná Brazil **142** F6
japa Ecuador **142** B4
Qu r. China **76** C2
uiricá Brazil **145** D1
uitaia Brazil **145** D2
', Wādī *watercourse* Egypt **85** A5
nīyāt, Shi'bān al *watercourse*
audi Arabia **85** D4
atol Tajik. **89** H2
r. India **70** A1
ft Iran **88** E4
iban Somalia **98** E3
vān Saudi Arabia **88** C6
van *well* Saudi Arabia **88** C6
ou China **77** F2
ash Shughūr Syria **85** C2
an China see **Lianshan**
a Malaysia **71** C6
r. Romania **59** J3
ding Shan *mt.* China **76** D2
iang *Jiangxi* China **77** G2
iang *Jiangxi* China **77** H2
ian China see **Mojiang**
ing Shan *mts* China **77** G2
ong *H.K.* China see **Kowloon**
ong *Sichuan* China **76** D2
qian China **77** F3
quan China **80** I4
u China **76** E3
zhou Jiang r. China **77** F4
ani Pak. **89** F5
en China **74** A2
Anhui China **77** H2
Heilong. China **74** C3
an China **74** C3
an China **77** G1
h, Ahrāmāt al *tourist site* Egypt see
yramids of Giza
n Saudi Arabia **86** F6
akh Uzbek. see **Jizzax**
ax Uzbek. **89** G1
çaba Brazil **145** A4
ma Brazil **145** C2
o Belo Moz. see **Xai-Xai**
o de Almeida Angola see **Chibia**
o Pessoa Brazil **143** L5
o Pinheiro Brazil **145** B2
quin V. González Arg. **144** D3
Peak U.S.A. **128** D2
eta Germany **53** M4
a India **83** F5
hpur India **82** C4
iya India **82** B5
nsuu Fin. **44** P5
tsu Japan **75** E5
ne Moz. **99** D6
re, Mount Canada **120** H5
bura Nepal **82** E3
eva Estonia **45** O7
jakarta Indon. see **Yogyakarta**
annesburg S. Africa **101** H4
annesburg U.S.A. **128** E4
an Peninsula Canada **119** K2
Pak. **89** G5
n Day U.S.A. **126** D3
n Day r. U.S.A. **126** C3
n D'Or Prairie Canada **120** H3
n F. Kennedy *airport* U.S.A. **135** I3
n H. Kerr Reservoir U.S.A. **135** F5
n Jay, Mount Canada/U.S.A. **120** D3
n o'Groats U.K. **50** F2
nson U.S.A. **130** C4
nsonburg U.S.A. **135** F3
nson City *NY* U.S.A. **135** H2
nson City *TN* U.S.A. **132** D4
nson City *TX* U.S.A. **131** D6
nsondale U.S.A. **128** D4
nson Draw *watercourse* U.S.A. **131** C6
nson's Crossing Canada **120** C2
nston, Lake *salt flat* Australia **109** C8
nston and Sand Islands *terr.*
. Pacific Ocean see **Johnston Atoll**

ohnston Atoll *terr.* N. Pacific Ocean
50 I4
nited States Unincorporated Territory.

nstone U.K. **50** E5
nstone Lake Canada see **Old Wives Lake**
nston Range *hills* Australia **109** B7
nstown Ireland **51** E5
nstown *NY* U.S.A. **135** H2
nstown *PA* U.S.A. **135** F3
or, Selat *strait* Malaysia/Sing. **71** [inset]
or, Sungai r. Malaysia **71** [inset]
or Bahru Malaysia **71** [inset]
ore Bahru Malaysia see **Johor Bahru**
vi Estonia **45** O7
ville Brazil **145** A4
ville France **56** G2
ville Island Antarctica **152** A2
smokk Sweden **44** K3
ulsá á Fjöllum r. Iceland **44** [inset]
ulsá í Fljótsdal r. Iceland **44** [inset]
a Iran **88** B2
et U.S.A. **134** A3
et, Lac *l.* Canada **122** F4
ette Canada **123** G5
Lake Canada **121** H1
Phil. **69** G5
i. Phil. **69** G5
da China **76** C2
ancy U.S.A. **134** D5
ava Lith. **45** N9
Jonê China **76** D1
Jonesboro *AR* U.S.A. **131** F5
Jonesboro *LA* U.S.A. **131** E5
Jones Sound *sea chan.* Canada **119** J2
Jonesville *MI* U.S.A. **134** C3
Jonesville *VA* U.S.A. **134** D5
Jonglei Canal Sudan **86** D8
Jönköping Sweden **45** I8
Jonquière Canada **123** H4
Joplin U.S.A. **131** E4
Joppa Israel see **Tel Aviv-Yafo**
Jora India **82** D4
Jordan *country* Asia **85** C4
Jordan r. Asia **85** B4
Jordan U.S.A. **126** G3
Jordan r. U.S.A. **126** D4
Jordânia Brazil **145** C1
Jordet Norway **45** H6
Jorhat India **83** H4
Jork Germany **53** J1
Jorm Afgh. **89** H2
Jörn Sweden **44** L4
Joroinen Fin. **44** O5
Jørpeland Norway **45** E7
Jos Nigeria **96** D4
José de San Martin Arg. **144** B6
Joseph, Lac *l.* Canada **123** I3
Joseph Bonaparte Gulf Australia **108** E3
Joseph City U.S.A. **129** H4
Joshimath India **82** D3
Joshipur India **84** E1
Joshua Tree National Park U.S.A. **129** F5
Jos Plateau Nigeria **96** D4
Jostedalsbreen Nasjonalpark *nat. park* Norway **45** E6
Jotunheimen Nasjonalpark *nat. park* Norway **45** F6
Jouaiya Lebanon **85** B3
Joubertina S. Africa **100** F7
Jouberton S. Africa **101** H4
Jõuga Estonia **45** O7
Joûnié Lebanon **85** B3
Joure Neth. **52** F2
Joutsa Fin. **45** O6
Joutseno Fin. **45** P6
Jouy-aux-Arches France **52** G5
Jovellanos Cuba **133** D8
Jowai India **83** H4
Jowr Deh Iran **88** C2
Jowzak Iran **89** F4
Joy, Mount Canada **120** C2
Joyce's Country *reg.* Ireland **51** C4
Joypurhat Bangl. **83** G4
Juan Aldama Mex. **131** C7
Juancheng China **77** G1
Juan de Fuca Strait Canada/U.S.A. **124** C2
Juan Fernández, Archipiélago *is* S. Pacific Ocean **151** O8
Juan Fernández Islands S. Pacific Ocean see **Juan Fernández, Archipiélago**
Juanjuí Peru **142** C5
Juankoski Fin. **44** P5
Juan Mata Ortíz Mex. **127** F7
Juaréz Mex. **131** C7
Juárez, Sierra de *mts* Mex. **127** D6
Juàzeiro Brazil **143** J5
Juàzeiro do Norte Brazil **143** K5
Juba r. Somalia see **Jubba**
Juba Sudan **97** G4
Jubany *research station* Antarctica **152** A2
Jubba r. Somalia **98** E4
Jubbah Saudi Arabia **91** F5
Jubbulpore India see **Jabalpur**
Jubilee Lake *salt flat* Australia **109** D7
Juby, Cap c. Morocco **96** B2
Júcar r. Spain **57** F4
Juchitán Mex. **136** E5
Jucuruçu Brazil **145** D2
Jucuruçu r. Brazil **145** D2
Judaberg Norway **45** D7
Judaidat al Hamir Iraq **91** F5
Judayyidat 'Ar'ar *well* Iraq **91** F5
Judenburg Austria **47** O7
Judian China **76** C3
Judith Gap U.S.A. **126** F3
Juegang China see **Rudong**
Juelsminde Denmark **45** G9
Juerana Brazil **145** D2
Jugar China see **Sêrxü**
Jugoslavija *country* Europe see **Yugoslavia**
Juigalpa Nicaragua **137** G6
Juillet, Lac *l.* Canada **123** J3
Juína Brazil **143** G6
Juist *i.* Germany **52** H1
Juiz de Fora Brazil **145** C3
Ju Ju Klu Turkm. **89** F2
Julaca Bol. **142** E8
Julesburg U.S.A. **130** C3
Julia Brazil **142** E4
Juliaca Peru **142** D7
Julia Creek Australia **110** C4
Julian U.S.A. **128** E5
Julian, Lac *l.* Canada **122** F3
Julianadorp Neth. **52** E2
Julian Alps *mts* Slovenia see **Julijske Alpe**
Julianatop *mt.* Indon. see **Mandala, Puncak**
Juliana Top *mt.* Suriname **143** G3
Julianehåb Greenland see **Qaqortoq**
Jülich Germany **52** G4
Julijske Alpe *mts* Slovenia **58** E1
Julimes Mex. **131** B6
Juliomagus France see **Angers**
Julius, Lake Australia **110** B4
Jullundur India see **Jalandhar**
Juma Uzbek. **89** G2
Jumbilla Peru **142** C5
Jumilla Spain **57** F4
Jumla Nepal **83** E3
Jümme r. Germany **53** H1
Jumna r. India see **Yamuna**
Jump r. U.S.A. **130** F2
Junagadh India **82** B5
Junagarh India **84** D2
Junan China **77** H1
Junayfah Egypt **85** A4
Junbuk Iran **88** E3
Junction *TX* U.S.A. **131** D6
Junction *UT* U.S.A. **129** G2
Junction City *KS* U.S.A. **130** D4
Junction City *KY* U.S.A. **134** C5
Junction City *OR* U.S.A. **126** C3
Jundiaí Brazil **145** B3
Jundian China **77** F1

▶Juneau *AK* U.S.A. **120** C3
Capital of Alaska.

Juneau *WI* U.S.A. **130** F3
Juneau Icefield Canada **120** C3
Junee Australia **112** C5
Jûn el Khudr *b.* Lebanon **85** B3
Jungar Qi China see **Shagedu**
Jungfrau *mt.* Switz. **56** H3
Junggar Pendi *basin* China **80** G2
Juniata r. U.S.A. **135** G3
Junín Arg. **144** D4
Junín Peru **142** C6
Junior U.S.A. **134** F4
Juniper Mountain U.S.A. **129** I1
Juniper Mountains U.S.A. **129** G4
Junipero Serro Peak U.S.A. **128** C3
Junlian China **76** E2
Junmenling China **77** G3
Juno U.S.A. **131** C6
Junsele Sweden **44** J5
Junshan Hu *l.* China **77** H2
Junxi China see **Datian**
Junxian China see **Danjiangkou**
Ju'nyung China **76** C1
Ju'nyunggoin China see **Ju'nyung**
Juodupė Lith. **45** N8
Jupiá Brazil **145** A3
Jupía, Represa *resr* Brazil **145** A3
Jupiter U.S.A. **133** D7
Juquiá r. Brazil **145** B4
Jur r. Sudan **86** C8
Jura *mts* France/Switz. **56** G4
Jura *i.* U.K. **50** D4
Jura, Sound of *sea chan.* U.K. **50** D5
Juraci Brazil **145** C1
Jurbarkas Lith. **45** M9
Jurf ad Darāwīsh Jordan **85** B4
Jürgenstorf Germany **53** M1
Jūrmala Latvia **45** M8
Jurmu Fin. **44** O4
Jurong Sing. **71** [inset]
Jurong, Sungai r. Sing. **71** [inset]
Jurong Island *reg.* Sing. **71** [inset]
Juruá r. Brazil **142** E4
Juruena r. Brazil **143** G5
Juruti Brazil **143** G4
Jurva Fin. **44** L5
Jūshqān Iran **88** E2
Jūsīyah Syria **85** C2
Jussara Brazil **145** A1
Justice U.S.A. **134** E5
Jutaí Brazil **142** E5
Jutaí r. Brazil **142** E4
Jüterbog Germany **53** N3
Jutiapa Guat. **136** G6
Juticalpa Hond. **137** G6
Jutis Sweden **44** J3
Jutland *pen.* Denmark **45** F8
Juuka Fin. **44** P5
Juva Fin. **44** O6
Juwain Afgh. **89** F4
Juye China **77** H1
Jūyom Iran **88** D4
Južnoukrajinsk Ukr. see **Yuzhnoukrayinsk**
Jwaneng Botswana **100** G3
Jylland *pen.* Denmark see **Jutland**
Jyväskylä Fin. **44** N5

K

▶K2 *mt.* China/Pakistan **82** D2
2nd highest mountain in Asia and in the world.

Ka r. Nigeria **96** D3
Kaafu Atoll Maldives see **Male Atoll**
Kaa-Iya del Gran Chaco, Parque Nacional *nat. park* Bol. **142** F7
Kaakhka Turkm. see **Kaka**
Ka'ala *mt.* U.S.A. **127** [inset]
Kaapstad S. Africa see **Cape Town**
Kaarina Fin. **45** M6
Kaarßen Germany **53** L1
Kaarst Germany **52** G3
Kaavi Fin. **44** P5
Kaba China see **Habahe**
Kabakly Turkm. see **Gabakly**
Kabala Sierra Leone **96** B4
Kabale Uganda **98** C4
Kabalega Falls National Park Uganda see **Murchison Falls National Park**
Kabalo Dem. Rep. Congo **99** C4
Kabambare Dem. Rep. Congo **99** C4
Kabanbay Kazakh. **80** F2
Kabangu Dem. Rep. Congo **99** C5
Kabanjahe Indon. **71** B7
Kabara *i.* Fiji **107** I3
Kabarega National Park Uganda see **Murchison Falls National Park**
Kabaw Valley Myanmar **70** A2
Kabbani r. India **84** C3
Kåbdalis Sweden **44** L3
Kabinakagami r. Canada **122** D4
Kabinakagami Lake Canada **122** D4
Kabinda Dem. Rep. Congo **99** C4
Kabīr r. Syria **85** B2
Kabīrkūh *mts* Iran **88** B3
Kabo Cent. Afr. Rep. **98** B3
Kābol Afgh. see **Kābul**
Kabompo r. Zambia **99** C5
Kabongo Dem. Rep. Congo **99** C4
Kabūdeh Iran **89** F3
Kabūd Gonbad Iran **89** E2
Kabūd Rāhang Iran **88** C3

▶Kābul Afgh. **89** H3
Capital of Afghanistan.

Kābul r. Afgh. **89** I3
Kabuli P.N.G. **69** L7
Kabunda Dem. Rep. Congo **99** C5
Kabunduk Indon. **108** B2
Kaburuang *i.* Indon. **69** H6
Kabūtar Khān Iran **88** E4
Kabwe Zambia **99** C5
Kacha Kuh *mts* Iran/Pak. **89** F4
Kachalinskaya Rus. Fed. **43** J6
Kachchh, Great Rann of *marsh* India see **Kachchh, Rann of**
Kachchh, Gulf of India **82** B5
Kachchh, Little Rann of *marsh* India **82** B5
Kachchh, Rann of *marsh* India **82** B4
Kachia Nigeria **96** D4
Kachiry Kazakh. **72** D2
Kachkanar Rus. Fed. **41** R4
Kachret'i Georgia **91** G2
Kachug Rus. Fed. **72** J2
Kaçkar Dağı *mt.* Turkey **91** F2
Kadaingti Myanmar **70** B3
Kadaiyanallur India **84** C4
Kadanai r. Afgh./Pak. **89** G4
Kadan Kyun *i.* Myanmar **71** B4
Kadavu *i.* Fiji **107** H3
Kadavu Passage Fiji **107** H3
Kaddam *l.* India **84** C2
Kade Ghana **96** C4
Kādhimain Iraq **91** G4
Kadi India **82** C5
Kadıköy Turkey **59** M4
Kadınhanı Turkey **90** D3
Kadiolo Mali **96** C3
Kadiri India **84** C3
Kadirli Turkey **90** E3
Kadirpur Pak. **89** I4
Kadiyevka Ukr. see **Stakhanov**
Kadmat *atoll* India **84** B4
Ka-do *i.* N. Korea **75** B5
Kadok Malaysia **71** C6
Kadoka U.S.A. **130** C3
Kadoma Zimbabwe **99** C5
Kadonkani Myanmar **70** A4
Kadu Myanmar **70** B1
Kadugli Sudan **86** C7
Kaduna Nigeria **96** D3
Kaduna r. Nigeria **96** D4
Kadusam *mt.* China/India **83** I3
Kaduy Rus. Fed. **42** H4
Kadyy Rus. Fed. **42** I4
Kadzherom Rus. Fed. **42** L2
Kaédi Mauritania **96** B3
Kaélé Cameroon **97** E3
Kaeng Krachan National Park Thai. **71** B4
Kaesŏng N. Korea **75** B5
Kāf Saudi Arabia **85** C4
Kafa Ukr. see **Feodosiya**
Kafakumba Dem. Rep. Congo **99** C4
Kafan Armenia see **Kapan**
Kafanchan Nigeria **96** D4

▶Kaffeklubben Ø *i.* Greenland **153** I1
Most northerly point of North America.

Kafireas, Akra *pt* Greece see **Ntoro, Kavo**
Kafiristan *reg.* Pak. **89** H3
Kafr ash Shaykh Egypt **90** C5
Kafr el Sheikh Egypt see **Kafr ash Shaykh**
Kafue Zambia **99** C5
Kafue r. Zambia **99** C5
Kafue National Park Zambia **99** C5
Kaga Japan **75** E5
Kaga Bandoro Cent. Afr. Rep. **98** B3
Kagan Pak. **89** I3
Kagan Uzbek. see **Kogon**
Kagang China **76** D1
Kaganovichabad Tajik. see **Kolkhozobod**
Kaganovichi Pervyye Ukr. see **Polis'ke**
Kagarlyk Ukr. see **Kaharlyk**
Kåge Sweden **44** L4
Kağızman Turkey **91** F2
Kagmar Sudan **86** D7
Kagoshima Japan **75** C7
Kagoshima *pref.* Japan **75** C7
Kagul Moldova see **Cahul**
Kahama Tanz. **98** D4
Kaharlyk Ukr. **43** F6
Kaherekoau Mountains N.Z. **113** A7
Kahla Germany **53** L4
Kahnūj Iran **88** E4
Kahoka U.S.A. **130** F3
Kaho'olawe *i.* U.S.A. **127** [inset]
Kahperusvaarat *mts* Fin. **44** L2
Kahramanmaraş Turkey **90** E3
Kahror Pak. **89** H4
Kâhta Turkey **90** E3
Kahuku U.S.A. **127** [inset]
Kahuku Point U.S.A. **127** [inset]
Kahulaui *i.* U.S.A. see **Kaho'olawe**
Kahurangi National Park N.Z. **113** D5
Kahurangi Point N.Z. **113** D5
Kahuta Pak. **89** I3
Kahuzi-Biega, Parc National du *nat. park* Dem. Rep. Congo **98** C4
Kai, Kepulauan *is* Indon. **69** I8
Kaiapoi N.Z. **113** D6
Kaibab U.S.A. **129** G3
Kaibab Plateau U.S.A. **129** G3
Kai Besar *i.* Indon. **69** I8
Kaibito Plateau U.S.A. **129** H3
Kaifeng *Henan* China **77** G1
Kaifeng *Henan* China **77** G1
Kaihua *Yunnan* China see **Wenshan**
Kaihua *Zhejiang* China **77** H2
Kaiingveld *reg.* S. Africa **100** E5
Kaijiang China **76** E2
Kai Kecil *i.* Indon. **69** I8
Kai Keung Leng *H.K.* China **77** [inset]
Kaikoura N.Z. **113** D6
Kailas *mt.* China see **Kangrinboqê Feng**
Kailasahar India see **Kailashahar**
Kailashahar India **83** H4
Kailas Range *mts* China see **Gangdisê Shan**
Kaili China **76** E3
Kailu China **73** M4
Kailua U.S.A. **127** [inset]
Kailua-Kona U.S.A. **127** [inset]
Kaimana Indon. **69** I7
Kaimanawa Mountains N.Z. **113** E4
Kaimar China **76** B1
Kaimur Range *hills* India **82** E4
Käina Estonia **45** M7
Kainan Japan **75** D6
Kainda Kyrg. see **Kayyngdy**
Kaindy Kyrg. see **Kayyngdy**
Kainji Lake National Park Nigeria **96** D4
Kaipara Harbour N.Z. **113** E3
Kaiparowits Plateau U.S.A. **129** H3
Kaiping China **77** G4
Kaipokok Bay Canada **123** K3
Kairana India **82** D3
Kairiru Island P.N.G. **69** K7
Kaironi Indon. **69** I7
Kairouan Tunisia **58** D7
Kaiserslautern Germany **53** H5
Kaiser Wilhelm II Land *reg.* Antarctica **152** E2
Kaitaia N.Z. **113** D2
Kaitangata N.Z. **113** B8
Kaitawa N.Z. **113** F4
Kaithal India **82** D3
Kaitum Sweden **44** L3
Kaiwatu Indon. **108** D2
Kaiwi Channel U.S.A. **127** [inset]
Kaixian China **77** F2
Kaiyang China **76** E3
Kaiyuan *Liaoning* China **74** B4
Kaiyuan *Yunnan* China **76** D4
Kajaani Fin. **44** O4
Kajabbi Australia **110** C4
Kajaki Afgh. **89** G3
Kajarabie, Lake Australia **112** D1
Kajrān Afgh. **89** G3
Kaka Turkm. **89** E2
Kakabeka Falls Canada **122** C4
Kakadu National Park Australia **108** F3
Kakagi Lake Canada **121** M5
Kakamas S. Africa **100** E5
Kakamega Kenya **98** D3
Kakana India **71** A5
Kakar Pak. **89** G5
Kakata Liberia **96** B4
Kake U.S.A. **120** C3
Kakenge Dem. Rep. Congo **99** C4
Kakerbeck Germany **53** L2
Kakhi Azer. see **Qax**
Kakhovka Ukr. **59** O1
Kakhovs'ke Vodoskhovyshche *resr* Ukr. **43** G7
Kakhul Moldova see **Cahul**
Kākī Iran **88** C4
Kakinada India **84** D2
Kakisa Canada **120** G2
Kakisa r. Canada **120** G2
Kakisa Lake Canada **120** G2
Kakogawa Japan **75** D6
Kakori India **82** E4
Kakshaal-Too *mts* China/Kyrg. **80** E3
Kaktovik U.S.A. **118** D2
Kakul Pak. **89** I3
Kakwa r. Canada **120** G4
Kala Pak. **89** H4
Kala Tanz. **99** D4
Kalaâ Kebira Tunisia **58** D7
Kalaallit Nunaat *terr.* N. America see **Greenland**
Kalabahi Indon. **108** D2
Kalabáka Greece see **Kalampaka**
Kalabgur India **84** C2
Kalabo Zambia **99** C5
Kalach Rus. Fed. **43** I6
Kalacha Dida Kenya **98** D3
Kalach-na-Donu Rus. Fed. **43** I6
Kaladan r. India/Myanmar **70** A2
Kaladar Canada **135** G1
Ka Lae *pt* U.S.A. **127** [inset]
Kalagwe Myanmar **70** B2
Kalahari Desert Africa **100** F2
Kalahari Gemsbok National Park S. Africa **100** E3
Kalaikhum Tajik. see **Qal'aikhum**
Kalai-Khumb Tajik. see **Qal'aikhum**
Kalajoki Fin. **44** M4
Kalalé Benin **96** D3
Kalam India **84** C1
Kalam Pak. **89** I3
Kalámai Greece see **Kalamata**
Kalamare Botswana **101** H2
Kalamaria Greece **59** J4
Kalamata Greece **59** J6
Kalamazoo U.S.A. **134** C2
Kalampaka Greece **59** I5
Kalanchak Ukr. **59** O1
Kalandi Pak. **89** F4
Kalandula Angola see **Calandula**
Kalannie Australia **109** B7
Kalanshiyū ar Ramlī al Kabīr, Sarīr *des.* Libya **86** B3
Kālān Zīād Iran **89** E5
Kalapana (abandoned) U.S.A. **127** [inset]
Kalār Iraq **91** G4
Kalasin Thai. **70** C3
Kalāt Afgh. **89** G3
Kalāt *Khorāsān* Iran see **Kabūd Gonbad**
Kalāt *Sīstān va Balūchestān* Iran **89** E5
Kalat *Balochistan* Pak. **89** G4
Kalat *Balochistan* Pak. **89** G5
Kalat, Kūh-e *mt.* Iran **88** E3
Kalaupapa U.S.A. **127** [inset]
Kalaus r. Rus. Fed. **43** J7
Kalaw Myanmar **70** B2
Kālbācār Azer. **91** G2
Kalbarri Australia **109** A6
Kalbarri National Park Australia **109** A6
Kalbe (Milde) Germany **53** L2
Kale Turkey **59** M6
Kalecik Turkey **90** D2
Kalefeld Germany **53** K3
Kaleindaung *inlet* Myanmar **70** A3
Kalemie Dem. Rep. Congo **99** C4
Kalemyo Myanmar **70** A2
Kāl-e Namak Iran **88** D3
Kalevala Rus. Fed. **44** Q4
Kalewa Myanmar **70** A2
Kaleybar Iran **88** B2
Kalgan China see **Zhangjiakou**
Kalghatgi India **84** B3
Kalgoorlie Australia **109** C7
Kāl Gūsheh Iran **88** E4
Kali Croatia **58** F2
Kali r. India/Nepal **82** E3
Kaliakra, Nos *pt* Bulg. **59** M3
Kali Gandaki r. Nepal **83** F4
Kaligiri India **84** C3
Kalikata India see **Kolkata**
Kalima Dem. Rep. Congo **98** C4
Kalimantan *reg.* Indon. **68** E7
Kálimnos *i.* Greece see **Kalymnos**
Kalinin Rus. Fed. see **Tver'**
Kalinin Adyndaky Tajik. see **Cheshtebe**
Kaliningrad Rus. Fed. **45** L9
Kalinino Armenia see **Tashir**
Kalinino Rus. Fed. **42** I4
Kalininsk Rus. Fed. **43** J6
Kalininskaya Rus. Fed. **43** H7
Kalinjara India **82** C5
Kalinkavichy Belarus **43** F5
Kalinkovichi Belarus see **Kalinkavichy**
Kalisch Poland see **Kalisz**
Kalispell U.S.A. **126** E2
Kalisz Poland **47** Q5
Kalitva r. Rus. Fed. **43** I6
Kaliua Tanz. **99** D4
Kaliujar India **82** E4
Kalix Sweden **44** M4
Kalkalighat India **83** H4
Kalkalpen, Nationalpark *nat. park* Austria **47** O7
Kalkan Turkey **59** M6
Kalkaska U.S.A. **134** C1
Kalkfeld Namibia **99** B6
Kalkfonteindam *dam* S. Africa **101** G5
Kalkudah Sri Lanka **84** D5
Kall Germany **52** G4
Kallang r. Sing. **71** [inset]
Kallaste Estonia **45** O7
Kallavesi *l.* Fin. **44** O5
Kallsedet Sweden **44** H5
Kallsjön *l.* Sweden **44** H5
Kallur India **84** C2
Kalmar Sweden **45** J8
Kalmarsund *sea chan.* Sweden **45** J8
Kalmit *hill* Germany **53** I5
Kalmūkh Qal'eh Iran **88** E2
Kalmunai Sri Lanka **84** D5
Kalmykia *aut. rep.* Rus. Fed. see **Kalmykiya-Khalm'g-Tangch, Respublika**
Kalmykiya-Khalm'g-Tangch, Respublika *aut. rep.* Rus. Fed. **91** G1
Kalmykovo Kazakh. see **Taypak**
Kalmytskaya Avtonomnaya Oblast' *aut. rep.* Rus. Fed. see **Kalmykiya-Khalm'g-Tangch, Respublika**
Kalnai India **83** E5
Kalodnaye Belarus **45** O11
Kalol India **82** C5
Kalomo Zambia **99** C5
Kalone Peak Canada **120** E4
Kalpa India **82** D3
Kalpeni *atoll* India **84** B4
Kalpetta India **84** C4
Kalpi India **82** D4
Kaltag U.S.A. **118** C3
Kaltensundheim Germany **53** K4
Kaltukatjara Australia **109** E6
Kalu India **89** I4
Kaluga Rus. Fed. **43** H5
Kalukalukuang *i.* Indon. **68** F8
Kalundborg Denmark **45** G9
Kalush Ukr. **43** E6
Kalvakol India **84** C2
Kälviä Fin. **44** M5
Kal'ya Rus. Fed. **41** R3
Kalyan India **84** B2
Kalyandurg India **87** M7
Kalyansingapuram India **84** D2
Kalyazin Rus. Fed. **42** H4
Kalymnos *i.* Greece **59** L6
Kama Dem. Rep. Congo **98** C4
Kama Myanmar **70** A3

▶Kama r. Rus. Fed. **42** L4
4th longest river in Europe.

Kamaishi Japan **75** F5
Kamalia Pak. **89** I4
Kaman Turkey **90** D3
Kamaniskeg Lake Canada **135** G1
Kamanjab Namibia **99** B5
Kamarān *i.* Yemen **86** F6
Kamaran Island Yemen see **Kamarān**
Kamard *reg.* Afgh. **89** G3
Kamarod Pak. **89** F5
Kamaron Sierra Leone **96** B4
Kamashi Uzbek. see **Qamashi**
Kamasin India **82** E4
Kambaiti Myanmar **70** B1
Kambalda Australia **109** C7
Kambam India **84** C4
Kambara *i.* Fiji see **Kabara**
Kambia Sierra Leone **96** B4
Kambing, Pulau *i.* East Timor see **Ataúro, Ilha de**
Kambo-san *mt.* N. Korea see **Kwanmo-bong**
Kambove Dem. Rep. Congo **99** C5
Kambūt Libya **90** B5
Kamchatka, Poluostrov *pen.* Rus. Fed. see **Kamchatka Peninsula**
Kamchatka Basin *sea feature* Bering Sea **150** H2
Kamchatka Peninsula Rus. Fed. **65** Q4
Kamchiya r. Bulg. **59** L3
Kameia, Parque Nacional de *nat. park* Angola see **Cameia, Parque Nacional da**
Kamelik r. Rus. Fed. **43** K5
Kamen Germany **53** H3
Kamen', Gory *mt.* Rus. Fed. **64** K3
Kamenets-Podol'skiy Ukr. see **Kam"yanets'-Podil's'kyy**
Kamenitsa *mt.* Bulg. **59** J4
Kamenjak, Rt *pt* Croatia **58** E2
Kamenka Kazakh. **41** Q5
Kamenka *Arkhangel'skaya Oblast'* Rus. Fed. **42** J2
Kamenka *Penzenskaya Oblast'* Rus. Fed. **43** J5
Kamenka *Primorskiy Kray* Rus. Fed. **74** E3
Kamenka-Bugskaya Ukr. see **Kam"yanka-Buz'ka**
Kamenka-Strumilovskaya Ukr. see **Kam"yanka-Buz'ka**
Kamen'-na-Obi Rus. Fed. **72** E2
Kamennogorsk Rus. Fed. **45** P6
Kamennomostskiy Rus. Fed. **91** F1
Kamenolomni Rus. Fed. **43** I7
Kamenongue Angola see **Camanongue**
Kamen'-Rybolov Rus. Fed. **74** D3
Kamenskoye Rus. Fed. **65** R3

Kamenskoye Ukr. see Dniprodzerzhyns'k
Kamensk-Shakhtinskiy Rus. Fed. 43 I6
Kamensk-Ural'skiy Rus. Fed. 64 H4
Kamet mt. China 82 D3
Kamiesberge mts S. Africa 100 D6
Kamieskroon S. Africa 100 C6
Kamileroi Australia 110 C3
Kamilukuak Lake Canada 121 K2
Kamina Dem. Rep. Congo 99 C4
Kaminak Lake Canada 121 M2
Kaminuriak Lake Canada see Qamanirjuaq Lake
Kamishihoro Japan 74 F4
Kamloops Canada 120 F5
Kamo Armenia see Gavarr
Kamoke Pak. 89 I4
Kamonia Dem. Rep. Congo 99 C4

▶Kampala Uganda 98 D3
Capital of Uganda.

Kampar r. Indon. 68 C6
Kampar Malaysia 71 C6
Kampara India 84 D1
Kampen Neth. 52 F2
Kampene Dem. Rep. Congo 98 C4
Kamphaeng Phet Thai. 70 B3
Kampinoski Park Narodowy nat. park Poland 47 R4
Kâmpóng Cham Cambodia 71 D5
Kâmpóng Chhnăng Cambodia 71 D4
Kâmpóng Khleăng Cambodia 71 D4
Kâmpóng Saôm Cambodia see Sihanoukville
Kâmpóng Spœ Cambodia 71 D5
Kâmpóng Thum Cambodia 71 D4
Kâmpóng Trâbêk Cambodia 71 D5
Kâmpôt Cambodia 71 D5
Kampuchea country Asia see Cambodia
Kamrau, Teluk b. Indon. 69 I7
Kamsack Canada 121 K5
Kamskoye Vodokhranilishche resr Rus. Fed. 41 R4
Kamsuuma Somalia 98 E3
Kamuchawie Lake Canada 121 K3
Kamuli Uganda 98 D3
Kam"yanets'-Podil's'kyy Ukr. 43 E6
Kam"yanka-Buz'ka Ukr. 43 E6
Kamyanyets Belarus 45 M10
Kāmyārān Iran 88 B3
Kamyshin Rus. Fed. 43 J6
Kamystybas, Ozero l. Kazakh. 80 B2
Kamyzyak Rus. Fed. 43 K7
Kamzar Oman 88 E5
Kanaaupscow r. Canada 122 F3
Kanab U.S.A. 129 G3
Kanab Creek r. U.S.A. 129 G3
Kanairiktok r. Canada 123 K3
Kanak Pak. 89 G4
Kananga Dem. Rep. Congo 99 C4
Kanangio, Mount vol. P.N.G. 69 L7
Kanangra-Boyd National Park Australia 112 E4
Kanarak India see Konarka
Kanarraville U.S.A. 129 G3
Kanas watercourse Namibia 100 C4
Kanash Rus. Fed. 42 J5
Kanauj India see Kannauj
Kanazawa Japan 75 E5
Kanbalu Myanmar 70 A2
Kanchanaburi Thai. 71 B4
Kanchanjanga mt. India/Nepal see Kangchenjunga
Kanchipuram India 84 C3
Kand mt. Pak. 89 G4
Kanda Pak. 89 G4
Kandahār Afgh. 89 G4
Kandalaksha Rus. Fed. 44 R3
Kandalakshskiy Zaliv g. Rus. Fed. 44 R3
Kandang Indon. 71 B7
Kandar Indon. 108 E2
Kandavu i. Fiji see Kadavu
Kandavu Passage Fiji see Kadavu Passage
Kandé Togo 96 D4
Kandh Kot Pak. 89 H4
Kandi Benin 96 D3
Kandi India 84 C2
Kandiaro Pak. 89 H5
Kandıra Turkey 59 N4
Kandos Australia 112 D4
Kandreho Madag. 99 E5
Kandrian P.N.G. 69 L8
Kandukur India 84 C3
Kandy Sri Lanka 84 D5
Kandyagash Kazakh. 80 A2
Kane U.S.A. 135 F3
Kane Bassin b. Greenland 153 K1
Kaneh watercourse Iran 88 D5
Kāne'ohe U.S.A. 127 [inset]
Kaneti Pak. 89 G4
Kanevskaya Rus. Fed. 43 H7
Kang Afgh. 89 F4
Kang Botswana 100 F2
Kangaamiut Greenland 119 M3
Kangaarsussuaq c. Greenland 119 K2
Kangaba Mali 96 C3
Kangal Turkey 90 E3
Kangān Būshehr Iran 88 D5
Kangān Hormozgan Iran 88 E5
Kangandala, Parque Nacional de nat. park Angola see Cangandala, Parque Nacional de
Kangar Malaysia 71 C6
Kangaroo Island Australia 111 B7
Kangaroo Point Australia 110 B3
Kangaslampi Fin. 44 P5
Kangasniemi Fin. 44 O6
Kangāvar Iran 88 B3

▶Kangchenjunga mt. India/Nepal 83 G4
3rd highest mountain in Asia and in the world.

Kangding China 76 D2
Kangean, Kepulauan is Indon. 68 F8
Kangen r. Sudan 97 G4
Kangerlussuaq Greenland 119 M3
Kangerlussuaq inlet Greenland 119 M3
Kangerlussuaq inlet Greenland 153 J2
Kangersuatsiaq Greenland 119 M2
Kangertittivaq sea chan. Greenland 119 P2
Kanggye N. Korea 74 B4
Kanghwa S. Korea 75 B5
Kangikajik c. Greenland 119 P2
Kangiqsualujjuaq Canada 123 I2
Kangirsuk Canada 123 H1
Kang Krung National Park Thai. 71 B5
Kangle Gansu China 76 D1
Kangle Jiangxi China see Wanzai
Kanglong China 76 C1
Kangmar China 83 F3
Kangnŭng S. Korea 75 C5
Kango Gabon 98 B3
Kangping China 74 A4
Kangri Karpo Pass China/India 83 I3
Kangrinboqê Feng mt. China 82 E3
Kangsangdobdê China see Xainza
Kangto mt. China/India 83 H4
Kangtog China 83 F2
Kangxian China 76 E1
Kanibongan Sabah Malaysia 68 F5
Kanifing Gambia 96 B3
Kanigiri India 84 C3
Kanin, Poluostrov pen. Rus. Fed. 42 J2
Kanin Nos Rus. Fed. 153 G2
Kanin Nos, Mys c. Rus. Fed. 42 I1
Kaninskiy Bereg coastal area Rus. Fed. 42 I2
Kanjiroba mt. Nepal 83 E3
Kankaanpää Fin. 45 M6
Kankakee U.S.A. 134 B3
Kankan Guinea 96 C3
Kanker India 84 D1
Kankesanturai Sri Lanka 84 D4
Kankossa Mauritania 96 B3
Kanmaw Kyun i. Myanmar 71 B5
Kannauj India 82 D4
Kanniya Kumari c. India see Comorin, Cape
Kannonkoski Fin. 44 N5
Kannur India see Cannanore
Kannus Fin. 44 M5
Kano Nigeria 96 D3
Kanonpunt pt S. Africa 100 E8
Kanosh U.S.A. 129 G2
Kanovlei Namibia 99 B5
Kanoya Japan 75 C7
Kanpur Orissa India 84 E1
Kanpur Uttar Prad. India 82 E4
Kanrach reg. Pak. 89 G5
Kansai airport Japan 75 D6
Kansas U.S.A. 134 B4
Kansas r. U.S.A. 130 E4
Kansas state U.S.A. 130 D4
Kansas City KS U.S.A. 130 E4
Kansas City MO U.S.A. 130 E4
Kansk Rus. Fed. 65 K4
Kansu prov. China see Gansu
Kantang Thai. 71 B6
Kantara hill Cyprus 85 A2
Kantaralak Thai. 71 D4
Kantavu i. Fiji see Kadavu
Kantchari Burkina 96 D3
Kantemirovka Rus. Fed. 43 H6
Kanthi India 83 F5
Kantishna r. U.S.A. 118 C3
Kanton atoll Kiribati 107 I2
Kantulong Myanmar 70 B3
Kanturk Ireland 51 D5
Kanuku Mountains Guyana 143 G3
Kanur India 84 C3
Kanus Namibia 100 D4
Kanyakubja India see Kannauj
Kanyamazane S. Africa 101 J3
Kanye Botswana 101 G3
Kaôh Pring i. Cambodia 71 C5
Kaohsiung Taiwan 77 I4
Kaôh Smăch i. Cambodia 71 C5
Kaôh Tang i. Cambodia 71 C5
Kaokoveld plat. Namibia 99 B5
Kaolack Senegal 96 B3
Kaoma Zambia 99 C5
Kaouadja Cent. Afr. Rep. 98 C3
Kapa S. Africa see Cape Town
Kapa'a U.S.A. 127 [inset]
Kapa'au U.S.A. 127 [inset]
Kapan Armenia 91 G3
Kapanga Dem. Rep. Congo 99 C4
Kaparhā Iran 88 C4
Kapatu Zambia 99 D4
Kapchagay Kazakh. 80 E3
Kapchagayskoye Vodokhranilishche resr Kazakh. 80 E3
Kap Dan Greenland see Kulusuk
Kapellen Belgium 52 E3
Kapello, Akra pt Attiki Greece see Kapello, Akrotirio
Kapello, Akrotirio pt Greece 59 J6
Kapellskär Sweden 45 K7
Kapelskär Sweden see Kapellskär
Kapili r. India 83 G4
Kapingamarangi atoll Micronesia 150 G5
Kapingamarangi Rise sea feature N. Pacific Ocean 150 G5
Kapıorman Dağları mts Turkey 59 N4
Kapip Pak. 89 H4
Kapiri Mposhi Zambia 99 C5
Kapisillit Greenland 119 M3
Kapiskau r. Canada 122 E3
Kapit Sarawak Malaysia 68 E6
Kapiti Island N.Z. 113 E5
Kaplankyr, Chink hills Asia 91 I2
Kaplankyr Döwlet Gorugy nature res. Turkm. 88 E1
Kapoeta Sudan 97 G4
Kapondai, Tanjung pt Indon. 69 G8
Kaposvár Hungary 58 G1
Kappel Germany 53 H5
Kappeln Germany 47 L3
Kapsukas Lith. see Marijampolė
Kaptai Bangl. 83 H5
Kapuas r. Indon. 68 D7
Kapuriya India 82 C4
Kapurthala India 82 C3
Kapuskasing Canada 122 E4
Kapustin Yar Rus. Fed. 43 J6
Kaputar mt. Australia 112 E3
Kaputir Kenya 98 D3
Kapuvár Hungary 58 G1
Kapydzhik, Gora mt. Armenia/Azer. see Qazangödağ
Kapyl' Belarus 45 O10
Kaqung China 89 J2
Kara India 82 E4
Kara Togo 96 D4
Kara r. Turkey 91 F3
Kara Art Pass China 89 I2
Kara-Balta Kyrg. 80 D3
Karabalyk Kazakh. 78 F1
Karabekaul' Turkm. see Garabekewül
Karabiga Turkey 59 L4
Karabil', Vozvyshennost' hills Turkm. see Garabil Belentligi
Kara-Bogaz-Gol, Proliv sea chan. Turkm. see Garabogazköl Bogazy
Kara-Bogaz-Gol'skiy Zaliv b. Turkm. see Garabogazköl Aÿlagy
Karabük Turkey 90 D2
Karaburun Turkey 59 L5
Karabutak Kazakh. 80 B2
Karacabey Turkey 59 M4
Karacaköy Turkey 59 M4
Karacalı Dağ mt. Turkey 91 E3
Karaçal Tepe mt. Turkey 85 A1
Karacasu Turkey 59 M6
Karaca Yarımadası pen. Turkey 59 N6
Karachayevsk Rus. Fed. 91 F2
Karachev Rus. Fed. 43 G5
Karachi Pak. 89 G5
Karacurun Turkey see Hilvan
Karad India 84 B2
Kara Dağ hill Turkey 85 D1
Kara Dağ mt. Turkey 90 D3
Kara-Dar'ya Uzbek. see Payshanba
Kara Deniz sea Asia/Europe see Black Sea
Karagan Rus. Fed. 74 A1
Karaganda Kazakh. 80 D2
Karagayly Kazakh. 80 E2
Karaginskiy Zaliv b. Rus. Fed. 65 R4
Karagiye, Vpadina depr. Kazakh. 91 H2
Karagola India 83 F4
Karahallı Turkey 59 M5
Karahasanlı Turkey 90 D3
Karaikal India 84 C4
Karaikkudi India 84 C4
Karaisalı Turkey 90 D3
Karaj Iran 88 C3
Karak Jordan see Al Karak
Karakalli Turkey see Özalp
Karakax China see Moyu
Karakax He r. China 82 E1
Karakax Shan mts China 82 E2
Karakelong i. Indon. 69 H6
Karaki China 82 E1
Karaklis Armenia see Vanadzor
Karakoçan Turkey 91 F3
Kara-Köl Kyrg. 79 G2
Karakol Kyrg. 80 E3
Karakoram Pass China/India 82 D2
Karakoram Range mts Asia 79 G3
Karakoram Range mts Asia 89 I2
Kara K'orē Eth. 98 D2
Karakorum Range mts Asia see Karakoram Range
Karakorum Range mts Asia see Karakoram Range
Karaköse Turkey see Ağrı
Kara Kul' Kyrg. see Kara-Köl
Karakul', Ozero l. Tajik. see Qarokŭl
Kara Kum des. Turkm. see Garagum
Kara Kum des. Turkm. see Karakum Desert
Karakum, Peski Kazakh. see Karakum Desert
Karakum Desert Kazakh. 78 E2
Karakum Desert Turkm. see Garagum
Karakum Desert Turkm. 88 F2
Karakumskiy Kanal canal Turkm. see Garagum Kanaly
Kara Kumy des. Turkm. see Garagum
Karakurt Turkey 91 F2
Karakuş Dağı ridge Turkey 59 N5
Karal Chad 97 E3
Karala Estonia 45 L7
Karalundi Australia 109 B6
Karama r. Indon. 68 F7
Karaman Turkey 90 D3
Karaman prov. Turkey 85 A1
Karamanlı Turkey 59 M6
Karamay China 80 F2
Karambar Pass Afgh./Pak. 89 I2
Karamea N.Z. 113 D5
Karamea Bight b. N.Z. 113 C5
Karamendy Kazakh. 80 B1
Karamiran China 83 F1
Karamiran Shankou pass China 83 F1
Karamürsel Turkey 59 M4
Karamyshevo Rus. Fed. 45 P8
Karān i. Saudi Arabia 88 C5
Karangasem Indon. 108 A2
Karanja India 84 C1
Karanjia India 82 E5
Karapınar Gaziantep Turkey 85 C1
Karapınar Konya Turkey 90 D3
Karas admin. reg. Namibia 100 C4
Karasay China 83 E1
Karasburg Namibia 100 D5
Kara Sea Rus. Fed. 64 I2
Kárášjohka Finnmark Norway see Karasjok
Karasjok Norway 44 N2
Kara Strait Rus. Fed. see Karskiye Vorota, Proliv
Karasu r. Syria/Turkey 85 C1
Karasu Bitlis Turkey see Hizan
Karasu Sakarya Turkey 59 N4
Karasu r. Turkey 91 F3
Karasubazar Ukr. see Bilohirs'k
Karasuk Rus. Fed. 64 I4
Karāt Iran 89 F3
Karataş Turkey 85 B1
Karataş Burnu hd Turkey see Fener Burnu
Karatau Kazakh. 80 D3
Karatau, Khrebet mts Kazakh. 80 C3
Karatepe Turkey 85 A1
Karathuri Myanmar 71 B5
Karativu i. Sri Lanka 84 C4
Karatsu Japan 75 C6
Karaudanawa Guyana 143 G3
Karauli India 82 D4
Karavan Kyrg. see Kerben
Karavostasi Cyprus 85 A2
Karawang Indon. 68 D8
Karayılan Turkey 85 C1
Karayulgan China 80 F3
Karazhal Kazakh. 80 D2
Karbalā' Iraq 91 G4
Karben Germany 53 I4
Karcag Hungary 59 I1
Karden Germany 53 H4
Kardhítsa Greece see Karditsa
Karditsa Greece 59 I5
Kärdla Estonia 45 M7
Karee S. Africa 101 H5
Kareeberge mts S. Africa 100 E6
Kareima Sudan 86 D6
Kareli India 82 D5
Karelia aut. rep. Rus. Fed. see Kareliya, Respublika
Kareliya, Respublika aut. rep. Rus. Fed. 44 R5
Karel'skaya A.S.S.R. aut. rep. Rus. Fed. see Kareliya, Respublika
Karel'skiy Bereg coastal area Rus. Fed. 44 R3
Karema Tanz. 99 D4
Karera India 82 D4
Karesuando Sweden 44 M2
Kārevāndar Iran 89 F5
Kargalinskaya Rus. Fed. 91 G2
Kargalinski Rus. Fed. see Kargalinskaya
Kargapazarı Dağları mts Turkey 91 F3
Karghalik China see Yecheng
Kargı Turkey 90 D2
Kargil India 82 D2
Kargilik China see Yecheng
Kargıpınarı Turkey 85 B1
Kargopol' Rus. Fed. 42 H3
Kari Nigeria 96 E3
Karīān Iran 88 E5
Kariba Zimbabwe 99 C5
Kariba, Lake resr Zambia/Zimbabwe 99 C5
Kariba Dam Zambia/Zimbabwe 99 C5
Kariba-yama vol. Japan 74 E4
Karibib Namibia 100 B1
Karigasniemi Fin. 44 N2
Karijini National Park Australia 109 B5
Karijoki Fin. 44 L5
Karikachi-tōge pass Japan 74 F4
Karikari, Cape N.Z. 113 D2
Karimata, Pulau-pulau is Indon. 68 D7
Karimata, Selat strait Indon. 68 D7
Karimganj India 83 H4
Karimnagar India 84 C2
Karimun Besar i. Indon. 71 C7
Karimunjawa, Pulau-pulau is Indon. 68 E8
Káristos Greece see Karystos
Karjat Mahar. India 84 B2
Karjat Mahar. India 84 B2
Karkaralinsk Kazakh. 80 E2
Karkar Island P.N.G. 69 L7
Karkh Pak. 89 G5
Karkinits'ka Zatoka g. Ukr. 59 O2
Kärkölä Fin. 45 N6
Karkonoski Park Narodowy nat. park Czech Rep./Poland see Krkonošský národní park
Karksi-Nuia Estonia 45 N7
Karkük Iraq see Kirkūk
Karlachi Pak. 89 H3
Karlholmsbruk Sweden 45 J6
Karlik Shan mt. China 80 H3
Karlıova Turkey 91 F3
Karlivka Ukr. 43 G6
Karl Marks, Qullai mt. Tajik. 89 I2
Karl-Marx-Stadt Germany see Chemnitz
Karlovac Croatia 58 F2
Karlovka Ukr. see Karlivka
Karlovo Bulg. 59 K3
Karlovy Vary Czech Rep. 53 M4
Karlsbad Germany 53 I6
Karlsborg Sweden 45 I7
Karlsburg Romania see Alba Iulia
Karlshamn Sweden 45 I8
Karlskoga Sweden 45 I7
Karlskrona Sweden 45 I8
Karlsruhe Germany 53 I5
Karlstad Sweden 45 H7
Karlstad U.S.A. 130 D1
Karlstadt Germany 53 J5
Karluk U.S.A. 118 C4
Karlyk Turkm. 89 G2
Karmala India 84 B2
Karmel, Har hill Israel see Carmel, Mount
Karmona Spain see Córdoba
Karmøy i. Norway 45 D7
Karmpur Pak. 89 I4
Karnafuli Reservoir Bangl. 83 H5
Karnal India 82 D3
Karnataka state India 84 B3
Karnavati India see Ahmadabad
Karnes City U.S.A. 131 D6
Karnobat Bulg. 59 L3
Karodi Pak. 89 G5
Karoi Zimbabwe 99 C5
Karokpi Myanmar 70 B4
Karo La pass China 83 G3
Karong India 83 H4
Karonga Malawi 99 D4
Karonie Australia 109 C7
Karoo National Park S. Africa 100 F7
Karoonda Australia 111 B7
Karora Eritrea 86 E6
Káros i. Greece see Keros
Karossa Indon. 68 F7
Karossa, Tanjung pt Indon. 108 B2
Karow Germany 53 M1
Karpasia pen. Cyprus 85 B2
Karpas Peninsula Cyprus see Karpasia
Karpathos i. Greece 59 L7
Karpathou, Steno sea chan. Greece 59 L6
Karpaty mts Europe see Carpathian Mountains
Karpenisi Greece 59 I5
Karpilovka Belarus see Aktsyabrski
Karpinsk Rus. Fed. 41 S4
Karpogory Rus. Fed. 42 J2
Karpuz r. Turkey 85 A1
Karratha Australia 108 B5
Karroo plat. S. Africa see Great Karoo
Karrychirla Turkm. see Garryçyrla
Kars Turkey 91 F2
Kärsämäki Fin. 44 N5
Kārsava Latvia 45 O8
Karshi Qashqadaryo Uzbek. see Qarshi
Karskiye Vorota, Proliv strait Rus. Fed. 64 G3
Karskoye More sea Rus. Fed. see Kara Sea
Karstädt Germany 53 L1
Karstula Fin. 44 N5
Karsu Turkey 85 C1
Karsun Rus. Fed. 43 J5
Kartal Turkey 59 M4
Kartaly Rus. Fed. 64 H4
Kartayel' Rus. Fed. 42 L2
Karttula Fin. 44 O5
Karumba Australia 110 C3
Karumbhar Island India 82 B5
Karun, Kūh-e hill Iran 88 C4
Kārūn, Rūd-e r. Iran 88 C4
Karuni Indon. 108 B2
Karur India 84 C4
Karvia Fin. 44 M5
Karviná Czech Rep. 47 Q6
Karwar India 84 B3
Karyagino Azer. see Füzuli
Karymskoye Rus. Fed. 73 K2
Karynzharyk, Peski des. Kazakh. 91 I2
Karystos Greece 59 K5
Kaş Turkey 59 M6
Kasa India 84 B2
Kasaba Turkey see Turgutlu
Kasabonika Canada 122 C3
Kasabonika Lake Canada 122 C3
Kasaï r. Dem. Rep. Congo 98 B4
also known as Kwa
Kasaï, Plateau du Dem. Rep. Congo 99 C4
Kasaji Dem. Rep. Congo 99 C5
Kasama Zambia 99 D5
Kasan Uzbek. see Koson
Kasane Botswana 99 C5
Kasaragod India 84 B3
Kasargod India see Kasaragod
Kasargode India see Kasaragod
Kasatkino Rus. Fed. 74 C2
Kasba Lake Canada 121 K2
Kasba Tadla Morocco 54 C5
Kasenga Dem. Rep. Congo 99 C5
Kasengu Dem. Rep. Congo 99 C4
Kasese Dem. Rep. Congo 98 C4
Kasese Uganda 98 D3
Kasevo Rus. Fed. see Neftekamsk
Kasganj India 82 D4
Kasha China 76 C2
Kashabowie Canada 122 C4
Kāshān Iran 88 C3
Kashary Rus. Fed. 43 I6
Kashechewan Canada 122 E3
Kashgar China see Kashi
Kashi China 80 E4
Kashihara Japan 75 D6
Kashima-nada b. Japan 75 F5
Kashin Rus. Fed. 42 H4
Kashipur India 82 D3
Kashira Rus. Fed. 43 H5
Kashiwazaki Japan 75 E5
Kashkarantsy Rus. Fed. 42 H2
Kashku'iyeh Iran 88 D4
Kāshmar Iran 88 E3
Kashmir terr. Asia see Jammu and Kashmir
Kashmir, Vale of reg. India 82 C2
Kashyukulu Dem. Rep. Congo 99 C4
Kasi India see Varanasi
Kasigar Afgh. 89 H3
Kasimov Rus. Fed. 43 I5
Kaskattama r. Canada 121 N3
Kaskinen Fin. 44 L5
Kas Klong i. Cambodia see Kŏng, Kaôh
Kaskö Fin. see Kaskinen
Kaslo Canada 120 G5
Kasmere Lake Canada 121 K3
Kasongo Dem. Rep. Congo 99 C4
Kasongo-Lunda Dem. Rep. Congo 99 B4
Kasos i. Greece 59 L7
Kaspīy Mangy Oypaty lowland Kazakh./Rus. Fed. see Caspian Lowland
Kaspiysk Rus. Fed. 91 G2
Kaspiyskiy Rus. Fed. see Lagan'
Kaspiyskoye More l. Asia/Europe see Caspian Sea
Kassa Slovakia see Košice
Kassala Sudan 86 E6
Kassandras, Akra pt Greece see Kassandras, Akrotirio
Kassandras, Akrotirio pt Greece 59 J5
Kassandras, Kolpos b. Greece 59 J4
Kassel Germany 53 J3
Kasserine Tunisia 58 C7
Kastag Pak. 89 F5
Kastamonu Turkey 90 D2
Kastellaun Germany 53 H4
Kastelli Kriti Greece see Kissamos
Kastéllion Greece see Kissamos
Kastéllion Kriti Greece see Kissamos
Kastellorizon i. Greece see Megisti
Kasterlee Belgium 52 E3
Kastoria Greece 59 I4
Kastornoye Rus. Fed. 43 H6
Kastsyukovichy Belarus 43 G5
Kasulu Tanz. 99 D4
Kasumkent Rus. Fed. 91 H2
Kasungu Malawi 99 D5
Kasungu National Park Malawi 99 D5
Kasur Pak. 89 I4
Katādtlit Nunāt terr. N. America see Greenland
Katahdin, Mount U.S.A. 132 G2
Kataklik India 82 D2
Katako-Kombe Dem. Rep. Congo 98 C4
Katakwi Uganda 98 D3
Katana India 82 C5
Katangi India 82 D5
Katanning Australia 109 B8
Katavi National Park Tanz. 99 D4
Katawaz reg. Afgh. 89 G3
Katchall i. India 71 A6
Katea Dem. Rep. Congo 99 C4
Katerini Greece 59 J4
Katesh Tanz. 99 D4
Kate's Needle mt. Canada/U.S.A. 120 C3
Katete Zambia 99 D5
Katherîna, Gebel mt. Egypt see Kātrīnā, Jabal
Katherine Australia 108 F3
Katherine Gorge National Park Australia see Nitmiluk National Park
Kathi India 89 I6
Kathiawar pen. India 82 B5
Kathihar India see Katihar
Kathiraveli Sri Lanka 84 D4
Kathiwara India 82 C5
Kathleen Falls Australia 108 E3

▶Kathmandu Nepal 83 F4
Capital of Nepal.

Kathu S. Africa 100 F4
Kathua India 82 C2
Kati Mali 96 C3
Katihar India 83 F4
Katikati S. Africa 101 H7
Katima Mulilo Namibia 99 C5
Katimik Lake Canada 121 L4
Katiola Côte d'Ivoire 96 C4
Kā Tiritiri o te Moana mts N.Z. see Southern Alps
Katkop Hills S. Africa 100 E6
Katlehong S. Africa 101 I4
Katmai National Park and Preserve U.S.A. 118 C4
Katmandu Nepal see Kathmandu
Kato Achaïa Greece 59 I5
Kat O Chau H.K. China see Crooked Island
Kat O Hoi b. H.K. China see Crooked Harbour
Katoomba Australia 112 E4
Katowice Poland 47 Q5
Katoya India 83 G5
Katrancık Dağı mts Turkey 59 M6
Kātrīnā, Jabal mt. Egypt 90 D5
Katrine, Loch l. U.K. 50 E4
Katrineholm Sweden 45 J7
Katse Dam Lesotho 101 I5
Katsina Nigeria 96 D3
Katsina-Ala Nigeria 96 D4
Katsuura Japan 75 F6
Kattaktoc, Cap c. Canada 123 I2
Kattamudda Well Australia 108 D5
Kattaqo'rg'on Uzbek. 89 G2
Kattaqŭrghon Uzbek. see Kattaqo'rg'on
Kattasang Hills Afgh. 89 G3
Kattegat strait Denmark/Sweden 45 G8
Kattowitz Poland see Katowice
Katumbar India 82 D4
Katunino Rus. Fed. 42 J4
Katuri Pak. 89 H4
Katwa India see Katoya
Katwijk aan Zee Neth. 52 E2
Katzenbuckel hill Germany 53 J5
Kaua'i i. U.S.A. 127 [inset]
Kaua'i Channel U.S.A. 127 [inset]
Kaub Germany 53 H4
Kaufungen Germany 53 J3
Kauhajoki Fin. 44 M5
Kauhava Fin. 44 M5
Kaukauna U.S.A. 134 A1
Kaukkwè Hills Myanmar 70 B1
Kaukonen Fin. 44 N3
Ka'ula i. U.S.A. 127 [inset]
Kaulakahi Channel U.S.A. 127 [inset]
Kaumajet Mountains Canada 123 J2
Kaunakakai U.S.A. 127 [inset]
Kaunas Lith. 45 M9
Kaunata Latvia 45 O8
Kaundy, Vpadina depr. Kazakh. 91 I2
Kaunia Bangl. 83 G4
Kaura-Namoda Nigeria 96 D3
Kau Sai Chau i. H.K. China 77 [inset]
Kaustinen Fin. 44 M5
Kautokeino Norway 44 M2
Kau-ye Kyun i. Myanmar 71 B5
Kavadarci Macedonia 59 J4
Kavak Turkey 90 E2
Kavaklıdere Turkey 59 M6
Kavala Greece 59 K4
Kavalas, Kolpos b. Greece 59 K4
Kavalerovo Rus. Fed. 74 D3
Kavali India 84 D3
Kavār Iran 88 D4
Kavaratti India 84 B4
Kavaratti atoll India 84 B4
Kavarna Bulg. 59 M3
Kavendou, Mont mt. Guinea 96 B3
Kaveri r. India 84 C4
Kavīr Iran 88 C3
Kavīr, Dasht-e des. Iran 88 D3
Kavīr Kūshk well Iran 88 E3
Kavkasioni mts Asia/Europe see Caucasus
Kawa Myanmar 70 B3
Kawagama Lake Canada 135 F1
Kawagoe Japan 75 E6
Kawaguchi Japan 75 E6
Kawaihae U.S.A. 127 [inset]
Kawaikini U.S.A. 127 [inset]
Kawakawa N.Z. 113 E2
Kawambwa Zambia 99 C4
Kawana Zambia 99 C5
Kawardha India 82 E5
Kawartha Lakes Canada 135 F1
Kawasaki Japan 75 E6
Kawau Island N.Z. 113 E3
Kawawachikamach Canada 123 I3
Kawdut Myanmar 70 B4
Kawerau N.Z. 113 F4
Kawhia N.Z. 113 E4
Kawhia Harbour N.Z. 113 E4
Kawich Peak U.S.A. 128 E3
Kawich Range mts U.S.A. 128 E3
Kawinaw Lake Canada 121 L4
Kaw Lake U.S.A. 131 D4
Kawlin Myanmar 70 A2
Kawm Umbū Egypt 86 D5
Kawngmeum Myanmar 70 B2
Kawthaung Myanmar 71 B5
Kaxgar China see Kashi
Kaxgar He r. China 80 E4
Kax He r. China 80 F3
Kaxtax Shan mts China 83 E1
Kaya Burkina 96 C3

ɣadibi Turkey **90** E3
ɣan r. Indon. **68** F6
ɣankulam India **84** C4
ɣar India **84** C2
ɣcee U.S.A. **126** G4
ɣdak, Sor *dry lake* Kazakh. **91** I1
ɣdanovo Belarus *see* **Dzyarzhynsk**
ɣembe-Mukulu Dem. Rep. Congo
9 C4
ɣenta U.S.A. **129** H3
ɣes Mali **96** B3
ɣmaz Turkey **59** N5
ɣnar Kazakh. **80** E2
ɣnar Turkey **90** E3
ɣseri Turkey **90** D3
ɣuyu Dem. Rep. Congo **98** C4
ɣyngdy Kyrg. **80** D3
zach'ye Rus. Fed. **65** O2
zakh Azer. *see* **Qazax**
zakhskaya S.S.R. *country* Asia *see*
Kazakhstan
zakhskiy Melkosopochnik *plain* Kazakh.
0 D1
zakhskiy Zaliv *b.* Kazakh. **91** I2

▶**Kazakhstan** *country* Asia **78** F2
th largest country in Asia, and 9th in the world.

akhstan Kazakh. *see* **Aksay**
akstan *country* Asia *see* **Kazakhstan**
an *r.* Canada **121** M2
an' Rus. Fed. **42** K5
andzhik Turkm. *see* **Bereket**
anka *r.* Rus. Fed. **42** K5
anlı Turkey **85** B1
anlŭk Bulg. **59** K3
an-rettō *is* Japan *see* **Volcano Islands**
atin Ukr. *see* **Kozyatyn**

▶**azbek** *mt.* Georgia/Rus. Fed. **43** J8
h highest mountain in Europe.

Dağı *mts* Turkey **59** L5
erūn Iran **88** C4
him Rus. Fed. **42** K3
idi Tajik. *see* **Qozideh**
i Magomed Azer. *see* **Qazımämmäd**
incbarcika Hungary **43** D6
iranga National Park India **83** H4
ret'i Georgia **91** G2
talovka Kazakh. **41** P6
y Turkm. **88** E2
ym *r.* Rus. Fed. **41** T3
ymskiy Mys Rus. Fed. **41** T3
i. Notio Aigaio Greece *see* **Tzia**
i. Notio Aigaio Greece *see* **Tzia**
dy U.K. **51** F3
ms Canyon U.S.A. **129** H4
mu *i.* Vanuatu *see* **Anatom**
rney U.S.A. **130** D3
rny U.S.A. **129** H5
an Turkey **90** E3
an Barajı *resr* Turkey **90** E3
émèr Senegal **96** B3
ili Tunisia **54** F5
īr, Nahr al *r.* Lebanon/Syria **85** B2
kabiya Sudan **97** F3
nekaise *mt.* Sweden **44** K3
ock Head *hd* U.K. **50** C2
rī Dehar Eth. **98** E3
h *reg.* Pak. **89** F5
hika *r.* Canada **120** E3
iborlu Turkey **59** N6
skemét Hungary **59** H1
ia Georgia **91** F2
ainiai Lith. **45** M9
airu Passage Fiji *see* **Kadavu Passage**
gwick Canada **123** I5
ian China **77** G2
ong China **74** B3
va *r.* Rus. Fed. **42** L2
zierzyn-Koźle Poland **47** Q5
le *r.* Canada **120** E1
le Peak Canada **120** D2
ler U.S.A. **128** E3
ley Lake Canada **121** I4
ing Islands *terr.* Indian Ocean *see*
ocos Islands
n, Mount *hill* U.K. **50** G4
ne *CA* U.S.A. **128** D4
ne *KY* U.S.A. **134** C5
ne *NH* U.S.A. **135** I2
ne *OH* U.S.A. **134** E3
per Hill *hill* Ireland **51** D5
pit, Lake *resr* Australia **112** E3
p River National Park Australia **108** E3
rbergen Belgium **52** E3
r-weer, Cape Australia **110** C2
tmanshoop Namibia **100** D4
watin Canada **121** M5
allinía *i.* Greece *see* **Cephalonia**
allonia *i.* Greece *see* **Cephalonia**
amenanu Indon. **108** D2
e Ukr. *see* **Feodosiya**
ī Nigeria **96** D4
avík Iceland **44** [inset]
ia, Mui *pt* Vietnam **71** E5
alla Sri Lanka **84** D5
en Kazakh. **80** E3
lo, Baie de *b.* Canada **123** I2
River Canada **120** G3
ul'ta Rus. Fed. **43** J7
ra Estonia **45** N7
hley U.K. **48** F5
a Estonia **45** N7
noes S. Africa **100** E5
ele Fin. **44** O5
ele *l.* Fin. **44** O5
h Australia **111** C8
h U.K. **50** G3
h Arm *b.* Canada **120** F1
nkujik National Park Canada **123** I5
aha U.S.A. **127** [inset]
es *mt.* Hungary **47** R7
i India **82** C4
afo Eth. **98** E3
i *i.* Maldives **84** B5
erg Germany **52** G4
eim Germany **53** L6
bia Tunisia **58** D6

Kelif Uzboýy *marsh* Turkm. **89** F2
Kelīrī Iran **88** E5
Kelkheim (Taunus) Germany **53** I4
Kelkit Turkey **91** E2
Kelkit *r.* Turkey **90** E2
Kéllé Congo **98** B4
Keller Lake Canada **120** F2
Kellett, Cape Canada **118** F2
Kelleys Island U.S.A. **134** D3
Kelliher Canada **121** K5
Kelloselkä Fin. **44** P3
Kells Ireland **51** F4
Kells *r.* U.K. **51** F3
Kelly U.S.A. **134** B5
Kelly Lake Canada **120** E1
Kelly Range *hills* Australia **109** C6
Kelmė Lith. **45** M9
Kelmis Belgium **52** G4
Kélo Chad **97** E4
Kelowna Canada **120** G5
Kelp Head *hd* Canada **120** E5
Kelseyville U.S.A. **128** B2
Kelso U.K. **50** G5
Kelso *CA* U.S.A. **129** F4
Kelso *WA* U.S.A. **126** C3
Keluang Malaysia **71** C7
Kelvington Canada **121** K4
Kem' Rus. Fed. **42** G2
Kem' *r.* Rus. Fed. **42** G2
Ke Macina Mali *see* **Massina**
Kemah Turkey **90** E3
Kemaliye Turkey **90** E3
Kemalpaşa Turkey **59** L5
Kemano (abandoned) Canada **120** E4
Kembé Cent. Afr. Rep. **98** C3
Kemeneshát *hills* Hungary **58** G1
Kemer *Antalya* Turkey **59** N6
Kemer *Muğla* Turkey **59** M6
Kemer Barajı *resr* Turkey **59** M6
Kemerovo Rus. Fed. **64** J4
Kemi Fin. **44** N4
Kemijärvi Fin. **44** O3
Kemijärvi *l.* Fin. **44** O3
Kemijoki *r.* Fin. **44** N4
Kemiö Fin. *see* **Kimito**
Kemir Turkm. *see* **Keymir**
Kemmerer U.S.A. **126** F4
Kemnath Germany **53** L5
Kemnay U.K. **50** G3
Kemp Coast *reg.* Antarctica *see*
Kemp Land
Kempele Fin. **44** N4
Kempen Germany **52** G3
Kempisch Kanaal *canal* Belgium **52** F3
Kemp Land *reg.* Antarctica **152** D2
Kemp Peninsula Antarctica **152** A2
Kemp's Bay Bahamas **133** E7
Kempsey Australia **112** F3
Kempt, Lac *l.* Canada **122** G5
Kempten (Allgäu) Germany **47** M7
Kempton U.S.A. **134** B3
Kempton Park S. Africa **101** I4
Kemptville Canada **135** H1
Kemujan *i.* Indon. **68** E8
Ken *r.* India **82** E4
Kenai U.S.A. **118** C3
Kenai Fiords National Park U.S.A. **118** C4
Kenai Mountains U.S.A. **118** C4
Kenamu *r.* Canada **123** K3
Kenansville U.S.A. **133** E5
Kenâyis, Râs el *pt* Egypt *see*
Ḥikmah, Ra's al
Kenbridge U.S.A. **135** F5
Kendal U.K. **48** E4
Kendall Australia **112** F3
Kendall, Cape Canada **119** J3
Kendallville U.S.A. **134** C3
Kendari Indon. **69** G7
Kendawangan Indon. **68** E7
Kendégué Chad **97** E3
Kendrapara India **83** F5
Kendraparha India *see* **Kendrapara**
Kendrick Peak U.S.A. **129** H4
Kendujhar India *see* **Keonjhar**
Kendujhargarh India *see* **Keonjhar**
Kendyrli-Kayasanskoye, Plato *plat.*
Kazakh. **91** I2
Kendyrlisor, Solonchak *salt l.* Kazakh. **91** I2
Kenebri Australia **112** D3
Kenedy U.S.A. **131** D6
Kenema Sierra Leone **96** B4
Kenge Dem. Rep. Congo **99** B4
Keng Lap Myanmar **70** C2
Kengtung Myanmar **70** B2
Kenhardt S. Africa **100** E5
Kéniéba Mali **96** B3
Kénitra Morocco **54** C5
Kenmare Ireland **51** C6
Kenmare U.S.A. **130** C1
Kenmare River *inlet* Ireland **51** B6
Kenmore U.S.A. **135** F2
Kenn Germany **52** G5
Kenna U.S.A. **131** C5
Kennebec U.S.A. **130** D3
Kennebec *r.* U.S.A. **132** G2
Kennebunkport U.S.A. **135** J2
Kennedy, Cape U.S.A. *see* **Canaveral, Cape**
Kennedy Range National Park
Australia **109** A6
Kennedy Town H.K. China **77** [inset]
Kenner U.S.A. **131** F6
Kennet *r.* U.K. **49** G7
Kenneth Range *hills* Australia **109** B5
Kennett U.S.A. **131** F4
Kennewick U.S.A. **126** D3
Kenn Reef Australia **110** F4
Kenogami *r.* Canada **122** D4
Keno Hill Canada **120** C2
Kenora Canada **121** M5
Kenosha U.S.A. **134** B2
Kenozero, Ozero *l.* Rus. Fed. **42** H3
Kent *r.* U.K. **48** E4
Kent *OH* U.S.A. **134** E3
Kent *TX* U.S.A. **131** B6
Kent *VA* U.S.A. **134** E5
Kent *WA* U.S.A. **126** C3
Kentani S. Africa **101** I7
Kent Group *is* Australia **111** [inset]
Kentland U.S.A. **134** B3
Kenton U.S.A. **134** D3
Kent Peninsula Canada **118** H3
Kentucky *state* U.S.A. **134** C5

Kentucky Lake U.S.A. **131** F4
Kenya *country* Africa **98** D3

▶**Kenya, Mount** Kenya **98** D4
2nd highest mountain in Africa.

Kenyir, Tasik *resr* Malaysia **71** C6
Keokuk U.S.A. **130** F3
Keoladeo National Park India **82** D4
Keonjhar India **83** F5
Keonjhargarh India *see* **Keonjhar**
Keosauqua U.S.A. **130** F3
Keowee, Lake *resr* U.S.A. **133** D5
Kepina *r.* Rus. Fed. **42** I2
Keppel Bay Australia **110** E4
Kepsut Turkey **59** M5
Kera India **83** F5
Kerāh Iran **88** E4
Kerala *state* India **84** B4
Kerang Australia **112** A5
Kerava Fin. **45** N6
Kerba Alg. **57** G5
Kerbela Iraq *see* **Karbalā'**
Kerben Kyrg. **80** D3
Kerbi *r.* Rus. Fed. **74** E1
Kerbodot, Lac *l.* Canada **123** I3
Kerch Ukr. **90** E1
Kerchem'ya Rus. Fed. **42** L3
Kerema P.N.G. **69** L8
Keremeos Canada **120** G5
Kerempe Burun *pt* Turkey **90** D2
Keren Eritrea **86** E6
Kerewan Gambia **96** B3
Kergeli Turkm. **88** E2
Kerguélen, Îles *is* Indian Ocean **149** M9
Kerguelen Islands Indian Ocean *see*
Kerguélen, Îles
Kerguelen Plateau *sea feature* Indian Ocean
149 M9
Kericho Kenya **98** D4
Kerikeri N.Z. **113** D2
Kerimäki Fin. **44** P6
Kerinci, Gunung *vol.* Indon. **68** C7
Kerinci Seblat, Taman Nasional
Indon. **68** C7
Kerintji *vol.* Indon. *see* **Kerinci, Gunung**
Keriya He *watercourse* China **72** E5
Keriya Shankou *pass* China **83** E2
Kerken Germany **52** G3
Kerkennah, Îles *is* Tunisia **58** D7
Kerkiçi Turkm. **89** G2
Kerkini, Limni *l.* Greece **59** J4
Kerkinitis, Limni *l.* Greece *see*
Kerkini, Limni
Kérkira *i.* Greece *see* **Corfu**
Kerkouane *tourist site* Tunisia **58** D6
Kerkyra Greece **59** H5
Kerkyra *i.* Greece *see* **Corfu**
Kerma Sudan **86** D6
Kermadec Islands S. Pacific Ocean **107** I5

▶**Kermadec Trench** *sea feature*
S. Pacific Ocean **150** I8
4th deepest trench in the world.

Kermān Iran **88** E4
Kerman U.S.A. **128** C3
Kermān, Bīābān-e Iran **88** E4
Kermānshāh Iran **88** B3
Kermānshāhān Iran **88** D4
Kermine Uzbek. *see* **Navoiy**
Kermit U.S.A. **131** C6
Kern *r.* U.S.A. **128** D4
Kernertut, Cap *c.* Canada **123** I2
Keros *i.* Greece **59** K6
Keros Rus. Fed. **42** L3
Kérouané Guinea **96** C4
Kerpen Germany **52** G4
Kerr, Cape Antarctica **152** H1
Kerrobert Canada **121** I5
Kerrville U.S.A. **131** D6
Kerry Head *hd* Ireland **51** C5
Kerteminde Denmark **45** G9
Kerulen *r.* China/Mongolia *see*
Herlen Gol
Kerur India **84** B2
Keryneia Cyprus *see* **Kyrenia**
Kerzaz Alg. **96** C2
Kerzhenets *r.* Rus. Fed. **42** J4
Kesagami Lake Canada **122** E4
Kesälahti Fin. **44** P6
Keşan Turkey **59** L4
Keşap Turkey **43** H8
Kesariya India **83** F4
Kesennuma Japan **75** F5
Keshan China **74** B2
Keshem Afgh. **89** H2
Keshena U.S.A. **134** A1
Keshendeh-ye Bala Afgh. **89** G2
Keshod India **82** B5
Keshvar Iran **88** C3
Keskin Turkey **90** D3
Keskozero Rus. Fed. **42** G3
Kesova Gora Rus. Fed. **42** H4
Kessel Neth. **52** G3
Kestell S. Africa **101** I5
Kesten'ga Rus. Fed. **44** Q4
Kestilä Fin. **44** O4
Keswick Canada **134** F1
Keswick U.K. **48** D4
Keszthely Hungary **58** G1
Ketapang Indon. **68** E7
Ketchikan U.S.A. **120** D4
Keti Bandar Pak. **89** G5
Ketmen', Khrebet *mts* China/Kazakh. **80** F3
Kettering U.K. **49** G6
Kettering U.S.A. **134** C4
Kettle *r.* Canada **120** G5
Kettle Creek *r.* U.S.A. **135** G3
Kettle Falls U.S.A. **126** D2
Kettleman City U.S.A. **128** D3
Kettle River Range *mts* U.S.A. **126** D2
Keuka U.S.A. **135** G2
Keuka Lake U.S.A. **135** G2
Keumgang, Mount N. Korea *see*
Kumgang-san
Keumsang, Mount N. Korea *see*
Kumgang-san
Keuruu Fin. **44** N5
Kew Turks and Caicos Is **133** F8
Kewanee U.S.A. **130** F3
Kewaunee U.S.A. **134** B1

Keweenaw Bay U.S.A. **130** F2
Keweenaw Peninsula U.S.A. **130** F2
Keweenaw Point U.S.A. **132** C2
Key, Lough *l.* Ireland **51** D3
Keyala Sudan **97** G4
Keyano Canada **123** G3
Keya Paha *r.* U.S.A. **130** D3
Key Harbour Canada **122** E5
Keyihe China **74** A2
Key Largo U.S.A. **133** D7
Keymir Turkm. **88** D2
Keynsham U.K. **49** E7
Keyser U.S.A. **135** F4
Keystone Lake U.S.A. **131** D4
Keystone Peak U.S.A. **129** H6
Keysville U.S.A. **135** F5
Keytesville U.S.A. **130** E4
Keyvy, Vozvyshennost' *hills*
Rus. Fed. **42** H2
Key West U.S.A. **133** D7
Kez Rus. Fed. **41** Q4
Kezi Zimbabwe **99** C6
Kgalagadi *admin. dist.* Botswana **100** E3
Kgalagadi Transfrontier National Park
101 D2
Kgalazadi *admin. dist.* Botswana *see*
Kgalagadi
Kgatlen *admin. dist.* Botswana *see* **Kgatleng**
Kgatleng *admin. dist.* Botswana **101** H3
Kgomofatshe Pan *salt pan*
Botswana **100** E2
Kgoro Pan *salt pan* Botswana **100** G3
Kgotsong S. Africa **101** H4
Khabab Syria **85** C3
Khabar Iran **88** D4
Khabarikha Rus. Fed. **42** L2
Khabarovsk Rus. Fed. **74** D2
Khabarovskiy Kray *admin. div.*
Rus. Fed. **74** D2
Khabarovsk Kray *admin. div.* Rus. Fed. *see*
Khabarovskiy Kray
Khabary Rus. Fed. **72** D2
Khabis Iran *see* **Shahdād**
Khabody Pass Afgh. **89** F3
Khachmas Azer. *see* **Xaçmaz**
Khadar, Jabal *mt.* Oman **88** E6
Khadro Pak. **89** H5
Khadzhiolen Turkm. **88** E2
Khafs Banbān *well* Saudi Arabia **88** B5
Khagaria India **83** F4
Khagrachari Bangl. **83** G5
Khagrachhari Bangl. *see* **Khagrachari**
Khairgarh Pak. **89** H4
Khairpur *Punjab* Pak. **89** I4
Khairpur *Sindh* Pak. **89** H5
Khāīz, Kūh-e *mt.* Iran **88** C4
Khaja Du Koh *hill* Afgh. **89** G2
Khajuha India **82** E4
Khāk-e Jabbar Afgh. **89** H3
Khakhea Botswana **100** F3
Khak-rēz Afgh. **89** G4
Khakriz *reg.* Afgh. **89** G4
Khalajestan *reg.* Iran **88** C3
Khalatse India **82** D2
Khalifat *mt.* Pak. **89** G4
Khalīj Surt *g.* Libya *see* **Sirte, Gulf of**
Khalilabad India **83** E4
Khalīlī Iran **88** D5
Khalkabad Turkm. **89** F1
Khalkhāl Iran **88** C2
Khálki *i.* Greece *see* **Chalki**
Khalkís Greece *see* **Chalkida**
Khallikot India **84** E2
Khalturin Rus. Fed. *see* **Orlov**
Khamar-Daban, Khrebet *mts*
Rus. Fed. **72** I2
Khamaria India **84** D1
Khambhat India **82** C5
Khambhat, Gulf of India **84** A2
Khamgaon India **84** C1
Khamir Yemen **86** F6
Khamis Mushayṭ Saudi Arabia **86** F6
Khamkkeut Laos **70** D3
Khamma *well* Saudi Arabia **88** B5
Khammam India **84** D2
Khammouan Laos *see* **Thakèk**
Khamra Rus. Fed. **65** M3
Khamseh *reg.* Iran **88** C3
Khan Afgh. **89** H3
Khan, Nam *r.* Laos **70** C3
Khānābād Afgh. **89** H2
Khān al Baghdādī Iraq **91** F4
Khān al Mashāhidah Iraq **91** G4
Khān al Muṣallá Iraq **91** G4
Khanapur India **84** B2
Khān ar Raḥbah Iraq **91** G5
Khanasur Pass Iran/Turkey **91** G3
Khanbalik China *see* **Beijing**
Khānch Iran **88** B2
Khandu India **89** I6
Khandwa India **82** D5
Khandyga Rus. Fed. **65** O3
Khanewal Pak. **89** H4
Khan Hung Vietnam *see* **Soc Trăng**
Khaniá Greece *see* **Chania**
Khān-i Yek Iran **88** D4
Khanka, Lake China/Rus. Fed. **74** D3
Khanka, Ozero *l.* China/Rus. Fed. *see*
Khanka, Lake
Khankendi Azer. *see* **Xankändi**
Khanna India **82** D3
Khannā, Qā' *salt pan* Jordan **85** C3
Khanpur Pak. **89** H4
Khanpur Pak. **89** H4
Khān Ruḥābah Iraq *see* **Khān ar Raḥbah**
Khansar Pak. **89** H4
Khān Shaykhūn Syria **85** C2
Khantayskoye, Ozero *l.* Rus. Fed. **64** K3
Khanthabouli Laos *see* **Savannakhét**
Khanty-Mansiysk Rus. Fed. **64** H3
Khān Yūnis Gaza **85** B4
Khanzi *admin. dist.* Botswana *see* **Ghanzi**
Khao Ang Rua Nai Wildlife Reserve
nature res. Thai. **71** C4
Khao Banthat Wildlife Reserve *nature res.*
Thai. **71** B6
Khao Chum Thong Thai. **71** B5
Khaoen Si Nakarin National Park Thai.
71 B4
Khao Laem, Ang Kep Nam Thai. **70** B4
Khao Laem National Park Thai. **70** B4
Khao Luang National Park Thai. **71** B5

Khao Pu-Khao Ya National Park
Thai. **71** B6
Khao Soi Dao Wildlife Reserve *nature res.*
Thai. **71** C4
Khao Sok National Park Thai. **71** B5
Khao Yai National Park Thai. **71** C4
Khaplu Pak. **80** E4
Khaptad National Park Nepal **82** E3
Kharabali Rus. Fed. **43** J7
Kharagpur *Bihar* India **83** F4
Kharagpur *W. Bengal* India **83** F5
Khārān *r.* Iran **87** I4
Kharari India *see* **Abu Road**
Kharda India **84** B2
Khardi India **82** C6
Khardong La *pass* India *see*
Khardung La
Khardung La *pass* India **82** D2
Kharez Ilias Afgh. **89** F3
Kharfiyah Iraq **91** G5
Kharga Egypt *see* **Al Khārijah**
Kharga *r.* Rus. Fed. **74** D1
Khârga, El Wâḥât el *oasis* Egypt *see*
Khārijah, Wāḥāt al
Kharga Oasis Egypt *see*
Khārijah, Wāḥāt al
Kharg Islands Iran **88** C4
Khargon India **82** C5
Khari *r. Rajasthan* India **82** C4
Khari *r. Rajasthan* India **82** C4
Kharian Pak. **89** I3
Khariar India **84** D1
Khārijah, Wāḥāt al *oasis* Egypt **86** D5
Kharīm, Gebel *hill* Egypt *see*
Kharīm, Jabal
Kharīm, Jabal *hill* Egypt **85** A4
Kharkhara *r.* India **82** E5
Kharkiv Ukr. **43** H6
Khar'kov Ukr. *see* **Kharkiv**
Khār Kūh *mt.* Iran **88** D4
Kharlovka Rus. Fed. **42** H1
Kharlu Rus. Fed. **44** Q6
Kharmanli Bulg. **59** K4
Kharoti *reg.* Afgh. **89** H3
Kharovsk Rus. Fed. **42** I4
Kharsia India **83** E5

▶**Khartoum** Sudan **86** D6
Capital of Sudan. 4th most populous city in Africa.

Kharwar *reg.* Afgh. **89** H3
Khasavyurt Rus. Fed. **91** G2
Khash Afgh. **89** F4
Khāsh Iran **89** F4
Khāsh, Dasht-e Afgh. **89** F4
Khashgort Rus. Fed. **41** T2
Khashm el Girba Sudan **86** E7
Khashm Ṣana' Saudi Arabia **90** E6
Khash Rūd *r.* Afgh. **89** F4
Khashuri Georgia **91** F2
Khasi Hills India **83** G4
Khaskovo Bulg. **59** K4
Khatanga Rus. Fed. **65** L2
Khatanga, Gulf of Rus. Fed. *see*
Khatangskiy Zaliv
Khatangskiy Zaliv *b.* Rus. Fed. **65** L2
Khatayakha Rus. Fed. **42** M2
Khatinza Pass Pak. **89** H2
Khatmat al Malāha Oman **88** E5
Khatyrka Rus. Fed. **65** S3
Khāvāk, Khowtal-e Afgh. **89** H3
Khavda India **82** B5
Khayamnandi S. Africa **101** G6
Khaybar Saudi Arabia **86** E4
Khayelitsha S. Africa **100** D8
Khayrān, Ra's al *pt* Oman **88** E6
Khedrī Iran **88** E3
Khefa Israel *see* **Haifa**
Khehuene, Ponta *pt* Moz. **101** L2
Khemis Miliana Alg. **57** H5
Khemmarat Thai. **70** D3
Khenchela Alg. **58** B7
Khenifra Morocco **54** C5
Kherāmeh Iran **88** D4
Kherrata Alg. **57** I5
Kherreh Iran **88** D5
Khersan *r.* Iran **88** C4
Kherson Ukr. **59** O1
Kheta *r.* Rus. Fed. **65** L2
Kheyrābād Iran **88** D4
Khezerābād Iran **88** D2
Khiching India **83** F5
Khilok Rus. Fed. **73** K2
Khilok *r.* Rus. Fed. **73** J2
Khinganskiy Zapovednik *nature res.*
Rus. Fed. **74** C2
Khinsar Pak. **89** H5
Khíos *i.* Greece *see* **Chios**
Khipro Pak. **89** H5
Khirbat Isrīyah Syria **85** C2
Khitai Dawan Aksai Chin **82** D2
Khīyāv Iran **88** B2
Khiytola Rus. Fed. **45** P6
Khlevnoye Rus. Fed. **43** H5
Khlong, Mae *r.* Thai. **71** C4
Khlong Saeng Wildlife Reserve *nature res.*
Thai. **71** B5
Khlong Wang Chao National Park
Thai. **70** B3
Khlung Thai. **71** C4
Khmel'nik Ukr. *see* **Khmil'nyk**
Khmel'nitskiy Ukr. *see* **Khmel'nyts'kyy**
Khmel'nyts'kyy Ukr. **43** E6
Khmer Republic *country* Asia *see*
Cambodia
Khmil'nyk Ukr. **43** E6
Khoai, Hon *i.* Vietnam **71** D5
Khobda Kazakh. **80** A1
Khobi Georgia **91** F2
Khodā Āfarīd *spring* Iran **88** E3
Khodzha-Kala Turkm. *see* **Hojagala**
Khodzhambaz Turkm. *see* **Hojambaz**
Khodzhent Tajik. *see* **Khŭjand**
Khodzheyli *Qoraqalpog'iston Respublikasi*
Uzbek. *see* **Xo'jayli**
Khojand Tajik. *see* **Khŭjand**
Khokhowe Pan *salt pan* Botswana **100** E3
Khokhropar Pak. **89** H5
Khoksar India **82** D2
Kholm Afgh. **89** G2
Kholm Poland *see* **Chełm**

Kholm Rus. Fed. **42** F4
Kholmsk Rus. Fed. **74** F3
Kholon Israel *see* **Ḥolon**
Khomas *admin. reg.* Namibia **100** C2
Khomas Highland *hills*
Namibia **100** B2
Khomeyn Iran **88** C3
Khomeynīshahr Iran **88** C3
Khong, Mae Nam *r.* Asia **70** D4 *see*
Mekong
Khonj Iran **88** D5
Khonj, Kūh-e *mts* Iran **88** D5
Khon Kaen Thai. **70** C3
Khon Kriel Cambodia *see*
Phumĭ Kon Kriel
Khonsa India **83** H4
Khonuu Rus. Fed. **65** P3
Khoper *r.* Rus. Fed. **43** I6
Khor Rus. Fed. **74** D3
Khor *r.* Rus. Fed. **74** D3
Khorat Plateau Thai. **70** C3
Khorda India *see* **Khurda**
Khordha India *see* **Khurda**
Khoreyver Rus. Fed. **42** M2
Khorinsk Rus. Fed. **73** J2
Khorixas Namibia **99** B6
Khormūj, Kūh-e *mt.* Iran **88** C4
Khorog Tajik. *see* **Khorugh**
Khorol Rus. Fed. **74** D3
Khorol Ukr. **43** G6
Khoroslū Dāgh *hills* Iran **88** B2
Khorramābād Iran **88** C3
Khorramshahr Iran **88** C4
Khorugh Tajik. **89** H2
Khosheutovo Rus. Fed. **43** J7
Khōst *reg.* Afgh./Pak. **89** H3
Khōst *Khōst* **89** H3
Khosūyeh Iran **88** D4
Khotan China *see* **Hotan**
Khouribga Morocco **54** C5
Khovaling Tajik. **89** H2
Khowrjān Iran **88** D4
Khowrnag, Kūh-e *mt.* Iran **88** D3
Khreum Myanmar **70** A2
Khroma *r.* Rus. Fed. **65** P2
Khromtau Kazakh. **80** A1
Khrushchev Ukr. *see* **Svitlovods'k**
Khrysokhou Bay Cyprus *see*
Chrysochou Bay
Khrystynivka Ukr. **43** F6
Khuar Pak. **89** I3
Khudumelapye Botswana **100** G2
Khudzhand Tajik. *see* **Khŭjand**
Khufaysah, Khashm al *hill*
Saudi Arabia **88** B6
Khugiana Afgh. *see* **Pirzada**
Khuis Botswana **100** E4
Khŭjand Tajik. **80** C3
Khŭjayli *Qoraqalpog'iston Respublikasi*
Uzbek. *see* **Xo'jayli**
Khŭjayli Uzbek. *see* **Xo'jayli**
Khu Khan Thai. **71** D4
Khulays Saudi Arabia **86** E5
Khulkhuta Rus. Fed. **43** J7
Khulm *r.* Afgh. **89** G2
Khulna Bangl. **83** G5
Khulo Georgia **91** F2
Khuma S. Africa **101** H4
Khŭm Batheay Cambodia **71** D5
Khunayzīr, Jabal al *mts* Syria **85** C2
Khūnīk Bālā Iran **88** E3
Khūnīnshahr Iran *see* **Khorramshahr**
Khunjerab Pass China/Pakistan **82** C1
Khunsar Iran **88** C3
Khun Yuam Thai. **70** B3
Khūr Iran **88** E3
Khūran *sea chan.* Iran **88** D5
Khurayṣ Saudi Arabia **86** G4
Khurd, Koh-i- *mt.* Afgh. **89** G3
Khurda India **84** E1
Khurdha India *see* **Khurda**
Khurja India **82** D3
Khurmalik Afgh. **89** F3
Khurmuli Rus. Fed. **74** E2
Khūrrāb Iran **88** D4
Khurz Iran **88** D3
Khushab Pak. **89** I3
Khushalgarh Pak. **89** H3
Khushshah, Wādī al *watercourse*
Jordan/Saudi Arabia **85** C5
Khust Ukr. **43** D6
Khutse Game Reserve *nature res.*
Botswana **100** G2
Khutsong S. Africa **101** H4
Khutu *r.* Rus. Fed. **74** E2
Khuzdar Pak. **89** G5
Khvāf Iran **89** F3
Khvāf *reg.* Iran **89** F3
Khvājeh Iran **88** B2
Khvalynsk Rus. Fed. **43** K5
Khvodrān Iran **88** D4
Khvord Nārvan Iran **88** E3
Khvormūj Iran **88** C4
Khvoy Iran **88** B2
Khvoynaya Rus. Fed. **42** G4
Khwaja Amran *mt.* Pak. **89** G4
Khwaja Muhammad Range *mts*
Afgh. **89** H2
Khyber Pass Afgh./Pak. **89** H3
Kiama Australia **112** E5
Kiamichi *r.* U.S.A. **131** E5
Kiangsi *prov.* China *see* **Jiangxi**
Kiangsu *prov.* China *see* **Jiangsu**
Kiantajärvi *l.* Fin. **44** P4
Kīāseh Iran **88** D2
Kiatassuaq *i.* Greenland **119** M2
Kibaha Tanz. **99** D4
Kibali *r.* Dem. Rep. Congo **98** C3
Kibangou Congo **98** B4
Kibaya Tanz. **99** D4
Kiboga Uganda **98** D3
Kibombo Dem. Rep. Congo **98** C4
Kibondo Tanz. **98** D4
Kibre Mengist Eth. **97** G4
Kıbrıs *country* Asia *see* **Cyprus**
Kibungo Rwanda **98** D4
Kičevo Macedonia **59** I4
Kichmengskiy Gorodok Rus. Fed. **42** J4
Kiçik Qafqaz *mts* Asia *see*
Lesser Caucasus
Kicking Horse Pass Canada **120** G5
Kidal Mali **96** D3

Kidderminster U.K. 49 E6
Kidepo Valley National Park Uganda 98 D3
Kidira Senegal 96 B3
Kidmang India 82 D2
Kidnappers, Cape N.Z. 113 F4
Kidsgrove U.K. 49 E5
Kiel Germany 47 M3
Kiel U.S.A. 134 A2
Kiel Canal Germany 47 L3
Kielce Poland 47 R5
Kielder Water resr U.K. 48 E3
Kieler Bucht b. Germany 47 M3
Kienge Dem. Rep. Congo 99 C5
Kierspe Germany 53 H3

▶Kiev Ukr. 43 F6
Capital of Ukraine.

Kiffa Mauritania 96 B3
Kifisia Greece 59 J5
Kifrī Iraq 91 G4

▶Kigali Rwanda 98 D4
Capital of Rwanda.

Kiğı Turkey 91 F3
Kiglapait Mountains Canada 123 J2
Kigoma Tanz. 99 C4
Kihlanki Fin. 44 M3
Kihniö Fin. 44 M5
Kīholo U.S.A. 127 [inset]
Kiiminki Fin. 44 N4
Kii-sanchi mts Japan 75 D6
Kii-suidō sea chan. Japan 75 D6
Kikerino Rus. Fed. 45 P7
Kikinda Serbia 59 I2
Kikki Pak. 89 F5
Kikládhes is Greece see Cyclades
Kiknur Rus. Fed. 42 J4
Kikonai Japan 74 F4
Kikori P.N.G. 69 K8
Kikori r. P.N.G. 69 K8
Kikwit Dem. Rep. Congo 99 B4
Kilafors Sweden 45 J6
Kilar India 82 D2
Kilauea U.S.A. 127 [inset]
Kilauea Crater U.S.A. 127 [inset]
Kilchu N. Korea 74 C4
Kilcoole Ireland 51 F4
Kilcormac Ireland 51 E4
Kilcoy Australia 112 F1
Kildare Ireland 51 F4
Kil'dinstroy Rus. Fed. 44 R2
Kilemary Rus. Fed. 42 J4
Kilembe Dem. Rep. Congo 99 B4
Kilfinan U.K. 50 D5
Kilgore U.S.A. 131 E5
Kilham U.K. 48 E3
Kilia Ukr. see Kiliya
Kılıç Dağı mt. Syria/Turkey see Aqra', Jabal al
Kilifi Kenya 98 D4
Kilik Pass China 82 C1

▶Kilimanjaro vol. Tanz. 98 D4
Highest mountain in Africa.

Kilimanjaro National Park Tanz. 98 D4
Kilinailau Islands P.N.G. 106 F2
Kilindoni Tanz. 99 D4
Kilingi-Nõmme Estonia 45 N7
Kilis Turkey 85 C1
Kilis prov. Turkey 85 C1
Kiliya Ukr. 59 M2
Kilkee Ireland 51 C5
Kilkeel U.K. 51 G3
Kilkenny Ireland 51 E5
Kilkhampton U.K. 49 C8
Kilkis Greece 59 J4
Killala Ireland 51 C3
Killala Bay Ireland 51 C3
Killaloe Ireland 51 D5
Killam Canada 121 I4
Killarney N.T. Australia 108 E4
Killarney Qld Australia 112 F2
Killarney Canada 122 E5
Killarney Ireland 51 C5
Killarney National Park Ireland 51 C6
Killary Harbour b. Ireland 51 C4
Killbuck U.S.A. 134 E3
Killeen U.S.A. 131 D6
Killenaule Ireland 51 E5
Killimor Ireland 51 D4
Killin U.K. 50 E4
Killinchy U.K. 51 G3
Killini mt Greece see Kyllini
Killinick Ireland 51 F5
Killorglin Ireland 51 C5
Killurin Ireland 51 F5
Killybegs Ireland 51 D3
Kilmacrenan Ireland 51 E2
Kilmaine Ireland 51 C4
Kilmallock Ireland 51 D5
Kilmaluag U.K. 50 C3
Kilmarnock U.K. 50 E5
Kilmelford U.K. 50 D4
Kil'mez' Rus. Fed. 42 K4
Kil'mez' r. Rus. Fed. 42 K4
Kilmona Ireland 51 D6
Kilmore Australia 112 B6
Kilmore Quay Ireland 51 F5
Kilosa Tanz. 99 D4
Kilpisjärvi Fin. 44 L2
Kilrea U.K. 51 F3
Kilrush Ireland 51 C5
Kilsyth U.K. 50 E5
Kiltan atoll India 84 B4
Kiltullagh Ireland 51 D4
Kilwa Masoko Tanz. 99 D4
Kilwinning U.K. 50 E5
Kim U.S.A. 131 C4
Kimba Australia 109 G8
Kimba Congo 98 B4
Kimball U.S.A. 130 C3
Kimball, Mount U.S.A. 118 D3
Kimbe P.N.G. 106 F2
Kimberley S. Africa 100 G5
Kimberley Plateau Australia 108 D4
Kimberley Range hills Australia 109 B6
Kimch'aek N. Korea 75 C4
Kimch'ŏn S. Korea 75 C5
Kimhae S. Korea 75 C6
Kimhandu mt. Tanz. 99 D4
Kimhwa S. Korea 75 B5
Kími Greece see Kymi
Kimito Fin. 45 M6
Kimmirut Canada 119 L3
Kimolos i. Greece 59 K6
Kimovsk Rus. Fed. 43 H5
Kimpese Dem. Rep. Congo 99 B4
Kimpoku-san mt. Japan see Kinpoku-san
Kimry Rus. Fed. 42 H4
Kimsquit Canada 120 E4
Kimvula Dem. Rep. Congo 99 B4
Kinabalu, Gunung mt. Sabah Malaysia 68 F5
Kinango Kenya 99 D4
Kinaskan Lake Canada 120 D3
Kinbasket Lake Canada 120 G4
Kinbrace U.K. 50 F2
Kincaid Canada 121 J5
Kincardine Canada 134 E1
Kincardine U.K. 50 F4
Kinchega National Park Australia 111 C7
Kincolith Canada 120 D4
Kinda Dem. Rep. Congo 99 C4
Kindat Myanmar 70 A2
Kinde U.S.A. 134 D2
Kinder Scout hill U.K. 48 F5
Kindersley Canada 121 I5
Kindia Guinea 96 B3
Kindu Dem. Rep. Congo 98 C4
Kinel' Rus. Fed. 43 K5
Kineshma Rus. Fed. 42 I4
Kingaroy Australia 112 E1
King Christian Island Canada 119 H2
King City U.S.A. 128 C3
King Edward VII Land pen. Antarctica see Edward VII Peninsula
Kingfield U.S.A. 135 J1
Kingfisher U.S.A. 131 D5
King George U.S.A. 135 G4
King George, Mount Canada 126 E2
King George Island Antarctica 152 A2
King George Islands Canada 122 F2
King George Islands Fr. Polynesia see Roi Georges, Îles du
King Hill hill Australia 108 C5
Kingisepp Rus. Fed. 45 P7
King Island Australia 111 [inset]
King Island Canada 120 E4
King Island Myanmar see Kadan Kyun
Kingisseppa Estonia see Kuressaare
Kinglake National Park Australia 112 B6
King Leopold and Queen Astrid Coast Antarctica 152 E2
King Leopold Range National Park Australia 108 D4
King Leopold Ranges hills Australia 108 D4
Kingman U.S.A. 129 F4

▶Kingman Reef terr. N. Pacific Ocean 150 J5
United States Unincorporated Territory.

King Mountain Canada 120 D3
King Mountain hill U.S.A. 131 C6
Kingoonya Australia 111 A6
King Peak Antarctica 152 L1
King Peninsula Antarctica 152 K2
Kingri Pak. 89 H4
Kings r. Ireland 51 E5
Kings r. CA U.S.A. 128 C3
Kings r. NV U.S.A. 126 D4
King Salmon U.S.A. 118 C4
Kingsbridge U.K. 49 D8
Kingsburg U.S.A. 128 D3
Kings Canyon National Park U.S.A. 128 D3
Kingscliff Australia 112 F2
Kingscote Australia 111 B7
Kingscourt Ireland 51 F4
King Sejong research station Antarctica 152 A2
King's Lynn U.K. 49 H6
Kingsmill Group is Kiribati 107 H2
Kingsnorth U.K. 49 H7
King Sound b. Australia 108 C4
Kings Peak U.S.A. 129 H1
Kingsport U.S.A. 132 D4
Kingston Australia 111 [inset]
Kingston Canada 135 G1

▶Kingston Jamaica 137 I5
Capital of Jamaica.

▶Kingston Norfolk I. 107 G4
Capital of Norfolk Island.

Kingston MO U.S.A. 130 E4
Kingston NY U.S.A. 135 H3
Kingston OH U.S.A. 134 D4
Kingston PA U.S.A. 135 H3
Kingston Peak U.S.A. 129 F4
Kingston South East Australia 111 B8
Kingston upon Hull U.K. 48 G5

▶Kingstown St Vincent 137 L6
Capital of St Vincent.

Kingstree U.S.A. 133 E5
Kingsville U.S.A. 131 D7
Kingswood U.K. 49 E7
Kington U.K. 49 D6
Kingungi Dem. Rep. Congo 99 B4
Kingurutik r. Canada 123 J2
Kingussie U.K. 50 E3
King William U.S.A. 135 G5
King William Island Canada 119 I3
King William's Town S. Africa 101 H7
Kingwood TX U.S.A. 131 E6
Kingwood WV U.S.A. 134 F4
Kinloch N.Z. 113 B7
Kinloss U.K. 50 F3
Kinmen Taiwan see Chinmen
Kinmen i. Taiwan see Chinmen Tao
Kinmount Canada 135 F1
Kinna Sweden 45 H8
Kinnegad Ireland 51 E4
Kinneret, Yam l. Israel see Galilee, Sea of
Kinniyai Sri Lanka 84 D4
Kinnula Fin. 44 N5
Kinoje r. Canada 122 E3
Kinoosao Canada 121 K3
Kinpoku-san mt. Japan 75 E5
Kinross U.K. 50 F4
Kinsale Ireland 51 D6
Kinsale U.S.A. 135 G4

▶Kinshasa Dem. Rep. Congo 99 B4
Capital of the Democratic Republic of the Congo. 3rd most populous city in Africa.

Kinsley U.S.A. 130 D4
Kinsman U.S.A. 134 E3
Kinston U.S.A. 133 E5
Kintore U.K. 50 G3
Kintyre pen. U.K. 50 D5
Kin-U Myanmar 70 A2
Kinushseo r. Canada 122 E3
Kinyeti mt. Sudan 97 G4
Kinzig r. Germany 53 I4
Kiowa CO U.S.A. 126 G5
Kiowa KS U.S.A. 131 D4
Kipahigan Lake Canada 121 K4
Kiparissía Greece see Kyparissia
Kipawa, Lac l. Canada 122 F5
Kipling Canada 121 K5
Kipling Station Canada see Kipling
Kipnuk U.S.A. 118 B4
Kiptopeke U.S.A. 135 H5
Kipungo Angola see Quipungo
Kipushi Dem. Rep. Congo 99 C5
Kirakira Solomon Is 107 G3
Kirandul India 84 D2
Kirchdorf Germany 53 I2
Kirchheim-Bolanden Germany 53 I5
Kirchheim unter Teck Germany 53 J6
Kircubbin U.K. 51 G3
Kirdimi Chad 97 E3
Kirenga r. Rus. Fed. 73 J1
Kirensk Rus. Fed. 65 L4
Kireyevsk Rus. Fed. 43 H5
Kirghizia country Asia see Kyrgyzstan
Kirghiz Range mts Kazakh./Kyrg. 80 D3
Kirgizskaya S.S.R. country Asia see Kyrgyzstan
Kirgizskiy Khrebet mts Kazakh./Kyrg. see Kirghiz Range
Kirgizstan country Asia see Kyrgyzstan
Kiri Dem. Rep. Congo 98 B4
Kiribati country Pacific Ocean 150 I6
Kırıkhan Turkey 85 C1
Kırıkkale Turkey 90 D3
Kirillov Rus. Fed. 42 H4
Kirillovo Rus. Fed. 74 F3
Kirin China see Jilin
Kirin prov. China see Jilin
Kirinda Sri Lanka 84 D5
Kirinyaga mt. Kenya see Kenya, Mount
Kirishi Rus. Fed. 42 G4
Kirishima-Yaku Kokuritsu-kōen nat. park Japan 75 C7
Kirishima-yama vol. Japan 75 C7
Kiritimati atoll Kiribati 151 J5
Kiriwina Islands P.N.G. see Trobriand Islands
Kırkağaç Turkey 59 L5
Kirk Bulāg Dāgi mt. Iran 88 B2
Kirkby U.K. 48 E5
Kirkby in Ashfield U.K. 49 F5
Kirkby Lonsdale U.K. 48 E4
Kirkby Stephen U.K. 48 E4
Kirkcaldy U.K. 50 F4
Kirkcolm U.K. 50 D6
Kirkcudbright U.K. 50 E6
Kirkenær Norway 45 H6
Kirkenes Norway 44 Q2
Kirkfield Canada 135 F1
Kirkintilloch U.K. 50 E5
Kirkkonummi Fin. 45 N6
Kirkland U.S.A. 129 G4
Kirkland Lake Canada 122 E4
Kırklareli Turkey 59 L4
Kirklin U.S.A. 134 B3
Kirk Michael Isle of Man 48 C4
Kirkoswald U.K. 48 E4
Kirkpatrick, Mount Antarctica 152 H1
Kirksville U.S.A. 130 E3
Kirkūk Iraq 91 G4
Kirkwall U.K. 50 G2
Kirkwood S. Africa 101 G7
Kirman Iran see Kermān
Kirn Germany 53 H5
Kirov Kaluzhskaya Oblast' Rus. Fed. 43 G5
Kirov Kirovskaya Oblast' Rus. Fed. 42 K4
Kirova, Zaliv b. Azer. see Qızılağac Körfäzi
Kirovabad Azer. see Gäncä
Kirovabad Tajik. see Panj
Kirovakan Armenia see Vanadzor
Kirovo Ukr. see Kirovohrad
Kirovo-Chepetsk Rus. Fed. 42 K4
Kirovo-Chepetskiy Rus. Fed. see Kirovo-Chepetsk
Kirovograd Ukr. see Kirovohrad
Kirovohrad Ukr. 43 G6
Kirovsk Leningradskaya Oblast' Rus. Fed. 42 F4
Kirovsk Murmanskaya Oblast' Rus. Fed. 44 R3
Kirovsk Turkm. see Badabaýhan
Kirovs'ke Ukr. 90 D1
Kirovskiy Rus. Fed. 74 D3
Kirovskoye Ukr. see Kirovs'ke
Kırpaşa pen. Cyprus see Karpasia
Kirpili Turkm. 88 E2
Kirriemuir U.K. 50 F4
Kirs Rus. Fed. 42 L4
Kirsanov Rus. Fed. 43 I5
Kırşehir Turkey 90 D3
Kirthar National Park Pak. 89 G5
Kirthar Range mts Pak. 89 G5
Kirtland U.S.A. 129 I3
Kirtorf Germany 53 J4
Kiruna Sweden 44 L3
Kirundu Dem. Rep. Congo 98 C4
Kirwan Escarpment Antarctica 152 B2
Kiryū Japan 75 E5
Kisa Sweden 45 I8
Kisama, Parque Nacional de nat. park Angola see Quiçama, Parque Nacional do
Kisandji Dem. Rep. Congo 99 B4
Kisangani Dem. Rep. Congo 98 C3
Kisantu Dem. Rep. Congo 99 B4
Kisar i. Indon. 108 D2
Kisaran Indon. 71 B7
Kiselevsk Rus. Fed. 72 F2
Kisel'ovka Rus. Fed. 74 E2
Kish i. Iran 88 D5
Kishanganj India 83 F4
Kishangarh Madh. Prad. India 82 D4
Kishangarh Rajasthan India 82 B4
Kishi Nigeria 96 D4
Kishinev Moldova see Chişinău
Kishkenekol' Kazakh. 79 G1
Kishoreganj Bangl. 83 G4
Kishorganj Bangl. see Kishoreganj
Kisi Nigeria see Kishi
Kisii Kenya 98 D4
Kiska Island U.S.A. 65 S4
Kiskittogisu Lake Canada 121 L4
Kiskitto Lake Canada 121 L4
Kiskunfélegyháza Hungary 59 H1
Kiskunhalas Hungary 59 H1
Kiskunsági nat. park Hungary 59 H1
Kislovodsk Rus. Fed. 91 F2
Kismaayo Somalia 98 E4
Kismayu Somalia see Kismaayo
Kisoro Uganda 97 F5
Kispiox Canada 120 E4
Kispiox r. Canada 120 E4
Kissamos Greece 59 J7
Kisseraing Island Myanmar see Kanmaw Kyun
Kissidougou Guinea 96 B4
Kissimmee U.S.A. 133 D6
Kissimmee, Lake U.S.A. 133 D7
Kississing Lake Canada 121 K4
Kistendey Rus. Fed. 43 I5
Kistigan Lake Canada 121 M4
Kistna r. India see Krishna
Kisumu Kenya 98 D4
Kisykkamys Kazakh. see Dzhangala
Kita Mali 96 C3
Kitab Uzbek. see Kitob
Kita-Daitō-jima i. Japan 73 O7
Kitaibaraki Japan 75 F5
Kita-Iō-jima vol. Japan 69 K1
Kitakami Japan 75 F5
Kita-Kyūshū Japan 75 C6
Kitale Kenya 98 D3
Kitami Japan 74 F4
Kit Carson U.S.A. 130 C4
Kitchener Canada 134 E2
Kitchigama r. Canada 122 F4
Kitee Fin. 44 Q5
Kitgum Uganda 98 D3
Kíthira i. Greece see Kythira
Kíthnos i. Greece see Kythnos
Kiti, Cape Cyprus see Kition, Cape
Kitimat Canada 120 D4
Kitinen r. Fin. 44 O3
Kition, Cape Cyprus 85 A2
Kitiou, Akra c. Cyprus see Kition, Cape
Kitkatla Canada 120 D4
Kitob Uzbek. 89 G2
Kitsault Canada 120 D4
Kittanning U.S.A. 134 F3
Kittatinny Mountains hills U.S.A. 135 H3
Kittery U.S.A. 135 J2
Kittilä Fin. 44 N3
Kittur India 84 B3
Kitty Hawk U.S.A. 132 F4
Kitui Kenya 98 D4
Kitwanga Canada 120 D4
Kitwe Zambia 99 C5
Kitzbüheler Alpen mts Austria 47 N7
Kitzingen Germany 53 K5
Kitzscher Germany 53 M3
Kiu Lom, Ang Kep Nam Thai. 70 B3
Kiunga P.N.G. 69 K8
Kiuruvesi Fin. 44 O5
Kivalina U.S.A. 118 B3
Kivijärvi Fin. 44 N5
Kiviõli Estonia 45 O7
Kivu, Lake Dem. Rep. Congo/Rwanda 98 C4
Kiwaba N'zogi Angola 99 B4
Kiwai Island P.N.G. 69 K8
Kiyev Ukr. see Kiev
Kiyevskoye Vodokhranilishche resr Ukr. see Kyyivs'ke Vodoskhovyshche
Kıyıköy Turkey 59 M4
Kizel Rus. Fed. 41 R4
Kizema Rus. Fed. 42 J3
Kızılcadağ Turkey 59 M6
Kızılca Dağ mt. Turkey 90 C3
Kızılcahamam Turkey 90 D2
Kızıldağ mt. Turkey 85 A1
Kızıldağ mt. Turkey 85 B1
Kızıl Dağı mt. Turkey 90 E3
Kızılırmak Turkey 90 D2
Kızılırmak r. Turkey 90 D2
Kızıltepe Turkey 91 F3
Kizilyurt Rus. Fed. 91 G2
Kızkalesi Turkey 85 B1
Kizlyar Rus. Fed. 91 G2
Kizlyarskiy Zaliv b. Rus. Fed. 91 G1
Kizner Rus. Fed. 42 K4
Kizyl-Arbat Turkm. see Serdar
Kizyl-Atrek Turkm. see Etrek
Kjøllefjord Norway 44 O1
Kjøpsvik Norway 44 J2
Kladno Czech Rep. 47 O5
Klagenfurt Austria 47 O7
Klagetoh U.S.A. 129 I4
Klaipėda Lith. 45 L9
Klaksvík Faroe Is 44 [inset]
Klamath U.S.A. 126 B4
Klamath r. U.S.A. 118 F5
Klamath Falls U.S.A. 126 C4
Klamath Mountains U.S.A. 126 C4
Klang Malaysia 71 C7
Klarälven r. Sweden 45 H7
Klatovy Czech Rep. 47 N6
Klawer S. Africa 100 D6
Klazienaveen Neth. 52 G2
Kleides Islands Cyprus 85 B2
Kleinbegin S. Africa 100 E5
Klein Karas Namibia 100 D4
Klein Nama Land reg. S. Africa see Namaqualand
Klein Roggeveldberge mts S. Africa 100 E7
Kleinsee S. Africa 100 C5
Klemtu Canada 120 D4
Klerksdorp S. Africa 101 H4
Kletnya Rus. Fed. 43 G5
Kletsk Belarus see Klyetsk
Kletskaya Rus. Fed. 43 I6
Kletskiy Rus. Fed. see Kletskaya
Kleve Germany 52 G3
Klidhes Islands Cyprus see Kleides Islands
Klimkovka Rus. Fed. 42 K4
Klimovo Rus. Fed. 43 G5
Klin Rus. Fed. 42 H4
Klingenberg am Main Germany 53 J5
Klingenthal Germany 53 M4
Klingkang, Banjaran mts Indon./Malaysia 68 E6
Klink Germany 53 M1
Klínovec mt. Czech Rep. 53 N4
Klintehamn Sweden 45 K8
Klintsy Rus. Fed. 43 G5
Ključ Bos.-Herz. 58 G2
Kłodzko Poland 47 P5
Klondike r. Canada 120 B1
Klondike Gold Rush National Historical Park nat. park U.S.A. 120 C3
Kloosterhaar Neth. 52 G2
Klosterneuburg Austria 47 P6
Klötze (Altmark) Germany 53 L2
Kluane Lake Canada 120 B2
Kluane National Park Canada 120 B2
Kluang Malaysia see Keluang
Kluczbork Poland 47 Q5
Klukhori Rus. Fed. see Karachayevsk
Klukhorskiy, Pereval Georgia/Rus. Fed. 91 F2
Klukhorskiy, Pereval Georgia/Rus. Fed. 91 F2
Klukwan U.S.A. 120 C3
Klyetsk Belarus 45 O10
Klyuchevskaya, Sopka vol. Rus. Fed. 65 R4
Klyuchi Rus. Fed. 74 B2
Knåda Sweden 45 I6
Knaresborough U.K. 48 F4
Knee Lake Man. Canada 121 M4
Knee Lake Sask. Canada 121 J4
Knetzgau Germany 53 K5
Knife r. U.S.A. 130 C2
Knight Inlet Canada 120 E5
Knighton U.K. 49 D6
Knights Landing U.S.A. 128 C2
Knightstown U.S.A. 134 C4
Knin Croatia 58 G2
Knittelfeld Austria 47 O7
Knjaževac Serbia 59 J3
Knob Lake Canada see Schefferville
Knob Lick U.S.A. 134 C5
Knob Peak hill Australia 108 E3
Knock Ireland 51 D4
Knockalongy hill Ireland 51 D3
Knockalough Ireland 51 C5
Knockanaffrin hill Ireland 51 E5
Knockboy hill Ireland 51 C6
Knock Hill hill U.K. 50 G3
Knockmealdown Mts hills Ireland 51 D5
Knocknaskagh hill Ireland 51 D5
Knokke-Heist Belgium 52 D3
Knorrendorf Germany 53 N1
Knowle U.K. 49 F6
Knowlton Canada 135 I1
Knox IN U.S.A. 134 B3
Knox PA U.S.A. 134 F3
Knox, Cape Canada 120 C4
Knox Coast Antarctica 152 F2
Knoxville GA U.S.A. 133 D5
Knoxville TN U.S.A. 132 D5
Knud Rasmussen Land reg. Greenland 119 L2
Knysna S. Africa 100 F8
Ko, Gora mt. Rus. Fed. 74 E3
Koartac Canada see Quaqtaq
Koba Indon. 68 D7
Kobbfoss Norway 44 P2
Kōbe Japan 75 D6
København Denmark see Copenhagen
Kobenni Mauritania 96 C3
Koblenz Germany 53 H4
Koboldo Rus. Fed. 74 D1
Kobrin Belarus see Kobryn
Kobroör i. Indon. 69 I8
Kobryn Belarus 45 N10
Kobuk Valley National Park U.S.A. 118 C3
K'obulet'i Georgia 91 F2
Kocaeli Turkey see İzmit
Kocaeli Yarımadası pen. Turkey 59 M4
Kočani Macedonia 59 J4
Kocasu r. Turkey 59 M4
Kočevje Slovenia 58 F2
Koch Bihar India 83 G4
Kocher r. Germany 53 J5
Kochevo Rus. Fed. 41 Q4
Kochi India see Cochin
Kōchi Japan 75 D6
Koçhisar Turkey see Kızıltepe
Koch Island Canada 119 K3
Kochkor Kyrg. 80 E3
Kochkorka Kyrg. see Kochkor
Kochkurovo Rus. Fed. 43 J5
Kochubeyevskoye Rus. Fed. 91 F1
Kod India 84 B3
Kodala India 84 E2
Kodarma India 83 F4
Koderma India see Kodarma
Kodiak U.S.A. 118 C4
Kodiak Island U.S.A. 118 C4
Kodibeleng Botswana 101 H2
Kodino Rus. Fed. 42 H3
Kodiyakkarai India 84 C4
Kodok Sudan 86 D8
Kodyma Ukr. 43 F6
Kodzhaele mt. Bulg./Greece 59 K4
Koedoesberg mts S. Africa 100 E7
Koegrabie S. Africa 100 E5
Koekenaap S. Africa 100 D6
Koersel Belgium 52 F3
Koës Namibia 100 D3
Kofa Mountains U.S.A. 129 G5
Koffiefontein S. Africa 100 G5
Koforidua Ghana 96 C4
Kōfu Japan 75 E6
Kogaluc r. Canada 122 F2
Kogaluc, Baie de b. Canada 122 F2
Kogaluk r. Canada 123 J2
Kogan Australia 112 E1
Køge Denmark 45 H9
Kogon r. Guinea 96 B3
Kogon Uzbek. 89 G2
Kohan Pak. 89 G5
Kohat Pak. 89 H3
Kohestānāt Afgh. 89 G3
Kohila Estonia 45 N7
Kohima India 83 H4
Kohistan reg. Afgh. 89 H3
Kohistan reg. Pak. 89 I3
Kohler Range mts Antarctica 152 K2
Kohlu Pak. 89 H4
Kohsan Afgh. 89 F3
Kohtla-Järve Estonia 45 O7
Kohŭng S. Korea 75 B6
Koidern Mountain Canada 120 A2
Koidu Sierra Leone see Sefadu
Koihoa India 71 A5
Koilkonda India 84 C2
Koin N. Korea 75 B4
Koin r. Rus. Fed. 42 K3
Koi Sanjaq Iraq 91 G3
Kŏje-do i. S. Korea 75 C6
Kojonup Australia 109 B8
Kokand Farg'ona Uzbek. see Qo'qon
Kökar Fin. 45 L7
Kokchetav Kazakh. see Kokshetau
Kokemäenjoki r. Fin. 45 L6
Kokerboom Namibia 100 D5
Ko Kha Thai. 70 B3
Kokkilai Sri Lanka 84 D4
Kokkola Fin. 44 M5
Koko Nigeria 96 D3
Kokomo U.S.A. 134 B3
Kokong Botswana 100 F3
Kokos i. Indon. 71 A7
Kokosi S. Africa 101 H4
Kokpekti Kazakh. 80 F2
Koksan N. Korea 75 B5
Kokshaal-Tau, Khrebet mts China/Kyrg. see Kakshaal-Too
Koksharka Rus. Fed. 42 J4
Kokshetau Kazakh. 79 F1
Koksoak r. Canada 123 H2
Kokstad S. Africa 101 I6
Koktal Kazakh. 80 E3
Kokterek Kazakh. 43 K6
Koktokay China see Fuyun
Kola i. Indon. 69 I8
Kola Rus. Fed. 44 R2
Kolachi r. Pak. 89 G5
Kolahoi mt. India 82 C2
Kolaka Indon. 69 G7
Ko Lanta Thai. 71 B6
Kola Peninsula Rus. Fed. 42 H2
Kolar Chhattisgarh India 84 D2
Kolar Karnataka India 84 C3
Kolaras India 82 D4
Kolar Gold Fields India 84 C3
Kolari Fin. 44 M3
Kolarovgrad Bulg. see Shumen
Kolasib India 83 H4
Kolayat India 82 C4
Kolberg Poland see Kołobrzeg
Kol'chugino Rus. Fed. 42 H4
Kolda Senegal 96 B3
Kolding Denmark 45 F9
Kole Kasaï-Oriental Dem. Rep. Congo 98 C
Kole Orientale Dem. Rep. Congo 98 C3
Koléa Alg. 57 H5
Kolekole mt. U.S.A. 127 [inset]
Koler Sweden 44 L4
Kolguyev, Ostrov i. Rus. Fed. 42 K1
Kolhan reg. India 83 F5
Kolhapur India 84 B2
Kolhumadulu Atoll Maldives 81 D11
Kolikata India see Kolkata
Kõljala Estonia 45 M7
Kolkasrags pt Latvia 45 M8

▶Kolkata India 83 G5
5th most populous city in Asia and 8th in the world.

Kolkhozabad Khatlon Tajik. see Vose
Kolkhozabad Khatlon Tajik. see Kolkhozobod
Kolkhozobod Tajik. 89 H2
Kollam India see Quilon
Kolleru Lake India 84 D2
Kollum Neth. 52 G1
Kolmanskop (abandoned) Namibia 100 B4
Köln Germany see Cologne
Köln-Bonn airport Germany 53 H4
Kołobrzeg Poland 47 O3
Kologriv Rus. Fed. 42 J4
Kolokani Mali 96 C3
Kolombangara i. Solomon Is 107 F2
Kolomea Ukr. see Kolomyya
Kolomna Rus. Fed. 43 H5
Kolomyja Ukr. see Kolomyya
Kolomyya Ukr. 43 E6
Kolondiéba Mali 96 C3
Kolonedale Indon. 69 G7
Koloni Cyprus 85 A2
Kolonkwaneng Botswana 100 E4
Kolozsvár Romania see Cluj-Napoca
Kolpashevo Rus. Fed. 64 J4
Kolpos Messaras b. Greece 59 K7
Kol'skiy Poluostrov pen. Rus. Fed. see Kola Peninsula
Kölük Turkey see Kâhta
Koluli Eritrea 86 F7
Kolumadulu Atoll Maldives see Kolhumadulu Atoll
Kolva r. Rus. Fed. 42 M2
Kolvan India 84 B2
Kolvereid Norway 44 G4
Kolvik Norway 44 N1
Kolvitskoye, Ozero l. Rus. Fed. 44 R3
Kolwa reg. Pak. 89 G5
Kolwezi Dem. Rep. Congo 99 C5
Kolyma r. Rus. Fed. 65 R3
Kolyma Lowland Rus. Fed. see Kolymskaya Nizmennost'

lyma Range mts Rus. Fed. see Kolymskiy, Khrebet
lymskaya Nizmennost' lowland Rus. Fed. 65 Q3
lymskiy, Khrebet mts Rus. Fed. 65 R3
lyshley Rus. Fed. 43 J5
m mt. Bulg. 59 J3
madugu-gana watercourse Nigeria 96 E3
maggas S. Africa 100 C5
maio P.N.G. 69 K8
maki Japan 75 E6
mandnaya, Gora mt. Rus. Fed. 74 E2
mandorskiye Ostrova is Rus. Fed. 65 R4
márno Slovakia 47 Q7
mati r. Swaziland 101 J3
matipoort S. Africa 101 J3
matsu Japan 75 E5
mba i. Indon. 108 C1
mga S. Africa 101 H7
mintern Ukr. see Marhanets'
minternivs'ke Ukr. 59 N1
miža Croatia 58 G3
mló Hungary 58 H1
mmunarsk Ukr. see Alchevs'k
modo, Taman Nasional ndon. 108 B2
m Ombo Egypt see Kawm Umbū
mono Congo 98 B4
moran i. Indon. 69 J8
motini Greece 59 K4
mpong Cham Cambodia see Kâmpóng Cham
mpong Chhnang Cambodia see Kâmpóng Chhnăng
mpong Kleang Cambodia see Kâmpóng Khleăng
mpong Som Cambodia see Sihanoukville
mpong Speu Cambodia see Kâmpóng Spœ
mpong Thom Cambodia see Kâmpóng Thum
mrat Moldova see Comrat
msberg mts S. Africa 100 E7
msomol Kazakh. see Karabalyk
msomolabad Tajik. see Komsomolobod
msomolets Kazakh. see Karabalyk
msomolets, Ostrov i. Rus. Fed. 64 K1
msomolobod Tajik. 89 H2
msomol's'k Ukr. 43 G6
msomol'skiy Chukotskiy Avtonomnyy Okrug Rus. Fed. 153 C2
msomol'skiy Khanty-Mansiyskiy Avtonomnyy Okrug Rus. Fed. see Yugorsk
msomol'skiy Respublika Kalmykiya - Khalm'g-Tangch Rus. Fed. 43 J7
msomol'sk-na-Amure Rus. Fed. 74 E2
msomol'skoye Kazakh. 80 B1
msomol'skoye Rus. Fed. 43 J6
mürlü Turkey 91 F2
n India 83 E4
nacık Turkey 85 B1
nada India 84 D2
narak India see Konarka
narka India 83 F6
nch India 82 D4
ndagaon India 84 D2
ndinin Australia 109 B8
ndinskoye Rus. Fed. see Oktyabr'skoye
ndoa Tanz. 99 D4
ndol' Rus. Fed. 43 J5
ndopoga Rus. Fed. 42 G3
ndoz Afgh. see Kunduz
ndrovo Rus. Fed. 43 G5
neürgenç Turkm. 87 I1
neürgenç Turkm. see Köneürgenç
ng Cameroon 96 E4
ng, Kaôh i. Cambodia 71 C5
ng, Tônlé r. Cambodia 71 D4
ng, Xé r. Laos 70 D4
ng Christian IX Land reg. Greenland 119 O3
ng Christian X Land reg. Greenland 119 P2
ngelab atoll Marshall Is see Rongelap
ng Frederik IX Land reg. Greenland 119 M3
ng Frederik VI Kyst coastal area Greenland 119 N3
ngolo Dem. Rep. Congo 99 C4
ngor Sudan 97 G4
ng Oscars Fjord inlet Greenland 119 P2
ngoussi Burkina 96 C3
ngsberg Norway 45 F7
ngsvinger Norway 45 H6
ngur Shan mt. China 80 E4
nigsberg Rus. Fed. see Kaliningrad
nigsee Germany 53 L4
nigswinter Germany 53 H4
nigs Wusterhausen Germany 53 N2
nimekh Uzbek. see Konimex
nimex Uzbek. 89 G1
nin Poland 47 Q4
njic Bos.-Herz. 58 G3
nkiep watercourse Namibia 100 C5
nnern Germany 53 L3
nnevesi Fin. 44 O5
nosha Rus. Fed. 42 I3
notop Ukr. 43 G6
npara India 83 E5
n Plông Vietnam 71 E4
nqi He r. China 80 G3
nso Eth. 98 D3
nstantinograd Ukr. see Krasnohrad
nstantinovka Rus. Fed. 74 B2
nstantinovka Ukr. see Kostyantynivka
nstantinovy Lázně Czech Rep. 53 M5
nstanz Germany 47 L7
ntha Myanmar 70 B2
ntiolahti Fin. 44 P5
nttila Fin. 44 O4
n Tum Vietnam 71 D4
n Tum, Cao Nguyên Vietnam 71 E4
Könugard Ukr. see Kiev
Konushin, Mys pt Rus. Fed. 42 I2
Konya Turkey 90 D3
Konz Germany 52 G5
Konzhakovskiy Kamen', Gora mt. Rus. Fed. 41 R4
Koocanusa, Lake resr Canada/U.S.A. 120 H5
Kooch Bihar India see Koch Bihar
Kookynie Australia 109 C7
Koolyanobbing Australia 109 B7
Koondrook Australia 112 B5
Koorawatha Australia 112 D5
Koordarrie Australia 108 A5
Kootenay r. Canada 120 G5
Kootenay Lake Canada 120 G5
Kootenay National Park Canada 120 G5
Kootjieskolk S. Africa 100 E6
Kópasker Iceland 44 [inset]
Kopbirlik Kazakh. 80 E2
Koper Slovenia 58 E2
Kopet Dag mts Iran/Turkm. 88 E2
Kopet-Dag, Khrebet mts Iran/Turkm. see Kopet Dag
Köpetdag Gershi mts Iran/Turkm. see Kopet Dag
Köping Sweden 45 J7
Köpmanholmen Sweden 44 K5
Kopong Botswana 101 G3
Koppal India 84 C3
Koppang Norway 45 G6
Kopparberg Sweden 45 I7
Koppeh Dāgh mts Iran/Turkm. see Kopet Dag
Köppel hill Germany 53 H4
Koppi r. Rus. Fed. 74 F2
Koppies S. Africa 101 H4
Koppieskraal Pan salt pan S. Africa 100 E4
Koprivnica Croatia 58 G1
Köprülü Turkey 85 A1
Köprülü Kanyon Milli Parkı nat. park Turkey 59 N6
Kopyl' Belarus see Kapyl'
Kora India 82 E4
Korablino Rus. Fed. 43 I5
K'orahē Eth. 98 E3
Korak Pak. 89 G5
Koramlik China 83 F1
Korangal India 84 C2
Korangi Pak. 89 G5
Korān va Monjan Afgh. 89 H2
Koraput India 84 D2
Korat Thai. see Nakhon Ratchasima
Koratla India 84 C2
Korba India 83 E5
Korbach Germany 53 I3
Korçë Albania 59 I4
Korčula Croatia 58 G3
Korčula i. Croatia 58 G3
Korčulanski Kanal sea chan. Croatia 58 G3
Korday Kazakh. 80 D3
Kord Küy Iran 88 D2
Kords reg. Iran 89 F5
Korea, North country Asia 75 B5
Korea, South country Asia 75 B5
Korea Bay g. China/N. Korea 75 B5
Korea Strait Japan/S. Korea 75 C6
Koregaon India 84 B2
Korenovsk Rus. Fed. 91 E1
Korenovskaya Rus. Fed. see Korenovsk
Korepino Rus. Fed. 41 R3
Korets' Ukr. 43 E6
Körfez Turkey 59 M4
Korff Ice Rise Antarctica 152 L1
Korfovskiy Rus. Fed. 74 D2
Korgalzhyn Kazakh. 80 D1
Korgen Norway 44 H3
Korhogo Côte d'Ivoire 96 C4
Koribundu Sierra Leone 96 B4
Kori Creek inlet India 82 B5
Korinthiakos Kolpos sea chan. Greece see Corinth, Gulf of
Korinthos Greece see Corinth
Kőris-hegy hill Hungary 58 G1
Koritnik mt. Albania 59 I3
Koritsa Albania see Korçë
Kōriyama Japan 75 F5
Korkuteli Turkey 59 N6
Korla China 80 G3
Kormakitis, Cape Cyprus 85 A2
Körmend Hungary 58 G1
Kornat nat. park Croatia 58 F3
Korneyevka Rus. Fed. 43 K6
Koro Côte d'Ivoire 96 C4
Koro i. Fiji 107 H3
Koro Mali 96 C3
Koroc r. Canada 123 I2
Köroğlu Dağları mts Turkey 59 O4
Köroğlu Tepesi mt. Turkey 90 D2
Korogwe Tanz. 99 D4
Koroneia, Limni l. Greece 59 J4
Korong Vale Australia 112 A6
Koronia, Limni l. Greece see Koroneia, Limni

▶Koror Palau 69 I5
Former capital of Palau.

Koro Sea b. Fiji 107 H3
Korosten' Ukr. 43 F6
Korostyshiv Ukr. 43 F6
Koro Toro Chad 97 E3
Korpilahti Fin. 44 N5
Korpo Fin. 45 L6
Korppoo Fin. see Korpo
Korsakov Rus. Fed. 74 F3
Korsnäs Fin. 44 L5
Korsør Denmark 45 G9
Korsun'-Shevchenkivs'kyy Ukr. 43 F6
Korsun'-Shevchenkovskiy Ukr. see Korsun'-Shevchenkivs'kyy
Korsze Poland 47 R3
Kortesjärvi Fin. 44 M5
Korti Sudan 86 D6
Kortkeros Rus. Fed. 42 K3
Kortrijk Belgium 52 D4
Korvala Fin. 44 O3
Koryakskaya, Sopka vol. Rus. Fed. 65 Q4
Koryakskoye Nagor'ye mts Rus. Fed. 65 S3
Koryazhma Rus. Fed. 42 J3
Koryŏng S. Korea 75 C6
Kos i. Greece 59 L6
Kosa Rus. Fed. 41 Q4
Kosam India 82 E4
Kosan N. Korea 75 B5
Kościan Poland 47 P4
Kosciusko, Mount Australia see Kosciuszko, Mount
Kosciuszko, Mount Australia 112 D6
Kosciuszko National Park Australia 112 D6
Köse Turkey 91 E2
Köseçobanlı Turkey 85 A1
Kosgi India 84 C2
Kosh-Agach Rus. Fed. 80 G2
Koshikijima-rettō is Japan 75 C7
Koshk Afgh. 89 F3
Koshk-e Kohneh Afgh. 89 F3
Koshki Rus. Fed. 43 K5
Kosi Bay S. Africa 101 K4
Košice Slovakia 43 D6
Kosigi India 84 C3
Koskullskulle Sweden 44 L3
Köslin Poland see Koszalin
Kosma r. Rus. Fed. 42 K2
Koson Uzbek. 89 G2
Kosŏng N. Korea 75 C5
Kosova prov. Europe see Kosovo

▶Kosovo country Europe 59 I3
World's newest independent country. Gained independence from Serbia in February 2008.

Kosovo-Metohija prov. Europe see Kosovo
Kosovska Mitrovica Kosovo see Mitrovicë
Kosrae atoll Micronesia 150 G5
Kosrap China 89 J2
Kösseine hill Germany 53 L5
Kosta-Khetagurovo Rus. Fed. see Nazran'
Kostanay Kazakh. 78 F1
Kostenets Bulg. 59 J3
Kosti Sudan 86 D7
Kostinbrod Bulg. 59 J3
Kostino Rus. Fed. 64 J3
Kostomuksha Rus. Fed. 44 Q4
Kostopil' Ukr. 43 E6
Kostopol' Ukr. see Kostopil'
Kostroma Rus. Fed. 42 I4
Kostrzyn Poland 47 O4
Kostyantynivka Ukr. 43 H6
Kostyukovichi Belarus see Kastsyukovichy
Kos'yu Rus. Fed. 41 R2
Koszalin Poland 47 P3
Kőszeg Hungary 58 G1
Kota Andhra Prad. India 84 D3
Kota Chhattisgarh India 83 E5
Kota Rajasthan India 82 C4
Kota Baharu Malaysia see Kota Bharu
Kotabaru Aceh Indon. 71 B7
Kotabaru Kalimantan Selatan Indon. 68 F7
Kota Bharu Malaysia 71 C6
Kotabumi Indon. 68 C7
Kot Addu Pak. 89 H4
Kota Kinabalu Sabah Malaysia 68 F5
Kotamobagu Indon. 69 G6
Kotaneelee Range mts Canada 120 E2
Kotaparh India 84 D2
Kotapinang Indon. 71 C7
Kotatengah Indon. 71 C7
Kota Tinggi Malaysia 71 C7
Kotcho r. Canada 120 F3
Kotcho Lake Canada 120 F3
Kot Diji Pak. 89 H5
Kotel'nich Rus. Fed. 42 K4
Kotel'nikovo Rus. Fed. 43 I7
Kotel'nyy, Ostrov i. Rus. Fed. 65 O2
Kotgar India 84 D2
Kotgarh India 82 D3
Kothagudem India see Kottagudem
Köthen (Anhalt) Germany 53 L3
Kotido Uganda 97 G4
Kotikovo Rus. Fed. 74 D3
Kot Imamgarh Pak. 89 H5
Kotka Fin. 45 O6
Kot Kapura India 82 C3
Kotkino Rus. Fed. 42 K2
Kotlas Rus. Fed. 42 J3
Kotli Pak. 89 I3
Kotlik U.S.A. 118 B3
Kötlutangi pt Iceland 44 [inset]
Kotly Rus. Fed. 45 P7
Kotorkoshi Nigeria 96 D3
Kotovo Rus. Fed. 43 J6
Kotovsk Rus. Fed. 43 I5
Kotra India 82 C4
Kotra Pak. 89 G4
Kotri r. India 84 D2
Kot Sarae Pak. 89 G6
Kottagudem India 84 D2
Kottarakara India 84 C4
Kottayam India 84 C4
Kotte Sri Lanka see Sri Jayewardenepura Kotte
Kotto r. Cent. Afr. Rep. 98 C3
Kotturu India 84 C3
Kotuy r. Rus. Fed. 65 L2
Kotzebue U.S.A. 118 B3
Kotzebue Sound sea chan. U.S.A. 118 B3
Kötzting Germany 53 M5
Kouango Cent. Afr. Rep. 98 C3
Koubia Guinea 96 B3
Kouchibouguac National Park Canada 123 I5
Koudougou Burkina 96 C3
Kouebokkeveld mts S. Africa 100 D7
Koufey Niger 96 E3
Koufonisi i. Greece 59 L7
Kougaberge mts S. Africa 100 F7
Koukourou r. Cent. Afr. Rep. 98 B3
Koulen Cambodia see Kulen
Koulikoro Mali 96 C3
Koumac New Caledonia 107 G4
Koumpentoum Senegal 96 B3
Koundâra Guinea 96 B3
Kountze U.S.A. 131 E6
Koupéla Burkina 96 C3
Kourou Fr. Guiana 143 H2
Kouroussa Guinea 96 C3
Kousséri Cameroon 97 E3
Koutiala Mali 96 C3
Kouvola Fin. 45 O6
Kovallberget Sweden 44 J4
Kovdor Rus. Fed. 44 Q3
Kovdozero, Ozero l. Rus. Fed. 44 R3
Kovel' Ukr. 43 E6
Kovernino Rus. Fed. 42 I4
Kovilpatti India 84 C4
Kovno Lith. see Kaunas
Kovriga, Gora hill Rus. Fed. 42 K2
Kovrov Rus. Fed. 42 I4
Kovylkino Rus. Fed. 43 I5
Kovzhskoye, Ozero l. Rus. Fed. 42 H3
Kowanyama Australia 110 C2
Kowloon H.K. China 77 [inset]
Kowloon Peak hill H.K. China 77 [inset]
Kowloon Peninsula H.K. China 77 [inset]
Kowŏn N. Korea 75 B5
Kōyama-misaki pt Japan 75 C6
Köyceğiz Turkey 59 M6
Koygorodok Rus. Fed. 42 K3
Koyna Reservoir India 84 B2
Köýtendag Turkm. 89 G2
Koyuk U.S.A. 118 B3
Koyukuk r. U.S.A. 118 C3
Koyulhisar Turkey 90 E2
Kozağacı Turkey see Günyüzü
Kō-zaki pt Japan 75 C6
Kozan Turkey 90 D3
Kozani Greece 59 I4
Kozara mts Bos.-Herz. 58 G2
Kozara nat. park Bos.-Herz. 58 G2
Kozarska Dubica Bos.-Herz. see Bosanska Dubica
Kozelets' Ukr. 43 F6
Kozel'sk Rus. Fed. 43 G5
Kozhikode India see Calicut
Kozhva Rus. Fed. 42 M2
Kozlu Turkey 59 N4
Koz'modem'yansk Rus. Fed. 42 J4
Kožuf mts Greece/Macedonia 59 J4
Kōzu-shima i. Japan 75 E6
Kozyatyn Ukr. 43 F6
Kpalimé Togo 96 D4
Kpandae Ghana 96 C4
Kpungan Pass India/Myanmar 70 B1
Kra, Isthmus of Thai. 71 B5
Krabi Thai. 71 B5
Kra Buri Thai. 71 B5
Krâchéh Cambodia 71 D4
Kraddsele Sweden 44 J4
Kragerø Norway 45 F7
Kraggenburg Neth. 52 F2
Kragujevac Serbia 59 I2
Krakatau vol. Indon. 68 D8
Krakau Poland see Kraków
Kraków Poland 47 Q5
Krakower See l. Germany 53 M1
Krâlănh Cambodia 71 C4
Kralendijk Neth. Antilles 137 K6
Kramators'k Ukr. 43 H6
Kramfors Sweden 44 J5
Krammer est. Neth. 52 E3
Kranidi Greece 59 J6
Kranj Slovenia 58 F1
Kranji Reservoir Sing. 71 [inset]
Kranskop S. Africa 101 J5
Krasavino Rus. Fed. 42 J3
Krasilov Ukr. see Krasyliv
Krasino Rus. Fed. 64 G2
Kraskino Rus. Fed. 74 C4
Krāslava Latvia 45 O9
Kraslice Czech Rep. 53 M4
Krasnaya Gorbatka Rus. Fed. 42 I5
Krasnaya Zarya Rus. Fed. 43 H5
Krasnoarmeysk Rus. Fed. 43 J6
Krasnoarmeysk Ukr. see Krasnoarmiys'k
Krasnoarmiys'k Ukr. 43 H6
Krasnoborsk Rus. Fed. 42 J3
Krasnodar Rus. Fed. 90 E1
Krasnodar Kray admin. div. Rus. Fed. see Krasnodarskiy Kray
Krasnodarskiy Kray admin. div. Rus. Fed. 90 E1
Krasnodon Ukr. 43 H6
Krasnogorodskoye Rus. Fed. 45 P8
Krasnogorsk Rus. Fed. 74 F2
Krasnogorskoye Rus. Fed. 42 L4
Krasnograd Ukr. see Krasnohrad
Krasnogvardeysk Uzbek. see Bulung'ur
Krasnogvardeyskoye Rus. Fed. 43 I7
Krasnohrad Ukr. 43 G6
Krasnohvardiys'ke Ukr. 43 G7
Krasnokamsk Rus. Fed. 41 R4
Krasnoperekops'k Ukr. 43 G7
Krasnopol'ye Rus. Fed. 74 F2
Krasnorechenskiy Rus. Fed. 74 D3
Krasnoslobodsk Rus. Fed. 43 I5
Krasnotur'insk Rus. Fed. 41 S4
Krasnoufimsk Rus. Fed. 41 R4
Krasnovishersk Rus. Fed. 41 R3
Krasnovodsk Turkm. see Türkmenbaşy
Krasnovodsk, Mys pt Turkm. 88 D2
Krasnovodskoye Plato plat. Turkm. 91 I2
Krasnowodsk Aylagy b. Turkm. see Türkmenbaşy Aýlagy
Krasnoyarovo Rus. Fed. 74 C2
Krasnoyarsk Rus. Fed. 64 K4
Krasnoyarskoye Vodokhranilishche resr Rus. Fed. 72 G2
Krasnoye Lipetskaya Oblast' Rus. Fed. 43 H5
Krasnoye Respublika Kalmykiya - Khalm'g-Tangch Rus. Fed. see Ulan Erge
Krasnoznamenskiy Kazakh. see Yegindykol'
Krasnoznamenskoye Kazakh. see Yegindykol'
Krasnyy Rus. Fed. 43 F5
Krasnyy Chikoy Rus. Fed. 73 J2
Krasnyye Baki Rus. Fed. 42 J4
Krasnyy Kamyshanik Rus. Fed. see Komsomol'skiy
Krasnyy Kholm Rus. Fed. 42 H4
Krasnyy Kut Rus. Fed. 43 J6
Krasnyy Luch Ukr. 43 H6
Krasnyy Lyman Ukr. 43 H6
Krasnyy Yar Rus. Fed. 43 K7
Krasyliv Ukr. 43 E6
Kratie Cambodia see Krâchéh
Kratke Range mts P.N.G. 69 L8
Kraulshavn Greenland see Nuussuaq
Krâvanh, Chuŏr Phnum mts Cambodia/Thai. see Cardamom Range
Kraynovka Rus. Fed. 91 G2
Krefeld Germany 52 G3
Kremenchug Ukr. see Kremenchuk
Kremenchugskoye Vodokhranilishche resr Ukr. see Kremenchuts'ka Vodoskhovyshche
Kremenchuk Ukr. 43 G6
Kremenchuts'ka Vodoskhovyshche resr Ukr. 43 G6
Křemešník hill Czech Rep. 47 O6
Kremges Ukr. see Svitlovods'k
Kremmidi, Akra pt Greece see Kremmydi, Akrotirio
Kremmydi, Akrotirio pt Greece 59 J6
Krems Austria see Krems an der Donau
Krems an der Donau Austria 47 O6
Kresta, Zaliv g. Rus. Fed. 65 T3
Kresttsy Rus. Fed. 42 G4
Kretinga Lith. 45 L9
Kreuzau Germany 52 G4
Kreuztal Germany 53 H4
Kreva Belarus 45 O9
Kribi Cameroon 96 D4
Krichev Belarus see Krychaw
Kriel S. Africa 101 I4
Krikellos Greece 59 I5
Kril'on, Mys c. Rus. Fed. 74 F3
Krishna India 84 C2
Krishna r. India 84 D2
Krishnanagar India 83 G5
Krishnaraja Sagara l. India 84 C3
Kristiania Norway see Oslo
Kristiansand Norway 45 E7
Kristianstad Sweden 45 I8
Kristiansund Norway 44 E5
Kristiinankaupunki Fin. see Kristinestad
Kristinehamn Sweden 45 I7
Kristinestad Fin. 44 L5
Kristinopol' Ukr. see Chervonohrad
Kriti i. Greece see Crete
Kritiko Pelagos sea Greece 59 K6
Krivoy Rog Ukr. see Kryvyy Rih
Križevci Croatia 58 G1
Krk i. Croatia 58 F2
Krkonošský narodní park nat. park Czech Rep./Poland 47 O5
Krokom Sweden 44 I5
Krokstadøra Norway 44 F5
Krokstranda Norway 44 I3
Krolevets' Ukr. 43 G6
Kronach Germany 53 L4
Krŏng Kaôh Kŏng Cambodia 71 C5
Kronoby Fin. 44 M5
Kronprins Christian Land reg. Greenland 153 I1
Kronprins Frederik Bjerge nunataks Greenland 119 O3
Kronshtadt Rus. Fed. 45 P7
Kronstadt Romania see Braşov
Kronstadt Rus. Fed. see Kronshtadt
Kronwa Myanmar 70 B4
Kroonstad S. Africa 101 H4
Kropotkin Rus. Fed. 91 F1
Kropstädt Germany 53 M3
Krosno Poland 43 D6
Krotoszyn Poland 47 P5
Kruger National Park S. Africa 101 J2
Kruglikovo Rus. Fed. 74 D2
Kruglyakov Rus. Fed. see Oktyabr'skiy
Krui Indon. 68 C8
Kruisfontein S. Africa 100 G8
Kruja Albania see Krujë
Krujë Albania 59 H4
Krumovgrad Bulg. 59 K4
Krungkao Thai. see Ayutthaya
Krung Thep Thai. see Bangkok
Krupa Bos.-Herz. see Bosanska Krupa
Krupa na Uni Bos.-Herz. see Bosanska Krupa
Krupki Belarus 43 F5
Krusenstern, Cape U.S.A. 118 B3
Kruševac Serbia 59 I3
Krušné hory mts Czech Rep. 53 M4
Kruzof Island U.S.A. 120 C3
Krychaw Belarus 43 F5
Krylov Seamount sea feature N. Atlantic Ocean 148 G4
Krym' pen. Ukr. see Crimea
Krymsk Rus. Fed. 90 E1
Krymskaya Rus. Fed. see Krymsk
Kryms'kyy Pivostriv pen. Ukr. see Crimea
Krystynopol Ukr. see Chervonohrad
Krytiko Pelagos sea Greece see Kritiko Pelagos
Kryvyy Rih Ukr. 43 G7
Ksabi Alg. 54 D6
Ksar Chellala Alg. 57 H6
Ksar el Boukhari Alg. 57 H6
Ksar el Kebir Morocco 57 D6
Ksar-es-Souk Morocco see Er Rachidia
Ksenofontova Rus. Fed. 41 R3
Kshirpai India 83 F5
Ksour Essaf Tunisia 58 D7
Kstovo Rus. Fed. 42 J4
Kū', Jabal al hill Saudi Arabia 86 G4
Kuah Malaysia 71 B6
Kuaidamao China see Tonghua
Kuala Belait Brunei 68 E6
Kuala Dungun Malaysia see Dungun
Kuala Kangsar Malaysia 71 C6
Kualakapuas Indon. 68 E7
Kuala Kerai Malaysia 71 C6
Kuala Lipis Malaysia 71 C6

▶Kuala Lumpur Malaysia 71 C7
Joint capital (with Putrajaya) of Malaysia.

Kuala Nerang Malaysia 71 C6
Kuala Pilah Malaysia 71 C7
Kuala Rompin Malaysia 71 C7
Kuala Selangor Malaysia 71 C7
Kualasimpang Indon. 71 B6
Kuala Terengganu Malaysia 71 C6
Kualatungal Indon. 68 C7
Kuamut Sabah Malaysia 68 F5
Kuandian China 74 B4
Kuantan Malaysia 71 C7
Kuba Azer. see Quba
Kuban' r. Rus. Fed. 43 H7
Kubār Syria 91 E4
Kubaybāt Syria 85 C2
Kubaysah Iraq 91 F4
Kubenskoye, Ozero l. Rus. Fed. 42 H4
Kubrat Bulg. 59 L3
Kubuang Indon. 68 F6
Kuchaman Road India 89 I5
Kuchema Rus. Fed. 42 I2
Kuching Sarawak Malaysia 68 E6
Kucing Sarawak Malaysia see Kuching
Kuçovë Albania 59 H4
Kuda India 82 B5
Kudal India 84 B3
Kudap Indon. 71 C7
Kudat Sabah Malaysia 68 F5
Kudligi India 84 C3
Kudremukh mt. India 84 B3
Kudus Indon. 68 E8
Kudymkar Rus. Fed. 41 Q4
Kueishan Tao i. Taiwan 77 I3
Kūfah Iraq 91 G4
Kufstein Austria 47 N7
Kugaaruk Canada 119 J3
Kugesi Rus. Fed. 42 J4
Kugka Lhai China 83 G3
Kugluktuk Canada 118 G3
Kugmallit Bay Canada 153 A2
Kūh, Ra's-al- pt Iran 88 E5
Kūhak Iran 89 F5
Kuhanbokano mt. China 83 E3
Kuhbier Germany 53 M1
Kūhdasht Iran 88 B3
Kūhīn Iran 88 C2
Kūhīrī Iran 89 F5
Kuhmo Fin. 44 P4
Kuhmoinen Fin. 45 N6
Kūhpāyeh mt. Iran 88 E4
Kūhrān, Kūh-e mt. Iran 88 E5
Kühren Germany 53 M3
Kui Buri Thai. 71 B4
Kuis Namibia 100 C3
Kuiseb watercourse Namibia 100 B2
Kuitan China 77 G4
Kuito Angola 99 B5
Kuitun China see Kuytun
Kuiu Island U.S.A. 120 C3
Kuivaniemi Fin. 44 N4
Kujang N. Korea 75 B5
Kuji Japan 75 F4
Kujū-san vol. Japan 75 C6
Kukālār, Kūh-e hill Iran 88 C4
Kukan Rus. Fed. 74 D2
Kukës Albania 59 I3
Kukesi Albania see Kukës
Kukmor Rus. Fed. 42 K4
Kukshi India 82 C5
Kukunuru India 84 D2
Kükürtli Turkm. 88 E2
Kūl r. Iran 88 D5
Kula Turkey 59 M5
Kulaisila India 83 F5
Kula Kangri mt. China/Bhutan 83 G3
Kulandy Kazakh. 80 A2
Kulaneh reg. Pak. 89 F5
Kular Rus. Fed. 65 O2
Kuldīga Latvia 45 L8
Kuldja China see Yining
Kul'dur Rus. Fed. 74 C2
Kule Botswana 100 E2
Kulebaki Rus. Fed. 43 I5
Kulen Cambodia 71 D4
Kulgera Australia 109 F6
Kulikovo Rus. Fed. 42 J3
Kulim Malaysia 71 C6
Kulin Australia 109 B8
Kulja Australia 109 B7
Kulkyne watercourse Australia 112 B3
Kullu India 82 D3
Kulmbach Germany 53 L4
Kŭlob Tajik. 89 H2
Kuloy Rus. Fed. 42 I3
Kuloy r. Rus. Fed. 42 I2
Kulp Turkey 91 F3
Kul'sary Kazakh. 78 E2
Külsheim Germany 53 J5
Kulu India see Kullu
Kulu Turkey 90 D3
Kulunda Rus. Fed. 72 D2
Kulundinskaya Step' plain Kazakh./Rus. Fed. 72 D2
Kulundinskoye, Ozero salt l. Rus. Fed. 72 D2
Kulusuk Greenland 119 O3
Kulwin Australia 111 C7
Kulyab Tajik. see Kŭlob
Kuma r. Rus. Fed. 43 J7
Kumagaya Japan 75 E5
Kumai, Teluk b. Indon. 68 E7
Kumalar Dağı mts Turkey 59 N5
Kumamoto Japan 75 C6
Kumano Japan 75 E6
Kumanovo Macedonia 59 I3
Kumara Rus. Fed. 74 B1
Kumasi Ghana 96 C4
Kumayri Armenia see Gyumri
Kumba Cameroon 96 D4
Kumbakonam India 84 C4
Kumbe Indon. 69 K8
Kümbet Turkey 59 N5
Kumbharli Ghat mt. India 84 B2
Kumbla India 84 B3
Kumchuru Botswana 100 F2
Kum-Dag Turkm. see Gumdag
Kumdah Saudi Arabia 86 G5
Kumel well Iran 88 D3
Kumeny Rus. Fed. 42 K4
Kumertau Rus. Fed. 64 G4
Kumgang-san mt. N. Korea 75 C5
Kumguri India 83 G4
Kumi S. Korea 75 C5
Kumi Uganda 97 G4
Kumla Sweden 45 I7
Kumlu Turkey 85 C1
Kummersdorf-Alexanderdorf Germany 53 N2
Kumo Nigeria 96 E3
Kŭmo-do i. S. Korea 75 B6
Kumon Range mts Myanmar 70 B1
Kumphawapi Thai. 70 C3
Kums Namibia 100 D5
Kumta India 84 B3

Kumu Dem. Rep. Congo 98 C3
Kumukh Rus. Fed. 91 G2
Kumul China see Hami
Kunmund India 84 D1
Kumylzhenskaya Rus. Fed. see Kumylzhenskiy
Kumylzhenskiy Rus. Fed. 43 I6
Kun r. Myanmar 70 B3
Kunar r. Afgh. 89 H3
Kunashir, Ostrov i. Rus. Fed. 74 G3
Kunashirskiy Proliv sea chan. Japan/Rus. Fed. see Nemuro-kaikyō
Kunchaung Myanmar 70 B2
Kunchuk Tso salt l. China 83 E2
Kunda Estonia 45 O7
Kunda India 83 E4
Kundapura India 84 B3
Kundelungu, Parc National de nat. park Dem. Rep. Congo 99 C5
Kundelungu Ouest, Parc National de nat. park Dem. Rep. Congo 99 C5
Kundia India 82 C4
Kundur i. Indon. 68 C6
Kunduz Afgh. 89 H2
Kunene r. Angola see Cunene
Kuneneng admin. dist. Botswana see Kweneng
Künes China see Xinyuan
Kungälv Sweden 45 G8
Kunghit Island Canada 120 D4
Kungsbacka Sweden 45 H8
Kungshamn Sweden 45 G7
Kungu Dem. Rep. Congo 98 B3
Kungur mt. China see Kongur Shan
Kungur Rus. Fed. 41 R4
Kunhing Myanmar 70 B2
Kuni r. India 84 C2
Kūnīch Iran 88 E5
Kunié i. New Caledonia see Pins, Île des
Kunigai India 84 C3
Kunimi-dake mt. Japan 75 C6
Kunkavav India 82 B5
Kunlong Myanmar 70 B2

▶Kunlun Shan mts China 82 D1
Location of highest active volcano in Asia.

Kunlun Shankou pass China 83 H2
Kunming China 76 D3
Kunsan S. Korea 75 B6
Kunshan China 77 I2
Kununurra Australia 108 E3
Kunwak r. Canada 121 L2
Kun'ya Rus. Fed. 42 F4
Kunyang Yunnan China see Jinning
Kunyang Zhejiang China see Pingyang
Kunya-Urgench Turkm. see Köneürgenç
Künzelsau Germany 53 J5
Künzels-Berg hill Germany 53 L3
Kuocang Shan mts China 77 I2
Kuohijärvi l. Fin. 45 N6
Kuolayarvi Rus. Fed. 44 P3
Kuopio Fin. 44 O5
Kuortane Fin. 44 M5
Kupa r. Croatia/Slovenia 58 G2
Kupang Indon. 108 C2
Kupari India 83 F5
Kupiškis Lith. 45 N9
Kupreanof Island U.S.A. 120 C3
Kupwara India 82 C2
Kup"yans'k Ukr. 43 H6
Kuqa China 80 F3
Kur r. Rus. Fed. 74 D2
also known as Kür (Georgia), Kura
Kura r. Georgia 91 G2
also known as Kur (Russian Federation), Kura
Kuragino Rus. Fed. 72 G2
Kurakh Rus. Fed. 43 J8
Kurama Range mts Asia 87 K1
Kuraminskiy Khrebet mts Asia see Kurama Range
Kūrān Dap Iran 89 E5
Kurashiki Japan 75 D6
Kurasia India 83 E5
Kurayn i. Saudi Arabia 88 C5
Kurayoshi Japan 75 D6
Kurchatov Rus. Fed. 43 G6
Kurchum Kazakh. 80 F2
Kürdämir Azer. 91 H2
Kŭrdzhali Bulg. 59 K4
Kure Japan 75 D6
Küre Turkey 90 D2
Kure Atoll U.S.A. 150 I4
Kuressaare Estonia 45 M7
Kurgal'dzhino Kazakh. see Korgalzhyn
Kurgal'dzhinskiy Kazakh. see Korgalzhyn
Kurgan Rus. Fed. 64 H4
Kurganinsk Rus. Fed. 91 F1
Kurgannaya Rus. Fed. see Kurganinsk
Kurgantyube Tajik. see Qūrghonteppa
Kuri Afgh. 89 H2
Kuri India 82 B4
Kuria Muria Islands Oman see Ḥalāniyāt, Juzur al
Kuridala Australia 110 C4
Kurigram Bangl. 83 G4
Kurikka Fin. 44 M5
Kuril Basin sea feature Sea of Okhotsk 150 F2
Kuril Islands Rus. Fed. 74 H3
Kurilovka Rus. Fed. 43 K6
Kuril'sk Rus. Fed. 74 G3
Kuril'skiye Ostrova is Rus. Fed. see Kuril Islands
Kuril Trench sea feature N. Pacific Ocean 150 F3
Kurkino Rus. Fed. 43 H5
Kurmashkino Kazakh. see Kurchum
Kurmuk Sudan 86 D7
Kurnool India 84 C3
Kuroiso Japan 75 F5
Kurort Schmalkalden Germany 53 K4
Kurovskiy Rus. Fed. 74 B1
Kurow N.Z. 113 C7
Kurram Pak. 89 H3
Kurri Kurri Australia 112 E4
Kursavka Rus. Fed. 91 F1
Kürshim Kazakh. see Kurchum
Kurshskiy Zaliv b. Lith./Rus. Fed. see Courland Lagoon
Kuršių marios b. Lith./Rus. Fed. see Courland Lagoon
Kursk Rus. Fed. 43 H6
Kurskaya Rus. Fed. 91 G1
Kurskiy Zaliv b. Lith./Rus. Fed. see Courland Lagoon
Kurşunlu Turkey 90 D2
Kurtalan Turkey 91 F3
Kurtoğlu Burnu pt Turkey 59 M6
Kurtpınar Turkey 85 B1
Kurucaşile Turkey 90 D2
Kuruçay Turkey 90 E3
Kurukshetra India 82 D3
Kuruktag mts China 80 G3
Kuruman S. Africa 100 F4
Kuruman watercourse S. Africa 100 E4
Kurume Japan 75 C6
Kurumkan Rus. Fed. 73 K2
Kurunegala Sri Lanka 84 D5
Kurupam India 84 D2
Kurush, Jebel hills Sudan 86 D5
Kur'ya Rus. Fed. 41 R3
Kuryk Kazakh. 91 H2
Kuşadası Turkey 59 L6
Kuşadası Körfezi b. Turkey 59 L6
Kusaie atoll Micronesia see Kosrae
Kusary Azer. see Qusar
Kuşcenneti nature res. Turkey 85 B1
Kuschke Nature Reserve S. Africa 101 I3
Kusel Germany 53 H5
Kuş Gölü l. Turkey 59 L4
Kushalgarh India 82 C5
Kushchevskaya Rus. Fed. 43 H7
Kushimoto Japan 75 D6
Kushiro Japan 74 G4
Kushka Turkm. see Serhetabat
Kushkopola Rus. Fed. 42 J3
Kushmurun Kazakh. 78 F1
Kushtagi India 84 C3
Kushtia Bangl. 83 G5
Kushtih Iran 89 E4
Kuskan Turkey 85 A1
Kuskokwim r. U.S.A. 118 B3
Kuskokwim Bay U.S.A. 118 B4
Kuskokwim Mountains U.S.A. 118 C3
Kuşluyan Turkey see Gölköy
Kusŏng N. Korea 75 B5
Kustanay Kazakh. see Kostanay
Küstence Romania see Constanța
Küstenkanal canal Germany 53 H1
Kustia Bangl. see Kushtia
Kut Iran 88 C4
Kut, Ko i. Thai. 71 C5
Kuta Bali Indon. 68 F8
Küt 'Abdollāh Iran 88 C4
Kutacane Indon. 71 B7
Kütahya Turkey 59 M5
K'ut'aisi Georgia 91 F2
Kut-al-Imara Iraq see Al Küt
Kutan Rus. Fed. 91 G1
Kutanibong Indon. 71 B7
Kutaraja Indon. see Banda Aceh
Kutayfat Ţurayf vol. Saudi Arabia 85 D4
Kutch, Gulf of India see Kachchh, Gulf of
Kutch, Rann of marsh India see Kachchh, Rann of
Kutchan Japan 74 F4
Kutina Croatia 58 G2
Kutjevo Croatia 58 G2
Kutkai Myanmar 70 B2
Kutno Poland 47 Q4
Kutru India 84 D2
Kutu Dem. Rep. Congo 98 B4
Kutubdia Island Bangl. 83 G5
Kutum Sudan 97 F3
Kutztown U.S.A. 135 H3
Kuujjua r. Canada 118 G2
Kuujjuaq Canada 123 H2
Kuujjuarapik Canada 122 F3
Kuusamo Fin. 44 P4
Kuusankoski Fin. 45 O6
Kuvango Angola 99 B5
Kuvshinovo Rus. Fed. 42 G4
Kuwait country Asia 88 B4

▶Kuwait Kuwait 88 B4
Capital of Kuwait.

Kuwajleen atoll Marshall Is see Kwajalein
Kuybyshev Novosibirskaya Oblast' Rus. Fed. 64 I4
Kuybyshev Respublika Tatarstan Rus. Fed. see Bolgar
Kuybyshev Samarskaya Oblast' Rus. Fed. see Samara
Kuybysheve Ukr. 43 H7
Kuybyshevka-Vostochnaya Rus. Fed. see Belogorsk
Kuybyshevskoye Vodokhranilishche resr Rus. Fed. 43 K5
Kuyeda Rus. Fed. 41 R4
Kuygan Kazakh. 80 D2
Kuytun China 80 F3
Kuytun Rus. Fed. 72 I2
Kuyucak Turkey 59 M6
Kuzino Rus. Fed. 41 R4
Kuznechnoye Rus. Fed. 45 P6
Kuznetsk Rus. Fed. 43 J5
Kuznetsovo Rus. Fed. 74 E3
Kuznetsovs'k Ukr. 43 E6
Kuzovatovo Rus. Fed. 43 J5
Kvænangen sea chan. Norway 44 L1
Kvaløya i. Norway 44 K2
Kvalsund Norway 44 M1
Kvarnerić sea chan. Croatia 58 F2
Kvitøya ice feature Svalbard 64 E2
Kwa r. Dem. Rep. Congo see Kasaï
Kwabhaca S. Africa see Mount Frere
Kwadelen atoll Marshall Is see Kwajalein
Kwajalein atoll Marshall Is 150 H5
Kwale Nigeria 96 D4
KwaMashu S. Africa 101 J5
KwaMhlanga S. Africa 101 I3
Kwa Mtoro Tanz. 99 D4
Kwangch'ŏn S. Korea 75 B5
Kwangchow China see Guangzhou
Kwangju S. Korea 75 B6
Kwangsi Chuang Autonomous Region aut. reg. China see Guangxi Zhuangzu Zizhiqu
Kwangtung prov. China see Guangdong
Kwanmo-bong mt. N. Korea 74 C4
Kwanobuhle S. Africa 101 G7
KwaNojoli S. Africa 101 G7
Kwanonqubela S. Africa 101 H7
KwaNonzame S. Africa 100 G6
Kwanza r. Angola see Cuanza
Kwatinidubu S. Africa 101 H7
KwaZamokuhle S. Africa 101 I4
KwaZamukucinga S. Africa 100 G7
Kwazamuxolo S. Africa 100 G6
KwaZanele S. Africa 101 I4
KwaZulu-Natal prov. S. Africa 101 J5
Kweichow prov. China see Guizhou
Kweiyang China see Guiyang
Kwekwe Zimbabwe 99 C5
Kweneng admin. dist. Botswana 100 G2
Kwenge r. Dem. Rep. Congo 99 B4
Kwetabohigan r. Canada 122 E4
Kwezi-Naledi S. Africa 101 H6
Kwidzyn Poland 47 Q4
Kwikila P.N.G. 69 L8
Kwilu r. Angola/Dem. Rep. Congo 99 B4
Kwo Chau Kwan To is H.K. China see Ninepin Group
Kwoka mt. Indon. 69 I7
Kyabra Australia 111 C5
Kyabram Australia 112 B6
Kyadet Myanmar 70 A2
Kyaikkami Myanmar 70 B3
Kyaiklat Myanmar 70 A3
Kyaikto Myanmar 70 B3
Kyakhta Rus. Fed. 72 J2
Kyalite Australia 112 A5
Kyancutta Australia 109 F8
Kyangin Myanmar 70 B3
Kyangngoin China 76 B2
Kyaukhnyat Myanmar 70 B3
Kyaukkyi Myanmar 70 B3
Kyaukme Myanmar 70 B2
Kyaukpadaung Myanmar 70 A2
Kyaukpyu Myanmar 70 A3
Kyaukse Myanmar 70 B2
Kyauktaw Myanmar 70 A2
Kyaunggon Myanmar 70 A3
Kybartai Lith. 45 M9
Kyebogyi Myanmar 70 B3
Kyêbxang Co l. China 83 G2
Kyeikdon Myanmar 70 B3
Kyeikywa Myanmar 70 B3
Kyeintali Myanmar 70 A3
Kyela Tanz. 99 D4
Kyelang India 82 D2
Kyidaunggan Myanmar 70 B3
Kyiv Ukr. see Kiev
Kyklades is Greece see Cyclades
Kyle Canada 121 I5
Kyle of Lochalsh U.K. 50 D3
Kyll r. Germany 52 G5
Kyllini mt. Greece 59 J6
Kymi Greece 59 K5
Kymis, Akra pt Greece see Kymis, Akrotirio
Kymis, Akrotirio pt Greece 59 K5
Kyneton Australia 112 B6
Kynuna Australia 110 C4
Kyoga, Lake Uganda 98 D3
Kyōga-misaki pt Japan 75 D6
Kyogle Australia 112 F2
Kyong Myanmar 70 B2
Kyŏngju S. Korea 75 C6
Kyonpyaw Myanmar 70 A3
Kyōto Japan 75 D6
Kyparissia Greece 59 I6
Kypros country Asia see Cyprus
Kypshak, Ozero salt l. Kazakh. 79 F1
Kyra Rus. Fed. 73 K3
Kyra Panagia i. Greece 59 K5
Kyrenia Cyprus 85 A2
Kyrenia Mountains Cyprus see Pentadaktylos Range
Kyrgyz Ala-Too mts Kazakh./Kyrg. see Kirghiz Range
Kyrgyzstan country Asia 80 D3
Kyritz Germany 53 M2
Kyrksæterøra Norway 44 F5
Kyrta Rus. Fed. 41 R3
Kyssa Rus. Fed. 42 J2
Kytalyktakh Rus. Fed. 65 O3
Kythira i. Greece 59 J6
Kythnos i. Greece 59 K6
Kyunglung China 82 E3
Kyunhla Myanmar 70 A2
Kyun Pila i. Myanmar 71 B5
Kyuquot Canada 120 E5
Kyurdamir Azer. see Kürdämir
Kyūshū i. Japan 75 C7
Kyushu-Palau Ridge sea feature N. Pacific Ocean 150 F4
Kyustendil Bulg. 59 J3
Kywebwe Myanmar 70 B3
Kywong Australia 112 C5
Kyyev Ukr. see Kiev
Kyyiv Ukr. see Kiev
Kyyivs'ke Vodoskhovyshche resr Ukr. 43 F6
Kyyjärvi Fin. 44 N5
Kyzyl Rus. Fed. 80 H1
Kyzyl-Art, Pereval pass Kyrg./Tajik. see Kyzylart Pass
Kyzylart Pass Kyrg./Tajik. 89 I2
Kyzyl-Burun Azer. see Siyäzän
Kyzyl-Kiya Kyrg. see Kyzyl-Kyya
Kyzylkum, Peski des. Kazakh./Uzbek see Kyzylkum Desert
Kyzylkum Desert Kazakh./Uzbek. 80 B3
Kyzyl-Kyya Kyrg. 80 D3
Kyzyl-Mazhalyk Rus. Fed. 80 H1
Kyzylorda Kazakh. 80 C3
Kyzylrabot Tajik. see Qizilrabot
Kyzylsay Kazakh. 91 I2
Kyzylysor Kazakh. 91 H1
Kyzylzhar Kazakh. 80 C2
Kzyl-Dzhar Kazakh. see Kyzylzhar
Kzyl-Orda Kazakh. see Kyzylorda
Kzyltu Kazakh. see Kishkenekol'

Laagri Estonia 45 N7
Laam Atoll Maldives see Hadhdhunmathi Atoll
La Angostura, Presa de resr Mex. 136 F5
Laanila Fin. 44 O2
Laascaanood Somalia 98 E3
La Ascensión, Bahía de b. Mex. 137 G5
Laasgoray Somalia 98 E2

▶Laâyoune W. Sahara 96 B2
Capital of Western Sahara.

La Babia Mex. 131 C6
La Baie Canada 123 H4
La Baleine, Grande Rivière de r. Canada 122 F3
La Baleine, Petite Rivière de r. Canada 122 F3
La Baleine, Rivière à r. Canada 123 I2
La Banda Arg. 144 D3
La Barge U.S.A. 126 F4
Labasa Fiji 107 H3
La Baule-Escoublac France 56 C3
Labazhskoye Rus. Fed. 42 L2
Labe r. Germany see Elbe
Labé Guinea 96 B3
La Belle U.S.A. 133 D7
La Bénoué, Parc National de nat. park Cameroon 97 E4
Laberge, Lake Canada 120 C2
Labian, Tanjung pt Malaysia 68 F5
La Biche, Lac l. Canada 121 H4
Labinsk Rus. Fed. 91 F1
Labis Malaysia 71 C7
La Boquilla Mex. 131 B7
La Boucle du Baoulé, Parc National de nat. park Mali 96 C3
Labouheyre France 56 D4
Laboulaye Arg. 144 D4
Labrador reg. Canada 123 J3
Labrador City Canada 123 I3
Labrador Sea Canada/Greenland 119 M3
Labrang China see Xiahe
Lábrea Brazil 142 F5
Labuan Malaysia 68 F5
Labudalin China see Ergun
Labuhanbilik Indon. 71 C7
Labuhanruku Indon. 71 B7
Labuna Indon. 69 H7
Labutta Myanmar 70 A3
Labyrinth, Lake salt flat Australia 111 A6
Labytnangi Rus. Fed. 64 H3
Laç Albania 59 H4
La Cabrera, Sierra de mts Spain 57 C2
La Cadena Mex. 131 B7
Lac-Allard Canada 123 J4
La Calle Alg. see El Kala
La Cañiza Spain see A Cañiza
La Capelle France 52 D5
La Carlota Arg. 144 D4
La Carolina Spain 57 E4
Lăcăuți, Vârful mt. Romania 59 L2
Laccadive, Minicoy and Amindivi Islands union terr. India see Lakshadweep
Laccadive Islands India 84 B4
Lac du Bonnet Canada 121 L5
Lacedaemon Greece see Sparti
La Ceiba Hond. 137 G5
Lacepede Bay Australia 111 B8
Lacepede Islands Australia 108 C4
Lacha, Ozero l. Rus. Fed. 42 H3
Lachendorf Germany 53 K2
Lachine U.S.A. 134 D1

▶Lachlan r. Australia 112 A5
5th longest river in Oceania.

La Chorrera Panama 137 I7
Lachute Canada 122 G5
Laçın Azer. 91 G3
La Ciotat France 56 G5
Lac La Biche Canada 121 I4
Lac la Martre Canada see Whatî
Lacolle Canada 135 I1
La Colorada Sonora Mex. 127 F7
La Colorada Zacatecas Mex. 131 C8
Lacombe Canada 120 H4
La Comoé, Parc National de nat. park Côte d'Ivoire 96 C4
Laconi Sardinia Italy 58 C5
Laconia U.S.A. 135 J2
La Corey Canada 121 I4
La Coruña Spain see A Coruña
La Corvette, Lac de l. Canada 122 G3
La Coubre, Pointe de pt France 56 D4
La Crete Canada 120 G3
La Crosse KS U.S.A. 130 D4
La Crosse VA U.S.A. 135 F5
La Crosse WI U.S.A. 130 F3
La Cruz Mex. 136 C4
La Cuesta Mex. 131 C6
La Culebra, Sierra de mts Spain 57 C3
La Cygne U.S.A. 130 E4
Ladainha Brazil 145 C2
Ladakh reg. India/Pak. 82 D2
Ladakh Range mts India 82 D2
Ladang, Ko i. Thai. 71 B6
La Demajagua Cuba 133 D8
La Demanda, Sierra de mts Spain 57 E2
La Déroute, Passage de strait Channel Is/France 49 E9
Ladik Turkey 90 D2
Lādīz Iran 89 F4
Ladnun India 82 C4

▶Ladoga, Lake Rus. Fed. 42 F3
2nd largest lake in Europe.

Ladong China 77 F3
Ladozhskoye Ozero l. Rus. Fed. see Ladoga, Lake
Ladrones terr. N. Pacific Ocean see Northern Mariana Islands
Ladu mt. India 83 H4
Ladue r. Canada/U.S.A. 120 A2
Ladva-Vetka Rus. Fed. 42 G3
Ladybank U.K. 50 F4
Ladybrand S. Africa 101 H5
Lady Frere S. Africa 101 H6
Lady Grey S. Africa 101 H6
Ladysmith S. Africa 101 I5
Ladysmith U.S.A. 130 F2
Ladzhanurges Georgia see Lajanurpekhi
Lae P.N.G. 69 L8
Laem Ngop Thai. 71 C4
Lærdalsøyri Norway 45 E6
La Esmeralda Bol. 142 F8
Læsø i. Denmark 45 G8
Lafayette Alg. see Bougaa
La Fayette AL U.S.A. 133 C5
Lafayette IN U.S.A. 134 B3
Lafayette LA U.S.A. 131 E6
Lafayette TN U.S.A. 134 B5
Lafé Cuba 133 C8
La Fère France 52 D5
Laferte r. Canada 120 G2
La Ferté-Gaucher France 52 D6
La-Ferté-Milon France 52 D5
La Ferté-sous-Jouarre France 52 D6
Lafia Nigeria 96 D4
Lafiagi Nigeria 96 D4
Laflamme r. Canada 122 F4
Lafleche Canada 121 J5
La Flèche France 56 D3
La Follette U.S.A. 134 C5
La Forest, Lac l. Canada 123 H3
Laforge Canada 123 G3
Laforge r. Canada 123 G3
La Frégate, Lac de l. Canada 122 G3
Lāft Iran 88 D5
Laful India 71 A6
La Galissonnière, Lac l. Canada 123 J4

▶La Galite i. Tunisia 58 C6
Most northerly point of Africa.

La Galite, Canal de sea chan. Tunisia 58 C6
La Gallega Mex. 131 B7
Lagan' Rus. Fed. 43 J7
Lagan r. U.K. 51 G3
La Garamba, Parc National de nat. park Dem. Rep. Congo 98 C3
Lagarto Brazil 143 K6
Lage Germany 53 I3
Lågen r. Norway 45 G7
Lage Vaart canal Neth. 52 F2
Lagg U.K. 50 D5
Laggan U.K. 50 E3
Lagh Bor watercourse Kenya/Somalia 98 E3
Laghouat Alg. 54 E5
Lagkor Co salt l. China 83 F2
La Gloria Mex. 131 D7
Lago Agrio Ecuador 142 C3
Lagoa Santa Brazil 145 C2
Lagoa Vermelha Brazil 145 A5
Lagodekhi Georgia 91 G2
Lagolândia Brazil 145 A1
La Gomera i. Canary Is 96 B2
La Gonâve, Île de i. Haiti 137 J5
Lagong i. Indon. 71 E7

▶Lagos Nigeria 96 D4
Former capital of Nigeria. Most populous city in Africa.

Lagos Port. 57 B5
Lagosa Tanz. 99 C4
La Grande r. Canada 122 F3
La Grande U.S.A. 126 D3
La Grande 3, Réservoir resr Canada 122 G3
La Grande 4, Réservoir resr Que. Canada 123 G3
La Grange Australia 108 C4
La Grange CA U.S.A. 128 C3
La Grange GA U.S.A. 133 C5
Lagrange U.S.A. 134 C3
La Grange KY U.S.A. 132 C4
La Grange TX U.S.A. 131 D6
La Gran Sabana plat. Venez. 142 F2
La Grita Venez. 142 D2
La Guajira, Península de pen. Col. 142 D1
Laguna Brazil 145 A5
Laguna, Picacho de la mt. Mex. 136 B4
Laguna Dam U.S.A. 129 F5
Laguna Mountains U.S.A. 128 E5
Lagunas Chile 144 C2
Laguna San Rafael, Parque Nacional nat. park Chile 144 B7
Laha China 74 B2
La Habana Cuba see Havana
La Habra U.S.A. 128 E5
Lahad Datu Sabah Malaysia 68 F5
La Hague, Cap de c. France 56 D2
Laharpur India 82 E4
Lahat Indon. 68 C7
Lahe Myanmar 70 A1
Lahemaa rahvuspark nat. park Estonia 45 N7
La Hève, Cap de c. France 49 H9
Lahewa Indon. 71 B7
Laḥij Yemen 86 F7
Lāhījān Iran 88 C2
Lahn r. Germany 53 H4
Lahnstein Germany 53 H4
Laholm Sweden 45 H8
Lahontan Reservoir U.S.A. 128 D2
Lahore Pak. 89 I4
Lahri Pak. 89 H4
Lahti Fin. 45 N6
Laï Chad 97 E4
Lai'an China 77 H1
Laibach Slovenia see Ljubljana
Laibin China 77 F4
Laidley Australia 112 F1
Laifeng China 77 F2
L'Aigle France 56 E2
Laihia Fin. 44 M5
Lai-hka Myanmar 70 B2
Lai-Hsak Myanmar 70 B2
Laimakuri India 83 H4
Laimos, Akrotirio pt Greece 59 J5
Laingsburg S. Africa 100 E7
Laingsburg U.S.A. 134 C2
Lainioälven r. Sweden 44 M3
Lair U.S.A. 134 C4
L'Aïr, Massif de mts Niger 96 D3
Lairg U.K. 50 E2
La Isabela Cuba 133 D8
Laishevo Rus. Fed. 42 K5
Laitila Fin. 45 L6
Laives Italy 58 D1
Laiwu China 73 L5
Laiwui Indon. 69 H7
Laiyang China 73 M5
Laizhou China 73 L5
Laizhou Wan b. China 73 L5
Lajamanu Australia 108 E4
Lajanurpekhi Georgia 91 F2
Lajeado Brazil 145 A5
Lajes Rio Grande do Norte Brazil 143 K5
Lajes Santa Catarina Brazil 145 A4
La Junta Mex. 127 G7
La Junta U.S.A. 130 C4
La Juventud, Isla de i. Cuba 137 H4
Lakadiya India 82 B5
L'Akagera, Parc National de nat. park Rwanda see Akagera National Park
La Kagera, Parc National de nat. park Rwanda see Akagera National Park
Lake U.S.A. 134 D5
Lake Andes U.S.A. 130 D3
Lakeba i. Fiji 107 I3
Lake Bardawil Reserve nature res. Egypt 85 A4
Lake Bolac Australia 112 A6
Lake Butler U.S.A. 133 D6
Lake Cargelligo Australia 112 C4
Lake Cathie Australia 112 F3
Lake Charles U.S.A. 131 E6
Lake City CO U.S.A. 129 J3
Lake City FL U.S.A. 133 D6
Lake City MI U.S.A. 134 C1
Lake Clark National Park and Preserve U.S.A. 118 C3
Lake Clear U.S.A. 135 H1
Lake District National Park U.K. 48 D4
Lake Eyre National Park Australia 111 B6
Lakefield Australia 110 D2
Lakefield Canada 135 F1
Lakefield National Park Australia 110 D2
Lake Forest U.S.A. 134 B2
Lake Gairdner National Park Australia 111 B7
Lake Geneva U.S.A. 130 F3
Lake George MI U.S.A. 134 C2
Lake George NY U.S.A. 135 I2
Lake Grace Australia 109 B8
Lake Harbour Canada see Kimmirut
Lake Havasu City U.S.A. 129 F4
Lakehurst U.S.A. 135 H3
Lake Isabella U.S.A. 128 D4
Lake Jackson U.S.A. 131 E6
Lake King Australia 109 B8
Lake Kopiago P.N.G. 69 K8
Lakeland FL U.S.A. 133 D7
Lakeland GA U.S.A. 133 D6
Lake Louise Canada 120 G5
Lakemba i. Fiji see Lakeba
Lake Mills U.S.A. 130 E3
Lake Nash Australia 110 B4
Lake Odessa U.S.A. 134 C2
Lake Paringa N.Z. 113 B6
Lake Placid FL U.S.A. 133 D7
Lake Placid NY U.S.A. 135 I1
Lake Pleasant U.S.A. 135 H2
Lakeport CA U.S.A. 128 B2
Lakeport MI U.S.A. 134 D2
Lake Providence U.S.A. 131 F5
Lake Range mts U.S.A. 128 D1
Lake River Canada 122 E3
Lakes Entrance Australia 112 D6
Lakeside AZ U.S.A. 129 I4
Lakeside VA U.S.A. 135 G5
Lake Tabourie Australia 112 E5
Lake Tekapo N.Z. 113 C7
Lake Torrens National Park Australia 111 B6
Lakeview MI U.S.A. 134 C2
Lakeview OH U.S.A. 134 D3
Lakeview OR U.S.A. 126 C4
Lake Village U.S.A. 131 F5
Lake Wales U.S.A. 133 D7
Lakewood CO U.S.A. 126 G5
Lakewood NJ U.S.A. 135 H3
Lakewood NY U.S.A. 134 F2
Lakewood OH U.S.A. 134 E3
Lake Worth U.S.A. 133 D7
Lakha India 82 B4
Lakhdenpokh'ya Rus. Fed. 44 Q6
Lakhimpur Assam India see North Lakhimpur
Lakhimpur Uttar Prad. India 82 E4
Lakhisarai India 83 F4
Lakhish r. Israel 85 B4
Lakhnadon India 82 D5
Lakhpat India 82 B5
Lakhtar India 82 B5
Lakin U.S.A. 130 C4
Lakitusaki r. Canada 122 E3
Lakki Marwat Pak. 89 H3
Lakonikos Kolpos b. Greece 59 J6
Lakor i. Indon. 108 E2
Lakota Côte d'Ivoire 96 C4
Lakota U.S.A. 130 D1
Laksefjorden sea chan. Norway 44 O1
Lakselv Norway 44 N1
Lakshadweep is India see Laccadive Islands
Lakshadweep union terr. India 84 B4
Lakshettipet India 84 C2
Lakshmipur Bangl. 83 G5
Laksmipur Bangl. see Lakshmipur
Lalaghat India 83 H4
Lalbara India 84 D1
L'Alcora Spain 57 F3
Lāleh Zār, Kūh-e mt. Iran 88 E4
Lalganj India 83 F4
Lālī Iran 88 C3
La Ligua Chile 144 B4
Laliki Indon. 108 D1
Lalin China 74 B3
Lalín Spain 57 B2
La Línea de la Concepción Spain 57 D5
Lalin He r. China 74 B3
Lalitpur India 82 D4
Lalitpur Nepal see Patan
Lalmanirhat Bangl. see Lalmonirhat
Lalmonirhat Bangl. 83 G4
La Loche Canada 121 I3
La Loche, Lac l. Canada 121 I3
La Louvière Belgium 52 E4
Lal'sk Rus. Fed. 42 J3
Lalung La pass China 83 F3
Lama Bangl. 83 H5

a Macarena, Parque Nacional *nat. park* Col. **142** D3
a Maddalena *Sardinia* Italy **58** C4
a Madeleine, Îles de *is* Canada **123** J5
a Madeleine, Monts de *mts* France **56** F3
amadian China **74** B3
amadianzi China *see* **Lamadian**
a Maiko, Parc National de *nat. park* Dem. Rep. Congo **98** C4
a Malbaie Canada **123** H5
amam Laos **70** D4
a Mancha Mex. **131** C7
a Mancha *reg.* Spain **57** E4
a Manche *strait* France/U.K. *see* **English Channel**
a Máquina Mex. **131** B6
amar *CO* U.S.A. **130** C4
amar *MO* U.S.A. **131** E4
amard Iran **88** D5
a Margeride, Monts de *mts* France **56** F4
a Marmora, Punta *mt. Sardinia* Italy **58** C5
a Marne au Rhin, Canal de France **52** G6
a Marque U.S.A. **131** E6
a Martre, Lac *l.* Canada **120** G2
amas *r.* Turkey **85** B1
a Mauricie, Parc National de *nat. park* Canada **123** G5
ambaréné Gabon **98** B4
ambasa Fiji *see* **Labasa**
ambayeque Peru **142** C5
ambay Island Ireland **51** G4
ambert *atoll* Marshall Is *see* **Ailinglaplap**

Lambert Glacier Antarctica **152** E2
Largest series of glaciers in the world.

ambert's Bay S. Africa **100** D7
ambeth Canada **134** E2
ambi India **82** C3
ambourn Downs *hills* U.K. **49** F7
ame Indon. **71** B7
a Medjerda, Monts de *mts* Alg. **58** B6
amego Port. **57** C3
amèque, Île *i.* Canada **123** I5
a Merced Arg. **144** C3
a Merced Peru **142** C6
ameroo Australia **111** C7
a Mesa U.S.A. **128** E5
amesa U.S.A. **131** C5
amia Greece **59** J5
amington National Park Australia **112** F2
a Misión Mex. **128** E5
amma Island *H.K.* China **77** [inset]
ammerlaw Range *mts* N.Z. **113** B7
ammermuir Hills U.K. **50** G5
ammhult Sweden **45** I8
ammi Fin. **45** N6
amont *CA* U.S.A. **128** D4
amont *WY* U.S.A. **126** G4
a Montagne d'Ambre, Parc National de *nat. park* Madag. **99** E5
a Montaña de Covadonga, Parque Nacional de *nat. park* Spain *see* **Los Picos de Europa, Parque Nacional de**
a Mora Mex. **131** C7
a Morita *Chihuahua* Mex. **131** B6
a Morita *Coahuila* Mex. **131** C6
amotrek *atoll* Micronesia **69** L5
a Moure U.S.A. **130** D2
ampang Thai. **70** B3
am Pao, Ang Kep Nam Thai. **70** C3
ampasas U.S.A. **131** D6
ampazos Mex. **131** C7
ampedusa, Isola di *i. Sicily* Italy **58** E7
ampeter U.K. **49** C6
amphun Thai. **70** B3
ampsacus Turkey *see* **Lâpseki**
am Tin *H.K.* China **77** [inset]
amu Kenya **98** E4
amu Myanmar **70** A3
ana'i *i.* U.S.A. **127** [inset]
ana'i City U.S.A. **127** [inset]
a Nao, Cabo de *c.* Spain **57** G4
anao, Lake Phil. **69** G5
anark Canada **135** G1
anark U.K. **50** F5
anbi Kyun *i.* Myanmar **71** B5
ancang China **76** C4
ancang Jiang *r.* China **76** C2
ancaster Canada **135** H1
ancaster U.K. **48** E4
ancaster *CA* U.S.A. **128** D4
ancaster *KY* U.S.A. **134** C5
ancaster *MO* U.S.A. **130** E3
ancaster *NH* U.S.A. **135** J1
ancaster *OH* U.S.A. **134** D4
ancaster *PA* U.S.A. **135** G3
ancaster *SC* U.S.A. **133** D5
ancaster *VA* U.S.A. **135** G5
ancaster *WI* U.S.A. **130** F3
ancaster Canal U.K. **48** E5
ancaster Sound *strait* Canada **119** J2
anchow China *see* **Lanzhou**
andana Angola *see* **Cacongo**
andau an der Isar Germany **53** M6
andau in der Pfalz Germany **53** I5
andeck Austria **47** M7
ander *watercourse* Australia **108** E5
ander U.S.A. **126** F4
andesbergen Germany **53** J2
andfall Island India **71** A4
andhi Pak. **89** G5
andis Canada **121** I4
andor Australia **109** B6
andsberg Poland *see* **Gorzów Wielkopolski**
andsberg am Lech Germany **47** M6
and's End *pt* U.K. **49** B8
andshut Germany **53** M6
andskrona Sweden **45** H9
andstuhl Germany **53** H5
and Wursten *reg.* Germany **53** I1
anesborough Ireland **51** E4
'nga Co *l.* China **82** E3
angao China **77** F1
angar Afgh. **89** H3
angberg *mts* S. Africa **100** F5
angdon U.S.A. **130** D1
angeac France **56** E4
angeberg *mts* S. Africa **100** D7
angeland *i.* Denmark **45** G9
angelmäki Fin. **45** N6
Langelsheim Germany **53** K3
Langen Germany **53** I1
Langenburg Canada **121** K5
Langenhagen Germany **53** J2
Langenhahn Germany **53** H4
Langenlonsheim Germany **53** H5
Langenthal Switz. **56** H3
Langenweddingen Germany **53** L2
Langeoog Germany **53** H1
Langesund Norway **45** F7
Langfang China **73** L5
Langgapayung Indon. **71** B7
Langgar China **76** B2
Langgöns Germany **53** I4
Langjan Nature Reserve S. Africa **101** I2
Langjökull *ice cap* Iceland **44** [inset]
Langka Indon. **71** B6
Langkawi *i.* Malaysia **71** B6
Lang Kha Toek, Khao *mt.* Thai. **71** B5
Langklip S. Africa **100** E5
Langley Canada **120** F5
Langley U.S.A. **134** D5
Langlo Crossing Australia **111** D5
Langmusi China *see* **Dagcanglhamo**
Langong, Xé *r.* Laos **70** D3
Langøya *i.* Norway **44** I2
Langphu *mt.* China **83** F3
Langport U.K. **49** E7
Langqên Zangbo *r.* China **82** D3
Langqi China **77** H3
Langres France **56** G3
Langres, Plateau de France **56** G3
Langru China **82** D1
Langsa Indon. **71** B6
Langsa, Teluk *b.* Indon. **71** B6
Långsele Sweden **44** J5
Lang Sơn Vietnam **70** D2
Langtang National Park Nepal **83** F3
Langtao Myanmar **70** B1
Langting India **83** H4
Langtoft U.K. **48** G4
Langtry U.S.A. **131** C6
Languan China *see* **Lantian**
Languedoc *reg.* France **56** E5
Långvattnet Sweden **44** L4
Langwedel Germany **53** J2
Langxi China **77** H2
Langzhong China **76** E2
Lanigan Canada **121** J5
Lanín, Parque Nacional *nat. park* Arg. **144** B5
Lanín, Volcán *vol.* Arg./Chile **144** B5
Lanji India **82** E5
Lanka *country* Asia *see* **Sri Lanka**
Länkäran Azer. **91** H3
Lannion France **56** C2
Lanping China **76** C3
Lansån Sweden **44** M3
L'Anse U.S.A. **130** F2
Lanshan China **77** G3

▶Lansing U.S.A. **134** C2
Capital of Michigan.

Lanta, Ko *i.* Thai. **71** B6
Lantau Island *H.K.* China **77** [inset]
Lantau Peak *hill H.K.* China **77** [inset]
Lantian China **77** F1
Lanxi *Heilong.* China **74** B3
Lanxi *Zhejiang* China **77** H2
Lan Yü *i.* Taiwan **77** I4
Lanzarote *i.* Canary Is **96** B2
Lanzhou China **72** I5
Lanzijing China **74** A3
Laoag Phil. **69** G3
Laoang Phil. **69** H4
Laobie Shan *mts* China **76** C4
Laobukou China **77** F3
Lao Cai Vietnam **70** C2
Laodicea Syria *see* **Latakia**
Laodicea Turkey *see* **Denizli**
Laodicea ad Lycum Turkey *see* **Denizli**
Laodicea ad Mare Syria *see* **Latakia**
Laohekou China **77** F1
Laohupo China *see* **Logpung**
Laojie China *see* **Yongping**
Laojunmiao China *see* **Yumen**
La Okapi, Parc National de *nat. park* Dem. Rep. Congo **98** C3
Lao Ling *mts* China **74** B4
Laon France **52** D5
La Oroya Peru **142** C6
Laos *country* Asia **70** C3
Laotougou China **74** C4
Laotuding Shan *hill* China **74** B4
Laowohi *pass* India *see* **Khardung La**
Laoye Ling *mts Heilongjiang/Jilin* China **74** B4
Laoye Ling *mts Heilongjiang/Jilin* China **74** C4
Lapa Brazil **145** A4
La Palma *i.* Canary Is **96** B2
La Palma Panama **137** I7
La Palma U.S.A. **129** H5
La Palma del Condado Spain **57** C5
La Panza Range *mts* U.S.A. **128** C4
La Paragua Venez. **142** F2
La Parilla Mex. **131** B8
La Paya, Parque Nacional *nat. park* Col. **142** D3
La Paz Arg. **144** E4

▶La Paz Bol. **142** E7
Official capital of Bolivia.

La Paz Hond. **136** G6
La Paz Mex. **136** B4
La Pedrera Col. **142** E4
Lapeer U.S.A. **134** D2
La Pendjari, Parc National de *nat. park* Benin **96** D3
La Perla Mex. **131** B6
La Pérouse Strait Japan/Rus. Fed. **74** F3
La Pesca Mex. **131** D8
Lapinlahti Fin. **44** O5
Lapithos Cyprus **85** A2
Lap Lae Thai. **70** C3
La Plant U.S.A. **130** C2
La Plata Arg. **144** E4
La Plata *MD* U.S.A. **135** G4
La Plata *MO* U.S.A. **130** E3
La Plata, Isla *i.* Ecuador **142** B4

▶La Plata, Río de *sea chan.* Arg./Uruguay **144** E4
Part of the Río de la Plata - Paraná, 2nd longest river in South America, and 9th in the world.

La Plonge, Lac *l.* Canada **121** J4
Lapmežciems Latvia **45** M8
Lapominka Rus. Fed. **42** I2
La Porte U.S.A. **134** B3
Laporte U.S.A. **135** G3
Laporte, Mount Canada **120** E2
La Potherie, Lac *l.* Canada **123** G2
La Poza Grande Mex. **127** E8
Lappajärvi Fin. **44** M5
Lappajärvi *l.* Fin. **44** M5
Lappeenranta Fin. **45** P6
Lappersdorf Germany **53** M5
Lappi Fin. **45** L6
Lappland *reg.* Europe **44** K3
La Pryor U.S.A. **131** D6
Lâpseki Turkey **59** L4
Laptevo Rus. Fed. *see* **Yasnogorsk**
Laptev Sea Rus. Fed. **65** N2
Lapua Fin. **44** M5
Lapurdum France *see* **Bayonne**
La Purísima Mex. **127** E8
Laqiya Arbain *well* Sudan **86** C5
La Quiaca Arg. **144** C2
L'Aquila Italy **58** E3
La Quinta U.S.A. **128** E5
Lār Iran **88** D5
Larache Morocco **57** C6
Lārak *i.* Iran **88** E5
Laramie U.S.A. **126** G4
Laramie *r.* U.S.A. **126** G4
Laramie Mountains U.S.A. **126** G4
Laranda Turkey *see* **Karaman**
Laranjal Paulista Brazil **145** B3
Laranjeiras do Sul Brazil **144** F3
Laranjinha *r.* Brazil **145** A3
Larantuka Indon. **108** C2
Larat Indon. **108** E1
Larat *i.* Indon. **108** E1
Larba Alg. **57** H5
Lärbro Sweden **45** K8
L'Archipélago de Mingan, Réserve du Parc National de *nat. park* Canada **123** J4
L'Ardenne, Plateau de *plat.* Belgium *see* **Ardennes**
Laredo Spain **57** E2
Laredo U.S.A. **131** D7
La Reina Adelaida, Archipiélago de *is* Chile **144** B8
Largeau Chad *see* **Faya**
Largo U.S.A. **133** D7
Largs U.K. **50** E5
Lārī Iran **88** B2
L'Ariana Tunisia **58** D6
Larimore U.S.A. **130** D2
La Rioja Arg. **144** C3
La Rioja *aut. comm.* Spain **57** E2
Larisa Greece **59** J5
Larissa Greece *see* **Larisa**
Laristan *reg.* Iran **88** E5
Larkana Pak. **89** H5
Lark Harbour Canada **123** K4
Lar Koh *mt.* Afgh. **89** F3
Lark Passage Australia **110** D2
L'Arli, Parc National de *nat. park* Burkina **96** D3
Larnaca Cyprus **85** A2
Larnaka Cyprus *see* **Larnaca**
Larnaka Bay Cyprus **85** A2
Larnakos, Kolpos *b.* Cyprus *see* **Larnaka Bay**
Larne U.K. **51** G3
Larned U.S.A. **130** D4
La Robe Noire, Lac de *l.* Canada **123** J4
La Robla Spain **57** D2
La Roche-en-Ardenne Belgium **52** F4
La Rochelle France **56** D3
La Roche-sur-Yon France **56** D3
La Roda Spain **57** E4
La Romana Dom. Rep. **137** K5
La Ronge Canada **121** J4
La Ronge, Lac *l.* Canada **121** J4
La Rosa Mex. **131** C7
La Rosita Mex. **131** C6
Larrey Point Australia **108** B4
Larrimah Australia **108** F3
Lars Christensen Coast Antarctica **152** E2
Larsen Ice Shelf Antarctica **152** L2
Larsmo Fin. **44** M5
Larvik Norway **45** G7
Las Adjuntas, Presa de *resr* Mex. **131** D8
La Sal U.S.A. **129** I2
LaSalle Canada **135** I1
La Salle U.S.A. **122** C6
La Salonga Nord, Parc National de *nat. park* Dem. Rep. Congo **98** C4
La Sambre à l'Oise, Canal de France **52** D5
Las Animas U.S.A. **130** C4
Las Anod Somalia *see* **Laascaanood**
La Sarre Canada **122** F4
Las Avispas Mex. **127** F7
La Savonnière, Lac *l.* Canada **123** G3
La Scie Canada **123** L4
Las Cruces *CA* U.S.A. **128** C4
Las Cruces *NM* U.S.A. **127** G6
La Selle, Pic *mt.* Haiti **137** J5
La Serena Chile **144** B3
Las Esperanças Mex. **131** C7
La Seu d'Urgell Spain **57** G2
Las Flores Arg. **144** E5
Las Guacamatas, Cerro *mt.* Mex. **127** F7
Lāshār *r.* Iran **89** F5
Lashburn Canada **121** I4
Las Heras Arg. **144** C4
Lashio Myanmar **70** B2
Lashkar India **82** D4
Lashkar Gāh Afgh. **89** G4
Las Juntas Chile **144** C3
Las Lomitas Arg. **144** D2
Las Marismas *marsh* Spain **57** C5
Las Martinetas Arg. **144** C7
Las Mesteñas Mex. **131** B6
Las Minas, Cerro de *mt.* Hond. **136** G6
Las Nopaleras, Cerro *mt.* Mex. **131** C7
La Société, Archipel de *is* Fr. Polynesia *see* **Society Islands**
La Somme, Canal de France **52** C5
Las Palmas *watercourse* Mex. **128** E5

▶Las Palmas de Gran Canaria Canary Is **96** B2
Joint capital of the Canary Islands.

Las Petas Bol. **143** G7
La Spezia Italy **58** C2
Las Piedras, Río de *r.* Peru **142** E6
Las Plumas Arg. **144** C6
Laspur Pak. **89** I2
Lassance Brazil **145** B2
Lassen Peak *vol.* U.S.A. **128** C1
Lassen Volcanic National Park U.S.A. **128** C1
Las Tablas Panama **137** H7
Las Tablas de Daimiel, Parque Nacional de *nat. park* Spain **57** E4
Last Chance U.S.A. **130** C4
Las Termas Arg. **144** D3
Last Mountain Lake Canada **121** J5
Las Tórtolas, Cerro *mt.* Chile **144** C3
Lastoursville Gabon **98** B4
Lastovo *i.* Croatia **58** G3
Las Tres Vírgenes, Volcán *vol.* Mex. **127** E8
Lastrup Germany **53** H2
Las Tunas Cuba **137** I4
Las Varas *Chihuahua* Mex. **127** G7
Las Varas *Nayarit* Mex. **136** C4
Las Varillas Arg. **144** D4
Las Vegas *NM* U.S.A. **127** G6
Las Vegas *NV* U.S.A. **129** F3
Las Viajas, Isla de *i.* Peru **142** C6
Las Villuercas *mt.* Spain **57** D4
La Tabatière Canada **123** K4
Latacunga Ecuador **142** C4
Latady Island Antarctica **152** L2
Latakia Syria **85** B2
La Teste-de-Buch France **56** D4
Latham Australia **109** B7
Lathen Germany **53** H2
Latheron U.K. **50** F2
Lathi India **82** B4
Latho India **82** D2
Lathrop U.S.A. **128** C3
Latina Italy **58** E4
La Tortuga, Isla *i.* Venez. **142** E1
Latrobe U.S.A. **134** F3
Latrun West Bank **85** B4
Lattaquié Syria *see* **Latakia**
Lattrop Neth. **52** G2
La Tuque Canada **123** G5
Latur India **84** C2
Latvia *country* Europe **45** N8
Latvija *country* Europe *see* **Latvia**
Latviyskaya S.S.R. *country* Europe *see* **Latvia**
Lauca, Parque Nacional *nat. park* Chile **142** E7
Lauchhammer Germany **47** N5
Lauder U.K. **50** G5
Laudio Spain *see* **Llodio**
Lauenbrück Germany **53** J1
Lauenburg (Elbe) Germany **53** K1
Lauf an der Pegnitz Germany **53** L5
Laufen Switz. **56** H3
Lauge Koch Kyst *reg.* Greenland **119** L2
Laughlen, Mount Australia **109** F5
Laughlin Peak U.S.A. **127** G5
Lauka Estonia **45** M7
Launceston Australia **111** [inset]
Launceston U.K. **49** C8
Laune *r.* Ireland **51** C5
Launggyaung Myanmar **70** B1
Launglon Myanmar **71** B4
Launglon Bok Islands Myanmar **71** B4
La Unión Bol. **142** F7
Laura Australia **110** D2
Laurel *DE* U.S.A. **135** H4
Laurel *MS* U.S.A. **131** F6
Laurel *MT* U.S.A. **126** F3
Laureldale U.S.A. **135** H3
Laurel Hill *hills* U.S.A. **134** F4
Laurencekirk U.K. **50** G4
Laurieton Australia **112** F3
Laurinburg U.S.A. **133** E5
Lauru *i.* Solomon Is *see* **Choiseul**
Lausanne Switz. **56** H3
Laut *i.* Indon. **68** F7
Laut *i.* Indon. **71** E6
Lautem East Timor **108** D2
Lautersbach (Hessen) Germany **53** J4
Laut Kecil, Kepulauan *is* Indon. **68** F8
Lautoka Fiji **107** H3
Lauvuskylä Fin. **44** P5
Lauwersmeer *l.* Neth. **52** G1
Lava Beds National Monument *nat. park* U.S.A. **126** C4
Laval Canada **122** G5
Laval France **56** D2
La Vall d'Uixó Spain **57** F4
Lāvān *i.* Iran **88** D5
La Vanoise, Massif de *mts* France **56** H4
La Vanoise, Parc National de *nat. park* France **56** H4
Lavapié, Punta *pt* Chile **144** B5
Lāvar Iran **88** C4
Laveaga Peak U.S.A. **128** C3
La Vega Dom. Rep. **137** J5
Laverne U.S.A. **131** D4
Laverton Australia **109** C7
La Víbora Mex. **131** C7
La Vila Joíosa Spain *see* **Villajoyosa-La Vila Joíosa**
La Viña Peru **142** C5
Lavongai *i.* P.N.G. *see* **New Hanover**
Lavras Brazil **145** B3
Lavumisa Swaziland **101** J4
Lavushi-Manda National Park Zambia **99** D5
Lawa India **82** C4
Lawa Myanmar **70** B1
Lawa Pak. **89** H3
Lawashi *r.* Canada **122** E3
Law Dome *ice feature* Antarctica **152** F2
Lawit, Gunung *mt.* Malaysia **71** C6
Lawksawk Myanmar **70** B2
Lawn Hill National Park Australia **110** B3
La Woëvre, Plaine de *plain* France **52** F5
Lawra Ghana **96** C3
Lawrence *IN* U.S.A. **134** B4
Lawrence *KS* U.S.A. **130** E4
Lawrence *MA* U.S.A. **135** J2
Lawrenceburg *IN* U.S.A. **134** C4
Lawrenceburg *KY* U.S.A. **134** C4
Lawrenceburg *TN* U.S.A. **132** C5
Lawrenceville *GA* U.S.A. **133** D5
Lawrenceville *IL* U.S.A. **134** B4
Lawrenceville *VA* U.S.A. **135** G5
Lawrence Wells, Mount *hill* Australia **109** C6
Lawton U.S.A. **131** D5
Lawz, Jabal al *mt.* Saudi Arabia **90** D5
Laxå Sweden **45** I7
Laxey Isle of Man **48** C4
Laxgalts'ap Canada **120** D4
Lax Kw'alaams Canada **120** D4
Laxo U.K. **50** [inset]
Laya *r.* Rus. Fed. **42** M2
Laydennyy, Mys *c.* Rus. Fed. **42** J1
Laylá Saudi Arabia **86** G5
Layla *salt pan* Saudi Arabia **85** D4
Laysan Island U.S.A. **150** I4
Laytonville U.S.A. **128** B2
Layyah Pak. **89** H4
Laza Myanmar **70** B1
Lazarev Rus. Fed. **74** F1
Lazarevac Serbia **59** I2
Lázaro Cárdenas Mex. **136** D5
Lazcano Uruguay **144** F4
Lazdijai Lith. **45** M9
Lazikou China **76** D1
Lazo *Primorskiy Kray* Rus. Fed. **74** D4
Lazo *Respublika Sakha (Yakutiya)* Rus. Fed. **65** O3
Lead U.S.A. **130** C2
Leader Water *r.* U.K. **50** G5
Leadville Australia **112** D4
Leaf *r.* U.S.A. **131** F6
Leaf Bay Canada *see* **Tasiujaq**
Leaf Rapids Canada **121** K3
Leakey U.S.A. **131** D6
Leaksville U.S.A. *see* **Eden**
Leamington Canada **134** D2
Leamington Spa, Royal U.K. **49** F6
Leane, Lough *l.* Ireland **51** C5
Leap Ireland **51** C6
Leatherhead U.K. **49** G7
L'Eau Claire, Lac à *l.* Canada **122** G2
L'Eau Claire, Rivière à *r.* Canada **122** G2
L'Eau d'Heure *l.* Belgium **52** E4
Leavenworth *IN* U.S.A. **134** B4
Leavenworth *KS* U.S.A. **130** E4
Leavenworth *WA* U.S.A. **126** C3
Leavitt Peak U.S.A. **128** D2
Lebach Germany **52** G5
Lebanon *country* Asia **85** B2
Lebanon *IN* U.S.A. **134** B3
Lebanon *KY* U.S.A. **134** C5
Lebanon *MO* U.S.A. **130** E4
Lebanon *NH* U.S.A. **135** I2
Lebanon *OH* U.S.A. **134** C4
Lebanon *OR* U.S.A. **126** C3
Lebanon *PA* U.S.A. **135** G3
Lebanon *TN* U.S.A. **132** C4
Lebanon *VA* U.S.A. **134** D5
Lebanon Junction U.S.A. **134** C5
Lebanon Mountains Lebanon *see* **Liban, Jebel**
Lebbeke Belgium **52** E3
Lebec U.S.A. **128** D4
Lebedyan' Rus. Fed. **43** H5
Lebel-sur-Quévillon Canada **122** F4
Le Blanc France **56** E3
Lębork Poland **47** P3
Lebowakgomo S. Africa **101** I3
Lebrija Spain **57** C5
Łebsko, Jezioro *lag.* Poland **47** P3
Lebu Chile **144** B5
Lebyazh'ye Kazakh. *see* **Akku**
Lebyazh'ye Rus. Fed. **42** K4
Le Caire Egypt *see* **Cairo**
Le Cateau-Cambrésis France **52** D4
Le Catelet France **52** D4
Lecce Italy **58** H4
Lecco Italy **58** C2
Lech *r.* Austria/Germany **47** M7
Lechaina Greece **59** I6
Lechang China **77** G3
Le Chasseron *mt.* Switz. **56** H3
Le Chesne France **52** E5
Lechtaler Alpen *mts* Austria **47** M7
Leck Germany **47** L3
Lecompte U.S.A. **131** E6
Le Creusot France **56** G3
Le Crotoy France **52** B4
Lectoure France **56** E5
Ledang, Gunung *mt.* Malaysia **71** C7
Ledbury U.K. **49** E6
Ledesma Spain **57** D3
Ledmore U.K. **50** E2
Ledmozero Rus. Fed. **44** R4
Ledong *Hainan* China **70** E3
Ledong *Hainan* China **77** F5
Le Dorat France **56** E3
Leduc Canada **120** H4
Lee *r.* Ireland **51** D6
Lee *IN* U.S.A. **134** B3
Lee *MA* U.S.A. **135** I2
Leech Lake U.S.A. **130** E2
Leeds U.K. **48** F5
Leedstown U.K. **49** B8
Leek Neth. **52** G1
Leek U.K. **49** E5
Leende Neth. **52** F3
Leer (Ostfriesland) Germany **53** H1
Leesburg *FL* U.S.A. **133** D6
Leesburg *GA* U.S.A. **133** C6
Leesburg *OH* U.S.A. **134** D4
Leesburg *VA* U.S.A. **135** G4
Leese Germany **53** J2
Lee Steere Range *hills* Australia **109** C6
Leesville U.S.A. **131** E6
Leesville Lake *OH* U.S.A. **134** E3
Leesville Lake *VA* U.S.A. **134** F5
Leeton Australia **112** C5
Leeu-Gamka S. Africa **100** E7
Leeuwarden Neth. **52** F1
Leeuwin, Cape Australia **109** A8
Leeuwin-Naturaliste National Park Australia **109** A8
Lee Vining U.S.A. **128** D3
Leeward Islands Caribbean Sea **137** L5
Lefka Cyprus **85** A2
Lefkada Greece **59** I5
Lefkada *i.* Greece **59** I5
Lefkás Greece *see* **Lefkada**
Lefke Cyprus *see* **Lefka**
Lefkimmi Greece **59** I5
Lefkoniko Cyprus *see* **Lefkonikon**
Lefkonikon Cyprus **85** A2
Lefkoşa Cyprus *see* **Nicosia**
Lefkosia Cyprus *see* **Nicosia**
Lefroy *r.* Canada **123** H2
Lefroy, Lake *salt flat* Australia **109** C7
Legarde *r.* Canada **122** D4
Legaspi Phil. **69** G4
Legden Germany **52** H2
Legges Tor *mt.* Australia **111** [inset]
Leghorn Italy *see* **Livorno**
Legnago Italy **58** D2
Legnica Poland **47** P5
Le Grand U.S.A. **128** C3
Legune Australia **108** E3
Leh India **82** D2
Le Havre France **56** E2
Lehi U.S.A. **129** H1
Lehighton U.S.A. **135** H3
Lehmo Fin. **44** P5
Lehre Germany **53** K2
Lehrte Germany **53** J2
Lehtimäki Fin. **44** M5
Lehututu Botswana **100** E2
Leibnitz Austria **47** O7
Leicester U.K. **49** F6
Leichhardt *r.* Australia **106** B3
Leichhardt Falls Australia **110** B3
Leichhardt Range *mts* Australia **110** D4
Leiden Neth. **52** E2
Leie *r.* Belgium **52** D3
Leigh N.Z. **113** E3
Leigh U.K. **48** E5
Leighton Buzzard U.K. **49** G7
Leiktho Myanmar **70** B3
Leimen Germany **53** I5
Leine *r.* Germany **53** J2
Leinefelde Germany **53** K3
Leinster Australia **109** C6
Leinster *reg.* Ireland **51** F4
Leinster, Mount *hill* Ireland **51** F5
Leipsic U.S.A. **134** D3
Leipsoi *i.* Greece **59** L6
Leipzig Germany **53** M3
Leipzig-Halle *airport* Germany **53** M3
Leiranger Norway **44** I3
Leiria Port. **57** B4
Leirvik Norway **45** D7
Leishan China **77** F3
Leisler, Mount *hill* Australia **109** E5
Leisnig Germany **53** M3
Leitchfield U.S.A. **134** B5
Leith Hill *hill* U.K. **49** G7
Leiva, Cerro *mt.* Col. **142** D3
Leixlip Ireland **51** F4
Leiyang China **77** G3
Leizhou China **77** F4
Leizhou Bandao *pen.* China **77** F4
Leizhou Wan *b.* China **77** F4
Lek *r.* Neth. **52** E3
Leka Norway **44** G4
Lékana Congo **98** B4
Le Kef Tunisia **58** C6
Lekhainá Greece *see* **Lechaina**
Lekitobi Indon. **69** G7
Lekkersing S. Africa **100** C5
Lékoni Gabon **98** B4
Leksand Sweden **45** I6
Leksozero, Ozero *l.* Rus. Fed. **44** Q5
Lelai, Tanjung *pt* Indon. **69** H6
Leland U.S.A. **134** C1
Leli China *see* **Tianlin**
Lélouma Guinea **96** B3
Lelystad Neth. **52** F2
Le Maire, Estrecho de *sea chan.* Arg. **144** C9
Léman, Lac *l.* France/Switz. *see* **Geneva, Lake**
Le Mans France **56** E2
Le Mars U.S.A. **130** D3
Lemberg France **53** H5
Lemberg Ukr. *see* **L'viv**
Lembruch Germany **53** I2
Lemdiyya Alg. *see* **Médéa**
Leme Brazil **145** B3
Lemele Neth. **52** G2
Lemesos Cyprus *see* **Limassol**
Lemgo Germany **53** I2
Lemhi Range *mts* U.S.A. **126** E3
Lemi Fin. **45** O6
Lemieux Islands Canada **119** L3
Lemmenjoen kansallispuisto *nat. park* Fin. **44** N2
Lemmer Neth. **52** F2
Lemmon U.S.A. **130** C2
Lemmon, Mount U.S.A. **129** H5
Lemnos *i.* Greece *see* **Limnos**
Lemoncove U.S.A. **128** D3
Lemoore U.S.A. **128** D3
Le Moyne, Lac *l.* Canada **123** H2
Lemro *r.* Myanmar **70** A2
Lemtybozh Rus. Fed. **41** R3
Le Murge *hills* Italy **58** G4
Lemvig Denmark **45** F8
Lem"yu *r.* Rus. Fed. **42** M3
Lena *r.* Rus. Fed. **72** J1
Lena U.S.A. **134** A1
Lena, Mount U.S.A. **129** I1
Lenadoon Point Ireland **51** C3
Lenchung Tso *salt l.* China **83** E2
Lencóis Brazil **145** C1
Lençóis Maranhenses, Parque Nacional dos *nat. park* Brazil **143** J4
Lendeh Iran **88** C4
Lendery Rus. Fed. **44** Q5
Le Neubourg France **49** H9
Lengerich Germany **53** H2
Lengshan Ling *mts* China **72** I5
Lengshuijiang China **77** F3
Lengshuitan China **77** F3
Lenham U.K. **49** H7
Lenhovda Sweden **45** I8
Lenin Tajik. **89** H2
Lenin, Qullai *mt.* Kyrg./Tajik. *see* **Lenin Peak**
Lenina, Pik *mt.* Kyrg./Tajik. *see* **Lenin Peak**
Leninabad Tajik. *see* **Khŭjand**
Leninakan Armenia *see* **Gyumri**

Lenin Atyndagy Choku *mt.* Kyrg./Tajik. *see* Lenin Peak
Lenine Ukr. 90 D1
Leningrad Rus. Fed. *see* St Petersburg
Leningrad Tajik. 89 H2
Leningrad *admin. div.* Rus. Fed. *see* Leningradskaya Oblast'
Leningradskaya Rus. Fed. 43 H7
Leningradskaya Oblast' *admin. div.* Rus. Fed. 45 R7
Leningradskiy Rus. Fed. 65 S3
Leningradskiy Tajik. *see* Leningrad
Lenino Ukr. *see* Lenine
Leninobod Tajik. *see* Khŭjand
Lenin Peak Kyrg./Tajik. 89 I2
Leninsk Kazakh. *see* Baykonyr
Leninsk Rus. Fed. 43 J6
Leninskiy Rus. Fed. 43 H5
Leninsk-Kuznetskiy Rus. Fed. 64 J4
Leninskoye Kazakh. 43 K6
Leninskoye *Kirovskaya Oblast'* Rus. Fed. 42 J4
Leninskoye *Yevreyskaya Avtonomnaya Oblast'* Rus. Fed. 74 D3
Lenkoran' Azer. *see* Länkäran
Lenne *r.* Germany 53 H3
Lennoxville Canada 135 J1
Lenoir U.S.A. 132 D5
Lenore U.S.A. 134 D5
Lenore Lake Canada 121 J4
Lenox U.S.A. 135 I2
Lens France 52 C4
Lensk Rus. Fed. 65 M3
Lenti Hungary 58 G1
Lentini *Sicily* Italy 58 F6
Lenya Myanmar 71 B5
Lenzen Germany 53 L1
Léo Burkina 96 C3
Leoben Austria 47 O7
Leodhais, Eilean *i.* U.K. *see* Lewis, Isle of
Leominster U.K. 49 E6
Leominster U.S.A. 135 J2
León Mex. 136 D4
León Nicaragua 137 G6
León Spain 57 D2
Leon *r.* U.S.A. 131 D6
Leonardtown U.S.A. 135 G4
Leonardville Namibia 100 D2
Leongatha Australia 112 B7
Leonidi *Peloponnisos* Greece *see* Leonidio
Leonidio Greece 59 J6
Leonidovo Rus. Fed. 74 F2
Leonora Australia 109 C7
Leopold U.S.A. 134 E4
Leopold and Astrid Coast Antarctica *see* King Leopold and Queen Astrid Coast
Léopold II, Lac *l.* Dem. Rep. Congo *see* Mai-Ndombe, Lac
Leopoldina Brazil 145 C3
Leopoldo de Bulhões Brazil 145 A2
Léopoldville Dem. Rep. Congo *see* Kinshasa
Leoti U.S.A. 130 C4
Leoville Canada 121 J4
Lepalale S. Africa *see* Lephalale
Lepaya Latvia *see* Liepāja
Lepel' Belarus *see* Lyepyel'
Lepellé *r.* Canada 123 H1
Lephalala *r.* S. Africa 101 H2
Lephalale S. Africa 101 H2
Lephepe Botswana 101 G2
Lephoi S. Africa 101 G6
Leping China 77 H2
Lepontine, Alpi *mts* Italy/Switz. 58 C1
Leppävirta Fin. 44 O5
Lepreau, Point Canada 123 I5
Lepsa Kazakh. *see* Lepsy
Lepsy Kazakh. 80 E2
Le Puy France *see* Le Puy-en-Velay
Le Puy-en-Velay France 56 F4
Le Quesnoy France 52 D4
Lerala Botswana 101 H2
Leratswana S. Africa 101 H5
Léré Mali 96 C3
Lereh Indon. 69 J7
Leribe Lesotho *see* Hlotse
Lérida Col. 142 D4
Lérida Spain *see* Lleida
Lerik Azer. 91 H3
Lerma Spain 57 E2
Lermontov Rus. Fed. 91 F1
Lermontovka Rus. Fed. 74 D3
Lermontovskiy Rus. Fed. *see* Lermontov
Leros *i.* Greece 59 L6
Le Roy U.S.A. 135 G2
Le Roy, Lac *l.* Canada 122 G2
Lerum Sweden 45 H8
Lerwick U.K. 50 [inset]
Les Amirantes *is* Seychelles *see* Amirante Islands
Lesbos *i.* Greece 59 K5
Les Cayes Haiti 137 J5
Leshan China 76 D2
Leshukonskoye Rus. Fed. 42 J2
Lesi *watercourse* Sudan 97 F4
Leskhimstroy Ukr. *see* Syeverodonets'k
Leskovac Serbia 59 I3
Leslie U.S.A. 134 C2
Lesneven France 56 B2
Lesnoy *Kirovskaya Oblast'* Rus. Fed. 42 L4
Lesnoy *Murmanskaya Oblast'* Rus. Fed. *see* Umba
Lesnoye Rus. Fed. 42 G4
Lesogorsk Rus. Fed. 74 F2
Lesopil'noye Rus. Fed. 74 D3
Lesosibirsk Rus. Fed. 64 K4
Lesotho *country* Africa 101 I5
Lesozavodsk Rus. Fed. 74 D3
L'Espérance Rock *i.* Kermadec Is 107 I5
Les Pieux France 49 F9
Les Sables-d'Olonne France 56 D3
Lesse *r.* Belgium 52 E4
Lesser Antarctica *reg.* Antarctica *see* West Antarctica
Lesser Antilles *is* Caribbean Sea 137 K6
Lesser Caucasus *mts* Asia 91 F2
Lesser Himalaya *mts* India/Nepal 82 D3
Lesser Khingan Mountains China *see* Xiao Hinggan Ling
Lesser Slave Lake Canada 120 H4
Lesser Tunb *i.* The Gulf 88 D5
Lessines Belgium 52 D4
L'Est, Canal de France 52 G6
L'Est, Île de *i.* Canada 123 J5
L'Est, Pointe de *pt* Canada 123 J4
Lester U.S.A. 134 E5
Lestijärvi Fin. 44 N5
Les Vans France 56 G4
Lesvos *i.* Greece *see* Lesbos
Leszno Poland 47 P5
Letaba S. Africa 101 J2
Letchworth Garden City U.K. 49 G7
Le Télégraphe *hill* France 56 G3
Leteri India 82 D4
Letha Range *mts* Myanmar 70 A2
Lethbridge *Alta* Canada 121 H5
Lethbridge *Nfld. and Lab.* Canada 123 L4
Leti *i.* Indon. 108 D2
Leti, Kepulauan *is* Indon. 108 D2
Leticia Col. 142 E4
Letlhakeng Botswana 101 G3
Letnerechenskiy Rus. Fed. 42 G2
Letniy Navolok Rus. Fed. 42 H2
Le Touquet-Paris-Plage France 52 B4
Letpadan Myanmar 70 A3
Le Tréport France 52 B4
Letsitele S. Africa 101 J2
Letsopa S. Africa 101 G4
Letterkenny Ireland 51 E3
Letung Indon. 71 D7
Lëtzebuerg *country* Europe *see* Luxembourg
Letzlingen Germany 53 L2
Léua Angola 99 C5
Leucas Greece *see* Lefkada
Leucate, Étang de *l.* France 56 F5
Leuchars U.K. 50 G4
Leukas Greece *see* Lefkada
Leung Shuen Wan Chau *i.* H.K. China *see* High Island
Leunovo Rus. Fed. 42 I2
Leupp U.S.A. 129 H4
Leupung Indon. 71 A6
Leura Australia 110 E4
Leusden Neth. 52 F2
Leuser, Gunung *mt.* Indon. 71 B7
Leutershausen Germany 53 K5
Leuven Belgium 52 E4
Levadeia *Sterea Ellada* Greece *see* Livadeia
Levan U.S.A. 129 H2
Levanger Norway 44 G5
Levante, Riviera di *coastal area* Italy 58 C2
Levanto Italy 58 C2
Levashi Rus. Fed. 91 G2
Levelland U.S.A. 131 C5
Leven *England* U.K. 48 G5
Leven *Scotland* U.K. 50 G4
Leven, Loch *l.* U.K. 50 F4
Lévêque, Cape Australia 108 C4
Leverkusen Germany 52 G3
Lévézou *mts* France 56 F4
Levice Slovakia 47 Q6
Levin N.Z. 113 E5
Lévis Canada 123 H5
Levitha *i.* Greece 59 L6
Levittown *NY* U.S.A. 135 I3
Levittown *PA* U.S.A. 135 H3
Levkás *i.* Greece *see* Lefkada
Levkímmi Greece *see* Lefkimmi
Levskigrad Bulg. *see* Karlovo
Lev Tolstoy Rus. Fed. 43 H5
Lévy, Cap *c.* France 49 F9
Lewe Myanmar 70 B3
Lewerberg *mt.* S. Africa 100 C5
Lewes U.K. 49 H8
Lewes U.S.A. 135 H4
Lewis *CO* U.S.A. 129 I3
Lewis *IN* U.S.A. 134 B4
Lewis *KS* U.S.A. 130 D4
Lewis, Isle of *i.* U.K. 50 C2
Lewis, Lake *salt flat* Australia 108 F5
Lewisburg *KY* U.S.A. 134 B5
Lewisburg *PA* U.S.A. 135 G3
Lewisburg *WV* U.S.A. 134 E5
Lewis Cass, Mount Canada/U.S.A. 120 D3
Lewis Hills *hill* Canada 123 K4
Lewis Pass N.Z. 113 D6
Lewis Range *hills* Australia 108 E5
Lewis Range *mts* U.S.A. 126 E2
Lewis Smith, Lake U.S.A. 133 C5
Lewiston *ID* U.S.A. 126 D3
Lewiston *ME* U.S.A. 135 J1
Lewistown *IL* U.S.A. 130 F3
Lewistown *MT* U.S.A. 126 F3
Lewistown *PA* U.S.A. 135 G3
Lewisville U.S.A. 131 E5
Lexington *KY* U.S.A. 134 C4
Lexington *MI* U.S.A. 134 D2
Lexington *NC* U.S.A. 132 D5
Lexington *NE* U.S.A. 130 D3
Lexington *TN* U.S.A. 131 F5
Lexington *VA* U.S.A. 134 F5
Lexington Park U.S.A. 135 G4
Leyden Neth. *see* Leiden
Leye China 76 E3
Leyla Dāgh *mt.* Iran 88 B2
Leyte *i.* Phil. 69 G4
Lezha Albania *see* Lezhë
Lezhë Albania 59 H4
Lezhi China 76 E2
Lezhu China 77 G4
L'gov Rus. Fed. 43 G6
Lhagoi Kangri *mt.* China 83 F3
Lharigarbo China 83 G2
Lhasa China 83 G3
Lhasoi China 76 B2
Lhatog China 76 C2
Lhaviyani Atoll Maldives *see* Faadhippolhu Atoll
Lhazê *Xizang* China 76 B2
Lhazê *Xizang* China 83 F3
Lhazhong China 83 F3
Lhokkruet Indon. 71 A6
Lhokseumawe Indon. 71 B6
Lhoksukon Indon. 71 B6
Lhomar China 83 G3
Lhorong China 76 B2
▶Lhotse *mt.* China/Nepal 83 F4
4th highest mountain in the world and in Asia.
Lhozhag China 83 G3
Lhuntshi Bhutan 83 G4
Lhünzê China *see* Xingba
Lhünzhub China *see* Gaindainqoinkor
Liakoura *mt.* Greece 59 J5
Liancheng China *see* Guangnan
Liancourt France 52 C5
Liancourt Rocks *i.* Asia 75 C5
Liandu China *see* Lishui
Liangdang China 76 E1
Liangdaohe China 83 G3
Lianghe *Chongqing* China *see* Liangre
Lianghe *Yunnan* China 76 C3
Lianghekou *Chongqing* China *see* Liangre
Lianghekou *Gansu* China 76 E1
Lianghekou *Sichuan* China 76 D2
Liangping China 76 E2
Liangshan China *see* Liangping
Liang Shan *mt.* Myanmar 70 B1
Liangshi China *see* Shaodong
Liangtian China 77 F4
Liangyuan China *see* Shangqiu
Liangzhou China *see* Wuwei
Liangzi Hu *l.* China 77 G2
Lianhe China *see* Qianjiang
Lianhua China 77 G3
Lianhua Shan *mts* China 77 G4
Lianjiang *Fujian* China 77 H3
Lianjiang *Jiangxi* China *see* Xingguo
Liannan China 77 G3
Lianping China 77 G3
Lianran China *see* Anning
Lianshan *Guangdong* China 77 G3
Lianshan *Liaoning* China 73 M4
Lianshui China 77 H1
Liant, Cape *i.* Thai. *see* Samae San, Ko
Liantang China *see* Nanchang
Lianxian China *see* Lianzhou
Lianyin China 74 A1
Lianyungang China 77 H1
Lianzhou *Guangdong* China 77 G3
Lianzhou *Guangxi* China *see* Hepu
Liaocheng China 73 L5
Liaodong Bandao *pen.* China 73 M4
Liaodong Wan *b.* China 73 M4
Liaogao China *see* Songtao
Liao He *r.* China 74 A4
Liaoning *prov.* China 74 A4
Liaoyang China 74 A4
Liaoyuan China 74 B4
Liaozhong China 74 A4
Liapades Greece 59 H5
Liard *r.* Canada 120 F2
Liard Highway Canada 120 F2
Liard Plateau Canada 120 E2
Liard River Canada 120 E3
Liari Pak. 89 G5
Liathach *mt.* U.K. 50 D3
Liban *country* Asia *see* Lebanon
Liban, Jebel *mts* Lebanon 85 C2
Libau Latvia *see* Liepāja
Libby U.S.A. 126 E2
Libenge Dem. Rep. Congo 98 B3
Liberal U.S.A. 131 C4
Liberdade Brazil 145 B3
Liberec Czech Rep. 47 O5
Liberia *country* Africa 96 C4
Liberia Costa Rica 137 G6
Liberty *IN* U.S.A. 134 C4
Liberty *KY* U.S.A. 134 C5
Liberty *ME* U.S.A. 135 K1
Liberty *MO* U.S.A. 130 E4
Liberty *MS* U.S.A. 131 F6
Liberty *NY* U.S.A. 135 H3
Liberty *TX* U.S.A. 131 E6
Liberty Lake U.S.A. 135 G4
Libin Belgium 52 F5
Libni, Gebel *hill* Egypt *see* Libnī, Jabal
Libnī, Jabal *hill* Egypt 85 A4
Libo China 76 E3
Libobo, Tanjung *pt* Indon. 69 H7
Libode S. Africa 101 I6
Libong, Ko *i.* Thai. 71 B6
Libourne France 56 D4
Libral Well Australia 108 D5
Libre, Sierra *mts* Mex. 127 F7
▶Libreville Gabon 98 A3
Capital of Gabon.
▶Libya *country* Africa 97 E2
4th largest country in Africa.
Libyan Desert Egypt/Libya 86 C5
Libyan Plateau Egypt 90 B5
Licantén Chile 144 B4
Licata *Sicily* Italy 58 E6
Lice Turkey 91 F3
Lich Germany 53 I4
Lichas *pen.* Greece 59 J5
Licheng *Guangxi* China *see* Lipu
Licheng *Jiangsu* China *see* Jinhu
Lichfield U.K. 49 F6
Lichinga Moz. 99 D5
Lichte Germany 53 L4
Lichtenau Germany 53 I3
Lichtenburg S. Africa 101 H4
Lichtenfels Germany 53 L4
Lichtenvoorde Neth. 52 G3
Lichuan *Hubei* China 77 F2
Lichuan *Jiangxi* China 77 H3
Lida Belarus 45 N10
Liddel Water *r.* U.K. 50 G5
Lidfontein Namibia 100 D3
Lidköping Sweden 45 H7
Lidsjöberg Sweden 44 I4
Liebenau Germany 53 J2
Liebenburg Germany 53 K2
Liebenwalde Germany 53 N2
Liebig, Mount Australia 109 E5
Liechtenstein *country* Europe 56 I3
Liège Belgium 52 F4
Liegnitz Poland *see* Legnica
Lieksa Fin. 44 Q5
Lielupe *r.* Latvia 45 N8
Lielvārde Latvia 45 N8
Lienart Dem. Rep. Congo 98 C3
Lienchung *i.* Taiwan *see* Matsu Tao
Liên Nghia Vietnam 71 E5
Liên Sơn Vietnam 71 E4
Lienz Austria 47 N7
Liepāja Latvia 45 L8
Liepaya Latvia *see* Liepāja
Lier Belgium 52 E3
Lierre Belgium *see* Lier
Lieshout Neth. 52 F3
Lietuva *country* Europe *see* Lithuania
Liévin France 52 C4
Lièvre, Rivière du *r.* Canada 122 G5
Liezen Austria 47 O7
Liffey *r.* Ireland 51 F4
Lifford Ireland 51 E3
Lifi Mahuida *mt.* Arg. 144 C6
Lifou *i.* New Caledonia 107 G4
Lifu *i.* New Caledonia *see* Lifou
Līgatne Latvia 45 N8
Lightning Ridge Australia 112 C2
Ligny-en-Barrois France 52 F6
Ligonha *r.* Moz. 99 D5
Ligonier U.S.A. 134 C3
Ligui Mex. 127 F8
Ligure, Mar *sea* France/Italy *see* Ligurian Sea
Ligurian Sea France/Italy 58 C3
Ligurienne, Mer *sea* France/Italy *see* Ligurian Sea
Ligurta U.S.A. 129 F5
Lihir Group *is* P.N.G. 106 F2
Lihou Reef and Cays Australia 110 E3
Liivi laht *b.* Estonia/Latvia *see* Riga, Gulf of
Lijiang *Yunnan* China 76 D3
Lijiang *Yunnan* China *see* Yuanjiang
Lijiazhai China 77 G2
Lika *reg.* Croatia 58 F2
Likasi Dem. Rep. Congo 99 C5
Likati Dem. Rep. Congo 98 C3
Likely Canada 120 F4
Likhachevo Ukr. *see* Pervomays'kyy
Likhachyovo Ukr. *see* Pervomays'kyy
Likhapani India 83 H4
Likhás *pen.* Greece *see* Lichas
Likhoslavl' Rus. Fed. 42 G4
Liku Indon. 68 D6
Likurga Rus. Fed. 42 I4
L'Île-Rousse *Corsica* France 56 I5
Lilienthal Germany 53 I1
Liling China 77 G3
Lilla Pak. 89 I3
Lilla Edet Sweden 45 H7
Lille Belgium 52 E3
Lille France 52 D4
Lille (Lesquin) *airport* France 52 D4
Lille Bælt *sea chan.* Denmark *see* Little Belt
Lillebonne France 49 H9
Lillehammer Norway 45 G6
Lillers France 52 C4
Lillesand Norway 45 F7
Lillestrøm Norway 45 G7
Lilley U.S.A. 134 C2
Lillholmsjö Sweden 44 I5
Lillian, Point *hill* Australia 109 D6
Lillington U.S.A. 133 E5
Lillooet Canada 120 F5
Lillooet *r.* Canada 120 F5
Lillooet Range *mts* Canada 120 F5
▶Lilongwe Malawi 99 D5
Capital of Malawi.
Lilydale Australia 111 B7
▶Lima Peru 142 C6
Capital of Peru. 5th most populous city in South America.
Lima *MT* U.S.A. 126 E3
Lima *NY* U.S.A. 135 G2
Lima *OH* U.S.A. 134 C3
Lima Duarte Brazil 145 C3
Lima Islands China *see* Wanshan Qundao
Liman Rus. Fed. 43 J7
Limar Indon. 108 D1
Limassol Cyprus 85 A2
Limavady U.K. 51 F2
Limay *r.* Arg. 144 C5
Limbaži Latvia 45 N8
Limbunya Australia 108 E4
Limburg an der Lahn Germany 53 I4
Lim Chu Kang *hill* Sing. 71 [inset]
Lime Acres S. Africa 100 F5
Limeira Brazil 145 B3
Limerick Ireland 51 D5
Limestone Point Canada 121 L4
Limingen Norway 44 H4
Limingen *l.* Norway 44 H4
Limington U.S.A. 135 J2
Liminka Fin. 44 N4
Limmen Bight *b.* Australia 110 B2
Limnos *i.* Greece 59 K5
Limoeiro Brazil 143 K5
Limoges Canada 135 H1
Limoges France 56 E4
Limón Costa Rica *see* Puerto Limón
Limon U.S.A. 130 C4
Limonlu Turkey 85 B1
Limonum France *see* Poitiers
Limousin *reg.* France 56 E4
Limoux France 56 F5
Limpopo *prov.* S. Africa 101 I2
Limpopo *r.* S. Africa/Zimbabwe 101 K3
Limpopo National Park *nat. park* 101 J2
Limu China 77 F3
Līnah *well* Saudi Arabia 91 F5
Linakhamari Rus. Fed. 44 Q2
Lin'an China *see* Jianshui
Linares Chile 144 B5
Linares Mex. 131 D7
Linares Spain 57 E4
Lincang China 76 D4
Lincheng *Hainan* China *see* Lingao
Lincheng *Hunan* China *see* Huitong
Linchuan China *see* Fuzhou
Linck Nunataks *nunataks* Antarctica 152 K1
Lincoln Arg. 144 D4
Lincoln U.K. 48 G5
Lincoln *CA* U.S.A. 128 C2
Lincoln *IL* U.S.A. 130 F3
Lincoln *MI* U.S.A. 134 D1
▶Lincoln *NE* U.S.A. 130 D3
Capital of Nebraska.
Lincoln City *IN* U.S.A. 134 B4
Lincoln City *OR* U.S.A. 126 B3
Lincoln Island Paracel Is 68 E3
Lincoln National Park Australia 111 A7
Lincoln Sea Canada/Greenland 153 J1
Lincolnshire Wolds *hills* U.K. 48 G5
Lincolnton U.S.A. 133 D5
Linda, Serra *hills* Brazil 145 C1
Linda Creek *watercourse* Australia 110 B4
Lindau Germany 53 M2
Lindau (Bodensee) Germany 47 L7
Lindeman Group *is* Australia 110 E4
Linden Canada 120 H5
Linden Germany 53 I4
Linden Guyana 143 G2
Linden *AL* U.S.A. 133 C5
Linden *MI* U.S.A. 134 D2
Linden *TN* U.S.A. 132 C5
Linden *TX* U.S.A. 131 E5
Linden Grove U.S.A. 130 E2
Lindern (Oldenburg) Germany 53 H2
Lindesnes *c.* Norway 45 E7
Líndhos Greece *see* Lindos
Lindi *r.* Dem. Rep. Congo 98 C3
Lindi Tanz. 99 D4
Lindian China 74 B3
Lindisfarne *i.* U.K. *see* Holy Island
Lindley S. Africa 101 H4
Lindos Greece 55 J4
Lindos, Akra *pt Notio Aigaio* Greece *see* Gkinas, Akrotirio
Lindsay Canada 135 F1
Lindsay *CA* U.S.A. 128 D3
Lindsay *MT* U.S.A. 126 G3
Lindsborg U.S.A. 130 D4
Lindside U.S.A. 134 E5
Lindum U.K. *see* Lincoln
Line Islands Kiribati 151 J5
Linesville U.S.A. 134 E3
Linfen China 73 K5
Lingampet India 84 C2
Linganamakki Reservoir India 84 B3
Lingao China 77 F5
Lingayen Phil. 69 G3
Lingbi China 77 H1
Lingcheng *Anhui* China *see* Lingbi
Lingcheng *Guangxi* China *see* Lingshan
Lingcheng *Hainan* China *see* Lingshui
Lingchuan *Guangxi* China 77 F3
Lingchuan *Shanxi* China 77 G1
Lingelethu S. Africa 101 H7
Lingen (Ems) Germany 53 H2
Lingga, Kepulauan *is* Indon. 68 D7
Lingle U.S.A. 126 G4
Lingomo Dem. Rep. Congo 98 C3
Lingshan China 77 F4
Lingshui China 77 F5
Lingshui Wan *b.* China 77 F5
Lingsugur India 84 C2
Lingtai China 76 E1
Linguère Senegal 96 B3
Lingui China 77 F3
Lingxi China *see* Yongshun
Lingxian China *see* Yanling
Lingxiang China 77 G2
Lingyang China *see* Cili
Lingyun China 76 E3
Lingzi Tang *reg.* Aksai Chin 82 D2
Linhai China 77 I2
Linhares Brazil 145 C2
Linhe China 73 J4
Linhpa Myanmar 70 A1
Linjiang China 74 B4
Linjin China 77 F1
Linköping Sweden 45 I7
Linkou China 74 C3
Linli China 77 F2
Linlithgow U.K. 50 F5
Linn *MO* U.S.A. 130 F4
Linn *TX* U.S.A. 131 D7
Linn, Mount U.S.A. 128 B1
Linnansaaren kansallispuisto *nat. park* Fin. 44 P5
Linnhe, Loch *inlet* U.K. 50 D4
Linnich Germany 52 G4
Linosa, Isola di *i. Sicily* Italy 58 E7
Linpo Myanmar 70 B2
Linquan China 77 G1
Linru China *see* Ruzhou
Linruzhen China 77 G1
Lins Brazil 145 A3
Linshu China 77 H1
Linshui China 76 E2
Lintan China 76 D1
Lintao China 76 D1
Linton *IN* U.S.A. 134 B4
Linton *ND* U.S.A. 130 C2
Linwu China 77 G3
Linxi China 73 L4
Linxia China 76 D1
Linxiang China 77 G2
Linyi *Shandong* China 73 L5
Linyi *Shandong* China 77 H1
Linying China 77 G1
Linz Austria 47 O6
Lion, Golfe du *g.* France 56 F5
Lions, Gulf of France *see* Lion, Golfe du
Lions Bay Canada 120 F5
Lioua Chad 97 E3
Lipari *Sicily* Italy 58 F5
Lipari, Isole *is* Italy 58 F5
Lipetsk Rus. Fed. 43 H5
Lipin Bor Rus. Fed. 42 H3
Liping China 77 F3
Lipova Romania 59 I1
Lipovtsy Rus. Fed. 74 C3
Lippe *r.* Germany 53 G3
Lippstadt Germany 53 I3
Lipsoi *i.* Greece *see* Leipsoi
Lipti Lekh *pass* Nepal 82 E3
Liptrap, Cape Australia 112 B7
Lipu China 77 F3
Lira Uganda 98 D3
Liranga Congo 98 B4
Lircay Peru 142 D6
Lisala Dem. Rep. Congo 98 C3
L'Isalo, Massif de *mts* Madag. 99 E6
L'Isalo, Parc National de *nat. park* Madag. 99 E6
Lisbellaw U.K. 51 E3
Lisboa Port. *see* Lisbon
▶Lisbon Port. 57 B4
Capital of Portugal.
Lisbon *ME* U.S.A. 135 J1
Lisbon *NH* U.S.A. 135 J1
Lisbon *OH* U.S.A. 134 E3
Lisburn U.K. 51 F3
Liscannor Bay Ireland 51 C5
Lisdoonvarna Ireland 51 C4
Lishan Taiwan 77 I3
Lishe Jiang *r.* China 76 D3
Lishi *Jiangxi* China *see* Dingnan
Lishi *Shanxi* China 73 K5
Lishu China 74 B4
Lishui China 77 H2
Li Shui *r.* China 77 F2
Lisichansk Ukr. *see* Lysychans'k
Lisieux France 56 E2
Liskeard U.K. 49 C8
Liski Rus. Fed. 43 H6
L'Isle-Adam France 52 C5
Lismore Australia 112 F2
Lismore Ireland 51 E5
Lisnarrick U.K. 51 E3
Lisnaskea U.K. 51 E3
Liss *mt.* Saudi Arabia 85 D4
Lissa Poland *see* Leszno
Lister, Mount Antarctica 152 H1
Listowel Canada 134 E2
Listowel Ireland 51 C5
Lit Sweden 44 I5
Litang *Guangxi* China 77 F4
Litang *Sichuan* China 76 D2
Līṭānī, Nahr el *r.* Lebanon 85 B3
Litchfield *CA* U.S.A. 128 C1
Litchfield *CT* U.S.A. 135 I3
Litchfield *IL* U.S.A. 130 F4
Litchfield *MI* U.S.A. 134 C2
Litchfield *MN* U.S.A. 130 E2
Lit-et-Mixe France 56 D4
Lithgow Australia 112 E4
Lithino, Akra *pt Kriti* Greece *see* Lithino, Akrotirio
Lithino, Akrotirio *pt* Greece 59 K7
Lithuania *country* Europe 45 M9
Lititz U.S.A. 135 G3
Litoměřice Czech Rep. 47 O5
Litovko Rus. Fed. 74 D2
Litovskaya S.S.R. *country* Europe *see* Lithuania
Little *r.* U.S.A. 131 E6
Little Abaco *i.* Bahamas 133 E7
Little Abitibi *r.* Canada 122 E4
Little Abitibi Lake Canada 122 E4
Little Andaman *i.* India 71 A5
Little Bahama Bank *sea feature* Bahamas 133 E7
Little Barrier *i.* N.Z. 113 E3
Little Belt *sea chan.* Denmark 45 F9
Little Belt Mountains U.S.A. 126 F3
Little Bitter Lake Egypt 85 A4
Little Cayman *i.* Cayman Is 137 H5
Little Churchill *r.* Canada 121 M3
Little Chute U.S.A. 134 A1
Little Coco Island Cocos Is 71 A4
Little Colorado *r.* U.S.A. 129 H3
Little Creek Peak U.S.A. 129 G3
Little Current Canada 122 E5
Little Current *r.* Canada 122 D4
Little Desert National Park Australia 111 C8
Little Egg Harbor *inlet* U.S.A. 135 H4
Little Exuma *i.* Bahamas 133 F8
Little Falls U.S.A. 130 E2
Littlefield *AZ* U.S.A. 129 G3
Littlefield *TX* U.S.A. 131 C5
Little Fork *r.* U.S.A. 130 E1
Little Grand Rapids Canada 121 M4
Littlehampton U.K. 49 G8
Little Inagua Island Bahamas 133 F8
Little Karas Berg *plat.* Namibia 100 D4
Little Karoo *plat.* S. Africa 100 E7
Little Lake U.S.A. 128 E4
Little Mecatina Island Canada *see* Petit Mécatina, Île du
Little Minch *sea chan.* U.K. 50 B3
Little Missouri *r.* U.S.A. 130 C2
Little Namaqualand *reg.* S. Africa *see* Namaqualand
Little Nicobar *i.* India 71 A6
Little Ouse *r.* U.K. 49 H6
Little Pamir *mts* Asia 89 I2
Little Rancheria *r.* Canada 120 D2
Little Red River Canada 120 H3
▶Little Rock U.S.A. 131 E5
Capital of Arkansas.
Littlerock U.S.A. 128 E4
Little Sable Point U.S.A. 134 B2
Little Salmon Lake Canada 120 C2
Little Salt Lake U.S.A. 129 G3
Little Sandy Desert Australia 109 B5
Little San Salvador *i.* Bahamas 133 F7
Little Smoky Canada 120 G4
Little Tibet *reg.* India/Pak. *see* Ladakh
Littleton U.S.A. 126 G5
Little Valley U.S.A. 135 F2
Little Wind *r.* U.S.A. 126 F4
Litunde Moz. 99 D5
Liu'an China *see* Lu'an
Liuba China 76 E1
Liucheng China 77 F3
Liuchiu Yü *i.* Taiwan 77 I4
Liuchong He *r.* China 76 E3
Liuchow China *see* Liuzhou
Liuhe China 74 B4
Liuheng Dao *i.* China 77 I2
Liujiachang China 77 F2
Liujiaxia Shuiku *resr* China 76 D1
Liukesong China 74 B3
Liulin China *see* Jonê
Liupan Shan *mts* China 76 E1
Liupanshui China *see* Lupanshui
Liuquan China 77 H1
Liuwa Plain National Park Zambia 99 C5

ıyang China 77 G2
ızhan China 74 B2
ızhou China 77 F3
adeia Greece 59 J5
vāni Latvia 45 O8
e Oak U.S.A. 133 D6
eringa Australia 106 C3
ermore CA U.S.A. 128 C3
ermore KY U.S.A. 134 B5
ermore, Mount U.S.A. 131 B6
ermore Falls U.S.A. 135 J1
erpool Australia 112 E4
erpool Canada 123 I5
erpool U.K. 48 E5
erpool Bay Canada 118 E3
erpool Plains Australia 112 E3
erpool Range mts Australia 112 D3
ia U.S.A. 134 B5
ingston U.K. 50 F5
ingston AL U.S.A. 131 F5
ingston KY U.S.A. 134 C5
ingston MT U.S.A. 126 F3
ingston TN U.S.A. 134 C5
ingston TX U.S.A. 131 E6
ingston, Lake U.S.A. 131 E6
ingstone Zambia 99 C5
ingston Island Antarctica 152 L2
ingston Manor U.S.A. 135 H3
no Bos.-Herz. 58 G3
ny Rus. Fed. 43 H5
ojoki r. Fin. 44 O4
onia MI U.S.A. 134 D2
onia NY U.S.A. 135 G2
orno Italy 58 D3
ramento do Brumado Brazil 145 C1
vā Oman 88 E5
vā', Wādī al watercourse Syria 85 C3
vale Tanz. 99 D4
ian Gansu China 76 E1
ian Sichuan China 76 D2
us Morocco see Larache
ang China see Hexian
uan China see Sangzhi
ard U.K. 49 B9
arda Brazil 143 I5
ard Point U.K. 49 B9
arra Spain see Estella
emores U.S.A. 134 E4
iping China 76 D2
y-sur-Ourcq France 52 D5
uwert Neth. see Leeuwarden

jubljana Slovenia 58 F1
Capital of Slovenia.

garn Sweden 45 K8
ngan r. Sweden 44 J5
ngaverk Sweden 44 J5
ngby Sweden 45 H8
sdal Sweden 45 J6
snan r. Sweden 45 J6
sne Sweden 45 J6
ima, Volcán vol. Chile 144 B5
nandras U.K. see Presteigne
nbadarn Fawr U.K. 49 C6
nbedr Pont Steffan U.K. see Lampeter
nbister U.K. 49 D6
ndeilo U.K. 49 D7
ndissilio U.K. 49 C7
ndovery U.K. 49 D7
ndrindod Wells U.K. 49 D6
ndudno U.K. 48 D5
ndysul U.K. 49 C6
negwad U.K. 49 C7
nelli U.K. 49 C7
nfair Caereinion U.K. 49 D6
nfair-ym-Muallt U.K. see
Builth Wells
ngefni U.K. 48 C5
ngollen U.K. 49 D6
ngurig U.K. 49 D6
nllyfni U.K. 49 C5
nnerch-y-medd U.K. 48 C5
nnor U.K. 49 C6
no Mex. 127 F7
no U.S.A. 131 D6
no r. U.S.A. 131 D6
no Estacado plain U.S.A. 131 C5
nos plain Col./Venez. 142 E2
nquihue, Lago l. Chile 144 B6
nrhystud U.K. 49 C6
ntrisant U.K. 49 D7
nuwchllyn U.K. 49 D6
nwnog U.K. 49 D6
nymddyfri U.K. see Llandovery
y U.K. 49 D5
ida Spain 57 G3
rena Spain 57 C4
ia Spain 57 F4
dio Spain 57 E2
yd George, Mount Canada 120 E3
yd Lake Canada 121 I3
ydminster Canada 121 I4
chmayor Spain see Llucmajor
cmajor Spain 57 H4

lullaillaco, Volcán vol. Chile 144 C2
Highest active volcano in the world and
outh America.

Sông r. China/Vietnam 70 D2
r. Chile 144 B2
U.S.A. 129 H2
an' r. Rus. Fed. 42 K4
atejo mt. Spain 57 D5
atse Botswana 101 G3
aye r. Cent. Afr. Rep. 98 B3
ejün Germany 53 L3
enberg hill Germany 53 M3
eria Arg. 144 E5
ito Angola 99 B5
os Arg. 144 E5
os, Cabo c. Mex. 127 E7
os, Isla i. Mex. 127 F8
os de Tierra, Isla i. Peru 142 B5
burg Germany 53 M2
Binh Vietnam 70 D2
chaline U.K. 50 D4
Chau H.K. China see
Beaufort Island
h Baghasdail U.K. see
Lochboisdale

Lochboisdale U.K. 50 B3
Lochcarron U.K. 50 D3
Lochearnhead U.K. 50 E4
Lochem Neth. 52 G2
Lochern National Park Australia 110 C5
Loches France 56 E3
Loch Garman Ireland see Wexford
Lochgelly U.K. 50 F4
Lochgilphead U.K. 50 D4
Lochinver U.K. 50 D2
Loch Lomond and Trossachs National Park U.K. 50 E4
Lochmaddy U.K. 50 B3
Lochnagar mt. U.K. 50 F4
Loch nam Madadh U.K. see Lochmaddy
Loch Raven Reservoir U.S.A. 135 G4
Lochy, Loch l. U.K. 50 E4
Lock Australia 111 A7
Lockerbie U.K. 50 F5
Lockhart Australia 112 C5
Lockhart U.S.A. 131 D6
Lock Haven U.S.A. 135 G3
Löcknitz r. Germany 53 L1
Lockport U.S.A. 135 F2
Lôc Ninh Vietnam 71 D5
Lod Israel 85 B4
Loddon r. Australia 112 A5
Lodève France 56 F5
Lodeynoye Pole Rus. Fed. 42 G3
Lodge, Mount Canada/U.S.A. 120 B3
Lodhikheda India 82 D5
Lodhran Pak. 89 H4
Lodi Italy 58 C2
Lodi CA U.S.A. 128 C2
Lodi OH U.S.A. 134 D3
Lødingen Norway 44 I2
Lodja Dem. Rep. Congo 98 C4
Lodomeria Rus. Fed. see Vladimir
Lodrani India 82 B5
Lodwar Kenya 98 D3
Łódź Poland 47 Q5
Loei Thai. 70 C3
Loeriesfontein S. Africa 100 D6
Lofoten is Norway 44 H2
Lofusa Sudan 97 G4
Log Rus. Fed. 43 I6
Loga Niger 96 D3
Logan IA U.S.A. 130 E3
Logan OH U.S.A. 134 D4
Logan UT U.S.A. 126 F4
Logan WV U.S.A. 134 E5

Logan, Mount Canada 120 A2
2nd highest mountain in North America.

Logan, Mount U.S.A. 126 C2
Logan Creek r. Australia 110 D4
Logan Lake Canada 120 F5
Logan Mountains Canada 120 D2
Logansport IN U.S.A. 134 B3
Logansport LA U.S.A. 131 E6
Logatec Slovenia 58 F2
Logpung China 76 D1
Logroño Spain 57 E2
Logtak Lake India 83 H4
Lohardaga India 83 F5
Loharu India 82 C3
Lohatlha S. Africa 100 F5
Lohawat India 82 C4
Lohfelden Germany 53 J3
Lohil r. China/India see Zayü Qu
Lohiniva Fin. 44 N3
Lohjanjärvi l. Fin. 45 M6
Löhne Germany 53 I2
Lohne (Oldenburg) Germany 53 I2
Lohtaja Fin. 44 M4
Loi, Nam r. Myanmar 70 C2
Loikaw Myanmar 70 B3
Loi Lan mt. Myanmar/Thai. 70 B3
Loi-lem Myanmar 70 B2
Loi Lun Myanmar 70 B2
Loimaa Fin. 45 M6
Loipyet Hills Myanmar 70 B1
Loire r. France 56 C3
Loi Sang mt. Myanmar 70 B2
L'Oise à l'Aisne, Canal de France 52 D5
Loi Song mt. Myanmar 70 B2
Loja Ecuador 142 C4
Loja Spain 57 D5
Lokan tekojärvi l. Fin. 44 O3
Lokchim r. Rus. Fed. 42 K3
Lokeren Belgium 52 E3
Lokgwabe Botswana 100 E3
Lokichar Kenya 78 C6
Lokichokio Kenya 98 D3
Lokilalaki, Gunung mt. Indon. 69 G7
Løkken Denmark 45 F8
Løkken Norway 44 F5
Loknya Rus. Fed. 42 F4
Lokoja Nigeria 96 D4
Lokolama Dem. Rep. Congo 98 B4
Lokossa Benin 96 D4
Lokot' Rus. Fed. 43 G5
Lol Sudan 97 F4
Lola Guinea 96 C4
Lola, Mount U.S.A. 128 C2
Loleta U.S.A. 128 A1
Lolland i. Denmark 45 G9
Lollondo Tanz. 98 D4
Lolo U.S.A. 126 E3
Loloda Indon. 69 H6
Lolo Pass U.S.A. 126 E3
Lolowau Indon. 71 B7
Lolwane S. Africa 100 F4
Lom Bulg. 59 J3
Lom Norway 45 F6
Loma U.S.A. 129 I2
Lomami r. Dem. Rep. Congo 98 C3
Lomar Pass Afgh. 89 G3
Lomas, Bahía de b. Chile 144 C8
Lomas de Zamora Arg. 144 E4
Lombarda, Serra hills Brazil 143 H3
Lomblen i. Indon. 108 C2
Lombok Indon. 108 B2
Lombok i. Indon. 108 B2
Lombok, Selat sea chan. Indon. 108 A2

Lomé Togo 96 D4
Capital of Togo.

Lomela Dem. Rep. Congo 98 C4
Lomela r. Dem. Rep. Congo 97 F5
Lomira U.S.A. 134 A2
Lomme France 52 C4
Lommel Belgium 52 F3
Lomond Canada 123 K4
Lomond, Loch l. U.K. 50 E4
Lomonosov Rus. Fed. 45 P7
Lomonosov Ridge sea feature Arctic Ocean 153 B1
Lomovoye Rus. Fed. 42 I2
Lomphat Cambodia see Lumphăt
Lompoc U.S.A. 128 C4
Lom Sak Thai. 70 C3
Łomża Poland 47 S4
Lon, Hon i. Vietnam 71 E4
Lonar India 84 C2
Londa Bangl. 83 G5
Londa India 84 B3
Londinières France 52 B5
Londinium U.K. see London
Londoko Rus. Fed. 74 D2
London Canada 134 E2

London U.K. 49 G7
Capital of the United Kingdom and of England. 4th most populous city in Europe.

London KY U.S.A. 134 C5
London OH U.S.A. 134 D4
Londonderry U.K. 51 E3
Londonderry OH U.S.A. 134 D4
Londonderry VT U.S.A. 135 I2
Londonderry, Cape Australia 108 D3
Londrina Brazil 145 A3
Lone Pine U.S.A. 128 D3
Long Thai. 70 B3
Longa Angola 99 B5
Longa, Proliv sea chan. Rus. Fed. 65 S2
Long'an China 76 E4
Long Ashton U.K. 49 E7
Long Bay U.S.A. 133 E5
Longbeach N.Z. 113 C7
Long Beach U.S.A. 128 D5
Longbo China see Shuangpai
Long Branch U.S.A. 135 I3
Longchang China 76 E2
Longcheng Anhui China see Xiaoxian
Longcheng Guangdong China see Longmen
Longcheng Yunnan China see Chenggong
Longchuan China see Nanhua
Longchuan Jiang r. China 76 C4
Long Creek r. Canada 121 K5
Long Creek U.S.A. 126 D3
Long Eaton U.K. 49 F6
Longford Ireland 51 E4
Longgang Chongqing China see Dazu
Longgang Guangdong China 77 G4
Longhoughton U.K. 48 F3
Longhui China 77 F3
Longhurst, Mount Antarctica 152 H1
Long Island Bahamas 133 F8
Long Island N.S. Canada 123 I5
Long Island Nunavut Canada 122 F3
Long Island India 71 A4
Long Island P.N.G. 69 L8
Long Island U.S.A. 135 I3
Long Island Sound sea chan. U.S.A. 135 I3
Longjiang China 74 A3
Longjin China see Qingliu
Longju China 76 B2
Longlac Canada 122 D4
Long Lake l. Canada 122 D4
Long Lake U.S.A. 135 H2
Long Lake l. ME U.S.A. 132 G2
Long Lake l. MI U.S.A. 134 D1
Long Lake l. ND U.S.A. 130 C2
Long Lake l. NY U.S.A. 135 H1
Longli China 76 E3
Longlin China 76 E3
Longling China 76 C3
Longmeadow U.S.A. 135 I2
Long Melford U.K. 49 H6
Longmen Guangdong China 77 G4
Longmen Heilong. China 74 B2
Longmen Shan hill China 77 F1
Longmen Shan mts China 76 E1
Longming China 76 E4
Longmont U.S.A. 126 G4
Longnan China 76 E1
Longnan China 77 G3
Long Phu Vietnam 71 D5
Longping China see Luodian
Long Point Ont. Canada 134 E2
Long Point Man. Canada 121 L4
Long Point Ont. Canada 134 E2
Long Point N.Z. 113 B8
Long Point Bay Canada 134 E2
Long Prairie U.S.A. 130 E2
Long Preston U.K. 48 E4
Longquan Guizhou China see Danzhai
Longquan Guizhou China see Fenggang
Longquan Hunan China see Xintian
Longquan Xi r. China 77 I2
Long Range Mountains Nfld. and Lab. Canada 123 K4
Long Range Mountains Nfld. and Lab. Canada 123 K5
Longreach Australia 110 D4
Longriba China 76 D1
Longshan Guizhou China see Longli
Longshan Hunan China 77 F2
Longshan Yunnan China see Longling
Long Shan mts China 76 E1
Longsheng China 77 F3
Longs Peak U.S.A. 126 G4
Long Stratton U.K. 49 I6
Longtom Lake Canada 120 G1
Longtown U.K. 48 E3
Longue-Pointe-de-Mingan Canada 123 I4
Longueuil Canada 122 G5
Longuyon France 52 F5
Longvale U.S.A. 128 B2
Longview TX U.S.A. 131 E5
Longview WA U.S.A. 126 C3
Longwangmiao China 74 D3
Longwei Co l. China 83 G2
Longxi China 76 E1
Longxian Guangdong China see Wengyuan
Longxian Shaanxi China 76 E1
Longxingchang China see Wuyuan
Longxi Shan mt. China 77 H3
Longxu China see Cangwu
Long Xuyên Vietnam 71 D5
Longyan China 77 H3

Longyearbyen Svalbard 64 C2
Capital of Svalbard.

Longzhen China 74 B2
Longzhou China 76 E4
Longzhouping China see Changyang
Löningen Germany 53 H2
Lonoke U.S.A. 131 F5
Lönsboda Sweden 45 I8
Lons-le-Saunier France 56 G3
Lonton Myanmar 70 B1
Looc Phil. 69 G4
Loochoo Islands Japan see Ryukyu Islands
Loogootee U.S.A. 134 B4
Lookout, Cape Canada 122 E3
Lookout, Cape U.S.A. 133 E5
Lookout, Point Australia 112 F1
Lookout, Point U.S.A. 134 D1
Lookout Mountain U.S.A. 129 I4
Lookout Point Australia 109 B8
Loolmalasin vol. crater Tanz. 98 D4
Loon Canada 122 C4
Loon r. Canada 120 H3
Loongana Australia 109 D7
Loon Lake Canada 121 I4
Loop Head hd Ireland 51 C5
Lop China 82 E1
Lopasnya Rus. Fed. see Chekhov
Lopatina, Gora mt. Rus. Fed. 74 F2
Lop Buri Thai. 70 C4
Lopez Phil. 69 G4
Lopez, Cap c. Gabon 98 A4
Lop Nur salt flat China 80 H3
Lopphavet b. Norway 44 L1
Loptyuga Rus. Fed. 42 K3
Lora Pak. 89 G5
Lora r. Venez. 142 D2
Lora del Río Spain 57 D5
Lorain U.S.A. 134 D3
Loralai Pak. 89 H4
Loralai r. Pak. 89 H4
Loramie, Lake U.S.A. 134 C3
Lorca Spain 57 F5
Lorch Germany 53 H4
Lordegān Iran 88 C4
Lord Howe Atoll Solomon Is see Ontong Java Atoll
Lord Howe Island Australia 107 F5
Lord Howe Rise sea feature S. Pacific Ocean 150 G7
Lord Loughborough Island Myanmar 71 B5
Lordsburg U.S.A. 129 I5
Lore East Timor 108 D2
Lore Lindu, Taman Nasional Indon. 68 G7
Lorena Brazil 145 B3
Lorengau P.N.G. 69 L7
Lorentz, Taman Nasional Indon. 69 J7
Loreto Brazil 143 I5
Loreto Mex. 127 F8
Lorient France 56 C3
Lorillard r. Canada 121 N1
Loring U.S.A. 126 G2
Lorn, Firth of est. U.K. 50 D4
Lorne Australia 110 D5
Lorne watercourse Australia 110 B3
Lorrain, Plateau France 53 G6
Lorraine Australia 110 B3
Lorraine admin. reg. France 52 G6
Lorraine reg. France 52 F5
Lorsch Germany 53 I5
Lorup Germany 53 H2
Losal India 82 C4
Los Alamos CA U.S.A. 128 C4
Los Alamos NM U.S.A. 127 G6
Los Alerces, Parque Nacional nat. park Arg. 144 B6
Los Ángeles Chile 144 B5

Los Angeles U.S.A. 128 D4
3rd most populous city in North America.

Los Angeles Aqueduct canal U.S.A. 128 D4
Los Arabos Cuba 133 D8
Los Banos U.S.A. 128 C3
Los Blancos Arg. 144 D2
Los Canarreos, Archipiélago de is Cuba 137 H4
Los Cerritos watercourse Mex. 127 F8
Los Chonos, Archipiélago de is Chile 144 A6
Los Coronados, Islas is Mex. 128 E5
Los Desventurados, Islas de is S. Pacific Ocean 151 O7
Los Estados, Isla de i. Arg. 144 D8
Los Gigantes, Llanos de plain Mex. 131 B6
Los Glaciares, Parque Nacional nat. park Arg. 144 B8
Losheim Germany 52 G5
Los Hoyos Mex. 127 F7
Lošinj i. Croatia 58 F2
Los Jardines de la Reina, Archipiélago de is Cuba 137 I4
Los Juríes Arg. 144 D3
Los Katios, Parque Nacional nat. park Col. 137 I7
Loskop Dam S. Africa 101 I3
Los Lunas U.S.A. 127 G6
Los Menucos Arg. 144 C6
Los Mochis Mex. 127 F8
Los Molinos U.S.A. 128 B1
Losombo Dem. Rep. Congo 98 B3
Los Palacios Cuba 133 D8
Los Picos de Europa, Parque Nacional de nat. park Spain 57 D2
Los Remedios r. Mex. 131 B7
Los Roques, Islas is Venez. 142 E1
Losser Neth. 52 G2
Lossie r. U.K. 50 F3
Lossiemouth U.K. 50 F3
Lößnitz Germany 53 M4
Lost Creek KY U.S.A. 134 D5
Lost Creek WV U.S.A. 134 E4
Los Teques Venez. 142 E1
Los Testigos is Venez. 142 F1
Lost Hills U.S.A. 128 D4
Lost Trail Pass U.S.A. 126 E3
Lostwithiel U.K. 49 C8
Los Vidrios Mex. 129 G6
Los Vilos Chile 144 B4
Lot r. France 56 E4
Lota Chile 144 B5
Loṭfābād Turkm. 88 E2
Lothringen reg. France see Lorraine
Lotikipi Plain Kenya/Sudan 98 D3
Loto Dem. Rep. Congo 98 C4
Lotsane r. Botswana 101 I2
Lot's Wife i. Japan see Sōfu-gan
Lotta r. Fin./Rus. Fed. 44 Q2
also known as Lutto
Lotte Germany 53 H2
Louangnamtha Laos 70 C2
Louangphabang Laos 70 C3
Loubomo Congo 99 B4
Loudéac France 56 C2
Loudi China 77 F3
L'Ouest, Pointe de pt Canada 123 I4
Louga Senegal 96 B3
Loughborough U.K. 49 F6
Lougheed Island Canada 119 H2
Loughor r. U.K. 49 C7
Loughrea Ireland 51 D4
Loughton U.K. 49 H7
Louhans France 56 G3
Louisa KY U.S.A. 134 D4
Louisa VA U.S.A. 135 G4
Louisbourg Canada 123 K5
Louisburg Canada see Louisbourg
Louisburgh Ireland 51 C4
Louise Falls Canada 120 G2
Louis-Gentil Morocco see Youssoufia
Louisiade Archipelago is P.N.G. 110 F1
Louisiana U.S.A. 130 F4
Louisiana state U.S.A. 131 F6
Louis Trichardt S. Africa see Makhado
Louisville GA U.S.A. 133 D5
Louisville IL U.S.A. 130 F4
Louisville KY U.S.A. 134 C4
Louisville MS U.S.A. 131 F5
Louisville Ridge sea feature S. Pacific Ocean 150 I8
Louis-XIV, Pointe pt Canada 122 F3
Loukhi Rus. Fed. 44 R3
Loukoléla Congo 98 B4
Loukouo Congo 97 E5
Loulé Port. 57 B5
Loum Cameroon 96 D4
Louny Czech Rep. 47 N5
Loup r. U.S.A. 130 D3
Loups Marins, Lacs des lakes Canada 122 G2
Loups Marins, Petit lac des l. Canada 123 G2
Lourdes Canada 123 K4
Lourdes France 56 D5
Lourenço Marques Moz. see Maputo
Lousã Port. 57 B3
Loushan China 74 C3
Loushanguan China see Tongzi
Louth Australia 112 B3
Louth U.K. 48 G5
Loutra Aidipsou Greece 59 J5
Louvain Belgium see Leuven
Louviers France 52 B5
Louwater-Suid Namibia 100 C2
Louwsburg S. Africa 101 J4
Lövånger Sweden 44 L4
Lovat' r. Rus. Fed. 42 F4
Lovech Bulg. 59 K3
Lovell U.S.A. 135 J1
Lovelock U.S.A. 128 D1
Lovendegem Belgium 52 D3
Lovers' Leap mt. U.S.A. 134 E5
Loviisa Fin. 45 O6
Lovington U.S.A. 131 C5
Lovozero Rus. Fed. 42 G1
Lóvua Angola 99 C4
Lóvua Angola 99 C5
Low, Cape Canada 119 J3
Lowa Dem. Rep. Congo 98 C4
Lowa r. Dem. Rep. Congo 98 C4
Lowarai Pass Pak. 89 H3
Lowell IN U.S.A. 134 B3
Lowell MA U.S.A. 135 J2
Lower Arrow Lake Canada 120 G5
Lower California pen. Mex. see Baja California
Lower Glenelg National Park Australia 111 C8
Lower Granite Gorge U.S.A. 129 G4
Lower Hutt N.Z. 113 E5
Lower Laberge Canada 120 C2
Lower Lake U.S.A. 128 B2
Lower Lough Erne l. U.K. 51 E3
Lower Post Canada 120 D3
Lower Red Lake U.S.A. 130 E2
Lower Saxony land Germany see Niedersachsen
Lower Tunguska r. Rus. Fed. see Nizhnyaya Tunguska
Lower Zambezi National Park Zambia 99 C5
Lowestoft U.K. 49 I6
Łowicz Poland 47 Q4
Low Island Kiribati see Starbuck Island
Lowkhi Afgh. 89 F4
Lowther Hills U.K. 50 F5
Lowville U.S.A. 135 H2
Loxstedt Germany 53 I1
Loxton Australia 111 C7
Loyal, Loch l. U.K. 50 E2
Loyalsock Creek r. U.S.A. 135 G3
Loyalton U.S.A. 128 C2
Loyalty Islands New Caledonia see Loyauté, Îles
Loyang China see Luoyang
Loyauté, Îles is New Caledonia 107 G4
Loyev Belarus see Loyew
Loyew Belarus 43 F6
Lozère, Mont mt. France 56 F4
Loznica Serbia 59 H2
Lozova Ukr. 43 H6
Lozovaya Ukr. see Lozova
Lua r. Dem. Rep. Congo 98 B3
Luacano Angola 99 C5
Lu'an China 77 H2
Luân Châu Vietnam 70 C2
Luanchuan China 77 F1

Luanda Angola 99 B4
Capital of Angola.

Luang, Khao mt. Thai. 71 B5
Luang, Thale lag. Thai. 71 C6
Luang Namtha Laos see Louangnamtha
Luang Phrabang, Thiu Khao mts Laos/Thai. 70 C3
Luang Prabang Laos see Louangphabang
Luanhaizi China 76 B1
Luanshya Zambia 99 C5
Luanza Dem. Rep. Congo 99 C4
Luao Angola see Luau
Luarca Spain 57 C2
Luashi Dem. Rep. Congo 99 C5
Luau Angola 99 C5
Luba Equat. Guinea 96 D4
Lubaczów Poland 43 D6
Lubalo Angola 99 B4
Lubānas ezers l. Latvia 45 O8
Lubang Islands Phil. 68 F4
Lubango Angola 99 B5
Lubao Dem. Rep. Congo 99 C4
Lubartów Poland 43 D6
Lübbecke Germany 53 I2
Lubbeskolk salt pan S. Africa 100 D5
Lubbock U.S.A. 131 C5
Lübbow Germany 53 L2
Lübeck Germany 47 M4
Lubeck U.S.A. 134 E4
Lubefu Dem. Rep. Congo 99 C4
Lubei China 73 M4
Lüben Poland see Lubin
Lubersac France 56 E4
Lubin Poland 47 P5
Lublin Poland 43 D6
Lubnān country Asia see Lebanon
Lubnān, Jabal mts Lebanon see Liban, Jebel
Lubny Ukr. 43 G6
Lubok Antu Sarawak Malaysia 68 E6
Lübtheen Germany 53 L1
Lubudi Dem. Rep. Congo 99 C4
Lubuklinggau Indon. 68 C7
Lubukpakam Indon. 71 B7
Lubuksikaping Indon. 68 C6
Lubumbashi Dem. Rep. Congo 99 C5
Lubutu Dem. Rep. Congo 98 C4
Lübz Germany 53 M1
Lucala Angola 99 B4
Lucan Canada 134 E2
Lucan Ireland 51 F4
Lucania, Mount Canada 120 A2
Lucapa Angola 99 C4
Lucas U.S.A. 134 B5
Lucasville U.S.A. 134 D4
Lucca Italy 58 D3
Luce Bay U.K. 50 E6
Lucedale U.S.A. 131 F6
Lucélia Brazil 145 A3
Lucena Phil. 69 G4
Lucena Spain 57 D5
Lučenec Slovakia 47 Q6
Lucera Italy 58 F4
Lucerne Switz. 56 I3
Lucerne Valley U.S.A. 128 E4
Lucero Mex. 127 G7
Luchegorsk Rus. Fed. 74 D3
Lucheng Guangxi China see Luchuan
Lucheng Sichuan China see Kangding
Luchuan China 77 F4
Lüchun China 76 D4
Lucipara, Kepulauan is Indon. 69 H8
Luck Ukr. see Luts'k
Luckeesarai India see Lakhisarai
Luckenwalde Germany 53 N2
Luckhoff S. Africa 100 G5
Lucknow Canada 134 E2
Lucknow India 82 E4
Lücongpo China 77 F2
Lucrecia, Cabo c. Cuba 137 I4
Lucusse Angola 99 C5
Lucy Creek Australia 110 B4
Lüda China see Dalian
Lüdenscheid Germany 53 H3
Lüderitz Namibia 100 B4
Ludewa Tanz. 99 D5
Ludhiana India 82 C3
Ludian China 76 D3
Luding China 76 D2
Ludington U.S.A. 134 B2
Ludlow U.K. 49 E6
Ludlow U.S.A. 128 E4
Ludogorie reg. Bulg. 59 L3
Ludowici U.S.A. 133 D6
Ludvika Sweden 45 I6
Ludwigsburg Germany 53 J6
Ludwigsfelde Germany 53 N2
Ludwigshafen am Rhein Germany 53 I5
Ludwigslust Germany 53 L1
Ludza Latvia 45 O8
Luebo Dem. Rep. Congo 99 C4
Luena Angola 99 B5
Luena Flats plain Zambia 99 C5
Lüeyang China 76 E1
Lufeng Guangdong China 77 G4
Lufeng Yunnan China 76 D3
Lufkin U.S.A. 131 E6
Lufu China see Shilin
Luga Rus. Fed. 45 P7
Luga r. Rus. Fed. 45 P7
Lugano Switz. 56 I3
Lugansk Ukr. see Luhans'k
Lugau Germany 53 M4
Lügde Germany 53 J3
Lugdunum France see Lyon
Lugg r. U.K. 49 E6
Luggudontsen mt. China 83 G3
Lugnaquilla hill Ireland 51 F5
Lugo Italy 58 D2
Lugo Spain 57 C2
Lugoj Romania 59 I2
Luhans'k Ukr. 43 H6
Luhe China 77 H1
Luhe r. Germany 53 K1
Luḩfī, Wādī watercourse Jordan 85 C3
Luhit r. China/India see Zayü Qu
Luhit r. India 83 H4
Luhua China see Heishui
Luhuo China 76 D2

Luhyny Ukr. 43 F6
Luia Angola 99 C4
Luiana Angola 99 C5
Luichow Peninsula China see Leizhou Bandao
Luik Belgium see Liège
Luimneach Ireland see Limerick
Luiro r. Fin. 44 O3
Luis Echeverría Álvarez Mex. 128 E5
Luitpold Coast Antarctica 152 A1
Luiza Dem. Rep. Congo 99 C4
Lujiang China 77 H2
Lüjing China 76 E1
Lukachek Rus. Fed. 74 D1
Lukapa Angola see Lucapa
Lukavac Bos.-Herz. 58 H2
Lukenga, Lac l. Dem. Rep. Congo 99 C4
Lukenie r. Dem. Rep. Congo 98 B4
Lukh r. Rus. Fed. 42 I4
Lukhovitsy Rus. Fed. 43 H5
Luk Keng H.K. China 77 [inset]
Lukou China see Zhuzhou
Lukovit Bulg. 59 K3
Łuków Poland 43 D6
Lukoyanov Rus. Fed. 43 J5
Lukusuzi National Park Zambia 99 D5
Luleå Sweden 44 M4
Luleälven r. Sweden 44 M4
Lüleburgaz Turkey 59 L4
Luliang China 76 D3
Lüliang Shan mts China 73 K5
Lulimba Dem. Rep. Congo 99 C4
Luling U.S.A. 131 D6
Lulonga r. Dem. Rep. Congo 98 B3
Luluabourg Dem. Rep. Congo see Kananga
Lülung China 83 F3
Lumachomo China 83 F3
Lumajang Indon. 68 E8
Lumajangdong Co salt l. China 82 E2
Lumbala Moxico Angola see Lumbala Kaquengue
Lumbala Moxico Angola see Lumbala N'guimbo
Lumbala Kaquengue Angola 99 C5
Lumbala N'guimbo Angola 99 C5
Lumberton U.S.A. 133 E5
Lumbini Nepal 83 E4
Lumbis Indon. 68 F6
Lumbrales Spain 57 C3
Lumezzane Italy 58 D2
Lumi P.N.G. 69 K7
Lumphăt Cambodia 71 D4
Lumpkin U.S.A. 133 C5
Lumsden Canada 121 J5
Lumsden N.Z. 113 B7
Lumut Malaysia 71 C6
Lumut, Tanjung pt Indon. 68 D7
Luna U.S.A. 129 I5
Lunan China see Shilin
Lunan Bay U.K. 50 G4
Lunan Lake Canada 121 M1
Lunan Shan mts China 76 D3
Luna Pier U.S.A. 134 D3
Lund Pak. 89 H5
Lund Sweden 45 H9
Lund NV U.S.A. 129 F2
Lund UT U.S.A. 129 G2
Lundar Canada 121 L5
Lundy U.K. 49 C7
Lune r. Germany 53 I1
Lune r. U.K. 48 E4
Lüneburg Germany 53 K1
Lüneburger Heide reg. Germany 53 K1
Lünen Germany 53 H3
Lunenburg U.S.A. 135 F5
Lunéville France 56 H2
Lunga r. Zambia 99 C5
Lungdo China 83 E2
Lunggar China 83 E3
Lung Kwu Chau i. H.K. China 77 [inset]
Lungleh India see Lunglei
Lunglei India 83 H5
Lungmari mt. China 83 F3
Lungmu Co salt l. China 82 E2
Lung-tzu Xizang China see Xingba
Lung-tzu Xizang China see Xingba
Lungwebungu r. Zambia 99 C5
Lunh Nepal 83 E3
Luni India 82 C4
Luni r. India 82 B4
Luni r. Pak. 89 H4
Luninets Belarus see Luninyets
Luning U.S.A. 128 D2
Luninyets Belarus 45 O10
Lunkaransar India 82 C3
Lunkha India 82 C3
Lünne Germany 53 H2
Lunsar Sierra Leone 96 B4
Lunsklip S. Africa 101 I3
Luntai China 80 F3
Luobei China 74 C3
Luobuzhuang China 80 G4
Luocheng Fujian China see Hui'an
Luocheng Guangxi China 77 F3
Luodian China 76 E3
Luoding China 77 F4
Luodou Sha i. China 77 F4
Luohe China 77 G1
Luo He r. China 77 G1
Luonan China 77 F1
Luoning China 77 F1
Luoping China 76 E3
Luotian China 77 G2
Luoto Fin. see Larsmo
Luoxiao Shan mts China 77 G3
Luoxiong China see Luoping
Luoyang Guangdong China see Boluo
Luoyang Henan China 77 G1
Luoyang Zhejiang China see Taishun
Luoyuan China 77 H3
Luozigou China 74 C4
Lupane Zimbabwe 99 C5
Lupanshui China 76 E3
L'Upemba, Parc National de nat. park Dem. Rep. Congo 99 C4
Lupeni Romania 59 J2
Lupilichi Moz. 99 D5
Lupton U.S.A. 129 I4
Luqiao China see Luding
Luqu China 76 D1
Lu Qu r. China see Tao He
Luquan China 70 C1
Luray U.S.A. 135 F4
Luremo Angola 99 B4
Lurgan U.K. 51 F3
Luring China see Oma
Lúrio Moz. 99 E5
Lurio r. Moz. 99 E5

▶Lusaka Zambia 99 C5
Capital of Zambia.

Lusambo Dem. Rep. Congo 99 C4
Lusancay Islands and Reefs P.N.G. 106 F2
Lusangi Dem. Rep. Congo 99 C4
Luseland Canada 121 I4
Lush, Mount hill Australia 108 D4
Lushi China 77 F1
Lushnja Albania see Lushnjë
Lushnjë Albania 59 H4
Lushui China see Luzhang
Lushuihe China 74 B4
Lüsi China 77 I1
Lusikisiki S. Africa 101 I6
Lusk U.S.A. 126 G4
Luso Angola see Luena
Lussvale Australia 112 C1
Lut, Bahrat salt l. Asia see Dead Sea
Lut, Dasht-e des. Iran 88 E4
Lü Tao i. Taiwan 77 I4
Lutetia France see Paris
Lüt-e Zangī Aḥmad des. Iran 88 E4
Luther U.S.A. 134 C1
Luther Lake Canada 134 E2
Lutherstadt Wittenberg Germany 53 M3
Luton U.K. 49 G7
Lutselk'e Canada 121 I2
Luts'k Ukr. 43 E6
Luttelgeest Neth. 52 F2
Luttenberg Neth. 52 G2
Lutto r. Fin./Rus. Fed. see Lotta
Lutz U.S.A. 133 D6
Lützelbach Germany 53 J5
Lützow-Holm Bay Antarctica 152 D2
Lutzputs S. Africa 100 E5
Lutzville S. Africa 100 D6
Luumäki Fin. 45 O6
Luuq Somalia 98 E3
Luverne AL U.S.A. 133 C6
Luverne MN U.S.A. 130 D3
Luvuei Angola 99 C5
Luvuvhu r. S. Africa 101 J2
Luwero Uganda 98 D3
Luwingu Zambia 99 C5
Luwuk Indon. 69 G7
Luxembourg country Europe 52 G5

▶Luxembourg Lux. 52 G5
Capital of Luxembourg.

Luxemburg country Europe see Luxembourg
Luxeuil-les-Bains France 56 H3
Luxi Hunan China see Wuxi
Luxi Yunnan China 76 C3
Luxi Yunnan China 76 D3
Luxolweni S. Africa 101 G6
Luxor Egypt 86 D4
Luyi China 77 G1
Luyksgestel Neth. 52 F3
Luza Rus. Fed. 42 J3
Luza r. Rus. Fed. 42 J3
Luza r. Rus. Fed. 42 M2
Luzern Switz. see Lucerne
Luzhai China 77 F3
Luzhang China 76 C3
Luzhi China 76 E3
Luzhou China 76 E2
Luziânia Brazil 145 B2
Luzon i. Phil. 69 G3
Luzon Strait Phil. 69 G2
Luzy France 56 F3
L'viv Ukr. 43 E6
L'vov Ukr. see L'viv
Lwów Ukr. see L'viv
Lyady Rus. Fed. 45 P7
Lyakhavichy Belarus 45 O10
Lyakhovichi Belarus see Lyakhavichy
Lyallpur Pak. see Faisalabad
Lyamtsa Rus. Fed. 42 H2
Lycia reg. Turkey 59 M6
Lyck Poland see Ełk
Lycksele Sweden 44 K4
Lycopolis Egypt see Asyūţ
Lydd U.K. 49 H8
Lydda Israel see Lod
Lyddan Island Antarctica 152 B2
Lydia reg. Turkey 59 L5
Lydney U.K. 49 E7
Lyel'chytsy Belarus 43 F6
Lyell, Mount U.S.A. 128 D3
Lyell Brown, Mount hill Australia 109 E5
Lyell Island Canada 120 D4
Lyepyel' Belarus 45 P9
Lykens U.S.A. 135 G3
Lyman U.S.A. 126 F4
Lyme Bay U.K. 49 E8
Lyme Regis U.K. 49 E8
Lymington U.K. 49 F8
Lynchburg OH U.S.A. 134 D4
Lynchburg TN U.S.A. 132 C5
Lynchburg VA U.S.A. 134 F5
Lynchville U.S.A. 135 J1
Lyndhurst N.S.W. Australia 112 D4
Lyndhurst Qld Australia 110 D3
Lyndhurst S.A. Australia 111 B6
Lyndon Australia 109 A5
Lyndon r. Australia 109 A5
Lyndonville U.S.A. 135 I1
Lyne r. U.K. 48 D4
Lyness U.K. 50 F2
Lyngdal Norway 45 E7
Lynn U.K. see King's Lynn
Lynn IN U.S.A. 134 C3
Lynn MA U.S.A. 135 J2
Lynndyl U.S.A. 129 G2
Lynn Lake Canada 121 K3
Lynton U.K. 49 D7
Lynx Lake Canada 121 J2
Lyon France 56 G4
Lyon r. U.K. 50 F4
Lyon Mountain U.S.A. 135 I1
Lyons Australia 109 F7
Lyons France see Lyon
Lyons GA U.S.A. 133 D5
Lyons NY U.S.A. 135 G2
Lyons Falls U.S.A. 135 H2
Lyozna Belarus 43 F5
Lyra Reef P.N.G. 106 F2
Lys r. France 52 D4
Lysekil Sweden 45 G7
Lyskovo Rus. Fed. 42 J4
Ly Sơn, Đao i. Vietnam 70 E4
Lys'va Rus. Fed. 41 R4
Lysychans'k Ukr. 43 H6
Lysyye Gory Rus. Fed. 43 J6
Lytham St Anne's U.K. 48 D5
Lytton Canada 120 F5
Lyuban' Belarus 45 P10
Lyubertsy Rus. Fed. 41 N4
Lyubeshiv Ukr. 43 E6
Lyubim Rus. Fed. 42 I4
Lyubytino Rus. Fed. 42 G4
Lyudinovo Rus. Fed. 43 G5
Lyunda r. Rus. Fed. 42 J4
Lyzha r. Rus. Fed. 42 M2

Ma r. Myanmar 70 B2
Ma, Nam r. Laos 70 C2
Ma'agan Israel 85 B3
Maale Maldives see Male
Maale Atholhu atoll Maldives see Male Atoll
Maalhosmadulu Atholhu Uthuruburi atoll Maldives see North Maalhosmadulu Atoll
Maalhosmadulu Atoll Maldives 84 B5
Ma'ān Jordan 85 B4
Maan Turkey see Nusratiye
Maaninka Fin. 44 O5
Maaninkavaara Fin. 44 P3
Ma'anshan China 77 H2
Maardu Estonia 45 N7
Maarianhamina Fin. see Mariehamn
Ma'arrat an Nu'mān Syria 85 C2
Maarssen Neth. 52 F2
Maas r. Neth. 52 E3
also known as Meuse (Belgium/France)
Maaseik Belgium 52 F3
Maasin Phil. 69 G4
Maasmechelen Belgium 52 F4
Maas-Schwalm-Nette nat. park Germany/Neth. 52 F3
Maastricht Neth. 52 F4
Maaza Plateau Egypt 90 C6
Maba Guangdong China see Qujiang
Maba Jiangsu China 77 H1
Mabai China see Maguan
Mabalane Moz. 101 K2
Mabana Dem. Rep. Congo 98 C3
Mabaruma Guyana 142 G2
Mabein Myanmar 70 B2
Mabel Creek Australia 109 F7
Mabel Downs Australia 108 D4
Mabella Canada 122 C4
Mabel Lake Canada 120 G5
Maberly Canada 135 G1
Mabian China 76 D2
Mablethorpe U.K. 48 H5
Mabopane S. Africa 101 I3
Mabote Moz. 101 L2
Mabou Canada 123 J5
Mabrak, Jabal mt. Jordan 85 B4
Mabuasehube Game Reserve nature res. Botswana 100 F3
Mabule Botswana 100 G3
Mabutsane Botswana 100 F3
Macá, Monte mt. Chile 144 B7
Macadam Plains Australia 109 B6
Macaé Brazil 145 C3
Macajuba Brazil 145 C1
Macaloge Moz. 99 D5
MacAlpine Lake Canada 119 H3
Macamic Canada 122 F4
Macandze Moz. 101 K2
Macao China 77 G4
Macao aut. reg. China 77 G4
Macapá Brazil 143 H3
Macará Ecuador 142 C4
Macarani Brazil 145 C1
Macas Ecuador 142 C4
Macassar Indon. see Makassar
Macau Brazil 143 K5
Macau China see Macao
Macau aut. reg. China see Macao
Macaúba Brazil 143 H6
Macauley Island N.Z. 107 I5
Maccaretane Moz. 101 K3
Macclenny U.S.A. 133 D6
Macclesfield U.K. 48 E5
Macdiarmid Canada 122 C4
Macdonald, Lake salt flat Australia 109 E5
Macdonald Range hills Australia 108 D3
Macdonnell Ranges mts Australia 109 E5
MacDowell Lake Canada 121 M4
Macduff U.K. 50 G3
Macedo de Cavaleiros Port. 57 C3
Macedon mt. Australia 112 B6
Macedon country Europe see Macedonia
Macedonia country Europe 59 I4
Maceió Brazil 143 K5
Macenta Guinea 96 C4
Macerata Italy 58 E3
Macfarlane, Lake salt flat Australia 111 B7
Macgillycuddy's Reeks mts Ireland 51 C6
Machachi Ecuador 142 C4
Machaila Moz. 101 K2
Machakos Kenya 98 D4
Machala Ecuador 142 C4
Machali China see Madoi
Machanga Moz. 99 D6
Machar Marshes Sudan 86 D8
Machattie, Lake salt flat Australia 110 B5
Machatuine Moz. 101 K3
Machault France 52 E5
Machaze Moz. see Chitobe
Macheng China 77 G2
Macherla India 84 C2
Machhagan India 83 F5
Machias ME U.S.A. 132 H2
Machias NY U.S.A. 135 F2
Machilipatnam India 84 D2
Machiques Venez. 142 D1
Māch Kowr Iran 89 F5
Machrihanish U.K. 50 D5
Machu Picchu tourist site Peru 142 D6
Machynlleth U.K. 49 D6
Macia Moz. 101 K3
Macias Nguema i. Equat. Guinea see Bioco
Măcin Romania 59 M2
Macintyre r. Australia 112 E2
Macintyre Brook r. Australia 112 E2
Mack U.S.A. 129 I2
Maçka Turkey 91 E2
Mackay Australia 110 E4
MacKay r. Canada 121 I3
Mackay U.S.A. 126 E3
Mackay, Lake salt flat Australia 108 E5
MacKay Lake Canada 121 I2
Mackenzie r. Australia 110 E4
Mackenzie Canada 120 F4

▶Mackenzie r. Canada 120 F2
Part of the Mackenzie-Peace-Finlay, the 2nd longest river in North America.

Mackenzie Guyana see Linden
Mackenzie atoll Micronesia see Ulithi
Mackenzie Bay Antarctica 152 E2
Mackenzie Bay Canada 118 E3
Mackenzie Highway Canada 120 G2
Mackenzie King Island Canada 119 G2
Mackenzie Mountains Canada 120 C1

▶Mackenzie-Peace-Finlay r. Canada 118 E3
2nd longest river in North America.

Mackillop, Lake salt flat Australia see Yamma Yamma, Lake
Mackintosh Range hills Australia 109 D6
Macklin Canada 121 I4
Macksville Australia 112 F3
Maclean Australia 112 F2
Maclear S. Africa 101 I6
MacLeod Canada see Fort Macleod
MacLeod, Lake imp. l. Australia 109 A6
Macmillan r. Canada 120 C2
Macmillan Pass Canada 120 D2
Macomb U.S.A. 130 F3
Macomer Sardinia Italy 58 C4
Mâcon France 56 G3
Macon GA U.S.A. 133 D5
Macon MO U.S.A. 130 E4
Macon MS U.S.A. 131 F5
Macon OH U.S.A. 134 D4
Macondo Angola 99 C5
Macoun Lake Canada 121 K3
Macpherson Robertson Land reg. Antarctica see Mac. Robertson Land
Macpherson's Strait India 71 A5
Macquarie r. Australia 112 C3
Macquarie, Lake b. Australia 112 E4

▶Macquarie Island S. Pacific Ocean 150 G9
Part of Australia. Most southerly point of Oceania.

Macquarie Marshes Australia 112 C3
Macquarie Mountain Australia 112 D4
Macquarie Ridge sea feature S. Pacific Ocean 150 G9
MacRitchie Reservoir Sing. 71 [inset]
Mac. Robertson Land reg. Antarctica 152 E2
Macroom Ireland 51 D6
Macumba Australia 111 A5
Macumba watercourse Australia 111 B5
Macuzari, Presa resr Mex. 127 F8
Mādabā Jordan 85 B4
Madadeni S. Africa 101 J4

▶Madagascar country Africa 99 E6
Largest island in Africa and 4th in the world.

Madagascar Basin sea feature Indian Ocean 149 L7
Madagascar Ridge sea feature Indian Ocean 149 K8
Madagasikara country Africa see Madagascar
Madakasira India 84 C3
Madama Niger 97 E2
Madan Bulg. 59 K4
Madanapalle India 84 C3
Madang P.N.G. 69 L8
Madaoua Niger 96 D3
Madaripur Bangl. 83 G5
Madau Turkm. see Madaw
Madaw Turkm. 88 D2
Madawaska Canada 135 G1
Madawaska r. Canada 135 G1
Madaya Myanmar 70 B2
Madded India 84 D2

▶Madeira r. Brazil 142 G4
4th longest river in South America.

▶Madeira terr. N. Atlantic Ocean 96 B1
Autonomous Region of Portugal.

Madeira, Arquipélago da terr. N. Atlantic Ocean see Madeira
Maden Turkey 91 E3
Madera Mex. 127 F7
Madera U.S.A. 128 C3
Madgaon India 84 B3
Madha India 84 B2
Madhavpur India 82 B5
Madhepura India 83 F4
Madhipura India see Madhepura
Madhubani India 83 F4
Madhya Pradesh state India 82 D5
Madibogo S. Africa 101 G4
Madidi r. Bol. 142 E6
Madikeri India 84 B3
Madikwe Game Reserve nature res. S. Africa 101 H3
Madill U.S.A. 131 D5
Madīnat ath Thawrah Syria 85 D2
Madingo-Kayes Congo 99 B4
Madingou Congo 99 B4
Madison FL U.S.A. 133 D6
Madison GA U.S.A. 133 D5
Madison IN U.S.A. 134 C4
Madison ME U.S.A. 135 K1
Madison NE U.S.A. 130 D3
Madison SD U.S.A. 130 D2
Madison VA U.S.A. 135 F4

▶Madison WI U.S.A. 130 F3
Capital of Wisconsin.

Madison WV U.S.A. 134 E4
Madison r. U.S.A. 126 F3
Madison Heights U.S.A. 134 F5
Madisonville KY U.S.A. 134 B5
Madisonville TX U.S.A. 131 E6
Madiun Indon. 68 E8
Madley, Mount hill Australia 109 C6
Madoc Canada 135 G1
Mado Gashi Kenya 98 D3
Madoi China 76 C1
Madona Latvia 45 O8
Madpura India 82 B4
Madra Dağı mts Turkey 59 L5
Madrakah Saudi Arabia 86 E5
Madrakah, Ra's c. Oman 87 I6
Madras India see Chennai
Madras state India see Tamil Nadu
Madras U.S.A. 126 C3
Madre, Laguna lag. Mex. 131 D7
Madre, Laguna lag. U.S.A. 131 D7
Madre de Dios r. Peru 142 E6
Madre de Dios, Isla i. Chile 144 A8
Madre del Sur, Sierra mts Mex. 136 D5
Madre Mountain U.S.A. 129 J4
Madre Occidental, Sierra mts Mex. 127 F7
Madre Oriental, Sierra mts Mex. 131 C7

▶Madrid Spain 57 E3
Capital of Spain. 5th most populous city in Europe.

Madridejos Spain 57 E4
Madruga Cuba 133 D8
Madugula India 84 D2
Madura i. Indon. 68 E8
Madura, Selat sea chan. Indon. 68 E8
Madurai India 84 C4
Madurantakam India 84 C3
Madvār, Kūh-e mt. Iran 88 D4
Madwas India 83 E4
Maé i. Vanuatu see Émaé
Maebashi Japan 75 E5
Mae Hong Son Thai. 70 B3
Mae Ping National Park Thai. 70 B3
Mae Ramat Thai. 70 B3
Mae Sai Thai. 70 B2
Mae Sariang Thai. 70 B3
Mae Sot Thai. 70 B3
Mae Suai Thai. 70 B3
Mae Tuen Wildlife Reserve nature res. Thai. 70 B3
Maevatanana Madag. 99 E5
Maéwo i. Vanuatu 107 G3
Mae Wong National Park Thai. 70 B4
Mae Yom National Park Thai. 70 C3
Mafeking Canada 121 K4
Mafeking S. Africa see Mafikeng
Mafeteng Lesotho 101 H5
Maffra Australia 112 C6
Mafia Island Tanz. 99 D4
Mafikeng S. Africa 101 G3
Mafinga Tanz. 99 D4
Mafra Brazil 145 A4
Mafraq Jordan see Al Mafraq
Magabeni S. Africa 101 J6
Magadan Rus. Fed. 65 Q4
Magadi Kenya 98 D4
Magaiza Moz. 101 K2
Magallanes Chile see Punta Arenas
Magallanes, Estrecho de Chile see Magellan, Strait of
Magangue Col. 142 D2
Mağara Dağı mt. Turkey 85 A1
Magaramkent Rus. Fed. 91 H2
Magaria Niger 96 D3
Magarida P.N.G. 110 E1
Magas Rus. Fed. 91 G2
Magazine Mountain hill U.S.A. 131 E5
Magdagachi Rus. Fed. 74 B1
Magdalena Bol. 142 F6
Magdalena r. Col. 142 D1
Magdalena Baja California Sur Mex. 127 E8
Magdalena Sonora Mex. 127 F7
Magdalena r. Mex. 127 F7
Magdalena, Bahía b. Mex. 136 B4
Magdalena, Isla i. Chile 144 B6
Magdeburg Germany 53 L2
Magdelaine Cays atoll Australia 110 E3
Magellan, Strait of Chile 144 B8
Magellan Seamounts sea feature N. Pacific Ocean 150 F4
Magenta, Lake salt flat Australia 109 B8
Magerøya i. Norway 44 N1
Maggiorasca, Monte mt. Italy 58 C2
Maggiore, Lago Italy see Maggiore, Lake
Maggiore, Lake Italy 58 C2
Maghâgha Egypt see Maghāghah
Maghāghah Egypt 90 C5
Maghama Mauritania 96 B3
Maghâra, Gebel hill Egypt see Maghārah, Jabal
Maghārah, Jabal hill Egypt 85 A4
Maghera U.K. 51 F3
Magherafelt U.K. 51 F3
Maghnia Alg. 57 F6
Maghor Afgh. 89 F3
Maghull U.K. 48 E5
Magilligan Point U.K. 51 F2
Magma U.S.A. 129 H5
Magna Grande mt. Sicily Italy 58 F6
Magnetic Island Australia 110 D3
Magnetic Passage Australia 110 D3
Magnetity Rus. Fed. 44 R2
Magnitogorsk Rus. Fed. 64 G4
Magnolia AR U.S.A. 131 E5
Magnolia MS U.S.A. 131 F6
Magny-en-Vexin France 52 B5
Mago Rus. Fed. 74 F1
Màgoé Moz. 99 D5
Magog Canada 135 I1
Mago National Park Eth. 98 D3
Magosa Cyprus see Famagusta
Magpie r. Canada 123 I4
Magpie, Lac l. Canada 123 I4
Magta' Laḥjar Mauritania 96 B3
Magu Tanz. 98 D4
Magu, Khrebet mts Rus. Fed. 74 E1
Maguan China 76 E4
Magude Moz. 101 K3
Magueyal Mex. 131 C7
Magura Bangl. 83 G5
Maguse Lake Canada 121 M2
Magway Myanmar see Magwe
Magwe Myanmar 70 A2
Magyar Köztársaság country Europe see Hungary
Magyichaung Myanmar 70 A2
Mahābād Iran 88 B2
Mahabharat Range mts Nepal 83 F4
Mahaboobnagar India see Mahbubnagar
Mahad India 84 B2
Mahadeo Hills India 82 D5
Mahaffey U.S.A. 135 F3
Mahajan India 82 C3
Mahajanga Madag. 99 E5
Mahakam r. Indon. 68 F7
Mahalapye Botswana 101 H2
Mahale Mountains National Park Tanz. 99 C4
Mahalevona Madag. 99 E5
Mahallāt Iran 88 C3
Māhān Iran 88 E4
Mahanadi r. India 84 E1
Mahanoro Madag. 99 E5
Maha Oya Sri Lanka 84 D5
Maharashtra state India 84 B2
Maha Sarakham Thai. 70 C3
Mahasham, Wâdi el watercourse Egypt see Muhashsham, Wādī al
Mahaxai Laos 70 D3
Mahbubabad India 84 D2
Mahbubnagar India 84 C2
Mahd adh Dhahab Saudi Arabia 86 F5
Mahdia Alg. 57 G6
Mahdia Guyana 143 G2
Mahdia Tunisia 58 D7
Mahe China 76 E1
Mahé i. Seychelles 149 L6
Mahendragiri mt. India 84 E2
Mahenge Tanz. 99 D4
Mahesana India 82 C5
Mahi r. India 82 C5
Mahia Peninsula N.Z. 113 F4
Mahilyow Belarus 43 F5
Mahim India 84 B2
Mah Jān Iran 88 D4
Mahlabatini S. Africa 101 J5
Mahlsdorf Germany 53 L2
Maḥmūdābād Iran 88 D2
Maḥmūd-e 'Erāqī Afgh. see Maḥmūd-e Rāqī
Maḥmūd-e Rāqī Afgh. 89 H3
Mahnomen U.S.A. 130 D2
Maho Sri Lanka 84 D5
Mahoba India 82 D4
Maholi India 82 E4
Mahón Spain 57 I4
Mahony Lake Canada 120 E1
Mahrauni India 82 D4
Mahrès Tunisia 58 D7
Māhrūd Iran 89 F3
Mahsana India see Mahesana
Mahudaung mts Myanmar 70 A2
Māhukona U.S.A. 127 [inset]
Mahur India 84 C2
Mahuva India 82 B5
Mahwa India 82 D4
Mahya Dağı mt. Turkey 59 L4
Mai i. Vanuatu see Émaé
Maiaia Moz. see Nacala
Maibang India 70 A1
Maicao Col. 142 D1
Maicasagi r. Canada 122 F4
Maicasagi, Lac l. Canada 122 F4
Maichen China 77 F4
Maidenhead U.K. 49 G7
Maidstone Canada 121 I4
Maidstone U.K. 49 H7
Maiduguri Nigeria 96 E3
Maiella, Parco Nazionale della nat. park Italy 58 F3
Mai Gudo mt. Eth. 98 D3
Maigue r. Ireland 51 D5
Maihar India 82 E4
Maiji Shan mt. China 76 E1
Maikala Range hills India 82 E5
Maiko r. Dem. Rep. Congo 98 C3
Mailan Hill mt. India 83 E5
Mailly-le-Camp France 52 E6
Mailsi Pak. 89 I4
Main r. Germany 53 I4
Main r. U.K. 51 F3
Main Brook Canada 123 L4
Mainburg Germany 53 L6
Main Channel lake channel Canada 134 E1
Maindargi India 84 C2
Mai-Ndombe, Lac l. Dem. Rep. Congo 98 B4
Main-Donau-Kanal canal Germany 53 K5
Maindong Xizang China see Coqên
Main Duck Island Canada 135 G2
Maine state U.S.A. 135 K1
Maine, Gulf of Canada/U.S.A. 135 K2
Mainé Hanari, Cerro hill Col. 142 D4
Maïné-Soroa Niger 96 E3
Maingkaing Myanmar 70 A1
Maingkwan Myanmar 70 B1
Maingy Island Myanmar 71 B4
Mainhardt Germany 53 J5
Mainkung China 76 C2
Mainland i. Scotland U.K. 50 F1
Mainland i. Scotland U.K. 50 [inset]
Mainleus Germany 53 L4
Mainoru Australia 108 F3

ainpat reg. India 83 E5
ainpuri India 82 D4
ain Range National Park
Australia 112 F2
aintenon France 52 B6
aintirano Madag. 99 E5
ainz Germany 53 I4
aio i. Cape Verde 96 [inset]
aipú Arg. 144 E5
aiskhal Island Bangl. 83 G5
aisons-Laffitte France 52 C6
aitengwe Botswana 99 C6
aitland N.S.W. Australia 112 E4
aitland S.A. Australia 111 B7
aitland r. Australia 108 B5
aitri research station Antarctica 152 C2
aiwo i. Vanuatu see Maéwo
aiyu, Mount hill Australia 108 E4
aíz, Islas del is Nicaragua 137 H6
aizar Pak. 89 H3
aizuru Japan 75 D6
aja Jezercë mt. Albania 59 H3
ajdel Aanjar tourist site Lebanon 85 B3
ajene Indon. 68 F7
ajestic U.S.A. 134 D5
ajḥūd well Saudi Arabia 88 C6
ajī Eth. 98 D3
ajiang Guangxi China 77 F4
ajiang Guizhou China 76 E3
ajiazi China 74 B2
ajöl country N. Pacific Ocean see
Marshall Islands
ajor, Puig mt. Spain 57 H4
ajorca i. Spain 57 H4
ajro atoll Marshall Is see Majuro
ajunga Madag. see Mahajanga
ajuro atoll Marshall Is 150 H5
ajwemasweu S. Africa 101 H5
akabana Congo 98 B4
akale Indon. 69 F7

Makalu mt. China/Nepal 83 F4
5th highest mountain in the world and
n Asia.

akalu Barun National Park Nepal 83 F4
akanchi Kazakh. 80 F2
akanpur India 82 E4
akari Mountain National Park Tanz. see
Mahale Mountains National Park
akarov Rus. Fed. 74 F2
akarov Basin sea feature
Arctic Ocean 153 B1
akarska Croatia 58 G3
akarwal Pak. 89 H3
akar'ye Rus. Fed. 42 K4
akar'yev Rus. Fed. 42 I4
akasar, Selat strait Indon. see
Makassar, Selat
akassar Indon. 68 F8
akassar, Selat strait Indon. 68 F7
akassar Strait Indon. see Makassar, Selat
akat Kazakh. 78 E2
akatini Flats lowland S. Africa 101 K4
akedonija country Europe see Macedonia
akeni Sierra Leone 96 B4
akete Tanz. 99 D4
akeyevka Ukr. see Makiyivka
akgadikgadi depr. Botswana 99 C6
akgadikgadi Pans National Park
Botswana 99 C6
akhachkala Rus. Fed. 91 G2
akhad Pak. 89 H3
akhado S. Africa 101 I2
akhāzin, Kathīb al des. Egypt 85 A4
akhâzin, Kathîb el des. Egypt see
Makhāzin, Kathīb al
akhazine, Barrage El dam
Morocco 57 D6
akhmūr Iraq 91 F4
akhtal India 84 C2
akin atoll Kiribati see Butaritari
akindu Kenya 98 D4
akinsk Kazakh. 79 G1
akira i. Solomon Is see San Cristobal
akiyivka Ukr. 43 H6
akkah Saudi Arabia see Mecca
akkovik Canada 123 K3
akkovik, Cape Canada 123 K3
akkum Neth. 52 F1
akó Hungary 59 I1
akokou Gabon 98 B3
akopong Botswana 100 F3
akotipoko Congo 97 E5
akran reg. Iran/Pak. 89 F5
akrana India 82 C4
akran Coast Range mts Pak. 89 F5
akri India 84 D2
aksatikha Rus. Fed. 42 G4
aksi India 82 D5
aksimovka Rus. Fed. 74 E3
aksotag Iran 89 F4
aksudangarh India 82 D5
akū Iran 88 B2
akunguwiro Tanz. 99 D5
akurdi Nigeria 96 D4
akwassie S. Africa 101 G4
al India 83 G4
ala Ireland see Mallow
ala i. Solomon Is see Malaita
ala Sweden 44 K4
ala, Punta pt Panama 137 H7
alabar Coast India 84 B3

Malabo Equat. Guinea 96 D4
Capital of Equatorial Guinea.

alaca Spain see Málaga
alacca Malaysia see Melaka
alacca, Strait of Indon./Malaysia 71 B6
alad City U.S.A. 126 E4
aladzyechna Belarus 45 O9
alá Fatra nat. park Slovakia 47 Q6
álaga Spain 57 D5
alaga U.S.A. 131 B5
alagasy Republic country Africa see
Madagascar
alainn Mhóir Ireland 51 D3
alaita i. Solomon Is 107 G2
alakal Sudan 86 D8
alakanagiri India see Malkangiri
alakheti Nepal 82 E3

Malakula i. Vanuatu 107 G3
Malan, Ras pt Pak. 89 G5
Malang Indon. 68 E8
Malangana Nepal see Malangwa
Malange Angola see Malanje
Malangwa Nepal 83 F4
Malanje Angola 99 B4
Malappuram India 84 C4
Mälaren l. Sweden 45 J7
Malargüe Arg. 144 C5
Malartic Canada 122 F4
Malaspina Glacier U.S.A. 120 A3
Malatya Turkey 90 E3
Malavalli India 84 C3
Malawi country Africa 99 D5
Malawi, Lake Africa see Nyasa, Lake
Malawi National Park Zambia see
Nyika National Park
Malaya pen. Malaysia see
Peninsular Malaysia
Malaya Pera Rus. Fed. 42 L2
Malaya Vishera Rus. Fed. 42 G4
Malaybalay Phil. 69 H5
Maläyer Iran 88 C3
Malay Peninsula Asia 71 B4
Malay Reef Australia 110 E3
Malaysia country Asia 68 D5
Malaysia, Semenanjung pen. Malaysia see
Peninsular Malaysia
Malazgirt Turkey 91 F3
Malbon Australia 110 C4
Malbork Poland 47 Q3
Malborn Germany 52 G5
Malchin Germany 47 N4
Malcolm Australia 109 C7
Malcolm, Point Australia 109 C8
Malcolm Island Myanmar 71 B5
Maldegem Belgium 52 D3
Malden U.S.A. 131 F4
Malden Island Kiribati 151 J6
Maldives country Indian Ocean 81 D10
Maldon Australia 112 B6
Maldon U.K. 49 H7
Maldonado Uruguay 144 F4

▶Male Maldives 81 D11
Capital of the Maldives.

Maleas, Akra pt Peloponnisos Greece see
Maleas, Akrotirio
Maleas, Akrotirio pt Greece 59 J6
Male Atoll Maldives 81 D11
Malebogo S. Africa 101 G5
Malegaon Mahar. India 84 B1
Malegaon Mahar. India 84 C2
Malé Karpaty hills Slovakia 47 P6
Malek Sīāh, Kūh-e mt. Afgh. 89 F4
Malele Dem. Rep. Congo 99 B4
Maler Kotla India 82 C3
Maleševske Planine mts Bulg./Macedonia
59 J4
Malgobek Rus. Fed. 91 G2
Malgomaj l. Sweden 44 J4
Malḥa, Naqb mt. Egypt see
Māliḥah, Naqb
Malhada Brazil 145 C1
Malheur r. U.S.A. 126 D3
Malheur Lake U.S.A. 126 D4
Mali country Africa 96 C3
Mali Dem. Rep. Congo 98 C4
Mali Guinea 96 B3
Maliana East Timor 108 D2
Malianjing China 80 I3
Māliḥah, Naqb mt. Egypt 85 A5
Malik Naro mt. Pak. 89 F4
Mali Kyun i. Myanmar 71 B4
Malili Indon. 69 G7
Malin Ukr. see Malyn
Malindi Kenya 98 E4
Malines Belgium see Mechelen
Malin Head hd Ireland 51 E2
Malipo China 76 E4
Mali Raginac mt. Croatia 58 F2
Malita Phil. 69 H5
Malka r. Rus. Fed. 91 G2
Malkangiri India 84 D2
Malkapur India 84 B2
Malkara Turkey 59 L4
Mal'kavichy Belarus 45 O10
Malko Tŭrnovo Bulg. 59 L4
Mallacoota Australia 112 D6
Mallacoota Inlet b. Australia 112 D6
Mallaig U.K. 50 D4
Mallani reg. India 89 H5
Mallawī Egypt 90 C6
Mallee Cliffs National Park Australia
111 C7
Mallery Lake Canada 121 L1
Mallét Brazil 145 A4
Mallorca i. Spain see Majorca
Mallow Ireland 51 D5
Mallowa Well Australia 108 D5
Mallwyd U.K. 49 D6
Malm Norway 44 G4
Malmberget Sweden 44 L3
Malmédy Belgium 52 G4
Malmesbury S. Africa 100 D7
Malmesbury U.K. 49 E7
Malmö Sweden 45 H9
Malmyzh Rus. Fed. 42 K4
Maloca Brazil 143 G3
Malone U.S.A. 135 H1
Malonje mt. Tanz. 99 D4
Maloshuyka Rus. Fed. 42 H3
Malosmadulu Atoll Maldives see
Maalhosmadulu Atoll
Måløy Norway 44 D6
Maloyaroslavets Rus. Fed. 43 H5
Malozemel'skaya Tundra lowland
Rus. Fed. 42 K2
Malpelo, Isla de i. N. Pacific Ocean 137 H8
Malprabha r. India 84 C2
Malta country Europe 58 F7
Malta Latvia 45 O8
Malta ID U.S.A. 126 E4
Malta MT U.S.A. 126 G2
Malta Channel Italy/Malta 58 F6
Maltahöhe Namibia 100 C3
Maltby U.K. 48 F5
Maltby le Marsh U.K. 48 H5
Malton U.K. 48 G4
Maluku is Indon. see Moluccas

Maluku, Laut sea Indon. 69 H6
Ma'lūlā, Jabal mts Syria 85 C3
Malung Sweden 45 H6
Maluti Mountains Lesotho 101 I5
Malu'u Solomon Is 107 G2
Malvan India 84 B2
Malvasia Greece see Monemvasia
Malvern U.K. see Great Malvern
Malvern U.S.A. 131 E5
Malvérnia Moz. see Chicualacuala
Malvinas, Islas terr. S. Atlantic Ocean see
Falkland Islands
Malyn Ukr. 43 F6
Malyy Anyuy r. Rus. Fed. 65 R3
Malyye Derbety Rus. Fed. 43 J7
Malyy Kavkaz mts Asia see
Lesser Caucasus
Malyy Lyakhovskiy, Ostrov i.
Rus. Fed. 65 P2
Malyy Uzen' r. Kazakh./Rus. Fed. 43 K6
Mamadysh Rus. Fed. 42 K5
Mamafubedu S. Africa 101 I4
Mamatān Nāvar l. Afgh. 89 G4
Mamba China 76 B2
Mambai Brazil 145 B1
Mambasa Dem. Rep. Congo 98 C3
Mamburao Phil. 69 G4
Mamelodi S. Africa 101 I3
Mamfe Cameroon 96 D4
Mamit India 83 H5
Mammoth U.S.A. 129 H5
Mammoth Cave National Park U.S.A.
134 B5
Mammoth Reservoir U.S.A. 128 D3
Mamonas Brazil 145 C1
Mamoré r. Bol./Brazil 142 E6
Mamou Guinea 96 B3
Mampikony Madag. 99 E5
Mampong Ghana 96 C4
Mamuju Indon. 68 F7
Mamuno Botswana 100 E2
Man Côte d'Ivoire 96 C4
Man India 84 B2
Man r. India 84 B2
Man U.S.A. 134 E5

▶Man, Isle of terr. Irish Sea 48 C4
United Kingdom Crown Dependency.

Manacapuru Brazil 142 F4
Manacor Spain 57 H4
Manado Indon. 69 G6

▶Managua Nicaragua 137 G6
Capital of Nicaragua.

Manakara Madag. 99 E6
Manakau mt. N.Z. 113 D6
Manākhah Yemen 86 F6

▶Manama Bahrain 88 C5
Capital of Bahrain.

Manamadurai India 84 C4
Mana Maroka National Park
S. Africa 101 H5
Manamelkudi India 84 C4
Manam Island P.N.G. 69 L7
Mananara Avaratra Madag. 99 E5
Manangoora Australia 110 B3
Mananjary Madag. 99 E6
Manantali, Lac de l. Mali 96 B3
Manantenina Madag. 99 E6
Mana Pass China/India 82 D3
Mana Pools National Park Zimbabwe
99 C5

▶Manapouri, Lake N.Z. 113 A7
Deepest lake in Oceania.

Manasa India 82 C4
Manas He r. China 80 G2
Manas Hu l. China 80 G2
Manāṣīr reg. U.A.E. 88 D6

▶Manaslu mt. Nepal 83 F3
8th highest mountain in the world and
in Asia.

Manassas U.S.A. 135 G4
Manastir Macedonia see Bitola
Manas Wildlife Sanctuary nature res.
Bhutan 83 G4
Man-aung Myanmar 70 A3
Man-aung Kyun Myanmar 70 A3
Manaus Brazil 142 F4
Manavgat Turkey 90 C3
Manbazar India 83 F5
Manbij Syria 85 C1
Manby U.K. 48 H5
Mancelona U.S.A. 134 C1
Manchar India 84 B2
Manchester U.K. 48 E5
Manchester CT U.S.A. 135 I3
Manchester IA U.S.A. 130 F3
Manchester KY U.S.A. 134 D5
Manchester MD U.S.A. 135 G4
Manchester MI U.S.A. 134 C2
Manchester NH U.S.A. 135 J2
Manchester OH U.S.A. 134 D4
Manchester TN U.S.A. 132 C5
Manchester VT U.S.A. 135 I2
Mancılık Turkey 90 E3
Mand Pak. 89 F5
Mand, Rūd-e r. Iran 88 C4
Manda Tanz. 99 D4
Manda, Jebel mt. Sudan 97 F4
Manda, Parc National de nat. park
Chad 97 E4
Mandabe Madag. 99 E6
Mandai Sing. 71 [inset]
Mandal Norway 45 E7

▶Mandala, Puncak mt. Indon. 69 K7
3rd highest mountain in Oceania.

Mandalay Myanmar 70 B2
Mandale Myanmar see Mandalay
Mandalgovĭ Mongolia 72 J3
Mandalī Iraq 91 G4
Mandal-Ovoo Mongolia 72 I4
Mandalt China 73 K4

Mandan U.S.A. 130 C2
Mandas Sardinia Italy 58 C5
Mandasa India 84 E2
Mandasor India see Mandsaur
Mandav Hills India 82 B5
Mandel Afgh. 89 F3
Mandera Kenya 98 E3
Manderfield U.S.A. 129 G2
Manderscheid Germany 52 G4
Mandeville Jamaica 137 I5
Mandeville N.Z. 113 B7
Mandha India 82 B4
Mandhoúdhion Greece see Mantoudi
Mandi India 82 D3
Mandiana Guinea 96 C3
Mandi Burewala Pak. 89 I4
Mandié Moz. 99 D5
Mandini S. Africa 101 J5
Mandira Dam India 83 F5
Mandla India 82 E5
Mandleshwar India 82 C5
Mandrael India 82 D4
Mandritsara Madag. 99 E5
Mandsaur India 82 C4
Mandurah Australia 109 A8
Manduria Italy 58 G4
Mandvi India 82 B5
Mandya India 84 C3
Manerbio Italy 58 D2
Manevychi Ukr. 43 E6
Manfalūṭ Egypt 90 C6
Manfredonia Italy 58 F4
Manfredonia, Golfo di g. Italy 58 G4
Manga Brazil 145 C1
Manga Burkina 96 C3
Mangabeiras, Serra das hills Brazil 143 I6
Mangai Dem. Rep. Congo 98 B4
Mangaia i. Cook Is 151 J7
Mangakino N.Z. 113 E4
Mangalagiri India 84 D2
Mangaldai India 70 A1
Mangaldoi India see Mangaldai
Mangalia Romania 59 M3
Mangalmé Chad 97 E3
Mangalore India 84 B3
Mangaon India 84 B2
Mangareva Islands Fr. Polynesia see
Gambier, Îles
Mangaung Free State S. Africa 101 H5
Mangaung Free State S. Africa see
Bloemfontein
Mangawan India 83 E4
Ma'ngê China see Luqu
Mangea i. Cook Is see Mangaia
Mangghyshlaq Kazakh. see Mangystau
Mangghystaū Kazakh. see Mangystau
Mangghystaū admin. div. Kazakh. see
Mangistauskaya Oblast'
Mangghyt Uzbek. see Mang'it
Manghit Uzbek. see Mang'it
Mangin Range mts Myanmar see
Mingin Range
Mangistau Kazakh. see Mangystau
Mangistauskaya Oblast' admin. div.
Kazakh. 91 I2
Mang'it Uzbek. 80 B3
Mangla Bangl. see Mongla
Mangla China see Guinan
Mangla Pak. 89 I3
Manglaqiongtuo China see Guinan
Mangnai China 80 H4
Mangnai Zhen China 80 H4
Mangochi Malawi 99 D5
Mangoky r. Madag. 99 E6
Mangole i. Indon. 69 H7
Mangoli India 84 B2
Mangotsfield U.K. 49 E7
Mangqystaū Shyghanaghy b. Kazakh. see
Mangyshlakskiy Zaliv
Mangra China see Guinan
Mangrol India 82 B5
Mangrul India 84 C1
Mangshi China see Luxi
Mangualde Port. 57 C3
Manguéni, Plateau du Niger 96 E2
Mangui China 74 A2
Mangula Zimbabwe see Mhangura
Mangum U.S.A. 131 D5
Mangyshlak Kazakh. see Mangystau
Mangyshlak, Poluostrov pen. Kazakh.
91 H1
Mangyshlak Oblast admin. div. Kazakh. see
Mangistauskaya Oblast'
Mangyshlakskaya Oblast' admin. div.
Kazakh. see Mangistauskaya Oblast'
Mangyshlakskiy Zaliv b. Kazakh. 91 H1
Mangystau Kazakh. 91 H2
Manhã Brazil 145 B1
Manhattan U.S.A. 130 D4
Manhica Moz. 101 K3
Manhoca Moz. 101 K4
Manhuaçu Brazil 145 C3
Manhuaçu r. Brazil 145 C2
Mani China 83 F2
Mania r. Madag. 99 E5
Maniago Italy 58 E1
Manicouagan Canada 123 H4
Manicouagan r. Canada 123 H4
Manicouagan, Réservoir resr
Canada 123 H4
Manic Trois, Réservoir resr Canada 123 H4
Manīfah Saudi Arabia 88 C5
Maniganggo China 76 C2
Manigotagan Canada 121 L5
Manihiki atoll Cook Is 150 J6
Maniitsoq Greenland 119 M3
Manikchhari Bangl. 83 H5
Manikgarh India see Rajura

▶Manila Phil. 69 G4
Capital of the Philippines.

Manila U.S.A. 126 F4
Manildra Australia 112 D4
Manilla Australia 112 E3
Maningrida Australia 108 F3
Manipur India see Imphal
Manipur state India 83 H4
Manisa Turkey 59 L5
Manistee U.S.A. 134 B1
Manistee r. U.S.A. 134 B1
Manistique U.S.A. 132 C2

Manitoba prov. Canada 121 L4
Manitoba, Lake Canada 121 L5
Manito Lake Canada 121 I4
Manitou Canada 121 L5
Manitou, Lake U.S.A. 134 B3
Manitou Beach U.S.A. 135 G2
Manitou Falls Canada 121 M5
Manitou Islands U.S.A. 134 B1
Manitoulin Island Canada 122 E5
Manitouwadge Canada 122 D4
Manitowoc U.S.A. 134 B1
Maniwaki Canada 122 G5
Manizales Col. 142 C2
Manja Madag. 99 E6
Manjarabad India 84 B3
Manjeri India 84 C4
Manjhand Pak. 89 H5
Manjhi India 83 F4
Manjra r. India 84 C2
Man Kabat Myanmar 70 B1
Mankaiana Swaziland see Mankayane
Mankato KS U.S.A. 130 D4
Mankato MN U.S.A. 130 E2
Mankayane Swaziland 101 J4
Mankera Pak. 89 H4
Mankono Côte d'Ivoire 96 C4
Mankota Canada 121 J5
Manlay Mongolia 72 J4
Manley Hot Springs U.S.A. 118 C3
Manmad India 84 B1
Mann r. Australia 108 F3
Mann, Mount Australia 109 E6
Manna Indon. 68 C7
Man Na Myanmar 70 B2
Mannahill Australia 111 B7
Mannar Sri Lanka 84 C4
Mannar, Gulf of India/Sri Lanka 84 C4
Manneru r. India 84 D3
Mannessier, Lac l. Canada 123 H3
Mannheim Germany 53 I5
Mannicolo Islands Solomon Is see
Vanikoro Islands
Manning r. Australia 112 F3
Manning Canada 120 G3
Manning U.S.A. 133 D5
Mannington U.S.A. 134 E4
Manningtree U.K. 49 I7
Mann Ranges mts Australia 109 E6
Mannsville KY U.S.A. 134 C5
Mannsville NY U.S.A. 135 G2
Mannu, Capo c. Sardinia Italy 58 C4
Mannville Canada 121 I4
Man-of-War Rocks is U.S.A. see
Gardner Pinnacles
Manoharpur India 82 D4
Manohar Thana India 82 D4
Manokotak U.S.A. 118 C4
Manokwari Indon. 69 I7
Manoron Myanmar 71 B5
Manosque France 56 G5
Manouane r. Canada 123 H4
Manouane, Lac l. Canada 123 H4
Man Pan Myanmar 70 B2
Manp'o N. Korea 74 B4
Manra i. Kiribati 107 I2
Manresa Spain 57 G3
Mansa Gujarat India 82 C5
Mansa Punjab India 82 C3
Mansa Zambia 99 C5
Mansa Konko Gambia 96 B3
Man Sam Myanmar 70 B2
Mansehra Pak. 87 L3
Mansel Island Canada 119 K3
Mansfield Australia 112 C6
Mansfield U.K. 49 F5
Mansfield LA U.S.A. 131 E5
Mansfield OH U.S.A. 134 D3
Mansfield PA U.S.A. 135 G3
Mansfield, Mount U.S.A. 135 I1
Man Si Myanmar 70 B1
Mansi Myanmar 70 A1
Manso r. Brazil see Mortes, Rio das
Manta Ecuador 142 B4
Mantaro r. Peru 142 D6
Manteca U.S.A. 128 C3
Mantena Brazil 145 C2
Manteo U.S.A. 132 F5
Mantes-la-Jolie France 52 B6
Mantiqueira, Serra da mts Brazil 145 B3
Manton U.S.A. 134 C1
Mantoudi Greece 59 J5
Mantova Italy see Mantua
Mäntsälä Fin. 45 N6
Mänttä Fin. 44 N5
Mantua Cuba 133 C8
Mantua Italy 58 D2
Mantuan Downs Australia 110 D5
Manturovo Rus. Fed. 42 J4
Mäntyharju Fin. 45 O6
Mäntyjärvi Fin. 44 O3
Manú Peru 142 D6
Manu, Parque Nacional nat. park
Peru 142 D6
Manuae atoll Fr. Polynesia 151 J7
Manu'a Islands American Samoa 107 I3
Manuel Ribas Brazil 145 A4
Manuel Vitorino Brazil 145 C1
Manuelzinho Brazil 143 H5
Manui i. Indon. 69 G7
Manukau N.Z. 113 E3
Manukau Harbour N.Z. 113 E3
Manunda watercourse Australia 111 B7
Manusela, Taman Nasional Indon. 69 H7
Manus Island P.N.G. 69 L7
Manvi India 84 C3
Many U.S.A. 131 E6
Manyana Botswana 101 G3
Manyas Turkey 59 L4
Manyas Gölü l. Turkey see Kuş Gölü
Manych-Gudilo, Ozero l. Rus. Fed. 43 I7
Many Island Lake Canada 121 I5
Manyoni Tanz. 99 D4
Manzai Pak. 89 H3
Manzanares Spain 57 E4
Manzanillo Cuba 137 I4
Manzanillo Mex. 136 D5
Manzhouli China 73 L3
Manzini Swaziland 101 J4
Mao Chad 97 E3
Maó Spain see Mahón
Maoba Guizhou China 76 E3
Maoba Hubei China 77 F2

Maocifan China 77 G2
Mao'ergai China 76 D1
Maoke, Pegunungan mts Indon. 69 J7
Maokeng S. Africa 101 H4
Maokui Shan mt. China 74 A4
Maolin China 74 A4
Maoming China 77 F4
Ma On Shan hill H.K. China 77 [inset]
Maopi T'ou c. Taiwan 77 I4
Maopora i. Indon. 108 D1
Maotou Shan mt. China 76 D3
Mapai Moz. 101 J2
Mapam Yumco l. China 83 E3
Mapanza Zambia 99 C5
Maphodi S. Africa 101 G6
Mapimí Mex. 131 C7
Mapinhane Moz. 101 L2
Mapiri Bol. 142 E7
Maple r. MI U.S.A. 134 C2
Maple r. ND U.S.A. 130 D2
Maple Creek Canada 121 I5
Maple Heights U.S.A. 134 E3
Maple Peak U.S.A. 129 I5
Mapmakers Seamounts sea feature
N. Pacific Ocean 150 H4
Mapoon Australia 110 C1
Mapor i. Indon. 71 D7
Mapoteng Lesotho 101 H5
Maprik P.N.G. 69 K7
Mapuera r. Brazil 143 G4
Mapulanguene Moz. 101 K3
Mapungubwe National Park
S. Africa 101 I2

▶Maputo Moz. 101 K3
Capital of Mozambique.

Maputo prov. Moz. 101 K3
Maputo r. Moz./S. Africa 101 K4
Maputo, Baía de b. Moz. 101 K4
Maputsoe Lesotho 101 H5
Maqanshy Kazakh. see Makanchi
Maqar an Na'am well Iraq 91 F5
Maqat Kazakh. see Makat
Maqên China 76 D1
Maqên Kangri mt. China 76 C1
Maqnā Saudi Arabia 90 D5
Maqteïr reg. Mauritania 96 B2
Maqu China 76 D1
Ma Qu r. China see Yellow River
Maquan He r. China 83 F3
Maquela do Zombo Angola 99 B4
Maquinchao Arg. 144 C6
Mar r. Pak. 89 G5
Mar, Serra do mts Rio de Janeiro/São Paulo
Brazil 145 B3
Mar, Serra do mts Rio Grande do Sul/Santa
Catarina Brazil 145 A5
Mara r. Canada 121 I1
Mara India 83 E5
Mara S. Africa 101 I2
Maraã Brazil 142 E4
Marabá Brazil 143 I5
Maraboon, Lake resr Australia 110 E4
Maracá, Ilha de i. Brazil 143 H3
Maracaibo Venez. 142 D1
Maracaibo, Lago de Venez. see
Maracaibo, Lake
Maracaibo, Lake Venez. 142 D2
Maracaju Brazil 144 E2
Maracaju, Serra de hills Brazil 144 E2
Maracanda Uzbek. see Samarqand
Maracás Brazil 145 C1
Maracás, Chapada de hills Brazil 145 C1
Maracay Venez. 142 E1
Marādah Libya 97 E2
Maradi Niger 96 D3
Marāgheh Iran 88 B2
Marahuaca, Cerro mt. Venez. 142 E3
Marajó, Baía de est. Brazil 143 I4
Marajó, Ilha de i. Brazil 143 H4
Marakele National Park S. Africa 101 H3
Maralal Kenya 98 D3
Maralbashi China see Bachu
Maralinga Australia 109 E7
Maralwexi China see Bachu
Maramasike i. Solomon Is 107 G2
Maramba Zambia see Livingstone
Marambio research station
Antarctica 152 A2
Maran Malaysia 71 C7
Maran mt. Pak. 89 G4
Marana U.S.A. 129 H5
Marand Iran 88 B2
Marandellas Zimbabwe see Marondera
Marang Malaysia 71 C6
Marang Myanmar 71 B5
Maranhão r. Brazil 145 A1
Maranoa r. Australia 112 D1
Marañón r. Peru 142 D4
Marão Moz. 101 L3
Marão mt. Port. 57 C3
Mara Rosa Brazil 145 A1
Maraş Turkey see Kahramanmaraş
Marathon Canada 122 D4
Marathon FL U.S.A. 133 D7
Marathon NY U.S.A. 135 G2
Marathon TX U.S.A. 131 C6
Maratua i. Indon. 68 F6
Maraú Brazil 145 D1
Maravillas Creek watercourse U.S.A. 131 C6
Mārāzā Azer. 91 H2
Marbella Spain 57 D5
Marble Bar Australia 108 B5
Marble Canyon U.S.A. 129 H3
Marble Canyon gorge U.S.A. 129 H3
Marble Hall S. Africa 101 I3
Marble Hill U.S.A. 131 F4
Marble Island Canada 121 N2
Marbul Pass India 82 C2
Marburg S. Africa 101 J6
Marburg Slovenia see Maribor
Marburg an der Lahn Germany 53 I4
Marca, Ponta do pt Angola 99 B5
Marcali Hungary 58 G1
Marcelino Ramos Brazil 145 A4
March U.K. 49 H6
Marche reg. France 56 E3
Marche-en-Famenne Belgium 52 F4
Marchena Spain 57 D5
Marchinbar Island Australia 110 B1
Mar Chiquita, Laguna l. Arg. 144 D4

Marchtrenk Austria 47 O6
Marco U.S.A. 133 D7
Marcoing France 52 D4
Marcona Peru 142 C7
Marcopeet Islands Canada 122 F2
Marcus Baker, Mount U.S.A. 118 D3
Marcy, Mount U.S.A. 135 I1
Mardan Pak. 89 I3
Mar del Plata Arg. 144 E5
Mardīān Afgh. 89 G2
Mardın Turkey 91 F3
Maré i. New Caledonia 107 G4
Maree, Loch l. U.K. 50 D3
Mareh Iran 89 E5
Marengo IA U.S.A. 130 E3
Marengo IN U.S.A. 134 B4
Marevo Rus. Fed. 42 G4
Marfa U.S.A. 131 B6
Marganets Ukr. see Marhanets'
Margao India see Madgaon
Margaret r. Australia 108 D4
Margaret watercourse Australia 111 B6
Margaret, Mount hill Australia 108 B5
Margaret Lake Alta Canada 120 H3
Margaret Lake N.W.T. Canada 120 G1
Margaret River Australia 109 A8
Margaretville U.S.A. 135 H2
Margarita, Isla de i. Venez. 142 F1
Margaritovo Rus. Fed. 74 D4
Margate U.K. 49 I7
Margherita, Lake Eth. see Abaya, Lake

▶Margherita Peak
Dem. Rep. Congo/Uganda 98 C3
3rd highest mountain in Africa.

Marghilon Uzbek. see Marg'ilon
Marg'ilon Uzbek. 80 D3
Mārgo, Dasht-i des. Afgh. see Māragow, Dasht-e
Margog Caka l. China 83 F2
Mārgow, Dasht-e des. Afgh. 89 F4
Margraten Neth. 52 F4
Marguerite Canada 120 F4
Marguerite, Pic mt.
Dem. Rep. Congo/Uganda see Margherita Peak
Marguerite Bay Antarctica 152 L2
Margyang China 83 G3
Marhaj Khalīl Iraq 91 G4
Marhanets' Ukr. 43 G7
Marhoum Alg. 54 D5
Mari Myanmar 70 B1
Maria atoll Fr. Polynesia 151 J7
María Elena Chile 144 C2
Maria Island Australia 110 A2
Maria Island Myanmar 71 B5
Maria Island National Park Australia 111 [inset]
Mariala National Park Australia 111 D5
Mariana Brazil 145 C3
Marianao Cuba 133 D8
Mariana Ridge sea feature N. Pacific Ocean 150 F4

▶Mariana Trench sea feature
N. Pacific Ocean 150 F5
Deepest trench in the world.

Mariani India 83 H4
Mariánica, Cordillera mts Spain see Morena, Sierra
Marian Lake Canada 120 G2
Marianna AR U.S.A. 131 F5
Marianna FL U.S.A. 133 C6
Mariano Machado Angola see Ganda
Mariánské Lázně Czech Rep. 53 M5
Marias r. U.S.A. 126 F3
Marías, Islas is Mex. 136 C4

▶Mariato, Punta pt Panama 137 H7
Most southerly point of North America.

Maria van Diemen, Cape N.Z. 113 D2
Ma'rib Yemen 86 G6
Maribor Slovenia 58 F1
Marica r. Bulg. see Maritsa
Maricopa AZ U.S.A. 129 G5
Maricopa CA U.S.A. 128 D4
Maricopa Mountains U.S.A. 129 G5
Maridi Sudan 97 F4
Marie Byrd Land reg. Antarctica 152 J1
Marie-Galante i. Guadeloupe 137 L5
Mariehamn Fin. 45 K6
Mariembero r. Brazil 145 A1
Marienbad Czech Rep. see Mariánské Lázně
Marienberg Germany 53 N4
Marienburg Poland see Malbork
Marienhafe Germany 53 H1
Mariental Namibia 100 C3
Marienwerder Poland see Kwidzyn
Mariestad Sweden 45 H7
Mariet r. Canada 122 F2
Marietta GA U.S.A. 133 C5
Marietta OH U.S.A. 134 E4
Marietta OK U.S.A. 131 D5
Marignane France 56 G5
Mariinsk Rus. Fed. 64 J4
Mariinskiy Posad Rus. Fed. 42 J4
Marijampolė Lith. 45 M9
Marília Brazil 145 A3
Marillana Australia 108 B5
Marimba Angola 99 B4
Marín Spain 57 B2
Marina U.S.A. 128 C3
Marina di Gioiosa Ionica Italy 58 G5
Mar'ina Gorka Belarus see Mar"ina Horka
Mar"ina Horka Belarus 45 P10
Marinduque i. Phil. 69 G4
Marinette U.S.A. 134 B1
Maringá Brazil 145 A3
Maringa r. Dem. Rep. Congo 98 B3
Maringo U.S.A. 134 D3
Marinha Grande Port. 57 B4
Marion AL U.S.A. 133 C5
Marion AR U.S.A. 131 F5
Marion IL U.S.A. 130 F4
Marion IN U.S.A. 134 C3
Marion KS U.S.A. 130 D4
Marion MI U.S.A. 134 C1
Marion NY U.S.A. 135 G2
Marion OH U.S.A. 134 D3
Marion SC U.S.A. 133 E5
Marion VA U.S.A. 134 E5
Marion, Lake U.S.A. 133 D5
Marion Reef Australia 110 F3
Maripa Venez. 142 E2
Mariposa U.S.A. 128 D3
Marisa Indon. 69 G6
Mariscal José Félix Estigarribia Para. 144 D2
Maritime Alps mts France/Italy 56 H4
Maritime Kray admin. div. Rus. Fed. see Primorskiy Kray
Maritimes, Alpes mts France/Italy see Maritime Alps
Maritsa r. Bulg. 59 L4
also known as Euros (Greece), Marica (Bulgaria), Meriç (Turkey)
Marittime, Alpi mts France/Italy see Maritime Alps
Mariupol' Ukr. 43 H7
Mariusa nat. park Venez. 142 F2
Marīvān Iran 88 B3
Marjan Afgh. see Wazi Khwa
Marjayoûn Lebanon 85 B3
Marka Somalia 98 E3
Markala Mali 96 C3
Markam China 76 C2
Markaryd Sweden 45 H8
Markdale Canada 134 E1
Marken S. Africa 101 I2
Markermeer l. Neth. 52 F2
Market Deeping U.K. 49 G6
Market Drayton U.K. 49 E6
Market Harborough U.K. 49 G6
Markethill U.K. 51 F3
Market Weighton U.K. 48 G5
Markha r. Rus. Fed. 65 M3
Markham Canada 134 F2
Markit China 80 E4
Markkleeberg Germany 53 M3
Markleeville U.S.A. 128 D2
Marklohe Germany 53 J2
Markog Qu r. China 76 D1
Markounda Cent. Afr. Rep. 98 B3
Markovo Rus. Fed. 65 S3
Markranstädt Germany 53 M3
Marks Rus. Fed. 43 J6
Marks U.S.A. 131 F5
Marksville U.S.A. 131 E6
Marktheidenfeld Germany 53 J5
Marktredwitz Germany 53 M4
Marl Germany 52 H3
Marla Australia 109 F6
Marlborough Downs hills U.K. 49 F7
Marle France 52 D5
Marlette U.S.A. 134 D2
Marlin U.S.A. 131 D6
Marlinton U.S.A. 134 E4
Marlo Australia 112 D6
Marmagao India 84 B3
Marmande France 56 E4
Marmara, Sea of g. Turkey 59 M4
Marmara Denizi g. Turkey see Marmara, Sea of
Marmara Gölü l. Turkey 59 M5
Marmarica reg. Libya 90 B5
Marmaris Turkey 59 M6
Marmarth U.S.A. 130 C2
Marmet U.S.A. 134 E4
Marmion, Lake salt l. Australia 109 C7
Marmion Lake Canada 121 N5
Marmolada mt. Italy 58 D1
Marne r. France 52 C6
Marne-la-Vallée France 52 C6
Marnitz Germany 53 L1
Maroantsetra Madag. 99 E5
Maroc country Africa see Morocco
Marol Pak. 89 I4
Marol Pak. 82 D2
Maroldsweisach Germany 53 K4
Maromokotro mt. Madag. 99 E5
Marondera Zimbabwe 99 D5
Maroochydore Australia 112 F1
Maroonah Australia 109 A5
Maroon Peak U.S.A. 126 G5
Marosvásárhely Romania see Târgu Mureș
Maroua Cameroon 97 E3
Marovoay Madag. 99 E5
Marqādah Syria 91 F4
Mar Qu r. China see Markog Qu
Marquard S. Africa 101 H5
Marquesas Islands Fr. Polynesia 151 K6
Marquesas Keys is U.S.A. 133 D7
Marquês de Valença Brazil 145 C3
Marquette U.S.A. 132 C2
Marquez U.S.A. 131 D6
Marquion France 52 D4
Marquise France 52 B4
Marquises, Îles is Fr. Polynesia see Marquesas Islands
Marra Australia 112 A3
Marra r. Australia 112 C3
Marra, Jebel mt. Sudan 97 F3
Marra, Jebel Sudan 97 F3
Marracuene Moz. 101 K3
Marrakech Morocco 54 C5
Marrakesh Morocco see Marrakech
Marrangua, Lagoa l. Moz. 101 L3
Marrar Australia 112 C5
Marrawah Australia 111 [inset]
Marrawah Tas. Australia 111 [inset]
Marree Australia 111 B6
Marrowbone U.S.A. 134 C5
Marruecos country Africa see Morocco
Marrupa Moz. 99 D5
Marryat Australia 109 F6
Marsá al 'Alam Egypt 86 D4
Marsa 'Alam Egypt see Marsá al 'Alam
Marsa al Burayqah Libya 97 E1
Marsabit Kenya 98 D3
Marsala Sicily Italy 58 E6
Marsá Maṭrūḥ Egypt 90 B5
Marsberg Germany 53 I3
Marsciano Italy 58 E3
Marsden Australia 112 C4
Marsden Canada 121 I4
Marsdiep sea chan. Neth. 52 E2
Marseille France 56 G5
Marseilles France see Marseille
Marsfjället mt. Sweden 44 I4
Marshall watercourse Australia 110 B4
Marshall AR U.S.A. 131 E5
Marshall IL U.S.A. 134 B4
Marshall MI U.S.A. 134 C2
Marshall MN U.S.A. 130 E2
Marshall MO U.S.A. 130 E4
Marshall TX U.S.A. 131 E5
Marshall Islands country N. Pacific Ocean 150 H5
Marshalltown U.S.A. 130 E3
Marshfield MO U.S.A. 131 E4
Marshfield WI U.S.A. 130 F2
Marsh Harbour Bahamas 133 E7
Mars Hill U.S.A. 132 H2
Marsh Island U.S.A. 131 F6
Marsh Peak U.S.A. 129 I1
Marsh Point Canada 121 M3
Marsing U.S.A. 126 D4
Märsta Sweden 45 J7
Marsyaty Rus. Fed. 41 S3
Martaban, Gulf of g. Myanmar see Mottama, Gulf of
Martapura Indon. 68 E7
Marten River Canada 122 F5
Marte R. Gómez, Presa resr Mex. 131 D7
Martha's Vineyard i. U.S.A. 135 J3
Martigny Switz. 56 H3
Martim Vaz, Ilhas is S. Atlantic Ocean see Martin Vas, Ilhas
Martin r. Canada 120 F2
Martin Slovakia 47 Q6
Martin MI U.S.A. 134 C2
Martin SD U.S.A. 130 C3
Martinez Lake U.S.A. 129 F5
Martinho Campos Brazil 145 B2

▶Martinique terr. West Indies 137 L6
French Overseas Department.

Martinique Passage Dominica/Martinique 137 L5
Martin Peninsula Antarctica 152 K2
Martinsburg U.S.A. 135 G4
Martins Ferry U.S.A. 134 E3
Martinsville IL U.S.A. 134 B4
Martinsville IN U.S.A. 134 B4
Martinsville VA U.S.A. 134 F5

▶Martin Vas, Ilhas is S. Atlantic Ocean 148 G7
Most easterly point of South America.

Martin Vaz Islands S. Atlantic Ocean see Martin Vas, Ilhas
Martök Kazakh. see Martuk
Marton N.Z. 113 E5
Martorell Spain 57 G3
Martos Spain 57 E5
Martuk Kazakh. 78 E1
Martuni Armenia 91 G2
Maruf Afgh. 89 G4
Maruim Brazil 143 K6
Marukhis Ugheltekhili pass Georgia/Rus. Fed. 91 F2
Marulan Australia 112 D5
Marusthali reg. India 89 H5
Marvast Iran 88 D4
Marv Dasht Iran 88 D4
Marvejols France 56 F4
Marvine, Mount U.S.A. 129 H2
Marwayne Canada 121 I4
Mary r. Australia 108 E3
Mary Turkm. 89 F2
Maryborough Qld Australia 111 F5
Maryborough Vic. Australia 112 A6
Marydale S. Africa 100 F5
Mary Frances Lake Canada 121 J2
Mary Lake Canada 121 K2
Maryland state U.S.A. 135 G4
Maryport U.K. 48 D4
Mary's Harbour Canada 123 L3
Marysvale U.S.A. 129 G2
Marysville CA U.S.A. 128 C2
Marysville KS U.S.A. 130 D4
Marysville OH U.S.A. 134 D3
Maryvale N.T. Australia 109 F6
Maryvale Qld Australia 110 D3
Maryville MO U.S.A. 130 E3
Maryville TN U.S.A. 132 D5
Marzagão Brazil 145 A2
Marzahna Germany 53 M2
Masada tourist site Israel 85 B4
Masāhūn, Kūh-e mt. Iran 88 D4
Masai Steppe plain Tanz. 99 D4
Masaka Uganda 98 D4
Masakhane S. Africa 101 H6
Masalembu Besar i. Indon. 68 E8
Masallı Azer. 91 H3
Masan S. Korea 75 C6
Masasi Tanz. 99 D5
Masavi Bol. 142 F7
Masbate Phil. 69 G4
Masbate i. Phil. 69 G4
Mascara Alg. 57 G6
Mascarene Basin sea feature Indian Ocean 149 L7
Mascarene Plain sea feature Indian Ocean 149 L7
Mascarene Ridge sea feature Indian Ocean 149 L6
Mascote Brazil 145 D1
Masein Myanmar 70 A2
Masela Indon. 108 E2
Masela i. Indon. 108 E2

▶Maseru Lesotho 101 H5
Capital of Lesotho.

Mashai Lesotho 101 I5
Mashan China 77 F4
Masherbrum mt. Pak. 82 D2
Mashhad Iran 89 E2
Mashishing S. Africa 101 J3
Mashket r. Pak. 89 F5
Mashki Chah Pak. 89 F4
Masi Norway 44 M2
Masiáca Mex. 127 F8
Masibambane S. Africa 101 H6
Masīlah, Wādī al watercourse Yemen 86 H6
Masilo S. Africa 101 H5
Masi-Manimba Dem. Rep. Congo 99 B4
Masindi Uganda 98 D3
Masinyusane S. Africa 100 F6
Masira, Gulf of Oman see Maşīrah, Khalīj
Maşīrah, Jazīrat i. Oman 87 I5
Maşīrah, Khalīj b. Oman 87 I6
Masira Island Oman see Maşīrah, Jazīrat
Masjed Soleymān Iran 88 C4
Mask, Lough l. Ireland 51 C4
Maskūtān Iran 89 E5
Maslovo Rus. Fed. 41 S3
Masoala, Tanjona c. Madag. 99 F5
Mason MI U.S.A. 134 C2
Mason OH U.S.A. 134 C4
Mason TX U.S.A. 131 D6
Mason, Lake salt flat Australia 109 B6
Mason Bay N.Z. 113 A8
Mason City U.S.A. 130 E3
Masontown U.S.A. 134 F4
Masqaţ Oman see Muscat
Masqaţ reg. Oman see Muscat
'Masrūg well Oman 88 D6
Massa Italy 58 D2
Massachusetts state U.S.A. 135 I2
Massachusetts Bay U.S.A. 135 J2
Massadona U.S.A. 129 I1
Massafra Italy 58 G4
Massakory Chad 97 E3
Massa Marittimo Italy 58 D3
Massangena Moz. 99 D6
Massango Angola 99 B4
Massawa Eritrea 86 E6
Massawippi, Lac l. Canada 135 I1
Massena U.S.A. 135 H1
Massenya Chad 97 E3
Masset Canada 120 C4
Massieville U.S.A. 134 D4
Massif Central mts France 56 F4
Massilia France see Marseille
Massillon U.S.A. 134 E3
Massina Mali 96 C3
Massinga Moz. 101 L2
Massingir Moz. 101 K2
Massingir, Barragem de resr Moz. 101 K2
Masson Island Antarctica 152 F2
Mastchoh Tajik. 89 H2
Masterton N.Z. 113 E5
Masticho, Akra pt Voreio Aigaio Greece see Oura, Akrotirio
Mastung Pak. 78 F4
Mastūrah Saudi Arabia 86 E5
Masty Belarus 45 N10
Masuda Japan 75 C6
Masuku Gabon see Franceville
Masulipatam India see Machilipatnam
Masulipatnam India see Machilipatnam
Masuna i. American Samoa see Tutuila
Masvingo Zimbabwe 99 D6
Masvingo prov. Zimbabwe 101 J1
Maswa Tanz. 98 D4
Maswaar i. Indon. 69 I7
Maşyāf Syria 85 C2
Mat, Nam r. Laos 70 D3
Mata Myanmar 70 B1
Matabeleland South prov. Zimbabwe 101 I1
Matachewan Canada 122 E5
Matad Dornod Mongolia 73 L3
Matadi Dem. Rep. Congo 99 B4
Matador U.S.A. 131 C5
Matagalpa Nicaragua 137 G6
Matagami Canada 122 F4
Matagami, Lac l. Canada 122 F4
Matagorda Island U.S.A. 131 D6
Matak i. Indon. 71 D7
Matakana Island N.Z. 113 F3
Matala Angola 99 B5
Maţāli', Jabal hill Saudi Arabia 91 F6
Matam Senegal 96 B3
Matamey Niger 96 D3
Matamoros U.S.A. 135 H3
Matamoros Coahuila Mex. 131 C7
Matamoros Tamaulipas Mex. 131 D7
Matandu r. Tanz. 99 D4
Matane Canada 123 I4
Matanzas Cuba 137 H4
Matapan, Cape pt Greece see Tainaro, Akrotirio
Matapédia, Lac l. Canada 123 I4
Maţār well Saudi Arabia 88 B5
Matara Sri Lanka 84 D5
Mataram Indon. 108 B2
Matarani Peru 142 D7
Mataranka Australia 108 F3
Mataripe Brazil 145 D1
Mataró Spain 57 H3
Matasiri i. Indon. 68 F7
Matatiele S. Africa 101 I6
Matatila Reservoir India 82 D4
Mataura N.Z. 113 B8

▶Matā'utu Wallis and Futuna Is 107 I3
Capital of Wallis and Futuna Islands.

Mata-Utu Wallis and Futuna Is see Matā'utu
Matawai N.Z. 113 F4
Matay Kazakh. 80 E2
Matcha Tajik. see Mastchoh
Mat Con, Hon i. Vietnam 70 D3
Mategua Bol. 142 F6
Matehuala Mex. 131 C8
Matemanga Tanz. 99 D5
Matera Italy 58 G4
Mateur Tunisia 58 C6
Mathaji India 82 B4
Matheson Canada 122 E4
Mathews U.S.A. 135 G5
Mathis U.S.A. 131 D6
Mathoura Australia 112 B5
Mathura India 82 D4
Mati Phil. 69 H5
Matiali India 83 G4
Matias Cardoso Brazil 145 C1
Matías Romero Mex. 136 E5
Matimekosh Canada 123 I3
Matin India 83 E5
Matinenda Lake Canada 122 E5
Matizi China 76 D1
Matla r. India 83 G5
Matlabas r. S. Africa 101 H2
Matli Pak. 89 H5
Matlock U.K. 49 F5
Mato, Cerro mt. Venez. 142 E2
Matobo Hills Zimbabwe 99 C6
Mato Grosso Brazil 142 G7
Mato Grosso state Brazil 145 A1
Matopo Hills Zimbabwe see Matobo Hills
Matos Costa Brazil 145 A4
Matosinhos Port. 57 B3
Mato Verde Brazil 145 C1
Maṭraḥ Oman 88 E6
Matroosberg mt. S. Africa 100 D7
Matsesta Rus. Fed. 91 E2
Matsue Japan 75 D6
Matsumoto Japan 75 E5
Matsu Tao i. Taiwan 77 I3
Matsuyama Japan 75 D6
Mattagami r. Canada 122 E4
Mattamuskeet, Lake U.S.A. 132 E5
Mattawa Canada 122 F5
Matterhorn mt. Italy/Switz. 58 B2
Matterhorn mt. U.S.A. 126 E4
Matthew Town Bahamas 137 J4
Maṭṭī, Sabkhat salt pan Saudi Arabia 88 D6
Mattoon U.S.A. 130 F4
Matturai Sri Lanka see Matara
Matuku i. Fiji 107 H3
Matumbo Angola 99 B5
Maturín Venez. 142 F2
Matusadona National Park Zimbabwe 99 C5
Matwabeng S. Africa 101 H5
Maty Island P.N.G. see Wuvulu Island
Mau India see Maunath Bhanjan
Maúa Moz. 99 D5
Maubeuge France 52 D4
Maubin Myanmar 70 A3
Ma-ubin Myanmar 70 B1
Maubourguet France 56 E5
Mauchline U.K. 50 E5
Maudaha India 82 E4
Maude Australia 111 D7
Maud Seamount sea feature S. Atlantic Ocean 148 I10
Mau-é-ele Moz. see Marão
Maués Brazil 143 G4
Maughold Head hd Isle of Man 48 C4
Maug Islands N. Mariana Is 69 L2
Maui i. U.S.A. 127 [inset]
Maukkadaw Myanmar 70 A2
Maulbronn Germany 53 I6
Maule r. Chile 144 B5
Maulvi Bazar Bangl. see Moulvibazar
Maumee U.S.A. 134 D3
Maumee Bay U.S.A. 134 D3
Maumere Indon. 108 C2
Maumturk Mts hills Ireland 51 C4
Maun Botswana 99 C5
Mauna Kea vol. U.S.A. 127 [inset]
Mauna Loa vol. U.S.A. 127 [inset]
Maunath Bhanjan India 83 E4
Maunatlala Botswana 101 H2
Maungaturoto N.Z. 113 E3
Maungdaw Myanmar 70 A2
Maungmagan Islands Myanmar 71 B4
Maurepas, Lake U.S.A. 131 F6
Mauriac France 56 F4
Maurice country Indian Ocean see Mauritius
Maurice, Lake salt flat Australia 109 E7
Maurik Neth. 52 F3
Mauritania country Africa 96 B3
Mauritanie country Africa see Mauritania
Mauritius country Indian Ocean 149 L7
Maurs France 56 F4
Mauston U.S.A. 130 F3
Mava Dem. Rep. Congo 98 C3
Mavago Moz. 99 D5
Mavan, Kūh-e hill Iran 88 E3
Mavanza Moz. 101 L2
Mavinga Angola 99 C5
Mavrovo nat. park Macedonia 59 I4
Mavume Moz. 101 L2
Mavuya S. Africa 101 H6
Ma Wan i. H.K. China 77 [inset]
Māwān, Khashm hill Saudi Arabia 88 B6
Mawana India 82 D3
Mawanga Dem. Rep. Congo 99 B4
Ma Wang Dui tourist site China 77 G2
Mawei China 77 H3
Mawjib, Wādī al r. Jordan 85 B4
Mawkmai Myanmar 70 B2
Mawlaik Myanmar 70 A2
Mawlamyaing Myanmar 70 B3
Mawlamyine Myanmar see Mawlamyaing
Mawqaq Saudi Arabia 91 F6
Mawson research station Antarctica 152 E2
Mawson Coast Antarctica 152 E2
Mawson Escarpment Antarctica 152 E2
Mawson Peninsula Antarctica 152 H2
Maw Taung mt. Myanmar 71 B5
Mawza Yemen 86 F7
Maxán Arg. 144 C3
Maxhamish Lake Canada 120 F3
Maxia, Punta mt. Sardinia Italy 58 C5
Maxixe Moz. 101 L2
Maxmo Fin. 44 M5
May, Isle of i. U.K. 50 G4
Maya r. Rus. Fed. 65 O3
Mayaguana i. Bahamas 133 F8
Mayaguana Passage Bahamas 133 F8
Mayagüez Puerto Rico 137 K5
Mayahi Niger 96 D3
Mayak Rus. Fed. 74 E2
Mayakovskiy, Qullai mt. Tajik. 89 H2
Mayakovskogo, Pik mt. Tajik. see Mayakovskiy, Qullai
Mayama Congo 98 B4
Maya Mountains Belize/Guat. 136 G5
Mayan China see Mayanhe
Mayang China 77 F3
Mayanhe China 76 E1
Mayar hill U.K. 50 F4
Maybeury U.S.A. 134 E5
Maybole U.K. 50 E5
Maych'ew Eth. 98 D2
Maydān Shahr Afgh. see Meydān Shahr
Maydh Somalia 86 G7
Maydos Turkey see Eceabat
Mayen Germany 53 H4
Mayenne France 56 D2
Mayenne r. France 56 D3
Mayer U.S.A. 129 G4
Mayêr Kangri mt. China 83 F2
Mayersville U.S.A. 131 F5
Mayerthorpe Canada 120 H4
Mayfield N.Z. 113 C6
Mayi He r. China 74 C3
Maykop Rus. Fed. 91 F1
Maymanah Afgh. 89 G3
Mayna Respublika Khakasiya Rus. Fed. 64 K4
Mayna Ul'yanovskaya Oblast' Rus. Fed. 43 J5
Mayni India 84 B2
Maynooth Canada 135 G1
Mayo Canada 120 C2
Mayo U.S.A. 133 D6
Mayo Alim Cameroon 96 E4
Mayoko Congo 98 B4
Mayo Lake Canada 120 C2
Mayo Landing Canada see Mayo
Mayor, Puig mt. Spain see Major, Puig
Mayor Island N.Z. 113 F3
Mayor Pablo Lagerenza Para. 144 D1

▶Mayotte terr. Africa 99 E5
French Departmental Collectivity.

Mayskiy Amurskaya Oblast' Rus. Fed. 74 C1
Mayskiy Kabardino-Balkarskaya Respublika Rus. Fed. 91 G2
Mays Landing U.S.A. 135 H4
Mayson Lake Canada 121 J3
Maysville U.S.A. 134 D4
Mayumba Gabon 98 B4
Mayum La pass China 83 E3
Mayuram India 84 C4
Mayville MI U.S.A. 134 D2
Mayville ND U.S.A. 130 D2
Mayville NY U.S.A. 134 F2
Mayville WI U.S.A. 134 A2
Mazabuka Zambia 99 C5
Mazaca Turkey see Kayseri
Mazagan Morocco see El Jadida
Mazar China 82 D1
Mazar, Koh-i- mt. Afgh. 89 G3
Mazara, Val di valley Sicily Italy 58 E6
Mazara del Vallo Sicily Italy 58 E6
Mazār-e Sharīf Afgh. 89 G2
Mazārī' reg. U.A.E. 88 D6
Mazatán Mex. 127 F7
Mazatlán Mex. 136 C4
Mazatzal Peak U.S.A. 129 H4
Mazdaj Iran 91 H4
Mažeikiai Lith. 45 M8
Maẓhūr, 'Irq al des. Saudi Arabia 88 A5
Mazīm Oman 88 E6
Mazocahui Mex. 127 F7
Mazocruz Peru 142 E7
Mazomora Tanz. 99 D4
Mazu Dao i. Taiwan see Matsu Tao
Mazunga Zimbabwe 99 C6
Mazyr Belarus 43 F5
Mazzouna Tunisia 58 C7

▶Mbabane Swaziland 101 J4
Capital of Swaziland.

Mbahiakro Côte d'Ivoire 96 C4
Mbaïki Cent. Afr. Rep. 98 B3
Mbakaou, Lac de l. Cameroon 96 E4
Mbala Zambia 99 D4
Mbale Uganda 98 D3
Mbalmayo Cameroon 96 E4
Mbam r. Cameroon 96 E4
Mbandaka Dem. Rep. Congo 98 B4
M'banza Congo Angola 99 B4
Mbarara Uganda 97 G5
Mbari r. Cent. Afr. Rep. 98 C3
Mbaswana S. Africa 101 K4
Mbemkuru r. Tanz. 99 D4
Mbeya Tanz. 99 D4
Mbinga Tanz. 99 D5
Mbini Equat. Guinea 96 D4
Mbizi Zimbabwe 99 D6
Mboki Cent. Afr. Rep. 98 C3
Mbomo Congo 98 B3
Mbouda Cameroon 96 E4
Mbour Senegal 96 B3
Mbout Mauritania 96 B3
Mbozi Tanz. 99 D4
Mbrès Cent. Afr. Rep. 98 B3
Mbuji-Mayi Dem. Rep. Congo 99 C4
Mbulu Tanz. 98 D4
Mburucuyá Arg. 144 E3
McAdam Canada 123 I5
McAlester U.S.A. 131 E5
McAlister mt. Australia 112 D5
McAllen U.S.A. 131 D7
McArthur r. Australia 110 B2
McArthur U.S.A. 134 D4
McArthur Mills Canada 135 G1
McBain U.S.A. 134 C1
McBride Canada 120 F4
McCall U.S.A. 126 D3
McCamey U.S.A. 131 C6
McCammon U.S.A. 126 E4
McCauley Island Canada 120 D4
McClintock, Mount Antarctica 152 H1
McClintock Channel Canada 119 H2
McClintock Range hills Australia 108 D4
McClure, Lake U.S.A. 128 C3
McClure Strait Canada 118 G2
McClusky U.S.A. 130 C2
McComb U.S.A. 131 F6
McConaughy, Lake U.S.A. 130 C3
McConnellsburg U.S.A. 135 G4
McConnelsville U.S.A. 134 E4
McCook U.S.A. 130 C3
McCormick U.S.A. 133 D5
McCrea r. Canada 120 H2
McCreary Canada 121 L5
McDame Canada 120 D3
McDermitt U.S.A. 126 D4
McDonald Islands Indian Ocean 149 M9
McDonald Peak U.S.A. 126 E3
McDonough U.S.A. 133 C5
McDougall's Bay S. Africa 100 C5
McDowell Peak U.S.A. 129 H5
McFarland U.S.A. 128 D4
McGill U.S.A. 129 F2
McGivney Canada 123 I5
McGrath AK U.S.A. 118 C3
McGrath MN U.S.A. 130 E2

Graw U.S.A. 135 G2
Gregor r. Canada 120 F4
Gregor S. Africa 100 D7
Gregor, Lake Canada 120 H5
Gregor Range hills Australia 111 C5
Guire, Mount U.S.A. 126 E3
hinga Tanz. 99 D4
hinji Malawi 99 D5
Ilwraith Range hills Australia 110 C2
Innes Lake Canada 121 M4
Intosh U.S.A. 130 C2
Kay Range hills Australia 108 C5
Kean i. Kiribati 107 I2
Kee U.S.A. 134 C5
Kenzie r. U.S.A. 126 C3
Kinlay r. Australia 110 C4

McKinley, Mount U.S.A. 118 C3
Highest mountain in North America.

Kinney U.S.A. 131 D5
Kittrick U.S.A. 128 D4
Laughlin U.S.A. 130 C2
Leansboro U.S.A. 130 F4
Lennan Canada 120 G4
Leod r. Canada 120 H4
Leod Bay Canada 121 I2
Leod Lake Canada 120 F4
Loughlin, Mount U.S.A. 126 C4
Millan, Lake U.S.A. 131 B5
Minnville OR U.S.A. 126 C3
Minnville TN U.S.A. 132 C5
Murdo research station Antarctica 52 H1
Murdo Sound b. Antarctica 152 H1
Nary U.S.A. 129 I4
Naughton Lake Canada see Kinbasket Lake
Pherson U.S.A. 130 D4
Questen r. Canada 120 B2
Rae U.S.A. 133 D5
Tavish Arm b. Canada 120 G1
Veytown U.S.A. 135 G3
Vicar Arm b. Canada 120 F1
antsane S. Africa 101 H7
Daourouch Alg. 58 B6
Đrak Vietnam 71 E4
, Hon i. Vietnam 70 D3
ad, Lake resr U.S.A. 129 F3
ade U.S.A. 131 C4
ade r. U.S.A. 118 C2
adow Australia 109 A6
adow SD U.S.A. 130 C2
adow UT U.S.A. 129 G2
adow Lake Canada 121 I4
adville MS U.S.A. 131 F6
adville PA U.S.A. 134 E3
aford Canada 134 E1
aken-dake vol. Japan 74 G4
alhada Port. 57 B3
aly Mountains Canada 123 K3
andarra Australia 112 D1
ander River Canada 120 G3
aux France 52 C6
cca Saudi Arabia 86 E5
cca CA U.S.A. 128 E5
cca OH U.S.A. 134 E3
chanic Falls U.S.A. 135 J1
chanicsville U.S.A. 135 G5
chelen Belgium 52 E3
chelen Neth. 52 F4
cherchar i. Palau see Eil Malk
cheria Alg. 54 D5
chernich Germany 52 G4
citözü Turkey 90 D2
ckenheim Germany 52 H4
cklenburger Bucht b. Germany 47 M3
cklenburg-Vorpommern land Germany 53 M1
cklenburg - West Pomerania land Germany see Mecklenburg-Vorpommern
da r. Australia 108 C4
da Port. 57 C3
dak India 84 C2
dan Indon. 71 B7
danosa, Punta pt Arg. 144 C7
danos de Coro, Parque Nacional nat. park Venez. 142 E1
dawachchiya Sri Lanka 84 D4
déa Alg. 57 H5
debach Germany 53 I3
dellín Col. 142 C2
den r. U.K. 48 G5
denine Tunisia 54 G5
derdra Mauritania 96 B3
dford NY U.S.A. 135 I3
dford OK U.S.A. 131 D4
dford OR U.S.A. 126 C4
dford WI U.S.A. 130 F2
dgidia Romania 59 M2
dia U.S.A. 135 H4
diaș Romania 59 K1
dicine Bow r. U.S.A. 126 G4
dicine Bow Mountains U.S.A. 126 G4
dicine Bow Peak U.S.A. 126 G4
dicine Hat Canada 121 I5
dicine Lake U.S.A. 126 G2
dicine Lodge U.S.A. 131 D4
dina Brazil 145 C2
dina Saudi Arabia 86 E5
dina ND U.S.A. 130 D2
dina NY U.S.A. 135 F2
dina OH U.S.A. 134 E3
dinaceli Spain 57 E3
dina del Campo Spain 57 D3
dina de Rioseco Spain 57 D3
dina Lake U.S.A. 131 D6
dinipur India 83 F5
diolanum Italy see Milan
diterranean Sea 54 K5
dnyy, Ostrov i. Rus. Fed. 150 H2
doc reg. France 56 D4
dog China 76 B2
dora U.S.A. 130 C2
dstead Canada 121 I4
duro atoll Marshall Is see Majuro
dvedevo Rus. Fed. 42 J4
dveditsa r. Rus. Fed. 43 I6
dvednica mts Croatia 58 F2
dvezh'i, Ostrova is Rus. Fed. 65 R2
dvezh'ya vol. Rus. Fed. 74 H3
dvezh'ya, Gora mt. Rus. Fed. 74 E3

Medvezh'yegorsk Rus. Fed. 42 G3
Medway r. U.K. 49 H7
Meekatharra Australia 109 B6
Meeker CO U.S.A. 129 J1
Meeker OH U.S.A. 134 D3
Meelpaeg Reservoir Canada 123 K4
Meemu Atoll Maldives see Mulaku Atoll
Meerane Germany 53 M4
Meerlo Neth. 52 G3
Meerut India 82 D3
Mega Escarpment Eth./Kenya 98 D3
Megalopoli Greece 59 J6
Megamo Indon. 69 I7
Mégantic, Lac l. Canada 123 H5
Megara Greece 59 J5
Megezez mt. Eth. 98 D3

▶Meghalaya state India 83 G4
Highest mean annual rainfall in the world.

Meghasani mt. India 83 F5
Meghri Armenia 91 G3
Megin Turkm. 88 E2
Megisti i. Greece 59 M6
Megri Armenia see Meghri
Mehamn Norway 44 O1
Mehar Pak. 89 G5
Meharry, Mount Australia 109 B5
Mehbubnagar India see Mahbubnagar
Mehdia Tunisia see Mahdia
Meherpur Bangl. 83 G5
Meherrin U.S.A. 135 F5
Meherrin r. U.S.A. 135 G5
Mehlville U.S.A. 130 F4
Mehrakān salt marsh Iran 88 D5
Mehrān Hormozgan Iran 88 D5
Mehrān Īlām Iran 88 B3
Mehren Germany 52 G4
Mehriz Iran 88 D4
Mehsana India see Mahesana
Mehtar Lām Afgh. 89 H3
Meia Ponte r. Brazil 145 A2
Meicheng China see Minqing
Meiganga Cameroon 97 E4
Meighen Island Canada 119 I2
Meigu China 76 D2
Meihekou China 74 B4
Meikeng China 77 G3
Meikle r. Canada 120 G3
Meikle Says Law hill U.K. 50 G5
Meiktila Myanmar 70 A2
Meilin China see Ganxian
Meilleur r. Canada 120 E2
Meilu China 77 F4
Meine Germany 53 K2
Meinersen Germany 53 K2
Meiningen Germany 53 K4
Meishan Anhui China see Jinzhai
Meishan Sichuan China 76 D2
Meishan Shuiku resr China 77 G2
Meißen Germany 47 N5
Meister r. Canada 120 D2
Meitan China 76 E3
Meixi China 74 C3
Meixian China see Meizhou
Meixing China see Xiaojin
Meizhou China 77 H3
Mej r. India 82 D4
Mejicana mt. Arg. 144 C3
Mejillones Chile 144 B2
Mékambo Gabon 98 B3
Mek'elē Eth. 98 D2
Mekelle Eth. see Mek'elē
Mékhé Senegal 96 B3
Mekhtar Pak. 89 H4
Meknassy Tunisia 58 C7
Meknès Morocco 54 C5
Mekong r. Asia 70 D4
also known as Mènam Khong (Laos/Thailand)
Mekong, Mouths of the Vietnam 71 D5
Mekoryuk U.S.A. 118 B3
Melaka Malaysia 71 C7
Melanau, Gunung hill Indon. 71 E7
Melanesia is Pacific Ocean 150 G6
Melanesian Basin sea feature Pacific Ocean 150 G5

▶Melbourne Australia 112 B6
Capital of Victoria. 2nd most populous city in Oceania.

Melbourne U.S.A. 133 D6
Melby U.K. 50 [inset]
Meldorf Germany 47 L3

▶Melekeok Palau 69 I5
Capital of Palau.

Melekess Rus. Fed. see Dimitrovgrad
Melenki Rus. Fed. 43 I5
Melet Turkey see Mesudiye
Mélèzes, Rivière aux r. Canada 123 H2
Melfa U.S.A. 135 H5
Melfi Chad 97 E3
Melfi Italy 58 F4
Melfort Canada 121 J4
Melhus Norway 44 G5
Meliadine Lake Canada 121 M2
Melide Spain 57 C2

▶Melilla N. Africa 57 E6
Autonomous Community of Spain.

Melimoyu, Monte mt. Chile 144 B6
Meliskerke Neth. 52 D3
Melita Canada 121 K5
Melitene Turkey see Malatya
Melitopol' Ukr. 43 G7
Melk Austria 47 O6
Melka Guba Eth. 98 D3
Melksham U.K. 49 E7
Mellakoski Fin. 44 N3
Mellansel Sweden 44 K5
Melle Germany 53 I2
Mellerud Sweden 45 H7
Mellette U.S.A. 130 D2
Mellid Spain see Melide
Mellilia N. Africa see Melilla
Mellor Glacier Antarctica 152 E2
Mellrichstadt Germany 53 K4
Mellum i. Germany 53 I1

Melmoth S. Africa 101 J5
Mel'nichoye Rus. Fed. 74 D3
Melo Uruguay 144 F4
Meloco Moz. 99 D5
Melolo Indon. 108 C2
Melozitna r. U.S.A. 118 C3
Melrhir, Chott salt l. Alg. 54 F5
Melrose Australia 109 C6
Melrose U.K. 50 G5
Melrose U.S.A. 130 E2
Melsungen Germany 53 J3
Melton Australia 112 B6
Melton Mowbray U.K. 49 G6
Melun France 56 F2
Melville Canada 121 K5
Melville, Cape Australia 110 D2
Melville, Lake Canada 123 K3
Melville Bugt b. Greenland see Qimusseriarsuaq
Melville Island Australia 108 E2
Melville Island Canada 119 H2
Melville Peninsula Canada 119 J3
Melvin U.S.A. 134 A3
Melvin, Lough l. Ireland/U.K. 51 D3
Mêmar Co salt l. China 83 E2
Memba Moz. 99 E5
Memberamo r. Indon. 69 J7
Memel Lith. see Klaipėda
Memel S. Africa 101 I4
Memmelsdorf Germany 53 K5
Memmingen Germany 47 M7
Mempawah Indon. 68 D6
Memphis tourist site Egypt 90 C5
Memphis MI U.S.A. 134 D2
Memphis TN U.S.A. 131 F5
Memphis TX U.S.A. 131 C5
Memphrémagog, Lac l. Canada 135 I1
Mena Ukr. 43 G6
Mena U.S.A. 131 E5
Menado Indon. see Manado
Ménaka Mali 96 D3
Menard U.S.A. 131 D6
Menasha U.S.A. 134 A1
Mendanha Brazil 145 C2
Mendarik i. Indon. 71 D7
Mende France 56 F4
Mendefera Eritrea 86 E7
Mendeleyev Ridge sea feature Arctic Ocean 153 B1
Mendeleyevsk Rus. Fed. 42 L5
Mendenhall U.S.A. 131 F6
Mendenhall, Cape U.S.A. 118 B4
Mendenhall Glacier U.S.A. 120 C3
Méndez Mex. 131 D7
Mendī Eth. 98 D3
Mendi P.N.G. 69 K8
Mendip Hills U.K. 49 E7
Mendocino U.S.A. 128 B2
Mendocino, Cape U.S.A. 128 A1
Mendocino, Lake U.S.A. 128 B2
Mendooran Australia 112 D3
Mendota CA U.S.A. 128 C3
Mendota IL U.S.A. 130 F3
Mendoza Arg. 144 C4
Menemen Turkey 59 L5
Ménerville Alg. see Thenia
Mengban China 76 D4
Mengcheng China 77 H1
Menghai China 76 D4
Mengjin China 77 G1
Mengla China 76 D4
Menglang China see Lancang
Menglie China see Jiangcheng
Mengyang China see Mingshan
Mengzi China 76 D4
Menihek Canada 123 I3
Menihek Lakes Canada 123 I3
Menindee Australia 111 C7
Menindee, Lake Australia 111 C7
Ménistouc, Lac l. Canada 123 I3
Menkere Rus. Fed. 65 N3
Mennecy France 52 C6
Menominee U.S.A. 134 B1
Menomonee Falls U.S.A. 134 A2
Menomonie U.S.A. 130 F2
Menongue Angola 99 B5
Menorca i. Spain see Minorca
Mentawai, Kepulauan is Indon. 68 B7
Mentawai, Selat sea chan. Indon. 68 C7
Menteroda Germany 53 K3
Mentmore U.S.A. 129 I4
Menton France 56 H5
Mentone U.S.A. 131 C6
Menuf Egypt see Minūf
Menzel Bourguiba Tunisia 58 C6
Menzelet Barajı resr Turkey 90 E3
Menzelinsk Rus. Fed. 41 Q4
Menzel Temime Tunisia 58 D6
Menzies Australia 109 C7
Menzies, Mount Antarctica 152 E2
Meobbaai b. Namibia 100 B3
Meoqui Mex. 131 B6
Meppel Neth. 52 G2
Meppen Germany 53 H2
Mepuze Moz. 101 K2
Meqheleng S. Africa 101 H5
Mequon U.S.A. 134 B2
Merak Indon. 68 D8
Meråker Norway 44 G5
Merano Italy 58 D1
Meratswe r. Botswana 100 G2
Merauke Indon. 69 K8
Merca Somalia see Marka
Mercantour, Parc National du nat. park France 56 H4
Merced U.S.A. 128 C3
Merced r. U.S.A. 128 C3
Mercedes Arg. 144 E3
Mercedes Uruguay 144 E4
Mercer ME U.S.A. 135 K1
Mercer PA U.S.A. 134 E3
Mercer WI U.S.A. 130 F2
Mercês Brazil 145 C3
Mercury Islands N.Z. 113 E3
Mercy, Cape Canada 119 L3
Merdenik Turkey see Göle
Mere Belgium 52 D4
Mere U.K. 49 E7
Meredith U.S.A. 135 J2
Meredith, Lake U.S.A. 131 C5
Merefa Ukr. 43 H6
Merga Oasis Sudan 86 C6

Mergui Myanmar see Myeik
Mergui Archipelago is Myanmar 71 B5
Meriç r. Turkey 59 L4
also known as Evros (Greece), Marica, Maritsa (Bulgaria)
Mérida Mex. 136 G4
Mérida Spain 57 C4
Mérida Venez. 142 D2
Mérida, Cordillera de mts Venez. 142 D2
Meriden U.S.A. 135 I3
Meridian MS U.S.A. 131 F5
Meridian TX U.S.A. 131 D6
Mérignac France 56 D4
Merijärvi Fin. 44 N4
Merikarvia Fin. 45 L6
Merimbula Australia 112 D6
Merín, Laguna l. Brazil/Uruguay see Mirim, Lagoa
Meringur Australia 111 C7
Merir i. Palau 69 I6
Merjayoun Lebanon see Marjayoûn
Merkel U.S.A. 131 C5
Merluna Australia 110 C2
Mermaid Reef Australia 108 B4
Meron, Har mt. Israel 85 B3
Merowe Sudan 86 D6
Mêrqung Co l. China 83 F3
Merredin Australia 109 B7
Merrick hill U.K. 50 E5
Merrickville Canada 135 H1
Merrill MI U.S.A. 134 C2
Merrill WI U.S.A. 130 F2
Merrill, Mount Canada 120 E2
Merrillville U.S.A. 134 B3
Merriman U.S.A. 130 C3
Merritt Canada 120 F5
Merritt Island U.S.A. 133 D6
Merriwa Australia 112 E4
Merrygoen Australia 112 D3
Mersa Fatma Eritrea 86 F7
Mersa Maṭrûḥ Egypt see Marsá Maṭrūḥ
Mersch Lux. 52 G5
Merseburg (Saale) Germany 53 L3
Mersey est. U.K. 48 E5
Mersin Turkey 85 B1
Mersin prov. Turkey 85 A1
Mersing Malaysia 71 C7
Mērsrags Latvia 45 M8
Merta India 82 C4
Merthyr Tydfil U.K. 49 D7
Mértola Port. 57 C5
Mertz Glacier Antarctica 152 G2
Mertz Glacier Tongue Antarctica 152 G2
Mertzon U.S.A. 131 C6
Méru France 52 C5

▶Meru vol. Tanz. 98 D4
4th highest mountain, and highest active volcano, in Africa.

Merui Pak. 89 F4
Merv Turkm. see Mary
Merweville S. Africa 100 E7
Merzifon Turkey 90 D2
Merzig Germany 52 G5
Merz Peninsula Antarctica 152 L2
Mesa AZ U.S.A. 129 H5
Mesa NM U.S.A. 127 G6
Mesabi Range hills U.S.A. 130 E2
Mesagne Italy 58 G4
Mesa Negra mt. U.S.A. 129 J4
Mesara, Ormos b. Kriti Greece see Kolpos Messaras
Mesara, Ormos b. Kriti Greece see Kolpos Messaras
Mesa Verde National Park U.S.A. 129 I3
Meschede Germany 53 I3
Mese Myanmar 70 B3
Meselefors Sweden 44 J4
Mesgouez, Lac Canada 122 G4
Meshed Iran see Mashhad
Meshkān Iran 88 E2
Meshra'er Req Sudan 86 C8
Mesick U.S.A. 134 C1
Mesimeri Greece 59 J4
Mesolongi Greece 59 I5
Mesolóngion Greece see Mesolongi
Mesopotamia reg. Iraq 91 F4
Mesquita Brazil 145 C2
Mesquite NV U.S.A. 129 F3
Mesquite TX U.S.A. 131 D5
Mesquite Lake U.S.A. 129 F4
Messaad Alg. 54 E5
Messana Sicily Italy see Messina
Messina Sicily Italy 58 F5
Messina, Strait of Italy 58 F5
Messina, Stretta di Italy see Messina, Strait of
Messini Greece 59 J6
Messiniakos Kolpos b. Greece 59 J6
Mesta r. Bulg. 59 K4
Mesta r. Greece see Nestos
Mesta, Akrotirio pt Greece 59 K5
Mestghanem Alg. see Mostaganem
Mestlin Germany 53 L1
Meston, Akra pt Voreio Aigaio Greece see Mesta, Akrotirio
Mestre Italy 58 E2
Mesudiye Turkey 90 E2
Meta r. Col./Venez. 142 E2
Métabetchouan Canada 123 H4
Meta Incognita Peninsula Canada 119 L3
Metairie U.S.A. 131 F6
Metallifere, Colline mts Italy 58 D3
Metán Arg. 144 C3
Meteghan Canada 123 I5
Meteor Depth sea feature S. Atlantic Ocean 148 G9
Methoni Greece 59 I6
Methuen U.S.A. 135 J2
Methven U.K. 50 F4
Metionga Lake Canada 122 C4
Metković Croatia 58 G3
Metlaoui Tunisia 54 F5
Metoro Moz. 99 D5
Metro Indon. 68 D8
Metropolis U.S.A. 131 F4
Metsada tourist site Israel see Masada
Metter U.S.A. 133 D5
Mettet Belgium 52 E4
Mettingen Germany 53 H2
Mettler U.S.A. 128 D4

Mettur India 84 C4
Metu Eth. 98 D3
Metz France 52 G5
Metz U.S.A. 134 C3
Meulaboh Indon. 71 B6
Meureudu Indon. 71 B6
Meuse r. Belgium/France 52 F3
also known as Maas (Netherlands)
Meuselwitz Germany 53 M3
Mevagissey U.K. 49 C8
Mêwa China 76 D1
Mexia U.S.A. 131 D6
Mexiana, Ilha i. Brazil 143 I3
Mexicali Mex. 129 F5
Mexican Hat U.S.A. 129 I3
Mexicanos, Lago de los l. Mex. 127 G7
Mexican Water U.S.A. 129 I3

▶Mexico country Central America 136 D4
2nd most populous and 3rd largest country in North America.

México Mex. see Mexico City
Mexico ME U.S.A. 135 J1
Mexico MO U.S.A. 130 F4
Mexico NY U.S.A. 135 G2
Mexico, Gulf of Mex./U.S.A. 125 H6

▶Mexico City Mex. 136 E5
Capital of Mexico. Most populous city in North America, and 2nd in the world.

Meybod Iran 88 D3
Meydanī, Ra's-e pt Iran 88 E5
Meydān Shahr Afgh. 89 H3
Meyenburg Germany 53 M1
Meyersdale U.S.A. 134 F4
Meymeh Iran 88 C3
Meynypil'gyno Rus. Fed. 153 C2
Mezada tourist site Israel see Masada
Mezdra Bulg. 59 J3
Mezen' Rus. Fed. 42 J2
Mezen' r. Rus. Fed. 42 J2
Mézenc, Mont mt. France 56 G4
Mezenskaya Guba b. Rus. Fed. 42 I2
Mezhdurechensk Kemerovskaya Oblast' Rus. Fed. 72 F2
Mezhdurechensk Respublika Komi Rus. Fed. 42 K3
Mezhdurechnye Rus. Fed. see Shali
Mezhdusharskiy, Ostrov i. Rus. Fed. 64 G2
Mezitli Turkey 85 B1
Mezőtúr Hungary 59 I1
Mežvidi Latvia 45 O8
Mhàil, Rubh' a' pt U.K. 50 C5
Mhangura Zimbabwe 99 D5
Mhlume Swaziland 101 J4
Mhow India 82 C5
Mi r. Myanmar 83 H5
Miahuatlán Mex. 136 E5
Miajadas Spain 57 D4
Miaméré Cent. Afr. Rep. 98 B3
Miami AZ U.S.A. 129 H5

▶Miami FL U.S.A. 133 D7
5th most populous city in North America.

Miami OK U.S.A. 131 E4
Miami Beach U.S.A. 133 D7
Miancaowan China 76 C1
Mīāndehī Iran 88 E3
Mīāndowāb Iran 88 B2
Miandrivazo Madag. 99 E5
Mīāneh Iran 88 B2
Miang, Phu mt. Thai. 70 C3
Miani India 89 I4
Miani Hor b. Pak. 89 G5
Mianjoi Afgh. 89 G3
Mianning China 76 D2
Mianwali Pak. 89 H3
Mianxian China 76 E1
Mianyang Hubei China see Xiantao
Mianyang Shaanxi China see Mianxian
Mianyang Sichuan China 76 E2
Mianzhu China 76 E2
Miaoli Taiwan 77 I3
Miarinarivo Madag. 99 E5
Miarritze France see Biarritz
Miass Rus. Fed. 64 H4
Mica Creek Canada 120 G4
Mica Mountain U.S.A. 129 H5
Micang Shan mts China 76 E1
Michalovce Slovakia 43 D6
Michel Canada 121 I4
Michelau in Oberfranken Germany 53 L4
Michelson, Mount U.S.A. 118 D3
Michelstadt Germany 53 J5
Michendorf Germany 53 N2
Micheng China see Midu
Michigan state U.S.A. 134 C2

▶Michigan, Lake U.S.A. 134 B2
3rd largest lake in North America, and 5th in the world.

Michigan City U.S.A. 134 B3
Michinberi India 84 D2
Michipicoten Bay Canada 122 D5
Michipicoten Island Canada 122 D5
Michipicoten River Canada 122 D5
Michurin Bulg. see Tsarevo
Michurinsk Rus. Fed. 43 I5
Micronesia country N. Pacific Ocean see Micronesia, Federated States of
Micronesia is Pacific Ocean 150 F5
Micronesia, Federated States of country N. Pacific Ocean 150 G5
Midai i. Indon. 71 D7
Mid-Atlantic Ridge sea feature Atlantic Ocean 148 E4
Mid-Atlantic Ridge sea feature Atlantic Ocean 148 G8
Middelburg Neth. 52 D3
Middelburg E. Cape S. Africa 101 G6
Middelburg Mpumalanga S. Africa 101 I3
Middelfart Denmark 45 F9
Middelharnis Neth. 52 E3
Middelwit S. Africa 101 H3
Middle Alkali Lake U.S.A. 126 C4

Middle America Trench sea feature N. Pacific Ocean 151 N5
Middle Andaman i. India 71 A4
Middle Atlas mts Morocco see Moyen Atlas
Middle Bay Canada 123 K4
Middlebourne U.S.A. 134 E4
Middleburg U.S.A. 135 G3
Middleburgh U.S.A. 135 H2
Middlebury IN U.S.A. 134 C3
Middlebury VT U.S.A. 135 I1
Middle Caicos i. Turks and Caicos Is 133 G8
Middle Concho r. U.S.A. 131 C6
Middle Congo country Africa see Congo
Middle Island Thai. see Tasai, Ko
Middle Loup r. U.S.A. 130 D3
Middlemarch N.Z. 113 C7
Middlemount Australia 110 E4
Middle River U.S.A. 135 G4
Middlesbrough U.K. 48 F4
Middle Strait India see Andaman Strait
Middleton Australia 110 C4
Middleton Canada 123 I5
Middleton Island atoll American Samoa see Rose Island
Middletown CA U.S.A. 128 B2
Middletown CT U.S.A. 135 I3
Middletown NY U.S.A. 135 H3
Middletown VA U.S.A. 135 F4
Midelt Morocco 54 D5
Midhurst U.K. 49 G8
Midi, Canal du France 56 F5
Mid-Indian Basin sea feature Indian Ocean 149 N6
Mid-Indian Ridge sea feature Indian Ocean 149 M7
Midland Canada 135 F1
Midland CA U.S.A. 129 F5
Midland IN U.S.A. 134 B4
Midland MI U.S.A. 134 C2
Midland SD U.S.A. 130 C2
Midland TX U.S.A. 131 C5
Midleton Ireland 51 D6
Midnapore India see Medinipur
Midnapur India see Medinipur
Midongy Atsimo Madag. 99 E6
Mid-Pacific Mountains sea feature N. Pacific Ocean 150 G4
Midu China 76 D3
Miðvágur Faroe Is 44 [inset]
Midway Oman see Thamarīt

▶Midway Islands terr. N. Pacific Ocean 150 I4
United States Unincorporated Territory.

Midway Well Australia 109 C5
Midwest U.S.A. 126 G4
Midwest City U.S.A. 131 D5
Midwoud Neth. 52 F2
Midyat Turkey 91 F3
Midye Turkey see Kıyıköy
Mid Yell U.K. 50 [inset]
Midzhur mt. Bulg./Serbia 90 A2
Miehikkälä Fin. 45 O6
Miekojärvi l. Fin. 44 N3
Mielec Poland 43 D6
Mienhua Yü i. Taiwan 77 I3
Mieraslompolo Fin. 44 O2
Mierašluoppal Fin. see Mieraslompolo
Miercurea-Ciuc Romania 59 K1
Mieres Spain 57 D2
Mieres del Camín Spain see Mieres
Mī'ēso Eth. 98 E3
Mieste Germany 53 L2
Mifflinburg U.S.A. 135 G3
Mifflintown U.S.A. 135 G3
Migang Shan mt. China 76 E1
Migdol S. Africa 101 G4
Miging India 76 B2
Migriggyangzham Co l. China 83 G2
Miguel Auza Mex. 131 C7
Miguel Hidalgo, Presa resr Mex. 127 F8
Mihalıççık Turkey 59 N5
Mihara Japan 75 D6
Mihintale Sri Lanka 84 D4
Mihmandar Turkey 85 B1
Mijares r. Spain see Millárs
Mijdrecht Neth. 52 E2
Mikhaylov Rus. Fed. 43 H5
Mikhaylovgrad Bulg. see Montana
Mikhaylov Island Antarctica 152 E2
Mikhaylovka Amurskaya Oblast' Rus. Fed. 74 C2
Mikhaylovka Primorskiy Kray Rus. Fed. 74 D4
Mikhaylovka Tul'skaya Oblast' Rus. Fed. see Kimovsk
Mikhaylovka Volgogradskaya Oblast' Rus. Fed. 43 I6
Mikhaylovskiy Rus. Fed. 80 E1
Mikhaylovskoye Rus. Fed. see Shpakovskoye
Mikhrot Timna Israel 85 B5
Mikir Hills India 83 H4
Mikkeli Fin. 45 O6
Mikkelin mlk Fin. 45 O6
Mikkwa r. Canada 120 H3
Mikonos i. Greece see Mykonos
Mikoyan Armenia see Yeghegnadzor
Mikulkin, Mys c. Rus. Fed. 42 J2
Mikumi National Park Tanz. 99 D4
Mikun' Rus. Fed. 42 K3
Mikuni-sanmyaku mts Japan 75 E5
Mikura-jima i. Japan 75 E6
Milaca U.S.A. 130 E2
Miladhunmadulu Atoll Maldives 84 B5
Miladummadulu Atoll Maldives see Miladhunmadulu Atoll
Milan Italy 58 C2
Milan MI U.S.A. 134 D2
Milan MO U.S.A. 130 E3
Milan OH U.S.A. 134 D3
Milange Moz. 99 D5
Milano Italy see Milan
Milas Turkey 59 L6
Milazzo Sicily Italy 58 F5
Milazzo, Capo di c. Sicily Italy 58 F5
Milbank U.S.A. 130 D2
Milbridge U.S.A. 132 H2
Milde r. Germany 53 L2

Mildenhall U.K. 49 H6
Mildura Australia 111 C7
Mile China 76 D3
Mileiz, Wâdi el watercourse Egypt see Mulayz, Wādī al
Miles Australia 112 E1
Miles City U.S.A. 126 G3
Milestone Ireland 51 D5
Miletto, Monte mt. Italy 58 F4
Mileura Australia 109 B6
Milford Ireland 51 E2
Milford DE U.S.A. 135 H4
Milford IL U.S.A. 134 B3
Milford MA U.S.A. 135 J2
Milford MI U.S.A. 134 D2
Milford NE U.S.A. 130 D3
Milford NH U.S.A. 135 J2
Milford PA U.S.A. 135 H3
Milford UT U.S.A. 129 G2
Milford VA U.S.A. 135 G4
Milford Haven U.K. 49 B7
Milford Sound N.Z. 113 A7
Milford Sound inlet N.Z. 113 A7
Milgarra Australia 110 C3
Milḥ, Baḥr al l. Iraq see Razāzah, Buḥayrat ar
Miliana Alg. 57 H5
Milid Turkey see Malatya
Milikapiti Australia 108 E2
Miling Australia 109 B7
Milk r. U.S.A. 126 G2
Milk, Wadi el watercourse Sudan 86 D6
Mil'kovo Rus. Fed. 65 Q4
Millaa Millaa Australia 110 D3
Millárs r. Spain 57 F4
Millau France 56 F4
Millbrook Canada 135 F1
Mill Creek r. U.S.A. 128 B1
Milledgeville U.S.A. 133 D5
Mille Lacs lakes U.S.A. 130 E2
Mille Lacs, Lac des l. Canada 119 I5
Millen U.S.A. 133 D5
Millennium Island atoll Kiribati see Caroline Island
Miller U.S.A. 130 D2
Miller Lake Canada 134 E1
Millerovo Rus. Fed. 43 I6
Millersburg OH U.S.A. 134 E3
Millersburg PA U.S.A. 135 G3
Millers Creek U.S.A. 134 D5
Millersville U.S.A. 135 G4
Millerton Lake U.S.A. 128 D3
Millet Canada 120 H4
Milleur Point U.K. 50 D5
Mill Hall U.S.A. 135 G3
Millicent Australia 111 C8
Millington MI U.S.A. 134 D2
Millington TN U.S.A. 131 F5
Millinocket U.S.A. 132 G2
Mill Island Canada 119 K3
Millmerran Australia 112 E1
Millom U.K. 48 D4
Millport U.K. 50 E5
Millsboro U.S.A. 135 H4
Mills Creek watercourse Australia 110 C4
Mills Lake Canada 120 G2
Millstone KY U.S.A. 134 D5
Millstone WV U.S.A. 134 E4
Millstream-Chichester National Park Australia 108 B5
Millthorpe Australia 112 D4
Milltown Canada 123 I5
Milltown U.S.A. 126 E3
Milltown Malbay Ireland 51 C5
Millungera Australia 110 C3
Millville U.S.A. 135 H4
Millwood U.S.A. 134 B5
Millwood Lake U.S.A. 131 E5
Milly Milly Australia 109 B6
Milne Land i. Greenland see Ilimananngip Nunaa
Milner U.S.A. 129 J1
Milo r. Guinea 96 C3
Milogradovo Rus. Fed. 74 D4
Miloli'i U.S.A. 127 [inset]
Milos i. Greece 59 K6
Milparinka Australia 111 C6
Milpitas U.S.A. 128 C3
Milroy U.S.A. 135 G3
Milton N.Z. 113 B8
Milton DE U.S.A. 135 H4
Milton NH U.S.A. 135 J2
Milton WV U.S.A. 134 D4
Milton Keynes U.K. 49 G6
Miluo China 77 G2
Milverton Canada 134 E2
Milwaukee U.S.A. 134 B2

▶Milwaukee Deep sea feature Caribbean Sea 148 D4
Deepest point in the Puerto Rico Trench and in the Atlantic.

Mimbres watercourse U.S.A. 129 J5
Mimili Australia 109 F6
Mimisal India 84 C4
Mimizan France 56 D4
Mimongo Gabon 98 B4
Mimosa Rocks National Park Australia 112 E6
Mina Mex. 131 C7
Mina U.S.A. 128 D2
Mīnāb Iran 88 E5
Minaçu Brazil 145 A1
Minahasa, Semenanjung pen. Indon. 69 G6
Minahassa Peninsula Indon. see Minahasa, Semenanjung
Minaker Canada see Prophet River
Mīnakh Syria 85 C1
Minaki Canada 121 M5
Minamia Australia 108 F3
Minami-Daitō-jima i. Japan 73 O7
Minami-lō-jima vol. Japan 69 K2
Min'an China see Longshan
Minaret of Jam tourist site Afgh. 89 G3
Minas Indon. 71 C7
Minas Uruguay 144 E4
Minas de Matahambre Cuba 133 D8
Minas Gerais state Brazil 145 B2
Minas Novas Brazil 145 C2
Minatitlán Mex. 136 F5
Minbu Myanmar 70 A2
Minbya Myanmar 70 A2
Minchinmávida vol. Chile 144 B6
Mindanao i. Phil. 69 H5
Mindanao Trench sea feature N. Pacific Ocean see Philippine Trench
Mindelo Cape Verde 96 [inset]
Minden Canada 135 F1
Minden Germany 53 I2
Minden LA U.S.A. 131 E5
Minden NE U.S.A. 124 H3
Minden NV U.S.A. 128 D2
Mindon Myanmar 70 A3
Mindoro i. Phil. 69 G4
Mindoro Strait Phil. 69 F4
Mindouli Congo 98 B4
Mine Head hd Ireland 51 E6
Minehead U.K. 49 D7
Mineola U.S.A. 135 I3
Mineral U.S.A. 135 G4
Mineral'nyye Vody Rus. Fed. 91 F1
Mineral Wells U.S.A. 131 D5
Mineralwells U.S.A. 134 E4
Minersville PA U.S.A. 135 G3
Minersville UT U.S.A. 129 G2
Minerva U.S.A. 134 E3
Minerva Reefs Fiji 107 I4
Minfeng China 83 E1
Minga Dem. Rep. Congo 99 C5
Mingäçevir Azer. 91 G2
Mingäçevir Su Anbarı resr Azer. 91 G2
Mingala Cent. Afr. Rep. 98 C3
Mingan, Îles de is Canada 123 J4
Mingan Archipelago National Park Reserve Canada see L'Archipélago de Mingan, Réserve du Parc National de
Mingbuloq Uzbek. 80 B3
Mingechaur Azer. see Mingäçevir
Mingechaurskoye Vodokhranilishche resr Azer. see Mingäçevir Su Anbarı
Mingenew Australia 109 A7
Mingfeng China see Yuan'an
Minggang China 77 G1
Mingguang China 77 H1
Mingin Range mts Myanmar 70 A2
Minglanilla Spain 57 F4
Mingoyo Tanz. 99 D5
Mingshan China 76 D2
Mingshui Gansu China 80 I3
Mingshui Heilong. China 74 B3
Mingteke China 82 C1
Mingulay i. U.K. 50 B4
Mingxi China 77 H3
Mingzhou China see Suide
Minhe China see Jinxian
Minhla Magwe Myanmar 70 A3
Minhla Pegu Myanmar 70 A3
Minho r. Port./Spain see Miño
Minicoy atoll India 84 B4
Minigwal, Lake salt flat Australia 109 C7
Minilya Australia 109 A5
Minilya r. Australia 109 A5
Minipi Lake Canada 123 J3
Miniss Lake Canada 121 N5
Minitonas Canada 121 K4
Minjian China see Mabian
Min Jiang r. Sichuan China 76 E2
Min Jiang r. China 77 H3
Minna Nigeria 96 D4
Minna Bluff pt Antarctica 152 H1
Minne Sweden 44 I5
Minneapolis KS U.S.A. 130 D4
Minneapolis MN U.S.A. 130 E2
Minnedosa Canada 121 L5
Minnehaha Springs U.S.A. 134 F4
Minneola U.S.A. 131 C4
Minnesota r. U.S.A. 130 E2
Minnesota state U.S.A. 130 E2
Minnewaukan U.S.A. 130 D1
Minnitaki Lake Canada 121 N5
Miño r. Port./Spain 57 B3
also known as Minho
Minorca i. Spain 57 H3
Minot U.S.A. 130 C1
Minqār, Ghadīr imp. l. Syria 85 C3
Minqing China 77 H3
Minquan China 77 G1
Min Shan mts China 76 D1
Minsin Myanmar 70 A1

▶Minsk Belarus 45 O10
Capital of Belarus.

Mińsk Mazowiecki Poland 47 R4
Minsterley U.K. 49 E6
Mintaka Pass China/Pakistan 82 C1
Minto, Lac l. Canada 122 G2
Minto, Mount Antarctica 152 H2
Minto Inlet Canada 118 G2
Minton Canada 121 J5
Mīnudasht Iran 88 D2
Minūf Egypt 90 C5
Minusinsk Rus. Fed. 72 G2
Minvoul Gabon 98 B3
Minxian China 76 E1
Minya Konka mt. China see Gongga Shan
Minywa Myanmar 70 A2
Minzong India 83 I4
Mio U.S.A. 134 C1
Miquelon Canada 122 F4
Miquelon i. St Pierre and Miquelon 123 K5
Mirabad Afgh. 89 F4
Mirabela Brazil 145 B2
Mirador, Parque Nacional de nat. park Brazil 143 I5
Mīrah, Wādī al watercourse Iraq/Saudi Arabia 91 F4
Miraí Brazil 145 C3
Miraj India 84 B2
Miramar Arg. 144 E5
Miramichi Canada 123 I5
Miramichi Bay Canada 123 I5
Mirampelou, Kolpos b. Greece 59 K7
Mirampelou, Kolpos b. Kriti Greece see Mirampellou, Kolpos
Miranda Brazil 144 E2
Miranda Moz. see Macaloge
Miranda U.S.A. 128 B1
Miranda, Lake salt flat Australia 109 C6
Miranda de Ebro Spain 57 E2
Mirandela Port. 57 C3
Mirandola Italy 58 D2
Mirante Brazil 145 C1
Mirante, Serra do hills Brazil 145 A3
Mirassol Brazil 145 A3
Mir-Bashir Azer. see Tärtär
Mirbāṭ Oman 87 H6
Mirboo North Australia 112 C7
Mirepoix France 56 E5
Mirgarh Pak. 89 I4
Mirgorod Ukr. see Myrhorod
Miri Sarawak Malaysia 68 E6
Miri mt. Pak. 89 F4
Mirialguda India 84 C2
Miri Hills India 83 H4
Mirim, Lagoa l. Brazil/Uruguay 144 F4
Mirim, Lagoa do l. Brazil 145 A5
Mirintu watercourse Australia 112 A2
Mirjan India 84 B3
Mirny research station Antarctica 152 F2
Mirnyy Arkhangel'skaya Oblast' Rus. Fed. 42 I3
Mirnyy Respublika Sakha (Yakutiya) Rus. Fed. 65 M3
Mirond Lake Canada 121 K4
Mironovka Ukr. see Myronivka
Mirow Germany 53 M1
Mirpur Khas Pak. 89 H5
Mirpur Sakro Pak. 89 G5
Mirs Bay H.K. China 77 [inset]
Mirtoan Sea Greece see Myrtoo Pelagos
Mirtoö Pelagos sea Greece see Myrtoo Pelagos
Miryalaguda India see Mirialguda
Miryang S. Korea 75 C6
Mirzachirla Turkm. see Murzechirla
Mirzachul Uzbek. see Guliston
Mirzapur India 83 E4
Mirzawal India 82 C3
Misaw Lake Canada 121 K3
Miscou Island Canada 123 I5
Misehkow r. Canada 122 C4
Mīsh, Kūh-e hill Iran 88 E3
Misha India 71 A6
Mishāsh al Ashāwī well Saudi Arabia 88 C5
Mishāsh az̧ Zuayyinī well Saudi Arabia 88 C5
Mishawaka U.S.A. 134 B3
Mishicot U.S.A. 134 B1
Mi-shima i. Japan 75 C6
Mishmi Hills India 83 H3
Mishvan' Rus. Fed. 42 L2
Misima Island P.N.G. 110 F1
Misis Dağ hills Turkey 85 B1
Miskin Oman 88 E6
Miskitos, Cayos is Nicaragua 137 H6
Miskolc Hungary 43 D6
Mismā, Tall al hill Jordan 85 C3
Misoöl i. Indon. 69 I7
Misquah Hills U.S.A. 130 F2
Misr country Africa see Egypt
Misraç Turkey see Kurtalan
Miṣrātah Libya 97 E1
Missinaibi r. Canada 122 E4
Mission Beach Australia 110 D3
Mission Viejo U.S.A. 128 E5
Missisa r. Canada 122 D3
Missisa Lake Canada 122 D3
Missisicabi r. Canada 122 F4
Mississauga Canada 134 F2
Mississinewa Lake U.S.A. 134 C3

▶Mississippi r. U.S.A. 131 F6
4th longest river in North America, and a major part of the longest (Mississippi-Missouri).

Mississippi state U.S.A. 131 F5
Mississippi Delta U.S.A. 131 F6
Mississippi Lake Canada 135 G1

▶Mississippi-Missouri r. U.S.A. 125 I4
Longest river in North America, and 4th in the world.

Mississippi Sound sea chan. U.S.A. 131 F6
Missolonghi Greece see Mesolongi
Missoula U.S.A. 126 E3

▶Missouri r. U.S.A. 130 F4
3rd longest river in North America, and a major part of the longest (Mississippi-Missouri).

Missouri state U.S.A. 130 E4
Mistanipisipou r. Canada 123 J4
Mistassibi r. Canada 119 K5
Mistassini r. Canada 123 G4
Mistassini, Lac l. Canada 122 G4
Mistastin Lake Canada 123 J3
Mistelbach Austria 47 P6
Mistinibi, Lac l. Canada 123 J2
Mistissini Canada 122 G4
Misty Fiords National Monument Wilderness nat. park U.S.A. 120 D4
Misumba Dem. Rep. Congo 99 C4
Misuratah Libya see Miṣrātah
Mitchell Australia 111 D5
Mitchell r. N.S.W. Australia 112 F2
Mitchell r. Qld Australia 110 C2
Mitchell r. Vic. Australia 112 C6
Mitchell Canada 134 E2
Mitchell IN U.S.A. 134 B4
Mitchell OR U.S.A. 126 C3
Mitchell SD U.S.A. 130 D3
Mitchell, Lake Australia 110 D3
Mitchell, Mount U.S.A. 132 D5
Mitchell and Alice Rivers National Park Australia 110 C2
Mitchell Island Cook Is see Nassau
Mitchell Island atoll Tuvalu see Nukulaelae
Mitchell Point Australia 108 E2
Mitchelstown Ireland 51 D5
Mīt Ghamr Egypt 90 C5
Mīt Ghamr Egypt see Mīt Ghamr
Mithi Pak. 89 H5
Mithrau Pak. 89 H5
Mithri Pak. 89 G4
Mitilíni Greece see Mytilini
Mitkof Island U.S.A. 120 C3
Mito Japan 75 F5
Mitole Tanz. 99 D4
Mitre mt. N.Z. 113 E5
Mitre Island Solomon Is 107 H3
Mitrofanovka Rus. Fed. 43 H6
Mitrovica Kosovo see Mitrovicë
Mitrovicë Kosovo 59 I3
Mitsinjo Madag. 99 E5
Mits'iwa Eritrea see Massawa
Mitta Mitta Australia 112 C6
Mittellandkanal canal Germany 53 I2
Mitterteich Germany 53 M5
Mittimatalik Canada see Pond Inlet
Mittweida Germany 53 M4
Mitú Col. 142 D3
Mitumba, Chaîne des mts Dem. Rep. Congo 99 C5
Mitzic Gabon 98 B3
Miughalaigh i. U.K. see Mingulay
Miura Japan 75 E6
Mixian China see Xinmi
Miyake-jima i. Japan 75 E6
Miyako Japan 75 F5
Miyakonojō Japan 75 C7
Miyang China see Mile
Miyani India 82 B5
Miyazaki Japan 75 C7
Miyazu Japan 75 D6
Miyi China 76 D3
Miyoshi Japan 75 D6
Mīzāni Afgh. 89 G3
Mīzan Teferī Eth. 98 D3
Mizdah Libya 97 E1
Mizen Head hd Ireland 51 C6
Mizhhir"ya Ukr. 43 D6
Mizo Hills state India see Mizoram
Mizoram state India 83 H5
Miẓpé Ramon Israel 85 B4
Mizusawa Japan 75 F5
Mjölby Sweden 45 I7
Mkata Tanz. 99 D4
Mkushi Zambia 99 C5
Mladá Boleslav Czech Rep. 47 O5
Mladenovac Serbia 59 I2
Mława Poland 47 R4
Mlilwane Nature Reserve Swaziland 101 J4
Mljet i. Croatia 58 G3
Mlungisi S. Africa 101 H6
Mmabatho S. Africa 101 G3
Mmamabula Botswana 101 H2
Mmathethe Botswana 101 G3
Mo Norway 45 D6
Moa i. Indon. 108 E2
Moab reg. Jordan 85 B4
Moab U.S.A. 129 I2
Moa Island Australia 110 C1
Moala i. Fiji 107 H3
Mo'alla Iran 88 D3
Moamba Moz. 101 K3
Moanda Gabon 98 B4
Moapa U.S.A. 129 F3
Moate Ireland 51 E4
Mobārakeh Iran 88 C3
Mobayembongo Dem. Rep. Congo see Mobayi-Mbongo
Mobayi-Mbongo Dem. Rep. Congo 98 C3
Moberly U.S.A. 130 E4
Moberly Lake Canada 120 F4
Mobha India 82 C5
Mobile AL U.S.A. 131 F6
Mobile AZ U.S.A. 129 G5
Mobile Bay U.S.A. 131 F6
Mobile watercourse Australia 112 B1
Mobridge U.S.A. 130 C2
Mobutu, Lake Dem. Rep. Congo/Uganda see Albert, Lake
Mobutu Sese Seko, Lake Dem. Rep. Congo/Uganda see Albert, Lake
Moca Geçidi pass Turkey 85 A1
Moçambique country Africa see Mozambique
Moçambique Moz. 99 E5
Moçâmedes Angola see Namibe
Môc Châu Vietnam 70 D2
Mocha Yemen 86 F7
Mocha, Isla i. Chile 144 B5
Mochirma, Parque Nacional nat. park Venez. 142 F1
Mochudi Botswana 101 H3
Mochudi admin. dist. Botswana see Kgatleng
Mocimboa da Praia Moz. 99 E5
Möckern Germany 53 L2
Möckmühl Germany 53 J5
Mockträsk Sweden 44 L4
Mocoa Col. 142 C3
Mococa Brazil 145 B3
Mocoduene Moz. 101 L2
Mocorito Mex. 127 G8
Moctezuma Chihuahua Mex. 127 G7
Moctezuma San Luis Potosí Mex. 136 D4
Moctezuma Sonora Mex. 127 F7
Mocuba Moz. 99 D5
Mocun China 77 G4
Modan Indon. 69 I7
Modane France 56 H4
Modder r. S. Africa 101 G5
Modena Italy 58 D2
Modena U.S.A. 129 G3
Modesto U.S.A. 128 C3
Modesto Lake U.S.A. 128 C3
Modimolle S. Africa 101 I3
Modung China 76 C2
Moe Australia 112 C7
Moel Sych hill U.K. 49 D6
Moelv Norway 45 G6
Moen Norway 44 K2
Moenkopi U.S.A. 129 H3
Moenkopi Wash r. U.S.A. 129 H4
Moeraki Point N.Z. 113 C7
Moero, Lake Dem. Rep. Congo/Zambia see Mweru, Lake
Moers Germany 52 G3
Moffat U.K. 50 F5
Moga India 82 C3

▶Mogadishu Somalia 98 E3
Capital of Somalia.

Mogador Morocco see Essaouira
Mogadore Reservoir U.S.A. 134 E3
Moganyaka S. Africa 101 I3
Mogaung Myanmar 70 B1
Mogdy Rus. Fed. 74 D2
Mögelin Germany 53 M2
Mogilev Belarus see Mahilyow
Mogilev Podol'skiy Ukr. see Mohyliv Podil's'kyy
Mogi-Mirim Brazil 145 B3
Mogiquiçaba Brazil 145 D2
Mogocha Rus. Fed. 73 L2
Mogod mts Tunisia 58 C6
Mogoditshane Botswana 101 G3
Mogollon Mountains U.S.A. 129 I5
Mogollon Plateau U.S.A. 129 H4
Mogontiacum Germany see Mainz
Mogroum Chad 97 E3
Moguqi China 74 A3
Mogwadi S. Africa 101 I2
Mogwase S. Africa 101 H3
Mogzon Rus. Fed. 73 K2
Mohács Hungary 58 H2
Mohaka r. N.Z. 113 F4
Mohala India 84 D1
Mohale Dam Lesotho 101 I5
Mohale's Hoek Lesotho 101 H6
Mohall U.S.A. 130 C1
Mohammad Iran 88 E3
Mohammadia Alg. 57 G6
Mohan r. India/Nepal 82 E3
Mohana India 82 D4
Mohave, Lake U.S.A. 129 F4
Mohawk r. U.S.A. 135 I2
Mohawk Mountains U.S.A. 129 G5
Mohenjo Daro tourist site Pak. 89 H5
Moher, Cliffs of Ireland 51 C5
Mohill Ireland 51 E4
Möhne r. Germany 53 H3
Möhnetalsperre resr Germany 53 I3
Mohon Peak U.S.A. 129 G4
Mohoro Tanz. 99 D4
Mohyliv Podil's'kyy Ukr. 43 E6
Moi Norway 45 E7
Moijabana Botswana 101 H2
Moincêr China 82 E3
Moinda China 83 G3
Moine Moz. 101 K3
Moinești Romania 59 L1
Mointy Kazakh. see Moyynty
Mo i Rana Norway 44 I3
Moirang India 76 B3
Mõisaküla Estonia 45 N7
Moisie Canada 123 I4
Moisie r. Canada 123 I4
Moissac France 56 E4
Mojave U.S.A. 128 D4
Mojave r. U.S.A. 128 E4
Mojave Desert U.S.A. 128 E4
Mojiang China 76 D4
Moji das Cruzes Brazil 145 B3
Mojos, Llanos de plain Bol. 142 E6
Moju r. Brazil 143 I4
Mokama India 83 F4
Mokau N.Z. 113 E4
Mokau r. N.Z. 113 E4
Mokelumne r. U.S.A. 128 C2
Mokelumne Aqueduct canal U.S.A. 128 C2
Mokhoabong Pass Lesotho 101 I5
Mokhotlong Lesotho 101 I5
Mokhtārān Iran 88 E3
Moknine Tunisia 58 D7
Mokohinau Islands N.Z. 113 E2
Mokokchung India 83 H4
Mokolo Cameroon 97 E3
Mokolo r. S. Africa 101 H2
Mokopane S. Africa 101 I3
Mokp'o S. Korea 75 B6
Mokrous Rus. Fed. 43 J6
Moksha r. Rus. Fed. 43 I5
Mokshan Rus. Fed. 43 J5
Möksy Fin. 44 N5
Môktama Myanmar see Mottama
Môktama, Gulf of g. Myanmar see Mottama, Gulf of
Mokundurra India see Mukandwara
Mokwa Nigeria 96 D4
Molatón mt. Spain 57 F4
Moldavia country Europe see Moldova
Moldavskaya S.S.R. country Europe see Moldova
Molde Norway 44 E5
Moldjord Norway 44 I3
Moldova country Europe 43 F7
Moldoveanu, Vârful mt. Romania 59 K2
Moldovei de Sud, Cîmpia plain Moldova 59 M1
Molega Lake Canada 123 I5
Molen r. S. Africa 101 I4
Mole National Park Ghana 96 C4
Molepolole Botswana 101 G3
Molėtai Lith. 45 N9
Molfetta Italy 58 G4
Molière Alg. see Bordj Bounaama
Molihong Shan mt. China see Morihong Shan
Molina de Aragón Spain 57 F3
Moline U.S.A. 131 D4
Molkom Sweden 45 H7
Mollagara Turkm. 88 D2
Mollakara Turkm. see Mollagara
Mol Len mt. India 83 H4
Möllenbeck Germany 53 N1
Mollendo Peru 142 D7
Mölln Germany 53 K1
Mölnlycke Sweden 45 H8
Molochnyy Rus. Fed. 44 R2
Molodechno Belarus see Maladzyechna
Molodezhnaya research station Antarctica 152 D2
Moloka'i i. U.S.A. 127 [inset]
Moloma r. Rus. Fed. 42 K4
Molong Australia 112 D4
Molopo watercourse Botswana/S. Africa 100 E5
Molotov Rus. Fed. see Perm'
Molotovsk Kyrg. see Kayyngdy
Molotovsk Arkhangel'skaya Oblast' Rus. Fed. see Severodvinsk
Molotovsk Kirovskaya Oblast' Rus. Fed. see Nolinsk
Moloundou Cameroon 97 E4
Molson Lake Canada 121 L4
Molu i. Indon. 69 I8
Moluccas is Indon. 69 H7
Molucca Sea sea Indon. see Maluku, Laut
Moma Moz. 99 D5
Moma r. Rus. Fed. 65 P3
Momba Australia 112 A3
Mombaça Brazil 143 K5
Mombasa Kenya 98 D4
Mombetsu Hokkaidō Japan see Monbetsu
Mombi New India 83 H4
Mombum Indon. 69 J8
Momchilgrad Bulg. 59 K4
Momence U.S.A. 134 B3
Momi, Ra's pt Yemen 87 H7
Mompós Col. 142 D2
Møn i. Denmark 45 H9
Mon India 83 H4
Mona terr. Irish Sea see Isle of Man
Mona U.S.A. 129 H2
Monaca U.S.A. 134 E3
Monach, Sound of sea chan. U.K. 50 B3
Monach Islands U.K. 50 B3
Monaco country Europe 56 H5
Monaco Basin sea feature N. Atlantic Ocean 148 G4
Monadhliath Mountains U.K. 50 E3
Monaghan Ireland 51 F3
Monahans U.S.A. 131 C6
Mona Passage Dom. Rep./Puerto Rico 137 K5
Monapo Moz. 99 E5
Monar, Loch l. U.K. 50 D3
Monarch Mountain Canada 120 E5
Monarch Pass U.S.A. 127 G5
Mona Reservoir U.S.A. 129 H2
Monashee Mountains Canada 120 G5
Monastir Macedonia see Bitola
Monastir Tunisia 58 D7
Monastyrishche Ukr. see Monastyryshche
Monastyryshche Ukr. 43 F6
Monbetsu Hokkaidō Japan 74 F3
Monbetsu Hokkaidō Japan 74 F4
Moncalieri Italy 58 B2
Monchegorsk Rus. Fed. 44 R3
Mönchengladbach Germany 52 G3
Monchique Port. 57 B5
Moncks Corner U.S.A. 133 D5
Monclova Mex. 131 C7
Moncouche, Lac l. Canada 123 H4
Moncton Canada 123 I5
Mondego r. Port. 57 B3
Mondlo S. Africa 101 J4
Mondo Chad 97 E3
Mondovì Italy 58 B2
Mondragone Italy 58 E4
Mondy Rus. Fed. 72 I2
Monemvasia Greece 59 J6
Monessen U.S.A. 134 F3
Moneta U.S.A. 126 G4
Moneygall Ireland 51 E5
Moneymore U.K. 51 F3
Monfalcone Italy 58 E2
Monfalut Egypt see Manfalūṭ
Monforte de Lemos Spain 57 C2
Monga Dem. Rep. Congo 98 C3
Mongala r. Dem. Rep. Congo 98 B3
Mongar Bhutan 83 G4
Mongbwalu Dem. Rep. Congo 98 D3
Mông Cai Vietnam 70 D2
Mongers Lake salt flat Australia 109 B7
Mong Hang Myanmar 70 B2
Mong Hkan Myanmar 70 C2
Mong Hpayak Myanmar 70 B2
Mong Hsat Myanmar 70 B2
Mong Hsawk Myanmar 70 B2
Mong Hsu Myanmar 70 B2
Monghyr India see Munger
Mong Kung Myanmar 70 B2
Mong Kyawt Myanmar 70 B3
Mongla Bangl. 83 G5
Mong Lin Myanmar 70 C2
Mong Loi Myanmar 70 C2
Mong Long Myanmar 70 B2
Mong Nai Myanmar 70 B2
Mong Nawng Myanmar 70 B2
Mongo Chad 97 E3
Mongolia country Asia 72 I3
Mongol Uls country Asia see Mongolia
Mongonu Nigeria 96 E3
Mongora Pak. 89 I3
Mongour hill U.K. 50 G4
Mong Pan Myanmar 70 B2
Mong Ping Myanmar 70 B2
Mong Pu Myanmar 70 B2
Mong Pu-awn Myanmar 70 B2
Mong Si Myanmar 70 B2
Mongu Zambia 99 C5
Mong Un Myanmar 70 C2
Mong Yai Myanmar 70 B2
Mong Yang Myanmar 70 B2
Mong Yawn Myanmar 70 B2
Mong Yawng Myanmar 70 C2
Mönhaan Mongolia 73 K3
Mönh Hayrhan Uul mt. Mongolia 80 H2
Moniaive U.K. 50 F5
Monitor Mountain U.S.A. 128 E2
Monitor Range mts U.S.A. 128 E2
Monivea Ireland 51 D4
Monkey Bay Malawi 99 D5
Monkira Australia 110 C5
Monkton Canada 134 E2
Monmouth U.K. 49 E7
Monmouth U.S.A. 130 F3
Monmouth Mountain Canada 120 F5
Monnow r. U.K. 49 E7
Mono, Punta del pt Nicaragua 137 H6
Mono Lake U.S.A. 128 D2
Monolithos Greece 59 L6
Monomoy Point U.S.A. 135 J3
Monon U.S.A. 134 B3
Monopoli Italy 58 G4
Monreal del Campo Spain 57 F3
Monreale Sicily Italy 58 E5
Monroe IN U.S.A. 134 C3

nroe LA U.S.A. 131 E5
nroe MI U.S.A. 134 D3
nroe NC U.S.A. 133 D5
nroe WI U.S.A. 130 F3
nroe Center U.S.A. 130 F2
nroe Lake U.S.A. 134 B4
nroeton U.S.A. 135 G3
'lonrovia Liberia 96 B4
apital of Liberia.
ns Belgium 52 D4
nschau Germany 52 G4
nselice Italy 58 D2
ntabaur Germany 53 H4
ntagu S. Africa 100 E7
ntague Canada 123 J5
ntague MI U.S.A. 134 B2
ntague TX U.S.A. 131 D5
ntague Range hills Australia 109 B6
ntalto mt. Italy 58 F5
ntalto Uffugo Italy 58 G5
ntana Bulg. 59 J3
ntana state U.S.A. 126 F3
ntanhas do Tumucumaque, Parque
acional nat. park 143 H3
ntargis France 56 F3
ntauban France 56 E4
ntauk U.S.A. 135 J3
ntauk Point U.S.A. 135 J3
nt-aux-Sources mt. Lesotho 101 I5
ntbard France 56 G3
ont Blanc mt. France/Italy 56 H4
h highest mountain in Europe.
ntblanc Spain 57 G3
ntblanch Spain see Montblanc
ntbrison France 56 G4
ntceau-les-Mines France 56 G3
ntcornet France 52 E5
nt-de-Marsan France 56 D5
ntdidier France 52 C5
nte Alegre Brazil 143 H4
nte Alegre de Goiás Brazil 145 B1
nte Alegre de Minas Brazil 145 A2
nte Azul Brazil 145 C1
nte Azul Paulista Brazil 145 A3
ntebello Canada 122 G5
ntebello Islands Australia 108 A5
ntebelluna Italy 58 E2
nte-Carlo Monaco 56 H5
nte Cristi Dom. Rep. 137 J5
nte Cristo S. Africa 101 H2
nte Dourado Brazil 143 H4
nte Falterona, Campigna e delle
oreste Casentinesi, Parco Nazionale del
at. park Italy 58 D3
ntego Bay Jamaica 137 I5
ntélimar France 56 G4
nte Lindo r. Para. 144 E2
ntello U.S.A. 130 F3
ntemorelos Mex. 131 D7
ntemor-o-Novo Port. 57 B4
ntenegro country Europe 58 H3
ntepulciano Italy 58 D3
nte Quemado Arg. 144 D3
ntereau-Fault-Yonne France 56 F2
nterey Mex. see Monterrey
nterey CA U.S.A. 128 C3
nterey VA U.S.A. 134 F4
nterey Bay U.S.A. 128 B3
ntería Col. 142 C2
nteros Arg. 144 C3
nterrey Baja California Mex. 129 F5
nterrey Nuevo León Mex. 131 C7
ntesano U.S.A. 126 C3
ntesano sulla Marcellana Italy 58 F4
nte Santo Brazil 143 K6
nte Santu, Capo di c. Sardinia
aly 58 C4
ntes Claros Brazil 145 C2
ntesilvano Italy 58 F3
ntevarchi Italy 58 D3
ontevideo Uruguay 144 E4
apital of Uruguay.
ntevideo U.S.A. 130 E2
ntezuma U.S.A. 130 E3
ntezuma Creek U.S.A. 129 I3
ntezuma Peak U.S.A. 128 E3
ntfort Neth. 52 F3
ntgomery U.K. 49 D6
ontgomery AL U.S.A. 133 C5
apital of Alabama.
ntgomery WV U.S.A. 134 E4
ntgomery Islands Australia 108 C3
nthey Switz. 56 H3
nticello AR U.S.A. 131 F5
nticello FL U.S.A. 133 D6
nticello IN U.S.A. 134 B3
nticello KY U.S.A. 134 C5
nticello MO U.S.A. 130 F3
nticello NY U.S.A. 135 H3
nticello UT U.S.A. 129 I3
ntignac France 56 E4
ntignies-le-Tilleul Belgium 52 E4
ntigny-lès-Metz France 52 G5
ntilla Spain 57 D5
nti Sibillini, Parco Nazionale dei
t. park Italy 58 E3
ntividiu Brazil 145 A2
ntivilliers France 49 H9
nt-Joli Canada 123 H4
nt-Laurier Canada 122 G5
ntluçon France 56 F3
ntmagny Canada 123 H5
ntmédy France 52 F5
ntmirail France 52 D6
ntmorillon France 56 E3
ntmort-Lucy France 52 D6
nto Australia 110 E5
ntour Falls U.S.A. 135 G2
ntoursville U.S.A. 135 G3
ntpelier ID U.S.A. 126 F4
ontpelier VT U.S.A. 135 I1
apital of Vermont.

Montpellier France 56 F5
Montréal Canada 122 G5
Montreal r. Ont. Canada 122 D5
Montreal r. Ont. Canada 122 F5
Montreal Lake Canada 121 J4
Montreal Lake l. Canada 121 J4
Montréal-Mirabel airport Canada 122 G5
Montreal River Canada 122 D5
Montréal-Trudeau airport Canada 122 G5
Montreuil France 52 B4
Montreux Switz. 56 H3
Montrose well S. Africa 100 E4
Montrose U.K. 50 G4
Montrose CO U.S.A. 129 J2
Montrose PA U.S.A. 135 H3
Montross U.S.A. 135 G4
Monts, Pointe des pt Canada 123 I4
Mont-St-Aignan France 49 I9
▶Montserrat terr. West Indies 137 L5
United Kingdom Overseas Territory.
Montviel, Lac l. Canada 123 H3
Monument Valley reg. U.S.A. 129 H3
Monywa Myanmar 70 A2
Monza Italy 58 C2
Monze, Cape pt Pak. see Muari, Ras
Monzón Spain 57 G3
Mooi r. S. Africa 101 J5
Mooifontein Namibia 100 C4
Mookane Botswana 101 H2
Mookgopong S. Africa see Naboomspruit
Moolawatana Australia 111 B6
Moomba Australia 111 C6
Moomin Creek r. Australia 112 D2
Moonaree Australia 111 A6
Moonbi Range mts Australia 112 E3
Moonda Lake salt flat Australia 111 C5
Moonie Australia 112 E1
Moonie r. Australia 112 D2
Moora Australia 109 B7
Mooraberree Australia 110 C5
Moorcroft U.S.A. 126 G3
Moore r. Australia 109 A7
Moore U.S.A. 126 F3
Moore, Lake salt flat Australia 109 B7
Moore Embayment b. Antarctica 152 H1
Moorefield U.S.A. 135 F4
Moore Haven U.S.A. 133 D7
Moore Reef Australia 110 E3
Moore Reservoir U.S.A. 135 J1
Moore River National Park Australia 109 A7
Moores Island Bahamas 133 E7
Moorfoot Hills U.K. 50 F5
Moorhead U.S.A. 130 D2
Moorman U.S.A. 134 B5
Moornanyah Lake imp. l. Australia 112 A4
Mooroopna Australia 112 B6
Moorreesburg S. Africa 100 D7
Moorrinya National Park Australia 110 D4
Moose r. Canada 122 E4
Moose Factory Canada 122 E4
Moosehead Lake U.S.A. 132 G2
Moose Jaw Canada 121 J5
Moose Jaw r. Canada 121 J5
Moose Lake U.S.A. 130 E2
Mooselookmeguntic Lake U.S.A. 135 J1
Moose Mountain Creek r. Canada 121 K5
Moosilauke, Mount U.S.A. 135 J1
Moosomin Canada 121 K5
Moosonee Canada 122 E4
Mootwingee National Park Australia 111 C6
Mopane S. Africa 101 I2
Mopeia Moz. 99 D5
Mopipi Botswana 99 C6
Mopti Mali 96 C3
Moqor Afgh. 89 G3
Moquegua Peru 142 D7
Mora Cameroon 97 E3
Mora Spain 57 E4
Mora Sweden 45 I6
Mora MN U.S.A. 130 E2
Mora NM U.S.A. 127 G6
Mora r. U.S.A. 127 G6
Moradabad India 82 D3
Morada Nova Brazil 143 K5
Moraine Lake Canada 121 J1
Moraleda, Canal sea chan. Chile 144 B6
Moram India 84 C2
Moramanga Madag. 99 E5
Moran U.S.A. 126 F4
Moranbah Australia 110 E4
Morang Nepal see Biratnagar
Morar, Loch l. U.K. 50 D4
Morari, Tso l. India 82 D2
Moratuwa Sri Lanka 84 C5
Morava reg. Czech Rep. 47 P6
Moravia U.S.A. 135 G2
Morawa Australia 109 A7
Moray Firth b. U.K. 50 E3
Moray Range hills Australia 108 E3
Morbach Germany 52 H5
Morbeng S. Africa see Soekmekaar
Morbi India 82 B5
Morcenx France 56 D4
Morcillo Mex. 131 B7
Mordaga China 73 M2
Mor Dağı mt. Turkey 91 G3
Morden Canada 121 L5
Mordovo Rus. Fed. 43 I5
Moreau r. U.S.A. 130 C2
Moreau, South Fork r. U.S.A. 130 C2
Morecambe U.K. 48 E4
Morecambe Bay U.K. 48 D4
Moree Australia 112 D2
Morehead P.N.G. 69 K8
Morehead U.S.A. 134 D4
Morehead City U.S.A. 137 I2
Moreland U.S.A. 134 C5
More Laptevykh sea Rus. Fed. see Laptev Sea
Morelia Mex. 136 D5
Morella Australia 110 C4
Morella Spain 57 F3
Morelos Mex. 127 G8
Morena India 82 D4
Morena, Sierra mts Spain 57 C5

Morenci AZ U.S.A. 129 I5
Morenci MI U.S.A. 134 C3
Moreni Romania 59 K2
Moreno Mex. 127 F7
Moreno Valley U.S.A. 128 E5
Moresby, Mount Canada 120 C4
Moresby Island Canada 120 C4
Moreswe Pan salt pan Botswana 100 G2
Moreton Bay Australia 112 F1
Moreton-in-Marsh U.K. 49 F7
Moreton Island Australia 112 F1
Moreton Island National Park Australia 112 F1
Moreuil France 52 C5
Morez France 56 H3
Morfou Cyprus 85 A2
Morfou Bay Cyprus 85 A2
Morgan U.S.A. 126 F4
Morgan City U.S.A. 131 F6
Morgan Hill U.S.A. 128 C3
Morganton U.S.A. 132 D5
Morgantown KY U.S.A. 134 B5
Morgantown WV U.S.A. 134 F4
Morgenzon S. Africa 101 I4
Morges Switz. 56 H3
Morgh, Kowtal-e Afgh. 89 H3
Morghāb r. Afgh. 89 F3
Morghāb reg. Afgh. 89 F3
Morhar r. India 83 F4
Mori China 80 H3
Mori Japan 74 F4
Moriah, Mount U.S.A. 129 F2
Moriarty's Range hills Australia 112 B2
Morice Lake Canada 120 E4
Morichal Col. 142 D3
Morihong Shan mt. China 74 B4
Morija Lesotho 101 H5
Morin Dawa China see Nirji
Moringen Germany 53 J3
Morioka Japan 75 F5
Moris Mex. 127 F7
Morisset Australia 112 E4
Moriyoshi-zan vol. Japan 75 F5
Morjärv Sweden 44 M3
Morjen r. Pak. 89 F4
Morki Rus. Fed. 42 K4
Morlaix France 56 C2
Morley U.K. 48 F5
Mormam Flat Dam U.S.A. 129 H5
Mormant France 52 C6
Mormon Lake U.S.A. 129 H4
Mormugao India see Marmagao
Morne Diablotins vol. Dominica 137 L5
Morney watercourse Australia 110 C5
Mornington, Isla i. Chile 144 A7
Mornington Abyssal Plain sea feature S. Atlantic Ocean 148 C9
Mornington Island Australia 110 B3
Mornington Peninsula National Park Australia 112 B7
Moro Pak. 89 G5
Moro U.S.A. 126 C3
Morobe P.N.G. 69 L8
Morocco country Africa 96 C1
Morocco U.S.A. 134 B3
Morococala mt. Bol. 142 E7
Morogoro Tanz. 99 D4
Moro Gulf Phil. 69 G5
Morojaneng S. Africa 101 H5
Morokweng S. Africa 100 F4
Morombe Madag. 99 E6
Morón Cuba 133 E8
Mörön Mongolia 80 J2
Morondava Madag. 99 E6
Morón de la Frontera Spain 57 D5
▶Moroni Comoros 99 E5
Capital of the Comoros.
Moroni U.S.A. 129 H2
Moron Us He r. China see Tongtian He
Morotai i. Indon. 69 H6
Moroto Uganda 98 D3
Morozovsk Rus. Fed. 43 I6
Morpeth Canada 134 E2
Morpeth U.K. 48 F3
Morphou Cyprus see Morfou
Morrill U.S.A. 134 C5
Morrilton U.S.A. 131 E5
Morrin Canada 121 H5
Morrinhos Brazil 145 A2
Morris Canada 121 L5
Morris IL U.S.A. 130 F3
Morris MN U.S.A. 130 E2
Morris PA U.S.A. 135 G3
Morris Jessup, Kap c. Greenland 153 I1
Morrison U.S.A. 130 F3
Morristown AZ U.S.A. 129 G5
Morristown NJ U.S.A. 135 H3
Morristown NY U.S.A. 135 H1
Morristown TN U.S.A. 132 D4
Morrisville U.S.A. 135 H2
Morro Brazil 145 B2
Morro Bay U.S.A. 128 C4
Morro d'Anta Brazil 145 D2
Morro do Chapéu Brazil 143 J6
Morro Grande hill Brazil 143 H4
Morrosquillo, Golfo de b. Col. 142 C2
Morrumbene Moz. 101 L2
Morschen Germany 53 J3
Morse Canada 121 J5
Morse U.S.A. 131 C4
Morse, Cape Antarctica 152 G2
Morse Reservoir U.S.A. 134 B3
Morshanka Rus. Fed. 43 I5
Morshansk Rus. Fed. see Morshanka
Morsott Alg. 58 C7
Mort watercourse Australia 110 C4
Mortagne-au-Perche France 56 E2
Mortagne-sur-Sèvre France 56 D3
Mortara Italy 58 C2
Mortehoe U.K. 49 C7
Morteros Arg. 144 D4
Mortes, Rio das r. Brazil 145 A1
Mortimer's Bahamas 133 F8
Mortlake Australia 112 A7
Mortlock Islands Micronesia 150 G5
Mortlock Islands P.N.G. see Takuu Islands
Morton U.K. 49 G6
Morton TX U.S.A. 131 C5
Morton WA U.S.A. 126 C3

Morton National Park Australia 112 E5
Morundah Australia 112 C5
Morupule Botswana 101 H2
Moruroa atoll Fr. Polynesia see Mururoa
Moruya Australia 112 E5
Morven Australia 111 D5
Morven hill U.K. 50 F2
Morvern reg. U.K. 50 D4
Morvi India see Morbi
Morwell Australia 112 C7
Morzhovets, Ostrov i. Rus. Fed. 42 I2
Mosbach Germany 53 J5
Mosborough U.K. 48 F5
Mosby U.S.A. 126 G3
▶Moscow Rus. Fed. 42 H5
Capital of the Russian Federation. Most populous city in Europe.
Moscow ID U.S.A. 126 D3
Moscow PA U.S.A. 135 H3
Moscow University Ice Shelf Antarctica 152 G2
Mosel r. Germany 53 H4
Moselebe watercourse Botswana 100 F3
Moselle r. France 52 G5
Möser Germany 53 L2
Moses, Mount U.S.A. 128 E1
Moses Lake U.S.A. 126 D3
Mosgiel N.Z. 113 C7
Moshaweng watercourse S. Africa 100 F4
Moshchnyy, Ostrov i. Rus. Fed. 45 O7
Moshi Tanz. 98 D4
Mosh'yuga Rus. Fed. 42 L2
Mosi-oa-Tunya waterfall Zambia/Zimbabwe see Victoria Falls
Mosjøen Norway 44 H4
Moskal'vo Rus. Fed. 74 F1
Moskenesøy i. Norway 44 H3
Moskva Rus. Fed. see Moscow
Moskva Tajik. 89 H2
Mosonmagyaróvár Hungary 47 P7
Mosquera Col. 142 C3
Mosquero U.S.A. 127 G6
Mosquito r. Brazil 145 C1
Mosquito Creek Lake U.S.A. 134 E3
Mosquito Lake Canada 121 K2
Mosquitos, Golfo de los b. Panama 137 H7
Moss Norway 45 G7
Mossâmedes Angola see Namibe
Mossat U.K. 50 G3
Mossburn N.Z. 113 B7
Mosselbaai S. Africa see Mossel Bay
Mossel Bay S. Africa 100 F8
Mossel Bay b. S. Africa 100 F8
Mossgiel Australia 112 B4
Mossman Australia 110 D3
Mossoró Brazil 143 K5
Moss Vale Australia 112 E5
Mossy r. Canada 121 K4
Most Czech Rep. 47 N5
Mostaganem Alg. 57 G6
Mostar Bos.-Herz. 58 G3
Mostoos Hills Canada 121 I4
Mostovskoy Rus. Fed. 91 F1
Mosty Belarus see Masty
Mosul Iraq 91 F3
Møsvatnet l. Norway 45 F7
Motala Sweden 45 I7
Motaze Moz. 101 K3
Motetema S. Africa 101 I3
Moth India 82 D4
Motherwell U.K. 50 F5
Motian Ling hill China 74 A4
Motihari India 83 F4
Motilla del Palancar Spain 57 F4
Motiti Island N.Z. 113 F3
Motokwe Botswana 100 F3
Motril Spain 57 E5
Motru Romania 59 J2
Mott U.S.A. 130 C2
Mottama Myanmar 70 B3
Mottama, Gulf of Myanmar 70 B3
Motu Ihupuku i. N.Z. see Campbell Island
Motul Mex. 136 G4
Mouaskar Alg. see Mascara
Mouding China 76 D3
Moudjéria Mauritania 96 B3
Moudros Greece 59 K5
Mouhijärvi Fin. 45 M6
Mouila Gabon 98 B4
Moulamein Australia 112 B5
Moulamein Creek r. Australia 112 A5
Moulavibazar Bangl. see Moulvibazar
Mould Bay Canada 118 G2
Moulèngui Binza Gabon 98 B4
Moulins France 56 F3
Moulmein Myanmar see Mawlamyaing
Moulouya r. Morocco 54 D4
Moultrie U.S.A. 133 D6
Moultrie, Lake U.S.A. 133 E5
Moulvibazar Bangl. 83 G4
Mound City KS U.S.A. 130 E4
Mound City SD U.S.A. 130 C2
Moundou Chad 97 E4
Moundsville U.S.A. 134 E4
Moŭng Roessei Cambodia 71 C4
Mount Abu India 82 C4
Mountain r. Canada 120 D1
Mountainair U.S.A. 127 G6
Mountain Brook U.S.A. 133 C5
Mountain City U.S.A. 134 E5
Mountain Home AR U.S.A. 131 E4
Mountain Home ID U.S.A. 126 E4
Mountain Home UT U.S.A. 129 H1
Mountain Lake Park U.S.A. 134 F4
Mountain View U.S.A. 131 E5
Mountain Zebra National Park S. Africa 101 G7
Mount Airy U.S.A. 134 E5
Mount Aspiring National Park N.Z. 113 B7
Mount Assiniboine Provincial Park Canada 120 H5
Mount Ayliff S. Africa 101 I6
Mount Ayr U.S.A. 130 E3
Mountbellew Ireland 51 D4
Mount Buffalo National Park Australia 112 C6
Mount Carmel U.S.A. 134 B4
Mount Carmel Junction U.S.A. 129 G3
Mount Coolon Australia 110 D4

Mount Darwin Zimbabwe 99 D5
Mount Denison Australia 108 F5
Mount Desert Island U.S.A. 132 G2
Mount Dutton Australia 111 A5
Mount Eba Australia 111 A6
Mount Elgon National Park Uganda 98 D3
Mount Fletcher S. Africa 101 I6
Mount Forest Canada 134 E2
Mount Frankland National Park Australia 109 B8
Mount Frere S. Africa 101 I6
Mount Gambier Australia 111 C8
Mount Gilead U.S.A. 134 D3
Mount Hagen P.N.G. 69 K8
Mount Holly U.S.A. 135 H4
Mount Hope Australia 112 B4
Mount Hope U.S.A. 134 E5
Mount Howitt Australia 111 C5
Mount Isa Australia 110 B4
Mount Jackson U.S.A. 135 F4
Mount Jewett U.S.A. 135 F3
Mount Joy U.S.A. 135 G3
Mount Kaputar National Park Australia 112 E3
Mount Keith Australia 109 C6
Mount Lofty Range mts Australia 111 B7
Mount Magnet Australia 109 B7
Mount Manara Australia 112 A4
Mount McKinley National Park U.S.A. see Denali National Park and Preserve
Mount Meadows Reservoir U.S.A. 128 C1
Mountmellick Ireland 51 E4
Mount Moorosi Lesotho 101 H6
Mount Morgan Australia 110 E4
Mount Morris MI U.S.A. 134 D2
Mount Morris NY U.S.A. 135 G2
Mount Murchison Australia 112 A3
Mount Nebo U.S.A. 134 E4
Mount Olivet U.S.A. 134 C4
Mount Pearl Canada 123 L5
Mount Pleasant Canada 123 I5
Mount Pleasant IA U.S.A. 130 F3
Mount Pleasant MI U.S.A. 134 C2
Mount Pleasant TX U.S.A. 131 E5
Mount Pleasant UT U.S.A. 129 H2
Mount Rainier National Park U.S.A. 126 C3
Mount Remarkable National Park Australia 111 B7
Mount Revelstoke National Park Canada 120 G5
Mount Robson Provincial Park Canada 120 G4
Mount Rogers National Recreation Area park U.S.A. 134 E5
Mount St Helens National Volcanic Monument nat. park U.S.A. 126 C3
Mount Sanford Australia 108 E4
Mount's Bay U.K. 49 B8
Mount Shasta U.S.A. 126 C4
Mountsorrel U.K. 49 F6
Mount Sterling U.S.A. 134 D4
Mount Swan Australia 110 A4
Mount Union U.S.A. 135 G3
Mount Vernon Australia 109 B6
Mount Vernon IL U.S.A. 130 F4
Mount Vernon IN U.S.A. 132 C4
Mount Vernon KY U.S.A. 134 C5
Mount Vernon MO U.S.A. 131 E4
Mount Vernon OH U.S.A. 134 D3
Mount Vernon TX U.S.A. 131 E5
Mount Vernon WA U.S.A. 126 C2
Mount William National Park Australia 111 [inset]
Mount Willoughby Australia 109 F6
Moura Australia 110 E5
Moura Brazil 142 F4
Moura Port. 57 C4
Mourdi, Dépression du depr. Chad 97 F3
Mourdiah Mali 96 C3
Mourne r. U.K. 51 E3
Mourne Mountains hills U.K. 51 F3
Mousa i. U.K. 50 [inset]
Mouscron Belgium 52 D4
Mousgougou Chad 98 B2
Moussafoyo Chad 97 E4
Moussoro Chad 97 E3
Moutamba Congo 98 B4
Mouth of the Yangtze China 77 I2
Moutong Indon. 69 G6
Mouy France 52 C5
Mouydir, Monts du plat. Alg. 96 D2
Mouzon France 52 F5
Movas Mex. 127 F7
Mowbullan, Mount Australia 112 E1
Moxey Town Bahamas 133 E7
Moy r. Ireland 51 C3
Moyale Eth. 98 D3
Moyen Atlas mts Morocco 54 C5
Moyen Congo country Africa see Congo
Moyeni Lesotho 101 H6
Moynalyk Rus. Fed. 80 I1
Moynaq Uzbek. see Mo'ynoq
Mo'ynoq Uzbek. 80 A3
Moyo i. Indon. 108 B2
Moyobamba Peru 142 C5
Moyock U.S.A. 135 G5
Moyola r. U.K. 51 F3
Moyu China 82 D1
Moyynkum Kazakh. 80 D3
Moyynkum, Peski des. Kazakh. 80 C3
Moyynty Kazakh. 80 D2
Mozambique country Africa 99 D6
Mozambique Channel Africa 99 E6
Mozambique Ridge sea feature Indian Ocean 149 K7
Mozdok Rus. Fed. 91 G2
Mozdūrān Iran 89 F2
Mozhaysk Rus. Fed. 43 H5
Mozhga Rus. Fed. 42 L4
Mozhnābād Iran 89 F3
Mozo Myanmar 76 B4
Mozyr' Belarus see Mazyr
Mpaathutlwa Pan salt pan Botswana 100 E3
Mpanda Tanz. 99 D4
Mpen India 83 I4
Mpika Zambia 99 D5
Mpolweni S. Africa 101 J5
Mporokoso Zambia 99 D4

Mpulungu Zambia 99 D4
Mpumalanga prov. S. Africa 101 I4
Mpunde mt. Tanz. 99 D4
Mpwapwa Tanz. 99 D4
Mqanduli S. Africa 101 I6
Mqinvartsveri mt. Georgia/Rus. Fed. see Kazbek
Mrauk-U Myanmar 70 A2
Mrewa Zimbabwe see Murehwa
Mrkonjić-Grad Bos.-Herz. 58 G2
M'Saken Tunisia 58 D7
Mshinskaya Rus. Fed. 45 P7
M'Sila Alg. 57 I6
Msta r. Rus. Fed. 42 F4
Mstislavl' Belarus see Mstsislaw
Mstsislaw Belarus 43 F5
Mtelo Kenya 98 D3
Mtoko Zimbabwe see Mutoko
Mtorwi Tanz. 99 D4
Mtsensk Rus. Fed. 43 H5
Mts'ire Kavkasioni Asia see Lesser Caucasus
Mtubatuba S. Africa 101 K5
Mtunzini S. Africa 101 J5
Mtwara Tanz. 99 E5
Mu r. Myanmar 70 A2
Mu'āb, Jibāl reg. Jordan see Moab
Muanda Dem. Rep. Congo 99 B4
Muang Ham Laos 70 D2
Muang Hiam Laos 70 C2
Muang Hinboun Laos 70 D3
Muang Hôngsa Laos 70 C3
Muang Khi Laos 70 C3
Muang Không Laos 71 D4
Muang Khoua Laos 70 C2
Muang Lamam Laos see Lamam
Muang Mok Laos 70 D3
Muang Ngoy Laos 70 C2
Muang Ou Nua Laos 70 C2
Muang Pakbeng Laos 70 C3
Muang Paktha Laos 70 C2
Muang Pakxan Laos see Pakxan
Muang Phalan Laos 68 D3
Muang Phin Laos 70 D3
Muang Sam Sip Thai. 70 D4
Muang Sing Laos 70 C2
Muang Soum Laos 70 C3
Muang Souy Laos 70 C3
Muang Thadua Laos 70 C3
Muang Thai country Asia see Thailand
Muang Va Laos 70 C2
Muang Vangviang Laos 70 C3
Muang Xon Laos 70 C2
Muar Malaysia 71 C7
Muarabungo Indon. 68 C7
Muarateweh Indon. 68 E7
Muari, Ras pt Pak. 89 G5
Mu'aysil, Khashm al hill Saudi Arabia 88 C5
Mubarek Uzbek. see Muborak
Mubarraz well Saudi Arabia 91 F5
Mubende Uganda 98 D3
Mubi Nigeria 96 E3
Muborak Uzbek. 89 G2
Mubur i. Indon. 71 D7
Mucajaí, Serra do mts Brazil 142 F3
Mucalic r. Canada 123 I2
Muccan Australia 108 C5
Much Germany 53 H4
Muchinga Escarpment Zambia 99 D5
Muchuan China 76 D2
Muck i. U.K. 50 C4
Mucojo Moz. 99 E5
Muconda Angola 99 C5
Mucubela Moz. 99 D5
Mucugê Brazil 145 C1
Mucur Turkey 90 D3
Mucuri Brazil 145 D2
Mucuri r. Brazil 145 D2
Mudabidri India 84 B3
Mudan China see Heze
Mudanjiang China 74 C3
Mudan Jiang r. China 74 C3
Mudan Ling mts China 74 B4
Mudanya Turkey 59 M4
Mudaybī Oman 88 E6
Mudaysīsāt, Jabal al hill Jordan 85 C4
Muddus nationalpark nat. park Sweden 44 K3
Muddy r. U.S.A. 129 F3
Muddy Gap U.S.A. 126 G4
Muddy Peak U.S.A. 129 F3
Mūd-e Dahanāb Iran 88 E3
Mudersbach Germany 53 H4
Mudgal India 84 C3
Mudgee Australia 112 D4
Mudhol India 84 B2
Mudigere India 84 B3
Mudjatik r. Canada 121 J3
Mud Lake U.S.A. 128 E3
Mudraya country Africa see Egypt
Mudurnu Turkey 59 N4
Mud'yuga Rus. Fed. 42 H3
Mueda Moz. 99 D5
Mueller Range hills Australia 108 D4
Muertos Cays is Bahamas 133 D7
Muftyuga Rus. Fed. 42 J2
Mufulira Zambia 99 C5
Mufumbwe Zambia 99 C5
Mufu Shan mts China 77 G2
Muğan Düzü lowland Azer. 91 H3
Mugarripug China 83 F2
Mughalbhin Pak. see Jati
Mughal Kot Pak. 89 H4
Mughal Sarai India 83 E4
Mūghār Iran 88 D3
Mughayrā' Saudi Arabia 85 C5
Mughayrā' well Saudi Arabia 88 B5
Muğla Turkey 59 M6
Mugodzhary, Gory mts Kazakh. 80 A2
Mugxung China 76 B1
Mūḩ, Sabkhat imp. l. Syria 85 D2
Muhammad Ashraf Pak. 89 H5
Muhammad Qol Sudan 86 E5
Muhammarah Iran see Khorramshahr
Muhashsham, Wādī al watercourse Egypt 85 B4
Muḩaysh, Wādī al watercourse Jordan 85 C5
Muhaysin Syria 85 D1
Mühlanger Germany 53 M3
Mühlberg Germany 53 N3

Mühlhausen (Thüringen) Germany 53 K3
Mühlig-Hofmann Mountains Antarctica 152 C2
Muhos Fin. 44 N4
Muḩradah Syria 85 C2
Mui Bai Bung c. Vietnam see Mui Ca Mau
Mui Ba Lang An pt Vietnam 70 E4
Mui Ca Mau c. Vietnam 71 D5
Mui Đốc pt Vietnam 70 D3
Muié Angola 99 C5
Muineachán Ireland see Monaghan
Muir U.S.A. 134 C2
Muirkirk U.K. 50 E5
Muir of Ord U.K. 50 E3
Mui Ron hd Vietnam 70 D3
Muite Moz. 99 D5
Muji China 82 D1
Muju S. Korea 75 B5
Mukacheve Ukr. 43 D6
Mukachevo Ukr. see Mukacheve
Mukah Sarawak Malaysia 68 E6
Mukalla Yemen 86 G7
Mukandwara India 82 D4
Mukdahan Thai. 70 D3
Mukden China see Shenyang
Muketei r. Canada 122 D3
Mukhen Rus. Fed. 74 E2
Mukhino Rus. Fed. 74 B1
Mukhtuya Rus. Fed. see Lensk
Mukinbudin Australia 109 B7
Mu Ko Chang Marine National Park Thai. 71 C5
Mukojima-rettō is Japan 75 F8
Mukry Turkm. 89 G2
Muktsar India 82 C3
Mukutawa r. Canada 121 L4
Mukwonago U.S.A. 134 A2
Mula r. India 84 B2
Mulakatholhu atoll Maldives see Mulaku Atoll
Mulaku Atoll Maldives 81 D11
Mulan China 74 C3
Mulanje, Mount Malawi 99 D5
Mulapula, Lake salt flat Australia 111 B6
Mulatos Mex. 127 F7
Mulayḩ Saudi Arabia 88 B5
Mulayḩah, Jabal hill U.A.E. 88 D5
Mulayz, Wādī al watercourse Egypt 85 A4
Mulchatna r. U.S.A. 118 C3
Mulde r. Germany 53 M3
Mule Creek NM U.S.A. 129 I5
Mule Creek WY U.S.A. 126 G4
Mulegé Mex. 127 E8
Mules i. Indon. 108 C2
Muleshoe U.S.A. 131 C5
Mulga Park Australia 109 E6
Mulgathing Australia 109 F7
Mulhacén mt. Spain 57 E5
Mülhausen France see Mulhouse
Mülheim an der Ruhr Germany 52 G3
Mulhouse France 56 H3
Muli China 76 D3
Muli Rus. Fed. see Vysokogorniy
Mulia Indon. 69 J7
Muling Heilong. China 74 C3
Muling He r. China 74 D3
Mull i. U.K. 50 D4
Mull, Sound of sea chan. U.K. 50 C4
Mullaghcleevaun hill Ireland 51 F4
Mullaittivu Sri Lanka 84 D4
Mullaley Australia 112 D3
Mullengudgery Australia 112 C3
Mullens U.S.A. 134 E5
Muller watercourse Australia 108 F5
Muller, Pegunungan mts Indon. 68 E6
Mullett Lake U.S.A. 134 C1
Mullewa Australia 109 A7
Mullica r. U.S.A. 135 H4
Mullingar Ireland 51 E4
Mullion Creek Australia 112 D4
Mull of Galloway c. U.K. 50 E6
Mull of Kintyre hd U.K. 50 D5
Mull of Oa hd U.K. 50 C5
Mullumbimby Australia 112 F2
Mulobezi Zambia 99 C5
Mulshi Lake India 84 B2
Multai India 82 D5
Multan Pak. 89 H4
Multia Fin. 44 N5
Multien reg. France 52 C6
Mulug India 84 C2

▶Mumbai India 84 B2
2nd most populous city in Asia and 3rd in the world.

Mumbil Australia 112 D4
Mumbwa Zambia 99 C5
Muminabad Tajik. see Leningrad
Mū'minobod Tajik. see Leningrad
Mun, Mae Nam r. Thai. 70 D4
Muna i. Indon. 69 G8
Muna Mex. 136 G4
Muna r. Rus. Fed. 65 N3
Munabao Pak. 89 H5
Munaðarnes Iceland 44 [inset]
Münchberg Germany 53 L4
München Germany see Munich
München-Gladbach Germany see Mönchengladbach
Münchhausen Germany 53 I4
Muncho Lake Canada 120 E3
Muncie U.S.A. 134 C3
Muncoonie West, Lake salt flat Australia 110 B5
Muncy U.S.A. 135 G3
Munda Pak. 89 H4
Mundel Lake Sri Lanka 84 C5
Mundesley U.K. 49 I6
Mundford U.K. 49 H6
Mundiwindi Australia 109 C5
Mundra India 82 B5
Mundrabilla Australia 106 C5
Munds Park U.S.A. 129 H4
Mundubbera Australia 111 E5
Mundwa India 82 C4
Munfordville U.S.A. 134 C5
Mungallala Australia 111 D5
Mungana Australia 110 D3
Mungári Moz. 99 D5
Mungbere Dem. Rep. Congo 98 C3
Mungeli India 83 E5
Munger India 83 F4
Mu Nggava i. Solomon Is see Rennell
Mungindi Australia 112 D2
Mungla Bangl. see Mongla
Mungo Angola 99 B5
Mungo, Lake Australia 112 A4
Mungo National Park Australia 112 A4
Munich Germany 47 M6
Munising U.S.A. 132 C2
Munjpur India 82 B5
Munkács Ukr. see Mukacheve
Munkebakken Norway 44 P2
Munkedal Sweden 45 G7
Munkfors Sweden 45 H7
Munkhafaḑ al Qaţţārah depr. Egypt see Qattara Depression
Munku-Sardyk, Gora mt. Mongolia/Rus. Fed. 72 I2
Münnerstadt Germany 53 K4
Munnik S. Africa 101 I2
Munroe Lake Canada 121 L3
Munsan S. Korea 75 B5
Münster Hessen Germany 53 I5
Münster Niedersachsen Germany 53 K2
Münster Nordrhein-Westfalen Germany 53 H3
Munster reg. Ireland 51 D5
Münsterland reg. Germany 53 H3
Muntadgin Australia 109 B7
Muntervary hd Ireland 51 C6
Munyal-Par sea feature India see Bassas de Pedro Padua Bank
Munzur Vadisi Milli Parkı nat. park Turkey 55 L4
Muojärvi l. Fin. 44 P4
Mương Nhe Vietnam 70 C2
Muong Sai Laos see Oudômxai
Muonio Fin. 44 M3
Muonioälven r. Fin./Sweden 44 M3
Muonionjoki r. Fin./Sweden see Muonioälven
Mupa, Parque Nacional da nat. park Angola 99 B5
Muping China see Baoxing
Muqaynimah well Saudi Arabia 88 C6
Muqdisho Somalia see Mogadishu
Muquem Brazil 145 A1
Muqui Brazil 145 C3
Mur r. Austria 47 P7
also known as Mura (Croatia/Slovenia)
Mura r. Austria see Mur
Murai, Tanjong pt Sing. 71 [inset]
Murai Reservoir Sing. 71 [inset]
Murakami Japan 75 E5
Murallón, Cerro mt. Chile 144 B7
Muramvya Burundi 98 C4
Murashi Rus. Fed. 42 K4
Murat r. Turkey 91 E3
Muratlı Turkey 59 L4
Muraysah, Ra's al pt Libya 90 B5
Murchison watercourse Australia 109 A6
Murchison, Mount Antarctica 152 H2
Murchison, Mount hill Australia 109 B6
Murchison Falls National Park Uganda 98 D3
Murcia Spain 57 F5
Murcia aut. comm. Spain 57 F5
Murdo U.S.A. 130 C3
Murehwa Zimbabwe 99 D5
Mureşul r. Romania 59 I1
Muret France 56 E5
Murewa Zimbabwe see Murehwa
Murfreesboro AR U.S.A. 131 E5
Murfreesboro TN U.S.A. 132 C5
Murg r. Germany 53 I6
Murgab Tajik. see Murghob
Murgab Turkm. see Murgap
Murgab r. Turkm. see Murgap
Murgap Turkm. 89 F2
Murgap r. Turkm. 87 J2
Murgha Kibzai Pak. 89 H4
Murghob Tajik. 89 I2
Murgon Australia 111 E5
Murgoo Australia 109 B6
Muri India 83 F5
Muriaé Brazil 145 C3
Murid Pak. 89 G4
Muriege Angola 99 C4
Müritz l. Germany 53 M1
Müritz, Nationalpark nat. park Germany 53 N1
Murmansk Rus. Fed. 44 R2
Murmanskaya Oblast' admin. div. Rus. Fed. 44 S2
Murmanskiy Bereg coastal area Rus. Fed. 42 G1
Murmansk Oblast admin. div. Rus. Fed. see Murmanskaya Oblast'
Muro, Capo di c. Corsica France 56 I6
Murom Rus. Fed. 42 I5
Muroran Japan 74 F4
Muros Spain 57 B2
Muroto Japan 75 D6
Muroto-zaki pt Japan 75 D6
Murphy ID U.S.A. 126 D4
Murphy NC U.S.A. 133 D5
Murphysboro U.S.A. 130 F4
Murrah reg. Saudi Arabia 88 C6
Murrah al Kubrá, Al Buḩayrah al l. Egypt see Great Bitter Lake
Murrah aş Şughrá, Al Buḩayrah al l. Egypt see Little Bitter Lake
Murramarang National Park nat. park N.S.W. 112 I5
Murra Murra Australia 112 C2
Murrat el Kubra, Buheirat l. Egypt see Great Bitter Lake
Murrat el Sughra, Buheirat l. Egypt see Little Bitter Lake

▶Murray r. S.A. Australia 111 B7
3rd longest river in Oceania, and a major part of the longest (Murray-Darling).

Murray r. W.A. Australia 109 A8
Murray KY U.S.A. 131 F4
Murray UT U.S.A. 129 H1
Murray, Lake P.N.G. 69 K8
Murray, Lake U.S.A. 133 D5
Murray, Mount Canada 120 D2
Murray Bridge Australia 111 B7

▶Murray-Darling r. Australia 106 E5
Longest river in Oceania.

Murray Downs Australia 108 F5
Murray Range hills Australia 109 E6
Murraysburg S. Africa 100 F6
Murray Sunset National Park Australia 111 C7
Murrhardt Germany 53 J6
Murrieta U.S.A. 128 E5
Murringo Australia 112 D5
Murrisk reg. Ireland 51 C4
Murroogh Ireland 51 C4

▶Murrumbidgee r. Australia 112 A5
4th longest river in Oceania.

Murrumburrah Australia 112 D5
Murrurundi Australia 112 E3
Mursan India 82 D4
Murshidabad India 83 G4
Murska Sobota Slovenia 58 G1
Mürt Iran 89 F5
Murtoa Australia 111 C8
Murua i. P.N.G. see Woodlark Island
Murud India 84 B2
Murud, Gunung mt. Indon. 68 F6
Murunkan Sri Lanka 84 D4
Murupara N.Z. 113 F4
Mururoa atoll Fr. Polynesia 151 K7
Murviedro Spain see Sagunto
Murwara India 82 E5
Murwillumbah Australia 112 F2
Murzechirla Turkm. 89 F2
Murzūq Libya 97 E2
Mürzzuschlag Austria 47 O7
Muş Turkey 91 F3
Mūsā, Khowr-e b. Iran 88 C4
Musakhel Pak. 89 H4
Musala mt. Bulg. 59 J3
Musala i. Indon. 71 B7
Musan N. Korea 74 C4
Musandam Peninsula Oman/U.A.E. 38 E5
Mūsá Qal'eh, Rūd-e r. Afgh. 89 G3
Musay'īd Qatar see Umm Sa'id

▶Muscat Oman 88 E6
Capital of Oman.

Muscat reg. Oman 88 E5
Muscat and Oman country Asia see Oman
Muscatine U.S.A. 130 F3
Musgrave Australia 110 C2
Musgrave Harbour Canada 123 L4
Musgrave Ranges mts Australia 109 E6
Mushāsh al Kabid well Jordan 85 C5
Mushayyish, Wādī al watercourse Jordan 85 C4
Mushie Dem. Rep. Congo 98 B4
Mushkaf Pak. 89 G4
Music Mountain U.S.A. 129 G4
Musina S. Africa 101 J2
Musinia Peak U.S.A. 129 H2
Muskeg r. Canada 120 F2
Muskeget Channel U.S.A. 135 J3
Muskegon MI U.S.A. 132 C3
Muskegon MI U.S.A. 134 B2
Muskegon r. U.S.A. 134 B2
Muskegon Heights U.S.A. 134 B2
Muskeg River Canada 120 G4
Muskogee U.S.A. 131 E5
Muskoka, Lake Canada 134 F1
Muskrat Dam Lake Canada 121 N4
Musmar Sudan 86 E6
Musoma Tanz. 98 D4
Musquanousse, Lac l. Canada 123 J4
Musquaro, Lac l. Canada 123 J4
Mussau Island P.N.G. 69 L7
Musselburgh U.K. 50 F5
Musselkanaal Neth. 52 H2
Musselshell r. U.S.A. 126 G3
Mussende Angola 99 B5
Mustafakemalpaşa Turkey 59 M4
Mustjala Estonia 45 M7
Mustvee Estonia 45 O7
Musu-dan pt N. Korea 74 C4
Muswellbrook Australia 112 E4
Mūţ Egypt 86 C4
Mut Turkey 85 A1
Mutá, Ponta do pt Brazil 145 D1
Mutare Zimbabwe 99 D5
Mutayr reg. Saudi Arabia 88 B5
Mutina Italy see Modena
Muting Indon. 69 K8
Mutis Col. 142 C2
Mutnyy Materik Rus. Fed. 42 L2
Mutoko Zimbabwe 99 D5
Mutsamudu Comoros 99 E5
Mutsu Japan 74 F4
Muttaburra Australia 110 D4
Mutton Island Ireland 51 C5
Muttukuru India 84 D3
Muttupet India 84 C4
Mutum Brazil 145 C2
Mutunópolis Brazil 145 A1
Mutur Sri Lanka 84 D4
Mutusjärvi r. Fin. 44 O2
Muurola Fin. 44 N3
Mu Us Shamo des. China 73 J5
Muxaluando Angola 99 B4
Muxi China see Muchuan
Muxima Angola 99 B4
Muyezerskiy Rus. Fed. 44 R5
Muyinga Burundi 98 D4
Müynoq Uzbek. see Mo'ynoq
Muyumba Dem. Rep. Congo 99 C4
Muyunkum, Peski des. Kazakh. see Moyynkum, Peski
Muyuping China 77 F2
Muzaffarabad Pak. 89 I3
Muzaffargarh Pak. 89 H4
Muzaffarnagar India 82 D3
Muzaffarpur India 83 F4
Muzamane Moz. 101 K2
Muzhi Rus. Fed. 41 S2
Mūzīn Iran 89 F5
Muzon, Cape U.S.A. 120 C4
Múzquiz Mex. 131 C7
Muztag mt. China 82 E2
Muz Tag mt. China 83 F1
Muztagata mt. China 89 I2
Muztor Kyrg. see Toktogul
Mvadi Gabon 98 B3
Mvolo Sudan 97 F4
Mvuma Zimbabwe 99 D5
Mwanza Malawi 99 D5
Mwanza Tanz. 98 D4
Mweelrea hill Ireland 51 C4
Mweka Dem. Rep. Congo 99 C4
Mwene-Ditu Dem. Rep. Congo 99 C4
Mwenezi Zimbabwe 99 D6
Mwenga Dem. Rep. Congo 98 C4
Mweru, Lake Dem. Rep. Congo/Zambia 99 C4
Mweru Wantipa National Park Zambia 99 C4
Mwimba Dem. Rep. Congo 99 C4
Mwinilunga Zambia 99 C5
Myadaung Myanmar 70 B2
Myadzyel Belarus 45 O9
Myajlar India 82 B4
Myall Lakes National Park Australia 112 F4
Myanaung Myanmar 70 A3
Myanmar country Asia 70 A2
Myauk-U Myanmar see Mrauk-U
Myaungmya Myanmar 70 A3
Myawadi Thai. 70 B3
Mybster U.K. 50 F2
Myebon Myanmar 70 A2
Myede Myanmar see Aunglan
Myeik Myanmar 71 B4
Myingyan Myanmar 70 A2
Myinkyado Myanmar 70 B2
Myinmoletkat mt. Myanmar 71 B4
Myitkyina Myanmar 70 B1
Myitson Myanmar 70 B2
Myitta Myanmar 71 B4
Myittha Myanmar 70 B2
Mykolayiv Ukr. 59 O1
Mykonos i. Greece 59 K6
Myla Rus. Fed. 42 K2
Myla r. Rus. Fed. 42 K2
Mylae Sicily Italy see Milazzo
Mylasa Turkey see Milas
Mymensing Bangl. see Mymensingh
Mymensingh Bangl. 83 G4
Mynämäki Fin. 45 M6
Myŏnggan N. Korea 74 C4
Myory Belarus 45 O9
My Phước Vietnam 71 D5
Mýrdalsjökull ice cap Iceland 44 [inset]
Myre Norway 44 I2
Myrheden Sweden 44 L4
Myrhorod Ukr. 43 G6
Myrnam Canada 121 I4
Myronivka Ukr. 43 F6
Myrtle Beach U.S.A. 133 E5
Myrtleford Australia 112 C6
Myrtle Point U.S.A. 126 B4
Myrtoo Pelagos sea Greece 59 J6
Mys Articheskiy c. Rus. Fed. 153 E1
Mysia reg. Turkey 59 L5
Mys Lazareva Rus. Fed. see Lazarev
Myślibórz Poland 47 O4
My Son Sanctuary tourist site Vietnam 70 E4
Mysore India 84 C3
Mysore state India see Karnataka
Mys Shmidta Rus. Fed. 65 T3
Mysy Rus. Fed. 42 L3
My Tho Vietnam 71 D5
Mytikas mt. Greece see Olympus, Mount
Mytilene i. Greece see Lesbos
Mytilini Greece 59 L5
Mytilini Strait Greece/Turkey 59 L5
Mytishchi Rus. Fed. 42 H5
Myton U.S.A. 129 H1
Myyeldino Rus. Fed. 42 L3
Mzamomhle S. Africa 101 H6
Mže r. Czech Rep. 53 M5
Mzimba Malawi 99 D5
Mzuzu Malawi 99 D5

N

Naab r. Germany 53 M5
Nā'ālehu U.S.A. 127 [inset]
Naantali Fin. 45 M6
Naas Ireland 51 F4
Naba Myanmar 70 B1
Nababeep S. Africa 100 C5
Nababganj Bangl. see Nawabganj
Nabadwip India see Navadwip
Nabarangapur India 84 D2
Nabarangpur India see Nabarangapur
Nabari Japan 75 E6
Nabatîyé et Tahta Lebanon 85 B3
Nabatiyet et Tahta Lebanon see Nabatîyé et Tahta
Nabberu, Lake salt flat Australia 109 C6
Nabburg Germany 53 M5
Naberera Tanz. 99 D4
Naberezhnyye Chelny Rus. Fed. 41 Q4
Nabesna U.S.A. 120 A2
Nabeul Tunisia 58 D6
Nabha India 82 D3
Nabil'skiy Zaliv lag. Rus. Fed. 74 F2
Nabire Indon. 69 J7
Nabi Younés, Ras en pt Lebanon 85 B3
Nāblus West Bank 85 B3
Naboomspruit S. Africa 101 I3
Nabq Reserve nature res. Egypt 90 D5
Nābulus West Bank see Nāblus
Nacala Moz. 99 E5
Nachalovo Rus. Fed. 43 K7
Nachicapau, Lac l. Canada 123 I2
Nachingwea Tanz. 99 D5
Nachna India 82 B4
Nachuge India 71 A5
Nacimiento Reservoir U.S.A. 128 C4
Naco U.S.A. 127 F7
Nacogdoches U.S.A. 131 E6
Nada China see Danzhou
Nadaleen r. Canada 120 C2
Nådendal Fin. see Naantali
Nadezhdinskoye Rus. Fed. 74 D2
Nadiad India 82 C5
Nadol India 82 C4
Nador Morocco 57 E6
Nadqān, Qalamat well Saudi Arabia 88 C6
Nadūshan Iran 88 D3
Nadvirna Ukr. 43 E6
Nadvoitsy Rus. Fed. 42 G3
Nadvornaya Ukr. see Nadvirna
Nadym Rus. Fed. 64 I3
Næstved Denmark 45 G9
Nafarroa aut. comm. Spain see Navarra
Nafas, Ra's an mt. Egypt 85 B5
Nafḩa, Har hill Israel 85 B4
Nafpaktos Greece 59 I5
Nafplio Greece 59 J6
Naftalan Azer. 91 G2
Naft-e Safīd Iran 88 C4
Naft-e Shāh Iran see Naft Shahr
Naft Shahr Iran 88 B3
Nafūd ad Daḩl des. Saudi Arabia 88 B6
Nafūd al Ghuwayţah des. Saudi Arabia 85 D5
Nafūd al Jur'ā des. Saudi Arabia 88 B5
Nafūd as Sirr des. Saudi Arabia 88 B5
Nafūd as Surrah des. Saudi Arabia 88 A6
Nafūd Qunayfidhah des. Saudi Arabia 88 B5
Nafūsah, Jabal hills Libya 96 E1
Nafy Saudi Arabia 86 F4
Nag, Co l. China 83 G2
Naga Phil. 69 G4
Nagagami r. Canada 122 D4
Nagagami Lake Canada 122 D4
Nagahama Japan 75 D6
Naga Hills India 83 H4
Naga Hills state India see Nagaland
Nagaland state India 83 H4
Nagamangala India 84 C3
Nagambie Australia 112 B6
Nagano Japan 75 E5
Nagaoka Japan 75 E5
Nagaon India 83 H4
Nagapatam India see Nagappattinam
Nagappattinam India 84 C4
Nagar Hima. Prad. India 87 M3
Nagar Karnataka India 84 B3
Nagaram India 84 D2
Nagari Hills India 84 C3
Nagarjuna Sagar Reservoir India 84 C2
Nagar Parkar Pak. 89 H5
Nagar Untari India 83 E4
Nagasaki Japan 75 C6
Nagato Japan 75 C6
Nagaur India 82 C4
Nagbhir India 84 C1
Nagda India 82 C5
Nageezi U.S.A. 129 J3
Nagercoil India 84 C4
Nagha Kalat Pak. 89 G5
Nag' Ḩammādī Egypt see Naj' Ḩammādī
Nagina India 82 D3
Nagold r. Germany 53 I6
Nagong Chu r. China see Parlung Zangbo
Nagorno-Karabakh aut. reg. Azer. see Dağlıq Qarabağ
Nagornyy Karabakh aut. reg. Azer. see Dağlıq Qarabağ
Nagorsk Rus. Fed. 42 K4
Nagoya Japan 75 E6
Nagpur India 82 D5
Nagqu China 76 B2
Nag Qu r. China 76 B2
Nagurskoye Rus. Fed. 64 F1
Nagyatád Hungary 58 G1
Nagybecskerek Serbia see Zrenjanin
Nagyenyed Romania see Aiud
Nagykanizsa Hungary 58 G1
Nagyvárad Romania see Oradea
Naha Japan 73 N7
Nahan India 82 D3
Nahanni Butte Canada 120 F2
Nahanni National Park Reserve Canada 120 E2
Nahanni Range mts Canada 120 F2
Naharāyim Jordan 85 B3
Nahariyya Israel 85 B3
Nahāvand Iran 88 C3
Nahr Dijlah r. Asia 91 G5 see Tigris
Nahuel Huapi, Parque Nacional nat. park Arg. 144 B6
Nahunta U.S.A. 133 D6
Naica Mex. 131 B7
Nai Ga Myanmar 76 C3
Naij Tal China 83 H2
Naikliu Indon. 108 C2
Nain Canada 123 J2
Nā'īn Iran 88 D3
Nainital India 82 D3
Naini Tal India see Nainital
Nairn U.K. 50 F3
Nairn r. U.K. 50 F3

▶Nairobi Kenya 98 D4
Capital of Kenya.

Naissus Serbia see Niš
Naivasha Kenya 98 D4
Najaf Iraq 91 G5
Najafābād Iran 88 C3
Na'jān Saudi Arabia 88 B5
Najd reg. Saudi Arabia 86 F4
Nájera Spain 57 E2
Naj' Ḩammādī Egypt 86 D4
Naji China 74 A2
Najibabad India 82 D3
Najin N. Korea 74 C4
Najitun China see Naji
Najrān Saudi Arabia 86 F6
Nakadōri-shima i. Japan 75 C6
Na Kae Thai. 70 D3
Nakambé r. Burkina/Ghana see White Volta
Nakanbe r. Burkina/Ghana see White Volta
Nakanno Rus. Fed. 65 L3
Nakano-shima i. Japan 75 D5
Nakasongola Uganda 97 G4
Nakatsu Japan 75 C6
Nakatsugawa Japan 75 E6
Nakfa Eritrea 86 E6
Nakhichevan' Azer. see Naxçıvan
Nakhl Egypt 85 A5
Nakhodka Rus. Fed. 74 D4
Nakhola India 83 H4
Nakhon Nayok Thai. 71 C4
Nakhon Pathom Thai. 71 C4
Nakhon Phanom Thai. 70 D3
Nakhon Ratchasima Thai. 70 C4
Nakhon Sawan Thai. 70 C4
Nakhon Si Thammarat Thai. 71 B5
Nakhtarana India 82 B5
Nakina Canada 122 D4
Nakina r. Canada 120 C3
Naknek U.S.A. 118 C4
Nakonde Zambia 99 D4
Nakskov Denmark 45 G9
Naktong-gang r. S. Korea 75 C6
Nakuru Kenya 98 D4
Nakusp Canada 120 G5
Nal Pak. 89 G5
Nal r. Pak. 89 G5
Na-lang Myanmar 70 B2
Nalázi Moz. 101 K3
Nalbari India 83 G4
Nal'chik Rus. Fed. 91 F2
Naldurg India 84 C2
Nalgonda India 84 C2
Naliya India 82 B5
Nallamala Hills India 84 C3
Nallıhan Turkey 59 N4
Nālūt Libya 96 E1
Namaacha Moz. 101 K3
Namacurra Moz. 99 D5
Namadgi National Park Australia 112 D5
Namahadi S. Africa 101 I4
Namak, Daryācheh-ye salt flat Iran 88 C3
Namak, Kavīr-e salt flat Iran 88 E3
Namakkal India 84 C4
Namakwaland reg. Namibia see Great Namaqualand
Namakzar-e Shadad salt flat Iran 88 E4
Namaland reg. Namibia see Great Namaqualand
Namangan Uzbek. 80 D3
Namaqualand reg. Namibia see Great Namaqualand
Namaqualand reg. S. Africa 100 C5
Namaqua National Park S. Africa 100 C6
Namas Indon. 69 K8
Namatanai P.N.G. 106 F2
Nambour Australia 112 F1
Nambucca Heads Australia 112 F3
Nambung National Park Australia 109 A7
Năm Căn Vietnam 71 D5
Namcha Barwa mt. China see Namjagbarwa Feng
Namche Bazar Nepal 83 F4
Nam Co salt l. China 83 G3
Namdalen valley Norway 44 H4
Namdalseid Norway 44 G4
Nam Đinh Vietnam 70 D2
Namen Belgium see Namur
Nam-gang r. N. Korea 75 B5
Namhae-do i. S. Korea 75 B6
Namhsan Myanmar 70 B2
Namib Desert Namibia 100 B3
Namibe Angola 99 B5
Namibia country Africa 99 B6
Namibia Abyssal Plain sea feature N. Atlantic Ocean 148 I8
Namib-Naukluft Game Park nature res. Namibia 100 B3
Namie Japan 75 F5
Namīn Iran 91 H3
Namjagbarwa Feng mt. China 76 B2
Namlan Myanmar 70 B2
Namlang r. Myanmar 70 B2
Nam Loi r. China see Nanlei He
Nam Nao National Park Thai. 70 C3
Nam Ngum Reservoir Laos 70 C3
Namoi r. Australia 112 D3
Namonuito atoll Micronesia 69 L5
Nampa mt. Nepal 82 E3
Nampa U.S.A. 126 D4
Nampala Mali 96 C3
Nam Phong Thai. 70 C3
Namp'o N. Korea 75 B5
Nampula Moz. 99 D5
Namsai Myanmar 70 B1
Namsang Myanmar 70 B2
Namsen r. Norway 44 G4
Nam She Tsim hill H.K. China see Sharp Peak
Namsos Norway 44 G4
Namti Myanmar 70 B1
Namtok Myanmar 70 B3
Namtok Chattakan National Park Thai. 70 C3
Namton Myanmar 70 B2
Namtsy Rus. Fed. 65 N3
Namtu Myanmar 70 B2
Namu Canada 120 E5
Namuli, Monte mt. Moz. 99 D5
Namuno Moz. 99 D5
Namur Belgium 52 E4
Namutoni Namibia 99 B5
Namwŏn S. Korea 75 B6
Namya Ra Myanmar 70 B1
Namyit Island S. China Sea 68 E4
Nan Thai. 70 C3
Nana Bakassa Cent. Afr. Rep. 98 B3
Nanaimo Canada 120 F5
Nanam N. Korea 74 C4
Nan'an China 77 H3
Nanango Australia 112 F1
Nananib Plateau Namibia 100 C3
Nanao Japan 75 E5
Nanatsu-shima i. Japan 75 E5
Nanbai China see Zunyi
Nanbin China see Shizhu
Nanbu China 76 E2
Nancha China 74 C3
Nanchang Jiangxi China 77 G2
Nanchang Jiangxi China 77 G2
Nanchong China 76 E2
Nanchuan China 76 E2
Nancowry i. India 71 A6
Nancun China 77 G1
Nancy France 52 G6
Nancy (Essey) airport France 52 G6
Nanda Devi mt. India 82 E3
Nanda Kot mt. India 82 E3
Nandan China 76 E3
Nandapur India 84 D2
Nanded India 84 C2
Nander India see Nanded
Nandewar Range mts Australia 112 E3
Nandod India 84 B1
Nandurbar India 82 C5
Nandyal India 84 C3

nfeng Guangdong China 77 F4
nfeng Jiangxi China 77 H3
ng China 76 B2
nga Eboko Cameroon 96 E4
langa Parbat mt. Pak. 82 C2
th highest mountain in the world and Asia.
ngar National Park Australia 112 D4
ngatayap Indon. 68 E7
ngin Myanmar 71 B5
ngnim-sanmaek mts N. Korea 75 B4
ngqên China 76 C1
ngulangwa Tanz. 99 D4
nguneri India 84 C4
nhua China 76 D3
nhui China 77 I2
njian China 76 D3
njiang China 76 E1
njing China 77 H1
nji Shan i. China 77 I3
nka Jiang r. China 76 C4
nkang China 77 G3
nking China see Nanjing
nkova Angola 99 B5
nlei He r. China 76 C4
so known as Nam Loi (Myanmar)
nling China 77 H2
Ling mts China 77 F3
nliu Jiang r. China 77 F4
nlong China see Nanbu
nnilam India 84 C4
nnine Australia 109 B6
nning China 77 F4
nnup Australia 109 A8
Noi Thai. 70 C3
nortalik Greenland 119 N3
nouki atoll Kiribati see Nonouti
nouti atoll Kiribati see Nonouti
npan Jiang r. China 76 E3
nping China 77 H3
npu China see Pucheng
nri Dao i. China 77 H3
sei-shotō is Japan see Ryukyu Islands
sei-shotō Trench sea feature . Pacific Ocean see Ryukyu Trench
sen Basin sea feature ctic Ocean 153 H1
sen Sound sea chan. Canada 119 I1
-sha Ch'ün-tao is S. China Sea see ratly Islands
shan Island S. China Sea 68 F4
sha Qundao is S. China Sea see ratly Islands
sio Tanz. 98 D4
tes France 56 D3
tes à Brest, Canal de France 56 C3
teuil-le-Haudouin France 52 C5
thi Kadal lag. Sri Lanka 84 D4
ticoke Canada 134 E2
ticoke U.S.A. 135 H4
tong China 77 I2
tou China 77 [inset]
t'ou Taiwan 77 I4
tucket U.S.A. 135 J3
tucket Island U.S.A. 135 K3
tucket Sound g. U.S.A. 135 J3
twich U.K. 49 E5
umaga i. Tuvalu see Nanumanga
umanga i. Tuvalu 107 H2
umea atoll Tuvalu 107 H2
uque Brazil 145 C2
usa, Kepulauan is Indon. 69 H6
xi China 76 E2
xian China 77 G2
xiong China 77 G3
yang China 77 G1
yuki Kenya 98 D4
zhang China 77 F2
zhao China see Zhao'an
zhou China see Nanxian
cocane, Lac l. Canada 123 H3
ero country S. Pacific Ocean see Nauru
gaon Bangl. 83 G4
li He r. China 74 D3
mid, Dasht-e des. Afgh./Iran 89 F3
shera India 82 C2
a U.S.A. 128 B2
aktulik Lake Canada 121 H1
anee Canada 135 G1
asoq Greenland 119 M3
erville U.S.A. 134 A3
ier N.Z. 113 F4
ier Range hills Australia 108 D4
erville Canada 135 I1
les Italy 58 F4
les FL U.S.A. 133 D7
les ME U.S.A. 135 J2
les TX U.S.A. 131 E5
les UT U.S.A. 129 I1
o China 76 E4
oleon IN U.S.A. 134 C4
oleon ND U.S.A. 130 D2
oleon OH U.S.A. 134 C3
oli Italy see Naples
adeh Iran 88 B2
India 82 B5
Japan 75 D6
Mali 96 C3
ach Belarus 45 O9
coorte Australia 111 C8
adhan Australia 112 C4
inpur India 84 D2
lua India 83 F4
njal Ecuador 142 C4
njo Mex. 127 F8
sapur India 84 D2
saraopet India 84 D2
singhapur India 84 E1
thiwat Thai. 71 C6
Visa U.S.A. 131 C5
yanganj Bangl. 83 G5
yanganj India 82 E5
yangarh India 82 C4
ada r. India see Narmada
erth U.K. 49 C7
o France see Narbonne
onne France 56 F5
orough Island Galápagos Ecuador see rnandina, Isla
ea r. Spain 57 C2
Narcondam Island India 71 A4
Nardò Italy 58 H4
Narechi r. Pak. 89 H4
Narembeen Australia 109 B8
Nares Abyssal Plain sea feature S. Atlantic Ocean 148 D4
Nares Deep sea feature N. Atlantic Ocean 148 D4
Nares Strait Canada/Greenland 119 K2
Naretha Australia 109 D7
Narew r. Poland 47 R4
Narib Namibia 100 C3
Narikel Jinjira i. Bangl. see St Martin's Island
Narimanov Rus. Fed. 43 J7
Narimskiy Khrebet mts Kazakh. see Narymskiy Khrebet
Narin Afgh. 89 H2
Narin reg. Afgh. 89 H2
Narince Turkey 90 E3
Narin Gol watercourse China 83 H1
Narizon, Punta pt Mex. 127 F8
Narkher India 82 D5
Narmada r. India 82 C5
Narman Turkey 91 F2
Narnaul India 82 D3
Narni Italy 58 E3
Narnia Italy see Narni
Narodnaya, Gora mt. Rus. Fed. 41 S3
Naro-Fominsk Rus. Fed. 43 H5
Narok Kenya 98 D4
Narooma Australia 112 E6
Narovchat Rus. Fed. 43 I5
Narowlya Belarus 43 F6
Närpes Fin. 44 L5
Narrabri Australia 112 D3
Narragansett Bay U.S.A. 135 J3
Narran r. Australia 112 C2
Narrandera Australia 112 C5
Narran Lake Australia 112 C2
Narrogin Australia 109 B8
Narromine Australia 112 D4
Narrows U.S.A. 134 E5
Narrowsburg U.S.A. 135 H3
Narsapur India 84 C2
Narsaq Greenland 119 N3
Narshingdi Bangl. see Narsingdi
Narsimhapur India see Narsinghpur
Narsingdi Bangl. 83 G5
Narsinghpur India 82 D5
Narsipatnam India 84 D2
Nartkala Rus. Fed. 91 F2
Naruto Japan 75 D6
Narva Estonia 45 P7
Narva Bay Estonia/Rus. Fed. 45 O7
Narva laht b. Estonia/Rus. Fed. see Narva Bay
Narva Reservoir resr Estonia/Rus. Fed. see Narvskoye Vodokhranilishche
Narva veehoidla resr Estonia/Rus. Fed. see Narvskoye Vodokhranilishche
Narvik Norway 44 J2
Narvskiy Zaliv b. Estonia/Rus. Fed. see Narva Bay
Narvskoye Vodokhranilishche resr Estonia/Rus. Fed. 45 P7
Narwana India 82 D3
Nar'yan-Mar Rus. Fed. 42 L2
Narymskiy Khrebet mts Kazakh. 80 F2
Naryn Kyrg. 80 E3
Näsåker Sweden 44 J5
Nashik India 84 B1
Nashua U.S.A. 135 J2
Nashville AR U.S.A. 131 E5
Nashville GA U.S.A. 133 D6
Nashville IN U.S.A. 134 B4
Nashville NC U.S.A. 132 E5
Nashville OH U.S.A. 134 D3

▶Nashville TN U.S.A. 132 C4
Capital of Tennessee.

Naşib Syria 85 C3
Näsijärvi l. Fin. 45 M6
Nasik India see Nashik
Nasir Pak. 89 H4
Nasir Sudan 86 D8
Nasirabad Bangl. see Mymensingh
Nasirabad India 82 C4
Nāşirīyah Iraq 91 G5
Naskaupi r. Canada 123 J3
Naşr Egypt 90 C5
Nasratabad Iran see Zābol
Naşrīān-e Pā'īn Iran 88 B3
Nass r. Canada 120 D4
Nassau r. Australia 110 C2

▶Nassau Bahamas 133 E7
Capital of The Bahamas.

Nassau i. Cook Is 107 J3
Nassau U.S.A. 135 I2
Nassawadox U.S.A. 135 H5
Nasser, Lake resr Egypt 86 D5
Nässjö Sweden 45 I8
Nassuttooq inlet Greenland 119 M3
Nastapoca r. Canada 122 F2
Nastapoka Islands Canada 122 F2
Nasugbu Phil. 69 G4
Nasva Rus. Fed. 42 F4
Nata Botswana 99 C6
Natal Brazil 143 K5
Natal Indon. 68 B6
Natal prov. S. Africa see KwaZulu-Natal
Natal Basin sea feature Indian Ocean 149 K8
Naţanz Iran 88 C3
Natashquan Canada 123 J4
Natashquan r. Canada 123 J4
Natchez U.S.A. 131 F6
Natchitoches U.S.A. 131 E6
Nathalia Australia 112 B6
Nathia Gali Pak. 89 I3
Nati, Punta pt Spain 57 H3
Natillas Mex. 131 C7
National City U.S.A. 128 E5
National West Coast Tourist Recreation Area park Namibia 100 B2
Natitingou Benin 96 D3
Natividad, Isla i. Mex. 127 E8
Natividade Brazil 143 I6
Natkyizin Myanmar 70 B4
Natla r. Canada 120 D2
Natmauk Myanmar 70 A2
Nator Bangl. see Natore
Nátora Mex. 127 F7
Natore Bangl. 83 G4
Natori Japan 75 F5
Natron, Lake salt l. Tanz. 98 D4
Nattai National Park Australia 112 E5
Nattalin Myanmar 70 A3
Nattaung mt. Myanmar 70 B3
Na'tū Iran 89 F3
Natuashish Nfld. and Lab. 123 J3
Natuna, Kepulauan is Indon. 71 D6
Natuna Besar i. Indon. 71 E6
Natural Bridges National Monument nat. park U.S.A. 129 H3
Naturaliste, Cape Australia 109 A8
Naturaliste Plateau sea feature Indian Ocean 149 P8
Naturita U.S.A. 129 I2
Nauchas Namibia 100 C2
Nau Co l. China 83 E2
Nauen Germany 53 M2
Naufragados, Ponta dos pt Brazil 145 A4
Naujoji Akmenė Lith. 45 M8
Naukh India 82 C4
Naukot Pak. 89 H5
Naumburg (Hessen) Germany 53 J3
Naumburg (Saale) Germany 53 L3
Naunglon Myanmar 70 B3
Naungpale Myanmar 70 B3
Naupada India 84 E2
Na'ūr Jordan 85 B4
Nauroz Kalat Pak. 89 G4
Naurskaya Rus. Fed. 91 G2
Nauru i. Nauru 107 G2
Nauru country S. Pacific Ocean 107 G2
Naustdal Norway 45 D6
Nauta Peru 142 D4
Nautaca Uzbek. see Qarshi
Naute Dam Namibia 100 C4
Nauzad Afgh. 89 G3
Nava Mex. 131 C6
Navadwip India 83 G5
Navahrudak Belarus 45 N10
Navajo Lake U.S.A. 129 J3
Navajo Mountain U.S.A. 129 H3
Navalmoral de la Mata Spain 57 D4
Navalvillar de Pela Spain 57 D4
Navan Ireland 51 F4
Navangar India see Jamnagar
Navapolatsk Belarus 45 P9
Nāvar, Dasht-e depr. Afgh. 89 G3
Navarin, Mys c. Rus. Fed. 65 S3
Navarra aut. comm. Spain 57 F2
Navarra, Comunidad Foral de aut. comm. Spain see Navarra
Navarre Australia 112 A6
Navarre aut. comm. Spain see Navarra
Navarro r. U.S.A. 128 B2
Navashino Rus. Fed. 42 I5
Navasota U.S.A. 131 D6

▶Navassa Island terr. West Indies 137 I5
United States Unincorporated Territory.

Naver r. U.K. 50 E2
Näverede Sweden 44 I5
Navi Mumbai Mahar. 87 L6
Navlakhi India 82 B5
Navlya Rus. Fed. 43 G5
Năvodari Romania 59 M2
Navoi Uzbek. see Navoiy
Navoiy Uzbek. 89 G1
Navojoa Mex. 127 F8
Navolato Mex. 136 C4
Návpaktos Greece see Nafpaktos
Návplion Greece see Nafplio
Navşar Turkey see Şemdinli
Navsari India 84 B1
Nawá Syria 85 C3
Nawabganj Bangl. 83 G4
Nawabshah Pak. 89 H5
Nawada India 83 F4
Nāwah Afgh. 89 G3
Nawalgarh India 82 C4
Nawanshahr India 82 D3
Nawan Shehar India see Nawanshahr
Nawar, Dasht-i depr. Afgh. see Nāvar, Dasht-e
Nawarangpur India see Nabarangapur
Nawngcho Myanmar see Nawnghkio
Nawnghkio Myanmar 70 B2
Nawng Hpa Myanmar 70 B2
Nawngleng Myanmar 70 B2
Nawoiy Uzbek. see Navoiy
Naxçıvan Azer. 91 G3
Naxos i. Greece 59 K6
Nayagarh India 84 E1
Nayak Afgh. 89 G3
Nayar Mex. 136 D4
Nāy Band, Kūh-e mt. Iran 88 E3
Nayong China 76 E3
Nayoro Japan 74 F3

▶Nay Pyi Taw Myanmar 70 B3
Joint capital (with Rangoon) of Myanmar.

Nazaré Brazil 145 D1
Nazareno Mex. 131 C7
Nazareth Israel 85 B3
Nazário Brazil 145 A2
Nazas Mex. 131 B7
Nazas r. Mex. 131 B7
Nazca Peru 142 D6
Nazca Ridge sea feature S. Pacific Ocean 151 O7
Nāzīl Iran 89 F4
Nazilli Turkey 59 M6
Nazimabad Pak. 89 G5
Nazımiye Turkey 91 E3
Nazir Hat Bangl. 83 G5
Nazko Canada 120 F4
Nazran' Rus. Fed. 91 G2
Nazrēt Eth. 98 D3
Nazwá Oman 88 E6
Ncojane Botswana 100 E2
N'dalatando Angola 99 B4
Ndélé Cent. Afr. Rep. 98 C3
Ndendé Gabon 98 B4
Ndende i. Solomon Is see Ndeni
Ndeni i. Solomon Is 107 G3

▶Ndjamena Chad 97 E3
Capital of Chad.

N'Djamena Chad see Ndjamena
Ndjouani i. Comoros see Nzwani
Ndoi i. Fiji see Doi
Ndola Zambia 99 C5
Nduke i. Solomon Is see Kolombangara
Ndwedwe S. Africa 101 J5
Ne, Hon i. Vietnam 70 D3
Neabul Creek r. Australia 112 C1
Neagh, Lough l. U.K. 51 F3
Neah Bay U.S.A. 126 B2
Neale, Lake salt flat Australia 109 E6
Nea Liosia Greece 59 J5
Neapoli Greece 59 J6
Neapolis Italy see Naples
Nea Roda Greece 59 J4
Neath U.K. 49 D7
Neath r. U.K. 49 D7
Nebbi Uganda 98 D3
Nebine Creek r. Australia 112 C2
Neblina, Pico da mt. Brazil 142 E3
Nebo Australia 110 E4
Nebo, Mount U.S.A. 129 H2
Nebolchi Rus. Fed. 42 G4
Nebraska state U.S.A. 130 C3
Nebraska City U.S.A. 130 E3
Nebrodi, Monti mts Sicily Italy 58 F6
Neches r. U.S.A. 131 E6
Nechisar National Park Eth. 98 D3
Nechranice, Vodní nádrž resr Czech Rep. 53 N4
Neckar r. Germany 53 I5
Neckarsulm Germany 53 J5
Necker Island U.S.A. 150 J4
Necochea Arg. 144 E5
Nederland country Europe see Netherlands
Nederlandse Antillen terr. West Indies see Netherlands Antilles
Neder Rijn r. Neth. 52 F3
Nedlouc, Lac l. Canada 123 G2
Nedluk Lake Canada see Nedlouc, Lac
Nêdong China see Zêtang
Nedre Soppero Sweden 44 L2
Nédroma Alg. 57 F6
Needle Mountain U.S.A. 126 F3
Needles U.S.A. 129 F4
Neemach India see Neemuch
Neemuch India 82 C4
Neenah U.S.A. 134 A1
Neepawa Canada 121 L5
Neergaard Lake Canada 119 J2
Neerijnen Neth. 52 F3
Neerpelt Belgium 52 F3
Neftçala Azer. 91 H3
Neftechala Azer. see Uzboy
Neftechala Azer. see Neftçala
Neftegorsk Sakhalinskaya Oblast' Rus. Fed. 74 F1
Neftegorsk Samarskaya Oblast' Rus. Fed. 43 K5
Neftekamsk Rus. Fed. 41 Q4
Neftekumsk Rus. Fed. 91 G1
Nefteyugansk Rus. Fed. 64 I3
Neftezavodsk Turkm. see Seýdi
Neftezawodsk Turkm. see Seýdi
Nefyn U.K. 49 C6
Nefza Tunisia 58 C6
Negage Angola 99 B4
Negār Iran 88 E4
Negara Indon. 108 A2
Negēlē Eth. 98 D3
Negev des. Israel 85 B4
Negomane Moz. 99 D5
Negombo Sri Lanka 84 C5
Negotino Macedonia 59 J4
Negra, Cordillera mts Peru 142 C5
Negra, Punta pt Peru 142 B5
Negra, Serra mts Brazil 145 C2
Negrais, Cape Myanmar 70 A4
Négrine Alg. 58 B7
Negro r. Arg. 144 D6
Negro r. Brazil 143 G7
Negro r. Brazil 145 A4
Negro r. S. America 142 G4
Negro, Cabo c. Morocco 57 D6
Negroponte i. Greece see Evvoia
Negros i. Phil. 69 G5
Negru Vodă, Podişul plat. Romania 59 M3
Nehbandān Iran 89 F4
Nehe China 74 B2
Neijiang China 76 E2
Neilburg Canada 121 I4
Neimenggu aut. reg. China see Nei Mongol Zizhiqu
Nei Mongol Zizhiqu aut. reg. China 74 A2
Neinstedt Germany 53 L3
Neiva Col. 142 C3
Neixiang China 77 F1
Nejanilini Lake Canada 121 L3
Nejd reg. Saudi Arabia see Najd
Neka Iran 88 D2
Nek'emtē Eth. 98 D3
Nekrasovskoye Rus. Fed. 42 I4
Neksø Denmark 45 I9
Nelang India 82 D3
Nelia Australia 110 C4
Nelidovo Rus. Fed. 42 G4
Neligh U.S.A. 130 D3
Nel'kan Rus. Fed. 65 P3
Nellore India 84 C3
Nelluz watercourse Turkey 85 D1
Nel'ma Rus. Fed. 74 E3
Nelson Canada 120 G5
Nelson r. Canada 121 M3
Nelson N.Z. 113 D5
Nelson U.K. 48 E5
Nelson U.S.A. 129 G4
Nelson, Cape Australia 111 C8
Nelson, Cape P.N.G. 69 L8
Nelson, Estrecho strait Chile 144 A8
Nelson Bay Australia 112 F4
Nelson Forks Canada 120 F3
Nelsonia U.S.A. 135 H5
Nelson Lakes National Park N.Z. 113 D6
Nelson Reservoir U.S.A. 126 G2
Nelspruit S. Africa 101 J3
Néma Mauritania 96 C3
Nema Rus. Fed. 42 K4
Neman r. Belarus/Lith. see Nyoman
Neman Rus. Fed. 45 M9
Nemausus France see Nîmes
Nemawar India 82 D5
Nemed Rus. Fed. 42 L3
Nementcha, Monts des mts Alg. 58 B7
Nemetocenna France see Arras
Nemetskiy, Mys c. Rus. Fed. 44 Q2
Nemirov Ukr. see Nemyriv
Nemiscau r. Canada 122 F4
Nemiscau, Lac l. Canada 122 F4
Nemor He r. China 74 B2
Nemours Alg. see Ghazaouet
Nemours France 56 F2
Nemrut Dağı mt. Turkey 91 F3
Nemunas r. Belarus/Lith. see Nyoman
Nemuro Japan 74 G4
Nemuro-kaikyō sea chan. Japan/Rus. Fed. 74 G4
Nemyriv Ukr. 43 F6
Nenagh Ireland 51 D5
Nenana U.S.A. 118 D3
Nene r. U.K. 49 H6
Nenjiang China 74 B2
Nen Jiang r. China 74 B3
Neosho U.S.A. 131 E4
Nepal country Asia 83 E3
Nepalganj Nepal 83 E3
Nepean Canada 135 H1
Nepean, Point Australia 112 B7
Nephi U.S.A. 129 H2
Nephin hill Ireland 51 C3
Nephin Beg Range hills Ireland 51 C3
Nepisiguit r. Canada 123 I5
Nepoko r. Dem. Rep. Congo 98 C3
Nérac France 56 E4
Nerang Australia 112 F1
Nera Tso l. China 83 H3
Nerchinsk Rus. Fed. 73 L2
Nerekhta Rus. Fed. 42 I4
Néret, Lac l. Canada 123 H3
Neretva r. Bos.-Herz./Croatia 58 G3
Nêri Pünco l. China 83 G3
Neriquinha Angola 99 C5
Neris r. Lith. 45 M9
also known as Viliya (Belarus/Lithuania)
Nerl' r. Rus. Fed. 42 H4
Nerópolis Brazil 145 A2
Neryungri Rus. Fed. 65 N4
Nes Neth. 52 F1
Nes Norway 45 F6
Nes' Rus. Fed. 42 J2
Nesbyen Norway 45 F6
Neskaupstaður Iceland 44 [inset]
Nesle France 52 C5
Nesna Norway 44 H3
Nesri India 84 B2
Ness r. U.K. 50 E3
Ness, Loch l. U.K. 50 E3
Ness City U.S.A. 130 D4
Nesse r. Germany 53 K4
Nesselrode, Mount Canada/U.S.A. 120 C3
Nestor Falls Canada 121 M5
Nestos r. Greece 59 K4
also known as Mesta
Nesvizh Belarus see Nyasvizh
Netanya Israel 85 B3
Netherlands country Europe 52 F2

▶Netherlands Antilles terr. West Indies 137 K6
Self-governing Netherlands Territory.

Netphen Germany 53 I4
Netrakona Bangl. 83 G4
Netrokona Bangl. see Netrakona
Nettilling Lake Canada 119 K3
Neubrandenburg Germany 53 N1
Neuburg an der Donau Germany 53 L6
Neuchâtel Switz. 56 H3
Neuchâtel, Lac de l. Switz. 56 H3
Neuendettelsau Germany 53 K5
Neuenhaus Germany 52 G2
Neuenkirchen Germany 53 J1
Neuenkirchen (Oldenburg) Germany 53 I2
Neufchâteau Belgium 52 F5
Neufchâteau France 56 G2
Neufchâtel-en-Bray France 52 B5
Neufchâtel-Hardelot France 52 B4
Neuharlingersiel Germany 53 H1
Neuhausen Rus. Fed. see Gur'yevsk
Neuhof Germany 53 J4
Neu Kaliß Germany 53 L1
Neukirchen Hessen Germany 53 J4
Neukirchen Sachsen Germany 53 M4
Neukuhren Rus. Fed. see Pionerskiy
Neumarkt in der Oberpfalz Germany 53 L5
Neumayer research station Antarctica 152 B2
Neumünster Germany 47 L3
Neunburg vorm Wald Germany 53 M5
Neunkirchen Austria 47 P7
Neunkirchen Germany 53 H5
Neuquén Arg. 144 C5
Neuruppin Germany 53 M2
Neu Sandez Poland see Nowy Sącz
Neuse r. U.S.A. 133 E5
Neusiedler See l. Austria/Hungary 47 P7
Neusiedler See Seewinkel, Nationalpark nat. park Austria 47 P7
Neuss Germany 52 G3
Neustadt (Wied) Germany 53 H4
Neustadt am Rübenberge Germany 53 J2
Neustadt an der Aisch Germany 53 K5
Neustadt an der Hardt Germany see Neustadt an der Weinstraße
Neustadt an der Waldnaab Germany 53 M5
Neustadt an der Weinstraße Germany 53 I5
Neustadt bei Coburg Germany 53 L4
Neustadt-Glewe Germany 53 L1
Neustrelitz Germany 53 N1
Neutraubling Germany 53 M6
Neuville-lès-Dieppe France 52 B5
Neuwied Germany 53 H4
Neu Wulmstorf Germany 53 J1
Nevada IA U.S.A. 130 E3
Nevada MO U.S.A. 130 E4
Nevada state U.S.A. 126 D5
Nevada, Sierra mts Spain 57 E5
Nevada, Sierra mts U.S.A. 128 C1
Nevada City U.S.A. 128 C2
Nevado, Cerro mt. Arg. 144 C5
Nevado, Sierra del mts Arg. 144 C5
Nevasa India 84 B2
Nevatim Israel 85 B4
Nevdubstroy Rus. Fed. see Kirovsk
Nevel' Rus. Fed. 42 F4
Nevel'sk Rus. Fed. 74 F3
Never Rus. Fed. 74 B1
Nevers France 56 F3
Nevertire Australia 112 C3
Nevesinje Bos.-Herz. 58 H3
Nevinnomyssk Rus. Fed. 91 F1
Nevşehir Turkey 90 D3
Nevskoye Rus. Fed. 74 D3
New r. CA U.S.A. 129 F5
New r. WV U.S.A. 134 E5
Newala Tanz. 99 D5
New Albany IN U.S.A. 134 C4
New Albany MS U.S.A. 131 F5
New Amsterdam Guyana 143 G2
New Amsterdam U.S.A. see New York
New Angledool Australia 112 C2
Newark DE U.S.A. 135 H4
Newark NJ U.S.A. 135 H3
Newark NY U.S.A. 135 G2
Newark OH U.S.A. 134 D3
Newark airport U.S.A. 132 F3
Newark Lake U.S.A. 129 F2
Newark-on-Trent U.K. 49 G5
New Bedford U.S.A. 135 J3
Newberg U.S.A. 126 C3
New Berlin U.S.A. 135 H2
New Bern U.S.A. 133 E5
Newberry IN U.S.A. 134 B4
Newberry MI U.S.A. 132 C2
Newberry SC U.S.A. 133 D5
Newberry National Volcanic Monument nat. park U.S.A. 126 C4
Newberry Springs U.S.A. 128 E4
New Bethlehem U.S.A. 134 F3
Newbiggin-by-the-Sea U.K. 48 F3
New Bight Bahamas 133 F7
New Bloomfield U.S.A. 135 G3
Newboro Canada 135 G1
New Boston OH U.S.A. 134 D4
New Boston TX U.S.A. 131 E5
New Braunfels U.S.A. 131 D6
Newbridge Ireland 51 F4
New Britain i. P.N.G. 69 L8
New Britain U.S.A. 135 I3
New Britain Trench sea feature S. Pacific Ocean 150 G6
New Brunswick prov. Canada 123 I5
New Brunswick U.S.A. 135 H3
New Buffalo U.S.A. 134 B3
Newburgh Canada 135 G1
Newburgh U.K. 50 G3
Newburgh U.S.A. 135 H3
Newbury U.K. 49 F7
Newburyport U.S.A. 135 J2
Newby Bridge U.K. 48 E4

▶New Caledonia terr. S. Pacific Ocean 107 G4
French Overseas Collectivity.

New Caledonia Trough sea feature Tasman Sea 150 G7
New Carlisle Canada 123 I4
Newcastle Australia 112 E4
Newcastle Canada 135 F2
Newcastle Ireland 51 F4
Newcastle S. Africa 101 I4
Newcastle U.K. 51 G3
New Castle CO U.S.A. 129 J2
New Castle IN U.S.A. 134 C4
New Castle KY U.S.A. 134 C4
New Castle PA U.S.A. 134 E3
Newcastle UT U.S.A. 129 G3
New Castle VA U.S.A. 134 E5
Newcastle WY U.S.A. 126 G4
Newcastle Emlyn U.K. 49 C6
Newcastle-under-Lyme U.K. 49 E5
Newcastle upon Tyne U.K. 48 F4
Newcastle Waters Australia 108 F4
Newcastle West Ireland 51 C5
Newchwang China see Yingkou
New City U.S.A. 135 I3
Newcomb U.S.A. 129 I3
New Concord U.S.A. 134 E4
New Cumberland U.S.A. 134 E3
New Cumnock U.K. 50 E5
New Deer U.K. 50 G3

▶New Delhi India 82 D3
Capital of India.

New Don Pedro Reservoir U.S.A. 128 C3
Newell U.S.A. 130 C2
Newell, Lake salt flat Australia 109 D6
Newell, Lake Canada 121 I5
New England National Park Australia 112 F3
New England Range mts Australia 112 E3
New England Seamounts sea feature N. Atlantic Ocean 148 E3
Newenham, Cape U.S.A. 118 B4
Newent U.K. 49 E7
New Era U.S.A. 134 B2
Newfane NY U.S.A. 135 F2
Newfane VT U.S.A. 135 I2
New Forest National Park nat. park England 49 F8
Newfoundland i. Canada 123 K4
Newfoundland prov. Canada see Newfoundland and Labrador
Newfoundland and Labrador prov. Canada 123 K3
Newfoundland Evaporation Basin salt l. U.S.A. 129 G1
New Galloway U.K. 50 E5
New Georgia i. Solomon Is 107 F2
New Georgia Islands Solomon Is 107 F2
New Georgia Sound sea chan. Solomon Is 107 F2
New Glasgow Canada 123 J5

▶New Guinea i. Indon./P.N.G. 69 K8
Largest island in Oceania, and 2nd in the world.

New Halfa Sudan 86 E6
New Hampshire state U.S.A. 135 J1
New Hampton U.S.A. 130 E3
New Hanover i. P.N.G. 106 F2
New Haven CT U.S.A. 135 I3
New Haven IN U.S.A. 134 C3
New Haven WV U.S.A. 134 E4
New Hebrides country S. Pacific Ocean see Vanuatu
New Hebrides Trench sea feature S. Pacific Ocean 150 H7
New Holstein U.S.A. 134 A2
New Iberia U.S.A. 131 F6
Newington S. Africa 101 J3
Newinn Ireland 51 E5
New Ireland i. P.N.G. 106 F2
New Jersey state U.S.A. 135 H4
New Kensington U.S.A. 134 F3
New Kent U.S.A. 135 G5
Newkirk U.S.A. 131 D4
New Lanark U.K. 50 F5
Newland Range hills Australia 109 C7
New Lexington U.S.A. 134 D4
New Liskeard Canada 122 F5
New London CT U.S.A. 135 I3
New London MO U.S.A. 130 F4
New Madrid U.S.A. 131 F4
Newman Australia 109 B5
Newman U.S.A. 128 C3
Newmarket Canada 134 F1
Newmarket Ireland 51 C5
Newmarket U.K. 49 H6
New Market U.S.A. 135 F4
Newmarket-on-Fergus Ireland 51 D5
New Martinsville U.S.A. 134 E4
New Meadows U.S.A. 126 D3
New Mexico state U.S.A. 127 G6
New Miami U.S.A. 134 C4
New Milford U.S.A. 135 H3
Newnan U.S.A. 133 C5
New Orleans U.S.A. 131 F6
New Paris IN U.S.A. 134 C3
New Paris OH U.S.A. 134 C4
New Philadelphia U.S.A. 134 E3
New Pitsligo U.K. 50 G3
New Plymouth N.Z. 113 E4
Newport Mayo Ireland 51 C4
Newport Tipperary Ireland 51 D5
Newport England U.K. 49 E6
Newport England U.K. 49 F8
Newport Wales U.K. 49 D7
Newport AR U.S.A. 131 F5
Newport IN U.S.A. 134 B4
Newport KY U.S.A. 134 C4
Newport MI U.S.A. 134 D3
Newport NH U.S.A. 135 I2
Newport NJ U.S.A. 135 H4
Newport OR U.S.A. 126 B3
Newport RI U.S.A. 135 J3
Newport VT U.S.A. 135 I1
Newport WA U.S.A. 126 D2
Newport Beach U.S.A. 128 E5
Newport News U.S.A. 135 G5
Newport Pagnell U.K. 49 G6
New Port Richey U.S.A. 133 D6
New Providence i. Bahamas 133 E7
Newquay U.K. 49 B8
New Roads U.S.A. 131 F6
New Rochelle U.S.A. 135 I3
New Rockford U.S.A. 130 D2
New Romney U.K. 49 H8
New Ross Ireland 51 F5
Newry Australia 108 E4
Newry U.K. 51 F3
New Siberia Islands Rus. Fed. 65 P2
New Smyrna Beach U.S.A. 133 D6
New South Wales state Australia 112 C4
New Stanton U.S.A. 134 F3
Newton U.K. 48 E5
Newton GA U.S.A. 133 C6
Newton IA U.S.A. 130 E3
Newton IL U.S.A. 130 F4
Newton KS U.S.A. 130 D4
Newton MA U.S.A. 135 J2
Newton MS U.S.A. 131 F5
Newton NC U.S.A. 132 D5
Newton NJ U.S.A. 135 H3
Newton TX U.S.A. 131 E6
Newton Abbot U.K. 49 D8
Newton Mearns U.K. 50 E5
Newton Stewart U.K. 50 E6
Newtown Ireland 51 D5
Newtown England U.K. 49 E6
Newtown Wales U.K. 49 D6
Newtown U.S.A. 134 C4
New Town U.S.A. 130 C1
Newtownabbey U.K. 51 G3
Newtownards U.K. 51 G3
Newtownbarry Ireland see Bunclody
Newtownbutler U.K. 51 E3
Newtown Mount Kennedy Ireland 51 F4
Newtown St Boswells U.K. 50 G5
Newtownstewart U.K. 51 E3
New Ulm U.S.A. 130 E2
Newville U.S.A. 135 G3
New World Island Canada 123 L4

▶New York U.S.A. 135 I3
2nd most populous city in North America, and 5th in the world.

New York state U.S.A. 135 H2

▶New Zealand country Oceania 113 D5
3rd largest and 3rd most populous country in Oceania.

Neya Rus. Fed. 42 I4
Ney Bīd Iran 88 E4
Neyrīz Iran 88 D4
Neyshābūr Iran 88 E2
Nezhin Ukr. see Nizhyn
Nezperce U.S.A. 126 D3
Ngabé Congo 98 B4
Nga Chong, Khao mt. Myanmar/Thai. 70 B4
Ngagahtawng Myanmar 76 C3
Ngagau mt. Tanz. 99 D4
Ngalu Indon. 108 C2
Ngamring China 83 F3
Ngangla Ringco salt l. China 83 E3
Nganglong Kangri mt. China 82 E2
Nganglong Kangri mts China 82 E2
Ngangzê Co salt l. China 83 F3
Ngangzê Shan mts China 83 F3
Ngân Sơn Vietnam 70 D2
Ngaoundal Cameroon 96 E4
Ngaoundéré Cameroon 97 E4
Ngape Myanmar 70 A2
Ngaputaw Myanmar 70 A3
Ngarrab China see Gyaca
Ngathainggyaung Myanmar 70 A3
Ngau i. Fiji see Gau
Ngawa China see Aba
Ngeaur i. Palau see Angaur
Ngeruangel i. Palau 69 I5
Ngga Pulu mt. Indon. see Jaya, Puncak
Ngiap r. Laos 70 C3
Ngilmina Indon. 108 D2
Ngiva Angola see Ondjiva
Ngo Congo 98 B4
Ngoako Ramalepe S. Africa see Duiwelskloof
Ngoin, Co salt l. China 83 G3
Ngok Linh mt. Vietnam 70 D4
Ngoko r. Cameroon/Congo 97 E4
Ngola Shankou pass China 76 C1
Ngom Qu r. China see Ji Qu
Ngong Shuen Chau pen. H.K. China see Stonecutters' Island
Ngoqumaima China 83 F2
Ngoring China 76 C1
Ngoring Hu l. China 76 C1
Ngourti Niger 96 E3
Nguigmi Niger 96 E3
Nguiu Australia 108 E2
Ngükang China 76 B2
Ngukurr Australia 108 F3
Ngulu atoll Micronesia 69 J5
Ngunza Angola see Sumbe
Ngunza-Kabolu Angola see Sumbe
Nguru Nigeria 96 E3
Ngwaketse admin. dist. Botswana see Southern
Ngwane country Africa see Swaziland
Ngwathe S. Africa 101 H4
Ngwavuma r. S. Africa/Swaziland 101 K4
Ngwelezana S. Africa 101 J5
Nhachengue Moz. 101 L2
Nhamalabué Moz. 99 D5
Nha Trang Vietnam 71 E4
Nhecolândia Brazil 143 G7
Nhill Australia 111 C8
Nhlangano Swaziland 101 J4
Nho Quan Vietnam 70 D2
Nhow i. Fiji see Gau
Nhulunbuy Australia 110 B2
Niacam Canada 121 J4
Niafounké Mali 96 C3
Niagara U.S.A. 132 C2
Niagara Falls Canada 134 F2
Niagara Falls U.S.A. 134 F2
Niagara-on-the-Lake Canada 134 F2
Niagzu Aksai Chin 82 D2
Niah Sarawak Malaysia 68 E6
Niakaramandougou Côte d'Ivoire 96 C4

▶Niamey Niger 96 D3
Capital of Niger.

Nīām Kand Iran 88 E5
Niampak Indon. 69 H6
Niangara Dem. Rep. Congo 98 C3
Niangay, Lac l. Mali 96 C3
Nianzishan China 74 A3
Nias i. Indon. 71 B7
Niassa, Lago l. Africa see Nyasa, Lake
Niaur i. Palau see Angaur
Nīāzābād Iran 89 F3
Nibil Well Australia 108 D5
Nīca Latvia 45 L8

▶Nicaragua country Central America 137 G6
5th largest country in North America.

Nicaragua, Lago de Nicaragua 137 G6
Nicastro Italy 58 G5
Nice France 56 H5
Nice U.S.A. 128 B2
Nicephorium Syria see Ar Raqqah
Niceville U.S.A. 133 C6
Nichicun, Lac l. Canada 123 H3
Nicholas Channel Bahamas/Cuba 133 D8
Nicholasville U.S.A. 134 C5
Nichols U.S.A. 134 A1
Nicholson r. Australia 110 B3
Nicholson Lake Canada 121 K2
Nicholson Range hills Australia 109 B6
Nicholville U.S.A. 135 H1
Nicobar Islands India 71 A5
Nicolaus U.S.A. 128 C2
Nicomedia Kocaeli Turkey see İzmit

▶Nicosia Cyprus 85 A2
Capital of Cyprus.

Nicoya, Península de pen. Costa Rica 137 G7
Nida Lith. 45 L9
Nidagunda India 84 C2
Nidd r. U.K. 48 F4
Nidda Germany 53 J4
Nidder r. Germany 53 I4
Nidzica Poland 47 R4
Niebüll Germany 47 L3
Nied r. France 52 G5
Niederanven Lux. 52 G5
Niederaula Germany 53 J4
Niedere Tauern mts Austria 47 N7
Niedersachsen land Germany 53 I2
Niedersächsisches Wattenmeer, Nationalpark nat. park Germany 52 G1
Niefang Equat. Guinea 96 E4
Niellé Côte d'Ivoire 96 C3
Nienburg (Weser) Germany 53 J2
Niers r. Germany 52 F3
Nierstein Germany 53 I5
Nieuwe-Niedorp Neth. 52 E2
Nieuwerkerk aan de IJssel Neth. 52 E3
Nieuw Nickerie Suriname 143 G2
Nieuwolda Neth. 52 G1
Nieuwoudtville S. Africa 100 D6
Nieuwpoort Belgium 52 C3
Nieuw-Vossemeer Neth. 52 E3
Niğde Turkey 90 D3
Niger country Africa 96 D3

▶Niger r. Africa 96 D4
3rd longest river in Africa.

Niger, Mouths of the Nigeria 96 D4
Niger Cone sea feature S. Atlantic Ocean 148 I5

▶Nigeria country Africa 96 D4
Most populous country in Africa, and 8th in the world.

Nighthawk Lake Canada 122 E4
Nigrita Greece 59 J4
Nihing Pak. 89 G4
Nihon country Asia see Japan
Niigata Japan 75 E5
Niihama Japan 75 D6
Ni'ihau i. U.S.A. 127 [inset]
Nii-jima i. Japan 75 E6
Niimi Japan 75 D6
Niitsu Japan 75 E5
Nijil, Wādī watercourse Jordan 85 B4
Nijkerk Neth. 52 F2
Nijmegen Neth. 52 F3
Nijverdal Neth. 52 G2
Nikel' Rus. Fed. 44 Q2
Nikki Benin 96 D4
Nikkō Kokuritsu-kōen nat. park Japan 75 E5
Nikolayev Ukr. see Mykolayiv
Nikolayevka Rus. Fed. 43 J5
Nikolayevsk Rus. Fed. 43 J6
Nikolayevskiy Rus. Fed. see Nikolayevsk
Nikolayevsk-na-Amure Rus. Fed. 74 F1
Nikol'sk Rus. Fed. 42 J4
Nikol'skiy Kazakh. see Satpayev
Nikol'skoye Kamchatskaya Oblast' Rus. Fed. 65 R4
Nikol'skoye Vologod. Obl. Rus. Fed. see Sheksna
Nikopol' Ukr. 43 G7
Niksar Turkey 90 E2
Nīkshahr Iran 89 F5
Nikšić Montenegro 58 H3
Nīkū Jahān Iran 89 F5
Nikumaroro atoll Kiribati 107 I2
Nikunau i. Kiribati 107 H2
Nīl, Bahr el r. Africa see Nile
Nilagiri India 83 F5
Niland U.S.A. 129 F5
Nilande Atoll Maldives see Nilandhoo Atoll
Nilandhe Atoll Maldives see Nilandhoo Atoll
Nilandhoo Atoll Maldives 81 D11
Nilang India see Nelang
Nilanga India 84 C2
Nilaveli Sri Lanka 84 D4

▶Nile r. Africa 90 C5
Longest river in the world.

Niles MI U.S.A. 134 B3
Niles OH U.S.A. 134 E3
Nilgiri Hills India 84 C4
Nīlī Dāykundī 89 G3
Nīl Kowtal Afgh. 89 G3
Nilphamari Bangl. 83 G4
Nilsiä Fin. 44 P5
Nimach India see Neemuch
Niman r. Rus. Fed. 74 D2
Nimba, Monts mts Africa see Nimba, Mount
Nimba, Mount Africa 96 C4
Nimbal India 84 B2
Nimberra Well Australia 109 C5
Nimelen r. Rus. Fed. 74 E1
Nîmes France 56 G5
Nimmitabel Australia 111 E8
Nimrod Glacier Antarctica 152 H1
Nimu India 82 D2
Nimule Sudan 97 G4
Nimwegen Neth. see Nijmegen
Nindigully Australia 112 D2
Nine Degree Channel India 84 B4
Nine Islands P.N.G. see Kilinailau Islands
Ninepin Group is H.K. China 77 [inset]
Ninetyeast Ridge sea feature Indian Ocean 149 N8
Ninety Mile Beach Australia 112 C7
Ninety Mile Beach N.Z. 113 D2
Nineveh U.S.A. 135 H2
Ning'an China 74 C3
Ningbo China 77 I2
Ningde China 77 H3
Ning'er China see Pu'er
Ningguo China 77 H2
Ninghai China 77 I2
Ninghsia Hui Autonomous Region aut. reg. China see Ningxia Huizu Zizhiqu
Ninghua China 77 H3
Ninging India 83 H3
Ningjiang China see Songyuan
Ningjing Shan mts China 76 C2
Ninglang China 76 D3
Ningming China 76 E4
Ningnan China 76 D3
Ningqiang China 76 E1
Ningwu China 73 K5
Ningxia aut. reg. China see Ningxia Huizu Zizhiqu
Ningxia Huizu Zizhiqu aut. reg. China 76 E1
Ningxian China 73 J5
Ningxiang China 77 G2
Ningzhou China see Huaning
Ninh Binh Vietnam 70 D2
Ninh Hoa Vietnam 71 E4
Ninigo Group atolls P.N.G. 69 K7
Ninnis Glacier Antarctica 152 G2
Ninnis Glacier Tongue Antarctica 152 H2
Ninohe Japan 75 F4
Niobrara r. U.S.A. 130 D3
Niokolo Koba, Parc National du nat. park Senegal 96 B3
Niono Mali 96 C3
Nioro Mali 96 C3
Niort France 56 D3
Nipani India 84 B2
Nipawin Canada 121 J4
Niphad India 84 B1
Nipigon Canada 119 J5
Nipigon, Lake Canada 119 J5
Nipishish Lake Canada 123 J3
Nipissing, Lake Canada 122 F5
Nippon country Asia see Japan
Nippon Hai sea N. Pacific Ocean see Japan, Sea of
Nipton U.S.A. 129 F4
Niquelândia Brazil 145 A1
Nir Ardabīl Iran 88 B2
Nir Yazd Iran 88 D4
Nira r. India 84 B2
Nirji China 74 B2
Nirmal India 84 C2
Nirmali India 83 F4
Nirmal Range hills India 84 C2
Niš Serbia 59 I3
Nisa Port. 57 C4
Nisarpur India 84 B1
Niscemi Sicily Italy 58 F6
Nīshāpūr Iran see Neyshābūr
Nishino-shima vol. Japan 75 F8
Nishi-Sonogi-hantō pen. Japan 75 C6
Nisibis Turkey see Nusaybin
Nísiros i. Greece see Nisyros
Niskibi r. Canada 121 N3
Nisling r. Canada 120 B2
Nispen Neth. 52 E3
Nissan r. Sweden 45 H8
Nistru r. Ukr. 59 N1 see Dniester
Nisutlin r. Canada 120 C2
Nisyros i. Greece 59 L6
Niṭā Saudi Arabia 88 C5
Nitchequon Canada 123 H3
Nitendi i. Solomon Is see Ndeni
Niterói Brazil 145 C3
Nith r. U.K. 50 F5
Nitibe East Timor 108 D2
Niti Pass China/India 82 D3
Niti Shankou pass China/India see Niti Pass
Nitmiluk National Park Australia 108 F3
Nitra Slovakia 47 Q6
Nitro U.S.A. 134 E4
Niuafo'ou i. Tonga 107 I3
Niuatoputopu i. Tonga 107 I3

▶Niue terr. S. Pacific Ocean 107 J3
Self-governing New Zealand Overseas Territory.

Niujing China see Binchuan
Niulakita i. Tuvalu 107 H3
Niutao i. Tuvalu 107 H2
Niutoushan China 77 H2
Nivala Fin. 44 N5
Nive watercourse Australia 110 D5
Nivelles Belgium 52 E4
Niwai India 82 C4
Niwas India 82 E5
Nixia China see Sêrxü
Nixon U.S.A. 128 D2
Niya China see Minfeng
Niya He r. China 83 E1
Nizamabad India 84 C2
Nizam Sagar l. India 84 C2
Nizhnedevitsk Rus. Fed. 43 H6
Nizhnekamsk Rus. Fed. 42 K5
Nizhnekamskoye Vodokhranilishche resr Rus. Fed. 41 Q4
Nizhnekolymsk Rus. Fed. 65 R3
Nizhnetambovskoye Rus. Fed. 74 E2
Nizhneudinsk Rus. Fed. 72 H2
Nizhnevartovsk Rus. Fed. 64 I3
Nizhnevolzhsk Rus. Fed. see Narimanov
Nizhneyansk Rus. Fed. 65 O2
Nizhniy Baskunchak Rus. Fed. 43 J6
Nizhniye Kresty Rus. Fed. see Cherskiy
Nizhniy Lomov Rus. Fed. 43 I5
Nizhniy Novgorod Rus. Fed. 42 I4
Nizhniy Odes Rus. Fed. 42 L3
Nizhniy Pyandzh Tajik. see Panji Poyon
Nizhniy Tagil Rus. Fed. 41 R4
Nizhnyaya Mola Rus. Fed. 42 J2
Nizhnyaya Omra Rus. Fed. 42 L3
Nizhnyaya Pirenga, Ozero l. Rus. Fed. 44 R3
Nizhnyaya Tunguska r. Rus. Fed. 64 J3
Nizhnyaya Tura Rus. Fed. 41 R4
Nizhyn Ukr. 43 F6
Nizina r. U.S.A. 120 A2
Nizina Mazowiecka reg. Poland 47 R4
Nizip Turkey 85 C1
Nízke Tatry nat. park Slovakia 47 Q6
Nizwā Oman see Nazwá
Nizza France see Nice
Njallavarri mt. Norway 44 L2
Njavve Sweden 44 K3
Njazidja i. Comoros 99 E5
Njombe Tanz. 99 D4
Njurundabommen Sweden 44 J5
Nkambe Cameroon 96 E4
Nkandla S. Africa 101 J5
Nkawkaw Ghana 96 C4
Nkhata Bay Malawi 99 D5
Nkhotakota Malawi 99 D5
Nkondwe Tanz. 99 D4
Nkongsamba Cameroon 96 D4
Nkululeko S. Africa 101 H6
Nkwenkwezi S. Africa 101 H7
Noakhali Bangl. 83 G5
Noatak r. U.S.A. 118 B3
Nobber Ireland 51 F4
Nobeoka Japan 75 C6
Noblesville U.S.A. 134 B3
Noboribetsu Japan 74 F4
Noccundra Australia 111 C5
Nockatunga Australia 111 C5
Nocona U.S.A. 131 D5
Noel Kempff Mercado, Parque Nacional nat. park Bol. 142 F6
Noelville Canada 122 E5
Nogales Mex. 127 F7
Nogales U.S.A. 127 F7
Nōgata Japan 75 C6
Nogent-le-Rotrou France 56 E2
Nogent-sur-Oise France 52 C5
Noginsk Rus. Fed. 42 H5
Nogliki Rus. Fed. 74 F2
Nogoa r. Australia 110 E4
Nohar India 82 C3
Noheji Japan 74 F4
Nohfelden Germany 52 H5
Noida India 82 D3
Noirmoutier, Île de i. France 56 C3
Noirmoutier-en-l'Île France 56 C3
Noisseville France 52 G5
Nokhowch, Kūh-e mt. Iran 89 F5
Nōkis Uzbek. see Nukus
Nok Kundi Pak. 89 F4
Nokomis Canada 121 J5
Nokomis Lake Canada 121 K3
Nokou Chad 97 E3
Nokrek Peak India 83 G4
Nola Cent. Afr. Rep. 98 B3
Nolin River Lake U.S.A. 134 B5
Nolinsk Rus. Fed. 42 K4
No Mans Land i. U.S.A. 135 J3
Nome U.S.A. 118 B3
Nomgon Mongolia 72 J4
Nomhon China 80 I4
Nomoi Islands Micronesia see Mortlock Islands
Nomonde S. Africa 101 H6
Nomzha Rus. Fed. 42 I4
Nonacho Lake Canada 121 I2
Nondweni S. Africa 101 J5
Nong'an China 74 B3
Nông Hèt Laos 70 D3
Nonghui China see Guang'an
Nong Khai Thai. 70 C3
Nongoma S. Africa 101 J4
Nongstoin India 83 G4
Nonidas Namibia 100 B2
Nonni r. China see Nen Jiang
Nonning Australia 111 B7
Nonnweiler Germany 52 G5
Nonoava Mex. 127 G8
Nonouti atoll Kiribati 107 H2
Nonthaburi Thai. 71 C4
Nonzwakazi S. Africa 100 G6
Noolyeanna Lake salt flat Australia 111 B5
Noondie, Lake salt flat Australia 109 B7
Noonkanbah Australia 108 D4
Noonthorangee Range hills Australia 111 C6
Noorama Creek watercourse Australia 112 B1
Noordbeveland i. Neth. 52 D3
Noorderhaaks i. Neth. 52 E2
Noordoost Polder Neth. 52 F2
Noordwijk-Binnen Neth. 52 E2
Nootka Island Canada 120 E5
Nora r. Rus. Fed. 74 C2
Norak Tajik. 89 H2
Norak, Obanbori resr Tajik. 89 H2
Norala Phil. 69 G5
Noranda Canada 122 F4
Nor-Bayazet Armenia see Gavarr
Norberg Sweden 45 I6
Nord Greenland see Station Nord
Nord, Canal du France 52 D4
Nordaustlandet i. Svalbard 64 D2
Nordegg Canada 120 G4
Norden Germany 53 H1
Nordenshel'da, Arkhipelag is Rus. Fed. 64 K2
Nordenskjold Archipelago is Rus. Fed. see Nordenshel'da, Arkhipelag
Norderney Germany 53 H1
Norderstedt Germany 53 K1
Nordfjordeid Norway 44 D6
Nordfold Norway 44 I3
Nordfriesische Inseln Germany see North Frisian Islands
Nordhausen Germany 53 K3
Nordholz Germany 53 I1
Nordhorn Germany 52 H2
Nordkapp c. Norway see North Cape
Nordkinnhalvøya i. Norway 44 O1
Nordkjosbotn Norway 44 K2
Nordli Norway 44 H4
Nördlingen Germany 53 K6
Nordmaling Sweden 44 K5
Nord- og Østgrønland, Nationalparken i nat. park Greenland 119 O2

▶Nordøstrundingen c. Greenland 153 I1
Most easterly point of North America.

Nord-Ostsee-Kanal Germany see Kiel Canal
Norðoyar i. Faroe Is 40 E3
Nord-Pas-de-Calais admin. reg. France 52 C4
Nordpfälzer Bergland reg. Germany 53 H5
Nordre Strømfjord inlet Greenland see Nassuttooq
Nordrhein-Westfalen land Germany 53 H3
Nordvik Rus. Fed. 65 M2
Nore r. Ireland 51 F5
Nore, Pic de mt. France 56 F5
Noreg country Europe see Norway
Norfolk NE U.S.A. 130 D3
Norfolk NY U.S.A. 135 H1
Norfolk VA U.S.A. 135 G5

▶Norfolk Island terr. S. Pacific Ocean 107 G4
Territory of Australia.

Norfolk Island Ridge sea feature Tasman Sea 150 H7
Norfork Lake U.S.A. 131 E4
Norg Neth. 52 G1
Norge country Europe see Norway
Norheimsund Norway 45 E6
Noril'sk Rus. Fed. 64 J3
Norkyung China 83 G3
Norland Canada 135 F1
Norma Co l. China 83 G2
Norman U.S.A. 131 D5
Norman, Lake resr U.S.A. 132 D5
Normanby Island P.N.G. 110 E1
Normandes, Îles is English Chan. see Channel Islands
Normandia Brazil 143 G3
Normandie reg. France see Normandy
Normandie, Collines de hills France 56 D2
Normandy reg. France 56 D2
Normanton Australia 110 C3
Norquay Canada 121 K5
Ñorquinco Arg. 144 B6
Norra Kvarken strait Fin./Sweden 44 L5
Norra Storfjället mts Sweden 44 I4
Norrent-Fontes France 52 C4
Norris Lake U.S.A. 134 D5
Norristown U.S.A. 135 H3
Norrköping Sweden 45 J7
Norrtälje Sweden 45 K7
Norseman Australia 109 C8
Norsjö Sweden 44 K4
Norsk Rus. Fed. 74 C1
Norsup Vanuatu 107 G3
Norte, Punta pt Arg. 144 E5
Norte, Serra do hills Brazil 143 G6
Nortelândia Brazil 143 G6
Nörten-Hardenberg Germany 53 J3
North, Cape Antarctica 152 H2
North, Cape Canada 123 J5
Northallerton U.K. 48 F4
Northam Australia 109 B7
Northampton Australia 106 B4
Northampton U.K. 49 G6
Northampton MA U.S.A. 135 I2
Northampton PA U.S.A. 135 H3
North Andaman i. India 71 A4
North Anna r. U.S.A. 135 G5
North Arm b. Canada 120 H2
North Atlantic Ocean Atlantic Ocean 125 O4
North Augusta U.S.A. 133 D5
North Aulatsivik Island Canada 123 J2
North Australian Basin sea feature Indian Ocean 149 P6
North Baltimore U.S.A. 134 D3
North Battleford Canada 121 I4
North Bay Canada 122 F5
North Belcher Islands Canada 122 F2
North Berwick U.K. 50 G4
North Berwick U.S.A. 135 J2
North Bourke Australia 112 B3
North Branch U.S.A. 130 E2
North Caicos i. Turks and Caicos Is 133
North Canton U.S.A. 134 E3
North Cape Canada 123 I5
North Cape Norway 44 N1
North Cape N.Z. 113 D2
North Cape U.S.A. 118 A4
North Caribou Lake Canada 121 N4
North Carolina state U.S.A. 132 E4
North Cascades National Park U.S.A. 126 C2
North Channel lake channel Canada 12
North Channel U.K. 51 G2
North Charleston U.S.A. 133 E5
North Chicago U.S.A. 134 B2
Northcliffe Glacier Antarctica 152 F2
North Collins U.S.A. 135 F2
North Concho r. U.S.A. 131 C6
North Conway U.S.A. 135 J1
North Dakota state U.S.A. 130 C2
North Downs hills U.K. 49 G7
North East U.S.A. 134 F2
Northeast Foreland c. Greenland see Nordøstrundingen
North-East Frontier Agency state India see Arunachal Pradesh
Northeast Pacific Basin sea feature N. Pacific Ocean 151 J4
Northeast Point Bahamas 133 F8
Northeast Providence Channel Bahamas 133 E7
North Edwards U.S.A. 128 E4
Northeim Germany 53 J3
Northern prov. S. Africa see Limpopo
Northern Areas admin. div. Pak. 89 I2
Northern Cape prov. S. Africa 100 D5
Northern Donets r. Rus. Fed./Ukr. see Severskiy Donets
Northern Dvina r. Rus. Fed. see Severnaya Dvina
Northern Indian Lake Canada 121 L3
Northern Ireland prov. U.K. 51 F3
Northern Lau Group is Fiji 107 I3
Northern Light Lake Canada 122 C4

▶Northern Mariana Islands terr. N. Pacific Ocean 69 K3
United States Commonwealth.

Northern Rhodesia country Africa see Zambia
Northern Sporades is Greece see Voreies Sporades
Northern Territory admin. div. Australia 106 D3
Northern Transvaal prov. S. Africa see Limpopo
North Esk r. U.K. 50 G4
Northfield MN U.S.A. 130 E2
Northfield VT U.S.A. 135 I1
North Foreland c. U.K. 49 I7
North Fork U.S.A. 128 D3
North Fork Pass Canada 118 E3
North French r. Canada 122 E4
North Frisian Islands Germany 47 L3
North Geomagnetic Pole (2008) Arctic Ocean 119 K1
North Grimston U.K. 48 G4
North Haven U.S.A. 135 I3
North Head hd N.Z. 113 E3
North Henik Lake Canada 121 L2
North Hero U.S.A. 135 I1
North Horr Kenya 98 D3
North Island India 84 B4

▶North Island N.Z. 113 D4
3rd largest island in Oceania.

North Jadito Canyon gorge U.S.A. 129
North Judson U.S.A. 134 B3
North Kingsville U.S.A. 134 E3
North Knife r. Canada 121 M3
North Knife Lake Canada 121 L3
North Korea country Asia 75 B5
North Lakhimpur India 83 H4
North Las Vegas U.S.A. 129 F3
North Little Rock U.S.A. 131 E5
North Loup r. U.S.A. 130 D3
North Luangwa National Park Zambia 99 D5

orth Maalhosmadulu Atoll Maldives 84 B5
orth Magnetic Pole (2008) Arctic Ocean 153 A1
orth Malosmadulu Atoll Maldives see North Maalhosmadulu Atoll
orth Mam Peak U.S.A. 129 J2
orth Muskegon U.S.A. 134 B2
orth Palisade mt. U.S.A. 128 D3
orth Perry U.S.A. 134 E3
orth Platte U.S.A. 130 C3
orth Platte r. U.S.A. 130 C3
orth Pole Arctic Ocean 153 I1
orth Port U.S.A. 133 D7
orth Reef Island India 71 A4
orth Rhine - Westphalia land Germany see Nordrhein-Westfalen
orth Rim U.S.A. 129 G3
orth Rona i. U.K. see Rona
orth Ronaldsay i. U.K. 50 G1
orth Ronaldsay Firth sea chan. U.K. 50 G1
orth Saskatchewan r. Canada 121 J4
orth Schell Peak U.S.A. 129 F2
orth Sea Europe 46 H2
orth Seal r. Canada 121 L3
orth Sentinel Island India 71 A5
orth Shields U.K. 48 F3
orth Shoal Lake Canada 121 L5
orth Shoshone Peak U.S.A. 128 E2
orth Siberian Lowland Rus. Fed. 64 L2
orth Simlipal National Park India 83 F5
orth Sinai governorate Egypt see Shamāl Sīnā'
orth Slope plain U.S.A. 118 D3
orth Somercotes U.K. 48 H5
orth Spirit Lake Canada 121 M4
orth Stradbroke Island Australia 112 F1
orth Sunderland U.K. 48 F3
orth Syracuse U.S.A. 135 G2
orth Taranaki Bight b. N.Z. 113 E4
orth Terre Haute U.S.A. 134 B4
orthton U.K. 50 B3
orth Tonawanda U.S.A. 135 F2
orth Trap reef N.Z. 113 A8
orth Troy U.S.A. 135 I1
orth Tyne r. U.K. 48 E4
orth Uist i. U.K. 50 B3
orthumberland National Park U.K. 48 E3
orthumberland Strait Canada 123 I5
orth Vancouver Canada 120 F5
orth Vernon U.S.A. 134 C4
orthville U.S.A. 135 H2
orth Wabasca Lake Canada 120 H3
orth Walsham U.K. 49 I6
orthway Junction U.S.A. 120 A2
orth West prov. S. Africa 100 G4
orthwest Atlantic Mid-Ocean Channel N. Atlantic Ocean 148 E1
orth West Cape Australia 108 A5
orth West Frontier prov. Pak. 89 H3
orth West Nelson Forest Park nat. park N.Z. see Kahurangi National Park
orthwest Pacific Basin sea feature N. Pacific Ocean 150 G3
orthwest Providence Channel Bahamas 133 E7
orth West River Canada 123 K3
orthwest Territories admin. div. Canada 120 J2
orthwich U.K. 48 E5
orth Wildwood U.S.A. 135 H4
orth Windham U.S.A. 135 J2
orthwind Ridge sea feature Arctic Ocean 153 B1
orthwood U.S.A. 135 J2
orth York Canada 134 F2
orth York Moors moorland U.K. 48 G4
orth York Moors National Park U.K. 48 G4
orton U.K. 48 G4
orton KS U.S.A. 130 D4
orton VA U.S.A. 134 D5
orton VT U.S.A. 135 J1
orton de Matos Angola see Balombo
orton Shores U.S.A. 134 B2
orton Sound sea chan. U.S.A. 118 B3
ortonville U.S.A. 134 B5
orvegia, Cape Antarctica 152 B2
orwalk CT U.S.A. 135 I3
orwalk OH U.S.A. 134 D3
orway country Europe 44 E6
orway U.S.A. 135 J1
orway House Canada 121 L4
orwegian Basin sea feature N. Atlantic Ocean 148 H1
orwegian Bay Canada 119 I2
orwegian Sea N. Atlantic Ocean 153 H2
orwich Canada 134 E2
orwich U.K. 49 I6
orwich CT U.S.A. 135 I3
orwich NY U.S.A. 135 H2
orwood CO U.S.A. 129 I2
orwood NY U.S.A. 135 H1
orwood OH U.S.A. 134 C4
ose Lake Canada 121 I1
oshiro Japan 75 F4
osovaya Rus. Fed. 42 L1
osratābād Iran 89 E4
oss, Isle of i. U.K. 50 [inset]
ossebro Sweden 45 H7
ossen Germany 53 N3
ossob watercourse Africa 100 D2 also known as Nosop
ossob watercourse Africa 100 D2 also known as Nossob
otakwanon r. Canada 123 J2
otch Peak U.S.A. 129 G2
oteć r. Poland 47 O4
otikewin r. Canada 120 G3
oto, Golfo di g. Sicily Italy 58 F6
otodden Norway 45 F7
oto-hantō pen. Japan 75 E5
otre-Dame, Monts mts Canada 123 H5
otre Dame Bay Canada 123 L4
otre-Dame-de-Koartac Canada see Quaqtaq
ottawasaga Bay Canada 134 E1
ottaway r. Canada 122 F4
ottingham U.K. 49 F6
ottingham Island Canada 119 K3
ottoway r. U.S.A. 135 G5
Nottuln Germany 53 H3
Notukeu Creek r. Canada 121 J5
Nouabalé-Ndoki, Parc National nat. park Congo 98 B3
Nouâdhibou Mauritania 96 B2
Nouâdhibou, Râs c. Mauritania 96 B2
▶Nouakchott Mauritania 96 B3 Capital of Mauritania.
Nouâmghâr Mauritania 96 B3
Nouei Vietnam 70 D4
▶Nouméa New Caledonia 107 G4 Capital of New Caledonia.
Nouna Burkina 96 C3
Noupoort S. Africa 100 G6
Nousu Fin. 44 P3
Nouveau-Brunswick prov. Canada see New Brunswick
Nouveau-Comptoir Canada see Wemindji
Nouvelle Calédonie i. S. Pacific Ocean 107 G4
Nouvelle Calédonie terr. S. Pacific Ocean see New Caledonia
Nouvelle-France, Cap de c. Canada 119 K3
Nouvelles Hébrides country S. Pacific Ocean see Vanuatu
Nova América Brazil 145 A1
Nova Chaves Angola see Muconda
Nova Freixa Moz. see Cuamba
Nova Friburgo Brazil 145 C3
Nova Gaia Angola see Cambundi-Catembo
Nova Goa India see Panaji
Nova Gradiška Croatia 58 G2
Nova Iguaçu Brazil 145 C3
Nova Kakhovka Ukr. 59 O1
Nova Lima Brazil 145 C2
Nova Lisboa Angola see Huambo
Novalukoml' Belarus 43 F5
Nova Mambone Moz. 99 D6
Nova Nabúri Moz. 99 D5
Nova Odesa Ukr. 43 F7
Nova Paraiso Brazil 142 F3
Nova Pilão Arcado Brazil 143 J5
Nova Ponte Brazil 145 B2
Nova Ponte, Represa resr Brazil 145 B2
Novara Italy 58 C2
Nova Roma Brazil 145 B1
Nova Scotia prov. Canada 123 I6
Nova Sento Sé Brazil 143 J5
Novato U.S.A. 128 B2
Nova Trento Brazil 145 A4
Nova Venécia Brazil 145 C2
Nova Xavantino Brazil 143 H6
Novaya Kakhovka Ukr. see Nova Kakhovka
Novaya Kazanka Kazakh. 41 P6
Novaya Ladoga Rus. Fed. 42 G3
Novaya Lyalya Rus. Fed. 41 S4
Novaya Odessa Ukr. see Nova Odesa
Novaya Sibir', Ostrov i. Rus. Fed. 65 P2
Novaya Ussura Rus. Fed. 74 E2
▶Novaya Zemlya is Rus. Fed. 64 G2 3rd largest island in Europe.
Nova Zagora Bulg. 59 L3
Novelda Spain 57 F4
Nové Zámky Slovakia 47 Q7
Novgorod Rus. Fed. see Velikiy Novgorod
Novgorod-Severskiy Ukr. see Novhorod-Sivers'kyy
Novgorod-Volynskiy Ukr. see Novohrad-Volyns'kyy
Novhorod-Sivers'kyy Ukr. 43 G6
Novi Grad Bos.-Herz. see Bosanski Novi
Novi Iskŭr Bulg. 59 J3
Novikovo Rus. Fed. 74 F3
Novi Kritsim Bulg. see Stamboliyski
Novi Ligure Italy 58 C2
Novi Pazar Bulg. 59 L3
Novi Pazar Serbia 59 I3
Novi Sad Serbia 59 H2
Novo Acre Brazil 145 C1
Novoalekseyevka Kazakh. see Khobda
Novoaltaysk Rus. Fed. 72 E2
Novoanninskiy Rus. Fed. 43 I6
Novo Aripuanã Brazil 142 F5
Novoazovs'k Ukr. 43 H7
Novocheboksarsk Rus. Fed. 42 J4
Novocherkassk Rus. Fed. 43 I7
Novo Cruzeiro Brazil 145 C2
Novodugino Rus. Fed. 42 G5
Novodvinsk Rus. Fed. 42 I2
Novoekonomicheskoye Ukr. see Dymytrov
Novogeorgiyevka Rus. Fed. 74 B2
Novogrudok Belarus see Navahrudak
Novo Hamburgo Brazil 145 A5
Novohradské hory mts Czech Rep. 47 O6
Novohrad-Volyns'kyy Ukr. 43 E6
Novokhopersk Rus. Fed. 43 I6
Novokiyevskiy Uval Rus. Fed. 74 C2
Novokubansk Rus. Fed. 91 F1
Novokubanskiy Rus. Fed. see Novokubansk
Novokuybyshevsk Rus. Fed. 43 K5
Novokuznetsk Rus. Fed. 72 F2
Novolazarevskaya research station Antarctica 152 C2
Novolukoml' Belarus see Novalukoml'
Novo Mesto Slovenia 58 F2
Novomikhaylovskiy Rus. Fed. 90 E1
Novomoskovsk Rus. Fed. 43 H5
Novomoskovs'k Ukr. 43 G6
Novonikolayevsk Rus. Fed. see Novosibirsk
Novonikolayevskiy Rus. Fed. 43 I6
Novooleksiyivka Ukr. 43 G7
Novopashiyskiy Rus. Fed. see Gornozavodsk
Novopokrovka Rus. Fed. 74 D3
Novopokrovskaya Rus. Fed. 43 I7
Novopolotsk Belarus see Navapolatsk
Novopskov Ukr. 43 H6
Novo Redondo Angola see Sumbe
Novorossiyka Rus. Fed. 74 C1
Novorossiysk Rus. Fed. 90 E1
Novorybnaya Rus. Fed. 65 L2
Novorzhev Rus. Fed. 42 F4
Novoselovo Rus. Fed. 72 G1
Novoselskoye Rus. Fed. see Achkhoy-Martan
Novosel'ye Rus. Fed. 45 P7
Novosergiyevka Rus. Fed. 41 Q5
Novoshakhtinsk Rus. Fed. 43 H7
Novosheshminsk Rus. Fed. 42 K5
Novosibirsk Rus. Fed. 64 J4
Novosibirskiye Ostrova is Rus. Fed. see New Siberia Islands
Novosil' Rus. Fed. 43 H5
Novosokol'niki Rus. Fed. 42 F4
Novospasskoye Rus. Fed. 43 J5
Novotroyits'ke Ukr. 43 G7
Novoukrainka Ukr. see Novoukrayinka
Novoukrayinka Ukr. 43 F6
Novouzensk Rus. Fed. 43 K6
Novovolyns'k Ukr. 43 E6
Novovoronezh Rus. Fed. 43 H6
Novovoronezhskiy Rus. Fed. see Novovoronezh
Novovoskresenovka Rus. Fed. 74 B1
Novozybkov Rus. Fed. 43 F5
Nový Jičín Czech Rep. 47 P6
Novyy Afon Georgia see Akhali Ap'oni
Novyy Bor Rus. Fed. 42 L2
Novyy Donbass Ukr. see Dymytrov
Novyye Petushki Rus. Fed. see Petushki
Novyy Kholmogory Rus. Fed. see Archangel
Novyy Margelan Uzbek. see Farg'ona
Novyy Nekouz Rus. Fed. 42 H4
Novyy Oskol Rus. Fed. 43 H6
Novyy Port Rus. Fed. 64 I3
Novyy Urengoy Rus. Fed. 64 I3
Novyy Urgal Rus. Fed. 74 D2
Novyy Uzen' Kazakh. see Zhanaozen
Novyy Zay Rus. Fed. 42 L5
Now Iran 88 D4
Nowabganj Bangl. see Nawabganj
Nowata U.S.A. 131 E4
Nowdī Iran 88 C2
Nowgong India see Nagaon
Now Kharegan Iran 88 D2
Nowleye Lake Canada 121 K2
Nowogard Poland 47 O4
Noworadomsk Poland see Radomsko
Nowra Australia 112 E5
Nowrangapur India see Nabarangapur
Nowshera Pak. 89 I3
Nowyak Lake Canada 121 L2
Nowy Sącz Poland 47 R6
Nowy Targ Poland 47 R6
Noxen U.S.A. 135 G3
Noy, Xé r. Laos 70 D3
Noyabr'sk Rus. Fed. 64 I3
Noyes Island U.S.A. 120 C4
Noyon France 52 C5
Noyon Mongolia 80 J3
Nozizwe S. Africa 101 G6
Nqamakwe S. Africa 101 H7
Nqutu S. Africa 101 J5
Nsanje Malawi 99 D5
Nsombo Zambia 99 C5
Nsukka Nigeria 96 D4
Nsumbu National Park Zambia see Sumbu National Park
Ntambu Zambia 99 C5
Ntha S. Africa 101 H4
Ntoro, Kavo pt Greece 59 K5
Ntoum Gabon 98 A3
Ntungamo Uganda 98 D4
Nuanetsi Zimbabwe see Mwenezi
Nu'aym reg. Oman 88 D6
Nuba Mountains Sudan 86 D7
Nubian Desert Sudan 86 D5
Nudo Coropuna mt. Peru 142 D7
Nueces r. U.S.A. 131 D7
Nueltin Lake Canada 121 L2
Nueva Ciudad Guerrero Mex. 131 D7
Nueva Gerona Cuba 137 H4
Nueva Harberton Arg. 144 C8
Nueva Imperial Chile 144 B5
Nueva Loja Ecuador see Lago Agrio
Nueva Rosita Mex. 131 C7
Nueva San Salvador El Salvador 136 G6
Nueva Villa de Padilla Mex. 131 D7
Nueve de Julio Arg. see 9 de Julio
Nuevitas Cuba 137 I4
Nuevo, Golfo g. Arg. 144 D6
Nuevo Casas Grandes Mex. 127 G7
Nuevo Ideal Mex. 131 B7
Nuevo Laredo Mex. 131 D7
Nuevo León Mex. 129 F5
Nuevo León state Mex. 131 D7
Nuevo Rocatuerte Ecuador 142 C4
Nugaal watercourse Somalia 98 E3
Nugget Point N.Z. 113 B8
Nugur India 84 D2
Nuguria Islands P.N.G. 106 F2
Nuh, Ras pt Pak. 89 F5
Nuhaka N.Z. 113 F4
Nui atoll Tuvalu 107 H2
Nui Con Voi r. Vietnam see Red
Nuiqsut U.S.A. 118 C2
Nui Thanh Vietnam 70 E4
Nui Ti On mt. Vietnam 70 D4
Nujiang China 76 C2
Nu Jiang r. China/Myanmar see Salween
Nukey Bluff hill Australia 111 A7
Nukha Azer. see Şäki
▶Nuku'alofa Tonga 107 I4 Capital of Tonga.
Nukufetau atoll Tuvalu 107 H2
Nukuhiva i. Fr. Polynesia see Nuku Hiva
Nuku Hiva i. Fr. Polynesia 151 K6
Nukuhu P.N.G. 69 L8
Nukulaelae atoll Tuvalu 107 H2
Nukulailai atoll Tuvalu see Nukulaelae
Nukumanu Islands P.N.G. 107 F2
Nukunau i. Kiribati see Nikunau
Nukunono atoll Tokelau see Nukunonu
Nukunonu atoll Tokelau 107 I2
Nukus Uzbek. 80 A3
Nulato U.S.A. 118 C3
Nullagine Australia 108 C5
Nullarbor Australia 109 E7
Nullarbor National Park Australia 109 E7
Nullarbor Plain Australia 109 E7
Nullarbor Regional Reserve park Australia 109 E7
Nuluarniavik, Lac l. Canada 122 F2
Nulu'erhu Shan mts China 73 L4
Num i. Indon. 69 J7
Numalla, Lake salt flat Australia 112 B2
Numan Nigeria 98 B3
Numanuma P.N.G. 110 E1
Numazu Japan 75 E6
Numbulwar Australia 110 A2
Numedal valley Norway 45 F6
Numfoor i. Indon. 69 I7
Numin He r. China 74 B3
Numurkah Australia 112 B6
Nunaksaluk Island Canada 123 J3
Nunakuluut i. Greenland 119 N3
Nunap Isua c. Greenland see Farewell, Cape
Nunarsuit i. Greenland see Nunakuluut
Nunavik reg. Canada 122 G1
Nunavut admin. div. Canada 121 L2
Nunda U.S.A. 135 G2
Nundle Australia 112 E3
Nuneaton U.K. 49 F6
Nungba India 83 H4
Nungesser Lake Canada 121 M5
Nungnain Sum China 73 L3
Nunivak Island U.S.A. 118 B4
Nunkapasi India 84 E1
Nunkun mt. India 82 D2
Nunligran Rus. Fed. 65 T3
Nuñomoral Spain 57 C3
Nunspeet Neth. 52 F2
Nuojiang China see Tongjiang
Nuoro Sardinia Italy 58 C4
Nupani i. Solomon Is 107 G3
Nuqrah Saudi Arabia 86 F4
Nur r. Iran 88 D2
Nūrābād Iran 88 C4
Nurakita i. Tuvalu see Niulakita
Nurata Uzbek. see Nurota
Nur Dağları mts Turkey 85 B1
Nurek Tajik. see Norak
Nurek Reservoir Tajik. see Norak, Obanbori
Nurekskoye Vodokhranilishche resr Tajik. see Norak, Obanbori
Nuremberg Germany 53 L5
Nuri Mex. 127 F7
Nurla India 82 D2
Nurlat Rus. Fed. 43 K5
Nurmes Fin. 44 P5
Nurmo Fin. 44 M5
Nürnberg Germany see Nuremberg
Nurota Uzbek. 80 C3
Nurri, Mount hill Australia 112 C3
Nusawulan Indon. 69 I7
Nusaybin Turkey 91 F3
Nu Shan mts China 76 C3
Nushki Pak. 89 G4
Nusratiye Turkey 85 D1
Nutak Canada 123 J2
Nutarawit Lake Canada 121 L2
Nutrioso U.S.A. 129 I5
Nuttal Pak. 89 H4
Nutwood Downs Australia 108 F3
Nutzotin Mountains U.S.A. 120 A2
▶Nuuk Greenland 119 M3 Capital of Greenland.
Nuupas Fin. 44 O3
Nuussuaq Greenland 119 M2
Nuussuaq pen. Greenland 119 M2
Nuwaybi' al Muzayyinah Egypt 90 D5
Nuweiba el Muzeina Egypt see Nuwaybi' al Muzayyinah
Nuwerus S. Africa 100 D6
Nuweveldberge mts S. Africa 100 E7
Nuyts, Point Australia 109 B8
Nuyts Archipelago is Australia 109 F8
Nuzvid India 84 D2
Nwanedi Nature Reserve S. Africa 101 J2
Nxai Pan National Park Botswana 99 C5
Nyagan' Rus. Fed. 41 T3
Nyagquka China see Yajiang
Nyagrong China see Xinlong
Nyahururu Kenya 98 D3
Nyah West Australia 112 A5
Nyainqêntanglha Feng mt. China 83 G3
Nyainqêntanglha Shan mts China 83 G3
Nyainrong China 76 B1
Nyainronglung China see Nyainrong
Nyåker Sweden 44 K5
Nyakh Rus. Fed. see Nyagan'
Nyaksimvol' Rus. Fed. 41 S3
Nyala Sudan 97 F3
Nyalam China see Congdü
Nyalikungu Tanz. see Maswa
Nyamandhiovu Zimbabwe 99 C5
Nyamtumbo Tanz. 99 D5
Nyande Zimbabwe see Masvingo
Nyandoma Rus. Fed. 42 I3
Nyandomskiy Vozvyshennost' hills Rus. Fed. 42 H3
Nyanga Congo 98 B4
Nyanga Zimbabwe 99 D5
Nyangbo China 76 B2
Nyarling r. Canada 120 H2
▶Nyasa, Lake Africa 99 D4 3rd largest lake in Africa, and 9th in the world.
Nyasaland country Africa see Malawi
Nyashabozh Rus. Fed. 42 L2
Nyasvizh Belarus 45 O10
Nyaungdon Myanmar see Yandoon
Nyaunglebin Myanmar 70 B3
Nyborg Denmark 45 G9
Nyborg Norway 44 P1
Nybro Sweden 45 I8
Nyeboe Land reg. Greenland 119 M1
Nyêmo China 83 G3
Nyenchen Tanglha Range mts China see Nyainqêntanglha Shan
Nyeri Kenya 98 D4
Nyi, Co l. China 83 F2
Nyika National Park Zambia 99 D5
Nyima China 83 F3
Nyimba Zambia 99 D5
Nyingchi China 76 B2
Nyinma China see Maqu
Nyíregyháza Hungary 43 D7
Nyiru, Mount Kenya 98 D3
Nykarleby Fin. 44 M5
Nykøbing Denmark 45 G9
Nykøbing Sjælland Denmark 45 G9
Nyköping Sweden 45 J7
Nyland Sweden 44 J5
Nylsvley nature res. S. Africa 101 I3
Nymagee Australia 112 C4
Nymboida National Park Australia 112 F2
Nynäshamn Sweden 45 J7
Nyngan Australia 112 C3
Nyogzê China 83 E3
Nyoman r. Belarus/Lith. 45 M10 also known as Neman or Nemunas
Nyon Switz. 56 H3
Nyons France 56 G4
Nýřany Czech Rep. 53 N5
Nyrob Rus. Fed. 41 R3
Nysa Poland 47 P5
Nysh Rus. Fed. 74 F2
Nyssa U.S.A. 126 D4
Nystad Fin. see Uusikaupunki
Nytva Rus. Fed. 41 R4
Nyuksenitsa Rus. Fed. 42 J3
Nyunzu Dem. Rep. Congo 99 C4
Nyurba Rus. Fed. 65 M3
Nyyskiy Zaliv lag. Rus. Fed. 74 F1
Nzambi Congo 98 B4
Nzega Tanz. 99 D4
Nzérékoré Guinea 96 C4
N'zeto Angola 99 B4
Nzwani i. Comoros 99 E5

Oahe, Lake U.S.A. 130 C2
O'ahu i. U.S.A. 127 [inset]
Oaitupu i. Tuvalu see Vaitupu
Oak Bluffs U.S.A. 135 J3
Oak City U.S.A. 129 G2
Oak Creek U.S.A. 129 J1
Oakdale U.S.A. 131 E6
Oakes U.S.A. 130 D2
Oakey Australia 112 E1
Oak Grove KY U.S.A. 134 B5
Oak Grove LA U.S.A. 131 F5
Oak Grove MI U.S.A. 134 C1
Oakham U.K. 49 G6
Oak Harbor U.S.A. 134 D3
Oak Hill OH U.S.A. 134 D4
Oak Hill WV U.S.A. 134 E5
Oakhurst U.S.A. 128 D3
Oak Lake Canada 121 K5
Oakland CA U.S.A. 128 B3
Oakland MD U.S.A. 134 F4
Oakland ME U.S.A. 135 K1
Oakland NE U.S.A. 130 D3
Oakland OR U.S.A. 126 C4
Oakland airport U.S.A. 128 B3
Oakland City U.S.A. 134 B4
Oaklands Australia 112 C5
Oak Lawn U.S.A. 134 B3
Oakley U.S.A. 130 C4
Oakover r. Australia 108 C5
Oak Park IL U.S.A. 134 B3
Oak Park MI U.S.A. 134 C2
Oak Park Reservoir U.S.A. 129 I1
Oakridge U.S.A. 126 C4
Oak Ridge U.S.A. 132 C4
Oakvale Australia 111 C7
Oak View U.S.A. 128 D4
Oakville Canada 134 F2
Oakwood OH U.S.A. 134 C3
Oakwood TN U.S.A. 134 B5
Oamaru N.Z. 113 C7
Oaro N.Z. 113 D6
Oasis CA U.S.A. 128 E3
Oasis NV U.S.A. 126 E4
Oates Coast reg. Antarctica see Oates Land
Oates Land reg. Antarctica 152 H2
Oaxaca Mex. 136 E5
Oaxaca de Juárez Mex. see Oaxaca
▶Ob' r. Rus. Fed. 72 E2 Part of the Ob'-Irtysh, the 2nd longest river in Asia.
Ob, Gulf of sea chan. Rus. Fed. see Obskaya Guba
Oba Canada 122 D4
Oba i. Vanuatu see Aoba
Obala Cameroon 96 E4
Obama Japan 75 D6
Oban U.K. 50 D4
O Barco Spain 57 C2
Obbia Somalia see Hobyo
Obdorsk Rus. Fed. see Salekhard
Óbecse Serbia see Bečej
Obed Canada 120 G4
Oberaula Germany 53 J4
Oberdorla Germany 53 K3
Oberhausen Germany 52 G3
Oberlin KS U.S.A. 130 C4
Oberlin LA U.S.A. 131 E6
Oberlin OH U.S.A. 134 D3
Obermoschel Germany 53 H5
Oberon Australia 112 D4
Oberpfälzer Wald mts Germany 53 M5
Obersinn Germany 53 J4
Oberthulba Germany 53 J4
Obertshausen Germany 53 I4
Oberwälder Land reg. Germany 53 J3
Obi i. Indon. 69 H7
Óbidos Brazil 143 G4
Obihiro Japan 74 F4
Obil'noye Rus. Fed. 43 J7
▶Ob'-Irtysh r. Rus. Fed. 64 H3 2nd longest river in Asia, and 5th in the world.
Obluch'ye Rus. Fed. 74 C2
Obninsk Rus. Fed. 43 H5
Obo Cent. Afr. Rep. 98 C3
Obock Djibouti 86 F7
Ŏbŏk N. Korea 74 C4
Obokote Dem. Rep. Congo 98 C4
Obo Liang China 80 H4
Obouya Congo 98 B4
Oboyan' Rus. Fed. 43 H6
Obozerskiy Rus. Fed. 42 I3
Obregón, Presa resr Mex. 127 F8
Obrenovac Serbia 59 I2
Obruk Turkey 90 D3
Observatory Hill hill Australia 109 F7
Obshchiy Syrt hills Rus. Fed. 41 Q5
Obskaya Guba sea chan. Rus. Fed. 64 I3
Obuasi Ghana 96 C4
Ob"yachevo Rus. Fed. 42 K3
Ocala U.S.A. 133 D6
Ocampo Mex. 131 C7
Ocaña Col. 142 D2
Ocaña Spain 57 E4
Occidental, Cordillera mts Chile 142 E7
Occidental, Cordillera mts Col. 142 C3
Occidental, Cordillera mts Peru 142 D7
Oceana U.S.A. 134 E5
Ocean Cay i. Bahamas 133 E7
Ocean City MD U.S.A. 135 H4
Ocean City NJ U.S.A. 135 H4
Ocean Falls Canada 120 E4
Ocean Island Kiribati see Banaba
Ocean Island atoll U.S.A. see Kure Atoll
Oceanside U.S.A. 128 E5
Ocean Springs U.S.A. 131 F6
Ochakiv Ukr. 59 N1
Och'amch'ire Georgia 91 F2
Ocher Rus. Fed. 41 Q4
Ochiishi-misaki pt Japan 74 G4
Ochil Hills U.K. 50 F4
Ochrida, Lake Albania/Macedonia see Ohrid, Lake
Ochsenfurt Germany 53 K5
Ochtrup Germany 53 H2
Ocilla U.S.A. 133 D6
Ockelbo Sweden 45 J6
Ocolașul Mare, Vârful mt. Romania 59 K1
Oconomowoc U.S.A. 134 A2
Oconto U.S.A. 134 B1
Octeville-sur-Mer France 49 H9
October Revolution Island Rus. Fed. see Oktyabr'skoy Revolyutsii, Ostrov
Ocussi enclave East Timor 108 D2
Ocussi-Ambeno enclave East Timor see Ocussi
Oda, Jebel mt. Sudan 86 E5
Ódáðahraun lava field Iceland 44 [inset]
Ŏdaejin N. Korea 74 C4
Odae-san National Park S. Korea 75 C5
Ōdate Japan 75 F4
Odawara Japan 75 E6
Odda Norway 45 E6
Odei r. Canada 121 L3
Odell U.S.A. 134 B3
Odem U.S.A. 131 D7
Odemira Port. 57 B5
Ödemiş Turkey 59 L5
Ödenburg Hungary see Sopron
Odense Denmark 45 G9
Odenwald reg. Germany 53 I5
Oder r. Germany 53 J3 also known as Odra (Poland)
Oderbucht b. Germany 47 O3
Oder-Havel-Kanal canal Germany 53 N2
Ödeshog Sweden 45 I7
Odessa Ukr. 59 N1
Odessa TX U.S.A. 131 C6
Odessa WA U.S.A. 126 D3
Odessus Bulg. see Varna
Odiel r. Spain 57 C5
Odienné Côte d'Ivoire 96 C4
Odintsovo Rus. Fed. 42 H5
Ŏdŏngk Cambodia 71 D5
Odra r. Germany/Pol. 47 Q6 also known as Oder (Germany)
Odzala, Parc National d' nat. park Congo 98 B3
Oea Libya see Tripoli
Oé-Cusse enclave East Timor see Ocussi
Oecussi enclave East Timor see Ocussi
Oeiras Brazil 143 J5
Oekussi enclave East Timor see Ocussi
Oelsnitz Germany 53 M4
Oenkerk Neth. 52 F1
Oenpelli Australia 108 F3
Oesel i. Estonia see Hiiumaa
Oeufs, Lac des l. Canada 123 G3
Of Turkey 91 F2
O'Fallon r. U.S.A. 126 G3
Ofanto r. Italy 58 G4
Ofaqim Israel 85 B4
Offa Nigeria 96 D4
Offenbach am Main Germany 53 I4
Offenburg Germany 47 K6
Oga Japan 75 E5
Ogadēn reg. Eth. 98 E3
Oga-hantō pen. Japan 75 E5
Ōgaki Japan 75 E6
Ogallala U.S.A. 130 C3
Ogasawara-shotō is Japan see Bonin Islands
Ogbomosho Nigeria 96 D4
Ogbomoso Nigeria see Ogbomosho
Ogden IA U.S.A. 130 E3
Ogden UT U.S.A. 126 F4
Ogden, Mount Canada 120 C3
Ogdensburg U.S.A. 135 H1
Ogidaki Canada 122 D5
Ogilvie r. Canada 118 E3
Ogilvie Mountains Canada 118 D3
Oglethorpe, Mount U.S.A. 133 C5
Oglio r. Italy 58 D2
Oglongi Rus. Fed. 74 E1
Ogmore Australia 110 E4
Ogoamas, Gunung mt. Indon. 69 G6
Ogodzha Rus. Fed. 74 D1
Ogoja Nigeria 96 D4
Ogoki r. Canada 122 D4
Ogoki Lake Canada 130 G1
Ogoki Reservoir Canada 122 C4
Ogoron Rus. Fed. 74 C1
Ogosta r. Bulg. 59 J3
Ogre Latvia 45 N8
Ogulin Croatia 58 F2
Ogurchinskiy, Ostrov i. Turkm. see Ogurjaly Adasy
Ogurjaly Adasy i. Turkm. 88 D2
Oğuzeli Turkey 85 C1
Ohai N.Z. 113 A7
Ohakune N.Z. 113 E4
Ohanet Alg. 96 D2
Ōhata Japan 74 F4

Ohcejohka Fin. see Utsjoki
O'Higgins (Chile) research station Antarctica 152 A2
O'Higgins, Lago l. Chile 144 B7
Ohio r. U.S.A. 134 A5
Ohio state U.S.A. 134 D3
Ohm r. Germany 53 I4
Ohrdruf Germany 53 K4
Ohře r. Czech Rep. 53 N4
Ohre r. Germany 53 L2
Ohrid Macedonia 59 I4
Ohrid, Lake Albania/Macedonia 59 I4
Ohridsko Ezero l. Albania/Macedonia see Ohrid, Lake
Ohrigstad S. Africa 101 J3
Öhringen Germany 53 J5
Ohrit, Liqeni i l. Albania/Macedonia see Ohrid, Lake
Ohura N.Z. 113 E4
Oich r. U.K. 50 E3
Oiga China 76 B2
Oignies France 52 C4
Oil City U.S.A. 134 F3
Oise r. France 52 C6
Ōita Japan 75 C6
Oiti mt. Greece 59 J5
Ojai U.S.A. 128 D4
Ojalava i. Samoa see 'Upolu
Ojinaga Mex. 131 B6
Ojiya Japan 75 E5
Ojo Caliente U.S.A. 127 G5
Ojo de Laguna Mex. 127 G7

►Ojos del Salado, Nevado mt. Arg./Chile 144 C3
2nd highest mountain in South America.

Oka r. Rus. Fed. 43 I4
Oka r. Rus. Fed. 72 I1
Okahandja Namibia 100 C1
Okahukura N.Z. 113 E4
Okakarara Namibia 99 B6
Okak Islands Canada 123 J2
Okanagan Lake Canada 120 G5
Okanda Sri Lanka 84 D5
Okano r. Gabon 98 B4
Okanogan U.S.A. 126 D2
Okanogan r. U.S.A. 126 D2
Okara Pak. 89 I4
Okarem Turkm. see Ekerem
Okataina vol. N.Z. see Tarawera, Mount
Okaukuejo Namibia 99 B5
Okavango r. Africa 99 C5

►Okavango Delta swamp Botswana 99 C5
Largest oasis in the world.

Okavango Swamps Botswana see Okavango Delta
Okaya Japan 75 E5
Okayama Japan 75 D6
Okazaki Japan 75 E6
Okeechobee U.S.A. 133 D7
Okeechobee, Lake U.S.A. 133 D7
Okeene U.S.A. 131 D4
Okefenokee Swamp U.S.A. 133 D6
Okehampton U.K. 49 C8
Okemah U.S.A. 131 D5
Oker r. Germany 53 K2
Okha India 82 B5
Okha Rus. Fed. 74 F1
Okha Rann marsh India 82 B5
Okhotsk Rus. Fed. 65 P4
Okhotsk, Sea of Japan/Rus. Fed. 74 G3
Okhotskoye More sea Japan/Rus. Fed. see Okhotsk, Sea of
Okhtyrka Ukr. 43 G6
Okinawa i. Japan 75 B8
Okinawa-guntō is Japan see Okinawa-shotō
Okinawa-shotō is Japan 75 B8
Okino-Daitō-jima i. Japan 73 O8
Okino-Tori-shima i. Japan 73 P8
Oki-shotō is Japan 73 O5
Oki-shotō is Japan 75 D5
Okkan Myanmar 70 A3
Oklahoma state U.S.A. 131 D5

►Oklahoma City U.S.A. 131 D5
Capital of Oklahoma.

Okmulgee U.S.A. 131 D5
Okolona KY U.S.A. 134 C4
Okolona MS U.S.A. 131 F5
Okondja Gabon 98 B4
Okovskiy Les for. Rus. Fed. 42 G5
Okoyo Congo 98 B4
Øksfjord Norway 44 M1
Oktemberyan Armenia see Armavir
Oktwin Myanmar 70 B3
Oktyabr' Kazakh. see Kandyagash
Oktyabr'sk Kazakh. see Kandyagash
Oktyabr'skiy Belarus see Aktsyabrski
Oktyabr'skiy Amurskaya Oblast' Rus. Fed. 74 C1
Oktyabr'skiy Arkhangel'skaya Oblast' Rus. Fed. 42 I3
Oktyabr'skiy Kamchatskaya Oblast' Rus. Fed. 65 Q4
Oktyabr'skiy Respublika Bashkortostan Rus. Fed. 41 Q5
Oktyabr'skiy Volgogradskaya Oblast' Rus. Fed. 43 I7
Oktyabr'skoye Rus. Fed. 41 T3
Oktyabr'skoy Revolyutsii, Ostrov i. Rus. Fed. 65 K2
Okulovka Rus. Fed. 42 G4
Okushiri-tō i. Japan 74 E4
Okusi enclave East Timor see Ocussi
Okuta Nigeria 96 D4
Okwa watercourse Botswana 100 G1
Ólafsvík Iceland 44 [inset]
Olakkur India 84 C3
Olancha U.S.A. 128 D3
Olancha Peak U.S.A. 128 D3
Öland i. Sweden 45 J8
Olary Australia 111 C7
Olathe CO U.S.A. 129 J2
Olathe KS U.S.A. 130 E4
Olavarría Arg. 144 D5
Oława Poland 47 P5
Olbernhau Germany 53 N4
Olbia Sardinia Italy 58 C4
Old Bahama Channel Bahamas/Cuba 133 E8
Old Bastar India 84 D2
Oldcastle Ireland 51 E4
Old Cork Australia 110 C4
Old Crow Canada 118 E3
Oldeboorn Neth. see Aldeboarn
Oldenburg Germany 53 I1
Oldenburg in Holstein Germany 47 M3
Oldenzaal Neth. 52 G2
Olderdalen Norway 44 L2
Old Forge U.S.A. 135 H2
Old Gidgee Australia 109 B6
Oldham U.K. 48 E5
Old Harbor U.S.A. 118 C4
Old Head of Kinsale hd Ireland 51 D6
Oldman r. Canada 120 I5
Oldmeldrum U.K. 50 G3
Old Perlican Canada 123 L5
Old River U.S.A. 128 D4
Olds Canada 120 H5
Old Speck Mountain U.S.A. 135 J1
Old Station U.S.A. 128 C1
Old Wives Lake Canada 121 J5
Olean U.S.A. 135 F2
Olecko Poland 47 S3
Olekma r. Rus. Fed. 65 N3
Olekminsk Rus. Fed. 65 N3
Olekminskiy Stanovik mts Rus. Fed. 73 M2
Oleksandrivs'k Ukr. see Zaporizhzhya
Oleksandriya Ukr. 43 G6
Ølen Norway 45 D7
Olenegorsk Rus. Fed. 44 R2
Olenek Rus. Fed. 65 M3
Olenek r. Rus. Fed. 65 M2
Olenek Bay Rus. Fed. see Olenekskiy Zaliv
Olenekskiy Zaliv b. Rus. Fed. 65 N2
Olenino Rus. Fed. 42 G4
Olenitsa Rus. Fed. 42 G2
Olenivs'ki Kar"yery Ukr. see Dokuchayevs'k
Olenya Rus. Fed. see Olenegorsk
Oleshky Ukr. see Tsyurupyns'k
Olevs'k Ukr. 43 E6
Ol'ga Rus. Fed. 74 D4
Olga, Lac l. Canada 122 F4
Olga, Mount Australia 109 E6
Ol'ginsk Rus. Fed. 74 D1
Olginskoye Rus. Fed. see Kochubeyevskoye
Ölgiy Mongolia 80 G2
Olhão Port. 57 C5
Olia Chain mts Australia 109 E6
Olifants r. Moz./S. Africa 101 J3
also known as Elefantes
Olifants watercourse Namibia 100 D3
Olifants S. Africa 101 J2
Olifants r. W. Cape S. Africa 100 D6
Olifants r. W. Cape S. Africa 100 E7
Olifantshoek S. Africa 100 F4
Olifantsrivierberge mts S. Africa 100 D7
Olimarao atoll Micronesia 69 L5
Olimbos hill Cyprus see Olympos
Olimbos mt. Greece see Olympus, Mount
Olimpos Beydağları Milli Parkı nat. park Turkey 59 N6
Olinda Brazil 143 L5
Olinga Moz. 99 D5
Olio Australia 110 C4
Oliphants Drift S. Africa 101 H3
Olisipo Port. see Lisbon
Oliva Spain 57 F4
Oliva, Cordillera de mts Arg./Chile 144 C3
Olivares, Cerro de mt. Arg./Chile 144 C4
Olive Hill U.S.A. 134 D4
Olivehurst U.S.A. 128 C2
Oliveira dos Brejinhos Brazil 145 C1
Olivença Moz. see Lupilichi
Olivenza Spain 57 C4
Oliver Lake Canada 121 K3
Olivet MI U.S.A. 134 C2
Olivet SD U.S.A. 130 D3
Olivia U.S.A. 130 E2
Ol'khovka Rus. Fed. 43 J6
Ollagüe Chile 144 C2
Ollombo Congo 98 B4
Olmaliq Uzbek. 80 C3
Olmos Peru 142 C5
Olmütz Czech Rep. see Olomouc
Olney U.K. 49 G6
Olney IL U.S.A. 130 F4
Olney MD U.S.A. 135 G4
Olney TX U.S.A. 131 D5
Olofström Sweden 45 I8
Olomane r. Canada 123 J4
Olomouc Czech Rep. 47 P6
Olonets Rus. Fed. 42 G3
Olongapo Phil. 69 G4
Oloron-Ste-Marie France 56 D5
Olosenga atoll American Samoa see Swains Island
Olot Spain 57 H2
Olot Uzbek. 89 F2
Olovyannaya Rus. Fed. 73 L2
Oloy r. Rus. Fed. 65 Q3
Oloy, Qatorkŭhi mts Asia see Alai Range
Olpe Germany 53 H3
Olsztyn Poland 47 R4
Olt r. Romania 59 K3
Olten Switz. 56 H3
Olteniţa Romania 59 L2
Oltu Turkey 91 F2
Oluan Pi c. Taiwan 77 I4
Ol'viopol' Ukr. see Pervomays'k
Olymbos hill Cyprus see Olympos

►Olympia U.S.A. 126 C3
Capital of Washington state.

Olympic National Park U.S.A. 126 C3
Olympos hill Cyprus 85 A2
Olympos Greece see Olympus, Mount
Olympos mt. Greece see Olympus, Mount
Olympos nat. park Greece see Olympou, Ethnikos Drymos
Olympou, Ethnikos Drymos nat. park Greece 59 J4
Olympus, Mount Greece 59 J4
Olympus, Mount U.S.A. 126 C3
Olyutorskiy Rus. Fed. 65 R3
Olyutorskiy, Mys c. Rus. Fed. 65 S4
Olyutorskiy Zaliv b. Rus. Fed. 65 R4
Olzheras Rus. Fed. see Mezhdurechensk
Oma China 83 E2
Oma r. Rus. Fed. 42 J2
Omagh U.K. 51 E3
Omaha U.S.A. 130 E3
Omaheke admin. reg. Namibia 100 D2
Omal'skiy Khrebet mts Rus. Fed. 74 E1
Oman country Asia 87 I6
Oman, Gulf of Asia 88 E5
Omaruru Namibia 99 B6
Omate Peru 142 D7
Omaweneno Botswana 100 F3
Omba i. Vanuatu see Aoba
Ombai, Selat sea chan. Indon. 108 D2
Ombalantu Namibia see Uutapi
Omboué Gabon 98 A4
Ombu China 83 F3
Omdraaisvlei S. Africa 100 F6
Omdurman Sudan 86 D6
Omeo Australia 112 C6
Omer U.S.A. 134 D1
Ometepec Mex. 136 E5
Omgoy Wildlife Reserve nature res. Thai. 70 B3
Om Hajēr Eritrea 86 E7
Omīdīyeh Iran 88 C4
Omineca Mountains Canada 120 E3
Omitara Namibia 100 C2
Ōmiya Japan 75 E6
Ommaney, Cape U.S.A. 120 C3
Ommen Neth. 52 G2
Omolon Rus. Fed. 65 R3
Omo National Park Eth. 98 D3
Omsk Rus. Fed. 64 I4
Omsukchan Rus. Fed. 65 Q3
Ōmū Japan 74 F3
O-mu Myanmar 70 B2
Omu, Vârful mt. Romania 59 K2
Ōmura Japan 75 C6
Omutninsk Rus. Fed. 42 L4
Onaman Lake Canada 122 D4
Onamia U.S.A. 130 E2
Onancock U.S.A. 135 H5
Onangué, Lac l. Gabon 98 B4
Onaping Lake Canada 122 E5
Onatchiway, Lac l. Canada 123 H4
Onavas Mex. 127 F7
Onawa U.S.A. 130 D3
Onaway U.S.A. 134 C1
Onbingwin Myanmar 71 B4
Oncativo Arg. 144 D4
Onchan Isle of Man 48 C4
Oncócua Angola 99 B5
Öncül Turkey 85 D1
Ondal India see Andal
Ondangwa Namibia 99 B5
Onderstedorings S. Africa 100 E6
Ondjiva Angola 99 B5
Ondo Nigeria 96 D4
Öndörhaan Mongolia 73 K3
Öndörshil Mongolia 73 J3
Ondozero Rus. Fed. 42 G3
One Botswana 100 E2
One and a Half Degree Channel Maldives 81 D11
Onega Rus. Fed. 42 H3
Onega r. Rus. Fed. 42 H3
Onega, Lake l. Rus. Fed. see Onezhskoye Ozero

►Onega, Lake Rus. Fed. 42 G3
3rd largest lake in Europe.

Onega Bay g. Rus. Fed. see Onezhskaya Guba
One Hundred and Fifty Mile House Canada see 150 Mile House
One Hundred Mile House Canada see 100 Mile House
Oneida NY U.S.A. 135 H2
Oneida TN U.S.A. 134 C5
Oneida Lake U.S.A. 135 H2
O'Neill U.S.A. 130 D3
Onekama U.S.A. 134 B1
Onekotan, Ostrov i. Rus. Fed. 65 Q5
Oneonta AL U.S.A. 133 C5
Oneonta NY U.S.A. 135 H2
Oneşti Romania 59 L1
Onezhskaya Guba g. Rus. Fed. 42 G2
Onezhskoye Ozero Rus. Fed. 41 N3
Onezhskoye Ozero l. Rus. Fed. see Onega, Lake
Ong r. India 84 D1
Onga Gabon 98 B4
Ongers watercourse S. Africa 100 F5
Ongiyn Gol r. Mongolia 80 J3
Ongjin N. Korea 75 B5
Ongole India 84 D3
Onida U.S.A. 130 C2
Onilahy r. Madag. 99 E6
Onistagane, Lac l. Canada 123 H4
Onitsha Nigeria 96 D4
Onjati Mountain Namibia 100 C2
Onjiva Angola see Ondjiva
Ono-i-Lau i. Fiji 107 I4
Onomichi Japan 75 D6
Onon atoll Micronesia see Namonuito
Onor, Gora mt. Rus. Fed. 74 F2
Onotoa atoll Kiribati 107 H2
Onseepkans S. Africa 100 D5
Onslow Australia 108 A5
Onslow Bay U.S.A. 133 E5
Onstwedde Neth. 52 H1
Ontake-san vol. Japan 75 E6
Ontario prov. Canada 134 E1
Ontario U.S.A. 126 D3
Ontario, Lake Canada/U.S.A. 135 G2
Ontong Java Atoll Solomon Is 107 F2
Onutu atoll Kiribati see Onotoa
Onverwacht Suriname 143 G2
Onyx U.S.A. 128 D4
Oodnadatta Australia 111 A5
Oodweyne Somalia 98 E3
Oolambeyan National Park nat. park N.S.W. 111 D7
Oolambeyan National Park nat. park N.S.W. 112 F5
Ooldea Australia 109 E7
Ooldea Range hills Australia 109 E7
Oologah Lake resr U.S.A. 131 E4
Ooratippra r. Australia 110 B4
Oos-Londen S. Africa see East London
Oostburg Neth. 52 D3
Oostende Belgium see Ostend
Oostendorp Neth. 52 F2
Oosterhout Neth. 52 E3
Oosterschelde est. Neth. 52 D3
Oosterwolde Neth. 52 G2
Oostvleteren Belgium 52 C4
Oost-Vlieland Neth. 52 F1
Ootacamund India see Udagamandalam
Ootsa Lake Canada 120 E4
Ootsa Lake l. Canada 120 E4
Opal Mex. 131 C7
Opala Dem. Rep. Congo 98 C4
Oparino Rus. Fed. 42 K4
Oparo i. Fr. Polynesia see Rapa
Opasatika r. Canada 122 E4
Opasatika Lake Canada 122 E4
Opasquia Canada 121 M4
Opataca, Lac l. Canada 122 G4
Opava Czech Rep. 47 P6
Opel hill Germany 53 H5
Opelika U.S.A. 133 C5
Opelousas U.S.A. 131 E6
Opeongo Lake Canada 122 F5
Opheim U.S.A. 126 G2
Opienge Dem. Rep. Congo 98 C3
Opinaca r. Canada 122 F3
Opinaca, Réservoir resr Canada 122 F3
Opinnagau r. Canada 122 E3
Opiscotéo, Lac l. Canada 123 H3
Op Luang National Park Thai. 70 B3
Opmeer Neth. 52 E2
Opochka Rus. Fed. 45 P8
Opocopa, Lac l. Canada 123 I3
Opodepe Mex. 136 B3
Opole Poland 47 P5
Oporto Port. 57 B3
Opotiki N.Z. 113 F4
Opp U.S.A. 133 C6
Oppdal Norway 44 F5
Oppeln Poland see Opole
Opportunity U.S.A. 126 D3
Opunake N.Z. 113 D4
Opuwo Namibia 99 B5
Oqsu r. Tajik. 89 I2
Oracle U.S.A. 129 H5
Oradea Romania 59 I1
Orahovac Kosovo see Rahovec
Orai India 82 D4
Oraibi U.S.A. 129 H4
Oraibi Wash watercourse U.S.A. 129 H4
Oral Kazakh. see Ural'sk
Oran Alg. 57 F6
Orán Arg. 144 D2
O Rang Cambodia 71 D4
Orang India 83 H4
Ŏrang N. Korea 74 C4
Orange Australia 112 D4
Orange France 56 G4
Orange r. Namibia/S. Africa 100 C5
Orange CA U.S.A. 128 E5
Orange MA U.S.A. 135 I2
Orange TX U.S.A. 131 E6
Orange VA U.S.A. 135 F4
Orange, Cabo c. Brazil 143 H3
Orangeburg U.S.A. 133 D5
Orange City U.S.A. 130 D3
Orange Cone sea feature S. Atlantic Ocean 148 I8
Orange Free State prov. S. Africa see Free State
Orangeville Canada 134 E2
Orange Walk Belize 136 G5
Oranienburg Germany 53 N2
Oranje r. Namibia/S. Africa see Orange
Oranje Gebergte hills Suriname 143 G3
Oranjemund Namibia 100 C5

►Oranjestad Aruba 137 J6
Capital of Aruba.

Oranmore Ireland 51 D4
Orapa Botswana 99 C6
Orăştie Romania 59 J2
Oraşul Stalin Romania see Braşov
Oravais Fin. 44 M5
Orba Co l. China 82 E2
Orbetello Italy 58 D3
Orbost Australia 112 D6
Orcadas research station S. Atlantic Ocean 152 A2
Orchard City U.S.A. 129 J2
Orchha India 82 D4
Orchila, Isla i. Venez. 142 E1
Orchy r. U.K. 50 D4
Orcutt U.S.A. 128 C4
Ord r. Australia 108 E3
Ord U.S.A. 130 D3
Ord, Mount hill Australia 108 D4
Ordenes Spain see Ordes
Orderville U.S.A. 129 G3
Ordes Spain 57 B2
Ordesa-Monte Perdido, Parque Nacional nat. park Spain 57 G2
Ord Mountain U.S.A. 128 E4
Ordos Nei Mongol China 73 K5
Ord River Dam Australia 108 E4
Ordu Hatay Turkey see Yayladağı
Ordu Ordu Turkey 90 E2
Ordubad Azer. 91 G3
Ordway U.S.A. 130 C4
Ordzhonikidze Rus. Fed. see Vladikavkaz
Ore Nigeria 96 D4
Oreana U.S.A. 128 D1
Örebro Sweden 45 I7
Oregon IL U.S.A. 130 F3
Oregon OH U.S.A. 134 D3
Oregon state U.S.A. 126 C4
Oregon City U.S.A. 126 C3
Orekhov Ukr. see Orikhiv
Orekhovo-Zuyevo Rus. Fed. 42 H5
Orel Rus. Fed. 43 H5
Orel, Gora mt. Rus. Fed. 74 E1
Orel', Ozero l. Rus. Fed. 74 E1
Orem U.S.A. 129 H1
Ore Mountains Czech Rep./Germany see Erzgebirge
Orenburg Rus. Fed. 64 G4
Orense Spain see Ourense
Oreor Palau see Koror
Orepuki N.Z. 113 A8
Öresund strait Denmark/Sweden 45 H9
Oretana, Cordillera mts Spain see Toledo, Montes de
Orewa N.Z. 113 E3
Oreye Belgium 52 F4
Orfanou, Kolpos b. Greece 59 J4
Orford Australia 111 [inset]
Orford U.K. 49 I6
Orford Ness hd U.K. 49 I6
Organabo Fr. Guiana 143 H2
Organ Pipe Cactus National Monument nat. park U.S.A. 129 G5
Orge r. France 52 C6
Orgūn Afgh. 89 H3
Orhaneli Turkey 59 M5
Orhangazi Turkey 59 M4
Orhon Gol r. Mongolia 80 J2
Orichi Rus. Fed. 42 K4
Oriental, Cordillera mts Bol. 142 E7
Oriental, Cordillera mts Col. 142 D2
Oriental, Cordillera mts Peru 142 E6
Orihuela Spain 57 F4
Orikhiv Ukr. 43 G7
Orillia Canada 134 F1
Orimattila Fin. 45 N6
Orin U.S.A. 126 G4
Orinoco r. Col./Venez. 142 F2
Orinoco Delta Venez. 142 F2
Orissa state India 84 E1
Orissaare Estonia 45 M7
Oristano Sardinia Italy 58 C5
Orivesi Fin. 45 N6
Orivesi l. Fin. 44 P5
Oriximiná Brazil 143 G4
Orizaba Mex. 136 E5

►Orizaba, Pico de vol. Mex. 136 E5
Highest active volcano and 3rd highest mountain in North America.

Orizona Brazil 145 A2
Orkanger Norway 44 F5
Örkelljunga Sweden 45 H8
Orkla r. Norway 44 F5
Orkney S. Africa 101 H4
Orkney Islands is U.K. 50 F1
Orla U.S.A. 131 C6
Orland U.S.A. 128 B2
Orlândia Brazil 145 B3
Orlando U.S.A. 133 D6
Orland Park U.S.A. 134 B3
Orleaes Brazil 145 A5
Orléans France 56 E3
Orleans IN U.S.A. 134 B4
Orleans VT U.S.A. 135 I1
Orléans, Île d' i. Canada 123 H5
Orléansville Alg. see Chlef
Orlik Rus. Fed. 72 H2
Orlov Rus. Fed. 42 K4
Orlov Gay Rus. Fed. 43 K6
Orlovskiy Rus. Fed. 43 I7
Ormara Pak. 89 G5
Ormara, Ras hd Pak. 89 G5
Ormiston Canada 121 J5
Ormoc Phil. 69 G4
Ormskirk U.K. 48 E5
Ormstown Canada 135 I1
Ornach Pak. 89 G5
Ornain r. France 52 E6
Orne r. France 56 D2
Ørnes Norway 44 H3
Örnsköldsvik Sweden 44 K5
Orobie, Alpi mts Italy 58 C1
Orobo, Serra do hills Brazil 145 C1
Orodara Burkina 96 C3
Orofino U.S.A. 126 D3
Oro Grande U.S.A. 128 E4
Orogrande U.S.A. 127 G6
Orol Dengizi salt l. Kazakh./Uzbek. see Aral Sea
Oromocto Canada 123 I5
Oromocto Lake Canada 123 I5
Oron Israel 85 B4
Orona atoll Kiribati 107 I2
Orono U.S.A. 132 G2
Orontes r. Asia 90 E3 see 'Āṣī, Nahr al
Orontes r. Lebanon/Syria 85 C2
Oroqen Zizhiqi China see Alihe
Oroquieta Phil. 69 G5
Orós, Açude resr Brazil 143 K5
Orosei, Golfo di b. Sardinia Italy 58 C4
Orosháza Hungary 59 I1
Oroville U.S.A. 128 C2
Oroville, Lake U.S.A. 128 C2
Orqohan China 74 A2
Orr U.S.A. 130 E1
Orsa Sweden 45 I6
Orsha Belarus 43 F5
Orshanka Rus. Fed. 42 J4
Orsk Rus. Fed. 64 G4
Ørsta Norway 44 E5
Orta Toroslar plat. Turkey 85 A1
Ortegal, Cabo c. Spain 57 C2
Orthez France 56 D5
Ortigueira Spain 57 C2
Ortíz Mex. 127 F7
Ortles mt. Italy 58 D1
Orton U.K. 48 E4
Ortona Italy 58 F3
Ortonville U.S.A. 130 D2
Ortospana Afgh. see Kābul
Orulgan, Khrebet mts Rus. Fed. 65 N3
Orumbo Namibia 100 C2
Orūmīyeh Iran see Urmia
Oruro Bol. 142 E7
Orūzgān Afgh. 89 G3
Orvieto Italy 58 E3
Orville Coast Antarctica 152 L1
Orwell OH U.S.A. 134 E3
Orwell VT U.S.A. 135 I2
Oryol Rus. Fed. see Orel
Os Norway 44 G5
Osa Rus. Fed. 41 R4
Osa, Península de pen. Costa Rica 137 H7
Osage IA U.S.A. 130 E3
Osage WV U.S.A. 134 E4
Osage WY U.S.A. 126 G3
Ōsaka Japan 75 D6
Osakarovka Kazakh. 80 D1
Osawatomie U.S.A. 130 E4
Osborne U.S.A. 130 D4
Osby Sweden 45 H8
Osceola IA U.S.A. 130 E3
Osceola MO U.S.A. 130 E4
Osceola NE U.S.A. 130 D3
Oschatz Germany 53 N3
Oschersleben (Bode) Germany 53 L2
Oschiri Sardinia Italy 58 C4
Ösel i. Estonia see Hiiumaa
Osetr r. Rus. Fed. 43 H5
Ōse-zaki pt Japan 75 C6
Osgoode Canada 135 H1
Osgood Mountains U.S.A. 126 D4
Osh Kyrg. 80 D3
Oshakati Namibia 99 B5
Oshawa Canada 135 F2
Oshika-hantō pen. Japan 75 F5
Ō-shima i. Japan 74 E4
Ō-shima i. Japan 75 E6
Oshkosh NE U.S.A. 130 C3
Oshkosh WI U.S.A. 134 A1
Oshmyany Belarus see Ashmyany
Oshnovīyeh Iran 88 B2
Oshogbo Nigeria 96 D4
Oshtorān Kūh mt. Iran 88 C3
Oshwe Dem. Rep. Congo 98 B4
Osijek Croatia 58 H2
Osilinka r. Canada 120 E3
Osimo Italy 58 E3
Osipenko Ukr. see Berdyans'k
Osipovichi Belarus see Asipovichy
Osiyan India 82 C4
Osizweni S. Africa 101 J4
Osječenica mts Bos.-Herz. 58 G2
Ösjön l. Sweden 44 I5
Oskaloosa U.S.A. 130 E3
Oskarshamn Sweden 45 J8
Öskemen Kazakh. see Ust'-Kamenogorsk

►Oslo Norway 45 G7
Capital of Norway.

Oslofjorden sea chan. Norway 45 G7
Osmanabad India 84 C2
Osmancık Turkey 90 D2
Osmaneli Turkey 59 M4
Osmaniye Turkey 90 E3
Osmannagar India 84 C2
Os'mino Rus. Fed. 45 P7
Osnabrück Germany 53 I2
Osnaburg atoll Fr. Polynesia see Mururoa
Osogbo Nigeria see Oshogbo
Osogovska Planina mts Bulg./Macedonia 59 J3
Osogovske Planine mts Bulg./Macedonia see Osogovska Planina
Osogovski Planini mts Bulg./Macedonia see Osogovska Planina
Osorno Chile 144 B6
Osorno Spain 57 D2
Osoyoos Canada 120 G5
Osøyri Norway 45 D6
Osprey Reef Australia 110 D2
Oss Neth. 52 F3
Ossa, Mount Australia 111 [inset]
Osseo U.S.A. 122 C5
Ossineke U.S.A. 134 D1
Ossining U.S.A. 135 I3
Ossipee U.S.A. 135 J2
Ossipee Lake U.S.A. 135 J2
Oßmannstedt Germany 53 L3
Ossokmanuan Lake Canada 123 I3
Ossora Rus. Fed. 65 R4
Ostashkov Rus. Fed. 42 G4
Ostbevern Germany 53 H2
Oste r. Germany 53 J1
Ostend Belgium 52 C3
Ostende Belgium see Ostend
Osterburg (Altmark) Germany 53 L2
Österbymo Sweden 45 I8
Österdalälven l. Sweden 45 H6
Østerdalen valley Norway 45 G5
Osterfeld Germany 53 L3
Osterholz-Scharmbeck Germany 53 I1
Osterode am Harz Germany 53 K3
Österreich country Europe see Austria
Östersund Sweden 44 I5
Osterwieck Germany 53 K3
Ostfriesische Inseln Germany see East Frisian Islands
Ostfriesland reg. Germany 53 H1
Östhammar Sweden 45 K6
Ostrava Czech Rep. 47 Q6
Ostróda Poland 47 Q4
Ostrogozhsk Rus. Fed. 43 H6
Ostrov Czech Rep. 53 M4
Ostrov Rus. Fed. 45 P8
Ostrovets Poland see Ostrowiec Świętokrzyski
Ostrovskoye Rus. Fed. 42 I4
Ostrov Vrangelya i. Rus. Fed. see Wrangel Island
Ostrów Poland see Ostrów Wielkopolski
Ostrowiec Poland see Ostrowiec Świętokrzyski
Ostrowiec Świętokrzyski Poland 43 D6
Ostrów Mazowiecka Poland 47 R4
Ostrowo Poland see Ostrów Wielkopolski
Ostrów Wielkopolski Poland 47 P5
O'Sullivan Lake Canada 122 D4
Osŭm r. Bulg. 59 K3
Ōsumi-shotō is Japan 75 C7
Osuna Spain 57 D5
Oswego KS U.S.A. 131 E4
Oswego NY U.S.A. 135 G2
Oswestry U.K. 49 D6
Otago Peninsula N.Z. 113 C7
Otahiti i. Fr. Polynesia see Tahiti
Otaki N.Z. 113 E5
Otanmäki Fin. 44 O4
Otaru Japan 74 F4
Otavi Namibia 99 B5
Ōtawara Japan 75 F5
Otdia atoll Marshall Is see Wotje
Otelnuc, Lac l. Canada 123 H2
Otematata N.Z. 113 C7
Otepää Estonia 45 O7
Otgon Tenger Uul mt. Mongolia 80 I2
Otinapa Mex. 131 B7
Otira N.Z. 113 C6
Otis U.S.A. 130 C3
Otish, Monts hills Canada 123 H4

ijinene Namibia 99 B6
tjiwarongo Namibia 99 B6
tjozondjupa admin. reg. Namibia 100 C1
sley U.K. 48 F5
torohanga N.Z. 113 E4
toskwin r. Canada 121 N5
tpan, Gora hill Kazakh. 91 H1
tpor Rus. Fed. see Zabaykal'sk
tradnoye Rus. Fed. see Otradnyy
tradnyy Rus. Fed. 43 K5
tranto Italy 58 H4
tranto, Strait of Albania/Italy 58 H4
rogovo Rus. Fed. see Stepnoye
trozhnyy Rus. Fed. 65 S3
sego Lake U.S.A. 135 H2
su Japan 75 D6
ta Norway 45 F6

Ottawa Canada 135 H1
Capital of Canada.

tawa r. Canada 122 G5
also known as Rivière des Outaouais
tawa IL U.S.A. 130 F3
tawa KS U.S.A. 130 E4
tawa OH U.S.A. 134 C3
tawa Islands Canada 122 E2
ter r. U.K. 49 D8
terbein U.S.A. 134 B3
terburn U.K. 48 E3
ter Rapids Canada 122 E4
tersberg Germany 53 J1
tignies Belgium 52 E4
tumwa U.S.A. 130 E3
tweiler Germany 53 H5
ukpo Nigeria 96 D4
urkpo Nigeria see Otukpo
uzco Peru 142 C5
way, Cape Australia 112 A7
way National Park Australia 112 A7
achita r. U.S.A. 131 F6
achita, Lake U.S.A. 131 E5
achita Mountains Arkansas/Oklahoma
J.S.A. 131 E5
adda Cent. Afr. Rep. 98 C3
addaï reg. Chad 97 F3

Ouagadougou Burkina 96 C3
Capital of Burkina.

ahigouya Burkina 96 C3
ahran Alg. see Oran
aka r. Cent. Afr. Rep. 98 B3
alâta Mauritania 96 C3
allam Niger 96 D3
anda-Djailé Cent. Afr. Rep. 98 C3
ando Cent. Afr. Rep. 98 C3
ango Cent. Afr. Rep. 98 C3
ara r. Cent. Afr. Rep. 98 C3
arâne reg. Mauritania 96 C2
argaye Burkina 96 D3
argla Alg. 54 F5
arogou Burkina see Ouargaye
arzazate Morocco 54 C5
asiemsca r. Canada 123 G4
bangui r.
Cent. Afr. Rep./Dem. Rep. Congo see
Ubangi
bergpas pass S. Africa 100 G7
denaarde Belgium 52 D4
dômxai Laos 70 C2
dtshoorn S. Africa 100 F7
d-Turnhout Belgium 52 E3
ed Tlélat Alg. 57 F6
ed Zem Morocco 54 C5
ed Zénati Alg. 58 B6
essant, Île d' i. France 56 B2
esso Congo 98 B3
ezzane Morocco 57 D6
ghter, Lough l. Ireland 51 E3
guati Namibia 100 B1
istreham France 49 G9
jda Morocco 57 F6
jeft Mauritania 96 B3
lainen Fin. 44 N4
langan kansallispuisto nat. park
in. 44 P3
led Djellal Alg. 57 I6
led Farès Alg. 57 G5
led Naïl, Monts des mts Alg. 57 H6
lu Fin. 44 N4
lujärvi l. Fin. 44 O4
lujoki r. Fin. 44 N4
lunsalo Fin. 44 N4
lx Italy 58 B2
m-Chalouba Chad 97 F3
m el Bouaghi Alg. 58 B7
m-Hadjer Chad 97 E3
nasjoki r. Fin. 44 N3
ndle U.K. 49 G6
ngre Canada 121 K5
nianga Kébir Chad 97 F3
peye Belgium 52 F4
r r. Lux. 52 G5
ra, Akrotirio pt Greece 59 L5
ray CO U.S.A. 129 J2
ray UT U.S.A. 129 I1
rcq r. France 52 D5
rense Spain 57 C2
ricurí Brazil 143 J5
rinhos Brazil 145 A3
ro r. Brazil 145 A1
ro Preto Brazil 145 C3
rthe r. Belgium 52 F4
Valley valley Germany/Lux. 52 G5
s Rus. Fed. 41 S3
se r. England U.K. 48 G5
se r. England U.K. 49 H8
taouais, Rivière des r. Canada 122 G5
e Ottawa
tardes, Rivière aux r.
anada 123 H4
tardes Quatre, Réservoir resr
anada 123 H4
ter Hebrides is U.K. 50 B3
ter Mongolia country Asia see
Mongolia
er Santa Barbara Channel
.S.A. 128 D5
jo Namibia 99 B6
look Canada 121 J5
okumpu Fin. 44 P5

Out Skerries is U.K. 50 [inset]
Ouvéa atoll New Caledonia 107 G4
Ouyanghai Shuiku resr China 77 G3
Ouyen Australia 111 C7
Ouzel r. U.K. 49 G6
Ovace, Punta d' mt. Corsica France 56 I6
Ovacık Turkey 85 A1
Ovada Italy 58 C2
Ovalle Chile 144 B4
Ovamboland reg. Namibia 99 B5
Ovan Gabon 98 B3
Ovar Port. 57 B3
Overath Germany 53 H4
Överkalix Sweden 44 M3
Overlander Roadhouse Australia 109 A6
Overland Park U.S.A. 130 E4
Overton U.S.A. 129 F3
Övertorneå Sweden 44 M3
Överum Sweden 45 J8
Overveen Neth. 52 E2
Ovid CO U.S.A. 130 C3
Ovid NY U.S.A. 135 G2
Oviedo Spain 57 D2
Øvre Anárjohka Nasjonalpark nat. park Norway 44 N2
Øvre Dividal Nasjonalpark nat. park Norway 44 K2
Øvre Rendal Norway 45 G6
Ovruch Ukr. 43 F6
Ovsyanka Rus. Fed. 74 B1
Owando Congo 98 B4
Owa Rafa i. Solomon Is see Santa Ana
Owasco Lake U.S.A. 135 G2
Owase Japan 75 E6
Owatonna U.S.A. 130 E2
Owbeh Afgh. 89 F3
Owego U.S.A. 135 G2
Owel, Lough l. Ireland 51 E4
Owen Island Myanmar 71 B5
Owenmore r. Ireland 51 C3
Owenreagh r. U.K. 51 E3
Owen River N.Z. 113 D5
Owens r. U.S.A. 128 E3
Owensboro U.S.A. 134 B5
Owen Sound Canada 134 E1
Owen Sound inlet Canada 134 E1
Owen Stanley Range mts P.N.G. 69 L8
Owenton U.S.A. 134 C4
Owerri Nigeria 96 D4
Owikeno Lake Canada 120 E5
Owingsville U.S.A. 134 D4
Owkal Afgh. 89 F3
Owl r. Canada 121 M3
Owl Creek Mountains U.S.A. 126 F4
Owo Nigeria 96 D4
Owosso U.S.A. 134 C2
Owyhee U.S.A. 126 D4
Owyhee r. U.S.A. 126 D4
Owyhee Mountains U.S.A. 126 D4
Öxarfjörður b. Iceland 44 [inset]
Oxbow Canada 121 K5
Ox Creek r. U.S.A. 130 C1
Oxelösund Sweden 45 J7
Oxford N.Z. 113 D6
Oxford U.K. 49 F7
Oxford IN U.S.A. 134 B3
Oxford MA U.S.A. 135 J2
Oxford MD U.S.A. 135 G4
Oxford MS U.S.A. 131 F5
Oxford NC U.S.A. 132 E4
Oxford NY U.S.A. 135 H2
Oxford OH U.S.A. 134 C4
Oxford House Canada 121 M4
Oxford Lake Canada 121 M4
Oxley Australia 112 B5
Oxleys Peak Australia 112 E3
Oxley Wild Rivers National Park Australia 112 F3
Ox Mountains hills Ireland 51 C4
Oxnard U.S.A. 128 D4
Oxtongue Lake Canada 135 F1
Oxus r. Asia see Amudar'ya
Øya Norway 44 H3
Oyama Japan 75 E5
Oyapock r. Brazil/Fr. Guiana 143 H3
Oyem Gabon 98 B3
Oyen Canada 121 I5
Oykel r. U.K. 50 E3
Oyo Nigeria 96 D4
Oyonnax France 56 G3
Oyster Rocks is India 84 B3
Oyten Germany 53 J1
Oytograk China 83 E1
Oyukludağı mt. Turkey 85 A1
Özalp Turkey 91 G3
Ozamiz Phil. 69 G5
Ozark AL U.S.A. 133 C6
Ozark AR U.S.A. 131 E5
Ozark MO U.S.A. 131 E4
Ozark Plateau U.S.A. 131 E4
Ozarks, Lake of the U.S.A. 130 E4
O'zbekiston country Asia see Uzbekistan
Özen Kazakh. see Kyzylsay
Ozernovskiy Rus. Fed. 65 Q4
Ozernyy Rus. Fed. 43 G5
Ozerpakh Rus. Fed. 74 F1
Ozersk Rus. Fed. 45 M9
Ozerskiy Rus. Fed. 74 F3
Ozery Rus. Fed. 43 H5
Ozeryane Rus. Fed. 74 C2
Ozieri Sardinia Italy 58 C4
Ozinki Rus. Fed. 43 K6
Oznachennoye Rus. Fed. see Sayanogorsk
Ozona U.S.A. 131 C6
Ozuki Japan 75 C6

P

Paamiut Greenland 119 N3
Pa-an Myanmar see Hpa-an
Paanopa i. Kiribati see Banaba
Paarl S. Africa 100 D7
Paatsjoki r. Europe see Patsoyoki
Paballelo S. Africa 100 E5
P'abal-li N. Korea 74 C4
Pabbay i. U.K. 50 B3
Pabianice Poland 47 Q5
Pabianitz Poland see Pabianice
Pabna Bangl. 83 G4
Pabradė Lith. 45 N9
Pab Range mts Pak. 89 G5
Pacaás Novos, Parque Nacional nat. park Brazil 142 F6
Pacaraimã, Serra mts S. America see Pakaraima Mountains
Pacasmayo Peru 142 C5
Pachagarh Bangl. see Panchagarh
Pacheco Chihuahua Mex. 127 F7
Pacheco Zacatecas Mex. 131 C7
Pachikha Rus. Fed. 42 J3
Pachino Sicily Italy 58 F6
Pachmarhi India 82 D5
Pachor India 82 D5
Pachora India 84 B1
Pachpadra India 82 C4
Pachuca Mex. 136 E4
Pachuca de Soto Mex. see Pachuca
Pacific-Antarctic Ridge sea feature S. Pacific Ocean 151 J9
Pacific Grove U.S.A. 128 C3

▶Pacific Ocean 150
Largest ocean in the world.

Pacific Rim National Park Canada 120 E5
Pacitan Indon. 68 E8
Packsaddle Australia 111 C6
Pacoval Brazil 143 H4
Pacuí r. Brazil 145 B2
Paczków Poland 47 P5
Padali Rus. Fed. see Amursk
Padampur India 82 C3
Padang Indon. 68 C7
Padang i. Indon. 71 C7
Padang Endau Malaysia 71 C7
Padangpanjang Indon. 68 C7
Padangsidimpuan Indon. 71 B7
Padany Rus. Fed. 42 G3
Padatha, Kūh-e mt. Iran 88 C3
Padaung Myanmar 70 A3
Padcaya Bol. 142 F8
Paddington Australia 112 B4
Paden City U.S.A. 134 E4
Paderborn Germany 53 I3
Paderborn/Lippstadt airport Germany 53 I3
Padeșu, Vârful mt. Romania 59 J2
Padibyu Myanmar 70 B2
Padilla Bol. 142 F7
Padjelanta nationalpark nat. park Sweden 44 J3
Padova Italy see Padua
Padrão, Ponta pt Angola 99 B4
Padrauna India 83 F4
Padre Island U.S.A. 131 D7
Padstow U.K. 49 C8
Padsvillye Belarus 45 O9
*Padua India 84 D2
Padua Italy 58 D2
Paducah KY U.S.A. 131 F4
Paducah TX U.S.A. 131 C5
Padum India 82 D2
Paegam N. Korea 74 C4
Paektu-san mt. China/N. Korea see Baotou Shan
Paengnyŏng-do i. S. Korea 75 B5
Pafos Cyprus see Paphos
Pafuri Moz. 101 J2
Pag Croatia 58 F2
Pag i. Croatia 58 F2
Paga Indon. 108 C2
Pagadian Phil. 69 G5
Pagai Selatan i. Indon. 68 C7
Pagalu i. Equat. Guinea see Annobón
Pagan i. N. Mariana Is 69 L3
Pagasitikos Kolpos b. Greece 59 J5
Pagatan Indon. 68 F7
Page U.S.A. 129 H3
Paget, Mount S. Georgia 144 I8
Paget Cay reef Australia 110 F3
Pagon i. N. Mariana Is see Pagan
Pagosa Springs U.S.A. 127 G5
Pagqên China see Gadê
Pagwa River Canada 122 D4
Pagwi P.N.G. 69 K7
Pāhala U.S.A. 127 [inset]
Pahang r. Malaysia 71 C7
Pahlgam India 82 C2
Pāhoa U.S.A. 127 [inset]
Pahokee U.S.A. 133 D7
Pahra Kariz Afgh. 89 F3
Pahranagat Range mts U.S.A. 129 F3
Pahrump U.S.A. 129 F3
Pahuj r. India 82 D4
Pahute Mesa plat. U.S.A. 128 E3
Pai Thai. 70 B3
Paicines U.S.A. 128 C3
Paide Estonia 45 N7
Paignton U.K. 49 D8
Päijänne l. Fin. 45 N6
Paikü Co l. China 83 F3
Pailin Cambodia 71 C4
Pailolo Channel U.S.A. 127 [inset]
Paimio Fin. 45 M6
Painel Brazil 145 A4
Painesville U.S.A. 134 E3
Pains Brazil 145 B3
Painted Desert U.S.A. 129 H3
Painted Rock Dam U.S.A. 129 G5
Paint Hills Canada see Wemindji
Paint Rock U.S.A. 131 D6
Paintsville U.S.A. 134 D5
Paisley U.K. 50 E5
Paita Peru 142 B5
Paitou China 77 I2
Paiva Couceiro Angola see Quipungo
Paizhou China 77 G2
Pajala Sweden 44 M3
Paka Malaysia 71 C6
Pakala India 84 C3
Pakanbaru Indon. see Pekanbaru
Pakangyi Myanmar 70 A2
Pakaraima Mountains S. America 142 F3
Pakaur India 83 F4
Pakesley Canada 122 E5
Pakhachi Rus. Fed. 65 R3
Pakhoi China see Beihai
Paki Nigeria 96 D3

▶Pakistan country Asia 89 H4
4th most populous country in Asia, and 6th in the world.

Pakkat Indon. 71 B7
Paknampho Thai. see Nakhon Sawan
Pakokku Myanmar 70 A2
Pakowki Lake imp. l. Canada 121 I5
Pakpattan Pak. 89 I4
Pak Phanang Thai. 71 C5
Pak Phayun Thai. 71 C6
Pakruojis Lith. 45 M9
Paks Hungary 58 H1
Pakse Laos see Pakxé
Pak Tam Chung H.K. China 77 [inset]
Pak Thong Chai Thai. 70 C4
Pakur India see Pakaur
Pakxan Laos 70 C3
Pakxé Laos 70 D4
Pakxeng Laos 70 C2
Pala Chad 97 E4
Pala Myanmar 71 B4
Palaestinia reg. Asia see Palestine
Palaiochora Greece 59 J7
Palaiseau France 52 C6
Palakkad India see Palghat
Palakkat India see Palghat
Palamakoloi Botswana 100 F2
Palamau India see Palamu
Palamós Spain 57 H3
Palamu India 83 F5
Palana Rus. Fed. 65 Q4
Palandur India 84 D1
Palangān, Kūh-e mts Iran 89 F4
Palangkaraya Indon. 68 E7
Palani India 84 C4
Palanpur India 82 C4
Palantak Pak. 89 G5
Palapye Botswana 101 H2
Palatka Rus. Fed. 65 Q3
Palatka U.S.A. 133 D6
Palau country N. Pacific Ocean 69 I5
Palau Islands Palau 69 I5
Palauk Myanmar 71 B4
Palaw Myanmar 71 B4
Palawan i. Phil. 68 F5
Palawan Passage strait Phil. 68 F5
Palawan Trough sea feature N. Pacific Ocean 150 D5
Palayankottai India 84 C4
Palchal Lake India 84 D2
Paldiski Estonia 45 N7
Palekh Rus. Fed. 42 I4
Palembang Indon. 68 C7
Palena Chile 144 B6
Palencia Spain 57 D2
Palermo Sicily Italy 58 E5
Palestine reg. Asia 85 B3
Palestine U.S.A. 131 E6
Paletwa Myanmar 70 A2
Palezgir Chauki Pak. 89 H4
Palghat India 84 C4
Palgrave, Mount hill Australia 109 A5
Palhoca Brazil 145 A4
Pali Chhattisgarh India 84 D1
Pali Mahar. India 84 B2
Pali Rajasthan India 82 C4

▶Palikir Micronesia 150 G5
Capital of Micronesia.

Palinuro, Capo c. Italy 58 F4
Paliouri, Akra pt Greece see Paliouri, Akrotirio
Paliouri, Akra pt Greece see Paliouri, Akrotirio
Paliouri, Akrotirio pt Greece 59 J5
Palisade U.S.A. 129 I2
Paliseul Belgium 52 F5
Palitana India 82 B5
Palivere Estonia 45 M7
Palk Bay Sri Lanka 84 C4
Palkino Rus. Fed. 45 P8
Palkonda Range mts India 84 C3
Palk Strait India/Sri Lanka 84 C4
Palla Bianca mt. Austria/Italy see Weißkugel
Pallamallawa Australia 112 E2
Pallas Green New Ireland 51 D5
Pallasovka Rus. Fed. 43 J6
Pallas-Yllästunturin kansallispuisto nat. park Fin. 44 M2
Pallavaram India 84 D3
Palliser, Cape N.Z. 113 E5
Palliser, Îles is Fr. Polynesia 151 K7
Palliser Bay N.Z. 113 E5
Pallu India 82 C3
Palma r. Brazil 145 B1
Palma del Río Spain 57 D5
Palma de Mallorca Spain 57 H4
Palmaner India 84 C3
Palmares Brazil 143 K5
Palmares do Sul Brazil 145 A5
Palmas Brazil 145 A4
Palmas Tocantins 142 I6
Palmas, Cape Liberia 96 C4
Palm Bay U.S.A. 133 D7
Palmdale U.S.A. 128 D4
Palmeira Brazil 145 A4
Palmeira das Missões Brazil 144 F3
Palmeira dos Índios Brazil 143 K5
Palmeirais Brazil 143 J5
Palmeiras Brazil 145 C1
Palmeirinhas, Ponta das pt Angola 99 B4
Palmer research station Antarctica 152 L2
Palmer r. Australia 110 C3
Palmer watercourse Australia 109 F6
Palmer U.S.A. 118 D3
Palmer Land reg. Antarctica 152 L2
Palmerston N.T. Australia 108 E3
Palmerston N.T. Australia see Darwin
Palmerston Canada 134 E2
Palmerston atoll Cook Is 107 J3
Palmerston N.Z. 113 C7
Palmerston North N.Z. 113 E5
Palmerton U.S.A. 135 H3
Palmerville Australia 110 D2
Palmetto Point Bahamas 133 E7
Palmi Italy 58 F5
Palmira Col. 142 C3
Palmira Cuba 133 D8
Palm Springs U.S.A. 128 E5
Palmyra Syria see Tadmur
Palmyra MO U.S.A. 130 F4
Palmyra PA U.S.A. 135 G3
Palmyra VA U.S.A. 135 F5

▶Palmyra Atoll terr. N. Pacific Ocean 150 J5
United States Unincorporated Territory.

Palmyras Point India 83 F5
Palni Hills India 84 C4
Palo Alto U.S.A. 128 B3
Palo Blanco Mex. 131 C7
Palo Chino watercourse Mex. 127 E7
Palo Duro watercourse U.S.A. 131 C5
Paloich Sudan 86 D7
Palojärvi Fin. 44 M2
Palojoensuu Fin. 44 M2
Palomaa Fin. 44 O2
Palomar Mountain U.S.A. 128 E5
Paloncha India 84 D2
Palo Pinto U.S.A. 131 D5
Palopo Indon. 69 G7
Palos, Cabo de c. Spain 57 F5
Palo Verde U.S.A. 129 F5
Paltamo Fin. 44 O4
Palu Indon. 68 F7
Palu i. Indon. 108 C2
Palu Turkey 91 E3
Pal'vart Turkm. 89 G2
Palwal India 82 D3
Palwancha India see Paloncha
Palyeskaya Nizina marsh Belarus/Ukr. see Pripet Marshes

▶Pamana i. Indon. 108 C2
Most southerly point of Asia.

Pambarra Moz. 101 L1
Pambula Australia 112 D6
Pamidi India 84 C3
Pamiers France 56 E5
Pamir mts Asia 89 I2
Pamlico Sound sea chan. U.S.A. 133 E5
Pamouscachiou, Lac l. Canada 123 H4
Pampa U.S.A. 131 C5
Pampa de Infierno Arg. 144 D3
Pampas reg. Arg. 144 D5
Pampeluna Spain see Pamplona
Pamphylia reg. Turkey 59 N6
Pamplin U.S.A. 135 F5
Pamplona Col. 142 D2
Pamplona Spain 57 F2
Pampow Germany 53 L1
Pamukova Turkey 59 N4
Pamzal India 82 D2
Pana U.S.A. 130 F4
Panaca U.S.A. 129 F3
Panache, Lake Canada 122 E5
Panagyurishte Bulg. 59 K3
Panaitan i. Indon. 68 D8
Panaji India 84 B3
Panama country Central America 137 H7
Panamá Panama see Panama City
Panamá, Gulf of Panama 137 I7
Panama, Isthmus of Panama 137 I7
Panamá, Istmo de Panama see Panama, Isthmus of
Panama Canal Panama 137 I7

▶Panama City Panama 137 I7
Capital of Panama.

Panama City U.S.A. 133 C6
Panamint Range mts U.S.A. 128 E3
Panamint Valley U.S.A. 128 E3
Panao Peru 142 C5
Panarea, Isola i. Italy 58 F5
Panarik Indon. 71 E7
Panay i. Phil. 69 G4
Panayarvi Natsional'nyy Park nat. park Rus. Fed. 44 Q3
Pancake Range mts U.S.A. 129 F2
Pančevo Serbia 59 I2
Panchagarh Bangl. 83 G4
Pancsova Serbia see Pančevo
Panda Moz. 101 L3
Pandan, Selat strait Sing. 71 [inset]
Pandan Reservoir Sing. 71 [inset]
Pandeiros r. Brazil 145 B1
Pandharpur India 84 B2
Pandy U.K. 49 E7
Paneas Syria see Bāniyās
Panevėžys Lith. 45 N9
Panfilov Kazakh. see Zharkent
Pang, Nam r. Myanmar 70 B2
Panghsang Myanmar 70 B2
Pangi Range mts Pak. 89 I3
Pangkalanbuun Indon. 68 E7
Pangkalansusu Indon. 71 B6
Pangkalpinang Indon. 68 D7
Pangkalsiang, Tanjung pt Indon. 69 G7
Panglang Myanmar 70 B1
Pangman Canada 121 J5
Pangnirtung Canada 119 L3
Pangody Rus. Fed. 64 I3
Pangong Tso salt l. China/India see Bangong Co
Pang Sida National Park Thai. 71 C4
Pang Sua, Sungai r. Sing. 71 [inset]
Pangtara Myanmar 76 C4
Pangu He r. China 74 B1
Panguitch U.S.A. 129 G3
Panhandle U.S.A. 131 C5
Panipat India 82 D3
Panir Pak. 89 G4
Panj Tajik. 89 H2
Panjāb Afgh. 89 G3
Panjakent Tajik. 89 G2
Panjang i. Indon. 71 E7
Panjang, Bukit Sing. 71 [inset]
Panjgur Pak. 89 G5
Panjim India see Panaji
Panji Poyon Tajik. 89 H2
Panjnad r. Pak. 89 H4
Panjshīr reg. Afgh. 89 H3
Pankakoski Fin. 44 Q5
Panlian China see Miyi
Panna India 82 E4
Panna reg. India 82 D4
Pannawonica Australia 108 B5
Pano Lefkara Cyprus 85 A2
Panorama Brazil 145 A3
Panormus Sicily Italy see Palermo
Panshi China 74 B4
Panshui China see Pu'an

▶Pantanal marsh Brazil 143 G7
Largest area of wetlands in the world.

Pantanal Matogrossense, Parque Nacional do nat. park Brazil 143 G7
Pantano U.S.A. 129 H6
Pantar i. Indon. 108 D2
Pantelaria Sicily Italy see Pantelleria
Pantelleria Sicily Italy 58 D6
Pantelleria, Isola di i. Sicily Italy 58 E6
Pantha Myanmar 70 A2
Panther r. U.S.A. 134 B5
Panth Piploda India 82 C5
Panticapaeum Ukr. see Kerch
Pantonlabu Indon. 71 B6
Pánuco Sinaloa Mex. 131 B8
Pánuco Veracruz Mex. 136 E4
Panwari India 82 D4
Panxian China 76 E3
Panyu China 77 G4
Panzhihua China 76 D3
Panzi Dem. Rep. Congo 99 B4
Paola Italy 58 G5
Paola U.S.A. 130 E4
Paoli U.S.A. 134 B4
Paoua Cent. Afr. Rep. 98 B3
Paôy Pêt Cambodia 71 C4
Pápa Hungary 58 G1
Papa, Monte del mt. Italy 58 F4
Papagni r. India 84 C3
Pāpa'ikou U.S.A. 127 [inset]
Papakura N.Z. 113 E3
Papanasam India 84 C4
Papantla Mex. 136 E4
Paparoa National Park N.Z. 113 C6
Papa Stour i. U.K. 50 [inset]
Papa Westray i. U.K. 50 G1
Papay i. U.K. see Papa Westray

▶Papeete Fr. Polynesia 151 K7
Capital of French Polynesia.

Papenburg Germany 53 H1
Paphos Cyprus 85 A2
Paphus Cyprus see Paphos
Papillion U.S.A. 130 D3
Papoose Lake U.S.A. 129 F3
Pappenheim Germany 53 K6
Papua, Gulf of P.N.G. 69 K8

▶Papua New Guinea country Oceania 106 E2
2nd largest and 2nd most populous country in Oceania.

Pa Qal'eh Iran 88 D4
Par U.K. 49 C8
Pará r. Brazil 145 B2
Pará, Rio do r. Brazil 143 I4
Paraburdoo Australia 109 B5
Paracatu Brazil 145 B2
Paracatu r. Brazil 145 B2
Paracel Islands S. China Sea 68 E3
Parachilna Australia 111 B6
Parachute U.S.A. 129 I2
Paraćin Serbia 59 I3
Paracuru Brazil 143 K4
Pará de Minas Brazil 145 B2
Paradis Canada 122 F4
Paradise r. Canada 123 K3
Paradise U.S.A. 128 C2
Paradise Hill Canada 121 I4
Paradise Peak U.S.A. 128 E2
Paradise River Canada 123 K3
Paradwip India 83 F5
Paraetonium Egypt see Marsá Maṭrūḥ
Paragominas Brazil 143 I4
Paragould U.S.A. 131 F4
Paragua i. Phil. see Palawan
Paraguaçu Paulista Brazil 145 A3
Paraguay r. Arg./Para. 144 E3
Paraguay country S. America 144 E2
Paraíba do Sul r. Brazil 145 C3
Parainen Fin. see Pargas
Paraíso do Norte Brazil 143 I6
Paraisópolis Brazil 145 B3
Parak Iran 88 D5
Parakou Benin 96 D4
Paralakhemundi India 84 E2
Paralkot India 84 D2
Paramagudi India see Paramakkudi
Paramakkudi India 84 C4

▶Paramaribo Suriname 143 G2
Capital of Suriname.

Paramillo, Parque Nacional nat. park Col. 142 C2
Paramirim Brazil 145 C1
Paramo Frontino mt. Col. 142 C2
Paramus U.S.A. 135 H3
Paramushir, Ostrov i. Rus. Fed. 65 Q4
Paran watercourse Israel 85 B4
Paraná Arg. 144 D4
Paranã Brazil 145 B1
Paraná r. Brazil 145 A1
Paraná state Brazil 145 A4

▶Paraná r. S. America 144 E4
Part of the Río de la Plata - Paraná, 2nd longest river in South America.

Paraná, Serra do hills Brazil 145 B1
Paranaguá Brazil 145 A4
Paranaíba Brazil 145 A2
Paranaíba r. Brazil 145 A3
Paranapiacaba, Serra mts Brazil 145 A4
Paranavaí Brazil 144 F2
Parangi Aru r. Sri Lanka 84 D4
Parang Pass India 82 D2
Parângul Mare, Vârful mt. Romania 59 J2
Paranthan Sri Lanka 84 D4
Paraopeba Brazil 145 B2
Pārapāra Iraq 91 G4
Paraparaumu N.Z. 113 E5

Paras Mex. 131 D7
Paras Pak. 89 I3
Paraspori, Akra *pt* Greece *see* **Paraspori, Akrotirio**
Paraspori, Akrotirio *pt* Greece 59 L7
Parateca Brazil 145 C1
Paratinga Brazil 145 C1
Parāū, Kūh-e *mt.* Iraq 91 G4
Paraúna Brazil 145 A2
Parbhani India 84 C2
Parchim Germany 53 L1
Parding China 83 G2
Pardo *r. Bahia* Brazil 145 D1
Pardo *r. Mato Grosso do Sul* Brazil 144 F2
Pardo *r. São Paulo* Brazil 145 A3
Pardoo Australia 108 B5
Pardubice Czech Rep. 47 O5
Parece Vela *i.* Japan *see* **Okino-Tori-shima**
Parecis, Serra dos *hills* Brazil 142 F6
Pareh Iran 88 B2
Parenda India 84 B2
Parent Canada 122 G5
Parent, Lac *l.* Canada 122 F4
Pareora N.Z. 113 C7
Parepare Indon. 68 F7
Parga Greece 59 I5
Pargas Fin. 45 M6
Parghelia Italy 58 F5
Pargi India 84 C2
Paria, Gulf of Trin. and Tob./Venez. 137 L6
Paria, Península de *pen.* Venez. 142 F1
Paria Plateau U.S.A. 129 G3
Parikkala Fin. 45 P6
Parikud Islands India 84 E2
Parima, Serra *mts* Brazil 142 F3
Parima-Tapirapecó, Parque Nacional *nat. park* Venez. 142 F3
Parintins Brazil 143 G4
Paris Canada 134 E2

▶**Paris** France 52 C6
Capital of France. 3rd most populous city in Europe.

Paris *IL* U.S.A. 134 B4
Paris *KY* U.S.A. 134 C4
Paris *MO* U.S.A. 130 E4
Paris *TN* U.S.A. 131 F4
Paris *TX* U.S.A. 131 E5
Paris (Charles de Gaulle) *airport* France 52 C5
Paris (Orly) *airport* France 52 C6
Paris Crossing U.S.A. 134 C4
Parit Buntar Malaysia 71 C6
Pārīz Iran 88 D4
Pārk Iran 89 F5
Park U.K. 51 E3
Parkano Fin. 45 M5
Park City U.S.A. 134 B5
Parke Lake Canada 123 K3
Parker *AZ* U.S.A. 129 F4
Parker *CO* U.S.A. 126 G5
Parker Dam U.S.A. 129 F4
Parker Lake Canada 121 M2
Parker Range *hills* Australia 109 B8
Parkersburg U.S.A. 134 E4
Parkers Lake U.S.A. 134 C5
Parkes Australia 112 D4
Park Falls U.S.A. 130 F2
Park Forest U.S.A. 134 B3
Parkhar Tajik. *see* **Farkhor**
Parkhill Canada 134 E2
Park Rapids U.S.A. 130 E2
Parkutta Pak. 82 D2
Park Valley U.S.A. 126 E4
Parla Kimedi India *see* **Paralakhemundi**
Parlakimidi India *see* **Paralakhemundi**
Parli Vaijnath India 84 C2
Parlung Zangbo *r.* China 76 B2
Parma Italy 58 D2
Parma *ID* U.S.A. 126 D4
Parma *OH* U.S.A. 134 E3
Parnaíba Brazil 143 J4
Parnaíba *r.* Brazil 143 J4
Parnassos *mt.* Greece *see* **Liakoura**
Parnassos *mt.* Greece *see* **Liakoura**
Parnassus N.Z. 113 D6
Parner India 84 B2
Parnon *mts* Greece *see* **Parnonas**
Parnon *mts* Greece *see* **Parnonas**
Parnonas *mts* Greece 59 J6
Pärnu Estonia 45 N7
Pärnu-Jaagupi Estonia 45 N7
Paro Bhutan 83 G4
Paroikia Greece 59 K6
Parona Turkey *see* **Fındık**
Paroo *watercourse* Australia 112 A3
Paroo Channel *watercourse* Australia 112 A3
Paroo-Darling National Park *nat. park N.S.W.* 111 C6
Paroo-Darling National Park *nat. park N.S.W.* 112 E3
Paros *Notio Aigaio* Greece *see* **Paroikia**
Paros *i.* Greece 59 K6
Parowan U.S.A. 129 G3
Parral Chile 144 B5
Parramatta Australia 112 E4
Parramore Island U.S.A. 135 H5
Parras Mex. 131 C7
Parrett *r.* U.K. 49 D7
Parry, Cape Canada 153 A2
Parry, Kap *c.* Greenland *see* **Kangaarsussuaq**
Parry, Lac *l.* Canada 122 G2
Parry Bay Canada 119 J3
Parry Channel Canada 119 G2
Parry Islands Canada 119 G2
Parry Range *hills* Australia 108 A5
Parry Sound Canada 134 E1
Parsnip Peak U.S.A. 129 F2
Parsons *KS* U.S.A. 131 E4
Parsons *WV* U.S.A. 134 F4
Parsons Range *hills* Australia 108 F3
Partabgarh India 84 B2
Partabpur India 83 E5
Partenstein Germany 53 J4
Parthenay France 56 D3
Partizansk Rus. Fed. 74 D4
Partney U.K. 48 H5
Partridge *r.* Canada 122 E4
Partry Ireland 51 C4
Partry Mts *hills* Ireland 51 C4
Paru *r.* Brazil 143 H4
Pārūd Iran 89 F5
Paryang China 83 E3
Parys S. Africa 101 H4
Pasa Dağı *mt.* Turkey 90 D3
Pasadena *CA* U.S.A. 128 D4
Pasadena *TX* U.S.A. 131 E6
Pasado, Cabo *c.* Ecuador 142 B4
Pa Sang Thai. 70 B3
Pasawng Myanmar 70 B3
Pascagama *r.* Canada 122 G4
Pascagoula U.S.A. 131 F6
Pascagoula *r.* U.S.A. 131 F6
Paşcani Romania 59 L1
Pasco U.S.A. 126 D3
Pascoal, Monte *hill* Brazil 145 D2
Pascua, Isla de *i.* S. Pacific Ocean *see* **Easter Island**
Pas de Calais *strait* France/U.K. *see* **Dover, Strait of**
Pasewalk Germany 47 O4
Pasfield Lake Canada 121 J3
Pasha Rus. Fed. 42 G3
Pashih Haihsia *sea chan.* Phil./Taiwan *see* **Bashi Channel**
Pashkovo Rus. Fed. 74 C2
Pashkovskiy Rus. Fed. 43 H7
Pashtun Zarghun Afgh. 89 F3
Pashū'īyeh Iran 88 E4
Pasi Ga Myanmar 70 B1
Pasighat India 83 H3
Pasinler Turkey 91 F3
Pasir Gudang Malaysia 71 [inset]
Pasir Mas Malaysia 71 C6
Pasir Putih Malaysia 71 C6
Paskūh Iran 89 F5
Pasni Pak. 149 M4
Paso de los Toros Uruguay 144 E4
Paso de San Antonio Mex. 131 C6
Pasok Myanmar 70 A2
Paso Robles U.S.A. 128 C4
Pasquia Hills Canada 121 K4
Passaic U.S.A. 135 H3
Passa Tempo Brazil 145 B3
Passau Germany 47 N6
Passo del San Gottardo Switz. *see* **St Gotthard Pass**
Passo Fundo Brazil 144 F3
Passos Brazil 145 B3
Passur *r.* Bangl. *see* **Pusur**
Passuri Nadi *r.* Bangl. *see* **Pusur**
Pastavy Belarus 45 O9
Pastaza *r.* Peru 142 C4
Pasto Col. 142 C3
Pastora Peak U.S.A. 129 I3
Pastos Bons Brazil 143 J5
Pasu Pak. 82 C1
Pasur Turkey *see* **Kulp**
Pasvalys Lith. 45 N8
Pasvikelva *r.* Europe *see* **Patsoyoki**
Patache, Punta *pt* Chile 144 B2
Patagonia *reg.* Arg. 144 B8
Pataliputra India *see* **Patna**
Patan *Gujarat* India *see* **Somnath**
Patan *Gujarat* India 82 C5
Patan *Mahar.* India 84 B2
Patan Nepal 83 F4
Patan Pak. 89 I3
Patandar, Koh-i- *mt.* Pak. 89 G5
Patavium Italy *see* **Padua**
Patea N.Z. 113 E4
Patea *inlet* N.Z. *see* **Doubtful Sound**
Pate Island Kenya 98 E4
Pateley Bridge U.K. 48 F4
Patensie S. Africa 100 G7
Patera India 82 D4
Paterson Australia 112 E4
Paterson *r.* Australia 112 C2
Paterson U.S.A. 135 H3
Paterson Range *hills* Australia 108 C5
Pathanamthitta India 84 C4
Pathankot India 82 C2
Pathari India 82 D5
Pathein Myanmar *see* **Bassein**
Pathfinder Reservoir U.S.A. 126 G4
Pathiu Thai. 71 B5
Pathum Thani Thai. 71 C4
Patía *r.* Col. 142 C3
Patiala India 82 D3
Patkai Bum *mts* India/Myanmar 83 H4
Patkaklik China 83 F1
Patmos *i.* Greece 59 L6
Patna India 83 F4
Patna *Orissa* India 83 F5
Patnagarh India 83 E5
Patnos Turkey 91 F3
Pato Branco Brazil 144 F3
Patoda India 84 B2
Patoka *r.* U.S.A. 134 B4
Patoka Lake U.S.A. 134 B4
Patos Albania 59 H4
Patos Brazil 143 K5
Patos, Lagoa dos *l.* Brazil 144 F4
Patos de Minas Brazil 145 B2
Patquía Arg. 144 C4
Patra Greece *see* **Patras**
Patrae Greece *see* **Patras**
Pátrai Greece *see* **Patras**
Patras Greece 59 I5
Patreksfjörður Iceland 44 [inset]
Patricio Lynch, Isla *i.* Chile 144 A7
Patrick Creek *watercourse* Australia 110 D4
Patrimônio Brazil 145 A2
Patrocínio Brazil 145 B2
Patrū Iran 89 E3
Patsoyoki *r.* Europe 44 Q2
Pattadakal *tourist site* India 84 B2
Pattani Thai. 71 C6
Pattaya Thai. 71 C4
Pattensen Germany 53 J2
Patterson *CA* U.S.A. 128 C3
Patterson *LA* U.S.A. 131 F6
Patterson, Mount Canada 120 C1
Patti India 83 E4
Pattijoki Fin. 44 N4
Pättikkä Fin. 44 L2
Patton U.S.A. 135 F3
Pattullo, Mount Canada 120 D3
Patu Brazil 143 K5
Patuakhali Bangl. 83 G5
Patuanak Canada 121 J4
Patuca, Punta *pt* Hond. 137 H5
Patur India 84 C1
Patuxent *r.* U.S.A. 135 G4
Patuxent Range *mts* Antarctica 152 L1
Patvinsuon kansallispuisto *nat. park* Fin. 44 Q5
Pau France 56 D5
Pauhunri *mt.* China/India 83 G4
Pauillac France 56 D4
Pauini Brazil 142 E5
Pauini *r.* Brazil 142 E5
Pauk Myanmar 70 A2
Paukkaung Myanmar 70 A3
Paulatuk Canada 153 A2
Paulden U.S.A. 129 G4
Paulding U.S.A. 134 C3
Paulicéia Brazil 145 A3
Paulis Dem. Rep. Congo *see* **Isiro**
Paul Island Canada 123 J2
Paulo Afonso Brazil 143 K5
Paulo de Faria Brazil 145 A3
Paulpietersburg S. Africa 101 J4
Paul Roux S. Africa 101 H5
Pauls Valley U.S.A. 131 D5
Paumotu, Îles *is* Fr. Polynesia *see* **Tuamotu Islands**
Paung Myanmar 70 B3
Paungbyin Myanmar 70 A1
Paungde Myanmar 70 A3
Pauni India 84 C1
Pauri India 82 D3
Pavagada India 84 C3
Pavão Brazil 145 C2
Pāveh Iran 88 B3
Pavia Italy 58 C2
Pāvilosta Latvia 45 L8
Pavino Rus. Fed. 42 J4
Pavlikeni Bulg. 59 K3
Pavlodar Kazakh. 80 E1
Pavlof Volcano U.S.A. 118 B4
Pavlograd Ukr. *see* **Pavlohrad**
Pavlohrad Ukr. 43 G6
Pavlovka Rus. Fed. 43 J5
Pavlovo Rus. Fed. 42 I5
Pavlovsk *Altayskiy Kray* Rus. Fed. 72 E2
Pavlovsk *Voronezhskaya Oblast'* Rus. Fed. 43 I6
Pavlovskaya Rus. Fed. 43 H7
Pawahku Myanmar 70 B1
Pawai India 82 E4
Pawnee U.S.A. 131 D4
Pawnee *r.* U.S.A. 130 D4
Pawnee City U.S.A. 130 D3
Paw Paw *MI* U.S.A. 134 C2
Paw Paw *WV* U.S.A. 135 F4
Pawtucket U.S.A. 135 J3
Pawut Myanmar 71 B4
Paxson U.S.A. 118 D3
Paxton U.S.A. 134 A3
Payakumbuh Indon. 68 C7
Paya Lebar Sing. 71 [inset]
Payette U.S.A. 126 D3
Pay-Khoy, Khrebet *hills* Rus. Fed. 64 H3
Payne Canada *see* **Kangirsuk**
Payne, Lac *l.* Canada 122 G2
Paynes Creek U.S.A. 128 C1
Payne's Find Australia 109 B7
Paynesville U.S.A. 130 E2
Paysandú Uruguay 144 E4
Pays de Bray *reg.* France 52 B5
Payshanba Uzbek. 89 G1
Payson U.S.A. 129 H4
Pazar Turkey 91 F2
Pazarcık Turkey 90 E3
Pazardzhik Bulg. 59 K3
Pazin Croatia 58 E2
Pe Myanmar 71 B4
Peabody *KS* U.S.A. 130 D4
Peabody *MA* U.S.A. 135 J2

▶**Peace** *r.* Canada 120 I3
Part of the Mackenzie-Peace-Finlay, the 2nd longest river in North America.

Peace Point Canada 121 H3
Peace River Canada 120 G3
Peach Creek U.S.A. 134 E5
Peach Springs U.S.A. 129 G4
Peacock Hills Canada 121 I1
Peak Charles *hill* Australia 109 C8
Peak Charles National Park Australia 109 C8
Peak District National Park U.K. 48 F5
Peake *watercourse* Australia 111 B6
Peaked Mountain *hill* U.S.A. 132 G2
Peak Hill *N.S.W.* Australia 112 D4
Peak Hill *W.A.* Australia 109 B6
Peale, Mount U.S.A. 129 I2
Peanut U.S.A. 128 B1
Pearce U.S.A. 129 I6
Pearce Point Australia 108 E3
Pearisburg U.S.A. 134 E5
Pearl *r.* U.S.A. 131 F6
Pearl Harbor *inlet* U.S.A. 127 [inset]
Pearsall U.S.A. 131 D6
Pearson U.S.A. 133 D6
Pearston S. Africa 101 G7
Peary Channel Canada 119 I2
Peary Land *reg.* Greenland 153 J1
Pease *r.* U.S.A. 131 D5
Peawanuck Canada 122 D3
Pebane Moz. 99 D5
Pebas Peru 142 D4
Peć Kosovo *see* **Pejë**
Peçanha Brazil 145 C2
Peças, Ilha das *i.* Brazil 145 A4
Pechenga Rus. Fed. 44 Q2
Pechora Rus. Fed. 42 M2
Pechora *r.* Rus. Fed. 42 L1
Pechora Sea Rus. Fed. *see* **Pechorskoye More**
Pechorskaya Guba *b.* Rus. Fed. 42 L1
Pechorskoye More *sea* Rus. Fed. 153 G2
Pechory Rus. Fed. 45 O8
Peck U.S.A. 134 D2
Pecos U.S.A. 131 C6
Pecos *r.* U.S.A. 131 C6
Pécs Hungary 58 H1
Pedda Vagu *r.* India 84 C2
Pedder, Lake Australia 111 [inset]
Peddie S. Africa 101 H7
Pedernales Dom. Rep. 137 J5
Pedersöre Fin. 44 M5
Pediaios *r.* Cyprus 85 A2
Pediva Angola 99 B5
Pedra Azul Brazil 145 C1
Pedra Preta, Serra da *mts* Brazil 145 A1
Pedras de Maria da Cruz Brazil 145 B1
Pedregulho Brazil 145 B3
Pedreiras Brazil 143 J4
Pedriceña Mex. 131 C7
Pedro, Point Sri Lanka 84 D4
Pedro Betancourt Cuba 133 D8
Pedro II, Ilha *reg.* Brazil/Venez. 142 E3
Pedro Juan Caballero Para. 144 E2
Peebles U.K. 50 F5
Peebles U.S.A. 134 D4
Pee Dee *r.* U.S.A. 133 E5
Peekskill U.S.A. 135 I3
Peel *r.* Australia 112 E3
Peel *r.* Canada 118 E3
Peel Isle of Man 48 C4
Peer Belgium 52 F3
Peera Peera Poolanna Lake *salt flat* Australia 111 B5
Peerless Lake Canada 120 H3
Peerless Lake *l.* Canada 120 H3
Peers Canada 120 G4
Peery Lake *salt flat* Australia 112 A3
Pegasus Bay N.Z. 113 D6
Pegnitz Germany 53 L5
Pegu Myanmar 70 B3
Pegu Yoma *mts* Myanmar 70 A3
Pegysh Rus. Fed. 42 K3
Pehuajó Arg. 144 D5
Peikang Taiwan 77 I4
Peine Chile 144 C2
Peine Germany 53 K2
Peint India 84 B1
Peipsi järv *l.* Estonia/Rus. Fed. *see* **Peipus, Lake**
Peipus, Lake Estonia/Rus. Fed. 45 O7
Peiraias Greece *see* **Piraeus**
Pei Shan *mts* China *see* **Bei Shan**
Peißen Germany 53 L3
Peixe Brazil 143 I6
Peixe *r.* Brazil 145 A1
Peixian *Jiangsu* China 77 H1
Peixian *Jiangsu* China *see* **Pizhou**
Peixoto de Azevedo Brazil 143 H6
Pejë Kosovo 59 I3
Pèk Laos *see* **Phônsavan**
Peka Lesotho 101 H5
Pekan Malaysia 71 C7
Pekanbaru Indon. 68 C6
Pekin U.S.A. 130 F3
Peking China *see* **Beijing**
Pekinga Benin 96 D3
Pelabohan Klang Malaysia *see* **Pelabuhan Klang**
Pelabuhan Klang Malaysia 71 C7
Pelagie, Isole *is Sicily* Italy 58 E7
Pelaihari Indon. 68 E7
Peleaga, Vârful *mt.* Romania 59 J2
Pelee Island Canada 134 D3
Pelee Point Canada 134 D3
Peles Rus. Fed. 42 K3
Pélican, Lac du *l.* Canada 123 G2
Pelican Lake Canada 121 K4
Pelican Lake U.S.A. 130 E1
Pelican Narrows Canada 121 K4
Pelkosenniemi Fin. 44 O3
Pella S. Africa 100 D5
Pellatt Lake Canada 121 I1
Pelleluhu Islands P.N.G. 69 K7
Pello Fin. 44 M3
Pelly *r.* Canada 120 C2
Pelly Crossing Canada 120 B2
Pelly Lake Canada 121 K1
Pelly Mountains Canada 120 C2
Peloponnese *admin. reg.* Greece 59 J6
Pelopónnesos *admin. reg.* Greece *see* **Peloponnese**
Peloponnisos *admin. reg.* Greece *see* **Peloponnese**
Pelotas Brazil 144 F4
Pelotas, Rio das *r.* Brazil 145 A4
Pelusium *tourist site* Egypt 85 A4
Pelusium, Bay of Egypt *see* **Tīnah, Khalīj aț**
Pemangkat Indon. 71 E7
Pematangsiantar Indon. 71 B7
Pemba Moz. 99 E5
Pemba Island Tanz. 99 D4
Pemberton Canada 120 F5
Pembina *r.* Canada 120 H4
Pembina *r.* U.S.A. 130 D1
Pembine U.S.A. 132 C2
Pembre Indon. 69 J8
Pembroke Canada 122 F5
Pembroke U.K. 49 C7
Pembroke U.S.A. 133 D5
Pembrokeshire Coast National Park U.K. 49 B7
Pen India 84 B2
Peña Cerredo *mt.* Spain *see* **Torrecerredo**
Peñalara *mt.* Spain 57 E3
Penamar Brazil 145 C1
Peña Nevada, Cerro *mt.* Mex. 136 E4
Penang Malaysia *see* **George Town**
Penang *i.* Malaysia *see* **Pinang**
Penápolis Brazil 145 A3
Peñaranda de Bracamonte Spain 57 D3
Penarie Australia 112 A5
Penarlâg U.K. *see* **Hawarden**
Peñarroya *mt.* Spain 57 F3
Peñarroya-Pueblonuevo Spain 57 D4
Penarth U.K. 49 D7
Peñas, Cabo de *c.* Spain 57 D2
Penas, Golfo de *g.* Chile 144 A7
Penasi, Pulau *i.* Indon. 71 A6
Peña Ubiña *mt.* Spain 57 D2
Pender U.S.A. 130 D3
Pendle Hill *hill* U.K. 48 E5
Pendleton U.S.A. 126 D3
Pendleton Bay Canada 120 E4
Pend Oreille *r.* U.S.A. 126 D2
Pend Oreille Lake U.S.A. 126 D2
Pendra India 83 E5
Penduv India 84 B2
Pendzhikent Tajik. *see* **Panjakent**
Penebangan *i.* Indon. 68 D7
Peneda Gerês, Parque Nacional da *nat. park* Port. 57 B3
Penetanguishene Canada 134 F1
Penfro U.K. *see* **Pembroke**
Peng'an China 76 E2
Penganga *r.* India 84 C2
Peng Chau *i. H.K.* China 77 [inset]
P'engchia Yü *i.* Taiwan 77 I3
Penge Dem. Rep. Congo 99 C4
Penge S. Africa 101 J3
P'enghu Ch'üntao *is* Taiwan 77 H4
P'enghu Liehtao *is* Taiwan *see* **P'enghu Ch'üntao**
P'enghu Tao *i.* Taiwan 77 H4
Peng Kang *hill* Sing. 71 [inset]
Penglaizhen China *see* **Daying**
Pengshan China 76 D2
Pengshui China 77 F2
Pengwa Myanmar 70 A2
Pengxi China 76 E2
Penha Brazil 145 A4
Penhoek Pass S. Africa 101 H6
Penhook U.S.A. 134 F5
Peniche Port. 57 B4
Penicuik U.K. 50 F5
Penig Germany 53 M4
Peninga Rus. Fed. 44 R5
Peninsular Malaysia Malaysia 71 D6
Penitente, Serra do *hills* Brazil 143 I5
Penn U.S.A. *see* **Penn Hills**
Pennell Coast Antarctica 152 H2
Penn Hills U.S.A. 134 F3
Pennine, Alpi *mts* Italy/Switz. 58 B2
Pennine Alps *mts* Italy/Switz. *see* **Pennine, Alpi**
Pennines *hills* U.K. 48 E4
Pennington Gap U.S.A. 134 D5
Pennsburg U.S.A. 135 H3
Penns Grove U.S.A. 135 H4
Pennsville U.S.A. 135 H4
Pennsylvania *state* U.S.A. 134 F3
Pennville U.S.A. 134 C3
Penn Yan U.S.A. 135 G2
Penny Icecap Canada 119 L3
Penny Point Antarctica 152 H1
Penola Australia 111 C8
Peñón Blanco Mex. 131 B7
Penong Australia 109 F7
Penonomé Panama 137 H7
Penrhyn *atoll* Cook Is 151 J6
Penrhyn Basin *sea feature* S. Pacific Ocean 151 J6
Penrith Australia 112 E4
Penrith U.K. 48 E4
Pensacola U.S.A. 133 C6
Pensacola Mountains Antarctica 152 L1
Pensi La *pass* India 82 D2
Pentadaktylos Range *mts* Cyprus 85 A2
Pentakota India 84 D2
Pentecost Island Vanuatu 107 G3
Pentecôte, Île *i.* Vanuatu *see* **Pentecost Island**
Penticton Canada 120 G5
Pentire Point U.K. 49 B8
Pentland Australia 110 D4
Pentland Firth *sea chan.* U.K. 50 F2
Pentland Hills U.K. 50 F5
Pentwater U.S.A. 134 B2
Penwegon Myanmar 70 B3
Pen-y-Bont ar Ogwr U.K. *see* **Bridgend**
Penygadair *hill* U.K. 49 D6
Penylan Lake Canada 121 J2
Penza Rus. Fed. 43 J5
Penzance U.K. 49 B8
Penzhinskaya Guba *b.* Rus. Fed. 65 R3
Peoria *AZ* U.S.A. 129 G5
Peoria *IL* U.S.A. 130 F3
Peotone U.S.A. 134 B3
Pequeña, Punta *pt* Mex. 127 E8
Pequop Mountains U.S.A. 129 F1
Peradeniya Sri Lanka 84 D5
Pera Head *hd* Australia 110 C2
Perak *i.* Malaysia 71 B6
Perales del Alfambra Spain 57 F3
Perambalur India 84 C4
Perämeren kansallispuisto *nat. park* Fin. 44 N4
Peräseinäjoki Fin. 44 M5
Percé Canada 123 I4
Percival Lakes *salt flat* Australia 108 D5
Percy U.S.A. 135 J1
Percy Isles Australia 110 E4
Percy Reach *l.* Canada 135 G1
Perdizes Brazil 145 B2
Perdu, Lac *l.* Canada 123 H4
Peregrebnoye Rus. Fed. 41 T3
Pereira Col. 142 C3
Pereira Barreto Brazil 145 A3
Pereira de Eça Angola *see* **Ondjiva**
Pere Marquette *r.* U.S.A. 134 B2
Peremul Par *reef* India 84 B4
Peremyshlyany Ukr. 43 E6
Perenjori Australia 109 B7
Pereslavl'-Zalesskiy Rus. Fed. 42 H4
Pereslavskiy Natsional'nyy Park *nat. park* Rus. Fed. 42 H4
Pereyaslavka Rus. Fed. 74 D3
Pereyaslav-Khmel'nitskiy Ukr. *see* **Pereyaslav-Khmel'nyts'kyy**
Pereyaslav-Khmel'nyts'kyy Ukr. 43 F6
Perforated Island Thai. *see* **Bon, Ko**
Pergamino Arg. 144 D4
Perhentian Besar, Pulau *i.* Malaysia 71 C6
Perho Fin. 44 N5
Péribonka, Lac *l.* Canada 123 H4
Perico Arg. 144 C2
Pericos Mex. 127 G8
Peridot U.S.A. 129 H5
Périgueux France 56 E4
Perijá, Parque Nacional *nat. park* Venez. 142 D2
Perija, Sierra de *mts* Venez. 142 D2
Periyar India *see* **Erode**
Perkasie U.S.A. 135 H3
Perlas, Punta de *pt* Nicaragua 137 H6
Perleberg Germany 53 L1
Perm' Rus. Fed. 41 R4
Permas Rus. Fed. 42 J4
Pernambuco Brazil *see* **Recife**
Pernambuco Plain *sea feature* S. Atlantic Ocean 148 G6
Pernatty Lagoon *salt flat* Australia 111 B6
Pernem India 84 B3
Pernik Bulg. 59 J3
Pernov Estonia *see* **Pärnu**
Perojpur Bangl. *see* **Pirojpur**
Peron Islands Australia 108 E3
Péronne France 52 C5
Perpignan France 56 F5
Perranporth U.K. 49 B8
Perrégaux Alg. *see* **Mohammadia**
Perris U.S.A. 128 E5
Perros-Guirec France 56 C2
Perrot, Île *i.* Canada 135 I1
Perry *FL* U.S.A. 133 D6
Perry *GA* U.S.A. 133 D5
Perry *MI* U.S.A. 134 C2
Perry *OK* U.S.A. 131 D4
Perry Lake U.S.A. 130 E4
Perryton U.S.A. 131 C4
Perryville *AK* U.S.A. 118 C4
Perryville *MO* U.S.A. 130 F4
Perseverancia Bol. 142 F6
Pershore U.K. 49 E6
Persia *country* Asia *see* **Iran**
Persian Gulf Asia *see* **The Gulf**
Pertek Turkey 91 E3

▶**Perth** Australia 109 A7
Capital of Western Australia. 4th most populous city in Oceania.

Perth Canada 135 G1
Perth U.K. 50 F4
Perth Amboy U.S.A. 135 H3
Perth-Andover Canada 123 I5
Perth Basin *sea feature* Indian Ocean 149 P7
Pertominsk Rus. Fed. 42 H2
Pertunmaa Fin. 45 O6
Pertusato, Capo *c. Corsica* France 56 I6
Peru *atoll* Kiribati *see* **Beru**

▶**Peru** *country* S. America 142 D6
3rd largest and 4th most populous country in South America.

Peru *IL* U.S.A. 130 F3
Peru *IN* U.S.A. 134 B3
Peru *NY* U.S.A. 135 I1
Peru-Chile Trench *sea feature* S. Pacific Ocean 151 O6
Perugia Italy 58 E3
Peruru India 84 C3
Perusia Italy *see* **Perugia**
Péruwelz Belgium 52 D4
Pervomaysk Rus. Fed. 43 I5
Pervomays'k Ukr. 43 F6
Pervomayskiy Kazakh. 80 F1
Pervomayskiy *Arkhangel'skaya Oblast'* Rus. Fed. *see* **Novodvinsk**
Pervomayskiy *Tambovskaya Oblast'* Rus. Fed. 43 I5
Pervomays'kyy Ukr. 43 H6
Pervorechenskiy Rus. Fed. 65 R3
Pesaro Italy 58 E3
Pescadores *is* Taiwan *see* **P'enghu Ch'üntao**
Pescara Italy 58 F3
Pescara *r.* Italy 58 F3
Peschanokopskoye Rus. Fed. 43 I7
Peschanoye Rus. Fed. *see* **Yashkul'**
Peschanyy, Mys *pt* Kazakh. 91 H2
Pesha *r.* Rus. Fed. 42 J2
Peshanjan Afgh. 89 F3
Peshawar Pak. 89 H3
Peshkopi Albania 59 I4
Peshtera Bulg. 59 K3
Peski Turkm. 89 F2
Peski Karakumy *des.* Turkm. *see* **Karakum Desert**
Peskovka Rus. Fed. 42 L4
Pesnica Slovenia 58 F1
Pessac France 56 D4
Pessin Germany 53 M2
Pestovo Rus. Fed. 42 G4
Pestravka Rus. Fed. 43 K5
Petaḥ Tiqwa Israel 85 B3
Petäjävesi Fin. 44 N5
Petaling Jaya Malaysia 71 C7
Petalion, Kolpos *sea chan.* Greece 59 K5
Petaluma U.S.A. 128 B2
Pétange Lux. 52 F5
Petatlán Mex. 136 D5
Petauke Zambia 99 D5
Petenwell Lake U.S.A. 130 F2
Peterbell Canada 122 E4
Peterborough Australia 111 B7
Peterborough Canada 135 F1
Peterborough U.K. 49 G6
Peterborough U.S.A. 135 J2
Peterculter U.K. 50 G3
Peterhead U.K. 50 H3
Peter I Island Antarctica 152 K2
Peter I Øy *i.* Antarctica *see* **Peter I Island**
Peter Lake Canada 121 M2
Peterlee U.K. 48 F4
Petermann Bjerg *nunatak* Greenland 119 P2
Petermann Ranges *mts* Australia 109 E6
Peter Pond Lake Canada 121 I4
Peters, Lac *l.* Canada 123 H2
Petersberg Germany 53 J4
Petersburg *AK* U.S.A. 120 C3
Petersburg *IL* U.S.A. 130 F4
Petersburg *IN* U.S.A. 134 B4
Petersburg *NY* U.S.A. 135 I2
Petersburg *VA* U.S.A. 135 G5
Petersburg *WV* U.S.A. 134 F4
Petersfield U.K. 49 G7
Petershagen Germany 53 I2
Petersville U.S.A. 118 C3
Peter the Great Bay Rus. Fed. *see* **Petra Velikogo, Zaliv**
Peth India 84 B2
Petilia Policastro Italy 58 G5
Petit Atlas *mts* Morocco *see* **Anti Atlas**
Petitcodiac Canada 123 I5
Petitjean Morocco *see* **Sidi Kacem**
Petit Lac Manicouagan *l.* Canada 123 I3
Petit Mécatina *r. Nfld. and Lab./Que.* Canada 123 K4
Petit Mécatina, Île du *i.* Canada 123 K4
Petit Morin *r.* France 52 D6
Petitot *r.* Canada 120 F2
Petit St-Bernard, Col du *pass* France 56 H

it Saut, Barrage du resr
r. Guiana 143 H3
to Mex. 136 G4
toskey U.S.A. 132 C2
tra tourist site Jordan 85 B4
tra Velikogo, Zaliv b. Rus. Fed. 74 C4
tre, Point Canada 135 G2
trich Bulg. 59 J4
trified Forest National Park
J.S.A. 129 I4
trikau Poland see Piotrków Trybunalski
trikov Belarus see Pyetrykaw
trinja Croatia 58 G2
troaleksandrovsk Uzbek. see To'rtko'l
trograd Rus. Fed. see St Petersburg
trokhanski Prokhod pass Bulg. 59 J3
trokov Poland see Piotrków Trybunalski
trolia Canada 134 D2
trolia U.S.A. 128 A1
trolina Brazil 143 J5
trolina de Goiás Brazil 145 A2
tropavl Kazakh. see Petropavlovsk
tropavlovsk Kazakh. 79 F1
tropavlovsk Rus. Fed. see
Petropavlovsk-Kamchatskiy
tropavlovsk-Kamchatskiy
Rus. Fed. 65 Q4
trópolis Brazil 145 C3
troșani Romania 59 J2
trovsk Rus. Fed. 43 J5
trovskoye Rus. Fed. see Svetlograd
trovsk-Zabaykal'skiy Rus. Fed. 73 J2
trozavodsk Rus. Fed. 42 E3
trus Steyn S. Africa 101 I4
trusville S. Africa 100 G6
tsamo Rus. Fed. see Pechenga
ttau Slovenia see Ptuj
tten Neth. 52 E2
ttigo U.K. 51 E3
ukhovo Rus. Fed. 64 H4
ushki Rus. Fed. 42 H5
tzeck mt. Austria 47 N7
uetsagu, Gunung vol. Indon. 71 B6
ureula Indon. 71 B6
vek Rus. Fed. 65 S3
zung China 76 B1
y Ostān Iran 88 E3
za r. Rus. Fed. 42 J2
zinok Slovakia 47 P6
zu Pak. 89 H3
alzer Wald hills Germany 53 H5
orzheim Germany 53 I6
ungstadt Germany 53 I5
agameng Limpopo S. Africa 101 I3
agwara India 82 C3
hameng Free State S. Africa 101 H5
alaborwa S. Africa 101 J2
alodi India 82 C4
alsund India 82 B4
alta India 83 G5
aluai, Ko i. Thai. 71 B5
alut Peak India/Nepal 83 G4
an Thai. 70 B3
anat Nikhom Thai. 71 C4
angan, Ko i. Thai. 71 C5
ang Hoei, San Khao mts Thai. 70 C3
angnga Thai. 71 B5
äng Xi Päng mt. Vietnam 70 C2
anom Dong Rak, Thiu Khao mts
Cambodia/Thai. 71 D4
an Rang-Thap Cham Vietnam 71 E5
an Thiêt Vietnam 71 E5
apon Myanmar see Pyapon
at Diêm Vietnam 70 D2
atthalung Thai. 71 C6
ayam, Ko i. Thai. 71 B5
ayao Thai. 70 B3
ayuhakhiri Thai. 70 C4
ek India 83 H4
elps Lake Canada 121 K3
en Thai. 70 C3
enix U.S.A. 135 F5
enix City U.S.A. 133 C5
et Buri Thai. 71 B4
etchabun Thai. 70 C3
afai Laos 70 D4
chai Thai. 70 C3
chit Thai. 70 C3
iladelphia Jordan see 'Ammān
iladelphia Turkey see Alașehir
iladelphia MS U.S.A. 131 F5
iladelphia NY U.S.A. 135 H1
iladelphia PA U.S.A. 135 H4
ilip U.S.A. 130 C2
ilip Atoll Micronesia see Sorol
ilippeville Alg. see Skikda
ilippeville Belgium 52 E4
ilippi U.S.A. 134 E4
ilippi, Lake salt flat Australia 110 B5
ilippine Neth. 52 D3
ilippine Basin sea feature
N. Pacific Ocean 150 E4
ilippines country Asia 69 G4
ilippine Sea N. Pacific Ocean 69 G3

Philippine Trench sea feature
N. Pacific Ocean 150 E4
3rd deepest trench in the world.

ilippolis S. Africa 101 G6
ilippopolis Bulg. see Plovdiv
ilippsburg Germany 53 I5
ilipsburg MT U.S.A. 126 E3
ilipsburg PA U.S.A. 135 F3
ilip Smith Mountains U.S.A. 118 D3
ilipstown S. Africa 100 G6
illip Island Australia 112 B7
illips ME U.S.A. 135 J1
illips WI U.S.A. 130 F2
illipsburg U.S.A. 130 D4
illips Range hills Australia 108 D4
ilmont U.S.A. 135 I2
ilomelium Turkey see Akșehir
iritona S. Africa 101 H4
tsanulok Thai. 70 C3

Phnom Penh Cambodia 71 D5
Capital of Cambodia.

num Pénh Cambodia see Phnom Penh
o, Laem pt Thai. 71 C6
oenicia U.S.A. 135 H2

▶Phoenix U.S.A. 127 E6
Capital of Arizona.

Phoenix Island Kiribati see Rawaki
Phoenix Islands Kiribati 107 I2
Phô Lu Vietnam 70 D2
Phon Thai. 70 C4
Phong Nha Vietnam 70 D3
Phôngsali Laos 70 C2
Phong Saly Laos see Phôngsali
Phong Thô Vietnam 70 C2
Phon Phisai Thai. 70 C3
Phônsavan Laos 70 C3
Phon Thong Thai. 70 C3
Phosphate Hill Australia 110 C4
Phrae Thai. 70 C3
Phra Nakhon Si Ayutthaya Thai. see Ayutthaya
Phrao Thai. 70 B3
Phra Saeng Thai. 71 B5
Phrom Phiram Thai. 70 C3
Phsar Ream Cambodia 71 C5
Phu Bai Vietnam 70 D3
Phuchong-Nayoi National Park Thai. 71 D4
Phu Cuong Vietnam see Thu Dâu Môt
Phuket Thai. 71 B6
Phuket, Ko i. Thai. 71 B6
Phu-khieo Wildlife Reserve nature res. Thai. 70 C3
Phulabani India see Phulbani
Phulbani India 84 E1
Phulchhari Ghat Bangl. see Fulchhari
Phulji Pak. 89 G5
Phu Lôc Vietnam 70 D3
Phu Lôc Vietnam 71 D5
Phu Luang National Park Thai. 70 C3
Phu Ly Vietnam 70 D2
Phumĭ Bŏeng Mealea Cambodia 71 D4
Phumĭ Chhlong Cambodia 71 D4
Phumĭ Kaôh Kŏng Cambodia 71 C5
Phumĭ Kon Kriel Cambodia 71 C4
Phumĭ Mlu Prey Cambodia 71 D4
Phumĭ Moŭng Cambodia 71 C4
Phumiphon, Khuan Thai. 70 B3
Phumĭ Prêk Kak Cambodia 71 D4
Phumĭ Sâmraông Cambodia 71 C4
Phumĭ Trâm Kak Cambodia 71 D5
Phumĭ Veal Renh Cambodia 71 C5
Phu My Vietnam 71 E4
Phung Hiêp Vietnam 71 D5
Phươc Bưu Vietnam 71 D5
Phươc Hai Vietnam 71 D5
Phu Phac Mo mt. Vietnam 70 C2
Phu Phan National Park Thai. 70 C3
Phu Quôc, Đao i. Vietnam 71 C5
Phu Quy, Đao i. Vietnam 71 E5
Phu Tho Vietnam 70 D2
Phu Vinh Vietnam see Tra Vinh
Phyu Myanmar 70 B3
Piaca Brazil 143 I5
Piacenza Italy 58 C2
Piacouadie, Lac l. Canada 123 H4
Piagochioui r. Canada 122 F3
Piai, Tanjung pt Malaysia 71 C7
Pian r. Australia 112 D3
Pianosa, Isola i. Italy 58 D3
Piatra Neamț Romania 59 L1
Piave r. Italy 58 E2
Pibor Post Sudan 97 G4
Pic r. Canada 122 D4
Picacho U.S.A. 129 H5
Picachos, Cerro dos mt. Mex. 127 E7
Picardie admin. reg. France 52 C5
Picardie reg. France see Picardy
Picardy admin. reg. France see Picardie
Picardy reg. France 52 B5
Picauville France 49 F9
Picayune U.S.A. 131 F6
Piceance Creek r. U.S.A. 129 I1
Pichanal Arg. 144 D2
Pichhor India 82 D4
Pichilemu Chile 144 B4
Pichilingue Mex. 136 B4
Pickens U.S.A. 134 E4
Pickering Canada 134 F2
Pickering U.K. 48 G4
Pickering, Vale of valley U.K. 48 G4
Pickle Lake Canada 119 I4
Pico da Neblina, Parque Nacional do nat. park Brazil 142 E3
Picos Brazil 143 J5
Pico Truncado Arg. 144 C7
Picton Australia 112 E5
Picton Canada 135 G2
Picton N.Z. 113 E5
Pictou Canada 123 J5
Picture Butte Canada 121 H5
Pidarak Pak. 89 F5
Pidurutalagala mt. Sri Lanka 84 D5
Piedade Brazil 145 B3
Piedra de Águila Arg. 144 B6
Piedras, Punta pt Arg. 144 E5
Piedras Blancas Point U.S.A. 128 C4
Piedras Negras Mex. 131 C6
Pie Island Canada 122 C4
Pieksämäki Fin. 44 O5
Pielavesi Fin. 44 O5
Pielinen l. Fin. 44 P5
Pieljekaise nationalpark nat. park Sweden 44 J3
Pienaarsrivier S. Africa 101 I3
Pieniński Park Narodowy nat. park Poland 47 R6
Pieninský nat. park Slovakia 47 R6
Pierce U.S.A. 130 D3
Pierce Lake Canada 121 M4
Pierceland Canada 121 I4
Pierceton U.S.A. 134 C3
Pieria mts Greece 59 J4
Pierowall U.K. 50 G1
Pierpont U.S.A. 134 E3

▶Pierre U.S.A. 130 C2
Capital of South Dakota.

Pierrelatte France 56 G4
Pietermaritzburg S. Africa 101 J5
Pietersaari Fin. see Jakobstad
Pietersburg Limpopo S. Africa see Polokwane
Pie Town U.S.A. 129 I4
Pietra Spada, Passo di pass Italy 58 G5
Piet Retief S. Africa 101 J4
Pietrosa mt. Romania 59 K1
Pigeon U.S.A. 134 D2
Pigeon Bay Canada 134 D3
Pigeon Lake Canada 120 H4
Piggott U.S.A. 131 F4
Pigg's Peak Swaziland 101 J3
Pigs, Bay of Cuba 133 D8
Pihij India 82 C5
Pihkva järv l. Estonia/Rus. Fed. see Pskov, Lake
Pihlajavesi l. Fin. 44 P6
Pihlava Fin. 45 L6
Pihtipudas Fin. 44 N5
Piippola Fin. 44 N4
Piispajärvi Fin. 44 P4
Pikalevo Rus. Fed. 42 G4
Pike U.S.A. 134 E4
Pike Bay Canada 134 E1
Pikelot i. Micronesia 69 L5
Pikes Peak U.S.A. 126 G5
Piketon U.S.A. 134 D4
Pikeville KY U.S.A. 134 D5
Pikeville TN U.S.A. 132 C5
Pikinni atoll Marshall Is see Bikini
Piła Poland 47 P4
Pilanesberg National Park S. Africa 101 H3
Pilar Arg. 144 E4
Pilar Para. 144 E3
Pilar de Goiás Brazil 145 A1
Pilaya r. Bol. 142 F8
Pilcomayo r. Bol./Para. 142 F8
Piler India 84 C3
Pili, Cerro mt. Chile 144 C2
Pilibangan India 82 C3
Pilibhit India 82 D3
Pilipinas country Asia see Philippines
Pillau Rus. Fed. see Baltiysk
Pillcopata Peru 142 D6
Pilliga Australia 112 D3
Pillsbury, Lake U.S.A. 128 B2
Pil'na Rus. Fed. 42 J5
Pil'nya, Ozero l. Rus. Fed. 42 M1
Pilões, Serra dos mts Brazil 145 B2
Pílos Greece see Pylos
Pilot Knob mt. U.S.A. 126 E3
Pilot Peak U.S.A. 128 E2
Pilot Station U.S.A. 118 B3
Pilsen Czech Rep. see Plzeň
Piltene Latvia 45 L8
Pil'tun, Zaliv lag. Rus. Fed. 74 F1
Pilu Pak. 89 H5
Pima U.S.A. 129 I5
Pimenta Bueno Brazil 142 F6
Pimento U.S.A. 134 B4
Pimpalner India 84 B1
Pin r. India 82 D2
Pin r. Myanmar 70 A2
Pinahat India 82 D4
Pinaleno Mountains U.S.A. 129 H5
Pinamar Arg. 144 E5
Pinang Malaysia see George Town
Pinang i. Malaysia 71 C6
Pınarbaşı Turkey 90 E3
Pinar del Río Cuba 137 H4
Pinarhisar Turkey 59 L4
Piñas Ecuador 142 C4
Pincher Creek Canada 120 H5
Pinckneyville U.S.A. 130 F4
Pinconning U.S.A. 134 D2
Pińczów Poland 47 R5
Pindaí Brazil 145 C1
Pindamonhangaba Brazil 145 B3
Pindar Australia 109 A7
Pindaré r. Brazil 143 J4
Píndhos Óros mts Greece see Pindus Mountains
Pindos mts Greece see Pindus Mountains
Pindrei India 82 E5
Pindus Mountains Greece 59 I5
Pine watercourse Australia 111 C7
Pine r. MI U.S.A. 134 C1
Pine r. MI U.S.A. 134 C2
Pine Bluff U.S.A. 131 E5
Pine Bluffs U.S.A. 126 G4
Pine Creek Australia 108 E3
Pine Creek r. U.S.A. 135 G3
Pinecrest U.S.A. 128 C2
Pinedale NM U.S.A. 129 I4
Pinedale WY U.S.A. 126 F4
Pine Dock Canada 121 L5
Pine Falls Canada 121 L5
Pine Flat Lake U.S.A. 128 D3
Pinega Rus. Fed. 42 I2
Pinega r. Rus. Fed. 42 I2
Pinegrove Australia 109 A6
Pine Grove U.S.A. 135 G3
Pine Hills FL U.S.A. 133 D6
Pinehouse Lake Canada 121 J4
Pinehouse Lake l. Canada 121 J4
Pineimuta r. Canada 121 N4
Pineios r. Greece 59 J5
Pine Island Bay Antarctica 151 N10
Pine Island Glacier Antarctica 152 K1
Pine Islands FL U.S.A. 133 D7
Pine Islands FL U.S.A. 133 D7
Pine Knot U.S.A. 134 C5
Pineland U.S.A. 131 E6
Pine Mountain U.S.A. 128 C4
Pine Peak U.S.A. 129 G4
Pine Point pt Canada 120 H2
Pine Point (abandoned) Canada 120 H2
Pineridge U.S.A. 128 D3
Pine Ridge U.S.A. 130 C3
Pinerolo Italy 58 B2
Pines, Akrotirio pt Greece 59 K4
Pines, Isle of i. Cuba see La Juventud, Isla de
Pines, Isle of i. New Caledonia see Pins, Île des
Pinetop U.S.A. 129 I4
Pinetown S. Africa 101 J5
Pine Valley U.S.A. 135 G2
Pineville KY U.S.A. 134 D5
Pineville MO U.S.A. 131 E4
Pineville WV U.S.A. 134 E5
Ping, Mae Nam r. Thai. 70 C4
Ping'an China 72 I5
Ping'anyi China see Ping'an
Pingba China 76 E3
Pingbian China 76 D4
Ping Dao i. China 77 H1
Pingdingbu China see Guyuan
Pingdingshan China 77 G1
Pingdong Taiwan see P'ingtung
Pingdu Jiangxi China see Anfu
Pingdu Shandong China 73 L5
Pinggang China 74 B4
Pinghe China 77 H3
Pinghu China see Pingtang
Pingjiang China 77 G2
Pingjinpu China 76 E2
Pingle China 77 F3
Pingli China 77 F1
Pingliang China 76 E1
Pinglu China 77 F1
Pingma China see Tiandong
Pingnan China 77 H3
Pingqiao China 77 G1
Pingshan Sichuan China 76 E2
Pingshan Yunnan China see Luquan
Pingshi China 77 G3
Pingtan China 77 H3
Pingtan Dao i. China see Haitan Dao
Pingtang China 76 E3
P'ingtung Taiwan 77 I4
Pingxi China see Yuping
Pingxiang Guangxi China 76 E4
Pingxiang Jiangxi China 77 G3
Pingyang Heilong. China 74 B3
Pingyang Zhejiang China 77 I3
Pingyi China 77 H1
Pingyu China 77 G1
Pingyuanjie China 76 D4
Pingzhai China 77 F3
Pinhal Brazil 145 B3
Pinheiro Brazil 143 I4
Pinhoe U.K. 49 D8
Pini i. Indon. 68 B6
Piniós r. Greece see Pineios
Pinjin Australia 109 C7
Pink Mountain Canada 120 F3
Pinlaung Myanmar 70 B2
Pinlebu Myanmar 70 A1
Pinnacle hill U.S.A. 135 F4
Pinnacles National Monument nat. park U.S.A. 128 C3
Pinnau r. Germany 53 J1
Pinneberg Germany 53 J1
Pinnes, Akra pt Greece see Pines, Akrotirio
Pinon Hills CA U.S.A. 128 E4
Pinos, Isla de i. Cuba see La Juventud, Isla de
Pinos, Mount U.S.A. 128 D4
Pinotepa Nacional Mex. 136 E5
Pins, Île des i. New Caledonia 107 G4
Pins, Pointe aux pt Canada 134 E2
Pinsk Belarus 45 O10
Pinta, Sierra hill U.S.A. 129 G5
Pintada Creek watercourse U.S.A. 127 G6
Pintados Chile 144 C2
Pintura U.S.A. 129 G3
Pioche U.S.A. 129 F3
Piodi Dem. Rep. Congo 99 C4
Pioneer Mountains U.S.A. 126 E3
Pioner, Ostrov i. Rus. Fed. 64 K2
Pionerskiy Kaliningradskaya Oblast' Rus. Fed. 45 L9
Pionerskiy Khanty-Mansiyskiy Avtonomnyy Okrug Rus. Fed. 41 S3
Pionki Poland 47 R5
Piopio N.Z. 113 E4
Piopiotahi inlet N.Z. see Milford Sound
Piorini, Lago l. Brazil 142 F4
Piotrków Trybunalski Poland 47 Q5
Pipa Dingzi mt. China 74 C4
Pipar India 82 C4
Pipar Road India 82 C4
Piperi i. Greece 59 K5
Piper Peak U.S.A. 128 E3
Pipestone Canada 121 K5
Pipestone r. Canada 121 N4
Pipestone U.S.A. 130 D3
Pipli India 82 C3
Pipmuacan, Réservoir resr Canada 123 H4
Piqua U.S.A. 134 C3
Piquiri r. Brazil 145 A4
Pira Benin 96 D4
Piracanjuba Brazil 145 A2
Piracicaba Brazil 145 B3
Piracicaba r. Brazil 145 C2
Piraçununga Brazil 145 B3
Piracuruca Brazil 143 J4
Piraeus Greece 59 J6
Piraí do Sul Brazil 145 A4
Piráievs Greece see Piraeus
Piraju Brazil 145 A3
Pirajuí Brazil 145 A3
Pirallahı Adası Azer. 91 H2
Piranhas Bahia Brazil 145 C1
Piranhas Goiás Brazil 143 H7
Piranhas r. Rio Grande do Norte Brazil 143 K5
Piranhas r. Brazil 145 A2
Pirapora Brazil 145 B2
Piraube, Lac l. Canada 123 H4
Pirawa India 82 D4
Pirenópolis Brazil 145 A1
Pires do Rio Brazil 145 A2
Pírgos Greece see Pyrgos
Pirin nat. park Bulg. 59 J4
Pirineos mts Europe see Pyrenees
Piripiri Brazil 143 J4
Pirlerkondu Turkey see Taşkent
Pirmasens Germany 53 H5
Pirojpur Bangl. 83 G5
Pir Panjal Pass India 82 C2
Pir Panjal Range mts India/Pak. 89 I3
Piryatin Ukr. see Pyryatyn
Pirzada Afgh. 89 G4
Pisa Italy 58 D3
Pisae Italy see Pisa
Pisagua Chile 142 D7
Pisang, Kepulauan is Indon. 69 I7
Pisaurum Italy see Pesaro
Pisco Peru 142 C6
Písek Czech Rep. 47 O6
Pisha China see Ningnan
Pishan China 82 D1
Pīshīn Iran 80 B6
Pishin Pak. 89 G4
Pishin Lora r. Pak. 89 G4
Pishpek Kyrg. see Bishkek
Pisidia reg. Turkey 90 C3

▶Pissis, Cerro Arg. 144 C3
4th highest mountain in South America.

Pisté Mex. 136 G4
Pisticci Italy 58 G4
Pistoia Italy 58 D3
Pistoriae Italy see Pistoia
Pisuerga r. Spain 57 D3
Pita Guinea 96 B3
Pitaga Canada 123 I3
Pitanga Brazil 145 A4
Pitangui Brazil 145 B2
Pitar India 82 B5
Pitarpunga Lake imp. l. Australia 112 A5
Pitcairn, Henderson, Ducie and Oeno Islands terr. S. Pacific Ocean see Pitcairn Islands
Pitcairn Island Pitcairn Is 151 L7

▶Pitcairn Islands terr. S. Pacific Ocean 151 L7
United Kingdom Overseas Territory.

Piteå Sweden 44 L4
Piteälven r. Sweden 44 L4
Pitelino Rus. Fed. 43 I5
Piterka Rus. Fed. 43 J6
Pitești Romania 59 K2
Pithoragarh India 82 E3
Pithra India 82 D5
Pitiquito Mex. 127 E7
Pitkyaranta Rus. Fed. 42 F3
Pitlochry U.K. 50 F4
Pitong China see Pixian
Pitsane Siding Botswana 101 G3
Pitti i. India 84 B4
Pitt Island Canada 120 D4
Pitt Island N.Z. 107 I6
Pitt Islands Solomon Is see Vanikoro Islands
Pittsboro U.S.A. 131 F5
Pittsburg KS U.S.A. 131 E4
Pittsburg TX U.S.A. 131 E5
Pittsburgh U.S.A. 134 F3
Pittsfield MA U.S.A. 135 I2
Pittsfield ME U.S.A. 135 K1
Pittsfield VT U.S.A. 135 I2
Pittston U.S.A. 135 H3
Pittsworth Australia 112 E1
Pitz Lake Canada 121 L2
Piumhí Brazil 145 B3
Piura Peru 142 B5
Piute Mountains U.S.A. 129 F4
Piute Peak U.S.A. 128 D4
Piute Reservoir U.S.A. 129 G2
Piuthan Nepal 83 E3
Pivabiska r. Canada 122 E4
Pivka Slovenia 58 F2
Pixariá mt. Greece see Pyxaria
Pixian China 76 D2
Pixley U.S.A. 128 D4
Piz Bernina mt. Italy/Switz. 58 C1
Piz Buin mt. Austria/Switz. 47 M7
Pizhanka Rus. Fed. 42 K4
Pizhi Nigeria 96 D4
Pizhma Rus. Fed. 42 J4
Pizhma r. Rus. Fed. 42 K4
Pizhma r. Rus. Fed. 42 L2
Pizhou China 77 H1
Placentia Canada 123 L5
Placentia Italy see Piacenza
Placentia Bay Canada 123 L5
Placerville CA U.S.A. 128 C2
Placerville CO U.S.A. 129 I2
Placetas Cuba 133 E8
Plácido de Castro Brazil 142 E6
Plain Dealing U.S.A. 131 E5
Plainfield CT U.S.A. 135 J3
Plainfield IN U.S.A. 134 B4
Plainfield VT U.S.A. 135 I1
Plains KS U.S.A. 131 C4
Plains TX U.S.A. 131 C5
Plainview U.S.A. 131 C5
Plainville IN U.S.A. 134 B4
Plainville KS U.S.A. 130 D4
Plainwell U.S.A. 134 C2
Plaka, Akra pt Kriti Greece see Plaka, Akrotirio
Plaka, Akrotirio pt Greece 59 L7
Plakoti, Cape Cyprus 85 B2
Plamondon Canada 121 H4
Planá Czech Rep. 53 M5
Plana Cays is Bahamas 133 F8
Planada U.S.A. 128 C3
Planaltina Brazil 145 B1
Plane r. Germany 53 M2
Plankinton U.S.A. 130 D3
Plano U.S.A. 131 D5
Planura Brazil 145 A3
Plaquemine U.S.A. 131 F6
Plasencia Spain 57 C3
Plaster City U.S.A. 129 F5
Plaster Rock Canada 123 I5
Plastun Rus. Fed. 74 E3
Platani r. Sicily Italy 58 E6
Platberg mt. S. Africa 101 I5

▶Plateau Antarctica
Lowest recorded annual mean temperature in the world.

Platina U.S.A. 128 B1
Platinum U.S.A. 153 B3
Plato Col. 142 D2
Platte r. U.S.A. 130 E3
Platte City U.S.A. 130 E4
Plattling Germany 53 M6
Plattsburgh U.S.A. 135 I1
Plattsmouth U.S.A. 130 E3
Plau Germany 53 M1
Plauen Germany 53 M4
Plauer See l. Germany 53 M1
Plavsk Rus. Fed. 43 H5
Playa Noriega, Lago l. Mex. 127 F7
Playas Ecuador 142 B4
Playas Lake U.S.A. 129 I6
Plây Ku Vietnam 71 E4
Pleasant, Lake U.S.A. 129 G5
Pleasant Bay U.S.A. 135 K3
Pleasant Grove U.S.A. 129 H1
Pleasant Hill Lake U.S.A. 134 D3
Pleasanton U.S.A. 131 D6
Pleasant Point N.Z. 113 C7
Pleasantville U.S.A. 135 H4
Pleasure Ridge Park U.S.A. 134 C4
Pleaux France 56 F4
Pledger Lake Canada 122 E4
Plei Doch Vietnam 71 D4
Plei Kân Vietnam 70 D4
Pleinfeld Germany 53 K5
Pleiße r. Germany 53 M3
Plenty watercourse Australia 110 B5
Plenty, Bay of g. N.Z. 113 F3
Plentywood U.S.A. 126 G2
Plesetsk Rus. Fed. 42 I3
Pleshchentsy Belarus see Plyeshchanitsy
Plétipi, Lac l. Canada 123 H4
Plettenberg Germany 53 H3
Plettenberg Bay S. Africa 100 F8
Pleven Bulg. 59 K3
Plevna Bulg. see Pleven
Pljevlja Montenegro 59 H3
Płock Poland 47 Q4
Pločno mt. Bos.-Herz. 58 G3
Plodovoye Rus. Fed. 42 F3
Ploemeur France 56 C3
Ploești Romania see Ploiești
Ploiești Romania 59 L2
Plomb du Cantal mt. France 56 F4
Ploskoye Rus. Fed. see Stanovoye
Płoty Poland 47 O4
Ploudalmézeau France 56 B2
Plouzané France 56 B2
Plovdiv Bulg. 59 K3
Plover Cove Reservoir H.K. China 77 [inset]
Plozk Poland see Płock
Plum U.S.A. 134 F3
Plumridge Lakes salt flat Australia 109 D7
Plungė Lith. 45 L9
Plutarco Elías Calles, Presa resr Mex. 127 F7
Pluto, Lac l. Canada 123 H3
Plyeshchanitsy Belarus 45 O9
Ply Huey Wati, Khao mt. Myanmar/Thai. 70 B3

▶Plymouth Montserrat 137 L5
Capital of Montserrat, abandoned in 1997 owing to volcanic activity. Temporary capital established at Brades.

Plymouth U.K. 49 C8
Plymouth CA U.S.A. 128 C2
Plymouth IN U.S.A. 134 B3
Plymouth MA U.S.A. 135 J3
Plymouth NC U.S.A. 132 E5
Plymouth NH U.S.A. 135 J2
Plymouth WI U.S.A. 134 B2
Plymouth Bay U.S.A. 135 J3
Plynlimon hill U.K. 49 D6
Plyussa Rus. Fed. 45 P7
Plzeň Czech Rep. 47 N6
Pô Burkina 96 C3
Po r. Italy 58 E2
Pô, Parc National de nat. park Burkina 96 C3
Pobeda Peak China/Kyrg. 80 F3
Pobedy, Pik mt. China/Kyrg. see Pobeda Peak
Pocahontas U.S.A. 131 F4
Pocatello U.S.A. 126 E4
Pochala Sudan 97 G4
Pochayiv Ukr. 43 E6
Pochep Rus. Fed. 43 G5
Pochinki Rus. Fed. 43 J5
Pochinok Rus. Fed. 43 G5
Pochutla Mex. 136 E5
Pocking Germany 47 N6
Pocklington U.K. 48 G5
Poções Brazil 145 C1
Pocomoke City U.S.A. 135 H4
Pocomoke Sound b. U.S.A. 135 H5
Poconé Brazil 143 G7
Pocono Mountains hills U.S.A. 135 H3
Pocono Summit U.S.A. 135 H3
Poços de Caldas Brazil 145 B3
Podanur India 84 C4
Poddor'ye Rus. Fed. 42 F4
Podgorenskiy Rus. Fed. 43 H6

▶Podgorica Montenegro 59 H3
Capital of Montenegro

Podgornoye Rus. Fed. 64 J4
Podile India 84 C3
Podișul Transilvaniei plat. Romania see Transylvanian Basin
Podkamennaya Tunguska r. Rus. Fed. 65 K3
Podocarpus, Parque Nacional nat. park Ecuador 142 C4
Podol'sk Rus. Fed. 43 H5
Podporozh'ye Rus. Fed. 42 G3
Podujevë Kosovo 59 I3
Podujevo Kosovo see Podujevë
Podz' Rus. Fed. 42 K3
Poelela, Lagoa l. Moz. 101 L3
Poeppel Corner salt flat Australia 111 B5
Poetovio Slovenia see Ptuj
Pofadder S. Africa 100 D5
Pogar Rus. Fed. 43 G5
Poggibonsi Italy 58 D3
Poggio di Montieri mt. Italy 58 D3
Pogradec Albania 59 I4
Pogranichnik Afgh. 89 F3
Pogranichnyy Rus. Fed. 74 C3
Po Hai g. China see Bo Hai
P'ohang S. Korea 75 C5
Pohnpei atoll Micronesia 150 G5
Pohri India 82 D4
Poi India 83 H4
Poiana Mare Romania 59 J3
Poinsett, Cape Antarctica 152 F2
Point Arena U.S.A. 128 B2
Point au Fer Island U.S.A. 131 F6
Pointe a la Hache U.S.A. 131 F6
Pointe-à-Pitre Guadeloupe 137 L5
Pointe-Noire Congo 99 B4
Point Hope U.S.A. 118 B3

Point Lake Canada 120 H1
Point of Rocks U.S.A. 126 F4
Point Pelee National Park Canada 134 D3
Point Pleasant NJ U.S.A. 135 H3
Point Pleasant WV U.S.A. 134 D4
Poitiers France 56 E3
Poitou reg. France 56 E3
Poix-de-Picardie France 52 B5
Pojuca r. Brazil 145 D1
Pokaran India 82 B4
Pokataroo Australia 112 D2
Pokcha Rus. Fed. 41 R3
Pokhara Nepal 83 E3
Pokhran Landi Pak. 89 G5
Pokhvistnevo Rus. Fed. 41 Q5
Pok Liu Chau i. H.K. China see Lamma Island
Poko Dem. Rep. Congo 98 C3
Pokosnoye Rus. Fed. 72 I1
P'ok'r Kovkas mts Asia see Lesser Caucasus
Pokrovka Chitinskaya Oblast' Rus. Fed. 74 A1
Pokrovka Primorskiy Kray Rus. Fed. 74 C4
Pokrovsk Respublika Sakha (Yakutiya) Rus. Fed. 65 N3
Pokrovsk Saratovskaya Oblast' Rus. Fed. see Engel's
Pokrovskoye Rus. Fed. 43 H7
Pokshen'ga r. Rus. Fed. 42 J3
Pol India 82 C5
Pola Croatia see Pula
Polacca Wash watercourse U.S.A. 129 H4
Pola de Lena Spain 57 D2
Pola de Siero Spain 57 D2
Poland country Europe 40 J5
Poland NY U.S.A. 135 H2
Poland OH U.S.A. 134 E3
Polar Plateau Antarctica 152 A1
Polatlı Turkey 90 D3
Polatsk Belarus 45 P9
Polavaram India 84 D2
Polcirkeln Sweden 44 L3
Pol-e 'Alam Lowgar 89 H3
Pol-e Fāsā Iran 88 D4
Pol-e Khatum Iran 89 F2
Pol-e Khomrī Afgh. 89 H3
Pol-e Safīd Iran 88 D2
Polessk Rus. Fed. 45 L9
Poles'ye marsh Belarus/Ukr. see Pripet Marshes
Polgahawela Sri Lanka 84 D5
Poli Cyprus see Polis
Políaigos i. Greece see Polyaigos
Police Poland 47 O4
Policoro Italy 58 G4
Poligny France 56 G3
Polikastron Greece see Polykastro
Polillo Islands Phil. 69 G3
Polis Cyprus 85 A2
Polis'ke Ukr. 43 F6
Polis'kyy Zapovidnyk nature res. Ukr. 43 F6
Politovo Rus. Fed. 42 K2
Políyiros Greece see Polygyros
Polkowice Poland 47 P5
Pollachi India 84 C4
Pollard Islands U.S.A. see Gardner Pinnacles
Polle Germany 53 J3
Pollino, Monte mt. Italy 58 G5
Pollino, Parco Nazionale del nat. park Italy 58 G5
Pollock Pines U.S.A. 128 C2
Pollock Reef Australia 109 C8
Polmak Norway 44 O1
Polnovat Rus. Fed. 41 T3
Polo Fin. 44 P4
Poloat atoll Micronesia see Puluwat
Pologi Ukr. see Polohy
Polohy Ukr. 43 H7
Polokwane S. Africa 101 I2
Polonne Ukr. 43 E6
Polonnoye Ukr. see Polonne
Polotsk Belarus see Polatsk
Polperro U.K. 49 C8
Polska country Europe see Poland
Polson U.S.A. 126 E3
Polta r. Rus. Fed. 42 I2
Poltava Ukr. 43 G6
Poltoratsk Turkm. see Aşgabat
Põltsamaa Estonia 45 N7
Polunochnoye Rus. Fed. 41 S3
Põlva Estonia 45 O7
Polvadera U.S.A. 127 G6
Polvijärvi Fin. 44 P5
Polyaigos i. Greece 59 K6
Polyanovgrad Bulg. see Karnobat
Polyarnyy Chukotskiy Avtonomnyy Okrug Rus. Fed. 65 S3
Polyarnyy Murmanskaya Oblast' Rus. Fed. 44 R2
Polyarnyye Zori Rus. Fed. 44 R3
Polyarnyy Ural mts Rus. Fed. 41 S2
Polygyros Greece 59 J4
Polykastro Greece 59 J4
Polynesia is Pacific Ocean 150 I6
Polynésie Française terr. S. Pacific Ocean see French Polynesia
Pom Indon. 69 J7
Pomarkku Fin. 45 M6
Pombal Pará Brazil 143 H4
Pombal Paraíba Brazil 143 K5
Pombal Port. 57 B4
Pomene Moz. 101 L2
Pomeranian Bay Poland 47 O3
Pomeroy S. Africa 101 J5
Pomeroy U.K. 51 F3
Pomeroy OH U.S.A. 134 D4
Pomeroy WA U.S.A. 126 D3
Pomezia Italy 58 E4
Pomfret S. Africa 100 F3
Pomona Namibia 100 B4
Pomona U.S.A. 128 E4
Pomorie Bulg. 59 L3
Pomorskie, Pojezierze reg. Poland 47 O4
Pomorskiy Bereg coastal area Rus. Fed. 42 G2
Pomorskiy Proliv sea chan. Rus. Fed. 42 K1
Pomos Point Cyprus 85 A2
Pomo Tso l. China see Puma Yumco
Pomou, Akra pt Cyprus see Pomos Point
Pomozdino Rus. Fed. 42 L3
Pompain China 76 B2
Pompano Beach U.S.A. 133 D7
Pompei Italy 58 F4
Pompéia Brazil 145 A3
Pompey France 52 G6
Pompeyevka Rus. Fed. 74 C2
Ponape atoll Micronesia see Pohnpei
Ponask Lake Canada 121 M4
Ponazyrevo Rus. Fed. 42 J4
Ponca City U.S.A. 131 D4
Ponce Puerto Rico 137 K5
Ponce de Leon Bay U.S.A. 133 D7
Poncheville, Lac l. Canada 122 F4
Pondicherry India see Puducherry
Pondicherry union terr. India see Puducherry
Pondichéry India see Puducherry
Pond Inlet Canada 153 K2
Ponds Bay Canada see Pond Inlet
Ponente, Riviera di coastal area Italy 58 B3
Poneto U.S.A. 134 C3
Ponferrada Spain 57 C2
Pongara, Pointe pt Gabon 98 A3
Pongaroa N.Z. 113 F5
Pongo watercourse Sudan 97 F4
Pongola r. S. Africa 101 K4
Pongolapoort Dam l. S. Africa 101 J4
Ponnagyun Myanmar 70 A2
Ponnaivar r. India 84 C4
Ponnampet India 84 B3
Ponnani India 84 B4
Ponnyadaung Range mts Myanmar 70 A2
Pono Indon. 69 I8
Ponoka Canada 120 H4
Ponoy r. Rus. Fed. 42 I2
Pons r. Canada 123 H2
▶Ponta Delgada Arquipélago dos Açores 148 G3
Capital of the Azores.
Ponta Grossa Brazil 145 A4
Pontal Brazil 145 A3
Pontalina Brazil 145 A2
Pont-à-Mousson France 52 G6
Ponta Porã Brazil 144 E2
Pontarfynach U.K. see Devil's Bridge
Pont-Audemer France 49 H9
Pontault-Combault France 52 C6
Pontax r. Canada 122 F4
Pontchartrain, Lake U.S.A. 131 F6
Pont-de-Loup Belgium 52 E4
Ponte Alta do Norte Brazil 143 I6
Ponte de Sor Port. 57 B4
Ponte Firme Brazil 145 B2
Pontefract U.K. 48 F5
Ponteix Canada 121 J5
Ponteland U.K. 48 F3
Ponte Nova Brazil 145 C3
Pontes-e-Lacerda Brazil 143 G7
Pontevedra Spain 57 B2
Ponthierville Dem. Rep. Congo see Ubundu
Pontiac IL U.S.A. 130 F3
Pontiac MI U.S.A. 134 D2
Pontiae is Italy see Ponziane, Isole
Pontianak Indon. 68 D7
Pontine Islands is Italy see Ponziane, Isole
Pont-l'Abbé France 56 B3
Pontoise France 52 C5
Ponton watercourse Australia 109 C7
Ponton Canada 121 L4
Pontotoc U.S.A. 131 F5
Pont-Ste-Maxence France 52 C5
Pontypool U.K. 49 D7
Pontypridd U.K. 49 D7
Ponza, Isola di i. Italy 58 E4
Ponziane, Isole is Italy 58 E4
Poochera Australia 109 F8
Poole U.K. 49 F8
Poole U.S.A. 134 B5
Poolowanna Lake salt flat Australia 111 B5
Poona India see Pune
Pooncarie Australia 111 C7
Poonch India see Punch
Poopelloe Lake salt l. Australia 112 B3
Poopó, Lago de l. Bol. 142 E7
Poor Knights Islands N.Z. 113 E2
Popayán Col. 142 C3
Poperinge Belgium 52 C4
Popigay r. Rus. Fed. 65 L2
Popiltah Australia 111 C7
Popilta Lake imp. l. Australia 111 C7
Poplar r. Canada 121 L4
Poplar U.S.A. 126 G2
Poplar Bluff U.S.A. 131 F4
Poplar Camp U.S.A. 134 E5
Poplarville U.S.A. 131 F6
▶Popocatépetl, Volcán vol. Mex. 136 E5
5th highest mountain in North America.
Popokabaka Dem. Rep. Congo 99 B4
Popondetta P.N.G. 69 L8
Popovichskaya Rus. Fed. see Kalininskaya
Popovo Bulg. 59 L3
Popovo Polje plain Bos.-Herz. 58 G3
Poppberg hill Germany 53 L5
Poppenberg hill Germany 53 K3
Poprad Slovakia 47 R6
Poquoson U.S.A. 135 G5
Porali r. Pak. 89 G5
Porangahau N.Z. 113 F5
Porangatu Brazil 145 A1
Porbandar India 82 B5
Porcher Island Canada 120 D4
Porcos r. Brazil 145 B1
Porcupine, Cape Canada 123 K3
Porcupine Abyssal Plain sea feature N. Atlantic Ocean 148 G2
Porcupine Gorge National Park Australia 110 D4
Porcupine Hills Canada 121 K4
Porcupine Mountains U.S.A. 130 F2
Poreč Croatia 58 E2
Porecatu Brazil 145 A3
Poretskoye Rus. Fed. 43 J5
Pori Fin. 45 L6
Porirua N.Z. 113 E5
Porkhov Rus. Fed. 45 P8
Porlamar Venez. 142 F1
Pormpuraaw Australia 110 C2
Pornic France 56 C3
Poronaysk Rus. Fed. 74 F2
Porong China 83 G3
Poros Greece 59 J6
Porosozero Rus. Fed. 42 G3
Porpoise Bay Antarctica 152 G2
Porsangerfjorden sea chan. Norway 44 N1
Porsangerhalvøya pen. Norway 44 N1
Porsgrunn Norway 45 F7
Porsuk r. Turkey 59 N5
Portadown U.K. 51 F3
Portaferry U.K. 51 G3
Portage MI U.S.A. 134 C2
Portage PA U.S.A. 135 F3
Portage WI U.S.A. 130 F3
Portage Lakes U.S.A. 134 E3
Portage la Prairie Canada 121 L5
Portal U.S.A. 130 C1
Port Alberni Canada 120 E5
Port Albert Australia 112 C7
Portalegre Port. 57 C4
Portales U.S.A. 131 C5
Port-Alfred Canada see La Baie
Port Alfred S. Africa 101 H7
Port Alice Canada 120 E5
Port Allegany U.S.A. 135 F3
Port Allen U.S.A. 131 F6
Port Alma Australia 110 E4
Port Angeles U.S.A. 126 C2
Port Antonio Jamaica 137 I5
Portarlington Ireland 51 E4
Port Arthur Australia 111 [inset]
Port Arthur U.S.A. 131 E6
Port Askaig U.K. 50 C5
Port Augusta Australia 111 B7
▶Port-au-Prince Haiti 137 J5
Capital of Haiti.
Port Austin U.S.A. 134 D1
Port aux Choix Canada 123 K4
Portavogie U.K. 51 G3
Port Beaufort S. Africa 100 E8
Port Blair India 71 A5
Port Bolster Canada 134 F1
Portbou Spain 57 H2
Port Burwell Canada 134 E2
Port Campbell Australia 112 A7
Port Campbell National Park Australia 112 A7
Port Carling Canada 134 F1
Port-Cartier Canada 123 I4
Port Chalmers N.Z. 113 C7
Port Charlotte U.S.A. 133 D7
Port Clements Canada 120 C4
Port Clinton U.S.A. 134 D3
Port Credit Canada 134 F2
Port-de-Paix Haiti 137 J5
Port Dickson Malaysia 71 C7
Port Douglas Australia 110 D3
Port Edward Canada 120 D4
Port Edward S. Africa 101 J6
Porteira Brazil 143 G4
Porteirinha Brazil 145 C1
Portel Brazil 143 H4
Port Elgin Canada 134 E1
Port Elizabeth S. Africa 101 G7
Port Ellen U.K. 50 C5
Port Erin Isle of Man 48 C4
Porter Lake N.W.T. Canada 121 J2
Porter Lake Sask. Canada 121 J3
Porter Landing Canada 120 D3
Porterville S. Africa 100 D7
Porterville U.S.A. 128 D3
Port Étienne Mauritania see Nouâdhibou
Port Everglades U.S.A. see Fort Lauderdale
Port Fitzroy N.Z. 113 E3
Port Francqui Dem. Rep. Congo see Ilebo
Port-Gentil Gabon 98 A4
Port Glasgow U.K. 50 E5
Port Harcourt Nigeria 96 D4
Port Harrison Canada see Inukjuak
Porthcawl U.K. 49 D7
Port Hedland Australia 108 B5
Port Henry U.S.A. 135 I1
Port Herald Malawi see Nsanje
Porthleven U.K. 49 B8
Porthmadog U.K. 49 C6
Port Hope Canada 135 F2
Port Hope Simpson Canada 123 L3
Port Hueneme U.S.A. 128 D4
Port Huron U.S.A. 134 D2
Portimão Port. 57 B5
Port Jackson Australia see Sydney
Port Jackson inlet Australia 112 E4
Port Keats Australia see Wadeye
Port Klang Malaysia see Pelabuhan Klang
Port Láirge Ireland see Waterford
Portland N.S.W. Australia 112 D4
Portland Vic. Australia 111 C8
Portland IN U.S.A. 134 C3
Portland ME U.S.A. 135 J2
Portland MI U.S.A. 134 C2
Portland OR U.S.A. 126 C3
Portland TN U.S.A. 134 B5
Portland, Isle of pen. U.K. 49 E8
Portland Bill hd U.K. see Bill of Portland
Portland Creek Pond l. Canada 123 K4
Portland Roads Australia 110 C2
Port-la-Nouvelle France 56 F5
Portlaoise Ireland 51 E4
Port Lavaca U.S.A. 131 D6
Portlaw Ireland 51 E5
Portlethen U.K. 50 G3
Port Lincoln Australia 111 A7
Port Loko Sierra Leone 96 B4
▶Port Louis Mauritius 149 L7
Capital of Mauritius.
Port-Lyautrey Morocco see Kénitra
Port Macquarie Australia 112 F3
Portmadoc U.K. see Porthmadog
Port McNeill Canada 120 E5
Port-Menier Canada 123 I4
▶Port Moresby P.N.G. 69 L8
Capital of Papua New Guinea.
Portnaguran U.K. 50 C2
Portnahaven U.K. 50 C5
Port nan Giúran U.K. see Portnaguran
Port Neill Australia 111 B7
Portneuf r. Canada 123 H4
Port Nis U.K. see Port of Ness
Port Nis Scotland U.K. see Port of Ness
Port Noarlunga Australia 111 B7
Port Nolloth S. Africa 100 C5
Port Norris U.S.A. 135 H4
Port-Nouveau-Québec Canada see Kangiqsualujjuaq
Porto Port. see Oporto
Porto Acre Brazil 142 E5
Porto Alegre Brazil 145 A5
Porto Alexandre Angola see Tombua
Porto Amboim Angola 99 B5
Porto Amélia Moz. see Pemba
Porto Artur Brazil 143 G6
Porto Belo Brazil 145 A4
Porto de Moz Brazil 143 H4
Porto de Santa Cruz Brazil 145 C1
Porto dos Gaúchos Óbidos Brazil 143 G6
Porto Esperança Brazil 143 G7
Porto Esperidião Brazil 143 G7
Portoferraio Italy 58 D3
Port of Ness U.K. 50 C2
Porto Franco Brazil 143 I5
▶Port of Spain Trin. and Tob. 137 L6
Capital of Trinidad and Tobago.
Porto Grande Brazil 143 H3
Portogruaro Italy 58 E2
Porto Jofre Brazil 143 G7
Portola U.S.A. 128 C2
Portomaggiore Italy 58 D2
Porto Mendes Brazil 144 F2
Porto Murtinho Brazil 144 E2
Porto Nacional Brazil 143 I6
▶Porto-Novo Benin 96 D4
Capital of Benin.
Porto Novo Cape Verde 96 [inset]
Porto Primavera, Represa resr Brazil 144 F2
Port Orchard U.S.A. 126 C3
Port Orford U.S.A. 126 B4
Porto Rico Angola 99 B4
Porto Santo, Ilha de i. Madeira 96 B1
Porto Seguro Brazil 145 D2
Porto Tolle Italy 58 E2
Porto Torres Sardinia Italy 58 C4
Porto União Brazil 145 A4
Porto-Vecchio Corsica France 56 I6
Porto Velho Brazil 142 F5
Portoviejo Ecuador 142 B4
Porto Wálter Brazil 142 D5
Portpatrick U.K. 50 D6
Port Perry Canada 135 F1
Port Phillip Bay Australia 112 B7
Port Pirie Australia 111 B7
Port Radium Canada see Echo Bay
Portreath U.K. 49 B8
Portree U.K. 50 C3
Port Rexton Canada 123 L4
Port Royal U.S.A. 135 G4
Port Royal Sound inlet U.S.A. 133 D5
Portrush U.K. 51 F2
Port Safaga Egypt see Būr Safājah
Port Said Egypt 85 A4
Port St Joe U.S.A. 133 C6
Port St Lucie City U.S.A. 133 D7
Port St Mary Isle of Man 48 C4
Portsalon Ireland 51 E2
Port Sanilac U.S.A. 134 D2
Port Severn Canada 134 F1
Port Shepstone S. Africa 101 J6
Port Simpson Canada see Lax Kw'alaams
Portsmouth U.K. 49 F8
Portsmouth NH U.S.A. 135 J2
Portsmouth OH U.S.A. 134 D4
Portsmouth VA U.S.A. 135 G5
Portsoy U.K. 50 G3
Port Stanley Falkland Is see Stanley
Port Stephens b. Australia 112 F4
Portstewart U.K. 51 F2
Port Sudan Sudan 86 E6
Port Swettenham Malaysia see Pelabuhan Klang
Port Talbot U.K. 49 D7
Porttipahdan tekojärvi l. Fin. 44 O2
Port Townsend U.S.A. 126 C2
Portugal country Europe 57 C4
Portugália Angola see Chitato
Portuguese East Africa country Africa see Mozambique
Portuguese Guinea country Africa see Guinea-Bissau
Portuguese Timor country Asia see East Timor
Portuguese West Africa country Africa see Angola
Portumna Ireland 51 D4
Portus Herculis Monoeci country Europe see Monaco
Port-Vendres France 56 F5
▶Port Vila Vanuatu 107 G3
Capital of Vanuatu.
Portville U.S.A. 135 F2
Port Vladimir Rus. Fed. 44 R2
Port Waikato N.Z. 113 E3
Port Washington U.S.A. 134 B2
Port William U.K. 50 E6
Porvenir Bol. 142 E6
Porvenir Chile 144 B8
Porvoo Fin. 45 N6
Posada Spain 57 D2
Posada de Llanera Spain see Posada
Posadas Arg. 144 E3
Posen Poland see Poznań
Posen U.S.A. 134 D1
Poseyville U.S.A. 134 B4
Poshekhon'ye Rus. Fed. 42 H4
Poshekon'ye-Volodarsk Rus. Fed. see Poshekhon'ye
Posht-e Badam Iran 88 D3
Poshteh-ye Chaqvīr hill Iran 88 E4
Posht-e Kūh mts Iran 88 B3
Posht-e Rūd-e Zamindavar reg. Afgh. see Zamīndāvar
Posht Kūh hill Iran 88 C2
Posio Fin. 44 P3
Poso Indon. 69 G7
Posof Turkey 91 F2
Posŏng S. Korea 75 B6
Possession Island Namibia 100 B4
Pößneck Germany 53 L4
Post U.S.A. 131 C5
Postavy Belarus see Pastavy
Poste-de-la-Baleine Canada see Kuujjuarapik
Poste Weygand Alg. 96 D2
Postmasburg S. Africa 100 F5
Poston U.S.A. 129 F4
Postville Canada 123 K3
Postville U.S.A. 122 C6
Postysheve Ukr. see Krasnoarmiys'k
Pota Indon. 108 C2
Pótam Mex. 127 F8
Poté Brazil 145 C2
Poteau U.S.A. 131 E5
Potegaon India 84 D2
Potentia Italy see Potenza
Potenza Italy 58 F4
Poth U.S.A. 131 D6
P'ot'i Georgia 91 F2
Potikal India 84 D2
Potiraguá Brazil 145 D1
Potiskum Nigeria 96 E3
Potlatch U.S.A. 126 D3
Pot Mountain U.S.A. 126 E3
Po Toi i. H.K. China 77 [inset]
Potomac r. U.S.A. 135 G4
Potosí Bol. 142 E7
Potosi U.S.A. 130 F4
Potosi Mountain U.S.A. 129 F4
Potrerillos Chile 144 C3
Potrero del Llano Mex. 131 B6
Potsdam Germany 53 N2
Potsdam U.S.A. 135 H1
Potter U.S.A. 130 C3
Potterne U.K. 49 E7
Potters Bar U.K. 49 G7
Potter Valley U.S.A. 128 B2
Pottstown U.S.A. 135 H3
Pottsville U.S.A. 135 G3
Pottuvil Sri Lanka 84 D5
Potwar reg. Pak. 89 I3
Pouch Cove Canada 123 L5
Poughkeepsie U.S.A. 135 I3
Poulin de Courval, Lac l. Canada 123 H4
Poulton-le-Fylde U.K. 48 E5
Pouso Alegre Brazil 145 B3
Poŭthĭsăt Cambodia 71 C4
Poŭthĭsăt, Stœng r. Cambodia 71 D4
Považská Bystrica Slovakia 47 Q6
Povenets Rus. Fed. 42 G3
Poverty Bay N.Z. 113 F4
Povlen mt. Serbia 59 H2
Póvoa de Varzim Port. 57 B3
Povorino Rus. Fed. 43 I6
Povorotnyy, Mys hd Rus. Fed. 74 D4
Poway U.S.A. 128 E5
Powder r. U.S.A. 126 G3
Powder, South Fork r. U.S.A. 126 G4
Powder River U.S.A. 126 G4
Powell r. U.S.A. 134 D5
Powell, Lake resr U.S.A. 129 H3
Powell Lake Canada 120 E5
Powell Mountain U.S.A. 128 D2
Powell Point Bahamas 133 E7
Powell River Canada 120 E5
Powhatan AR U.S.A. 131 F4
Powhatan VA U.S.A. 135 G5
Powo China 76 C1
Pöwrize Turkm. 88 E2
Poxoréu Brazil 143 H7
Poyang China see Boyang
Poyang Hu l. China 77 H2
Poyan Reservoir Sing. 71 [inset]
Poyarkovo Rus. Fed. 74 C2
Pozantı Turkey 90 D3
Požarevac Serbia 59 I2
Poza Rica Mex. 136 E4
Pozdeyevka Rus. Fed. 74 C2
Požega Croatia 58 G2
Požega Serbia 59 I3
Pozharskoye Rus. Fed. 74 D3
Poznań Poland 47 P4
Pozoblanco Spain 57 D4
Pozo Colorado Para. 144 E2
Pozsony Slovakia see Bratislava
Pozzuoli Italy 58 F4
Prabumulih Indon. 68 C7
Prachatice Czech Rep. 47 O6
Prachi r. India 83 F6
Prachin Buri Thai. 71 C4
Prachuap Khiri Khan Thai. 71 B5
Prades France 56 F5
Prado Brazil 145 D2
▶Prague Czech Rep. 47 O5
Capital of the Czech Republic.
Praha Czech Rep. see Prague
▶Praia Cape Verde 96 [inset]
Capital of Cape Verde.
Praia do Bilene Moz. 101 K3
Prainha Brazil 143 H4
Prairie Australia 110 D4
Prairie r. U.S.A. 130 E2
Prairie Dog Town Fork r. U.S.A. 131 C5
Prairie du Chien U.S.A. 130 F3
Prairie River Canada 121 K4
Pram, Khao mt. Thai. 71 B5
Pran r. Thai. 71 C4
Pran Buri Thai. 71 B4
Prapat Indon. 71 B7
Prasonisi, Akra pt Notio Aigaio Greece see Prasonisi, Akrotirio
Prasonisi, Akrotirio pt Greece 59 L7
Prata Brazil 145 A2
Prata r. Brazil 145 A2
Prat de Llobregat Spain see El Prat de Llobregat
Prathes Thai country Asia see Thailand
Prato Italy 58 D3
Pratt U.S.A. 130 D4
Prattville U.S.A. 133 C5
Pravdinsk Rus. Fed. 45 L9
Praya Indon. 108 B2
Preah, Prêk r. Cambodia 71 D4
Preăh Vihéar Cambodia 71 D4
Preble U.S.A. 135 G2
Prechistoye Smolenskaya Oblast' Rus. Fed. 43 G5
Prechistoye Yaroslavskaya Oblast' Rus. Fed. 42 I4
Precipice National Park Australia 110 E5
Preeceville Canada 121 K5
Pregolya r. Rus. Fed. 45 L9
Preiļi Latvia 45 O8
Prelate Canada 121 I5
Premer Australia 112 D3
Prémery France 56 F3
Premnitz Germany 53 M2
Prentiss U.S.A. 131 F6
Prenzlau Germany 47 N4
Preparis Island Cocos Is 68 A4
Preparis North Channel Cocos Is 68 A4
Preparis South Channel Cocos Is 68 A4
Přerov Czech Rep. 47 P6
Presa San Antonio Mex. 131 C7
Prescelly Mts hills U.K. see Preseli, Mynydd
Prescott Canada 135 H1
Prescott AR U.S.A. 131 E5
Prescott AZ U.S.A. 129 G4
Prescott Valley U.S.A. 129 G4
Preseli, Mynydd hills U.K. 49 C7
Preševo Serbia 59 I3
Presidencia Roque Sáenz Peña Arg. 144 D3
Presidente Dutra Brazil 143 J5
Presidente Hermes Brazil 142 F6
Presidente Olegário Brazil 145 B2
Presidente Prudente Brazil 145 A3
Presidente Venceslau Brazil 145 A3
Presidio U.S.A. 131 B6
Preslav Bulg. see Veliki Preslav
Prešov Slovakia 43 D6
Prespa, Lake Europe 59 I4
Prespansko Ezero l. Europe see Prespa, Lake
Prespes nat. park Greece 59 I4
Prespës, Liqeni i l. Europe see Prespa, Lake
Presque Isle ME U.S.A. 132 G2
Presque Isle MI U.S.A. 134 D1
Pressburg Slovakia see Bratislava
Presteigne U.K. 49 D6
Preston U.K. 48 E5
Preston ID U.S.A. 126 F4
Preston MN U.S.A. 130 E3
Preston MO U.S.A. 130 E4
Preston, Cape Australia 108 B5
Prestonpans U.K. 50 G5
Prestonsburg U.S.A. 134 D5
Prestwick U.K. 50 E5
Preto r. Bahia Brazil 143 J6
Preto r. Minas Gerais Brazil 145 B2
Preto r. Brazil 145 D1
▶Pretoria S. Africa 101 I3
Official capital of South Africa.
Pretoria-Witwatersrand-Vereeniging prov. S. Africa see Gauteng
Pretzsch Germany 53 M3
Preussisch-Eylau Rus. Fed. see Bagrationovsk
Preußisch Stargard Poland see Starogard Gdański
Preveza Greece 59 I5
Prewitt U.S.A. 129 I4
Prey Vêng Cambodia 71 D5
Priaral'skiye Karakumy, Peski des. Kazakh. 80 B2
Priargunsk Rus. Fed. 73 L2
Pribilof Islands U.S.A. 118 A4
Priboj Serbia 59 H3
Price r. Australia 108 E3
Price NC U.S.A. 134 F5
Price UT U.S.A. 129 H2
Price r. U.S.A. 129 H2
Price Island Canada 120 D4
Prichard AL U.S.A. 131 F6
Prichard WV U.S.A. 134 D4
Pridorozhnoye Rus. Fed. see Khulkhuta
Priekule Latvia 45 L8
Priekuļi Latvia 45 N8
Priel'brus'ye, Natsional'nyy Park nat. park Rus. Fed. 43 I8
Prienai Lith. 45 M9
Prieska S. Africa 100 F5
Prievidza Slovakia 47 Q6
Prignitz reg. Germany 53 M1
Prijedor Bos.-Herz. 58 G2
Prijepolje Serbia 59 H3
Prikaspiyskaya Nizmennost' lowland Kazakh./Rus. Fed. see Caspian Lowland
Prilep Macedonia 59 I4
Priluki Ukr. see Pryluky
Přimda Czech Rep. 53 M5
Primero de Enero Cuba 133 E8
Primorsk Rus. Fed. 45 P6
Primorsk Ukr. see Prymors'k
Primorskiy Kray admin. div. Rus. Fed. 74 D3
Primorsko-Akhtarsk Rus. Fed. 43 H7
Primo Tapia Mex. 128 E5
Primrose Lake Canada 121 I4
Prims r. Germany 52 G5
Prince Albert Canada 121 J4
Prince Albert S. Africa 100 F7
Prince Albert Mountains Antarctica 152 H1
Prince Albert National Park Canada 121 J4
Prince Albert Peninsula Canada 118 G2
Prince Albert Road S. Africa 100 E7
Prince Alfred, Cape Canada 118 F2
Prince Alfred Hamlet S. Africa 100 D7
Prince Charles Island Canada 119 K3
Prince Charles Mountains Antarctica 152 E2
Prince Edward Island prov. Canada 123 J5
▶Prince Edward Islands Indian Ocean 149 K9
Part of South Africa.
Prince Edward Point Canada 135 G2
Prince Frederick U.S.A. 135 G4
Prince George Canada 120 F4
Prince Harald Coast Antarctica 152 D2
Prince of Wales, Cape U.S.A. 118 B3
Prince of Wales Island Australia 110 C1

ince of Wales Island Canada **119** I2
ince of Wales Island U.S.A. **120** C4
ince of Wales Strait Canada **118** G2
ince Patrick Island Canada **118** G2
ince Regent Inlet *sea chan.* Canada **119** I2
ince Rupert Canada **120** D4
incess Anne U.S.A. **135** H4
incess Astrid Coast Antarctica **152** C2
incess Charlotte Bay Australia **110** C2
incess Elizabeth Land *reg.* Antarctica **152** E2
incess Mary Lake Canada **121** L1
incess Ragnhild Coast Antarctica **152** C2
incess Royal Island Canada **120** D4
inceton Canada **120** F5
inceton *CA* U.S.A. **128** B2
inceton *IL* U.S.A. **130** F3
inceton *IN* U.S.A. **134** B4
nceton *MO* U.S.A. **130** E3
inceton *NJ* U.S.A. **135** H3
nceton *WV* U.S.A. **134** E5
ince William Sound *b.* U.S.A. **118** D3
ncipe *i.* São Tomé and Príncipe **96** D4
ineville U.S.A. **126** C3
ins Harald Kyst *coastal area* Antarctica *see* **Prince Harald Coast**
nzapolca Nicaragua **137** H6
ozersk Rus. Fed. **45** Q6
ozyorsk Rus. Fed. *see* **Priozersk**
pet *r.* Belarus/Ukr. **43** F6
also spelt Pryp"yat' (Ukraine) or Prypyats' (Belarus)
pet Marshes Belarus/Ukr. **43** E6
rechnyy Rus. Fed. **44** Q2

▶**Prishtinë** Kosovo **59** I3
Capital of Kosovo

ština Kosovo *see* **Prishtinë**
tzier Germany **53** L1
tzwalk Germany **53** M1
vas France **56** G4
vlaka Croatia **58** F2
volzhsk Rus. Fed. **42** I4
volzhskaya Vozvyshennost' *hills* Rus. Fed. **43** J6
volzhskiy Rus. Fed. **43** J6
volzh'ye Rus. Fed. **43** K5
yutnoye Rus. Fed. **43** I7
zren Kosovo **59** I3
obolinggo Indon. **68** E8
obstzella Germany **53** L4
obus U.K. **49** C8
oddatur India **84** C3
ofessor van Blommestein Meer *resr* Suriname **143** G3
ogreso Hond. *see* **El Progreso**
ogreso Mex. **131** C7
ogress Rus. Fed. **74** C2
oject City U.S.A. **126** C4
okhladnyy Rus. Fed. **91** G2
okop'yevsk Rus. Fed. **72** F2
okuplje Serbia **59** I3
oletarsk Rus. Fed. **43** I7
oletarskaya Rus. Fed. *see* **Proletarsk**
ome Myanmar *see* **Pyè**
omissão Brazil **145** A3
omissão, Represa *resr* Brazil **145** A3
ophet *r.* Canada **120** F3
ophet River Canada **120** F3
opriá Brazil **143** K6
oskurov Ukr. *see* **Khmel'nyts'kyy**
osser U.S.A. **126** D3
otem S. Africa **100** E8
ovadiya Bulg. **59** L3
oven Greenland *see* **Kangersuatsiaq**
ovence *reg.* France **56** G5
ovidence *KY* U.S.A. **134** B5
ovidence *MD* U.S.A. *see* **Annapolis**

▶**Providence** *RI* U.S.A. **135** J3
Capital of Rhode Island.

ovidence, Cape N.Z. **113** A8
ovidencia, Isla de *i.* Caribbean Sea **137** H6
ovideniya Rus. Fed. **65** T3
ovincetown U.S.A. **135** J2
ovo U.S.A. **129** H1
ovost Canada **121** I4
udentópolis Brazil **145** A4
udhoe Bay U.S.A. **118** D2
üm Germany **52** G4
üm *r.* Germany **52** G5
unelli-di-Fiumorbo *Corsica* France **56** I5
untytown U.S.A. **134** E4
usa Turkey *see* **Bursa**
ushkov Poland *see* **Pruszków**
uszków Poland **47** R4
ut *r.* Europe **43** F7
ydz Bay Antarctica **152** E2
yluky Ukr. **43** G6
ymors'k Ukr. **43** H7
ymors'ke Ukr. *see* **Sartana**
yp"yat' *r.* Belarus/Ukr. **43** F6 *see* **Pripet**
ypyats' *r.* Belarus/Ukr. **41** L5 *see* **Pripet**
zemyśl Poland **43** D6
zheval'sk Kyrg. *see* **Karakol**
ara *i.* Greece **59** K5
ov Rus. Fed. **45** P8
kov, Lake Estonia/Rus. Fed. **45** O7
kov Oblast *admin. div.* Rus. Fed. *see* **Pskovskaya Oblast'**
kovskaya Oblast' *admin. div.* Rus. Fed. **45** P8
kovskoye Ozero *l.* Estonia/Rus. Fed. *see* **Pskov, Lake**
olemaïda Greece **59** I4
olemais Israel *see* **'Akko**
j Slovenia **58** F1
a Thai. **70** C3
aka *hill* Sing. **71** [inset]
an *Guizhou* China **76** E3
an *Sichuan* China **76** E2
an S. Korea **75** B6
callpa Peru **142** D5
cheng *Fujian* China **77** H3
cheng *Shaanxi* China **77** F1
chezh Rus. Fed. **42** I4
ch'ŏn S. Korea **75** B5
ck Poland **47** Q3

Pudai *watercourse* Afgh. *see* **Dor**
Pūdanū Iran **88** D3
Pudasjärvi Fin. **44** O4
Pudimoe S. Africa **100** G4
Pudong *Shanghai* China **66** E4
Pudozh Rus. Fed. **42** H3
Pudsey U.K. **48** F5
Pudu China *see* **Suizhou**
Puduchcheri India *see* **Puducherry**
Puducherry India **84** C4
Puducherry *union terr.* India **84** C4
Pudukkottai India **84** C4
Puebla *Baja California* Mex. **129** F5
Puebla *Puebla* Mex. **136** E5
Puebla de Sanabria Spain **57** C2
Puebla de Zaragoza Mex. *see* **Puebla**
Pueblo U.S.A. **127** G5
Pueblo Yaqui Mex. **127** F8
Puelches Arg. **144** C5
Puelén Arg. **144** C5
Puente-Genil Spain **57** D5
Pu'er China **76** D4
Puerco *watercourse* U.S.A. **129** H4
Puerto Acosta Bol. **142** E7
Puerto Alegre Bol. **142** F6
Puerto Ángel Mex. **136** E5
Puerto Armuelles Panama **137** H7
Puerto Ayacucho Venez. **142** E2
Puerto Bahía Negra Para. *see* **Bahía Negra**
Puerto Baquerizo Moreno *Galápagos* Ecuador **142** [inset]
Puerto Barrios Guat. **136** G5
Puerto Cabello Venez. **142** E1
Puerto Cabezas Nicaragua **137** H6
Puerto Carreño Col. **142** E2
Puerto Casado Para. **144** E2
Puerto Cavinas Bol. **142** E6
Puerto Coig Arg. **144** C8
Puerto Cortés Mex. **136** B4
Puerto de Lobos Mex. **127** E7
Puerto Escondido Mex. **136** E5
Puerto Francisco de Orellana *Orellana* Ecuador *see* **Coca**
Puerto Francisco de Orellana Ecuador *see* **Coca**
Puerto Frey Bol. **142** F6
Puerto Génova Bol. **142** E6
Puerto Guarani Para. **144** E2
Puerto Heath Bol. **142** E6
Puerto Huitoto Col. **142** D3
Puerto Inírida Col. **142** E3
Puerto Isabel Bol. **143** G7
Puerto Leguizamo Col. **142** D4
Puerto Lempira Hond. **137** H5
Puerto Libertad Mex. **127** E7
Puerto Limón Costa Rica **137** H6
Puertollano Spain **57** D4
Puerto Lobos Arg. **144** C6
Puerto Madryn Arg. **144** C6
Puerto Maldonado Peru **142** E6
Puerto Máncora Peru **142** B4
Puerto México Mex. *see* **Coatzacoalcos**
Puerto Montt Chile **144** B6
Puerto Natales Chile **144** B8
Puerto Nuevo Col. **142** E2
Puerto Peñasco Mex. **127** E7
Puerto Pirámides Arg. **144** D6
Puerto Plata Dom. Rep. **137** J5
Puerto Portillo Peru **142** D5
Puerto Prado Peru **142** D6
Puerto Princesa Phil. **68** F5
Puerto Rico Arg. **144** E3
Puerto Rico Bol. **142** E6

▶**Puerto Rico** *terr.* West Indies **137** K5
United States Commonwealth.

▶**Puerto Rico Trench** *sea feature* Caribbean Sea **148** D4
Deepest trench in the Atlantic Ocean.

Puerto Santa Cruz Arg. **144** C8
Puerto Sastre Para. **144** E2
Puerto Saucedo Bol. **142** F6
Puerto Suárez Bol. **143** G7
Puerto Supe Peru **142** C6
Puerto Vallarta Mex. **136** C4
Puerto Victoria Peru **142** D5
Puerto Visser Arg. **144** C7
Puerto Yartou Chile **144** B8
Puerto Ybapobó Para. **144** E2
Pugachev Rus. Fed. **43** K5
Pugal India **82** C3
Puge China **76** D3
Pūhāl-e Khamīr, Kūh-e *mts* Iran **88** D5
Puhiwaero *c.* N.Z. *see* **South West Cape**
Puigmal *mt.* France/Spain **56** F5
Pui O Wan *b. H.K.* China **77** [inset]
Puji China *see* **Puge**
Pukaki, Lake N.Z. **113** C7
Pukapuka *atoll* Cook Is **107** J3
Pukaskwa National Park Canada **122** D4
Pukatawagan Canada **121** K4
Pukchin N. Korea **75** B4
Pukch'ŏng N. Korea **75** C4
Pukekohe N.Z. **113** E3
Puketeraki Range *mts* N.Z. **113** D6
Pukeuri Junction N.Z. **113** C7
Puksubaek-san *mt.* N. Korea **74** B4
Pula China *see* **Nyingchi**
Pula Croatia **58** E2
Pula *Sardinia* Italy **58** C5
Pulap *atoll* Micronesia **69** L5
Pulaski *NY* U.S.A. **135** G2
Pulaski *VA* U.S.A. **134** E5
Pulaski *WI* U.S.A. **134** A1
Pulau Simeulue, Suaka Margasatwa *nature res.* Indon. **71** A7
Pulheim Germany **52** G3
Pulicat Lake *inlet* India **84** D3
Pulivendla India **84** C3
Pulkkila Fin. **44** N4
Pullman U.S.A. **126** D3
Pulo Anna *i.* Palau **69** I6
Pulozero Rus. Fed. **44** R2
Púlpito, Punta *pt* Mex. **127** F8
Pulu China **82** E1
Pülümür Turkey **91** E3
Pulusuk *atoll* Micronesia **69** L5
Puluwat *atoll* Micronesia **69** L5
Pulwama India **89** I3

Pumasillo, Cerro *mt.* Peru **142** D6
Puma Yumco *l.* China **83** G3
Pumiao China *see* **Yongning**
Puná, Isla *i.* Ecuador **142** B4
Punakha Bhutan **83** G4
Punch India **82** C2
Punchaw Canada **120** F4
Punda Maria S. Africa **101** J2
Pundri India **82** D3
Pune India **84** B2
P'ungsan N. Korea **74** C4
Puning China **77** H4
Punjab *state* India **82** C3
Punjab *prov.* Pak. **89** H4
Punmah Glacier China/Pakistan **82** D2
Puno Peru **142** D7
Punta, Cerro de *mt.* Puerto Rico **137** K5
Punta Abreojos Mex. **127** E8
Punta Alta Arg. **144** D5
Punta Arenas Chile **144** B8
Punta Balestrieri *mt.* Italy **58** C4
Punta del Este Uruguay **144** F5
Punta Delgada Arg. **144** D6
Punta Gorda Belize **136** G5
Punta Gorda U.S.A. **133** D7
Punta Norte Arg. **144** D6
Punta Prieta Mex. **127** E7
Puntarenas Costa Rica **137** H6
Punxsutawney U.S.A. **135** F3
Puokio Fin. **44** O4
Puolanka Fin. **44** O4
Puqi China *see* **Chibi**
Pur *r.* Rus. Fed. **64** I3
Puracé, Volcán de *vol.* Col. **142** C3
Purcell U.S.A. **131** D5
Purcell Mountains Canada **120** G5
Purgatoire *r.* U.S.A. **130** C4
Puri India **84** E2
Purmerend Neth. **52** E2
Purna *r. Mahar.* India **82** D5
Purna *r. Mahar.* India **84** C2
Purnea India *see* **Purnia**
Purnia India **83** F4
Purnululu National Park Australia **108** E4
Pursat Cambodia *see* **Poŭthĭsăt**
Puruliya India **83** F5

▶**Purus** *r.* Peru **142** F4
3rd longest river in South America.

Puruvesi *l.* Fin. **44** P6
Purwodadi Indon. **68** E8
Puryŏng N. Korea **74** C4
Pusad India **84** C2
Pusan S. Korea **75** C6
Pusatlı Dağı *mt.* Turkey **85** A1
Pushchino Rus. Fed. **43** H5
Pushemskiy Rus. Fed. **42** J3
Pushkin Rus. Fed. **45** Q7
Pushkino Azer. *see* **Biläsuvar**
Pushkinskaya, Gora *mt.* Rus. Fed. **74** F3
Pushkinskiye Gory Rus. Fed. **45** P8
Pusht-i-Rud *reg.* Afgh. *see* **Zamīndāvar**
Pustoshka Rus. Fed. **42** F4
Pusur *r.* Bangl. **83** G5
Putahow Lake Canada **121** K3
Putain Indon. **108** D2
Putao Myanmar **70** B1
Puteoli Italy *see* **Pozzuoli**
Puthein Myanmar *see* **Bassein**
Putian China **77** H3
Puting China *see* **De'an**
Puting, Tanjung *pt* Indon. **68** E7
Putlitz Germany **53** M1
Putna *r.* Romania **59** L2
Putney U.S.A. **135** I2
Putoi *i. H.K.* China *see* **Po Toi**
Putorana, Gory *mts* Rus. Fed. **153** E2

▶**Putrajaya** Malaysia **71** C7
Joint capital (with Kuala Lumpur) of Malaysia.

Putre Chile **142** E7
Putsonderwater S. Africa **100** E5
Puttalam Sri Lanka **84** C4
Puttalam Lagoon Sri Lanka **84** C4
Puttelange-aux-Lacs France **52** G5
Putten Neth. **52** F2
Puttershoek Neth. **52** E3
Puttgarden Germany **47** M3
Putumayo *r.* Col. **142** D4
also known as Ica (Peru)
Putuo China *see* **Shenjiamen**
Puumala Fin. **45** P6
Pu'uwai U.S.A. **127** [inset]
Puvirnituq Canada **122** F1
Puyallup U.S.A. **126** C3
Puyang China **77** G1
Puy de Sancy *mt.* France **56** F4
Puyehue, Parque Nacional *nat. park* Chile **144** B6
Puysegur Point N.Z. **113** A8
Puzak, Hāmūn-e *marsh* Afgh. **89** F4
Puzla Rus. Fed. **42** L3
Pweto Dem. Rep. Congo **99** C4
Pwinbyu Myanmar **70** A2
Pwllheli U.K. **49** C6
Pyal'ma Rus. Fed. **42** G3
Pyalo Myanmar **70** A3
Pyamalaw *r.* Myanmar **70** A4
Pyandzh Tajik. *see* **Panj**
Pyaozero, Ozero *l.* Rus. Fed. **44** Q3
Pyaozerskiy Rus. Fed. **44** Q4
Pyapali India **84** C3
Pyapon Myanmar **70** A3
Pyasina *r.* Rus. Fed. **64** J2
Pyatigorsk Rus. Fed. **91** F1
Pyatikhatki Ukr. *see* **P"yatykhatky**
P"yatykhatky Ukr. **43** G6
Pyay Myanmar *see* **Pyè**
Pychas Rus. Fed. **42** L4
Pyè Myanmar **70** A3
Pye, Mount *hill* N.Z. **113** B8
Pyetrykaw Belarus **43** F5
Pygmalion Point India **71** A6
Pyhäjoki Fin. **44** N4
Pyhäjoki *r.* Fin. **44** N4
Pyhäntä Fin. **44** O4
Pyhäsalmi Fin. **44** N5
Pyhäselkä *l.* Fin. **44** P5
Pyi Myanmar *see* **Pyè**

Pyin Myanmar *see* **Pyè**
Pyingaing Myanmar **70** A2
Pyinmana Myanmar **70** B3
Pyin-U-Lwin Myanmar **70** B2
Pyle U.K. **49** D7
Pyl'karamo Rus. Fed. **64** J3
Pylos Greece **59** I6
Pymatuning Reservoir U.S.A. **134** E3
Pyŏktong N. Korea **74** B4
P'yŏnggang N. Korea **75** B5
P'yŏnghae S. Korea **75** C5
P'yŏngsong N. Korea **75** B5
P'yŏngt'aek S. Korea **75** B5

▶**P'yŏngyang** N. Korea **75** B5
Capital of North Korea.

Pyramid Hill Australia **112** B6
Pyramid Lake U.S.A. **128** D1
Pyramid Peak U.S.A. **129** J1
Pyramid Range *mts* U.S.A. **128** D2
Pyramids of Giza *tourist site* Egypt **90** C5
Pyrenees *mts* Europe **57** H2
Pyrénées *mts* Europe *see* **Pyrenees**
Pyrénées, Parc National des *nat. park* France/Spain **56** D5
Pyrgos Greece **59** I6
Pyryatyn Ukr. **43** G6
Pyrzyce Poland **47** O4
Pyshchug Rus. Fed. **42** J4
Pytalovo Rus. Fed. **45** O8
Pyxaria *mt.* Greece **59** J5

Qaa Lebanon **85** C2
Qaanaaq Greenland *see* **Thule**
Qabātiya West Bank **85** B3
Qabnag China **76** B2
Qabqa China *see* **Gonghe**
Qacentina Alg. *see* **Constantine**
Qacha's Nek Lesotho **101** I6
Qādes Afgh. **89** F3
Qādisīyah, Sadd *dam* Iraq **91** F4
Qadisiyah Dam Iraq *see* **Qādisīyah, Sadd**
Qā'emābād Iran **89** F4
Qagan China **73** L3
Qagan Nur China **73** K4
Qagan Nur *l.* China **74** B3
Qagan Us *Nei Mongol* China **73** K4
Qagan Us *Qinghai* China *see* **Dulan**
Qagbasêrag China **76** B2
Qagca China **76** C1
Qagcaka China **83** E2
Qagchêng China *see* **Xiangcheng**
Qahremānshahr Iran *see* **Kermānshāh**
Qaidam He *r.* China **83** H1
Qaidam Pendi *basin* China **80** H4
Qainaqangma China **83** G2
Qaisar, Koh-i- *mt.* Afgh. *see* **Qeyṣār, Kūh-e**
Qakar China **82** E1
Qalā Diza Iraq **91** G3
Qalagai Afgh. **89** H3
Qala-i-Kang Afgh. *see* **Kang**
Qal'aikhum Tajik. **89** H2
Qala Jamal Afgh. **89** F3
Qalansīyah Yemen **87** H7
Qala Shinia Takht Afgh. **89** G3
Qalāt Afgh. *see* **Kalāt**
Qal'at al Ḥiṣn Syria **85** C2
Qal'at al Mu'aẓẓam Saudi Arabia **90** E6
Qal'at Bīshah Saudi Arabia **86** F5
Qal'at Muqaybirah, Jabal *mt.* Syria **85** D2
Qal'eh Dāgh *mt.* Iran **88** B2
Qal'eh Tirpul Afgh. **89** F3
Qal'eh-ye Bost Afgh. **89** G4
Qal'eh-ye Now Afgh. **89** F3
Qal'eh-ye Shūrak *well* Iran **88** E3
Qalhāt Oman **88** E6
Qalīb Bāqūr *well* Iraq **91** G5
Qalluviartuuq, Lac *l.* Canada **122** G2
Qalyûb Egypt *see* **Qalyūb**
Qalyūb Egypt **90** C5
Qamalung China **76** C1
Qamanirjuaq Lake Canada **121** M2
Qamanittuaq Canada *see* **Baker Lake**
Qamashi Uzbek. **89** G2
Qamata S. Africa **101** H6
Qamdo China **76** C2
Qandahar Afgh. *see* **Kandahār**
Qandarānbāshī, Kūh-e *mt.* Iran **88** B2
Qandyaghash Kazakh. *see* **Kandyagash**
Qangzê China **82** D3
Qapan Iran **88** D2
Qapshagay Kazakh. *see* **Kapchagay**
Qapshagay Bögeni *resr* Kazakh. *see* **Kapchagayskoye Vodokhranilishche**
Qapugtang China *see* **Zadoi**
Qaqortoq Greenland **119** N3
Qara Āghach *r.* Iran *see* **Mand, Rūd-e**
Qarabutaq Kazakh. *see* **Karabutak**
Qaraçala Azer. **88** C2
Qara Ertis *r.* China/Kazakh. *see* **Ertix He**
Qaraghandy Kazakh. *see* **Karaganda**
Qaraghayly Kazakh. *see* **Karagayly**
Qārah Egypt **90** B5
Qārah Saudi Arabia **91** F5
Qarah Bāgh Afgh. **89** H3
Qarak China **89** J2
Qaraqum *des.* Turkm. *see* **Garagum**
Qaraqum *des.* Turkm. *see* **Karakum Desert**
Qara Quzi Iran **88** D2
Qarasu Azer. **91** H2
Qara Şū Chāy *r.* Syria/Turkey *see* **Karasu**
Qara Tarai *mt.* Afgh. **89** G3
Qarataū Kazakh. *see* **Karatau**
Qarataū Zhotasy *mts* Kazakh. *see* **Karatau, Khrebet**
Qara Tikan Iran **88** C2
Qarazhal Kazakh. *see* **Karazhal**
Qardho Somalia **98** E3
Qareh Chāy *r.* Iran **88** C3
Qareh Sū *r.* Iran **88** B2
Qareh Tekān Iran **89** F2
Qarhan China **83** H1
Qarkilik China *see* **Ruoqiang**
Qarn al Kabsh, Jabal *mt.* Egypt **90** D5
Qarnayn *i.* U.A.E. **88** D5
Qarnein *i.* U.A.E. *see* **Qarnayn**

Qarn el Kabsh, Gebel *mt.* Egypt *see* **Qarn al Kabsh, Jabal**
Qarnobcho'l cho'li *plain* Uzbek. **89** G2
Qarokŭl *l.* Tajik. **89** I2
Qarqan China *see* **Qiemo**
Qarqan He *r.* China **80** G4
Qarqaraly Kazakh. *see* **Karkaralinsk**
Qarshi Uzbek. **89** G2
Qarshi cho'li *plain* Uzbek. **89** G2
Qarshi Chŭli *plain* Uzbek. *see* **Qarshi cho'li**
Qartaba Lebanon **85** B2
Qārūh, Jazīrat *i.* Kuwait **88** C4
Qārūn, Birkat *l.* Egypt **90** C5
Qârûn, Birket *l.* Egypt *see* **Qārūn, Birkat**
Qaryat al Gharab Iraq **91** G5
Qaryat al Ulyā Saudi Arabia **88** B5
Qasa Murg *mts* Afgh. **89** F3
Qāsemābād Iran **88** E3
Qash Qai *reg.* Iran **88** C4
Qasigiannguit Greenland **119** M3
Qaşr al Azraq Jordan **85** C4
Qaşr al Farāfirah Egypt **90** B6
Qaşr al Kharānah Jordan **85** C4
Qasr al Khubbāz Iraq **91** F4
Qaşr 'Amrah *tourist site* Jordan **85** C4
Qaşr Burqu' *tourist site* Jordan **85** C3
Qaşr-e Shīrīn Iran **88** B3
Qaşr Farâfra Egypt *see* **Qaşr al Farāfirah**
Qassimiut Greenland **119** N3
Qaţanā Syria **85** C3
Qatar *country* Asia **88** C5
Qaţmah Syria **85** C1
Qaţrūyeh Iran **88** D4
Qaţţāfī, Wādī al *watercourse* Jordan **85** C4
Qaţţâra, Râs *esc.* Egypt *see* **Qaţţārah, Ra's**
Qattara Depression Egypt **90** B5
Qaţţārah, Ra's *esc.* Egypt **90** B5
Qaţţīnah, Buḩayrat *resr* Syria **85** C2
Qax Azer. **91** G2
Qāyen Iran **88** E3
Qaynar Kazakh. *see* **Kaynar**
Qayşār Afgh. **89** G3
Qaysīyah, Qā' al *imp. l.* Jordan **85** C4
Qaysūm, Juzur *is* Egypt **90** D6
Qayyārah Iraq **91** F4
Qazangödağ *mt.* Armenia/Azer. **91** G3
Qazaq Shyghanaghy *b.* Kazakh. *see* **Kazakhskiy Zaliv**
Qazaqstan *country* Asia *see* **Kazakhstan**
Qazax Azer. **86** G1
Qazi Ahmad Pak. **89** H5
Qazımämmäd Azer. **91** H2
Qazvīn Iran **88** C2
Qeisûm, Gezâ'ir *is* Egypt *see* **Qaysūm, Juzur**
Qeisum Islands Egypt *see* **Qaysūm, Juzur**
Qena Egypt *see* **Qinā**
Qeqertarsuaq Greenland **119** M3
Qeqertarsuaq *i.* Greenland **119** M3
Qeqertarsuatsiaat Greenland **119** M3
Qeqertarsuup Tunua *b.* Greenland **119** M3
Qeshm Iran **88** E5
Qeydār Iran **88** C2
Qeydū Iran **88** C3
Qeyşār, Kūh-e *mt.* Afgh. **89** G3
Qezel Owzan, Rūdkhāneh-ye *r.* Iran **88** C2
Qeẕi'ot Israel **85** B4
Qian'an China **74** B3
Qian Gorlos China *see* **Qianguozhen**
Qianguozhen China **74** B3
Qianjiang *Chongqing* China **77** F2
Qianjiang *Hubei* China **77** G2
Qianjin *Heilong.* China **74** D3
Qianjin *Jilin* China **74** C3
Qianning China **76** D2
Qianqihao China **74** A3
Qian Shan *mts* China **74** A4
Qianxi China **76** E3
Qiaocheng China *see* **Bozhou**
Qiaojia China **76** D3
Qiaoshan China *see* **Huangling**
Qiaowa China *see* **Muli**
Qiaowan China **80** I3
Qiaozhuang China *see* **Qingchuan**
Qibā' Saudi Arabia **91** G6
Qibing S. Africa **101** H5
Qichun China **77** G2
Qidong China **77** G3
Qidukou China **76** B1
Qiemo China **80** G4
Qijiang China **76** E2
Qijiaojing China **80** H3
Qikiqtarjuaq Canada **119** L3
Qila Ladgasht Pak. **89** F5
Qila Saifullah Pak. **89** H4
Qilian China **80** J4
Qilian Shan *mts* China **80** I4
Qillak *i.* Greenland **119** O3
Qiman Tag *mts* China **83** G1
Qimusseriarsuaq *b.* Greenland **119** L2
Qinā Egypt **86** D4
Qin'an China **76** E1
Qincheng China *see* **Nanfeng**
Qing'an China **74** B3
Qingchuan China **76** E1
Qingdao China **73** M5
Qinggang China **74** B3
Qinggil China *see* **Qinghe**
Qinghai *prov.* China **76** B1
Qinghai Hu *salt l.* China **80** J4
Qinghai Nanshan *mts* China **80** I4
Qinghe *Heilong.* China **74** C3
Qinghe *Xinjiang* China **80** H2
Qinghecheng China **74** B4
Qinghua China *see* **Bo'ai**
Qingjiang *Jiangsu* China *see* **Huai'an**
Qingjiang *Jiangxi* China *see* **Zhangshu**
Qing Jiang *r.* China **77** F2
Qingkou China *see* **Ganyu**
Qinglan China **77** F5
Qingliu China **77** H3
Qinglung China **83** G3
Qingpu China **77** I2
Qingquan China *see* **Xishui**
Qingshan China *see* **Wudalianchi**
Qingshui China **76** E1
Qingshuihe *Nei Mongol* China **73** K5
Qingshuihe *Qinghai* China **76** C1
Qingtian China **77** I2
Qingyang *Anhui* China **77** H2
Qingyang *Gansu* China **76** E1
Qingyang *Jiangsu* China *see* **Sihong**

Qingyuan *Gansu* China *see* **Weiyuan**
Qingyuan *Guangdong* China **77** G4
Qingyuan *Guangxi* China *see* **Yizhou**
Qingyuan *Liaoning* China **74** B4
Qingyuan *Zhejiang* China **77** H3
Qingzang Gaoyuan *plat.* China *see* **Tibet, Plateau of**
Qingzhen China **76** E3
Qinhuangdao China **73** L5
Qinjiang China *see* **Shicheng**
Qin Ling *mts* China **76** E1
Qinshui China **77** G1
Qinting China *see* **Lianhua**
Qinzhou China **77** F4
Qionghai China **77** F5
Qiongjiexue China *see* **Qonggyai**
Qionglai China **76** D2
Qionglai Shan *mts* China **76** D2
Qiongxi China *see* **Hongyuan**
Qiongzhong China **77** F5
Qiongzhou Haixia *strait* China *see* **Hainan Strait**
Qiqian China **74** A1
Qiqihar China **74** A3
Qīr Iran **88** D4
Qira China **82** E1
Qîraîya, Wâdi *watercourse* Egypt *see* **Qurayyah, Wādī**
Qiryat Israel **85** B3
Qiryat Shemona Israel **85** B3
Qishan China **76** E1
Qishon *r.* Israel **85** B3
Qitab ash Shāmah *vol. crater* Saudi Arabia **85** C4
Qitaihe China **74** C3
Qiubei China **76** E3
Qiujin China **77** G2
Qixing He *r.* China **74** D3
Qiyang China **77** F3
Qizhou Liedao *i.* China **77** F5
Qızılağac Körfäzi *b.* Azer. **88** C2
Qizil-Art, Aghbai *pass* Kyrg./Tajik. *see* **Kyzylart Pass**
Qizilqum *des.* Kazakh./Uzbek. *see* **Kyzylkum Desert**
Qizilrabot Tajik. **89** I2
Qogir Feng *mt.* China/Pakistan *see* **K2**
Qog Qi China *see* **Sain Us**
Qom Iran **88** C3
Qomdo China *see* **Qumdo**
Qomīsheh Iran *see* **Shahrezā**
Qomolangma Feng *mt.* China/Nepal *see* **Everest, Mount**
Qomsheh Iran *see* **Shahrezā**
Qonāq, Kūh-e *hill* Iran **88** C3
Qondūz Afgh. *see* **Kunduz**
Qonggyai China **83** G3
Qo'ng'irot Uzbek. **80** A3
Qong Muztag *mt.* China **83** E2
Qongrat Uzbek. *see* **Qo'ng'irot**
Qoornoq Greenland **119** M3
Qoqek China *see* **Tacheng**
Qo'qon Uzbek. **80** D3
Qorako'l Uzbek. **89** F2
Qorghalzhyn Kazakh. *see* **Korgalzhyn**
Qornet es Saouda *mt.* Lebanon **85** C2
Qorovulbozor Uzbek. **89** G2
Qorowulbozor Uzbek. *see* **Qorovulbozor**
Qorveh Iran **88** B3
Qo'shrabot Uzbek. **89** G1
Qosh Tepe Iraq **91** F3
Qostanay Kazakh. *see* **Kostanay**
Qoubaiyat Lebanon **85** C2
Qowowuyag *mt.* China/Nepal *see* **Cho Oyu**
Qozideh Tajik. **89** H2
Quabbin Reservoir U.S.A. **135** I2
Quadra Island Canada **120** E5
Quadros, Lago dos *l.* Brazil **145** A5
Quaidabad Pak. **89** H3
Quail Mountains U.S.A. **128** E4
Quairading Australia **109** B8
Quakenbrück Germany **53** H2
Quakertown U.S.A. **135** H3
Quambatook Australia **112** A5
Quambone Australia **112** C3
Quamby Australia **110** C4
Quanah U.S.A. **131** D5
Quanbao Shan *mt.* China **77** F1
Quan Dao Hoang Sa *is* S. China Sea *see* **Paracel Islands**
Quân Đao Nam Du *i.* Vietnam **71** D5
Quan Dao Truong Sa *is* S. China Sea *see* **Spratly Islands**
Quang Ha Vietnam **70** D2
Quang Ngai Vietnam **70** E4
Quang Tri Vietnam **70** D3
Quan Hoa Vietnam **70** D2
Quan Long Vietnam *see* **Ca Mau**
Quannan China **77** G3
Quan Phu Quoc *i.* Vietnam *see* **Phu Quôc, Đao**
Quantock Hills U.K. **49** D7
Quanwan *H.K.* China *see* **Tsuen Wan**
Quanzhou *Fujian* China **77** H3
Quanzhou *Guangxi* China **77** F3
Qu'Appelle *r.* Canada **121** K5
Quaqtaq Canada **119** L3
Quarry Bay *H.K.* China **77** [inset]
Quartu Sant'Elena *Sardinia* Italy **58** C5
Quartzite Mountain U.S.A. **128** E3
Quartzsite U.S.A. **129** F5
Quba Azer. **91** H2
Quchan Iran **88** E2
Qudaym Syria **85** D2
Queanbeyan Australia **112** D5

▶**Québec** Canada **123** H5
Capital of Québec.

Québec *prov.* Canada **135** I1
Quebra Anzol *r.* Brazil **145** B2
Quedlinburg Germany **53** L3
Queen Adelaide Islands Chile *see* **La Reina Adelaida, Archipiélago de**
Queen Anne U.S.A. **135** H4
Queen Bess, Mount Canada **126** B2
Queen Charlotte Canada **120** C4
Queen Charlotte Islands Canada **120** C4
Queen Charlotte Sound *sea chan.* Canada **120** D5
Queen Charlotte Strait Canada **120** E5
Queen Creek U.S.A. **129** H5

Queen Elizabeth Islands Canada **119** H2
Queen Elizabeth National Park Uganda **98** C4
Queen Mary Land *reg.* Antarctica **152** F2
Queen Maud Gulf Canada **119** H3
Queen Maud Land *reg.* Antarctica **148** G10
Queen Maud Land *reg.* Antarctica **152** C2
Queen Maud Mountains Antarctica **152** J1
Queenscliff Australia **112** B7
Queensland *state* Australia **112** B1
Queenstown Australia **111** [inset]
Queenstown Ireland *see* **Cobh**
Queenstown N.Z. **113** B7
Queenstown S. Africa **101** H6
Queenstown Sing. **71** [inset]
Queets U.S.A. **126** B3
Queimada, Ilha *i.* Brazil **143** H4
Quelimane Moz. **99** D5
Quellón Chile **144** B6
Quelpart Island S. Korea *see* **Cheju-do**
Quemado U.S.A. **129** I4
Quemoy *i.* Taiwan *see* **Chinmen Tao**
Que Que Zimbabwe *see* **Kwekwe**
Querétaro Mex. **136** D4
Querétaro de Arteaga Mex. *see* **Querétaro**
Querfurt Germany **53** L3
Querobabi Mex. **127** F7
Quesnel Canada **120** F4
Quesnel Lake Canada **120** F4
Quetta Pak. **89** G4
Quetzaltenango Guat. **136** F6
Queuco Chile **144** B5
Quezaltenango Guat. *see* **Quetzaltenango**

▶**Quezon City** Phil. **69** G4
Former capital of the Philippines.

Qufu China **77** H1
Quibala Angola **99** B5
Quibaxe Angola **99** B4
Quibdó Col. **142** C2
Quiberon France **56** C3
Quiçama, Parque Nacional do *nat. park* Angola **99** B4
Qui Châu Vietnam **70** D3
Quiet Lake Canada **120** C2
Quilengues Angola **99** B5
Quillabamba Peru **142** D6
Quillacollo Bol. **142** E7
Quillan France **56** F5
Quill Lakes Canada **121** J5
Quilmes Arg. **144** E4
Quilon India **84** C4
Quilpie Australia **112** B1
Quilpué Chile **144** B4
Quimbele Angola **99** B4
Quimilí Arg. **144** D3
Quimper France **56** B3
Quimperlé France **56** C3
Quinag *hill* U.K. **50** D2
Quincy *CA* U.S.A. **128** C2
Quincy *FL* U.S.A. **133** C6
Quincy *IL* U.S.A. **130** F4
Quincy *IN* U.S.A. **134** B4
Quincy *MA* U.S.A. **135** J2
Quincy *MI* U.S.A. **134** C3
Quincy *OH* U.S.A. **134** D3
Quines Arg. **144** C4
Quinga Moz. **99** E5
Quinn Canyon Range *mts* U.S.A. **129** F3
Quinto Spain **57** F3
Quionga Moz. **99** E5
Quipungo Angola **99** B5
Quirima Angola **99** B5
Quirimbas, Parque Nacional das *nat. park* **99** E5
Quirindi Australia **112** E3
Quirinópolis Brazil **145** A2
Quissanga Moz. **99** E5
Quissico Moz. **101** L3
Quitapa Angola **99** B5
Quitilipi Arg. **144** D3
Quitman *GA* U.S.A. **133** D6
Quitman *MS* U.S.A. **131** F5

▶**Quito** Ecuador **142** C4
Capital of Ecuador.

Quitovac Mex. **127** E7
Quixadá Brazil **143** K4
Quixeramobim Brazil **143** K5
Qujiang *Guangdong* China **77** G3
Qujiang *Sichuan* China *see* **Quxian**
Qujie China **77** F4
Qujing China **76** D3
Qulandy Kazakh. *see* **Kulandy**
Qulbān Layyah *well* Iraq **88** B4
Qulin Gol *r.* China **74** A3
Qulsary Kazakh. *see* **Kul'sary**
Qulyndy Zhazyghy *plain* Kazakh./Rus. Fed. *see* **Kulundinskaya Step'**
Qulzum, Baḩr al Egypt *see* **Suez Bay**
Qumar He *r.* China **72** G6
Qumarheyan China **80** H4
Qumarlêb China *see* **Sêrwolungwa**
Qumarrabdün China **76** B1
Qumbu S. Africa **101** I6
Qumdo China **76** B2
Qumqo'rg'on Uzbek. **89** G2
Qumqŭrghon Uzbek. *see* **Qumqo'rg'on**
Qumrha S. Africa **101** H7
Qumulangma *mt.* China/Nepal *see* **Everest, Mount**
Qunayy *well* Saudi Arabia **88** B6
Qundūz Afgh. *see* **Kunduz**
Qŭnghirot Uzbek. *see* **Qo'ng'irot**
Quntamari China **83** G2
Qu'nyido China **76** C2
Quoich *r.* Canada **121** M1
Quoich, Loch *l.* U.K. **50** D3
Quoile *r.* U.K. **51** G3
Quoin Point S. Africa **100** D8
Quoxo *r.* Botswana **100** G2
Qŭqon Uzbek. *see* **Qo'qon**
Qurama, Qatorkŭhi *mts* Asia *see* **Kurama Range**
Qurama Tizmasi *mts* Asia *see* **Kurama Range**
Qurayyah, Wādī *watercourse* Egypt **85** B4
Qurayyat al Milḩ *l.* Jordan **85** C4
Qŭrghonteppa Tajik. **89** H2
Qusar Azer. **91** H2
Qushan China *see* **Beichuan**
Qŭshrabot Uzbek. *see* **Qo'shrabot**
Qusmuryn Kazakh. *see* **Kushmurun**
Qusum China **82** D2
Quthing Lesotho *see* **Moyeni**
Quttinirpaaq National Park Canada **119** K1
Quwayq, Nahr *r.* Syria/Turkey **85** C2
Quxar China *see* **Lhazê**
Quxian *Sichuan* China **76** E2
Quxian *Zhejiang* China *see* **Quzhou**
Quyang China *see* **Jingzhou**
Quyghan Kazakh. *see* **Kuygan**
Quy Nhơn Vietnam **71** E4
Quyon Canada **135** G1
Qüyün Eshek *i.* Iran **88** B2
Quzhou China **77** H2
Qypshaq Köli *salt l.* Kazakh. *see* **Kypshak, Ozero**
Qyrghyz Zhotasy *mts* Kazakh./Kyrg. *see* **Kirghiz Range**
Qyteti Stalin Albania *see* **Kuçovë**
Qyzylorda Kazakh. *see* **Kyzylorda**
Qyzylqum *des.* Kazakh./Uzbek. *see* **Kyzylkum Desert**
Qyzyltū Kazakh. *see* **Kishkenekol'**
Qyzylzhar Kazakh. *see* **Kyzylzhar**

Raa Atoll Maldives *see* **North Maalhosmadulu Atoll**
Raab *r.* Austria **47** P7
Raab Hungary *see* **Győr**
Raahe Fin. **44** N4
Rääkkylä Fin. **44** P5
Raalte Neth. **52** G2
Raanujärvi Fin. **44** N3
Raasay *i.* U.K. **50** C3
Raasay, Sound of *sea chan.* U.K. **50** C3
Raba Indon. **108** B2
Rabang China **82** E2
Rabat *Gozo* Malta *see* **Victoria**
Rabat Malta **58** F7

▶**Rabat** Morocco **54** C5
Capital of Morocco.

Rabaul P.N.G. **106** F2
Rabbath Ammon Jordan *see* **'Ammān**
Rabbit *r.* Canada **120** E3
Rabbit Flat Australia **108** E5
Rabbitskin *r.* Canada **120** F2
Rābigh Saudi Arabia **86** E5
Rabnabad Islands Bangl. **83** G5
Râbniţa Moldova *see* **Rîbniţa**
Rabocheostrovsk Rus. Fed. **42** G2
Racaka China **76** C2
Raccoon Cay *i.* Bahamas **133** F8
Race, Cape Canada **123** L5
Race Point U.S.A. **135** J2
Rachaïya Lebanon **85** B3
Rachal U.S.A. **131** D7
Rachaya Lebanon *see* **Rachaïya**
Rachel U.S.A. **129** F3
Rach Gia Vietnam **71** D5
Rach Gia, Vinh *b.* Vietnam **71** D5
Racibórz Poland **47** Q5
Racine *WI* U.S.A. **134** B2
Racine *WV* U.S.A. **134** E4
Rădăuţi Romania **43** E7
Radcliff U.S.A. **134** C5
Radde Rus. Fed. **74** C2
Radford U.S.A. **134** E5
Radisson *Que.* Canada **122** F3
Radisson *Sask.* Canada **121** J4
Radlinski, Mount Antarctica **152** K1
Radnevo Bulg. **59** K3
Radom Poland **47** R5
Radom Sudan **97** F4
Radomir Bulg. **59** J3
Radom National Park Sudan **97** F4
Radomsko Poland **47** Q5
Radoviš Macedonia **90** A2
Radstock U.K. **49** E7
Radstock, Cape Australia **109** F8
Radun' Belarus **45** N9
Radviliškis Lith. **45** M9
Radyvyliv Ukr. **43** E6
Rae Bareli India **82** E4
Raeside, Lake *salt flat* Australia **109** C7
Raetihi N.Z. **113** E4
Rāf *hill* Saudi Arabia **91** E5
Rafaela Arg. **144** D4
Rafaḩ Gaza *see* **Rafiah**
Rafaï Cent. Afr. Rep. **98** C3
Rafḩā' Saudi Arabia **91** F5
Rafiah Gaza **85** B4
Rafsanjān Iran **88** D4
Raft *r.* U.S.A. **126** E4
Raga Sudan **97** F4
Rāgelin Germany **53** M1
Ragged, Mount *hill* Australia **109** C8
Ragged Island Bahamas **133** F8
Rāgh Afgh. **89** H2
Rago Nasjonalpark *nat. park* Norway **44** J3
Ragösen Germany **53** M2
Ragueneau Canada **123** H4
Raguhn Germany **53** M3
Ragusa Croatia *see* **Dubrovnik**
Ragusa *Sicily* Italy **58** F6
Ra'gyagoinba China **76** D1
Raha Indon. **69** G7
Rahachow Belarus **43** F5
Rahad *r.* Sudan **86** D7
Rahaeng Thai. *see* **Tak**
Rahden Germany **53** I2
Rahimyar Khan Pak. **89** H4
Rahovec Kosovo **59** I3
Rahuri India **84** B2
Rai, Hon *i.* Vietnam **71** D5
Raiatea *i.* Fr. Polynesia **151** J7
Raibu *i.* Indon. *see* **Air**
Raichur India **84** C2
Raiganj India **83** G4
Raigarh *Chhattisgarh* India **83** E5
Raigarh *Orissa* India **84** D2
Raijua *i.* Indon. **108** C2
Railroad Pass U.S.A. **128** E2
Railroad Valley U.S.A. **129** F2
Raimangal *r.* Bangl. **83** G5
Raimbault, Lac *l.* Canada **123** H3
Rainbow Lake Canada **120** G3
Raine Island Australia **110** D1
Rainelle U.S.A. **134** E5
Raini *r.* Pak. **89** H4
Rainier, Mount *vol.* U.S.A. **126** C3
Rainy *r.* Canada/U.S.A. **121** M5
Rainy Lake Canada/U.S.A. **125** I2
Rainy River Canada **121** M5
Raipur *Chhattisgarh* India **83** E5
Raipur *W. Bengal* India **83** F5
Raisen India **82** D5
Raisio Fin. **45** M6
Raismes France **52** D4
Raitalai India **82** D5
Raivavae *i.* Fr. Polynesia **151** K7
Raiwind Pak. **89** I4
Raja, Ujung *pt* Indon. **71** B7
Rajaampat, Kepulauan *is* Indon. **69** H7
Rajahmundry India **84** D2
Raja-Jooseppi Fin. **44** P2
Rajanpur Pak. **89** H4
Rajapalaiyam India **84** C4
Rajapur India **84** B2
Rajasthan *state* India **82** C4
Rajasthan Canal India **82** C3
Rajauri India *see* **Rajouri**
Rajevadi India **84** B2
Rajgarh India **82** D4
Rájijovsset Fin. *see* **Raja-Jooseppi**
Rajkot India **82** B5
Raj Mahal India **82** C4
Rajmahal Hills India **83** F4
Raj Nandgaon India **82** E5
Rajouri India **82** C2
Rajpipla India **82** C5
Rajpur India **82** C5
Rajpura India **82** D3
Rajputana Agency *state* India *see* **Rajasthan**
Rajsamand India **82** C4
Rajshahi Bangl. **83** G4
Rājū Syria **85** C1
Rajula India **84** A1
Rajur India **84** C1
Rajura India **84** C2
Raka China **83** F3
Rakan, Ra's *pt* Qatar **88** C5
Rakaposhi *mt.* Pak. **82** C1
Raka Zangbo *r.* China *see* **Dogxung Zangbo**
Rakhiv Ukr. **43** E6
Rakhni Pak. **89** H4
Rakhni *r.* Pak. **89** H4
Rakhshan *r.* Pak. **89** F5
Rakitnoye *Belgorodskaya Oblast'* Rus. Fed. **43** G6
Rakitnoye *Primorskiy Kray* Rus. Fed. **74** D3
Rakiura *i.* N.Z. *see* **Stewart Island**
Rakke Estonia **45** O7
Rakkestad Norway **45** G7
Rakovski Bulg. **59** K3
Rakushechnyy, Mys *pt* Kazakh. **91** H2
Rakvere Estonia **45** O7

▶**Raleigh** U.S.A. **132** E5
Capital of North Carolina.

Ralston U.S.A. **135** G3
Ram *r.* Canada **120** F2
Ramādī Iraq **91** F4
Ramagiri India **84** E2
Ramah U.S.A. **129** I4
Ramalho, Serra do *hills* Brazil **145** B1
Rāmallāh West Bank **85** B4
Ramanagaram India **84** C3
Ramanathapuram India **84** C4
Ramapo Deep *sea feature* N. Pacific Ocean **150** F3
Ramapur India **84** D1
Ramas, Cape India **84** B3
Ramatlabama S. Africa **101** G3
Rambhapur India **82** C5
Rambouillet France **52** B6
Rambutyo Island P.N.G. **69** L7
Rame Head *hd* Australia **112** D6
Rame Head *hd* U.K. **49** C8
Rameshki Rus. Fed. **42** H4
Ramezān Kalak Iran **89** F5
Ramgarh *Jharkhand* India **83** F5
Ramgarh *Rajasthan* India **82** B4
Ramgarh *Rajasthan* India **82** C3
Ramgul *reg.* Afgh. **89** H3
Rāmhormoz Iran **88** C4
Ramingining Australia **108** F3
Ramitan Uzbek. *see* **Romiton**
Ramla Israel **85** B4
Ramlat Rabyānah *des.* Libya *see* **Rebiana Sand Sea**
Ramm, Jabal *mts* Jordan **85** B5
Ramnad India *see* **Ramanathapuram**
Râmnicu Sărat Romania **59** L2
Râmnicu Vâlcea Romania **59** K2
Ramon' Rus. Fed. **43** H6
Ramona U.S.A. **128** E5
Ramos *r.* Mex. **131** B7
Ramotswa Botswana **101** G3
Rampart of Genghis Khan *tourist site* Asia **73** K3
Rampur India **82** D3
Rampur Boalia Bangl. *see* **Rajshahi**
Ramree Myanmar **70** A3
Ramree Island Myanmar **70** A3
Rāmsar Iran **88** C2
Ramsele Sweden **44** J5
Ramsey Isle of Man **48** C4
Ramsey U.K. **49** G6
Ramsey U.S.A. **135** H3
Ramsey Bay Isle of Man **48** C4
Ramsey Island U.K. **49** B7
Ramsey Lake Canada **122** E5
Ramsgate U.K. **49** I7
Rāmshir Iran **88** C4
Ramsing *mt.* India **83** H3
Ramu Bangl. **83** H5
Ramusio, Lac *l.* Canada **123** J3
Ramygala Lith. **45** N9
Ranaghat India **83** G5
Ranai *i.* U.S.A. *see* **Lāna'i**
Rana Pratap Sagar *resr* India **82** C4
Ranapur India **82** C5
Ranasar India **82** B4
Rancagua Chile **144** B4
Rancharia Brazil **145** A3
Rancheria Canada **120** D2
Rancheria *r.* Canada **120** D2
Ranchi India **83** F5
Ranco, Lago *l.* Chile **144** B6
Rand Australia **112** C5
Randalstown U.K. **51** F3
Randers Denmark **45** G8
Randijaure *l.* Sweden **44** K3
Randolph *ME* U.S.A. **135** K1
Randolph *UT* U.S.A. **126** F4
Randolph *VT* U.S.A. **135** I2
Randsjö Sweden **44** H5
Råneå Sweden **44** M4
Ranérou Senegal **96** B3
Ranfurly N.Z. **113** C7
Rangae Thai. **71** C6
Rangamati Bangl. **83** H5
Rangapara India **83** H4
Rangeley Lake U.S.A. **135** J1
Rangely U.S.A. **129** I1
Ranger Lake Canada **122** E5
Rangiora N.Z. **113** D6
Rangitata *r.* N.Z. **113** C7
Rangitikei *r.* N.Z. **113** E5
Rangke China *see* **Zamtang**
Rangkŭl Tajik. **89** I2
Rangôn Myanmar *see* **Rangoon**

▶**Rangoon** Myanmar **70** B3
Joint capital (with Nay Pyi Taw) of Myanmar.

Rangoon *r.* Myanmar **70** B3
Rangpur Bangl. **83** G4
Rangsang *i.* Indon. **71** C7
Rangse Myanmar **70** A1
Ranibennur India **84** B3
Raniganj India **83** F5
Ranipur Pak. **89** H5
Raniwara India **82** C4
Rankin U.S.A. **131** C6
Rankin Inlet Canada **121** M2
Rankin's Springs Australia **112** C4
Ranna Estonia **45** O7
Rannes Australia **110** E5
Rannoch, Loch U.K. **50** E4
Ranong Thai. **71** B5
Ranot Thai. **71** C6
Ranpur India **82** B5
Rānsa Iran **88** C3
Ransby Sweden **45** H6
Rantasalmi Fin. **44** P5
Rantau *i.* Indon. **71** C7
Rantauprapat Indon. **71** B7
Rantoul U.S.A. **134** A3
Rantsila Fin. **44** N4
Ranua Fin. **44** O4
Rānya Iraq **91** G3
Ranyah, Wādī *watercourse* Saudi Arabia **86** F5
Rao Go *mt.* Laos/Vietnam **70** D3
Raohe China **74** D3
Raoul Island Kermadec Is **107** I4
Rapa *i.* Fr. Polynesia **151** K7
Rapa-iti *i.* Fr. Polynesia *see* **Rapa**
Rapallo Italy **58** C2
Rapar India **82** B5
Raphoe Ireland **51** E3
Rapidan *r.* U.S.A. **135** G4
Rapid City U.S.A. **130** C2
Rapid River U.S.A. **132** C2
Rapla Estonia **45** N7
Rapur *Andhra Prad.* India **84** C3
Rapur *Gujarat* India **82** B5
Raqqa Syria *see* **Ar Raqqah**
Raquette Lake U.S.A. **135** H2
Rara National Park Nepal **83** E3
Raritan Bay U.S.A. **135** H3
Rarkan Pak. **89** H4
Raroia *atoll* Fr. Polynesia **151** K7
Rarotonga *i.* Cook Is **151** J7
Ras India **82** C4
Rasa, Punta *pt* Arg. **144** D6
Ra's ad Daqm Oman **87** I6
Ra's al Ḩikmah Egypt **90** B5
Ras al Khaimah U.A.E. *see* **Ra's al Khaymah**
Ra's al Khaymah U.A.E. **88** D5
Ra's an Naqb Jordan **85** B4
Ras Dashen *mt.* Eth. *see* **Ras Dejen**

▶**Ras Dejen** *mt.* Eth. **98** D2
5th highest mountain in Africa.

Raseiniai Lith. **45** M9
Râs el Hikma Egypt *see* **Ra's al Ḩikmah**
Ra's Ghārib Egypt **90** D5
Rashad Sudan **86** D7
Rashīd Egypt **90** C5
Rashīd Egypt *see* **Rashīd**
Rashid Qala Afgh. **89** G4
Rashm Iran **88** D3
Rasht Iran **88** C2
Raskam *mts* China **82** C1
Ras Koh *mt.* Pak. **89** G4
Raskoh *mts* Pak. **89** G4
Raso, Cabo *c.* Arg. **144** C6
Raso da Catarina *hills* Brazil **143** K5
Rason Lake *salt flat* Australia **109** D7
Rasony Belarus **45** P9
Rasra India **83** E4
Rasshua, Ostrov *i.* Rus. Fed. **73** S3
Rass Jebel Tunisia **58** D6
Rasskazovo Rus. Fed. **43** I5
Rastatt Germany **53** I6
Rastede Germany **53** I1
Rastow Germany **53** L1
Rasūl *watercourse* Iran **88** D5
Rasul Pak. **89** I3
Ratae U.K. *see* **Leicester**
Rätan Sweden **44** I5
Ratanda S. Africa **101** I4
Ratangarh India **82** C3
Rätansbyn Sweden **44** I5
Rat Buri Thai. **71** B4
Rathangan Ireland **51** F4
Rathbun Lake U.S.A. **130** E3
Rathdowney Ireland **51** E5
Rathdrum Ireland **51** F5
Rathedaung Myanmar **70** A2
Rathenow Germany **53** M2
Rathfriland U.K. **51** F3
Rathkeale Ireland **51** D5
Rathlin Island U.K. **51** F2
Ratibor Poland *see* **Racibórz**
Ratingen Germany **52** G3
Ratisbon Germany *see* **Regensburg**
Ratiya India **82** C3
Rat Lake Canada **121** L3
Ratlam India **82** C5
Ratnagiri India **84** B2
Ratnapura Sri Lanka **84** D5
Ratne Ukr. **43** E6
Ratno Ukr. *see* **Ratne**
Raton U.S.A. **127** G5
Rattray Head *hd* U.K. **50** H3
Rättvik Sweden **45** I6
Ratz, Mount Canada **120** C3
Ratzeburg Germany **53** K1
Raub Malaysia **71** C7
Rauðamýri Iceland **44** [inset]
Raudhatain Kuwait **88** B4
Rauenstein Germany **53** L4
Raufarhöfn Iceland **44** [inset]
Raukumara Range *mts* N.Z. **113** F4
Raul Soares Brazil **145** C3
Rauma Fin. **45** L6
Raurkela India **83** F5
Rauschen Rus. Fed. *see* **Svetlogorsk**
Rausu Japan **74** G3
Rautavaara Fin. **44** P5
Rautjärvi Fin. **45** P6
Ravānsar Iran **88** B3
Rāvar Iran **88** E4
Ravat Kyrg. **89** H2
Ravels Belgium **52** E3
Ravena U.S.A. **135** I2
Ravenglass U.K. **48** D4
Ravenna Italy **58** E2
Ravenna *NE* U.S.A. **130** D3
Ravenna *OH* U.S.A. **134** E3
Ravensburg Germany **47** L7
Ravenshoe Australia **110** D3
Ravenswood Australia **110** D4
Ravi *r.* Pak. **89** H4
Ravnina Turkm. *see* **Rawnina**
Rāwah Iraq **91** F4
Rawaki *i.* Kiribati **107** I2
Rawalpindi Pak. **89** I3
Rawalpindi Lake Canada **120** H1
Ŗawāndiz Iraq **91** G3
Rawi, Ko *i.* Thai. **71** B6
Rawicz Poland **47** P5
Rawlinna Australia **109** D7
Rawlins U.S.A. **126** G4
Rawlinson Range *hills* Australia **109** E6
Rawnina *Maryyskaya Oblast'* Turkm. **89** F2
Rawnina *Maryyskaya Oblast'* Turkm. **89** F2
Rawson Arg. **144** C6
Rawu China **76** C2
Raxón, Cerro *mt.* Guat. **136** G5
Ray, Cape Canada **123** K5
Raya, Bukit *mt.* Indon. **68** E7
Rayachoti India **84** C3
Rayadurg India **84** C3
Rayagada India **84** D2
Rayagarha India *see* **Rayagada**
Rayak Lebanon **85** C3
Raychikhinsk Rus. Fed. **74** C2
Raydah Yemen **86** F6
Rayes Peak U.S.A. **128** D4
Rayevskiy Rus. Fed. **41** Q5
Rayleigh U.K. **49** H7
Raymond U.S.A. **135** J2
Raymond Terrace Australia **112** E4
Raymondville U.S.A. **131** D7
Raymore Canada **121** J5
Rayner Glacier Antarctica **152** D2
Rayong Thai. **71** C4
Raystown Lake U.S.A. **135** F3
Raz, Pointe du *pt* France **56** B2
Razan Iran **88** C3
Rāzān Iran **88** C3
Razani Pak. **89** H3
Razāzah, Buḩayrat ar *l.* Iraq **91** F4
Razdan Armenia *see* **Hrazdan**
Razdel'naya Ukr. *see* **Rozdil'na**
Razdol'noye Rus. Fed. **74** C4
Razeh Iran **88** C3
Razgrad Bulg. **59** L3
Razim, Lacul *lag.* Romania **59** M2
Razisi China **76** D1
Razlog Bulg. **59** J4
Razmak Pak. **89** H3
Raz"yezd 3km Rus. Fed. *see* **Novyy Urgal**
Ré, Île de *i.* France **56** D3
Reading U.K. **49** G7
Reading *MI* U.S.A. **134** C3
Reading *OH* U.S.A. **134** C4
Reading *PA* U.S.A. **135** H3
Reagile S. Africa **101** H3
Realicó Arg. **144** D5
Réalmont France **56** F5
Reăng Kesei Cambodia **71** C4
Reate Italy *see* **Rieti**
Rebais France **52** D6
Rebecca, Lake *salt flat* Australia **109** C7
Rebiana Sand Sea *des.* Libya **97** F2
Reboly Rus. Fed. **44** Q5
Rebrikha Rus. Fed. **72** E2
Rebun-tō *i.* Japan **74** F3
Recherche, Archipelago of the *is* Australia **109** C8
Rechitsa Belarus *see* **Rechytsa**
Rechna Doab *lowland* Pak. **89** I4
Rechytsa Belarus **43** F5
Recife Brazil **143** L5
Recife, Cape S. Africa **101** G8
Recklinghausen Germany **53** H3
Reconquista Arg. **144** E3
Recreo Arg. **144** C3
Rectorville U.S.A. **134** D4
Red *r.* Australia **110** C3
Red *r.* Canada **120** E3
Red *r.* Canada/U.S.A. **130** D1
Red *r. TN* U.S.A. **134** B5
Red *r.* U.S.A. **131** F6
Red *r.* Vietnam **70** D2
Redang *i.* Malaysia **71** C6
Red Bank *NJ* U.S.A. **135** H3
Red Bank *TN* U.S.A. **133** C5
Red Basin China *see* **Sichuan Pendi**
Red Bay Canada **123** K4
Redberry Lake Canada **121** J4
Red Bluff U.S.A. **128** B1
Red Bluff Lake U.S.A. **131** C6
Red Butte *mt.* U.S.A. **129** G4
Redcar U.K. **48** F4
Redcliff Canada **126** F2
Redcliffe, Mount *hill* Australia **109** C7
Red Cliffs Australia **111** C7
Red Cloud U.S.A. **130** D3
Red Deer Canada **120** H4
Red Deer *r. Alberta/Saskatchewan* Canada **121** I5
Red Deer *r. Man./Sask.* Canada **121** K4
Red Deer Lake Canada **121** K4
Reddersburg S. Africa **101** H5
Redding U.S.A. **128** B1
Redditch U.K. **49** F6
Rede *r.* U.K. **48** E3
Redenção Brazil **143** H5
Redeyef Tunisia **58** C7
Redfield U.S.A. **130** D2
Red Granite Mountain Canada **120** B2
Red Hills U.S.A. **131** D4
Red Hook U.S.A. **135** I3
Red Indian Lake Canada **123** K4
Redkey U.S.A. **134** C3
Redkino Rus. Fed. **42** H4
Redknife *r.* Canada **120** G2
Red Lake Canada **121** M5
Red Lake U.S.A. **129** G4
Red Lake *r.* U.S.A. **130** D2
Red Lake Falls U.S.A. **121** L6
Red Lakes U.S.A. **130** E1
Redlands U.S.A. **128** E4
Red Lion U.S.A. **135** G4
Red Lodge U.S.A. **126** F3
Redmesa U.S.A. **129** I3
Redmond *OR* U.S.A. **126** C3
Redmond *UT* U.S.A. **129** H2
Red Oak U.S.A. **130** E3
Redonda Island Canada **120** E5
Redondo Port. **57** C4
Redondo Beach U.S.A. **128** D5
Red Peak U.S.A. **126** E3
Red River, Mouths of the Vietnam **70** D2
Red Rock Canada **122** C4
Red Rock *AZ* U.S.A. **129** H5
Redrock U.S.A. **129** I5
Red Rock *PA* U.S.A. **135** G3
Redrock Lake Canada **120** H1
Red Sea Africa/Asia **86** D4
Redstone *r.* Canada **120** E1
Red Sucker Lake Canada **121** M4
Reduzum Neth. **52** F1
Redwater Canada **120** H4
Redway U.S.A. **128** B1
Red Wing U.S.A. **130** E2
Redwood City U.S.A. **128** B3
Redwood Falls U.S.A. **130** E2
Redwood National Park U.S.A. **126** B4
Redwood Valley U.S.A. **128** B2
Ree, Lough *l.* Ireland **51** E4
Reed U.S.A. **134** B5
Reed City U.S.A. **134** C2
Reedley U.S.A. **128** D3
Reedsport U.S.A. **126** B4
Reedsville U.S.A. **134** E4
Reedville U.S.A. **135** G5
Reedy U.S.A. **134** E4
Reedy Glacier Antarctica **152** J1
Reefton N.Z. **113** C6
Rees Germany **52** G3
Reese U.S.A. **134** D2
Reese *r.* U.S.A. **128** E1
Refahiye Turkey **90** E3
Refugio U.S.A. **131** D6
Regen Germany **53** N6
Regen *r.* Germany **53** M5
Regência Brazil **145** D2
Regensburg Germany **53** M5
Regenstauf Germany **53** M5
Reggane Alg. **96** D2
Reggio *Calabria* Italy *see* **Reggio di Calabria**
Reggio *Emilia-Romagna* Italy *see* **Reggio nell'Emilia**
Reggio di Calabria Italy **58** F5
Reggio Emilia Italy *see* **Reggio nell'Emilia**
Reggio nell'Emilia Italy **58** D2
Reghin Romania **59** K1
Regi Afgh. **89** G3

▶**Regina** Canada **121** J5
Capital of Saskatchewan.

Régina Fr. Guiana **143** H3
Registān *reg.* Afgh. **89** G4
Registro Brazil **144** G2
Registro do Araguaia Brazil **145** A1
Regium Lepidum Italy *see* **Reggio nell'Emilia**
Regozero Rus. Fed. **44** Q4
Rehau Germany **53** M4
Rehburg (Rehburg-Loccum) Germany **53** J2
Rehli India **82** D5
Rehoboth Namibia **100** C2
Rehoboth Bay U.S.A. **135** H4
Reḩovot Israel **85** B4
Reïbell Alg. *see* **Ksar Chellala**
Reibitz Germany **53** M3
Reichenbach Germany **53** M4
Reichshoffen France **53** H6
Reid Australia **109** E7
Reidh, Rubha *pt* U.K. **50** D3
Reidsville U.S.A. **132** E4
Reigate U.K. **49** G7
Reiley Peak U.S.A. **129** H5
Reims France **52** E5
Reinbek Germany **53** K1
Reindeer *r.* Canada **121** K4
Reindeer Island Canada **121** L4
Reindeer Lake Canada **121** K3
Reine Norway **44** H3
Reinosa Spain **57** D2
Reinsfeld Germany **52** G5
Reiphólsfjöll *hill* Iceland **44** [inset]
Reisaelva *r.* Norway **44** L2
Reisa Nasjonalpark *nat. park* Norway **44** M2

sjärvi Fin. 44 N5
tz S. Africa 101 I4
kapalle India 84 D2
ken Germany 52 H3
iance Canada 121 I2
lizane Alg. 57 G6
lano Mex. 131 B7
llingen Germany 53 J1
magen Germany 53 H4
markable, Mount hill Australia 111 B7
medios Cuba 133 E8
meshk Iran 88 E5
mhoogte Pass Namibia 100 C2
mi France see Reims
mmel Mountain U.S.A. 126 C2
mscheid Germany 53 H3
na Norway 45 G6
naix Belgium see Ronse
nam Myanmar 76 C3
napur India 84 C2
ndsburg Germany 47 L3
né-Levasseur, Île i. Canada 123 H4
news Canada 123 L5
nfrew Canada 135 G1
nfrew U.K. 50 E5
ngali Reservoir India 83 F5
ngat Indon. 68 C7
ngo Chile 144 B4
n He r. China 77 F1
nheji China 77 G2
nhua China 77 G3
ni Ukr. 59 M2
nick U.S.A. 134 E5
nland reg. Greenland see Tuttut Nunaat
nnell i. Solomon Is 107 G3
nerod Germany 53 I4
nnes France 56 D2
nnick Glacier Antarctica 152 H2
nnie Canada 121 M5
no r. Italy 58 E2
no U.S.A. 128 D2
novo U.S.A. 135 G3
nsselaer U.S.A. 134 B3
nswoude Neth. 52 F2
nton U.S.A. 126 C3
o Burkina 96 C3
o Indon. 108 C2
palle India 84 D2
petek Turkm. 89 F2
petek Döwlet Gorugy nature res.
urkm. 89 F2
polka Rus. Fed. 45 P7
public U.S.A. 126 D2
publican r. U.S.A. 130 D4

epublic of South Africa country Africa
00 F5
th most populous country in Africa.

pulse Bay b. Australia 110 E4
pulse Bay Canada 119 J3
quena Peru 142 D5
quena Spain 57 F4
şadiye Turkey 90 E2
serva Brazil 145 A4
serve U.S.A. 129 I5
shi China 77 F2
shteh-ye Alborz mts Iran see
lburz Mountains
sistencia Arg. 144 E3
şiţa Romania 59 I2
solute Canada 119 I2
solute Bay Nunavut Canada see Resolute
solution Island Canada 119 L3
solution Island N.Z. 113 A7
splendor Brazil 145 C2
stigouche r. Canada 123 I5
sülayn Turkey see Ceylanpınar
talhuleu Guat. 136 F6
ezat, Parcul Național nat. park
omania 59 J2
ford U.K. 48 G5
hel France 52 E5
hem (Aller) Germany 53 J2
himnon Greece see Rethymno
hymno Greece 59 K7
reat Australia 110 C5
tden Germany 53 M2

éunion terr. Indian Ocean 149 L7
rench Overseas Department.

us Spain 57 G3
usam, Pulau i. Indon. 71 B7
utlingen Germany 47 L6
val Estonia see Tallinn
vda Rus. Fed. 44 S3
vel Estonia see Tallinn
vel France 56 F5
velstoke Canada 120 G5
vigny-sur-Ornain France 52 E6
villagigedo, Islas is Mex. 136 B5
villagigedo Island U.S.A. 120 D4
vin France 52 E5
vivim Israel 85 B4
volyutsii, Pik mt. Tajik. see
evolyutsiya, Qullai
volyutsiya, Qullai mt. Tajik. 89 I2
wa India 82 E4
wari India 82 D3
xburg U.S.A. 126 F4
xton Canada 123 I5
yes, Point U.S.A. 128 B2
yhanlı Turkey 85 C1
ykir Iceland 44 [inset]
ykjanes Ridge sea feature
. Atlantic Ocean 148 F2
ykjanestá pt Iceland 44 [inset]

eykjavík Iceland 44 [inset]
Capital of Iceland.

yneke, Ostrov i. Rus. Fed. 74 E1
ynoldsburg U.S.A. 134 D4
ynolds Range mts Australia 108 F5
ynosa Mex. 131 D7
zā Iran 88 D3
zā'īyeh Iran see Urmia
zā'īyeh, Daryācheh-ye salt l. Iran see
rmia, Lake
zekne Latvia 45 O8
zvān Iran 89 F4

Rezvāndeh Iran see Rezvānshahr
Rezvānshahr Iran 88 C2
Rhaeader Gwy U.K. see Rhayader
Rhayader U.K. 49 D6
Rheda-Wiedenbrück Germany 53 I3
Rhede Germany 52 G3
Rhegium Italy see Reggio di Calabria
Rheims France see Reims
Rhein r. Germany 53 G3 see Rhine
Rheine Germany 53 H2
Rheinland-Pfalz land Germany 53 H5
Rheinsberg Germany 53 M1
Rheinstetten Germany 53 I6
Rhemilès well Alg. 96 C2
Rhin r. Germany 53 I6 see Rhine
Rhine r. Germany 53 G3
also spelt Rhein (Germany) or Rhin (France)
Rhinebeck U.S.A. 135 I3
Rhinelander U.S.A. 130 F2
Rhineland-Palatinate land Germany see
Rheinland-Pfalz
Rhinkanal canal Germany 53 M2
Rhinow Germany 53 M2
Rhiwabon U.K. see Ruabon
Rho Italy 58 C2
Rhode Island state U.S.A. 135 J3
Rhodes Greece 59 M6
Rhodes i. Greece 59 M6
Rhodesia country Africa see Zimbabwe
Rhodes Peak U.S.A. 126 E3
Rhodope Mountains Bulg./Greece 59 J4
Rhodus i. Greece see Rhodes
Rhône r. France/Switz. 56 G5
Rhum i. U.K. see Rum
Rhuthun U.K. see Ruthin
Rhydaman U.K. see Ammanford
Rhyl U.K. 48 D5
Riachão Brazil 143 I5
Riacho Brazil 145 C2
Riacho de Santana Brazil 145 C1
Riacho dos Machados Brazil 145 C1
Rialma Brazil 145 A1
Rialto U.S.A. 128 E4
Riasi India 82 C2
Riau, Kepulauan is Indon. 68 C6
Ribadeo Spain 57 C2
Ribadesella Spain 57 D2
Ribas do Rio Pardo Brazil 144 F2
Ribat Afgh. 89 H2
Ribat-i-Shur waterhole Iran 88 E3
Ribáuè Moz. 99 D5
Ribble r. U.K. 48 E5
Ribblesdale valley U.K. 48 E4
Ribe Denmark 45 F9
Ribécourt-Dreslincourt France 52 C5
Ribeira r. Brazil 145 B4
Ribeirão Preto Brazil 145 B3
Ribemont France 52 D5
Ribérac France 56 E4
Riberalta Bol. 142 E6
Rîbnița Moldova 43 F7
Ribnitz-Damgarten Germany 47 N3
Říčany Czech Rep. 47 O6
Rice U.S.A. 135 F5
Rice Lake Canada 135 F1
Richards Bay S. Africa 101 K5
Richards Inlet Antarctica 152 H1
Richards Island Canada 118 E3
Richardson r. Canada 121 I3
Richardson U.S.A. 131 D5
Richardson Island Canada 120 G1
Richardson Lakes U.S.A. 135 J1
Richardson Mountains Canada 118 E3
Richardson Mountains N.Z. 113 B7
Richfield U.S.A. 129 G2
Richfield Springs U.S.A. 135 H2
Richford NY U.S.A. 135 G2
Richford VT U.S.A. 135 I1
Richgrove U.S.A. 128 D4
Richland U.S.A. 126 D3
Richland Center U.S.A. 130 F3
Richmond N.S.W. Australia 112 E4
Richmond Qld Australia 110 C4
Richmond Canada 135 H1
Richmond N.Z. 113 D5
Richmond Kwazulu-Natal S. Africa 101 J5
Richmond N. Cape S. Africa 100 F6
Richmond U.K. 48 F4
Richmond CA U.S.A. 128 B3
Richmond IN U.S.A. 134 C4
Richmond KY U.S.A. 134 C5
Richmond MI U.S.A. 134 D2
Richmond MO U.S.A. 130 E4
Richmond TX U.S.A. 131 E6

▶Richmond VA U.S.A. 135 G5
Capital of Virginia.

Richmond Dale U.S.A. 134 D4
Richmond Hill U.S.A. 133 D6
Richmond Range hills Australia 112 F2
Richtersveld National Park S. Africa 100 C5
Richvale U.S.A. 128 C2
Richwood U.S.A. 134 E4
Rico U.S.A. 129 I3
Ricomagus France see Riom
Riddell Nunataks Antarctica 152 E2
Rideau Lakes Canada 135 G1
Ridge r. Canada 122 D4
Ridgecrest U.S.A. 128 E4
Ridge Farm U.S.A. 134 B4
Ridgeland MS U.S.A. 131 F5
Ridgeland SC U.S.A. 133 D5
Ridgetop U.S.A. 134 B5
Ridgetown Canada 134 E2
Ridgeway OH U.S.A. 134 D3
Ridgeway VA U.S.A. 134 F5
Ridgway CO U.S.A. 129 J2
Ridgway PA U.S.A. 135 F3
Riding Mountain National Park Canada
121 K5
Riecito Venez. 142 E1
Riemst Belgium 52 F4
Riesa Germany 53 N3
Riesco, Isla i. Chile 144 B8
Riet watercourse S. Africa 100 E6
Rietavas Lith. 45 L9
Rietfontein S. Africa 100 E4
Rieti Italy 58 E3
Rifā'ī, Tall mt. Jordan/Syria 85 C3
Rifeng China see Lichuan
Rifle U.S.A. 129 J2

Rifstangi pt Iceland 44 [inset]
Rift Valley Lakes National Park Eth. see
Abijatta-Shalla National Park

▶Rīga Latvia 45 N8
Capital of Latvia.

Riga, Gulf of Estonia/Latvia 45 M8
Rigain Pūnco l. China 83 F2
Rīgān Iran 88 E4
Rīgas jūras līcis b. Estonia/Latvia see
Riga, Gulf of
Rigby U.S.A. 126 F4
Rīgestān reg. Afgh. see Registān
Rigolet Canada 123 K3
Rigside U.K. 50 F5
Riia laht b. Estonia/Latvia see Riga, Gulf of
Riihimäki Fin. 45 N6
Riiser-Larsen Ice Shelf Antarctica 152 B2
Riito Mex. 129 F5
Rijau Nigeria 96 D3
Rijeka Croatia 58 F2
Rikā, Wādī ar watercourse Saudi Arabia
88 B6
Rikitgaib Indon. 71 B6
Rikor India 76 B2
Rikuchū-kaigan Kokuritsu-kōen nat. park
Japan 75 F5
Rikuzen-takata Japan 75 F5
Rila mts Bulg. 59 J3
Rila China 83 F3
Riley U.S.A. 126 D4
Rileyville U.S.A. 135 F4
Rillieux-la-Pape France 56 G4
Rillito U.S.A. 129 H5
Rimah, Wādī al watercourse Saudi Arabia
86 F4
Rimavská Sobota Slovakia 47 R6
Rimbey Canada 120 H4
Rimini Italy 58 E2
Rîmnicu Sărat Romania see Râmnicu Sărat
Rîmnicu Vîlcea Romania see
Râmnicu Vâlcea
Rimouski Canada 123 H4
Rimpar Germany 53 J5
Rimsdale, Loch l. U.K. 50 E2
Rinbung China 83 G3
Rincão Brazil 145 A3
Rindal Norway 44 F5
Ringarooma Bay Australia 111 [inset]
Ringas India 82 C4
Ringe Germany 52 G2
Ringebu Norway 45 G6
Ringhkung Myanmar 70 B1
Ringkøbing Denmark 45 F8
Ringsend U.K. 51 F2
Ringsted Denmark 45 G9
Ringtor China 83 E3
Ringvassøya i. Norway 44 K2
Ringwood Australia 112 B6
Ringwood U.K. 49 F8
Rinjani, Gunung vol. Indon. 68 F8
Rinns Point U.K. 50 C5
Rinqênzê China 83 G3
Rinteln Germany 53 J2
Río Abiseo, Parque Nacional nat. park
Peru 142 C5
Rio Azul Brazil 145 A4
Riobamba Ecuador 142 C4
Rio Blanco U.S.A. 129 J2
Rio Bonito Brazil 145 C3
Rio Branco Brazil 142 E6
Rio Branco, Parque Nacional do nat. park
Brazil 142 F3
Río Bravo, Parque Internacional del
nat. park Mex. 131 C6
Rio Brilhante Brazil 144 F2
Rio Casca Brazil 145 C3
Rio Claro Brazil 145 B3
Río Colorado Arg. 144 D5
Río Cuarto Arg. 144 D4
Rio das Pedras Moz. 101 L2
Rio de Contas Brazil 145 C1

▶Rio de Janeiro Brazil 145 C3
Former capital of Brazil. 3rd most
populous city in South America.

Rio de Janeiro state Brazil 145 C3

▶Río de la Plata-Paraná r. S. America
144 E4
2nd longest river in South America,
and 9th in the world.

Rio Dell U.S.A. 128 A1
Rio do Sul Brazil 145 A4
Río Gallegos Arg. 144 C8
Río Grande Arg. 144 C8
Rio Grande Brazil 144 F4
Río Grande Mex. 131 C8
Rio Grande r. Mex./U.S.A. 127 G5
also known as Río Bravo del Norte
Rio Grande City U.S.A. 131 D7
Rio Grande do Sul state Brazil 145 A5
Rio Grande Rise sea feature
S. Atlantic Ocean 148 F8
Ríohacha Col. 142 D1
Río Hondo, Embalse resr Arg. 144 C3
Rioja Peru 142 C5
Río Lagartos Mex. 133 B8
Rio Largo Brazil 143 K5
Riom France 56 F4
Rio Manso, Represa do resr Brazil 143 G6
Río Mulatos Bol. 142 E7
Río Muni reg. Equat. Guinea 96 E4
Río Negro, Embalse del resr
Uruguay 144 E4
Rioni r. Georgia 91 F2
Rio Novo Brazil 145 C3
Rio Pardo de Minas Brazil 145 C1
Rio Preto Brazil 145 C3
Rio Preto, Serra do hills Brazil 145 B2
Rio Rancho U.S.A. 127 G6
Río Tigre Ecuador 142 C4
Riou Lake Canada 121 J3
Rio Verde Brazil 145 A2
Rio Verde de Mato Grosso Brazil 143 H7
Rio Vista U.S.A. 128 C2
Ripky Ukr. 43 F6
Ripley England U.K. 48 F4
Ripley England U.K. 49 F5

Ripley NY U.S.A. 134 F2
Ripley OH U.S.A. 134 D4
Ripley WV U.S.A. 134 E4
Ripoll Spain 57 H2
Ripon U.K. 48 F4
Ripon U.S.A. 128 C3
Ripu India 83 G4
Risca U.K. 49 D7
Rishiri-tō i. Japan 74 F3
Rishon LeZiyyon Israel 85 B4
Rish Pish Iran 89 F5
Rising Sun IN U.S.A. 134 C4
Rising Sun MD U.S.A. 135 G4
Risle r. France 49 H9
Risør Norway 45 F7
Rissa Norway 44 F5
Ristiina Fin. 45 O6
Ristijärvi Fin. 44 P4
Ristikent Rus. Fed. 44 Q2
Risum China 82 D2
Ritchie S. Africa 100 G5
Ritchie's Archipelago is India 71 A4
Ritscher Upland mts Antarctica 152 B2
Ritsem Sweden 44 J3
Ritter, Mount U.S.A. 128 D3
Ritterhude Germany 53 I1
Ritzville U.S.A. 126 D3
Riu, Laem pt Thai. 71 B5
Riva del Garda Italy 58 D2
Rivas Nicaragua 137 G6
Rivera Arg. 144 D5
Rivera Uruguay 144 E4
River Cess Liberia 96 C4
Riverhead U.S.A. 135 I3
Riverhurst Canada 121 J5
Riverina Australia 109 C7
Riverina reg. Australia 112 B5
Riversdale S. Africa 100 E8
Riverside S. Africa 101 I6
Riverside U.S.A. 128 E5
Rivers Inlet Canada 120 E5
Riversleigh Australia 110 B3
Riverton N.Z. 113 B8
Riverton VA U.S.A. 135 F4
Riverton WY U.S.A. 126 F4
Riverview Canada 123 I5
Rivesaltes France 56 F5
Riviera Beach U.S.A. 133 D7
Rivière-du-Loup Canada 123 H5
Rivière-Pentecôte Canada 123 I4
Rivière-Pigou Canada 123 I4
Rivne Ukr. 43 E6
Rivungo Angola 99 C5
Riwaka N.Z. 113 D5
Riwoqê China see Racaka

▶Riyadh Saudi Arabia 86 G5
Capital of Saudi Arabia.

Riyan India 89 I5
Riza well Iran 88 D3
Rize Turkey 91 F2
Rizhao Shandong China see Donggang
Rizhao Shandong China 77 H1
Rizokarpaso Cyprus see Rizokarpason
Rizokarpason Cyprus 85 B2
Rīzū well Iran 88 E3
Rīzū'īyeh Iran 88 E4
Rjukan Norway 45 F7
Rjuvbrokkene mt. Norway 45 E7
Rkîz Mauritania 96 B3
Roa Norway 45 G6
Roachdale U.S.A. 134 B4
Roach Lake U.S.A. 129 F4
Roade U.K. 49 G6
Roads U.S.A. 134 D4

▶Road Town Virgin Is (U.K.) 137 L5
Capital of the British Virgin Islands.

Roan Fell hill U.K. 50 G5
Roan High Knob mt. U.S.A. 132 D4
Roanne France 56 G3
Roanoke IN U.S.A. 134 C3
Roanoke VA U.S.A. 134 F5
Roanoke r. U.S.A. 132 E4
Roanoke Rapids U.S.A. 132 E4
Roan Plateau U.S.A. 129 I2
Roaring Spring U.S.A. 135 F3
Roaringwater Bay Ireland 51 C6
Roatán Hond. 137 G5
Röbäck Sweden 44 L5
Robat r. Afgh. 89 F4
Robāţe Tork Iran 88 C3
Robāţ Karīm Iran 88 C3
Robāt-Sang Iran 88 E3
Robb Canada 120 G4
Robbins Island Australia 111 [inset]
Robbinsville U.S.A. 133 D5
Robe Australia 111 B8
Robe r. Australia 108 A5
Robe r. Ireland 51 C4
Röbel Germany 53 M1
Robert-Bourassa, Réservoir resr
Canada 122 F3
Robert Glacier Antarctica 152 D2
Robert Lee U.S.A. 131 C6
Roberts U.S.A. 126 E4
Roberts, Mount Australia 112 F2
Robertsburg U.S.A. 134 E4
Roberts Butte mt. Antarctica 152 H2
Roberts Creek Mountain U.S.A. 128 E2
Robertsfors Sweden 44 L4
Robertsganj India 83 E4
Robertson S. Africa 100 D7
Robertson, Lac l. Canada 123 K4
Robertson Bay Antarctica 152 H2
Robertson Island Antarctica 152 A2
Robertson Range hills Australia 109 C5
Robertsport Liberia 96 B4
Roberval Canada 123 G4
Robhanais, Rubha hd U.K. see
Butt of Lewis
Robin Hood's Bay U.K. 48 G4
Robin's Nest hill H.K. China 77 [inset]
Robinson Canada 120 C2
Robinson U.S.A. 134 B4
Robinson Range hills Australia 109 B6
Robinson River Australia 110 B3
Robles Pass U.S.A. 129 H5
Roblin Canada 121 K5
Robsart Canada 121 I5

Robson, Mount Canada 120 G4
Robstown U.S.A. 131 D7
Roby U.S.A. 131 C5
Roçadas Angola see Xangongo
Rocca Busambra mt. Sicily Italy 58 E6
Rocha Uruguay 144 F4
Rochdale U.K. 48 E5
Rochechouart France 56 E4
Rochefort Belgium 52 F4
Rochefort France 56 D4
Rochefort, Lac l. Canada 123 G2
Rochegda Rus. Fed. 42 I3
Rochester Australia 112 B6
Rochester U.K. 49 H7
Rochester IN U.S.A. 134 B3
Rochester MN U.S.A. 130 E2
Rochester NH U.S.A. 135 J2
Rochester NY U.S.A. 135 G2
Rochford U.K. 49 H7
Rochlitz Germany 53 M3
Roc'h Trévezel hill France 56 C2
Rock r. Canada 120 E2
Rockall i. N. Atlantic Ocean 40 D4
Rockall Bank sea feature
N. Atlantic Ocean 148 G2
Rock Creek Canada 120 B1
Rock Creek U.S.A. 134 E3
Rock Creek r. U.S.A. 126 G2
Rockdale U.S.A. 131 D6
Rockefeller Plateau Antarctica 152 J1
Rockford AL U.S.A. 133 C5
Rockford IL U.S.A. 130 F3
Rockford MI U.S.A. 134 C2
Rockglen Canada 121 J5
Rockhampton Australia 110 E4
Rockhampton Downs Australia 108 F4
Rock Hill U.S.A. 133 D5
Rockingham Australia 109 A8
Rockingham U.S.A. 133 E5
Rockingham Bay Australia 110 D3
Rockinghorse Lake Canada 121 H1
Rock Island Canada 135 I1
Rock Island U.S.A. 130 F3
Rocklake U.S.A. 130 D1
Rockland MA U.S.A. 135 J2
Rockland ME U.S.A. 132 G2
Rocknest Lake Canada 120 H1
Rockport IN U.S.A. 134 B5
Rockport TX U.S.A. 131 D7
Rock Rapids U.S.A. 130 D3
Rock River U.S.A. 126 G4
Rock Sound Bahamas 133 E7
Rock Springs MT U.S.A. 126 G3
Rocksprings U.S.A. 131 C6
Rock Springs WY U.S.A. 126 F4
Rockstone Guyana 143 G2
Rockville CT U.S.A. 135 I3
Rockville IN U.S.A. 134 B4
Rockville MD U.S.A. 135 G4
Rockwell City U.S.A. 130 E3
Rockwood MI U.S.A. 134 D2
Rockwood PA U.S.A. 134 F4
Rockyford Canada 120 H5
Rocky Harbour Canada 123 K4
Rocky Hill U.S.A. 134 D4
Rocky Island Lake Canada 122 E5
Rocky Lane Canada 120 G3
Rocky Mount U.S.A. 134 F5
Rocky Mountain House Canada 120 H4
Rocky Mountain National Park
U.S.A. 126 G4
Rocky Mountains Canada/U.S.A. 124 F3
Rocourt-St-Martin France 52 D5
Rocroi France 52 E5
Rodberg Norway 45 F6
Rødbyhavn Denmark 45 G9
Roddickton Canada 123 L4
Rodeio Brazil 145 A4
Rodel U.K. 50 C3
Roden Neth. 52 G1
Rödental Germany 53 L4
Rodeo Arg. 144 C4
Rodeo Mex. 131 B7
Rodeo U.S.A. 127 F7
Rodez France 56 F4
Ródhos i. Greece see Rhodes
Rodi i. Greece see Rhodes
Roding Germany 53 M5
Rodney, Cape U.S.A. 118 B3
Rodniki Rus. Fed. 42 I4
Rodolfo Sanchez Toboada Mex. 127 D7
Rodopi Planina mts Bulg./Greece see
Rhodope Mountains
Rodos Greece see Rhodes
Rodos i. Greece see Rhodes
Rodosto Turkey see Tekirdağ
Rodrigues Island Mauritius 149 M7
Roe r. U.K. 51 F2
Roebourne Australia 108 B5
Roebuck Bay Australia 108 C4
Roedtan S. Africa 101 I3
Roe Plains Australia 109 D7
Roermond Neth. 52 F3
Roeselare Belgium 52 D4
Roes Welcome Sound sea chan.
Canada 119 J3
Rogachev Belarus see Rahachow
Rogätz Germany 53 L2
Rogers U.S.A. 131 E4
Rogers, Mount U.S.A. 134 E5
Rogers City U.S.A. 134 D1
Rogers Lake U.S.A. 128 E4
Rogerson U.S.A. 126 E4
Rogersville U.S.A. 134 D5
Roggan r. Canada 122 F3
Roggan, Lac l. Canada 122 F3
Roggeveen Basin sea feature
S. Pacific Ocean 151 O8
Roggeveld plat. S. Africa 100 E7
Roggeveldberge esc. S. Africa 100 E7
Roghadal U.K. see Rodel
Rognan Norway 44 I3
Rögnitz r. Germany 53 K1
Rogue r. U.S.A. 126 B4
Roha India 84 B2
Rohnert Park U.S.A. 128 B2
Rohrbach in Oberösterreich Austria 47 N6
Rohrbach-lès-Bitche France 53 H5
Rohri Sangar Pak. 89 H5
Rohtak India 82 D3
Roi Et Thai. 70 C3
Roi Georges, Îles du is Fr. Polynesia 151 K6

Rois-Bheinn hill U.K. 50 D4
Roisel France 52 D5
Roja Latvia 45 M8
Rojas Arg. 144 D4
Rokeby Australia 110 C2
Rokeby National Park Australia 110 C2
Rokiškis Lith. 45 N9
Roknäs Sweden 44 L4
Rokytne Ukr. 43 E6
Rolagang China 83 G2
Rola Kangri mt. China 83 G2
Rolândia Brazil 145 A3
Rolim de Moura Brazil 142 F6
Roll AZ U.S.A. 129 G5
Roll IN U.S.A. 134 C3
Rolla MO U.S.A. 130 F4
Rolla ND U.S.A. 130 D1
Rollag Norway 45 F6
Rolleston Australia 110 E5
Rolleville Bahamas 133 F8
Rolling Fork U.S.A. 131 F5
Rollins U.S.A. 126 E3
Roma Australia 111 E5
Roma Italy see Rome
Roma Lesotho 101 H5
Roma Sweden 45 K8
Romain, Cape U.S.A. 133 E5
Romaine r. Canada 123 J4
Roman Romania 59 L1
Românâ, Câmpia plain Romania 59 J2
Romanche Gap sea feature
S. Atlantic Ocean 148 G6
Romanet, Lac l. Canada 123 I2
Romang, Pulau i. Indon. 108 D1
Romania country Europe 59 K2
Roman-Kosh mt. Ukr. 90 D1
Romano, Cape U.S.A. 133 D7
Romanovka Rus. Fed. 73 K2
Romans-sur-Isère France 56 G4
Romanzof, Cape U.S.A. 118 B3
Rombas France 52 G5
Romblon Phil. 69 G4

▶Rome Italy 58 E4
Capital of Italy.

Rome GA U.S.A. 133 C5
Rome ME U.S.A. 135 K1
Rome NY U.S.A. 135 H2
Rome TN U.S.A. 134 B5
Rome City U.S.A. 134 C3
Romeo U.S.A. 134 D2
Romford U.K. 49 H7
Romilly-sur-Seine France 56 F2
Romiton Uzbek. 89 G2
Romney U.S.A. 135 F4
Romney Marsh reg. U.K. 49 H7
Romny Ukr. 43 G6
Rømø i. Denmark 45 F9
Romodanovo Rus. Fed. 43 J5
Romorantin-Lanthenay France 56 E3
Rompin r. Malaysia 71 C7
Romsey U.K. 49 F8
Romulus U.S.A. 134 D2
Ron India 84 B3
Rona i. U.K. 50 D1
Ronas Hill hill U.K. 50 [inset]
Roncador, Serra do hills Brazil 143 H6
Roncador Reef Solomon Is 107 F2
Ronda Spain 57 D5
Ronda, Serranía de mts Spain 57 D5
Rondane Nasjonalpark nat. park
Norway 45 F6
Rondon Brazil 144 F2
Rondonópolis Brazil 143 H7
Rondout Reservoir U.S.A. 135 H3
Rongcheng Anhui China see Qingyang
Rongcheng Guangxi China see Rongxian
Rongcheng Hubei China see Jianli
Rong Chu r. China 83 G3
Rongelap atoll Marshall Is 150 H5
Rongjiang Guizhou China 77 F3
Rongjiang Jiangxi China see Nankang
Rongjiawan China see Yueyang
Rongklang Range mts Myanmar 70 A2
Rongmei China see Hefeng
Rongshui China 77 F3
Rongwo China see Tongren
Rongxian China 77 F4
Rongyul China 76 C2
Rongzhag China see Danba
Rönlap atoll Marshall Is see Rongelap
Rønne Denmark 45 I9
Ronneby Sweden 45 I8
Ronne Entrance strait Antarctica 152 L2
Ronne Ice Shelf Antarctica 152 L1
Ronnenberg Germany 53 J2
Ronse Belgium 52 D4
Roodeschool Neth. 52 G1
Rooke Island P.N.G. see Umboi
Roordahuizum Neth. see Reduzum
Roorkee India 82 D3
Roosendaal Neth. 52 E3
Roosevelt AZ U.S.A. 129 H5
Roosevelt UT U.S.A. 129 I1
Roosevelt, Mount Canada 120 E3
Roosevelt Island Antarctica 152 I1
Root r. Canada 120 F2
Root r. U.S.A. 130 F3
Ropar India see Rupnagar
Roper r. Australia 110 A2
Roper Bar Australia 108 F3
Roquefort France 56 D4
Roraima, Mount Guyana 142 F2
Rori India 82 C3
Rori Indon. 69 J7
Røros Norway 44 G5
Rørvik Norway 44 G4
Rosa, Punta pt Mex. 127 F8
Rosalia U.S.A. 126 D3
Rosamond U.S.A. 128 D4
Rosamond Lake U.S.A. 128 D4
Rosario Arg. 144 D4
Rosário Brazil 143 J4
Rosario Baja California Mex. 127 E7
Rosario Coahuila Mex. 131 C7
Rosario Sinaloa Mex. 136 C4
Rosario Sonora Mex. 124 F6
Rosario Zacatecas Mex. 131 C7
Rosario Venez. 142 D1
Rosário do Sul Brazil 144 F4
Rosário Oeste Brazil 143 G6

Rosarito Baja California Mex. 127 E7
Rosarito Baja California Mex. 128 E5
Rosarito Baja California Sur Mex. 127 F8
Rosarno Italy 58 F5
Roscoff France 56 C2
Roscommon Ireland 51 D4
Roscommon U.S.A. 134 C1
Roscrea Ireland 51 E5
Rose r. Australia 110 A2
Rose, Mount U.S.A. 128 D2
Rose Atoll American Samoa see Rose Island

▶Roseau Dominica 137 L5
Capital of Dominica.

Roseau U.S.A. 130 E1
Roseau r. U.S.A. 130 D1
Roseberth Australia 111 B5
Rose Blanche Canada 123 K5
Rosebud r. Canada 120 H5
Rosebud U.S.A. 126 G3
Roseburg U.S.A. 126 C4
Rose City U.S.A. 134 C1
Rosedale U.S.A. 131 F5
Rosedale Abbey U.K. 48 G4
Roseires Reservoir Sudan 86 D7
Rose Island atoll American Samoa 107 J3
Rosenberg U.S.A. 131 E6
Rosendal Norway 45 E7
Rosendal S. Africa 101 H5
Rosenheim Germany 47 N7
Rose Peak U.S.A. 129 I5
Rose Point Canada 120 D4
Roseto degli Abruzzi Italy 58 F3
Rosetown Canada 121 J5
Rosetta Egypt see Rashid
Rose Valley Canada 121 K4
Roseville CA U.S.A. 128 C2
Roseville MI U.S.A. 134 D2
Roseville OH U.S.A. 134 D4
Rosewood Australia 112 F1
Roshchino Rus. Fed. 45 P6
Rosh Pinah Namibia 100 C4
Roshtkala Tajik. see Roshtqal'a
Roshtqal'a Tajik. 89 H2
Rosignano Marittimo Italy 58 D3
Roșiori de Vede Romania 59 K2
Roskilde Denmark 45 H9
Roskruge Mountains U.S.A. 129 H5
Roslavl' Rus. Fed. 43 G5
Roslyakovo Rus. Fed. 44 R2
Roslyatino Rus. Fed. 42 J4
Ross N.Z. 113 C6
Ross, Mount hill N.Z. 113 E5
Rossano Italy 58 G5
Rossan Point Ireland 51 D3
Ross Barnett Reservoir U.S.A. 131 F5
Ross Bay Junction Canada 123 I3
Rosscarbery Ireland 51 C6
Ross Dependency reg. Antarctica 152 I2
Rosseau, Lake Canada 134 F1
Rossel Island P.N.G. 110 F1
Ross Ice Shelf Antarctica 152 I1
Rossignol, Lac l. Canada 122 G3
Rössing Namibia 100 B2
Ross Island Antarctica 152 H1
Rossiyskaya Sovetskaya Federativnaya Sotsialisticheskaya Respublika country Asia/Europe see Russian Federation
Rossland Canada 120 G5
Rosslare Ireland 51 F5
Rosslare Harbour Ireland 51 F5
Roßlau Germany 53 M3
Rosso Mauritania 96 B3
Ross-on-Wye U.K. 49 E7
Rossony Belarus see Rasony
Rossosh' Rus. Fed. 43 H6
Ross River Canada 120 C2
Ross Sea Antarctica 152 H1
Roßtal Germany 53 K5
Røssvatnet l. Norway 44 I4
Rossville U.S.A. 134 B3
Roßwein Germany 53 N3
Rosswood Canada 120 D4
Rostāq Afgh. 89 H2
Rostāq Iran 88 D5
Rosthern Canada 121 J4
Rostock Germany 47 N3
Rostov Rus. Fed. 42 H4
Rostov-na-Donu Rus. Fed. 43 H7
Rostov-on-Don Rus. Fed. see Rostov-na-Donu
Rosvik Sweden 44 L4
Roswell U.S.A. 127 G6
Rota i. N. Mariana Is 69 L4
Rot am See Germany 53 K5
Rotch Island Kiribati see Tamana
Rote i. Indon. 108 C2
Rotenburg (Wümme) Germany 53 J1
Roth Germany 53 L5
Rothaargebirge hills Germany 53 I4
Rothbury U.K. 48 F3
Rothenburg ob der Tauber Germany 53 K5
Rother r. U.K. 49 G8
Rothera research station Antarctica 152 L2
Rotherham U.K. 48 F5
Rothes U.K. 50 F3
Rothesay U.K. 50 D5
Rothwell U.K. 49 G6
Roti Indon. 108 C2
Roti i. Indon. see Rote
Roto Australia 112 B4
Rotomagus France see Rouen
Rotomanu N.Z. 113 C6
Rotondo, Monte mt. Corsica France 56 I5
Rotorua N.Z. 113 F4
Rotorua, Lake N.Z. 113 F4
Röttenbach Germany 53 L5
Rottendorf Germany 53 K5
Rottenmann Austria 47 O7
Rotterdam Neth. 52 E3
Rottleberode Germany 53 K3
Rottnest Island Australia 109 A8
Rottumeroog i. Neth. 52 G1
Rottweil Germany 47 L6
Rotuma i. Fiji 107 H3
Rotung India 76 B2
Rötviken Sweden 44 I5
Rötz Germany 53 M5
Roubaix France 52 D4
Rouen France 52 B5
Rough River Lake U.S.A. 134 B5
Roulers Belgium see Roeselare
Roumania country Europe see Romania
Roundeyed Lake Canada 123 H3
Round Hill hill U.K. 48 F4
Round Mountain Australia 112 F3
Round Rock AZ U.S.A. 129 I3
Round Rock TX U.S.A. 131 D6
Roundup U.S.A. 126 F3
Rousay i. U.K. 50 F1
Rouses Point U.S.A. 135 I1
Rouxville S. Africa 101 H6
Rouyn-Noranda Canada 122 F4
Rovaniemi Fin. 44 N3
Roven'ki Rus. Fed. 43 H6
Rovereto Italy 58 D2
Rôviěng Tbong Cambodia 71 D4
Rovigo Italy 58 D2
Rovinj Croatia 58 E2
Rovno Ukr. see Rivne
Rovnoye Rus. Fed. 43 J6
Rovuma r. Moz./Tanz. see Ruvuma
Rowena Australia 112 D2
Rowley Island Canada 119 K3
Rowley Shoals sea feature Australia 108 B4
Równe Ukr. see Rivne
Roxas Mindoro Phil. 69 G4
Roxas Palawan Phil. 68 F4
Roxas Panay Phil. 69 G4
Roxboro U.S.A. 132 E4
Roxburgh N.Z. 113 B7
Roxburgh Island Cook Is see Rarotonga
Roxby Downs Australia 111 B6
Roxo, Cabo c. Senegal 96 B3
Roy MT U.S.A. 126 F3
Roy NM U.S.A. 127 G5
Royal Canal Ireland 51 E4
Royal Chitwan National Park Nepal 83 F4
Royale, Île i. Canada see Cape Breton Island
Royale, Isle i. U.S.A. 130 F1
Royal Natal National Park S. Africa 101 I5
Royal National Park Australia 112 E5
Royal Oak U.S.A. 134 D2
Royal Sukla Phanta Wildlife Reserve Nepal 82 E3
Royan France 56 D4
Roye France 52 C5
Roy Hill Australia 108 B5
Royston U.K. 49 G6
Rozdil'na Ukr. 59 N1
Rozivka Ukr. 43 H7
Rtishchevo Rus. Fed. 43 I5
Ruabon U.K. 49 D6
Ruaha National Park Tanz. 99 D4
Ruahine Range mts N.Z. 113 F5
Ruanda country Africa see Rwanda

▶Ruapehu, Mount vol. N.Z. 113 E4
Highest active volcano in Oceania.

Ruapuke Island N.Z. 113 B8
Ruatoria N.Z. 113 G3
Ruba Belarus 43 F5

▶Rub' al Khālī des. Saudi Arabia 86 G6
Largest uninterrupted stretch of sand in the world.

Rubaydā reg. Saudi Arabia 88 C5
Rubtsovsk Rus. Fed. 80 F1
Ruby U.S.A. 118 C3
Ruby Dome mt. U.S.A. 129 F1
Ruby Mountains U.S.A. 129 F1
Rubys Inn U.S.A. 129 G3
Ruby Valley U.S.A. 129 F1
Rucheng China 77 G3
Ruckersville U.S.A. 135 F4
Rudall River National Park Australia 108 C5
Rudarpur India 83 E4
Ruda Śląska Poland 47 Q5
Rudauli India 83 E4
Rūdbār Iran 88 C2
Rudkøbing Denmark 45 G9
Rudnaya Pristan' Rus. Fed. 74 D3
Rudnichnyy Rus. Fed. 42 L4
Rudnik Ingichka Uzbek. see Ingichka
Rudnya Smolenskaya Oblast' Rus. Fed. 43 F5
Rudnya Volgogradskaya Oblast' Rus. Fed. 43 J6
Rudnyy Kazakh. 78 F1
Rudolf, Lake salt l. Eth./Kenya see Turkana, Lake

▶Rudol'fa, Ostrov i. Rus. Fed. 64 G1
Most northerly point of Europe.

Rudolph Island Rus. Fed. see Rudol'fa, Ostrov
Rudolstadt Germany 53 L4
Rudong China 77 I1
Rūdsar Iran 88 C2
Rue France 52 B4
Rufiji r. Tanz. 99 D4
Rufino Arg. 144 D4
Rufisque Senegal 96 B3
Rufrufua Indon. 69 I7
Rufunsa Zambia 99 C5
Rugao China 77 I1
Rugby U.K. 49 F6
Rugby U.S.A. 130 C1
Rugeley U.K. 49 F6
Rügen i. Germany 47 N3
Rugged Mountain Canada 120 E5
Rügland Germany 53 K5
Ruḩayyat al Ḩamr'ā' waterhole Saudi Arabia 88 B5
Ruhengeri Rwanda 98 C4
Ruhnu i. Estonia 45 M8
Ruhr r. Germany 53 G3
Ruhuna National Park Sri Lanka 84 D5
Rui'an China 77 I3
Rui Barbosa Brazil 145 C1
Ruicheng China 77 F1
Ruijin China 77 G3
Ruili China 76 C3
Ruin Point Canada 121 P2
Ruipa Tanz. 99 D4
Ruiz Mex. 136 C4
Ruiz, Nevado del vol. Col. 142 C3
Rujaylah, Ḩarrat ar lava field Jordan 85 C3
Rūjiena Latvia 45 N8
Ruk is Micronesia see Chuuk
Rukanpur Pak. 89 I4
Rukumkot Nepal 83 E3
Rukwa, Lake Tanz. 99 D4
Rulin China see Chengbu
Rulong China see Xinlong
Rum i. U.K. 50 C4
Rum, Jebel mts Jordan see Ramm, Jabal
Ruma Serbia 59 H2
Rumāh Saudi Arabia 86 G4
Rumania country Europe see Romania
Rumbek Sudan 97 F4
Rumberpon i. Indon. 69 I7
Rum Cay i. Bahamas 133 F8
Rum Jungle Australia 108 E3
Rummānā hill Syria 85 D3
Rumphi Malawi 99 D5
Runan China 77 G1
Runaway, Cape N.Z. 113 F3
Runcorn U.K. 48 E5
Rundu Namibia 99 B5
Rundvik Sweden 44 K5
Rũng, Kaôh i. Cambodia 71 C5
Rungwa Tanz. 99 D4
Rungwa r. Tanz. 99 D4
Runheji China 77 H1
Runing China see Runan
Runton Range hills Australia 109 C5
Ruokolahti Fin. 45 P6
Ruoqiang China 80 G4
Rupa India 83 H4
Rupat i. Indon. 71 C7
Rupert r. Canada 122 F4
Rupert ID U.S.A. 126 E4
Rupert WV U.S.A. 134 E5
Rupert Bay Canada 122 F4
Rupert Coast Antarctica 152 J1
Rupert House Canada see Waskaganish
Rupnagar India 82 D3
Rupshu reg. India 82 D2
Ruqqād, Wādī ar watercourse Israel 85 B3
Rural Retreat U.S.A. 134 E5
Rusaddir N. Africa see Melilla
Rusape Zimbabwe 99 D5
Ruschuk Bulg. see Ruse
Ruse Bulg. 59 K3
Rusera India 83 F4
Rush U.S.A. 134 D4
Rush Creek r. U.S.A. 130 C4
Rushden U.K. 49 G6
Rushinga Zimbabwe 99 D5
Rushville IL U.S.A. 130 F3
Rushville IN U.S.A. 134 C4
Rushville NE U.S.A. 130 C3
Rushworth Australia 112 B6
Rusk U.S.A. 131 E6
Russell Man. Canada 121 K5
Russell Ont. Canada 135 H1
Russell N.Z. 113 E2
Russell KS U.S.A. 130 D4
Russell PA U.S.A. 134 F3
Russell Bay Antarctica 152 J2
Russell Lake Man. Canada 121 K3
Russell Lake N.W.T. Canada 120 H2
Russell Lake Sask. Canada 121 J3
Russell Range hills Australia 109 C8
Russell Springs U.S.A. 134 C5
Russellville AL U.S.A. 131 G5
Russellville AR U.S.A. 131 E5
Russellville KY U.S.A. 134 B5
Rüsselsheim Germany 53 I4
Russia country Asia/Europe see Russian Federation
Russian r. U.S.A. 128 B2

▶Russian Federation country Asia/Europe 64 I3
Largest country in the world, Europe and Asia. Most populous country in Europe, 5th in Asia and 9th in the world.

Russian Soviet Federal Socialist Republic country Asia/Europe see Russian Federation
Russkiy, Ostrov i. Rus. Fed. 74 C4
Russkiy Kameshkir Rus. Fed. 43 J5
Rust'avi Georgia 91 G2
Rustburg U.S.A. 134 F5
Rustenburg S. Africa 101 H3
Ruston U.S.A. 131 E5
Rutanzige, Lake Dem. Rep. Congo/Uganda see Edward, Lake
Ruteng Indon. 108 C2
Ruth U.S.A. 129 F2
Rüthen Germany 53 I3
Rutherglen Australia 112 C6
Ruther Glen U.S.A. 135 G5
Ruthin U.K. 49 D5
Ruthiyai India 82 D4
Ruth Reservoir U.S.A. 128 B1
Rutka r. Rus. Fed. 42 J4
Rutland U.S.A. 135 I2
Rutland Water resr U.K. 49 G6
Rutledge Lake Canada 121 I2
Rutog Xizang China 76 B2
Rutög China see Dêrub
Rutog Xizang China 83 F3
Rutul Rus. Fed. 91 G2
Ruukki Fin. 44 N4
Ruvuma r. Moz./Tanz. 99 E5
also known as Rovuma
Ruwayshid, Wādī watercourse Jordan 85 C3
Ruwayṭah, Wādī watercourse Jordan 85 C5
Ruweis U.A.E. 88 D5
Ruwenzori National Park Uganda see Queen Elizabeth National Park
Ruza Rus. Fed. 42 H5
Ruzayevka Kazakh. 78 F1
Ruzayevka Rus. Fed. 43 J5
Ruzhou China 77 G1
Ružomberok Slovakia 47 Q6
Rwanda country Africa 98 C4
Ryābād Iran 88 D2
Ryan, Loch b. U.K. 50 D5
Ryazan' Rus. Fed. 43 H5
Ryazhsk Rus. Fed. 43 I5
Rybachiy, Poluostrov pen. Rus. Fed. 44 R2
Rybach'ye Kyrg. see Balykchy
Rybinsk Rus. Fed. 42 H4

▶Rybinskoye Vodokhranilishche resr Rus. Fed. 42 H4
5th largest lake in Europe

Rybnik Poland 47 Q5
Rybnitsa Moldova see Rîbnița
Rybnoye Rus. Fed. 43 H5
Rybreka Rus. Fed. 42 G3
Ryd Sweden 45 I8
Rydberg Peninsula Antarctica 152 L2
Ryde U.K. 49 F8
Rye U.K. 49 H8
Rye r. U.K. 48 G4
Rye Bay U.K. 49 H8
Ryegate U.S.A. 126 F3
Rye Patch Reservoir U.S.A. 128 D1
Rykovo Ukr. see Yenakiyeve
Ryl'sk Rus. Fed. 43 G6
Rylstone Australia 112 D4
Ryn-Peski des. Kazakh. 41 P6
Ryōtsu Japan 75 E5
Ryukyu Islands Japan 75 B8
Ryūkyū-rettō is Japan see Ryukyu Islands
Ryukyu Trench sea feature N. Pacific Ocean 150 E4
Rzeszów Poland 43 D6
Rzhaksa Rus. Fed. 43 I5
Rzhev Rus. Fed. 42 G4

Sa'ādah al Barṣā' pass Saudi Arabia 85 C5
Sa'ādatābād Iran 88 D4
Saal an der Donau Germany 53 L6
Saale r. Germany 53 L3
Saalfeld Germany 53 L4
Saanich Canada 120 F5
Saar land Germany see Saarland
Saar r. Germany 52 G5
Saarbrücken Germany 52 G5
Saaremaa i. Estonia 45 M7
Saarenkylä Fin. 44 N3
Saargau reg. Germany 52 G5
Saarijärvi Fin. 44 N5
Saari-Kämä Fin. 44 O3
Saarikoski Fin. 44 L2
Saaristomeren kansallispuisto nat. park Fin. see Skärgårdshavets nationalpark
Saarland land Germany 52 G5
Saarlouis Germany 52 G5
Saatlı Azer. 91 H3
Saatly Azer. see Saatlı
Sab'a Egypt see Saba'ah
Saba'ah Egypt 85 A4
Sab' Ābār Syria 85 C3
Šabac Serbia 59 H2
Sabadell Spain 57 H3
Sabae Japan 75 E6
Sabak Malaysia 71 C7
Sabalana i. Indon. 68 F8
Sabalana, Kepulauan is Indon. 68 F8
Sabana, Archipiélago de is Cuba 137 H4
Sabang Indon. 71 A6
Şabanözü Turkey 90 D2
Sabará Brazil 145 C2
Sabastiya West Bank 85 B3
Sab'atayn, Ramlat as des. Yemen 86 G6
Sabaudia Italy 58 E4
Sabaya Bol. 142 E7
Sabdê China 76 D2
Sabelo S. Africa 100 F6
Sāberi, Hāmūn-e marsh Afgh./Iran 89 F4
Şabḩā Jordan 85 C3
Sabhā Libya 97 E2
Şabḩā' Saudi Arabia 88 B6
Sabhrai India 82 B5
Sabi r. India 82 D3
Sabi r. Moz./Zimbabwe see Save
Sabie Moz. 101 K3
Sabie r. Moz./S. Africa 101 K3
Sabie S. Africa 101 J3
Sabina U.S.A. 134 D4
Sabinal Mex. 127 G7
Sabinal, Cayo i. Cuba 133 E8
Sabinas Mex. 131 C7
Sabinas r. Mex. 131 C7
Sabinas Hidalgo Mex. 131 C7
Sabine r. U.S.A. 131 E6
Sabine Lake U.S.A. 131 E6
Sabine Pass U.S.A. 131 E6
Sabini, Monti mts Italy 58 E3
Sabirabad Azer. 91 H2
Sabkhat al Bardawīl Reserve nature res. Egypt see Lake Bardawil Reserve
Sable, Cape Canada 123 I6
Sable, Cape U.S.A. 133 D7
Sable, Lac du l. Canada 123 I3
Sable Island Canada 123 K6
Sabon Kafi Niger 96 D3
Sabrina Coast Antarctica 152 F2
Sabugal Port. 57 C3
Sabzawar Afgh. see Shīndand
Sabzevār Iran 88 E2
Sabzvārān Iran see Jīroft
Sacalinul Mare, Insula i. Romania 59 M2
Sacaton U.S.A. 129 H5
Sac City U.S.A. 130 E3
Săcele Romania 59 K2
Sachigo r. Canada 121 N4
Sachigo Lake Canada 121 M4
Sachin India 82 C5
Sach'on S. Korea 75 C6
Sach Pass India 82 D2
Sachsen land Germany 53 N3
Sachsen-Anhalt land Germany 53 L2
Sachsenheim Germany 53 J6
Sachs Harbour Canada 118 F2
Sacirsuyu r. Syria/Turkey see Sājūr, Nahr
Sackpfeife hill Germany 53 I4
Sackville Canada 123 I5
Saco ME U.S.A. 135 J2
Saco MT U.S.A. 126 G2
Sacramento Brazil 145 B2

▶Sacramento U.S.A. 128 C2
Capital of California.

Sacramento r. U.S.A. 128 C2
Sacramento Mountains U.S.A. 127 G6
Sacramento Valley U.S.A. 128 B1
Sada S. Africa 101 H7
Sádaba Spain 57 F2
Sá da Bandeira Angola see Lubango
Şadad Syria 85 C2
Şa'dah Yemen 86 F6
Sadao Thai. 71 C6
Saddat al Hindīyah Iraq 91 G4
Saddleback Mesa mt. U.S.A. 131 C5
Saddle Hill hill Australia 110 D2
Saddle Peak hill India 71 A4
Sa Đec Vietnam 71 D5
Sadêng China 76 B2
Sadieville U.S.A. 134 C4
Sadīj watercourse Iran 88 E5
Sadiola Mali 96 B3
Sadiqabad Pak. 89 H4
Sad Istragh mt. Afgh./Pak. 89 I2
Sa'dīyah, Hawr as imp. l. Iraq 91 G4
Sa'diyyat i. U.A.E. 88 D5
Sado r. Port. 57 B4
Sadoga-shima i. Japan 75 E5
Sadot Egypt see Sadūt
Sadovoye Rus. Fed. 43 J7
Sa Dragonera i. Spain 57 H4
Sadras India 84 D3
Sadūt Egypt 85 B4
Sadût Egypt see Sadūt
Sæby Denmark 45 G8
Saena Julia Italy see Siena
Safad Israel see Ẕefat
Safāshahr Iran 88 D4
Safayal Maqūf well Iraq 91 G5
Safed Khirs mts Afgh. 89 H2
Safed Koh mts Afgh. 89 G3
Safed Koh mts Afgh./Pak. 89 H3
Saffānīyah, Ra's as pt Saudi Arabia 88 C4
Säffle Sweden 45 H7
Safford U.S.A. 129 I5
Saffron Walden U.K. 49 H6
Safi Morocco 54 C5
Safīdār, Kūh-e mt. Iran 88 D4
Safīd Kūh mts Afgh. 89 F3
Safīd Kūh mts Afgh. see Safīd Kūh
Safīd Sagak Iran 89 F3
Safiras, Serra das mts Brazil 145 C2
Şāfītā Syria 85 C2
Safonovo Arkhangel'skaya Oblast' Rus. Fed. 42 K2
Safonovo Smolenskaya Oblast' Rus. Fed. 43 G5
Safrā' al Asyāḩ esc. Saudi Arabia 88 A5
Safrā' as Sark esc. Saudi Arabia 86 F4
Safranbolu Turkey 90 D2
Saga China 83 F3
Saga Japan 75 C6
Saga Kazakh. 80 B1
Sagaing Myanmar 70 A2
Sagami-nada g. Japan 75 E6
Sagamore U.S.A. 134 F3
Saganthit Kyun i. Myanmar 71 B4
Sagar Karnataka India 84 B3
Sagar Karnataka India 84 C2
Sagar Madh. Prad. India 82 D5
Sagaredzho Georgia see Sagarejo
Sagarejo Georgia 91 G2
Sagar Island India 83 G5
Sagarmatha National Park Nepal 83 F4
Sagastyr Rus. Fed. 65 N2
Sagavanirktok r. U.S.A. 118 D2
Sage U.S.A. 126 F4
Saggi, Har mt. Israel 85 B4
Saghand Iran 88 D3
Saginaw U.S.A. 134 D2
Saginaw Bay U.S.A. 134 D2
Saglek Bay Canada 123 J2
Saglouc Canada see Salluit
Sagone, Golfe de b. Corsica France 56 I5
Sagres Port. 57 B5
Sagthale India 82 C5
Saguache U.S.A. 127 G5
Sagua la Grande Cuba 137 H4
Saguaro Lake U.S.A. 129 H5
Saguaro National Park U.S.A. 129 H5
Saguenay r. Canada 123 H4
Sagunt Spain see Sagunto
Sagunto Spain 57 F4
Saguntum Spain see Sagunto
Sahagún Spain 57 D2
Sahand, Kūh-e mt. Iran 88 B2

▶Sahara des. Africa 96 D3
Largest desert in the world.

Şahara el Gharbîya des. Egypt see Western Desert
Şahara el Sharqîya des. Egypt see Eastern Desert
Saharan Atlas mts Alg. see Atlas Saharien
Saharanpur India 82 D3
Sahara Well Australia 108 C5
Saharsa India 83 F4
Sahaswan India 82 D3
Sahat, Kūh-e hill Iran 88 D3
Sahatwar India 83 F4
Şahbuz Azer. 91 G3
Sahdol India see Shahdol
Sahebganj India see Sahibganj
Sahebgunj India see Sahibganj
Saheira, Wâdi el watercourse Egypt see Suhaymī, Wādī as
Sahel reg. Africa 96 C3
Sahibganj India 83 F4
Sahiwal Pak. 89 I4
Sahlābād Iran 89 E3
Şaḩm Oman 88 E5
Şaḩneh Iran 88 B3
Şaḩrā al Ḩijārah reg. Iraq 91 G5
Sahuaripa Mex. 127 F7
Sahuayo Mex. 136 D4
Sahuteng China see Zadoi
Sa Huynh Vietnam 71 E4
Sahyadri mts India see Western Ghats
Sahyadriparvat Range hills India 84 B1
Sai r. India 83 E4
Sai Buri Thai. 71 C6
Saïda Alg. 57 G6
Saïda Lebanon see Sidon
Sai Dao Tai, Khao mt. Thai. 71 C4
Saïdia Morocco 57 E6
Sa'īdīyeh Iran see Solṭānīyeh
Saidpur Bangl. 83 G4
Saiha India 83 H5
Saihan Tal China 73 K4
Saijō Japan 75 D6
Saikai Kokuritsu-kōen nat. park Japan 75 C6
Saiki Japan 75 C6
Sai Kung H.K. China 77 [inset]
Sailana India 82 C5
Saimaa l. Fin. 45 P6
Saimbeyli Turkey 90 E3
Saindak Pak. 89 F4
Sa'īndezh Iran 88 B2
Sa'in Qal'eh Iran see Sa'īndezh
St Abb's Head hd U.K. 50 G5
St Agnes U.K. 49 B8
St Agnes i. U.K. 49 A9
St Alban's Canada 123 L5
St Albans U.K. 49 G7
St Albans VT U.S.A. 135 I1
St Albans WV U.S.A. 134 E4
St Alban's Head hd England U.K. see St Aldhelm's Head
St Albert Canada 120 H4
St Aldhelm's Head hd U.K. 49 E8
St-Amand-les-Eaux France 52 D4
St-Amand-Montrond France 56 F3
St-Amour France 56 G3
St-André, Cap pt Madag. see Vilanandro, Tanjona
St Andrews U.K. 50 G4
St Andrew Sound inlet U.S.A. 133 D6
St Anne U.S.A. 134 B3
St Ann's Bay Jamaica 137 I5
St Anthony Canada 123 L4
St Anthony U.S.A. 126 F4
St-Arnaud Alg. see El Eulma
St Arnaud Australia 112 A6
St Arnaud Range mts N.Z. 113 D6
St-Arnoult-en-Yvelines France 52 B6
St-Augustin Canada 123 K4
St Augustin r. Canada 123 K4
St Augustine U.S.A. 133 D6
St Austell U.K. 49 C8
St-Avertin France 56 E3
St-Avold France 52 G5
St Barbe Canada 123 K4

▶St-Barthélemy i. West Indies 137 L5
French Overseas Collectivity.

St Bees U.K. 48 D4
St Bees Head hd U.K. 48 D4
St Bride's Bay U.K. 49 B7
St-Brieuc France 56 C2
St Catharines Canada 134 F2
St Catherines Island U.S.A. 133 D6
St Catherine's Point U.K. 49 F8
St-Céré France 56 E4
St-Chamond France 56 G4
St Charles ID U.S.A. 126 F4
St Charles MD U.S.A. 135 G4
St Charles MI U.S.A. 134 C2
St Charles MO U.S.A. 130 F4
St-Chély-d'Apcher France 56 F4
St Christopher and Nevis country West Indies see St Kitts and Nevis
St Clair r. Canada/U.S.A. 134 D2
St Clair, Lake Canada/U.S.A. 134 D2
St-Claude France 56 G3
St Clears U.K. 49 C7
St Cloud U.S.A. 130 E2
St Croix r. U.S.A. 122 B5
St Croix Falls U.S.A. 130 E2
St David U.S.A. 129 H6
St David's Head hd U.K. 49 B7
St-Denis France 52 C6

▶St-Denis Réunion 149 L7
Capital of Réunion.

St-Denis-du-Sig Alg. see Sig
St-Dié France 56 H2
St-Dizier France 52 E6
St-Domingue country West Indies see Hai
Sainte Anne Canada 121 L5
Ste-Anne, Lac l. Canada 123 I4
St Elias, Cape U.S.A. 118 D4

▶St Elias, Mount U.S.A. 120 A2
4th highest mountain in North America.

St Elias Mountains Canada 120 A2
Ste-Marguerite r. Canada 123 I4
Ste-Marie, Cap c. Madag. see Vohimena, Tanjona
Sainte-Marie, Île i. Madag. see Boraha, Nosy
Ste-Maxime France 56 H5
Sainte Rose du Lac Canada 121 L5
Saintes France 56 D4
Sainte Thérèse, Lac l. Canada 120 F1
St-Étienne France 56 G4
St-Étienne-du-Rouvray France 52 B5
St-Fabien Canada 123 H4
St-Félicien Canada 123 G4
Saintfield U.K. 51 G3
St-Florent Corsica France 56 I5
St-Florent-sur-Cher France 56 F3
St-Floris, Parc National nat. park Cent. Afr. Rep. 98 C3
St-Flour France 56 F4
St Francesville U.S.A. 131 F6
St Francis U.S.A. 130 C4
St Francis r. U.S.A. 131 F5
St Francis Isles Australia 109 F8
St-François r. Canada 123 G5
St-François, Lac l. Canada 123 H5
St-Gaudens France 56 E5
St George Australia 112 D2
St George r. Australia 110 D3
St George AK U.S.A. 118 B4
St George SC U.S.A. 133 D5
St George UT U.S.A. 129 G3
St George, Point U.S.A. 126 B4
St George Island U.S.A. 118 B4
St George Range hills Australia 108 D4
St-Georges Canada 123 H5

St George's Grenada 137 L6
Capital of Grenada.

George's Bay Nfld. and Lab.
Canada 123 K4
George's Bay N.S. Canada 123 J5
George's Channel Ireland/U.K. 51 F6
George's Channel P.N.G. 106 F2
George's Head hd Australia 112 E5
Gotthard Hungary see Szentgotthárd
Gotthard Pass Switz. 56 I3
Govan's Head hd U.K. 49 C7
Helen U.S.A. 134 C1
Helena i. S. Atlantic Ocean 148 H7
Helena U.S.A. 128 B2

St Helena and Dependencies terr.
S. Atlantic Ocean 148 H7
United Kingdom Overseas territory. Consists of St Helena, Ascension, Tristan da Cunha and Gough Island.

Helena Bay S. Africa 100 D7
Helens Australia 111 [inset]
Helens U.K. 48 E5
Helens U.S.A. 126 C3
Helens, Mount vol. U.S.A. 126 C3
Helens Point Australia 111 [inset]

St Helier Channel Is 49 E9
Capital of Jersey.

nthiya India 83 F5
Hubert Belgium 52 F4
Hyacinthe Canada 123 G5
gnace U.S.A. 132 C2
gnace Island Canada 122 D4
shmael U.K. 49 C7
ves England U.K. 49 B8
ves England U.K. 49 G6
Jacques, Cap Vietnam see Vung Tau
Jacques-de-Dupuy Canada 122 F4
James MN U.S.A. 130 E3
James MO U.S.A. 130 F4
James, Cape Canada 120 D5
Jean r. Canada 123 I4
Jean, Lac l. Canada 123 G4
Jean-d'Acre Israel see 'Akko
Jean-d'Angély France 56 D4
Jean-de-Monts France 56 C3
Jean-sur-Richelieu Canada 135 I1
Jérôme Canada 122 G5
Joe r. U.S.A. 126 D3
nt John Canada 123 I5
John U.S.A. 130 D4
John r. U.S.A. 132 H2
John, Cape Canada 123 L4
John Bay Canada 123 K4
John Island Canada 123 K4

St John's Antigua and Barbuda 137 L5
Capital of Antigua and Barbuda.

St John's Canada 123 L5
Capital of Newfoundland and Labrador.

Johns AZ U.S.A. 129 I4
Johns MI U.S.A. 134 C2
Johns OH U.S.A. 134 C3
Johns r. U.S.A. 133 D6
Johnsbury U.S.A. 135 I1
John's Chapel U.K. 48 E4
Joseph IL U.S.A. 134 A3
Joseph LA U.S.A. 131 F6
Joseph MI U.S.A. 134 B2
Joseph MO U.S.A. 130 E4
Joseph r. U.S.A. 134 C3
Joseph, Lake Canada 121 N5
Joseph-d'Alma Canada see Alma
Joseph Island Canada 122 E5
Junien France 56 E4
Just U.K. 49 B8
Just-en-Chaussée France 52 C5
Keverne U.K. 49 B8
Kilda i. U.K. 40 E4
Kilda is U.K. 46 C2
Kitts and Nevis country
West Indies 137 L5
Laurent inlet Canada see St Lawrence
Laurent, Golfe du g. Canada see
St Lawrence, Gulf of
Laurent-du-Maroni Fr. Guiana 143 H2
Lawrence Canada 123 L5
Lawrence inlet Canada 123 H4
Lawrence, Cape Canada 123 J5
Lawrence, Gulf of Canada 123 J4
Lawrence Island U.S.A. 118 B3
Lawrence Islands National Park
Canada 135 H1
Lawrence Seaway sea chan.
Canada/U.S.A. 135 H1
Léonard Canada 123 G5
Leonard U.S.A. 135 G4
Lewis r. Canada 123 K3
Lô France 56 D2
Louis Senegal 96 B3
Louis MI U.S.A. 134 C2
Louis MO U.S.A. 130 F4
Louis r. U.S.A. 122 B5
Lucia country West Indies 137 L6
Lucia, Lake S. Africa 101 K5
Lucia Estuary S. Africa 101 K5
Luke's Island Myanmar see
Zadetkale Kyun
Magnus Bay U.K. 50 [inset]
Maixent-l'École France 56 D3
Malo France 56 C2
Malo, Golfe de g. France 56 C2
Marc Haiti 137 J5
Maries U.S.A. 126 D3
Marks S. Africa 101 H7
Mark's S. Africa see Cofimvaba
Martin i. Neth. Antilles see Sint Maarten

St-Martin i. West Indies 137 L5
French Overseas Collectivity. The southern part of the island is the Dutch territory of Sint Maarten.

Martin, Cape S. Africa 100 C7
St Martin, Lake Canada 121 L5
St Martin's i. U.K. 49 A9
St Martin's Island Bangl. 70 A2
St Mary Peak Australia 111 B6
St Mary Reservoir Canada 120 H5
St Mary's Canada 134 E2
St Mary's U.K. 50 G2
St Mary's i. U.K. 49 A9
St Marys PA U.S.A. 135 F3
St Marys WV U.S.A. 134 E4
St Marys r. U.S.A. 134 C3
St Mary's, Cape Canada 123 L5
St Mary's Bay Canada 123 L5
St Marys City U.S.A. 135 G4
St Matthew Island U.S.A. 118 A3
St Matthews U.S.A. 134 C4
St Matthew's Island Myanmar see
Zadetkyi Kyun
St Matthias Group is P.N.G. 69 L7
St-Maurice r. Canada 123 G5
St Mawes U.K. 49 B8
St-Médard-en-Jalles France 56 D4
St Meinrad U.S.A. 134 B4
St Michaels U.S.A. 135 G4
St Michael's Bay Canada 123 L3
St-Mihiel France 52 F6
St-Nazaire France 56 C3
St Neots U.K. 49 G6
St-Nicolas Belgium see Sint-Niklaas
St-Nicolas, Mont hill Lux. 52 G5
St-Nicolas-de-Port France 56 H2
St-Omer France 52 C4
Saintonge reg. France 56 D4
St-Pacôme Canada 123 H5
St-Palais France 56 D5
St Paris U.S.A. 134 D3
St-Pascal Canada 123 H5
St Paul r. Canada 123 K3
St-Paul atoll Fr. Polynesia see Hérèhérétué
St Paul AK U.S.A. 118 A4

▶St Paul MN U.S.A. 130 E2
Capital of Minnesota.

St Paul NE U.S.A. 130 D3
St-Paul, Île i. Indian Ocean 149 N8
St Paul Island U.S.A. 118 A4
St Peter and St Paul Rocks is
N. Atlantic Ocean see
São Pedro e São Paulo

▶St Peter Port Channel Is 49 E9
Capital of Guernsey.

St Peter's N.S. Canada 123 J5
St Peters P.E.I. Canada 123 J5
St Petersburg Rus. Fed. 45 Q7
St Petersburg U.S.A. 133 D7
St-Pierre mt. France 56 G5

▶St-Pierre St Pierre and Miquelon 123 L5
Capital of St Pierre and Miquelon.

▶St Pierre and Miquelon terr. N. America 123 K5
French Territorial Collectivity.

St-Pierre-d'Oléron France 56 D4
St-Pierre-le-Moûtier France 56 F3
St-Pol-sur-Ternoise France 52 C4
St-Pourçain-sur-Sioule France 56 F3
St-Quentin France 52 D5
St Regis U.S.A. 126 E3
St Regis Falls U.S.A. 135 H1
St-Rémi Canada 135 I1
St-Saëns France 52 B5
St Sebastian Bay S. Africa 100 E8
St-Siméon Canada 123 H5
St Simons Island U.S.A. 133 D6
St Theresa Point Canada 121 M4
St Thomas Canada 134 E2
St-Trond Belgium see Sint-Truiden
St-Tropez France 56 H5
St-Tropez, Cap de c. France 56 H5
St-Vaast-la-Hougue France 49 F9
St-Valery-en-Caux France 49 H9
St-Véran France 56 H4
St Vincent U.S.A. 130 D1
St Vincent country West Indies see
St Vincent and the Grenadines
St Vincent, Cape Australia 111 [inset]
St Vincent, Cape Port. see
São Vicente, Cabo de
St Vincent, Gulf Australia 111 B7
St Vincent and the Grenadines country
West Indies 137 L6
St Vincent Passage St Lucia/St Vincent
137 L6
St-Vith Belgium 52 G4
St Walburg Canada 121 I4
St Williams Canada 134 E2
St-Yrieix-la-Perche France 56 E4
Sain Us China 72 J4
Saioa mt. Spain 57 F2
Saipal mt. Nepal 82 E3
Saipan i. N. Mariana Is 69 L3
Sai Pok Liu Hoi Hap H.K. China see
West Lamma Channel
Saiteli Turkey see Kadınhanı
Saitlai Myanmar 70 A2
Saittanulkki hill Fin. 44 N3
Sai Yok National Park Thai. 71 B4
Sajam Indon. 69 I7
Sajama, Nevado mt. Bol. 142 E7
Sājir Saudi Arabia 88 B5
Sājūr, Nahr r. Syria/Turkey 85 D1
Sajzī Iran 88 D3
Sak watercourse S. Africa 100 E5
Sakaide Japan 75 D6
Sakākah Saudi Arabia 91 F5
Sakakawea, Lake U.S.A. 130 C2
Sakami Canada 122 G3
Sakami r. Canada 122 F3
Sakami Lake Canada 122 F3
Sakar mts Bulg. 59 L4
Sakaraha Madag. 99 E6
Sak'art'velo country Asia see Georgia
Sakarya Sakarya Turkey see Adapazarı
Sakarya r. Turkey 59 N4
Sakassou Côte d'Ivoire 96 C4
Sakata Japan 75 E5
Sakchu N. Korea 75 B4
Sakesar Pak. 89 I3
Sakhalin i. Rus. Fed. 74 F2
Sakhalin Oblast admin. div. Rus. Fed. see
Sakhalinskaya Oblast'
Sakhalinskaya Oblast' admin. div.
Rus. Fed. 74 F2
Sakhalinskiy Zaliv b. Rus. Fed. 74 F1
Sakhi India 82 C3
Sakhile S. Africa 101 I4
Şäki Azer. 91 G2
Saki Nigeria see Shaki
Saki Ukr. see Saky
Šakiai Lith. 45 M9
Sakir mt. Pak. 89 G4
Sakishima-shotō is Japan 73 M8
Sakoli India 82 D5
Sakon Nakhon Thai. 70 D3
Sakrivier S. Africa 100 E6
Sakura Japan 75 F6
Saky Ukr. 90 D1
Säkylä Fin. 45 M6
Sal i. Cape Verde 96 [inset]
Sal r. Rus. Fed. 43 I7
Sala Sweden 45 J7
Salaberry-de-Valleyfield Canada 135 H1
Salacgrīva Latvia 45 N8
Sala Consilina Italy 58 F4
Salada, Laguna salt l. Mex. 129 F5
Saladas Arg. 144 E3
Salado r. Buenos Aires Arg. 144 E5
Salado r. Santa Fé Arg. 144 D4
Salado r. Arg. 144 C5
Salado r. Mex. 131 D7
Salaga Ghana 96 C4
Salairskiy Kryazh ridge Rus. Fed. 72 E2
Salajwe Botswana 100 G2
Şalālah Oman 87 H6
Salamanca Mex. 136 D4
Salamanca Spain 57 D3
Salamanca U.S.A. 135 F2
Salamanga Moz. 101 K4
Salamantica Spain see Salamanca
Salamat, Bahr r. Chad 97 E4
Salāmī Iran 89 E3
Salamina i. Greece 59 J6
Salamis tourist site Cyprus 85 A2
Salamís i. Greece see Salamina
Salamīyah Syria 85 C2
Salamonie r. U.S.A. 134 C3
Salamonie Lake U.S.A. 134 C3
Salang, Tūnel-e Afgh. 89 H3
Salantai Lith. 45 L8
Salar de Pocitos Arg. 144 C2
Salari Pak. 89 G5
Salas Spain 57 C2
Salaspils Latvia 45 N8
Salavan Laos 70 D4
Salawati i. Indon. 69 I7
Salawin, Mae Nam r. China/Myanmar see
Salween
Salaya India 82 B5
Salayar i. Indon. 69 G8

▶Sala y Gómez, Isla i. S. Pacific Ocean 151 M7
Most easterly point of Oceania.

Salazar Angola see N'dalatando
Salbris France 56 F3
Šalčininkai Lith. 45 N9
Salcombe U.K. 49 D8
Saldae Alg. see Bejaïa
Saldaña Spain 57 D2
Saldanha S. Africa 100 C7
Saldanha Bay S. Africa 100 C7
Saldus Latvia 45 M8
Sale Australia 112 C7
Saleh, Teluk b. Indon. 68 F8
Şāleḩābād Iran 88 C3
Salekhard Rus. Fed. 64 H3
Salem India 84 C4
Salem AR U.S.A. 131 F4
Salem IL U.S.A. 130 F4
Salem IN U.S.A. 134 B4
Salem MA U.S.A. 135 J2
Salem MO U.S.A. 130 F4
Salem NJ U.S.A. 135 H4
Salem NY U.S.A. 135 I2
Salem OH U.S.A. 134 E3

▶Salem OR U.S.A. 126 C3
Capital of Oregon.

Salem SD U.S.A. 130 D3
Salem VA U.S.A. 134 E5
Salen Scotland U.K. 50 D4
Salen Scotland U.K. 50 D4
Salerno Italy 58 F4
Salerno, Golfo di g. Italy 58 F4
Salernum Italy see Salerno
Salford U.K. 48 E5
Salgótarján Hungary 47 Q6
Salgueiro Brazil 143 K5
Salian Afgh. 89 F4
Salibabu i. Indon. 69 H6
Salida U.S.A. 127 G5
Salies-de-Béarn France 56 D5
Salihli Turkey 59 M5
Salihorsk Belarus 45 O10
Salima Malawi 99 D5
Salina KS U.S.A. 130 D4
Salina UT U.S.A. 129 H2
Salina, Isola i. Italy 58 F5
Salina Cruz Mex. 136 E5
Salinas Brazil 145 C2
Salinas Ecuador 142 B4
Salinas Mex. 136 D4
Salinas r. Mex. 131 D7
Salinas U.S.A. 128 C3
Salinas r. U.S.A. 128 C3
Salinas, Cabo de c. Spain see
Ses Salines, Cap de
Salinas, Ponta das pt Angola 99 B5
Salinas Peak U.S.A. 127 G6
Saline U.S.A. 134 D2
Saline r. U.S.A. 130 D4
Saline Valley depr. U.S.A. 128 E3
Salinópolis Brazil 143 I4
Salinosó Lachay, Punta pt Peru 142 C6
Salisbury U.K. 49 F7
Salisbury MD U.S.A. 135 H4
Salisbury NC U.S.A. 132 D5
Salisbury Zimbabwe see Harare
Salisbury Plain U.K. 49 E7
Şalkhad Syria 85 C3
Salla Fin. 44 P3
Sallisaw U.S.A. 131 E5
Salluit Canada 153 K2
Sallum, Khalīj as b. Egypt 90 B5
Sallyana Nepal 83 E3
Salmās Iran 88 B2
Salmi Rus. Fed. 42 F3
Salmo Canada 120 G5
Salmon U.S.A. 126 E3
Salmon r. U.S.A. 126 D3
Salmon Arm Canada 120 G5
Salmon Falls Creek r. U.S.A. 126 E4
Salmon Gums Australia 109 C8
Salmon Reservoir U.S.A. 135 H2
Salmon River Mountains U.S.A. 126 E3
Salmtal Germany 52 G5
Salo Fin. 45 M6
Salome U.S.A. 129 G5
Salon India 82 E4
Salon-de-Provence France 56 G5
Salonica Greece see Thessaloniki
Salonika Greece see Thessaloniki
Salpausselkä reg. Fin. 45 N6
Salqīn Syria 85 C1
Salses, Étang de l. France see
Leucate, Étang de
Sal'sk Rus. Fed. 43 I7
Salsomaggiore Terme Italy 58 C2
Salt Jordan see As Salṭ
Salt watercourse S. Africa 100 F7
Salt r. U.S.A. 129 G5
Salta Arg. 144 C2
Saltaire U.K. 48 F5
Saltash U.K. 49 C8
Saltcoats U.K. 50 E5
Saltee Islands Ireland 51 F5
Saltfjellet Svartisen Nasjonalpark nat. park
Norway 44 I3
Saltfjorden sea chan. Norway 44 H3
Salt Fork Arkansas r. U.S.A. 131 D4
Salt Fork Lake U.S.A. 134 E3
Saltillo Mex. 131 C7
Salt Lake India 89 I5

▶Salt Lake City U.S.A. 129 H1
Capital of Utah.

Salt Lick U.S.A. 134 D4
Salto Brazil 145 B3
Salto Uruguay 144 E4
Salto da Divisa Brazil 145 D2
Salto Grande Brazil 145 A3
Salton Sea salt l. U.S.A. 129 F5
Salto Santiago, Represa de resr
Brazil 144 F3
Salt Range hills Pak. 89 I3
Salt River Canada 121 H2
Saluda U.S.A. 135 G5
Salûm Egypt see As Sallūm
Salûm, Khalîg el b. Egypt see
Sallum, Khalīj as
Saluq, Kūh-e mt. Iran 88 E2
Salur India 84 D2
Saluzzo Italy 58 B2
Salvador Brazil 145 D1
Salvador country Central America see
El Salvador
Salvador, Lake U.S.A. 131 F6
Salvaleón de Higüey Dom. Rep. see Higüey
Salvation Creek r. U.S.A. 129 H2
Salwah Saudi Arabia 98 F1
Salwah, Dawḩat b. Qatar/Saudi Arabia
88 C5
Salween r. China/Myanmar 76 C5
also known as Mae Nam Khong or Mae Nam Salawin or Nu Jiang (China) or Thanlwin (Myanmar)
Salyan Azer. 91 H3
Salyan Nepal see Sallyana
Sal'yany Azer. see Salyan
Salyersville U.S.A. 134 D5
Salzbrunn Namibia 100 C3
Salzburg Austria 47 N7
Salzgitter Germany 53 K2
Salzhausen Germany 53 K1
Salzkotten Germany 53 I3
Salzmünde Germany 53 L3
Salzwedel Germany 53 L2
Sam India 82 B4
Samae San, Ko i. Thai. 71 C4
Samagaltay Rus. Fed. 80 H1
Samāh well Saudi Arabia 88 B4
Samaida Iran see Someydeh
Samaixung China 83 E2
Samakhixai Laos see Attapu
Samalanga Indon. 71 B6
Samalayuca Mex. 127 G7
Samalkot India 84 D2
Samālūṭ Egypt 90 C5
Samâlût Egypt see Samālūṭ
Samana Cay i. Bahamas 133 F8
Samanala mt. Sri Lanka see Adam's Peak
Samandağı Turkey 85 B1
Samangān Afgh. see Āybak
Samangān Iran 89 F3
Samani Japan 74 F4
Samanlı Dağları mts Turkey 59 M4
Samar Kazakh. see Samarskoye
Samar i. Phil. 69 H4
Samara Rus. Fed. 43 K5
Samara r. Rus. Fed. 41 Q5
Samarga Rus. Fed. 74 E3
Samarinda Indon. 68 F7
Samarka Rus. Fed. 74 D3
Samarkand Uzbek. see Samarqand
Samarkand, Pik mt. Tajik. see
Samarqand, Qullai
Samarobriva France see Amiens
Samarqand Uzbek. 89 G2
Samarqand, Qullai mt. Tajik. 89 H2
Sāmarrā' Iraq 91 F4
Samarskoye Kazakh. 80 F2
Samasata Pak. 89 H4
Samastipur India 83 F4
Şamaxı Azer. 91 H2
Samba India 82 C2
Sambaliung mts Indon. 68 F6
Sambalpur India 83 E5
Sambar, Tanjung pt Indon. 68 E7
Sambas Indon. 71 E7
Sambat Ukr. see Kiev
Sambava Madag. 99 F5
Sambha India 83 G4
Sambhajinagar India see Aurangabad
Sambhal India 82 D3
Sambhar Lake India 82 C4
Sambir Ukr. 43 D6
Sambito r. Brazil 143 J5
Sâmbor Cambodia 71 D4
Sambor Ukr. see Sambir
Samborombón, Bahía b. Arg. 144 E5
Sambre r. Belgium/France 52 E4
Samch'ŏk S. Korea 75 C5
Samch'ŏnp'o S. Korea see Sach'on
Same Tanz. 98 D4
Samer France 52 B4
Sami India 82 B5
Samīrah Saudi Arabia 86 F4
Samirum Iran see Yazd-e Khvāst
Samjiyŏn N. Korea 74 C4
Şämkir Azer. 91 G2
Sam Neua Laos see Xam Nua
Samoa country S. Pacific Ocean 107 I3
Samoa Basin sea feature
S. Pacific Ocean 150 I7
Samoa i Sisifo country S. Pacific Ocean see
Samoa
Samobor Croatia 58 F2
Samoded Rus. Fed. 42 I3
Samokov Bulg. 59 J3
Šamorín Slovakia 47 P6
Samos i. Greece 59 L6
Samosir i. Indon. 71 B7
Samothrace i. Greece see Samothraki
Samothraki i. Greece 59 K4
Samoylovka Rus. Fed. 43 I6
Sampê China see Xiangcheng
Sampit Indon. 68 E7
Sampit, Teluk b. Indon. 68 E7
Sam Rayburn Reservoir U.S.A. 131 E6
Samrong Cambodia see Phumĭ Sâmraông
Samsang China 83 E3
Sam Sao, Phou mts Laos/Vietnam 70 C2
Samson U.S.A. 133 C6
Sâm Sơn Vietnam 70 D3
Samsun Turkey 90 E2
Samti Afgh. 89 H2
Samui, Ko i. Thai. 71 C5
Samut Prakan Thai. 71 C4
Samut Sakhon Thai. 71 C4
Samut Songkhram Thai. 71 C4
Samyai China 83 G3
San Mali 96 C3
San, Phou mt. Laos 70 C3
San, Tônlé r. Cambodia 71 D4

▶Şan'ā' Yemen 86 F6
Capital of Yemen.

Sanaa Yemen see Şan'ā'
SANAE IV research station Antarctica
152 B2
San Agostín U.S.A. see St Augustine
San Agustin, Cape Phil. 69 H5
San Agustin, Plains of U.S.A. 129 I5
Sanak Island U.S.A. 118 B4
Sanandaj Iran 88 B3
San Andreas U.S.A. 128 C2
San Andrés, Isla de i.
Caribbean Sea 137 H6
San Andres Mountains U.S.A. 127 G6
San Angelo U.S.A. 131 C6
San Antonio Chile 144 B4
San Antonio NM U.S.A. 127 G6
San Antonio TX U.S.A. 131 D6
San Antonio r. U.S.A. 131 D6
San Antonio, Cabo c. Cuba 137 H4
San Antonio del Mar Mex. 127 D7
San Antonio Oeste Arg. 144 D6
San Antonio Reservoir U.S.A. 128 C4
San Augustín de Valle Fértil Arg. 144 C4
San Augustine U.S.A. 131 E6
San Benedetto del Tronto Italy 58 E3
San Benedicto, Isla i. Mex. 136 B5
San Benito U.S.A. 131 D7
San Benito r. U.S.A. 128 C3
San Benito Mountain U.S.A. 128 C3
San Bernardino U.S.A. 128 E4
San Bernardino Mountains U.S.A. 128 E4
San Bernardo Chile 144 B4
San Blas Mex. 127 F8
San Blas, Cape U.S.A. 133 C6
San Borja Bol. 142 E6
Sanbornville U.S.A. 135 J2
Sanbu China see Kaiping
San Buenaventura Mex. 131 C7
San Carlos Chile 144 B5
San Carlos Equat. Guinea see Luba
San Carlos Coahuila Mex. 131 C6
San Carlos Tamaulipas Mex. 131 D7
San Carlos Phil. 69 G3
San Carlos U.S.A. 129 H5
San Carlos Venez. 142 E2
San Carlos de Bariloche Arg. 144 B6
San Carlos de Bolívar Arg. 144 D5
San Carlos Lake U.S.A. 129 H5
Sancha China 76 E1
Sanchahe China see Fuyu
Sancha He r. China 76 E3
Sanchi India 82 D5
San Chien Pau mt. Laos 70 C2
Sanchor India 82 B4
San Clemente U.S.A. 128 E5
San Clemente Island U.S.A. 128 D5
Sanclêr U.K. see St Clears
San Cristóbal Arg. 144 D4
San Cristobal i. Solomon Is 107 G3
San Cristóbal Venez. 142 D2
San Cristóbal, Isla i. Galápagos
Ecuador 142 [inset]
San Cristóbal de las Casas Mex. 136 F5
Sancti Spíritus Cuba 137 I4
Sand r. S. Africa 101 J2
Sandagou Rus. Fed. 74 D4
Sanda Island U.K. 50 D5
Sandakan Sabah Malaysia 68 F5
Sândăn Cambodia 71 D4
Sandane Norway 44 E6
Sandanski Bulg. 59 J4
Sandaré Mali 96 B3
Sandau Germany 53 M2
Sanday i. U.K. 50 G1
Sandbach U.K. 49 E5
Sandborn U.S.A. 134 B4
Sand Cay reef India 84 B4
Sandefjord Norway 45 G7
Sandercock Nunataks Antarctica 152 D2
Sanders U.S.A. 129 I4
Sandersleben Germany 53 L3
Sanderson U.S.A. 131 C6
Sandfire Roadhouse Australia 108 C4
Sand Fork U.S.A. 134 E4
Sandgate Australia 112 F1
Sandhead U.K. 50 E6
Sand Hill r. U.S.A. 130 D2
Sand Hills U.S.A. 130 C3
Sandia Peru 142 E6
San Diego Mex. 131 B6
San Diego CA U.S.A. 128 E5
San Diego TX U.S.A. 131 D7
San Diego, Sierra mts Mex. 127 F7
Sandıklı Turkey 59 N5
Sandila India 82 E4
Sand Lake Canada 122 D5
Sand Lake l. Canada 121 M5
Sandnes Norway 45 D7
Sandnessjøen Norway 44 H3
Sandoa Dem. Rep. Congo 99 C4
Sandomierz Poland 43 D6
San Donà di Piave Italy 58 E2
Sandover watercourse Australia 110 B4
Sandovo Rus. Fed. 42 H4
Sandoway Myanmar see Thandwè
Sandown U.K. 49 F8
Sandoy i. Faroe Is 44 [inset]
Sand Point U.S.A. 118 B4
Sandpoint U.S.A. 126 D2
Sandray i. U.K. 50 B4
Sandringham Australia 110 B5
Şandrul Mare, Vârful mt. Romania 59 L1
Sandsjö Sweden 45 I6
Sandspit Canada 120 D4
Sand Springs U.S.A. 131 D4
Sand Springs Salt Flat U.S.A. 128 D2
Sandstone Australia 109 B6
Sandstone U.S.A. 130 E2
Sandu Guizhou China 76 E3
Sandu Hunan China 77 G3
Sandur Faroe Is 44 [inset]
Sandusky MI U.S.A. 134 D2
Sandusky OH U.S.A. 134 D3
Sandveld mts S. Africa 100 D6
Sandverhaar Namibia 100 C4
Sandvika Akershus Norway 45 G7
Sandvika Nord-Trøndelag Norway 44 H5
Sandviken Sweden 45 J6
Sandwich Bay Canada 123 K3
Sandwich Island Vanuatu see Éfaté
Sandwich Islands is N. Pacific Ocean see
Hawai'ian Islands
Sandwick U.K. 50 [inset]
Sandwip Bangl. 83 G5
Sandy U.S.A. 129 H1
Sandy r. U.S.A. 135 K1
Sandy Bay Canada 121 K4
Sandy Cape Qld Australia 110 F5
Sandy Cape Tas. Australia 111 [inset]
Sandy Hook U.S.A. 134 D4
Sandy Hook pt U.S.A. 135 H3
Sandy Island Australia 108 C3
Sandykachy Turkm. see Sandykgaçy
Sandykgaçy Turkm. 89 F2
Sandykly Gumy des. Turkm. 89 F2
Sandy Lake Alta Canada 120 H4
Sandy Lake Ont. Canada 121 M4
Sandy Lake l. Canada 121 M4
Sandy Springs U.S.A. 133 C5
San Estanislao Para. 144 E2
San Esteban, Isla i. Mex. 127 E7
San Felipe Chile 144 B4
San Felipe Baja California Mex. 127 E7
San Felipe Chihuahua Mex. 127 G8
San Felipe Venez. 142 E1
San Felipe, Cayos de is Cuba 133 D8
San Felipe de Puerto Plata Dom. Rep. see
Puerto Plata
San Fernando Chile 144 B4
San Fernando Mex. 131 D7
San Fernando watercourse Mex. 127 E7
San Fernando Phil. 69 G3
San Fernando Spain 57 C5
San Fernando Trin. and Tob. 137 L6
San Fernando U.S.A. 128 D4
San Fernando de Apure Venez. 142 E2
San Fernando de Atabapo Venez. 142 E3
San Fernando de Monte Cristi Dom. Rep.
see Monte Cristi
Sanford FL U.S.A. 133 D6
Sanford ME U.S.A. 135 J2
Sanford MI U.S.A. 134 C2
Sanford NC U.S.A. 132 E5
Sanford, Mount U.S.A. 118 D3
Sanford Lake U.S.A. 134 C2
San Francisco Arg. 144 D4
San Francisco U.S.A. 128 B3
San Francisco, Cabo de c. Ecuador 142 B3
San Francisco, Passo de pass Arg./Chile
144 C3
San Francisco Bay inlet U.S.A. 128 B3
San Francisco del Oro Mex. 131 B7
San Francisco de Paula, Cabo c.
Arg. 144 C7
San Francisco Javier Spain 57 G4
San Gabriel, Punta pt Mex. 127 E7
San Gabriel Mountains U.S.A. 128 D4
Sangachaly Azer. see Sanqaçal
Sangameshwar India 84 B2
Sangamon r. U.S.A. 130 F3
Sangan, Koh-i- mt. Afgh. see Sangān, Kūh-e
Sangān, Kūh-e mt. Afgh. 89 G3
Sangar Rus. Fed. 65 N3
Sangareddi India 84 C2
Sangareddy India see Sangareddi
San Gavino Monreale Sardinia Italy 58 C5
Sangay, Parque Nacional nat. park
Ecuador 142 C4
Sangbur Afgh. 89 F3
Sangeang i. Indon. 108 B2
Sanger U.S.A. 128 D3
Sangerfield U.S.A. 135 H2
Sangerhausen Germany 53 L3
Sang-e Surakh Iran 88 E2
Sanggarmai China 76 D1

Sanggau Indon. 68 E6
Sangilen, Nagor'ye mts Rus. Fed. 80 I1
San Giovanni in Fiore Italy 58 G5
Sangir India 82 C5
Sangir i. Indon. 69 H6
Sangir, Kepulauan is Indon. 69 G6
Sangkapura Indon. 68 E8
Sangkulirang Indon. 68 F6
Sangli India 84 B2
Sangmai China see Dêrong
Sangmélima Cameroon 96 E4
Sangngagqoiling China 76 B2
Sango Zimbabwe 99 D6
Sangole India 84 B2
San Gorgonio Mountain U.S.A. 128 E4
Sangpi China see Xiangcheng
Sangre de Cristo Range mts U.S.A. 127 G5
Sangrur India 82 C3
Sangu r. Bangl. 83 G5
Sanguem India 84 B3
Sangutane r. Moz. 101 K3
Sangzhi China 77 F2
Sanhe China see Sandu
San Hipólito, Punta pt Mex. 127 E8
Sanhûr Egypt see Sanhūr
Sanhūr Egypt 90 C5
San Ignacio Beni Bol. 142 E6
San Ignacio Santa Cruz Bol. 142 F7
San Ignacio Baja California Mex. 127 E7
San Ignacio Durango Mex. 131 C7
San Ignacio Sonora Mex. 127 F7
San Ignacio Para. 144 E3
San Ignacio, Laguna l. Mex. 127 E8
Sanikiluaq Canada 122 F2
Sanin-kaigan Kokuritsu-kōen nat. park Japan 75 D6
San Jacinto U.S.A. 128 E5
San Jacinto Peak U.S.A. 128 E5
San Javier Bol. 142 F7
Sanjiang Guangdong China see Liannan
Sanjiang Guangxi China 77 F3
Sanjiang Guizhou China see Jinping
Sanjiangkou China 74 A4
Sanjiaocheng China see Haiyan
Sanjiaoping China 77 F2
Sanjō Japan 75 E5
San Joaquin r. U.S.A. 128 C2
San Joaquin Valley U.S.A. 128 C3
Sanjoli India 82 C5
San Jon U.S.A. 131 C5
San Jorge, Golfo de g. Arg. 144 C7
San Jorge, Golfo de g. Spain see Sant Jordi, Golf de

▶San José Costa Rica 137 H7
Capital of Costa Rica.

San Jose Phil. 69 G3
San Jose CA U.S.A. 128 C3
San Jose NM U.S.A. 127 G6
San Jose watercourse U.S.A. 129 J4
San José, Isla i. Mex. 136 B4
San José de Amacuro Venez. 142 F2
San José de Bavicora Mex. 127 G7
San José de Buenavista Phil. 69 G4
San José de Chiquitos Bol. 142 F7
San José de Comondú Mex. 127 F8
San José de Gracia Mex. 127 E8
San Joséde la Brecha Mex. 127 F8
San José del Cabo Mex. 136 C4
San José del Guaviare Col. 142 D3
San José de Mayo Uruguay 144 E4
San José de Raíces Mex. 131 C7
San Juan Arg. 144 C4
San Juan r. Costa Rica/Nicaragua 137 H6
San Juan mt. Cuba 133 D8
San Juan Mex. 127 G8
San Juan r. Mex. 131 D7

▶San Juan Puerto Rico 137 K5
Capital of Puerto Rico.

San Juan U.S.A. 129 J5
San Juan r. U.S.A. 129 H3
San Juan, Cabo c. Arg. 144 D8
San Juan, Cabo c. Equat. Guinea 96 D4
San Juan Bautista Para. 144 E3
San Juan Bautista de las Misiones Para. see San Juan Bautista
San Juan de Guadalupe Mex. 131 C7
San Juan de los Morros Venez. 142 E2
San Juan Mountains U.S.A. 129 J3
San Juan y Martínez Cuba 133 D8
San Julián Arg. 144 C7
San Justo Arg. 144 D4
Sankari Drug India 84 C4
Sankh r. India 81 F7
Sankhu India 82 C3
Sankra Chhattisgarh India 84 D1
Sankra Rajasthan India 82 B4
Sankt Augustin Germany 53 H4
Sankt Gallen Switz. 56 I3
Sankt-Peterburg Rus. Fed. see St Petersburg
Sankt Pölten Austria 47 O6
Sankt Veit an der Glan Austria 47 O7
Sankt Vith Belgium see St-Vith
Sankt Wendel Germany 53 H5
Sanku India 82 D2
Şanlıurfa Turkey 90 E3
Şanlıurfa prov. Turkey 85 D1
San Lorenzo Arg. 144 D4
San Lorenzo Beni Bol. 142 E7
San Lorenzo Tarija Bol. 142 F8
San Lorenzo Ecuador 142 C3
San Lorenzo mt. Spain 57 E2
San Lorenzo, Cerro mt. Arg./Chile 144 B7
San Lorenzo, Isla i. Mex. 127 E7
Sanlúcar de Barrameda Spain 57 C5
San Lucas Baja California Sur Mex. 127 E8
San Lucas Baja California Sur Mex. 136 C4
San Lucas, Serranía de mts Col. 142 D2
San Luis Arg. 144 C4
San Luis AZ U.S.A. 129 F5
San Luis AZ U.S.A. 129 H5
San Luis CO U.S.A. 131 B4
San Luís, Isla i. Mex. 127 E7
San Luisito Mex. 127 E7
San Luis Obispo U.S.A. 128 C4
San Luis Obispo Bay U.S.A. 128 C4
San Luis Potosí Mex. 136 D4
San Luis Reservoir U.S.A. 128 C3
San Luis Río Colorado Mex. 129 F5
San Manuel U.S.A. 129 H5
San Marcial, Punta pt Mex. 127 F8
San Marcos U.S.A. 131 D6
San Marcos, Isla i. Mex. 127 E8
San Marino country Europe 58 E3

▶San Marino San Marino 58 E3
Capital of San Marino.

San Martín research station Antarctica 152 L2
San Martín Catamarca Arg. 144 C3
San Martín Mendoza Arg. 144 C4
San Martín, Lago l. Arg./Chile 144 B7
San Martín de los Andes Arg. 144 B6
San Mateo U.S.A. 128 B3
San Mateo Mountains U.S.A. 129 J4
San Matías Bol. 143 G7
San Matías, Golfo g. Arg. 144 D6
Sanmen China 77 I2
Sanmen Wan b. China 77 I2
Sanmenxia China 77 F1
San Miguel El Salvador 136 G6
San Miguel U.S.A. 128 C4
San Miguel r. U.S.A. 129 I2
San Miguel de Huachi Bol. 142 E7
San Miguel de Tucumán Arg. 144 C3
San Miguel do Araguaia Brazil 145 A1
San Miguel Island U.S.A. 128 C4
Sanming China 77 H3
Sanndatti India 84 B3
Sanndraigh i. U.K. see Sandray
Sannicandro Garganico Italy 58 F4
San Nicolás Durango Mex. 131 B7
San Nicolás Tamaulipas Mex. 131 D7
San Nicolas Island U.S.A. 128 D5
Sannieshof S. Africa 101 G4
Sanniquellie Liberia 96 C4
Sanok Poland 43 D6
San Pablo Bol. 142 E8
San Pablo Phil. 69 G4
San Pablo de Manta Ecuador see Manta
San Pedro Arg. 144 D2
San Pedro Bol. 142 F7
San Pedro Chile 144 C2
San-Pédro Côte d'Ivoire 96 C4
San Pedro Baja California Sur Mex. 124 E7
San Pedro Chihuahua Mex. 127 G7
San Pedro Para. see San Pedro de Ycuamandyyú
San Pedro watercourse U.S.A. 129 H5
San Pedro, Sierra de mts Spain 57 C4
San Pedro Channel U.S.A. 128 D5
San Pedro de Arimena Col. 142 D3
San Pedro de Atacama Chile 144 C2
San Pedro de las Colonias Mex. 131 C7
San Pedro de Macorís Dom. Rep. 137 K5
San Pedro de Ycuamandyyú Para. 144 E2
San Pedro Martir, Parque Nacional nat. park Mex. 127 E7
San Pedro Sula Hond. 136 G5
San Pierre U.S.A. 134 B3
San Pietro, Isola di i. Sardinia Italy 58 C5
San Pitch r. U.S.A. 129 H2
Sanqaçal Azer. 91 H2
Sanquhar U.K. 50 F5
Sanquianga, Parque Nacional nat. park Col. 142 C3
San Quintín, Cabo c. Mex. 127 D7
San Rafael Arg. 144 C4
San Rafael CA U.S.A. 128 B3
San Rafael NM U.S.A. 129 J4
San Rafael r. U.S.A. 129 H2
San Rafael Knob mt. U.S.A. 129 H2
San Rafael Mountains U.S.A. 128 C4
San Ramón Bol. 142 F6
Sanrao China 77 H3
San Remo Italy 58 B3
San Roque Spain 57 B2
San Roque, Punta pt Mex. 127 E8
San Saba U.S.A. 131 D6
San Salvador i. Bahamas 133 F7

▶San Salvador El Salvador 136 G6
Capital of El Salvador.

San Salvador, Isla i. Galápagos Ecuador 142 [inset]
San Salvador de Jujuy Arg. 144 C2
Sansanné-Mango Togo 96 D3
San Sebastián Arg. 144 C8
San Sebastián Spain see Donostia-San Sebastián
San Sebastián de los Reyes Spain 57 E3
Sansepolcro Italy 58 E3
San Severo Italy 58 F4
San Simon U.S.A. 129 I5
Sanski Most Bos.-Herz. 58 G2
Sansoral Islands Palau see Sonsorol Islands
Sansui China 77 F3
Santa r. Peru 142 C5
Santa Ana Bol. 142 E7
Santa Ana El Salvador 136 G6
Santa Ana Mex. 127 F7
Santa Ana i. Solomon Is 107 G3
Santa Ana U.S.A. 128 E5
Santa Ana de Yacuma Bol. 142 E6
Santa Anna U.S.A. 131 D6
Santa Bárbara Brazil 145 C2
Santa Bárbara Cuba see La Demajagua
Santa Bárbara Mex. 131 B7
Santa Barbara U.S.A. 128 D4
Santa Bárbara, Ilha i. Brazil 145 D2
Santa Barbara Channel U.S.A. 128 C4
Santa Bárbara d'Oeste Brazil 145 B3
Santa Barbara Island U.S.A. 128 D5
Santa Catalina, Gulf of U.S.A. 128 E5
Santa Catalina, Isla i. Mex. 127 F8
Santa Catalina de Armada Spain 57 B2
Santa Catalina Island U.S.A. 128 D5
Santa Catarina state Brazil 145 A4
Santa Catarina Baja California Mex. 127 E7
Santa Catarina Nuevo León Mex. 131 C7
Santa Catarina, Ilha de i. Brazil 145 A4
Santa Clara Col. 142 E4
Santa Clara Cuba 137 I4
Santa Clara Mex. 131 B6
Santa Clara CA U.S.A. 128 C3
Santa Clara UT U.S.A. 129 G3
Santa Clarita U.S.A. 128 D4
Santa Clotilde Peru 142 D4
Santa Comba Angola see Waku-Kungo
Santa Croce, Capo c. Sicily Italy 58 F6
Santa Cruz Bol. 142 F7
Santa Cruz Brazil 143 K5
Santa Cruz Costa Rica 142 A1
Santa Cruz U.S.A. 128 B3
Santa Cruz watercourse U.S.A. 129 G5
Santa Cruz, Isla i. Galápagos Ecuador 142 [inset]
Santa Cruz, Isla i. Mex. 127 F8
Santa Cruz Cabrália Brazil 145 D2
Santa Cruz de Goiás Brazil 145 A2
Santa Cruz de la Palma Canary Is 96 B2
Santa Cruz del Sur Cuba 137 I4
Santa Cruz de Moya Spain 57 F4

▶Santa Cruz de Tenerife Canary Is 96 B2
Joint capital of the Canary Islands.

Santa Cruz do Sul Brazil 144 F3
Santa Cruz Island U.S.A. 128 D4
Santa Cruz Islands Solomon Is 107 G3
Santa Elena, Bahía de b. Ecuador 142 B4
Santa Elena, Cabo c. Costa Rica 137 G6
Santa Elena, Punta pt Ecuador 142 B4
Santa Eudóxia Brazil 145 B3
Santa Eufemia, Golfo di g. Italy 58 G5
Santa Fé Arg. 144 D4
Santa Fé Cuba 133 D8

▶Santa Fe U.S.A. 127 G6
Capital of New Mexico.

Santa Fé de Bogotá Col. see Bogotá
Santa Fé de Minas Brazil 145 B2
Santa Fé do Sul Brazil 145 A3
Santa Helena Brazil 143 I4
Santa Helena de Goiás Brazil 145 A2
Santai Sichuan China 76 E2
Santai Yunnan China 76 D3
Santa Inês Brazil 143 I4
Santa Inés, Isla i. Chile 152 L3
Santa Isabel Arg. 144 C5
Santa Isabel Equat. Guinea see Malabo
Santa Isabel i. Solomon Is 107 F2
Santa Juliana Brazil 145 B2
Santalpur India 82 B5
Santa Lucia Range mts U.S.A. 128 C3
Santa Margarita U.S.A. 128 C4
Santa Margarita, Isla i. Mex. 136 B4
Santa María Arg. 144 C3
Santa Maria Amazonas Brazil 143 G4
Santa Maria Rio Grande do Sul Brazil 144 F3
Santa Maria Cape Verde 96 [inset]
Santa María r. Mex. 127 G7
Santa María Peru 142 D4
Santa Maria U.S.A. 128 C4
Santa Maria r. U.S.A. 129 G4
Santa Maria, Cabo de c. Moz. 101 K4
Santa Maria, Cabo de c. Port. 57 C5
Santa Maria, Chapadão de hills Brazil 145 B1
Santa María, Isla i. Galápagos Ecuador 142 [inset]
Santa Maria, Serra de hills Brazil 145 B1
Santa Maria da Vitória Brazil 145 B1
Santa María de Cuevas Mex. 131 B7
Santa Maria do Suaçuí Brazil 145 C2
Santa María Island Vanuatu 107 G3
Santa Maria Madalena Brazil 145 C3
Santa Maria Mountains U.S.A. 129 G4
Santa Marta Col. 142 D1
Santa Marta, Cabo de c. Angola 99 B5
Santa Marta Grande, Cabo de c. Brazil 145 A5
Santa Maura i. Greece see Lefkada
Santa Monica U.S.A. 128 D4
Santa Monica, Pico mt. Mex. 127 E8
Santa Monica Bay U.S.A. 128 D5
Santan Indon. 68 F7
Santana Brazil 145 C1
Santana r. Brazil 145 A2
Santana do Araguaia Brazil 143 H5
Santander Spain 57 E2
Santa Nella U.S.A. 128 C3
Santanilla, Islas is Caribbean Sea see Cisne, Islas del
Santan Mountain hill U.S.A. 129 H5
Sant'Antioco Sardinia Italy 58 C5
Sant'Antioco, Isola di i. Sardinia Italy 58 C5
Sant Antoni de Portmany Spain 57 G4
Santapilly India 84 D2
Santaquin U.S.A. 129 H2
Santa Quitéria Brazil 143 J4
Santarém Brazil 143 H4
Santarém Port. 57 B4
Santa Rita Mex. 131 C7
Santa Rosa Arg. 144 D5
Santa Rosa Acre Brazil 142 D5
Santa Rosa Rio Grande do Sul Brazil 144 F3
Santa Rosa Mex. 131 C7
Santa Rosa CA U.S.A. 128 B2
Santa Rosa NM U.S.A. 127 G6
Santa Rosa de Copán Hond. 136 G6
Santa Rosa de la Roca Bol. 142 F7
Santa Rosa Island U.S.A. 128 C5
Santa Rosalía Mex. 127 E8
Santa Rosa Range mts U.S.A. 126 D4
Santa Rosa Wash watercourse U.S.A. 129 G5
Santa Sylvina Arg. 144 D3
Santa Teresa Australia 109 F6
Santa Teresa r. Brazil 145 A1
Santa Teresa Mex. 131 D7
Santa Vitória Brazil 145 A2
Santa Ynez r. U.S.A. 128 C4
Santa Ysabel i. Solomon Is see Santa Isabel
Santee U.S.A. 128 E5
Santee r. U.S.A. 133 E5
Santiago Brazil 144 F3
Santiago i. Cape Verde 96 [inset]

▶Santiago Chile 144 B4
Capital of Chile.

Santiago Dom. Rep. 137 J5
Santiago Panama 137 H7
Santiago Phil. 69 G3
Santiago de Compostela Spain 57 B2
Santiago de Cuba Cuba 137 I4
Santiago del Estero Arg. 144 D3
Santiago de los Caballeros Dom. Rep. see Santiago
Santiago de Veraguas Panama see Santiago
Santiaguillo, Laguna de l. Mex. 131 B7
Santianna Point Canada 121 P2
Santipur India see Shantipur
Sant Jordi, Golf de g. Spain 57 G3
Santo Amaro Brazil 145 D1
Santo Amaro de Campos Brazil 145 C3
Santo Anastácio Brazil 145 A3
Santo André Brazil 145 B3
Santo Angelo Brazil 144 F3

▶Santo Antão i. Cape Verde 96 [inset]
Most westerly point of Africa.

Santo Antônio Brazil 142 F4
Santo Antônio r. Brazil 145 C2
Santo António São Tomé and Príncipe 96 D4
Santo Antônio, Cabo c. Brazil 145 D1
Santo Antônio da Platina Brazil 145 A3
Santo Antônio de Jesus Brazil 145 D1
Santo Antônio do Içá Brazil 142 E4
Santo Corazón Bol. 143 G7
Santo Domingo Cuba 133 D8

▶Santo Domingo Dom. Rep. 137 K5
Capital of the Dominican Republic.

Santo Domingo Baja California Mex. 127 E7
Santo Domingo Baja California Sur Mex. 127 F8
Santo Domingo country West Indies see Dominican Republic
Santo Domingo de Guzmán Dom. Rep. see Santo Domingo
Santo Hipólito Brazil 145 B2
Santorini i. Greece 59 K6
Santos Brazil 145 B3
Santos Dumont Brazil 145 C3
Santos Plateau sea feature S. Atlantic Ocean 148 E7
Santo Tomás Mex. 127 E7
Santo Tomás Peru 142 D6
Santo Tomé Arg. 144 E3
Sanup Plateau U.S.A. 129 G3
San Valentín, Cerro mt. Chile 144 B7
San Vicente El Salvador 136 G6
San Vicente Mex. 127 D7
San Vicente de Baracaldo Spain see Barakaldo
San Vicente de Cañete Peru 142 C6
San Vincenzo Italy 58 D3
San Vito, Capo c. Sicily Italy 58 E5
Sanwer India 82 C5
Sanxia Shuiku resr China see Three Gorges Reservoir
Sanya China 77 F5
Sanyuan China 77 F1
S. A. Nyýazow Adyndaky Turkm. 89 F2
Sanza Pombo Angola 99 B4
Sao, Phou mt. Laos 70 C3
São Bernardo do Campo Brazil 145 B3
São Borja Brazil 144 E3
São Carlos Brazil 145 B3
São Domingos Brazil 145 B1
São Felipe, Serra de hills Brazil 145 B1
São Félix Bahia Brazil 145 D1
São Félix Mato Grosso Brazil 143 H6
São Félix Pará Brazil 143 H5
São Fidélis Brazil 145 C3
São Francisco Brazil 145 B1

▶São Francisco r. Brazil 145 C1
5th longest river in South America.

São Francisco, Ilha de i. Brazil 145 A4
São Francisco de Paula Brazil 145 A5
São Francisco de Sales Brazil 145 A2
São Francisco do Sul Brazil 145 A4
São Gabriel Brazil 144 F4
São Gonçalo Brazil 145 C3
São Gonçalo do Abaeté Brazil 145 B2
São Gonçalo do Sapucaí Brazil 145 B3
São Gotardo Brazil 145 B2
São João, Ilhas de is Brazil 143 J4
São João da Barra Brazil 145 C3
São João da Boa Vista Brazil 145 B3
São João da Madeira Port. 57 B3
São João da Ponte Brazil 145 B1
São João del Rei Brazil 145 B3
São João do Paraíso Brazil 145 C1
São Joaquim Brazil 145 A5
São Joaquim da Barra Brazil 145 B3
São José Amazonas Brazil 142 E4
São José Santa Catarina Brazil 145 A4
São José do Rio Preto Brazil 145 A3
São José dos Campos Brazil 145 B3
São José dos Pinhais Brazil 145 A4
São Leopoldo Brazil 145 A5
São Lourenço Brazil 145 B3
São Lourenço r. Brazil 143 G7
São Luís Brazil 143 J4
São Luís Brazil 143 G4
São Luís de Montes Belos Brazil 145 A2
São Manuel Brazil 145 A3
São Marcos r. Brazil 145 B2
São Mateus Brazil 145 D2
São Mateus do Sul Brazil 145 A4
São Miguel i. Arquipélago dos Açores 148 G3
São Miguel r. Brazil 145 B2
São Miguel do Tapuio Brazil 143 J5
Saône r. France 56 G4
Saoner India 82 D5
São Nicolau i. Cape Verde 96 [inset]

▶São Paulo Brazil 145 B3
Most populous city in South America and 4th in the world.

São Paulo state Brazil 145 A3
São Paulo de Olivença Brazil 142 E4
São Pedro da Aldeia Brazil 145 C3
São Pedro e São Paulo is N. Atlantic Ocean 148 G5
São Pires r. Brazil see Teles Pires
São Raimundo Nonato Brazil 143 J5
São Romão Amazonas Brazil 142 E5
São Romão Minas Gerais Brazil 145 B2
São Roque Brazil 145 B3
São Roque, Cabo de c. Brazil 143 K5
São Salvador Angola see M'banza Congo
São Salvador do Congo Angola see M'banza Congo
São Sebastião Brazil 145 B3
São Sebastião, Ilha do i. Brazil 145 B3
São Sebastião do Paraíso Brazil 145 B3
São Sebastião dos Poções Brazil 145 B1
São Simão Minas Gerais Brazil 143 H7
São Simão São Paulo Brazil 145 B3
São Simão, Barragem de resr Brazil 145 A2
São Tiago i. Cape Verde see Santiago

▶São Tomé São Tomé and Príncipe 96 D4
Capital of São Tomé and Príncipe.

São Tomé i. São Tomé and Príncipe 96 D4
São Tomé, Cabo de c. Brazil 145 C3
São Tomé, Pico de mt. São Tomé and Príncipe 96 D4
São Tomé and Príncipe country Africa 96 D4
Saoura, Oued watercourse Alg. 54 D6
São Vicente Brazil 145 B3
São Vicente i. Cape Verde 96 [inset]
São Vicente, Cabo de c. Port. 57 B5
Sapanca Turkey 59 N4
Sapaul India see Supaul
Şaphane Dağı mt. Turkey 59 N5
Sapo National Park Liberia 96 C4
Sapouy Burkina 96 C3
Sapozhok Rus. Fed. 43 I5
Sappa Creek r. U.S.A. 130 D3
Sapporo Japan 74 F4
Sapulpa U.S.A. 131 D4
Sapulut Sabah Malaysia 68 F6
Saputang China see Zadoi
Sāqī Iran 88 E3
Saqqez Iran 88 B2
Sarā Iran 88 B2
Sarāb Iran 88 B2
Sara Buri Thai. 71 C4
Saradiya India 82 B5
Saragossa Spain see Zaragoza
Saragt Turkm. 89 F2
Saraguro Ecuador 142 C4
Sarahs Turkm. see Saragt
Sarai Afgh. 89 G3
Sarai Sidhu Pak. 89 I4

▶Sarajevo Bos.-Herz. 58 H3
Capital of Bosnia-Herzegovina.

Sarakhs Iran 89 F2
Saraktash Rus. Fed. 64 G4
Saraland U.S.A. 131 F6
Saramati mt. India/Myanmar 70 A1
Saran' Kazakh. 80 D2
Saranac U.S.A. 134 C2
Saranac r. U.S.A. 135 I1
Saranac Lake U.S.A. 135 H1
Saranda Albania see Sarandë
Sarandë Albania 59 I5
Sarandib country Asia see Sri Lanka
Sarangani Islands Phil. 69 H5
Sarangpur India 82 D5
Saransk Rus. Fed. 43 J5
Sara Peak Nigeria 96 D4
Saraphi Thai. 70 B3
Sarapul Rus. Fed. 41 Q4
Sarāqib Syria 85 C2
Sarasota U.S.A. 133 D7
Saraswati r. India 89 H6
Sarata Ukr. 59 M1
Saratoga CA U.S.A. 128 B3
Saratoga WY U.S.A. 126 G4
Saratoga Springs U.S.A. 132 F3
Saratok Sarawak Malaysia 68 E6
Saratov Rus. Fed. 43 J6
Saratovskoye Vodokhranilishche resr Rus. Fed. 43 J5
Saratsina, Akrotirio pt Greece 59 K5
Saravan Iran 89 F5
Saray Turkey 59 L4
Sarayköy Turkey 59 M6
Sarayönü Turkey 90 D3
Sarbāz Iran 87 J4
Sarbāz reg. Iran 89 F5
Sarbhang Bhutan 83 G4
Sarbīsheh Iran 87 I3
Sarda r. Nepal 83 E3
Sard Āb Afgh. 89 H2
Sardarshahr India 82 C3
Sar Dasht Iran 88 B2
Sardegna i. Sardinia Italy see Sardinia
Sardica Bulg. see Sofia
Sardinia i. Sardinia Italy 58 C4
Sardis MS U.S.A. 131 F5
Sardis WV U.S.A. 134 E4
Sardis Lake resr U.S.A. 131 F5
Sar-e Būm Afgh. 89 G3
Sareks nationalpark nat. park Sweden 44 J3
Sarektjåkkå mt. Sweden 44 J3
Sar-e Pol Afgh. 89 G2
Sar-e Pol-e Żahāb Iran 88 B3
Sar Eskandar Iran see Hashtrud
Sare Yazd Iran 88 D4
Sargasso Sea N. Atlantic Ocean 151 P4
Sargodha Pak. 89 I3
Sarh Chad 97 E4
Sarhad reg. Iran 89 F4
Sārī Iran 88 D2
Saria i. Greece 59 L7
Sar-i-Bum Afgh. see Sar-e Būm
Sáric Mex. 127 F7
Sarigan i. N. Mariana Is 69 L3
Sarigh Jilganang Kol salt l. Aksai Chin 82 D2
Sarıgöl Turkey 59 M5
Sarıkamış Turkey 91 F2
Sarikei Sarawak Malaysia 68 E6
Sarikūl, Qatorkŭhi mts China/Tajik. see Sarykol Range
Sarila India 82 D4
Sarina Australia 110 E4
Sarıoğlan Kayseri Turkey 90 D3
Sarıoğlan Konya Turkey see Belören
Sariqamish Kuli salt l. Turkm./Uzbek. see Sarykamyshskoye Ozero
Sarīr Tibesti des. Libya 97 E2
Sarita U.S.A. 131 D7
Sarıveliler Turkey 85 A1
Sariwŏn N. Korea 75 B5
Sarıyar Barajı resr Turkey 59 N5
Sarıyer Turkey 59 M4
Sarız Turkey 90 E3
Sark i. Channel Is 49 E9
Sarkand Kazakh. 80 E2
Şarkikaraağaç Turkey 59 N5
Şarkışla Turkey 90 E3
Şarköy Turkey 59 L4
Sarlath Range mts Afgh./Pak. 89 G4
Sarmi Indon. 69 J7
Särna Sweden 45 H6
Sarneh Iran 88 B3
Sarnen Switz. 56 I3
Sarni India see Amla
Sarnia Canada 134 D2
Sarny Ukr. 43 E6
Sarolangun Indon. 68 C7
Saroma-ko l. Japan 74 F3
Saronikos Kolpos g. Greece 59 J6
Saros Körfezi b. Turkey 59 L4
Sarova Rus. Fed. 43 I5
Sarowbī Afgh. 89 H3
Sarpa, Ozero l. Rus. Fed. 43 J6
Sarpan i. N. Mariana Is see Rota
Sarpsborg Norway 45 G7
Sarqant Kazakh. see Sarkand
Sarre r. France 52 H5
Sarrebourg France 52 H6
Sarreguemines France 52 H5
Sarria Spain 57 C2
Sarry France 52 E6
Sartana Ukr. 43 H7
Sartanahu Pak. 89 H5
Sartène Corsica France 56 I6
Sarthe r. France 56 D3
Sartu China see Daqing
Saruna Pak. 89 G5
Sarupsar India 82 C3
Şärur Azer. 91 G3
Saru Tara tourist site Afgh. 89 F4
Sarv Iran 88 D3
Sarvābād Iran 88 B3
Sárvár Hungary 58 G1
Sarwar India 82 C4
Sarygamysh Köli salt l. Turkm./Uzbek. see Sarykamyshskoye Ozero
Sary-Ishikotrau, Peski des. Kazakh. see Saryyesik-Atyrau, Peski
Sarykamyshskoye Ozero salt l. Turkm./Uzbek. 91 J2
Sarykol Range mts China/Tajik. 89 I2
Saryozek Kazakh. 80 E3
Saryshagan Kazakh. 80 D2
Sarysu watercourse Kazakh. 80 C2
Sarytash Kazakh. 91 H1
Sary-Tash Kyrg. 89 I2
Saryýazy Suw Howdany resr Turkm. 89 F
Saryyesik-Atyrau, Peski des. Kazakh. 80
Sarzha Kazakh. 91 H2
Sasar, Tanjung pt Indon. 108 B2
Sasaram India 83 F4
Sasebo Japan 75 C6
Saskatchewan prov. Canada 121 J4
Saskatchewan r. Canada 121 K4
Saskatoon Canada 121 J4
Saskylakh Rus. Fed. 65 M2
Saslaya mt. Nicaragua 137 H6
Sasoi r. India 82 B5
Sasolburg S. Africa 101 H4
Sasovo Rus. Fed. 43 I5
Sass r. Canada 120 H2
Sassandra Côte d'Ivoire 96 C4
Sassari Sardinia Italy 58 C4
Sassenberg Germany 53 I3
Sassnitz Germany 47 N3
Sass Town Liberia 96 C4
Sasykkol', Ozero l. Kazakh. 80 F2
Sasykoli Rus. Fed. 43 J7
Sasyqköl l. Kazakh. see Sasykkol', Ozero
Satahual i. Micronesia see Satawal
Sata-misaki c. Japan 75 C7
Satana India 84 B1
Satan Pass U.S.A. 129 I4
Satara India 84 B2
Satara S. Africa 101 J3
Satawal i. Micronesia 69 L5
Sätbaev Kazakh. see Satpayev
Satevó Mex. 131 B7
Satevo r. Mex. 127 G8
Satırlar Turkey see Yeşilova
Satkania Bangl. 83 H5
Satkhira Bangl. 83 G5
Satluj r. India/Pak. see Sutlej
Satmala Range hills India 84 C2
Satna India 82 E4
Satpayev Kazakh. 80 C2
Satpura Range mts India 82 C5
Satsuma-hantō pen. Japan 75 C7
Sattahip Thai. 71 C4
Satteldorf Germany 53 K5
Satthwa Myanmar 70 A3
Satu Mare Romania 43 D7
Satun Thai. 71 C6
Satwas India 82 D5
Sauceda Mountains U.S.A. 129 G5
Saucillo Mex. 131 B6
Sauda Norway 45 E7
Sauðárkrókur Iceland 44 [inset]

▶Saudi Arabia country Asia 86 F4
5th largest country in Asia.

Sauer r. France 53 I6
Saugatuck U.S.A. 134 B2
Saugeen r. Canada 134 E1
Säüjbolāgh Iran see Mahābād
Sauk Center U.S.A. 130 E2
Saulieu France 56 G3
Saulnois reg. France 52 G6
Sault Sainte Marie Canada 122 D5
Sault Sainte Marie U.S.A. 132 C2
Saumalkol' Kazakh. 78 F1
Saumarez Reef Australia 110 F4
Saumlakki Indon. 108 E2
Saumur France 56 D3
Saunders, Mount hill Australia 108 E3
Saunders Coast Antarctica 152 J1
Saurimo Angola 99 C4
Sautar Angola 99 B5
Sauvolles, Lac l. Canada 123 G3
Sava r. Europe 58 I2
Savage River Australia 111 [inset]

vai'i i. Samoa 107 I3
vala r. Rus. Fed. 43 I6
valou Benin 96 D4
vanat Iran see Eşţahbān
vane r. Canada 123 H4
vanna U.S.A. 130 F3
vannah GA U.S.A. 133 D5
vannah OH U.S.A. 134 D3
vannah TN U.S.A. 131 F5
vannah r. U.S.A. 133 D5
vannah Sound Bahamas 133 E7
vannakhét Laos 70 D3
vanna-la-Mar Jamaica 137 I5
vant Lake Canada 122 C4
vant Lake l. Canada 122 C4
vanur India 84 B3
var Sweden 44 L5
vaştepe Turkey 59 L5
vè Benin 96 D4
ve r. Moz./Zimbabwe 99 D6
veh Iran 88 C3
verne France 53 H6
verne, Col de pass France 53 H6
viaho Fin. 44 P5
vinskiy Rus. Fed. 42 I3
vitri r. India 84 B2
vli India 82 C5
voie reg. France see Savoy
vona Italy 58 C2
vonlinna Fin. 44 P6
vonranta Fin. 44 P5
voy reg. France 56 H3
vşat Turkey 91 F2
vsjö Sweden 45 I8
vu i. Indon. 108 C2
vukoski Fin. 44 P3
vur Turkey 91 F3
vu Sea Indon. see Sawu, Laut
w Myanmar 70 A2
wai Madhopur India 82 D4
wan Myanmar 70 B1
war India 82 C4
watch Range mts U.S.A. 126 G5
wel Mountain hill U.K. 51 E3
wi, Ao b. Thai. 71 B5
wn Myanmar 70 B2
wtell Australia 112 F3
wtooth Range mts U.S.A. 126 C2
wu Indon. 108 C2
wu i. Indon. see Savu
wu, Laut sea Indon. 108 C2
wye Myanmar 70 B2
wyer U.S.A. 134 B3
xilby U.K. 48 G5
xmundham U.K. 49 I6
xnäs Sweden 44 I4
xony land Germany see Sachsen
xony-Anhalt land Germany see Sachsen-Anhalt
xton U.S.A. 135 F3
y Niger 96 D3
yabouri Laos see Xaignabouli
yak Kazakh. 80 E2
yanogorsk Rus. Fed. 72 G2
yano-Shushenskoye Vodokhranilishche resr Rus. Fed. 72 G2
yansk Rus. Fed. 72 I2
yaq Kazakh. see Sayak
yat Turkm. see Saýat
ýat Turkm. 89 F2
ydā Lebanon see Sidon
yen Iran 88 D4
yer Island Thai. see Similan, Ko
yghān Afgh. 89 G3
yhan-Ovoo Mongolia 72 I3
yḥūt Yemen 86 H6
yingpan China 76 D3
ykhin Kazakh. 41 P6
ylac Somalia 97 H3
ylan country Asia see Sri Lanka
ynshand Mongolia 73 K4
yoa mt. Spain see Saioa
yot Turkm. see Saýat
yqal, Baḩr imp. l. Syria 85 C3
yqyn Kazakh. see Saykhin
yre OK U.S.A. 131 D5
yre PA U.S.A. 135 G3
yreville U.S.A. 135 H3
yula Mex. 136 F5
yyod Turkm. see Saýat
zdy Kazakh. 43 K7
zin Pak. 89 I3
aa Alg. 54 D6
eitla Tunisia 58 C7
addan Australia 109 C8
afell Pike hill U.K. 48 D4
alasaig U.K. 50 C4
alea Italy 58 F5
alloway U.K. 50 [inset]
alpaigh, Eilean i. U.K. see Scalpay
alpay i. U.K. 50 C3
apa Flow inlet U.K. 50 F2
arba i. U.K. 50 D4
arborough Canada 134 F2
arborough Trin. and Tob. 137 L6
arborough U.K. 48 G4
arborough Shoal sea feature S. China Sea 68 F3
ariff Island Ireland 51 B6
arp i. U.K. 50 B2
arpanto i. Greece see Karpathos
haale r. Germany 53 K1
haalsee l. Germany 53 K1
haerbeek Belgium 52 E4
haffhausen Switz. 56 I3
hafstädt Germany 53 L3
hagen Neth. 52 E2
hagerbrug Neth. 52 E2
hakalskuppe Namibia 100 C4
härding Austria 47 N6
harendijke Neth. 52 D3
harteberg hill Germany 52 G4
haumburg U.S.A. 134 A2
hebheim Germany 53 K5
heeßel Germany 53 J1
hefferville Canada 123 I3
heibbs Austria 47 O6
helde r. Belgium see Scheldt
heldt r. Belgium 52 E3
hell Creek Range mts U.S.A. 129 F2
hellerten Germany 53 K2
hellville U.S.A. 128 B2
Schenectady U.S.A. 135 I2
Schenefeld Germany 53 J1
Schermerhorn Neth. 52 E2
Schertz U.S.A. 131 D6
Schierling Germany 53 M6
Schiermonnikoog Neth. 52 G1
Schiermonnikoog i. Neth. 52 G1
Schiermonnikoog Nationaal Park nat. park Neth. 52 G1
Schiffdorf Germany 53 I1
Schinnen Neth. 52 F4
Schio Italy 58 D2
Schkeuditz Germany 53 M3
Schleiden Germany 52 G4
Schleiz Germany 53 L4
Schleswig Germany 47 L3
Schleswig-Holstein land Germany 53 K1
Schleswig-Holsteinisches Wattenmeer, Nationalpark nat. park Germany 47 L3
Schleusingen Germany 53 K4
Schlitz Germany 53 J4
Schloss Holte-Stukenbrock Germany 53 I3
Schloss Wartburg tourist site Germany 53 K3
Schlüchtern Germany 53 J4
Schlüsselfeld Germany 53 K5
Schmallenberg Germany 53 I3
Schmidt Island Rus. Fed. see Shmidta, Ostrov
Schmidt Peninsula Rus. Fed. see Shmidta, Poluostrov
Schneeberg Germany 53 M4
Schneidemühl Poland see Piła
Schneidlingen Germany 53 L3
Schneverdingen Germany 53 J1
Schoharie U.S.A. 135 H2
Schönebeck Germany 53 M1
Schönebeck (Elbe) Germany 53 L2
Schönefeld airport Germany 53 N2
Schöningen Germany 53 K2
Schöntal Germany 53 J5
Schoolcraft U.S.A. 134 C2
Schoonhoven Neth. 52 E3
Schopfloch Germany 53 K5
Schöppenstedt Germany 53 K2
Schortens Germany 53 H1
Schouten Island Australia 111 [inset]
Schouten Islands P.N.G. 69 K7
Schrankogel mt. Austria 47 M7
Schreiber Canada 122 D4
Schroon Lake U.S.A. 135 I2
Schröttersburg Poland see Płock
Schulenburg U.S.A. 131 D6
Schuler Canada 121 I5
Schull Ireland 51 C6
Schultz Lake Canada 121 L1
Schüttorf Germany 53 H2
Schuyler U.S.A. 130 D3
Schuyler Lake U.S.A. 135 H2
Schuylkill Haven U.S.A. 135 G3
Schwabach Germany 53 L5
Schwäbische Alb mts Germany 47 L7
Schwäbisch Gmünd Germany 53 J6
Schwäbisch Hall Germany 53 J5
Schwaförden Germany 53 I2
Schwalm r. Germany 53 J3
Schwalmstadt-Ziegenhain Germany 53 J4
Schwandorf Germany 53 M5
Schwaner, Pegunungan mts Indon. 68 E7
Schwanewede Germany 53 I1
Schwarmstedt Germany 53 J2
Schwarze Elster r. Germany 53 M3
Schwarzenbek Germany 53 K1
Schwarzenberg Germany 53 M4
Schwarzer Mann hill Germany 52 G4
Schwarzrand mts Namibia 100 C3
Schwarzwald mts Germany see Black Forest
Schwatka Mountains U.S.A. 118 C3
Schwaz Austria 47 M7
Schwedt an der Oder Germany 47 O4
Schwegenheim Germany 53 I5
Schweich Germany 52 G5
Schweinfurt Germany 53 K4
Schweinitz Germany 53 N3
Schweinrich Germany 53 M1
Schweiz country Europe see Switzerland
Schweizer-Reneke S. Africa 101 G4
Schwelm Germany 53 H3
Schwerin Germany 53 L1
Schweriner See l. Germany 53 L1
Schwetzingen Germany 53 I5
Schwyz Switz. 56 I3
Sciacca Sicily Italy 58 E6
Scicli Sicily Italy 58 F6
Science Hill U.S.A. 134 C5
Scilly, Île atoll Fr. Polynesia see Manuae
Scilly, Isles of U.K. 49 A9
Scioto r. U.S.A. 134 D4
Scipio U.S.A. 129 G2
Scobey U.S.A. 126 G2
Scodra Albania see Shkodër
Scofield Reservoir U.S.A. 129 H2
Scole U.K. 49 I6
Scone Australia 112 E4
Scone U.K. 50 F4
Scoresby Land reg. Greenland 119 P2
Scoresbysund Greenland see Ittoqqortoormiit
Scoresby Sund sea chan. Greenland see Kangertittivaq
Scorno, Punta dello pt Sardinia Italy see Caprara, Punta
Scorpion Bight b. Australia 109 D8
Scotia Ridge sea feature S. Atlantic Ocean 148 E9
Scotia Sea S. Atlantic Ocean 148 F9
Scotland Canada 134 E2
Scotland admin. div. U.K. 50 F3
Scotland U.S.A. 135 G4
Scotstown Canada 123 H5
Scott U.S.A. 134 C3
Scott, Cape Australia 108 E3
Scott, Cape Canada 120 D5
Scott, Mount hill U.S.A. 131 D5
Scott Base research station Antarctica 152 H1
Scottburgh S. Africa 101 J6
Scott City U.S.A. 130 C4
Scott Coast Antarctica 152 H1
Scott Glacier Antarctica 152 I1
Scott Island Antarctica 152 H2
Scott Islands Canada 120 D5
Scott Lake Canada 121 J3
Scott Mountains Antarctica 152 D2
Scott Reef Australia 108 C3
Scottsbluff U.S.A. 130 C3
Scottsboro U.S.A. 133 C5
Scottsburg U.S.A. 134 C4
Scottsville KY U.S.A. 134 B5
Scottsville VA U.S.A. 135 F5
Scourie U.K. 50 D2
Scousburgh U.K. 50 [inset]
Scrabster U.K. 50 F2
Scranton U.S.A. 135 H3
Scunthorpe U.K. 48 G5
Scuol Switz. 56 J3
Scupi Macedonia see Skopje
Scutari Albania see Shkodër
Scutari, Lake Albania/Montenegro 59 H3
Seaboard U.S.A. 135 G5
Seabrook, Lake salt flat Australia 109 B7
Seaford U.K. 49 H8
Seaforth Canada 134 E2
Seal r. Canada 121 M3
Seal, Cape S. Africa 100 F8
Sea Lake Australia 111 C7
Seal Lake Canada 123 J3
Sealy U.S.A. 131 D6
Seaman U.S.A. 134 D4
Seaman Range mts U.S.A. 129 F3
Seamer U.K. 48 G4
Searchlight U.S.A. 129 F4
Searcy U.S.A. 131 F5
Searles Lake U.S.A. 128 E4
Seaside CA U.S.A. 127 C5
Seaside OR U.S.A. 126 C3
Seaside Park U.S.A. 135 H4
Seattle U.S.A. 126 C3
Seaview Range mts Australia 110 D3
Seba Indon. 108 C2
Sebago Lake U.S.A. 135 J2
Sebastea Turkey see Sivas
Sebastian U.S.A. 133 D7
Sebastián Vizcaíno, Bahía b. Mex. 127 E7
Sebasticook r. U.S.A. 135 K1
Sebasticook Lake U.S.A. 135 K1
Sebastopol Ukr. see Sevastopol'
Sebastopol U.S.A. 128 B2
Sebatik i. Indon. 68 F6
Sebba Burkina 96 D3
Seben Turkey 59 N4
Sebenico Croatia see Šibenik
Sebeş Romania 59 J2
Sebewaing U.S.A. 134 D2
Sebezh Rus. Fed. 45 P8
Şebinkarahisar Turkey 90 E2
Sebree U.S.A. 134 B5
Sebring U.S.A. 133 D7
Sebrovo Rus. Fed. 43 I6
Sebta N. Africa see Ceuta
Sebuku i. Indon. 68 F7
Sechelt Canada 120 F5
Sechenovo Rus. Fed. 43 J5
Sechura Peru 142 B5
Sechura, Bahía de b. Peru 142 B5
Seckach Germany 53 J5
Second Mesa U.S.A. 129 H4
Secretary Island N.Z. 113 A7
Secunda S. Africa 101 I4
Secunderabad India 84 C2
Sedalia U.S.A. 130 E4
Sedam India 84 C2
Sedan France 52 E5
Sedan U.S.A. 131 D4
Sedan Dip Australia 110 C3
Seddon N.Z. 113 E5
Seddonville N.Z. 113 C5
Sedeh Iran 88 E3
Sederot Israel 85 B4
Sedlčany Czech Rep. 47 O6
Sedlets Poland see Siedlce
Sedom Israel 85 B4
Sedona U.S.A. 129 H4
Sédrata Alg. 58 B6
Šeduva Lith. 45 M9
Seedorf Germany 53 K1
Seehausen Germany 53 L2
Seehausen (Altmark) Germany 53 L2
Seeheim Namibia 100 C4
Seeheim-Jugenheim Germany 53 I5
Seelig, Mount Antarctica 152 K1
Seelze Germany 53 J2
Seenu Atoll Maldives see Addu Atoll
Sées France 56 E2
Seesen Germany 53 K3
Seevetal Germany 53 K1
Sefadu Sierra Leone 96 B4
Sefare Botswana 101 H2
Seferihisar Turkey 59 L5
Sefid, Kūh-e mt. Iran 88 C3
Sefophe Botswana 101 H2
Segalstad Norway 45 G6
Segamat Malaysia 71 C7
Ségbana Benin 96 D3
Segeletz Germany 53 M2
Segezha Rus. Fed. 42 G3
Seghnān Afgh. 89 H2
Segontia U.K. see Caernarfon
Segontium U.K. see Caernarfon
Segorbe Spain 57 F4
Ségou Mali 96 C3
Segovia r. Hond./Nicaragua see Coco
Segovia Spain 57 D3
Segozerskoye, Ozero resr Rus. Fed. 42 G3
Seguam Island U.S.A. 118 A4
Séguédine Niger 96 E2
Séguéla Côte d'Ivoire 96 C4
Seguin U.S.A. 131 D6
Segura r. Spain 57 F4
Segura, Sierra de mts Spain 57 E5
Sehithwa Botswana 99 C6
Sehlabathebe National Park Lesotho 101 I5
Sehore India 82 D5
Sehwan Pak. 89 G5
Seibert U.S.A. 130 C4
Seignelay r. Canada 123 H4
Seikphyu Myanmar 70 A2
Seiland i. Norway 44 M1
Seille r. France 52 G5
Seinäjoki Fin. 44 M5
Seine r. Canada 121 N5
Seine r. France 52 A5
Seine, Baie de b. France 56 D2
Seine, Val de valley France 56 F2
Seistan reg. Iran see Sīstān
Sejny Poland 45 M9
Sekayu Indon. 68 C7
Seke China see Sêrtar
Sekoma Botswana 100 F3
Sekondi Ghana 96 C4
Sek'ot'a Eth. 98 D2
Sekura Indon. 71 E7
Şela Rus. Fed. see Shali
Selama Malaysia 71 C6
Selaru i. Indon. 108 E2
Selassi Indon. 69 I7
Selatan, Tanjung pt Indon. 68 E7
Selat Makassar strait Indon. see Makassar, Selat
Selatpanjang Indon. 71 C7
Selawik U.S.A. 118 B3
Selb Germany 53 M4
Selbekken Norway 44 F5
Selbu Norway 44 G5
Selby U.K. 48 F5
Selby U.S.A. 130 C2
Selbyville U.S.A. 135 H4
Selden U.S.A. 130 C4
Selebi-Phikwe Botswana 99 C6
Selebi-Pikwe Botswana see Selebi-Phikwe
Selemdzha r. Rus. Fed. 74 C1
Selemdzhinsk Rus. Fed. 74 C1
Selemdzhinskiy Khrebet mts Rus. Fed. 74 D1
Selendi Turkey 59 M5

►Selenga r. Mongolia/Rus. Fed. 72 J2
Part of the Yenisey-Angara-Selenga, 3rd longest river in Asia. Also known as Selenga Mörön.

Selenga Mörön r. Mongolia/Rus. Fed. see Selenga
Seletar Sing. 71 [inset]
Seletar Reservoir Sing. 71 [inset]
Selety r. Kazakh. see Sileti
Seletyteniz, Ozero salt l. Kazakh. see Siletiteniz, Ozero
Seleucia Turkey see Silifke
Seleucia Pieria Turkey see Samandağı
Selfridge U.S.A. 130 C2
Sel'gon Stantsiya Rus. Fed. 74 D2
Selib Rus. Fed. 42 K3
Sélibabi Mauritania 96 B3
Selibe-Phikwe Botswana see Selebi-Phikwe
Seligenstadt Germany 53 I4
Seliger, Ozero l. Rus. Fed. 42 G4
Seligman U.S.A. 129 G4
Selikhino Rus. Fed. 74 E2
Selîma Oasis Sudan 86 C5
Selimiye Turkey 59 L6
Selinsgrove U.S.A. 135 G3
Selizharovo Rus. Fed. 42 G4
Seljord Norway 45 F7
Selkirk Canada 121 L5
Selkirk U.K. 50 G5
Selkirk Mountains Canada 120 G4
Sellafield U.K. 48 D4
Sellersburg U.S.A. 134 C4
Sellore Island Myanmar see Saganthit Kyun
Sells U.S.A. 129 H6
Selm Germany 53 H3
Selma AL U.S.A. 133 C5
Selma CA U.S.A. 128 D3
Selmer U.S.A. 131 F5
Selous, Mount Canada 120 C2
Selseleh-ye Pīr Shūrān mts Iran 89 F4
Selsey Bill hd U.K. 49 G8
Sel'tso Rus. Fed. 43 G5
Selty Rus. Fed. 42 L4
Selu i. Indon. 108 E1
Seluan i. Indon. 71 D6
Selvas reg. Brazil 142 D5
Selvin U.S.A. 134 B4
Selway r. U.S.A. 126 E3
Selwyn Lake Canada 121 J2
Selwyn Mountains Canada 120 D1
Selwyn Range hills Australia 110 B4
Selz r. Germany 53 I5
Semarang Indon. 68 E8
Semau i. Indon. 108 C2
Sembawang Sing. 71 [inset]
Sembé Congo 98 B3
Şemdinli Turkey 91 G3
Semendire Serbia see Smederevo
Semenivka Ukr. 43 G5
Semenov Rus. Fed. 42 J4
Semenovka Ukr. see Semenivka
Semey Kazakh. see Semipalatinsk
Semidi Islands U.S.A. 118 C4
Semikarakorsk Rus. Fed. 43 I7
Semiluki Rus. Fed. 43 H6
Seminoe Reservoir U.S.A. 126 G4
Seminole U.S.A. 131 C5
Semipalatinsk Kazakh. 80 F1
Semirara Islands Phil. 69 G4
Semīrom Iran 88 C4
Sem Kolodezey Ukr. see Lenine
Semnān Iran 88 D3
Semnān va Dāmghān reg. Iran 88 D3
Semois r. Belgium/France 52 E5
Semois, Vallée de la valley Belgium/France 52 E5
Semyonovskoye Arkhangel'skaya Oblast' Rus. Fed. see Bereznik
Semyonovskoye Kostromskaya Oblast' Rus. Fed. see Ostrovskoye
Sena Bol. 142 E6
Sena Madureira Brazil 142 E5
Senanga Zambia 99 C5
Sendai Kagoshima Japan 75 C7
Sendai Miyagi Japan 75 F5
Sêndo China 76 B2
Senebui, Tanjung pt Indon. 71 C7
Seneca KS U.S.A. 130 D4
Seneca OR U.S.A. 126 D3
Seneca Lake U.S.A. 135 G2
Seneca Rocks U.S.A. 134 F4
Senecaville Lake U.S.A. 134 E4
Senegal country Africa 96 B3
Sénégal r. Mauritania/Senegal 96 B3
Seney U.S.A. 130 G2
Senftenberg Germany 47 O5
Senga Hill Zambia 99 D4
Sengerema Tanz. 98 D4
Sengeyskiy, Ostrov i. Rus. Fed. 42 K1
Sengiley Rus. Fed. 43 K5
Sengirli, Mys pt Kazakh. see Syngyrli, Mys
Senhor do Bonfim Brazil 143 J6
Senigallia Italy 58 E3
Senj Croatia 58 F2
Senja i. Norway 44 J2
Sen'kina Rus. Fed. 42 K2
Şenköy Turkey 85 C1
Senlac S. Africa 100 F3
Senlin Shan mt. China 74 C4
Senlis France 52 C5
Senmonorom Cambodia 71 D4
Sennar Sudan 86 D7
Sennen U.K. 49 B8
Senneterre Canada 122 F4
Senqu r. Lesotho 101 H6
Sens France 56 F2
Sensuntepeque El Salvador 136 G6
Senta Serbia 59 I2
Senthal India 82 D3
Sentinel U.S.A. 129 G5
Sentinel Peak Canada 120 F4
Sentosa i. Sing. 71 [inset]
Senwabarwana S. Africa 101 I2
Şenyurt Turkey 91 F3
Seo de Urgell Spain see La Seu d'Urgell
Seonath r. India 84 D1
Seoni India 82 D5
Seorinarayan India 83 E5

►Seoul S. Korea 75 B5
Capital of South Korea.

Separation Well Australia 108 C5
Sepik r. P.N.G. 69 K7
Sep'o N. Korea 75 B5
Sepon India 83 H4
Seppa India 83 H4
Sept-Îles Canada 123 I4
Sequoia National Park U.S.A. 128 D3
Serafimovich Rus. Fed. 43 I6
Sêraitang China see Baima
Seram i. Indon. 69 H7
Seram, Laut sea Indon. 69 I7
Serang Indon. 68 D8
Serangoon Harbour b. Sing. 71 [inset]
Serapi, Gunung hill Indon. 71 E7
Serapong, Mount hill Sing. 71 [inset]
Serasan i. Indon. 71 E7
Serasan, Selat sea chan. Indon. 71 E7
Seraya i. Indon. 71 E7
Serbāl, Gebel mt. Egypt see Sirbāl, Jabal

►Serbia country Europe 59 I3
Formerly known as Yugoslavia and as Serbia and Montenegro. Up to 1993 included Bosnia-Herzegovina, Croatia, Macedonia, Montenegro and Slovenia. Became independent from Montenegro in June 2006. Kosovo declared independence in February 2008.

Sêrbug Co l. China 83 G2
Sêrca China 76 B2
Serchhip India 83 H5
Serdar Turkm. 88 E2
Serdica Bulg. see Sofia
Serdo Eth. 98 E2
Serdoba r. Rus. Fed. 43 J5
Serdobsk Rus. Fed. 43 J5
Serebryansk Kazakh. 80 F2
Seredka Rus. Fed. 45 P7
Şereflikoçhisar Turkey 90 D3
Seremban Malaysia 71 C7
Serengeti National Park Tanz. 98 D4
Serenje Zambia 99 D5
Serezha r. Rus. Fed. 42 I5
Sergach Rus. Fed. 42 J5
Sergeyevka Rus. Fed. 74 B2
Sergiyev Posad Rus. Fed. 42 H4
Sergo Ukr. see Stakhanov
Serh China 80 I4
Serhetabat Turkm. 89 F3
Serifos i. Greece 59 K6
Sérigny r. Canada 123 H3
Sérigny, Lac l. Canada 123 H3
Serik Turkey 90 C3
Seringapatam Reef Australia 108 C3
Sêrkang China see Nyainrong
Sermata i. Indon. 69 H8
Sermata, Kepulauan is Indon. 108 E2
Sermersuaq glacier Greenland 119 M2
Sermilik inlet Greenland 119 O3
Sernovodsk Rus. Fed. 43 K5
Sernur Rus. Fed. 42 K4
Sernyy Zavod Turkm. see Kükürtli
Seronga Botswana 99 C5
Serov Rus. Fed. 41 S4
Serowe Botswana 101 H2
Serpa Port. 57 C5
Serpa Pinto Angola see Menongue
Serpentine Lakes salt flat Australia 109 E7
Serpukhov Rus. Fed. 43 H5
Serra Brazil 145 C3
Serra Alta Brazil 145 A4
Serrachis r. Cyprus 85 A2
Serra da Bocaina, Parque Nacional da nat. park Brazil 145 B3
Serra da Canastra, Parque Nacional da nat. park Brazil 145 B3
Serra da Mesa, Represa resr Brazil 145 A1
Serra das Araras Brazil 145 B1
Serra do Divisor, Parque Nacional da nat. park Brazil 142 D5
Sérrai Greece see Serres
Serranía de la Neblina, Parque Nacional nat. park Venez. 142 E3
Serraria, Ilha i. Brazil see Queimada, Ilha
Serra Talhada Brazil 143 K5
Serre r. France 52 D5
Serres Greece 59 J4
Serrinha Brazil 143 K6
Sêrro Brazil 145 C2
Sers Tunisia 58 C6
Sertanópolis Brazil 145 A3
Sertãozinho Brazil 145 B3
Sêrtar China 76 D1
Sertavul Geçidi pass Turkey 85 A1
Sertolovo Rus. Fed. 45 Q6
Seruai Indon. 71 B6
Serui Indon. 69 J7
Serule Botswana 99 C6
Seruna India 82 C3
Sêrwolungwa China 76 B1
Sêrxü China 76 C1
Seryshevo Rus. Fed. 74 C2
Seseganaga Lake Canada 122 C4
Sese Islands Uganda 98 D4
Sesel country Indian Ocean see Seychelles
Sesfontein Namibia 99 B5
Seshachalam Hills India 84 C3
Sesheke Zambia 99 C5
Sesostris Bank sea feature India 84 A3
Ses Salines, Cap de c. Spain 57 H4
Sestri Levante Italy 58 C2
Sestroretsk Rus. Fed. 45 P6
Set, Phou mt. Laos 70 D4
Sète France 56 F5
Sete Lagoas Brazil 145 B2
Setermoen Norway 44 K2
Setesdal valley Norway 45 E7
Seti r. Nepal 82 E3
Sétif Alg. 54 F4
Seto Japan 75 E6
Seto-naikai sea Japan 73 O6
Seto-naikai Kokuritsu-kōen nat. park Japan 75 D6
Setsan Myanmar 70 A3
Settat Morocco 54 C5
Settepani, Monte mt. Italy 58 C2
Settle U.K. 48 E4
Setúbal Port. 57 B4
Setúbal, Baía de b. Port. 57 B4
Seul, Lac l. Canada 121 M5
Sevan Armenia 91 G2
Sevan, Lake Armenia 91 G2
Sevan, Ozero l. Armenia see Sevan, Lake
Sevana Lich l. Armenia see Sevan, Lake
Sevastopol' Ukr. 90 D1
Seven Islands Canada see Sept-Îles
Seven Islands Bay Canada 123 J2
Sevenoaks U.K. 49 H7
Seventy Mile House Canada see 70 Mile House
Sévérac-le-Château France 56 F4
Severn r. Australia 112 E2
Severn r. Canada 122 D3
Severn S. Africa 100 F4
Severn r. U.K. 49 E7
also known as Hafren
Severnaya Dvina r. Rus. Fed. 42 I2
Severnaya Sos'va r. Rus. Fed. 41 T3
Severnaya Zemlya is Rus. Fed. 65 L1
Severn Lake Canada 121 N4
Severnoye Rus. Fed. 41 Q5
Severnyy Nenetskiy Avtonomnyy Okrug Rus. Fed. 42 K1
Severnyy Respublika Komi Rus. Fed. 64 H3
Severobaykal'sk Rus. Fed. 73 J1
Severo-Baykal'skoye Nagor'ye mts Rus. Fed. 65 M4
Severodonetsk Ukr. see Syeverodonets'k
Severodvinsk Rus. Fed. 42 H2
Severo-Kuril'sk Rus. Fed. 65 Q4
Severomorsk Rus. Fed. 44 R2
Severoonezhsk Rus. Fed. 42 H3
Severo-Sibirskaya Nizmennost' lowland Rus. Fed. see North Siberian Lowland
Severoural'sk Rus. Fed. 41 R3
Severo-Yeniseyskiy Rus. Fed. 64 K3
Severskaya Rus. Fed. 90 E1
Severskiy Donets r. Rus. Fed./Ukr. 43 I7
also known as Northern Donets, Sivers'kyy Donets'
Sevier U.S.A. 129 G2
Sevier r. U.S.A. 129 G2
Sevier Desert U.S.A. 129 G2
Sevier Lake U.S.A. 129 G2
Sevierville U.S.A. 132 D5
Sevilla Col. 142 C3
Sevilla Spain see Seville
Seville Spain 57 D5
Sevlyush Ukr. see Vynohradiv
Sewani India 82 C3
Seward AK U.S.A. 118 D3
Seward NE U.S.A. 130 D3
Seward Mountains Antarctica 152 L2
Seward Peninsula U.S.A. 118 B3
Sexi Spain see Almuñécar
Sexsmith Canada 120 G4
Sextín Mex. 131 B7
Seyah Band Koh mts Afgh. 89 F3
Seyakha Rus. Fed. 153 F2
Seychelles country Indian Ocean 149 L6
Seydi Turkm. 89 F2
Seydişehir Turkey 90 C3
Seyðisfjörður Iceland 44 [inset]
Seyhan Turkey see Adana
Seyhan r. Turkey 85 B1
Seyitgazi Turkey 59 N5
Seym r. Rus. Fed./Ukr. 43 G6
Seymchan Rus. Fed. 65 Q3
Seymour Australia 112 B6
Seymour S. Africa 101 H7
Seymour IN U.S.A. 134 C4
Seymour TX U.S.A. 131 D5
Seymour Inlet Canada 120 E5
Seymour Range mts Australia 109 F6
Seypan i. N. Mariana Is see Saipan
Seyyedābād Afgh. 89 H3
Sézanne France 52 D6
Sfakia Kriti Greece see Chora Sfakion
Sfântu Gheorghe Romania 59 K2
Sfax Tunisia 58 D7
Sfikia, Limni resr Greece see Sfikias, Limni
Sfikias, Limni resr Greece 59 J4
Sfintu Gheorghe Romania see Sfântu Gheorghe
Sgiersch Poland see Zgierz
's-Graveland Neth. 52 F2
's-Gravenhage Neth. see The Hague
Sgurr Alasdair hill U.K. 50 C3
Sgurr Dhomhnuill hill U.K. 50 D4
Sgurr Mòr mt. U.K. 50 D3
Sgurr na Ciche mt. U.K. 50 D3
Shaanxi prov. China 76 F1
Shaartuz Tajik. see Shahrtuz
Shaban Pak. 89 G4
Shabani Zimbabwe see Zvishavane

Shabeelle, Webi r. Ehiopia/Somalia see **Shebelē Wenz, Wabē**
Shabestar Iran **88** B2
Shabībī, Jabal ash mt. Jordan **85** B5
Shabla, Nos pt Bulg. **59** M3
Shabogamo Lake Canada **123** I3
Shabunda Dem. Rep. Congo **98** C4
Shache China **80** E4
Shackleton Coast Antarctica **152** H1
Shackleton Glacier Antarctica **152** I1
Shackleton Ice Shelf Antarctica **152** F2
Shackleton Range mts Antarctica **152** A1
Shadaogou China **77** F2
Shadaw Myanmar **70** B3
Shādegān Iran **88** C4
Shadihar Pak. **89** G4
Shady Grove U.S.A. **126** C4
Shady Spring U.S.A. **134** E5
Shafer, Lake U.S.A. **134** B3
Shafer Peak Antarctica **152** H2
Shafter U.S.A. **128** D4
Shaftesbury U.K. **49** E7
Shagamu r. Canada **122** D3
Shagedu China **73** K5
Shageluk U.S.A. **118** C3
Shaghyray Üstirti plat. Kazakh. see **Shagyray, Plato**
Shagonar Rus. Fed. **80** H1
Shag Point N.Z. **113** C7
Shag Rocks is S. Georgia **144** H8
Shagyray, Plato plat. Kazakh. **80** A2
Shahabad Karnataka India **84** C2
Shahabad Rajasthan India **82** D4
Shahabad Uttar Prad. India **82** E4
Shāhābād Iran see **Eslāmābād-e Gharb**
Shah Alam Malaysia **71** C7
Shah Bandar Pak. **89** G5
Shahdād Iran **88** E4
Shahdol India **82** E5
Shahe China **77** F2
Shahejie China see **Jiujiang**
Shahezhen China see **Jiujiang**
Shah Fuladi mt. Afgh. **89** G3
Shah Ismail Afgh. **89** G4
Shahjahanpur India **82** D4
Shāh Jehān, Kūh-e mts Iran **88** E2
Shāh Jūy Afgh. **89** G3
Shāh Kūh mt. Iran **88** E4
Shāhpūr Iran see **Salmās**
Shahrak Afgh. **89** G3
Shāhrakht Iran **89** F3
Shahr-e Bābak Iran **88** D4
Shahr-e Kord Iran **88** C3
Shahr-e Ṣafā Afgh. **89** G4
Shahrezā Iran **88** C3
Shahrig Pak. **89** G4
Shahrisabz Uzbek. **89** G2
Shahriston Tajik. **89** H2
Shahr Rey Iran **88** C3
Shahr Sultan Pak. **89** H4
Shahrtuz Tajik. **89** H2
Shāhrūd Iran see **Emāmrūd**
Shāhrūd, Rūdkhāneh-ye r. Iran **88** C2
Shahrud Bustam reg. Iran **88** D3
Shāh Savārān, Kūh-e mts Iran **88** E4
Shāh Taqī Iran see **Emām Taqī**
Shaighalu Pak. **89** H4
Shaikh Husain mt. Pak. **89** G4
Shaikhpura India see **Sheikhpura**
Shā'īr, Jabal mts Syria **85** C2
Sha'īra, Gebel mt. Egypt see **Sha'īrah, Jabal**
Sha'īrah, Jabal mt. Egypt **85** B5
Shaj'ah, Jabal hill Saudi Arabia **88** C5
Shajapur India **82** D5
Shajianzi China **74** B4
Shakaville S. Africa **101** J5
Shakh Tajik. see **Shoh**
Shakhbuz Azer. see **Şahbuz**
Shākhen Iran **89** E3
Shakhovskaya Rus. Fed. **42** G4
Shakhrisabz Uzbek. see **Shahrisabz**
Shakhristan Tajik. see **Shahriston**
Shakhtinsk Kazakh. **80** D2
Shakhty Respublika Buryatiya Rus. Fed. see **Gusinoozersk**
Shakhty Rostovskaya Oblast' Rus. Fed. **43** I7
Shakhun'ya Rus. Fed. **42** J4
Shaki Nigeria **96** D4
Shakotan-hantō pen. Japan **74** F4
Shalakusha Rus. Fed. **42** I3
Shalang China **77** F4
Shali Rus. Fed. **91** G2
Shaliuhe China see **Gangca**
Shalkar India **82** D3
Shalkar Kazakh. **80** A2
Shalkarteniz, Solonchak salt marsh Kazakh. **80** B2
Shalqar Kazakh. see **Shalkar**
Shaluli Shan mts China **76** C2
Shaluni mt. India **83** I3
Shama r. Tanz. **99** D4
Shamâl Sînâ' governorate Egypt see **Shamāl Sīnā'**
Shamāl Sīnā' governorate Egypt **85** A4
Shamalzā'ī Afgh. **89** G4
Shāmat al Akbād des. Saudi Arabia **91** F5
Shamattawa Canada **121** N4
Shamattawa r. Canada **122** D3
Shambār Iran **88** C3
Shamgong Bhutan see **Shemgang**
Shamīl Iran **88** E5
Shāmīyah des. Iraq/Syria **85** D2
Shamkhor Azer. see **Şämkir**
Shamrock U.S.A. **131** C5
Shancheng Fujian China see **Taining**
Shancheng Shandong China see **Shanxian**
Shand Afgh. **89** F4
Shandan China **80** J4
Shandong prov. China **77** H1
Shandong Bandao pen. China **73** M5
Shandur Pass Pak. **89** I2
Shangchao China **77** F3
Shangcheng China **77** G2
Shangchuan Dao i. China **77** G4
Shangdu China **73** K4
Shangganling China **74** C3

▶**Shanghai** China **77** I2
4th most populous city in Asia and 7th in the world.

Shanghai municipality China **77** I2
Shangji China see **Xichuan**
Shangjie China see **Yangbi**
Shangjin China **77** F1
Shangluo China **77** F1
Shangmei China see **Xinhua**
Shangnan China **77** F1
Shangpa China see **Fugong**
Shangpai China see **Feixi**
Shangpaihe China see **Feixi**
Shangqiu Henan China **77** G1
Shangqiu Henan China see **Suiyang**
Shangrao China **77** H2
Shangshui China **77** G1
Shangyou China **77** G3
Shangyou Shuiku resr China **80** F3
Shangyu China **77** I2
Shangzhi China **74** B3
Shangzhou Shaanxi China see **Shangluo**
Shangzhou Shaanxi China see **Shangluo**
Shanhe China see **Zhengning**
Shanhetun China **74** B3
Shankou China **77** F4
Shanlaragh Ireland **51** C6
Shannon airport Ireland **51** D5
Shannon est. Ireland **51** D5
Shannon r. Ireland **51** D5
Shannon, Mouth of the Ireland **51** C5
Shannon National Park Australia **109** B8
Shannon Ø i. Greenland **153** I1
Shan Plateau Myanmar **70** B2
Shansi prov. China see **Shanxi**
Shan Teng hill H.K. China see **Victoria Peak**
Shantipur India **83** G5
Shantou China **77** H4
Shantung prov. China see **Shandong**
Shanwei China **77** G4
Shanxi prov. China **77** F1
Shanxian China **77** H1
Shanyang China **77** F1
Shaodong China **77** F3
Shaoguan China **77** G3
Shaowu China **77** H3
Shaoxing China **77** I2
Shaoyang China **77** F3
Shap U.K. **48** E4
Shapa China **77** F4
Shaping China see **Ebian**
Shapinsay i. U.K. **50** G1
Shapkina r. Rus. Fed. **42** L2
Shapshal'skiy Khrebet mts Rus. Fed. **80** G1
Shaqrā' Saudi Arabia **86** G4
Shār, Jabal mt. Saudi Arabia **90** D6
Sharaf well Iraq **91** F5
Sharan Paktīkā **89** H3
Sharan Jogizai Pak. **89** H4
Shārb Māh Iran **88** E4
Shardara Kazakh. **80** C3
Shardara, Step' plain Kazakh. see **Chardara, Step'**
Shari r. Cameroon/Chad see **Chari**
Shārī, Buḥayrat imp. l. Iraq **91** G4
Shari-dake vol. Japan **74** G4
Sharīfah Syria **85** C2
Sharjah U.A.E. **88** D5
Sharka-leb La pass China **83** G3
Sharkawshchyna Belarus **45** O9
Shark Bay Australia **109** A6
Shark Reef Australia **110** D2
Sharlyk Rus. Fed. **41** Q5
Sharm ash Shaykh Egypt **90** D6
Sharm el Sheikh Egypt see **Sharm ash Shaykh**
Sharon U.S.A. **134** E3
Sharon Springs U.S.A. **130** C4
Sharpe Lake Canada **121** M4
Sharp Peak hill H.K. China **77** [inset]
Sharqat Iraq see **Ash Sharqāṭ**
Sharqī, Jabal ash mts Lebanon/Syria **85** B3
Sharqiy Ustyurt Chink esc. Uzbek. **80** A3
Sharur Azer. see **Şärur**
Shar'ya Rus. Fed. **42** J4
Shashe r. Botswana/Zimbabwe **99** C6
Shashemenē Eth. **98** D3
Shashi China see **Jingzhou**
Shasta U.S.A. **128** B1
Shasta, Mount vol. U.S.A. **126** C4
Shasta Lake U.S.A. **128** B1
Shatilki Belarus see **Svyetlahorsk**
Sha Tin H.K. China **77** [inset]
Shatki Rus. Fed. **43** J5
Shaṭnat as Salmās, Wādī watercourse Syria **85** D2
Sha Tong Hau Shan H.K. China see **Bluff Island**
Shatoy Rus. Fed. **91** G2
Shatsk Rus. Fed. **43** I5
Shaṭṭ al 'Arab r. Iran/Iraq **91** H5
Shatura Rus. Fed. **43** H5
Shaubak Jordan see **Ash Shawbak**
Shaunavon Canada **121** I5
Shaver Lake U.S.A. **128** D3
Shaw r. Australia **108** B5
Shawangunk Mountains hills U.S.A. **135** H3
Shawano U.S.A. **134** A1
Shawano Lake U.S.A. **134** A1
Shawinigan Canada **123** G5
Shawnee OK U.S.A. **131** D5
Shawnee WY U.S.A. **126** G4
Shawneetown U.S.A. **130** F4
Shaxian China **77** H3
Shay Gap (abandoned) Australia **108** C5
Shaykh, Jabal ash mt. Lebanon/Syria see **Hermon, Mount**
Shaykh Miskīn Syria **85** C3
Shayṭūr Iran **88** D4
Shāzand Iran **88** C3
Shaẓāẓ, Jabal mt. Saudi Arabia **91** F6
Shazud Tajik. **89** I2
Shchekino Rus. Fed. **43** H5
Shchel'yayur Rus. Fed. **42** L2
Shcherbakov Rus. Fed. see **Rybinsk**
Shchigry Rus. Fed. **43** H6
Shchors Ukr. **43** F6
Shchuchin Belarus see **Shchuchyn**
Shchuchyn Belarus **45** N10
Shebalino Rus. Fed. **80** G1
Shebekino Rus. Fed. **43** H6

▶**Shebelē Wenz, Wabē** r. Ethiopia/Somalia **98** E3
5th longest river in Africa.

Sheberghān Afgh. **89** G2
Sheboygan U.S.A. **134** B2
Shebshi Mountains Nigeria **96** E4
Shebunino Rus. Fed. **74** F3
Shediac Canada **123** I5
Shedin Peak Canada **120** E4
Shedok Rus. Fed. **91** F1
Sheelin, Lough l. Ireland **51** E4
Sheep Haven b. Ireland **51** E2
Sheepmoor S. Africa **101** J4
Sheep Mountain U.S.A. **129** J2
Sheep Peak U.S.A. **129** F3
Sheep's Head hd Ireland see **Muntervary**
Sheerness U.K. **49** H7
Sheet Harbour Canada **123** J5
Shefar'am Israel **85** B3
Sheffield N.Z. **113** D6
Sheffield U.K. **48** F5
Sheffield AL U.S.A. **133** C5
Sheffield PA U.S.A. **134** F3
Sheffield TX U.S.A. **131** C6
Sheffield Lake Canada **123** K4
Shegah Afgh. **89** G4
Shegmas Rus. Fed. **42** K2
Shehong China **76** E2
Sheikh, Jebel esh mt. Lebanon/Syria see **Hermon, Mount**
Sheikhpura India **83** F4
Sheikhupura Pak. **89** I4
Shekak r. Canada **122** D4
Shekār Āb Iran **88** D3
Shekhawati reg. India **89** I5
Shekhem West Bank see **Nāblus**
Shekhpura India see **Sheikhpura**
Sheki Azer. see **Şäki**
Shekka Ch'ün-Tao H.K. China see **Soko Islands**
Shek Kwu Chau i. H.K. China **77** [inset]
Shekou China **77** [inset]
Sheksna Rus. Fed. **42** H4
Sheksninskoye Vodokhranilishche resr Rus. Fed. **42** H4
Shek Uk Shan mt. H.K. China **77** [inset]
Shela China **76** B2
Shelagskiy, Mys pt Rus. Fed. **65** S2
Shelbina U.S.A. **130** E4
Shelburn U.S.A. **134** B4
Shelburne N.S. Canada **123** I6
Shelburne Ont. Canada **134** E1
Shelburne Bay Australia **110** C1
Shelby MI U.S.A. **134** B2
Shelby MS U.S.A. **131** F5
Shelby MT U.S.A. **126** F2
Shelby NC U.S.A. **133** D5
Shelbyville IL U.S.A. **130** F4
Shelbyville IN U.S.A. **134** C4
Shelbyville KY U.S.A. **134** C4
Shelbyville TN U.S.A. **132** C5
Sheldon IA U.S.A. **130** E3
Sheldon IL U.S.A. **134** B3
Sheldrake Canada **123** I4
Shelek Kazakh. see **Chilik**
Shelikhova, Zaliv g. Rus. Fed. **65** Q3
Shelikof Strait U.S.A. **118** C4
Shell U.S.A. **130** B2
Shellbrook Canada **121** J4
Shelley U.S.A. **126** E4
Shellharbour Australia **112** E5
Shell Lake Canada **121** J4
Shell Lake U.S.A. **130** F2
Shell Mountain U.S.A. **128** B1
Shelter Bay Canada see **Port-Cartier**
Shelter Island U.S.A. **135** I3
Shelter Point N.Z. **113** B8
Shelton U.S.A. **126** C3
Shemakha Azer. see **Şamaxı**
Shemgang Bhutan **83** G4
Shemordan Rus. Fed. **42** K4
Shenandoah IA U.S.A. **130** E3
Shenandoah PA U.S.A. **135** G3
Shenandoah Mountains U.S.A. **134** F4
Shenandoah National Park U.S.A. **135** F4
Shendam Nigeria **96** D4
Shending Shan hill China **74** D3
Shengena mt. Tanz. **99** D4
Shengli China **77** G2
Shengli Feng mt. China/Kyrg. see **Pobeda Peak**
Shengping China **74** B3
Shengrenjian China see **Pinglu**
Shengsi China **77** I2
Shengsi Liedao is China **77** I2
Shenjiamen China **77** I2
Shen Khan Bandar Afgh. **89** H2
Shenkursk Rus. Fed. **42** I3
Shenmu China **73** K5
Shennong Ding mt. China **77** F2
Shennongjia China **77** F2
Shenqiu China **77** G1
Shenshu China **74** C3
Shensi prov. China see **Shaanxi**
Shentala Rus. Fed. **43** K5
Shenton, Mount hill Australia **109** C7
Shenyang China **74** A4
Shenzhen China **77** G4
Shenzhen Wan b. H.K. China see **Deep Bay**
Sheopur India **82** D4
Shepetivka Ukr. **43** E6
Shepetovka Ukr. see **Shepetivka**
Shepherd Islands Vanuatu **107** G3
Shepherdsville U.S.A. **134** C5
Shepparton Australia **112** B6
Sheppey, Isle of i. U.K. **49** H7
Sheqi China **77** G1
Sherabad Uzbek. see **Sherobod**
Sherborne U.K. **49** E8
Sherbro Island Sierra Leone **96** B4
Sherbrooke Canada **123** H5
Sherburne U.S.A. **135** H2
Shercock Ireland **51** F4
Shereiq Sudan **86** D6
Shergaon India **83** H4
Shergarh India **82** C4
Sheridan AR U.S.A. **131** E5
Sheridan WY U.S.A. **126** G3
Sheringham U.K. **49** I6
Sherman U.S.A. **131** D5
Sherman Mountain U.S.A. **129** F1
Sherobod Uzbek. **89** G2
Sherpur Dhaka Bangl. **83** G4
Sherpur Rajshahi Bangl. **83** G4
Sherridon Canada **121** K4
's-Hertogenbosch Neth. **52** F3
Sherwood Forest reg. U.K. **49** F5
Sherwood Lake Canada **121** K2
Sheslay Canada **120** D3
Sheslay r. Canada **120** C3
Shethanei Lake Canada **121** L3
Shetland Islands is U.K. **50** [inset]
Shetpe Kazakh. **78** E2
Sheung Shui H.K. China **77** [inset]
Sheung Sze Mun sea chan. H.K. China **77** [inset]
Shevchenko Kazakh. see **Aktau**
Shevli r. Rus. Fed. **74** D1
Shexian China **77** H2
Sheyang China **77** I1
Sheyenne r. U.S.A. **130** D2
Shey Phoksundo National Park Nepal **83** E3
Shiant Islands U.K. **50** C3
Shiashkotan, Ostrov i. Rus. Fed. **65** Q5
Shibām Yemen **86** G6
Shibar, Kowtal-e Afgh. **89** H3
Shibata Japan **75** E5
Shibazhan China **74** B1
Shibh Jazīrat Sīnā' pen. Egypt see **Sinai**
Shibīn al Kawm Egypt **90** C5
Shibîn el Kôm Egypt see **Shibīn al Kawm**
Shibogama Lake Canada **122** C3
Shibotsu-jima i. Rus. Fed. see **Zelenyy, Ostrov**
Shicheng Fujian China see **Zhouning**
Shicheng Jiangxi China **77** H3
Shidād al Mismā' hill Saudi Arabia **85** D4
Shidao China **73** M5
Shidian China **76** C3
Shiel, Loch l. U.K. **50** D4
Shield, Cape Australia **110** B2
Shīeli Kazakh. see **Chiili**
Shifa, Jabal ash mts Saudi Arabia **90** D5
Shifang China **76** E2
Shigatse China see **Xigazê**
Shiḥān mt. Jordan **85** B4
Shihezi China **80** G3
Shihkiachwang China see **Shijiazhuang**
Shijiao China see **Fogang**
Shijiazhuang China **73** K5
Shijiu Hu l. China **77** H2
Shijiusuo China see **Rizhao**
Shikag Lake Canada **122** C4
Shikar r. Pak. **89** F4
Shikarpur Pak. **89** H5
Shikengkong mt. China **77** G3
Shikhany Rus. Fed. **43** J5
Shikohabad India **82** D4
Shikoku i. Japan **75** D6
Shikoku-sanchi mts Japan **75** D6
Shikotan, Ostrov i. Rus. Fed. **74** G4
Shikotan-tō i. Rus. Fed. see **Shikotan, Ostrov**
Shikotsu-Tōya Kokuritsu-kōen nat. park Japan **74** F4
Shildon U.K. **48** F4
Shilega Rus. Fed. **42** J2
Shiliguri India **83** G4
Shilin China **76** D3
Shilipu China **77** G2
Shiliu China see **Changjiang**
Shilla mt. India **82** D2
Shillelagh Ireland **51** F5
Shillo r. Israel **85** B3
Shillong India **83** G4
Shilovo Rus. Fed. **43** I5
Shimada Japan **75** E6
Shimanovsk Rus. Fed. **74** B1
Shimbiris mt. Somalia **98** E2
Shimen Gansu China **76** D1
Shimen Hunan China **77** F2
Shimen Yunnan China see **Yunlong**
Shimla India **82** D3
Shimoga India **84** B3
Shimokita-hantō pen. Japan **74** F4
Shimoni Kenya **99** D4
Shimonoseki Japan **75** C6
Shimsk Rus. Fed. **42** F4
Shin, Loch l. U.K. **50** E2
Shināfiyah Iraq see **Ash Shanāfiyah**
Shinan China see **Xingye**
Shīndand Afgh. **89** F3
Shingbwiyang Myanmar **70** B1
Shing-gai Myanmar **70** B1
Shinghshal Pass Pak. **89** I2
Shingletown U.S.A. **128** C1
Shingū Japan **75** E6
Shingwedzi S. Africa **101** J2
Shingwedzi r. S. Africa **101** J2
Shīnkāy Afgh. **89** G4
Shīnkay Ghar Afgh. **89** H3
Shinnston U.S.A. **134** E4
Shinshār Syria **85** C2
Shinyanga Tanz. **98** D4
Shiocton U.S.A. **134** A1
Shiogama Japan **75** F5
Shiono-misaki c. Japan **75** D6
Shipai China **77** H2
Shiping China **76** D4
Shipki Pass China/India **82** D3
Shipman U.S.A. **135** F5
Shippegan Island Canada **123** I5
Shippensburg U.S.A. **135** G3
Shiprock U.S.A. **129** I3
Shiprock Peak U.S.A. **129** I3
Shipu China **77** I2
Shipunovo Rus. Fed. **72** E2
Shiqian China **77** F3
Shiqiao China see **Panyu**
Shiqizhen China see **Zhongshan**
Shiquan China **77** F1
Shiquanhe Xizang China see **Ali**
Shiquanhe Xizang China see **Gar**
Shiquan Shuiku resr China **77** F1
Shira Rus. Fed. **72** F2
Shīrābād Iran **88** C2
Shirakawa-go and Gokayama tourist site Japan **75** E5
Shirane-san vol. Japan **75** E5
Shirase Coast Antarctica **152** J1
Shirase Glacier Antarctica **152** D2
Shīrāz Iran **88** D4
Shire r. Malawi **99** D5
Shireza Pak. **89** G5
Shirīn Tagāb Afgh. **89** G2
Shiriya-zaki c. Japan **74** F4
Shirkala reg. Kazakh. **80** A2
Shīr Kūh mt. Iran **88** D4
Shiroro Reservoir Nigeria **96** D3
Shirpur India **82** C5
Shirten Holoy Gobi des. China **80** I3
Shīrvān Iran **88** E2
Shisanzhan China **74** B2
Shishaldin Volcano U.S.A. **118** B4
Shisha Pangma mt. China see **Xixabangma Feng**
Shishou China **77** G2
Shitan China **77** G3
Shitang China **77** I2
Shithāthah Iraq **91** F4
Shiv India **82** B4
Shiveluch, Sopka vol. Rus. Fed. **65** R4
Shivpuri India **82** D4
Shivwits U.S.A. **129** G3
Shivwits Plateau U.S.A. **129** G3
Shiwan Dashan mts China **76** E4
Shiwa Ngandu Zambia **99** D5
Shixing China **77** G3
Shiyan China **77** F1
Shizhu China **77** F2
Shizilu China see **Junan**
Shizipu China **77** H2
Shizong China **76** D3
Shizuishan China **72** J5
Shizuoka Japan **75** E6

▶**Shkhara** mt. Georgia/Rus. Fed. **91** F2
3rd highest mountain in Europe.

Shklov Belarus see **Shklow**
Shklow Belarus **43** F5
Shkodër Albania **59** H3
Shkodra Albania see **Shkodër**
Shkodrës, Liqeni i l. Albania/Montenegro see **Scutari, Lake**
Shmidta, Ostrov i. Rus. Fed. **64** K1
Shmidta, Poluostrov pen. Rus. Fed. **74** F1
Shoal Lake Canada **121** K5
Shoals U.S.A. **134** B4
Shōbara Japan **75** D6
Shoh Tajik. **89** H2
Shohi Pass Pak. see **Tal Pass**
Shokanbetsu-dake mt. Japan **74** F4
Sholakkorgan Kazakh. **80** C3
Sholapur India see **Solapur**
Sholaqorghan Kazakh. see **Sholakkorgan**
Shomba r. Rus. Fed. **44** R4
Shomvukva Rus. Fed. **42** K3
Shona Ridge sea feature S. Atlantic Ocean **148** I9
Shonzha Kazakh. see **Chundzha**
Shor India **82** D2
Shorap Pak. **89** G5
Shorapur India **84** C2
Shorawak reg. Afgh. **89** G4
Sho'rchi Uzbek. **89** G2
Shorewood IL U.S.A. **134** A3
Shorewood WI U.S.A. **134** B2
Shorkot Pak. **89** I4
Shorkozakhly, Solonchak salt flat Turkm. **91** J2
Shoshone CA U.S.A. **128** E4
Shoshone ID U.S.A. **126** E4
Shoshone r. U.S.A. **126** F3
Shoshone Mountains U.S.A. **128** E2
Shoshone Peak U.S.A. **128** E3
Shoshong Botswana **101** H2
Shoshoni U.S.A. **126** F4
Shostka Ukr. **43** G6
Shotor Khūn Afgh. **89** G3
Shouyang Shan mt. China **77** F1
Showak Sudan **86** E7
Show Low U.S.A. **129** H4
Shoyna Rus. Fed. **42** J2
Shpakovskoye Rus. Fed. **91** F1
Shpola Ukr. **43** F6
Shqipëria country Europe see **Albania**
Shreve U.S.A. **134** D3
Shreveport U.S.A. **131** E5
Shrewsbury U.K. **49** E6
Shri Lanka country Asia see **Sri Lanka**
Shri Mohangarh India **82** B4
Shrirampur India **83** G5
Shu Kazakh. **80** D3
Shū r. Kazakh./Kyrg. see **Chu**
Shu'ab, Ra's pt Yemen **87** H7
Shuajingsi China **76** D1
Shuangbai China **76** D3
Shuangcheng Fujian China see **Zherong**
Shuangcheng Heilong. China **74** B3
Shuanghe China **77** G2
Shuanghechang China **76** E2
Shuanghedagang China **74** C2
Shuangjiang Guizhou China see **Jiangkou**
Shuangjiang Hunan China see **Tongdao**
Shuangjiang Yunnan China see **Eshan**
Shuangliao China **74** A4
Shuangliu China **76** D2
Shuangpai China **77** F3
Shuangshipu China see **Fengxian**
Shuangxi China see **Shunchang**
Shuangyang China **74** B4
Shuangyashan China **74** C3
Shubarkuduk Kazakh. **80** A2
Shubayḥ well Saudi Arabia **85** D4
Shugozero Rus. Fed. **42** G4
Shuicheng China see **Lupanshui**
Shuidong China see **Dianbai**
Shuijing China **76** E1
Shuikou China **77** F3
Shuikouguan China **76** E4
Shuikoushan China **77** G3
Shuiluocheng China see **Zhuanglang**
Shuizhai China see **Wuhua**
Shulan China **74** B3
Shumagin Islands U.S.A. **118** B4
Shumba Zimbabwe **99** C5
Shumen Bulg. **59** L3
Shumerlya Rus. Fed. **42** J5
Shumilina Belarus **43** F5
Shumyachi Rus. Fed. **43** G5
Shunchang China **77** H3
Shuncheng China **74** A4
Shunde China **77** G4
Shuoxian China see **Shuozhou**
Shuozhou China **73** K5
Shuqrah Yemen **86** G7
Shūr r. Iran **88** D4
Shūr r. Iran **89** F3
Shūr watercourse Iran **88** D5
Shur watercourse Iran **88** E3
Shūr, Rūd-e watercourse Iran **88** E4
Shūr Āb watercourse Iran **88** D4
Shūrjestān Iran **88** D4
Shūrū Iran **89** F4
Shuryshkarskiy Sor, Ozero l. Rus. Fed. **41** T2
Shūsh Iran **88** C3
Shusha Azer. see **Şuşa**
Shushtar Iran **88** C3
Shutfah, Qalamat well Saudi Arabia **88** D
Shuwaysh, Tall ash hill Jordan **85** C4
Shuya Ivanovskaya Oblast' Rus. Fed. **42** I
Shuya Respublika Kareliya Rus. Fed. **42** G
Shuyskoye Rus. Fed. **42** I4
Shwebo Myanmar **70** A2
Shwedwin Myanmar **70** A1
Shwegun Myanmar **70** B3
Shwegyin Myanmar **70** B3
Shweudaung mt. Myanmar **70** B2
Shyghanaq Kazakh. see **Chiganak**
Shymkent Kazakh. **80** C3
Shyok India **82** D2
Shypuvate Ukr. **43** H6
Shyroke Ukr. **43** G7
Sia Indon. **69** I8
Siabu Indon. **71** B7
Siahan Range mts Pak. **89** F5
Sīāh Chashmeh Iran **88** B2
Siahgird Afgh. **89** G2
Siah Koh mts Afgh. **89** G3
Sialkot Pak. **89** I3
Siam country Asia see **Thailand**
Sian China see **Xi'an**
Sian Rus. Fed. **74** B1
Siang r. India see **Brahmaputra**
Siantan i. Indon. **71** D7
Siargao i. Phil. **69** H5
Siau i. Indon. **69** H6
Šiauliai Lith. **45** M9
Siazan' Azer. see **Siyäzän**
Si Bai, Lam r. Thai. **70** D4
Sibasa S. Africa **101** J2
Sibayi, Lake S. Africa **101** K4
Sibda China **76** C2
Šibenik Croatia **58** F3
Siberia reg. Rus. Fed. **65** M3
Siberut i. Indon. **68** B7
Siberut, Selat sea chan. Indon. **68** B7
Sibi Pak. **89** G4
Sibidiri P.N.G. **69** K8
Sibigo Indon. **71** A7
Sibiloi National Park Kenya **98** D3
Sibir' reg. Rus. Fed. see **Siberia**
Sibiti Congo **98** B4
Sibiu Romania **59** K2
Sibley U.S.A. **130** E3
Siboa Indon. **69** G6
Sibolga Indon. **71** B7
Siborongborong Indon. **71** B7
Sibsagar India **83** H4
Sibu Sarawak Malaysia **68** E6
Sibut Cent. Afr. Rep. **98** B3
Sibuyan i. Phil. **69** G4
Sibuyan Sea Phil. **69** G4
Sicamous Canada **120** G5
Sicca Veneria Tunisia see **Le Kef**
Siccus watercourse Australia **111** B6
Sicheng Anhui China see **Sixian**
Sicheng Guangxi China see **Lingyun**
Sichon Thai. **71** B5
Sichuan prov. China **76** D2
Sichuan Pendi basin China **76** E2
Sicié, Cap c. France **56** G5
Sicilia i. Italy see **Sicily**
Sicilian Channel Italy/Tunisia **58** E6
Sicily i. Italy **58** F5
Sicuani Peru **142** D6
Siddhapur India **82** C5
Siddipet India **84** C2
Sideros, Akra pt Kriti Greece see **Sideros, Akrotirio**
Sideros, Akrotirio pt Greece **59** L7
Sidesaviwa S. Africa **100** F7
Sidhauli India **82** E4
Sidhi India **83** E4
Sidhpur India see **Siddhapur**
Sidi Aïssa Alg. **57** H6
Sidi Ali Alg. **57** G5
Sīdī Barrānī Egypt **90** B5
Sidi Bel Abbès Alg. **57** F6
Sidi Bennour Morocco **54** C5
Sidi Bou Sa'id Tunisia see **Sidi Bouzid**
Sidi Bouzid Tunisia **58** C7
Sidi el Barrâni Egypt see **Sīdī Barrānī**
Sidi El Hani, Sebkhet de salt pan Tunisia **58** D7
Sidi Ifni Morocco **96** B2
Sidi Kacem Morocco **54** C5
Sidikalang Indon. **71** B7
Sidi Khaled Alg. **54** E5
Sid Lake Canada **121** J2
Sidlaw Hills U.K. **50** F4
Sidley, Mount Antarctica **152** J1
Sidli India **83** G4
Sidmouth U.K. **49** D8
Sidney IA U.S.A. **130** E3
Sidney MT U.S.A. **126** G3
Sidney NE U.S.A. **130** C3
Sidney OH U.S.A. **134** C3
Sidney Lanier, Lake U.S.A. **133** D5
Sidoktaya Myanmar **70** A2
Sidon Lebanon **85** B3
Sidr Egypt see **Sudr**
Siedlce Poland **43** D5
Sieg r. Germany **53** H4
Siegen Germany **53** I4
Siĕmréab Cambodia **71** C4

m Reap Cambodia see Siĕmréab
n China see Huanjiang
na Italy 58 D3
radz Poland 47 Q5
erdingka China 76 B2
rra Blanca U.S.A. 127 G7
rra Colorada Arg. 144 C6
rra Grande Arg. 144 C6
rra Leone country Africa 96 B4
rra Leone Basin sea feature
N. Atlantic Ocean 148 G5
rra Leone Rise sea feature
N. Atlantic Ocean 148 G5
rra Madre Mountains U.S.A. 128 C4
rra Mojada Mex. 131 C7
rra Nevada, Parque Nacional nat. park
Venez. 142 D2
rra Nevada de Santa Marta, Parque
Nacional nat. park Col. 142 D1
rraville U.S.A. 128 C2
rra Vista U.S.A. 127 F7
rre Switz. 56 H3
vi Fin. 44 N5
ang Ling mts China 76 E4
angtai China 74 B3
enī Eth. 98 E2
nos i. Greece 59 K6
Alg. 57 F6
guup Nunaa pen. Greenland 119 M2
hetu Marmației Romania 43 D7
hișoara Romania 59 K1
lap Sing. 71 [inset]
li Indon. 71 A6
ufjörður Iceland 44 [inset]
nal de Botrange hill Belgium 52 G4
nal de la Ste-Baume mt.
rance 56 G5
nal Peak U.S.A. 129 F5
ny-l'Abbaye France 52 E5
ourney U.S.A. 130 E3
ri, Akra pt Voreio Aigaio Greece see
aratsina, Akrotirio
sbee Deep sea feature G. of Mexico
51 N4
üenza Spain 57 E3
uiri Guinea 96 C3
ulda Latvia 45 N8
urd U.S.A. 129 H2
anoukville Cambodia 71 C5
aung Myauk Myanmar 70 A2
awa India 84 D1
ong China 77 H1
ora India 82 E5
ui China 77 G4
kajoki Fin. 44 N4
injärvi Fin. 44 O5
t Turkey 91 F3
wal Pak. 82 B4
aka Saudi Arabia see Sakākah
andra Rao India 82 D4
anni Chief Canada 120 F3
anni Chief r. Canada 120 F3
ar India 82 C4
aram mt. Afgh. 89 H3
asso Mali 96 C3
aw Myanmar 70 B2
eston U.S.A. 131 F4
hote-Alin' mts Rus. Fed. 74 D4
hote-Alinskiy Zapovednik nature res.
us. Fed. 74 E3
inos i. Greece 59 K6
ka India 82 B5
kim state India 83 G4
sjö Sweden 44 J4
r. Spain 57 C2
' i. Saudi Arabia 90 D6
alė Lith. 45 M9
anna National Park Thai. 70 B3
s U.S.A. 131 F6
avatturai Sri Lanka 84 C4
awaih Agam vol. Indon. 71 A6
berberg hill Germany 53 J1
char India 83 H4
e Turkey 59 M4
eru r. India 84 D2
esia reg. Czech Rep./Poland 47 P5
eti r. Kazakh. 72 C2
etiteniz, Ozero salt l. Kazakh. 79 G1
ghat India 83 H4
ana Tunisia 58 C6
fke Turkey 85 A1
guri India see Shiliguri
ng Co salt l. China 83 G3
pur India 82 D4
stra Bulg. 59 L2
stria Bulg. see Silistra
vri Turkey 59 M4
an l. Sweden 45 I6
keborg Denmark 45 F8
ajhuay mt. Chile 142 E7
amäe Estonia 45 O7
e Turkey 90 D3
i India 83 F5
od India 84 B1
obela S. Africa 101 J4
by Lake Canada 121 M4
U.S.A. 129 J2
aharju Fin. 44 O3
ip r. Iran 89 F5
atė Lith. 45 L9
an Turkey 91 F3
ânia Brazil 145 A2
assa India 84 B1
er Bank Passage Turks and Caicos Is
37 J4
er Bay U.S.A. 130 F2
er City NM U.S.A. 129 I5
er City NV U.S.A. 128 D2
er City (abandoned) Canada 120 B2
er Creek r. U.S.A. 129 H4
er Lake U.S.A. 126 C4
er Lake l. U.S.A. 128 E4
ermine Mts hills Ireland 51 D5
er Peak Range mts U.S.A. 128 E3
er Spring U.S.A. 135 G4
er Springs U.S.A. 128 D2
erthrone Mountain Canada 120 E5
ertip Mountain Canada 120 F5
erton U.K. 49 D8
erton CO U.S.A. 129 J3
erton TX U.S.A. 131 C5
a China 83 G3

Simanggang Sarawak Malaysia see
Sri Aman
Simao China 76 D4
Simard, Lac l. Canada 122 F5
Simaria India 83 F4
Simav Turkey 59 M5
Simav Dağları mts Turkey 59 M5
Simba Dem. Rep. Congo 98 C3
Simbirsk Rus. Fed. see Ul'yanovsk
Simcoe Canada 134 E2
Simcoe, Lake Canada 134 F1
Simdega India 84 E1
Simēn mts Eth. 98 D2
Simēn Mountains Eth. see Simēn
Simeulue i. Indon. 71 B7
Simferopol' Ukr. 90 D1
Simi i. Greece see Symi
Simikot Nepal 83 E3
Similan, Ko i. Thai. 71 B5
Simi Valley U.S.A. 128 D4
Simla India see Shimla
Simla U.S.A. 126 G5
Şimleu Silvaniei Romania 59 J1
Simmerath Germany 52 G4
Simmern (Hunsrück) Germany 53 H5
Simmesport U.S.A. 131 F6
Simms U.S.A. 126 F3
Simojärvi l. Fin. 44 O3
Simon Mex. 131 C7
Simonette r. Canada 120 G4
Simon Wash watercourse U.S.A. 129 I5
Simoom Sound Canada 120 E5
Simoon Sound Canada see Simoom Sound
Simpang Indon. 68 C7
Simpang Mangayau, Tanjung pt
Malaysia 68 F5
Simplício Mendes Brazil 143 J5
Simplon Pass Switz. 56 I3
Simpson Canada 121 J5
Simpson U.S.A. 126 F2
Simpson Desert Australia 110 B5
Simpson Desert National Park
Australia 110 B5
Simpson Desert Regional Reserve
nature res. Australia 111 B5
Simpson Islands Canada 121 H2
Simpson Park Mountains U.S.A. 128 E2
Simpson Peninsula Canada 119 J3
Simrishamn Sweden 45 I9
Simushir, Ostrov i. Rus. Fed. 73 S3
Sina r. India 84 B2
Sinabang Indon. 71 B7
Sinabung vol. Indon. 71 B7
Sinai pen. Egypt 85 A5
Sinai, Mont hill France 52 E5
Sinai al Janūbīya governorate Egypt see
Janūb Sīnā'
Sinai ash Shamālīya governorate Egypt see
Shamāl Sīnā'
Si Nakarin, Ang Kep Nam Thai. 70 B4
Sinaloa state Mex. 127 F8
Sinalunga Italy 58 D3
Sinan China 77 F3
Sinancha Rus. Fed. see Cheremshany
Sinbo Myanmar 70 B1
Sinbyubyin Myanmar 71 B4
Sinbyugyun Myanmar 70 A2
Sincan Turkey 90 E3
Sincelejo Col. 142 C2
Sinchu Taiwan see T'aoyüan
Sinclair Mills Canada 120 F4
Sincora, Serra do hills Brazil 145 C1
Sind r. India 82 D4
Sind Pak. see Thul
Sind prov. Pak. see Sindh
Sinda Rus. Fed. 74 E2
Sindari India 82 B4
Sindelfingen Germany 53 I6
Sindh prov. Pak. 89 H5
Sindhuli Garhi Nepal 83 F4
Sindhulimadi Nepal see Sindhuli Garhi
Sındırgı Turkey 59 M5
Sindor Rus. Fed. 42 K3
Sindou Burkina 96 C3
Sindri India 83 F5
Sind Sagar Doab lowland Pak. 89 H4
Sinel'nikovo Ukr. see Synel'nykove
Sines Port. 57 B5
Sines, Cabo de c. Port. 57 B5
Sinettä Fin. 44 N3
Sinfra Côte d'Ivoire 96 C4
Sing Myanmar 70 B2
Singa Sudan 86 D7
Singanallur India 84 C4
Singapore country Asia 71 [inset]

▶Singapore Sing. 71 [inset]
Capital of Singapore.

Singapore r. Sing. 71 [inset]
Singapore, Strait of Indon./Sing. 71 [inset]
Singapura country Asia see Singapore
Singapura Sing. see Singapore
Singapuru India 84 D2
Singaraja Indon. 108 A2
Sing Buri Thai. 70 C4
Singhampton Canada 134 E1
Singhana India 82 C3
Singida Tanz. 99 D4
Singidunum Serbia see Belgrade
Singkaling Hkamti Myanmar 70 A1
Singkawang Indon. 68 D6
Singkep i. Indon. 68 C7
Singkil Indon. 71 B7
Singkuang Indon. 71 B7
Singleton Australia 112 E4
Singleton, Mount hill N.T.
Australia 108 E5
Singleton, Mount hill W.A. Australia 109 B7
Singora Thai. see Songkhla
Sin'gosan N. Korea see Kosan
Singra India 83 G4
Singri India 83 H4
Singu Myanmar 76 B4
Singwara India 84 D1
Sin'gye N. Korea 75 B5
Sinhala country Asia see Sri Lanka
Sinhkung Myanmar 70 B1
Sining China see Xining
Siniscola Sardinia Italy 58 C4
Sinj Croatia 58 G3
Sinjai Indon. 69 G8

Sinjār, Jabal mt. Iraq 91 F3
Sinkat Sudan 86 E6
Sinkiang aut. reg. China see
Xinjiang Uygur Zizhiqu
Sinkiang Uighur Autonomous Region
aut. reg. China see
Xinjiang Uygur Zizhiqu
Sinmi-do i. N. Korea 75 B5
Sinn Germany 53 I4
Sinnamary Fr. Guiana 143 H2
Sinn Bishr, Gebel hill Egypt see
Sinn Bishr, Jabal
Sinn Bishr, Jabal hill Egypt 85 A5
Sinneh Iran see Sanandaj
Sinoia Zimbabwe see Chinhoyi
Sinop Brazil 143 G6
Sinop Turkey 90 D2
Sinope Turkey see Sinop
Sinp'a N. Korea 74 B4
Sinp'o N. Korea 75 C4
Sinsang N. Korea 75 B5
Sinsheim Germany 53 I5
Sintang Indon. 68 E6
Sint Eustatius i. Neth. Antilles 137 L5
Sint-Laureins Belgium 52 D3

▶Sint Maarten i. Neth. Antilles 137 L5
Part of the Netherlands Antilles. The
northern part of the island is the French
Overseas Collectivity of St Martin.

Sint-Niklaas Belgium 52 E3
Sinton U.S.A. 131 D6
Sintra Port. 57 B4
Sint-Truiden Belgium 52 F4
Sinŭiju N. Korea 75 B4
Sinzig Germany 53 H4
Siófok Hungary 58 H1
Sioma Ngwezi National Park
Zambia 99 C5
Sion Switz. 56 H3
Sion Mills U.K. 51 E3
Siorapaluk Greenland 119 K2
Sioux Center U.S.A. 125 H3
Sioux City U.S.A. 130 D3
Sioux Falls U.S.A. 130 D3
Sioux Lookout Canada 121 N5
Siphaqeni S. Africa see Flagstaff
Siping China 74 B4
Sipiwesk Canada 121 L4
Sipiwesk Lake Canada 121 L4
Siple, Mount Antarctica 152 J2
Siple Coast Antarctica 152 I1
Siple Island Antarctica 152 J2
Siponj Tajik. see Bartang
Sipsey r. U.S.A. 131 F5
Sipura i. Indon. 68 B7
Sīq, Wādī as watercourse Egypt 85 A5
Sir r. Pak. 89 H6
Sir, Dar"yoi r. Asia see Syrdar'ya
Sira India 84 C3
Sira r. Norway 45 E7
Şīr Abū Nu'āyr i. U.A.E. 88 D5
Siracusa Sicily Italy see Syracuse
Siraha Nepal see Sirha
Sirajganj Bangl. 83 G4
Sir Alexander, Mount Canada 120 F4
Şiran Turkey 91 E2
Sirbāl, Jabal mt. Egypt 90 D5
Şīr Banī Yās i. U.A.E. 88 D5
Sircilla India see Sirsilla
Sirdaryo r. Asia see Syrdar'ya
Sirdaryo Uzbek. 80 C3
Sirdingka China see Si'erdingka
Sir Edward Pellew Group is
Australia 110 B2
Sirha Nepal 83 F4
Sirhān, Wādī as watercourse
Jordan/Saudi Arabia 85 C4
Sirik, Tanjung pt Malaysia 68 E6
Siri Kit, Khuan Thai. 70 C3
Sirína i. Greece see Syrna
Sīrjā Iran 89 F5
Sir James MacBrien, Mount
Canada 120 E2
Sīrjān Iran 88 D4
Sīrjān salt flat Iran 88 D4
Sirkazhi India 84 C4
Sirmilik National Park Canada 119 K2
Şırnak Turkey 91 F3
Sirohi India 82 C4
Sirombu Indon. 71 B7
Sironj India 82 D4
Síros i. Greece see Syros
Sirpur India 84 C2
Sirretta Peak U.S.A. 128 D4
Sīrrī, Jazīreh-ye i. Iran 88 D5
Sirsa India 82 C3
Sir Sandford, Mount Canada 120 G5
Sirsi Karnataka India 84 B3
Sirsi Madh. Prad. India 82 D4
Sirsi Uttar Prad. India 82 D3
Sirsilla India 84 C2
Sirte Libya 97 E1
Sirte, Gulf of Libya 97 E1
Sir Thomas, Mount hill Australia 109 E6
Siruguppa India 84 C3
Sirur India 84 B2
Şirvan Turkey 91 F3
Sirvel India 84 C3
Širvintai Lith. see Širvintos
Širvintos Lith. 45 N9
Sīrwān r. Iraq 91 G4
Sir Wilfrid Laurier, Mount
Canada 120 G4
Sis Turkey see Kozan
Sisak Croatia 58 G2
Sisaket Thai. 70 D4
Siscia Croatia see Sisak
Sishen S. Africa 100 F4
Sishilipu China 76 E1
Sishuang Liedao is China 77 I3
Sisian Armenia 91 G3
Sisimiut Greenland 119 M3
Sisipuk Lake Canada 121 K4
Sisŏphŏn Cambodia 71 C4
Sissano P.N.G. 69 K7
Sisseton U.S.A. 130 D2
Sīstān reg. Iran 89 F4
Sisteron France 56 G4
Sisters is India 71 A5
Sīt Iran 88 E5

Sitamarhi India 83 F4
Sitang China see Sinan
Sitapur India 82 E4
Siteia Greece 59 L7
Siteki Swaziland 101 J4
Sithonia pen. Greece see
Sithonias, Chersonisos
Sithonias, Chersonisos pen. Greece 59 J4
Sitía Greece see Siteia
Sitidgi Lake Canada 118 E3
Sitila Moz. 101 L2
Siting China 76 E3
Sítio do Mato Brazil 145 C1
Sitka U.S.A. 120 C3
Sitka National Historical Park nat. park
U.S.A. 120 C3
Sitra oasis Egypt see Sitrah
Sitrah oasis Egypt 90 B5
Sittang r. Myanmar see Sittaung
Sittard Neth. 52 F4
Sittaung Myanmar 70 A1
Sittaung r. Myanmar 70 B3
Sittensen Germany 53 J1
Sittingbourne U.K. 49 H7
Sittoung r. Myanmar see Sittaung
Sittwe Myanmar 70 A2
Situbondo Indon. 68 E8
Siumpu i. Indon. 69 G8
Siuri India 83 F5
Sivaganga India 84 C4
Sivakasi India 84 C4
Sivaki Rus. Fed. 74 B1
Sivan India see Siwan
Sivas Turkey 90 E3
Sivaslı Turkey 59 M5
Siverek Turkey 91 E3
Siverskiy Rus. Fed. 45 Q7
Sivers'kyy Donets' r. Rus. Fed./Ukr. see
Severskiy Donets
Sivomaskinskiy Rus. Fed. 41 S2
Sivrice Turkey 91 E3
Sivrihisar Turkey 59 N5
Sivukile S. Africa 101 I4
Sīwa Egypt see Sīwah
Sīwah Egypt 90 B5
Sīwah, Wāḩāt oasis Egypt 90 B5
Siwalik Range mts India/Nepal 82 D3
Siwan India 83 F4
Siwana India 82 C4
Siwa Oasis oasis Egypt see Sīwah, Wāḩāt
Sixian China 77 H1
Sixmilecross U.K. 51 E3
Siyabuswa S. Africa 101 I3
Siyäzän Azer. 91 H2
Sīyunī Iran 88 D3
Siziwang Qi China see Ulan Hua
Sjælland i. Denmark see Zealand
Sjenica Serbia 59 I3
Sjöbo Sweden 45 H9
Sjøvegan Norway 44 J2
Skadarsko Jezero nat. park
Montenegro 59 H3
Skadovs'k Ukr. 59 O1
Skaftafell nat. park Iceland 44 [inset]
Skaftárós r. mouth Iceland 44 [inset]
Skagafjörður inlet Iceland 44 [inset]
Skagen Denmark 45 G8
Skagerrak strait Denmark/Norway 45 F8
Skagit r. U.S.A. 126 C2
Skagway U.S.A. 153 A3
Skaidi Norway 44 N1
Skaland Norway 44 J2
Skalmodal Sweden 44 I4
Skanderborg Denmark 45 F8
Skaneateles Lake U.S.A. 135 G2
Skara Sweden 45 H7
Skardarsko Jezero l. Albania/Montenegro
see Scutari, Lake
Skardu Pak. 82 C2
Skärgårdshavets nationalpark nat. park
Fin. 45 L7
Skarnes Norway 45 G6
Skarżysko-Kamienna Poland 47 R5
Skaulo Sweden 44 L3
Skawina Poland 47 Q6
Skeena r. Canada 120 D4
Skeena Mountains Canada 120 D3
Skegness U.K. 48 H5
Skellefteå Sweden 44 L4
Skellefteälven r. Sweden 44 L4
Skelleftehamn Sweden 44 L4
Skelmersdale U.K. 48 E5
Skerries Ireland 51 F4
Ski Norway 45 G7
Skiathos i. Greece 59 J5
Skibbereen Ireland 51 C6
Skibotn Norway 44 L2
Skiddaw hill U.K. 48 D4
Skien Norway 45 F7
Skiermûntseach Neth. see
Schiermonnikoog
Skiermûntseach i. Neth. see
Schiermonnikoog
Skierniewice Poland 47 R5
Skikda Alg. 58 B6
Skipsea U.K. 48 G5
Skipton Australia 112 A6
Skipton U.K. 48 E5
Skirlaugh U.K. 48 G5
Skíros i. Greece see Skyros
Skive Denmark 45 F8
Skjern Denmark 45 F9
Skjolden Norway 45 E6
Skobelev Uzbek. see Farg'ona
Skobeleva, Pik mt. Kyrg. 89 I2
Skodje Norway 44 E5
Skoganvarri Norway 44 N2
Skokie U.S.A. 134 B2
Skomer Island U.K. 49 B7
Skopelos i. Greece 59 J5
Skopin Rus. Fed. 43 H5

▶Skopje Macedonia 59 I4
Capital of Macedonia.

Skoplje Macedonia see Skopje
Skövde Sweden 45 H7
Skovorodino Rus. Fed. 74 A1
Skowhegan U.S.A. 135 K1
Skrunda Latvia 45 M8
Skukum, Mount Canada 120 C2
Skukuza S. Africa 101 J3

Skull Valley U.S.A. 129 G4
Skuodas Lith. 45 L8
Skurup Sweden 45 H9
Skutskär Sweden 45 J6
Skyvra Ukr. 43 F6
Skye i. U.K. 50 C3
Skylge i. Neth. see Terschelling
Skyring, Seno b. Chile 144 B8
Skyros Greece 59 K5
Skyros i. Greece 59 K5
Skytrain Ice Rise Antarctica 152 L1
Slættaratindur hill Faroe Is 44 [inset]
Slagelse Denmark 45 G9
Slagnäs Sweden 44 K4
Slane Ireland 51 F4
Slaney r. Ireland 51 F5
Slantsy Rus. Fed. 45 P7
Slapovi Krke nat. park Croatia 58 F3
Slashers Reefs Australia 110 D3
Slatina Croatia 58 G2
Slatina Romania 59 K2
Slaty Fork U.S.A. 134 E4
Slava Rus. Fed. 74 C1
Slave r. Canada 121 H2
Slave Coast Africa 96 D4
Slave Lake Canada 120 H4
Slave Point Canada 120 H2
Slavgorod Belarus see Slawharad
Slavgorod Rus. Fed. 72 D2
Slavkovichi Rus. Fed. 45 P8
Slavonska Požega Croatia see Požega
Slavonski Brod Croatia 58 H2
Slavuta Ukr. 43 E6
Slavutych Ukr. 43 F6
Slavyanka Rus. Fed. 74 C4
Slavyansk Ukr. see Slov"yans'k
Slavyanskaya Rus. Fed. see
Slavyansk-na-Kubani
Slavyansk-na-Kubani Rus. Fed. 90 E1
Slawharad Belarus 43 F5
Sławno Poland 47 P3
Slayton U.S.A. 130 E3
Sleaford U.K. 49 G5
Slea Head hd Ireland 51 B5
Sleat Neth. see Sloten
Sleat, Sound of sea chan. U.K. 50 D3
Sled Lake Canada 121 J4
Sleeper Islands Canada 122 F2
Sleeping Bear Dunes National Lakeshore
nature res. U.S.A. 134 B1
Slessor Glacier Antarctica 152 B1
Slick Rock U.S.A. 129 I2
Slide Mountain U.S.A. 135 H3
Slieve Bloom Mts hills Ireland 51 E5
Slieve Car hill Ireland 51 C3
Slieve Donard hill U.K. 51 G3
Slieve Mish Mts hills Ireland 51 B5
Slieve Snaght hill Ireland 51 E2
Sligachan U.K. 50 C3
Sligeach Ireland see Sligo
Sligo Ireland 51 D3
Sligo U.S.A. 134 F3
Sligo Bay Ireland 51 D3
Slinger U.S.A. 134 A2
Slippery Rock U.S.A. 134 E3
Slite Sweden 45 K8
Sliven Bulg. 59 L3
Sloan U.S.A. 129 F4
Sloat U.S.A. 128 C2
Sloboda Rus. Fed. see Ezhva
Slobodchikovo Rus. Fed. 42 K3
Slobodskoy Rus. Fed. 42 K4
Slobozia Romania 59 L2
Slochteren Neth. 52 G1
Slonim Belarus 45 N10
Slootdorp Neth. 52 E2
Sloten Neth. 52 F2
Slough U.K. 49 G7
Slovakia country Europe 40 J6
Slovenia country Europe 58 F2
Slovenija country Europe see Slovenia
Slovenj Gradec Slovenia 58 F1
Slovensko country Europe see Slovakia
Slovenský raj nat. park Slovakia 47 R6
Slov"yans'k Ukr. 43 H6
Słowiński Park Narodowy nat. park
Poland 47 P3
Sluch r. Ukr. 43 E6
S'Lung, B'Nom mt. Vietnam 71 D5
Słupsk Poland 47 P3
Slussfors Sweden 44 J4
Slutsk Belarus 45 O10
Slyne Head hd Ireland 51 B4
Slyudyanka Rus. Fed. 72 I2
Small Point U.S.A. 135 K2
Smallwood Reservoir Canada 123 I3
Smalyavichy Belarus 45 P9
Smalyenskaya Wzwyshsha hills
Belarus/Rus. Fed. see
Smolensko-Moskovskaya
Vozvyshennost'
Smarhon' Belarus 45 O9
Smeaton Canada 121 J4
Smederevo Serbia 59 I2
Smederevska Palanka Serbia 59 I2
Smela Ukr. see Smila
Smethport U.S.A. 135 F3
Smidovich Rus. Fed. 74 D2
Smila Ukr. 43 F6
Smilde Neth. 52 G2
Smiltene Latvia 45 N8
Smirnykh Rus. Fed. 74 F2
Smith Canada 120 H4
Smith Center U.S.A. 130 D4
Smithfield S. Africa 101 H6
Smithfield NC U.S.A. 132 E5
Smithfield UT U.S.A. 126 F4
Smith Glacier Antarctica 152 K1
Smith Island India 71 A4
Smith Island MD U.S.A. 135 G4
Smith Island VA U.S.A. 135 H5
Smith Mountain Lake U.S.A. 134 F5
Smith River Canada 120 E3
Smiths Falls Canada 135 G1
Smithton Australia 111 [inset]
Smithtown Australia 112 F3
Smithville OK U.S.A. 131 E5
Smithville WV U.S.A. 134 E4
Smoke Creek Desert U.S.A. 128 D1
Smoky Bay Australia 109 F8
Smoky Cape Australia 112 F3
Smoky Falls Canada 122 E4

Smoky Hill r. U.S.A. 130 C4
Smoky Hills KS U.S.A. 124 H4
Smoky Hills KS U.S.A. 130 D4
Smoky Lake Canada 121 H4
Smoky Mountains U.S.A. 126 E4
Smøla i. Norway 44 E5
Smolenka Rus. Fed. 43 K6
Smolensk Rus. Fed. 43 G5
Smolensk-Moscow Upland hills
Belarus/Rus. Fed. see
Smolensko-Moskovskaya
Vozvyshennost'
Smolensko-Moskovskaya Vozvyshennost'
hills Belarus/Rus. Fed. 43 G5
Smolevichi Belarus see Smalyavichy
Smolyan Bulg. 59 K4
Smooth Rock Falls Canada 122 E4
Smoothrock Lake Canada 122 C4
Smoothstone Lake Canada 121 J4
Smørfjord Norway 44 N1
Smorgon' Belarus see Smarhon'
Smyley Island Antarctica 152 L2
Smyrna Turkey see İzmir
Smyrna U.S.A. 135 H4
Smyth Island atoll Marshall Is see Taongi
Snæfell mt. Iceland 44 [inset]
Snaefell hill Isle of Man 48 C4
Snag (abandoned) Canada 120 A2
Snake r. Canada 120 C1
Snake r. U.S.A. 126 D3
Snake Island Australia 112 C7
Snake Range mts U.S.A. 129 F2
Snake River Canada 120 F3
Snake River Plain U.S.A. 126 E4
Snare r. Canada 120 G2
Snare Lake Canada 121 J3
Snare Lakes Canada see Wekweêtì
Snares Islands N.Z. 107 G6
Snåsa Norway 44 H4
Sneedville U.S.A. 134 D5
Sneek Neth. 52 F1
Sneem Ireland 51 C6
Sneeuberge mts S. Africa 100 G6
Snegamook Lake Canada 123 J3
Snegurovka Ukr. see Tetiyiv
Snelling U.S.A. 128 C3
Snettisham U.K. 49 H6
Snezhnogorsk Rus. Fed. 64 J3
Snežnik mt. Slovenia 58 F2
Sniečkus Lith. see Visaginas
Snihurivka Ukr. 43 G7
Snits Neth. see Sneek
Snizort, Loch b. U.K. 50 C3
Snoqualmie Pass U.S.A. 126 C3
Snøtinden mt. Norway 44 H3
Snoul Cambodia see Snuŏl
Snover U.S.A. 134 D2
Snovsk Ukr. see Shchors
Snowbird Lake Canada 121 K2
Snowcrest Mountain Canada 120 G5
Snowdon mt. U.K. 49 C5
Snowdonia National Park U.K. 49 D6
Snowdrift Canada see Łutselk'e
Snowdrift r. Canada 121 I2
Snowflake U.S.A. 129 H4
Snow Hill U.S.A. 135 H4
Snow Lake Canada 121 K4
Snowville U.S.A. 126 E4
Snow Water Lake U.S.A. 129 F1
Snowy r. Australia 112 D6
Snowy Mountain U.S.A. 135 H2
Snowy Mountains Australia 112 C6
Snowy River National Park
Australia 112 D6
Snug Corner Bahamas 133 F8
Snug Harbour Nfld. and Lab.
Canada 123 L3
Snug Harbour Ont. Canada 134 E1
Snuŏl Cambodia 71 D4
Snyder U.S.A. 131 C5
Soalala Madag. 99 E5
Soalara Madag. 99 E6
Soanierana-Ivongo Madag. 99 E5
Soan-kundo is S. Korea 75 B6
Soavinandriana Madag. 99 E5
Sobat r. Sudan 86 D8
Sobger r. Indon. 69 K7
Sobinka Rus. Fed. 42 I5
Sobradinho, Barragem de resr
Brazil 143 J6
Sobral Brazil 143 J4
Sochi Rus. Fed. 91 E2
Sŏch'ŏn S. Korea 75 B5
Society Islands Fr. Polynesia 151 J7
Socorro Brazil 145 B3
Socorro Col. 142 D2
Socorro U.S.A. 127 G6
Socorro, Isla i. Mex. 136 B5
Socotra i. Yemen 87 H7
Soc Trăng Vietnam 71 D5
Socuéllamos Spain 57 E4
Soda Lake CA U.S.A. 128 D4
Soda Lake CA U.S.A. 128 E4
Sodankylä Fin. 44 O3
Soda Plains Aksai Chin 82 D2
Soda Springs U.S.A. 126 F4
Söderhamn Sweden 45 J6
Söderköping Sweden 45 J7
Södertälje Sweden 45 J7
Sodiri Sudan 86 C7
Sodo Eth. 98 D3
Södra Kvarken strait Fin./Sweden 45 K6
Sodus U.S.A. 135 G2
Soë Indon. 69 G8
Soekarno, Puntjak mt. Indon. see
Jaya, Puncak
Soekmekaar S. Africa 101 I2
Soerabaia Indon. see Surabaya
Soerendonk Neth. 52 F3
Soest Germany 53 I3
Soest Neth. 52 F2
Sofala Australia 112 D4

▶Sofia Bulg. 59 J3
Capital of Bulgaria.

Sofiya Bulg. see Sofia
Sofiyevka Ukr. see Vil'nyans'k
Sofiysk Khabarovskiy Kray Rus. Fed. 74 D1
Sofiysk Khabarovskiy Kray
Rus. Fed. 74 E2
Sofporog Rus. Fed. 44 Q4

Sofrana i. Greece 59 L6
Softa Kalesi tourist site Turkey 85 A1
Sōfu-gan i. Japan 75 F7
Sog China 76 B2
Soğanlı Dağları mts Turkey 91 E2
Sogda Rus. Fed. 74 D2
Sögel Germany 53 H2
Sogma China 82 E2
Søgne Norway 45 E7
Sognefjorden inlet Norway 45 D6
Sogruma China 76 D1
Söğüt Turkey 59 N4
Söğüt Dağı mts Turkey 59 M6
Soh Iran 88 C3
Sohâg Egypt see Sūhāj
Sohagpur India 82 D5
Soham U.K. 49 H6
Sohan r. Pak. 89 H3
Sohano P.N.G. 106 F2
Sohar Oman see Şuḥār
Sohawal India 82 E4
Sohela India 83 E5
Sohng Gwe, Khao hill Myanmar/Thai. 71 B4
Sŏho-ri N. Korea 75 C4
Sohŭksan-do i. S. Korea 75 B6
Soignies Belgium 52 E4
Soila China 76 C2
Soini Fin. 44 N5
Soissons France 52 D5
Sojat India 82 C4
Sojat Road India 82 C4
Sok r. Rus. Fed. 43 K5
Sokal' Ukr. 43 E6
Sokch'o S. Korea 75 C5
Söke Turkey 59 L6
Sokhor, Gora mt. Rus. Fed. 72 J2
Sokhumi Georgia 91 F2
Sokiryany Ukr. see Sokyryany
Sokodé Togo 96 D4
Soko Islands H.K. China 77 [inset]
Sokol Rus. Fed. 42 I4
Sokolo Mali 96 C3
Sokolov Czech Rep. 53 M4
Sokoto Nigeria 96 D3
Sokoto r. Nigeria 96 D3
Sokyryany Ukr. 43 E6
Sola Cuba 133 E8
Sola i. Tonga see Ata
Solan India 82 D3
Solana Beach U.S.A. 128 E5
Solander Island N.Z. 113 A8
Solapur India 84 B2
Soldotna U.S.A. 118 C3
Soledad U.S.A. 128 C3
Soledade Brazil 144 F3
Solenoye Rus. Fed. 43 I7
Solfjellsjøen Norway 44 H3
Solginskiy Rus. Fed. 42 I3
Solhan Turkey 91 F3
Soligalich Rus. Fed. 42 I4
Soligorsk Belarus see Salihorsk
Solihull U.K. 49 F6
Solikamsk Rus. Fed. 41 R4
Sol'-Iletsk Rus. Fed. 64 G4
Solimões r. S. America see Amazon
Solingen Germany 52 H3
Solitaire Namibia 100 B2
Sol-Karmala Rus. Fed. see Severnoye
Şollar Azer. 91 H2
Sollefteå Sweden 44 J5
Söllichau Germany 53 M3
Solling hills Germany 53 J3
Sollstedt Germany 53 K3
Sollum, Gulf of Egypt see Sallum, Khalīj as
Solms Germany 53 I4
Solnechnogorsk Rus. Fed. 42 H4
Solnechnyy Amurskaya Oblast' Rus. Fed. 74 A1
Solnechnyy Khabarovskiy Kray Rus. Fed. 74 E2
Solok Indon. 68 C7
Solomon U.S.A. 129 I5
Solomon, North Fork r. U.S.A. 130 D4
▶Solomon Islands country S. Pacific Ocean 107 G2
4th largest and 5th most populous country in Oceania.
Solomon Sea S. Pacific Ocean 106 F2
Solon U.S.A. 135 K1
Solon Springs U.S.A. 130 F2
Solor i. Indon. 108 C2
Solor, Kepulauan is Indon. 108 C2
Solothurn Switz. 56 H3
Solovetskiye Ostrova is Rus. Fed. 42 G2
Solov'yevsk Rus. Fed. 74 B1
Šolta i. Croatia 58 G3
Solţānābād Kermān Iran 88 E4
Solţānābād Khorāsān Iran 89 E3
Solţānābād Iran 88 C3
Solţānīyeh Iran 88 C2
Soltau Germany 53 J2
Sol'tsy Rus. Fed. 42 F4
Solvay U.S.A. 135 G2
Sölvesborg Sweden 45 I8
Solway Firth est. U.K. 50 F6
Solwezi Zambia 99 C5
Soma Turkey 59 L5
Somain France 52 D4
Somalia country Africa 98 E3
Somali Basin sea feature Indian Ocean 149 L6
Somali Republic country Africa see Somalia
Sombo Angola 99 C4
Sombor Serbia 59 H2
Sombrero Channel India 71 A6
Sombrio, Lago do l. Brazil 145 A5
Somero Fin. 45 M6
Somerset KY U.S.A. 134 C5
Somerset MI U.S.A. 134 C2
Somerset OH U.S.A. 134 D4
Somerset PA U.S.A. 134 F4
Somerset, Lake Australia 112 F1
Somerset East S. Africa 101 G7
Somerset Island Canada 119 I2
Somerset Reservoir U.S.A. 135 I2
Somerset West S. Africa 100 D8
Somersworth U.S.A. 135 J2
Somerton U.S.A. 129 F5
Somerville NJ U.S.A. 135 H3
Somerville TN U.S.A. 131 F5
Someydeh Iran 88 B3
Somme r. France 52 B4
Sommen l. Sweden 45 I7
Sömmerda Germany 53 L3
Sommet, Lac du l. Canada 123 H3
Somnath India 82 B5
Somutu Myanmar 70 B1
Son r. India 83 F4
Sonag China see Zêkog
Sonapur India 84 D1
Sonar r. India 82 D4
Sŏnbong N. Korea 74 C4
Sŏnch'ŏn N. Korea 75 B5
Sønderborg Denmark 45 F9
Sondershausen Germany 53 K3
Søndre Strømfjord Greenland see Kangerlussuaq
Søndre Strømfjord inlet Greenland see Kangerlussuaq
Sondrio Italy 58 C1
Sonepat India see Sonipat
Sonepur India see Sonapur
Songbai China see Shennongjia
Songbu China 77 G2
Sông Câu Vietnam 71 E4
Songcheng China see Xiapu
Sông Đa, Hô resr Vietnam 70 D2
Songea Tanz. 99 D5
Songhua Hu resr China 74 B4
Songhua Jiang r. Heilongjiang/Jilin China 74 D3
Songhua Jiang r. Jilin China see Di'er Songhua Jiang
Songjiang China 77 I2
Songjianghe China 74 B4
Sŏngjin N. Korea see Kimch'aek
Songkan China 76 E2
Songkhla Thai. 71 C6
Songling China see Ta'erqi
Songlong Myanmar 70 B2
Sŏngnam S. Korea 75 B5
Songnim N. Korea 75 B5
Songo Angola 99 B4
Songo Moz. 99 D5
Songpan China 76 D1
Songshan China see Ziyun
Song Shan mt. China 77 G1
Songtao China 77 F2
Songxi China 77 H3
Songxian China 77 G1
Songyuan Fujian China see Songxi
Songyuan Jilin China 74 B3
Songzi China 77 F2
Sơn Hai Vietnam 71 E5
Sonid Youqi China see Saihan Tal
Sonid Zuoqi China see Mandalt
Sonipat India 82 D3
Sonkajärvi Fin. 44 O5
Sonkovo Rus. Fed. 42 H4
Sơn La Vietnam 70 C2
Sonmiani Pak. 89 G5
Sonmiani Bay Pak. 89 G5
Sonneberg Germany 53 L4
Sono r. Minas Gerais Brazil 145 B2
Sono r. Tocantins Brazil 143 I5
Sonoma U.S.A. 128 B2
Sonoma Peak U.S.A. 128 E1
Sonora r. Mex. 127 F7
Sonora state Mex. 127 F7
Sonora CA U.S.A. 128 C3
Sonora KY U.S.A. 134 C5
Sonora TX U.S.A. 131 C6
Sonoran Desert U.S.A. 129 G5
Sonoran Desert National Monument nat. park U.S.A. 127 E6
Sonqor Iran 88 B3
Sonsonate El Salvador 136 G6
Sonsorol Islands Palau 69 I5
Sơn Tây Vietnam 70 D2
Sonwabile S. Africa 101 I6
Soochow China see Suzhou
Soomaaliya country Africa see Somalia
Sopi, Tanjung pt Indon. 69 H6
Sopo watercourse Sudan 97 F4
Sopot Bulg. 59 K3
Sopot Poland 47 Q3
Sop Prap Thai. 70 B3
Sopron Hungary 58 G1
Sopur India 82 C2
Sora Italy 58 E4
Sorab India 84 B3
Sorada India 84 E2
Söråker Sweden 44 J5
Sŏrak-san mt. S. Korea 75 C5
Sorak-san National Park S. Korea 75 C5
Sorel Canada 123 G5
Soreq r. Israel 85 B4
Sorgun Turkey 90 D3
Sorgun r. Turkey 85 B1
Soria Spain 57 E3
Sorkh, Kūh-e mts Iran 88 D3
Sorkhān Iran 88 E4
Sorkheh Iran 88 D3
Sørli Norway 44 H4
Soro India 83 F5
Soroca Moldova 43 F6
Sorocaba Brazil 145 B3
Soroki Moldova see Soroca
Sorol atoll Micronesia 69 K5
Sorong Indon. 69 I7
Soroti Uganda 98 D3
Sørøya i. Norway 44 M1
Sorraia r. Port. 57 B4
Sørreisa Norway 44 K2
Sorrento Italy 58 F4
Sorsele Sweden 44 J4
Sorsogon Phil. 69 G4
Sortavala Rus. Fed. 44 Q6
Sortland Norway 44 I2
Sortopolovskaya Rus. Fed. 42 K3
Sorvizhi Rus. Fed. 42 K4
Sŏsan S. Korea 75 B5
Sosenskiy Rus. Fed. 43 G5
Soshanguve S. Africa 101 I3
Sosna r. Rus. Fed. 43 H5
Sosneado mt. Arg. 144 C4
Sosnogorsk Rus. Fed. 42 L3
Sosnovka Arkhangel'skaya Oblast' Rus. Fed. 42 J3
Sosnovka Kaliningradskaya Oblast' Rus. Fed. 41 K5
Sosnovka Murmanskaya Oblast' Rus. Fed. 42 I2
Sosnovka Tambovskaya Oblast' Rus. Fed. 43 I5
Sosnovo Rus. Fed. 45 Q6
Sosnovo-Ozerskoye Rus. Fed. 73 K2
Sosnovyy Rus. Fed. 44 R4
Sosnovyy Bor Rus. Fed. 45 P7
Sosnowiec Poland 47 Q5
Sosnowitz Poland see Sosnowiec
Sos'va Khanty-Mansiyskiy Avtonomnyy Okrug Rus. Fed. 41 S3
Sos'va Sverdlovskaya Oblast' Rus. Fed. 41 S4
Sotang China 76 B2
Sotara, Volcán vol. Col. 142 C3
Sotkamo Fin. 44 P4
Sotteville-lès-Rouen France 52 B5
Souanké Congo 98 B3
Soubré Côte d'Ivoire 96 C4
Souderton U.S.A. 135 H3
Soufflenheim France 53 H6
Soufli Greece 59 L4
Soufrière St Lucia 137 L6
Soufrière vol. St Vincent 137 L6
Sougueur Alg. 57 G6
Souillac France 56 E4
Souilly France 52 F5
Souk Ahras Alg. 58 B6
Souk el Arbaâ du Rharb Morocco 54 C5
Sŏul S. Korea see Seoul
Soulac-sur-Mer France 56 D4
Soulom France 56 D5
Sounding Creek r. Canada 121 I4
Souni Cyprus 85 A2
Soûr Lebanon see Tyre
Soure Brazil 143 I4
Sour el Ghozlane Alg. 57 H5
Souris Canada 121 K5
Souris r. Canada 121 L5
Souriya country Asia see Syria
Sousa Brazil 143 K5
Sousa Lara Angola see Bocoio
Sousse Tunisia 58 D7
Soustons France 56 D5
▶South Africa, Republic of country Africa 100 F5
5th most populous country in Africa.
Southampton Canada 134 E1
Southampton U.K. 49 F8
Southampton U.S.A. 135 I3
Southampton, Cape Canada 119 J3
Southampton Island Canada 119 J3
South Andaman i. India 71 A5
South Anna r. U.S.A. 135 G5
South Anston U.K. 48 F5
South Aulatsivik Island Canada 123 J2
South Australia state Australia 106 D5
South Australian Basin sea feature Indian Ocean 149 P8
Southaven U.S.A. 131 F5
South Baldy mt. U.S.A. 127 G6
South Bank U.K. 48 F4
South Bass Island U.S.A. 134 D3
South Bend IN U.S.A. 134 B3
South Bend WA U.S.A. 126 C3
South Bluff pt Bahamas 133 F8
South Boston U.S.A. 135 F5
South Brook Canada 123 K4
South Cape pt U.S.A. see Ka Lae
South Carolina state U.S.A. 133 D5
South Charleston OH U.S.A. 134 D4
South Charleston WV U.S.A. 134 E4
South China Sea N. Pacific Ocean 68 F4
South Coast Town Australia see Gold Coast
South Dakota state U.S.A. 130 C2
South Downs hills U.K. 49 G8
South-East admin. dist. Botswana 101 G3
South East Cape Australia 111 [inset]
Southeast Cape U.S.A. 118 B3
Southeast Indian Ridge sea feature Indian Ocean 149 N8
South East Isles Australia 109 C8
Southeast Pacific Basin sea feature S. Pacific Ocean 151 M10
South East Point Australia 112 C7
Southend Canada 121 K3
Southend U.K. 50 D5
Southend-on-Sea U.K. 49 H7
Southern admin. dist. Botswana 100 G3
Southern Alps mts N.Z. 113 C6
Southern Cross Australia 109 B7
Southern Indian Lake Canada 121 L3
Southern Lau Group is Fiji 107 I3
Southern National Park Sudan 97 F4
Southern Ocean 152 C2
Southern Pines U.S.A. 133 E5
Southern Rhodesia country Africa see Zimbabwe
Southern Uplands hills U.K. 50 E5
South Esk r. U.K. 50 F4
South Esk Tableland reg. Australia 108 D4
Southey Canada 121 J5
Southfield U.S.A. 134 D2
South Fiji Basin sea feature S. Pacific Ocean 150 H7
South Fork U.S.A. 128 B1
South Geomagnetic Pole (2008) Antarctica 152 F1
South Georgia i. S. Atlantic Ocean 144 I8
▶South Georgia and the South Sandwich Islands terr. S. Atlantic Ocean 144 I8
United Kingdom Overseas Territory
South Harris pen. U.K. 50 B3
South Haven U.S.A. 134 B2
South Henik Lake Canada 121 L2
South Hill U.S.A. 135 F5
South Honshu Ridge sea feature N. Pacific Ocean 150 F3
South Indian Lake Canada 121 L3
South Island India 84 B4
▶South Island N.Z. 113 D7
2nd largest island in Oceania.
South Junction Canada 121 M5
South Korea country Asia 75 B5
South Lake Tahoe U.S.A. 128 C2
South Luangwa National Park Zambia 99 D5
South Magnetic Pole (2008) Antarctica 152 G2
South Mills U.S.A. 135 G5
Southminster U.K. 49 H7
South Mountains hills U.S.A. 135 G4
South New Berlin U.S.A. 135 H2
South Orkney Islands S. Atlantic Ocean 148 F10
South Paris U.S.A. 135 J1
South Platte r. U.S.A. 130 C3
South Point Bahamas 133 F8
South Pole Antarctica 152 C1
Southport Qld Australia 112 F1
Southport Tas. Australia 111 [inset]
Southport U.K. 48 D5
Southport U.S.A. 135 G2
South Portland U.S.A. 135 J2
South Ronaldsay i. U.K. 50 G2
South Royalton U.S.A. 135 I2
South Salt Lake U.S.A. 129 H1
South Sand Bluff pt S. Africa 101 J6
▶South Sandwich Islands S. Atlantic Ocean 148 G9
United Kingdom Overseas Territory.
South Sandwich Trench sea feature S. Atlantic Ocean 148 G9
South San Francisco U.S.A. 128 B3
South Saskatchewan r. Canada 121 J4
South Seal r. Canada 121 L3
South Shetland Islands Antarctica 152 A2
South Shetland Trough sea feature S. Atlantic Ocean 152 L2
South Shields U.K. 48 F3
South Sinai governorate Egypt see Janūb Sīnā'
South Solomon Trench sea feature S. Pacific Ocean 150 G6
South Taranaki Bight b. N.Z. 113 E4
South Tasman Rise sea feature Southern Ocean 150 F9
South Tent mt. U.S.A. 129 H2
South Tons r. India 83 E4
South Twin Island Canada 122 F3
South Tyne r. U.K. 48 E4
South Uist i. U.K. 50 B3
South Wellesley Islands Australia 110 B3
South-West Africa country Africa see Namibia
South West Cape N.Z. 113 A8
South West Entrance sea chan. P.N.G. 110 E1
Southwest Indian Ridge sea feature Indian Ocean 149 K8
South West National Park Australia 111 [inset]
Southwest Pacific Basin sea feature S. Pacific Ocean 150 I8
Southwest Peru Ridge sea feature S. Pacific Ocean see Nazca Ridge
South West Rocks Australia 112 F3
South Whitley U.S.A. 134 C3
South Wichita r. U.S.A. 131 D5
South Windham U.S.A. 135 J2
Southwold U.K. 49 I6
Southwood National Park Australia 112 E1
Soutpansberg mts S. Africa 101 I2
Souttouf, Adrar mts W. Sahara 96 B2
Soverato Italy 58 G5
Sovetsk Kaliningradskaya Oblast' Rus. Fed. 45 L9
Sovetsk Kirovskaya Oblast' Rus. Fed. 42 K4
Sovetskaya Gavan' Rus. Fed. 74 F2
Sovetskiy Khanty-Mansiyskiy Avtonomnyy Okrug Rus. Fed. 41 S3
Sovetskiy Leningradskaya Oblast' Rus. Fed. 45 P6
Sovetskiy Respublika Mariy El Rus. Fed. 42 K4
Sovetskoye Chechenskaya Respublika Rus. Fed. see Shatoy
Sovetskoye Stavropol'skiy Kray Rus. Fed. see Zelenokumsk
Sovyets'kyy Ukr. 90 D1
Sowa China 76 C2
Soweto S. Africa 101 H4
So'x Tajik. 89 H2
Sōya-kaikyō strait Japan/Rus. Fed. see La Pérouse Strait
Sōya-misaki c. Japan 74 F3
Soyana r. Rus. Fed. 42 I2
Soyma r. Rus. Fed. 42 K2
Soyopa Mex. 127 F7
Sozh r. Europe 43 F6
Sozopol Bulg. 59 L3
Spa Belgium 52 F4
▶Spain country Europe 57 E3
4th largest country in Europe.
Spalato Croatia see Split
Spalatum Croatia see Split
Spalding U.K. 49 G6
Spanish Canada 122 E5
Spanish Fork U.S.A. 129 H1
Spanish Guinea country Africa see Equatorial Guinea
Spanish Netherlands country Europe see Belgium
Spanish Sahara terr. Africa see Western Sahara
Spanish Town Jamaica 137 I5
Sparks U.S.A. 128 D2
Sparta Greece see Sparti
Sparta GA U.S.A. 133 D5
Sparta KY U.S.A. 134 C4
Sparta MI U.S.A. 134 C2
Sparta NC U.S.A. 134 E5
Sparta TN U.S.A. 132 C5
Spartanburg U.S.A. 133 D5
Sparti Greece 59 J6
Spartivento, Capo c. Italy 58 G6
Spas-Demensk Rus. Fed. 43 G5
Spas-Klepiki Rus. Fed. 43 I5
Spassk-Dal'niy Rus. Fed. 74 D3
Spassk-Ryazanskiy Rus. Fed. 43 I5
Spatha, Akra pt Kriti Greece see Spatha, Akrotirio
Spatha, Akrotirio pt Greece 59 J7
Spearman U.S.A. 131 C4
Speedway U.S.A. 134 B4
Spence Bay Canada see Taloyoak
Spencer IA U.S.A. 130 E3
Spencer ID U.S.A. 126 E3
Spencer IN U.S.A. 134 B4
Spencer NE U.S.A. 130 D3
Spencer WV U.S.A. 134 E4
Spencer, Cape U.S.A. 120 B3
Spencer Bay Namibia 100 B3
Spencer Gulf est. Australia 111 B7
Spencer Range hills Australia 108 E3
Spennymoor U.K. 48 F4
Sperrin Mountains hills U.K. 51 E3
Sperryville U.S.A. 135 F4
Spessart reg. Germany 53 J5
Spétsai i. Greece see Spetses
Spetses i. Greece 59 J6
Spey r. U.K. 50 F3
Speyer Germany 53 I5
Spezand Pak. 89 G4
Spice Islands Indon. see Moluccas
Spijk Neth. 52 G1
Spijkenisse Neth. 52 E3
Spilimbergo Italy 58 E1
Spilsby U.K. 48 H5
Spīn Böldak Afgh. 89 G4
Spintangi Pak. 89 H4
Spirit Lake U.S.A. 130 E3
Spirit River Canada 120 G4
Spirovo Rus. Fed. 42 G4
Spišská Nová Ves Slovakia 43 D6
Spiti r. India 82 D3
▶Spitsbergen i. Svalbard 64 C2
5th largest island in Europe.
Spittal an der Drau Austria 47 N7
Spitzbergen i. Svalbard see Spitsbergen
Split Croatia 58 G3
Split Lake Canada 121 L3
Split Lake l. Canada 121 L3
Spokane U.S.A. 126 D3
Spoletium Italy see Spoleto
Spoleto Italy 58 E3
Spŏng Cambodia 71 D4
Spoon r. U.S.A. 130 F3
Spooner U.S.A. 130 F2
Spornitz Germany 53 L1
Spotsylvania U.S.A. 135 G4
Spotted Horse U.S.A. 126 G3
Spranger, Mount Canada 120 F4
Spratly Islands S. China Sea 68 E4
Spray U.S.A. 126 D3
Spree r. Germany 47 N4
Sprimont Belgium 52 F4
Springbok S. Africa 100 C5
Springdale Canada 123 L4
Springdale U.S.A. 134 C4
Springe Germany 53 J2
Springer U.S.A. 127 G5
Springerville U.S.A. 129 I4
Springfield CO U.S.A. 130 C4
▶Springfield IL U.S.A. 130 F4
Capital of Illinois.
Springfield KY U.S.A. 134 C5
Springfield MA U.S.A. 135 I2
Springfield MO U.S.A. 131 E4
Springfield OH U.S.A. 134 D4
Springfield OR U.S.A. 126 C3
Springfield TN U.S.A. 134 B5
Springfield VT U.S.A. 135 I2
Springfield WV U.S.A. 135 F4
Springfontein S. Africa 101 G6
Spring Glen U.S.A. 129 H2
Spring Grove U.S.A. 134 A2
Springhill Canada 123 I5
Spring Hill U.S.A. 133 D6
Springhouse Canada 120 F5
Spring Mountains U.S.A. 129 F3
Springs Junction N.Z. 113 D6
Springsure Australia 110 E5
Spring Valley MN U.S.A. 130 E3
Spring Valley NY U.S.A. 135 H3
Springview U.S.A. 130 D3
Springville CA U.S.A. 128 D3
Springville NY U.S.A. 135 F2
Springville PA U.S.A. 135 H3
Springville UT U.S.A. 129 H1
Sprowston U.K. 49 I6
Spruce Grove Canada 120 H4
Spruce Knob mt. U.S.A. 132 E4
Spruce Mountain CO U.S.A. 129 I2
Spruce Mountain NV U.S.A. 129 F1
Spurn Head hd U.K. 48 H5
Spuzzum Canada 120 F5
Squam Lake U.S.A. 135 J2
Square Lake U.S.A. 123 H5
Squillace, Golfo di g. Italy 58 G5
Squires, Mount hill Australia 109 D6
Srbija country Europe see Serbia
Srbinje Bos.-Herz. see Foča
Srê Âmbĕl Cambodia 71 C5
Srebrenica Republika Srpska 59 H2
Sredets Burgas Bulg. 59 L3
Sredets Sofiya-Grad Bulg. see Sofia
Sredinnyy Khrebet mts Rus. Fed. 65 Q4
Sredna Gora mts Bulg. 59 J3
Srednekolymsk Rus. Fed. 65 Q3
Sredne-Russkaya Vozvyshennost' hills Rus. Fed. see Central Russian Upland
Sredne-Sibirskoye Ploskogor'ye plat. Rus. Fed. see Central Siberian Plateau
Sredneye Kuyto, Ozero l. Rus. Fed. 44 Q4
Sredniy Ural mts Rus. Fed. 41 R4
Srednogorie Bulg. 59 K3
Srednyaya Akhtuba Rus. Fed. 43 J6
Sreepur Bangl. see Sripur
Sre Khtum Cambodia 71 D4
Srê Noy Cambodia 71 D4
Sretensk Rus. Fed. 73 L2
Sri Aman Sarawak Malaysia 68 E6
Sriharikota Island India 84 D3
▶Sri Jayewardenepura Kotte Sri Lanka 84 C5
Capital of Sri Lanka.
Srikakulam India 84 E2
Sri Kalahasti India 84 C3
Sri Lanka country Asia 84 D5
Srinagar India 82 C2
Sri Pada mt. Sri Lanka see Adam's Peak
Sripur Bangl. 83 G4
Srirangam India 84 C4
Sri Thep tourist site Thai. 70 C3
Srivardhan India 84 B2
Staaten r. Australia 110 C3
Staaten River National Park Australia 110 C3
Stabroek Guyana see Georgetown
Stade Germany 53 J1
Staden Belgium 52 D4
Stadskanaal Neth. 52 G2
Stadtallendorf Germany 53 J4
Stadthagen Germany 53 J2
Stadtilm Germany 53 L4
Stadtlohn Germany 52 G3
Stadtoldendorf Germany 53 J3
Stadtroda Germany 53 L4
Staffa i. U.K. 50 C4
Staffelberg hill Germany 53 L4
Staffelstein Germany 53 K4
Stafford U.K. 49 E6
Stafford U.S.A. 135 G4
Stafford Creek Bahamas 133 E7
Stafford Springs U.S.A. 135 I3
Stagg Lake Canada 120 H2
Staicele Latvia 45 N8
Staines U.K. 49 G7
Stakhanov Ukr. 43 H6
Stakhanovo Rus. Fed. see Zhukovskiy
Stalbridge U.K. 49 E8
Stalham U.K. 49 I6
Stalin Bulg. see Varna
Stalinabad Tajik. see Dushanbe
Stalingrad Rus. Fed. see Volgograd
Staliniri Georgia see Ts'khinvali
Stalino Ukr. see Donets'k
Stalinogorsk Rus. Fed. see Novomoskovs
Stalinogród Poland see Katowice
Stalinsk Rus. Fed. see Novokuznetsk
Stalowa Wola Poland 43 D6
Stamboliyski Bulg. 59 K3
Stamford Australia 110 C4
Stamford U.K. 49 G6
Stamford CT U.S.A. 135 I3
Stamford NY U.S.A. 135 H2
Stampalia i. Greece see Astypalaia
Stampriet Namibia 100 D3
Stamsund Norway 44 H2
Stanardsville U.S.A. 135 F4
Stanberry U.S.A. 130 E3
Stancomb-Wills Glacier Antarctica 152 B
Standard Canada 120 H5
Standdaarbuiten Neth. 52 E3
Standerton S. Africa 101 I4
Standish U.S.A. 134 D2
Stanfield U.S.A. 129 H5
Stanford KY U.S.A. 134 C5
Stanford MT U.S.A. 126 F3
Stanger S. Africa 101 J5
Stanislaus r. U.S.A. 128 C3
Stanislav Ukr. see Ivano-Frankivs'k
Stanke Dimitrov Bulg. see Dupnitsa
Staňkov Czech Rep. 53 N5
Stanley Australia 111 [inset]
Stanley H.K. China 77 [inset]
▶Stanley Falkland Is 144 E8
Capital of the Falkland Islands.
Stanley U.K. 48 F4
Stanley ID U.S.A. 126 E3
Stanley KY U.S.A. 134 B5
Stanley ND U.S.A. 130 C1
Stanley VA U.S.A. 135 F4
Stanley, Mount hill N.T. Australia 108 E5
Stanley, Mount hill Tas. Australia 111 [ins
Stanley, Mount Dem. Rep. Congo/Ugand see Margherita Peak
Stanleyville Dem. Rep. Congo see Kisangani
Stann Creek Belize see Dangriga
Stannington U.K. 48 F3
Stanovoye Rus. Fed. 43 H5
Stanovoye Nagor'ye mts Rus. Fed. 73 L1
Stanovoy Khrebet mts Rus. Fed. 65 N4
Stansmore Range hills Australia 108 E5
Stanthorpe Australia 112 E2
Stanton U.K. 49 H6
Stanton KY U.S.A. 134 D5
Stanton MI U.S.A. 134 C2
Stanton ND U.S.A. 130 C2
Stanton TX U.S.A. 131 C5
Stapleton U.S.A. 130 C3
Starachowice Poland 47 R5
Stara Planina mts Bulg./Serbia see Balkan Mountains
Staraya Russa Rus. Fed. 42 F4
Stara Zagora Bulg. 59 K3
Starbuck Island Kiribati 151 J6
Star City U.S.A. 134 B3
Starcke National Park Australia 110 D2
Stargard in Pommern Poland see Stargard Szczeciński
Stargard Szczeciński Poland 47 O4
Staritsa Rus. Fed. 42 G4
Starke U.S.A. 133 D6
Starkville U.S.A. 131 F5
Star Lake U.S.A. 135 H1
Starnberger See l. Germany 47 M7
Starobel'sk Ukr. see Starobil's'k
Starobil's'k Ukr. 43 H6
Starogard Gdański Poland 47 Q4
Starokonstantinov Ukr. see Starokostyantyniv
Starokostyantyniv Ukr. 43 E6
Starominskaya Rus. Fed. 43 H7
Staroshcherbinovskaya Rus. Fed. 43 H7
Star Peak U.S.A. 128 D1
Start Point U.K. 49 D8
Starve Island Kiribati see Starbuck Island
Staryya Darohi Belarus 43 F5
Staryye Dorogi Belarus see Staryya Darol
Staryy Kayak Rus. Fed. 65 L2
Staryy Oskol Rus. Fed. 43 H6
Staßfurt Germany 53 L3
State College U.S.A. 135 G3
State Line U.S.A. 131 F6

ten Island Arg. see Los Estados, Isla de
tenville U.S.A. 133 D6
tesboro U.S.A. 133 D5
tesville U.S.A. 132 D5
tia i. Neth. Antilles see Sint Eustatius
tion U.S.A. 134 C4
tion Nord Greenland 153 I1
uchitz Germany 53 N3
ufenberg Germany 53 I4
unton U.S.A. 134 F4
vanger Norway 45 D7
veley U.K. 48 F5
vropol' Rus. Fed. 91 F1
vropol Kray admin. div. Rus. Fed. see Stavropol'skiy Kray
vropol'-na-Volge Rus. Fed. see Tol'yatti
vropol'skaya Vozvyshennost' hills Rus. Fed. 91 F1
vropol'skiy Kray admin. div. Rus. Fed. 91 F1
yner Canada 134 E1
yton U.S.A. 126 C3
adville S. Africa 101 I5
amboat Springs U.S.A. 126 G4
arns U.S.A. 134 C5
bbins U.S.A. 118 B3
ele Island Antarctica 152 L2
elville U.S.A. 130 F4
en r. Canada 120 G3
enderen Neth. 52 G2
enkampsberge mts S. Africa 101 J3
en River Canada 120 G3
ens Mountain U.S.A. 126 D4
enstrup Gletscher glacier Greenland see ermersuaq
envoorde France 52 C4
enwijk Neth. 52 G2
fansson Island Canada 119 H2
gi Swaziland see Siteki
igerwald mts Germany 53 K5
in Germany 53 L5
inach Germany 53 L4
inaker Reservoir U.S.A. 129 I1
inbach Canada 121 L5
infeld (Oldenburg) Germany 53 I2
infurt Germany 53 H2
inhausen Namibia 99 B6
inheim Germany 53 J3
inkjer Norway 44 G4
inkopf S. Africa 100 C5
insdalen Norway 44 G4
lla S. Africa 100 G4
lla Maris Bahamas 133 F8
llenbosch S. Africa 100 D7
llo, Monte mt. Corsica France 56 I5
lvio, Parco Nazionale dello nat. park aly 58 D1
nay France 52 F5
ndal Germany 53 L2
nhousemuir U.K. 50 F4
nungsund Sweden 45 G7
ornabhagh U.K. see Stornoway
panakert Azer. see Xankändi
phens, Cape N.Z. 113 D5
phens City U.S.A. 135 F4
phens Lake Canada 121 M3
phenville U.S.A. 131 D5
pnoy Rus. Fed. see Elista
pnoye Rus. Fed. 43 J6
rkfontein Dam resr S. Africa 101 I5
rkstroom S. Africa 101 H6
rlet Lake Canada 121 I1
rlibashevo Rus. Fed. 41 R5
rling S. Africa 100 E6
rling CO U.S.A. 130 C3
rling IL U.S.A. 130 F3
rling MI U.S.A. 134 C1
rling UT U.S.A. 129 H2
rling City U.S.A. 131 C6
rling Heights U.S.A. 134 D2
rlitamak Rus. Fed. 64 G4
ttin Poland see Szczecin
ttler Canada 121 H4
ubenville KY U.S.A. 134 C5
ubenville OH U.S.A. 134 E3
venage U.K. 49 G7
venson U.S.A. 126 C3
venson Lake Canada 121 L4
vens Point U.S.A. 130 F2
vens Village U.S.A. 118 D3
vensville MI U.S.A. 134 B2
vensville PA U.S.A. 135 G3
wart Canada 120 D4
wart r. Canada 120 B2
wart, Isla i. Chile 144 B8
wart Crossing Canada 120 B2
wart Island N.Z. 113 A8
wart Islands Solomon Is 107 G2
wart Lake Canada 119 J3
warton U.K. 50 E5
warts Point U.S.A. 128 B2
wiacke Canada 123 J5
ynsburg S. Africa 101 G6
yr Austria 47 O6
ytlerville S. Africa 100 G7
ns Neth. 52 F1
Alg. see Sétif
ler U.S.A. 131 E5
ine r. Canada 120 C3
ine Plateau Canada 120 D3
ine Strait U.S.A. 120 C3
baai S. Africa 100 E8
es U.S.A. 134 A1
water MN U.S.A. 130 E2
water OK U.S.A. 131 D4
water Range mts U.S.A. 128 D2
well U.S.A. 134 B3
on U.K. 49 G6
well U.S.A. 131 E5
nett U.S.A. 131 C5
Macedonia 59 J4
ling Australia 108 F5
ling Canada 135 G1
ling U.K. 50 F4
ing Creek r. Australia 108 E4
ing Range National Park ustralia 109 B8
sville Canada 135 H1
rdalshalsen Norway 44 G5
ckbridge U.S.A. 134 C2
ckerau Austria 47 P6
ckheim Germany 53 L4

▶Stockholm Sweden 45 K7
Capital of Sweden.

Stockinbingal Australia 112 C5
Stockport U.K. 48 E5
Stockton CA U.S.A. 128 C3
Stockton KS U.S.A. 130 D4
Stockton MO U.S.A. 130 E4
Stockton UT U.S.A. 129 G1
Stockton Lake U.S.A. 130 E4
Stockton-on-Tees U.K. 48 F4
Stockville U.S.A. 130 C3
Stod Czech Rep. 53 N5
Stœng Trêng Cambodia 71 D4
Stoer, Point of U.K. 50 D2
Stoke-on-Trent U.K. 49 E5
Stokesley U.K. 48 F4
Stokes Point Australia 111 [inset]
Stokes Range hills Australia 108 E4
Stokkseyri Iceland 44 [inset]
Stokkvågen Norway 44 H3
Stokmarknes Norway 44 I2
Stolac Bos.-Herz. 58 G3
Stolberg (Rheinland) Germany 52 G4
Stolbovoy Rus. Fed. 153 G2
Stolbtsy Belarus see Stowbtsy
Stolin Belarus 45 O11
Stollberg Germany 53 M4
Stolp Poland see Słupsk
Stolzenau Germany 53 J2
Stone U.K. 49 E6
Stoneboro U.S.A. 134 E3
Stonecliffe Canada 122 F5
Stonecutters' Island pen. H.K. China 77 [inset]
Stonehaven U.K. 50 G4
Stonehenge Australia 110 C5
Stonehenge tourist site U.K. 49 F7
Stoner U.S.A. 129 I3
Stonewall Canada 121 L5
Stonewall Jackson Lake U.S.A. 134 E4
Stony Creek U.S.A. 135 G5
Stony Lake Canada 121 L3
Stony Point U.S.A. 135 G2
Stony Rapids Canada 121 J3
Stony River U.S.A. 118 C3
Stooping r. Canada 122 E3
Stora Lulevatten l. Sweden 44 K3
Stora Sjöfallets nationalpark nat. park Sweden 44 J3
Storavan l. Sweden 44 K4
Store Bælt sea chan. Denmark see Great Belt
Støren Norway 44 G5
Storfjordbotn Norway 44 O1
Storforshei Norway 44 I3
Storjord Norway 44 I3
Storkerson Peninsula Canada 119 H2
Storm Bay Australia 111 [inset]
Stormberg S. Africa 101 H6
Storm Lake U.S.A. 130 E3
Stornosa mt. Norway 44 E6
Stornoway U.K. 50 C2
Storozhevsk Rus. Fed. 42 L3
Storozhynets' Ukr. 43 E6
Storrs U.S.A. 135 I3
Storseleby Sweden 44 J4
Storsjön l. Sweden 44 I5
Storskrymten mt. Norway 44 F5
Storslett Norway 44 L2
Stortemelk sea chan. Neth. 52 F1
Storuman Sweden 44 J4
Storuman l. Sweden 44 J4
Storvik Sweden 45 J6
Storvorde Denmark 45 G8
Storvreta Sweden 45 J7
Story U.S.A. 126 G3
Stotfold U.K. 49 G6
Stoughton Canada 121 K5
Stour r. England U.K. 49 F6
Stour r. England U.K. 49 F8
Stour r. England U.K. 49 I7
Stour r. England U.K. 49 I7
Stourbridge U.K. 49 E6
Stourport-on-Severn U.K. 49 E6
Stout Lake Canada 121 M4
Stowbtsy Belarus 45 O10
Stowe U.S.A. 135 I1
Stowmarket U.K. 49 H6
Stoyba Rus. Fed. 74 C1
Strabane U.K. 51 E3
Stradbally Ireland 51 E4
Stradbroke U.K. 49 I6
Stradella Italy 58 C2
Strakonice Czech Rep. 47 N6
Stralsund Germany 47 N3
Strand S. Africa 100 D8
Stranda Norway 44 E5
Strangford U.K. 51 G3
Strangford Lough inlet U.K. 51 G3
Strangways r. Australia 108 F3
Stranraer U.K. 50 D6
Strasbourg France 56 H2
Strasburg Germany 53 N1
Strasburg U.S.A. 135 F4
Strassburg France see Strasbourg
Stratford Australia 112 C6
Stratford Canada 134 E2
Stratford CA U.S.A. 128 D3
Stratford TX U.S.A. 131 C4
Stratford-upon-Avon U.K. 49 F6
Strathaven U.K. 50 E5
Strathmore Canada 120 H5
Strathmore r. U.K. 50 E2
Strathnaver Canada 120 F4
Strathroy Canada 134 E2
Strathspey valley U.K. 50 F3
Strathy U.K. 50 F2
Stratton U.K. 49 C8
Stratton U.S.A. 135 J1
Stratton Mountain U.S.A. 135 I2
Straubing Germany 53 M6
Straumnes pt Iceland 44 [inset]
Strawberry U.S.A. 129 H4
Strawberry Mountain U.S.A. 126 D3
Strawberry Reservoir U.S.A. 129 H1
Streaky Bay Australia 109 F8
Streaky Bay b. Australia 109 F8
Streator U.S.A. 130 F3
Street U.K. 49 E7
Streetsboro U.S.A. 134 E3

Strehaia Romania 59 J2
Strehla Germany 53 N3
Streich Mound hill Australia 109 C7
Strelka Rus. Fed. 65 Q3
Strel'na r. Rus. Fed. 42 H2
Strenči Latvia 45 N8
Streymoy i. Faroe Is 44 [inset]
Stříbro Czech Rep. 53 M5
Strichen U.K. 50 G3
Strimonas r. Greece see Strymonas
Stroeder Arg. 144 D6
Strokestown Ireland 51 D4
Stroma, Island of U.K. 50 F2
Stromboli, Isola i. Italy 58 F5
Stromness S. Georgia 144 I8
Stromness U.K. 50 F2
Strömstad Sweden 45 G7
Strömsund Sweden 44 I5
Strongsville U.S.A. 134 E3
Stronsay i. U.K. 50 G1
Stroud Australia 112 E4
Stroud U.K. 49 E7
Stroud Road Australia 112 E4
Stroudsburg U.S.A. 135 H3
Struer Denmark 45 F8
Struga Macedonia 59 I4
Strugi-Krasnyye Rus. Fed. 45 P7
Struis Bay S. Africa 100 E8
Strullendorf Germany 53 K5
Struma r. Bulg. 59 J4
also known as Strymonas (Greece)
Strumble Head hd U.K. 49 B6
Strumica Macedonia 59 J4
Struthers U.S.A. 134 E3
Stryama r. Bulg. 59 K3
Strydenburg S. Africa 100 F5
Strymonas r. Greece 59 J4
also known as Struma (Bulgaria)
Stryn Norway 44 E6
Stryy Ukr. 43 D6
Strzelecki Desert Australia 111 B6
Strzelecki, Mount hill Australia 108 F5
Strzelecki Regional Reserve nature res. Australia 111 B6
Stuart FL U.S.A. 133 D7
Stuart NE U.S.A. 130 D3
Stuart VA U.S.A. 134 E5
Stuart Lake Canada 120 E4
Stuart Range hills Australia 111 A6
Stuarts Draft U.S.A. 134 F4
Stuart Town Australia 112 D4
Stuchka Latvia see Aizkraukle
Stučka Latvia see Aizkraukle
Studholme Junction N.Z. 113 C7
Studsviken Sweden 44 K5
Stukely, Lac l. Canada 135 I1
Stung Treng Cambodia see Stœng Trêng
Stupart r. Canada 121 M4
Stupino Rus. Fed. 43 H5
Sturge Island Antarctica 152 H2
Sturgeon r. Ont. Canada 122 F5
Sturgeon r. Sask. Canada 121 J4
Sturgeon Bay b. Canada 121 L4
Sturgeon Bay U.S.A. 134 B1
Sturgeon Bay Canal lake channel U.S.A. 134 B1
Sturgeon Falls Canada 122 F5
Sturgeon Lake Ont. Canada 121 N5
Sturgeon Lake Ont. Canada 135 F1
Sturgis MI U.S.A. 134 C3
Sturgis SD U.S.A. 130 C2
Sturt, Mount hill Australia 111 C6
Sturt Creek watercourse Australia 108 D4
Sturt National Park Australia 111 C6
Sturt Stony Desert Australia 111 C6
Stutterheim S. Africa 101 H7
Stuttgart Germany 53 J6
Stuttgart U.S.A. 131 F5
Stykkishólmur Iceland 44 [inset]
Styr r. Belarus/Ukr. 43 E5
Suaçuí Grande r. Brazil 145 C2
Suai East Timor 108 D2
Suakin Sudan 86 E6
Suao Taiwan 77 I3
Suaqui Grande Mex. 127 F7
Suau P.N.G. 110 E1
Subačius Lith. 45 N9
Subankhata India 83 G4
Subarnapur India see Sonapur
Sūbāshī Iran 88 C3
Subay reg. Saudi Arabia 88 B5
Şubayḩah Saudi Arabia 85 D4
Subei China 80 H4
Subi Besar i. Indon. 71 E7
Subi Kecil i. Indon. 71 E7
Sublette U.S.A. 131 C4
Subotica Serbia 59 H1
Success, Lake U.S.A. 128 D3
Succiso, Alpi di mts Italy 58 D2
Suceava Romania 43 E7
Suchan Rus. Fed. see Partizansk
Suck r. Ireland 51 D4
Suckling, Mount P.N.G. 110 E1
Suckow Germany 53 L1

▶Sucre Bol. 142 E7
Legislative capital of Bolivia.

Suczawa Romania see Suceava
Sud, Grand Récif du reef New Caledonia 107 G4
Suda Rus. Fed. 42 H4
Sudak Ukr. 90 D1

▶Sudan country Africa 97 F3
Largest country in Africa, and 10th largest in the world.

Suday Rus. Fed. 42 I4
Sudayr reg. Saudi Arabia 88 B5
Sudbury Canada 122 E5
Sudbury U.K. 49 H6
Sudd swamp Sudan 86 C8
Sude r. Germany 53 K1
Sudest Island P.N.G. see Tagula Island
Sudetenland mts Czech Rep./Poland see Sudety
Sudety mts Czech Rep./Poland 47 O5
Sudislavl' Rus. Fed. 42 I4
Sudlersville U.S.A. 135 H4
Süd-Nord-Kanal canal Germany 52 H2
Sudogda Rus. Fed. 42 I5

Sudr Egypt 85 A5
Suðuroy i. Faroe Is 44 [inset]
Sue watercourse Sudan 97 F4
Sueca Spain 57 F4
Suez Egypt 85 A5
Suez, Gulf of Egypt 85 A5
Suez Bay Egypt 85 A5
Suez Canal Egypt 85 A4
Suffolk U.S.A. 135 G5
Sugarbush Hill hill U.S.A. 130 F2
Sugarloaf Mountain U.S.A. 135 J1
Sugarloaf Point Australia 112 F4
Sugun China 80 E4
Sūhāj Egypt 86 D4
Şuḩār Oman 88 E5
Suhaymī, Wādī as watercourse Egypt 85 A4
Sühbaatar Mongolia 72 J2
Suheli Par i. India 84 B4
Suhl Germany 53 K4
Suhlendorf Germany 53 K2
Suhul reg. Saudi Arabia 88 B6
Suhūl al Kidan plain Saudi Arabia 88 D6
Şuhut Turkey 59 N5
Sui Pak. 89 H4
Sui, Laem pt Thai. 71 B5
Suibin China 74 C3
Suid-Afrika country Africa see Republic of South Africa
Suide China 73 K5
Suidzhikurmsy Turkm. see Madaw
Suifenhe China 74 C3
Suihua China 74 B3
Suileng China 74 B3
Suining Hunan China 77 F3
Suining Jiangsu China 77 H1
Suining Sichuan China 76 E2
Suippes France 52 E5
Suir r. Ireland 51 E5
Suisse country Europe see Switzerland
Sui Vehar Pak. 89 H4
Suixi China 77 H1
Suixian Henan China 77 G1
Suixian Hubei China see Suizhou
Suiyang Guizhou China 76 E3
Suiyang Henan China 77 G1
Suiza country Europe see Switzerland
Suizhong China 73 M4
Suizhou China 77 G2
Sujangarh India 82 C4
Sujawal Pak. 89 H5
Suk atoll Micronesia see Pulusuk
Sukabumi Indon. 68 D8
Sukagawa Japan 75 F5
Sukarnapura Indon. see Jayapura
Sukarno, Puncak mt. Indon. see Jaya, Puncak
Sukchŏn N. Korea 75 B5
Sukhinichi Rus. Fed. 43 G5
Sukhona r. Rus. Fed. 42 J3
Sukhothai Thai. 70 B3
Sukhumi Georgia see Sokhumi
Sukhum-Kale Georgia see Sokhumi
Sukkertoppen Greenland see Maniitsoq
Sukkozero Rus. Fed. 42 G3
Sukkur Pak. 89 H5
Sukma India 84 D2
Sukpay Rus. Fed. 74 E3
Sukpay r. Rus. Fed. 74 E3
Sukri r. India 82 C4
Sukri r. India 82 C4
Suktel r. India 84 D1
Sukun i. Indon. 108 C2
Sula i. Norway 45 D6
Sula r. Rus. Fed. 42 K2
Sula, Kepulauan is Indon. 69 H7
Sulaiman Range mts Pak. 89 H4
Sulak Rus. Fed. 91 G2
Sūlār Iran 88 C4
Sula Sgeir i. U.K. 50 C1
Sulawesi i. Indon. see Celebes
Sulaymān Beg Iraq 91 G4
Sulaymānīyah Iraq 91 G4
Sulayyimah Saudi Arabia 88 B6
Sulci Sardinia Italy see Sant'Antioco
Sulcis Sardinia Italy see Sant'Antioco
Suledeh Iran 88 C2
Sule Skerry i. U.K. 50 E1
Sule Stack i. U.K. 50 E1
Sulingen Germany 53 I2
Sulitjelma Norway 44 J3
Sulkava Fin. 44 P6
Sullana Peru 142 B4
Sullivan IL U.S.A. 130 F4
Sullivan IN U.S.A. 134 B4
Sullivan Bay Canada 120 E5
Sullivan Island Myanmar see Lanbi Kyun
Sullivan Lake Canada 121 I5
Sulmo Italy see Sulmona
Sulmona Italy 58 E3
Sulphur LA U.S.A. 131 E6
Sulphur OK U.S.A. 131 D5
Sulphur r. U.S.A. 131 E5
Sulphur Springs U.S.A. 131 E5
Sultan Canada 122 E5
Sultan, Koh-i- mts Pak. 89 F4
Sultanabad India see Osmannagar
Sultanabad Iran see Arāk
Sultan Dağları mts Turkey 59 N5
Sultanıye Turkey see Karapınar
Sultanpur India 83 E4
Sulu Archipelago is Phil. 69 G5
Sulu Basin sea feature N. Pacific Ocean 150 E5
Sülüklü Turkey 90 D3
Sülüktü Kyrg. 89 H2
Sulusaray Turkey 90 E3
Sulu Sea N. Pacific Ocean 68 F5
Suluvvaulik, Lac l. Canada 123 G2
Sulyukta Kyrg. see Sülüktü
Sulzbach-Rosenberg Germany 53 L5
Sulzberger Bay Antarctica 152 I1
Sumāil Oman 88 E6
Sumampa Arg. 144 D3
Sumapaz, Parque Nacional nat. park Col. 142 D3
Sūmār Iran 88 B3
Sumatera i. Indon. see Sumatra

▶Sumatra i. Indon. 71 B7
2nd largest island in Asia, and 6th in the world.

Šumava nat. park Czech Rep. 47 N6
Sumba i. Indon. 108 C2
Sumba, Selat sea chan. Indon. 108 B2
Sumbar r. Turkm. 88 D2
Sumbawa i. Indon. 108 B2
Sumbawabesar Indon. 108 B2
Sumbawanga Tanz. 99 D4
Sumbe Angola 99 B5
Sumbu National Park Zambia 99 D4
Sumburgh U.K. 50 [inset]
Sumburgh Head hd U.K. 50 [inset]
Sumdo China 76 D2
Sumdum, Mount U.S.A. 120 C3
Sume'eh Sarā Iran 88 C2
Sumeih Sudan 86 C8
Sumenep Indon. 68 E8
Sumgait Azer. see Sumqayıt
Sumisu-jima i. Japan 73 Q6
Summēl Iraq 91 F3
Summer Beaver Canada 122 C3
Summerford Canada 123 L4
Summer Island U.S.A. 132 C2
Summer Isles U.K. 50 D2
Summerland Canada 120 G5
Summersville U.S.A. 134 E4
Summit Lake Canada 120 F4
Summit Mountain U.S.A. 128 E2
Summit Peak U.S.A. 127 G5
Sumnal Aksai Chin 82 D2
Sumner N.Z. 113 D6
Sumner, Lake N.Z. 113 D6
Sumon-dake mt. Japan 75 E5
Šumperk Czech Rep. 47 P6
Sumpu Japan see Shizuoka
Sumqayıt Azer. 91 H2
Sumskiy Posad Rus. Fed. 42 G2
Sumter U.S.A. 133 D5
Sumur India 82 D2
Sumy Ukr. 43 G6
Sumzom China 76 C2
Suna Rus. Fed. 42 K4
Sunaj India 82 D4
Sunam India 82 C3
Sunamganj Bangl. 83 G4
Sunart, Loch inlet U.K. 50 D4
Şunaynah Oman 88 D6
Sunburst U.S.A. 126 F2
Sunbury Australia 112 B6
Sunbury OH U.S.A. 134 D3
Sunbury PA U.S.A. 135 G3
Sunch'ŏn S. Korea 75 B6
Sun City S. Africa 101 H3
Sun City AZ U.S.A. 129 G5
Sun City CA U.S.A. 128 E5
Sunda, Selat strait Indon. 68 C8
Sunda Kalapa Indon. see Jakarta
Sundance U.S.A. 126 G3
Sundarbans coastal area Bangl./India 83 G5
Sundarbans National Park Bangl./India 83 G5
Sundargarh India 83 F5
Sunda Shelf sea feature Indian Ocean 149 P5
Sunda Strait Indon. see Sunda, Selat
Sunda Trench sea feature Indian Ocean see Java Trench
Sunderland U.K. 48 F4
Sundern (Sauerland) Germany 53 I3
Sündiken Dağları mts Turkey 59 N5
Sundown National Park Australia 112 E2
Sundre Canada 120 H5
Sundridge Canada 122 F5
Sundsvall Sweden 44 J5
Sundukli, Peski des. Turkm. see Sandykly Gumy
Sundumbili S. Africa 101 J5
Sungaipenuh Indon. 68 C7
Sungai Petani Malaysia 71 C6
Sungari r. China see Songhua Jiang
Sungei Seletar Reservoir Sing. 71 [inset]
Sungkiang China see Songjiang
Sung Kong i. H.K. China 77 [inset]
Sungqu China see Songpan
Sungsang Indon. 68 C7
Sungurlu Turkey 90 D2
Sun Kosi r. Nepal 83 F4
Sunman U.S.A. 134 C4
Sunndal Norway 45 E6
Sunndalsøra Norway 44 F5
Sunne Sweden 45 H7
Sunnyside U.S.A. 126 D3
Sunnyvale U.S.A. 128 B3
Sun Prairie U.S.A. 130 F3
Sunset House Canada 120 G4
Sunset Peak hill H.K. China 77 [inset]
Suntar Rus. Fed. 65 M3
Suntsar Pak. 89 F5
Sunwi-do i. N. Korea 75 B5
Sunwu China 74 B2
Sunyani Ghana 96 C4
Suolijärvet l. Fin. 44 P3
Suomi country Europe see Finland
Suomussalmi Fin. 44 P4
Suō-nada b. Japan 75 C6
Suonenjoki Fin. 44 O5
Suong r. Laos 70 C3
Suoyarvi Rus. Fed. 42 G3
Supa India 84 B3
Supaul India 83 F4
Superior AZ U.S.A. 129 H5
Superior MT U.S.A. 126 E3
Superior NE U.S.A. 130 D3
Superior WI U.S.A. 130 E2

▶Superior, Lake Canada/U.S.A. 125 J2
Largest lake in North America, and 2nd in the world.

Suphan Buri Thai. 71 C4
Süphan Dağı mt. Turkey 91 F3
Supiori i. Indon. 69 J7
Suponevo Rus. Fed. 43 G5
Support Force Glacier Antarctica 152 A1
Sūq ash Shuyūkh Iraq 91 G5
Suqian China 77 H1
Suquṭrá i. Yemen see Socotra
Şūr Oman 89 E6
Sur, Point U.S.A. 128 C3
Sur, Punta pt Arg. 144 E5
Sura r. Rus. Fed. 43 J4
Şuraabad Azer. 91 H2

Surabaya Indon. 68 E8
Sūrak Iran 88 E5
Surakarta Indon. 68 E8
Sūran Iran 89 F5
Şūrān Syria 85 C2
Surat Australia 112 D1
Surat India 82 C5
Suratgarh India 82 C3
Surat Thani Thai. 71 B5
Surazh Rus. Fed. 43 G5
Surbiton Australia 110 D4
Surdulica Serbia 59 J3
Sûre r. Lux. 52 G5
Surendranagar India 82 B5
Surf U.S.A. 128 C4
Surgut Rus. Fed. 64 I3
Suri India see Siuri
Suriapet India 84 C2
Surigao Phil. 69 H5
Surin Thai. 70 C4
Surinam country S. America see Suriname
Suriname country S. America 143 G3
Surin Nua, Ko i. Thai. 71 B5
Surkhduz Afgh. 89 G4
Surkhet Nepal 83 E3
Surkhon Uzbek. see Surxon
Sürmene Turkey 91 F2
Surovikino Rus. Fed. 43 I6
Surpura India 82 C4
Surrey Canada 120 F5
Surry U.S.A. 135 G5
Surskoye Rus. Fed. 43 J5
Surt Libya see Sirte
Surtsey i. Iceland 44 [inset]
Sürü Hormozgan Iran 88 E5
Sürü Sīstān va Balūchestān Iran 88 E5
Suruç Turkey 85 D1
Surud, Raas pt Somalia 98 E2
Surud Ad mt. Somalia see Shimbiris
Suruga-wan b. Japan 75 E6
Surulangun Indon. 68 C7
Surwold Germany 53 H2
Surxon Uzbek. 89 G2
Suryapet India see Suriapet
Şuşa Azer. 91 G3
Susah Tunisia see Sousse
Susaki Japan 75 D6
Susan U.S.A. 135 G5
Süsangerd Iran 88 C4
Susanino Rus. Fed. 74 F1
Susanville U.S.A. 128 C1
Suşehri Turkey 90 E2
Suso Thai. 71 B6
Susong China 77 H2
Susquehanna U.S.A. 135 H3
Susquehanna r. U.S.A. 135 G4
Susquehanna, West Branch r. U.S.A. 135 G3
Susques Arg. 144 C2
Sussex U.S.A. 135 H3
Susuman Rus. Fed. 65 P3
Susupu Indon. 69 H6
Susurluk Turkey 59 M5
Sutak India 82 D2
Sutherland Australia 112 E5
Sutherland S. Africa 100 E7
Sutherland U.S.A. 130 C3
Sutherland Range hills Australia 109 D6
Sutjeska nat. park Bos.-Herz. 58 H3
Sutlej r. India/Pak. 82 B3
Sütlüce Turkey 85 A1
Sutter U.S.A. 128 C2
Sutterton U.K. 49 G6
Sutton Canada 135 I1
Sutton r. Canada 122 E3
Sutton U.K. 49 H6
Sutton NE U.S.A. 130 D3
Sutton WV U.S.A. 134 E4
Sutton Coldfield U.K. 49 F6
Sutton in Ashfield U.K. 49 F5
Sutton Lake Canada 122 D3
Sutton Lake U.S.A. 134 E4
Suttor r. Australia 110 D4
Suttsu Japan 74 F4
Sutwik Island U.S.A. 118 C4
Sutyr' r. Rus. Fed. 74 D2

▶Suva Fiji 107 H3
Capital of Fiji.

Suvadiva Atoll Maldives see Huvadhu Atoll
Suvalki Poland see Suwałki
Suvorov atoll Cook Is see Suwarrow
Suvorov Rus. Fed. 43 H5
Suwa Japan 75 E5
Suwałki Poland 43 D5
Suwannaphum Thai. 70 C4
Suwannee r. U.S.A. 133 D6
Suwanose-jima i. Japan 75 C7
Suwarrow atoll Cook Is 107 J3
Suwaylih Jordan 85 B3
Suwayr well Saudi Arabia 91 F5
Suways, Khalīj as g. Egypt see Suez, Gulf of
Suways, Qanāt as canal Egypt see Suez Canal
Suweilih Jordan see Suwaylih
Suweis, Khalîg el g. Egypt see Suez, Gulf of
Suweis, Qanâ el canal Egypt see Suez Canal
Suwŏn S. Korea 75 B5
Suyūl Ḩanīsh i. Yemen 86 F7
Suz, Mys pt Kazakh. 91 I2
Suzaka Japan 75 E5
Suzdal' Rus. Fed. 42 I4
Suzhou Anhui China 77 H1
Suzhou Gansu China see Jiuquan
Suzhou Jiangsu China 77 I2
Suzi He r. China 74 B4
Suzuka Japan 75 E6
Suzu-misaki pt Japan 75 E5
Sværholthalvøya pen. Norway 44 O1

▶Svalbard terr. Arctic Ocean 64 C2
Part of Norway.

Svappavaara Sweden 44 L3
Svartenhuk Halvø pen. Greenland see Sigguup Nunaa
Svatove Ukr. 43 H6

Svay Chék Cambodia 71 C4
Svay Riĕng Cambodia 71 D5
Svecha Rus. Fed. 42 J4
Sveg Sweden 45 I5
Sveķi Latvia 45 O8
Svelgen Norway 44 D6
Svellingen Norway 44 F5
Švenčionėliai Lith. 45 N9
Švenčionys Lith. 45 O9
Svendborg Denmark 45 G9
Svensbu Norway 44 K2
Svenstavik Sweden 44 I5
Sverdlovsk Rus. Fed. see Yekaterinburg
Sverdlovs'k Ukr. 43 H6
Sverdrup Islands Canada 119 I2
Sverige country Europe see Sweden
Sveti Nikole Macedonia 59 I4
Svetlaya Rus. Fed. 74 E3
Svetlogorsk Belarus see Svyetlahorsk
Svetlogorsk Kaliningradskaya Oblast' Rus. Fed. 45 L9
Svetlogorsk Krasnoyarskiy Kray Rus. Fed. 64 J3
Svetlograd Rus. Fed. 91 F1
Svetlovodsk Ukr. see Svitlovods'k
Svetlyy Kaliningradskaya Oblast' Rus. Fed. 45 L9
Svetlyy Orenburgskaya Oblast' Rus. Fed. 80 B1
Svetlyy Yar Rus. Fed. 43 J6
Svetogorsk Rus. Fed. 45 P6
Svíahnúkar vol. Iceland 44 [inset]
Svilaja mts Croatia 58 G3
Svilengrad Bulg. 59 L4
Svinecea Mare, Vârful mt. Romania 59 J2
Svir Belarus 45 O9
Svir' r. Rus. Fed. 42 G3
Svishtov Bulg. 59 K3
Svitava r. Czech Rep. 47 P6
Svitavy Czech Rep. 47 P6
Svitlovods'k Ukr. 43 G6
Sviyaga r. Rus. Fed. 42 K5
Svizzer, Parc Naziunal Switz. 58 D1
Svizzera country Europe see Switzerland
Svobodnyy Rus. Fed. 74 C2
Svolvær Norway 44 I2
Svrljiške Planine mts Serbia 59 J3
Svyatoy Nos, Mys c. Rus. Fed. 42 K2
Svyetlahorsk Belarus 43 F5
Swadlincote U.K. 49 F6
Swaffham U.K. 49 H6
Swain Reefs Australia 110 F4
Swainsboro U.S.A. 133 D5
Swains Island atoll American Samoa 107 I3
Swakop watercourse Namibia 100 B2
Swakopmund Namibia 100 B2
Swale r. U.K. 48 F4
Swallow Islands Solomon Is 107 G3
Swamihalli India 84 C3
Swampy r. Canada 123 H2
Swan r. Australia 109 A7
Swan r. Man./Sask. Canada 121 K4
Swan r. Ont. Canada 122 E3
Swanage U.K. 49 F8
Swandale U.S.A. 134 E4
Swan Hill Australia 112 A5
Swan Hills Canada 120 H4
Swan Lake B.C. Canada 120 D4
Swan Lake Man. Canada 121 K4
Swanley U.K. 49 H7
Swanquarter U.S.A. 133 E5
Swan Reach Australia 111 B7
Swan River Canada 121 K4
Swansea U.K. 49 D7
Swansea Bay U.K. 49 D7
Swanton CA U.S.A. 128 B3
Swanton VT U.S.A. 135 I1
Swartbergpas pass S. Africa 100 F7
Swart Nossob watercourse Namibia see Black Nossob
Swartruggens S. Africa 101 H3
Swartz Creek U.S.A. 134 D2
Swasey Peak U.S.A. 129 G2
Swat Kohistan reg. Pak. 89 I3
Swatow China see Shantou
Swayzee U.S.A. 134 C3
Swaziland country Africa 101 J4

▶Sweden country Europe 44 I5
5th largest country in Europe.

Sweet Home U.S.A. 126 C3
Sweet Springs U.S.A. 134 E5
Sweetwater U.S.A. 131 C5
Sweetwater r. U.S.A. 126 G4
Swellendam S. Africa 100 E8
Świdnica Poland 47 P5
Świdwin Poland 47 O4
Świebodzin Poland 47 O4
Świecie Poland 47 Q4
Swift Current Canada 121 J5
Swiftcurrent Creek r. Canada 121 J5
Swilly r. Ireland 51 E3
Swilly, Lough inlet Ireland 51 E2
Swindon U.K. 49 F7
Swinford Ireland 51 D4
Świnoujście Poland 47 O4
Swinton U.K. 50 G5
Swiss Confederation country Europe see Switzerland
Switzerland country Europe 56 I3
Swords Ireland 51 F4
Swords Range hills Australia 110 C4
Syamozero, Ozero l. Rus. Fed. 42 G3
Syamzha Rus. Fed. 42 I3
Syang Nepal 83 E3
Syas'troy Rus. Fed. 42 G3
Sychevka Rus. Fed. 42 G5
Sydenham atoll Kiribati see Nonouti

▶Sydney Australia 112 E4
Capital of New South Wales. Most populous city in Oceania.

Sydney Canada 123 J5
Sydney Island Kiribati see Manra
Sydney Lake Canada 121 M5
Sydney Mines Canada 123 J5
Syedra tourist site Turkey 85 A1
Syeverodonets'k Ukr. 43 H6
Syke Germany 53 I2
Sykesville U.S.A. 135 F3
Syktyvkar Rus. Fed. 42 K3
Sylarna mt. Norway/Sweden 44 H5
Sylhet Bangl. 83 G4
Syloga Rus. Fed. 42 I3
Sylt i. Germany 47 L3
Sylva U.S.A. 133 D5
Sylvania GA U.S.A. 133 D5
Sylvania OH U.S.A. 134 D3
Sylvan Lake Canada 120 H4
Sylvester U.S.A. 133 D6
Sylvester, Lake salt flat Australia 110 A3
Sylvia, Mount Canada 120 E3
Symerton U.S.A. 134 A3
Symi i. Greece 59 L6
Synel'nykove Ukr. 43 G6
Syngyrli, Mys pt Kazakh. 91 I2
Synya Rus. Fed. 41 R2
Syowa research station Antarctica 152 D2
Syracusae Sicily Italy see Syracuse
Syracuse Sicily Italy 58 F6
Syracuse KS U.S.A. 130 C4
Syracuse NY U.S.A. 135 G2
Syrdar'ya r. Asia 80 C3
Syrdar'ya Uzbek. see Sirdaryo
Syrdaryinskiy Uzbek. see Sirdaryo
Syria country Asia 90 E4
Syriam Myanmar see Thanlyin
Syrian Desert Asia 90 E4
Syrna i. Greece 59 L6
Syros i. Greece 59 K6
Syrskiy Rus. Fed. 43 H5
Sysmä Fin. 45 N6
Sysola r. Rus. Fed. 42 K3
Syumsi Rus. Fed. 42 K4
Syurkum Rus. Fed. 74 F2
Syurkum, Mys pt Rus. Fed. 74 F2
Syzran' Rus. Fed. 43 K5
Szabadka Serbia see Subotica
Szczecin Poland 47 O4
Szczecinek Poland 47 P4
Szczytno Poland 47 R4
Szechwan prov. China see Sichuan
Szeged Hungary 59 I1
Székesfehérvár Hungary 58 H1
Szekszárd Hungary 58 H1
Szentes Hungary 59 I1
Szentgotthárd Hungary 58 G1
Szigetvár Hungary 58 G1
Szolnok Hungary 59 I1
Szombathely Hungary 58 G1
Sztálinváros Hungary see Dunaújváros

Taagga Duudka reg. Somalia 98 E3
Tābah Saudi Arabia 86 F4
Tabajara Brazil 142 F5
Tabakhmela Georgia see Kazret'i
Tabalo P.N.G. 69 L7
Tabanan Indon. 108 A2
Tabankulu S. Africa 101 I6
Ţabaqah Ar Raqqah Syria 85 D2
Ţabaqah Ar Raqqah Syria see Madīnat ath Thawrah
Tabar Islands P.N.G. 106 F2
Tabarka Tunisia 58 C6
Ţabas Iran 89 F3
Tabāsin Iran 88 E4
Tābask, Kūh-e mt. Iran 88 C4
Tabatinga Amazonas Brazil 142 E4
Tabatinga São Paulo Brazil 145 A3
Tabatinga, Serra da hills Brazil 143 J6
Tabatsquri, Tba l. Georgia 91 F2
Tabayin Myanmar 70 A2
Tabbita Australia 112 B5
Tabelbala Alg. 54 D6
Taber Canada 121 H5
Tabet, Nam r. Myanmar 70 B1
Tabia Tsaka salt l. China 83 F3
Tabiteuea atoll Kiribati 107 H2
Tabivere Estonia 45 O7
Table Cape N.Z. 113 F4
Table Mountain Nature Reserve S. Africa 100 D8
Tabligbo Togo 96 D4
Tábor Czech Rep. 47 O6
Tabora Tanz. 99 D4
Tabou Côte d'Ivoire 96 C4
Tabrīz Iran 88 B2
Tabuaeran atoll Kiribati 151 J5
Tabūk Saudi Arabia 90 E5
Tabulam Australia 112 F2
Tabuyung Indon. 71 B7
Tabwémasana, Mount Vanuatu 107 G3
Täby Sweden 45 K7
Tacalé Brazil 143 H3
Tacheng China 80 F2
Tachie Canada 120 E4
Tachov Czech Rep. 53 M5
Tacloban Phil. 69 H4
Tacna Peru 142 D7
Tacoma U.S.A. 126 C3
Taco Pozo Arg. 144 D3
Tacuarembó Uruguay 144 E4
Tacupeto Mex. 127 F7
Tadcaster U.K. 48 F5
Tademaït, Plateau du Alg. 54 E6
Tadin New Caledonia 107 G4
Tadjikistan country Asia see Tajikistan
Tadjourah Djibouti 86 F7
Tadmur Syria 85 D2
Tadohae Haesang National Park S. Korea 75 B6
Tadoule Lake Canada 121 L3
Tadoussac Canada 123 H4
Tadpatri India 84 C3
Tadwale India 84 C2
Tadzhikskaya S.S.R. country Asia see Tajikistan
T'aean Haean National Park S. Korea 75 B5
Taech'ŏng-do i. S. Korea 75 B5
Taedasa-do N. Korea 75 B5
Taedong-man b. N. Korea 75 B5
Taegu S. Korea 75 C6
Taehan-min'guk country Asia see South Korea
Taehŭksan-kundo is S. Korea 75 B6
Taejŏn S. Korea 75 B5
Taejŏng S. Korea 75 B6
T'aepaek S. Korea 75 C5
Ta'erqi China 73 M3
Taf r. U.K. 49 C7
Tafahi i. Tonga 107 I3
Tafalla Spain 57 F2
Tafeng China see Lanshan
Tafila Jordan see Aţ Ţafīlah
Tafi Viejo Arg. 144 C3
Tafresh Iran 88 C3
Taft Iran 88 D4
Taft U.S.A. 128 D4
Taftān, Kūh-e mt. Iran 89 F4
Taftanāz Syria 85 C2
Tafwap India 71 A6
Taganrog Rus. Fed. 43 H7
Taganrog, Gulf of Rus. Fed./Ukr. 43 H7
Taganrogskiy Zaliv b. Rus. Fed./Ukr. see Taganrog, Gulf of
Tagarev, Gora mt. Iran/Turkm. 88 E2
Tagarkaty, Pereval pass Tajik. 89 I2
Tagaung Myanmar 70 B2
Tagchagpu Ri mt. China 83 E2
Tagdempt Alg. see Tiaret
Taghmon Ireland 51 F5
Tagish Canada 120 C2
Tagtabazar Turkm. 89 F3
Tagula P.N.G. 110 F1
Tagula Island P.N.G. 110 F1
Tagus r. Port. 57 B4
also known as Tajo (Portugal) or Tejo (Spain)
Taha China 74 B3
Tahaetkun Mountain Canada 120 G5
Tahan, Gunung mt. Malaysia 71 C6
Tahanroz'ka Zatoka b. Rus. Fed./Ukr. see Taganrog, Gulf of
Tahat, Mont mt. Alg. 96 D2
Tahaurawe i. U.S.A. see Kaho'olawe
Tahe China 74 B1
Taheke N.Z. 113 D2
Tahiti i. Fr. Polynesia 151 K7
Tahlab r. Iran/Pak. 89 F4
Tahlab, Dasht-i- plain Pak. 89 F4
Tahlequah U.S.A. 131 E5
Tahltan Canada 120 D3
Tahoe, Lake U.S.A. 128 C2
Tahoe Lake Canada 119 H3
Tahoe Vista U.S.A. 128 C2
Tahoka U.S.A. 131 C5
Tahoua Niger 96 D3
Tahrūd Iran 88 E4
Tahrūd r. Iran 88 E4
Tahtsa Peak Canada 120 E4
Tahulandang i. Indon. 69 H6
Tahuna Indon. 69 H6
Taï, Parc National de nat. park Côte d'Ivoire 96 C4
Tai'an China 73 L5
Taibai China 76 E1
Taibai Shan mt. China 76 E1
Taibei Taiwan see T'aipei
Taibus Qi China see Baochang
T'aichung Taiwan 77 I3
Taidong Taiwan see T'aitung
Taigong China see Taijiang
Taihang Shan mts Hebei China 73 K5
Taihang Shan mts China 73 K5
Taihape N.Z. 113 E4
Taihe Jiangxi China 77 G3
Taihe Sichuan China see Shehong
Taihezhen China see Shehong
Tai Ho Wan H.K. China 77 [inset]
Taihu China 77 H2
Tai Hu l. China 77 I2
Taijiang China 77 F3
Taikang China 74 B3
Tailai China 74 A3
Tai Lam Chung Shui Tong resr H.K. China 77 [inset]
Tailem Bend Australia 111 B7
Tai Long Wan b. H.K. China 77 [inset]
Taimani reg. Afgh. 89 F3
Tai Mo Shan hill H.K. China 77 [inset]
Tain U.K. 50 F2
T'ainan Taiwan 77 I4
T'ainan Taiwan see Hsinying
Tainaro, Akra pt Greece see Tainaro, Akrotirio
Tainaro, Akrotirio pt Greece 59 J6
Taining China 77 H3
Tai O H.K. China 77 [inset]
Taiobeiras Brazil 145 C1
Tai Pang Wan b. H.K. China see Mirs Bay

▶T'aipei Taiwan 77 I3
Capital of Taiwan.

Taiping Guangdong China see Shixing
Taiping Guangxi China see Chongzuo
Taiping Guangxi China 77 F4
Taiping Malaysia 71 C6
Taipingchuan China 74 A3
Tai Po H.K. China 77 [inset]
Tai Po Hoi b. H.K. China see Tolo Harbour
Tai Poutini National Park N.Z. see Westland National Park
Tairbeart U.K. see Tarbert
Tai Rom Yen National Park Thai. 71 B5
Tairuq Iran 88 B3
Tais P.N.G. 69 K8
Taishan China 77 G4
Taishun China 77 H3
Tai Siu Mo To is H.K. China see The Brothers
Taissy France 52 E5
Taitao, Península de pen. Chile 144 B7
Tai Tapu N.Z. 113 D6
Tai To Yan mt. H.K. China 77 [inset]
T'aitung Taiwan 77 I4
Tai Tung Shan hill H.K. China see Sunset Peak
Taivalkoski Fin. 44 P4
Taivaskero hill Fin. 44 N2
Taiwan country Asia 77 I4
T'aiwan Haihsia strait China/Taiwan see Taiwan Strait
Taiwan Haixia strait China/Taiwan see Taiwan Strait
Taiwan Shan mts Taiwan see Chungyang Shanmo
Taiwan Strait China/Taiwan 77 H4
Taixian China see Jiangyan
Taixing China 77 I1
Taiyuan China 73 K5
Tai Yue Shan i. H.K. China see Lantau Island
Taizhao China 76 B2
Taizhong Taiwan see T'aichung
Taizhong Taiwan see Fengyüan
Taizhou Jiangsu China 77 H1
Taizhou Zhejiang China 77 I2
Taizhou Liedao i. China 77 I2
Taizhou Wan b. China 77 I2
Taizi He r. China 74 B4
Ta'izz Yemen 86 F7
Tājābād Iran 88 E4
Tajal Pak. 89 H5
Tajamulco, Volcán de vol. Guat. 136 F5
Tajerouine Tunisia 58 C7
Tajikistan country Asia 89 H2
Tajitos Mex. 127 E7
Tajo r. Port. 57 C4 see Tagus
Tajrīsh Iran 88 C3
Tak Thai. 70 B3
Takāb Iran 88 B2
Takabba Kenya 98 E3
Takahashi Japan 75 D6
Takamatsu Japan 75 D6
Takaoka Japan 75 E5
Takapuna N.Z. 113 E3
Ta karpo China 83 G4
Takatokwane Botswana 100 G3
Takatshwaane Botswana 100 E2
Takatsuki-yama mt. Japan 75 D6
Takayama Japan 75 E5
Tak Bai Thai. 71 C6
Takefu Japan 75 E6
Takengon Indon. 71 B6
Takeo Cambodia see Takêv
Take-shima i. Asia see Liancourt Rocks
Takestān Iran 88 C2
Takêv Cambodia 71 D5
Takhemaret Alg. 57 G6
Takhini Hotspring Canada 120 C2
Ta Khli Thai. 70 C4
Ta Khmau Cambodia 71 D5
Takhta-Bazar Turkm. see Tagtabazar
Takht Apān, Kūh-e mt. Iran 88 C3
Takhteh Iran 88 D4
Takhteh Pol Afgh. 89 G4
Takht-e Soleymān mt. Iran 88 C2
Takht-e Soleymān tourist site Iran 88 B2
Takht-i-Bahi tourist site Pak. 89 H3
Takht-i-Sulaiman mt. Pak. 89 H4
Takijuq Lake Canada see Napaktulik Lake
Takingeun Indon. see Takengon
Takinoue Japan 74 F3
Takla Lake Canada 120 E4
Takla Landing Canada 120 E4
Takla Makan des. China see Taklimakan Desert
Taklimakan Desert China 82 E1
Taklimakan Shamo des. China see Taklimakan Desert
Takpa Shiri mt. China 76 B2
Taku Canada 120 C3
Takum Nigeria 96 D4
Takuu Islands P.N.G. 107 F2
Talachyn Belarus 43 F5
Talaja India 82 C5
Talakan Amurskaya Oblast' Rus. Fed. 74 C2
Talakan Khabarovskiy Kray Rus. Fed. 74 D2
Talandzha Rus. Fed. 74 C2
Talangbatu Indon. 68 D7
Talara Peru 142 B4
Talar-i-Band mts Pak. see Makran Coast Range
Talas Kyrg. 80 D3
Talas Ala-Too mts Kyrg. 80 D3
Talas Range mts Kyrg. see Talas Ala-Too
Talasskiy Alatau, Khrebet mts Kyrg. see Talas Ala-Too
Ţal'at Mūsá mt. Lebanon/Syria 85 C2
Talaud, Kepulauan is Indon. 69 H6
Talavera de la Reina Spain 57 D4
Talawgyi Myanmar 70 B1
Talaya Rus. Fed. 65 Q3
Talbehat India 82 D4
Talbīsah Syria 85 C2
Talbot, Mount hill Australia 109 D6
Talbotton U.S.A. 133 C5
Talbragar r. Australia 112 D4
Talca Chile 144 B5
Talcahuano Chile 144 B5
Taldan Rus. Fed. 74 B1
Taldom Rus. Fed. 42 H4
Taldykorgan Kazakh. 80 E3
Taldy-Kurgan Kazakh. see Taldykorgan
Taldyqorghan Kazakh. see Taldykorgan
Tālesh Iran see Hashtpar
Talgarth U.K. 49 D7
Talguppa India 84 B3
Talia Australia 111 A7
Taliabu i. Indon. 69 G7
Talikota India 84 C2
Talimardzhan Uzbek. see Tollimarjon
Talin Hiag China 74 B3
Taliparamba India 84 B3
Talisay Phil. 69 G4
Taliş Dağları mts Azer./Iran 88 C2
Talitsa Rus. Fed. 42 J4
Taliwang Indon. 108 B2
Talkeetna U.S.A. 118 C3
Talkeetna Mountains U.S.A. 118 D3
Talkh Āb Iran 88 E3
Tallacootra, Lake salt flat Australia 109 F7
Talladega U.S.A. 133 C5

▶Tallahassee U.S.A. 133 C6
Capital of Florida.

Tall al Aḩmar Syria 85 D1
Tall Baydar Syria 91 F3
Tall-e Ḩalāl Iran 88 D4

▶Tallinn Estonia 45 N7
Capital of Estonia.

Tall Kalakh Syria 85 C2
Tall Kayf Iraq 91 F3
Tall Kūjik Syria 91 F3
Tallow Ireland 51 D5
Tallulah U.S.A. 131 F5
Tall 'Uwaynāt Iraq 91 F3
Tallymerjen Uzbek. see Tollimarjon
Talmont-St-Hilaire France 56 D3
Tal'ne Ukr. 43 F6
Tal'noye Ukr. see Tal'ne
Taloda India 82 C5
Talodi Sudan 86 D7
Taloga U.S.A. 131 D4
Talon, Lac l. Canada 123 I3
Ta-long Myanmar 70 B2
Tāloqān Afgh. 89 H2
Talos Dome ice feature Antarctica 152 H2
Ta Loung San mt. Laos 70 C2
Talovaya Rus. Fed. 43 I6
Taloyoak Canada 119 I3
Tal Pass Pak. 89 I3
Talsi Latvia 45 M8
Tal Sīyāh Iran 89 F4
Taltal Chile 144 B3
Taltson r. Canada 121 H2
Talu China 76 B2
Talvik Norway 44 M1
Talwood Australia 112 D2
Talyshskiye Gory mts Azer./Iran see Taliş Dağları
Talyy Rus. Fed. 42 L2
Tamala Australia 109 A6
Tamala Rus. Fed. 43 I5
Tamale Ghana 96 C4
Tamana i. Kiribati 107 H2
Taman Negara National Park Malaysia 71 C6
Tamano Japan 75 D6
Tamanrasset Alg. 96 D2
Tamanthi Myanmar 70 A1
Tamaqua U.S.A. 135 H3
Tamar India 83 F5
Tamar Syria see Tadmur
Tamar r. U.K. 49 C8
Tamarugal, Pampa de plain Chile 142 E7
Tamasane Botswana 101 H2
Tamatave Madag. see Toamasina
Tamaulipas state Mex. 131 D7
Tambacounda Senegal 96 B3
Tambaqui Brazil 142 F5
Tambar Springs Australia 112 D3
Tambelan, Kepulauan is Indon. 71 D7
Tambelan Besar i. Indon. 71 D7
Tambo r. Australia 112 C6
Tambohorano Madag. 99 E5

▶Tambora, Gunung vol. Indon. 108 B2
Deadliest recorded volcanic eruption (1815).

Tamboritha mt. Australia 112 C6
Tambov Rus. Fed. 43 I5
Tambovka Rus. Fed. 74 C2
Tambura Sudan 97 F4
Tamburi Brazil 145 C1
Tâmchekket Mauritania 96 B3
Tamdybulak Uzbek. see Tomdibuloq
Tâmega r. Port. 57 B3
Tamenghest Alg. see Tamanrasset
Tamenglong India 83 H4
Tamerza Tunisia 58 B7
Tamgak, Adrar mt. Niger 96 D3
Tamgué, Massif du mt. Guinea 96 B3
Tamiahua, Laguna de lag. Mex. 136 E4
Tamiang, Ujung pt Indon. 71 B6
Tamil Nadu state India 84 C4
Tamitsa Rus. Fed. 42 H2
Ţâmîya Egypt see Ţāmīyah
Ţāmīyah Egypt 90 C5
Tamkuhi India 83 F4
Tam Ky Vietnam 70 E4
Tammarvi r. Canada 121 K1
Tammerfors Fin. see Tampere
Tammisaari Fin. see Ekenäs
Tampa U.S.A. 133 D7
Tampa Bay U.S.A. 133 D7
Tampere Fin. 45 M6
Tampico Mex. 136 E4
Tampin Malaysia 71 C7
Tampines Sing. 71 [inset]
Tamsagbulag Mongolia 73 L3
Tamsweg Austria 47 N7
Tamu Myanmar 70 A1
Tamworth Australia 112 E3
Tamworth U.K. 49 F6
Tana r. Fin./Norway see Tenojoki
Tana r. Kenya 98 E4
Tana Madag. see Antananarivo
Tana i. Vanuatu see Tanna
Tana, Lake Eth. 98 D2
Tanabe Japan 75 D6
Tanabi Brazil 145 A3
Tana Bru Norway 44 P1
Tanada Lake U.S.A. 120 A2
Tanafjorden inlet Norway 44 P1
Tanah, Tanjung pt Indon. 68 D8
T'ana Hāyk' l. Eth. see Tana, Lake
Tanahgrogot Indon. 68 F7
Tanah Merah Malaysia 71 C6
Tanahputih Indon. 71 C7
Tanakeke i. Indon. 68 F8
Tanami Australia 108 E4
Tanami Desert Australia 108 E4
Tân An Vietnam 71 D5
Tanana r. U.S.A. 120 A2
Tananarive Madag. see Antananarivo
Tanandava Madag. 99 E6
Tancheng China see Pingtan
Tanch'ŏn N. Korea 75 C4
Tanda Côte d'Ivoire 96 C4
Tanda Uttar Prad. India 82 D3
Tanda Uttar Prad. India 83 E4
Tandag Phil. 69 H5
Ţăndărei Romania 59 L2
Tandaué Angola 99 B5
Tandi India 82 D2
Tandil Arg. 144 E5
Tando Adam Pak. 89 H5
Tando Allahyar Pak. 89 H5
Tando Bago Pak. 89 H5
Tandou Lake imp. l. Australia 111 C7
Tandragee U.K. 51 F3
Tandur India 84 C2
Tanduri Pak. 89 G4
Tanega-shima i. Japan 75 C7
Tanen Taunggyi mts Thai. 70 B3
Tanezrouft reg. Alg./Mali 96 C2
Ţanf, Jabal aţ hill Syria 85 D3
Tang, Ra's-e pt Iran 89 E5
Tanga Tanz. 99 D4
Tangail Bangl. 83 G4
Tanga Islands P.N.G. 106 F2
Tanganyika country Africa see Tanzania

▶Tanganyika, Lake Africa 99 C4
Deepest and 2nd largest lake in Africa, and 6th largest in the world.

Tangará Brazil 145 A4
Tangasseri India 84 C4
Tangdan China 76 D3
Tangeli Iran 88 D2
Tanger Morocco see Tangier
Tangerhütte Germany 53 L2
Tangermünde Germany 53 L2
Tang-e Sarkheh Iran 89 E5
Tanggor China 76 D1
Tanggulashan China 76 B1
Tanggula Shan mt. China 83 G2
Tanggula Shan mts China 83 G2
Tanggula Shankou pass China 83 G2
Tangguo China 83 F3
Tanghe China 77 G1
Tangier Morocco 57 D6
Tangiers Morocco see Tangier
Tang La pass China 83 G4
Tangla India 83 G4
Tanglag China 76 C1
Tanglin Sing. 71 [inset]
Tangmai China 76 B2
Tangnag China 76 D1
Tangorin Australia 110 D4
Tangra Yumco salt l. China 83 F3
Tangse Indon. 71 A6
Tangshan Guizhou China see Shiqian
Tangshan Hebei China 73 L5
Tangte mt. Myanmar 70 B2
Tangtse India see Tanktse
Tangwan China 77 F3
Tangwanghe China 74 C2
Tangyuan China 74 C3
Tangyung Tso salt l. China 83 F3
Tanhaçu Brazil 145 C1
Tanhua Fin. 44 O3
Tani Cambodia 71 D5
Taniantaweng Shan mts China 76 B2
Tanimbar, Kepulauan is Indon. 108 E1
Taninthari Myanmar see Tenasserim
Tanintharyi Myanmar see Tenasserim
Taninthayi Myanmar see Tenasserim
Tanjah Morocco see Tangier
Tanjay Phil. 69 G5
Tanjore India see Thanjavur
Tanjung Indon. 68 F7
Tanjungbalai Indon. 71 B7
Tanjungkarang-Telukbetung Indon. see Bandar Lampung
Tanjungpandan Indon. 68 D7
Tanjungpinang Indon. 71 D7
Tanjungpura Indon. 71 B7
Tanjung Puting, Taman Nasional Indon. 68 E7
Tanjungredeb Indon. 68 F6
Tanjungselor Indon. 68 F6
Tankse India see Tanktse
Tanktse India 82 D2
Tankwa-Karoo National Park S. Africa 100 D7
Tanna i. Vanuatu 107 G3
Tannadice U.K. 50 G4
Tännäs Sweden 44 H5
Tanner, Mount Canada 120 G5
Tannu-Ola, Khrebet mts Rus. Fed. 80 H1
Tanot India 82 B4
Tanout Niger 96 D3
Tansen Nepal 83 E4
Tanshui Taiwan 77 I3
Ţanţā Egypt 90 C5
Tanta Egypt see Ţanţā
Tan-Tan Morocco 96 B2
Tantu China 74 A3
Tanuku India 84 D2
Tanumbirini Australia 108 F4
Tanumshede Sweden 45 G7
Tanzania country Africa 99 D4
Tanzilla r. Canada 120 D3
Tao, Ko i. Thai. 71 B5
Tao'an China see Taonan
Taobh Tuath U.K. see Northton
Taocheng China see Daxin
Tao He r. China 76 D1
Taohong China see Longhui
Taohuajiang China see Taojiang
Taohuaping China see Longhui
Taojiang China 77 G2
Taolanaro Madag. see Tôlañaro
Taonan China 74 A3
Taongi atoll Marshall Is 150 H5
Taos U.S.A. 127 G5
Taounate Morocco 54 D5
Taourirt Morocco 54 D5
Taoxi China 77 H3
Taoyang China see Lintao
Taoyuan China 77 F2
T'aoyüan Taiwan 77 I3
Tapa Estonia 45 N7
Tapachula Mex. 136 F6
Tapah Malaysia 71 C6
Tapajós r. Brazil 143 H4
Tapaktuan Indon. 71 B7
Tapauá Brazil 142 F5
Tapauá r. Brazil 142 F5
Taperoá Brazil 145 D1
Tapi r. India 82 C5
Tapiau Rus. Fed. see Gvardeysk
Tapis, Gunung mt. Malaysia 71 C6
Tapisuelas Mex. 127 F8
Taplejung Nepal 83 F4
Tap Mun Chau i. H.K. China 77 [inset]
Ta-pom Myanmar 70 B2
Tappahannock U.S.A. 135 G5
Tappeh, Kūh-e hill Iran 88 C3
Taprobane country Asia see Sri Lanka
Tapuaenuku mt. N.Z. 113 D5

pulonanjing mt. Indon. 71 B7
purucuara Brazil 142 E4
puteouea atoll Kiribati see Tabiteuea
qtaq Iraq 91 G4
quara Brazil 145 A5
quari Rio Grande do Sul Brazil 145 A5
quarí r. Brazil 143 G7
quaritinga Brazil 145 A3
r r. Ireland 51 E5
ra Australia 112 E1
rābulus Lebanon see Tripoli
rābulus Libya see Tripoli
rahuwan India 82 E4
rai reg. India 83 G4
rakan Indon. 68 F6
rakan i. Indon. 68 F6
rakki reg. Afgh. 89 G3
raklı Turkey 59 N4
ran, Mys pt Rus. Fed. 45 K9
rana Australia 112 D4
ranagar India 82 C3
ranaki, Mount vol. N.Z. 113 E4
rancón Spain 57 E3
rangambadi India 84 C4
rangire National Park Tanz. 98 D4
ranto Italy 58 G4
ranto, Golfo di g. Italy 58 G4
ranto, Gulf of Italy see
Taranto, Golfo di
rapoto Peru 142 C5
rapur India 84 D3
rarua Range mts N.Z. 113 E5
rascon-sur-Ariège France 56 E5
rasovskiy Rus. Fed. 43 I6
rauacá Brazil 142 D5
rauacá r. Brazil 142 E5
rawera N.Z. 113 F4
rawera, Mount vol. N.Z. 113 F4
raz Kazakh. 80 D3
razona Spain 57 F3
razona de la Mancha Spain 57 F4
rbagatay, Khrebet mts Kazakh. 80 F2
rbat Ness pt U.K. 50 F3
rbert Ireland 51 C5
rbert Scotland U.K. 50 C3
rbert Scotland U.K. 50 D5
rbes France 56 E5
rboro U.S.A. 132 E5
rcoola Australia 109 F7
rcoon Australia 112 C3
rcoonyinna watercourse
Australia 109 F6
rcutta Australia 112 C5
rdoki-Yani, Gora mt. Rus. Fed. 74 E2
ree Australia 112 F3
rella Australia 111 C6
rentum Italy see Taranto
rfā', Baṭn aṭ depr. Saudi Arabia 88 C6
rfaya Morocco 96 B2
ga well Niger 96 D3
gan China see Talin Hiag
ghee Pass U.S.A. 126 F3
rgoviște Romania 59 K2
rguist Morocco 57 D6
gu Jiu Romania 59 J2
gu Mureș Romania 59 K1
gu Neamț Romania 59 L1
gu Secuiesc Romania 59 L1
rgyailing China 83 F3
ri P.N.G. 69 K8
riat Mongolia 80 I2
rif U.A.E. 88 D5
rifa Spain 57 D5
rifa, Punta de pt Spain 57 D5
rija Bol. 142 F8
rikere India 84 B3
riku r. Indon. 69 J7
im Yemen 86 G6
im Basin China 80 F4
ime Tanz. 98 D4
im He r. China 80 G3
im Pendi basin China see
Tarim Basin
in Kowt Afgh. 89 G3
itatu r. Indon. 69 J7
ka r. S. Africa 101 G7
kastad S. Africa 101 H7
kio U.S.A. 130 E3
ko-Sale Rus. Fed. 64 I3
kwa Ghana 96 C4
lac Phil. 69 G3
lo River National Park
Australia 112 D5
ma Peru 142 C6
mstedt Germany 53 J1
n r. France 56 E4
naby Sweden 44 I4
nak r. Afgh. 89 G4
năveni Romania 59 K1
nobrzeg Poland 43 D6
nogskiy Gorodok Rus. Fed. 42 I3
nopol Ukr. see Ternopil'
nów Poland 43 D6
nowitz Poland see Tarnowskie Góry
nowskie Góry Poland 47 Q5
o Co salt l. China 83 E3
om Iran 88 D4
oom Australia 111 E5
oudannt Morocco 54 C5
paulin Swamp Australia 110 B3
q Iran 88 C3
quinia Italy 58 D3
quinii Italy see Tarquinia
rabool Lake salt flat Australia 110 A3
raco Spain see Tarragona
rafal Cape Verde 96 [inset]
ragona Spain 57 G3
rajaur Sweden 44 K3
ran Hills hill Australia 112 C4
rant Point Australia 110 B3
rega Spain 57 G3
rong China see Nyêmo
so Emissi mt. Chad 97 E2
sus Turkey 85 B1
t China 83 H1
tär Azer. 91 G2
tu Estonia 45 O7
ṭūs Syria 85 B2
umovka Rus. Fed. 91 G1
ung Hka r. Myanmar 70 B1
utao, Ko i. Thai. 71 B6
utao National Park Thai. 71 B6
Tarutung Indon. 71 B7
Tarvisium Italy see Treviso
Tarz Iran 88 E4
Tasai, Ko i. Thai. 71 B5
Taschereau Canada 122 F4
Taseko Mountain Canada 120 F5
Tashauz Turkm. see Daşoguz
Tashi Chho Bhutan see Thimphu
Tashigang Bhutan 83 G4
Tashino Rus. Fed. see Pervomaysk
Tashir Armenia 91 G2
Tashk, Daryācheh-ye l. Iran 88 D4
Tashkent Toshkent Uzbek. see Toshkent
Tāshqurghān Afgh. see Kholm
Tashtagol Rus. Fed. 72 F2
Tashtyp Rus. Fed. 72 F2
Tasialujjuaq, Lac l. Canada 123 G2
Tasiat, Lac l. Canada 122 G2
Tasiilap Karra c. Greenland 119 O3
Tasiilaq Greenland see Ammassalik
Tasīl Syria 85 B3
Tasiujaq Canada 123 H2
Tasiusaq Greenland 119 M2
Taşkent Turkey 85 A1
Tasker Niger 96 E3
Taskesken Kazakh. 80 F2
Taşköprü Turkey 90 D2
Tasman Abyssal Plain sea feature
Tasman Sea 150 G8
Tasman Basin sea feature Tasman Sea
150 G8
Tasman Bay N.Z. 113 D5

▶Tasmania state Australia 111 [inset]
4th largest island in Oceania.

Tasman Islands P.N.G. see
Nukumanu Islands
Tasman Mountains N.Z. 113 D5
Tasman Peninsula Australia 111 [inset]
Tasman Sea S. Pacific Ocean 106 H6
Taşova Turkey 90 E2
Tassara Niger 96 D3
Tassialouc, Lac l. Canada 122 G2
Tassili du Hoggar plat. Alg. 96 D2
Tassili n'Ajjer plat. Alg. 96 D2
Tasty Kazakh. 80 C3
Taşucu Turkey 85 A1
Tas-Yuryakh Rus. Fed. 65 M3
Tata Morocco 54 C6
Tatabánya Hungary 58 H1
Tatamailau, Foho mt.
East Timor 108 D2
Tataouine Tunisia 54 G5
Tatarbunary Ukr. 59 M2
Tatarsk Rus. Fed. 64 I4
Tatarskiy Proliv strait Rus. Fed. 74 F2
Tatar Strait Rus. Fed. see
Tatarskiy Proliv
Tate r. Australia 110 C3
Tateyama Japan 75 E6
Tathlina Lake Canada 120 G2
Tathlīth Saudi Arabia 86 F6
Tathlīth, Wādī watercourse
Saudi Arabia 86 F5
Tathra Australia 112 D6
Tatinnai Lake Canada 121 L2
Tatishchevo Rus. Fed. 43 J6
Tatkon Myanmar 70 B2
Tatla Lake Canada 120 E5
Tatla Lake l. Canada 120 E5
Tatlayoko Lake Canada 120 E5
Tatnam, Cape Canada 121 N3
Tatra Mountains Poland/Slovakia 47 Q6
Tatry mts Poland/Slovakia see
Tatra Mountains
Tatrzański Park Narodowy nat. park
Poland 47 Q6
Tatshenshini-Alsek Provincial Wilderness
Park Canada 120 B3
Tatsinskiy Rus. Fed. 43 I6
Tatuí Brazil 145 B3
Tatuk Mountain Canada 120 E4
Tatum U.S.A. 131 C5
Tatvan Turkey 91 F3
Tau Norway 45 D7
Taua Brazil 143 J5
Tauapeçaçu Brazil 142 F4
Taubaté Brazil 145 B3
Tauber r. Germany 53 J5
Tauberbischofsheim Germany 53 J5
Taucha Germany 53 M3
Taufstein hill Germany 53 J4
Taukum, Peski des. Kazakh. 80 D3
Taumarunui N.Z. 113 E4
Taumaturgo Brazil 142 D5
Taung S. Africa 100 G4
Taungdwingyi Myanmar 70 A2
Taunggyi Myanmar 70 B2
Taunglau Myanmar 70 B2
Taung-ngu Myanmar 70 B3
Taungnyo Range mts Myanmar 70 B3
Taungtha Myanmar 70 A2
Taungup Myanmar 76 B5
Taunton U.K. 49 D7
Taunton U.S.A. 135 J3
Taunus hills Germany 53 H4
Taupo N.Z. 113 F4
Taupo, Lake N.Z. 113 E4
Tauragė Lith. 45 M9
Tauranga N.Z. 113 F3
Taurasia Italy see Turin
Taureau, Réservoir resr Canada 122 G5
Taurianova Italy 58 G5
Tauroa Point N.Z. 113 D2
Taurus Mountains Turkey 85 A1
Taute r. France 49 F9
Tauz Azer. see Tovuz
Tavas Turkey 59 M6
Tavastehus Fin. see Hämeenlinna
Taverham U.K. 49 I6
Taveuni i. Fiji 107 I3
Tavildara Tajik. 89 H2
Tavira Port. 57 C5
Tavistock Canada 134 E2
Tavistock U.K. 49 C8
Tavoy Myanmar 71 B4
Tavoy r. mouth Myanmar 71 B4
Tavoy Island Myanmar see Mali Kyun
Tavoy Point Myanmar 71 B4
Tavşanlı Turkey 59 M5
Taw r. U.K. 49 C7
Tawang India 83 G4
Tawas City U.S.A. 134 D1
Tawau Sabah Malaysia 68 F6
Tawè Myanmar see Tavoy
Tawe r. U.K. 49 D7
Ṭawī Ḥafīr well U.A.E. 88 D5
Ṭawī Murra well U.A.E. 88 D5
Tawmaw Myanmar 70 B1
Tawu Taiwan 77 I4
Taxkorgan China 80 E4
Tay r. Canada 120 C2
Tay r. U.K. 50 F4
Tay, Firth of est. U.K. 50 F4
Tay, Lake salt flat Australia 109 C8
Tay, Loch l. U.K. 50 E4
Tayandu, Kepulauan is Indon. 69 I8
Taybola Rus. Fed. 44 R2
Taycheedah U.S.A. 134 A2
Tayinloan U.K. 50 D5
Taylor Canada 120 F3
Taylor AK U.S.A. 118 B3
Taylor MI U.S.A. 134 D2
Taylor NE U.S.A. 130 D3
Taylor TX U.S.A. 131 D6
Taylor, Mount U.S.A. 129 J4
Taylorsville U.S.A. 134 C4
Taylorville U.S.A. 130 F4
Taymā' Saudi Arabia 90 E6
Taymura r. Rus. Fed. 65 K3
Taymyr, Ozero l. Rus. Fed. 65 L2
Taymyr, Poluostrov pen. Rus. Fed. see
Taymyr Peninsula
Taymyr Peninsula Rus. Fed. 64 J2
Tây Ninh Vietnam 71 D5
Taypak Kazakh. 41 Q6
Taypaq Kazakh. see Taypak
Tayshet Rus. Fed. 72 H1
Taytay Phil. 68 F4
Tayuan China 74 B2
Tayyebād Iran 89 F3
Taz r. Rus. Fed. 64 I3
Taza Morocco 54 D5
Tāza Khurmātū Iraq 91 G4
Taze Myanmar 70 A2
Tazewell TN U.S.A. 134 D5
Tazewell VA U.S.A. 134 E5
Tazin r. Canada 121 I2
Tazin Lake Canada 121 I3
Tāzirbū Libya 97 F2
Tazmalt Alg. 57 I5
Tazovskaya Guba sea chan.
Rus. Fed. 64 I3
Tbessa Alg. see Tébessa

▶T'bilisi Georgia 91 G2
Capital of Georgia.

Tbilisskaya Rus. Fed. 43 I7
Tchabal Mbabo mt. Cameroon 96 E4
Tchad country Africa see Chad
Tchamba Togo 96 D4
Tchibanga Gabon 98 B4
Tchigaï, Plateau du Niger 97 E2
Tchin-Tabaradene Niger 96 D3
Tcholliré Cameroon 97 E4
Tchula U.S.A. 131 F5
Tczew Poland 47 Q3
Te, Prêk r. Cambodia 71 D4
Teague, Lake salt flat Australia 109 C6
Te Anau N.Z. 113 A7
Te Anau, Lake N.Z. 113 A7
Teapa Mex. 136 F5
Te Araroa N.Z. 113 G3
Teate Italy see Chieti
Te Awamutu N.Z. 113 E4
Teba Indon. 69 J7
Tébarat Niger 96 D3
Tebas Indon. 71 E7
Tebay U.K. 48 E4
Tebesjuak Lake Canada 121 L2
Tébessa Alg. 58 C7
Tébessa, Monts de mts Alg. 58 C7
Tebingtinggi Indon. 71 B7
Tébourba Tunisia 58 C6
Téboursouk Tunisia 58 C6
Tebulos Mt'a Georgia/Rus. Fed. 91 G2
Tecate Mex. 128 E5
Tece Turkey 85 B1
Techiman Ghana 96 C4
Tecka Arg. 144 B6
Tecklenburger Land reg. Germany 53 H2
Tecoripa Mex. 127 F7
Técpan Mex. 136 D5
Tecuala Mex. 136 C4
Tecuci Romania 59 L2
Tecumseh MI U.S.A. 134 D3
Tecumseh NE U.S.A. 130 D3
Tedzhen Turkm. see Tejen
Teec Nos Pos U.S.A. 129 I3
Tees r. U.K. 48 F4
Teeswater Canada 134 E1
Tefé r. Brazil 142 F4
Tefenni Turkey 59 M6
Tegal Indon. 68 D8
Tegel airport Germany 53 N2
Tegid, Llyn l. Wales U.K. see Bala Lake

▶Tegucigalpa Hond. 137 G6
Capital of Honduras.

Teguidda-n-Tessoumt Niger 96 D3
Tehachapi U.S.A. 128 D4
Tehachapi Mountains U.S.A. 128 D4
Tehachapi Pass U.S.A. 128 D4
Tehek Lake Canada 121 M1
Teheran Iran see Tehrān
Tehery Lake Canada 121 M1
Téhini Côte d'Ivoire 96 C4

▶Tehrān Iran 88 C3
Capital of Iran.

Tehri India see Tikamgarh
Tehuacán Mex. 136 E5
Tehuantepec, Gulf of Mex. 136 F5
Tehuantepec, Istmo de isthmus
Mex. 136 F5
Teide, Pico del vol. Canary Is 96 B2
Teifi r. U.K. 49 C6
Teignmouth U.K. 49 D8
Teixeira de Sousa Angola see Luau
Teixeiras Brazil 145 C3
Teixeira Soares Brazil 145 A4
Tejakula Indon. 108 A2
Tejen Turkm. 89 F2
Tejo r. Port. 57 B4 see Tagus
Tejon Pass U.S.A. 128 D4
Tekapo, Lake N.Z. 113 C6
Tekax Mex. 136 G4
Tekeli Kazakh. 80 E3
Tekes China 80 F3
Tekiliktag mt. China 82 E1
Tekin Rus. Fed. 74 D2
Tekirdağ Turkey 59 L4
Tekka India 84 D2
Tekkali India 84 E2
Teknaf Bangl. 83 H5
Tekong Kechil, Pulau i. Sing. 71 [inset]
Te Kuiti N.Z. 113 E4
Tel r. India 84 D1
Télagh Alg. 57 F6
Telanaipura Indon. see Jambi
Tel Ashqelon tourist site Israel 85 B4
Télataï Mali 96 D3
Tel Aviv-Yafo Israel 85 B3
Telč Czech Rep. 47 O6
Telchac Puerto Mex. 136 G4
Telekhany Belarus see Tsyelyakhany
Telêmaco Borba Brazil 145 A4
Teleorman r. Romania 59 K3
Telertheba, Djebel mt. Alg. 96 D2
Telescope Peak U.S.A. 128 E3
Teles Pires r. Brazil 143 G5
Telford U.K. 49 E6
Telgte Germany 53 H3
Télimélé Guinea 96 B3
Teljo, Jebel mt. Sudan 86 C7
Telkwa Canada 120 E4
Tell Atlas mts Alg. see Atlas Tellien
Tell City U.S.A. 134 B5
Teller U.S.A. 118 B3
Tell es Sultan West Bank see Jericho
Tellicherry India 84 B4
Tellin Belgium 52 F4
Telloh Iraq 91 G5
Telluride U.S.A. 129 J3
Tel'novskiy Rus. Fed. 74 F2
Telok Anson Malaysia see Teluk Intan
Telo Martius France see Toulon
Telpoziz, Gora mt. Rus. Fed. 41 R3
Telsen Arg. 144 C6
Telšiai Lith. 45 M9
Teltow Germany 53 N2
Teluk Anson Malaysia see Teluk Intan
Telukbetung Indon. see
Bandar Lampung
Teluk Cenderawasih, Taman Nasional
Indon. 69 I7
Teluk Intan Malaysia 71 C6
Temagami Lake Canada 122 F5
Temanggung Indon. 68 E8
Têmarxung China 83 G2
Temba S. Africa 101 I3
Tembagapura Indon. 69 J7
Tembenchi r. Rus. Fed. 65 K3
Tembilahan Indon. 68 C7
Tembisa S. Africa 101 I4
Tembo Aluma Angola 99 B4
Teme r. U.K. 49 E6
Temecula U.S.A. 128 E5
Temerloh Malaysia see Temerluh
Temerluh Malaysia 71 C7
Teminabuan Indon. 69 I7
Temirtau Kazakh. 80 D1
Témiscamie r. Canada 123 G4
Témiscamie, Lac l. Canada 123 G4
Témiscaming Canada 122 F5
Témiscamingue, Lac l. Canada 122 F5
Témiscouata, Lac l. Canada 123 H5
Temmes Fin. 44 N4
Temnikov Rus. Fed. 43 I5
Temora Australia 112 C5
Temósachic Mex. 127 G7
Tempe U.S.A. 129 H5
Tempe Downs Australia 109 F6
Tempelhof airport Germany 53 N2
Temple MI U.S.A. 134 C1
Temple TX U.S.A. 131 D6
Temple Bar U.K. 49 C6
Temple Dera Pak. 89 H4
Templemore Ireland 51 E5
Temple Sowerby U.K. 48 E4
Templeton watercourse Australia 110 B4
Templin Germany 53 N1
Tempué Angola 99 B5
Temryuk Rus. Fed. 90 E1
Temryukskiy Zaliv b. Rus. Fed. 43 H7
Temuco Chile 144 B5
Temuka N.Z. 113 C7
Temuli China see Butuo
Tena Ecuador 142 C4
Tenabo Mex. 136 F4
Tenabo, Mount U.S.A. 128 E1
Tenali India 84 D2
Tenasserim Myanmar 71 B4
Tenasserim r. Myanmar 71 B4
Tenbury Wells U.K. 49 E6
Tenby U.K. 49 C7
Tendaho Eth. 98 E2
Tende, Col de pass France/Italy 56 H4
Ten Degree Channel India 71 A5
Tendō Japan 75 F5
Tenedos i. Turkey see Bozcaada
Ténenkou Mali 96 C3
Ténéré reg. Niger 96 D2
Ténéré du Tafassâsset des. Niger 96 E2
Tenerife i. Canary Is 96 B2
Ténès Alg. 57 G5
Teng, Nam r. Myanmar 70 B3
Tengah, Kepulauan is Indon. 68 F8
Tengah, Sungai r. Sing. 71 [inset]
Tengcheng China see Tengxian
Tengchong China 76 C3
Tengeh Reservoir Sing. 71 [inset]
Tengger Shamo des. China 72 I5
Tenggul i. Malaysia 71 C6
Tengiz, Ozero salt l. Kazakh. 80 C1
Tengqiao China 77 F5
Tengréla Côte d'Ivoire 96 C3
Ten'gushevo Rus. Fed. 43 I5
Tengxian China 77 F4
Teni India see Theni
Teniente Jubany research station Antarctica
see Jubany
Tenille U.S.A. 133 D6
Tenke Dem. Rep. Congo 99 C5
Tenkeli Rus. Fed. 65 P2
Tenkodogo Burkina 96 C3
Ten Mile Lake salt flat
Australia 109 C6
Ten Mile Lake Canada 123 K4
Tennant Creek Australia 108 F4
Tennessee r. U.S.A. 131 F4
Tennessee state U.S.A. 134 C5
Tennessee Pass U.S.A. 126 G5
Tennevoll Norway 44 J2
Tenojoki r. Fin./Norway 44 P1
Tenosique Mex. 136 F5
Tenteno Indon. 69 G7
Tenterden U.K. 49 H7
Tenterfield Australia 112 F2
Ten Thousand Islands U.S.A. 133 D7
Tentudia mt. Spain 57 C4
Tentulia Bangl. see Tetulia
Teodoro Sampaio Brazil 144 F2
Teófilo Otôni Brazil 145 C2
Tepa Indon. 108 E1
Tepache Mex. 127 F7
Te Paki N.Z. 113 D2
Tepatitlán Mex. 136 D4
Tepehuanes Mex. 131 B7
Tepeköy Turkey see Karakoçan
Tepelenë Albania 59 I4
Tepelská vrchovina hills Czech Rep. 53 M5
Tepequem, Serra mts Brazil 137 L8
Tepic Mex. 136 D4
Te Pirita N.Z. 113 C6
Teplá r. Czech Rep. 53 M4
Teplice Czech Rep. 47 N5
Teplogorka Rus. Fed. 42 L3
Teploozersk Rus. Fed. 74 C2
Teploye Rus. Fed. 43 H5
Teploye Ozero Rus. Fed. see Teploozersk
Tepoca, Cabo c. Mex. 127 E7
Tepopa, Punta pt Mex. 127 E7
Tequila Mex. 136 D4
Téra Niger 96 D3
Teramo Italy 58 E3
Terang Australia 112 A7
Ter Apel Neth. 52 H2
Teratani r. Pak. 89 H4
Tercan Turkey 91 F3
Terebovlya Ukr. 43 E6
Terekty Kazakh. 80 G2
Teresa Cristina Brazil 145 A4
Tereshka r. Rus. Fed. 43 J6
Teresina Brazil 143 J5
Teresina de Goias Brazil 145 B1
Teresita Col. 142 E3
Teresópolis Brazil 145 C3
Teressa Island India 71 A5
Terezinha Brazil 143 H3
Tergeste Italy see Trieste
Tergnier France 52 D5
Teriberka Rus. Fed. 44 S2
Termez Uzbek. see Termiz
Termini Imerese Sicily Italy 58 E6
Términos, Laguna de lag. Mex. 136 F5
Termit-Kaoboul Niger 96 E3
Termiz Uzbek. 89 G2
Termo U.S.A. 128 C1
Termoli Italy 58 F4
Termonde Belgium see Dendermonde
Tern r. U.K. 49 E6
Ternate Indon. 69 H6
Terneuzen Neth. 52 D3
Terney Rus. Fed. 74 E3
Terni Italy 58 E3
Ternopil' Ukr. 43 E6
Ternopol' Ukr. see Ternopil'
Terpeniya, Mys c. Rus. Fed. 74 G2
Terpeniya, Zaliv g. Rus. Fed. 74 F2
Terra Alta U.S.A. 134 F4
Terra Bella U.S.A. 128 D4
Terrace Canada 120 D4
Terrace Bay Canada 122 D4
Terra Firma S. Africa 100 F3
Terråk Norway 44 H4
Terralba Sardinia Italy 58 C5
Terra Nova Bay Antarctica 152 H1
Terra Nova National Park Canada 123 L4
Terrebonne Bay U.S.A. 131 F6
Terre Haute U.S.A. 134 B4
Terre-Neuve prov. Canada see
Newfoundland and Labrador
Terre-Neuve-et-Labrador prov. Canada see
Newfoundland and Labrador
Terres Australes et Antarctiques Françaises
terr. Indian Ocean see
French Southern and Antarctic Lands
Terry U.S.A. 126 G3
Terschelling i. Neth. 52 F1
Terskiy Bereg coastal area Rus. Fed. 42 H2
Tertenia Sardinia Italy 58 C5
Terter Azer. see Tărtăr
Teruel Spain 57 F3
Tervola Fin. 44 N3
Tes Mongolia 80 I2
Tešanj Bos.-Herz. 58 G2
Teseney Eritrea 86 E6
Tesha r. Rus. Fed. 43 I5
Teshekpuk Lake U.S.A. 118 C2
Teshio Japan 74 F3
Teshio-gawa r. Japan 74 F3
Teslin Canada 120 C2
Teslin r. Canada 120 C2
Teslin Lake Canada 120 C2
Tesouras r. Brazil 145 A1
Tessalit Mali 96 D2
Tessaoua Niger 96 D3
Tessolo Moz. 101 L1
Test r. U.K. 49 F8
Testour Tunisia 58 C6
Tetachuck Lake Canada 120 E4
Tetas, Punta pt Chile 144 B2
Tete Moz. 99 D5
Te Teko N.Z. 113 F4
Teteriv r. Ukr. 43 F6
Teterow Germany 47 N4
Tetiyev Ukr. see Tetiyiv
Tetiyiv Ukr. 43 F6
Tetlin U.S.A. 120 A2
Tetlin Lake U.S.A. 120 A2
Tetney U.K. 48 G5
Teton r. U.S.A. 126 F3
Tétouan Morocco 57 D6
Tetovo Macedonia 59 I3
Tetuán Morocco see Tétouan
Tetulia Bangl. 83 G4
Tetulia sea chan. Bangl. 83 G5
Tetyukhe Rus. Fed. see Dal'negorsk
Tetyukhe-Pristan' Rus. Fed. see
Rudnaya Pristan'
Tetyushi Rus. Fed. 43 K5
Teuco r. Arg. 144 D2
Teufelsbach Namibia 100 C2
Teunom Indon. 71 A6
Teunom r. Indon. 71 A6
Teutoburger Wald hills Germany 53 I2
Teuva Fin. 44 L5
Tevere r. Italy see Tiber
Teverya Israel see Tiberias
Teviot r. U.K. 50 G5
Te Waewae Bay N.Z. 113 A8
Te Waipounamu i. N.Z. see South Island
Tewane Botswana 101 H2
Tewantin Australia 111 F5
Tewkesbury U.K. 49 E7
Têwo China 76 D1
Texarkana AR U.S.A. 131 E5
Texarkana TX U.S.A. 131 E5
Texas Australia 112 E2
Texas state U.S.A. 131 D6
Texel i. Neth. 52 E1
Texhoma U.S.A. 131 C4
Texoma, Lake U.S.A. 131 D5
Teyateyaneng Lesotho 101 H5
Teykovo Rus. Fed. 42 I4
Teza r. Rus. Fed. 42 I4
Tezpur India 83 H4
Tezu India 83 I4
Tha, Nam r. Laos 70 C2
Thaa Atoll Maldives see
Kolhumadulu Atoll
Tha-anne r. Canada 121 M2
Thabana-Ntlenyana mt. Lesotho 101 I5
Thaba Nchu S. Africa 101 H5
Thaba Putsoa mt. Lesotho 101 H5
Thaba-Tseka Lesotho 101 I5
Thabazimbi S. Africa 101 H3
Thab Lan National Park Thai. 71 C4
Tha Bo Laos 70 C3
Thabong S. Africa 101 H4
Thabyedaung Myanmar 76 C4
Thade r. Myanmar 70 A3
Thagyettaw Myanmar 71 B4
Tha Hin Thai. see Lop Buri
Thai Binh Vietnam 70 D2
Thailand country Asia 70 C4
Thailand, Gulf of Asia 71 C5
Thai Muang Thai. 71 B5
Thai Nguyên Vietnam 70 D2
Thaj Saudi Arabia 88 C5
Thakèk Laos 70 D3
Thakurgaon Bangl. 83 G4
Thakurtola India 82 E5
Thal Germany 53 K4
Thala Tunisia 58 C7
Thalang Thai. 71 B5
Thalassery India see Tellicherry
Thal Desert Pak. 89 H4
Thale (Harz) Germany 53 L3
Thaliparamba India see Taliparamba
Thallon Australia 112 D2
Thalo Pak. 89 G4
Thamaga Botswana 101 G3
Thamar, Jabal mt. Yemen 86 G7
Thamarīt Oman 87 H6
Thame r. U.K. 49 F7
Thames r. Ont. Canada 125 K3
Thames r. Ont. Canada 134 D2
Thames N.Z. 113 E3
Thames est. U.K. 49 H7
Thames r. U.K. 49 H7
Thamesford Canada 134 E2
Thana India see Thane
Thanatpin Myanmar 70 B3
Thandwè Myanmar 70 A3
Thane India 84 B2
Thanet, Isle of pen. U.K. 49 I7
Thangoo Australia 108 C4
Thangra India 82 D2
Thanh Hoa Vietnam 70 D3
Thanjavur India 84 C4
Than Kyun i. Myanmar 71 B5
Thanlwin r. China/Myanmar see Salween
Thanlyin Myanmar 70 B3
Thaolintoa Lake Canada 121 L2
Tha Pla Thai. 70 C3
Thap Put Thai. 71 B5
Thapsacus Syria see Dibsī
Thap Sakae Thai. 71 B5
Tharabwin Myanmar 71 B4
Tharad India 82 B4
Tharad India 82 B4
Thar Desert India/Pak. 89 H5
Thargomindah Australia 112 A1
Tharrawaw Myanmar 70 A3
Tharthār, Buḥayrat ath l. Iraq 91 F4
Tharwāniyyah U.A.E. 88 D6
Thasos i. Greece 59 K4
Thatcher U.S.A. 129 I5
Thât Khê Vietnam 70 D2
Thaton Myanmar 70 B3
Thatta Pak. 89 G5
Thaungdut Myanmar 70 A1
Tha Uthen Thai. 70 D3
Thayawthadangyi Kyun i. Myanmar 71 B4
Thayetmyo Myanmar 70 A3
Thazi Magwe Myanmar 70 A3
Thazi Mandalay Myanmar 83 I5
The Aldermen Islands N.Z. 113 F3
Theba U.S.A. 129 G5
The Bahamas country West Indies 133 E7
Thebes Greece see Thiva
The Bluff Bahamas 133 E7
The Broads nat. park U.K. 49 I6
The Brothers is H.K. China 77 [inset]
The Calvados Chain is P.N.G. 110 F1
The Cheviot hill U.K. 48 E3
The Dalles U.S.A. 126 C3
Thedford U.S.A. 130 C3
The Entrance Australia 112 E4
The Faither stack U.K. 50 [inset]
The Fens reg. U.K. 49 G6
The Gambia country Africa 96 B3
Thegon Myanmar 70 A3
The Grampians mts Australia 111 C8

The Great Oasis oasis Egypt see Khārijah, Wāḥāt al
The Grenadines is St Vincent 137 L6
The Gulf Asia 88 C4

▶The Hague Neth. 52 E2
Seat of government of the Netherlands.

The Hunters Hills N.Z. 113 C7
Thekulthili Lake Canada 121 I2
The Lakes National Park Australia 112 C6
Thelon r. Canada 121 L1
The Lynd Junction Australia 110 D3
Themar Germany 53 K4
Thembalihle S. Africa 101 I4
The Minch sea chan. U.K. 50 C2
The Naze c. Norway see Lindesnes
The Needles stack U.K. 49 F8
Theni India 84 C4
Thenia Alg. 57 H5
Theniet El Had Alg. 57 H6
The North Sound sea chan. U.K. 50 G1
Theodore Australia 110 E5
Theodore Canada 121 K5
Theodore Roosevelt Lake U.S.A. 129 H5
Theodore Roosevelt National Park U.S.A. 130 C2
Theodosia Ukr. see Feodosiya
The Old Man of Coniston hill U.K. 48 D4
The Paps hill Ireland 51 C5
The Pas Canada 121 K4
The Pilot mt. Australia 112 D6
Thera i. Greece see Santorini
Thérain r. France 52 C5
Theresa U.S.A. 135 H1
Thermaïkos Kolpos g. Greece 59 J4
Thermopolis U.S.A. 126 F4
The Rock Australia 112 C5
Thérouanne France 52 C4
The Salt Lake salt flat Australia 111 C6

▶The Settlement Christmas I. 68 D9
Capital of Christmas Island.

The Skaw spit Denmark see Grenen
The Skelligs is Ireland 51 B6
The Slot sea chan. Solomon Is see New Georgia Sound
The Solent strait U.K. 49 F8
Thessalon Canada 122 E5
Thessalonica Greece see Thessaloniki
Thessaloniki Greece 59 J4
The Storr hill U.K. 50 C3
Thet r. U.K. 49 H6
The Terraces hills Australia 109 C7
Thetford U.K. 49 H6
Thetford Mines Canada 123 H5
Thetkethaung r. Myanmar 70 A4
The Triangle mts Myanmar 70 B1
The Trossachs hills U.K. 50 E4
The Twins Australia 111 A6
Theva-i-Ra reef Fiji see Ceva-i-Ra

▶The Valley Anguilla 137 L5
Capital of Anguilla.

Thevenard Island Australia 108 A5
Thévenet, Lac l. Canada 123 H2
Theveste Alg. see Tébessa
The Wash b. U.K. 49 H6
The Weald reg. U.K. 49 H7
The Woodlands U.S.A. 131 E6
Thibodaux U.S.A. 131 F6
Thicket Portage Canada 121 L4
Thief River Falls U.S.A. 130 D1
Thiel Neth. see Tiel
Thiel Mountains Antarctica 152 K1
Thielsen, Mount U.S.A. 126 C4
Thielt Belgium see Tielt
Thiérache reg. France 52 D5
Thiers France 56 F4
Thiès Senegal 96 B3
Thika Kenya 98 D4
Thiladhunmathi Atoll Maldives 84 B5
Thiladunmathi Atoll Maldives see Thiladhunmathi Atoll
Thimbu Bhutan see Thimphu

▶Thimphu Bhutan 83 G4
Capital of Bhutan.

Thionville France 52 G5
Thira i. Greece see Santorini
Thirsk U.K. 48 F4
Thirty Mile Lake Canada 121 L2
Thiruvananthapuram India see Trivandrum
Thiruvannamalai India see Tiruvannamalai
Thiruvarur India 84 C4
Thiruvattiyur India see Tiruvottiyur
Thisted Denmark 45 F8
Thistle Creek Canada 120 B2
Thistle Lake Canada 121 I1
Thityabin Myanmar 70 A2
Thiu Khao Luang Phrabang mts Laos/Thai. see Luang Phrabang, Thiu Khao
Thiva Greece 59 J5
Thívai Greece see Thiva
Thlewiaza r. Canada 121 M2
Thoa r. Canada 121 I2
Thô Chu, Đao i. Vietnam 71 C5
Thoen Thai. 76 C5
Thoeng Thai. 70 C3
Thohoyandou S. Africa 101 J2
Tholen Neth. 52 E3
Tholen i. Neth. 52 E3
Tholey Germany 52 H5
Thomas Hill Reservoir U.S.A. 130 E4
Thomas Hubbard, Cape Canada 119 I1
Thomaston CT U.S.A. 135 I3
Thomaston GA U.S.A. 133 C5
Thomastown Ireland 51 E5
Thomasville AL U.S.A. 133 C6
Thomasville GA U.S.A. 133 D6
Thommen Belgium 52 G4
Thompson Canada 121 L4
Thompson r. Canada 120 F5
Thompson U.S.A. 129 I2
Thompson r. U.S.A. 124 I4
Thompson Falls U.S.A. 126 E3
Thompson Peak U.S.A. 127 G6
Thompson's Falls Kenya see Nyahururu
Thompson Sound Canada 120 E5
Thomson U.S.A. 133 D5
Thon Buri Thai. 71 C4
Thonokied Lake Canada 121 I1
Thoothukudi India see Tuticorin
Thoreau U.S.A. 129 I4
Thorn Neth. 52 F3
Thorn Poland see Toruń
Thornaby-on-Tees U.K. 48 F4
Thornapple r. U.S.A. 134 C2
Thornbury U.K. 49 E7
Thorne U.K. 48 G5
Thorne U.S.A. 128 D2
Thornton r. Australia 110 B3
Thorold Canada 134 F2
Thorshavnfjella reg. Antarctica see Thorshavnheiane
Thorshavnheiane reg. Antarctica 152 C2
Thota-ea-Moli Lesotho 101 H5
Thôt Nôt Vietnam 71 D5
Thouars France 56 D3
Thoubal India 83 H4
Thourout Belgium see Torhout
Thousand Islands Canada/U.S.A. 135 G1
Thousand Lake Mountain U.S.A. 129 H2
Thousand Oaks U.S.A. 128 D4
Thousandsticks U.S.A. 134 D5
Thrace reg. Europe 59 L4
Thraki reg. Europe see Thrace
Thrakiko Pelagos sea Greece 59 K4
Three Gorges Reservoir China 77 F2
Three Hills Canada 120 H5
Three Hummock Island Australia 111 [inset]
Three Kings Islands N.Z. 113 D2
Three Oaks U.S.A. 134 B3
Three Pagodas Pass Myanmar/Thai. 70 B4
Three Points, Cape Ghana 96 C4
Three Rivers U.S.A. 134 C3
Three Sisters mt. U.S.A. 126 C3
Three Springs Australia 109 A7
Thrissur India see Trichur
Throckmorton U.S.A. 131 D5
Throssell, Lake salt flat Australia 109 D6
Throssel Range hills Australia 108 C5
Thrushton National Park Australia 112 C1
Thu Ba Vietnam 71 D5
Thubun Lakes Canada 121 I2
Thu Dâu Môt Vietnam 71 D5
Thuddungra Australia 112 D5
Thu Đuc Vietnam 71 D5
Thuin Belgium 52 E4
Thul Pak. 89 H4
Thulaythawāt Gharbī, Jabal hill Syria 85 D2
Thule Greenland 119 L2
Thun Switz. 56 H3
Thunder Bay Canada 119 J5
Thunder Bay b. U.S.A. 134 D1
Thunder Creek r. Canada 121 J5
Thüngen Germany 53 J5
Thung Salaeng Luang National Park Thai. 70 C3
Thung Song Thai. 71 B5
Thung Yai Naresuan Wildlife Reserve nature res. Thai. 70 B4
Thüringen land Germany 53 K3
Thüringer Becken reg. Germany 53 L3
Thüringer Wald mts Germany 53 K4
Thuringia land Germany see Thüringen
Thuringian Forest mts Germany see Thüringer Wald
Thurles Ireland 51 E5
Thurn, Pass Austria 47 N7
Thursday Island Australia 110 C1
Thurso U.K. 50 F2
Thurso r. U.K. 50 F2
Thurston Island Antarctica 152 K2
Thurston Peninsula i. Antarctica see Thurston Island
Thüster Berg hill Germany 53 J2
Thuthukudi India see Tuticorin
Thwaite U.K. 48 E4
Thwaites Glacier Tongue Antarctica 152 K1
Thyatira Turkey see Akhisar
Thyborøn Denmark 45 F8
Thymerais reg. France 52 B6
Tianchang China 77 H1
Tiancheng China see Chongyang
Tianchi China see Lezhi
Tiandeng China 76 E4
Tiandong China 76 E4
T'ianet'i Georgia 91 G2
Tianfanjie China 77 H2
Tianjin China 73 L5
Tianjin municipality China 73 L5
Tianjun China 80 I4
Tianlin China 76 E3
Tianma China see Changshan
Tianmen China 77 G2
Tianqiaoling China 74 C4
Tianquan China 76 D2
Tianshan China 73 M4
Tian Shan mts China/Kyrg. see Tien Shan
Tianshui China 76 E1
Tianshuihai Aksai Chin 82 D2
Tiantai China 77 I2
Tiantang China see Yuexi
Tianyang China 76 E4
Tianzhou China see Tianyang
Tianzhu Gansu China 72 I5
Tianzhu Guizhou China 77 F3
Tiaret Alg. 57 G6
Tiassalé Côte d'Ivoire 96 C4
Tibagi Brazil 145 A4
Tibal, Wādī watercourse Iraq 91 F4
Tibati Cameroon 96 E4
Tibba Pak. 89 H4
Tibé, Pic de mt. Guinea 96 C4
Tiber r. Italy 58 E4
Tiberias Israel 85 B3
Tiberias, Lake Israel see Galilee, Sea of
Tiber Reservoir U.S.A. 126 F2
Tibesti mts Chad 97 E2
Tibet aut. reg. China see Xizang Zizhiqu
Tibet, Plateau of China 83 F2
Tibi India 89 I4
Tibooburra Australia 111 C6
Tibrikot Nepal 83 E3
Tibro Sweden 45 I7
Tibur Italy see Tivoli
Tiburón, Isla i. Mex. 127 E7
Ticehurst U.K. 49 H7
Tichborne Canada 135 G1
Tichégami r. Canada 123 G4
Tîchît Mauritania 96 C3
Tichla W. Sahara 96 B2
Ticinum Italy see Pavia
Ticonderoga U.S.A. 135 I2
Ticul Mex. 136 G4
Tidaholm Sweden 45 H7
Tiddim Myanmar 70 A2
Tiden India 71 A6
Tidjikja Mauritania 96 B3
Tiefa Liaoning China see Diaobingshan
Tiel Neth. 52 F3
Tieli China 74 B3
Tieling China 74 A4
Tielongtan Aksai Chin 82 D2
Tielt Belgium 52 D4
Tienen Belgium 52 E4
Tien Shan mts China/Kyrg. 72 D4
Tientsin municipality China see Tianjin
Tiên Yên Vietnam 70 D2
Tierp Sweden 45 J6
Tierra Amarilla U.S.A. 127 G5

▶Tierra del Fuego, Isla Grande de i. Arg./Chile 144 C8
Largest island in South America.

Tierra del Fuego, Parque Nacional nat. park Arg. 144 C8
Tiétar r. Spain 57 D4
Tiétar, Valle de valley Spain 57 D3
Tietê r. Brazil 145 A3
Tieyon Australia 109 F6
Tiffin U.S.A. 134 D3
Tiflis Georgia see T'bilisi
Tifton U.S.A. 133 D6
Tiga Reservoir Nigeria 96 D3
Tigen Kazakh. 91 H1
Tigh Āb Iran 89 F5
Tigheciului, Dealurile hills Moldova 59 M2
Tighina Moldova 59 M1
Tigiria India 84 E1
Tignère Cameroon 96 E4
Tignish Canada 123 I5
Tigranocerta Turkey see Siirt
Tigre r. Venez. 142 F2
Tigris r. Asia 91 G5
also known as Dicle (Turkey) or Nahr Dijlah (Iraq/Syria)
Tigrovaya Balka Zapovednik nature res. Tajik. 89 H2
Tiguidit, Falaise de esc. Niger 96 D3
Tīh, Gebel el plat. Egypt see Tīh, Jabal at
Tīh, Jabal at plat. Egypt 85 A5
Tijuana Mex. 128 E5
Tikamgarh India 82 D4
Tikanlik China 80 G3
Tikhoretsk Rus. Fed. 43 I7
Tikhvin Rus. Fed. 42 G4
Tikhvinskaya Gryada ridge Rus. Fed. 42 G4
Tiki Basin sea feature S. Pacific Ocean 151 L7
Tikokino N.Z. 113 F4
Tikopia i. Solomon Is 107 G3
Tikrīt Iraq 91 F4
Tikse India 82 D2
Tikshozero, Ozero l. Rus. Fed. 44 R3
Tiksi Rus. Fed. 65 N2
Tiladummati Atoll Maldives see Thiladhunmathi Atoll
Tilaiya Reservoir India 83 F4
Tilbeşar Ovasi plain Turkey 85 C1
Tilbooroo Australia 112 B1
Tilburg Neth. 52 F3
Tilbury Canada 134 D2
Tilbury U.K. 49 H7
Tilcara Arg. 144 C2
Tilcha Creek watercourse Australia 111 C6
Tilden U.S.A. 131 D6
Tilemsès Niger 96 D3
Tilemsi, Vallée du watercourse Mali 96 D3
Tilhar India 82 D4
Tilimsen Alg. see Tlemcen
Tilin Myanmar 70 A2
Tillabéri Niger 96 D3
Tillamook U.S.A. 126 C3
Tillanchong Island India 71 A5
Tillia Niger 96 D3
Tillicoultry U.K. 50 F4
Tillsonburg Canada 134 E2
Tillyfourie U.K. 50 G3
Tilonia India 89 I5
Tilos i. Greece 59 L6
Tilothu India 83 F4
Tilpa Australia 112 B3
Tilsit Rus. Fed. see Sovetsk
Tilt r. U.K. 50 F4
Tilton IL U.S.A. 134 B3
Tilton NH U.S.A. 135 J2
Tim Rus. Fed. 43 H6
Ţimā Egypt 86 D4
Timah, Bukit hill Sing. 71 [inset]
Timakara i. India 84 B4
Timanskiy Kryazh ridge Rus. Fed. 42 K2
Timar Turkey 91 F3
Timaru N.Z. 113 C7
Timashevsk Rus. Fed. 43 H7
Timashevskaya Rus. Fed. see Timashevsk
Timbedgha Mauritania 96 C3
Timber Creek Australia 106 D3
Timber Mountain U.S.A. 128 E3
Timberville U.S.A. 135 F4
Timbuktu Mali 96 C3
Timétrine reg. Mali 96 C3
Timiaouine Alg. 96 D2
Timimoun Alg. 54 E6
Timirist, Râs pt Mauritania 96 B3
Timiskaming, Lake Canada see Témiscamingue, Lac
Timişoara Romania 59 I2
Timmins Canada 122 E4
Timms Hill hill U.S.A. 130 F2
Timon Brazil 143 J5
Timor i. Indon. 108 D2
Timor-Leste country Asia see East Timor
Timor Loro Sae country Asia see East Timor
Timor Sea Australia/Indon. 106 C3
Timor Timur country Asia see East Timor
Timperley Range hills Australia 109 C6
Timrå Sweden 44 J5
Tīn, Ra's at pt Libya 90 A4
Ţīna, Khalīg el b. Egypt see Ţīnah, Khalīj at
Tīnah Syria 85 D1
Ţīnah, Khalīj aţ b. Egypt 85 A4
Tin Can Bay Australia 111 F5
Tindivanam India 84 C3
Tindouf Alg. 54 C6
Ti-n-Essako Mali 96 D3
Tinggi i. Malaysia 71 D7
Tingha Australia 112 E2
Tingis Morocco see Tangier
Tingo María Peru 142 C5
Tingréla Côte d'Ivoire see Tengréla
Tingsryd Sweden 45 I8
Tingvoll Norway 44 F5
Tingwall U.K. 50 F1
Tingzhou China see Changting
Tinharé, Ilha de i. Brazil 145 D1
Tinh Gia Vietnam 70 D3
Tinian i. N. Mariana Is 69 L4
Tini Heke is N.Z. see Snares Islands
Tinnelvelly India see Tirunelveli
Tinogasta Arg. 144 C3
Tinos Greece 59 K6
Tinos i. Greece 59 K6
Tinqueux France 52 D5
Tinrhert, Hamada de Alg. 96 D2
Tinsukia India 83 H4
Tintagel U.K. 49 C8
Ţînţâne Mauritania 96 B3
Tintina Arg. 144 D3
Tintinara Australia 111 C7
Tioga U.S.A. 130 C1
Tioman i. Malaysia 71 D7
Tionesta U.S.A. 134 F3
Tionesta Lake U.S.A. 134 F3
Tipasa Alg. 57 H5
Tiphsah Syria see Dibsī
Tipperary Ireland 51 D5
Tipton CA U.S.A. 128 D3
Tipton IA U.S.A. 130 F3
Tipton IN U.S.A. 134 B3
Tipton MO U.S.A. 130 E4
Tipton, Mount U.S.A. 129 F4
Tiptop U.S.A. 134 E5
Tip Top Hill hill Canada 122 D4
Tiptree U.K. 49 H7
Tiptur India 84 C3
Tipturi India see Tiptur
Tiracambu, Serra do hills Brazil 143 I4
Tirah reg. Pak. 89 H3

▶Tirana Albania 59 H4
Capital of Albania.

Tiranë Albania see Tirana
Tirano Italy 58 D1
Tirari Desert Australia 111 B5
Tiraspol Moldova 59 M1
Tiraz Mountains Namibia 100 C4
Tire Turkey 59 L5
Tirebolu Turkey 91 E2
Tiree i. U.K. 50 C4
Tîrgovişte Romania see Târgovişte
Tîrgu Jiu Romania see Târgu Jiu
Tîrgu Mureş Romania see Târgu Mureş
Tîrgu Neamţ Romania see Târgu Neamţ
Tîrgu Secuiesc Romania see Târgu Secuiesc
Tiri Pak. 89 G4
Tirich Mir mt. Pak. 89 H2
Tirlemont Belgium see Tienen
Tirna r. India 84 C2
Tîrnăveni Romania see Târnăveni
Tírnavos Greece see Tyrnavos
Tiros Brazil 145 B2
Tirourda, Col de pass Alg. 57 I5
Tirreno, Mare sea France/Italy see Tyrrhenian Sea
Tirso r. Sardinia Italy 58 C5
Tirthahalli India 84 B3
Tiruchchendur India 84 C4
Tiruchchirappalli India 84 C4
Tiruchengodu India 84 C4
Tirunelveli India 84 C4
Tirupati India 84 C3
Tiruppattur Tamil Nadu India 84 C3
Tiruppattur Tamil Nadu India 84 C4
Tiruppur India 84 C4
Tiruttani India 84 C3
Tirutturaippundi India 84 C4
Tiruvallur India 84 C3
Tiruvannamalai India 84 C3
Tiruvottiyur India 84 D3
Tiru Well Australia 108 D5
Tisa r. Serbia 59 I2
also known as Tisza (Hungary), Tysa (Ukraine)
Tisdale Canada 121 J4
Tishomingo U.S.A. 131 D5
Ţīsīyah Syria 85 C3
Tissemsilt Alg. 57 G6
Tisza r. Serbia see Tisa
Titalya Bangl. see Tetulia
Titan Dome ice feature Antarctica 152 H1
Titao Burkina 96 C3
Tit-Ary Rus. Fed. 65 N2
Titawin Morocco see Tétouan
Titicaca, Lago Bol./Peru see Titicaca, Lake

▶Titicaca, Lake Bol./Peru 142 E7
Largest lake in South America.

Titi Islands N.Z. 113 A8
Tititea mt. N.Z. see Aspiring, Mount
Titlagarh India 84 D1
Titograd Montenegro see Podgorica
Titova Mitrovica Kosovo see Mitrovicë
Titovo Užice Serbia see Užice
Titovo Velenje Slovenia see Velenje
Titov Veles Macedonia see Veles
Titov Vrbas Serbia see Vrbas
Ti Tree Australia 108 F5
Titu Romania 59 K2
Titusville FL U.S.A. 133 D6
Titusville PA U.S.A. 134 F3
Tiu Chung Chau i. H.K. China 77 [inset]
Tiumpain, Rubha an hd U.K. see Tiumpan Head
Tiumpan Head hd U.K. 50 C2
Tiva watercourse Kenya 98 D4
Tivari India 82 C4
Tiverton Canada 134 E1
Tiverton U.K. 49 D8
Tivoli Italy 58 E4
Ţīwī Oman 88 E6
Ti-ywa Myanmar 71 B4
Tizi El Arba hill Alg. 57 H5
Tizimín Mex. 136 G4
Tizi N'Koulal pass Alg. 57 I5
Tizi Ouzou Alg. 57 I5
Tiznap He r. China 82 D1
Tiznit Morocco 96 C2
Tiztoutine Morocco 57 E6
Tjaneni Swaziland 101 J3
Tjappsåive Sweden 44 K4
Tjeukemeer l. Neth. 52 F2
Tjirebon Indon. see Cirebon
Tjolotjo Zimbabwe see Tsholotsho
Tjorhom Norway 45 E7
Tkibuli Georgia see Tqibuli
Tlahualilo Mex. 131 C7
Tlaxcala Mex. 136 E5
Tl'ell Canada 120 D4
Tlemcen Alg. 57 F6
Tlhakalatlou S. Africa 100 F5
Tlholong S. Africa 101 I5
Tlokweng Botswana 101 G3
Tlyarata Rus. Fed. 91 G2
To r. Myanmar 70 B3
Toad r. Canada 120 E3
Toad River Canada 120 E3
Toamasina Madag. 99 E5
Toana mts U.S.A. 129 F1
Toano U.S.A. 135 G5
Toa Payoh Sing. 71 [inset]
Toba China 76 C2
Toba, Danau l. Indon. 71 B7
Toba, Lake Indon. see Toba, Danau
Toba and Kakar Ranges mts Pak. 89 G4
Toba Gargaji Pak. 89 I4
Tobago i. Trin. and Tob. 137 L6
Tobelo Indon. 69 H6
Tobercurry Ireland 51 D3
Tobermorey Australia 110 B4
Tobermory Australia 112 A1
Tobermory Canada 134 E1
Tobermory U.K. 50 C4
Tobi i. Palau 69 I6
Tobin, Lake salt flat Australia 108 D5
Tobin, Mount U.S.A. 128 E1
Tobin Lake Canada 121 K4
Tobin Lake l. Canada 121 K4
Tobi-shima i. Japan 75 E5
Tobol r. Kazakh./Rus. Fed. 78 F1
Tobol'sk Rus. Fed. 64 H4
Tobruk Libya see Tubruq
Tobseda Rus. Fed. 42 L1
Tobyl r. Kazakh./Rus. Fed. see Tobol
Tobysh r. Rus. Fed. 42 K2
Tocache Nuevo Peru 142 C5
Tocantinópolis Brazil 143 I5
Tocantins r. Brazil 145 A1
Tocantins state Brazil 145 A1
Tocantinzinha r. Brazil 145 A1
Toccoa U.S.A. 133 D5
Tochi r. Pak. 89 H3
Töcksfors Sweden 45 G7
Tocopilla Chile 144 B2
Tocumwal Australia 112 B5
Tod, Mount Canada 120 G5
Todd watercourse Australia 110 A5
Todi Italy 58 E3
Todoga-saki pt Japan 75 F5
Todos Santos Mex. 136 B4
Toe Head hd U.K. 50 B3
Tofino Canada 120 E5
Toft U.K. 50 [inset]
Tofua i. Tonga 107 I3
Togatax China 82 E2
Togian i. Indon. 69 G7
Togian, Kepulauan is Indon. 69 G7
Togliatti Rus. Fed. see Tol'yatti
Togo country Africa 96 D4
Togtoh China 73 K4
Togton He r. China 83 H2
Togton Heyan China see Tanggulashan
Tohatchi U.S.A. 129 I4
Toholampi Fin. 44 N5
Toiba China 83 G3
Toibalewe India 71 A5
Toijala Fin. 45 M6
Toili Indon. 69 G7
Toi-misaki pt Japan 75 C7
Toivakka Fin. 44 O5
Toiyabe Range mts U.S.A. 128 E2
Tojikiston country Asia see Tajikistan
Tok U.S.A. 120 A2
Tokar Sudan 86 E6
Tokara-rettō is Japan 75 C7
Tokarevka Rus. Fed. 43 I6
Tokat Turkey 90 E2
Tŏkchŏk-to i. S. Korea 75 B5
Tokdo i. Asia see Liancourt Rocks

▶Tokelau terr. S. Pacific Ocean 107 I2
New Zealand Overseas Territory.

Tokmak Kyrg. see Tokmok
Tokmak Ukr. 43 G7
Tokmok Kyrg. 80 E3
Tokomaru Bay N.Z. 113 G4
Tokoroa N.Z. 113 E4
Tokoza S. Africa 101 I4
Toksun China 80 G3
Tok-to i. Asia see Liancourt Rocks
Toktogul Kyrg. 80 D3
Tokto-ri i. Asia see Liancourt Rocks
Tokur Rus. Fed. 74 D1
Tokushima Japan 75 D6
Tokuyama Japan 75 C6

▶Tōkyō Japan 75 E6
Capital of Japan. Most populous city in the world and in Asia.

Tokzār Afgh. 89 G3
Tolaga Bay N.Z. 113 G4
Tôlañaro Madag. 99 E6
Tolbo Mongolia 80 H2
Tolbukhin Bulg. see Dobrich
Tolbuzino Rus. Fed. 74 B1
Toledo Brazil 144 F2
Toledo Spain 57 D4
Toledo IA U.S.A. 130 E3
Toledo OH U.S.A. 134 D3
Toledo OR U.S.A. 126 C3
Toledo, Montes de mts Spain 57 D4
Toledo Bend Reservoir U.S.A. 131 E6
Toletum Spain see Toledo
Toliara Madag. 99 E6
Tolitoli Indon. 69 G6
Tol'ka Rus. Fed. 64 J3
Tolleson U.S.A. 129 G5
Tollimarjon Uzbek. 89 G2
Tolmachevo Rus. Fed. 45 P7
Tolo Dem. Rep. Congo 98 B4
Tolo Channel H.K. China 77 [inset]
Tolochin Belarus see Talachyn
Tolo Harbour b. H.K. China 77 [inset]
Tolosa France see Toulouse
Tolosa Spain 57 E2
Toluca Mex. 136 E5
Toluca de Lerdo Mex. see Toluca
To-lun Nei Mongol China see Dolonnur
Tol'yatti Rus. Fed. 43 K5
Tom' r. Rus. Fed. 74 B2
Tomah U.S.A. 130 F3
Tomakomai Japan 74 F4
Tomales U.S.A. 128 B2
Tomali Indon. 69 G7
Tomamae Japan 74 F3
Tomanivi mt. Fiji 107 H3
Tomar Brazil 142 F4
Tomar Port. 57 B4
Tomari Rus. Fed. 74 F3
Tomarza Turkey 90 D3
Tomaszów Lubelski Poland 43 D6
Tomaszów Mazowiecki Poland 47 R5
Tomatin U.K. 50 F3
Tomatlán Mex. 136 C5
Tomazina Brazil 145 A3
Tombador, Serra do hills Brazil 143 G6
Tombigbee r. U.S.A. 133 C6
Tomboco Angola 99 B4
Tombouctou Mali see Timbuktu
Tombstone U.S.A. 127 F7
Tombua Angola 99 B5
Tom Burke S. Africa 101 H2
Tomdibuloq Uzbek. 80 B3
Tome Moz. 101 L2
Tomelilla Sweden 45 H9
Tomelloso Spain 57 E4
Tomi Romania see Constanţa
Tomingley Australia 112 D4
Tomini, Teluk g. Indon. 69 G7
Tominian Mali 96 C3
Tomintoul U.K. 50 F3
Tomislavgrad Bos.-Herz. 58 G3
Tomkinson Ranges mts Australia 109 E6
Tømmerneset Norway 44 I3
Tommot Rus. Fed. 65 N4
Tomo r. Col. 142 E2
Tomóchic Mex. 127 G7
Tomortei China 73 K4
Tompkinsville U.S.A. 134 C5
Tom Price Australia 108 B5
Tomra China 83 F3
Tomsk Rus. Fed. 64 J4
Toms River U.S.A. 135 H4
Tomtabacken hill Sweden 45 I8
Tomtor Rus. Fed. 65 P3
Tomur Feng mt. China/Kyrg. see Pobeda Peak
Tomuzlovka r. Rus. Fed. 43 J7
Tom White, Mount U.S.A. 118 D3
Tonalá Mex. 136 F5
Tonantins Brazil 142 E4
Tonb-e Bozorg, Jazīreh-ye i. The Gulf see Greater Tunb
Tonb-e Kūchek, Jazīreh-ye i. The Gulf see Lesser Tunb
Tonbridge U.K. 49 H7
Tondano Indon. 69 G6
Tønder Denmark 45 F9
Tondi India 84 C4
Tone r. U.K. 49 E7
Toney Mountain Antarctica 152 K1
Tonga country S. Pacific Ocean 107 I4
Tongaat S. Africa 101 J5
Tongariro National Park N.Z. 113 E4
Tongatapu Group is Tonga 107 I4

▶Tonga Trench sea feature S. Pacific Ocean 150 I7
2nd deepest trench in the world.

Tongbai Shan mts China 77 G1
Tongcheng China 77 H2
T'ongch'ŏn N. Korea 75 B5
Tongchuan Shaanxi China 77 F1
Tongchuan Sichuan China see Santai
Tongdao China 77 F3
Tongde China 76 D1
Tongduch'ŏn S. Korea 75 B5
Tongeren Belgium 52 F4
Tonggu China 77 G2
Tonggu Zui pt China 77 F5
Tonghae S. Korea 75 C5
Tonghai China 76 D3
Tonghe China 74 C3
Tonghua Jilin China 74 B4
Tonghua Jilin China 74 B4
Tongi Bangl. see Tungi
Tongjiang Heilong. China 74 D3
Tongjiang Sichuan China 76 E2
Tongking, Gulf of China/Vietnam 70 E2
Tongle China see Leye
Tongliang China 76 E2
Tongliao China 73 M4
Tongling China 77 H2
Tonglu China 77 H2
Tongo Australia 112 A3
Tongo Lake salt flat Australia 112 A3
Tongren Guizhou China 77 F3
Tongren Qinghai China 76 D1
Tongres Belgium see Tongeren
Tongsa Bhutan 83 G4

'ongshan *Jiangsu* China *see* **Xuzhou**
'ongshi *Hainan* China *see* **Wuzhishan**
ongta Myanmar 70 B2
ongtian He *r. Qinghai* China 76 B1
ongtian He *r. Qinghai* China 76 C1 *see* **Yangtze**
ongue U.K. 50 E2
ongue *r.* U.S.A. 126 G3
ongue of the Ocean *sea chan.* Bahamas 133 E7
ongxin China 72 J5
'ongyŏng S. Korea 75 C6
ongzi China 76 E2
ónichi Mex. 127 F7
onk India 82 C4
onkābon Iran 88 C2
onkin *reg.* Vietnam 70 D2
ônle Repou *r.* Laos 71 D4
ônlé Sab *l.* Cambodia *see* **Tonle Sap**

Tonle Sap *l.* Cambodia 71 C4
Largest lake in southeast Asia.

onopah *AZ* U.S.A. 129 G5
onopah *NV* U.S.A. 128 E2
ønsberg Norway 45 G7
onstad Norway 45 E7
onto Creek *watercourse* U.S.A. 129 H5
onvarjeh Iran 88 E3
onzang Myanmar 70 A2
onzi Myanmar 70 A1
oobeah Australia 112 D2
oobli Liberia 96 C4
ooele U.S.A. 129 G1
oogoolawah Australia 112 F1
ooma *r.* Australia 112 D6
oompine Australia 112 B1
oora Australia 112 C7
ooraweenah Australia 112 D3
oorberg *mt.* S. Africa 100 G7
oowoomba Australia 112 E1
ooxin Somalia 98 F2
op Afgh. 89 H3
op Boğazı Geçidi *pass* Turkey 85 C1

Topeka U.S.A. 130 E4
Capital of Kansas.

opia Mex. 127 G8
öplitz Germany 53 M2
opoľčany Slovakia 47 Q6
opolobampo Mex. 127 F8
opolovgrad Bulg. 59 L3
opozero, Ozero *l.* Rus. Fed. 44 R4
opsfield U.S.A. 132 H2
or Eth. 97 G4
or Baldak *mt.* Afgh. 89 G4
orbalı Turkey 59 L5
orbat-e Heydarīyeh Iran 88 E3
orbat-e Jām Iran 89 F3
orbay Bay Australia 109 B8
orbert, Mount U.S.A. 118 C3
orbeyevo Rus. Fed. 43 I5
orch *r.* Canada 121 K4
ordesillas Spain 57 D3
ordesilos Spain 57 F3
öre Sweden 44 M4
orelló Spain 57 H2
orenberg *hill* Neth. 52 F2
oretam Kazakh. *see* **Baykonyr**
orgau Germany 53 M3
orghay Kazakh. *see* **Turgay**
orgun *r.* Rus. Fed. 43 J6
orhout Belgium 52 D3
orino Italy *see* **Turin**
ori-shima *i.* Japan 75 F7
orit Sudan 97 G4
orkamān Iran 88 B2
orkovichi Rus. Fed. 42 F4
ornado Mountain Canada 120 H5
orneå Fin. *see* **Tornio**
orneälven *r.* Sweden 44 N4
orneträsk *l.* Sweden 44 K2
orngat, Monts *mts* Canada *see* **Torngat Mountains**
orngat Mountains Canada 123 I2
ornio Fin. 44 N4
oro Spain 57 D3
oro, Pico del *mt.* Mex. 131 C7
orom Rus. Fed. 74 D1

Toronto Canada 134 F2
Capital of Ontario.

oro Peak U.S.A. 128 E5
oropets Rus. Fed. 42 F4
ororo Uganda 98 D3
oros Dağları *mts* Turkey *see* **Taurus Mountains**
orphins U.K. 50 G3
orquay Australia 112 B7
orquay U.K. 49 D8
orrance U.S.A. 128 D5
orrão Port. 57 B4
orre *mt.* Port. 57 C3
orreblanca Spain 57 G3
orre Blanco, Cerro *mt.* Mex. 127 E6
orrecerredo *mt.* Spain 57 D2
orre del Greco Italy 58 F4
orre de Moncorvo Port. 57 C3
orrelavega Spain 57 D2
orremolinos Spain 57 D5

Torrens, Lake *imp. l.* Australia 111 B6
2nd largest lake in Oceania.

orrens Creek Australia 110 D4
orrent Spain 57 F4
orrente Spain *see* **Torrent**
orreón Mex. 131 C7
orres Brazil 145 A5
orres Mex. 127 F7
orres del Paine, Parque Nacional *nat. park* Chile 144 B8
orres Islands Vanuatu 107 G3
orres Novas Port. 57 B4
orres Strait Australia 106 E2
orres Vedras Port. 57 B4
orrevieja Spain 57 F5
orrey U.S.A. 129 H2
orridge *r.* U.K. 49 C8
orridon, Loch *b.* U.K. 50 D3

Torrijos Spain 57 D4
Torrington Australia 112 E2
Torrington *CT* U.S.A. 132 F3
Torrington *WY* U.S.A. 126 G4
Torsby Sweden 45 H6

▶**Tórshavn** Faroe Is 44 [inset]
Capital of the Faroe Islands.

Tortilla Flat U.S.A. 129 H5
To'rtko'l Uzbek. 80 B3
Törtköl Uzbek. *see* **To'rtko'l**
Tortolì *Sardinia* Italy 58 C5
Tortona Italy 58 C2
Tortosa Spain 57 G3
Tortum Turkey 91 F2
Ţorūd Iran 88 D3
Torugart, Pereval *pass* China/Kyrg. *see* **Turugart Pass**
Torul Turkey 91 E2
Toruń Poland 47 Q4
Tory Island Ireland 51 D2
Tory Sound *sea chan.* Ireland 51 D2
Torzhok Rus. Fed. 42 G4
Tosa Japan 75 D6
Tosbotn Norway 44 H4
Tosca S. Africa 100 F3
Toscano, Arcipelago *is* Italy 58 C3
Tosham India 82 C3
Tōshima-yama *mt.* Japan 75 F4

▶**Toshkent** Uzbek. 80 C3
Capital of Uzbekistan.

Tosno Rus. Fed. 42 F4
Toson Hu *l.* China 83 I1
Tostado Arg. 144 D3
Tostedt Germany 53 J1
Tosya Turkey 90 D2
Totapola *mt.* Sri Lanka 84 D5
Tôtes France 52 B5
Tot'ma Rus. Fed. 42 I4
Totness Suriname 143 G2
Tottenham Australia 112 C4
Totton U.K. 49 F8
Tottori Japan 75 D6
Touba Côte d'Ivoire 96 C4
Touba Senegal 96 B3
Toubkal, Jbel *mt.* Morocco 54 C5
Toubkal, Parc National du *nat. park* Morocco 54 C5
Touboro Cameroon 97 E4
Tougan Burkina 96 C3
Touggourt Alg. 54 F5
Tougué Guinea 96 B3
Touil Mauritania 96 B3
Toul France 52 F6
Touliu Taiwan 77 I4
Toulon France 56 G5
Toulon U.S.A. 130 F3
Toulouse France 56 E5
Toumodi Côte d'Ivoire 96 C4
Toupai China 77 F3
Tourane Vietnam *see* **Đa Năng**
Tourcoing France 52 D4
Tourgis Lake Canada 121 J1
Tourlaville France 49 F9
Tournai Belgium 52 D4
Tournon-sur-Rhône France 56 G4
Tournus France 58 A1
Touros Brazil 143 K5
Tours France 56 E3
Tousside, Pic *mt.* Chad 97 E2
Toussoro, Mont *mt.* Cent. Afr. Rep. 98 C3
Toutai China 74 B3
Touwsrivier S. Africa 100 E7
Toužim Czech Rep. 53 M4
Tovarkovo Rus. Fed. 43 G5
Tovil'-Dora Tajik. *see* **Tavildara**
Tovuz Azer. 91 G2
Towada Japan 74 F4
Towak Mountain *hill* U.S.A. 118 B3
Towanda U.S.A. 135 G3
Towaoc U.S.A. 129 I3
Towcester U.K. 49 G6
Tower Ireland 51 D6
Towner U.S.A. 130 C1
Townes Pass U.S.A. 128 E3
Townsend U.S.A. 126 F3
Townsend, Mount Australia 112 D6
Townshend Island Australia 110 E4
Townsville Australia 110 D3
Towot Sudan 97 G4
Towr Kham Afgh. 89 H3
Towson U.S.A. 135 G4
Towyn U.K. *see* **Tywyn**
Toy U.S.A. 128 D1
Toyah U.S.A. 131 C6
Toyama Japan 75 E5
Toyama-wan *b.* Japan 75 E5
Toyohashi Japan 75 E6
Toyokawa Japan 75 E6
Toyonaka Japan 75 D6
Toyooka Japan 75 D6
Toyota Japan 75 E6
Tozanlı Turkey *see* **Almus**
Tozê Kangri *mt.* China 83 E2
Tozeur Tunisia 54 F5
Tozi, Mount U.S.A. 118 C3
Tqibuli Georgia 91 F2
Traben Germany 52 H5
Trâblous Lebanon *see* **Tripoli**
Trabotivište Macedonia 59 J4
Trabzon Turkey 91 E2
Tracy *CA* U.S.A. 128 C3
Tracy *MN* U.S.A. 130 E2
Trading *r.* Canada 122 C4
Traer U.S.A. 130 E3
Trafalgar U.S.A. 134 B4
Trafalgar, Cabo *c.* Spain 57 C5
Traffic Mountain Canada 120 D2
Trail Canada 120 G5
Tràille, Rubha na *pt* U.K. 50 D5
Traill Island Greenland *see* **Traill Ø**
Traill Ø *i.* Greenland 119 P2
Trainor Lake Canada 120 F2
Trajectum Neth. *see* **Utrecht**
Trakai Lith. 45 N9
Tra Khuc, Sông *r.* Vietnam 70 E4
Trakiya *reg.* Europe *see* **Thrace**
Trakt Rus. Fed. 42 K3
Trakya *reg.* Europe *see* **Thrace**

Tralee Ireland 51 C5
Tralee Bay Ireland 51 C5
Trá Li Ireland *see* **Tralee**
Tramandaí Brazil 145 A5
Tramán Tepuí *mt.* Venez. 142 F2
Trá Mhór Ireland *see* **Tramore**
Tramore Ireland 51 E5
Tranås Sweden 45 I7
Trancas Arg. 144 C3
Trancoso Brazil 145 D2
Tranemo Sweden 45 H8
Tranent U.K. 50 G5
Trang Thai. 71 B6
Trangan *i.* Indon. 108 F1
Trangie Australia 112 C4
Trân Ninh, Cao Nguyên Laos 70 C3
Transantarctic Mountains Antarctica 152 H2
Trans Canada Highway Canada 121 H5
Transylvanian Alps *mts* Romania 59 J2
Transylvanian Basin *plat.* Romania 59 K1
Trapani *Sicily* Italy 58 E5
Trapezus Turkey *see* **Trabzon**
Trapper Peak U.S.A. 126 E3
Trappes France 52 C6
Traralgon Australia 112 C7
Trashigang Bhutan *see* **Tashigang**
Trasimeno, Lago *l.* Italy 58 E3
Trasvase, Canal de Spain 57 E4
Trat Thai. 71 C4
Traunsee *l.* Austria 47 N7
Traunstein Germany 47 N7
Travellers Lake *imp. l.* Australia 111 C7
Travers, Mount N.Z. 113 D6
Traverse City U.S.A. 134 C1
Tra Vinh Vietnam 71 D5
Travnik Bos.-Herz. 58 G2
Trbovlje Slovenia 58 F1
Tre, Hon *i.* Vietnam 71 E4
Treasury Islands Solomon Is 106 F2
Trebbin Germany 53 N2
Trebevič *nat. park* Bos.-Herz. 58 H3
Třebíč Czech Rep. 47 O6
Trebinje Bos.-Herz. 58 H3
Trebišov Slovakia 43 D6
Trebizond Turkey *see* **Trabzon**
Trebnje Slovenia 58 F2
Trebur Germany 53 I5
Tree Island India 84 B4
Trefaldwyn U.K. *see* **Montgomery**
Treffurt Germany 53 K3
Treffynnon U.K. *see* **Holywell**
Trefyclawdd U.K. *see* **Knighton**
Trefynwy U.K. *see* **Monmouth**
Tregosse Islets and Reefs Australia 110 E3
Treinta y Tres Uruguay 144 F4
Trelew Arg. 144 C6
Trelleborg Sweden 45 H9
Trélon France 52 E4
Tremblant, Mont *hill* Canada 122 G5
Trembleur Lake Canada 120 E4
Tremiti, Isole *is* Italy 58 F3
Tremont U.S.A. 135 G3
Tremonton U.S.A. 126 E4
Tremp Spain 57 G2
Trenance U.K. 49 B8
Trenary U.S.A. 132 C2
Trenche *r.* Canada 123 G5
Trenčín Slovakia 47 Q6
Trendelburg Germany 53 J3
Trêng Cambodia 71 C4
Trenque Lauquén Arg. 144 D5
Trent Italy *see* **Trento**
Trent *r.* U.K. 49 G5
Trento Italy 58 D1
Trenton Canada 135 G1
Trenton *FL* U.S.A. 133 D6
Trenton *GA* U.S.A. 133 C5
Trenton *KY* U.S.A. 134 B5
Trenton *MO* U.S.A. 130 E3
Trenton *NC* U.S.A. 133 E5
Trenton *NE* U.S.A. 130 C3

▶**Trenton** *NJ* U.S.A. 135 H3
Capital of New Jersey.

Treorchy U.K. 49 D7
Trepassey Canada 123 L5
Tres Arroyos Arg. 144 D5
Tresco *i.* U.K. 49 A9
Três Corações Brazil 145 B3
Tres Esquinas Col. 142 C3
Tres Forcas, Cabo *c.* Morocco *see* **Trois Fourches, Cap des**
Três Lagoas Brazil 145 A3
Três Marias, Represa *resr* Brazil 145 B2
Tres Picachos, Sierra *mts* Mex. 127 G7
Tres Picos, Cerro *mt.* Arg. 144 D5
Três Pontas Brazil 145 B3
Tres Puntas, Cabo *c.* Arg. 144 C7
Três Rios Brazil 145 C3
Tretten Norway 45 G6
Tretyy Severnyy Rus. Fed. *see* **3-y Severnyy**
Treuchtlingen Germany 53 K6
Treuenbrietzen Germany 53 M2
Treungen Norway 45 F7
Treves Germany *see* **Trier**
Treviglio Italy 58 C2
Treviso Italy 58 E2
Trevose Head *hd* U.K. 49 B8
Tri An, Hô *resr* Vietnam 71 D5
Triánda Greece *see* **Trianta**
Triangle U.S.A. 135 G4
Trianta Greece 59 M6
Tribal Areas *admin. div.* Pak. 89 H3
Tri Brata, Gora *hill* Rus. Fed. 74 F1
Tribune U.S.A. 130 C4
Tricase Italy 58 H5
Trichinopoly India *see* **Tiruchchirappalli**
Trichur India 84 C4
Tricot France 52 C5
Trida Australia 112 B4
Tridentum Italy *see* **Trento**
Trier Germany 52 G5
Trieste Italy 58 E2
Trieste, Golfo di *g.* Europe *see* **Trieste, Gulf of**
Trieste, Gulf of Europe 58 E2
Triglav *mt.* Slovenia 58 E1

Triglavski narodni park *nat. park* Slovenia 58 E1
Trikala Greece 59 I5
Trikkala Greece *see* **Trikala**

▶**Trikora, Puncak** *mt.* Indon. 69 J7
2nd highest mountain in Oceania.

Trim Ireland 51 F4
Trincomalee Sri Lanka 84 D4
Trindade Brazil 145 A2
Trindade, Ilha da *i.* S. Atlantic Ocean 148 G7
Trinidad Bol. 142 F6
Trinidad Cuba 137 I4
Trinidad *i.* Trin. and Tob. 137 L6
Trinidad Uruguay 144 E4
Trinidad U.S.A. 127 G5
Trinidad *country* West Indies *see* **Trinidad and Tobago**
Trinidad and Tobago *country* West Indies 137 L6
Trinity U.S.A. 131 E6
Trinity *r. CA* U.S.A. 126 B1
Trinity *r. TX* U.S.A. 131 E6
Trinity Bay Canada 123 L5
Trinity Islands U.S.A. 118 C4
Trinity Range *mts* U.S.A. 128 D1
Trinkat Island India 71 A5
Trionto, Capo *c.* Italy 58 G5
Tripa *r.* Indon. 71 B7
Tripkau Germany 53 L1
Tripoli Greece 59 J6
Tripoli Lebanon 85 B2

▶**Tripoli** Libya 97 E1
Capital of Libya.

Trípolis Greece *see* **Tripoli**
Tripolis Lebanon *see* **Tripoli**
Tripunittura India 84 C4
Tripura *state* India 83 G5

▶**Tristan da Cunha** *i.* S. Atlantic Ocean 148 H8
Dependency of St Helena.

Trisul *mt.* India 82 D3
Triton Canada 123 L4
Triton Island *atoll* Paracel Is 68 E3
Trittau Germany 53 K1
Trittenheim Germany 52 G5
Trivandrum India 84 C4
Trivento Italy 58 F4
Trnava Slovakia 47 P6
Trobriand Islands P.N.G. 106 F2
Trochu Canada 120 H5
Trofors Norway 44 H4
Trogir Croatia 58 G3
Troia Italy 58 F4
Troisdorf Germany 53 H4
Trois Fourches, Cap des *c.* Morocco 57 E6
Trois-Ponts Belgium 52 F4
Trois-Rivières Canada 123 G5
Troitsko-Pechorsk Rus. Fed. 41 R3
Troitskoye *Altayskiy Kray* Rus. Fed. 72 E2
Troitskoye *Khabarovskiy Kray* Rus. Fed. 74 E2
Troitskoye *Respublika Kalmykiya - Khalm'g-Tangch* Rus. Fed. 43 J7
Troll *research stn* 152 B2
Trollhättan Sweden 45 H7
Trombetas *r.* Brazil 143 G4
Tromelin, Île *i.* Indian Ocean 149 L7
Tromelin Island Micronesia *see* **Fais**
Tromen, Volcán *vol.* Arg. 144 B5
Tromie *r.* U.K. 50 E3
Trompsburg S. Africa 101 G6
Tromsø Norway 44 K2
Trona U.S.A. 128 E4
Tronador, Monte *mt.* Arg. 144 B6
Trondheim Norway 44 G5
Trondheimsfjorden *sea chan.* Norway 44 F5
Trongsa Bhutan *see* **Tongsa**
Troödos, Mount Cyprus 85 A2
Troödos Mountains Cyprus 85 A2
Troon U.K. 50 E5
Tropeiros, Serra dos *hills* Brazil 145 B1
Tropic U.S.A. 129 G3
Tropic of Cancer 131 B8
Tropic of Capricorn 110 G4
Trosh Rus. Fed. 42 L2
Trostan *hill* U.K. 51 F2
Trout *r. B.C.* Canada 120 E3
Trout *r. N.W.T.* Canada 120 G2
Trout Lake *Alta* Canada 120 H3
Trout Lake *N.W.T.* Canada 120 F2
Trout Lake *l. N.W.T.* Canada 120 F2
Trout Lake *l. Ont.* Canada 121 M5
Trout Peak U.S.A. 126 F3
Trout Run U.S.A. 135 G3
Trouville-sur-Mer France 49 H9
Trowbridge U.K. 49 E7
Troy *tourist site* Turkey 59 L5
Troy *AL* U.S.A. 133 C6
Troy *KS* U.S.A. 130 E4
Troy *MI* U.S.A. 134 D2
Troy *MO* U.S.A. 130 F4
Troy *MT* U.S.A. 126 E2
Troy *NH* U.S.A. 135 I2
Troy *NY* U.S.A. 135 I2
Troy *OH* U.S.A. 134 C3
Troy *PA* U.S.A. 135 G3
Troyan Bulg. 59 K3
Troyes France 56 G2
Troy Lake U.S.A. 128 E4
Troy Peak U.S.A. 129 F2
Trstenik Serbia 59 I3
Truc Giang Vietnam *see* **Bên Tre**
Trucial Coast *country* Asia *see* **United Arab Emirates**
Trucial States *country* Asia *see* **United Arab Emirates**
Trud Rus. Fed. 42 G4
Trufanovo Rus. Fed. 42 J2
Trujillo Hond. 137 G5
Trujillo Peru 142 C5
Trujillo Spain 57 D4
Trujillo Venez. 142 D2
Trujillo, Monte *mt.* Dom. Rep. *see* **Duarte, Pico**
Truk *is* Micronesia *see* **Chuuk**

Trulben Germany 53 H5
Trumbull, Mount U.S.A. 129 G3
Trumon Indon. 71 B7
Trundle Australia 112 C4
Trưng Hiệp Vietnam 70 D4
Trung Khanh Vietnam 70 D2
Truong Sa *is* S. China Sea *see* **Spratly Islands**
Truro Canada 123 J5
Truro U.K. 49 B8
Truskmore *hill* Ireland 51 D3
Trutch Canada 120 F3
Truth or Consequences U.S.A. 127 G6
Trutnov Czech Rep. 47 O5
Truuli Peak U.S.A. 118 C4
Truva *tourist site* Turkey *see* **Troy**
Trypiti, Akra *pt Kriti* Greece *see* **Trypiti, Akrotirio**
Trypiti, Akrotirio *pt* Greece 59 K7
Trysil Norway 45 H6
Trzebiatów Poland 47 O3
Tsagaannuur Mongolia 80 G2
Tsagaan-Uul Mongolia 80 I2
Tsagan Aman Rus. Fed. 43 J7
Tsagan-Nur Rus. Fed. 43 J7
Tsaidam Basin China *see* **Qaidam Pendi**
Tsaka La *pass* China/India 82 D2
Tsalenjikha Georgia 91 F2
Tsaratanana, Massif du *mts* Madag. 99 E5
Tsarevo Bulg. 59 L3
Tsaris Mountains Namibia 100 C3
Tsaritsyn Rus. Fed. *see* **Volgograd**
Tsaukaib Namibia 100 B4
Tsavo East National Park Kenya 98 D4
Tsavo West National Park Africa 98 D3
Tsefat Israel *see* **Ẕefat**
Tselinograd Kazakh. *see* **Astana**
Tsenhermandal Mongolia 73 J3
Tsenogora Rus. Fed. 42 J2
Tses Namibia 100 D3
Tsetseg Mongolia 80 H2
Tsetseng Botswana 100 F2
Tsetserleg *Arhangay* Mongolia 80 J2
Tsetserleg Mongolia 80 I2
Tshabong Botswana 100 F4
Tshad *country* Africa *see* **Chad**
Tshane Botswana 100 E3
Tshela Dem. Rep. Congo 99 B4
Tshibala Dem. Rep. Congo 99 C4
Tshikapa Dem. Rep. Congo 99 C4
Tshing S. Africa 101 H4
Tshipise S. Africa 101 J2
Tshitanzu Dem. Rep. Congo 99 C4
Tshofa Dem. Rep. Congo 99 C4
Tshokwane S. Africa 101 J3
Tsholotsho Zimbabwe 99 C5
Tshootsha Botswana 100 E2
Tshuapa *r.* Dem. Rep. Congo 97 F5
Tshwane S. Africa *see* **Pretoria**
Tsil'ma *r.* Rus. Fed. 42 K2
Tsimlyansk Rus. Fed. 43 I7
Tsimlyanskoye Vodokhranilishche *resr* Rus. Fed. 43 I7
Tsimmermanovka Rus. Fed. 74 E2
Tsinan China *see* **Jinan**
Tsineng S. Africa 100 F4
Tsinghai *prov.* China *see* **Qinghai**
Tsing Shan Wan *H.K.* China *see* **Castle Peak Bay**
Tsingtao China *see* **Qingdao**
Tsing Yi *i. H.K.* China 77 [inset]
Tsining China *see* **Jining**
Tsiombe Madag. 99 E6
Tsiroanomandidy Madag. 99 E5
Tsitsihar China *see* **Qiqihar**
Tsitsikamma Forest and Coastal National Park S. Africa 100 F8
Tsitsutl Peak Canada 120 E4
Tsivil'sk Rus. Fed. 42 J5
Tskhaltubo Georgia *see* **Tsqaltubo**
Ts'khinvali Georgia 91 F2
Tsna *r.* Rus. Fed. 43 I5
Tsnori Georgia 91 G2
Tsokar Chumo *l.* India 82 D2
Tsolo S. Africa 101 I6
Tsomo S. Africa 101 H7
Tsona China *see* **Cona**
Tsqaltubo Georgia 91 F2
Tsu Japan 75 E6
Tsuchiura Japan 75 F5
Tsuen Wan *H.K.* China 77 [inset]
Tsugarū-kaikyō *strait* Japan 74 F4
Tsugaru Strait Japan *see* **Tsugarū-kaikyō**
Tsumeb Namibia 99 B5
Tsumis Park Namibia 100 C2
Tsumkwe Namibia 99 C5
Tsuruga Japan 75 E6
Tsurugi-san *mt.* Japan 75 D6
Tsurukhaytuy Rus. Fed. *see* **Priargunsk**
Tsuruoka Japan 75 E5
Tsushima *is* Japan 75 C6
Tsushima-kaikyō *strait* Japan/S. Korea *see* **Korea Strait**
Tsuyama Japan 75 D6
Tswaane Botswana 100 E2
Tswaraganang S. Africa 101 G5
Tswelelang S. Africa 101 G4
Tsyelyakhany Belarus 45 N10
Tsyp-Navolok Rus. Fed. 44 R2
Tsyurupyns'k Ukr. 59 O1
Tthenaagoo Canada *see* **Nahanni Butte**
Tua Dem. Rep. Congo 98 B4
Tual Indon. 69 I8
Tuam Ireland 51 D4
Tuamotu, Archipel des *is* Fr. Polynesia *see* **Tuamotu Islands**
Tuamotu Islands Fr. Polynesia 151 K6
Tuân Giao Vietnam 70 C2
Tuangku *i.* Indon. 71 B7
Tuapse Rus. Fed. 90 E1
Tuas Sing. 71 [inset]
Tuath, Loch a' *b.* U.K. 50 C2
Tuba City U.S.A. 129 H3
Tubarão Brazil 145 A5
Tubarjal Saudi Arabia 85 D4
Tübingen Germany 47 L6
Tubmanburg Liberia 96 B4
Tubruq Libya 90 A4
Tubuai *i.* Fr. Polynesia 151 K7
Tubuai Islands Fr. Polynesia 151 J7
Tucano Brazil 143 K6
Tucavaca Bol. 143 G7

Tüchen Germany 53 M1
Tuchheim Germany 53 M2
Tuchitua Canada 120 D2
Tuchodi *r.* Canada 120 F3
Tuckerton U.S.A. 135 H4
Tucopia *i.* Solomon Is *see* **Tikopia**
Tucson U.S.A. 129 H5
Tucson Mountains U.S.A. 129 H5
Tuctuc *r.* Canada 123 I2
Tucumán Arg. *see* **San Miguel de Tucumán**
Tucumcari U.S.A. 131 C5
Tucupita Venez. 142 F2
Tucuruí Brazil 143 I4
Tucuruí, Represa *resr* Brazil 143 I4
Tudela Spain 57 F2
Tuder Italy *see* **Todi**
Tüdevtey Mongolia 80 I2
Tuela *r.* Port. 57 C3
Tuen Mun *H.K.* China 77 [inset]
Tuensang India 83 H4
Tufts Abyssal Plain *sea feature* N. Pacific Ocean 151 K2
Tugela *r.* S. Africa 101 J5
Tuglung China 76 B2
Tuguegarao Phil. 69 G3
Tugur Rus. Fed. 74 E1
Tuhemberua Indon. 71 B7
Tujiabu China *see* **Yongxiu**
Tukangbesi, Kepulauan *is* Indon. 69 G8
Tukarak Island Canada 122 F2
Ţukhmān, Banī *reg.* Saudi Arabia 88 C6
Tukituki *r.* N.Z. 113 F4
Tuktoyaktuk Canada 118 E3
Tuktut Nogait National Park Canada 118 F3
Tukums Latvia 45 M8
Tukuringra, Khrebet *mts* Rus. Fed. 74 B1
Tukuyu Tanz. 99 D4
Tula Rus. Fed. 43 H5
Tulach Mhór Ireland *see* **Tullamore**
Tulagt Ar Gol *r.* China 83 H1
Tulak Afgh. 89 F3
Tulameen Canada 120 F5
Tula Mountains Antarctica 152 D2
Tulancingo Mex. 136 E4
Tulare U.S.A. 128 D3
Tulare Lake Bed U.S.A. 128 D4
Tularosa Mountains U.S.A. 129 I5
Tulasi *mt.* India 84 D2
Tulbagh S. Africa 100 D7
Tulcán Ecuador 142 C3
Tulcea Romania 59 M2
Tule *r.* U.S.A. 131 C5
Tuléar Madag. *see* **Toliara**
Tulemalu Lake Canada 121 L2
Tulia U.S.A. 131 C5
Tulihe China 74 A2
Tulita Canada 120 E1
Ţulkarem West Bank *see* **Ţūlkarm**
Ţūlkarm West Bank 85 B3
Tulla Ireland 51 D5
Tullahoma U.S.A. 132 C5
Tullamore Australia 112 C4
Tullamore Ireland 51 E4
Tulle France 56 E4
Tulleråsen Sweden 44 I5
Tullibigeal Australia 112 C4
Tullow Ireland 51 F5
Tully Australia 110 D3
Tully *r.* Australia 110 D3
Tully U.K. 51 E3
Tulos Rus. Fed. 44 Q5
Tulqarem West Bank *see* **Ţūlkarm**
Tulsa U.S.A. 131 E4
Tulsipur Nepal 83 E3
Tuluá Col. 142 C3
Tuluksak U.S.A. 153 B2
Tulūl al Ashāqif *hills* Jordan 85 C3
Tulun Rus. Fed. 72 I2
Tulu-Tuloi, Serra *hills* Brazil 142 F3
Tulu Welel *mt.* Eth. 98 D3
Tuma Rus. Fed. 43 I5
Tumaco Col. 142 C3
Tumahole S. Africa 101 H4
Tumain China 83 G2
Tumannyy Rus. Fed. 44 S2
Tumasik Sing. *see* **Singapore**
Tumba Dem. Rep. Congo 98 C4
Tumba Sweden 45 J7
Tumba, Lac *l.* Dem. Rep. Congo 98 B4
Tumbarumba Australia 112 D5
Tumbes Peru 142 B4
Tumbler Ridge Canada 120 F4
Tumby Bay Australia 111 B7
Tumcha *r.* Fin./Rus. Fed. 44 Q3 *also known as Tuntsajoki*
Tumen *Jilin* China 74 C4
Tumen *Shaanxi* China 77 F1
Tumereng Guyana 142 F2
Tumindao *i.* Phil. 68 F6
Tumiritinga Brazil 145 C2
Tumkur India 84 C3
Tummel *r.* U.K. 50 F4
Tummel, Loch *l.* U.K. 50 F4
Tumnin *r.* Rus. Fed. 74 F2
Tump Pak. 89 F5
Tumpat Malaysia 71 C6
Tumpôr, Phnum *mt.* Cambodia 71 C4
Tumshuk Uzbek. 89 G2
Tumu Ghana 96 C3
Tumucumaque, Serra *hills* Brazil 143 G3
Tumudibandh India 84 D2
Tumut Australia 112 D5
Tuna India 82 B5
Ţunb al Kubrá *i.* The Gulf *see* **Greater Tunb**
Ţunb aş Şughrá *i.* The Gulf *see* **Lesser Tunb**
Tunbridge Wells, Royal U.K. 49 H7
Tunceli Turkey 91 E3
Tunchang China 77 F5
Tuncurry Australia 112 F4
Tundun-Wada Nigeria 96 D3
Tunduru Tanz. 99 D5
Tunes Tunisia *see* **Tunis**
Tunga Nigeria 96 D4
Tungabhadra Reservoir India 84 C3
Tungi Bangl. 83 G5
Tung Lung Island *H.K.* China 77 [inset]
Tungnaá *r.* Iceland 44 [inset]
Tungor Rus. Fed. 74 F1

Tung Pok Liu Hoi Hap H.K. China see East Lamma Channel
T'ung-shan Jiangsu China see Xuzhou
Tung-sheng Nei Mongol China see Ordos
Tungsten (abandoned) Canada 120 D2
Tung Wan b. H.K. China 77 [inset]
Tuni India 84 D2
Tunica U.S.A. 131 F5
Tūnis country Africa see Tunisia
▶Tunis Tunisia 58 D6
Capital of Tunisia.
Tunis, Golfe de g. Tunisia 58 D6
Tunisia country Africa 54 F5
Tunja Col. 142 D2
Tunkhannock U.S.A. 135 H3
Tunnsjøen l. Norway 44 H4
Tunstall U.K. 49 I6
Tuntsa Fin. 44 P3
Tuntsajoki r. Fin./Rus. Fed. see Tumcha
Tunulic r. Canada 123 I2
Tununak U.S.A. 118 B3
Tunungayualok Island Canada 123 J2
Tunxi China see Huangshan
Tuodian China see Shuangbai
Tuojiang China see Fenghuang
Tuŏl Khpos Cambodia 71 D5
Tuoniang Jiang r. China 76 E3
Tuotuo He r. China see Togton He
Tuotuoheyan China see Tanggulashan
Tüp Kyrg. 80 E3
Tupã Brazil 145 A3
Tupelo U.S.A. 131 F5
Tupik Rus. Fed. 73 L2
Tupinambarama, Ilha i. Brazil 143 G4
Tupiraçaba Brazil 145 A1
Tupiza Bol. 142 E8
Tupper Canada 120 F4
Tupper Lake U.S.A. 135 H1
Tupper Lake l. U.S.A. 135 H1
Tüpqaraghan Tübegi pen. Kazakh. see Mangyshlak, Poluostrov
▶Tupungato, Cerro mt. Arg./Chile 144 C4
5th highest mountain in South America.
Tuqayyid well Iraq 88 B4
Tuquan China 73 M3
Tuqu Wan b. China see Lingshui Wan
Tura China 83 F1
Tura India 83 G4
Tura Rus. Fed. 65 L3
Turabah Saudi Arabia 86 F5
Turakina N.Z. 113 E5
Turan Rus. Fed. 72 G2
Turana, Khrebet mts Rus. Fed. 74 C2
Turan Lowland Asia 80 A4
Turan Oypaty lowland Asia see Turan Lowland
Turan Pasttekisligi lowland Asia see Turan Lowland
Turan Pesligi lowland Asia see Turan Lowland
Turanskaya Nizmennost' lowland Asia see Turan Lowland
Ţurāq al 'Ilab hills Syria 85 D3
Turar Ryskulov Kazakh. 80 D3
Tura-Ryskulova Kazakh. see Turar Ryskulov
Ţurayf Saudi Arabia 85 D4
Turba Estonia 45 N7
Turbat Pak. 89 F5
Turbo Col. 142 C2
Turda Romania 59 J1
Türeh Iran 88 C3
Turfan China see Turpan
Turfan Basin depr. China see Turpan Pendi
Turfan Depression China see Turpan Pendi
Turgay Kazakh. 80 B2
Turgayskaya Dolina valley Kazakh. 80 B2
Türgovishte Bulg. 59 L3
Turgutlu Turkey 59 L5
Turhal Turkey 90 E2
Türi Estonia 45 N7
Turia r. Spain 57 F4
Turin Canada 121 H5
Turin Italy 58 B2
Turiy Rog Rus. Fed. 74 C3
▶Turkana, Lake salt l. Eth./Kenya 98 D3
5th largest lake in Africa.
Turkestan Kazakh. 80 C3
Turkestan Range mts Asia 89 G2
Turkey country Asia/Europe 90 D3
Turkey U.S.A. 134 D5
Turkey r. U.S.A. 130 F3
Turki Rus. Fed. 43 I6
Türkistan Kazakh. see Turkestan
Türkiye country Asia/Europe see Turkey
Türkmenabat Turkm. 89 F2
Türkmen Adasy i. Turkm. see Ogurjaly Adasy
Türkmen Aylagy b. Turkm. see Türkmen Aýlagy
Türkmen Aýlagy b. Turkm. 88 D2
Türkmenbaşy Turkm. 88 D1
Türkmenbaşy Aylagy b. Turkm. see Türkmenbaşy Aýlagy
Türkmenbaşy Aýlagy b. Turkm. 88 D2
Türkmenbaşy Döwlet Gorugy nature res. Turkm. 88 D2
Türkmen Dağı mt. Turkey 59 N5
Turkmenistan country Asia 87 I2
Turkmeniya country Asia see Turkmenistan
Türkmenostan country Asia see Turkmenistan
Turkmenskaya S.S.R. country Asia see Turkmenistan
Türkoğlu Turkey 90 E3
▶Turks and Caicos Islands terr. West Indies 137 J4
United Kingdom Overseas Territory.
Turks Island Passage Turks and Caicos Is 133 G8
Turks Islands Turks and Caicos Is 137 J4
Turku Fin. 45 M6
Turkwel watercourse Kenya 98 D3
Turlock U.S.A. 128 C3
Turlock Lake U.S.A. 128 C3
Turmalina Brazil 145 C2
Turnagain r. Canada 120 E3
Turnagain, Cape N.Z. 113 F5
Turnberry U.K. 50 E5
Turnbull, Mount U.S.A. 129 H5
Turneffe Islands atoll Belize 136 G5
Turner U.S.A. 134 D1
Turner Valley Canada 120 H5
Turnhout Belgium 52 E3
Turnor Lake Canada 121 I3
Tŭrnovo Bulg. see Veliko Tŭrnovo
Turnu Măgurele Romania 59 K3
Turnu Severin Romania see Drobeta-Turnu Severin
Turon r. Australia 112 D4
Turones France see Tours
Turovets Rus. Fed. 42 I4
Turpan China 80 G3
▶Turpan Pendi depr. China 80 G3
Lowest point in northern Asia.
Turquino, Pico mt. Cuba 137 I4
Turriff U.K. 50 G3
Turris Libisonis Sardinia Italy see Porto Torres
Tursāq Iraq 91 G4
Turtle Island Fiji see Vatoa
Turtle Lake Canada 121 I4
Turugart Pass China/Kyrg. 80 E3
Turugart Shankou pass China/Kyrg. see Turugart Pass
Turuvanur India 84 C3
Turvo r. Brazil 145 A2
Turvo r. Brazil 145 A2
Tusayan U.S.A. 129 G4
Tuscaloosa U.S.A. 133 C5
Tuscarawas r. U.S.A. 134 E3
Tuscarora Mountains hills U.S.A. 135 G3
Tuscola IL U.S.A. 130 F4
Tuscola TX U.S.A. 131 D5
Tuscumbia U.S.A. 133 C5
Tuskegee U.S.A. 133 C5
Tussey Mountains hills U.S.A. 135 F3
Tustin U.S.A. 134 C1
Tutak Turkey 91 F3
Tutayev Rus. Fed. 42 H4
Tutera Spain see Tudela
Tuticorin India 84 C4
Tutong Brunei 68 E6
Tuttle Creek Reservoir U.S.A. 130 D4
Tuttlingen Germany 47 L7
Tuttut Nunaat reg. Greenland 119 P2
Tutuala East Timor 108 D2
Tutubu P.N.G. 110 E1
Tutubu Tanz. 99 D4
Tutuila i. American Samoa 107 I3
Tutume Botswana 99 C6
Tutwiler U.S.A. 131 F5
Tuun-bong mt. N. Korea 74 B4
Tuupovaara Fin. 44 Q5
Tuusniemi Fin. 44 P5
Tuvalu country S. Pacific Ocean 107 H2
Tuwayq, Jabal hills Saudi Arabia 86 G4
Tuwayq, Jabal mts Saudi Arabia 86 G5
Ţuwayyil ash Shihāq mt. Jordan 85 C4
Tuwwal Saudi Arabia 86 E5
Tuxpan Mex. 136 E4
Tuxtla Gutiérrez Mex. 136 F5
Tuya Lake Canada 120 D3
Tuyên Quang Vietnam 70 D2
Tuy Hoa Vietnam 71 E4
Tuz, Lake salt l. Turkey 90 D3
Tuz Gölü salt l. Turkey see Tuz, Lake
Tuzha Rus. Fed. 42 J4
Tuz Khurmātū Iraq 91 G4
Tuzla Bos.-Herz. 58 H2
Tuzla Turkey 85 B1
Tuzla Gölü lag. Turkey 59 L4
Tuzlov r. Rus. Fed. 43 I7
Tuzu r. Myanmar 70 A1
Tvedestrand Norway 45 F7
Tver' Rus. Fed. 42 G4
Twain Harte U.S.A. 128 C2
Tweed Canada 135 G1
Tweed r. U.K. 50 G5
Tweed Heads Australia 112 F2
Tweedie Canada 121 I4
Tweefontein S. Africa 100 D7
Twee Rivier Namibia 100 D3
Twentekanaal canal Neth. 52 G2
Twentynine Palms U.S.A. 128 E4
Twin Bridges CA U.S.A. 128 C2
Twin Bridges MT U.S.A. 126 E3
Twin Buttes Reservoir U.S.A. 131 C6
Twin Falls Canada 123 I3
Twin Falls U.S.A. 126 E4
Twin Heads hill Australia 108 D5
Twin Peak U.S.A. 128 C2
Twistringen Germany 53 I2
Twitchen Reservoir U.S.A. 128 C4
Twitya r. Canada 120 D1
Twizel Canterbury 113 C7
Twofold Bay Australia 112 D6
Two Harbors U.S.A. 130 F2
Two Hills Canada 121 I4
Two Rivers U.S.A. 134 B1
Tyan' Shan' mts China/Kyrg. see Tien Shan
Tyao r. India/Myanmar 76 B4
Tyatya, Vulkan vol. Rus. Fed. 74 G3
Tydal Norway 44 G5
Tygart Valley U.S.A. 134 F4
Tygda Rus. Fed. 74 B1
Tygda r. Rus. Fed. 74 B1
Tyler U.S.A. 131 E5
Tylertown U.S.A. 131 F6
Tym' r. Rus. Fed. 74 F2
Tymovskoye Rus. Fed. 74 F2
Tynda Rus. Fed. 73 M1
Tyndall U.S.A. 130 D3
Tyndinskiy Rus. Fed. see Tynda
Tyne r. U.K. 50 G4
Tynemouth U.K. 48 F3
Tynset Norway 44 G5
Tyoploozyorsk Rus. Fed. see Teploozersk
Tyoploye Ozero Rus. Fed. see Teploozersk
Tyr Lebanon see Tyre
Tyras Ukr. see Bilhorod-Dnistrovs'kyy
Tyre Lebanon 85 B3
Tyree, Mount Antarctica 152 L1
Tyrma Rus. Fed. 74 D2
Tyrma r. Rus. Fed. 74 C2
Tyrnävä Fin. 44 N4
Tyrnavos Greece 59 J5
Tyrnyauz Rus. Fed. 91 F2
Tyrone U.S.A. 135 F3
Tyrrell r. Australia 112 A5
Tyrrell, Lake dry lake Australia 111 C7
Tyrrell Lake Canada 121 J2
Tyrrhenian Sea France/Italy 58 D4
Tyrus Lebanon see Tyre
Tysa r. Serbia see Tisa
Tyukalinsk Rus. Fed. 64 I4
Tyulen'i Ostrova is Kazakh. 91 H1
Tyumen' Rus. Fed. 64 H4
Tyup Kyrg. see Tüp
Tyuratam Kazakh. see Baykonyr
Tywi r. U.K. 49 C7
Tywyn U.K. 49 C6
Tzaneen S. Africa 101 J2
Tzia i. Greece 59 K6

Uaco Congo Angola see Waku-Kungo
Ualan atoll Micronesia see Kosrae
Uamanda Angola 99 C5
Uarc, Ras c. Morocco see Trois Fourches, Cap des
Uaroo Australia 109 A5
Uatumã r. Brazil 143 G4
Uauá Brazil 143 K5
Uaupés r. Brazil 142 E3
U'aylī, Wādī al watercourse Saudi Arabia 85 D4
U'aywij well Saudi Arabia 88 B4
U'aywij, Wādī al watercourse Saudi Arabia 91 F5
Ubá Brazil 145 C3
Ubaí Brazil 145 B2
Ubaitaba Brazil 145 D1
Ubangi r. Cent. Afr. Rep./Dem. Rep. Congo 98 B4
Ubangi-Shari country Africa see Central African Republic
Ubauro Pak. 89 H4
Ubayyiḑ, Wādī al watercourse Iraq/Saudi Arabia 91 F4
Ube Japan 75 C6
Úbeda Spain 57 E4
Uberaba Brazil 145 B2
Uberlândia Brazil 145 A2
Ubin, Pulau i. Sing. 71 [inset]
Ubly U.S.A. 134 D2
Ubolratna, Ang Kep Nam Thai. 70 C3
Ubombo S. Africa 101 K4
Ubon Ratchathani Thai. 70 D4
Ubstadt-Weiher Germany 53 I5
Ubundu Dem. Rep. Congo 97 F5
Üçajy Turkm. 89 F2
Ucar Azer. 91 G2
Uçarı Turkey 85 A1
Ucayali r. Peru 142 D4
Uch Pak. 89 H4
Üchajy Turkm. see Üçajy
Üchān Iran 88 C2
Ucharal Kazakh. 80 F2
Uchiura-wan b. Japan 74 F4
Uchkeken Rus. Fed. 91 F2
Uchkuduk Uzbek. see Uchquduq
Uchquduq Uzbek. 80 B3
Uchte Germany 53 I2
Uchte r. Germany 53 L2
Uchto r. Pak. 89 G5
Uchur r. Rus. Fed. 65 O4
Uckermark reg. Germany 53 N1
Uckfield U.K. 49 H8
Ucluelet Canada 120 E5
Ucross U.S.A. 126 G3
Uda r. Rus. Fed. 73 J2
Uda r. Rus. Fed. 74 D1
Udachnoye Rus. Fed. 43 J7
Udachnyy Rus. Fed. 153 E2
Udagamandalam India 84 C4
Udaipur Rajasthan India 82 C4
Udaipur Tripura India 83 G5
Udanti r. India/Myanmar 83 E5
Uday r. Ukr. 43 G6
'Udaynān well Saudi Arabia 88 C6
Uddevalla Sweden 45 G7
Uddingston U.K. 50 E5
Uddjaure l. Sweden 44 J4
'Udeid, Khōr al inlet Qatar 88 C5
Uden Neth. 52 F3
Udgir India 84 C2
Udhagamandalam India see Udagamandalam
Udhampur India 82 C2
Udia-Milai atoll Marshall Is see Bikini
Udimskiy Rus. Fed. 42 J3
Udine Italy 58 E1
Udit India 89 I5
Udjuktok Bay Canada 123 J3
Udmalaippettai India see Udumalaippettai
Udomlya Rus. Fed. 42 G4
Udon Thani Thai. 70 C3
Udskaya Guba b. Rus. Fed. 65 O4
Udskoye Rus. Fed. 74 D1
Udumalaippettai India 84 C4
Udupi India 84 B3
Udyl', Ozero l. Rus. Fed. 74 E1
Udzhary Azer. see Ucar
Udzungwa Mountains National Park Tanz. 99 D4
Uéa atoll New Caledonia see Ouvéa
Ueckermünde Germany 47 O4
Ueda Japan 75 E5
Uele r. Dem. Rep. Congo 98 C3
Uelen Rus. Fed. 65 U3
Uelzen Germany 53 K2
Uetersen Germany 53 J1
Uettingen Germany 53 J5
Uetze Germany 53 K2
Ufa Rus. Fed. 41 R5
Ufa r. Rus. Fed. 41 R5
Uffenheim Germany 53 K5
Uftyuga r. Rus. Fed. 42 J3
Ugab watercourse Namibia 99 B6
Ugalla r. Tanz. 99 D4
Uganda country Africa 98 D3
Ugie S. Africa 101 I6
Ūgīnak Iran 89 F5
Uglegorsk Rus. Fed. 74 F2
Uglich Rus. Fed. 42 H4
Ugljan i. Croatia 58 F2
Uglovoye Rus. Fed. 74 C2
Ugol'noye Rus. Fed. 65 P3
Ugolnyy Rus. Fed. see Beringovskiy
Ugol'nyye Kopi Rus. Fed. 65 S3
Ugra Rus. Fed. 43 G5
Uherské Hradiště Czech Rep. 47 P6
Úhlava r. Czech Rep. 53 N5
Uhrichsville U.S.A. 134 E3
Uibhist a' Deas i. U.K. see South Uist
Uibhist a' Tuath i. U.K. see North Uist
Uig U.K. 50 C3
Uíge Angola 99 B4
Ŭijŏngbu S. Korea 75 B5
Ŭiju N. Korea 75 B4
Uimaharju Fin. 44 Q5
Uinta Mountains U.S.A. 129 H1
Uis Mine Namibia 99 B6
Uitenhage S. Africa 101 G7
Uithoorn Neth. 52 E2
Uithuizen Neth. 52 G1
Uivak, Cape Canada 123 J2
Ujhani India 82 D4
Uji Japan 75 D6
Uji-guntō is Japan 75 C7
Ujiyamada Japan see Ise
Ujjain India 82 C5
Ujung Pandang Indon. see Makassar
Újvidék Serbia see Novi Sad
Ukal Sagar l. India 82 C5
Ukata Nigeria 96 D3
'Ukayrishah well Saudi Arabia 88 B5
uKhahlamba-Drakensberg Park nat. park S. Africa 101 I5
Ukholovo Rus. Fed. 43 I5
Ukhrul India 83 H4
Ukhta Respublika Kareliya Rus. Fed. see Kalevala
Ukhta Respublika Komi Rus. Fed. 42 L3
Ukiah CA U.S.A. 128 B2
Ukiah OR U.S.A. 126 D3
Ukkusiksalik National Park nat. park Nunavut 119 J3
Ukkusissat Greenland 119 M2
Ukmergė Lith. 45 N9
▶Ukraine country Europe 43 F6
2nd largest country in Europe.
Ukrainskaya S.S.R. country Europe see Ukraine
Ukrayina country Europe see Ukraine
Uku-jima i. Japan 75 C6
Ukwi Botswana 100 E2
Ukwi Pan salt pan Botswana 100 E2
Ulaanbaatar Mongolia see Ulan Bator
Ulaangom Mongolia 80 H2
Ulan Australia 112 D4
▶Ulan Bator Mongolia 72 J3
Capital of Mongolia.
Ulanbel' Kazakh. 80 D3
Ulan Erge Rus. Fed. 43 J7
Ulanhad China see Chifeng
Ulanhot China 74 A3
Ulan Hua China 73 K4
Ulan-Khol Rus. Fed. 43 J7
Ulan-Ude Rus. Fed. 73 J2
Ulan Ul Hu l. China 83 G2
Ulaş Turkey 90 E3
Ulawa Island Solomon Is 107 G2
Ulayyah reg. Saudi Arabia 88 B6
Ul'banskiy Zaliv b. Rus. Fed. 74 E1
Ulchin S. Korea 75 C5
Uldz r. Mongolia 73 L3
Uleåborg Fin. see Oulu
Ulefoss Norway 45 F7
Ülenurme Estonia 45 O7
Ulety Rus. Fed. 73 K2
Ulhasnagar India 84 B2
Uliastai China 73 L3
Uliastay Mongolia 80 I2
Uliatea i. Fr. Polynesia see Raiatea
Ulicoten Neth. 52 E3
Ulie atoll Micronesia see Woleai
Ulita r. Rus. Fed. 44 R2
Ulithi atoll Micronesia 69 J4
Ulladulla Australia 112 E5
Ullapool U.K. 50 D3
Ulla Ulla, Parque Nacional nat. park Bol. 142 E6
Ullava Fin. 44 M5
Ullersuaq c. Greenland 119 K2
Ullswater l. U.K. 48 E4
Ullŭng-do i. S. Korea 75 C5
Ulm Germany 47 L6
Ulmarra Australia 112 F2
Ulmen Germany 52 G4
Uloowaranie, Lake salt flat Australia 111 B5
Ulricehamn Sweden 45 H8
Ulrum Neth. 52 G1
Ulsan S. Korea 75 C6
Ulsberg Norway 44 F5
Ulster reg. Ireland/U.K. 51 E3
Ulster U.S.A. 135 G3
Ulster Canal Ireland/U.K. 51 E3
Ultima Australia 112 A5
Ulubat Gölü l. Turkey 59 M4
Ulubey Turkey 59 M5
Uluborlu Turkey 59 N5
Uludağ mt. Turkey 59 M4
Uludağ Milli Parkı nat. park Turkey 59 M4
Ulugqat China see Wuqia
Ulu Kali, Gunung mt. Malaysia 71 C7
Ulukhaktok Canada 118 G2
Ulukışla Turkey 90 D3
Ulundi S. Africa 101 J5
Ulungur Hu l. China 80 G2
Ulunkhan Rus. Fed. 73 K2
Uluqsaqtuuq Canada see Ulukhaktok
Uluṟu hill Australia 109 E6
Uluṟu-Kata Tjuṯa National Park Australia 109 E6
Uluru National Park Australia see Uluṟu-Kata Tjuṯa National Park
Ulutau Kazakh. see Ulytau
Ulutau, Gory mts Kazakh. see Ulytau, Gory
Uluyatır Turkey 85 C1
Ulva i. U.K. 50 C4
Ulvenhout Neth. 52 E3
Ulverston U.K. 48 D4
Ulvsjön Sweden 45 I6
Ül'yanov Kazakh. see Ul'yanovskiy
Ul'yanovsk Rus. Fed. 43 K5
Ul'yanovskiy Kazakh. 80 D1
Ul'yanovskoye Kazakh. see Ul'yanovskiy
Ulysses KS U.S.A. 130 C4
Ulysses KY U.S.A. 134 D5
Ulytau Kazakh. 80 C2
Ulytau, Gory mts Kazakh. 80 C2
Uma Rus. Fed. 74 A1
Umaltinskiy Rus. Fed. 74 D2
'Umān country Asia see Oman
Uman' Ukr. 43 F6
Umarao Pak. 89 G4
'Umarī, Qā' al salt pan Jordan 85 C4
Umaria India 82 E5
Umarkhed India 84 C2
Umarkot India 84 D2
Umarkot Pak. 89 H4
Umarkot Pak. 89 H5
Umaroona, Lake salt flat Australia 111 B5
Umarpada India 82 C5
Umatilla U.S.A. 126 D3
Umba Rus. Fed. 42 G2
Umbagog Lake U.S.A. 135 J1
Umbeara Australia 109 F6
Umboi i. P.N.G. 69 L8
Umeå Sweden 44 L5
Umeälven r. Sweden 44 L5
Umfolozi r. S. Africa 101 K5
Umfreville Lake Canada 121 M5
Umhlanga Rocks S. Africa 101 J5
Umiiviip Kangertiva inlet Greenland 119 N3
Umingmaktok (abandoned) Canada 153 L2
Umirzak Kazakh. 91 H2
Umiujaq Canada 122 F2
Umkomaas S. Africa 101 J6
Umlaiteng India 83 H4
Umlazi S. Africa 101 J5
Umm ad Daraj, Jabal mt. Jordan 85 B3
Umm al 'Amad Syria 85 C2
Umm al Jamājim well Saudi Arabia 88 B5
Umm al Qaywayn U.A.E. 88 D5
Umm al Qaiwain U.A.E. see Umm al Qaywayn
Umm ar Raqabah, Khabrat imp. l. Saudi Arabia 85 C5
Umm at Qalbān Saudi Arabia 91 F6
Umm az Zumūl well Oman 88 D6
Umm Bāb Qatar 88 C5
Umm Bel Sudan 86 C7
Umm Keddada Sudan 86 C7
Umm Lajj Saudi Arabia 86 E4
Umm Nukhaylah hill Saudi Arabia 85 D5
Umm Qaşr Iraq 91 G5
Umm Quşūr i. Saudi Arabia 90 D6
Umm Ruwaba Sudan 86 D7
Umm Sa'ad Libya 90 B5
Umm Sa'īd Qatar 88 C5
Umm Shugeira Sudan 86 C7
Umm Wa'āl hill Saudi Arabia 85 D4
Umm Wazīr well Saudi Arabia 88 B6
Umnak Island U.S.A. 118 B4
Um Phang Wildlife Reserve nature res. Thai. 70 B4
Umpqua r. U.S.A. 126 B4
Umpulo Angola 99 B5
Umraniye Turkey 59 N5
Umred India 84 C1
Umri India 82 D4
Umtali Zimbabwe see Mutare
Umtata S. Africa 101 I6
Umtentweni S. Africa 101 J6
Umuahia Nigeria 96 D4
Umuarama Brazil 144 F2
Umvuma Zimbabwe see Mvuma
Umzimkulu S. Africa 101 I6
Una r. Bos.-Herz./Croatia 58 G2
Una Brazil 145 D1
Una India 82 D3
'Unāb, Jabal al hill Jordan 85 C5
'Unāb, Wādī al watercourse Jordan 85 C4
Unaí Brazil 145 B2
Unalaska Island U.S.A. 118 B4
Unapool U.K. 50 D2
'Unayzah Saudi Arabia 86 F4
'Unayzah, Jabal hill Iraq 91 E4
Uncia Bol. 142 E7
Uncompahgre Peak U.S.A. 129 J2
Uncompahgre Plateau U.S.A. 129 I2
Undara National Park Australia 110 D3
Underberg S. Africa 101 I5
Underbool Australia 111 C7
Underwood U.S.A. 134 C4
Undur Indon. 69 I7
Unecha Rus. Fed. 43 G5
Ungama Bay Kenya see Ungwana Bay
Ungarie Australia 112 C4
Ungava, Baie d' b. Canada see Ungava Bay
Ungava, Péninsule d' pen. Canada 122 G1
Ungava Bay Canada 123 I2
Ungava Peninsula Canada see Ungava, Péninsule d'
Ungeny Moldova see Ungheni
Ungheni Moldova 59 L1
Unguana Moz. 101 L2
Unguja i. Tanz. see Zanzibar Island
Unguz, Solonchakovyye Vpadiny salt flat Turkm. 88 E2
Üngüz Angyrsyndaky Garagum des. Turkm. 88 E1
Ungvár Ukr. see Uzhhorod
Ungwana Bay Kenya 98 E4
Uni Rus. Fed. 42 K4
União Brazil 143 J4
União da Vitória Brazil 145 A4
União dos Palmares Brazil 143 K5
Unimak Island U.S.A. 118 B4
Unini r. Brazil 142 F4
Union MO U.S.A. 130 F4
Union WV U.S.A. 134 E5
Union, Mount U.S.A. 129 G4
Union City OH U.S.A. 134 C3
Union City PA U.S.A. 134 F3
Union City TN U.S.A. 131 F4
Uniondale S. Africa 100 F7
Unión de Reyes Cuba 133 D8
▶Union of Soviet Socialist Republics
Divided in 1991 into 15 independent nations: Armenia, Azerbaijan, Belarus, Estonia, Georgia, Latvia, Kazakhstan, Kyrgyzstan, Lithuania, Moldova, the Russi Federation, Tajikistan, Turkmenistan, Ukraine and Uzbekistan.
Union Springs U.S.A. 133 C5
Uniontown U.S.A. 134 F4
Unionville U.S.A. 135 G3
United Arab Emirates country Asia 88 D6
United Arab Republic country Africa see Egypt
▶United Kingdom country Europe 46 G3
4th most populous country in Europe.
United Provinces state India see Uttar Pradesh
▶United States of America country N. America 124 F3
Most populous country in North America, and 3rd most populous in the world. Also 3rd largest country in the world, and 2nd i North America.
United States Range mts Canada 119 L1
Unity Canada 121 I4
Unjha India 82 C5
Unna Germany 53 H3
Unnao India 82 E4
Ŭnp'a N. Korea 75 B5
Unsan N. Korea 75 B4
Ŭnsan N. Korea 75 B5
Unst i. U.K. 50 [inset]
Unstrut r. Germany 53 L3
Untor, Ozero l. Rus. Fed. 41 T3
Unuk r. Canada/U.S.A. 120 D3
Unuli Horog China 83 G2
Unzen-dake vol. Japan 75 C6
Unzha Rus. Fed. 42 J4
Upalco U.S.A. 129 H1
Upar Ghat reg. India 83 F5
Upemba, Lac l. Dem. Rep. Congo 99 C4
Uperbada India 83 F5
Upernavik Greenland 119 M2
Upington S. Africa 100 E5
Upland U.S.A. 128 E4
Upleta India 82 B5
Upoloksha Rus. Fed. 44 Q3
'Upolu i. Samoa 107 I3
Upper Arlington U.S.A. 134 D3
Upper Arrow Lake Canada 120 G5
Upper Chindwin Myanmar see Mawlaik
Upper Fraser Canada 120 F4
Upper Garry Lake Canada 121 K1
Upper Hutt N.Z. 113 E5
Upper Klamath Lake U.S.A. 126 C4
Upper Lough Erne l. U.K. 51 E3
Upper Marlboro U.S.A. 135 G4
Upper Mazinaw Lake Canada 135 G1
Upper Missouri Breaks National Monument nat. park U.S.A. 130 A2
Upper Peirce Reservoir Sing. 71 [inset]
Upper Red Lake U.S.A. 130 E1
Upper Sandusky U.S.A. 134 D3
Upper Saranac Lake U.S.A. 135 H1
Upper Seal Lake Canada see Iberville, Lac d'
Upper Tunguska r. Rus. Fed. see Angara
Upper Volta country Africa see Burkina
Upper Yarra Reservoir Australia 112 B6
Uppinangadi India 84 B3
Uppsala Sweden 45 J7
Upsala Canada 122 C4
Upshi India 82 D2
Upton U.S.A. 135 J2
'Uqayqah, Wādī watercourse Jordan 85 B4
'Uqayribāt Syria 85 C2
'Uqlat al 'Udhaybah well Iraq 91 G5
Uqturpan China see Wushi
Uracas vol. N. Mariana Is see Farallon de Pajaros
Urad Houqi China see Sain Us
Ūrāf Iran 88 E4
Urakawa Japan 74 F4
Ural hill Australia 112 C4
Ural r. Kazakh./Rus. Fed. 78 E2
Uralla Australia 112 E3
Ural Mountains Rus. Fed. 41 S2
Ural'sk Kazakh. 78 E1
Ural'skaya Oblast' admin. div. Kazakh. see Zapadnyy Kazakhstan
Ural'skiye Gory mts Rus. Fed. see Ural Mountains
Ural'skiy Khrebet mts Rus. Fed. see Ural Mountains
Urambo Tanz. 99 D4
Uran India 84 B2
Urana Australia 112 C5
Urana, Lake Australia 112 C5
Urandangi Australia 110 B4
Urandi Brazil 145 C1
Uranium City Canada 121 I3
Uranquinty Australia 112 C5
Uraricoera r. Brazil 142 F3
Urartu country Asia see Armenia
Ura-Tyube Tajik. see Üroteppa
Uravakonda India 84 C3
Uravan U.S.A. 129 I2
Urawa Japan 75 E6
'Urayf an Nāqah, Jabal hill Egypt 85 B4
'Uray'irah Saudi Arabia 88 C5
'Urayq ad Duḩūl des. Saudi Arabia 88 B5
'Urayq Sāqān des. Saudi Arabia 88 B5
Urbana IL U.S.A. 130 F3
Urbana OH U.S.A. 134 D3
Urbino Italy 58 E3
Urbinum Italy see Urbino
Urbs Vetus Italy see Orvieto
Urdoma Rus. Fed. 42 K3
Urdyuzhskoye, Ozero l. Rus. Fed. 42 K2
Urdzhar Kazakh. 80 F2

re r. U.K. **48** F4
reki Georgia **91** F2
ren' Rus. Fed. **42** J4
rengoy Rus. Fed. **64** I3
réparapara i. Vanuatu **107** G3
rewera National Park N.Z. **113** F4
rfa Turkey see **Şanlıurfa**
rfa prov. Turkey see **Şanlıurfa**
rga Mongolia see **Ulan Bator**
rgal r. Rus. Fed. **74** D2
rganch Uzbek. **80** B3
rgench Uzbek. see **Urganch**
rgüp Turkey **90** D3
rgut Uzbek. **89** G2
rho China **80** G2
rho Kekkosen kansallispuisto nat. park Fin. **44** O2
rie r. U.K. **50** G3
ril Rus. Fed. **74** C2
risino Australia **112** A2
rjala Fin. **45** M6
rk Neth. **52** F2
rkan Rus. Fed. **74** B1
rkan r. Rus. Fed. **74** B1
rla Turkey **59** L5
rlingford Ireland **51** E5
rluk Rus. Fed. **73** J2
rmā aş Şughrá Syria **85** C1
rmai China **83** F3
rmia Iran **88** B2
rmia, Lake salt l. Iran **88** B2
rmston Road sea chan. H.K. China **77** [inset]
romi Nigeria **96** D4
roševac Kosovo see **Ferijaz**
rosozero Rus. Fed. **42** G3
roteppa Tajik. **89** H2
rru Co salt l. China **83** F3
rt Moron China **80** H4
ruáchic Mex. **124** F6
ruaçu Brazil **145** A1
ruana Brazil **145** A1
ruapan Baja California Mex. **127** D7
ruapan Michoacán Mex. **136** D5
rubamba r. Peru **142** D6
rucara Brazil **143** G4
rucu r. Brazil **142** F4
ruçuca Brazil **145** D1
ruçuí Brazil **143** J5
ruçuí, Serra do hills Brazil **143** I5
rucuia Brazil **145** B2
rucurituba Brazil **143** G4
ruguai r. Arg./Uruguay see **Uruguay**
ruguaiana Brazil **144** E3
ruguay r. Arg./Uruguay **144** E4
also known as Uruguai
ruguay country S. America **144** E4
ruhe China **74** B2
rumchi China see **Ürümqi**
rümqi China **80** G3
rundi country Africa see **Burundi**
rup, Ostrov i. Rus. Fed. **73** S3
rusha Rus. Fed. **74** A1
rutaí Brazil **145** A2
ryl' Kazakh. **80** G2
ryupino Rus. Fed. **73** M2
ryupinsk Rus. Fed. **43** I6
rzhar Kazakh. see **Urdzhar**
rzhum Rus. Fed. **42** K4
rziceni Romania **59** L2
sa Japan **75** C6
sa r. Rus. Fed. **42** M2
şak Turkey **59** M5
sakos Namibia **100** B1
sarp Mountains Antarctica **152** H2
sborne, Mount hill Falkland Is **144** E8
shakova, Ostrov i. Rus. Fed. **64** I1
shant i. France see **Ouessant, Île d'**
sharal Kazakh. see **Ucharal**
sh-Bel'dyr Rus. Fed. **72** H2
shtobe Kazakh. **80** E2
sh-Tyube Kazakh. see **Ushtobe**
shuaia Arg. **144** C8
shumun Rus. Fed. **74** B1
singen Germany **53** I4
sinsk Rus. Fed. **41** R2
sk U.K. **49** E7
sk r. U.K. **49** E7
skhodni Belarus **45** O10
skoplje Bos.-Herz. see **Gornji Vakuf**
sküdar Turkey **59** M4
slar Germany **53** J3
sman' Rus. Fed. **43** H5
smanabad India see **Osmanabad**
smas ezers l. Latvia **45** M8
sogorsk Rus. Fed. **42** K3
sol'ye-Sibirskoye Rus. Fed. **72** I2
spenovka Rus. Fed. **74** B1
ssel France **56** F4
ssuri r. China/Rus. Fed. **74** D2
ssuriysk Rus. Fed. **74** C4
st'-Abakanskoye Rus. Fed. see **Abakan**
sta Muhammad Pak. **89** H4
st'-Balyk Rus. Fed. see **Nefteyugansk**
st'-Donetskiy Rus. Fed. **43** I7
st'-Dzheguta Rus. Fed. **91** F1
st'-Dzhegutinskaya Rus. Fed. see **Ust'-Dzheguta**
stica, Isola di i. Sicily Italy **58** E5
st'-Ilimsk Rus. Fed. **65** L4
st'-Ilimskiy Vodokhranilishche resr Rus. Fed. **65** L4
st'-Ilych Rus. Fed. **41** R3
stí nad Labem Czech Rep. **47** O5
stinov Rus. Fed. see **Izhevsk**
stirt plat. Kazakh./Uzbek. see **Ustyurt Plateau**
stka Poland **47** P3
st'-Kamchatsk Rus. Fed. **65** R4
st'-Kamenogorsk Kazakh. **80** F2
st'-Kan Rus. Fed. **80** F1
st'-Koksa Rus. Fed. **80** G1
st'-Kulom Rus. Fed. **42** L3
st'-Kut Rus. Fed. **65** L4
st'-Kuyga Rus. Fed. **65** O2
st'-Labinsk Rus. Fed. **91** E1
st'-Labinskaya Rus. Fed. see **Ust'-Labinsk**
st'-Lyzha Rus. Fed. **42** M2
st'-Maya Rus. Fed. **65** O3
st'-Nera Rus. Fed. **65** P3
st'-Ocheya Rus. Fed. **42** K3
st'-Olenek Rus. Fed. **65** M2

Ust'-Omchug Rus. Fed. **65** P3
Ust'-Ordynskiy Rus. Fed. **72** I2
Ust'-Penzhino Rus. Fed. see **Kamenskoye**
Ust'-Port Rus. Fed. **64** J3
Ustrem Rus. Fed. **41** T3
Ust'-Tsil'ma Rus. Fed. **42** L2
Ust'-Uda Rus. Fed. **72** I2
Ust'-Umalta Rus. Fed. **74** D2
Ust'-Undurga Rus. Fed. **73** L2
Ust'-Ura Rus. Fed. **42** J3
Ust'-Urgal Rus. Fed. **74** D2
Ust'-Usa Rus. Fed. **42** M2
Ust'-Vayen'ga Rus. Fed. **42** I3
Ust'-Voya Rus. Fed. **41** R3
Ust'-Vyyskaya Rus. Fed. **42** J3
Ust'ya r. Rus. Fed. **42** I3
Ust'ye Rus. Fed. **42** H4
Ustyurt, Plato plat. Kazakh./Uzbek. see **Ustyurt Plateau**
Ustyurt Plateau Kazakh./Uzbek. **78** E2
Ustyurt Platosi plat. Kazakh./Uzbek. see **Ustyurt Plateau**
Ustyuzhna Rus. Fed. **42** H4
Usulután El Salvador **136** G6
Usumbura Burundi see **Bujumbura**
Usvyaty Rus. Fed. **42** F5
Utah state U.S.A. **126** F5
Utah Lake U.S.A. **129** H1
Utajärvi Fin. **44** O4
Utashinai Rus. Fed. see **Yuzhno-Kuril'sk**
'Utaybah, Buḩayrat al imp. l. Syria **85** C3
Utena Lith. **45** N9
Uterlai India **82** B4
Uthai Thani Thai. **70** C4
Uthal Pak. **89** G5
'Uthmānīyah Syria **85** C2
Utiariti Brazil **143** G6
Utica NY U.S.A. **135** H2
Utica OH U.S.A. **134** D3
Utiel Spain **57** F4
Utikuma Lake Canada **120** H4
Utlwanang S. Africa **101** G4
Utrecht Neth. **52** F2
Utrecht S. Africa **101** J4
Utrera Spain **57** D5
Utsjoki Fin. **44** O2
Utsunomiya Japan **75** E5
Utta Rus. Fed. **43** J7
Uttaradit Thai. **70** C3
Uttarakhand state India see **Uttaranchal**
Uttaranchal state India **82** D3
Uttarkashi India **82** D3
Uttar Kashi India see **Uttarkashi**
Uttar Pradesh state India **82** D4
Uttoxeter U.K. **49** F6
Uttranchal state India see **Uttaranchal**
Utubulak China **80** G2
Utupua i. Solomon Is **107** G3
Uummannaq Greenland see **Dundas**
Uummannaq Fjord inlet Greenland **153** J2
Uummannarsuaq c. Greenland see **Farewell, Cape**
Uurainen Fin. **44** N5
Uusikaarlepyy Fin. see **Nykarleby**
Uusikaupunki Fin. **45** L6
Uutapi Namibia **99** B5
Uva Rus. Fed. **42** L4
Uvalde U.S.A. **131** D6
Uval Karabaur hills Kazakh./Uzbek. **91** I2
Uval Muzbel' hills Kazakh. **91** I2
Uvarovo Rus. Fed. **43** I6
Uvéa atoll New Caledonia see **Ouvéa**
Uvinza Tanz. **99** D4
Uvs Nuur salt l. Mongolia **80** H1
Uwajima Japan **75** D6
'Uwayriḑ, Ḩarrat al lava field Saudi Arabia **86** E4
Uwaysiţ well Saudi Arabia **85** D4
Uweinat, Jebel mt. Sudan **86** C5
Uwi i. Indon. **71** D7
Uxbridge Canada **134** F1
Uxbridge U.K. **49** G7
Uxin Qi China see **Dabqig**
Uyaly Kazakh. **80** B3
Uyar Rus. Fed. **72** G1
Uyo Nigeria **96** D4
Uyu Chaung r. Myanmar **70** A1
Uyuni Bol. **142** E8
Uyuni, Salar de salt flat Bol. **142** E8
Uza r. Rus. Fed. **43** J5
Uzbekistan country Asia **80** B3
Ŭzbekiston country Asia see **Uzbekistan**
Uzbekskaya S.S.R. country Asia see **Uzbekistan**
Uzbek S.S.R. country Asia see **Uzbekistan**
Uzboy Azer. **91** H3
Uzboy Turkm. **88** D2
Uzen' Kazakh. see **Kyzylsay**
Uzhgorod Ukr. see **Uzhhorod**
Uzhhorod Ukr. **43** D6
Užhorod Ukr. see **Uzhhorod**
Užice Serbia **59** H3
Uzlovaya Rus. Fed. **43** H5
Üzümlü Turkey **59** M6
Uzun Uzbek. **89** H2
Uzunköprü Turkey **59** L4
Uzynkair Kazakh. **80** B3

Vaaf Atoll Maldives see **Felidhu Atoll**
Vaajakoski Fin. **44** N5
Vaal r. S. Africa **101** F5
Vaala Fin. **44** O4
Vaalbos National Park S. Africa **100** G5
Vaal Dam S. Africa **101** I4
Vaalwater S. Africa **101** I3
Vaasa Fin. **44** L5
Vaavu Atoll Maldives see **Felidhu Atoll**
Vác Hungary **47** Q7
Vacaria Brazil **145** A5
Vacaria, Campo da plain Brazil **145** A5
Vacaville U.S.A. **128** C2
Vachon r. Canada **123** H1
Vad Rus. Fed. **42** J5
Vad r. Rus. Fed. **43** I5
Vada India **84** B2
Vadla Norway **45** E7
Vadodara India **82** C5
Vadsø Norway **44** P1

▶**Vaduz** Liechtenstein **56** I3
Capital of Liechtenstein.

Værøy i. Norway **44** H3
Vaga r. Rus. Fed. **42** I3
Vågåmo Norway **45** F6
Vaganski Vrh mt. Croatia **58** F2
Vágar i. Faroe Is **44** [inset]
Vägsele Sweden **44** K4
Vágur Faroe Is **44** [inset]
Váh r. Slovakia **47** Q7
Vähäkyrö Fin. **44** M5

▶**Vaiaku** Tuvalu **107** H2
Capital of Tuvalu, on Funafuti atoll.

Vaida Estonia **45** N7
Vaiden U.S.A. **131** F5
Vail U.S.A. **124** F4
Vailly-sur-Aisne France **52** D5
Vaitupu i. Tuvalu **107** H2
Vajrakarur India see **Kanur**
Vakhsh Tajik. **89** H2
Vakhsh r. Tajik. **89** H2
Vakhstroy Tajik. see **Vakhsh**
Vakīlābād Iran **88** E4
Valbo Sweden **45** J6
Valcheta Arg. **144** C6
Valdai Hills Rus. Fed. see **Valdayskaya Vozvyshennost'**
Valday Rus. Fed. **42** G4
Valdayskaya Vozvyshennost' hills Rus. Fed. **42** G4
Valdecañas, Embalse de resr Spain **57** D4
Valdemārpils Latvia **45** M8
Valdemarsvik Sweden **45** J7
Valdepeñas Spain **57** E4
Val-de-Reuil France **52** B5
Valdés, Península pen. Arg. **144** D6
Valdez U.S.A. **118** D3
Valdivia Chile **144** B5
Val-d'Or Canada **122** F4
Valdosta U.S.A. **133** D6
Valdres valley Norway **45** F6
Vale Georgia **91** F2
Vale U.S.A. **126** D3
Valemount Canada **120** G4
Valença Brazil **145** D1
Valence France **56** G4
Valencia Spain **57** F4
València Spain see **Valencia**
Valencia reg. Spain **57** F4
Valencia Venez. **142** E1
Valencia, Golfo de g. Spain **57** G4
Valencia de Don Juan Spain **57** D2
Valencia Island Ireland **51** B6
Valenciennes France **52** D4
Valensole, Plateau de France **56** H5
Valentia Spain see **Valencia**
Valentin Rus. Fed. **74** D4
Valentine U.S.A. **130** C3
Våler Norway **45** G6
Valera Venez. **142** D2
Vale Verde Brazil **145** D2
Val Grande, Parco Nazionale della nat. park Italy **58** C1
Valjevo Serbia **59** H2
Valka Latvia **45** O8
Valkeakoski Fin. **45** N6
Valkenswaard Neth. **52** F3
Valky Ukr. **43** G6
Valkyrie Dome ice feature Antarctica **152** D1
Valladolid Mex. **136** G4
Valladolid Spain **57** D3
Vallard, Lac l. Canada **123** H3
Valle Norway **45** E7
Vallecillos Mex. **131** D7
Vallecito Reservoir U.S.A. **129** J3
Valle de la Pascua Venez. **142** E2
Valledupar Col. **142** D1
Vallée-Jonction Canada **123** H5
Valle Fértil, Sierra de mts Arg. **144** C4
Valle Grande Bol. **142** F7
Valle Hermoso Mex. **131** D7
Vallejo U.S.A. **128** B2
Vallenar Chile **144** B3

▶**Valletta** Malta **58** F7
Capital of Malta.

Valley r. Canada **121** L5
Valley U.K. **48** C5
Valley City U.S.A. **130** D2
Valleyview Canada **120** G4
Valls Spain **57** G3
Val Marie Canada **121** J5
Valmiera Latvia **45** N8
Valmy U.S.A. **128** E1
Valnera mt. Spain **57** E2
Valognes France **49** F9
Valona Albania see **Vlorë**
Valozhyn Belarus **45** O9
Val-Paradis Canada **122** F4
Valparai India **84** C4
Valparaíso Chile **144** B4
Valparaiso U.S.A. **134** B3
Valpoi India **84** B3
Valréas France **56** G4
Vals, Tanjung c. Indon. **69** J8
Valsad India **84** B1
Valspan S. Africa **100** G4
Val'tevo Rus. Fed. **42** J2
Valtimo Fin. **44** P5
Valuyevka Rus. Fed. **43** I7
Valuyki Rus. Fed. **43** H6
Vammala Fin. **45** M6
Van Turkey **91** F3
Van, Lake salt l. Turkey **91** F3
Vanadzor Armenia **91** G2
Van Buren AR U.S.A. **131** E5
Van Buren MO U.S.A. **131** F4
Van Buren OH U.S.A. see **Kettering**
Vanceburg U.S.A. **134** D4
Vanch Tajik. see **Vanj**
Vancleve U.S.A. **134** D5
Vancouver Canada **120** F5
Vancouver U.S.A. **126** C3
Vancouver, Mount Canada/U.S.A. **120** B2
Vancouver Island Canada **120** E5

Vanda Fin. see **Vantaa**
Vandalia IL U.S.A. **130** F4
Vandalia OH U.S.A. **134** C4
Vandekerckhove Lake Canada **121** K3
Vanderbijlpark S. Africa **101** H4
Vanderbilt U.S.A. **134** C1
Vandergrift U.S.A. **134** F3
Vanderhoof Canada **120** E4
Vanderkloof Dam resr S. Africa **100** G6
Vanderlin Island Australia **110** B2
Vanderwagen U.S.A. **129** I4
Van Diemen, Cape N.T. Australia **108** E2
Van Diemen, Cape Qld Australia **110** B3
Van Diemen Gulf Australia **108** F2
Van Diemen's Land state Australia see **Tasmania**
Vändra Estonia **45** N7
Väner, Lake Sweden see **Vänern**

▶**Vänern** l. Sweden **45** H7
4th largest lake in Europe.

Vänersborg Sweden **45** H7
Vangaindrano Madag. **99** E6
Van Gia Vietnam **71** E4
Van Gölü salt l. Turkey see **Van, Lake**
Van Horn U.S.A. **127** G7
Vanikoro Islands Solomon Is **107** G3
Vanimo P.N.G. **69** K7
Vanino Rus. Fed. **74** F2
Vanivilasa Sagara resr India **84** C3
Vaniyambadi India **84** C3
Vanj Tajik. **89** H2
Vännäs Sweden **44** K5
Vannes France **56** C3
Vannes, Lac l. Canada **123** I3
Vannovka Kazakh. see **Turar Ryskulov**
Vannøya i. Norway **44** K1
Van Rees, Pegunungan mts Indon. **69** J7
Vanrhynsdorp S. Africa **100** D6
Vansant U.S.A. **134** D5
Vansbro Sweden **45** I6
Vansittart Island Canada **119** J3
Van Starkenborgh Kanaal canal Neth. **52** G1
Vantaa Fin. **45** N6
Van Truer Tableland reg. Australia **109** C6
Vanua Lava i. Vanuatu **107** G3
Vanua Levu i. Fiji **107** H3
Vanuatu country S. Pacific Ocean **107** G3
Van Wert U.S.A. **134** C3
Vanwyksvlei S. Africa **100** E6
Vanwyksvlei l. S. Africa **100** E6
Văn Yên Vietnam **70** D2
Van Zylsrus S. Africa **100** F4
Varadero Cuba **133** D8
Varahi India **82** B5
Varakļāni Latvia **45** O8
Varalé Côte d'Ivoire **96** C4
Varāmīn Iran **88** C3
Varanasi India **83** E4
Varandey Rus. Fed. **42** M1
Varangerfjorden sea chan. Norway **44** P1
Varangerhalvøya pen. Norway **41** L1
Varangerhalvøya pen. Norway **44** P1
Varaždin Croatia **58** G1
Varberg Sweden **45** H8
Vardar r. Macedonia **59** J4
Varde Denmark **45** F9
Vardenis Armenia **91** G2
Vardø Norway **44** Q1
Varel Germany **53** I1
Varėna Lith. **45** N9
Varese Italy **58** C2
Varfolomeyevka Rus. Fed. **74** D3
Vårgårda Sweden **45** H7
Varginha Brazil **145** B3
Varik Neth. **52** F3
Varillas Chile **144** B2
Varkana Iran see **Gorgān**
Varkaus Fin. **44** O5
Varna Bulg. **59** L3
Värnamo Sweden **45** I8
Värnäs Sweden **45** H6
Varnavino Rus. Fed. **42** J4
Várnjárg pen. Norway see **Varangerhalvøya**
Varpaisjärvi Fin. **44** O5
Várpalota Hungary **58** H1
Varsaj Afgh. **89** H2
Varsh, Ozero l. Rus. Fed. **42** J2
Varto Turkey **91** F3
Várzea da Palma Brazil **145** B2
Vasa Fin. see **Vaasa**
Vasai India **84** B2
Vashka r. Rus. Fed. **42** J2
Vasht Iran see **Khāsh**
Vasilkov Ukr. see **Vasyl'kiv**
Vasknarva Estonia **45** O7
Vaslui Romania **59** L1
Vassar U.S.A. **134** D2
Vas-Soproni-síkság hills Hungary **58** G1
Vastan Turkey see **Gevaş**
Västerås Sweden **45** J7
Västerdalälven r. Sweden **45** I6
Västerfjäll Sweden **44** J3
Västerhaninge Sweden **45** K7
Västervik Sweden **45** J8
Vasto Italy **58** F3
Vasyl'kiv Ukr. **43** F6
Vatan France **56** E3
Vaté i. Vanuatu see **Éfaté**
Vatersay i. U.K. **50** B4
Vathar India **84** B2
Vathí Greece see **Vathy**
Vathy Greece **59** L6

▶**Vatican City** Europe **58** E4
Independent papal state, the smallest country in the world.

Vaticano, Città del Europe see **Vatican City**
Vatnajökull ice cap Iceland **44** [inset]
Vatoa i. Fiji **107** I3
Vatra Dornei Romania **59** K1
Vätter, Lake Sweden see **Vättern**
Vättern l. Sweden **45** I7
Vaughn U.S.A. **127** G6
Vaupés r. Col. **142** E3
Vauquelin r. Canada **122** F3

Vauvert France **56** G5
Vauxhall Canada **121** H5
Vavatenina Madag. **99** E5
Vava'u Group is Tonga **107** I3
Vavitao i. Fr. Polynesia see **Raivavae**
Vavoua Côte d'Ivoire **96** C4
Vavozh Rus. Fed. **42** K4
Vavuniya Sri Lanka **84** D4
Vawkavysk Belarus **45** N10
Växjö Sweden **45** I8
Vay, Đao i. Vietnam **71** C5
Vayenga Rus. Fed. see **Severomorsk**
Vazante Brazil **145** B2
Vazáš Sweden see **Vittangi**
Veaikevárri Sweden see **Svappavaara**
Veal Vêng Cambodia **71** C4
Vecht r. Neth. **52** G2
also known as Vechte (Germany)
Vechta Germany **53** I2
Vechte r. Germany **52** G2
also known as Vecht (Netherlands)
Veckerhagen (Reinhardshagen) Germany **53** J3
Vedaranniyam India **84** C4
Vedasandur India **84** C4
Veddige Sweden **45** H8
Vedea r. Romania **59** K3
Veedersburg U.S.A. **134** B3
Veendam Neth. **52** G1
Veenendaal Neth. **52** F2
Vega i. Norway **44** G4
Vega U.S.A. **131** C5
Vegreville Canada **121** H4
Vehari Pak. **89** I4
Vehkalahti Fin. **45** O6
Vehoa Pak. **89** H4
Veinticinco de Mayo Buenos Aires Arg. see **25 de Mayo**
Veinticinco de Mayo La Pampa Arg. see **25 de Mayo**
Veirwaro Pak. **89** H5
Veitshöchheim Germany **53** J5
Vejle Denmark **45** F9
Vekil'bazar Turkm. see **Wekilbazar**
Velbert Germany **52** H3
Velbŭzhdki Prokhod pass Bulg./Macedonia **59** J3
Velddrif S. Africa **100** D7
Velebit mts Croatia **58** F2
Velen Germany **52** G3
Velenje Slovenia **58** F1
Veles Macedonia **59** I4
Vélez-Málaga Spain **57** D5
Vélez-Rubio Spain **57** E5
Velhas r. Brazil **145** B2
Velibaba Turkey see **Aras**
Velika Gorica Croatia **58** G2
Velika Plana Serbia **59** I2
Velikaya r. Rus. Fed. **42** K4
Velikaya r. Rus. Fed. **45** P8
Velikaya r. Rus. Fed. **65** S3
Velikaya Kema Rus. Fed. **74** E3
Veliki Preslav Bulg. **59** L3
Velikiye Luki Rus. Fed. **42** F4
Velikiy Novgorod Rus. Fed. **42** F4
Velikiy Ustyug Rus. Fed. **42** J3
Velikonda Range hills India **84** C3
Veliko Tŭrnovo Bulg. **59** K3
Velikoye Rus. Fed. **42** H4
Velikoye, Ozero l. Rus. Fed. **43** I5
Veli Lošinj Croatia **58** F2
Velizh Rus. Fed. **42** F5
Vella Lavella i. Solomon Is **107** F2
Vellar r. India **84** C4
Vellberg Germany **53** J5
Vellmar Germany **53** J3
Vellore India **84** C3
Velpke Germany **53** K2
Vel'sk Rus. Fed. **42** I3
Velsuna Italy see **Orvieto**
Velten Germany **53** N2
Veluwezoom, Nationaal Park nat. park Neth. **52** F2
Velykyy Tokmak Ukr. see **Tokmak**
Vel'yu r. Rus. Fed. **42** L3
Vemalwada India **84** C2
Vema Seamount sea feature S. Atlantic Ocean **148** I8
Vema Trench sea feature Indian Ocean **149** M6
Vempalle India **84** C3
Venado Tuerto Arg. **144** D4
Venafro Italy **58** F4
Venceslau Bráz Brazil **145** A3
Vendinga Rus. Fed. **42** J3
Vendôme France **56** E3
Venegas Mex. **131** C8
Venetia Italy see **Venice**
Venetie Landing U.S.A. **118** D3
Venev Rus. Fed. **43** H5
Venezia Italy see **Venice**
Venezia, Golfo di g. Europe see **Venice, Gulf of**

▶**Venezuela** country S. America **142** E2
5th most populous country in South America.

Venezuela, Golfo de g. Venez. **142** D1
Venezuelan Basin sea feature S. Atlantic Ocean **148** D4
Vengurla India **84** B3
Veniaminof Volcano U.S.A. **118** C4
Venice Italy **58** E2
Venice U.S.A. **133** D7
Venice, Gulf of Europe **58** E2
Vénissieux France **56** G4
Venkatapalem India **84** D2
Venkatapuram India **84** D2
Venlo Neth. **52** G3
Vennesla Norway **45** E7
Venray Neth. **52** F3
Venta r. Latvia/Lith. **45** M8
Venta Lith. **45** M8
Ventersburg S. Africa **101** H5
Ventersdorp S. Africa **101** H4
Venterstad S. Africa **101** G6
Ventnor U.K. **49** F8
Ventotene, Isola i. Italy **58** E4
Ventoux, Mont mt. France **56** G4
Ventspils Latvia **45** L8
Ventura U.S.A. **128** D4

Venus Bay Australia **112** B7
Venustiano Carranza Mex. **131** C7
Venustiano Carranza, Presa resr Mex. **131** C7
Vera Arg. **144** D3
Vera Spain **57** F5
Vera Cruz Brazil **145** A3
Veracruz Mex. **136** E5
Vera Cruz Mex. see **Veracruz**
Veraval India **82** B5
Verbania Italy **58** C2
Vercelli Italy **58** C2
Vercors reg. France **56** G4
Verdalsøra Norway **44** G5
Verde r. Goiás Brazil **145** A2
Verde r. Goiás Brazil **145** B2
Verde r. Minas Gerais Brazil **145** A2
Verde r. Mex. **127** G8
Verde r. U.S.A. **129** H5
Verden (Aller) Germany **53** J2
Verde Pequeno r. Brazil **145** C1
Verdi U.S.A. **128** D2
Verdon r. France **56** G5
Verdun France **52** F5
Vereeniging S. Africa **101** H4
Vereshchagino Rus. Fed. **41** Q4
Vergennes U.S.A. **135** I1
Véria Greece see **Veroia**
Verín Spain **57** C3
Veríssimo Brazil **145** A2
Verkhneimbatsk Rus. Fed. **64** J3
Verkhnekolvinsk Rus. Fed. **42** M2
Verkhnespasskoye Rus. Fed. **42** J4
Verkhnetulomskiy Rus. Fed. **44** Q2
Verkhnetulomskoye Vodokhranilishche resr Rus. Fed. **44** Q2
Verkhnevilyuysk Rus. Fed. **65** N3
Verkhneye Kuyto, Ozero l. Rus. Fed. **44** Q4
Verkhnezeysk Rus. Fed. **73** N2
Verkhniy Vyalozerskiy Rus. Fed. **42** G2
Verkhnyaya Khava Rus. Fed. **43** H6
Verkhnyaya Salda Rus. Fed. **41** S4
Verkhnyaya Tunguska r. Rus. Fed. see **Angara**
Verkhnyaya Tura Rus. Fed. **41** R4
Verkhoshizhem'ye Rus. Fed. **42** K4
Verkhovazh'ye Rus. Fed. **42** I3
Verkhov'ye Rus. Fed. **43** H5
Verkhoyansk Rus. Fed. **65** O3
Verkhoyanskiy Khrebet mts Rus. Fed. **65** N2
Vermand France **52** D5
Vermelho r. Brazil **145** A1
Vermilion Canada **121** I4
Vermilion Bay U.S.A. **131** F6
Vermilion Cliffs AZ U.S.A. **129** G3
Vermilion Cliffs UT U.S.A. **129** G3
Vermilion Cliffs National Monument nat. park U.S.A. **129** H3
Vermilion Lake U.S.A. **130** E2
Vermillion U.S.A. **130** D3
Vermillion Bay Canada **121** M5
Vermont state U.S.A. **135** I1
Vernadsky research station Antarctica **152** L2
Vernal U.S.A. **129** I1
Verner Canada **122** E5
Verneuk Pan salt pan S. Africa **100** E5
Vernon Canada **120** G5
Vernon France **52** B5
Vernon AL U.S.A. **131** F5
Vernon IN U.S.A. **134** C4
Vernon TX U.S.A. **131** D5
Vernon UT U.S.A. **129** G1
Vernon Islands Australia **108** E3
Vernoye Rus. Fed. **74** C2
Vernyy Kazakh. see **Almaty**
Vero Beach U.S.A. **133** D7
Veroia Greece **59** J4
Verona Italy **58** D2
Verona U.S.A. **134** F4
Versailles France **52** C6
Versailles IN U.S.A. **134** C4
Versailles KY U.S.A. **134** C4
Versailles OH U.S.A. **134** C3
Versec Serbia see **Vršac**
Versmold Germany **53** I2
Vert, Île i. Canada **123** H4
Vertou France **56** D3
Verulam S. Africa **101** J5
Verulamium U.K. see **St Albans**
Verviers Belgium **52** F4
Vervins France **52** D5
Verwood Canada **121** J5
Verzy France **52** E5
Vescovato Corsica France **56** I5
Vesele Ukr. **43** G7
Veselyy Rus. Fed. **43** I7
Veselyy Yar Rus. Fed. **74** D4
Veshenskaya Rus. Fed. **43** I6
Vesle r. France **52** D5
Veslyana r. Rus. Fed. **42** L3
Vesontio France see **Besançon**
Vesoul France **56** H3
Vessem Neth. **52** F3
Vesterålen is Norway **44** H2
Vesterålsfjorden sea chan. Norway **44** H2
Vestertana Norway **44** O1
Vestfjorddalen valley Norway **45** F7
Vestfjorden sea chan. Norway **44** H3
Vestia Brazil **145** A3
Vestmanna Faroe Is **44** [inset]
Vestmannaeyjar Iceland **44** [inset]
Vestmannaeyjar is Iceland **44** [inset]
Vestnes Norway **44** E5
Vesturhorn hd Iceland **44** [inset]
Vesuvio vol. Italy see **Vesuvius**
Vesuvius vol. Italy **58** F4
Ves'yegonsk Rus. Fed. **42** H4
Veszprém Hungary **58** G1
Veteli Fin. **44** M5
Veteran Canada **121** I4
Vetlanda Sweden **45** I8
Vetluga Rus. Fed. **42** J4
Vetluga r. Rus. Fed. **42** J4
Vetluzhskiy Kostromskaya Oblast' Rus. Fed. **42** J4
Vetluzhskiy Nizhegorodskaya Oblast' Rus. Fed. **42** J4
Vettore, Monte mt. Italy **58** E3
Veurne Belgium **52** C3

Vevay U.S.A. 134 C4
Vevey Switz. 56 H3
Vexin Normand reg. France 52 B5
Veyo U.S.A. 129 G3
Vézère r. France 56 E4
Vezirköprü Turkey 90 D2
Vialar Alg. see Tissemsilt
Viamao Brazil 145 A5
Viana Espírito Santo Brazil 145 C3
Viana Maranhão Brazil 143 J4
Viana do Castelo Port. 57 B3
Vianen Neth. 52 F3
Viangchan Laos see Vientiane
Viangphoukha Laos 70 C2
Viannos Greece 59 K7
Vianópolis Brazil 145 A2
Viareggio Italy 58 D3
Viborg Denmark 45 F8
Viborg Rus. Fed. see Vyborg
Vibo Valentia Italy 58 G5
Vic Spain 57 H3
Vicam Mex. 127 F8
Vicecomodoro Marambio research station Antarctica see Marambio
Vicente, Point U.S.A. 128 D5
Vicente Guerrero Mex. 127 D7
Vicenza Italy 58 D2
Vich Spain see Vic
Vichada r. Col. 142 E3
Vichadero Uruguay 144 F4
Vichy France 56 F3
Vicksburg AZ U.S.A. 129 G5
Vicksburg MS U.S.A. 131 F5
Viçosa Brazil 145 C3
Victor, Mount Antarctica 152 D2
Victor Harbor Australia 111 B7
Victoria Arg. 144 D4
Victoria r. Australia 108 E3
Victoria state Australia 112 B6

▶Victoria Canada 120 F5
Capital of British Columbia.

Victoria Chile 144 B5
Victoria Malaysia see Labuan
Victoria Malta 58 F6

▶Victoria Seychelles 149 L6
Capital of the Seychelles.

Victoria TX U.S.A. 131 D6
Victoria VA U.S.A. 135 F5
Victoria prov. Zimbabwe see Masvingo

▶Victoria, Lake Africa 98 D4
Largest lake in Africa, and 3rd in the world.

Victoria, Lake Australia 111 C7
Victoria, Mount Fiji see Tomanivi
Victoria, Mount Myanmar 70 A2
Victoria, Mount P.N.G. 69 L8
Victoria and Albert Mountains Canada 119 K2
Victoria Falls Zambia/Zimbabwe 99 C5
Victoria Harbour sea chan. H.K. China see Hong Kong Harbour

▶Victoria Island Canada 118 H2
3rd largest island in North America, and 9th in the world.

Victoria Land coastal area Antarctica 152 H2
Victoria Peak Belize 136 G5
Victoria Peak hill H.K. China 77 [inset]
Victoria Range mts N.Z. 113 D6
Victoria River Downs Australia 108 E4
Victoriaville Canada 123 H5
Victoria West S. Africa 100 F6
Victorica Arg. 144 C5
Victorville U.S.A. 128 E4
Victory Downs Australia 109 F6
Vidalia U.S.A. 131 F6
Vidal Junction U.S.A. 129 F4
Videle Romania 59 K2
Vidisha India 82 D5
Vidlin U.K. 50 [inset]
Vidlitsa Rus. Fed. 42 G3
Viechtach Germany 53 M5
Viedma Arg. 144 D6
Viedma, Lago l. Arg. 144 B7
Viejo, Cerro mt. Mex. 127 E7
Vielank Germany 53 L1
Vielsalm Belgium 52 F4
Vienenburg Germany 53 K3

▶Vienna Austria 47 P6
Capital of Austria.

Vienna MO U.S.A. 130 F4
Vienna WV U.S.A. 134 E4
Vienne France 56 G4
Vienne r. France 56 E3

▶Vientiane Laos 70 C3
Capital of Laos.

Vieques i. Puerto Rico 137 K5
Vieremä Fin. 44 O5
Viersen Germany 52 G3
Vierzon France 56 F3
Viesca Mex. 131 C7
Viesīte Latvia 45 N8
Vieste Italy 58 G4
Vietas Sweden 44 K3
Việt Nam country Asia see Vietnam
Vietnam country Asia 70 D3
Việt Quang Vietnam 70 D2
Việt Tri Vietnam 70 D2
Vieux Comptoir, Lac du l. Canada 122 F3
Vieux-Fort Canada 123 K4
Vieux Poste, Pointe du pt Canada 123 J4
Vigan Phil. 69 G3
Vigevano Italy 58 C2
Vigia Brazil 143 I4
Vignacourt France 52 C4
Vignemale mt. France 54 D3
Vignola Italy 58 D2
Vigo Spain 57 B2
Vihanti Fin. 44 N4
Vihti Fin. 45 N6
Viipuri Rus. Fed. see Vyborg
Viitasaari Fin. 44 N5
Vijayadurg India 84 B2
Vijayanagaram India see Vizianagaram
Vijayapati India 84 C4
Vijayawada India 84 D2
Vík Iceland 44 [inset]
Vikajärvi Fin. 44 O3
Vikeke East Timor see Viqueque
Viking Canada 121 I4
Vikna i. Norway 44 G4
Vikøyri Norway 45 E6
Vila Vanuatu see Port Vila
Vila Alferes Chamusca Moz. see Guija
Vila Bittencourt Brazil 142 E4
Vila Bugaço Angola see Camanongue
Vila Cabral Moz. see Lichinga
Vila da Ponte Angola see Kuvango
Vila de Aljustrel Angola see Cangamba
Vila de Almoster Angola see Chiange
Vila de João Belo Moz. see Xai-Xai
Vila de María Arg. 144 D3
Vila de Trego Morais Moz. see Chókwé
Vila Fontes Moz. see Caia
Vila Franca de Xira Port. 57 B4
Vilagarcía de Arousa Spain 57 B2
Vila Gomes da Costa Moz. 101 K3
Vilalba Spain 57 C2
Vila Luísa Moz. see Marracuene
Vila Marechal Carmona Angola see Uíge
Vila Miranda Moz. see Macaloge
Vilanandro, Tanjona pt Madag. 99 E5
Vilanculos Moz. 101 L1
Vila Nova de Gaia Port. 57 B3
Vilanova i la Geltrú Spain 57 G3
Vila Pery Moz. see Chimoio
Vila Real Port. 57 C3
Vilar Formoso Port. 57 C3
Vila Salazar Angola see N'dalatando
Vila Salazar Zimbabwe see Sango
Vila Teixeira de Sousa Angola see Luau
Vila Velha Brazil 145 C3
Vilcabamba, Cordillera mts Peru 142 D6
Vil'cheka, Zemlya i. Rus. Fed. 64 H1
Viled' r. Rus. Fed. 42 J3
Vileyka Belarus see Vilyeyka
Vil'gort Rus. Fed. 42 K3
Vilhelmina Sweden 44 J4
Vilhena Brazil 142 F6
Viliya r. Lith. see Neris
Viljandi Estonia 45 N7
Viljoenskroon S. Africa 101 H4
Vilkaviškis Lith. 45 M9
Vilkija Lith. 45 M9
Vil'kitskogo, Proliv strait Rus. Fed. 65 K2
Vilkovo Ukr. see Vylkove
Villa Abecia Bol. 142 E8
Villa Ahumada Mex. 127 G7
Villa Ángela Arg. 144 D3
Villa Bella Bol. 142 E6
Villa Bens Morocco see Tarfaya
Villablino Spain 57 C2
Villacañas Spain 57 E4
Villach Austria 47 N7
Villacidro Sardinia Italy 58 C5
Villa Cisneros W. Sahara see Ad Dakhla
Villa Constitución Mex. see Ciudad Constitución
Villa Dolores Arg. 144 C4
Villagarcía de Arosa Spain see Vilagarcía de Arousa
Villagrán Mex. 131 D7
Villaguay Arg. 144 E4
Villahermosa Mex. 136 F5
Villa Insurgentes Mex. 127 F8
Villajoyosa Spain see Villajoyosa-La Vila Joíosa
Villajoyosa-La Vila Joíosa Spain 57 F4
Villaldama Mex. 131 C7
Villa Mainero Mex. 131 D7
Villa María Arg. 144 D4
Villa Montes Bol. 142 F8
Villa Nora S. Africa 101 I2
Villanueva de la Serena Spain 57 D4
Villanueva de los Infantes Spain 57 E4
Villanueva-y-Geltrú Spain see Vilanova i la Geltrú
Villa Ocampo Arg. 144 E3
Villa Ocampo Mex. 131 B7
Villa Ojo de Agua Arg. 144 D3
Villaputzu Sardinia Italy 58 C5
Villa Regina Arg. 144 C5
Villarrica Para. 144 E3
Villarrica, Lago l. Chile 144 B5
Villarrica, Parque Nacional nat. park Chile 144 B5
Villarrobledo Spain 57 E4
Villas U.S.A. 135 H4
Villasalazar Zimbabwe see Sango
Villa San Giovanni Italy 58 F5
Villa Sanjurjo Morocco see Al Hoceima
Villa San Martín Arg. 144 D3
Villa Unión Arg. 144 C3
Villa Unión Coahuila Mex. 131 C6
Villa Unión Durango Mex. 131 B8
Villa Unión Sinaloa Mex. 136 C4
Villa Valeria Arg. 144 D4
Villavicencio Col. 142 D3
Villazon Bol. 142 E8
Villefranche-sur-Saône France 56 G4
Ville-Marie Canada see Montréal
Villena Spain 57 F4
Villeneuve-sur-Lot France 56 E4
Villeneuve-sur-Yonne France 56 F2
Villers-Cotterêts France 52 D5
Villers-sur-Mer France 49 G9
Villerupt France 52 F5
Villeurbanne France 56 G4
Villiers S. Africa 101 I4
Villingen Germany 47 L6
Villuppuram India see Viluppuram
Villupuram India 84 C4
Vilna Canada 121 I4
Vilna Lith. see Vilnius

▶Vilnius Lith. 45 N9
Capital of Lithuania.

Vil'nyans'k Ukr. 43 G7
Vilppula Fin. 44 N5
Vils r. Germany 53 L5
Vils r. Germany 53 N6
Vilvoorde Belgium 52 E4
Vilyeyka Belarus 45 O9
Vilyuy r. Rus. Fed. 65 N3
Vilyuyskoye Vodokhranilishche resr Rus. Fed. 65 M3
Vimmerby Sweden 45 I8
Vimy France 52 C4
Vina r. Cameroon 97 E4
Vina U.S.A. 128 B2
Viña del Mar Chile 144 B4
Vinalhaven Island U.S.A. 132 G2
Vinaròs Spain 57 G3
Vinaroz Spain see Vinaròs
Vincelotte, Lac l. Canada 123 G3
Vincennes U.S.A. 134 B4
Vincennes Bay Antarctica 152 F2
Vinchina Arg. 144 C3
Vindelälven r. Sweden 44 K5
Vindeln Sweden 44 K4
Vindhya Range hills India 82 C5
Vindobona Austria see Vienna
Vine Grove U.S.A. 134 C5
Vineland U.S.A. 135 H4
Vinh Vietnam 70 D3
Vinh Loc Vietnam 70 D2
Vinh Long Vietnam 71 D5
Vinh Thực, Đao i. Vietnam 70 D2
Vinita U.S.A. 131 E4
Vinjhan India 82 B5
Vinland i. Canada see Newfoundland
Vinnitsa Ukr. see Vinnytsya
Vinnytsya Ukr. 43 F6
Vinogradov Ukr. see Vynohradiv

▶Vinson Massif mt. Antarctica 152 L1
Highest mountain in Antarctica.

Vinstra Norway 45 F6
Vinton U.S.A. 130 E3
Vinukonda India 84 C2
Violeta Cuba see Primero de Enero
Vipperow Germany 53 M1
Viqueque East Timor 108 D2
Virac Phil. 69 G4
Viramgam India 82 C5
Viranşehir Turkey 91 E3
Virawah Pak. 89 H5
Virchow, Mount hill Australia 108 B5
Virdel India 82 C5
Virden Canada 121 K5
Virden U.S.A. 129 I5
Vire France 56 D2
Virei Angola 99 B5
Virgem da Lapa Brazil 145 C2
Virgilina U.S.A. 135 F5
Virgin r. U.S.A. 129 F3
Virginia Ireland 51 E4
Virginia S. Africa 101 H5
Virginia U.S.A. 130 F4
Virginia state U.S.A. 134 F5
Virginia Beach U.S.A. 135 H5
Virginia City MT U.S.A. 126 F3
Virginia City NV U.S.A. 128 D2
Virginia Falls Canada 120 E2

▶Virgin Islands (U.K.) terr. West Indies 137 L5
United Kingdom Overseas Territory.

▶Virgin Islands (U.S.A.) terr. West Indies 137 L5
United States Unincorporated Territory.

Virgin Mountains U.S.A. 129 F3
Virginópolis Brazil 145 C2
Virkkala Fin. 45 N6
Virôchey Cambodia 71 D4
Viroqua U.S.A. 130 F3
Virovitica Croatia 58 G2
Virrat Fin. 44 M5
Virton Belgium 52 F5
Virtsu Estonia 45 M7
Virudhunagar India 84 C4
Virudunagar India see Virudhunagar
Virunga, Parc National des nat. park Dem. Rep. Congo 98 C4
Vis i. Croatia 58 G3
Visaginas Lith. 45 O9
Visakhapatnam India see Vishakhapatnam
Visalia U.S.A. 128 D3
Visapur India 84 B2
Visayan Sea Phil. 69 G4
Visbek Germany 53 I2
Visby Sweden 45 K8
Viscount Melville Sound sea chan. Canada 119 G2
Visé Belgium 52 F4
Viseu Brazil 143 I4
Viseu Port. 57 C3
Vishakhapatnam India 84 D2
Vishera r. Rus. Fed. 41 R4
Vishera r. Rus. Fed. 42 L3
Višķi Latvia 45 O8
Visnagar India 82 C5
Viso, Monte mt. Italy 58 B2
Visoko Bos.-Herz. 58 H3
Visp Switz. 56 H3
Visselhövede Germany 53 J2
Vista U.S.A. 128 E5
Vista Lake U.S.A. 128 D4
Vistonida, Limni lag. Greece 59 K4
Vistula r. Poland 47 Q3
Vitebsk Belarus see Vitsyebsk
Viterbo Italy 58 E3
Vitichi Bol. 142 E8
Vitigudino Spain 57 C3
Viti Levu i. Fiji 107 H3
Vitimskoye Ploskogor'ye plat. Rus. Fed. 73 K2
Vitória Brazil 145 C3
Vitória da Conquista Brazil 145 C1
Vitoria-Gasteiz Spain 57 E2
Vitória Seamount sea feature S. Atlantic Ocean 148 F7
Vitré France 56 D2
Vitry-en-Artois France 52 C4
Vitry-le-François France 52 E6
Vitsyebsk Belarus 43 F5
Vittangi Sweden 44 L3
Vittel France 56 G2
Vittoria Sicily Italy 58 F6
Vittorio Veneto Italy 58 E2
Viveiro Spain 57 C2
Vivero Spain see Viveiro
Vivo S. Africa 101 I2
Vizagapatam India see Vishakhapatnam
Vizcaíno, Desierto de des. Mex. 127 E8
Vizcaíno, Sierra mts Mex. 127 E8
Vize Turkey 59 L4
Vize, Ostrov i. Rus. Fed. 64 I2
Vizhas r. Rus. Fed. 42 J2
Vizianagaram India 84 D2
Vizinga Rus. Fed. 42 K3
Vlaardingen Neth. 52 E3
Vlădeasa, Vârful mt. Romania 59 J1
Vladikavkaz Rus. Fed. 91 G2
Vladimir Primorskiy Kray Rus. Fed. 74 D4
Vladimir Vladimirskaya Oblast' Rus. Fed. 42 I4
Vladimiro-Aleksandrovskoye Rus. Fed. 74 D4
Vladimir-Volynskiy Ukr. see Volodymyr-Volyns'kyy
Vladivostok Rus. Fed. 74 C4
Vlakte S. Africa 101 I3
Vlasotince Serbia 59 J3
Vlas'yevo Rus. Fed. 74 F1
Vlieland i. Neth. 52 E1
Vlissingen Neth. 52 D3
Vlora Albania see Vlorë
Vlorë Albania 59 H4
Vlotho Germany 53 I2
Vlotslavsk Poland see Włocławek
Vltava r. Czech Rep. 47 O5
Vobkent Uzbek. 89 G1
Vöcklabruck Austria 47 N6
Vodlozero, Ozero l. Rus. Fed. 42 H3
Voe U.K. 50 [inset]
Voerendaal Neth. 52 F4
Vogelkop Peninsula Indon. see Doberai, Jazirah
Vogelsberg hills Germany 53 I4
Voghera Italy 58 C2
Vohburg an der Donau Germany 53 L6
Vohémar Madag. see Iharaña
Vohenstrauß Germany 53 M5
Vohibinany Madag. see Ampasimanolotra
Vohimarina Madag. see Iharaña
Vohimena, Tanjona c. Madag. 99 E6
Vohipeno Madag. 99 E6
Vöhl Germany 53 I3
Võhma Estonia 45 N7
Voinjama Liberia 96 C4
Vojens Denmark 45 F9
Vojvodina prov. Serbia 59 H2
Vokhma Rus. Fed. 42 J4
Voknavolok Rus. Fed. 44 Q4
Vol' r. Rus. Fed. 42 L3
Volcano Bay Japan see Uchiura-wan

▶Volcano Islands Japan 69 K2
Part of Japan.

Volda Norway 44 E5
Vol'dino Rus. Fed. 42 L3
Volendam Neth. 52 F2
Volga Rus. Fed. 42 H4

▶Volga r. Rus. Fed. 43 J7
Longest river in Europe.

Volga Upland hills Rus. Fed. see Privolzhskaya Vozvyshennost'
Volgodonsk Rus. Fed. 43 I7
Volgograd Rus. Fed. 43 J6
Volgogradskoye Vodokhranilishche resr Rus. Fed. 43 J6
Völkermarkt Austria 47 O7
Volkhov Rus. Fed. 42 G4
Volkhov r. Rus. Fed. 42 G3
Völklingen Germany 52 G5
Volkovysk Belarus see Vawkavysk
Volksrust S. Africa 101 I4
Vol'no-Nadezhdinskoye Rus. Fed. 74 C4
Volnovakha Ukr. 43 H7
Vol'nyansk Ukr. see Vil'nyans'k
Volochanka Rus. Fed. 64 K2
Volochisk Ukr. see Volochys'k
Volochys'k Ukr. 43 E6
Volodars'ke Ukr. 43 H7
Volodarskoye Kazakh. see Saumalkol'
Volodymyr-Volyns'kyy Ukr. 43 E6
Vologda Rus. Fed. 42 H4
Volokolamsk Rus. Fed. 42 G4
Volokovaya Rus. Fed. 42 K2
Volos Greece 59 J5
Volosovo Rus. Fed. 45 P7
Volot Rus. Fed. 42 F4
Volovo Rus. Fed. 43 H5
Volozhin Belarus see Valozhyn
Volsinii Italy see Orvieto
Vol'sk Rus. Fed. 43 J5

▶Volta, Lake resr Ghana 96 D4
4th largest lake in Africa.

Volta Blanche r. Burkina/Ghana see White Volta
Voltaire, Cape Australia 108 D3
Volta Redonda Brazil 145 B3
Volturno r. Italy 58 F4
Volubilis tourist site Morocco 54 C5
Volvi, Limni l. Greece 59 J4
Volzhsk Rus. Fed. 42 K5
Volzhskiy Samarskaya Oblast' Rus. Fed. 43 K5
Volzhskiy Volgogradskaya Oblast' Rus. Fed. 43 J6
Vondanka Rus. Fed. 42 J4
Vontimitta India 84 C3
Vopnafjörður Iceland 44 [inset]
Vopnafjörður b. Iceland 44 [inset]
Vörå Fin. 44 M5
Voranava Belarus 45 N9
Voreies Sporades is Greece 59 J5
Voreioi Sporades is Greece see Voreies Sporades
Voríai Sporádhes is Greece see Voreies Sporades
Voring Plateau sea feature N. Atlantic Ocean 148 I1
Vorjing mt. India 83 H3
Vorkuta Rus. Fed. 64 H3
Vormsi i. Estonia 45 M7
Vorona r. Rus. Fed. 43 I6
Voronezh Rus. Fed. 43 H6
Voronezh r. Rus. Fed. 43 H6
Voronov, Mys pt Rus. Fed. 42 I2
Vorontsovo-Aleksandrovskoye Rus. Fed. see Zelenokumsk
Voroshilov Rus. Fed. see Ussuriysk
Voroshilovgrad Ukr. see Luhans'k
Voroshilovsk Rus. Fed. see Stavropol'
Voroshilovsk Ukr. see Alchevs'k
Vorotynets Rus. Fed. 42 J4
Vorozhba Ukr. 43 G6
Vorpommersche Boddenlandschaft, Nationalpark nat. park Germany 47 N3
Vorskla r. Rus. Fed. 43 G6
Võrtsjärv l. Estonia 45 N7
Võru Estonia 45 O8
Vorukh Tajik. 89 H2
Vosburg S. Africa 100 F6
Vose Tajik. 89 H2
Vosges mts France 56 H3
Voskresensk Rus. Fed. 43 H5
Voskresenskoye Rus. Fed. 42 H4
Voss Norway 45 E6
Vostochno-Sakhalinskiy Gory mts Rus. Fed. 74 F2
Vostochno-Sibirskoye More sea Rus. Fed. see East Siberian Sea
Vostochnyy Kirovskaya Oblast' Rus. Fed. 42 L4
Vostochnyy Sakhalinskaya Oblast' Rus. Fed. 74 F2
Vostochnyy Sayan mts Rus. Fed. 72 G2

▶Vostok research station Antarctica 152 F1
Lowest recorded screen temperature in the world.

Vostok Primorskiy Kray Rus. Fed. 74 D3
Vostok Sakhalinskaya Oblast' Rus. Fed. see Neftegorsk
Vostok Island Kiribati 151 J6
Vostroye Rus. Fed. 42 J3
Votkinsk Rus. Fed. 41 Q4
Votkinskoye Vodokhranilishche resr Rus. Fed. 41 R4
Votuporanga Brazil 145 A3
Vouziers France 52 E5
Voves France 56 E2
Voyageurs National Park U.S.A. 130 E1
Voynitsa Rus. Fed. 44 Q4
Vöyri Fin. see Vörå
Voyvozh Rus. Fed. 42 L3
Vozhayel' Rus. Fed. 42 K3
Vozhe, Ozero l. Rus. Fed. 42 H3
Vozhega Rus. Fed. 42 I3
Vozhgaly Rus. Fed. 42 K4
Voznesens'k Ukr. 43 F7
Vozonin Trough sea feature Arctic Ocean 153 F1
Vozrozhdenya Island i. Uzbek. 80 A3
Vozzhayevka Rus. Fed. 74 C2
Vrangel' Rus. Fed. 74 D4
Vrangelya, Mys pt Rus. Fed. 74 E1
Vranje Serbia 59 I3
Vratnik pass Bulg. 59 L3
Vratsa Bulg. 59 J3
Vrbas Serbia 59 H2
Vrede S. Africa 101 I4
Vredefort S. Africa 101 H4
Vredenburg S. Africa 100 C7
Vredendal S. Africa 100 D6
Vresse Belgium 52 E5
Vriddhachalam India 84 C4
Vries Neth. 52 G1
Vrigstad Sweden 45 I8
Vršac Serbia 59 I2
Vryburg S. Africa 100 G4
Vryheid S. Africa 101 J4
Vsevidof, Mount vol. U.S.A. 118 B4
Vsevolozhsk Rus. Fed. 42 F3
Vu Ban Vietnam 70 D2
Vučitrn Kosovo see Vushtrri
Vukovar Croatia 59 H2
Vuktyl' Rus. Fed. 41 R3
Vukuzakhe S. Africa 101 I4
Vulcan Canada 120 H5
Vulcan Island P.N.G. see Manam Island
Vulcano, Isola i. Italy 58 F5
Vu Liêt Vietnam 70 D3
Vulture Mountains U.S.A. 129 G5
Vung Tau Vietnam 71 D5
Vuohijärvi Fin. 45 O6
Vuolijoki Fin. 44 O4
Vuollerim Sweden 44 L3
Vuostimo Fin. 44 O3
Vurnary Rus. Fed. 42 J5
Vushtrri Kosovo 59 I3
Vvedenovka Rus. Fed. 74 C2
Vyara India 82 C5
Vyarkhowye Belarus see Ruba
Vyatka Rus. Fed. see Kirov
Vyatka r. Rus. Fed. 42 K5
Vyatskiye Polyany Rus. Fed. 42 K4
Vyazemskiy Rus. Fed. 74 D3
Vyaz'ma Rus. Fed. 43 G5
Vyazniki Rus. Fed. 42 I4
Vyazovka Rus. Fed. 43 J5
Vyborg Rus. Fed. 45 P6
Vychegda r. Rus. Fed. 42 J3
Vychegodskiy Rus. Fed. 42 J3
Vyerkhnyadzvinsk Belarus 45 O9
Vyetryna Belarus 45 P9
Vygozero, Ozero l. Rus. Fed. 42 G3
Vyksa Rus. Fed. 43 I5
Vylkove Ukr. 59 M2
Vym' r. Rus. Fed. 42 K3
Vynohradiv Ukr. 43 D6
Vypin Island India 84 C4
Vypolzovo Rus. Fed. 42 G4
Vyritsa Rus. Fed. 45 Q7
Vyrnwy, Lake U.K. 49 D6
Vyselki Rus. Fed. 43 H7
Vysha Rus. Fed. 43 I5
Vyshhorod Ukr. 43 F6
Vyshnevolotskaya Gryada ridge Rus. Fed. 42 G4
Vyshniy-Volochek Rus. Fed. 42 G4
Vyškov Czech Rep. 47 P6
Vysokaya Gora Rus. Fed. 42 K5
Vysokogorniy Rus. Fed. 74 E2
Vystupovychi Ukr. 43 F6
Vytegra Rus. Fed. 42 H3
Vyya r. Rus. Fed. 42 J3
Vyžuona r. Lith. 45 N9

Wa Ghana 96 C3
Waal r. Neth. 52 E3
Waalwijk Neth. 52 F3
Waat Sudan 86 D8
Wabag P.N.G. 69 K8
Wabakimi Lake Canada 122 C4
Wabasca r. Canada 120 H3
Wabasca-Desmarais Canada 120 H4
Wabash U.S.A. 134 C3
Wabash r. U.S.A. 134 A5
Wabasha U.S.A. 130 E2
Wabassi r. Canada 122 D4
Wabatongushi Lake Canada 122 D4
Wabē Gestro r. Eth. 78 D6
Wabē Shebelē Wenz r. Eth. 98 E3
Wabigoon Lake Canada 121 M5
Wabowden Canada 121 L4
Wabrah well Saudi Arabia 88 B5
Wabu China 77 H1
Wabuk Point Canada 122 D3
Wabush Canada 123 I3
Waccasassa Bay U.S.A. 133 D6
Wächtersbach Germany 53 J4
Waco Canada 123 I4
Waco U.S.A. 131 D6
Waconda Lake U.S.A. 130 D4
Wadbilliga National Park Australia 112 D6
Waddān Libya 55 H6
Waddell Dam U.S.A. 129 G5
Waddeneilanden Neth. 52 E1
Waddenzee sea chan. Neth. 52 E2
Waddington, Mount Canada 120 E5
Waddinxveen Neth. 52 E2
Wadebridge U.K. 49 C8
Wadena Canada 121 K5
Wadena U.S.A. 130 E2
Wadern Germany 52 G5
Wadesville U.S.A. 134 B4
Wadeye Australia 108 E3
Wadgassen Germany 52 G5
Wadh Pak. 89 G5
Wadhwan India see Surendranagar
Wadi India 84 C2
Wādī as Sīr Jordan 85 B4
Wadi Halfa Sudan 86 D5
Wad Medani Sudan 86 D7
Wad Rawa Sudan 86 D6
Wadsworth U.S.A. 128 D2
Waenhuiskrans S. Africa 100 E8
Wafangdian China 73 M5
Wafra Kuwait see Al Wafrah
Wagenfeld Germany 53 I2
Wagenhoff Germany 53 K2
Wagga Wagga Australia 112 C5
Wagner U.S.A. 130 D3
Wagoner U.S.A. 131 E4
Wagon Mound U.S.A. 127 G5
Wah Pak. 89 I3
Wahai Indon. 69 H7
Wāḥāt Jālū Libya 97 F2
Wahemen, Lac l. Canada 123 H3
Wahiawā U.S.A. 127 [inset]
Wahlhausen Germany 53 J3
Wahpeton U.S.A. 130 D2
Wahran Alg. see Oran
Wah Wah Mountains U.S.A. 129 G2
Wai India 84 B2
Waialua U.S.A. 127 [inset]
Waiau N.Z. see Franz Josef Glacier
Waiau r. N.Z. 113 D6
Waiblingen Germany 53 J6
Waidhofen an der Ybbs Austria 47 O7
Waigeo i. Indon. 69 I7
Waiheke Island N.Z. 113 E3
Waikabubak Indon. 108 B2
Waikaia r. N.Z. 113 B7
Waikari N.Z. 113 D6
Waikerie Australia 111 B7
Waikouaiti N.Z. 113 C7
Wailuku U.S.A. 127 [inset]
Waimangaroa N.Z. 113 C5
Waimarama N.Z. 113 F4
Waimate N.Z. 113 C7
Waimea U.S.A. 127 [inset]
Wainganga r. India 84 C2
Waingapu Indon. 108 C2
Wainhouse Corner U.K. 49 C8
Waini Point Guyana 143 G2
Wainwright Canada 121 I4
Wainwright U.S.A. 118 C2
Waiouru N.Z. 113 E4
Waipahi N.Z. 113 B8
Waipaoa r. N.Z. 113 F4
Waipara N.Z. 113 D6
Waipawa N.Z. 113 F4
Waipukurau N.Z. 113 F4
Wairarapa, Lake N.Z. 113 E5
Wairau r. N.Z. 113 E5
Wairoa N.Z. 113 F4
Wairoa r. N.Z. 113 F4
Waitahanui N.Z. 113 F4
Waitahuna N.Z. 113 B7
Waitakaruru N.Z. 113 E3
Waitaki r. N.Z. 113 C7
Waitangi N.Z. 107 I6
Waite River Australia 108 F5
Waiuku N.Z. 113 E3
Waiwera South N.Z. 113 B8
Waiyang China 77 H3
Wajima Japan 75 E5
Wajir Kenya 98 E3
Waka Indon. 108 C2
Wakasa-wan b. Japan 75 D6
Wakatipu, Lake N.Z. 113 B7
Wakaw Canada 121 J4
Wakayama Japan 75 D6
Wake Atoll terr. N. Pacific Ocean see Wake Island
WaKeeney U.S.A. 130 D4
Wakefield N.Z. 113 D5
Wakefield U.K. 48 F5

/akefield *MI* U.S.A. **130** F2
/akefield *RI* U.S.A. **135** J3
/akefield *VA* U.S.A. **135** G5

▶Wake Island *terr.* N. Pacific Ocean **150** H4
United States Unincorporated Territory.

/akema Myanmar **70** A3
'akhan *reg.* Afgh. **89** I2
/akkanai Japan **74** F3
/akkerstroom S. Africa **101** J4
/akool Australia **112** B5
/akool *r.* Australia **112** A5
/akuach, Lac *l.* Canada **123** I3
/aku-Kungo Angola **99** B5
/ałbrzych Poland **47** P5
/alcha Australia **112** E3
/alcott U.S.A. **126** G4
/alcourt Belgium **52** E4
/ałcz Poland **47** P4
/aldburg Range *mts* Australia **109** B6
/alden U.S.A. **135** H3
/aldenbuch Germany **53** J6
/aldenburg Poland *see* **Wałbrzych**
'aldkraiburg Germany **47** N6
'aldo U.S.A. **134** D3
'aldoboro U.S.A. **135** K1
'aldorf U.S.A. **135** G4
'aldport U.S.A. **126** B3
'aldron U.S.A. **131** E5
'aldron, Cape Antarctica **152** F2
'alebing Australia **109** B7
'alêg China **76** D2
'ales *admin. div.* U.K. **49** D6
'algaon India **82** D5
'algett Australia **112** D3
'algreen Coast Antarctica **152** K1
'alhalla *MI* U.S.A. **134** B2
'alhalla *ND* U.S.A. **130** D1
'alikale Dem. Rep. Congo **97** F5
'alingai P.N.G. **69** L8
'alker *r.* Australia **110** A2
'alker *watercourse* Australia **109** F6
'alker *MI* U.S.A. **134** C2
'alker *MN* U.S.A. **130** E2
'alker *r.* U.S.A. **128** D2
'alker Bay S. Africa **100** D8
'alker Creek *r.* Australia **110** C3
'alker Lake Canada **121** L4
'alker Lake U.S.A. **128** D2
'alker Pass U.S.A. **128** D4
'alkersville U.S.A. **135** G4
'alkerton Canada **134** E1
'alkerton U.S.A. **134** B3
'all, Mount *hill* Australia **108** B5
'allaby Island Australia **110** C2
'allace *ID* U.S.A. **126** D3
'allace *NC* U.S.A. **133** E5
'allace *VA* U.S.A. **134** D5
'allaceburg Canada **134** D2
'allal Downs Australia **108** C4
'allangarra Australia **112** E2
'allaroo Australia **111** B7
'allasey U.K. **48** D5
'alla Walla Australia **112** C5
'alla Walla U.S.A. **126** D3
'alldürn Germany **53** J5
'allekraal S. Africa **100** C6
'allendbeen Australia **112** D5
'allingford U.K. **49** F7
'allis, Îles *is* Wallis and Futuna Is **107** I3

Wallis and Futuna Islands *terr.* S. Pacific Ocean **107** I3
French Overseas Collectivity.

'allis et Futuna, Îles *terr.* S. Pacific Ocean *see* **Wallis and Futuna Islands**
'allis Islands Wallis and Futuna Is *see* **Wallis, Îles**
'allis Lake *inlet* Australia **112** F4
'allops Island U.S.A. **135** H5
'allowa Mountains U.S.A. **126** D3
'alls U.K. **50** [inset]
'alls of Jerusalem National Park Australia **111** [inset]
'allumbilla Australia **111** E5
'almsley Lake Canada **121** I2
'alney, Isle of *i.* U.K. **48** D4
'alnut Creek U.S.A. **128** B3
'alnut Grove U.S.A. **128** C2
'alnut Ridge U.S.A. **131** F4
'along India **83** I3
'alpole U.S.A. **135** I2
'alsall U.K. **49** F6
'alsenburg U.S.A. **127** G5
'alsh U.S.A. **131** C4
'alsrode Germany **53** J2
'altair India **84** D2
'alterboro U.S.A. **133** D5
'alters U.S.A. **131** D5
'alter's Range *hills* Australia **112** B2
'althall U.S.A. **131** F5
'altham U.S.A. **135** J2
'alton *IN* U.S.A. **134** B3
'alton *KY* U.S.A. **134** C4
'alton *NY* U.S.A. **135** H2
'alton *WV* U.S.A. **134** E4
'alvisbaai Namibia *see* **Walvis Bay**
'alvisbaai *b.* Namibia *see* **Walvis Bay**
'alvis Bay Namibia **100** B2
'alvis Bay *b.* Namibia **100** B2
'alvis Ridge *sea feature* S. Atlantic Ocean **148** H8
'ama Afgh. **89** H3
'amba *Équateur* Dem. Rep. Congo **97** F5
'amba *Orientale* Dem. Rep. Congo **98** C3
'amba Nigeria **96** D4
'ampum U.S.A. **134** E3
'ampusirpi Hond. **137** H5
'amsutter U.S.A. **126** G4
'ana Pak. **89** H3
'anaaring Australia **112** B2
'anaka N.Z. **113** B7
'anaka, Lake N.Z. **113** B7
'an'an China **77** G3
'anapitei Lake Canada **122** E5
'anbi Australia **111** C7
'anbrow, Cape N.Z. **113** C7
'anda Shan *mts* China **74** D3
'andering River Canada **121** H4

Wandersleben Germany **53** K4
Wandlitz Germany **53** N2
Wando S. Korea **75** B6
Wandoan Australia **111** E5
Wanganui N.Z. **113** E4
Wanganui *r.* N.Z. **113** E4
Wangaratta Australia **112** C6
Wangcang China **76** E1
Wangda China *see* **Zogang**
Wangdain China **83** G3
Wangdi Phodrang Bhutan **83** G4
Wanggamet, Gunung *mt.* Indon. **108** C2
Wanggao China **77** F3
Wang Gaxun China **83** I1
Wangguan China **76** E1
Wangiwangi *i.* Indon. **69** G8
Wangkui China **74** B3
Wangmo China **76** E3
Wangqing China **74** C4
Wangwu Shan *mts* China **77** F1
Wangying China *see* **Huaiyin**
Wanham Canada **120** G4
Wan Hsa-la Myanmar **70** B2
Wanie-Rukula Dem. Rep. Congo **98** C3
Wankaner India **82** B5
Wankie Zimbabwe *see* **Hwange**
Wanlaweyn Somalia **98** E3
Wanna Germany **53** I1
Wanna Lakes *salt flat* Australia **109** E7
Wannian China **77** H2
Wanning China **77** F5
Wanroij Neth. **52** F3
Wanshan China **77** F3
Wanshan Qundao *is* China **77** G4
Wansheng China **76** E2
Wanshengchang China *see* **Wansheng**
Wantage U.K. **49** F7
Wanxian *Chongqing* China **77** F2
Wanxian *Chongqing* China *see* **Shahe**
Wanyuan China **77** F1
Wanzai China **77** G2
Wanze Belgium **52** F4
Wapakoneta U.S.A. **134** C3
Wapawekka Lake Canada **121** J4
Wapello U.S.A. **130** F3
Wapikaimaski Lake Canada **122** C4
Wapikopa Lake Canada **122** C3
Wapiti *r.* Canada **120** G4
Wapusk National Park Canada **121** M3
Waqên China **76** D1
Waqf aş Şawwān, Jibāl *hills* Jordan **85** C4
War U.S.A. **134** E5
Warab Sudan **86** C8
Warangal India **84** C2
Waranga Reservoir Australia **112** B6
Waratah Bay Australia **112** B7
Warbreccan Australia **110** C5
Warburg Germany **53** J3
Warburton Australia **109** D6
Warburton *watercourse* Australia **111** B5
Warburton Bay Canada **121** I2
Warche *r.* Belgium **52** F4
Ward, Mount N.Z. **113** B6
Warden S. Africa **101** I4
Wardenburg Germany **53** I1
Wardha India **84** C1
Wardha *r.* India **84** C2
Ward Hill *hill* U.K. **50** F2
Ward Hunt, Cape P.N.G. **69** L8
Ware Canada **120** E3
Ware U.S.A. **135** I2
Wareham U.K. **49** E8
Waremme Belgium **52** F4
Waren Germany **53** M1
Warendorf Germany **53** H3
Warginburra Peninsula Australia **110** E4
Wargla Alg. *see* **Ouargla**
Warialda Australia **112** E2
Warin Chamrap Thai. **70** D4
Warkum Neth. *see* **Workum**
Warkworth U.K. **48** F3
Warli China *see* **Walêg**
Warloy-Baillon France **52** C4
Warman Canada **121** J4
Warmbad Namibia **100** D5
Warmbad S. Africa **101** I3
Warmbaths S. Africa *see* **Warmbad**
Warminster U.K. **49** E7
Warminster U.S.A. **135** H3
Warmond Neth. **52** E2
Warm Springs *NV* U.S.A. **128** E2
Warm Springs *VA* U.S.A. **134** F4
Warmwaterberg *mts* S. Africa **100** E7
Warner Canada **121** H5
Warner Lakes U.S.A. **126** D4
Warner Mountains U.S.A. **126** C4
Warnes Bol. **142** F7
Warning, Mount Australia **112** F2
Waronda India **84** C2
Warora India **84** C1
Warra Australia **112** E1
Warragamba Reservoir Australia **112** E5
Warragul Australia **112** B7
Warrambool *r.* Australia **112** C3
Warrandirinna, Lake *salt flat* Australia **111** B5
Warrandyte Australia **112** B6
Warrawagine Australia **108** C5
Warrego *r.* Australia **112** B3
Warrego Range *hills* Australia **110** D5
Warren Australia **112** C3
Warren *AR* U.S.A. **131** E5
Warren *MI* U.S.A. **134** D2
Warren *MN* U.S.A. **130** D1
Warren *OH* U.S.A. **134** E3
Warren *PA* U.S.A. **134** F3
Warren Hastings Island Palau *see* **Merir**
Warren Island U.S.A. **120** C4
Warrenpoint U.K. **51** F3
Warrensburg *MO* U.S.A. **130** E4
Warrensburg *NY* U.S.A. **135** I2
Warrenton S. Africa **100** G5
Warrenton *GA* U.S.A. **133** D5
Warrenton *MO* U.S.A. **130** F4
Warrenton *VA* U.S.A. **135** G4
Warri Nigeria **96** D4
Warriners Creek *watercourse* Australia **111** B6
Warrington N.Z. **113** C7
Warrington U.K. **48** E5
Warrington U.S.A. **133** C6

Warrnambool Australia **111** C8
Warroad U.S.A. **130** E1
Warrumbungle National Park Australia **112** D3

▶Warsaw Poland **47** R4
Capital of Poland.

Warsaw *IN* U.S.A. **134** C3
Warsaw *KY* U.S.A. **134** C4
Warsaw *MO* U.S.A. **130** E4
Warsaw *NY* U.S.A. **135** F2
Warsaw *VA* U.S.A. **135** G5
Warshiikh Somalia **98** E3
Warstein Germany **53** I3
Warszawa Poland *see* **Warsaw**
Warta *r.* Poland **47** O4
Warwick Australia **112** F2
Warwick U.K. **49** F6
Warwick U.S.A. **135** J3
Warzhong China **76** D2
Wasaga Beach Canada **134** E1
Wasatch Range *mts* U.S.A. **126** F5
Wasbank S. Africa **101** J5
Wasco U.S.A. **128** D4
Washburn *ND* U.S.A. **130** C2
Washburn *WI* U.S.A. **130** F2
Washim India **84** C1

▶Washington *DC* U.S.A. **135** G4
Capital of the United States of America.

Washington *GA* U.S.A. **133** D5
Washington *IA* U.S.A. **130** F3
Washington *IN* U.S.A. **134** B4
Washington *MO* U.S.A. **130** F4
Washington *NC* U.S.A. **132** E5
Washington *NJ* U.S.A. **135** H3
Washington *PA* U.S.A. **134** E3
Washington *UT* U.S.A. **129** G3
Washington *state* U.S.A. **126** C3
Washington, Cape Antarctica **152** H2
Washington, Mount U.S.A. **135** J1
Washington Court House U.S.A. **134** D4
Washington Island U.S.A. **132** C2
Washington Land *reg.* Greenland **119** L2
Washir Afgh. **89** F3
Washita *r.* U.S.A. **131** D5
Washpool National Park Australia **112** F2
Washtucna U.S.A. **126** D3
Washuk Pak. **89** G5
Wasi India **84** B2
Wasi' Saudi Arabia **88** B5
Wasi' *well* Saudi Arabia **88** C6
Waskaganish Canada **122** F4
Waskagheganish Canada *see* **Waskaganish**
Waskaiowaka Lake Canada **121** L3
Waskey, Mount U.S.A. **118** C4
Wassenaar Neth. **52** E2
Wasser Namibia **100** D4
Wasserkuppe *hill* Germany **53** J4
Wassertrüdingen Germany **53** K5
Wassuk Range *mts* U.S.A. **128** D2
Wasua P.N.G. **69** K8
Wasum P.N.G. **69** L8
Waswanipi *r.* Canada **122** F4
Waswanipi, Lac *l.* Canada **122** F4
Watam P.N.G. **69** K7
Watampone Indon. **69** G7
Watapi Lake Canada **121** I4
Watarrka National Park Australia **109** E6
Watenstadt-Salzgitter Germany *see* **Salzgitter**
Waterbury *CT* U.S.A. **135** I3
Waterbury *VT* U.S.A. **135** I1
Waterbury Lake Canada **121** J3
Water Cays *i.* Bahamas **133** E8
Waterdown Canada **134** F2
Wateree *r.* U.S.A. **133** D5
Waterfall U.S.A. **120** C4
Waterford Ireland **51** E5
Waterford *PA* U.S.A. **134** F3
Waterford *WI* U.S.A. **134** A2
Waterford Harbour Ireland **51** F5
Watergrasshill Ireland **51** D5
Waterhen Lake Canada **121** L4
Waterloo Australia **108** E4
Waterloo Belgium **52** E4
Waterloo *Ont.* Canada **134** E2
Waterloo *Que.* Canada **135** I1
Waterloo *IA* U.S.A. **130** E3
Waterloo *IL* U.S.A. **130** F4
Waterloo *NY* U.S.A. **135** G2
Waterlooville U.K. **49** F8
Waterton Lakes National Park Canada **120** H5
Watertown *NY* U.S.A. **135** H2
Watertown *SD* U.S.A. **130** D2
Watertown *WI* U.S.A. **130** F3
Waterval Boven S. Africa **101** J3
Water Valley U.S.A. **131** F5
Waterville *ME* U.S.A. **135** K1
Waterville *WA* U.S.A. **126** C3
Watford Canada **134** E2
Watford U.K. **49** G7
Watford City U.S.A. **130** C2
Wathaman *r.* Canada **121** K3
Wathaman Lake Canada **121** K3
Watheroo National Park Australia **109** A7
Wathlingen Germany **53** K2
Watino Canada **120** G4
Watīr, Wādī *watercourse* Egypt **85** B5
Watkins Glen U.S.A. **135** G2
Watling Island Bahamas *see* **San Salvador**
Watmuri Indon. **108** E1
Watonga U.S.A. **131** D5
Watrous Canada **121** J5
Watrous U.S.A. **127** G6
Watseka U.S.A. **134** B3
Watsi Kengo Dem. Rep. Congo **97** F5
Watson *r.* Australia **110** C2
Watson Canada **121** J4
Watson Lake Canada **120** D2
Watsontown U.S.A. **135** G3
Watsonville U.S.A. **128** C3
Watten U.K. **50** F2
Watterson Lake Canada **121** L2
Watton U.K. **49** H6
Watts Bar Lake *resr* U.S.A. **132** C5
Wattsburg U.S.A. **134** F2
Watubela, Kepulauan *is* Indon. **69** I7

Wau P.N.G. **69** L8
Wau Sudan **86** C8
Waubay Lake U.S.A. **130** D2
Wauchope *N.S.W.* Australia **112** F3
Wauchope *N.T.* Australia **108** F5
Waukaringa (abandoned) Australia **111** B7
Waukarlycarly, Lake *salt flat* Australia **108** C5
Waukegan U.S.A. **134** B2
Waukesha U.S.A. **134** A2
Waupaca U.S.A. **130** F2
Waupun U.S.A. **130** F3
Waurika U.S.A. **131** D5
Wausau U.S.A. **130** F2
Wausaukee U.S.A. **132** C2
Wauseon U.S.A. **134** C3
Wautoma U.S.A. **130** F2
Wave Hill Australia **108** E4
Waveney *r.* U.K. **49** I6
Waverly *IA* U.S.A. **130** E3
Waverly *NY* U.S.A. **135** G2
Waverly *OH* U.S.A. **134** D4
Waverly *TN* U.S.A. **132** C4
Waverly *VA* U.S.A. **135** G5
Wavre Belgium **52** E4
Waw Myanmar **70** B3
Wawa Canada **122** D5
Wawalalindu Indon. **69** G7
Wāw al Kabīr Libya **97** E2
Wawasee, Lake U.S.A. **134** C3
Wawo Indon. **69** G7
Waxahachie U.S.A. **131** D5
Waxü China **76** D1
Waxxari China **80** G4
Way, Lake *salt flat* Australia **109** C6
Waycross U.S.A. **133** D6
Wayland *KY* U.S.A. **134** D5
Wayland *MI* U.S.A. **134** C2
Wayne *NE* U.S.A. **130** D3
Wayne *WV* U.S.A. **134** D4
Waynesboro *GA* U.S.A. **133** D5
Waynesboro *MS* U.S.A. **131** F6
Waynesboro *TN* U.S.A. **132** C5
Waynesboro *VA* U.S.A. **135** F4
Waynesburg U.S.A. **134** E4
Waynesville *MO* U.S.A. **130** E4
Waynesville *NC* U.S.A. **132** D5
Waynoka U.S.A. **131** D4
Waza, Parc National de *nat. park* Cameroon **97** E3
Wāzah Khwāh Afgh. *see* **Wazi Khwa**
Wazi Khwa Afgh. **89** H3
Wazirabad Pak. **89** I3
W du Niger, Parcs Nationaux du *nat. park* Niger **96** D3
We, Pulau *i.* Indon. **71** A6
Weagamow Lake Canada **121** N4
Weam P.N.G. **69** K8
Wear *r.* U.K. **48** F4
Weare U.S.A. **135** J2
Weatherford U.S.A. **131** D5
Weaver Lake Canada **121** L4
Weaverville U.S.A. **126** C4
Webb, Mount *hill* Australia **108** E5
Webequie Canada **122** D3
Weber, Mount Canada **120** D4
Weber Basin *sea feature* Laut Banda **150** E6
Webster *IN* U.S.A. **134** C4
Webster *MA* U.S.A. **135** J2
Webster *SD* U.S.A. **130** D2
Webster City U.S.A. **130** E3
Webster Springs U.S.A. **134** E4
Wecho Lake Canada **120** H2
Wedau P.N.G. **110** E1
Weddell Abyssal Plain *sea feature* Southern Ocean **152** A2
Weddell Island Falkland Is **144** D8
Weddell Sea Antarctica **152** A2
Wedderburn Australia **112** A6
Weddin Mountains National Park Australia **112** D4
Wedel (Holstein) Germany **53** J1
Wedge Mountain Canada **120** F5
Wedowee U.S.A. **133** C5
Weedville U.S.A. **135** F3
Weenen S. Africa **101** J5
Weener Germany **53** H1
Weert Neth. **52** F3
Weethalle Australia **112** C4
Wee Waa Australia **112** D3
Wegberg Germany **52** G3
Węgorzewo Poland **47** R3
Weichang China **73** L4
Weida Germany **53** M4
Weidenberg Germany **53** L5
Weiden in der Oberpfalz Germany **53** M5
Weidongmen China *see* **Qianjin**
Weifang China **73** L5
Weihai China **73** M5
Wei He *r. Shaanxi* China **76** F1
Wei He *r.* China **77** G1
Weilburg Germany **53** I4
Weilmoringle Australia **112** C2
Weimar Germany **53** L4
Weinan China **77** F1
Weinheim Germany **53** I5
Weining China **76** E3
Weinsberg Germany **53** J5
Weipa Australia **110** C2
Weiqu China *see* **Chang'an**
Weir *r.* Australia **112** D2
Weir River Canada **121** M3
Weirton U.S.A. **134** E3
Weiser U.S.A. **126** D3
Weishan China **76** D3
Weishan Hu *l.* China **77** H1
Weishi China **77** G1
Weiße Elster *r.* Germany **53** L3
Weißenburg in Bayern Germany **53** K5
Weißenfels Germany **53** L3
Weißkugel *mt.* Austria/Italy **47** M7
Weissrand Mountains Namibia **100** D3
Weiterstadt Germany **53** I5
Weitzel Lake Canada **121** J3
Weixi China **76** C3
Weixin China **76** E3
Weiya China **80** H3
Weiyuan *Gansu* China **76** E1
Weiyuan *Sichuan* China **76** E2

Weiyuan *Yunnan* China *see* **Jinggu**
Weiyuan Jiang *r.* China **76** D4
Weiz Austria **47** O7
Weizhou China *see* **Wenchuan**
Weizhou Dao *i.* China **77** F4
Wejherowo Poland **47** Q3
Wekilbazar Turkm. **89** F2
Wekusko Canada **121** L4
Wekusko Lake Canada **121** L4
Wekweêtì Canada **120** H1
Welatam Myanmar **70** B1
Welbourn Hill Australia **109** F6
Welch U.S.A. **134** E5
Weld U.S.A. **135** J1
Weldiya Eth. **98** D2
Welford National Park Australia **110** C5
Welk'īt'ē Eth. **98** D3
Welkom S. Africa **101** H4
Welland Canada **134** F2
Welland *r.* U.K. **49** G6
Welland Canal Canada **134** F2
Wellesley Canada **134** E2
Wellesley Islands Australia **110** B3
Wellesley Lake Canada **120** B2
Wellfleet U.S.A. **135** J3
Wellin Belgium **52** F4
Wellingborough U.K. **49** G6
Wellington Australia **112** D4
Wellington Canada **135** G2

▶Wellington N.Z. **113** E5
Capital of New Zealand.

Wellington S. Africa **100** D7
Wellington *England* U.K. **49** D8
Wellington *England* U.K. **49** E6
Wellington *CO* U.S.A. **126** G4
Wellington *IL* U.S.A. **134** B3
Wellington *KS* U.S.A. **131** D4
Wellington *NV* U.S.A. **128** D2
Wellington *OH* U.S.A. **134** D3
Wellington *TX* U.S.A. **131** C5
Wellington *UT* U.S.A. **129** H2
Wellington, Isla *i.* Chile **144** B7
Wellington Range *hills N.T.* Australia **108** F3
Wellington Range *hills W.A.* Australia **109** C6
Wells Canada **120** F4
Wells U.K. **49** E7
Wells U.S.A. **126** E4
Wells, Lake *salt flat* Australia **109** C6
Wellsboro U.S.A. **135** G3
Wellsburg U.S.A. **134** E3
Wellsford N.Z. **113** E3
Wells-next-the-Sea U.K. **49** H6
Wellston U.S.A. **134** C1
Wellsville U.S.A. **135** G2
Wellton U.S.A. **129** F5
Wels Austria **47** O6
Welshpool U.K. **49** D6
Welsickendorf Germany **53** N3
Welwitschia Namibia *see* **Khorixas**
Welwyn Garden City U.K. **49** G7
Welzheim Germany **53** J6
Wem U.K. **49** E6
Wembesi S. Africa **101** I5
Wembley Canada **120** G4
Wemindji Canada **122** F3
Wenatchee U.S.A. **126** C3
Wenatchee Mountains U.S.A. **126** C3
Wenbu China *see* **Nyima**
Wenchang *Hainan* China **77** F5
Wenchang *Sichuan* China *see* **Zitong**
Wenchow China *see* **Wenzhou**
Wenchuan China **76** D2
Wendelstein Germany **53** L5
Wenden Germany **53** H4
Wenden Latvia *see* **Cēsis**
Wenden U.S.A. **129** G5
Wendover U.S.A. **129** F1
Weng'an China **76** E3
Wengshui China **76** C2
Wengyuan China **77** G3
Wenhua China *see* **Weishan**
Wenlan China *see* **Mengzi**
Wenling China **77** I2
Wenlock *r.* Australia **110** C2
Wenping China *see* **Ludian**
Wenquan *Guizhou* China **76** E2
Wenquan *Henan* China *see* **Wenxian**
Wenquan *Hubei* China *see* **Yingshan**

▶Wenquan *Qinghai* China **83** G2
Highest settlement in the world.

Wenquan *Xinjiang* China **80** F3
Wenshan China **76** E4
Wenshui China **76** E2
Wensum *r.* U.K. **49** I6
Wentorf bei Hamburg Germany **53** K1
Wentworth Australia **111** C7
Wenxi China **77** F1
Wenxian *Gansu* China **76** E1
Wenxian *Henan* China **77** G1
Wenxing China *see* **Xiangyin**
Wenzhou China **77** I3
Wenzlow Germany **53** M2
Wepener S. Africa **101** H5
Wer India **82** D4
Werben (Elbe) Germany **53** L2
Werda Botswana **100** F3
Werdau Germany **53** M4
Werdër Eth. **98** E3
Werder Germany **53** M2
Werdohl Germany **53** H3
Werl Germany **53** H3
Wernberg-Köblitz Germany **53** M5
Werne Germany **53** H3
Wernecke Mountains Canada **120** B1
Wernigerode Germany **53** K3
Werra *r.* Germany **53** J3
Werris Creek Australia **112** E3
Wertheim Germany **53** J5
Wervik Belgium **52** D4
Wesel Germany **52** G3
Wesel-Datteln-Kanal *canal* Germany **52** G3
Wesenberg Germany **53** M1
Wesendorf Germany **53** K2
Weser *r.* Germany **53** I1
Weser *sea chan.* Germany **53** I1

Wesergebirge *hills* Germany **53** I2
Weslaco U.S.A. **131** D7
Weslemkoon Lake Canada **135** G1
Wesleyville Canada **123** L4
Wessel, Cape Australia **110** B1
Wessel Islands Australia **110** B1
Wesselsbron S. Africa **101** H4
Wesselton S. Africa **101** I4
Wessington Springs U.S.A. **130** D2
Westall, Point Australia **109** F8
West Allis U.S.A. **134** A2
West Antarctica *reg.* Antarctica **152** J1
West Australian Basin *sea feature* Indian Ocean **149** O7

▶West Bank *terr.* Asia **85** B3
Territory occupied by Israel.

West Bay Canada **123** K3
West Bay *inlet* U.S.A. **133** C6
West Bend U.S.A. **134** A2
West Bengal *state* India **83** F5
West Branch U.S.A. **134** C1
West Bromwich U.K. **49** F6
Westbrook U.S.A. **135** J2
West Burke U.S.A. **135** J1
West Burra *i.* U.K. *see* **Burra**
Westbury U.K. **49** E7
West Caicos *i.* Turks and Caicos Is **133** F8
West Cape Howe Australia **109** B8
West Caroline Basin *sea feature* N. Pacific Ocean **150** F5
West Chester U.S.A. **135** H4
Westcliffe U.S.A. **127** G5
West Coast National Park S. Africa **100** D7
West End Bahamas **133** E7
Westerburg Germany **53** H4
Westerholt Germany **53** H1
Westerland Germany **47** L3
Westerlo Belgium **52** E3
Westerly U.S.A. **135** J3
Western *r.* Canada **121** J1
Western Australia *state* Australia **109** C6
Western Cape *prov.* S. Africa **100** E7
Western Desert Egypt **90** C6
Western Dvina *r.* Europe *see* **Zapadnaya Dvina**
Western Ghats *mts* India **84** B3
Western Port *b.* Australia **112** B7

▶Western Sahara *terr.* Africa **96** B2
Disputed territory (Morocco).

Western Samoa *country* S. Pacific Ocean *see* **Samoa**
Western Sayan Mountains *reg.* Rus. Fed. *see* **Zapadnyy Sayan**
Westerschelde *est.* Neth. **52** D3
Westerstede Germany **53** H1
Westerville U.S.A. **134** D3
Westerwald *hills* Germany **53** H4
West Falkland *i.* Falkland Is **144** D8
West Fargo U.S.A. **130** D2
West Fayu *atoll* Micronesia **69** L5
Westfield *IN* U.S.A. **134** B3
Westfield *MA* U.S.A. **135** I2
Westfield *NY* U.S.A. **134** F2
Westfield *PA* U.S.A. **135** G3
West Frisian Islands Neth. *see* **Waddeneilanden**
Westgat *sea chan.* Neth. **52** G1
Westgate Australia **112** C1
West Glacier U.S.A. **126** E2
West Grand Lake U.S.A. **132** H2
West Hartford U.S.A. **135** I3
Westhausen Germany **53** K6
West Haven U.S.A. **135** I3
Westhill U.K. **50** G3
Westhope U.S.A. **130** C1
West Ice Shelf Antarctica **152** E2
West Indies *is* Caribbean Sea **137** J4
West Island India **71** A4
Westkapelle Neth. **52** D3
West Kazakhstan Oblast *admin. div.* Kazakh. *see* **Zapadnyy Kazakhstan**
West Kingston U.S.A. **135** J3
West Lafayette U.S.A. **134** B3
West Lamma Channel *H.K.* China **77** [inset]
Westland Australia **110** C4
Westland National Park N.Z. **113** C6
Westleigh S. Africa **101** H4
Westleton U.K. **49** I6
West Liberty U.S.A. **134** D5
West Linton U.K. **50** F5
West Loch Roag *b.* U.K. **50** C2
Westlock Canada **120** H4
West Lorne Canada **134** E2
West Lunga National Park Zambia **99** C5
West MacDonnell National Park Australia **109** F5
West Malaysia *pen.* Malaysia *see* **Peninsular Malaysia**
Westmalle Belgium **52** E3
Westmar Australia **112** D1
West Mariana Basin *sea feature* N. Pacific Ocean **150** F4
West Memphis U.S.A. **131** F5
Westminster U.S.A. **135** G4
Westmoreland Australia **110** B3
Westmoreland U.S.A. **134** B5
Westmorland U.S.A. **129** F5
Weston *OH* U.S.A. **134** D3
Weston *WV* U.S.A. **134** E4
Weston-super-Mare U.K. **49** E7
West Palm Beach U.S.A. **133** D7
West Plains U.S.A. **131** F4
West Point *pt* Australia **111** [inset]
West Point *CA* U.S.A. **128** C2
West Point *KY* U.S.A. **134** C5
West Point *MS* U.S.A. **131** F5
West Point *NE* U.S.A. **130** D3
West Point *VA* U.S.A. **135** G5
West Point Lake *resr* U.S.A. **133** C5
Westport Canada **135** G1
Westport Ireland **51** C4
Westport N.Z. **113** C5
Westport *CA* U.S.A. **128** B2
Westport *KY* U.S.A. **134** C4
Westport *NY* U.S.A. **135** I1
Westray Canada **121** K4

Westray i. U.K. 50 F1
Westray Firth sea chan. U.K. 50 F1
Westree Canada 122 E5
West Rutland U.S.A. 135 I2
West Salem U.S.A. 134 D3
West Siberian Plain Rus. Fed. 64 J3
West-Skylge Neth. see West-Terschelling
West Stewartstown U.S.A. 135 J1
West-Terschelling Neth. 52 F1
West Topsham U.S.A. 135 I1
West Union IA U.S.A. 130 F3
West Union IL U.S.A. 134 B4
West Union OH U.S.A. 134 D4
West Union WV U.S.A. 134 E4
West Valley City U.S.A. 129 H1
Westville U.S.A. 134 B3
West Virginia state U.S.A. 134 E4
Westwood U.S.A. 128 C1
West Wyalong Australia 112 C4
West York U.S.A. 135 G4
Westzaan Neth. 52 E2
Wetar i. Indon. 108 D1
Wetar, Selat sea chan. Indon. 108 D2
Wetaskiwin Canada 120 H4
Wete Tanz. 99 D4
Wetter r. Germany 53 I4
Wettin Germany 53 L3
Wetumpka U.S.A. 133 C5
Wetwun Myanmar 70 B2
Wetzlar Germany 53 I4
Wewahitchka U.S.A. 133 C6
Wewak P.N.G. 69 K7
Wewoka U.S.A. 131 D5
Wexford Ireland 51 F5
Wexford Harbour b. Ireland 51 F5
Weyakwin Canada 121 J4
Weybridge U.K. 49 G7
Weyburn Canada 121 K5
Weyhe Germany 53 I2
Weymouth U.K. 49 E8
Weymouth U.S.A. 135 J2
Wezep Neth. 52 G2
Whakaari i. N.Z. 113 F3
Whakatane N.Z. 113 F3
Whalan Creek r. Australia 112 D2
Whale r. Canada see La Baleine, Rivière à
Whalsay i. U.K. 50 [inset]
Whampoa China see Huangpu
Whangamata N.Z. 113 E3
Whanganui National Park N.Z. 113 E4
Whangarei N.Z. 113 E2
Whapmagoostui Canada 122 F3
Wharfe r. U.K. 48 F5
Wharfedale valley U.K. 48 F4
Wharton U.S.A. 131 D6
Wharton Lake Canada 121 L1
Whatî Canada 120 G2
Wheatland IN U.S.A. 134 B4
Wheatland WY U.S.A. 126 G4
Wheaton IL U.S.A. 134 A3
Wheaton MN U.S.A. 130 D2
Wheaton-Glenmont U.S.A. 135 G4
Wheeler U.S.A. 131 C5
Wheeler Lake Canada 120 H2
Wheeler Lake resr U.S.A. 133 C5
Wheeler Peak NM U.S.A. 127 G5
Wheeler Peak NV U.S.A. 129 F2
Wheelersburg U.S.A. 134 D4
Wheeling U.S.A. 134 E3
Whernside hill U.K. 48 E4
Whinham, Mount Australia 109 E6
Whiskey Jack Lake Canada 121 K3
Whitburn U.K. 50 F5
Whitby Canada 135 F2
Whitby U.K. 48 G4
Whitchurch U.K. 49 E6
Whitchurch-Stouffville Canada 134 F2
White r. Canada 122 D4
White r. Canada/U.S.A. 120 B2
White r. AR U.S.A. 125 I5
White r. AR U.S.A. 131 F5
White r. CO U.S.A. 129 I1
White r. IN U.S.A. 134 B4
White r. MI U.S.A. 134 B2
White r. NV U.S.A. 129 F3
White r. SD U.S.A. 130 D3
White r. VT U.S.A. 135 I2
White watercourse U.S.A. 129 H5
White, Lake salt flat Australia 108 E5
White Bay Canada 123 K4
White Butte mt. U.S.A. 130 C2
White Canyon U.S.A. 129 H3
White Cloud U.S.A. 134 C2
Whitecourt Canada 120 H4
Whiteface Mountain U.S.A. 135 I1
Whitefield U.S.A. 135 J1
Whitefish r. Canada 120 E1
Whitefish U.S.A. 126 E2
Whitefish Bay U.S.A. 134 B1
Whitefish Lake Canada 121 J2
Whitefish Point U.S.A. 132 C2
Whitehall Ireland 51 E5
Whitehall U.K. 50 G1
Whitehall NY U.S.A. 135 I2
Whitehall WI U.S.A. 130 F2
Whitehaven U.K. 48 D4
Whitehead U.K. 51 G3
White Hill hill Canada 123 J5
Whitehill U.K. 49 G7

▶Whitehorse Canada 120 C2
Capital of Yukon Territory.

White Horse U.S.A. 129 J4
White Horse, Vale of valley U.K. 49 F7
White Horse Pass U.S.A. 129 F1
White House U.S.A. 134 B5
White Island Antarctica 152 D2
White Island N.Z. see Whakaari
White Lake Ont. Canada 122 D4
White Lake Ont. Canada 135 G1
White Lake LA U.S.A. 131 E6
White Lake MI U.S.A. 134 B2
Whitemark Australia 111 [inset]
White Mountain Peak U.S.A. 128 D3
White Mountains U.S.A. 135 J1
White Mountains National Park Australia 110 D4
Whitemouth Lake Canada 121 M5
Whitemud r. Canada 120 G3
White Nile r. Sudan/Uganda 86 D6
also known as Bahr el Abiad or Bahr el Jebel
White Nossob watercourse Namibia 100 D2
White Oak U.S.A. 134 D5
White Otter Lake Canada 121 N5
White Pass Canada/U.S.A. 120 C3
White Pine Range mts U.S.A. 129 F2
White Plains U.S.A. 135 I3
White River Canada 122 D4
Whiteriver U.S.A. 129 I5
White River U.S.A. 130 C3
White River Valley U.S.A. 129 F2
White Rock Peak U.S.A. 129 F2
White Russia country Europe see Belarus
Whitesail Lake Canada 120 E4
White Salmon U.S.A. 126 C3
Whitesand r. Canada 120 H2
White Sands National Monument nat. park U.S.A. 127 G6
Whitesburg U.S.A. 134 D5
White Sea Rus. Fed. 42 H2
White Stone U.S.A. 135 G5
White Sulphur Springs MT U.S.A. 126 F3
White Sulphur Springs WV U.S.A. 134 E5
Whitesville U.S.A. 134 E5
Whiteville U.S.A. 133 E5
White Volta r. Burkina/Ghana 96 C4
also known as Nakambé or Nakanbe or Volta Blanche
Whitewater U.S.A. 129 I2
Whitewater Baldy mt. U.S.A. 129 I5
Whitewater Lake Canada 122 C4
Whitewood Australia 110 C4
Whitewood Canada 121 K5
Whitfield U.K. 49 I7
Whithorn U.K. 50 E6
Whitianga N.Z. 113 E3
Whitland U.K. 49 C7
Whitley Bay U.K. 48 F3
Whitmore Mountains Antarctica 152 K1
Whitney Canada 135 F1
Whitney, Mount U.S.A. 128 D3
Whitney Point U.S.A. 135 H2
Whitstable U.K. 49 I7
Whitsunday Group is Australia 110 E4
Whitsunday Island National Park Australia 110 E4
Whitsun Island Vanuatu see Pentecost Island
Whittemore U.S.A. 134 D1
Whittlesea Australia 112 B6
Whittlesey U.K. 49 G6
Whitton Australia 112 C5
Wholdaia Lake Canada 121 J2
Why U.S.A. 129 G5
Whyalla Australia 111 B7
Wiang Sa Thai. 70 C3
Wiarton Canada 134 E1
Wibaux U.S.A. 126 G3
Wichelen Belgium 52 D3
Wichita U.S.A. 130 D4
Wichita r. U.S.A. 131 D5
Wichita Falls U.S.A. 131 D5
Wichita Mountains U.S.A. 131 D5
Wick U.K. 50 F2
Wick r. U.K. 50 F2
Wickenburg U.S.A. 129 G5
Wickes U.S.A. 131 E5
Wickford U.K. 49 H7
Wickham r. Australia 108 E4
Wickham, Cape Australia 111 [inset]
Wickham, Mount hill Australia 108 E4
Wickliffe U.S.A. 131 F4
Wicklow Ireland 51 F5
Wicklow Head hd Ireland 51 G5
Wicklow Mountains Ireland 51 F5
Wicklow Mountains National Park Ireland 51 F4
Widerøe, Mount Antarctica 152 C2
Widerøefjellet mt. Antarctica see Widerøe, Mount
Widgeegoara watercourse Australia 112 B1
Widgiemooltha Australia 109 C7
Widnes U.K. 48 E5
Wi-do i. S. Korea 75 B6
Wied r. Germany 53 H4
Wiehengebirge hills Germany 53 I2
Wiehl Germany 53 H4
Wielkopolskie, Pojezierze reg. Poland 47 O4
Wielkopolski Park Narodowy nat. park Poland 47 P4
Wieluń Poland 47 Q5
Wien Austria see Vienna
Wiener Neustadt Austria 47 P7
Wierden Neth. 52 G2
Wieren Germany 53 K2
Wieringerwerf Neth. 52 F2
Wiesbaden Germany 53 I4
Wiesenfelden Germany 53 M5
Wiesentheid Germany 53 K5
Wiesloch Germany 53 I5
Wiesmoor Germany 53 H1
Wietze Germany 53 J2
Wietzendorf Germany 53 J2
Wieżyca hill Poland 47 Q3
Wigan U.K. 48 E5
Wiggins U.S.A. 131 F6
Wight, Isle of i. England U.K. 49 F8
Wigierski Park Narodowy nat. park Poland 45 M9
Wignes Lake Canada 121 J2
Wigston U.K. 49 F6
Wigton U.K. 48 D4
Wigtown U.K. 50 E6
Wigtown Bay U.K. 50 E6
Wijchen Neth. 52 F3
Wijhe Neth. 52 G2
Wilberforce, Cape Australia 110 B1
Wilbur U.S.A. 126 D3
Wilburton U.S.A. 131 E5
Wilcannia Australia 112 A3
Wilcox U.S.A. 135 F3
Wilczek Land i. Rus. Fed. see Vil'cheka, Zemlya
Wildberg Germany 53 M2
Wildcat Peak U.S.A. 128 E2
Wild Coast S. Africa 101 I6
Wilderness National Park S. Africa 100 F8
Wildeshausen Germany 53 I2
Wild Horse Hill mt. U.S.A. 130 C3
Wildspitze mt. Austria 47 M7
Wildwood FL U.S.A. 133 D6
Wildwood NJ U.S.A. 135 H4
Wilge r. S. Africa 101 I4
Wilge r. S. Africa 101 I3
Wilgena Australia 109 F7

▶Wilhelm, Mount P.N.G. 69 L8
5th highest mountain in Oceania.

Wilhelm II Land reg. Antarctica see Kaiser Wilhelm II Land
Wilhelmina Gebergte mts Suriname 143 G3
Wilhelmina Kanaal canal Neth. 52 F3
Wilhelmshaven Germany 53 I1
Wilhelmstal Namibia 100 C1
Wilkes-Barre U.S.A. 135 H3
Wilkesboro U.S.A. 132 D4
Wilkes Coast Antarctica 152 G2
Wilkes Land reg. Antarctica 152 G2
Wilkie Canada 121 I4
Wilkins Coast Antarctica 152 L2
Wilkins Ice Shelf Antarctica 152 L2
Wilkinson Lakes salt flat Australia 109 F7
Will, Mount Canada 120 D3
Willand U.K. 49 D8
Willandra Billabong watercourse Australia 112 B4
Willandra National Park Australia 112 B4
Willapa Bay U.S.A. 126 B3
Willard Mex. 127 F7
Willard NM U.S.A. 127 G6
Willard OH U.S.A. 134 D3
Willcox U.S.A. 129 I5
Willcox Playa salt flat U.S.A. 129 I5
Willebadessen Germany 53 J3
Willebroek Belgium 52 E3

▶Willemstad Neth. Antilles 137 K6
Capital of the Netherlands Antilles.

Willeroo Australia 108 E3
Willette U.S.A. 134 C5
William, Mount Australia 111 C8
William Creek Australia 111 B6
William Lake Canada 121 L4
Williams AZ U.S.A. 129 G4
Williams CA U.S.A. 128 B2
Williamsburg KY U.S.A. 134 C5
Williamsburg OH U.S.A. 134 C4
Williamsburg VA U.S.A. 135 G5
Williams Lake Canada 120 F4
William Smith, Cap c. Canada 123 I1
Williamson NY U.S.A. 135 G2
Williamson WV U.S.A. 134 D5
Williamsport IN U.S.A. 134 B3
Williamsport PA U.S.A. 135 G3
Williamston U.S.A. 132 E5
Williamstown KY U.S.A. 134 C4
Williamstown NJ U.S.A. 135 H4
Willimantic U.S.A. 135 I3
Willis Group atolls Australia 110 E3
Williston S. Africa 100 E6
Williston ND U.S.A. 130 C1
Williston SC U.S.A. 133 D5
Williston Lake Canada 120 F4
Williton U.K. 49 D7
Willits U.S.A. 128 B2
Willmar U.S.A. 130 E2
Willoughby, Lake U.S.A. 135 I1
Willow Beach U.S.A. 129 F4
Willow Bunch Canada 121 J5
Willow Hill U.S.A. 135 G3
Willow Lake Canada 120 G2
Willowlake r. Canada 120 F2
Willowmore S. Africa 100 F7
Willowra Australia 108 F5
Willows U.S.A. 128 B2
Willow Springs U.S.A. 131 F4
Willowvale S. Africa 101 I7
Wills, Lake salt flat Australia 108 E5
Wilma U.S.A. 133 C6
Wilmington DE U.S.A. 135 H4
Wilmington NC U.S.A. 133 E5
Wilmington OH U.S.A. 134 D4
Wilmore U.S.A. 134 C5
Wilmslow U.K. 48 E5
Wilno Lith. see Vilnius
Wilnsdorf Germany 53 I4
Wilpattu National Park Sri Lanka 84 D4
Wilseder Berg hill Germany 53 J1
Wilson watercourse Australia 111 C5
Wilson atoll Micronesia see Ifalik
Wilson KS U.S.A. 130 D4
Wilson NC U.S.A. 132 E5
Wilson NY U.S.A. 135 F2
Wilson, Mount CO U.S.A. 129 J3
Wilson, Mount NV U.S.A. 129 F2
Wilson, Mount OR U.S.A. 126 C3
Wilsonia U.S.A. 128 D3
Wilson's Promontory pen. Australia 112 C7
Wilson's Promontory National Park Australia 112 C7
Wilsum Germany 52 G2
Wilton r. Australia 108 F3
Wilton U.S.A. 135 J1
Wiltz Lux. 52 F5
Wiluna Australia 109 C6
Wimereux France 52 B4
Wina r. Cameroon see Vina
Winamac U.S.A. 134 B3
Winbin watercourse Australia 111 D5
Winburg S. Africa 101 H5
Wincanton U.K. 49 E7
Winchester Canada 135 H1
Winchester U.K. 49 F7
Winchester IN U.S.A. 134 C3
Winchester KY U.S.A. 134 C5
Winchester NH U.S.A. 135 I2
Winchester TN U.S.A. 133 C5
Winchester VA U.S.A. 135 F4
Wind r. Canada 120 C1
Wind r. U.S.A. 126 F4
Windau Latvia see Ventspils
Windber U.S.A. 135 F3
Wind Cave National Park U.S.A. 130 C3
Windermere U.K. 48 E4
Windermere l. U.K. 48 E4
Windham U.S.A. 120 C3

▶Windhoek Namibia 100 C2
Capital of Namibia.

Windigo Lake Canada 121 N4
Windlestraw Law hill U.K. 50 G5
Wind Mountain U.S.A. 127 G6
Windom U.S.A. 130 E3
Windom Peak U.S.A. 129 J3
Windorah Australia 110 C5
Window Rock U.S.A. 129 I4
Wind Point U.S.A. 134 B2
Wind River Range mts U.S.A. 126 F4
Windrush r. U.K. 49 F7
Windsbach Germany 53 K5
Windsor Australia 112 E4
Windsor N.S. Canada 123 I5
Windsor Ont. Canada 134 D2
Windsor U.K. 49 G7
Windsor NC U.S.A. 132 E4
Windsor NY U.S.A. 135 H2
Windsor VA U.S.A. 135 G5
Windsor VT U.S.A. 135 I2
Windsor Locks U.S.A. 135 I3
Windward Islands Caribbean Sea 137 L5
Windward Passage Cuba/Haiti 137 J5
Windy U.S.A. 118 D3
Winefred Lake Canada 121 I4
Winfield KS U.S.A. 131 D4
Winfield WV U.S.A. 134 E4
Wingate U.K. 48 F4
Wingen Australia 112 E3
Wingene Belgium 52 D3
Wingen-sur-Moder France 53 H6
Wingham Australia 112 F3
Wingham Canada 134 E2
Winisk r. Canada 122 D3
Winisk (abandoned) Canada 122 D3
Winisk Lake Canada 122 D3
Winkana Myanmar 70 B4
Winkelman U.S.A. 129 H5
Winkler Canada 121 L5
Winlock U.S.A. 126 C3
Winneba Ghana 96 C4
Winnebago, Lake U.S.A. 134 A1
Winnecke Creek watercourse Australia 108 E4
Winnemucca U.S.A. 128 E1
Winnemucca Lake U.S.A. 128 D1
Winner U.S.A. 130 C3
Winnett U.S.A. 126 F3
Winnfield U.S.A. 131 E6
Winnibigoshish, Lake U.S.A. 130 E2
Winnie U.S.A. 131 E6
Winning Australia 109 A5

▶Winnipeg Canada 121 L5
Capital of Manitoba.

Winnipeg r. Canada 121 L5
Winnipeg, Lake Canada 121 L5
Winnipegosis Canada 121 L5
Winnipegosis, Lake Canada 121 K4
Winnipesaukee, Lake U.S.A. 135 J2
Winona AZ U.S.A. 129 H4
Winona MN U.S.A. 130 F2
Winona MO U.S.A. 131 F4
Winona MS U.S.A. 131 F5
Winschoten Neth. 52 H1
Winsen (Aller) Germany 53 J2
Winsen (Luhe) Germany 53 K1
Winsford U.K. 48 E5
Winslow AZ U.S.A. 129 H4
Winslow ME U.S.A. 135 K1
Winsop, Tanjung pt Indon. 69 I7
Winsted U.S.A. 135 I3
Winston-Salem U.S.A. 132 D4
Winterberg Germany 53 I3
Winter Haven U.S.A. 133 D6
Winters CA U.S.A. 128 C2
Winters TX U.S.A. 131 D6
Wintersville U.S.A. 134 E3
Winterswijk Neth. 52 G3
Winterthur Switz. 56 I3
Winterton S. Africa 101 I5
Winthrop U.S.A. 135 K1
Winton Australia 110 C4
Winton N.Z. 113 B8
Winton U.S.A. 132 E4
Winwick U.K. 49 G6
Wirral pen. U.K. 48 D5
Wirrulla Australia 111 A7
Wisbech U.K. 49 H6
Wiscasset U.S.A. 135 K1
Wisconsin r. U.S.A. 130 F3
Wisconsin state U.S.A. 134 A1
Wisconsin Rapids U.S.A. 130 F2
Wise U.S.A. 134 D5
Wiseman U.S.A. 118 C3
Wishaw U.K. 50 F5
Wisher U.S.A. 130 D2
Wisil Dabarow Somalia 98 E3
Wisła r. Poland see Vistula
Wismar Germany 47 M4
Wistaria Canada 120 E4
Witbank S. Africa 101 I3
Witbooisvlei Namibia 100 D3
Witham U.K. 49 H7
Witham r. U.K. 49 H6
Witherbee U.S.A. 135 I1
Withernsea U.K. 48 H5
Witjira National Park Australia 111 A5
Witmarsum Neth. 52 F1
Witney U.K. 49 F7
Witrivier S. Africa 101 J3
Witry-lès-Reims France 52 E5
Witteberg mts S. Africa 101 H6
Wittenberg Germany see Lutherstadt Wittenberg
Wittenberge Germany 53 L2
Wittenburg Germany 53 L1
Wittingen Germany 53 K2
Wittlich Germany 52 G5
Wittmund Germany 53 H1
Wittstock Germany 53 M1
Witu Islands P.N.G. 69 L7
Witvlei Namibia 100 D2
Witzenhausen Germany 53 J3
Wivenhoe, Lake Australia 112 F1
Władysławowo Poland 47 Q3
Włocławek Poland 47 Q4
Wobkent Uzbek. see Vobkent
Wodonga Australia 112 C6
Wœrth France 53 H6
Wohlthat Mountains Antarctica 152 C2
Woippy France 52 G5
Wōjjā atoll Marshall Is see Wotje
Wokam i. Indon. 69 I8
Woken He r. China 74 C3
Wokha India 83 H4
Woking U.K. 49 G7
Wokingham watercourse Australia 110 C4
Wokingham U.K. 49 G7
Woko National Park Australia 112 E3
Wolcott IN U.S.A. 134 B3
Wolcott NY U.S.A. 135 G2
Woldegk Germany 53 N1
Wolea atoll Micronesia see Woleai
Woleai atoll Micronesia 69 K5
Wolf r. Canada 120 C2
Wolf r. TN U.S.A. 131 F5
Wolf r. WI U.S.A. 130 F2
Wolf Creek MT U.S.A. 126 E3
Wolf Creek OR U.S.A. 126 C4
Wolf Creek Pass U.S.A. 127 G5
Wolfen Germany 53 M3
Wolfenbüttel Germany 53 K2
Wolfhagen Germany 53 J3
Wolf Lake Canada 120 D2
Wolf Point U.S.A. 126 G2
Wolfsberg Austria 47 O7
Wolfsburg Germany 53 K2
Wolfstein Germany 53 H5
Wolfville Canada 123 I5
Wolgast Germany 47 N3
Wolin Poland 47 O4
Wollaston Lake Canada 121 K3
Wollaston Lake l. Canada 121 K3
Wollaston Peninsula Canada 118 G3
Wollemi National Park Australia 112 E4
Wollongong Australia 112 E5
Wolmaransstad S. Africa 101 G4
Wolmirstedt Germany 53 L2
Wolong Reserve nature res. China 76 D2
Wolseley Australia 111 C8
Wolseley S. Africa 100 D7
Wolsey U.S.A. 130 D2
Wolsingham U.K. 48 F4
Wolvega Neth. 52 G2
Wolvegea Neth. see Wolvega
Wolverhampton U.K. 49 E6
Wolverine U.S.A. 134 C1
Wommelgem Belgium 52 E3
Womrather Höhe hill Germany 53 H5
Wonarah Australia 110 B3
Wonay, Kowtal-e Afgh. 89 H3
Wondai Australia 111 E5
Wongalarroo Lake salt l. Australia 112 B3
Wongarbon Australia 112 D4
Wong Chuk Hang H.K. China 77 [inset]
Wong Leng hill H.K. China 77 [inset]
Wong Wan Chau H.K. China see Double Island
Wŏnju S. Korea 75 B5
Wonowon Canada 120 F3
Wŏnsan N. Korea 75 B5
Wonthaggi Australia 112 B7
Wonyulgunna, Mount hill Australia 109 B6
Woocalla Australia 111 B6
Wood, Mount Canada 120 A2
Woodbine GA U.S.A. 133 D6
Woodbine NJ U.S.A. 135 H4
Woodbridge U.K. 49 I6
Woodbridge U.S.A. 135 G4
Wood Buffalo National Park Canada 120 H3
Woodburn U.S.A. 126 C3
Woodbury NJ U.S.A. 135 H4
Woodbury TN U.S.A. 131 G5
Wooded Bluff hd Australia 112 F2
Wood Lake Canada 121 K4
Woodlake U.S.A. 128 D3
Woodland CA U.S.A. 128 C2
Woodland PA U.S.A. 135 F3
Woodland WA U.S.A. 126 C3
Woodlands Sing. 71 [inset]
Woodlark Island P.N.G. 106 F2
Woodridge Canada 121 L5
Woodroffe watercourse Australia 110 B4
Woodroffe, Mount Australia 109 E6
Woodruff UT U.S.A. 126 F4
Woodruff WI U.S.A. 130 F2
Woods, Lake salt flat Australia 108 F4
Woods, Lake of the Canada/U.S.A. 125 I2
Woodsfield U.S.A. 134 E4
Woodside Australia 112 C7
Woodstock N.B. Canada 123 I5
Woodstock Ont. Canada 134 E2
Woodstock IL U.S.A. 130 F3
Woodstock VA U.S.A. 135 F4
Woodstock VT U.S.A. 135 I2
Woodsville U.S.A. 135 I1
Woodville Canada 135 F1
Woodville MS U.S.A. 131 F6
Woodville OH U.S.A. 134 D3
Woodville TX U.S.A. 131 E6
Woodward U.S.A. 131 D4
Woody U.S.A. 128 D4
Wooler U.K. 48 E3
Woolgoolga Australia 112 F3
Wooli Australia 112 F2
Woollard, Mount Antarctica 152 K1
Woollett, Lac l. Canada 122 G4
Woolyeenyer Hill hill Australia 109 C8
Woomera Australia 111 B6
Woomera Prohibited Area Australia 109 F7
Woonsocket RI U.S.A. 135 J2
Woonsocket SD U.S.A. 130 D2
Woorabinda Australia 110 E5
Wooramel r. Australia 109 A6
Wooster U.S.A. 134 E3
Worbis Germany 53 K3
Worbody Point Australia 110 C2
Worcester S. Africa 100 D7
Worcester U.K. 49 E6
Worcester MA U.S.A. 135 J2
Worcester NY U.S.A. 135 H2
Wörgl Austria 47 N7
Workai i. Indon. 69 I8
Workington U.K. 48 D4
Worksop U.K. 48 F5
Workum Neth. 52 F2
Worland U.S.A. 126 G3
Wörlitz Germany 53 M3
Wormerveer Neth. 52 E2
Worms Germany 53 I5
Worms Head hd U.K. 49 C7
Wortel Namibia 100 C2
Wörth am Rhein Germany 53 I5
Worthing U.K. 49 G8
Worthington IN U.S.A. 134 B4
Worthington MN U.S.A. 130 E3
Wotje atoll Marshall Is 150 H5
Wotu Indon. 69 G7
Woudrichem Neth. 52 E3
Woustviller France 52 H5
Wowoni i. Indon. 69 G7
Wozrojdeniye Oroli i. Uzbek. see Vozrozhdenya Island
Wrangel Island Rus. Fed. 65 T2
Wrangell Island U.S.A. 120 C3
Wrangell Mountains U.S.A. 153 B3
Wrangell-St Elias National Park and Preserve U.S.A. 120 A2
Wrath, Cape U.K. 50 D2
Wray U.S.A. 130 C3
Wreake r. U.K. 49 F6
Wreck Point S. Africa 100 C5
Wreck Reef Australia 110 F4
Wrecsam U.K. see Wrexham
Wrestedt Germany 53 K2
Wrexham U.K. 49 E5
Wrightmyo India 71 A5
Wrightson, Mount U.S.A. 127 F7
Wrightwood U.S.A. 128 E4
Wrigley Canada 120 F2
Wrigley U.S.A. 134 D4
Wrigley Gulf Antarctica 152 J2
Wrocław Poland 47 P5
Września Poland 47 P4
Wu'an China see Changtai
Wubin Australia 109 B7
Wuchang Heilong. China 74 B3
Wuchang Hubei China see Jiangxia
Wuchow China see Wuzhou
Wuchuan Guangdong China see Meilu
Wuchuan Guizhou China 76 E2
Wudalianchi China 74 B2
Wuḍām 'Alwā Oman 88 E6
Wudang Shan mt. China 77 F1
Wudaoliang China 76 B1
Wuding China 76 D3
Wudinna Australia 109 F8
Wufeng Hubei China 77 F2
Wufeng Yunnan China see Zhenxiong
Wugang China 77 F3
Wuhai China 72 J5
Wuhan China 77 G2
Wuhe China 77 H1
Wuhu China 77 H2
Wuhua China 77 G4
Wuhubei China 77 H2
Wüjang China 82 D2
Wu Jiang r. China 76 E2
Wujin Jiangsu China see Changzhou
Wujin Sichuan China see Xinjin
Wukari Nigeria 96 D4
Wulang China 76 B2
Wuli China 76 B1
Wulian Feng mts China 76 D2
Wuliang Shan mts China 76 D3
Wuliaru i. Indon. 108 E1
Wuli Jiang r. China 77 F4
Wuling Shan mts China 77 F2
Wulong China 76 E2
Wulongji China see Huaibin
Wulur Indon. 108 E1
Wumeng Shan mts China 76 D3
Wuming China 77 F4
Wümme r. Germany 53 I1
Wundwin Myanmar 70 B2
Wungda China 76 D2
Wuning China 77 G2
Wünnenberg Germany 53 I3
Wunnummin Lake Canada 119 J4
Wunsiedel Germany 53 M4
Wunstorf Germany 53 J2
Wupatki National Monument nat. park U.S.A. 129 H4
Wuping China 77 H3
Wuppertal Germany 53 H3
Wuppertal S. Africa 100 D7
Wuqi China 73 J5
Wuqia China 80 D4
Wuquan China see Wuyang
Wuranga Australia 109 B7
Wurno Nigeria 96 D3
Würzburg Germany 53 J5
Wurzen Germany 53 M3
Wushan Chongqing China 77 F2
Wushan Gansu China 76 E1
Wu Shan mts China 77 F2
Wushi Guangdong China 77 F4
Wushi Xinjiang China 80 E3
Wüstegarten hill Germany 53 J3
Wusuli Jiang r. China/Rus. Fed. see Ussur
Wuvulu Island P.N.G. 69 K7
Wuwei China 72 I5
Wuxi Chongqing China 77 F2
Wuxi Hunan China 77 F2
Wuxi Hunan China see Qiyang
Wuxi Jiangsu China 77 I2
Wuxia China see Wushan
Wuxian China see Suzhou
Wuxing China see Huzhou
Wuxu China 77 F4
Wuxuan China 77 F4
Wuxue China 77 G2
Wuyang Guizhou China see Zhenyuan
Wuyang Henan China 77 G1
Wuyang Zhejiang China see Wuyi
Wuyi China 77 H2
Wuyiling China 74 C2
Wuyi Shan mts China 77 H3
Wuyuan Jiangxi China 77 H2
Wuyuan Nei Mongol China 73 J4
Wuyuan Zhejiang China see Haiyan
Wuyun China see Jinyun
Wuzhishan China 77 F5
Wuzhi Shan mts China 77 F5

uzhong China 72 J5
uzhou China 77 F4
yalkatchem Australia 109 B7
yalong Australia 112 C4
yandra Australia 112 B1
yangala Reservoir Australia 112 D4
yara, Lake *salt flat* Australia 112 B2
ycheproof Australia 112 A6
ylliesburg U.S.A. 135 F5
yloo Australia 108 B5
ylye *r.* U.K. 49 F7
ymondham U.K. 49 I6
ymore U.S.A. 130 D3
ynbring Australia 109 F7
yndham Australia 108 E3
yndham-Werribee Australia 112 B6
nne U.S.A. 131 F5
nyard Canada 121 J5
ola Lake *salt flat* Australia 109 E7
yoming U.S.A. 134 C2
yoming *state* U.S.A. 126 G4
yoming Peak U.S.A. 126 F4
yoming Range *mts* U.S.A. 126 F4
yong Australia 112 E4
yperfeld National Park Australia 111 C7
ysox U.S.A. 135 G3
yszków Poland 47 R4
ythall U.K. 49 F6
ytheville U.S.A. 134 E5
ytmarsum Neth. *see* Witmarsum

afuun Somalia 98 F2

Xaafuun, Raas *pt* Somalia 86 H7
Most easterly point of Africa.

byaisamba China 76 C2
çmaz Azer. 91 H2
go China 83 G3
gquka China 76 B2
idulla China 82 D1
ignabouli Laos 70 C3
ignabouri Laos *see* Xaignabouli
inza China 83 G3
i-Xai Moz. 101 K3
lapa Mex. *see* Jalapa
mbioa Brazil 143 I5
n Nua Laos 70 D2
Muteba Angola 99 B4
n *r.* Laos 70 C3
nagas Botswana 100 E2
ngda China *see* Nangqên
ngdin Hural China 73 K4
ngdoring China 83 E2
ngongo Angola 99 B5
nkändi Azer. 91 G3
nlar Azer. 91 G2
nthi Greece 59 K4
rag China 83 I1
rardheere Somalia 98 E3
tiva Spain 57 F4
vantes, Serra dos *hills* Brazil 143 I6
ka China 83 E2
yar China 80 F3
a Guat. *see* Quetzaltenango
va Spain *see* Chelva
nia U.S.A. 134 D4
ro Potamos *r.* Cyprus *see* Xeros
ros *r.* Cyprus 85 A2
ora S. Africa *see* Elliotdale
bole Shan *mt.* China 74 B2
chuan Dao *i.* China 77 G4
guan China *see* Dali
he China 76 D1
men China 77 H3
an China 77 F1
nfeng China 77 F2
ngcheng *Sichuan* China 76 C2
ngcheng *Yunnan* China *see* Jiangyun
ngfan China 77 G1
ngfeng China *see* Laifeng
nggang *H.K.* China *see* Hong Kong
nggang Tebie Xingzhengqu *aut. reg.* China *see* Hong Kong
nggelila China 76 C3
ngjiang China *see* Huichang
ngkou China *see* Wulong
ngning China 73 K5
ngquan He *r.* China *see* Nangqên Zangbo
ngride China 83 I2
ngshan China *see* Menghai
ngshui China 77 H1
ngshuiba China 77 F3
ngtan China 77 G3
ngxiang China 77 G3
ngyang China *see* Xiangfan
ngyang Hu *l.* China 83 G2
ngyin China 77 G2
ngyun China 76 D3
nju China 77 I2
nning China 77 G2
nnümiao China *see* Jiangdu
nshui He *r.* China 76 D2
ntao China 77 G2
nxia Ling *mts* China 77 H3
nyang China 77 F1
ocaohu China 80 G3
odong China 77 F4
odongliang China 76 C1
o'ergou China 74 A2
ogan China 77 G2
ogang China *see* Dongxiang
o Hinggan Ling *mts* China 74 B2
ojin China 76 D2
onanchuan China 83 H2
osanjiang China 77 G3
oshan China 77 I2
o Shan *mts* China 77 F1
oshi China *see* Benxi
o Surmang China 76 C1
otao China 77 H3
oxi China *see* Pinghe
oxian China 77 H1

Xiaoxiang Ling *mts* China 76 D2
Xiaoxita China *see* Yiling
Xiapu China 77 I3
Xiaqiong China *see* Batang
Xiashan China *see* Zhanjiang
Xiayang China *see* Yanling
Xiayanjing China *see* Yanjing
Xiayingpan *Guizhou* China *see* Lupanshui
Xiayingpan *Guizhou* China *see* Luzhi
Xiayukou China 77 F1
Xiazhuang China *see* Linshu
Xibdê China 76 C2
Xibing China 77 H3
Xibu China *see* Dongshan
Xichang China 76 D3
Xichou China 76 E4
Xichuan China 77 F1
Xide China 76 D2
Xidu China *see* Hengyang
Xiemahe' China 77 F2
Xieng Khouang Laos *see* Phônsavan
Xiêng Lam Vietnam 70 D3
Xieyang Dao *i.* China 77 F4
Xifeng *Guizhou* China 76 E3
Xifeng *Liaoning* China 74 B4
Xifengzhen China *see* Qingyang
Xigazê China 83 G3
Xihan Shui *r.* China 76 E1
Xi He *r.* China 76 E2
Xi Jiang *r.* China 77 G4
Xijir China 83 G2
Xijir Ulan Hu *salt l.* China 83 G2
Xiliao He *r.* China 74 A4
Xilin China 76 E3
Xilinhot China 73 L4
Ximiao China 80 J3
Xin'an *Anhui* China *see* Lai'an
Xin'an *Guizhou* China *see* Anlong
Xin'an *Henan* China 77 G1
Xin'anjiang China 77 H2
Xin'anjiang Shuiku *resr* China 77 H2
Xinavane Moz. 101 K3
Xin Barag Zuoqi China *see* Amgalang
Xincai China 77 G1
Xinchang *Jiangxi* China *see* Yifeng
Xinchang *Zhejiang* China 77 I2
Xincheng *Fujian* China *see* Gutian
Xincheng *Guangdong* China *see* Xinxing
Xincheng *Guangxi* China 77 F3
Xincheng *Sichuan* China *see* Zhaojue
Xincun China *see* Dongchuan
Xindi *Guangxi* China 77 F4
Xindi *Hubei* China *see* Honghu
Xindian China 74 B3
Xindu *Guangxi* China 77 F4
Xindu *Sichuan* China *see* Luhuo
Xindu *Sichuan* China 76 E2
Xinduqiao China 76 D2
Xinfeng *Guangdong* China 77 G3
Xinfeng *Jiangxi* China 77 G3
Xinfengjiang Shuiku *resr* China 77 G4
Xing'an *Guangxi* China 77 F3
Xingan China 77 G3
Xing'an *Shaanxi* China *see* Ankang
Xingba China 76 B2
Xingguo *Gansu* China *see* Qin'an
Xingguo *Hubei* China *see* Yangxin
Xingguo *Jiangxi* China 77 G3
Xinghai China 80 I4
Xinghua China 77 H1
Xinghua Wan *b.* China 77 H3
Xingkai China 74 D3
Xingkai Hu *l.* China/Rus. Fed. *see* Khanka, Lake
Xinglong China 74 B2
Xinglongzhen *Gansu* China 76 E1
Xinglongzhen *Heilong.* China 74 B3
Xingning *Guangdong* China 77 G3
Xingning *Hunan* China 77 G3
Xingou China 77 G2
Xingping China 77 F1
Xingqêngoin China 76 D2
Xingren China 76 E3
Xingsagoinba China 76 D1
Xingshan *Guizhou* China *see* Majiang
Xingshan *Hubei* China 77 F2
Xingtai China 73 K5
Xingu *r.* Brazil 143 H4
Xingu, Parque Indígena do *res.* Brazil 143 H6
Xinguara Brazil 143 H5
Xingye China 77 F4
Xingyi China 76 E3
Xinhua *Guangdong* China *see* Huadu
Xinhua *Hunan* China 77 F3
Xinhua *Yunnan* China *see* Qiaojia
Xinhua *Yunnan* China *see* Funing
Xinhuang China 77 F3
Xinhui China 77 G4
Xining China 72 I5
Xinjian China 77 G2
Xinjiang China 77 F1
Xinjiang *aut. reg.* China *see* Xinjiang Uygur Zizhiqu
Xinjiangkou China *see* Songzi
Xinjiang Uygur Zizhiqu *aut. reg.* China 82 E1
Xinjie *Qinghai* China 76 D1
Xinjie *Yunnan* China 76 C3
Xinjie *Yunnan* China 76 D4
Xinjin China 76 D2
Xinjing China *see* Jingxi
Xinkai He *r.* China 74 A4
Xinling China *see* Badong
Xinlitun China 74 B2
Xinlong China 76 D2
Xinmi China 77 G1
Xinmin China 74 B2
Xinning *Gansu* China *see* Ningxian
Xinning *Hunan* China 77 F3
Xinning *Jiangxi* China *see* Wuning
Xinning *Sichuan* China *see* Kaijiang
Xinping China 76 D3
Xinqiao China 77 G1
Xinqing China 74 C2
Xinquan China 77 H3
Xinshan China *see* Anyuan
Xinshiba China *see* Ganluo
Xinsi China 76 E1
Xintai China 73 L5

Xintanpu China 77 G2
Xintian China 77 G3
Xinxiang China 77 G1
Xinxing China 77 G4
Xinyang *Henan* China 77 G1
Xinyang *Henan* China *see* Pingqiao
Xinye China 77 G1
Xinyi *Guangdong* China 77 F4
Xinyi *Jiangsu* China 77 H1
Xinying China 77 F5
Xinying Taiwan *see* Hsinying
Xinyu China 77 G3
Xinyuan *Qinghai* China *see* Tianjun
Xinyuan *Xinjiang* China 80 F3
Xinzhangfang China 74 A2
Xinzhou *Guangxi* China *see* Longlin
Xinzhou *Hubei* China 77 G2
Xinzhou *Shanxi* China 73 K5
Xinzhu Taiwan *see* Hsinchu
Xinzo de Limia Spain 57 C2
Xiongshan China *see* Zhenghe
Xiongshi China *see* Guixi
Xiongzhou China *see* Nanxiong
Xiping *Henan* China 77 F1
Xiping *Henan* China 77 G1
Xiqing Shan *mts* China 76 D1
Xique Xique Brazil 143 J6
Xisa China *see* Xichou
Xisha Qundao *is* S. China Sea *see* Paracel Islands
Xishuangbanna *reg.* China 76 D4
Xishui *Guizhou* China 76 E2
Xishui *Hubei* China 77 G2
Xitianmu Shan *mt.* China 77 H2
Xiugu China *see* Jinxi
Xi Ujimqin Qi China *see* Bayan Ul Hot
Xiuning China 77 H2
Xiushan *Chongqing* China 77 F2
Xiushan *Yunnan* China *see* Tonghai
Xiushui China 77 G2
Xiuwen China 76 E3
Xiuwu China 77 G1
Xiuying China 77 F4
Xiwu China 76 C1
Xixabangma Feng *mt.* China 83 F3
Xixia China 77 F1
Xixiang China 76 E1
Xixiu China *see* Anshun
Xixón Spain *see* Gijón-Xixón
Xiyang Dao *i.* China 77 I3
Xiyang Jiang *r.* China 76 E3
Xizang *aut. reg.* China *see* Xizang Zizhiqu
Xizang Gaoyuan *plat.* China *see* Tibet, Plateau of
Xizang Zizhiqu *aut. reg.* China 83 G3
Xo'japiryox tog'i *mt.* Uzbek. 89 G2
Xo'jayli Uzbek. 80 A3
Xorkol China 80 H4
Xuancheng China 77 H2
Xuan'en China 77 F2
Xuanhua China 73 L4
Xuân Lôc Vietnam 71 D5
Xuanwei China 76 E3
Xuanzhou China *see* Xuancheng
Xuchang China 77 G1
Xucheng China *see* Xuwen
Xuddur Somalia 98 E3
Xuefeng China *see* Mingxi
Xuefeng Shan *mts* China 77 F3
Xue Shan *mts* China 76 C3
Xugui China 80 I4
Xuguit Qi China *see* Yakeshi
Xujiang China *see* Guangchang
Xümatang China 76 C1
Xunde Qundao *is* Paracel Is *see* Amphitrite Group
Xungba China *see* Xangdoring
Xungmai China 83 G3
Xunhe China 74 B2
Xun He *r.* China 74 C2
Xun Jiang *r.* China 77 F4
Xunwu China 77 G3
Xunyi China 77 F1
Xúquer, Riu *r.* Spain 57 F4
Xuru Co *salt l.* China 83 F3
Xuwen China 68 E2
Xuyi China 77 H1
Xuyong China 76 E2
Xuzhou China 77 H1

Y

Ya'an China 76 D2
Yabanabat Turkey *see* Kızılcahamam
Yabēlo Eth. 98 D3
Yablonovyy Khrebet *mts* Rus. Fed. 73 J2
Yabrīn *reg.* Saudi Arabia 88 C6
Yabuli China 74 C3
Yacha China *see* Baisha
Yacheng China 77 F5
Yachi He *r.* China 76 E3
Yacuma *r.* Bol. 142 E6
Yadgir India 84 C2
Yadrin Rus. Fed. 42 J5
Yaeyama-rettō *is* Japan 73 M8
Yafa Israel *see* Tel Aviv-Yafo
Yagaba Ghana 96 C3
Yagan China 72 I4
Yağda Turkey *see* Erdemli
Yaghan Basin *sea feature* S. Atlantic Ocean 148 D9
Yagman Turkm. 88 D2
Yagodnoye Rus. Fed. 65 P3
Yagodnyy Rus. Fed. 74 E2
Yagoua Cameroon 97 E3
Yagra China 83 E3
Yagradagzê Shan *mt.* China 76 B1
Yaguajay Cuba 133 E8
Yaha Thai. 71 C6
Yahk Canada 120 G5
Yahualica Mex. 136 D4
Yahyalı Turkey 55 L4
Yai Myanmar *see* Ye
Yai, Khao *mt.* Thai. 71 B4
Yaizu Japan 75 E6
Yajiang China 76 D2
Yakacık Turkey 85 C1
Yakeshi China 73 M3

Yakhab *waterhole* Iran 88 E3
Yakhehal Afgh. 89 G4
Yakima U.S.A. 126 C3
Yakima *r.* U.S.A. 126 D3
Yakmach Pak. 89 F4
Yako Burkina 96 C3
Yakovlevka Rus. Fed. 74 D3
Yaku-shima *i.* Japan 75 C7
Yakutat U.S.A. 120 B3
Yakutat Bay U.S.A. 120 A3
Yakutsk Rus. Fed. 65 N3
Yakymivka Ukr. 43 G7
Yala Thai. 71 C6
Yalai China 83 F3
Yala National Park Sri Lanka *see* Ruhuna National Park
Yalan Dünya Mağarası *tourist site* Turkey 85 A1
Yale Canada 120 F5
Yale U.S.A. 134 D2
Yalgoo Australia 109 B7
Yalleroi Australia 110 D5
Yaloké Cent. Afr. Rep. 98 B3
Yalova Turkey 59 M4
Yalta Ukr. 90 D1
Yalu Jiang *r.* China/N. Korea 74 B4
Yalujiang Kou *r. mouth* China/N. Korea 75 B5
Yalvaç Turkey 59 N5
Yamagata Japan 75 F5
Yamaguchi Japan 75 C6
Yamal, Poluostrov *pen.* Rus. Fed. *see* Yamal Peninsula
Yam-Alin', Khrebet *mts* Rus. Fed. 74 D1
Yamal Peninsula Rus. Fed. 64 H2
Yamanie Falls National Park Australia 110 D3
Yamba Australia 112 F2
Yamba Lake Canada 121 I1
Yambarran Range *hills* Australia 108 E3
Yambi, Mesa de *hills* Col. 142 D3
Yambio Sudan 97 F4
Yambol Bulg. 59 L3
Yamdena *i.* Indon. 108 E1
Yamethin Myanmar 70 B2

▶Yamin, Puncak *mt.* Indon. 69 J7
4th highest mountain in Oceania.

Yamkanmardi India 84 B2
Yamkhad Syria *see* Aleppo
Yamm Rus. Fed. 45 P7
Yamma Yamma, Lake *salt flat* Australia 111 C5

▶Yamoussoukro Côte d'Ivoire 96 C4
Capital of Côte d'Ivoire.

Yampa *r.* U.S.A. 129 I1
Yampil' Ukr. 43 F6
Yampol' Ukr. *see* Yampil'
Yamuna *r.* India 82 E4
Yamunanagar India 82 D3
Yamzho Yumco *l.* China 83 G3
Yana *r.* Rus. Fed. 65 O2
Yanam India 84 D2
Yan'an China 73 J5
Yanaoca Peru 142 D6
Yanaon India *see* Yanam
Yanaul Rus. Fed. 41 Q4
Yanbu' al Baḩr Saudi Arabia 86 E5
Yanceyville U.S.A. 132 E4
Yancheng *Henan* China 77 G1
Yancheng *Jiangsu* China 77 I1
Yanchep Australia 109 A7
Yanco Australia 112 C5
Yanco Creek *r.* Australia 112 B5
Yanco Glen Australia 111 C6
Yanda *watercourse* Australia 112 B3
Yandama Creek *watercourse* Australia 111 C6
Yandao China *see* Yingjing
Yandoon Myanmar 70 A3
Yandun China 80 H3
Yanfolila Mali 96 C3
Ya'ngamdo China 76 B2
Yangbi China 76 C3
Yangcheng *Guangdong* China *see* Yangshan
Yangcheng *Shanxi* China 77 G1
Yangchuan China *see* Suiyang
Yangchun China 77 F4
Yangcun China 77 G4
Yangdok N. Korea 75 B5
Yang Hu *l.* China 83 F2
Yangi Nishon Uzbek. 89 G2
Yangī Qal'ah Afgh. 89 H2
Yangiqishloq Uzbek. 80 C3
Yangirabot Uzbek. 89 G1
Yangiyo'l Uzbek. 80 C3
Yangjiajiang China 77 G2
Yangjiang China 77 F4
Yangming China *see* Heping
Yangôn Myanmar *see* Rangoon
Yangping China 77 F2
Yangquan China 73 K5
Yangshan China 77 G3
Yang Talat Thai. 70 C3
Yangtouyan China 76 D3

▶Yangtze *r.* China 76 E2
Longest river in Asia and 3rd in the world. Also known as Chang Jiang or Jinsha Jiang or Tongtian He or Yangtze Kiang or Zhi Qu.

Yangtze Kiang *r.* China *see* Yangtze
Yangudi Rassa National Park Eth. 98 E2
Yangweigang China 77 H1
Yangxi China 77 F4
Yangxian China 76 E1
Yangxin China 77 G2
Yangyang S. Korea 75 C5
Yangzhou *Jiangsu* China 77 H1
Yangzhou *Shaanxi* China *see* Yangxian
Yanhe China 77 F2
Yanhuqu China 83 E2
Yanishpole Rus. Fed. 42 G3
Yanis"yarvi, Ozero *l.* Rus. Fed. 44 Q5
Yanji China 74 C4
Yanjiang China *see* Ziyang
Yanjin *Henan* China 77 G1
Yanjin *Yunnan* China 76 E2

Yanjing *Sichuan* China *see* Yanyuan
Yanjing *Xizang* China 76 C2
Yanjing *Yunnan* China *see* Yanjin
Yankara National Park Nigeria 96 E4
Yankton U.S.A. 130 D3
Yanling *Hunan* China 77 G3
Yanling *Sichuan* China *see* Weiyuan
Yannina Greece *see* Ioannina
Yano-Indigirskaya Nizmennost' *lowland* Rus. Fed. 65 P2
Yanovski, Mount U.S.A. 120 C3
Yanrey *r.* Australia 109 A5
Yanshan *Jiangxi* China 77 H2
Yanshan *Yunnan* China 76 E4
Yanshi China 77 G1
Yanshiping China 76 B1
Yanskiy Zaliv *g.* Rus. Fed. 65 O2
Yantabulla Australia 112 B2
Yantai China 73 M5
Yanting China 76 E2
Yantongshan China 74 B4
Yantou China 77 I2
Yanwa China 76 C3
Yany-Kurgan Kazakh. *see* Zhanakorgan
Yanyuan China 76 D3
Yao Chad 97 E3
Yao'an China 76 D3
Yaodu China *see* Dongzhi
Yaoli China 77 H2

▶Yaoundé Cameroon 96 E4
Capital of Cameroon.

Yaoxian *Shaanxi* China *see* Yaozhou
Yaoxiaoling China 74 B2
Yao Yai, Ko *i.* Thai. 71 B6
Yaozhou China 77 F1
Yap *i.* Micronesia 69 J5
Yapen *i.* Indon. 69 J7
Yappar *r.* Australia 110 C3
Yap Trench *sea feature* N. Pacific Ocean 150 F5
Yaqui *r.* Mex. 127 F8
Yar Rus. Fed. 42 L4
Yaradzha Turkm. *see* Ýarajy
Ýarajy Turkm. 88 E2
Yaraka Australia 110 D5
Yarangüme Turkey *see* Tavas
Yaransk Rus. Fed. 42 J4
Yardea Australia 111 A7
Yardımcı Burnu *pt* Turkey 59 N6
Yardımlı Azer. 91 H3
Yardymly Azer. *see* Yardımlı
Yare *r.* U.K. 49 I6
Yarega Rus. Fed. 42 L3

▶Yaren Nauru 107 G2
Capital of Nauru.

Yarensk Rus. Fed. 42 K3
Yariga-take *mt.* Japan 75 E5
Yarīm Yemen 86 F7
Yarımca Turkey *see* Körfez
Yarkand China *see* Shache
Yarkant China *see* Shache
Yarkant He *r.* China 80 E4
Yarker Canada 135 G1
Yarkhun *r.* Pak. 89 I2
Yarlung Zangbo *r.* China 76 B2 *see* Brahmaputra
Yarmouth Canada 123 I6
Yarmouth *England* U.K. 49 F8
Yarmouth *England* U.K. *see* Great Yarmouth
Yarmouth U.S.A. 135 J2
Yarmuk *r.* Asia 85 B3
Yarnell U.S.A. 129 G4
Yaroslavl' Rus. Fed. 42 H4
Yaroslavskiy Rus. Fed. 74 D3
Yarra *r.* Australia 112 B6
Yarra Junction Australia 112 B6
Yarram Australia 112 C7
Yarraman Australia 112 E1
Yarrawonga Australia 112 B6
Yarra Yarra Lakes *salt flat* Australia 109 A7
Yarronvale Australia 112 B1
Yarrowmere Australia 110 D4
Yartö Tra La *pass* China 83 H3
Yartsevo *Krasnoyarskiy Kray* Rus. Fed. 64 J3
Yartsevo *Smolenskaya Oblast'* Rus. Fed. 43 G5
Yarumal Col. 142 C2
Yarwa China 76 C2
Yarzhong China 76 C2
Yaş Romania *see* Iaşi
Yasawa Group *is* Fiji 107 H3
Yashilkŭl *l.* Tajik. 89 I2
Yashkul' Rus. Fed. 43 J7
Yasin Pak. 82 C1
Yasnogorsk Rus. Fed. 43 H5
Yasnyy Rus. Fed. 74 C1
Yasothon Thai. 70 D4
Yass Australia 112 D5
Yass *r.* Australia 112 D5
Yassı Burnu *c.* Cyprus *see* Plakoti, Cape
Yāsūj Iran 88 C4
Yasuní, Parque Nacional *nat. park* Ecuador 142 C4
Yatağan Turkey 59 M6
Yaté New Caledonia 107 G4
Yates *r.* Canada 120 H2
Yates Center U.S.A. 130 E4
Yathkyed Lake Canada 121 L2
Yatsushiro Japan 75 C6
Yaṭṭa West Bank 85 B4
Yatton U.K. 49 E7
Yauca Peru 142 D7
Yau Tong *b.* H.K. China 77 [inset]
Yavan Tajik. *see* Yovon
Yavari *r.* Brazil/Peru 142 E4
also known as Javari (Brazil/Peru)
Yávaros Mex. 127 F8
Yavatmal India 84 C1
Yavi Turkey 91 F3
Yaví, Cerro *mt.* Venez. 142 E2
Yavoriv Ukr. 43 D6
Yavuzlu Turkey 85 C1
Yawatongguzlangar China 83 E1
Yaw Chaung *r.* Myanmar 76 B4
Yaxian China *see* Sanya
Yay Myanmar *see* Ye
Yayladağı Turkey 85 C2
Yazd Iran 88 D4

Yazdān Iran 89 F3
Yazd-e Khvāst Iran 88 D4
Yazıhan Turkey 90 E3
Yazoo City U.S.A. 131 F5
Y Bala U.K. *see* Bala
Yding Skovhøj *hill* Denmark 47 L3
Ydra *i.* Greece 59 J6
Y Drenewydd U.K. *see* Newtown
Ye Myanmar 70 B4
Yea Australia 112 B6
Yealmpton U.K. 49 D8
Yebawmi Myanmar 70 A1
Yebbi-Bou Chad 97 E2
Yecheng China 80 E4
Yécora Mex. 127 F7
Yedashe Myanmar 70 B3
Yedatore India 84 C3
Yedi Burun Başı *pt* Turkey 59 M6
Yeeda River Australia 108 C4
Yefremov Rus. Fed. 43 H5
Yêgainnyin China *see* Henan
Yeghegnadzor Armenia 91 G3
Yegindykol' Kazakh. 80 C1
Yegorlykskaya Rus. Fed. 43 I7
Yegorova, Mys *pt* Rus. Fed. 74 E3
Yegor'yevsk Rus. Fed. 43 H5
Yei Sudan 97 G4
Yei *r.* Sudan 97 G4
Yeji China 77 G2
Yejiaji China *see* Yeji
Yekaterinburg Rus. Fed. 64 H4
Yekaterinodar Rus. Fed. *see* Krasnodar
Yekaterinoslav Ukr. *see* Dnipropetrovs'k
Yekaterinoslavka Rus. Fed. 74 C2
Yekhegnadzor Armenia *see* Yeghegnadzor
Ye Kyun *i.* Myanmar 70 A3
Yelabuga *Khabarovskiy Kray* Rus. Fed. 74 D2
Yelabuga *Respublika Tatarstan* Rus. Fed. 42 K5
Yelan' Rus. Fed. 43 I6
Yelan' *r.* Rus. Fed. 43 I6
Yelandur India 84 C3
Yelantsy Rus. Fed. 72 J2
Yelarbon Australia 112 E2
Yelbarsli Turkm. 89 F2
Yelenovskiye Kar'yery Ukr. *see* Dokuchayevs'k
Yelets Rus. Fed. 43 H5
Yélimané Mali 96 B3
Yelizavetgrad Ukr. *see* Kirovohrad
Yelkhovka Rus. Fed. 43 K5
Yell *i.* U.K. 50 [inset]
Yellabina Regional Reserve *nature res.* Australia 109 F7
Yellandu India 84 D2
Yellapur India 84 B3
Yellowhead Pass Canada 120 G4

▶Yellowknife Canada 120 H2
Capital of the Northwest Territories.

Yellowknife *r.* Canada 120 H2
Yellow Mountain *hill* Australia 112 C4

▶Yellow *r.* China 77 G1
4th longest river in Asia, and 7th in the world.

Yellow Sea N. Pacific Ocean 73 N5
Yellowstone *r.* U.S.A. 130 C2
Yellowstone Lake U.S.A. 126 F3
Yellowstone National Park U.S.A. 126 F3
Yell Sound *strait* U.K. 50 [inset]
Yeloten Turkm. *see* Ýolöten
Yelovo Rus. Fed. 41 Q4
Yel'sk Belarus 43 F6
Yelva *r.* Rus. Fed. 42 K3
Yematan China 76 C1
Yemen *country* Asia 86 G6
Yemetsk Rus. Fed. 42 I3
Yemişenbükü Turkey *see* Taşova
Yemmiganur India *see* Emmiganuru
Yemtsa Rus. Fed. 42 I3
Yemva Rus. Fed. 42 K3
Yena Rus. Fed. 44 Q3
Yenagoa Nigeria 96 D4
Yenakiyeve Ukr. 43 H6
Yenakiyevo Ukr. *see* Yenakiyeve
Yenangyat Myanmar 70 A2
Yenangyaung Myanmar 70 A2
Yenanma Myanmar 70 A3
Yenda Australia 112 C5
Yêndum China *see* Zhag'yab
Yengisar China 80 E4
Yengo National Park Australia 112 E4
Yenice Turkey 59 L5
Yenidamlar Turkey *see* Demirtaş
Yenihan Turkey *see* Yıldızeli
Yenije-i-Vardar Greece *see* Giannitsa
Yenişehir Greece *see* Larisa
Yenişehir Turkey 59 M4

▶Yenisey *r.* Rus. Fed. 64 J2
Part of the Yenisey-Angara-Selenga, 3rd longest river in Asia.

▶Yenisey-Angara-Selenga *r.* Rus. Fed. 64 J2
3rd longest river in Asia, and 6th in the world.

Yeniseysk Rus. Fed. 64 K4
Yeniseyskiy Kryazh *ridge* Rus. Fed. 64 K4
Yeniseyskiy Zaliv *inlet* Rus. Fed. 153 F2
Yeniyol Turkey *see* Borçka
Yên Minh Vietnam 70 D2
Yenotayevka Rus. Fed. 43 J7
Yeola India 84 B1
Yeo Lake *salt flat* Australia 109 D6
Yeotmal India *see* Yavatmal
Yeoval Australia 112 D4
Yeovil U.K. 49 E8
Yeo Yeo *r.* Australia *see* Bland
Yeppoon Australia 110 E4
Yeraliyev Kazakh. *see* Kuryk
Yerbent Turkm. 88 E2
Yerbogachen Rus. Fed. 65 L3
Yercaud India 84 C4

▶Yerevan Armenia 91 G2
Capital of Armenia.

Yereymentau Kazakh. 80 D1
Yergara India 84 C2
Yergeni *hills* Rus. Fed. 43 J7
Yergoğu Romania *see* **Giurgiu**
Yeriḥo West Bank *see* **Jericho**
Yerilla Australia 109 C7
Yerington U.S.A. 128 D2
Yerköy Turkey 90 D3
Yerla *r.* India 84 B2
Yermak Kazakh. *see* **Aksu**
Yermakovo Rus. Fed. 74 B1
Yermak Plateau *sea feature* Arctic Ocean 153 H1
Yermentau Kazakh. *see* **Yereymentau**
Yermo Mex. 131 B7
Yermo U.S.A. 128 E4
Yerofey Pavlovich Rus. Fed. 74 A1
Yerres *r.* France 52 C6
Yersa *r.* Rus. Fed. 42 L2
Yershov Rus. Fed. 43 K6
Yertsevo Rus. Fed. 42 I3
Yeruḥam Israel 85 B4
Yerupaja *mt.* Peru 142 C6
Yerushalayim Israel/West Bank *see* **Jerusalem**
Yeruslan *r.* Rus. Fed. 43 J6
Yesagyo Myanmar 70 A2
Yesan S. Korea 75 B5
Yesil' Kazakh. 78 F1
Yeşilhisar Turkey 90 D3
Yeşilırmak *r.* Turkey 90 E2
Yeşilova *Burdur* Turkey 59 M6
Yeşilova *Yozgat* Turkey *see* **Sorgun**
Yessentuki Rus. Fed. 91 F1
Yessey Rus. Fed. 65 L3
Yes Tor *hill* U.K. 49 C8
Yêtatang China *see* **Baqên**
Yetman Australia 112 E2
Ye-U Myanmar 70 A2
Yeu, Île d' *i.* France 56 C3
Yevdokimovskoye Rus. Fed. *see* **Krasnogvardeyskoye**
Yevlakh Azer. *see* **Yevlax**
Yevlax Azer. 91 G2
Yevpatoriya Ukr. 90 D1
Yevreyskaya Avtonomnaya Oblast' *admin. div.* Rus. Fed. 74 D2
Yexian China *see* **Laizhou**
Yeyik China 83 E1
Yeysk Rus. Fed. 43 H7
Yeyungou China 80 G3
Yezhou China *see* **Jianshi**
Yezhuga *r.* Rus. Fed. 42 J2
Yezo *i.* Japan *see* **Hokkaidō**
Yezyaryshcha Belarus 42 F5
Y Fenni U.K. *see* **Abergavenny**
Y Fflint U.K. *see* **Flint**
Y Gelli Gandryll U.K. *see* **Hay-on-Wye**
Yialí *i.* Greece *see* **Gyali**
Yi'allaq, Gebel *mt.* Egypt *see* **Yu'alliq, Jabal**
Yialousa Cyprus *see* **Aigialousa**
Yi'an China 74 B3
Yianisádha *i.* Greece *see* **Gianisada**
Yianisádha *i. Kriti* Greece *see* **Gianisada**
Yiannitsá Greece *see* **Giannitsa**
Yibin *Sichuan* China 76 E2
Yibin *Sichuan* China 76 E2
Yibug Caka *salt l.* China 83 F2
Yichang *Hubei* China 77 F2
Yicheng *Henan* China *see* **Zhumadian**
Yicheng *Hubei* China 77 G2
Yicheng *Shanxi* China 77 F1
Yichun *Heilong.* China 74 C3
Yichun *Jiangxi* China 77 G3
Yidu China *see* **Zhicheng**
Yidun China 76 C2
Yifeng China 77 G2
Yi He *r. Henan* China 77 G1
Yi He *r. Shandong* China 77 H1
Yihuang China 77 H3
Yijun China 77 F1
Yilaha China 74 B2
Yilan China 74 C3
Yilan Taiwan *see* **Ilan**
Yıldız Dağları *mts* Turkey 59 L4
Yıldızeli Turkey 90 E3
Yilehuli Shan *mts* China 74 A2
Yiliang China 76 E3
Yiling *Hubei* China 77 F2
Yilong *Heilong.* China 74 B3
Yilong *Sichuan* China 76 E2
Yilong *Yunnan* China *see* **Shiping**
Yilong Hu *l.* China 76 D4
Yimianpo China 74 C3
Yinbaing Myanmar 70 B3
Yincheng China *see* **Dexing**
Yinchuan China 72 J5
Yindarlgooda, Lake *salt flat* Australia 109 C7
Yingcheng China 77 G2
Yingde China 77 G3
Yinggehai China 77 F5
Yinggen China *see* **Qiongzhong**
Ying He *r.* China 77 H1
Yingjing China 76 D2
Yingkou China 73 M4
Yingshan China 77 G2
Yingtan China 77 H2
Yining *Jiangxi* China *see* **Xiushui**
Yining *Xinjiang* China 80 F3
Yinjiang China 77 F3
Yinkeng China *see* **Yinkengxu**
Yinkengxu China 77 G3
Yinmabin Myanmar 70 A2
Yinnyein Myanmar 70 B3
Yin Shan *mts* China 73 J4
Yinxian China *see* **Ningbo**
Yipinglang China 76 D3
Yiquan China *see* **Meitan**
Yirga Alem Eth. 98 D3
Yirol Sudan 97 G4
Yisa China *see* **Honghe**
Yishan *Guangxi* China *see* **Yizhou**
Yishan *Jiangsu* China *see* **Guanyun**
Yishui China 73 L5
Yishun Sing. 71 [inset]
Yíthion Greece *see* **Gytheio**
Yitiaoshan China *see* **Jingtai**
Yitong He *r.* China 74 B3
Yi Tu, Nam *r.* Myanmar 70 B2
Yitulihe China 74 A2
Yiwu China 76 D4
Yixing China 77 H2
Yiyang China 77 G2
Yizheng China 77 H1
Yizhou China 77 F3
Yizra'el *country* Asia *see* **Israel**
Yläne Fin. 45 M6
Ylihärmä Fin. 44 M5
Yli-Ii Fin. 44 N4
Yli-Kärppä Fin. 44 N4
Ylikiiminki Fin. 44 O4
Yli-Kitka *l.* Fin. 44 P3
Ylistaro Fin. 44 M5
Ylitornio Fin. 44 M3
Ylivieska Fin. 44 N4
Ylöjärvi Fin. 45 M6
Ymer Ø *i.* Greenland 119 P2
Ynys Enlli *i.* U.K. *see* **Bardsey Island**
Ynys Môn *i.* U.K. *see* **Anglesey**
Yoakum U.S.A. 131 D6
Yoder U.S.A. 134 C3
Yogan, Cerro *mt.* Chile 144 B8
Yogyakarta Indon. 68 E8
Yoho National Park Canada 120 G5
Yokadouma Cameroon 97 E4
Yokkaichi Japan 75 E6
Yoko Cameroon 96 E4
Yokohama Japan 75 E6
Yokosuka Japan 75 E6
Yokote Japan 75 F5
Yola Nigeria 96 E4
Yolo U.S.A. 128 C2
Yolombo Dem. Rep. Congo 98 C4
Yolöten Turkm. 89 F2
Yoluk Mex. 133 C8
Yom, Mae Nam *r.* Thai. 70 C4
Yomou Guinea 96 C4
Yomuka Indon. 69 J8
Yonaguni-jima *i.* Japan 77 I3
Yŏnan N. Korea 75 B5
Yonezawa Japan 75 F5
Yong'an *Chongqing* China *see* **Fengjie**
Yong'an *Fujian* China 77 H3
Yongbei China *see* **Yongsheng**
Yongcong China 77 F3
Yongding *Fujian* China 77 H3
Yongding *Yunnan* China *see* **Yongren**
Yongding *Yunnan* China *see* **Fumin**
Yongfeng China 77 G3
Yongfu China 77 F3
Yŏnghŭng N. Korea 75 B5
Yŏnghŭng-man *b.* N. Korea 75 B5
Yŏngil-man *b.* S. Korea 75 C6
Yongjing *Guizhou* China *see* **Xifeng**
Yongjing *Liaoning* China *see* **Xifeng**
Yŏngju S. Korea 75 C5
Yongkang *Yunnan* China 76 C3
Yongkang *Zhejiang* China 77 I2
Yongle China *see* **Zhen'an**
Yongning *Guangxi* China 77 F4
Yongning *Jiangxi* China *see* **Tonggu**
Yongning *Sichuan* China *see* **Xuyong**
Yongping China 76 C3
Yongqing China *see* **Qingshui**
Yongren China 76 D3
Yongsheng China 76 D3
Yongshou China 77 F1
Yongshun China 77 F2
Yongtai China 77 H3
Yongxi China *see* **Nayong**
Yongxing *Hunan* China 77 G3
Yongxing *Jiangxi* China 77 G3
Yongxiu China 77 G2
Yongyang China *see* **Weng'an**
Yongzhou China 77 F3
Yonkers U.S.A. 135 I3
Yopal Col. 142 D2
Yopurga China 80 E4
Yordu India 82 C2
York Australia 109 B7
York Canada 134 F2
York U.K. 48 F5
York *AL* U.S.A. 131 F5
York *NE* U.S.A. 130 D3
York *PA* U.S.A. 135 G4
York, Cape Australia 110 C1
York, Kap *c.* Greenland *see* **Innaanganeq**
York, Vale of *valley* U.K. 48 F4
Yorke Peninsula Australia 111 B7
Yorkshire Dales National Park U.K. 48 E4
Yorkshire Wolds *hills* U.K. 48 G5
Yorkton Canada 121 K5
Yorktown U.S.A. 135 G5
Yorkville U.S.A. 130 F3
Yorosso Mali 96 C3
Yosemite U.S.A. 134 C5
Yosemite National Park U.S.A. 128 D3
Yoshkar-Ola Rus. Fed. 42 J4
Yos Sudarso *i.* Indon. *see* **Dolok, Pulau**
Yŏsu S. Korea 75 B6
Yotvata Israel 85 B5
Youbou Canada 120 E5
Youghal Ireland 51 E6
Young Australia 112 D5
Young U.S.A. 129 H4
Younghusband, Lake *salt flat* Australia 111 B6
Younghusband Peninsula Australia 111 B7
Young Island Antarctica 152 H2
Youngstown Canada 121 I5
Youngstown U.S.A. 134 E3
You Shui *r.* China 77 F2
Youssoufia Morocco 54 C5
Youvarou Mali 96 C3
Youxi China 77 H3
Youxian China 77 G3
Youyang China 77 F2
Youyi China 74 C3
Youyi Feng *mt.* China/Rus. Fed. 80 G2
Yovon Tajik. 89 H2
Yowah *watercourse* Australia 112 B2
Yozgat Turkey 90 D3
Ypres Belgium *see* **Ieper**
Yreka U.S.A. 126 C4
Yrghyz Kazakh. *see* **Irgiz**
Yr Wyddfa *mt.* U.K. *see* **Snowdon**
Yser *r.* France 52 C4
also known as IJzer (Belgium)
Ysselsteyn Neth. 52 F3
Ystad Sweden 45 H9
Ystwyth *r.* U.K. 49 C6
Ysyk-Köl Kyrg. *see* **Balykchy**
▶**Ysyk-Köl** *salt l.* Kyrg. 80 E3
5th largest lake in Asia.
Ythan *r.* U.K. 50 G3
Y Trallwng U.K. *see* **Welshpool**
Ytyk-Kyuyel' Rus. Fed. 65 O3
Yu'alliq, Jabal *mt.* Egypt 85 A4
Yuan'an China 77 F2
Yuanbao Shan *mt.* China 77 F3
Yuanjiang *Hunan* China 77 G2
Yuanjiang *Yunnan* China 76 D4
Yuan Jiang *r. Hunan* China 77 F2
Yuan Jiang *r. Yunnan* China 76 D4
Yuanjiazhuang China *see* **Foping**
Yuanlin China 74 A2
Yuanling China 77 F2
Yuanma China *see* **Yuanmou**
Yuanmou China 76 D3
Yuanquan China *see* **Anxi**
Yuanshan China *see* **Lianping**
Yuanyang China *see* **Xinjie**
Yub'ā *i.* Saudi Arabia 90 D6
Yuba City U.S.A. 128 C2
Yubei China 76 E2
Yuben' Tajik. 89 I2
Yucatán *pen.* Mex. 136 F5
Yucatan Channel Cuba/Mex. 137 G4
Yucca U.S.A. 129 F4
Yucca Lake U.S.A. 128 E3
Yucca Valley U.S.A. 128 E4
Yucheng *Henan* China 77 G1
Yucheng *Sichuan* China *see* **Ya'an**
Yuci China *see* **Jinzhong**
Yudi Shan *mt.* China 74 A1
Yudu China 77 G3
Yuelai China *see* **Huachuan**
Yueliang Pao *l.* China 74 A3
Yuendumu Australia 108 E5
Yuen Long *H.K.* China 77 [inset]
Yueqing China 77 I2
Yuexi China 77 H2
Yueyang *Hunan* China 77 G2
Yueyang *Hunan* China 77 G2
Yueyang *Sichuan* China *see* **Anyue**
Yug *r.* Rus. Fed. 42 J3
Yugan China 77 H2
Yugorsk Rus. Fed. 41 S3
▶**Yugoslavia** *country* Europe 59 I2
Former European country. Up to 1993 included Bosnia-Herzegovina, Croatia, Macedonia and Slovenia. Renamed as Serbia and Montenegro in 2003. Serbia and Montenegro became separate independent countries in June 2006. Kosovo became independent from Serbia in February 2008.
Yuhang China 77 I2
Yuhu China *see* **Eryuan**
Yuhuan China 77 I2
Yuin Australia 109 B6
Yu Jiang *r.* China 77 F4
Yukagirskoye Ploskogor'ye *plat.* Rus. Fed. 65 Q3
Yukamenskoye Rus. Fed. 42 L4
Yukarı Sakarya Ovaları *plain* Turkey 59 N5
Yukarısarıkaya Turkey 90 D3
▶**Yukon** *r.* Canada/U.S.A. 120 B2
5th longest river in North America.
Yukon Crossing (abandoned) Canada 120 B2
Yukon Territory *admin. div.* Canada 120 C2
Yüksekova Turkey 91 G3
Yulara Australia 109 E6
Yule *r.* Australia 108 B5
Yuleba Australia 112 D1
Yulee U.S.A. 133 D6
Yulin *Guangxi* China 77 F4
Yulin *Shaanxi* China 73 J5
Yulong Xueshan *mt.* China 76 D3
Yuma *AZ* U.S.A. 129 F5
Yuma *CO* U.S.A. 130 C3
Yuma Desert U.S.A. 129 F5
Yumen China 80 I4
Yumenguan China 80 H3
Yumurtalık Turkey 85 B1
Yuna Australia 109 A7
Yunak Turkey 90 C3
Yunan China 77 F4
Yunaska Island U.S.A. 118 A4
Yuncheng China 77 F1
Yundamindera Australia 109 C7
Yunfu China 77 G4
Yungas *reg.* Bol. 142 E7
Yungui Gaoyuan *plat.* China 76 D3
Yunhe *Jiangsu* China *see* **Pizhou**
Yunhe *Yunnan* China *see* **Heqing**
Yunhe *Zhejiang* China 77 H2
Yunjinghong China *see* **Jinghong**
Yunkai Dashan *mts* China 77 F4
Yünlin Taiwan *see* **Touliu**
Yunling China *see* **Yunxiao**
Yun Ling *mts* China 76 C3
Yunlong China 76 C3
Yunmeng China 77 G2
Yunmenling China *see* **Junmenling**
Yunnan *prov.* China 76 D3
Yunta Australia 111 B7
Yunt Dağı *mt.* Turkey 85 A1
Yunxi *Hubei* China 77 F1
Yunxi *Sichuan* China *see* **Yanting**
Yunxian *Hubei* China 77 F1
Yunxian *Yunnan* China 76 D3
Yunxiao China 77 H4
Yunyang *Chongqing* China 77 F2
Yunyang *Henan* China 77 G1
Yuping *Guizhou* China *see* **Libo**
Yuping *Guizhou* China 77 F3
Yuping *Yunnan* China *see* **Pingbian**
Yuqing China 76 E3
Yuraygir National Park Australia 112 F2
Yurba Co *l.* China 83 F2
Yürekli Turkey 85 B1
Yurga Rus. Fed. 64 J4
Yuriria Mex. 136 D4
Yurungkax He *r.* China 82 E1
Yur'ya Rus. Fed. 42 K4
Yur'yakha *r.* Rus. Fed. 42 L2
Yuryev Estonia *see* **Tartu**
Yur'yevets Rus. Fed. 42 I4
Yur'yev-Pol'skiy Rus. Fed. 42 H4
Yushan China 77 H2
Yü Shan *mt.* Taiwan 77 I4
Yushino Rus. Fed. 42 L1
Yushkozero Rus. Fed. 44 R4
Yushu *Jilin* China 74 B3
Yushu *Qinghai* China 76 C1
Yushuwan China *see* **Huaihua**
Yusufeli Turkey 91 F2
Yus'va Rus. Fed. 41 Q4
Yuta West Bank *see* **Yaṭṭa**
Yutai China 77 H1
Yutan China *see* **Ningxiang**
Yuxi *Guizhou* China *see* **Daozhen**
Yuxi *Hubei* China 77 F2
Yuxi *Yunnan* China 76 D3
Yuyangguan China 77 F2
Yuyao China 77 I2
Yuzawa Japan 75 F5
Yuzha Rus. Fed. 42 I4
Yuzhno-Kamyshovyy Khrebet *ridge* Rus. Fed. 74 F3
Yuzhno-Kuril'sk Rus. Fed. 74 G3
Yuzhno-Muyskiy Khrebet *mts* Rus. Fed. 73 K1
Yuzhno-Sakhalinsk Rus. Fed. 74 F3
Yuzhno-Sukhokumsk Rus. Fed. 91 G1
Yuzhnoukrayinsk Ukr. 43 F7
Yuzhnyy Rus. Fed. *see* **Adyk**
Yuzhou *Chongqing* China *see* **Chongqing**
Yuzhou *Henan* China 77 G1
Yuzovka Ukr. *see* **Donets'k**
Yverdon Switz. 56 H3
Yvetot France 56 E2
Ywamun Myanmar 70 A2

Z

Zaamin Uzbek. *see* **Zomin**
Zaandam Neth. 52 E2
Zab, Monts du *mts* Alg. 57 I6
Zabānābād Iran 88 E3
Zabaykal'sk Rus. Fed. 73 L3
Zabīd Yemen 86 F7
Zābol Iran 89 F4
Zacapa Guat. 136 G5
Zacatecas Mex. 136 D4
Zacatecas *state* Mex. 131 C8
Zacharo Greece 59 I6
Zacoalco Mex. 136 D4
Zacynthus *i.* Greece *see* **Zakynthos**
Zadar Croatia 58 F2
Zadetkale Kyun *i.* Myanmar 71 B5
Zadetkyi Kyun *i.* Myanmar 71 B5
Zadi Myanmar 71 B4
Zadoi China 76 B1
Zadonsk Rus. Fed. 43 H5
Zadran *reg.* Afgh. 89 H3
Za'farâna Egypt *see* **Za'farānah**
Za'farānah Egypt 90 D5
Zafer Adaları *is* Cyprus *see* **Kleides Islands**
Zafer Burnu *c.* Cyprus *see* **Apostolos Andreas, Cape**
Zafora *i.* Greece *see* **Sofrana**
Zafra Spain 57 C4
Zagazig Egypt *see* **Az Zaqāzīq**
Zaghdeh *well* Iran 88 E3
Zaghouan Tunisia 58 D6
Zagorsk Rus. Fed. *see* **Sergiyev Posad**
▶**Zagreb** Croatia 58 F2
Capital of Croatia.
Zagros, Kūhhā-ye *mts* Iran *see* **Zagros Mountains**
Zagros Mountains Iran 88 B3
Zagunao China *see* **Lixian**
Za'gya Zangbo *r.* China 83 G3
Zāhedān Iran 89 F4
Zahir Pir Pak. 89 H4
Zaḥlah Lebanon *see* **Zahlé**
Zahlé Lebanon 85 B3
Zähmet Turkm. 89 F2
Ẓahrān Saudi Arabia 86 F6
Zahrez Chergui *salt pan* Alg. 57 H6
Zahrez Rharbi *salt pan* Alg. 57 H6
Zainlha China *see* **Xiaojin**
Zainsk Rus. Fed. *see* **Novyy Zay**
Zaire *country* Africa *see* **Congo, Democratic Republic of the**
Zaïre *r.* Congo/Dem. Rep. Congo *see* **Congo**
Zaječar Serbia 59 J3
Zaka Zimbabwe 99 D6
Zakamensk Rus. Fed. 80 J1
Zakataly Azer. *see* **Zaqatala**
Zakháro Greece *see* **Zacharo**
Zakhmet Turkm. *see* **Zähmet**
Zākhō Iraq 91 F3
Zakhodnyaya Dzvina *r.* Europe *see* **Zapadnaya Dvina**
Zákinthos *i.* Greece *see* **Zakynthos**
Zakopane Poland 47 Q6
Zakouma, Parc National de *nat. park* Chad 97 E3
Zakwaski, Mount Canada 120 F5
Zakynthos Greece 59 I6
Zakynthos *i.* Greece 59 I6
Zala China 76 B2
Zalaegerszeg Hungary 58 G1
Zalai-domsag *hills* Hungary 58 G1
Zalamea de la Serena Spain 57 D4
Zalantun China 74 A3
Zalari Rus. Fed. 72 I2
Zalău Romania 59 J1
Zaleski U.S.A. 134 D4
Ẓalim Saudi Arabia 86 F5
Zalingei Sudan 97 F3
Ẓalmā, Jabal aẓ *mt.* Saudi Arabia 86 E4
Zama City Canada 120 G3
Zambeze *r.* Africa 99 C5 *see* **Zambezi**
▶**Zambezi** *r.* Africa 99 C5
4th longest river in Africa. Also known as Zambeze.
Zambezi Zambia 99 C5
Zambia *country* Africa 99 C5
Zamboanga Phil. 69 G5
Zamfara *watercourse* Nigeria 96 D3
Zamīndāvar *reg.* Afgh. 89 F4
Zamkog China *see* **Zamtang**
Zamora Ecuador 142 C4
Zamora Spain 57 D3
Zamora de Hidalgo Mex. 136 D5
Zamość Poland 43 D6
Zamost'ye Poland *see* **Zamość**
Zamtang China 76 D1
Zamuro, Sierra del *mts* Venez. 142 F3
Zanaga Congo 98 B4
Zancle *Sicily* Italy *see* **Messina**
Zandamela Moz. 101 L3
Zandvliet Belgium 52 E3
Zanesville U.S.A. 134 D4
Zangguy China 82 D1
Zangsêr Kangri *mt.* China 83 F2
Zangskar *reg.* India *see* **Zanskar**
Zangskar Mountains India *see* **Zanskar Mountains**
Zanjān Iran 88 C2
Zanjān Rūd *r.* Iran 88 B2
Ẓannah, Jabal aẓ *hill* U.A.E. 88 D5
Zanskar *reg.* India 82 D2
Zanskar Mountains India 82 D2
Zante *i.* Greece *see* **Zakynthos**
Zanthus Australia 109 C7
Zanughān Iran 88 E3
Zanzibar Tanz. 99 D4
Zanzibar Island Tanz. 99 D4
Zaoshi *Hubei* China 77 G2
Zaoshi *Hunan* China 77 G3
Zaouatallaz Alg. 96 D2
Zaouet el Kahla Alg. *see* **Bordj Omer Driss**
Zaoyang China 77 G1
Zaoyangzhan China 77 G1
Zaozernyy Rus. Fed. 65 K4
Zaozhuang China 77 H1
Zapadnaya Dvina *r.* Europe 42 F5
also known as Dvina or Zakhodnyaya Dzvina. English form Western Dvina
Zapadnaya Dvina Rus. Fed. 42 G4
Zapadni Rodopi *mts* Bulg. 59 J4
Zapadno-Kazakhstanskaya Oblast' *admin. div.* Kazakh. *see* **Zapadnyy Kazakhstan**
Zapadno-Sakhalinskiy Khrebet *mts* Rus. Fed. 74 F2
Zapadno-Sibirskaya Nizmennost' *plain* Rus. Fed. *see* **West Siberian Plain**
Zapadno-Sibirskaya Ravnina *plain* Rus. Fed. *see* **West Siberian Plain**
Zapadnyy Chink Ustyurta *esc.* Kazakh. 91 I2
Zapadnyy Kazakhstan *admin. div.* Kazakh. 41 Q6
Zapadnyy Kil'din Rus. Fed. 44 S2
Zapadnyy Sayan *reg.* Rus. Fed. 72 F2
Zapata U.S.A. 131 D7
Zapata, Península de *pen.* Cuba 133 D8
Zapiga Chile 142 E7
Zapolyarnyy Rus. Fed. 44 Q2
Zapol'ye Rus. Fed. 42 H4
Zaporizhzhya Ukr. 43 G7
Zaporozh'ye Ukr. *see* **Zaporizhzhya**
Zapug China 82 E2
Zaqatala Azer. 91 G2
Zaqên China 76 B1
Zaqāzīq Egypt *see* **Az Zaqāzīq**
Za Qu *r.* China 76 C2
Zaqungngomar *mt.* China 83 G2
Zara China *see* **Moinda**
Zara Croatia *see* **Zadar**
Zara Turkey 90 E3
Zarafshan Uzbek. *see* **Zarafshon**
Zarafshon Uzbek. 80 B3
Zarafshon, Qatorkŭhi *mts* Tajik. 89 G2
Zaragoza Spain 57 F3
Zarand Iran 88 E4
Zarang China 82 D3
Zaranikh Reserve *nature res.* Egypt 85 B4
Zaranj Afgh. 89 F4
Zarasai Lith. 45 O9
Zárate Arg. 144 E4
Zaraysk Rus. Fed. 43 H5
Zaraza Venez. 142 E2
Zarbdor Uzbek. 89 H1
Zārdab Azer. 43 J8
Zarechensk Rus. Fed. 44 Q3
Zāreh Iran 88 C3
Zarembo Island U.S.A. 120 C3
Zargun *mt.* Pak. 89 G4
Zari Afgh. 89 G3
Zaria Nigeria 96 D3
Zarichne Ukr. 43 E6
Zarifête, Col des *pass* Alg. 57 F6
Zaring China *see* **Liangdaohe**
Zarinsk Rus. Fed. 72 E2
Zarmardan Afgh. 89 F3
Zarneh Iran 88 B3
Zărneşti Romania 59 K2
Zarqā' Jordan *see* **Az Zarqā'**
Zarqā', Nahr az *r.* Jordan 85 B3
Zarubino Rus. Fed. 74 C4
Żary Poland 47 O5
Zarzis Tunisia 54 G5
Zasheyek Rus. Fed. 44 Q3
Zaskar *reg.* India *see* **Zanskar**
Zaskar Range *mts* India *see* **Zanskar Mountains**
Zaslawye Belarus 45 O9
Zastron S. Africa 101 H6
Za'tarī, Wādī az *watercourse* Jordan 85 C3
Zaterechnyy Rus. Fed. 43 J7
Zauche *reg.* Germany 53 M2
Zaunguzskiye Karakumy *des.* Turkm. *see* **Üngüz Angyrsyndaky Garagum**
Zavalla U.S.A. 131 E6
Zavetnoye Rus. Fed. 43 I7
Zavety Il'icha Rus. Fed. 74 F2
Zavidovići Bos.-Herz. 58 H2
Zavitaya Rus. Fed. *see* **Zavitinsk**
Zavitinsk Rus. Fed. 74 C2
Zavolzhsk Rus. Fed. 42 I4
Zavolzh'ye Rus. Fed. *see* **Zavolzhsk**
Závora, Ponta *pt* Moz. 101 L3
Zawiercie Poland 47 Q5
Zawīlah Libya 97 E2
Zāwīyah, Jabal az *hills* Syria 85 C2
Zaydī, Wādī az *watercourse* Syria 85 C3
Zaysan Kazakh. 80 F2
Zaysan, Lake Kazakh. 80 F2
Zaysan, Ozero *l.* Kazakh. *see* **Zaysan, Lake**
Zayü China *see* **Gyigang**
Zayü Qu *r.* China/India 83 I3
Žďár nad Sázavou Czech Rep. 47 O6
Zdolbuniv Ukr. 43 E6
Zdolbunov Ukr. *see* **Zdolbuniv**
Zealand *i.* Denmark 45 G9
Zēbāk Afgh. 82 B1
Zebulon U.S.A. 134 D5
Zedelgem Belgium 52 D3
Zeebrugge Belgium 52 D3
Zeeland U.S.A. 134 B2
Zeerust S. Africa 101 H3
Ẓefat Israel 85 B3
Zehdenick Germany 53 N2
Zeil, Mount Australia 109 F5
Zeil am Main Germany 53 K4
Zeist Neth. 52 F2
Zeitz Germany 53 M3
Zêkog China 76 D1
Zela Turkey *see* **Zile**
Zelennik Rus. Fed. 42 J3
Zelenoborsk Rus. Fed. 41 S3
Zelenoborskiy Rus. Fed. 44 R3
Zelenodol'sk Rus. Fed. 42 K5
Zelenogorsk Rus. Fed. 45 P6
Zelenograd Rus. Fed. 42 H4
Zelenogradsk Rus. Fed. 45 L9
Zelenokumsk Rus. Fed. 91 F1
Zelentsovo Rus. Fed. 42 J4
Zelenyy, Ostrov *i.* Rus. Fed. 74 G4
Zell am See Austria 47 N7
Zellingen Germany 53 J5
Zelzate Belgium 52 D3
Žemaitijos nacionalinis parkas *nat. park* Lith. 45 L8
Zêmdasam China 76 D1
Zemetchino Rus. Fed. 43 I5
Zémio Cent. Afr. Rep. 98 C3
Zemmora Alg. 57 G6
Zempoaltépetl, Nudo de *mt.* Mex. 136 E5
Zengcheng China 77 G4
Zenica Bos.-Herz. 58 G2
Ẓenifim *watercourse* Israel 85 B4
Zennor U.K. 49 B8
Zenta Serbia *see* **Senta**
Zenzach Alg. 57 H6
Zeravshanskiy Khrebet *mts* Tajik. *see* **Zarafshon, Qatorkŭhi**
Zerbst Germany 53 M3
Zerenike Reserve *nature res.* Egypt *see* **Zaranikh Reserve**
Zerf Germany 52 G5
Zernien Germany 53 K1
Zernitz Germany 53 M2
Zernograd Rus. Fed. 43 I7
Zernovoy Rus. Fed. *see* **Zernograd**
Zêtang China 83 G3
Zetel Germany 53 H1
Zeulenroda Germany 53 L4
Zeven Germany 53 J1
Zevenaar Neth. 52 G3
Zevgari, Cape Cyprus 85 A2
Zeya Rus. Fed. 74 B1
Zeya *r.* Rus. Fed. 74 B2
Zeydar Iran 88 E2
Zeydī Iran 89 F5
Zeyskiy Zapovednik *nature res.* Rus. Fed. 74 B1
Zeysko-Bureinskaya Vpadina *depr.* Rus. Fed. 74 C2
Zeyskoye Vodokhranilishche *resr* Rus. Fed. 74 B1
Zeytin Burnu *c.* Cyprus *see* **Elaia, Cape**
Zêzere *r.* Port. 57 B4
Zgharta Lebanon 85 B2
Zghorta Lebanon *see* **Zgharta**
Zgierz Poland 47 Q5
Zhabdün China *see* **Zhongba**
Zhabinka Belarus 45 N10
Zhaggo China *see* **Luhuo**
Zhaglag China 76 C1
Zhag'yab China 76 C2
Zhaksy Sarysu *watercourse* Kazakh. *see* **Sarysu**
Zhalanash Kazakh. *see* **Damdy**
Zhalpaktal Kazakh. 41 P6
Zhalpaqtal Kazakh. *see* **Zhalpaktal**
Zhaltyr Kazakh. 80 C1
Zhambyl *Karagandinskaya Oblast'* Kazakh. 80 D2
Zhambyl *Zhambylskaya Oblast'* Kazakh. *see* **Taraz**
Zhamo China *see* **Bomi**
Zhanakorgan Kazakh. 80 C3
Zhanaozen Kazakh. 78 E2
Zhanatas Kazakh. 80 C3
Zhanbei China 74 B2
Zhangaözen Kazakh. *see* **Zhanaozen**
Zhanga Qazan Kazakh. *see* **Novaya Kazan**
Zhangaqorghan Kazakh. *see* **Zhanakorgan**
Zhangatas Kazakh. *see* **Zhanatas**
Zhangbei China 73 K4
Zhangcheng China *see* **Yongtai**
Zhangcunpu China 77 H1
Zhangde China *see* **Anyang**
Zhangdian China *see* **Zibo**
Zhanggu China *see* **Danba**
Zhangguangcai Ling *mts* China 74 C3
Zhanghua Taiwan *see* **Changhua**
Zhangjiabang China 77 G2
Zhangjiajie China 77 F2
Zhangjiakou China 73 K4
Zhangjiang China *see* **Taoyuan**
Zhangjiapan China *see* **Jingbian**
Zhangla China 76 D1
Zhangling China 74 A1
Zhanglou China 77 H1
Zhangping China 77 H3
Zhangqiangzhen China 74 A4
Zhangqiao China 77 H1
Zhangshu China 77 G2
Zhangxian China 76 E1
Zhangye China 80 J4
Zhangzhou China 77 H3
Zhanhe China *see* **Zhanbei**
Zhanibek Kazakh. 41 P6
Zhanjiang China 77 F4
Zhanjiang Bei China *see* **Chikan**

ao'an China **77** H4
aodong China **74** B3
aojue China **76** D2
aoliqiao China **77** G2
aoping China **77** F3
aoqing China **77** G4
aotong China **76** D3
aoyuan China **74** B3
aozhou China **74** B3
ari Namco *salt l.* China **83** F3
arkamys Kazakh. **80** A2
arkent Kazakh. **80** F3
arkovskiy Rus. Fed. **42** G5
arma Kazakh. **80** F2
ashkiv Ukr. **43** F6
ashkov Ukr. *see* **Zhashkiv**
aslyk Uzbek. *see* **Jasliq**
axi China *see* **Weixin**
axi Co *salt l.* China **83** F2
axigang China **82** D2
axizê China **76** C2
axizong China **83** F3
ayü China **76** C2
ayyq *r.* Kazakh./Rus. Fed. *see* **Ural**
danov Ukr. *see* **Mariupol'**
danovsk Azer. *see* **Beyläqan**
edao China *see* **Lianghe**
êhor China **76** D2
ejiang *prov.* China **77** I2
elaniya, Mys *c.* Rus. Fed. **64** H2
eleznodorozhnyy Rus. Fed. *see* **Yemva**
eleznodorozhnyy Uzbek. *see* **Qo'ng'irot**
eleznogorsk Rus. Fed. **43** G5
elou China *see* **Ceheng**
eltyye Vody Ukr. *see* **Zhovti Vody**
em Kazakh. *see* **Emba**
en'an China **77** F1
enba China **76** E1
enghe China **77** H3
engjiatun China *see* **Shuangliao**
engning China **77** F1
engyang China **77** G1
engyangguan China **77** H1
engzhou China **77** G1
enhai China **77** I2
enjiang China **77** H1
enjiangguan China **76** D1
enlai China **74** A3
enning China **76** E3
enping China **77** F2
enxi China **74** A3
enxiong China **76** E3
enyang China *see* **Zhengyang**
enyuan China **77** F3
erdevka Rus. Fed. **43** I6
Zherong China **77** H3
Zheshart Rus. Fed. **42** K3
Zhetikara Kazakh. *see* **Zhitikara**
Zhêxam China **83** F3
Zhexi Shuiku *resr* China **77** F2
Zhezkazgan Kazakh. **80** C2
Zhezqazghan Kazakh. *see* **Zhezkazgan**
Zhicheng *Hubei* China **77** F2
Zhicheng *Zhejiang* China *see* **Changxing**
Zhidoi China **76** B1
Zhifang China *see* **Jiangxia**
Zhigalovo Rus. Fed. **72** J2
Zhigansk Rus. Fed. **65** N3
Zhigung China **83** G3
Zhijiang *Hubei* China **77** F2
Zhijiang *Hunan* China **70** E1
Zhijin China **76** E3
Zhilong China *see* **Yangxi**
Zhi Qu *r.* China *see* **Yangtze**
Zhitikara Kazakh. **78** F1
Zhitkovichi Belarus *see* **Zhytkavichy**
Zhitkur Rus. Fed. **43** J6
Zhitomir Ukr. *see* **Zhytomyr**
Zhīvār Iran **88** B3
Zhiziluo China **76** C3
Zhlobin Belarus **43** F5
Zhmerinka Ukr. *see* **Zhmerynka**
Zhmerynka Ukr. **43** F6
Zhob Pak. **89** H4
Zhob *r.* Pak. **89** H3
Zhong'an China *see* **Fuyuan**
Zhongba *Guangdong* China **77** G4
Zhongba *Sichuan* China *see* **Jiangyou**
Zhongba *Xizang* China **83** F3
Zhongduo China *see* **Youyang**
Zhongguo *country* Asia *see* **China**
Zhongguo Renmin Gongheguo *country* Asia *see* **China**
Zhonghe China *see* **Xiushan**
Zhongping China *see* **Huize**
Zhongshan *research station* Antarctica **152** E2
Zhongshan *Guangdong* China **77** G4
Zhongshan *Guangxi* China **77** F3
Zhongshan *Guizhou* China *see* **Lupanshui**
Zhongshu *Yunnan* China *see* **Luxi**
Zhongshu *Yunnan* China *see* **Luliang**
Zhongtai China *see* **Lingtai**
Zhongtiao Shan *mts* China **77** F1
Zhongwei China **72** J5
Zhongxin *Guangdong* China **77** G3
Zhongxin *Yunnan* China *see* **Xianggelila**
Zhongxin *Yunnan* China *see* **Huaping**
Zhongxingji China **77** H2
Zhongyaozhan China **74** B2
Zhongyicun China **76** D3
Zhongyuan China **77** F5
Zhongzhai China **76** E1
Zhosaly Kazakh. *see* **Dzhusaly**
Zhoujiajing China **72** I5
Zhoukou *Henan* China **77** G1
Zhoukou *Sichuan* China *see* **Peng'an**
Zhouning China **77** H3
Zhoushan China **77** I2
Zhoushan Dao *i.* China **77** I2
Zhoushan Qundao *is* China **77** I2
Zhouzhi China **77** F1
Zhovti Vody Ukr. **43** G6
Zhuanghe China **75** A5
Zhuanglang China **76** E1
Zhubgyügoin China **76** C1
Zhudong Taiwan *see* **Chutung**
Zhugla China **76** B2
Zhugqu China **76** E1
Zhuhai China **77** G4
Zhuji *Henan* China *see* **Shangqiu**
Zhuji *Zhejiang* China **77** I2
Zhujing China **77** I2
Zhukeng China **77** G4
Zhukovka Rus. Fed. **43** G5
Zhukovskiy Rus. Fed. **43** H5
Zhumadian China **77** G1
Zhuokeji China **76** D2
Zhushan *Hubei* China **77** F1
Zhushan *Hubei* China *see* **Xuan'en**
Zhuxi China **77** F1
Zhuxiang China **77** H1
Zhuyang China *see* **Dazhu**
Zhuzhou *Hunan* China **77** G3
Zhuzhou *Hunan* China **77** G3
Zhydachiv Ukr. **43** E6
Zhympity Kazakh. **41** Q5
Zhytkavichy Belarus **45** O10
Zhytomyr Ukr. **43** F6
Zīā'ābād Iran **88** C3
Žiar nad Hronom Slovakia **47** Q6
Zibā *salt pan* Saudi Arabia **85** D4
Zibo China **73** L5
Zicheng China *see* **Zijin**
Zidi Pak. **89** G5
Ziel, Mount Australia *see* **Zeil, Mount**
Zielona Góra Poland **47** O5
Ziemelkursas augstiene *hills* Latvia **45** M8
Zierenberg Germany **53** J3
Ziesar Germany **53** M2
Ziftá Egypt **90** C5
Zīghan Libya **97** F2
Zigong China **76** E2
Ziguey Chad **97** E3
Ziguinchor Senegal **96** B3
Žīguri Latvia **45** O8
Zihuatanejo Mex. **136** D5
Zijin China **77** G4
Zijpenberg *hill* Neth. **52** G2
Ziketan China *see* **Xinghai**
Zile Turkey **90** D2
Žilina Slovakia **47** Q6
Zillah Libya **97** E2
Zima Rus. Fed. **72** I2
Zimba Zambia **99** C5
Zimbabwe *country* Africa **99** C5
Zimi Sierra Leone *see* **Zimmi**
Zimmerbude Rus. Fed. *see* **Svetlyy**
Zimmi Sierra Leone **96** B4
Zimnicea Romania **59** K3
Zimniy Bereg *coastal area* Rus. Fed. **42** H2
Zimovniki Rus. Fed. **43** I7
Zimrīn Syria **85** B2
Ẕin *watercourse* Israel **85** B4
Zin Pak. **89** H4
Zinave, Parque Nacional de *nat. park* Moz. **99** D6
Zinder Niger **96** D3
Zindo China **76** D2
Ziniaré Burkina **96** C3
Zinjibār Yemen **86** G7
Zinoyevsk Ukr. *see* **Kirovohrad**
Zion U.S.A. **134** B2
Zion National Park U.S.A. **129** G3
Zionz Lake Canada **121** N5
Zippori Israel **85** B3
Ziqudukou China **76** B1
Zirc Hungary **58** G1
Zirkel, Mount U.S.A. **126** G4
Zirkūh *i.* U.A.E. **88** D5
Zirndorf Germany **53** K5
Ziro India **83** H4
Zirreh Afgh. **89** F4
Zīr Rūd Iran **88** C4
Zi Shui *r.* China **73** K7
Zistersdorf Austria **47** P6
Zitácuaro Mex. **136** D5
Zito China *see* **Lhorong**
Zitong China **76** E2
Zittau Germany **47** O5
Zixi China **77** H3
Zixing China *see* **Xingning**
Ziyang *Jiangxi* China *see* **Wuyuan**
Ziyang *Shaanxi* China **77** F1
Ziyang *Sichuan* China **76** E2
Ziyaret Dağı *hill* Turkey **85** B1
Ziyuan China **77** F3
Ziyun China **76** E3
Ziz, Oued *watercourse* Morocco **54** D5
Zizhong China **76** E2
Zlatoustovsk Rus. Fed. **74** D1
Zlín Czech Rep. **47** P6
Zmeinogorsk Rus. Fed. **80** F1
Zmiyevka Rus. Fed. **43** H5
Znamenka Rus. Fed. **43** I5
Znamenka Ukr. *see* **Znam"yanka**
Znam"yanka Ukr. **43** G6
Znojmo Czech Rep. **47** P6
Zoar S. Africa **100** E7
Zoetermeer Neth. **52** E2
Zogainrawar China *see* **Huashixia**
Zogang China **76** C2
Zogqên China **76** C1
Zoigê China **76** D1
Zoji La *pass* India **82** C2
Zola S. Africa **101** H7
Zolder Belgium **52** F3
Zolochev *Kharkivs'ka Oblast'* Ukr. *see* **Zolochiv**
Zolochev *L'vivs'ka Oblast'* Ukr. *see* **Zolochiv**
Zolochiv *Kharkivs'ka Oblast'* Ukr. **43** G6
Zolochiv *L'vivs'ka Oblast'* Ukr. **43** E6
Zolotonosha Ukr. **43** G6
Zolotoye Rus. Fed. **43** J6
Zolotukhino Rus. Fed. **43** H5

▶**Zomba** Malawi **99** D5
Former capital of Malawi.

Zombor Serbia *see* **Sombor**
Zomin Uzbek. **89** H2
Zongga China *see* **Gyirong**
Zonguldak Turkey **59** N4
Zongxoi China **83** G3
Zörbig Germany **53** M3
Zorgho Burkina **96** C3
Zorgo Burkina *see* **Zorgho**
Zorn *r.* France **53** I6
Żory Poland **47** Q5
Zossen Germany **53** N2
Zottegem Belgium **52** D4
Zouar Chad **97** E2
Zoucheng China **77** H1
Zouérat Mauritania **96** B2
Zousfana, Oued *watercourse* Alg. **54** D5
Zoushi China **77** F2
Zouxian China *see* **Zoucheng**
Zrenjanin Serbia **59** I2
Zschopau Germany **53** N4
Zschopau *r.* Germany **53** N3
Zschornewitz Germany **53** M3
Zubālah, Birkat *waterhole* Saudi Arabia **91** F5
Zubillaga Arg. **144** D5
Zubova Polyana Rus. Fed. **43** I5
Zubtsov Rus. Fed. **42** G4
Zuénoula Côte d'Ivoire **96** C4
Zug Switz. **56** I3
Zugdidi Georgia **91** F2
Zugspitze *mt.* Austria/Germany **47** M7
Zugu Nigeria **96** D3
Zuider Zee *l.* Neth. *see* **IJsselmeer**
Zuidhorn Neth. **52** G1
Zuid-Kennemerland Nationaal Park *nat. park* Neth. **52** E2
Zuitai China *see* **Kangxian**
Zuitaizi China *see* **Kangxian**
Zuitou China *see* **Taibai**
Zújar *r.* Spain **57** D4
Zülpich Germany **52** G4
Zumba Ecuador **142** C4
Zunheboto India **83** H4
Zuni U.S.A. **129** I4
Zuni *watercourse* U.S.A. **129** I4
Zuni Mountains U.S.A. **129** I4
Zunyi *Guizhou* China **76** E3
Zunyi *Guizhou* China **76** E3
Zuo Jiang *r.* China/Vietnam **70** E2
Županja Croatia **58** H2
Zūrābād *Āžarbāyjān-e Gharbī* Iran **88** B2
Zūrābād *Khorāsān* Iran **89** F3
Zurhen Ul Shan *mts* China **83** G2
Zürich Switz. **56** I3
Zurmat *reg.* Afgh. **89** H3
Zuru Nigeria **96** D3
Zurzuna Turkey *see* **Çıldır**
Zutphen Neth. **52** G2
Zuwārah Libya **96** E1
Zuyevka Rus. Fed. **42** K4
Zūzan Iran **89** E3
Zvishavane Zimbabwe **99** D6
Zvolen Slovakia **47** Q6
Zvornik Bos.-Herz. **59** H2
Zwedru Liberia **96** C4
Zweeloo Neth. **52** G2
Zweibrücken Germany **53** H5
Zweletemba S. Africa **100** D7
Zwelitsha S. Africa **101** H7
Zwethau Germany **53** N3
Zwettl Austria **47** O6
Zwickau Germany **53** M4
Zwochau Germany **53** M3
Zwolle Neth. **52** G2
Zwönitz Germany **53** M4
Zyablovo Rus. Fed. **42** L4
Zygi Cyprus **85** A2
Zyryan Kazakh. *see* **Zyryanovsk**
Zyryanka Rus. Fed. **65** Q3
Zyryanovsk Kazakh. **80** F2
Zyyi Cyprus *see* **Zygi**

Acknowledgements

Maps and data

Maps, design and origination by Collins Geo, HarperCollins Reference, Glasgow.
Illustrations created by HarperCollins Publishers unless otherwise stated.

Earthquake data (pp14–15): United States Geological Survey (USGS) National Earthquakes Information Center, Denver, USA.

Population map (pp20-21): 2005. Gridded Population of the World Version 3 (GPWv3). Palisades, NY: Socioeconomic Data and Applications Center (SEDAC), Columbia University. Available at http://sedac.ciesn.columbia.edu/plue/gpw http://www.ciesin.columbia.edu

Company sales figures (p29): Reprinted by permission of Forbes Magazine ©2008Forbes Inc.

Coral reefs data (p35): UNEP World Conservation Monitoring Centre, Cambridge, UK, and World Resources Institute (WRI), Washington D.C., USA.

Terrorism data (pp30–31): MIPT Terrorism Knowledge Base, and National Counterterrorism Center *2007 Report on Terrorism.*

Desertification data(p35): U.S. Department of Agriculture Natural Resources Conservation Service.

Antarctica (p152): Antarctic Digital Database (versions1 and 2), ©Scientific Committee on Antarctic research (SCAR), Cambridge, UK (1993,1998).

Photographs and images

Page	Image	Satellite/ Sensor	Credit
5	Amsterdam	IKONOS	Space Imaging Europe/ Science Photo Library
	The Alps	MODIS	MODIS/NASA
6	Cyprus	MODIS	MODIS/NASA
	Bhutan	ASTER	ASTER/NASA
7	Victoria Falls		Roger De La Harpe, Gallo Images/Corbis
8	Sydney	IKONOS	IKONOS image courtesy of GeoEye
	Uluru (Ayers Rock)		ImageState
	Aoraki (Mt Cook)		Mike Schroder/Still Pictures
9	The Pentagon	IKONOS	IKONOS image courtesy of GeoEye
	Cuba	MODIS	MODIS/NASA
10–11	Vatican City	IKONOS	IKONOS image courtesy of GeoEye
12–13	Greenland	MODIS	MODIS/NASA
16–17	Tropical Cyclone Dina	MODIS	MODIS/NASA/GSFC
18–19	Tokyo	ASTER	ASTER/NASA
	Cropland.Consuegra		© Rick Barrentine/Corbis
	Mojave Desert		Keith Moore
	Larsen Ice Shelf	MODIS	MODIS/NASA
20–21	Singapore		Courtesy of USGS EROS Data Center
	Kuna Indians		Danny Lehman/Corbis
22–23	Hong Kong		IKONOS satellite imagery courtesy of GeoEye
28–29	Sudan Village		Mark Edwards/Still Pictures
30–31	Refugee Camp		Thomas Coex/AFP/Getty Images
32–33	Drugs		Fredy Amariles/Getty Images
	Water		Harmut Schwarzbach/ Still Pictures
34–35	Itaipu Dam/ Iguaçu Falls	Landsat ETM	UNEP/USGS
	Aral Sea	Landsat	Images reproduced by kind permission of UNEP
	Great Barrier Reef	MODIS	MODIS/NASA
36–37	Iceland	MODIS	MODIS/NASA
38–39	Bosporus	ISS	NASA/Johnson Space Center
60–61	Caspian Sea	MODIS	MODIS/NASA
	Yangtze	MODIS	MODIS/NASA
62–63	Timor	MODIS	MODIS/NASA
	Beijing	IKONOS	IKONOS satellite imagery courtesy of GeoEye
92–93	Congo	Shuttle	NASA
	Lake Victoria	MODIS	MODIS/NASA
94–95	Cape Town	IKONOS	IKONOS image courtesy of GeoEye
102–103	Heron Island	IKONOS	IKONOS satellite imagery courtesy of GeoEye
	Banks Peninsula	Space shuttle	NASA
104–105	Nouméa	ISS	NASA/Johnson Space Center
	Wellington		NZ Aerial Mapping Ltd www.nzam.com
114–115	Mississippi	ASTER	ASTER/NASA
	Panama Canal	Landsat	Clifton-Campbell Imaging Inc.
116–117	The Bahamas	MODIS	MODIS/NASA
	Mexicali	ASTER	NASA
138–139	Tierra del Fuego	MODIS	MODIS/NASA
	Amazon/ Rio Negro	Terra/ MISR	NASA
140–141	Galapagos Islands	MODIS	MODIS/NASA
	Falkland Islands	MODIS	MODIS/NASA
146–147	Larsen Ice Shelf	MODIS	MODIS/NASA